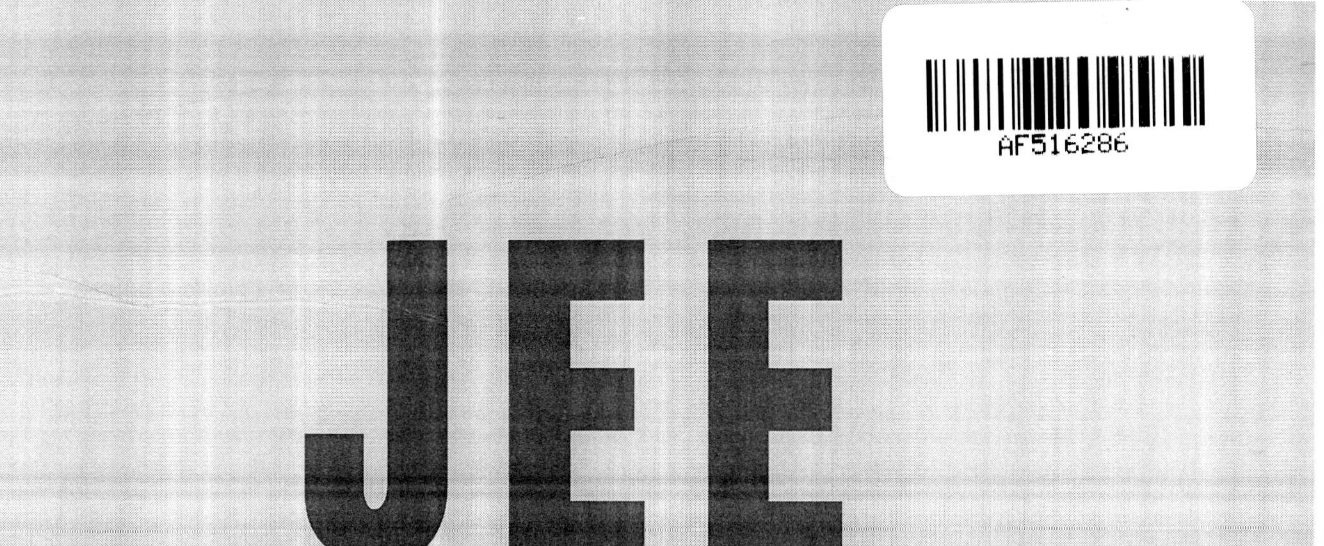

Foundation Mathematics

for

Class IX & X

A Bridge & Foundation for
Preparation of JEE Main & Advanced

ANUJA ARORA
Mentor, Counsellor & Academic Methodologist
for School and Competitive Examinations

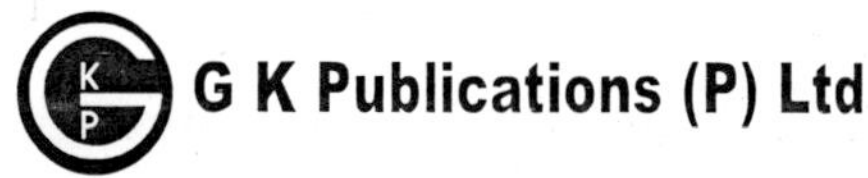

Title : JEE Foundation Mathematics for Class IX & X

Language : English

Editor's Name : Amit Singh

Typeset & Published by :

Career Launcher Infrastructure (P) Ltd.

A-45, Mohan Cooperative Industrial Area, Near Mohan Estate Metro Station, New Delhi - 110044

Marketed by :

G.K. Publications (P) Ltd.

Plot No. 63, Sector-27A, Near Sector - 28 Metro Station, Faridabad, Haryana-121003

ISBN : **978-93-56813-33-5**

Printer's Details: Printed in India, New Delhi.

For product information :

Visit ***www.gkpublications.com*** or email to ***gkp@gkpublications.com***

Dedicated

to

My Parents My Husband

& My Kids

PREFACE

JEE Main & Advanced are the competitive exams which are giving most promising career options of engineering to the students of science with maths stream. For these exams students mainly prepare after class 10. Mathematics upto class 10 plays very important role in preparation of these exams. In JEE both the subjects Physics & Maths require a fair understanding of concepts of mathematics covered in class 9 & 10 to a decent level of in-depth knowledge and applications.

This book covers all the topics of mathematics of class 9 and 10 with a detailed in-depth understanding with applications in variety of concepts. The format of this book is planned in a way that students gain most of aspects of the subject on which conceptual applications will be required in class 11 & 12 while preparing for above exams. For students preparing for NTSE (Stage I and II) also this book gave a complete hands-on practice experience of all the topics in syllabus until 2020 when NTSE was in place and considered as one of the most promising benchmarking exam for JEE aspirants.

In this book an exercise exclusively based on previously asked NTSE question is kept to boost the confidence level of students while preparing on topics of class 9 and 10. This book builds a strong foundation for prepaation of class 9 and 10 mathematics as well as for JEE Main & Advanced in upcoming years. This book also acts as a bridge course between classes 10 & 11 for all science stream students.

I am very much thankful to my better half, my guide, my mentor Ashish for inspiring me, to write this book. I can never imagine, without his constant support to complete this book in such a proper format. I am very grateful to my parents for believing in me and always encouraging me to do what I always want to do. I also want to thank my brother and sister for their unconditional support and love. I also want to thank my uncle - Raju Chacha, who inculcated in me the habit of reading and thus introduced me to this magical world of Education.

I would also like to thank my Guru VK Bansal Sir, who inspired me a lot and because of him I am at this position and he opened a new window of life for me.

I can't forget to thank my two little angels Aakash and Aashi, they unknowingly supported me in completing this book on time. Finally I would like to thank our Sr manager, Mr. Dayashankar Prajapati for completing the type setting of this book in such an appealing style and format.

At the End, I just want to say that this is the first edition of the book. I've tried my level best to make this book error-free. But I also know, To err is human, So there is possibility of some errors left untouched. I shall be grateful to the readers, if they point out some errors, they can also help me in improving this book by their valuable and constructive suggestions.

Date : *August, 2023* **Anuja Arora**

B-80, Model Town, Malviya Nagar, Jaipur-302017
e-mail: *anujapremy@yahoo.co.in*

CONTENTS

* * * * *

Real Number

1

- A number is called a rational number, if it can be written in the form $\frac{p}{q}$, where p and q are integers and $q \neq 0$.

- There are infinitely many rational numbers between any two given rational numbers.

- A number is called an irrational number if it cannot be written in the form $\frac{p}{q}$, where p and q are integers and $q \neq 0$.

- All the rational and irrational numbers together are called set of real numbers.

- Every real number is represented by a unique point on the number line. Also, every point on the number line represents a unique real number.

- The decimal expansion of a rational number is either terminating or non-terminating repeating. Moreover, a number whose decimal expansion is terminating or non-terminating repeating, is rational.

- The decimal expansion of an irrational number is non terminating non repeating. Moreover, a number whose decimal expansion is non terminating non-repeating, is irrational.

- The sum or difference of a rational number and an irrational number is always irrational.

- The product or quotient of a non-zero rational number with an irrational number is irrational.

- If we add, subtract, multiply or divide two irrationals, the result may be rational or irrational.

- For positive real numbers a and b, the following identities hold:

(i) $\sqrt{ab} = \sqrt{a}\,\sqrt{b}$

(ii) $\sqrt{\frac{a}{b}} = \frac{\sqrt{a}}{\sqrt{b}}$

(iii) $(\sqrt{a}+\sqrt{b})\,(\sqrt{a}-\sqrt{b}) = a-b$

(iv) $(a+\sqrt{b})\,(a-\sqrt{b}) = a^2-b$

(v) $(\sqrt{a}+\sqrt{b})^2 = a+2\sqrt{ab}+b$

- When the denominator of an expression contains a term with a square root (or a number under a radical sign), the process of converting it to an equivalent expression whose denominator is a rational number is called rationalising the denominator.

- To rationalise the denominator of $\frac{1}{\sqrt{a}+b}$, we multiply this by $\frac{\sqrt{a}-b}{\sqrt{a}-b}$, where a and b are integers.

Note :

$\sqrt{a}-b$ is called the conjugate of $\sqrt{a}+b$

- Let $a > 0$ be a real number and p and q be rational numbers. Then

(a) $a^p \cdot a^q = a^{p+q}$ (b) $(a^p)^q = a^{pq}$

(c) $\frac{a^p}{a^q} = a^{p-q}$ (d) $a^p\,b^p = (ab)^p$

- Given positive integers a and b, there exist unique integers q and r satisfying $a = bq + r$, $0 \leq r < b$. This result is known as **Euclid's division lemma.**

- An algorithm is a series of well defined steps which gives a procedure for solving a type of problem.

- A lemma is a proven statement used for proving another statement.

- HCF of two positive integers a and b is the largest positive integer d that divides both a and b exactly without leaving any remainder.

Basically there two methods of finding the HCF.

(i) Factor Method

(ii) Long division Method

- **HCF with Remainders:**

In case-1 : The remainders are different.

Greatest number that will divide x, y and z leaving remainder p, q and r respectively. Required number

$= \text{HCF of } (x-p), (y-q), (z-r)$

In case-2 : The remainders are same in each case. Greatest number that will divide x, y and z leaving remainder r, in each case. Required number

$= \text{HCF of } (x-r), (y-r), (z-r)$

In case-3 : The remainders are same in each case, but the value of remainder is unknown.

Greatest number that will divide x, y and z leaving the same remainder in each case. Required number

$= \text{HCF of } |x-y|, |y-z| \text{ and } |z-x|$

- HCF of fractions $= \dfrac{\text{HCF of numerators}}{\text{LCM of denominators}}$

- If a and b be any two positive integers then

  HCF $(a, b) \times$ LCM $(a, b) = a \times b$

- **L.C.M. (Least Common Multiple) :**

The least number which is exactly divisible by each one of the given numbers is called their LCM.

Basically there two methods of finding the HCF.

(i) Factor Method

(ii) Long division Method

- **L.C.M. with remainder :**

Case-1 : When the remainders are same for all the divisors.

Least number which when divided by x, y and z leaves the remainder r in each case.

Required number = (LCM of x, y and z) + r.

Case-2 : When the remainders are different for different divisors but the respective difference between the divisors and the remainders remain constant.

Least number which when divided by x, y and z leaves the remainder p, q and r respectively and $x-p=y-q=z-r=k$.

Required number = (LCM of x, y and z) $- k$.

Case-3 : When neither the remainder is same nor the difference between divisors and the remainders are same.

- **Euclid's Division Algorithm :**

To obtain the HCF of two positive integers, say c and d with $c > d$, we follow the steps below :

Step-1 : Apply Euclid's division lemma to find q and r where $c = dq + r, 0 = r < d$.

Step-2 : If $r = 0$, then, d is the HCF of c and d. If $r \neq 0$, then apply Euclid's division lemma to d and r.

Step-3 : Continue this process till the remainder is zero. The divisor at this stage will be the required HCF.

- **The Fundamental Theorem of Arithmetic :**

Every composite number can be expressed (factorised) as a product of primes, and this factorisation is unique, apart from the order in which the prime factors occur. Or the prime factorisation of a natural number is unique, except for the order of its factors.

- Let p be a prime number. If p divides a^2, then p divides a, where a is a positive integer.

- The sum or difference of a rational and an irrational number is irrational.

- The product and quotient of a non-zero rational number and an irrational number is irrational.

- Let x be a rational number whose decimal expansion terminates. Then x can be expressed in the form $\dfrac{p}{q}$ where p and q are coprime and the prime factorisation of q is of the form $2^n 5^m$, where n and m are non negative integers. Then, x has a decimal expansion which terminates.

- If $x = \dfrac{p}{q}$ is a rational number, such that the prime factorisation of q is of the form $2^m 5^n$, where m and n are whole numbers. If $m = n$, then the decimal expansion of x will terminate after m places of decimal. If $m > n$, then the decimal expansion of x will terminate after m places of decimal. If $n > m$, then the decimal expansion of x will terminate after n places of decimal.

- Let $x = \dfrac{p}{q}$ be a rational number, such that the prime factorisation of q is not of the form $2^n 5^m$, where n and m are non negative integers. Then x has a decimal expansion which is non terminating repeating (recurring).

- The decimal expansion of every rational number is either terminating or non-terminating repeating.

- **Fermat's Theorem :**

If p is a prime and a is an integer then $a^p - a$ is divisible by p.

- $\dfrac{a^{p-1}}{p}$ leaves a remainder 1 when divided by p. Where (a, p) are coprime.

- If N is composite number then N can be expressed as

$N = a^p \cdot b^q \cdot c^r \ldots$

(where $a, b, c \ldots$ are prime numbers and p, q, r are non negative integers) then total numbers of factors of

$N = (p+1)\cdot(q+1)\cdot(r+1)\ldots$

○ To find the last digit or digit at the unit's place of a^n :

Case-1 : If the last digit or digit at the unit's place of a is 1, 5 or 6, whatever be the value of n, it will have the same digit at unit's place, i.e. the cyclicity of digits 1, 5, 6 is 1.

$(\ldots 1)^n = (\ldots 1)$

$(\ldots 5)^n = (\ldots 5)$

$(\ldots 6)^n = (\ldots 6)$

Case-2 : If the last digit or digit at the unit's place of a is 2, 3, 7 or 8, then the last digit of a^n depends upon the value of n as the cyclicity of these digits is 4 and follows a repeating pattern in terms of 4 as given below :

n	last digit of $(\ldots 2)^n$	last digit of $(\ldots 3)^n$	last digit of $(\ldots 7)^n$	last digit of $(\ldots 8)^n$
$4x+1$	2	3	7	8
$4x+2$	4	9	9	4
$4x+3$	8	7	3	2
$4x$	6	1	1	6

Case-3 : If the last digit or digit at the unit's place of a is either 4 or 9, then the last digit of a^n depends upon the value of n as the cyclicity of these two digits is 2 and follows repeating pattern in terms of 2 as given below :

$n =$	last digit of $(\ldots 4)^n$	last digit of $(\ldots 9)^n$
$2x$	6	1
$2x+1$	4	9

* * * * *

PRACTICE EXERCISE - 1.1

1-1 The value of x, if $5^{x-3}.3^{2x-8} = 225$ is :
(A) 5 (B) 4
(C) 3 (D) 2

1-2 If $x = 7 + 4\sqrt{3}$, then $\sqrt{x} + \frac{1}{\sqrt{x}}$ equals :
(A) 6 (B) 4
(C) $2\sqrt{3}$ (D) $4\sqrt{3}$

1-3 If $\frac{1}{a+b} + \frac{1}{a^{-1}+b^{-1}} = 12^{-1}(1+ab)$. Then the maximum value of $a^2 + b^2$ for non negative integer values of a & b is :
(A) 22 (B) 256
(C) 144 (D) 90

1-4 If $4^x = 3^y = 12^{-z}$ then $\left(\frac{1}{x}+\frac{1}{y}+\frac{1}{z}\right)$ is equal to :
(A) 0 (B) 1
(C) $\frac{3}{2}$ (D) $-\frac{1}{2}$

1-5 If $x^{x\sqrt{x}} = (x\sqrt{x})^x$, find the value of x :
(A) $\frac{3}{2}$ (B) $\frac{2}{9}$
(C) $\frac{9}{4}$ (D) $\frac{4}{9}$

1-6 Which one is not correct in the following :
(A) There are infinitely many irrational numbers
(B) The sum of two irrational numbers is always irrational
(C) The sum of a rational number and an irrational number is irrational
(D) Zero is a rational number

1-7 $\sqrt{n}$ in an irrational number, if n is :
(A) A natural number (B) A prime number
(C) An even number (D) An odd number

1-8 If p be a prime number and a and b integers such that $p|ab$, then :
(A) $p|a$ as well as $p|b$ (B) $p|a$ or $p|b$
(C) $p|(a+b)$ (D) $p|(a-b)$

1-9 A number in the form $15q+7$ can be written as :
(A) $3m+3$ (B) $5m+2$
(C) $5m+3$ (D) $3m+2$

1-10 The length, breadth and height of a room are 8 m 25 cm, 6 m 75 cm and 4 m 50 cm respectively, then the longest rod which can measure the three dimensions of the room exactly :
(A) 65 cm (B) 70 cm
(C) 75 cm (D) 80 cm

1-11 Find the difference of second and third remainders of (13, 99) :
(A) 2 (B) 3
(C) 1 (D) 0

1-12 If LCM of 404 and 96 is 9696, then their HCF will be :
(A) 4 (B) 6
(C) 8 (D) 12

1-13 Two numbers are in the ratio of 9 : 5. If their LCM is 900, then HCF is :
(A) 30 (B) 20
(C) 15 (D) 60

1-14 Find HCF of 0.84, 7.2 and 1.440 :
(A) 1.2 (B) 0.0012
(C) 0.012 (D) 0.12

1-15 The greatest number that will divide 290, 460 and 552 leaving respectively 4, 5, 6 as remainders is:
(A) 11 (B) 13
(C) 12 (D) 14

1-16 If p is a prime number, then the LCM of p and $(p+1)$:
(A) p^2 (B) $\frac{p(p+1)}{2}$
(C) $(p+1)^2$ (D) $p(p+1)$

1-17 Five bells begin to toll together and toll respectively at intervals of 6, 7, 8 and 12 second. What time they will toll together :
(A) 168 (B) 170
(C) 169 (D) 182

1-18 The least perfect square which is divisible by 3, 4, 5, 6, 8 is :
(A) 900 (B) 1200
(C) 2500 (D) 3600

1-19 Which of the following rule is not followed by rational numbers in subtraction :
(A) Associative law (B) Commutative Property
(C) Existence of left identity (D) All of above

1-20 The division of two rational numbers is always :
(A) Rational
(B) Irrational
(C) May be rational or may be irrational
(D) None of these

1-21 Which of the following is a true statement?
(A) Every real number is rational
(B) Every real number is irrational
(C) A real number is neither rational nor irrational
(D) None of these

1-22 HCF of $2^3 \times 3^2 \times 5$, $2^2 \times 3^3 \times 5^2$ and $2^4 \times 3 \times 5^3 \times 7$ is :
(A) 30 (B) 48
(C) 60 (D) 105

1-23 Which of the following is a pair of co-primes :
(A) (14, 35) (B) (18, 25)
(C) (31, 93) (D) (32, 62)

1-24 Three pieces of timber 42 m, 49 m and 63 m long have to be divided into planks of the same length. What is the greatest possible length of each plank :
(A) 7 m (B) 14 m
(C) 42 m (D) 63 m

1-25 The greatest number of four digits which is divisible by each one of the numbers 12, 18, 21 & 28 is :
(A) 9848 (B) 9864
(C) 9828 (D) 9636

1-26 A seminar, the number of participants in Hindi, English and science are 60, 84 and 108 respectively. Find the minimum number of rooms required if in each room the same number of participants are to be seated and all of them being in the same subject :
(A) 18 (B) 6
(C) 24 (D) 21

1-27 If $(\sqrt{2})^x + (\sqrt{3})^x = (\sqrt{13})^{\frac{x}{2}}$ then the number of values of x is :
(A) 1 (B) 2
(C) 4 (D) 0

1-28 If $\frac{2A}{3} = \frac{3B}{4} = \frac{5C}{6}$ then find $A:B:C$
(A) $6:8:9$ (B) $45:40:36$
(C) $40:45:36$ (D) $12:15:20$

1-29 If $p > q$ where p, q and r are real numbers. Then which of the following is always true :
(A) $p.r > r - q$ (B) $\frac{p}{r} > \frac{q}{r}$
(C) $p + r > q + r$ (D) All of these

1-30 There is one number which is formed by writing one digit 6 times (e.g 222222, 333333 etc.). Such a number is always divisible by :
(A) 7 only (B) 11 only
(C) 13 only (D) All of these

1-31 If x and y are any positive integers, then $(x^2 - x) + (y^2 - y)$ is always :
(A) Even number
(B) Odd number
(C) Can't say
(D) Both even and odd are possible

1-32 If $x = \sqrt{1 + \sqrt{1 + \sqrt{1 + \ldots}}}$, then :
(A) $x = 1$ (B) $0 < x < 1$
(C) x is infinite (D) $1 < x < 2$

1-33 Which of the following statements is correct ?
(A) If n is odd, $(10)^n - 1$ is divisible by 11
(B) If n is even, $(10)^n - 1$ is divisible by 11
(C) If n is odd, $(5)^n - 1$ is divisible by 5
(D) If n is even, $(5)^n - 1$ is divisible by 5

1-34 Find the sum of
$$\frac{1}{3\times7} + \frac{1}{7\times11} + \frac{1}{11\times15} + \ldots + \frac{1}{99\times103}$$
(A) $\frac{100}{309}$ (B) $\frac{101}{309}$
(C) $\frac{25}{309}$ (D) $\frac{105}{309}$

1-35 $\left(1+\frac{1}{2}\right)\left(1+\frac{1}{3}\right)\left(1+\frac{1}{4}\right)\ldots\left(1+\frac{1}{n}\right) =$
(A) n (B) $\frac{n-1}{2}$
(C) $\frac{n+1}{2}$ (D) $\frac{n}{2}$

1-36 The product of two numbers is 4107. If the HCF of these numbers is 37, then the greater number is :
(A) 101 (B) 107
(C) 111 (D) 185

1-37 Find the greatest number that will divide 46, 91 and 181 so as to leave the same remainder in each case :
(A) 4 (B) 7
(C) 9 (D) 45

1-38 The least multiple of 7. Which leaves a remainder of 4, when divided by 6, 9, 15 and 18 is :

(A) 74 (B) 94
(C) 184 (D) 364

1-39 Find the least multiple of 23, which when divided by 18, 21 and 24 leaves remainder 7, 10 and 13 respectively :

(A) 3002 (B) 3013
(C) 3024 (D) 3036

1-40 Four different electronic devices make a beep after every 30 minutes, 1 hour, 1½ hour and 1 hour 45 minutes respectively. All the devices beeped together at 12 noon. They will again beep together at :

(A) 12 mid night (B) 3 am
(C) 6.9 am (D) 9 am

1-41 $\sqrt{3+2\sqrt{2}} + \sqrt{3-2\sqrt{2}}$ is :

(A) A rational number (B) An irrational number
(C) Zero (D) None of these

1-42 The unit's digit of $3^{1001}.7^{1002}.(13)^{1003}$ is :

(A) 9 (B) 7
(C) 5 (D) 3

1-43 The greater among $\sqrt{11}-\sqrt{6}$ and $\sqrt{17}-\sqrt{12}$ is :

(A) $\sqrt{17}-\sqrt{12}$ (B) $\sqrt{11}-\sqrt{6}$
(C) Both are equal (D) Can't say

1-44 LCM and HCF of two numbers are 180 and 6 respectively. If one number lies between 25 and 35 then find the numbers :

(A) (25, 36) (B) (28, 32)
(C) (30, 32) (D) (30, 36)

1-45 $4^{61}+4^{62}+4^{63}+4^{64}$ is divisible by ?

(A) 3 (B) 10
(C) 11 (D) 13

1-46 The number of prime factors of $(3\times5)^{12}(2\times7)^{10}(10)^{25}$ is :

(A) 47 (B) 60
(C) 72 (D) None of these

1-47 If $5x+11y$ is a prime number for positive integral values of x and y, then what is the least value of $x+y$?

(A) 2 (B) 3
(C) 4 (D) 5

1-48 Pick up the irrational numbers from

$$\frac{3}{2}, (\pi-1), (3+\sqrt{2})-\sqrt{3}, -7, \sqrt{4}, 8, \frac{-9}{8} \ \& \ \pi$$

(A) $\sqrt{4}, 8$

(B) $\frac{3}{2}, \sqrt{4}, -7, \frac{-9}{8}$

(C) $\pi, (\pi-1), (3+\sqrt{2})-\sqrt{3}$

(D) None of these

1-49 Which one is divisible by 3 in the following (for $n\in N$) :

(A) n (B) $n+2$
(C) $n+4$ (D) n or $(n+2)$ or $(n+4)$

1-50 If $x=\frac{\sqrt{3}+1}{2}$, find the value of $4x^3+2x^2-8x+7$:

(A) 0 (B) 1
(C) 10 (D) $7\sqrt{3}$

* * * * *

PRACTICE EXERCISE - 1.2

1-1 If a and x are any positive integers, then $(a^x + a)^x + (a^x - a)^x$ is always :
(A) Even number
(B) Odd number
(C) Can't say
(D) Both even and odd are possible

1-2 Two numbers are such that their difference, their sum and their product are to one another as 1 : 7 : 24. The product of two numbers is :
(A) 12 (B) 24
(C) 48 (D) 96

1-3 If n is any even number, then $n(n^2 + 20)$ is always divisible by :
(A) 15 (B) 20
(C) 24 (D) 32

1-4 If n is any odd number then, $n^5 - n$ is always divisible by :
(A) 120 (B) 140
(C) 260 (D) 320

1-5 If x and y are two odd numbers such that $x > y$, then the largest number which divides all possible numbers of the form $x^2 - y^2$ is :
(A) 2 (B) 4
(C) 6 (D) 8

1-6 Let x, y and z be distinct odd positive integers. Then find which of the following statements can't be true ?
(A) xyz^2 is odd
(B) $(x - y)^2 z$ is even
(C) $(x + y - z)^2 (x + y)$ is even
(D) $(x - y)(y + z)(x + y - z)$ is odd

1-7 The remainder when 7^{63} is divided by 25 is :
(A) 13 (B) 24
(C) 18 (D) 17

1-8 The remainder when 13^{55} is divided by 85 is :
(A) 16 (B) 72
(C) 77 (D) 54

1-9 There is a three-digit number, $N = xyz$; x, y, z are three different digits. If $x^2 + y^2 = 41$, $x^2 + z^2 = 89$ and $y^2 + z^2 = 80$, find N:
(A) 458 (B) 854
(C) 548 (D) 485

1-10 N is a four-digit number. All the digits of N are odd. If another four-digit number M is formed by reversing the digits of N, P is the positive difference of numbers M and N, then which of the following statements is necessarily correct ?
(A) $M + N + P$ is an odd number
(B) P lies between M and N
(C) $M + N - P$ is an even number
(D) None of these

1-11 $N = abcd$ is a four-digit number where a, b, c and d are four consecutive even digits. $M = 1.5\,N$ and $P = \frac{1}{2}(dcba)$. Then which of the following statements is wrong?
(A) $P > M > N$ (B) $\frac{N}{2} + P < 2N$
(C) $\frac{N}{2} + P = 5555$ (D) All are correct

1-12 $N = a^2 + b^2$ is a three-digit number divisible by 5. Also, $a = 10x + y$ and $b = 10x + z$ where z is a prime number, and z and y are natural numbers. If $a + b = 31$, find the value of N:
(A) 565 (B) 485
(C) 505 (D) 485 or 505

1-13 $N = 10x + 10y + z$, where x, y and z are non-zero digits. If $z > y > x$ and $(z - x) = 2(y - x)$ and the unit's digits of N^2 is 4, find the value of N:
(A) 678 (B) 578
(C) 468 (D) Can't be found

1-14 $N = 1a9b7c$ is a six-digit number where $A = 1a9$ and $B = b7c$ are three-digit perfect squares of two-digit nos. If $\sqrt{B} = 2\sqrt{A}$, which of the following statements is/are true ?
(1) $a = b = c$ (2) $b = c \neq a$
(3) $N = 169676$ is one of the two possible values
(4) $A + B = 5A$
(A) Only 1 alone (B) Either 1 or 2
(C) Only 1 and 3 (D) Only 1 and 4

1-15 $20 \times 21 \times 22 \times \ldots \times 30 = A$. If A is divisible by 10^x, find the maximum value of x:
(A) 3 (B) 4
(C) 5 (D) 6

1-16 How many zeros exist at the end of the product of $10^4 \times 12^3 \times 15^4 \times 21^3 \times 16^3 \times 25^4$?
(A) 12 (B) 14
(C) 16 (D) 18

1-17 What digit exists at the unit's place of $(39)^{42} \times (27)^{23} \times (36)^{12}$?

(A) 2 (B) 4
(C) 6 (D) 8

1-18 What unit's digit exists in the product of all prime numbers between 10 and 30 ?

(A) 5 (B) 4
(C) 3 (D) 2

1-19 What digit will exist at the unit's place of $(347)^{42} - (763219)^2 \times (53213)^4$?

(A) 8 (B) 10
(C) 12 (D) 14

1-20 It is given that the number $(189)^{53}$ is divisible by all the elements in set S. How many prime numbers are elements of the set S?

(A) 0 (B) 1
(C) 2 (D) 3

1-21 The cube of any positive integer can be in the form of :

(A) $9q, 9q+1, 9q+2$ (B) $9q, 9q+3, 9q+5$
(C) $9q, 9q+1, 9q+8$ (D) $9q, 9q+5, 9q+7$

1-22 If $a^m \cdot a^n = a^{mn}$, then $m(n-2)+n(m-2)$ is :

(A) 1 (B) -1
(C) 0 (D) 1/2

1-23 If $a^x = b^y = c^z$ and $b^2 = ac$, then y equals :

(A) $\frac{xz}{x+z}$ (B) $\frac{xz}{2(x-z)}$
(C) $\frac{xz}{2(z-x)}$ (D) $\frac{2xz}{x+z}$

1-24 If the sum of two numbers is 90 and their HCF is 6 then how many such pairs of numbers are there ?

(A) 5 (B) 2
(C) 3 (D) 4

1-25 The sum of three non-zero prime numbers is 100. One of them exceeds the other by 36. Then the largest number is :

(A) 73 (B) 91
(C) 67 (D) 57

* * * * *

PRACTICE EXERCISE - 1.3

1-1 There are 540 students in a school. For a P.T. drill They have to stand in such a manner that the number of rows is equal to number of Column. How many minimum students would be left out in this arrangements : **[NTSE-2012 (Stage-I) Rajasthan]**

(A) 22 Students (B) 11 Students
(C) 40 Students (D) 29 Students

1-2 Find the smallest square number that is divisible by each of the numbers 4, 9 and 10 : **[NTSE-2012 (Stage-I) Rajasthan]**

(A) 600 (B) 3600
(C) 900 (D) 8100

1-3 Find the value of m for which $5^m \div 5^{-3} = 5^5$: **[NTSE-2012 (Stage-I) Rajasthan]**

(A) $m=2$ (B) $m=-2$
(C) $m=3$ (D) $m=8$

1-4 If $21x5$ is a multiple of 9, Where 'x' is a digit. What is the value of 'x'? **[NTSE-2012 (Stage-I) Rajasthan]**

(A) 6 (B) 3
(C) 0 (D) 1

1-5 Find the value of $\dfrac{30^n \times 3^{2n} \times 2^n}{6^n \times 2^n \times 3^{3n}}$ **[NTSE-2012 (Stage-I) Rajasthan]**

(A) $\left(\dfrac{3}{10}\right)^n$ (B) $\left(\dfrac{5}{3}\right)^n$
(C) $\left(\dfrac{10}{8}\right)^n$ (D) $\left(\dfrac{10}{3}\right)^n$

1-6 Rationalising the denominator of $\dfrac{5}{\sqrt{3}-\sqrt{5}}$ is : **[NTSE-2013 (Stage-I) Rajasthan]**

(A) $\left(\dfrac{5}{2}\right)(\sqrt{3}+\sqrt{5})$ (B) $\left(-\dfrac{5}{2}\right)(\sqrt{3}+\sqrt{5})$
(C) $\left(\dfrac{5}{2}\right)(\sqrt{3}-\sqrt{5})$ (D) $\left(-\dfrac{5}{2}\right)(\sqrt{3}-\sqrt{5})$

1-7 Value of $\dfrac{2^{100}}{2}$ is : **[NTSE-2013 (Stage-I) Rajasthan]**

(A) 1 (B) 50^{100}
(C) 2^{50} (D) 2^{99}

1-8 If 3 is the least prime factor of number a and 7 is the least prime factor of number b, then the least prime factor of $a+b$ is : **[NTSE-2014 (Stage-I) Rajasthan]**

(A) 2 (B) 3
(C) 5 (D) 10

1-9 If x, y, z are positive real numbers and a, b, c are rational numbers, then the value of

$$\frac{1}{1+x^{b-a}+x^{c-a}}+\frac{1}{1+x^{a-b}+x^{c-b}}+\frac{1}{1+x^{b-c}+x^{a-c}} \text{ is :}$$

[NTSE-2014 (Stage-I) Rajasthan]

(A) –1 (B) 0
(C) 1 (D) None of these

1-10 The value of $\left(\dfrac{x^b}{x^c}\right)^{\frac{1}{bc}} \cdot \left(\dfrac{x^c}{x^a}\right)^{\frac{1}{ca}} \cdot \left(\dfrac{x^a}{x^b}\right)^{\frac{1}{ab}}$ is equal to : **[NTSE-2015 (Stage-I) Rajasthan]**

(A) 1 (B) –1
(C) 0 (D) abc

1-11 The HCF of any two prime numbers a and b, is : **[NTSE-2015 (Stage-I) Rajasthan]**

(A) a (B) ab
(C) b (D) 1

1-12 The total two-digit numbers which are divisible by 5, are : **[NTSE-2015 (Stage-I) Rajasthan]**

(A) 17 (B) 18
(C) 19 (D) 20

1-13 The value of $\sqrt{5-2\sqrt{6}}$ is : **[NTSE-2015 (Stage-I) West Bengal]**

(A) $\pm(\sqrt{3}-\sqrt{2})$ (B) $\sqrt{3}-\sqrt{2}$
(C) $\sqrt{2}-\sqrt{3}$ (D) All of the above

1-14 If $x=ay, y=bx$, the value of $\dfrac{1}{a+1}+\dfrac{1}{1+b}$ is : **[NTSE-2015 (Stage-I) West Bengal]**

(A) 0 (B) $x+y$
(C) $\dfrac{1}{x+y}$ (D) 1

1-15 Among the numbers 2^{250}, 3^{200}, 4^{150} and 5^{100}, the greatest is : **[NTSE-2015 (Stage-I) West Bengal]**

(A) 2^{250} (B) 3^{200}
(C) 4^{150} (D) 5^{100}

1-16 If $a * b = a + b - ab$, the value of $4 * 5 + 5 * 6$ is : **[NTSE-2015 (Stage-I) West Bengal]**

(A) 20 (B) -20
(C) 30 (D) -30

1-17 If the LCM of 12 and 42 is $(10m + 4)$ then the value of 'm' is : **[NTSE-2015 (Stage-I) West Bengal]**

(A) 50 (B) 8
(C) $\frac{1}{5}$ (D) 1

1-18 If a, b and c are any positive real number then the value of $\sqrt{a^{-1}b} \cdot \sqrt{b^{-1}c} \cdot \sqrt{c^{-1}a}$ is : **[NTSE-2015 (Stage-I) UP]**

(A) 1/2 (B) 0
(C) 1 (D) -1

1-19 If a numbers is divided by 6, the remainder is 3 then what will be the remainder when the square of the same numbers is divided by 6 again : **[NTSE-2015 (Stage-I) UP]**

(A) 0 (B) 1
(C) 2 (D) 3

1-20 If $\left(\frac{a}{b}\right)^{x-1} = \left(\frac{b}{a}\right)^{x-3}$ then the value of x will be : **[NTSE-2015 (Stage-I) UP]**

(A) -1 (B) 1
(C) 2 (D) 3

1-21 If $x^a = y$, $y^b = z$, $z^c = x$ then the correct statement will be : **[NTSE-2015 (Stage-I) Chhatisgarh]**

(A) $a.\,b.\,c = 1$ (B) $a.\,b.\,c = 0$
(C) $a + b + c = 1$ (D) $a + b + c = 0$

1-22 One Rational number between $\frac{1}{5}$ and $\frac{1}{4}$ is : **[NTSE-2015 (Stage-I) Chhatisgarh]**

(A) $\frac{18}{100}$ (B) $\frac{22}{100}$
(C) $\frac{26}{100}$ (D) $\frac{27}{100}$

1-23 The value of $\sqrt{10 + \sqrt{25 + \sqrt{108 + \sqrt{154 + \sqrt{225}}}}}$ will be : **[NTSE-2015 (Stage-I) Chandigarh]**

(A) 4 (B) 6
(C) 8 (D) 10

1-24 $\sqrt{m^4n^4} \times \sqrt[6]{m^2n^2} \times \sqrt[3]{m^2n^2} = (m, n)^k$, then find the value of k : **[NTSE-2015 (Stage-I) Maharashtra]**

(A) 6 (B) 3
(C) 2 (D) 1

1-25 The LCM of a^3b^2, abc is : **[NTSE-2015 (Stage-I) TN]**

(A) c (B) a^4b^3c
(C) ab (D) a^3b^2c

1-26 The GCD of $(x^3 - 1)$ and $(x^4 - 1)$ is : **[NTSE-2015 (Stage-I) TN]**

(A) $x^3 - 1$ (B) $x^2 + 1$
(C) $x^2 - 1$ (D) $x - 1$

1-27 $F_1 = F_2 = 1$ and $F_n = F_{n-1} + F_{n-2}$ then the value of F_5 is : **[NTSE-2015 (Stage-I) TN]**

(A) 3 (B) 2
(C) 8 (D) 5

1-28 If $\frac{32}{500} = \frac{2^3}{5^m}$, then the value of m is : **[NTSE-2015 (Stage-I) TN]**

(A) 2 (B) 3
(C) 4 (D) 0

1-29 If $\frac{9}{y} + \frac{4}{x} = \frac{12}{\sqrt{xy}}$ where $x > 0, y > 0$ then $3\sqrt{x} - 2\sqrt{y} =$ **[NTSE-2015 (Stage-I) TN]**

(A) 5 (B) 1
(C) 2 (D) 0

1-30 The rational form of $0.\overline{24}$ is : **[NTSE-2015 (Stage-I) TN]**

(A) $\frac{24}{100}$ (B) $\frac{8}{33}$
(C) $\frac{24}{1000}$ (D) $\frac{0.24}{100}$

1-31 If $P = \frac{x}{x+y}$, $Q = \frac{y}{x+y}$ then the value of $\frac{1}{P-Q} - \frac{2Q}{P^2 - Q^2}$ is : **[NTSE-2015 (Stage-I) TN]**

(A) $\frac{x+y}{x-y}$ (B) 0
(C) 1 (D) $\frac{x-y}{x+y}$

1-32 If $2^m - 2^{m-1} - 4 = 0$. Then value of m^m is : **[NTSE-2015 (Stage-I) Delhi]**

(A) 4 (B) 27
(C) 6 (D) 29

1-33 If $a + b = 3$, $ab = 2$ and $a > b$, then what is the value of $2^{a^3 - b^3}$? **[NTSE-2016 (Stage-I) Odisha]**

(A) 32 (B) 64

(C) 128 (D) 256

1-34 $\overline{AB}$ is a diameter of the circle shown in the figure and O is the centre of it. If $m\angle A = 30°$ and $m\angle POQ = 60°$, what is the ratio between the areas of ΔPOQ and ΔABC ?

[NTSE-2016 (Stage-I) Odisha]

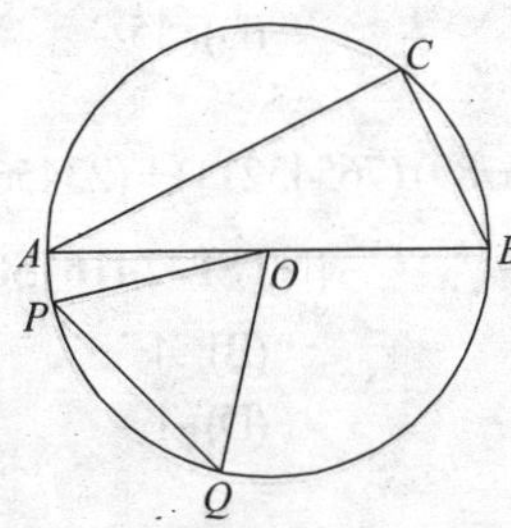

Figure 1.1

(A) $\sqrt{3}:2$ (B) $\sqrt{3}:1$

(C) $3:2$ (D) $1:2$

1-35 The cube root of $x + y + 3x^{1/3}\, y^{1/3}\, (x^{1/3} + y^{1/3})$ is : **[NTSE-2016 (Stage-I) Rajasthan]**

(A) $x+y$ (B) $x^{1/3} + y^{1/3}$

(C) $(x+y)^{1/3}$ (D) $(x+y)^3$

1-36 Expressing $0.\overline{23}+0.2\overline{3}$ as a single decimal, we get :

[NTSE-2016 (Stage-I) Rajasthan]

(A) $0.46\overline{5}$ (B) $0.4\overline{65}$

(C) $0.\overline{465}$ (D) $0.465\overline{4}$

1-37 What is the least number which when divided by 42, 72 and 84 leaves the remainder 25, 55 and 67 respectively : **[NTSE-2016 (Stage-I) Bihar]**

(A) 521 (B) 512

(C) 504 (D) 487

1-38 If the sum of two numbers is 22 and sum of their squares is 404 then the product of the number is :

[NTSE-2016 (Stage-I) Bihar]

(A) 40 (B) 44

(C) 80 (D) 88

1-39 If $1^3 + 2^3 + \ldots + 10^3 = 3025$ then $4 + 32 + 108 + \ldots + 4000$ is equal to : **[NTSE-2016 (Stage-I) Bihar]**

(A) 1200 (B) 12100

(C) 12200 (D) 12400

1-40 What is the square root of $9+2\sqrt{14}$?

[NTSE-2016 (Stage-I) Bihar]

(A) $1+2\sqrt{2}$ (B) $\sqrt{3}+\sqrt{6}$

(C) $\sqrt{2}+\sqrt{7}$ (D) $\sqrt{2}+\sqrt{5}$

1-41 $\sqrt[3]{1-\frac{127}{343}}$ is equal to : **[NTSE-2016 (Stage-I) Bihar]**

(A) $\frac{5}{9}$ (B) $1-\frac{1}{7}$

(C) $\frac{4}{7}$ (D) $1-\frac{2}{7}$

1-42 What is the value of $2.\overline{6}-1.\overline{9}$?

[NTSE-2016 (Stage-I) Bihar]

(A) $0.\overline{6}$ (B) $0.\overline{9}$

(C) $0.\overline{7}$ (D) 0.7

1-43 How many numbers lie between 10 to 300, which when divided by 4 leave a remainder 3 :

[NTSE-2016 (Stage-I) Jharkhand]

(A) 71 (B) 72

(C) 73 (D) 74

1-44 **Statement-A :** The rationalising factor of $\sqrt[3]{a}+\sqrt[3]{b}$ is $-\sqrt[3]{b}$.

Statement-B : The product of $(\sqrt[3]{a}-\sqrt[3]{b})$ and $(\sqrt[3]{a^2}+\sqrt[3]{b^2}+\sqrt[3]{ab})$ is $(a-b)$: **[NTSE-2016 (Stage-I) Karnatka]**

(A) Both A and B statements are true

(B) Both A and B statements are false

(C) A is true and B is false

(D) A is false and B is true

1-45 If $(-1)^n + (-1)^{4n} = 0$, then n is :

[NTSE-2016 (Stage-I) Chandigarh]

(A) Any positive

(B) Any negative

(C) Any odd natural number

(D) Any even natural number

1-46 Four positive integers sum to 125. If the first of these numbers is increased by 4, the second is decreased by 4. The third is multiplied by 4 and the fourth is divided by 4 we find four equal numbers then four original integers are :

[NTSE-2016 (Stage-I) Delhi]

(A) 16, 24, 5, 80 (B) 8, 22, 38, 57

(C) 7, 19, 46, 53 (D) 12, 28, 40, 45

1-47 The first term of a sequence is 2005. Each succeeding term is the sum of the cubes of the digits of the previous term.

What is the 2005th term of the sequence?

[NTSE-2016 (Stage-I) Telangana]

(A) 29 (B) 85
(C) 250 (D) 133

1-48 Suppose that

$4^{x_1} = 5, 5^{x_2} = 6,$

$6^{x_3} = 7, \ldots (127)^{x_{124}} = 128$

what is $x_1, x_2, x_3, \ldots x_{124}$? **[NTSE-2016 (Stage-I) Telangana]**

(A) 2 (B) $\frac{5}{2}$
(C) 3 (D) $\frac{7}{2}$

1-49 Let a, b, c, d, e, f, g and h be distinct elements in the set $\{-7, -5, -3, -2, 2, 4, 6, 13\}$. What is the minimum possible value of $(a+b+c+d)^2 + (e+f+g+h)^2 = ?$

[NTSE-2016 (Stage-I) Telangana]

(A) 30 (B) 32
(C) 34 (D) 40

1-50 A positive integer n has 60 divisors and $7n$ has 80 divisors what is the greatest integer k such that 7^k divides n?

[NTSE-2016 (Stage-I) Telangana]

(A) 0 (B) 1
(C) 2 (D) 3

1-51 What is the largest integer that is a divisor of $(n+1)(n+3)(n+5)(n+7)(n+9)$ for all positive even integers n? **[NTSE-2016 (Stage-I) Telangana]**

(A) 3 (B) 5
(C) 11 (D) 15

1-52 The sum of 18 consecutive positive integers is a perfect square. The smallest possible value of this sum is :

[NTSE-2016 (Stage-I) Telangana]

(A) 169 (B) 225
(C) 289 (D) 361

1-53 Let A, M and C be non-negative integers such that $A + M + C = 12$; what is the maximum value of AMC + AM + MC + CA?

[NTSE-2016 (Stage-I) Telangana]

(A) 112 (B) 62
(C) 72 (D) 92

1-54 $2^{3x} = 64^{-1}$ and $10y = 0.01$, then the value of $(50x)^{-1}(10y)^{-1}$ is : **[NTSE-2016 (Stage-I) Telangana]**

(A) 1 (B) -1
(C) 2 (D) -2

1-55 If $4^{18} - 1 = 687194a6735$, then the value of a is…

[NTSE-2016 (Stage-I) Telangana]

(A) 6 (B) 3
(C) 7 (D) 5

1-56 If $xyz + xy + xz + yz + x + y + z = 384$, where x, y, z are positive integers, then find the value of $x + y + z$:

[NTSE-2016 (Stage-I) Telangana]

(A) 20 (B) 17
(C) 25 (D) 15

1-57 If $x = (123456789)(76543211) + (23456789)^2$, then find the number of zeros in $\sqrt[4]{x}$? **[NTSE-2016 (Stage-I) Telangana]**

(A) 3 (B) 4
(C) 5 (D) 1

1-58 Express $1 - \frac{1}{1+\sqrt{3}} + \frac{1}{1-\sqrt{3}}$ in the form $a + b\sqrt{3}$, where a and b are rational numbers, then the values of a and b are …

[NTSE-2016 (Stage-I) Telangana]

(A) 1, 2 (B) 1, −1
(C) 3, 1 (D) 2, 1

1-59 The altitude of a triangle are 12, 15 and 20. What is the measure of the largest angle in this triangle?

[NTSE-2016 (Stage-I) Telangana]

(A) 90° (B) 60°
(C) 45° (D) 72°

1-60 If $(a+b+c+d+e+f+g+h+i)^2$ is expanded and simplified, how many different terms are in the final answer?

[NTSE-2016 (Stage-I) Telangana]

(A) 45 (B) 36
(C) 42 (D) 28

1-61 The G.C.D. of the numbers $2^{100} - 1$ and $2^{120} - 1$ is :

[NTSE-2016 (Stage-I) Telangana]

(A) $2^{60} - 1$ (B) $2^{20} - 1$
(C) 2^{20} (D) 2^{10}

1-62 The sum of the digits in $(10^{4n^2+8} + 1)^2$, where n is a positive integer, is : **[NTSE-2016 (Stage-I) Telangana]**

(A) 4 (B) $4n$
(C) $2 + 2n$ (D) $4n^2$

1-63 If 30, 72 and x are three integers, such that the product of any two of them is divisible by the third, then the least value of x is : **[NTSE-2016 (Stage-I) Telangana]**

(A) 45 (B) 60
(C) 48 (D) 24

1-64 Let a, b and c be real numbers, such that $a-7b+8c=4$ and $8a+4b-c=7$ then the value of $a^2-b^2+c^2=$ **[NTSE-2016 (Stage-I) Telangana]**

(A) -1 (B) 4
(C) -2 (D) 1

1-65 If $a<b<c<d<e$ are consecutive positive integers, such that $b+c+d$ is a perfect square and $a+b+c+d+e$ is a perfect cube. What is the smallest possible value of c? **[NTSE-2016 (Stage-I) Telangana]**

(A) 675 (B) 576
(C) 475 (D) 384

1-66 $3^9+3^{12}+3^{15}+3^n$ is a perfect cube, $n \in N$, then the value of $n = \ldots$ **[NTSE-2016 (Stage-I) Telangana]**

(A) 18 (B) 17
(C) 14 (D) 16

1-67 A four digit number has the following properties :
(i) It is a perfect square
(ii) Its first two digits are equal to each other
(ii) Its last two digits are equal to each other
Then the four digit number is… **[NTSE-2016 (Stage-I) Telangana]**

(A) 5566 (B) 7744
(C) 2288 (D) 3399

1-68 When 31513 and 34369 are divided by a certain three digit number, the remainders are equal, then the remainder is : **[NTSE-2017 (Stage-I) Andhra Pradesh]**

(A) 86 (B) 97
(C) 374 (D) 113

1-69 The greatest number of four digits which when divided by 3, 5, 7, 9 leaves the remainders 1, 3, 5, 7 respectively, is : **[NTSE-2017 (Stage-I) Andhra Pradesh]**

(A) 9763 (B) 6973
(C) 9367 (D) 9969

1-70 $efgh$ is a four digit number. One hundredth of $efgh$ is the mean of ef and gh, then the four digit number is : **[NTSE-2017 (Stage-I) Andhra Pradesh]**

(A) 3648 (B) 4950
(C) 4590 (D) 3468

1-71 If $(\sqrt[3]{2})^{12} \times (\sqrt{5})^8 = [(2\times 5)^2]^x$ then the value of x is : **[NTSE-2017 (Stage-I) Chandigarh]**

(A) 4 (B) 2
(C) 10 (D) 12

1-72 The sum of squares of two consecutive even numbers added by 4 is always divisible by : **[NTSE-2017 (Stage-I) Chandigarh]**

(A) 24 (B) 16
(C) 8 (D) 32

1-73 If $\dfrac{6^6+6^6+6^6+6^6+6^6+6^6}{2^6+2^6} \times \dfrac{5^6+5^6+5^6+5^6+5^6}{3^6+3^6+3^6} = 5^n$ then the value of n is … **[NTSE-2017 (Stage-I) Chandigarh]**

(A) 6 (B) 0
(C) 12 (D) 7

1-74 If $x^m . y^n = 7889$, where x and y are prime numbers, the value of $x+y$ is : **[NTSE-2017 (Stage-I) Chandigarh]**

(A) 30 (B) 60
(C) 100 (D) 300

1-75 If $a=\dfrac{p-q}{p+q}$, $b=\dfrac{q-r}{q+r}$, $c=\dfrac{r-p}{r+p}$, then the value of $\dfrac{(1+a)(1+b)(1+c)}{(1-a)(1-b)(1-c)}$ is … **[NTSE-2017 (Stage-I) Chandigarh]**

(A) 1 (B) 0
(C) 121 (D) 11

1-76 The value of $\dfrac{1}{1+\sqrt{2}}+\dfrac{1}{\sqrt{2}+\sqrt{3}}+\dfrac{1}{\sqrt{3}+\sqrt{4}}+\dfrac{1}{\sqrt{4}+\sqrt{5}}+\dfrac{1}{\sqrt{5}+\sqrt{6}}+\dfrac{1}{\sqrt{6}+\sqrt{7}}+\dfrac{1}{\sqrt{7}+\sqrt{8}}+\dfrac{1}{\sqrt{8}+\sqrt{9}}$ is : **[NTSE-2017 (Stage-I) Delhi]**

(A) 4 (B) 2
(C) 0 (D) 1

1-77 Divisor is 10 times of quotient and 10 times of remainder. If quotient is 10 then what is dividend ? **[NTSE-2017 (Stage-I) Delhi]**

(A) 1010 (B) 1100
(C) 1001 (D) 101

1-78 If n is a natural number then $9^{2n}-4^{2n}$ is always divisible by : **[NTSE-2017 (Stage-I) Delhi]**

(A) 13 (B) Both 5 and 13
(C) 5 (D) None of the above

1-79 If sum of LCM and HCF of two number is 50 and their LCM is 20 more than their HCF, then the product of two numbers will be : **[NTSE-2017 (Stage-I) Delhi]**

(A) 525 (B) 425
(C) 625 (D) 325

1-80 In how many ways 144 can be expressed as a product of it's two different factors ? **[NTSE-2017 (Stage-I) Goa]**

(A) 10 (B) 9
(C) 8 (D) 7

1-81 If both 5^2 and 3^3 are factors of $n \times 6^2 \times 7^3$, then what is the smallest possible value of n ? **[NTSE-2017 (Stage-I) Goa]**

(A) 75 (B) 65
(C) 55 (D) 45

1-82 If LCM of first 40 natural numbers is x, LCM of first 50 natural numbers is kx and LCM of $\frac{(k-27)}{10000}$ first Natural numbers is a kx then the value of a is : **[NTSE-2017 (Stage-I) Goa]**

(A) 59 (B) 53
(C) 47 (D) 61

1-83 0.235 is a — number : **[NTSE-2017 (Stage-I) Gujarat]**

(A) Natural (B) Integer
(C) Rational (D) Irrational

1-84 *G.C.D.* of 4 and 19 is — : **[NTSE-2017 (Stage-I) Gujarat]**

(A) 1 (B) 4
(C) 19 (D) 76

1-85 A number when divided by 5, 3 and 2 leaves remainders 4, 2 and 1 respectively. Find the total of all three digit such numbers : **[NTSE-2017 (Stage-I) Haryana]**

(A) 28 (B) 29
(C) 30 (D) 31

1-86 **Statement-I :** If $\sqrt{5+\sqrt{24}} = \sqrt{x}+\sqrt{y}$ then $x+y=5$ and $xy=24$.

Statement-II : Then square root of $(5-\sqrt{24})$ is $(\sqrt{3}-\sqrt{2})$: **[NTSE-2017 (Stage-I) Karnataka]**

(A) Both statement-I and II are wrong
(B) Statement-I is wrong, but statement-II is right
(C) Both statement-I and II are right
(D) Statement-I is right, but statement-II is wrong

1-87 Which rational expression should be added to $\frac{x-x^2+2}{x(x^2-1)}$ to get $\frac{x+1}{x^2-1}$? **[NTSE-2017 (Stage-I) Madhya Pradesh]**

(A) $\frac{x}{2}$ (B) $\frac{2}{x}$
(C) $2x$ (D) x^2

1-88 If $\sqrt{(0.04\times 0.4x)} = 0.4 \times 0.04\sqrt{y}$. Then the value of $\frac{x}{y}$ is : **[NTSE-2017 (Stage-I) Punjab]**

(A) 0.0016 (B) 0.16
(C) 0.016 (D) 1.6

1-89 If $x = \sqrt[3]{2\frac{93}{125}}$, then the value of x is : **[NTSE-2017 (Stage-I) Punjab]**

(A) $2\frac{1}{2}$ (B) $1\frac{2}{5}$
(C) $3\frac{4}{5}$ (D) $4\frac{1}{5}$

1-90 If $\frac{3+2\sqrt{3}}{3-\sqrt{3}} = a+\sqrt{3}b$, then the value of $\sqrt{a+b}$ where a and b are rational number is : **[NTSE-2017 (Stage-I) Rajasthan]**

(A) 5 (B) 8
(C) 2 (D) 16

1-91 Which is unit digit of $6^{18} - 5^{10}$? **[NTSE-2017 (Stage-I) Rajasthan]**

(A) 5 (B) 8
(C) 1 (D) 9

1-92 If $128 - 8^x = 2^6$, then the value of x is : **[NTSE-2017 (Stage-I) Tamilnadu]**

(A) 2 (B) –2
(C) $\frac{1}{2}$ (D) 4

1-93 Value of $\sqrt{10+\sqrt{25+\sqrt{121}}}$ in the following is : **[NTSE-2017 (Stage-I) Uttar Pradesh]**

(A) 5 (B) 3
(C) 4 (D) 6

1-94 x in the following is $\frac{\sqrt{a+x}+\sqrt{a-x}}{\sqrt{a+x}-\sqrt{a-x}} = b$: **[NTSE-2017 (Stage-I) Uttar Pradesh]**

(A) $\frac{2ab}{(b^2+1)}$ (B) $\frac{2ab}{a+b}$
(C) $\frac{a+b}{2ab}$ (D) $\frac{b^2+1}{2ab}$

1-95 If $5^p = 7^q = 35^{-r}$ then value of $\frac{1}{p}+\frac{1}{q}+\frac{1}{r}$ is : **[NTSE-2017 (Stage-I) Uttar Pradesh]**

(A) 1 (B) –1
(C) 0 (D) $\frac{2}{3}$

1-96 If $0.\overline{6} = \frac{p}{q}$ where p and q are relatively prime integers, then value of q is : **[NTSE-2017 (Stage-I) Uttar Pradesh]**

(A) 10 (B) 3
(C) 1 (D) 9

1-97 The *H.C.F.* and *L.C.M.* of two numbers are 12 and 240 respectively. If one of these numbers is 48 what the other number will be : **[NTSE-2017 (Stage-I) Uttrakhand]**

(A) 58 (B) 60
(C) 70 (D) 80

1-98 What least number must be added to each of the numbers 6, 15, 20 and 43 to make them proportional : **[NTSE-2017 (Stage-I) Uttrakhand]**

(A) 3 (B) 4
(C) 2 (D) 1

1-99 If $\sqrt{13-a\sqrt{10}}=\sqrt{8}+\sqrt{5}$ then value of '*a*' will be : **[NTSE-2017 (Stage-I) Uttrakhand]**

(A) -6 (B) -4
(C) -8 (D) -5

1-100 If $\frac{3^{2x-8}}{225}=\frac{5^3}{5^x}$ then the value of *x* will be : **[NTSE-2017 (Stage-I) Uttrakhand]**

(A) 4 (B) 2
(C) 5 (D) None of these

1-101 The identity $\sqrt{(x+4)^2}=x+4$ is possible, when : **[NTSE-2017 (Stage-I) West Bengal]**

(A) $x\le-4$ (B) $x\ge-4$
(C) $x\le-16$ (D) Not possible

1-102 The solution of the equation $9^x+6^x=2.4^x$: **[NTSE-2017 (Stage-I) West Bengal]**

(A) 0 (B) 1
(C) ±2 (D) -1

1-103 What is the smallest number which leaves the same remainder 1 on division by 18, 24, 30, 42 ? **[NTSE-2017 (Stage-I) Kerala]**

(A) 2519 (B) 2520
(C) 2521 (D) 2522

1-104 What is the sum of all factors of 256 ? **[NTSE-2017 (Stage-I) Kerala]**

(A) 511 (B) 512
(C) 1023 (D) 1024

1-105 The difference of the squares of two consecutive natural numbers is 101. What is the sum of the numbers ? **[NTSE-2017 (Stage-I) Kerala]**

(A) 102 (B) 101
(C) 100 (D) 99

1-106 The sum of two numbers is 40 and their difference is 10. What is their product ? **[NTSE-2017 (Stage-I) Kerala]**

(A) 325 (B) 350
(C) 375 (D) 400

1-107 The sum of two numbers and the difference of their squares are both 10. What is the larger of these two numbers ? **[NTSE-2017 (Stage-I) Kerala]**

(A) 4 (B) $4\frac{1}{2}$
(C) 5 (D) $5\frac{1}{2}$

1-108 Which of the following is not an irrational number : **[NTSE-2018 (Stage-I) Rajasthan]**

(A) $2+\sqrt{5}$ (B) $\sqrt{2}$
(C) $\frac{7}{\sqrt{5}}$ (D) $\frac{2\sqrt{11}}{7\sqrt{11}}$

1-109 The sum of the digits of a two-digit number is 14. If 18 is subtracted from the number, digits are reversed. Find the number : **[NTSE-2018 (Stage-I) Rajasthan]**

(A) 86 (B) 77
(C) 68 (D) 76

1-110 The multiplication of all prime numbers between 1 and 10 is : **[NTSE-2018 (Stage-I) Rajasthan]**

(A) 105 (B) 945
(C) 210 (D) 1890

1-111 A positive integer n when divided by 9, gives 7 as remainder. What will be the remainder when $(3n-1)$ is divided by 9 ? **[NTSE-2018 (Stage-I) Bihar]**

(A) 1 (B) 2
(C) 3 (D) 4

1-112 Which one of the following decimal expansion is not terminating : **[NTSE-2018 (Stage-I) Bihar]**

(A) $\frac{3}{8}$ (B) $\frac{6}{15}$
(C) $\frac{17}{512}$ (D) $\frac{29}{343}$

1-113 If $x:y=3:5$ and $x:z=5:7$, then what is $(y-z)(y+z)$ equal to : **[NTSE-2018 (Stage-I) Chandigarh]**

(A) 2/23 (B) 27/46
(C) 18/46 (D) 15/46

1-114 If a natural number '*a*' is divided by 7, the remainder is 5. If a natural number '*b*' is divided by 7, the remainder is 3. The remainder is 'r' if $a+b$ is divided by 7. Find the value of $\frac{3r+5}{4}$:

[NTSE-2018 (Stage-I) Chandigarh]

(A) 7 (B) 2
(C) 8 (D) 11

1-115 If $a:b=2:3$ and $x:y=3:4$, then $\frac{2ax-25by}{3ay+4bx}$ is :

[NTSE-2018 (Stage-I) Delhi]

(A) $\frac{24}{5}$ (B) $\frac{5}{24}$
(C) $-\frac{24}{5}$ (D) $\frac{12}{13}$

1-116 If x, y and z are positive real numbers and a, b and c are rational numbers, then value of

$$\frac{1}{1+x^{b-a}+x^{c-a}}+\frac{1}{1+x^{a-b}+x^{c-b}}+\frac{1}{1+x^{b-c}+x^{a-c}} \text{ is :}$$

[NTSE-2018 (Stage-I) Delhi]

(A) -1 (B) 1
(C) 0 (D) 2

1-117 If $\frac{1}{y+z}+\frac{1}{z+x}=\frac{2}{x+y}$, then what is the value of x^2+y^2 :

[NTSE-2018 (Stage-I) Delhi]

(A) 1 (B) $-2z^2$
(C) $2z^2$ (D) y^2+z^2

1-118 If $x^2=y+z$, $y^2=z+x$ and $z^2=x+y$, then what is the value of $\frac{1}{x+1}+\frac{1}{y+1}+\frac{1}{z+1}$?

[NTSE-2018 (Stage-I) Delhi]

(A) 1 (B) 0
(C) -1 (D) 2

1-119 The expression 14^m-6^m will always divisible by :

[NTSE-2018 (Stage-I) Delhi]

(A) 8 (B) 20
(C) 14 (D) 6

1-120 The supplementary angle of the complementary angle having measure 23 has measure____.

[NTSE-2018 (Stage-I) Gujarat]

(A) 67 (B) 90
(C) 113 (D) 23

1-121 If G.C.D of two numbers is 8 and their product is 384, then their L.C.M. is _____ : **[NTSE-2018 (Stage-I) Gujarat]**

(A) 24 (B) 16
(C) 32 (D) 48

1-122 If in a two digit number, the digit at unit place is y and the digit at tens place is 7, then the number is ___:

[NTSE-2018 (Stage-I) Gujarat]

(A) $70y+7$ (B) $y+7$
(C) $y+70$ (D) $10y+7$

1-123 $\frac{317}{3125}$ represents____ : **[NTSE-2018 (Stage-I) Gujarat]**

(A) A terminating decimal (B) A non-recurring decimal
(C) A recurring decimal (D) An Integer

1-124 The decimal expansion of the number $\frac{14588}{8750}$ will :

[NTSE-2018 (Stage-I) Haryana]

(A) Terminate after two decimal places
(B) Terminate after three decimal places
(C) Terminate after four decimal places
(D) Not terminate

1-125 The largest number which divides 72 and 127 leaving remainders 7 and 10 respectively is :

[NTSE-2018 (Stage-I) Haryana]

(A) 845 (B) 458
(C) 65 (D) 13

1-126 $8.3\overline{1}+0.\overline{6}+0.00\overline{2}$ is equal to :

[NTSE-2018 (Stage-I) Himachal Pradesh]

(A) $8.9\overline{12}$ (B) $8.\overline{912}$
(C) $8.9\overline{79}$ (D) $8.97\overline{9}$

1-127 The HCF of two numbers is 15 and their LCM is 225. If one of the numbers is 75, find the another number :

[NTSE-2018 (Stage-I) Jharkhand]

(A) 105 (B) 90
(C) 60 (D) 45

1-128 Simplify $6-[9\{18-(15-\overline{(12-9)})\}]$

[NTSE-2018 (Stage-I) Jharkhand]

(A) 1 (B) -4
(C) 5 (D) 3

1-129 The product of two numbers is 12960 and their HCF is 36. Number of pairs of such numbers that can be formed is :

[NTSE-2018 (Stage-I) Jharkhand]

(A) 2 (B) 3
(C) 6 (D) 5

1-130 The value of $\left(\sqrt[2010]{2\sqrt{7}-3\sqrt{3}}\right)\left(\sqrt[4020]{55+12\sqrt{21}}\right)$ is :

[NTSE-2018 (Stage-I) Karnataka]

(A) –1
(B) 0
(C) 1
(D) 2

1-131 Number r is termed as rational number if it can be expresses as $\frac{p}{q}$, where p and q are integers and :
[NTSE-2018 (Stage-I) Madhya Prasesh]

(A) $p=0$
(B) $p\neq 0$
(C) $q=0$
(D) $q\neq 0$

1-132 Product of any three consecutive even numbers is divisible by: **[NTSE-2018 (Stage-I) Madhya Prasesh]**

(A) 12
(B) 4
(C) 16
(D) All of these

1-133 Choose false statement from following :
[NTSE-2018 (Stage-I) Madhya Prasesh]

(A) All equilateral triangles are isosceles triangle
(B) Some rational numbers are integers
(C) All integers are not rational number
(D) Some Isosceles triangles are equilateral triangles

1-134 How many natural numbers between 15 to 500 when divided by 6 leave remainder 5 :
[NTSE-2018 (Stage-I) Maharashtra]

(A) 80
(B) 81
(C) 82
(D) 83

1-135 Read the following statements carefully and choose the correct alternative : **[NTSE-2018 (Stage-I) Maharashtra]**

(a) The ratio of the circumference of a circle to its diameter is denoted by the Greek letter π
(b) π is non terminating, recurring decimal fraction and its exact value is $\frac{22}{7}\left(\pi=\frac{22}{7}\right)$

(A) Statements a and b false
(B) Statements a and b correct
(C) Statements a correct but b false
(D) Statements a false but b correct

1-136 The value of $\left[9\left(\frac{1}{64^{\frac{-1}{3}}}+125^{\frac{1}{3}}\right)\right]^{\frac{1}{4}}$ is :
[NTSE-2018 (Stage-I) Tamil Nadu]

(A) 9
(B) 3
(C) 81
(D) $9\sqrt[4]{9}$

1-137 If $\sqrt{m}+\sqrt{n}-\sqrt{p}=0$, then the value of $(m+n-p)^2$ is :
[NTSE-2018 (Stage-I) Tamil Nadu]

(A) mn
(B) $-mn$
(C) $2mn$
(D) $4mn$

1-138 If the HCF of 55 and 22 is expressed in the form of $55m-22\times 2$ then the value of m is :
[NTSE-2018 (Stage-I) Tamil Nadu]

(A) 2
(B) 1
(C) 11
(D) 22

1-139 The remainder when x^n+n divided by $x-1$ is :
[NTSE-2018 (Stage-I) Tamil Nadu]

(A) n
(B) Cannot be determined
(C) $n+1$
(D) 0

1-140 Which of the following statement are not true :

(a) Sum of two irrational numbers always irrational
(b) Difference between two irrational numbers is irrational
(c) Product of two irrational numbers irrational
(d) Quotient of two irrational numbers is irrational

[NTSE-2018 (Stage-I) Tamil Nadu]

(A) a and b only
(B) a, b, c, and d
(C) a, b, and c only
(D) none of the above

1-141 If $10^{2017}-2017$ is expressed as integer, what is the sum of its digits : **[NTSE-2018 (Stage-I) Telangana]**

(A) 18, 144
(B) 17, 468
(C) 16, 466
(D) 18, 564

1-142 If $3^9+3^{12}+3^{15}+3^n$ is a perfect cube (of an integer) where $n\in N$, then find the value of n :
[NTSE-2018 (Stage-I) Telangana]

(A) 18
(B) 14
(C) 16
(D) 17

1-143 Compute $\frac{\text{L.C.M. of }(1,2,3......200)}{\text{L.C.M. of }(102,103,104......200)}$
[NTSE-2018 (Stage-I) Telangana]

(A) 101
(B) 106
(C) 184
(D) 176

1-144 If $x=\frac{1}{3-2\sqrt{2}}$ and $y=\frac{1}{3+2\sqrt{2}}$ then find the value of $x+y$: **[NTSE-2018 (Stage-I) Uttar Pradesh]**

(A) 3
(B) 0
(C) 6
(D) 1

1-145 If a and b are odd integers, then which of the following is an even integer : **[NTSE-2018 (Stage-I) Uttar Pradesh]**

(A) ab
(B) $2a+b$
(C) $ab+1$
(D) $a+2b$

1-146 The sum of $0.\overline{6}$ and $0.\overline{7}$ is :
[NTSE-2018 (Stage-I) Uttar Pradesh]

(A) $1.\overline{3}$
(B) 1.3
(C) $1.\overline{4}$
(D) an irrational number

1-147 Given a number $x = 2^{48} - 1$. Then between 5 and 10, x has/have : **[NTSE-2012 (Stage-II)]**

(A) no factor (B) only one factor
(C) two factors (D) three factors

1-148 Given two 4-digit numbers $abcd$ and $dcba$. If $a+d=b+c=7$, then their sum is not divisible by : **[NTSE-2012 (Stage-II)]**

(A) 7 (B) 11
(C) 101 (D) 111

1-149 Unit's digit of the number $3^{1001} \times 7^{1002} \times 13^{1003}$ is : **[NTSE-2012 (Stage-II)]**

(A) 1 (B) 3
(C) 7 (D) 9

1-150 If the square root of a number is between 6 and 7, then its cube root lies between : **[NTSE-2012 (Stage-II)]**

(A) 2 and 3 (B) 2.5 and 3
(C) 3 and 4 (D) 4 and 4.5

1-151 Which of the following is an irrational number? **[NTSE-2013 (Stage-II)]**

(A) $\sqrt{41616}$ (B) 23.232323
(C) $\frac{(1+\sqrt{3})^3-(1-\sqrt{3})^3}{\sqrt{3}}$ (D) 23.10100100010000...

1-152 Rs 1 and Rs 5 coins are available (as many required). Find the smallest payment which cannot be made by these coins, if not more than 5 coins are allowed : **[NTSE-2013 (Stage-II)]**

(A) 3 (B) 12
(C) 14 (D) 18

1-153 $\sqrt{(a-b)^2}+\sqrt{(b-a)^2}$ is : **[NTSE-2013 (Stage-II)]**

(A) Always zero
(B) Never zero
(C) Positive if and only if $a > b$
(D) Positive only if $a \neq b$

1-154 Which of the following numbers is the fourth power of a natural number? **[NTSE-2013 (Stage-II)]**

(A) 6765201 (B) 6765206
(C) 6765207 (D) 6765209

1-155 The square of an odd integer must be of the form : **[NTSE-2013 (Stage-II)]**

(A) $6n+1$
(B) $6n+3$
(C) $8n+1$
(D) $4n+1$ but may not be $8n+1$

1-156 Which of the number can be expressed as the sum of squares of two positive integers, as well three positive integers? **[NTSE-2014 (Stage-II)]**

(A) 75 (B) 192
(C) 250 (D) 100

1-157 The number of integers $n(< 20)$ for which $n^2 - 3n + 3$ is a perfect square is : **[NTSE-2014 (Stage-II)]**

(A) 0 (B) 1
(C) 2 (D) 3

1-158 For positive x and y, the LCM is 225 and HCF is 15. There : **[NTSE-2014 (Stage-II)]**

(A) is exactly one such pair
(B) are exactly two such pairs
(C) are exactly three such pairs
(D) are exactly four such pairs

1-159 The value of the expression $\frac{1}{\sqrt{11-2\sqrt{30}}}-\frac{3}{\sqrt{7-2\sqrt{10}}}-\frac{4}{\sqrt{8+4\sqrt{3}}}$ after simplification is : **[NTSE-2014 (Stage-II)]**

(A) $\sqrt{30}$ (B) $2\sqrt{10}$
(C) 1 (D) 0

1-160 On dividing a natural number by 13, the remainder is 3 and on dividing the same number by 21, the remainder is 11. If the number lies between 500 and 600, then the remainder on dividing the number by 19 is : **[NTSE-2015 (Stage-II)]**

(A) 4 (B) 6
(C) 9 (D) 13

1-161 Expressing $0.3\overline{4}+0.3\overline{4}$ as a single decimal, we get : **[NTSE-2015 (Stage-II)]**

(A) $0.6\overline{788}$ (B) $0.6\overline{89}$
(C) $0.6\overline{878}$ (D) $0.68\overline{7}$

1-162 The sum of all the possible remainders, which can be obtained when the cube of a natural number is divided by 9, is : **[NTSE-2016 (Stage-II)]**

(A) 5 (B) 6
(C) 8 (4) 9

1-163 On dividing 2272 as well as 875 by a 3-digit number N, we get the same remainder in each case. The sum of the digits of N is : **[NTSE-2016 (Stage-II)]**

(A) 10 (B) 11
(C) 12 (D) 13

1-164 Given that $\frac{1}{7} = 0.\overline{142857}$, which is a repeating decimal having six different digits. If x is the sum of such first three positive integers n such that $0.\overline{abcdef}$, where a, b, c, d, e and f are different digits, then the value of x is :

[NTSE-2017 (Stage-II)]

(A) 20 (B) 21

(C) 41 (D) 42

1-165 Which of the following digits is ruled out in the units place of $12^n + 1$ for every positive integer n ?

[NTSE-2017 (Stage-II)]

(A) 1 (B) 3

(C) 5 (D) 7

* * * * *

ANSWERS

PRACTICE EXERCISE-1.1

1	(A)	**2**	(B)	**3**	(C)
4	(A)	**5**	(C)	**6**	(B)
7	(B)	**8**	(B)	**9**	(B)
10	(C)	**11**	(A)	**12**	(A)
13	(B)	**14**	(D)	**15**	(B)
16	(D)	**17**	(A)	**18**	(D)
19	(D)	**20**	(A)	**21**	(D)
22	(C)	**23**	(B)	**24**	(A)
25	(C)	**26**	(D)	**27**	(C)
28	(B)	**29**	(D)	**30**	(D)
31	(A)	**32**	(D)	**33**	(B)
34	(C)	**35**	(C)	**36**	(C)
37	(A)	**38**	(D)	**39**	(B)
40	(D)	**41**	(B)	**42**	(A)
43	(B)	**44**	(D)	**45**	(B)
46	(D)	**47**	(D)	**48**	(C)
49	(D)	**50**	(C)		

PRACTICE EXERCISE-1.2

1	(A)	**2**	(C)	**3**	(C)
4	(A)	**5**	(D)	**6**	(D)
7	(C)	**8**	(B)	**9**	(C)
10	(C)	**11**	(B)	**12**	(D)
13	(D)	**14**	(D)	**15**	(B)
16	(C)	**17**	(D)	**18**	(C)
19	(A)	**20**	(C)	**21**	(C)
22	(C)	**23**	(D)	**24**	(D)
25	(C)				

PRACTICE EXERCISE-1.3

1	(B)	**2**	(C)	**3**	(A)
4	(D)	**5**	(B)	**6**	(B)
7	(D)	**8**	(A)	**9**	(C)
10	(A)	**11**	(D)	**12**	(B)
13	(D)	**14**	(D)	**15**	(B)
16	(D)	**17**	(B)	**18**	(C)
19	(D)	**20**	(C)	**21**	(A)
22	(B)	**23**	(A)	**24**	(B)
25	(D)	**26**	(D)	**27**	(D)
28	(B)	**29**	(D)	**30**	(B)
31	(C)	**32**	(B)	**33**	(C)
34	(D)	**35**	(B)	**36**	(B)
37	(D)	**38**	(A)	**39**	(B)
40	(C)	**41**	(B)	**42**	(A)
43	(B)	**44**	(D)	**45**	(C)
46	(A)	**47**	(C)	**48**	(D)
49	(C)	**50**	(C)	**51**	(D)
52	(B)	**53**	(A)	**54**	(B)
55	(C)	**56**	(A)	**57**	(B)
58	(B)	**59**	(A)	**60**	(A)
61	(B)	**62**	(A)	**63**	(B)
64	(D)	**65**	(A)	**66**	(C)
67	(B)	**68**	(B)	**69**	(A)
70	(B)	**71**	(B)	**72**	(C)
73	(D)	**74**	(A)	**75**	(A)
76	(B)	**77**	(A)	**78**	(B)
79	(A)	**80**	(D)	**81**	(A)
82	(B)	**83**	(C)	**84**	(A)
85	(C)	**86**	(B)	**87**	(B)
88	(C)	**89**	(B)	**90**	(C)
91	(C)	**92**	(A)	**93**	(C)
94	(A)	**95**	(C)	**96**	(B)
97	(B)	**98**	(A)	**99**	(B)
100	(C)	**101**	(B)	**102**	(A)
103	(C)	**104**	(A)	**105**	(B)
106	(C)	**107**	(D)	**108**	(D)
109	(A)	**110**	(C)	**111**	(B)
112	(D)	**113**	(A)	**114**	(B)
115	(C)	**116**	(B)	**117**	(C)
118	(A)	**119**	(A)	**120**	(C)
121	(D)	**122**	(C)	**123**	(A)
124	(C)	**125**	(D)	**126**	(D)
127	(D)	**128**	(C)	**129**	(A)
130	(C)	**131**	(D)	**132**	(D)
133	(C)	**134**	(B)	**135**	(C)
136	(B)	**137**	(D)	**138**	(B)
139	(C)	**140**	(B)	**141**	(A)
142	(B)	**143**	(A)	**144**	(C)
145	(C)	**146**	(C)	**147**	(C)
148	(D)	**149**	(D)	**150**	(C)
151	(D)	**152**	(C)	**153**	(D)
154	(A)	**155**	(C)	**156**	(C)
157	(C)	**158**	(B)	**159**	(D)
160	(A)	**161**	(D)	**162**	(D)
163	(A)	**164**	(C)	**165**	(A)

Solutions of PRACTICE EXERCISE-1.1

Sol. 1 (A) $5^{x-3}.3^{2x-8} = 225$

$\Rightarrow \quad 5^{x-3}.3^{2x-8} = 3^2 \times 5^2$

$\Rightarrow \quad \dfrac{5^{x-3}}{5^2} \times \dfrac{3^{2x-8}}{3^2} = 1$

$\Rightarrow \quad 5^{x-5} \times 3^{2x-8-2} = 1$

$\Rightarrow \quad 5^{x-5} \times 3^{2x-10} = 1$

$\Rightarrow \quad 5^{x-5} = 1$ and $3^{2x-10} = 1$

When $\quad 5^{x-5} = 1$

$\Rightarrow \quad x - 5 = 0$

$\Rightarrow \quad x = 5$

and when $\quad 3^{2x-10} = 1$

$\Rightarrow \quad 2x - 10 = 0$

$x = 5$

Hence Ans is (A)

Sol. 2 (B) Given

$x = 7 + 4\sqrt{3}$

$\Rightarrow \quad x = 4 + 3 + 4\sqrt{3}$

$\Rightarrow \quad x = 2^2 + (\sqrt{3})^2 + 2 \cdot 2\sqrt{3}$

$\Rightarrow \quad x = (2+\sqrt{3})^2$

$\Rightarrow \quad \sqrt{x} = 2+\sqrt{3}$

To find $\sqrt{x} + \dfrac{1}{\sqrt{x}}$

$= 2+\sqrt{3} + \dfrac{1}{2+\sqrt{3}}$

$= 2+\sqrt{3} + \dfrac{2-\sqrt{3}}{(2+\sqrt{3})(2-\sqrt{3})}$

$= 2+\sqrt{3} + \dfrac{2-\sqrt{3}}{4-3}$

$= 2+\sqrt{3} + 2-\sqrt{3}$

$=4$

Hence Ans is (B)

Sol. 3 (C) $\dfrac{1}{a+b} + \dfrac{1}{\frac{1}{a}+\frac{1}{b}} = \dfrac{1}{12}(1+ab)$

$\Rightarrow \quad \dfrac{1}{a+b} + \dfrac{ab}{a+b} = \dfrac{1}{12}(1+ab)$

$\Rightarrow \quad \dfrac{1+ab}{a+b} = \dfrac{1}{12}(1+ab)$

$\Rightarrow \quad a+b=12$

If $\quad a=0 \;\&\; b=12$

Maximum value

$0^2+12^2=144$

of a^2+b^2

Hence Ans is (C)

Sol. 4 (A) Let

$4^x = 3^y = 12^{-z} = k$

$\Rightarrow \quad 4^x = k;\; 3^y = k;\; 12^{-z} = k$

$\Rightarrow \quad 4 = k^{1/x};\; 3 = k^{1/y};\; 12 = k^{-1/z}$

We know $4\times 3=12$

$k^{1/x} \times k^{1/y} = k^{-1/z}$

$\Rightarrow \quad k^{\frac{1}{x}+\frac{1}{y}} = k^{\frac{-1}{z}}$

$\Rightarrow \quad \dfrac{1}{x}+\dfrac{1}{y} = \dfrac{-1}{z}$

$\Rightarrow \quad \dfrac{1}{x}+\dfrac{1}{y}+\dfrac{1}{z} = 0$

Hence Ans is (A)

Sol. 5 (C) Given

$x^{x^{3/2}} = x^{3x/2}$

$\Rightarrow \quad x^{3/2} = \dfrac{3x}{2}$

$\Rightarrow \quad x^3 = \dfrac{9x^2}{4}$

$\Rightarrow \quad x = \dfrac{9}{4}$

Hence Ans is (C)

Sol. 6 (B) For option (B) as the sum at $4+\sqrt{15}$ & $4-\sqrt{15}$ is a rational number.

Hence Ans is (B)

Sol. 7 (B) $\sqrt{n}$ is irrational if n is prime.

Hence Ans is (B)

Sol. 8 (B) Consider $p=5$ & $a=3, b=5$ and check all options

Hence Ans is (B)

Sol. 9 (B) Given $15q+7$

$\Rightarrow \quad 5(3q+1)+2$

$\Rightarrow \quad 5(m)+2 \qquad$ [when $m=3q+1$]

Hence Ans is (B)

Sol. 10 (C) Given $l=825$ cm, $b=675, h=450$

Size of the longest rod. Which can measure the dimension of the room is

HCF of(825, 675, 450)

Hence Ans is (C)

Sol. 11 (A) Use long division method of finding HCF

```
13) 99 (7
    91
    8) 13 (1
        8
       5) 8 (1
          5
          3
```

$|3-5| = |-2| = 2$

Hence Ans is (A)

Sol. 12 (A) HCF × LCM

= Product of two numbers

$\Rightarrow \quad 9696 \times \text{HCF} = 404\times 96$

$\Rightarrow \quad \text{HCF} = \dfrac{404\times 96}{96\times 101}$

$\text{HCF} = 4$

Hence Ans is (A)

Sol. 13 (B) Let the HCF of the numbers be x

Given LCM is 900

Then 1st Number $\equiv 9 \times x$

2nd Number $= 5 \times x$

So LCM $= 9 \times 5 \times x$

$\Rightarrow 9 \times 5 \times x = 900$

$x = 20$

HCF $= 20$

Hence Ans is (B)

Sol. 14 (D) HCF of (0.84, 07.2, 1.44)

HCF of $\left(\frac{84}{100}, \frac{72}{10}, \frac{144}{100}\right)$

HCF of fraction $= \frac{\text{HCF of numerator}}{\text{LCM of denominator}}$

$\Rightarrow \frac{\text{HCF of (84, 72, 144)}}{\text{LCM of (100, 10, 100)}} = \frac{12}{100}$

Hence Ans is (D)

Sol. 15 (B) Greatest number satisfying the given condition.

$=$ HCF of [(290 − 4), (460 − 5), (552 − 6)]

$=$ HCF of [286, 455, 546]

$= 13$

Hence Ans is (B)

Sol. 16 (D) LCM of two consecutive number is

$p(p+1)$

Hence Ans is (D)

Sol. 17 (A) They began toll simultaneously at the LCM of (6, 7, 8, 12) sec

$\Rightarrow$ 168 sec

2	6,7,8,12
2	3,7,4,6
2	3,7,2,3
3	3,7,1,3
7	1,7,1,7
	1,1,1,1

After every 168 sec they toll together

Hence Ans is (A)

Sol. 18 (D) The least number which is divisible by 3, 4, 5, 6, 8 is

The LCM of (3, 4, 5, 6, 8)

$2 \times 2 \times 2 \times 3 \times 5 = 120$

Now least perfect square will be

$\Rightarrow 2 \times 2 \times 2 \times 3 \times 5 \times (2 \times 3 \times 5) = 3600$

2	3,4,5,6,8
2	3,2,5,3,4
2	3,1,5,3,2
3	3,1,5,3,1
5	1,1,5,1,1
	1,1,1,1,1

Hence Ans is (D)

Sol. 19 (D) Take an example. You will see none of the rules followed

Hence Ans is (D)

Sol. 20 (A) By definition

Hence Ans is (A)

Sol. 21 (D) By definition

Hence Ans is (D)

Sol. 22 (C) Let

$A = 2^3 \times 3^2 \times 5$

$B = 2^2 \times 3^3 \times 5^2$

$C = 2^4 \times 3 \times 5^3 \times 7$

HCF of $A, B, C = 2^2 \times 3^1 \times 5 = 60$

Hence the Ans is (C)

Sol. 23 (B) Since HCF of coprime number is 1 hence

Hence Ans is (B)

Sol. 24 (A) HCF of (42m, 49m, 63m)

will be greatest length of the plank

$= 7m$

Hence Ans is (A)

Sol. 25 (C) Least number which is divisible by all 12, 18, 21, & 28 is LCM of (2, 18, 21, 28)

2	12,18,21,28
2	6,9,21,14
3	3,9,21,7
3	1,3,7,7
7	1,1,7,7
	1,1,1,1

$= 2 \times 2 \times 3 \times 3 \times 7$

$= 252$

Now greatest four digit number will be

$$\begin{array}{r} 252\overline{)9999}(39 \\ 756 \\ \hline 2439 \\ 2268 \\ \hline 171 \end{array}$$

So greatest 4 digit no which is divisible by

$$252 = (9999 - 171)$$
$$= 9828$$

Hence Ans is (C)

Sol. 26 (D) HCF of $(60, 84, 108) = 12$

Now minimum number of rooms

$$= \frac{60+84+108}{12} = 5+7+9$$
$$= 21$$

Hence Ans is (D)

Sol. 27 (C) Given

$$(\sqrt{2})^x + (\sqrt{3})^x = (\sqrt{13})^{\frac{x}{2}}$$
$$((2^2)^{1/2})^{x/2} + ((3^2)^{1/2})^{x/2} = (13)^{x/4}$$
$$(4)^{x/4} + (9)^{x/4} = (13)^{x/4}$$

Clearly $x = 4$ satisfies

Hence Ans is (C)

Sol. 28 (B) $\frac{2A}{3} = \frac{3B}{4} = \frac{5C}{6} = k$

$$A = \frac{3}{2}k \quad B = \frac{4}{3}k \quad C = \frac{6}{5}k$$
$$A:B:C = \frac{3}{2}k : \frac{4}{3}:k\frac{6}{5}k$$
$$= \frac{3}{2}:\frac{4}{3}:\frac{6}{5}$$
$$= 45:40:36$$

Hence Ans is (B)

Sol. 29 (D) Take p, q and r any three number satisfying the given condition and then check each option

Hence Ans is (D)

Sol. 30 (D) A number of the form

aaaaaa is always divisible by 7, 11 & 13

Hence Ans is (D)

Sol. 31 (A) It is obvious from the property of even and odd numbers that

$$(x^2 + x) + (y^2 - y)$$

is always an even number or you can take any two numbers and verify

Hence Ans is (A)

Sol. 32 (D) Let

$$x = \sqrt{1+\sqrt{1+\sqrt{1+\ldots}}}$$
$$\Rightarrow \quad x = \sqrt{1+x}$$

On squaring both sides we get

$$x^2 = 1 + x$$
$$\Rightarrow \quad x^2 - x - 1 = 0$$

Use quadratic formula

$$x = \frac{-(-1) \pm \sqrt{(-1)^2 - 4\times1\times-1}}{2}$$
$$= \frac{1\pm\sqrt{5}}{2}$$
$$= \frac{1+\sqrt{5}}{2}$$

Hence Ans is (D)

Sol. 33 (B) $x^n - a^n$ is divisible by $(x-a)$ if n is odd & $x^n - a^n$ is divisible by $(x+a)\,(x-a)$ if n is even

Hence Ans is (B)

Sol. 34 (C) Multiply both the side by 4

$$\Rightarrow \quad 4S = \left[\frac{1}{3\times7} + \frac{1}{7\times11} + \ldots + \frac{1}{99\times103}\right]$$
$$\Rightarrow \quad S = \frac{1}{4}\left[\frac{1}{3\times7} + \frac{1}{7\times11} + \frac{1}{11\times15} + \ldots \frac{1}{99\times103}\right]$$
$$\Rightarrow \quad S = \frac{1}{4}\left[\frac{4}{3\times7} + \frac{4}{7\times11} + \frac{4}{11\times15} + \ldots \frac{4}{99\times103}\right]$$
$$\Rightarrow \quad S = \frac{1}{4}\left[\frac{7-3}{7\times3} + \frac{11-7}{11\times7} + \frac{15-11}{11\times15} + \ldots \frac{103-99}{99\times103}\right]$$
$$\Rightarrow \quad S = \frac{1}{4}\left[\frac{1}{3} - \frac{1}{7} + \frac{1}{7} - \frac{1}{11} + \frac{1}{11} - \frac{1}{15} + \ldots \frac{1}{99} - \frac{1}{103}\right].$$
$$\Rightarrow \quad S = \frac{1}{4}\left[\frac{1}{3} - \frac{1}{103}\right] = \frac{25}{309}$$

Hence Ans is (C)

Sol. 35 (C) Let

$$S = \left(1+\frac{1}{2}\right)\left(1+\frac{1}{3}\right)\left(1+\frac{1}{4}\right)\ldots\left(1+\frac{1}{n}\right)$$
$$\Rightarrow \quad S = \frac{n+1}{2}$$

Hence Ans is (C)

Sol. 36 (C) Given product of tow numbers = 4107

& their HCF = 37

So numbers will be $37x$ & $37y$

$\Rightarrow \quad 37x \times 37y = 4107$

$\Rightarrow \quad xy = \frac{4107}{37 \times 37}$

$\Rightarrow \quad xy = 3$

$\Rightarrow \quad x = 3 \;\&\; y = 1$

or vice versa

So greater number will be

$= 37 \times 3$

$= 111$

Hence Ans is (C)

Sol. 37 (A) Let the number be

$a = 46 \quad b = 91 \quad \& c = 181$

they are leaving same remainder after dividing by the largest number

So then largest number is

HCF of $[(a \sim b), (b \sim c), (c \sim a)]$

HCF of $[(91 - 46), (181 - 91), (181 - 46)]$

HCF of $(45, 90, 135)$

$= 45$

Hence Ans is (D)

Sol. 38 (D) The required number will be of the form

$7k = \text{LCM of } (6, 9, 15, 18)\, m + 4$

$7k = 90m + 4$

LCM of (6, 9, 15, 18)

2	6,9,15,18
3	3,9,15,9
3	1,3,5,3
5	1,1,5,1
	1,1,1,1

put $m = 4$

to get a multiple of $7 = 364$

Hence Ans is (D)

Sol. 39 (B) As given in question number when divided by 18 leaves a remainder 7 &number when divided by 21 leaves a remainder 10 number when divided by 24 leaves a remainder 13. Here the difference between remainder & divisor is same in each case $(18 - 7 = 21 - 10 = 24 - 13 = 11)$

So least number will be

LCM of $(18, 21, 24)m - 11$

$\Rightarrow \quad 504m - 11$

LCM of 18, 21, 24 is

2	18,21,24
2	9,21,12
2	9,21,6
3	9,21,3
3	3,7,1
7	1,7,1
	1,1,1

As given the required number will be of the form

$504m - 11 = 23k$

$m = 6$

Satisfies the condition

Hence number is 3013

Hence the is (B)

Sol. 40 (D) 1st bell beep after every $\frac{1}{2}$ hour

2nd bell beep after very 1 hour

3rd bell beep after very $\frac{3}{2}$ hour

4th bell beep after very $\frac{7}{4}$ hour

All of them beep together after

$\text{LCM}\left(\frac{1}{2}, \frac{1}{1}, \frac{3}{2}, \frac{7}{4}\right) = 21 \text{ hour}$

$\Rightarrow$ Time will be 9 am

Hence Ans is (D)

Sol. 41 (B) $\sqrt{3 + 2\sqrt{2}} + \sqrt{3 - 2\sqrt{2}}$

$\sqrt{(\sqrt{2} + \sqrt{1})^2} + \sqrt{(\sqrt{2} - \sqrt{1})^2}$

$\sqrt{2} + \sqrt{1} + \sqrt{2} - \sqrt{1} = 2\sqrt{2}$

Hence Ans is (B)

Sol. 42 (A) The digits cyclicity of 3 & 7 is 4. So unit digit repeat after every 4 cycle

To find unit digit of $3^{1001} \times 7^{1002} \times (13)^{1003}$

$= 3^{1000} . 3^1 \times 7^{1000} \times 7^2 \times (3)^{1000} \times 3^3$

$= (3^4)^{250} \times (3^4)^{250} \times 3^1 \times 3^3 \times (7^4)^{250} \times 7^2$

$= (\ldots 1)^{250} (\ldots 1)^{250} \times 3 \times 27 \times (\ldots 1)^{250} \times 49$

$= 1 \times 3 \times 27 \times 49$ (consider only digit)

We get $1 \times 49 = 9$

Hence Ans is (A)

Sol. 43 (B) Let

$$x = \sqrt{11} - \sqrt{6} \;\&\; y = \sqrt{17} - \sqrt{12}$$

$$\frac{1}{x} = \frac{1}{\sqrt{11}-\sqrt{6}} \;\&\; \frac{1}{y} = \frac{1}{\sqrt{17}-\sqrt{12}}$$

$$\frac{1}{x} = \frac{\sqrt{11}+\sqrt{6}}{5} \;\&\; \frac{1}{y} = \frac{\sqrt{17}+\sqrt{12}}{5}$$

$$\Rightarrow \quad \frac{1}{y} > \frac{1}{x}$$

$$\Rightarrow \quad x > y$$

$$\Rightarrow \quad \sqrt{11} - \sqrt{6}$$

Hence Ans is (B)

Sol. 44 (D) Given LCM = 180

HCF = 6

Let the numbers be $6x$ & $6y$

$6x\,6y = 180 \times 6$

$xy = 30$ (x & y are co-prime)

$xy = 1 \times 30$ (so possible cases are)

$= 2 \times 15$

$= 3 \times 10$

$= 5 \times 6$

Hence Ans is (D)

Sol. 45 (B) Given $4^{61} + 4^{62} + 4^{63} + 4^{64}$

$= 4^{61}(1 + 4 + 4^2 + 4^3)$

$= 4^{61}(1 + 4 + 16 + 64)$

$= 4^{61}(85)$

$= 4^{60}.\,4(5 \times 17)$

$= 4^{60} \times 17 \times 20$

$\Rightarrow$ It is dividing by 10

Hence Ans is (B)

Sol. 46 (D) $(3 \times 5)^{12}\,(2 \times 7)^{10}$

$= 3^{12} \times 5^{12} \times 2^{10} \times 7^{10}$

Total no of prime factors are 4

Hence Ans is (D)

Sol. 47 (D) $5x + 11y$ is a prime no

Put $x = \text{odd}|_{\text{even}}$ & $y = \text{even}|_{\text{odd}}$ both value x & y can't be taken as odd or even then expression will be an even no.

Put $x = 2, y = 3$

$2 \times 5 + 3 \times 11 = 10 + 33 = 43$

So min value of $x + y = 5$

Hence Ans is (D)

Sol. 48 (C) By definition of irrational number, we can observe option (C) is the valid answer

Hence Ans is (C)

Sol. 49 (D) Any number of the for $3k$, $3k + 1$ or $3k + 2$ is divisible by 3

Hence Ans is (D)

Sol. 50 (C) Given

$$x = \frac{\sqrt{3}+1}{2}$$

$$\Rightarrow \quad 2x = \sqrt{3} + 1$$

$$\Rightarrow \quad 2x - 1 = \sqrt{3}$$

Squaring on both the sides, we get

$$(2x - 1)^2 = (\sqrt{3})^2$$

$$\Rightarrow \quad 4x^2 - 4x + 1 = 3$$

$$\Rightarrow \quad 4x^2 - 4x = 2$$

$$\Rightarrow \quad 2x^2 - 2x = 1$$

$$\Rightarrow \quad 2x^2 - 2x - 1 = 0 \qquad \ldots(1)$$

We have to find the value of

$$4x^3 + 2x^2 - 8x + 7$$

So

$$\begin{array}{r|l} & 2x+3 \\ 2x^2 - 2x - 1 & 4x^3 + 2x^2 - 8x + 7 \\ & -(4x^3 - 4x^2 - 2x) \\ \hline & 6x^2 - 6x + 7 \\ & -(6x^2 - 6x - 3) \\ \hline & 10 \end{array}$$

Now $4x^3 + 2x^2 - 8x + 7 = (2x^2 - 2x - 1) \times (2x + 3) + 10$

Using (1) $4x^3 + 2x^2 - 8x + 7 = 10$

Hence Ans is (C)

Solutions of PRACTICE EXERCISE-1.2

Sol. 1 (A) By property of even and odd numbers it is obvious that $(a^x + a)^x + (a^x - a)^x$ is even whatever be the value of a and x

Hence Ans is (A)

Sol. 2 (C) Let the two numbers be a & b

Given $\quad a - b = x \qquad \ldots(1)$

$a + b = 7x \qquad \ldots(2)$

$ab = 24x \qquad \ldots(3)$

$(1) + (2)$

$2a = 8x$

$\Rightarrow \quad a = 4x$

$\Rightarrow \quad b = 3x$

Using (3)

$$4x \times 3x = 24x$$

$\Rightarrow$ $x = 2$

So $ab = 24x = 24 \times 2 = 48$

Hence Ans is (C)

Sol. 3 (C) Using the property of even number $n(n^2 + 20)$ is always divisible by 48, if n is even number.

$\Rightarrow$ It will be divisible by 24

Hence Ans is (C)

Sol. 4 (A) Given 'n' is an odd number

Let $E = n^5 - n$

$= n(n^4 - 1)$

$= n(n^2 - 1)(n^2 + 1)$

$= (n - 1).n.(n + 1)(n^2 + 1)$

Now, by using property of odd & even we can say it is divisible by 120

Hence Ans is (A)

Sol. 5 (D) Let $x = 2m + 1, y = 2n + 1$

Then $x^2 - y^2$

$= (2m + 1)^2 - (2n + 1)^2$

$= 4m^2 + 1 + 4m - 4n^2 - 1 - 4n$

$= 4(m^2 - n^2) + 4(m - n)$

$= 4(m - n)(m + n) + 4(m - n)$

$= 4(m + n + 1)(m - n)$

If m and n are either both even or both odd, then $(m - n)$ is even and therefore divisible by 2.

If one of them (m or n) is even and the other is odd, then $(m + n + 1)$ is even and therefore divisible by 2.

Therefore $x^2 - y^2$ is always divisible by 8.

Hence Ans is (D)

Sol. 6 (D) Using property of even & odd we can say that $(x - y)$ is even

$(x + y)$ is even, $(x + y - z)$ is odd, and the product of even and odd numbers is always even.

Hence $(x - y)(y + z)(x + y - z)$ is even

Hence Ans is (D)

Sol. 7 (C) Let

$$R = \frac{7^{63}}{25}$$

$$= \frac{(7^2)^{31} \times 7}{25}$$

$$= \frac{(49)^{31} \times 7}{25}$$

$$= \frac{(50-1)^{31}}{25} \times 7$$

$$= \frac{(-1)^{31}}{25} \times 7$$

$$= \frac{-7}{25}$$

Hence remainder = 18

Hence Ans is (C)

Sol. 8 (B) Let

$$R = \frac{13^{55}}{85}$$

$$= \frac{(13^2)^{29} \times 13}{85}$$

$$= \frac{(169)^{27} \times 13}{85}$$

$$= \frac{(170-1)^{27} \times 13}{85}$$

$$= \frac{(-1)^{27} \times 13}{85}$$

$$= \frac{-13}{85}$$

$= 72$

Hence Ans is (B)

Sol. 9 (C) $x^2 + y^2 = 41$

$\Rightarrow$ $(x, y) = (4, 5), (5, 4);$

$x^2 + z^2 = 89$

$\Rightarrow$ $(x, z) = (5, 8), (8, 5); y^2 + z^2 = 80$

$\Rightarrow$ $(y, z) = (4, 8), (8, 4)$

All the three sets of solution

$\Rightarrow$ $(x, y, z) = (5, 4, 8)$

Hence Ans is (C)

Sol. 10 (C) Using even & odd number property or by taking on example we can verify all options

Hence Ans is (C)

Sol. 11 (B) Let us take

$N = 2468$

Given $M = 1.5\text{N}$

$$= \frac{3}{2}(2468) = 3702$$

$$P = \frac{1}{2}(8642)$$

$$= 4321$$

Now we have to go by option check (B)

$$\frac{N}{2} + P < 2N$$

$$1234 + 4321$$

$$\Rightarrow \quad < 4936$$

$$5555 < 4936$$

⇒ Not possible

Hence Ans is (B)

Sol. 12 (D) Here $a + b = 31$

⇒ $(a, b) = (16, 15), (14, 17), (13, 18), (12, 19),$

$(11, 20), (10, 21)$

We have to consider only for two-digit numbers.

Now $a^2 + b^2$ is divisible by 5

$(a, b) = (14, 17), (12, 19)$

Both are correct as $17 = 10 + 7$ (a prime number)

and $12 = 10 + 2$ (a prime number)

Hence Ans is (D)

Sol. 13 (D) Given,

$$z - x = 2(y - x) = 2(z - y)$$

$$\Rightarrow \quad y = \frac{z + x}{2}$$

⇒ y is the average of z and x

⇒ y lies exactly in the middle of z and x in the series (1, 2, 3, 4, 5, 6, 7, 8, 9)

Now, unit's digit of N^2 is 4

⇒ $z = 2$ or 8

or As we can't get further information about 'z' can't find x & y

Hence Ans is (D)

Sol. 14 (D) Here $A = 169$ and $B = 676$

($\because 26 = 2 \times 13$ or $\sqrt{B} = 2\sqrt{A}$ is satisfied only if $B = 676$ and not 576)

(3) is not true because $N = 169676$ is the only possible value.

$a = b = c = 6$

⇒ (1) is true and (4) is true

Hence Ans is (D)

Sol. 15 (B) Here $20 \times 21 \times 22 \times \ldots \times 30 = A$

When 2 is multiplied by 5 it gives zero.

In the above multiplication there are four 5's, two in 25 and one each in 20 and 30.

And more than four 2's.

⇒ There are 4 zeroes at the end of the product. Therefore maximum value of $x = 4$

Hence Ans is (B)

Sol. 16 (C) When we change all the terms in the powers of 2 and 5 we get $2^{22} \times 5^{16}$.

Power of 5 is less than that of 2. Thus it can be concluded that there will be 16 zeroes at the end of the result since 2 and 5 constitute zero when they are multiplied

Hence Ans is (C)

Sol. 17 (D) $(39)^{42} \times (27)^{23} \times (36)^{12}$

$$= [(39)^2]^{21} \times [(27)^4]^5 \times (27)^3 \times 36^{12}$$

$$= (\ldots 1) \times (\ldots 1) \times (\ldots 3) \times (\ldots 6) = (\ldots 8)$$

Hence Ans is (D)

Sol. 18 (C) Given to just multiply the unit's digit to get the unit's digit in the product

$$11 \times 13 \times 17 \times 19 \times 23 \times 29$$

We have

$$\Rightarrow \quad (\ldots 1) \times (\ldots 3) \times (\ldots 7) \times (\ldots 9) \times (\ldots 3) \times (\ldots 9)$$

$$= (\ldots 3)$$

Hence Ans is (C)

Sol. 19 (A) $(347)^{40}(347)^2 - (763219)^2 \times (53213)^4$

⇒ $(\ldots 1)^{10}(\ldots 9) - (\ldots 1) \times (\ldots 1)$

⇒ $9 - 1 = 8$

Hence Ans is (A)

Sol. 20 (C) Set S contains two prime numbers 3 and 7

Hence Ans is (C)

Sol. 21 (C) Let the number be of the form $3q + r$ then $0 \le r < 3$

If $N = 3q \quad \Rightarrow \quad N^3 = 3(9q^3) = 9m$

If $N = 3q + 1 \quad \Rightarrow \quad N^3 = (3q + 1)^3 = 9m + 1$

$N = 3q + 2 \quad \Rightarrow \quad N^3 = (3q + 2)^3 = 9m + 8$

Hence Ans is (C)

Sol. 22 (C) Given

$$a^m \cdot a^n = a^{mn}$$

We know $a^m a^n = a^{m+n}$

$\Rightarrow \quad mn = m + n$

$\Rightarrow \quad mn - m - n = 0$

$\Rightarrow \quad mn - m - n + 1 = 1$

$\Rightarrow \quad (m-1)(n-1) = 1$

$\Rightarrow$ either $\quad m - 1 = 1 \;\&\; n - 1 = 1$

$m = 2 \;\&\; n = 2$

or $\quad (m-1) = -1 \;\&\; (n-1) = -1$

$m = 0$

$n = 0$

Hence Ans is (C)

Sol. 23 (D) $a^x = b^y = c^z = k$

$a = (k)^{1/x} \quad b = (k)^{1/y} \quad c = (k)^{1/z}$

$\Rightarrow \quad b^2 = ac$

$\Rightarrow \quad (k)^{2/y} = (k)^{1/x}(k)^{1/z}$

$\Rightarrow \quad \frac{2}{y} = \frac{1}{x} + \frac{1}{z}$

$\Rightarrow \quad y = \frac{2xz}{x+z}$

Hence Ans is (D)

Sol. 24 (D) Let the numbers be x & y

given $x + y = 90$

& HCF is 6

$\Rightarrow$ $x = 6a$ & $y = 6b$ where a & b

arc co-prime

$\Rightarrow \quad 6a + 6b = 90$

$a + b = 15$ (a & b are co-prime)

possible values of a & b are

1, 14 √

2, 13 √

3, 12 ×

4, 11√

5, 10 ×

6, 9 ×

7, 8√

So 4 pair exists when n & 3 coprime

Hence Ans is (D)

Sol. 25 (C) Let number be a, b & c

Given $a + b + c = 100$ & $b = c + 36$

Since sum of three prime is an even number

then one has to be 2

$\Rightarrow \quad b + c = 98$

$\Rightarrow \quad c + 36 + c = 98$

$\Rightarrow \quad 2c = 98 - 36 = 62$

$c = 31, b = 67$

Hence Ans is (C)

Solutions of PRACTICE EXERCISE-1.3

Sol. 1 (B) Nearest perfect square to 540 is 529 hence minimum number of students left 540 – 529 = 11 students

Hence Ans is (B)

Sol. 2 (C) L.C.M = (4, 9, 10) = 2 × 2 × 5 × 3 × 3.

So that number is = 900

Hence Ans is (C)

Sol. 3 (A) Given

$$\frac{5^m}{5^{-3}} = 5^5$$

$$5^{m+3} = 5^5$$

$$m = 2$$

Hence Ans is (A)

Sol. 4 (D) Number will be a multiple of 9 if the sum of the digits of number is a multiple of 9

$2 + 1 + x + 5 \;\; = 8 + x$

hence least value of x which make $8 + x$ a multiple of 9 is 1

i.e. $x = 1$

Hence Ans is (D)

Sol. 5 (B) Given expression can be written as

$$\frac{2^n \times 3^n \times 5^n \times 3^{2n} \times 2^n}{2^n \times 3^n \times 2^n \times 3^{3n}}$$

$$\Rightarrow \left(\frac{5}{3}\right)^n$$

Hence Ans is (B)

Sol. 6 (B) Consider $\frac{5}{\sqrt{3} - \sqrt{5}} \times \frac{\sqrt{3} + \sqrt{5}}{\sqrt{3} + \sqrt{5}}$

$$= \frac{-5}{2}(\sqrt{3} + \sqrt{5})$$

Hence Ans is (B)

Sol. 7 (D) Consider

$$\frac{2^{100}}{2} = 2^{99}$$

Hence Ans is (D)

Sol. 8 (A) a & b are odd numbers so $a + b$ is even, so least prime factor of $a + b$ is 2

Hence Ans is (A)

Sol. 9 (C) Consider

$$\frac{1}{1+x^{b-a}+x^{c-a}} + \frac{1}{1+x^{a-b}+x^{c-b}} + \frac{1}{1+x^{c-b}+x^{a-c}} = \frac{x^a}{x^a+x^b+x^c} + \frac{c^b}{x^a+x^b+x^c} + \frac{c^x}{x^a+x^b+x^c} = 1$$

$$\Rightarrow \frac{x^a+x^b+x^c}{x^a+x^b+x^c} = 1$$

Hence Ans is (C)

Sol. 10 (A) Consider

$$x^{\frac{b-c}{bc}} \times x^{\frac{c-a}{ca}} \times x^{\frac{a-b}{ab}} = x^{\frac{b-c}{bc}+\frac{c-a}{ca}+\frac{a-b}{ab}}$$

$$= x^{\frac{ab-ac+bc-ab+ac-bc}{abc}} = x^{\frac{0}{abc}} = 1$$

Hence Ans is (A)

Sol. 11 (D) HCF of two prime number is always 1

Hence Ans is (D)

Sol. 12 (B) Total two digit numbers digit divisible by 5 are 10, 15, 20, 25, 30, 35, 40, 45, 50, 55, 60, 65, 70, 75, 80, 85, 90, 95

i.e. 18

Hence Ans is (B)

Sol. 13 (D) Given $\sqrt{5-2\sqrt{6}}$

$$= \pm(\sqrt{3}-\sqrt{2})$$

Hence Ans is (D)

Sol. 14 (D) Given $x = ay$

& $y = bx$

$$\Rightarrow x + y = (a+1)y$$

$$\Rightarrow \frac{1}{a+1} = \frac{y}{x+y}$$

Similarly $\frac{1}{b+1} = \frac{x}{x+y}$

$$\Rightarrow \frac{1}{a+1} + \frac{1}{b+1} = \frac{x+y}{x+y} = 1$$

Hence Ans is (D)

Sol. 15 (B) Given $2^{250}, 3^{200}, 4^{150}$ and 5^{100}

$$(2^5)^{50}, (3^4)^{50}, (4^3)^{50}, (5^2)^{50}$$

$$(32)^{50}, (81)^{50}, (64)^{50}, (25)^{50}$$

$\Rightarrow$ 3^{200} is greatest

Hence Ans is (B)

Sol. 16 (D) Given $a * b = (a + b - ab)$

$$\Rightarrow 4 * 5 + 5 * 6$$

$$(4+5-4\times 5)+(5+6-5\times 6)$$

$$20-50=-30$$

Hence Ans is (D)

Sol. 17 (B) L.C.M. of 12 & 42

2	12, 42
2	6, 21
3	3, 21
7	1, 7
	1, 1

L.C.M. of 12 & 42 $= 2 \times 2 \times 3 \times 7$

$$= 84$$

$$\Rightarrow 10m + 4 = 84$$

$$\Rightarrow m = 8$$

Hence Ans is (B)

Sol. 18 (C) Given $\sqrt{a^{-1}b} \times \sqrt{b^{-1}c} \times \sqrt{c^{-1}a}$

$$= \sqrt{\frac{\not{b}}{\not{a}} \times \frac{\not{c}}{\not{b}} \times \frac{\not{a}}{\not{c}}}$$

$$= \sqrt{1} = 1$$

Hence Ans is (C)

Sol. 19 (D) Let P be the number

$$P = 6q + 3$$

$$P^2 = (6q+3)^2$$

$$= 36q^2 + 36q + 9 = 36q^2 + 36q + 6 + 3$$

$$= 6(6q^2 + 6q + 1) + 3$$

$\Rightarrow$ Remainder $= 3$

Hence Ans is (D)

Sol. 20 (C) Given $\left(\frac{a}{b}\right)^{x-1} = \left(\frac{b}{a}\right)^{x-3}$

$$\Rightarrow \quad \left(\frac{a}{b}\right)^{x-1} = \left(\frac{a}{b}\right)^{3-x}$$

On comparing the exponent, as base is same

$$x-1=3-x$$

$$\Rightarrow \quad 2x=4$$

$$\Rightarrow \quad x=2$$

Hence Ans is (C)

Sol. 21 (A) Given $x^a = y$ ...(1)

$y^b = z$ ...(2)

$z^c = x$ ...(3)

Using equation-(2) in equation-(3)

$$\Rightarrow \quad (y^b)^c = x$$

$(y)^{bc} = x$ ...(4)

Now using equation-(1) in equation-(4)

$$\Rightarrow \quad (x^a)^{bc} = x$$

$$\Rightarrow \quad (x)^{abc} = x^1$$

$$\Rightarrow \quad abc = 1$$

Hence Ans is (A)

Sol. 22 (B) Given two numbers

$$\frac{1}{5}, \frac{1}{4}$$

In the options we have denominator 100 so convert the given number with denominator 100

$$\frac{20}{100}, \frac{25}{100}$$

Hence Ans is (B)

Sol. 23 (A) Given

$$\sqrt{10+\sqrt{25+\sqrt{108+\sqrt{154+\sqrt{225}}}}}$$

$$= \sqrt{10+\sqrt{25+\sqrt{108+\sqrt{154+15}}}}$$

$$= \sqrt{10+\sqrt{25+\sqrt{108+\sqrt{169}}}}$$

$$= \sqrt{10+\sqrt{25+\sqrt{108+13}}}$$

$$= \sqrt{10+\sqrt{25+\sqrt{121}}}$$

$$= \sqrt{10+\sqrt{25+11}}$$

$$= \sqrt{10+\sqrt{36}} = \sqrt{10+6} = \sqrt{16} = 4$$

Hence Ans is (A)

Sol. 24 (B) Given,

$$(m^4 n^4)^{1/2} \times (m^2 n^2)^{1/6} \times (m^2 n^2)^{1/3} = (mn)^k$$

$$\Rightarrow \quad m^2 n^2 \times m^{2/6}.n^{2/6} \times m^{2/3}.\ n^{2/3} = (mn)^k$$

$$\Rightarrow \quad m^2 n^2 \times m^{1/3}.\ n^{1/3}\ .\ m^{2/3}\ .\ n^{2/3} = (mn)^k$$

$$\Rightarrow \quad m^{2+\frac{1}{3}+\frac{2}{3}}.n^{2+\frac{1}{3}+\frac{2}{3}} = (mn)^k$$

$$\Rightarrow \quad m^3\ .\ n^3 = (mn)^k$$

Hence Ans is (B)

Sol. 25 (D) LCM of a^3b^2 & abc

LCM will be a^3b^2c

Hence Ans is (D)

Sol. 26 (D) GCD of (x^3-1) & (x^4-1)

We can write

$$x^3-1=(x-1)(x^2+x+1)$$

$$x^4-1=(x-1)(x+1)(x^2+1)$$

So GCD $= (x-1)$

Hence Ans is (D)

Sol. 27 (D) Given

$$F_1 = F_2 = 1$$

& $F_n = F_{n-1} + F_{n-2}$

$$F_3 = F_2 + F_1 = 1+1 = 2$$

$$F_4 = F_3 + F_2 = 2+1 = 3$$

$$F_5 = F_4 + F_3 = 3+2 = 5$$

Hence Ans is (D)

Sol. 28 (B) Given

$$\frac{32}{500} = \frac{2^3}{5^m}$$

$$\Rightarrow \quad \frac{8}{125} = \frac{2^3}{5^m}$$

$$\Rightarrow \quad 5^m = 125$$

$$\Rightarrow \quad 5^m = 5^3$$

$$\Rightarrow \quad m = 3$$

Hence Ans is (B)

Sol. 29 (D) Given

$$\frac{9}{y}+\frac{4}{x} = \frac{12}{\sqrt{xy}}$$

$$\Rightarrow \quad \frac{9}{y}+\frac{4}{x} = \frac{12}{\sqrt{xy}} = 0$$

$$\Rightarrow \quad \left(\frac{3}{\sqrt{y}}\right)^2 + \left(\frac{2}{\sqrt{x}}\right)^2 - \frac{12}{\sqrt{xy}} = 0$$

$$\Rightarrow \quad \left(\frac{3}{\sqrt{y}}-\frac{2}{\sqrt{x}}\right)^2 = 0$$

$$\Rightarrow \quad \frac{3}{\sqrt{y}}-\frac{2}{\sqrt{x}} = 0$$

$$\Rightarrow \quad 3\sqrt{x}-2\sqrt{y} = 0$$

Hence Ans is (D)

Sol. 30 (B) Given $0.\overline{24}$

Rational form is

$$\frac{24}{99}=\frac{8}{33}$$

Hence Ans is (B)

Sol. 31 (C) Given

$$P=\frac{x}{x+y}, Q=\frac{y}{x+y}$$

$$\frac{1}{P-Q}-\frac{2Q}{P^2-Q^2}=\frac{P+Q-2Q}{P^2-Q^2}=\frac{P-Q}{P^2-Q^2}$$

$$=\frac{1}{P+Q}=\frac{1}{\frac{x}{x+y}+\frac{y}{x+y}}$$

$$=\frac{1}{\frac{x+y}{x+y}}=1$$

Hence Ans is (C)

Sol. 32 (B) $2^m-2^{m-1}-4=0$

$$\Rightarrow \quad 2^m-\frac{1}{2}2^m=4$$

$$\Rightarrow \quad \frac{1}{2}2^m=4$$

$$\Rightarrow \quad 2^m=8$$

$$\Rightarrow \quad m=3$$

$$\Rightarrow \quad m^m=3^3=27$$

Hence Ans is (B)

Sol. 33 (C) On solving we get

$$a=2, b=1$$

$$2^{a^3-b^3}=128$$

Hence Ans is (C)

Sol. 34 (D) From the figure area of $\Delta POQ=\frac{\sqrt{3}}{4}r^2$

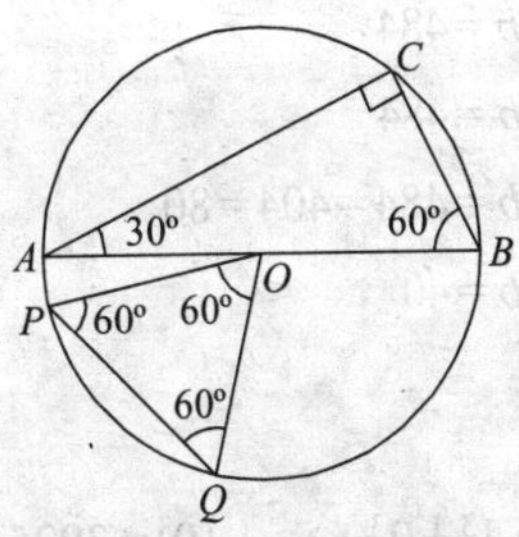

Area of $\Delta ACB=\frac{\sqrt{3}}{2}r^2$

$$\frac{\text{Area of } POQ}{\text{Area of } ACB}=\frac{1}{2}$$

Hence Ans is (D)

Sol. 35 (B) Let

$$A=\sqrt[3]{(x^{1/3})^3+(y^{1/3})^3+3x^{1/3}y^{1/3}(x^{1/3}+y^{1/3})}$$

$$=\sqrt[3]{\left[(x^{1/3})+(y^{1/3})\right]^3}$$

$$=(x)^{1/3}+(y)^{1/3}$$

Hence Ans is (B)

Sol. 36 (B) $0.\overline{23}+0.2\overline{3}$

$$=\frac{23}{99}+\frac{23-2}{90}$$

$$=\frac{23\times10}{99\times10}+\frac{21\times11}{90\times11}$$

$$=\frac{230+231}{990}$$

$$=0.4656565\ldots$$

$$=0.4\overline{65}$$

Hence Ans is (B)

Sol. 37 (D) Here the difference between remainder & divisor is same & is equal to 17

So the least number is

LCM of $(47, 72, 84)m-17$

$504m-17$

$$=504-17=487$$

Hence Ans is (D)

Sol. 38 (A) Let number be a & b

then as per question

$$a+b=22 \qquad \ldots(1)$$

& $$a^2+b^2=404 \qquad \ldots(2)$$

$$(a+b)^2=(22)^2$$

$\Rightarrow \quad a^2+b^2+2ab=484$

$\Rightarrow \quad 404+2ab=484$

$\Rightarrow \quad 2ab=484-404=80$

$\Rightarrow \quad ab=40$

Hence Ans is (A)

Sol. 39 (B) Given $1^3+2^3+\ldots+10^3=3025$ ...(1)

then consider $4+32+108+\ldots+4000$

$=4[1+8+27+\ldots+1000]$

$=4[1+2^3+3^3+\ldots+10^3]$

$=4\times 3025$ using (1)

$=12100$

Hence Ans is (B)

Sol. 40 (C) Given

$$x=9+2\sqrt{14}$$

$$\Rightarrow \sqrt{x}=\sqrt{9+2\sqrt{14}}$$

$$=\sqrt{(\sqrt{7})^2+(\sqrt{2})^2+2\sqrt{14}}$$

$$=\sqrt{7}+\sqrt{2}$$

Hence Ans is (C)

Sol. 41 (B) Given

$$\sqrt[3]{1-\frac{127}{343}}=\sqrt[3]{\frac{343-127}{343}}$$

$$=\sqrt[3]{\frac{216}{343}}$$

$$=\left(\frac{6}{7}\right)=1-\frac{1}{7}$$

Hence Ans is (B)

Sol. 42 (A) Given $2.\overline{6}-1.\overline{9}$

$=2+0.\overline{6}-1.\overline{9}$

$=2+0.\overline{6}-1-1$

$=0.\overline{6}$

Hence Ans is (A)

Sol. 43 (B) We need to find number of the form

$4x+3$

So first number be

$15, 19, 23, \ldots 299$

by A.P.

$T_n=a+(n-1)d$

$299=15+(n-1)\times 4$

$299-15=(n-1)\times 4$

$284=(n-1)\times 4$

$(n-1)=\frac{284}{4}=71$

$n=72$

Hence Ans is (B)

Sol. 44 (D) Hence Ans is (D)

Sol. 45 (C) Given

$$(-1)^n+(-1)^{4n}=0$$

$$\Rightarrow (-1)^n+(1)^n=0$$

This expansion will be zero if n is odd natural number

Hence Ans is (C)

Sol. 46 (A) Let number of x, y, z, t

Now given

$$x+y+z+t=125$$

Given $x+4=y-4=4z=\frac{t}{4}=k$

$\Rightarrow \quad x=k-4; y=k+4;$

$\Rightarrow \quad z=\frac{k}{4}\cdot t=4k$

So $k-4+k+4+\frac{k}{4}+4k=125$

$\Rightarrow \frac{1}{4}(8k+k+16k)=125$

$\Rightarrow k=20$

$\Rightarrow x=16, y=24, z=5; t=80$

Hence Ans is (A)

Sol. 47 (C) Given

$T_1\equiv 2005$

$T_2\equiv 2^3+0^3+0^3+5^3=8+125=133$

$T_3\equiv 1^3+3^3+3^3=55$

$T_4\equiv 5^3+5^3=125+125=250$

$T_5\equiv 133$

$T_6\equiv 55$

$T_7\equiv 250$

$\Rightarrow$ here is a cycle of 3 except 1st term.

So after dividing the term by 3 if we get 1 as a remainder the T_2 will be the term and if we get 2 as remainder then T_3 will be term & if we get 0 as remainder then T_4 will be term here we need to find the value of T_{2005} so we have to divide 2004 by 3 here we are getting 0 as remainder so answer will be T_4.

Hence 250 will be the 2005th term

Hence Ans is (C)

Sol. 48 (D) Given

$$4^{x_1}=5 \quad \ldots(1)$$
$$5^{x_2}=6 \quad \ldots(2)$$
$$6^{x_3}=7 \quad \ldots(3)$$
$$7^{x_4}=8 \quad \ldots(4)$$

$$127^{x_{124}}=128 \quad \ldots(A)$$

$\Rightarrow$ Using (1) & (2) we can have.

$$\Rightarrow \quad 6=(4)^{x_1x_2} \quad \ldots(5)$$

Using equation-(5) & equation-(3) & equation-(4)

$$8=(4)^{x_1x_2x_3x_4}$$

Similarly we can write

$$\Rightarrow \quad 128=(4)^{x_1x_2x_3\ldots x_{124}}$$
$$\Rightarrow \quad 2^7=(2)^{2x_1x_2x_3\ldots x_{124}}$$
$$\Rightarrow \quad 2(x_1,x_2,x_3\ldots x_{124})=7$$
$$\Rightarrow \quad x_1,x_2,x_3\ldots x_{124}=\frac{7}{2}$$

Hence Ans is (D)

Sol. 49 (C) Given

$a,b,c,d,e,f,g,h\in\{-7,-5,-3,-2,2,4,6,13\}$

to get

Let $E=(a+b+c+d)^2+(e+f+g+h)^2$

To find minimum value of E

Let $a+b+c+d=x \quad \ldots(1)$

Since $a+b+c+d+e+f+g+h=8$

$$\Rightarrow \quad e+f+g=8-h \quad \ldots(2)$$

$$E=x^2+(8-x)^2 \text{ [from (1) \& (2)]}$$
$$=x^2+64+x^2-16x$$
$$=2x^2-16x+64$$
$$=2x^2-16x+32+32$$
$$=2(x^2-8x+16)+32$$
$$=2(x-4)^2+32$$
$$\Rightarrow \quad E\geq 32$$

Hence Ans is (C)

Sol. 50 (C) Let $n=7^{k_1}\prod_{i=2}^{m}p_i^{k_i}$

Where p_i are the prime divisor of n then

$$7n=7^{k_1+1}\prod_{i=2}^{m}p_i^{k_i}$$

The number of factors of n is

$$(k_1+1)\prod_{i=2}^{m}(k_i+1)=60 \quad \ldots(1)$$

Then number of factors of $7n$ is

$$(k_1+2)\prod_{i=2}^{m}(k_i+1)=80 \quad \ldots(2)$$

Equation-(1) $\div$ equation-(2)

$$\frac{k_1+1}{k_1+2}=\frac{60}{80}=\frac{3}{4}$$
$$4(k_1+1)=3(k_1+2)$$
$$k_1=2$$

Hence Ans is (C)

Sol. 51 (D) Product of first 5 odd natural number is always divisible by 3 as well as 5

Hence Ans is (D)

Aliter

Product of first n odd natural number is

$$\frac{(2n)!}{2^n\cdot n!}$$

Here $\quad n=5$

$$\Rightarrow \quad \frac{10!}{2^5\times 5!}=\frac{10.9.8.7.6.5!}{32\times 5!}$$
$$=3.5.7.9$$

Clearly it is divisible by 15

Hence Ans is (D)

Sol. 52 (B) Let the number be

$$a,a+1,a+2,\ldots a+17$$

Now sum will be

$$=18a+(1+2+\ldots 17)$$
$$=18a+\frac{17\times 18}{2}$$
$$=18a+153 \quad \ldots(1)$$

Now the smallest value of a which make equation-(1) a perfect square will be at $a=4$

Hence Ans is (B)

Sol. 53 (A) If the sum is constant then product will be maximum when all are equal

$\Rightarrow$ Given $A+M+C=12$

$\Rightarrow$ $A=M=C=4$

So maximum value of

$$AMC+AM+MC+CA$$

$= (A+1)(M+1)(C+1) - (A+M+C) - 1$

$= 5 \times 5 \times 5 - 12 - 1$

$= 125 - 13$

$= 112$

Hence Ans is (A)

Sol. 54 (B) Given

$2^{3x} = (64)^{-1} \quad \& \quad 10y = 0.01$

$2^{3x} = 2^{-6} \quad \& \quad y = \dfrac{1}{1000}$

$3x = -6 \quad \& \quad y = 10^{-3}$

$x = -2$

$\Rightarrow (50x)^{-1}(10y)^{-1}$

$\Rightarrow (50 \times -2)^{-1}(10.10^{-3})^{-1}$

$\Rightarrow \dfrac{1}{-100} \times 100 = -1$

Hence Ans is (B)

Sol. 55 (C) Given $4^{18} - 1 = 687194a6735$

Since LHS is a multiple of 3 so RHS has to be.

Therefore sum of digit of RHS should be a multiple of 3

$56 + a$

So if $a = 7$ we get 63 as sum which is multiple of 3.

Hence Ans is (C)

Sol. 56 (A) Given $x, y, z \in I^+$

& $xyz + xy + yz + zx + x + y + z = 384$

Now

$xyz + xy + yz + zx + x + y + z = 1 = 385$

$(x+1)(y+1)(z+1) = 5 \times 11 \times 7$

$\Rightarrow x = 4 \quad y = 10 \;\&\; z = 6$

So sum of $x + y + z = 20$

Hence Ans is (A)

Sol. 57 (B) Given

$x = (123456789)(76543211) + (23456789)^2$

$x = (100000000 + 23456789)(76543211) + (23456789)^2$

Let $a = 23456789$

$x = (100000000 + a)(100000000 - a) + a^2$

$x = (10^8)^2 - a^2 + a^2$

$x = (10^8)^2$

$x = 10^{16}$

$\sqrt[4]{x} = (16^{15})^{1/4} = 10^4$

So number of zeroes will be 4

Hence Ans is (B)

Sol. 58 (B) Given

$$1 - \frac{1}{1+\sqrt{3}} + \frac{1}{1-\sqrt{3}} = a + b\sqrt{3}$$

$$1 - \frac{1}{(1+\sqrt{3})} \times \frac{(1-\sqrt{3})}{(1-\sqrt{3})} + \frac{1}{(1-\sqrt{3})} \times \frac{(1+\sqrt{3})}{(1+\sqrt{3})} = a + b\sqrt{3}$$

$$1 - \frac{(1-\sqrt{3})}{(1-3)} + \frac{(1+\sqrt{3})}{1-3} = a + b\sqrt{3}$$

$$1 + \frac{(1-\sqrt{3})}{2} - \frac{(1+\sqrt{3})}{2} = a + b\sqrt{3}$$

$$\frac{2 + (1-\sqrt{3}) - (1+\sqrt{3})}{2} = a + b\sqrt{3}$$

$$\frac{2 + 1 - \sqrt{3} - 1 - \sqrt{3}}{2} = a + b\sqrt{3}$$

$$\frac{2 - 2\sqrt{3}}{2} = a + b\sqrt{3}$$

$$1 - \sqrt{3} = a + b\sqrt{3}$$

$a = 1;\ b = -1$

Hence Ans is (B)

Sol. 59 (B)

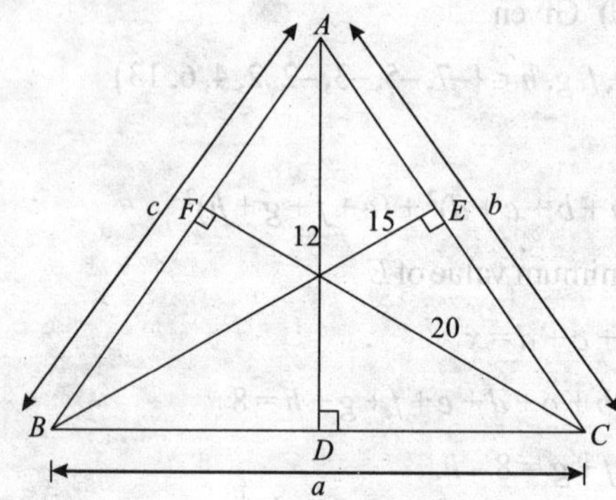

Given $AD = 12$

$BE = 15$

$CF = 20$

Now area of $\Delta = \dfrac{1}{2} a \times AD = \dfrac{1}{2} b \times BE$

$= \dfrac{1}{2} \times c \times CF$

$\Rightarrow \quad \dfrac{1}{2} a \times 12 = \dfrac{1}{2} \times b \times 15 = \dfrac{1}{2} \times c \times 20$

$\Rightarrow \quad 12a = 15b = 20c$

$\Rightarrow \quad \dfrac{9}{5} = \dfrac{b}{4} = \dfrac{c}{3}$

$\Rightarrow \quad a = 5k;\ c = 4k;\ c = 3k$

$\Rightarrow$ Δ is right angle Δ so largest angle $= 90°$

Hence Ans is (A)

Sol. 60 (A) $(a+b+c+d+e+f+g+h+i)^2$

$=(a+b+c+d+e+f+g+h+i)$

$\times(a+b+c+d+e+f+g+h+i)$

Now if a of first bracket multiply each term of second bracket, then we will get 9 different term similarly when b of first bracket multiply each term of second bracket we will get-8 term so this way we can have total number of terms as

$9+8+7+6+5+4+3+2+1=45$

Hence Ans is (A)

Sol. 61 (B) GCD of $(2^{100}-1)$ & $(2^{120}-1)$

$((2^{20})^5-1)$ & $[(2^{20})^6-1]$

Now we know that

x^n-a^n is divisible by $(x-a)$

if n is any positive integer.

$\Rightarrow$ GCD of $(2^{100}-1)$ & $(2^{120}-1)$ is $(2^{20}-1)$

Hence Ans is (B)

Sol. 62 (A) Given $(10^{4n^2+8}+1)^2$

$(10^{4n^2+8})^2+2.\,10^{4n^2+8}+(1)^2$

$10^{8n^2+16}+2.\,10^{4n^2+8}+1$

Now sum of digit $=1+2+1=4$

Hence Ans is (A)

Sol. 63 (B) Given 30, 72 and x

LCM $-$ 30, 72 = 360

HCF $-$ 30, 72 = 6

The third number = LCM/HCF = 360/6 = 60

$x=60$

Hence Ans is (B)

Sol. 64 (D) Given $a-7b+8c=4$

$8a+4b-c=7$

Consider $c=k$

$a-7b=4-8k$

$a=\dfrac{5k-13}{12},\ b=\dfrac{5-13k}{12}$

$$a^2-b^2+c^2=\left(\frac{5k-13}{12}\right)^2-\left(\frac{5-13k}{12}\right)^2+k^2$$

$=1$

Aliter : $a+8c=4+7b$ ...(1)

$8a-c=7-4b$ ...(2)

Equation-(1) & equation-(2) & then adding.

Hence Ans is (D)

Sol. 65 (A) $a<b<c<d<e$

$a=x-2,\ b=x-1,\ c=x,\ d=x+1,$

$e=x+2$

$b+c+d=$ perfect square

$3x=$ perfect square

$a+b+c+d+e=$ perfect cube

$5x=$ perfect cube

$x=675=5\times5\times3\times3\times3$

$3x=$ perfect square

$5x=$ perfect cube

Hence Ans is (A)

Sol. 66 (C) $3^9+3^{12}+3^{15}+3^n$

$=3^9(1+3^3+3^6+3^{n-9})$

$=3^9$ is a perfect cube

$=3^9(757+3^{n-9})$

If $n=14$

$\Rightarrow$ $3^{n-9}=3^{14-9}=3^5=243$

$\Rightarrow$ $757+243=1000$ is a perfect cube

$\Rightarrow$ $n=14$

Hence Ans is (C)

Sol. 67 (B) 7744 is a perfect square

$7744=(88)^2$

Hence Ans is (B)

Sol. 68 (B) When 31513 and 34369 are divided by a certain three digit number, the remainders are equal, then the remainder is

$34369=xp+r$ ...(1)

$31513=xq+r$ ...(2)

from (1) - (2) $x(p-q)=2856$ by prime factorization

$x(p-q)=119\,X24$

Since x is three digit number let $x=119$ which leaves reminder 97 when divides 34369, 31513.

Hence Ans is (B)

Sol. 69 (A) Let the greatest four digit number be 9999

LCM of (3, 5, 7, 9) = 315.

When 9999 divided by 315 it leaves reminder 234 hence $9999-234=9765$ is exactly divisible by 315.

Which means it is also divisible by 3, 5, 7, 9 exactly but given the number leaves reminders 1, 3, 5, 7 when divided by 3, 5, 7, 9 difference between reminder and divisor = 2,

So required number = 9765 − 2 = 9763

Hence Ans is (A)

Sol. 70 (B) $\frac{efgh}{100} = \frac{ef+gh}{2}$ from given options $efgh = 4950$ then condition satisfied.

Hence Ans is (B)

Sol. 71 (B) $(\sqrt[3]{2})^{12} \times (\sqrt{5})^8 = [(2\times 5)^2]^x$

$\Rightarrow \quad (2^{1/3})^{12} \times (5^{1/2})^8 = [(2\times 5)^2]^x$

$\Rightarrow \quad 2^{12/3} \times 5^{8/2} = (2\times 5)^{2x}$ [using $(a^m)^n = a^{mn}$]

$\Rightarrow \quad 2^4 \times 5^4 = (2\times 5)^{2x}$

$\Rightarrow \quad 4 = 2x$

$\Rightarrow \quad x = 2$

Hence Ans is (B)

Sol. 72 (C) Let the two consecutive even numbers be $2n$ and $(2n+2)$ for some integer

$$(2n)^2 + (2n+2)^2 + 4$$
$$= 4n^2 + 4n^2 + 8n + 4 + 4$$
$$= 8n^2 + 8n + 8$$
$$= 8(n^2 + n + 1)$$

Thus always divisible by 8

Hence Ans is (C)

Sol. 73 (D) $\frac{6^6+6^6+6^6+6^6+6^6+6^6}{2^6+2^6} \times \frac{5^6+5^6+5^6+5^6+5^6}{3^6+3^6+3^6} = 5^n$

$\Rightarrow \quad \frac{6(6^6)}{2(2^6)} \times \frac{5(5^6)}{3(3^6)} = 5^n$

$\Rightarrow \quad \frac{6^7 \times 5^7}{2^7 \times 3^7} = 5^n$

$\Rightarrow \quad 5^7 = 5^n$

$\Rightarrow \quad n = 7$

Hence Ans is (D)

Sol. 74 (A) $x^m . y^n = 7889$

$x^m . y^n = 7^3 \times 23^1$

$\Rightarrow$ x and y are 7 and 23

Thus $x + y = 30$

Hence Ans is (A)

Sol. 75 (A) $a = \frac{p-q}{p+q}$

Thus $\frac{1+a}{1-a} = \frac{1+\frac{p-q}{p+q}}{1-\frac{p-q}{p+q}}$

$\Rightarrow \quad \frac{1+a}{1-a} = \frac{\frac{2p}{p+q}}{\frac{2q}{p+q}} = \frac{p}{q}$

Similarly $\frac{1+b}{1-b} = \frac{q}{r}, \frac{1+c}{1-c} = \frac{r}{p}$

$\Rightarrow \quad \left(\frac{(1+a)(1+b)(1+c)}{(1-a)(1-b)(1-c)}\right) = \frac{p}{q} \times \frac{q}{r} \times \frac{r}{p} = 1$

Hence Ans is (A)

Sol. 76 (B) $\frac{1}{\sqrt{2}+1} + \frac{1}{\sqrt{3}+\sqrt{2}} + \frac{1}{\sqrt{4}+\sqrt{3}} + \ldots \frac{1}{\sqrt{9}+\sqrt{8}}$

$\sqrt{2} - 1 + \sqrt{3} - \sqrt{2} + \sqrt{4} - \sqrt{3} + \ldots$

$\sqrt{8} - \sqrt{7} + \sqrt{9} - \sqrt{8}$

$= \sqrt{9} - 1 = 2$

Hence Ans is (B)

Sol. 77 (A) Divisor = $10Q$

Divisor = $10R$

$Q = 10$

Divisor = 100

$R = 10$

Dividend = $100 \times 10 + 10 = 1010$

Hence Ans is (A)

Sol. 78 (B) $9^{2n} - 4^{2n}$

$81^n - 16^n$

$\Rightarrow$ $a^n - b^n$ is always divisible by $(a-b)$

$(81 - 16) = 65$

$\Rightarrow$ So factors of 65 are 5 and 13

Hence Ans is (B)

Sol. 79 (A) LCM + HCF = 50

LCM = HCF + 20

HCF + 20 + HCF = 50

2HCF = 30

HCF = 15

$\Rightarrow$ LCM = 35

$\Rightarrow$ Product of two numbers $= 35 \times 15 = 525$

Hence Ans is (A)

Sol. 80 (D) $xy = 144 = 2^4 \times 3^2$

Total number of factors $= (4+1)(2+1) = 15$

Number of way in which 144 can be expressed as of product of two of its distinct factor $= \frac{15-1}{2}$

Hence Ans is (D)

Sol. 81 (A) If 5^2 and 3^3 are factors, then number be

$5^2 \times 3^2 \times \ldots$

But 3^2 be present in $n \times 3^2 \times 2^2 \times 7^3$

Factor missing $5^2 \times 3 = 25 \times 3 = 75$

So minimum value of $n = 75$

Hence Ans is (A)

Sol. 82 (B)

LCM of first 40 naturals $= x$

LCM of first 50 naturals $= x \times 41 \times 43 \times 47 \times 7 = kx$

Hence, $k = 580027$

Therefore $(k-27)/10000 = 58$

Hence, $a = 53$

Hence Ans is (B)

Sol. 83 (C) $0.235 = \frac{235}{1000}$

Hence Ans is (C)

Sol. 84 (A) 4 & 19 are co-prime

Hence Ans is (A)

Sol. 85 (C) Here $x_1 = 5k_1 + 4, x_2 = 3k_2 + 2, x_3 = 2k_3 + 1$

The smallest such number

$= 1\,\text{cm}$ or $(5, 3, 2)\,m - 1$

$\Rightarrow 30\text{m} - 1$

So smallest three digit such number will be

$30 \times 4 - 1 = 119$

These numbers forms *AP*. Whose common differences is l cm

$(5, 3, 2)$ i.e. 30

First term is 119 (By observation) then *AP* will be

$119, 149, 179, \ldots (a_n)$

$a_n \leq 999$

$a + (n-1)d \leq 999$

$119 + (n-1)30 \leq 999$

$n = 30$

Hence total such numbers = 30

Hence Ans is (C)

Sol. 86 (B) $\sqrt{5+\sqrt{24}} = \sqrt{x} + \sqrt{y}$

$\Rightarrow \sqrt{5+2\sqrt{6}} = \sqrt{x} + \sqrt{y}$

$\Rightarrow \sqrt{3} + \sqrt{2} = \sqrt{x} + \sqrt{y}$

$x = 3 \quad y = 2$

$x + y = 3 + 2 = 5$

$xy = 3.2 = 6$

Statement-I is false; statement-II is true.

Hence Ans is (B)

Sol. 87 (B) Let $\frac{x - x^2 + 2}{x(x^2-1)} + K = \frac{x+1}{x^2-1}$

$$K = \frac{x+1}{x^2-1} - \frac{x - x^2 + 2}{x(x^2-1)}$$

$$= \frac{x^2 + x - x + x^2 - 2}{x(x^2-1)}$$

$$= \frac{2x^2 - 2}{x(x^2-1)}$$

Hence Ans is (B)

Sol. 88 (C) $\sqrt{0.04 \times 0.4x} = 0.4 \times 0.04\sqrt{y}$

Squaring both sides

$0.04 \times 0.4x = (0.4)^2 \times (0.04)^2 \times y$

$\frac{x}{y} = 0.4 \times 0.04 = 0.016$

Hence Ans is (C)

Sol. 89 (B) $x = \sqrt[3]{2\frac{93}{125}} = \sqrt[3]{2 + \frac{93}{125}} = \sqrt[3]{\frac{343}{125}}$

$$x = \sqrt[3]{\frac{7^3}{5^3}} = \frac{7}{5} = 1\frac{2}{5}$$

Hence Ans is (B)

Sol. 90 (C) $\frac{3+2\sqrt{3}}{3-\sqrt{3}} \times \frac{3+\sqrt{3}}{3+\sqrt{3}} = \frac{(3+2\sqrt{3})(3+\sqrt{3})}{9-3}$

$$= \frac{9+6\sqrt{3}+3\sqrt{3}+6}{6}$$

$$= \frac{15+9\sqrt{3}}{6}$$

$$= \frac{15}{6} + \frac{9}{6}\sqrt{3}$$

$$= \frac{5}{2} + \frac{3}{2}\sqrt{3}$$

$$a = \frac{5}{2}, b = \frac{3}{2}$$

$$\sqrt{a+b} = \sqrt{\frac{5}{2}+\frac{3}{2}}$$

$$= \sqrt{\frac{8}{2}} = \sqrt{4} = 2$$

Hence Ans is (C)

Sol. 91 (C) $6^{18} \downarrow \quad 5^{10} \downarrow$

$6 - 5 = ①$

Hence Ans is (C)

Sol. 92 (A) $128 - 64 = 8^x$

$64 = 8^x$

$2 = x$

Hence Ans is (A)

Sol. 93 (C) $\sqrt{10+\sqrt{25+\sqrt{121}}} = \sqrt{10+\sqrt{25+11}}$

$= \sqrt{10+\sqrt{36}}$

$= \sqrt{10+6} = 4$

Hence Ans is (C)

Sol. 94 (A) Given $\dfrac{\sqrt{a+x}+\sqrt{a-x}}{\sqrt{a+x}-\sqrt{a-x}} = \dfrac{b}{1}$

Apply Componendo and Dividendo

$$\Rightarrow \frac{\sqrt{a+x}}{\sqrt{a-x}} = \frac{b+1}{b-1}$$

$$\Rightarrow \frac{a+x}{a-x} = \frac{(b+1)^2}{(b-1)^2}$$

Again Apply Componendo and Dividendo

$$\Rightarrow \frac{a}{x} = \frac{(b^2+1)}{2b} \Rightarrow x = \frac{2ab}{(b^2+1)}$$

Hence Ans is (A)

Sol. 95 (C) $5^p = 7^q = 35^{-r} = k \Rightarrow 5 = k^{\frac{1}{p}}$

$\Rightarrow 7 = k^{\frac{1}{q}} \Rightarrow 35 = k^{\frac{1}{r}}$

Since $35 = 5 \times 7$

$$k^{\frac{-1}{r}} = k^{\frac{1}{p}} \cdot k^{\frac{1}{q}}$$

$$k^{\frac{-1}{r}} = k^{\frac{1}{p}+\frac{1}{q}}$$

$$\frac{1}{p} + \frac{1}{q} + \frac{1}{r} = 0$$

Hence Ans is (C)

Sol. 96 (B) $0.\bar{6} = \dfrac{p}{q}$

Clearly, $\dfrac{p}{q} = \dfrac{2}{3}$

$\Rightarrow \quad q = 3$

Hence Ans is (B)

Sol. 97 (B) H.C.F. of two numbers = 12

L.C.M of two numbers = 240

One number = 48

LCM × HCF = Product of two number

Let the second number be x

$12 \times 240 = 48 \times (x)$

$x = 60$

Hence Ans is (B)

Sol. 98 (A) Let number added be x

$$\Rightarrow \frac{6+x}{15+x} = \frac{20+x}{43+x}$$

$(6+x)(43+x) = (15+x)(20+x)$

$258 + 6x + 43x + x^2 = 300 + 15x + 20x + x^2$

$14x = 42$

$x = 3$

Hence Ans is (A)

Sol. 99 (B) $\sqrt{13 - a\sqrt{10}} = \sqrt{8} + \sqrt{5}$

on squaring both sides we get

$13 - a\sqrt{10} = 8 + 5 + 2\sqrt{40}$

$\Rightarrow \quad -a\sqrt{10} = 2\sqrt{40}$

$-a\sqrt{10} = 2 \times 2\sqrt{10}$

$\Rightarrow \quad a = -4$

Hence Ans is (B)

Sol. 100 (C) $\frac{3^{2x-8}}{225} = \frac{5^3}{5^x}$

$3^{2x-8}.5^x = 5^3.(225)$

$3^{2x-8}.5^x = 5^3.3^2.5^2$ $[225 = 3^2.5^2]$

$3^{2x-8}.5^x = 5^5 3^2$

On comparing both sides

$\Rightarrow$ $2x - 8 = 2$

$2x = 10$

$x = 5$

Hence Ans is (C)

Sol. 101 (B) $x \geq -4$, since square root of a number is always non-negative

Hence Ans is (B)

Sol. 102 (A) Let $3^x = p, 2^x = q$

$\Rightarrow$ $9^x + 6^x = 2.4^x$

$\Rightarrow$ $p^2 + pq = 2q^2$

$\Rightarrow$ $(p-q)(p+2q) = 0$

$\Rightarrow$ $p - q = 0$ $[p \neq -2q]$

$\Rightarrow$ $3^x - 2^x = 0$

$\Rightarrow$ $x = 0$

Hence Ans is (A)

Sol. 103 (C) L.C.M. of $(18, 24, 30, 42)\, m + 1$

$2520\, m + 1$

$= 2521$

Hence Ans is (C)

Sol. 104 (A) $256 \equiv 2^8$

Sum of all factor of 256

$= \frac{2^9 - 1}{2 - 1} = 511$

Hence Ans is (A)

Sol. 105 (B) Let the number be x & $(x + 1)$

given $(x+1)^2 - x^2 = 101$

$(x + 1 - x)(x + 1 + x) = 101$

$2x + 1 = 101$

Hence Ans is (B)

Sol. 106 (C) Let two number be a & b

given $a + b = 40$ & $a - b = 10$

We know $4ab = (a+b)^2 - (a-b)^2$

$= (42)^2 - (10)^2$

$= 50 \times 30$

$4ab = 1500$

$ab = \frac{1500}{4}$

$ab = 375$

Hence Ans is (C)

Sol. 107 (D) Let number be a & b

given $a + b = 10$

& $a^2 - b^2 = 10$

$\Rightarrow$ $(a-b)(a+b) = 10$

$\Rightarrow$ $(a - b) = 1$ ...(1)

& $a + b = 10$ ...(2)

Adding (1) & (2)

$2a = 11$

$a = \frac{11}{2} = 5\frac{1}{2}$

Hence Ans is (D)

Sol. 108 (D) $\frac{2\sqrt{11}}{7\sqrt{11}} \Rightarrow \frac{2}{7}$ = Rational number

Hence Ans is (D)

Sol. 109 (A) Let the unit digit be x

Ten's digit $= 14 - x$

Number $= 10\,(14 - x) + x$

So, $10\,(14 - x) + x - 18 = 10x + (14 - x)$

$\Rightarrow$ $140 - 9x - 18 = 9x + 14$

$\Rightarrow$ $140 - 14 - 18 = 18x$

$\Rightarrow$ $126 - 18 = 18x$

$\Rightarrow$ $x = 6$

$14 - x = 8$

So, Number $= 86$

Hence Ans is (A)

Sol. 110 (C) $2 \times 3 \times 5 \times 7 = 210$

Hence Ans is (C)

Sol. 111 (B) Given a positive integer n is divided by 9 gives 7 as the remainder

Let a be quotient

$n = 9a + 7$

$(3n - 1) = 3\,(9a + 7) - 1$

$= 27a + 20$

$\Rightarrow \quad 27a+18+2$

$\Rightarrow \quad 9(3a+6)+2$

When divided by 9 remainder will be 2

Hence Ans is (B)

Sol. 112 (D) $\dfrac{29}{343}$

For termination, denominator must be in the form of $2^n \times 5^m$

Hence Ans is (D)

Sol. 113 (A) Let $x=3a,\ y=5a$

$$x:z=3a:z=5:7$$

$$\frac{3a}{z}=\frac{5}{7},z=\frac{21a}{5}$$

$$\frac{y-z}{y+z}=\frac{5a-\frac{21a}{5}}{5a+\frac{21a}{5}}=\frac{4}{46}=\frac{2}{23}$$

Hence Ans is (A)

Sol. 114 (B) $a=7k_1+5$

$$b=7k_2+3$$

$$a+b=7(k_1+k_2)+8$$

$$=7(k_1+k_2)+7+1$$

$$=7(k_1+k_2+1)+1$$

$\Rightarrow \quad r=1$

So, $\dfrac{3r+5}{4}=\dfrac{3+5}{4}=2$

Hence Ans is (B)

Sol. 115 (C) Let

$a=2k \qquad x=3p$

$b=3k \qquad y=4p$

$$\frac{2ax-25by}{3ay+4bx}$$

$$\frac{2.2k.3p-25.3k.4p}{3.2k.4p+4.3k.3p}$$

$$\frac{kp(12-300)}{kp(24+36)}=-\frac{24}{5}$$

Hence Ans is (C)

Sol. 116 (B)

$$\frac{1}{1+x^{b-a}+x^{c-a}}+\frac{1}{1+x^{a-b}+x^{c-b}}+\frac{1}{1+x^{b-c}+x^{a-c}}$$

$$=\frac{1}{1+\frac{x^b}{x^a}+\frac{x^c}{x^a}}+\frac{1}{1+\frac{x^a}{x^b}+\frac{x^c}{x^b}}+\frac{1}{1+\frac{x^b}{x^c}+\frac{x^a}{x^c}}$$

$$=\frac{x^a}{x^a+x^b+x^c}+\frac{x^b}{x^a+x^b+x^c}+\frac{x^c}{x^a+x^b+x^c}$$

$$=\frac{x^a+x^b+x^c}{x^a+x^b+x^c}=1$$

Hence Ans is (B)

Sol. 117 (C) $\dfrac{1}{y+z}+\dfrac{1}{z+x}=\dfrac{2}{x+y}$

$$\frac{x+z+y+z}{(y+z)(x+z)}=\frac{2}{x+y}$$

$$\frac{x+y+2z}{(y+z)(x+z)}=\frac{2}{x+y}$$

$$(x+y+2z)(x+y)=2(y+z)(x+z)$$

$$(x+y)^2+2z(x+y)=2[xy+yz+zx+z^2]$$

$$x^2+y^2+2xy+2xz+2zy=2xy+2yz+2zx+2z^2$$

$$x^2+y^2=2z^2$$

Hence Ans is (C)

Sol. 118 (A) $x^2=y+z \quad y^2=x+z \qquad z^2=y+x$

$$=\frac{1}{x+1}+\frac{1}{y+1}+\frac{1}{z+1}$$

$$=\frac{1+x-x}{x+1}+\frac{1+y-y}{y+1}+\frac{1+z-z}{z+1}$$

$$=3-\left\{\frac{x^2}{x+x^2}+\frac{y^2}{y+y^2}+\frac{z^2}{z+z^2}\right\}$$

$$=3-\left\{\frac{2(x+y+z)}{x+y+z}\right\}$$

$$=3-\left\{\frac{2(x+y+z)}{x+y+z}\right\}$$

$$=3-2=1$$

Hence Ans is (A)

Sol. 119 (A) $\because a^m-b^m$

Always divisible by $(a-b)$

So, 14^m-6^m divisible by $(14-6)=8$

Hence Ans is (A)

Sol. 120 (C) Complementary of $23=90-23=67$

Supplementary of $67=180-67=113$

Hence Ans is (C)

Sol. 121 (D) Product of two numbers = G.C.D. × L.C.M

$$384 = 8 \times \text{L.C.M}$$

$$\text{L.C.M} = \frac{384}{8} = 48$$

Hence Ans is (D)

Sol. 122 (C) Two digit number is given by 10 (Ten digit) + Unit digit = $10(7) + y = 70 + y = y + 70$.

Hence Ans is (C)

Sol. 123 (A) $\frac{317}{3125} = \frac{317}{5^5}$

As denominator has only factor of 5, it will be having a terminating decimal expansion.

Hence Ans is (A)

Sol. 124 (C) $\frac{14588}{8750} = \frac{1042}{625} = \frac{1042}{5^4} = \frac{1042 \times 2^4}{(5 \times 2)^4}$

⇒ The given fraction will terminate after four decimal places.

Hence Ans is (C)

Sol. 125 (D) According to the question

$$72 = aq_1 + 7$$

$$127 = aq_2 + 10$$

$$65 = aq_1$$

$$117 = aq_2$$

$$\Rightarrow \quad a = \text{HCF}(65, 117) = 13$$

Hence Ans is (D)

Sol. 126 (D) $8.3\overline{1} + 0.\overline{6} + 0.00\overline{2}$

$$8 + \left(\frac{28}{90} + \frac{6}{9} + \frac{2}{900}\right)$$

$$8 + \frac{280 + 600 + 2}{900}$$

$$= 8 + \left(\frac{882}{900}\right) = 8.98$$

$$= 8.97\overline{9} \qquad [\because \text{ as } 0.\overline{9} = 1]$$

Hence Ans is (D)

Sol. 127 (D) We know that numbers x and y

HCF (x, y) × LCM (x, y) = product of numbers

$$\Rightarrow \quad 15 \times 225 = 75 \times x$$

$$\Rightarrow \quad x = \frac{225 \times 15}{75} = 45$$

Hence Ans is (D)

Sol. 128 (C) $6 - [9\{18 - (15 - (\overline{12 - 9}))\}]$

$$= 6 - [9 - \{18 - 12\}]$$

$$= 6 - [9 - 6] = 3$$

Hence Ans is (C)

Sol. 129 (A) Clearly the no will be $36x$ & $36y$. Then $36x \times 36y = 12690$

$$\Rightarrow \quad xy = 10$$

So possible pair of (x, y) can be (1, 10), (2, 5)

Hence 2 pairs are possible.

Hence Ans is (A)

Sol. 130 (C) $(\sqrt[2010]{2\sqrt{7} - 3\sqrt{3}})\,(\sqrt[4020]{55 + 12\sqrt{21}})$

$$\Rightarrow \quad [(2\sqrt{7} - 3\sqrt{3})^2 (55 + 12\sqrt{21})]^{1/4020}$$

$$\Rightarrow \quad [(28 + 27 - 12\sqrt{21})(55 + 12\sqrt{21})]^{1/4020}$$

$$\Rightarrow \quad [(55)^2 - 144 \times 21]^{1/4020}$$

$$= 1$$

Hence Ans is (C)

Sol. 131 (D) $r = \frac{p}{q}$, p & q are integers and $q \neq 0$

Hence Ans is (D)

Sol. 132 (D) Product of any three consecutive even numbers

$$= 2n(2n + 2)(2n + 4)$$

$$= 8[n(n + 1)(n + 2)]$$

⇒ Its divisible by 2, 4, 12 and 16 also

[∴ $n(n+1)(n+2)$ are always divisible of 6]

⇒ Product minimum value of the product is 48 and 48 is divisible by 2, 4, 12, 16. Therefore all options are correct.

Hence Ans is (D)

Sol. 133 (C) All integers are not rational number

Hence Ans is (C)

Sol. 134 (B) Natural number = (15 to 500)

$AP - 17, 23, 29 \ldots\ldots 497$

$$a = 17, d = 6\; a_n = 497$$

$$\Rightarrow \quad a_n = a + (n - 1)d$$

$$497 = 17 + (n - 1)6$$

$$\Rightarrow \quad 6(n - 1) = 480$$

$$\Rightarrow \quad n = 81$$

Hence Ans is (B)

Sol. 135 (C) Given $A : \frac{C}{D} = \pi$

$B : \pi$ is non terminating, recurring (False)

Hence Ans is (C)

Sol. 136 (B) $= \left[9\left(\frac{1}{64^{\frac{-1}{3}}} + 125^{\frac{1}{3}}\right)\right]^{\frac{1}{4}}$

$= [9[4+5]]^{\frac{1}{4}}$

$= 3$

Hence Ans is (B)

Sol. 137 (D) $\sqrt{m} + \sqrt{n} - \sqrt{p} = 0$

$\Rightarrow \quad \sqrt{m} + \sqrt{n} = \sqrt{p}$

$\Rightarrow$ Squaring both sides :

$(m+n-p)^2 = (-2\sqrt{mn})^2$

$\Rightarrow \quad (m+n-p)^2 = 4\,\text{mn}$

Hence Ans is (D)

Sol. 138 (B) HCF of 55 & 22 = 11

Given :

$55m - 2 \times 22 = 11$

$\Rightarrow \quad m = 1$

Hence Ans is (B)

Sol. 139 (C) Conceptual

Sol. 140 (B) Conceptual

Sol. 141 (A) $= 10^{2017} - 2017$

$= \underbrace{(1000....)}_{\text{NO. of digit 2018}} - 2017$

$= \underbrace{(9999....7983)}_{2013\,\text{times}}$

$= 9 \times 2013 + 7 + 9 + 8 + 3 = 18117 + 27 = 18144$

Hence Ans is (A)

Sol. 142 (B) $3^9 + 3^{12} + 3^{15} + 3^n$ should be a perfect cube

$= 3^9(1 + 3^3 + 3^6 + 3^{n-9}) \quad \ldots(1)$

To be a perfect cube $= 3^9[1 + 3^2]^3$

$= 3^9(1 + 3^3 + 3^6 + 3^5) \quad \ldots(2)$

By comparing (1) and (2), we get

$3^{n-9} = 3^5$

$n = 14$

Hence Ans is (B)

Sol. 143 (A) 101 is the only prime number whose multiple does not exist till 200

$$\frac{\text{L.C.M. of }(1,2,3......200)}{\text{L.C.M. of }(102,103,104......200)} = 101$$

Hence Ans is (A)

Sol. 144 (C) If $x = \frac{1}{3-2\sqrt{2}} \times \frac{3+2\sqrt{2}}{3+2\sqrt{2}}$

and $y = \frac{1}{3+2\sqrt{2}} \times \frac{3-2\sqrt{2}}{3-2\sqrt{2}}$

After rationalization we get $x = 3 + 2\sqrt{2}$ and $y = 3 - 2\sqrt{2}$

Therefore $x + y = 6$

Hence Ans is (C)

Sol. 145 (C) Product of two odd number is odd therefore $a \times b =$ odd

Since 1 is odd

Sum of two odd numbers is even

Therefore $ab + 1$ even

Hence Ans is (C)

Sol. 146 (C) $0.\overline{6} = \frac{2}{3}$ and $0.\overline{7} = \frac{7}{9}$

$0.\overline{6} + 0.\overline{7} = \frac{2}{3} + \frac{7}{9} = \frac{13}{9} = 1.\overline{4}$

Hence Ans is (C)

Sol. 147 (C) Given $x = 2^{48} - 1$

[using identity $(a^2 - b^2) = (a-b)(a+b)$]

$x = (2^{24}+1)(2^{24}-1)$

$= (2^{24}+1)(2^{12}+1)(2^{12}-1)$

$= (2^{24}+1)(2^{12}+1)(2^6+1)(2^6-1)$

$= (2^{24}+1)(2^{12}+1)(2^6+1)(2^3+1)(2^3-1)$

$= (2^{24}+1)(2^{12}+1)(2^6+1)\,8 \times 7$

Hence two factors are there between 5 & 10 which are 7 & 8

Hence Ans is (C)

Sol. 148 (D) Consider $abcd + dcba$

On adding

$1000a + 100b + 10c + d$

$+ 1000\text{d} + 100\text{c} + 10b + a$

$= 1001a + 110b + 110c + 1001d$

$= 1001(a+d) + 110(b+c)$

$= 1001 \times 7 + 110 \times 7$

$= 7 \times 11 \times 13 \times 7 + 11 \times 10 \times 7$

$= 11 \times 7 [91 + 10]$

$= 11 \times 7 \times [101]$

Hence Ans is (D)

Sol. 149 (D) Consider

$3^{1001} \times 7^{1002} \times 3^{1003}$

$= 3^{2004} \times 7^{1002}$

$= (3^4)^{501} \times (7^4)^{250}. 7^2$

$= (......1)^{501} . (......1)^{250} \times 49$

$= 1 \times 1 \times 49$

$= 9$

Hence Ans is (D)

Sol. 150 (C) Let the number be 'x'

$6 < \sqrt{x} < 7$

$36 < x < 49$

$\sqrt[3]{36} < \sqrt[3]{x} < \sqrt[3]{49}$

Hence Ans is (C)

Sol. 151 (D) 23.10100100010000... will be irrational number because it's non terminating non repeating

Hence Ans is (D)

Sol. 152 (C) 14 is the required number because

$14 = 5 + 5 + 1 + 1 + 1 + 1 = 6$ coins are required

Hence Ans is (C)

Sol. 153 (D) Consider

$\sqrt{(a-b)^2} + \sqrt{(b-a)^2}$

$|a-b| + |b-a|$

This will be positive if $a \neq b$

Hence Ans is (D)

Sol. 154 (A) We know $6765201 = (51)^4$

Hence Ans is (A)

Sol. 155 (C) Let the odd number will be of the form $4q + 1$ or $4q + 3$ then

$(4q+1)^2 = 16q^2 + 1 + 8q$

$= 8(2q^2 + q) + 1$

$= 8n + 1$

$\Rightarrow \quad (4q+3)^2 = 16q^2 + 9 + 24q$

$= 8[2q^2 + 3q + 1] + 1$

$= 8n + 1$

Hence Ans is (C)

Sol. 156 (C) Let us verify each option

$250 = 25 + 225$

$= 25 + 144 + 81$

Hence Ans is (C)

Sol. 157 (C) Let us verify each option

$n = 1$ and 2

Hence Ans is (C)

Sol. 158 (B) Let the numbers are $15a$ and $15b$, here a and b are coprime integers

i.e. L.C.M is $15\,ab = 225$

$ab = 15$

So that $\quad a = 1, b = 15$ and $a = 3, b = 5$

There are exactly two such pairs

Hence Ans is (B)

Sol. 159 (D) Consider

$$\frac{1}{\sqrt{11-2\sqrt{30}}} - \frac{3}{\sqrt{7-2\sqrt{10}}} - \frac{4}{\sqrt{8+4\sqrt{3}}}$$

$$\Rightarrow \frac{1}{(\sqrt{6}-\sqrt{5})} - \frac{3}{(\sqrt{5}-\sqrt{2})} - \frac{4}{\sqrt{2}(\sqrt{3}+1)}$$

$$\Rightarrow (\sqrt{6}+\sqrt{5}) - (\sqrt{5}+\sqrt{2}) - \frac{4(\sqrt{3}-1)}{2\sqrt{2}}$$

$$\Rightarrow \sqrt{6} - \sqrt{2} - \frac{2(\sqrt{3}-1)}{\sqrt{2}}$$

$$\Rightarrow \sqrt{6} - \sqrt{2} - \sqrt{6} + \sqrt{2} = 0$$

Hence Ans is (D)

Sol. 160 (A) Let

$N = 13q_1 + 3$

$N = 21q_2 + 11$

$\text{LCM}(13, 21) = 273$

Number is $273 \times 2 - 10 = 536$

$536 = 19q_3 + 4$

Remainder is 4

Hence Ans is (A)

Sol. 161 (D) Consider

$$0.\overline{34} + 0.3\overline{4} = \frac{34}{99} + \frac{34-3}{90} = \frac{34}{99} + \frac{31}{90}$$

$= \frac{1}{9}\left[\frac{34}{11}+\frac{31}{10}\right] = \frac{1}{9}\left[\frac{34\times 10+31\times 11}{11\times 10}\right]$

$= \frac{1}{9}\left[\frac{340+341}{110}\right] = \frac{681}{990} = 0.687878787\ldots$

$= 0.6\overline{87}$

Hence Ans is (D)

Sol. 162 (D) Let a be any positive integer. Then, it is of the form $3q$ or $3q+1$ or $3q+2$ for some integer q.

Here, following three cases arise

Case-1 When $a = 3q$

$\Rightarrow a^3 = (3q)^3 \Rightarrow a^3 = 27q^3$

$\Rightarrow a^3 = 9(3q^3) = 9m$, where $m = 3q^3$

Case-2 When $a = 3q+1$

$\Rightarrow a^3 = (3q+1)^3$

$\Rightarrow a^3 = 27q^3 + 27q^2 + 9q + 1$

$\Rightarrow a^3 = 9q(3q^2 + 3q + 1) + 1$

$\Rightarrow a^3 = 9m + 1$, where $m = q(3q^2 + 3q + 1)$

Case-3 When $a = 3q+2$

$\Rightarrow a^3 = (3q+2)^3$

$\Rightarrow a^3 = 27q^3 + 54q^2 + 36q + 8$

$\Rightarrow a^3 = 9q(3q^2 + 6q + 4) + 8$

$\Rightarrow a^3 = 9m + 8$, where $m = q(3q^2 + 6q + 4)$

So, a^3 is of the form $9m$, $9m+1$ or $9m+8$

Hence, the cube of any positive integer is either of the form $9m$, $9m+1$ or $9m+8$

Sum of reminder are $0+1+8=9$

Hence Ans is (D)

Sol. 163 (A) Consider

$$2272 = Nq_1 + r \quad \ldots(1)$$

$$875 = Nq_2 + r \quad \ldots(2)$$

Subtract (2) from (1)

$\Rightarrow \quad 1397 = N(q_2 - q_1)$

$\Rightarrow \quad 11 \times 127 = N(q_2 - q_1)$

$\Rightarrow \quad N = 127$

Sum of digits of N is $= 1+2+7 = 10$

Hence Ans is (A)

Sol. 164 (C) Consider

$$\frac{1}{7} = 0.\overline{142857}$$

$$\frac{1}{13} = 0.\overline{076923}$$

$$\frac{1}{21} = 0.\overline{047619}$$

$\Rightarrow \quad x = 7 + 13 + 21$

$\Rightarrow \quad x = 41$

Hence Ans is (C)

Sol. 165 (A) Consider $12^n + 1$

Unit's digit of $12^n + 1$ can be 3, 5, 7, 9

$\Rightarrow$ 1 cannot be the unit digit of $12n + 1$

Hence Ans is (A)

* * * * *

Polynomial

2

❍ An algebraic expression $f(x)$ of the form $f(x) = a_0 + a_1x + a_2x^2 + \ldots + a_nx^n$, where $a_0, a_1, a_2 \ldots a_n$ are real numbers and all the indices of x are non negative integers is called a polynomial in x and the highest index n is called the degree of the polynomial, if $a_n \neq 0$. Here $a_0, a_1x, a_2x^2 \ldots, a_nx^n$ are called the terms of the polynomial and $a_0, a_1, a_2, \ldots a_n$ are called various co-efficients of the polynomial $f(x)$. A polynomial in x is said to be in standard form when the terms are written either in increasing order or decreasing order of the indices of x in various terms.

❍ A polynomial of degree zero is called a zero degree polynomial or **constant polynomial**.

For example : $4 = 4x^0$

❍ A polynomial of degree one is called a linear polynomial. The general form of a **linear polynomial** is $ax + b$, where a and b are any real numbers and $a \neq 0$

For example : $4x + 5, 2x + 3, 5x + 3$ etc.

❍ A polynomial of degree two is called a **quadratic polynomial**. The general form of a quadratic polynomial is $ax^2 + bx + c$ where $a \neq 0$

For example : $x^2 + x + 1, 2x^2 + 1, 3x^2 + 2x + 1$ etc.

❍ A polynomial of degree three is called a **cubic polynomial**. The general form of a cubic polynomial is $ax^3 + bx^2 + cx + d$, where $a \neq 0$

For example : $x^3 + x^2 + x + 1, x^3 + 2x + 1, 2x^3 + 1$ etc.

❍ A polynomial of degree four is called a **biquadratic** or **quartic polynomial**. The general form of biquadratic polynomial is $ax^4 + bx^3 + cx^2 + dx + e$ where $a \neq 0$

For example : $x^4 + x^3 + x^2 + x + 1, x^4 + x^2 + 1$ etc.

❍ A polynomial is said to be a **monomial** if it has only one term. For example, $x, 9x^2, -5x^2$ are all monomials

❍ A polynomial is said to be a **binomial** if it contains two terms.

For example $2x^2 + 3x, \sqrt{3}\,x + 5x^4, -8x^3 + 3$ etc are all binomials.

❍ A polynomial is said to be a **trinomial** if it contains three terms.

For example $3x^3 - 8x + \frac{5}{2}, \sqrt{7}\,x^{10} + 8x^4 - 3x^2$ etc are all trinomials.

Note :

1. A polynomial having four or more than four terms does not have any particular name. They are simply called polynomials.

2. A polynomial of degree greater than or equal to 5 does not have any particular name. They are simply called a polynomial of degree 5 or degree 6 etc.

3. A polynomial whose co-efficients are all zero is called a zero polynomial, degree of a zero polynomial is not defined.

❍ If $p(x)$ is a polynomial in variable x then the values of x for which, it becomes zero are called the zeroes of the polynomial $p(x)$. i.e. α is any value such that $p(\alpha) = 0$ then α is called a zero of $p(x)$.

❍ A polynomial of degree n can have at most n real zeroes.

❍ If $p(x)$ is a polynomial and α is any real number, then the real number obtained by replacing x by α in $p(x)$, is called the value of $p(x)$ at $x = \alpha$ and is denoted by $p(\alpha)$.

❍ Mathematically we know that zeroes of a polynomial means, the values of variable which satisfied the given polynomial i.e. the value of polynomial at those values of variable becomes zero.

❍ Geometrically the zeroes of a polynomial $p(x)$ are the x-coordinates of the points, where the graph of $p(\alpha) = 0$ intersects x-axis.

❍ Let $y = ax + b$ is any linear polynomial, where $p(x) = y$. If we replace x by $-\frac{b}{a}$ then $y = 0$ i.e. value of $p(x)$ is zero so by definition we can say $-\frac{b}{a}$ is a zero of $y = ax + b$.

❍ Let α & β are two zeroes of a quadratic polynomial

$$p(x) = ax^2 + bx + c \qquad \ldots(1)$$

$$\Rightarrow \quad p(x) = a(x - \alpha)(x - \beta), \qquad \ldots(2)$$

On comparing (1) & (2)

$$\Rightarrow \quad \alpha + \beta = -\frac{b}{a}$$

$$\Rightarrow \quad \alpha\beta = \frac{c}{a}$$

i.e. Sum of zeroes $= S = \alpha + \beta = -\frac{b}{a}$

Product of zeroes $= P = \alpha \times \beta = \frac{c}{a}$

$\Rightarrow$ Sum of zeroes $= -\frac{\text{Coefficient of } x}{\text{Coefficient of } x^2} = \frac{-b}{a}$

and Product of zeroes $= \frac{\text{Constant term}}{\text{Coefficient of } x^2} = \frac{c}{a}$

❍ Let α, β and γ are the zeroes of a cubic polynomial, $p(x) = ax^3 + bx^2 + cx + d$ ...(1)

$$p(x) = a(x-\alpha)(x-\beta)(x-\gamma) \quad \text{...(2)}$$

On comparing (1) & (2)

$\Rightarrow \quad \alpha + \beta + \gamma = -\frac{b}{a}$

$\Rightarrow \quad \alpha\beta + \beta\gamma + \gamma\alpha = \frac{c}{a}$

$\Rightarrow \quad \alpha\beta\gamma = -\frac{d}{a}$

S_1 = Sum of zeroes $(\alpha + \beta + \gamma)$

$$= -\frac{b}{a} = \frac{\text{Coefficient of } x^2}{\text{Coefficient of } x^3}$$

S_2 = Sum of product of zeroes taken two at a time $(\alpha\beta + \beta\gamma + \gamma\alpha)$

$$= \frac{c}{a} = \frac{\text{Coefficient of } x}{\text{Coefficient of } x^3}$$

S_3 = Product of zeroes $(\alpha\beta\gamma)$

$$= -\frac{d}{a} = \frac{-\text{Constant term}}{\text{Coefficient of } x^3}$$

❍ A quadratic polynomial whose zeroes are α, β is given by

$$p(x) = x^2 - (\alpha + \beta)x + \alpha\beta$$

$= x^2$ – (sum of the zeroes) x + (product of the zeroes)

❍ A cubic polynomial whose zeroes are α, β, γ is given by

$$p(x) = x^3 - (\alpha + \beta + \gamma)x^2 + (\alpha\beta + \beta\gamma + \gamma\alpha)x - \alpha\beta\gamma$$

$= x^3$ – (sum of the zeroes)x^2 + (sum of the products of the zeroes taken two at a time)x – (product of the zeroes)

❍ If $p(x)$ and $g(x)$ are any two polynomials of degree m and n respectively such that $m < n$ then we can find two unique polynomials $q(x)$ and $r(x)$ such that

$$g(x) = p(x) \times q(x) + r(x)$$

Where either $\quad r(x) = 0$ or $\deg r(x) < \deg p(x)$.

Here $g(x)$ is dividend, $p(x)$ divisor, $q(x)$ quotient and $r(x)$ is remainder. This rule is called division rule or division algorithm of polynomials.

❍ If a polynomial $p(x)$ is divided by $d(x) = x - a$, then the remainder is given by $p(a)$.

[degree of $p(x) \geq$ degree of $d(x)$].

❍ **Factor Theorem :**

Let $f(x)$ be a polynomial of degree $n > 1$ and let a be any real number.

If $f(a) = 0$, then $(x - a)$ is a factor of $f(x)$ and converse is also true i.e.

If $(x - a)$ is a factor of $f(x)$, then $f(a) = 0$.

❍ Following results are known as identities as they are true for all values of the variables a, b and c.

(i) $(a + b)^2 = a^2 + 2ab + b^2$

(ii) $(a - b)^2 = a^2 - 2ab + b^2$

(iii) $(a + b)(a - b) = a^2 - b^2$

(iv) $(a + b + c)^2 = a^2 + b^2 + c^2 + 2ab + 2bc + 2ca$

(v) $(a + b)^3 = a^3 + b^3 + 3ab(a + b)$

(vi) $(a - b)^3 = a^3 - b^3 - 3ab(a - b)$

(vii) $a^3 + b^3 = (a + b)(a^2 - ab + b^2)$

(viii) $a^3 - b^3 = (a - b)(a^2 + ab + b^2)$

(ix) $a^3 + b^3 + c^3 - 3abc = (a + b + c)(a^2 + b^2 + c^2 - ab - bc - ca)$

Remember, in this identify

If $\quad a + b + c = 0$

$\Rightarrow \quad a^3 + b^3 + c^3 = 3abc$

* * * * *

PRACTICE EXERCISE - 2.1

2-1 For $x \neq 0, \pm 1$, the expression $\left[\dfrac{\frac{1}{x^{2007}} - \frac{1}{x^{2009}}}{\frac{1}{x^{2008}} - x^{2010}}\right]$ is equivalent to :

(A) x (B) $x-1$

(C) x^2-1 (D) $\frac{1}{x}$

2-2 If $x + \frac{1}{x} = 5$, the value of $\frac{x^4+1}{x^2}$ is :

(A) 21 (B) 23

(C) 25 (D) 30

2-3 Which two of the following cannot be factorised with integral coefficients ?

I x^4+x^2+1 II x^4+2x+2

III x^4-2x^2+1 IV $x^4=x+1$

(A) I and II (B) I and IV

(C) II and III (D) II and IV

2-4 A factor of x^3-6x^2-6x+1, is :

(A) $x+1$ (B) $x-1$

(C) $x-2$ (D) $2x+1$

2-5 Let $x = (2008)^{1004} + (2008)^{-1004}$ and $y = (2008)^{1004} - (2008)^{-1004}$ then the value of (x^2-y^2) is equal to :

(A) 4 (B) -4

(C) 0 (D) None

2-6 Two non zero real numbers, a and b, satisfy $ab = a - b$. A possible value of the expression $\frac{a}{b} + \frac{b}{a} - ab$, is :

(A) 2 (B) $\frac{1}{2}$

(C) -2 (D) $-\frac{1}{2}$

2-7 If $a+1 = b+2 = c+3 = d+4 = a+b+c+d+5$, then $(a+b+c+d)$ is equal to :

(A) -5 (B) $-10/3$

(C) $-7/3$ (D) $5/3$

2-8 Evaluate: $\frac{(a-b)^2}{(b-c)(c-a)} + \frac{(b-c)^2}{(a-b)(c-a)} + \frac{(c-a)^2}{(a-b)(b-c)}$:

(A) 0 (B) 1

(C) 2 (D) 3

2-9 If $(a^2+b^2)^3 = (a^3+b^3)^2$ then $\frac{a}{b} + \frac{b}{a} =$

(A) $\frac{2}{3}$ (B) $\frac{3}{2}$

(C) $\frac{5}{6}$ (D) $\frac{6}{5}$

2-10 If $x = \sqrt{2+\sqrt{2}}$, then $x^4 + \frac{4}{x^4}$ is :

(A) $2(3-\sqrt{2})$ (B) $6\sqrt{2}-2$

(C) $6-\sqrt{2}$ (D) 12

2-11 $\dfrac{x^{-3}-y^{-3}}{x^{-3}y^{-1}+(xy)^{-2}+y^{-3}+x^{-1}} =$

(A) $x+y$ (B) $y-x$

(C) $\frac{1}{x}-\frac{1}{y}$ (D) $\frac{1}{x}+\frac{1}{y}$

2-12 If $\dfrac{(\sqrt{a}-\sqrt{b})^2+4\sqrt{ab}}{a-b} = \dfrac{5}{3}$, then the value of $a:b$ is :

(A) $1:16$ (B) $1:4$

(C) $4:1$ (D) $16:1$

2-13 If $\dfrac{1}{\dfrac{1}{\dfrac{1}{\frac{1}{x}+\frac{1}{2}}+\dfrac{1}{\frac{1}{x}+\frac{1}{2}}}+\dfrac{1}{\dfrac{1}{\frac{1}{x}+\frac{1}{2}}+\dfrac{1}{\frac{1}{x}+\frac{1}{2}}}} = \dfrac{x}{36}$, then x is equal to :

(A) 70 (B) 72

(C) 36 (D) 68

2-14 Find the number of real zeros of $P(x) = (x-1)^2 + 1$:

(A) 1 (B) 0

(C) 2 (D) None of these

2-15 If both roots of quadratic equation $ax^2 + bx + c = 0$ are zero then :

(A) $a=0, b=0$ (B) $b=0, c=0$

(C) only $c=0$ (D) $a=0, b=0, c=0$

2-16 If α, β are the zeros of polynomial $f(x) = x^2 - p(x+1) - c$, then $(\alpha+1)(\beta+1) =$

(A) $c-1$ (B) $1-c$

(C) c (D) $1+c$

2-17 On dividing a cubic polynomial by a quadratic polynomial, the quotient obtained is always :

(A) A constant
(B) A linear polynomial
(C) A quadratic polynomial
(D) Either a constant or a linear polynomial

2-18 If one zero of the polynomial $f(x) = ax^2 + bx + c$, be twice of the other, then :

(A) $2b^2 = 3ac$ (B) $9b^2 = 2ac$
(C) $b^2 = 6ac$ (D) $2b^2 = 9ac$

2-19 What must be subtracted from $4x^4 - 2x^3 - 6x^2 + x - 5$ so that the result is exactly divisible by $2x^2 + x - 2$:

(A) $-3x - 5$ (B) $3x - 5$
(C) $-3x + 5$ (D) None of these

2-20 If 'a' is one of the zero of the polynomial $x^2 - 2px + p$, then the other root is :

(A) $\frac{a}{2a-1}$ (B) $\frac{2a-1}{a}$
(C) $\frac{a}{2a+1}$ (D) $\frac{2a+1}{a}$

2-21 The condition that the zeros of the polynomial $lx^2 + mx + n$ may be in the ratio 3 : 4 is :

(A) $14n^2 = 49\,ml$ (B) $m^2 = 9nl$
(C) $12m^2 = 49nl$ (D) $4l^2 = 49ml$

2-22 If $x^y = y^x$, then $\left(\frac{x}{y}\right)^{\frac{x}{y}}$ is equal to :

(A) $x^{\frac{x}{y}+1}$ (B) $x^{\frac{1}{y}}$
(C) $x^{\frac{1}{x}}$ (D) $x^{\frac{x}{y}-1}$

2-23 Factors of $2(a+b)^2 - 9(a+b) - 5$ are :

(A) $a+b+5, 2a+2b-1$ (B) $a+b-5, 2a+2b+1$
(C) $a-b+5, 2a-2b+5$ (D) None of these

2-24 If $a^x = b, b^y = c, c^z = a$, then $xyz =$

(A) 0 (B) 1
(C) $\frac{1}{abc}$ (D) abc

2-25 If α, β are the zeros of the polynomial $f(x) = 2x^2 + 5x + k$ satisfying the relation $\alpha^2 + \beta^2 + \alpha\beta = \frac{21}{4}$, then the value of $k =$

(A) 2 (B) -2
(C) 0 (D) $\frac{23}{2}$

2-26 If α, β, γ are the zeros of the polynomial $f(x) = x^3 - px^2 + qx - r$, then $\frac{1}{\alpha\beta} + \frac{1}{\beta\gamma} + \frac{1}{\gamma\alpha} =$

(A) $\frac{r}{p}$ (B) $-\frac{p}{r}$
(C) $\frac{p}{r}$ (D) $-\frac{r}{p}$

2-27 If α and β are zeros of the quadratic polynomial $f(x) = x^2 + 3x - 2$ then a polynomial whose zeros are $(3\alpha + 2\beta)$ and $(2\alpha + 3\beta)$ is :

(A) $x^2 + 15x - 52$ (B) $x^2 + 15x + 52$
(C) $x^2 + 15x - 10$ (D) $x^2 + 15x + 10$

2-28 If α, β, γ are the zeroes of the polynomial for $= ax^3 + bx^2 + cx + d$, then $\frac{1}{\alpha} + \frac{1}{\beta} + \frac{1}{\gamma} =$

(A) $-b/d$ (B) c/d
(C) $-c/d$ (D) $-c/a$

2-29 The number of real zeros of the polynomial $x^4 + 4x^2 + 5$ is :

(A) One real zero (B) Two real zero
(C) Third real zero (D) No real zero

2-30 If the polynomials $2x^3 + ax^2 + 3x - 5$ and $x^3 + x^2 - 4x + a$ leave the same remainder when divided by $x - 2$ then the value of a is :

(A) $\frac{3}{13}$ (B) $\frac{3}{17}$
(C) $\frac{-13}{3}$ (D) $\frac{-3}{13}$

2-31 If $(x+1)$ and $(x-1)$ are the factors of $px^3 + x^2 - 2x + q$ then the value of p and q are :

(A) $p = -1, q = 2$ (B) $p = 2, q = -1$
(C) $p = 2, q = 1$ (D) $p = -2, q = -2$

2-32 For graph shown in figure-2.1 $y = p(x)$, the number of zeros are :

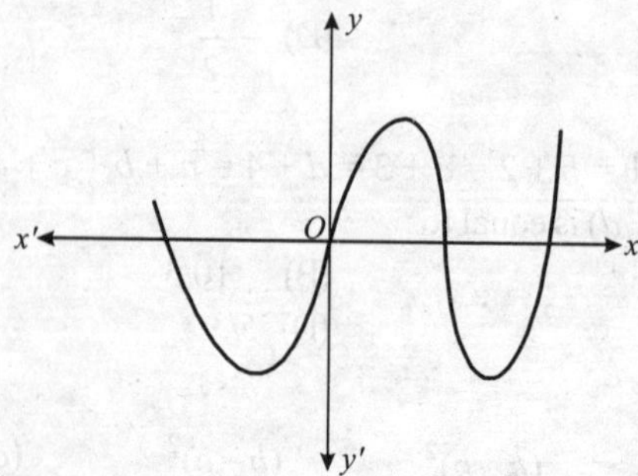

Figure 2.1

(A) 2 (B) 3
(C) 4 (D) 0

2-33 For graph shown in figure-2.2 $y = p(x)$, the number of zeros are :

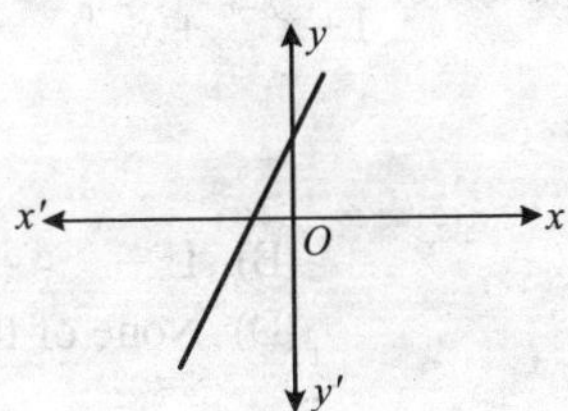

Figure 2.2

(A) 1 (B) 21
(C) 0 (D) 3

2-34 If $a < 0$, then graph of $y = ax^2 + bx + c$ is :

(A) 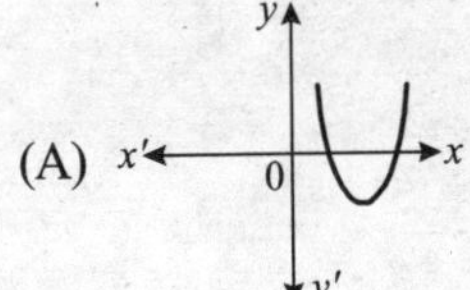

(B) 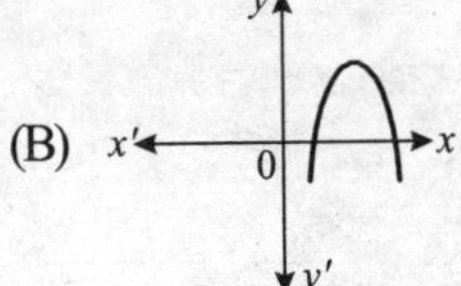

(C) 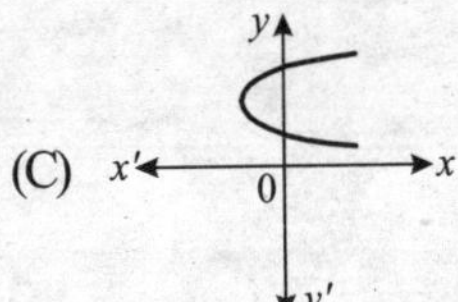

(D) 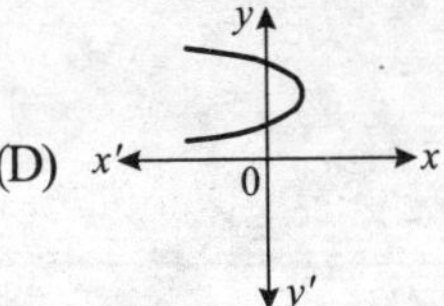

2-35 If zeros of polynomial $f(x) = x^3 - 12x^2 + 39x + k$ are in A.P., then value of K is :

(A) 28 (B) –28
(C) 27 (D) –27

2-36 A cubic polynomial with sum, sum of product of its zeros taken two at a time, and product of its zeros as 3, –1 and –3 respectively is :

(A) $k(x^3 - x^2 + 3)$ (B) $k(x^3 - 3x^2 - x + 3)$
(C) $k(x^3 + 3x^2 + x + 3)$ (D) None of these

2-37 Which of following sentence is NOT true :

(A) If α is zero of polynomial $f(x)$, then $f(\alpha) = 0$

(B) If $f(x) = g(x) \times q(x) + r(x)$, where $r(x) = 0$ or degree $r(x) <$ degree $q(x)$

(C) If α, β, γ are zeros of $f(x) = ax^3 + bx^2 + cx + d$, then $\alpha + \beta + \gamma = -b/a$, $\alpha\beta + \beta\gamma + \gamma\alpha = c/a$ and $\alpha\beta\gamma = -d/a$

(D) None of these

2-38 Remainder when we divide $x^3 + 3x^2 - 5x + 4$ by $(x - 1)$ is :

(A) 3 (B) –3
(C) 0 (D) 4

2-39 If a, b and c are real numbers such that $a^2 + b^2 + c^2 = 1$, then $ab + bc + ca$ is equal to :

(A) $\le -\frac{1}{2}$ (B) $\ge -\frac{1}{2}$
(C) ≥ 1 (D) ≤ 1

2-40 How many times the polynomial $p(x) = (x + 1)^2 + 2$ will cut x-axis :

(A) 1 (B) 2
(C) 3 (D) 0

2-41 Which of the following is the graph of $p(x) = x^2 + x - 6$:

(A) 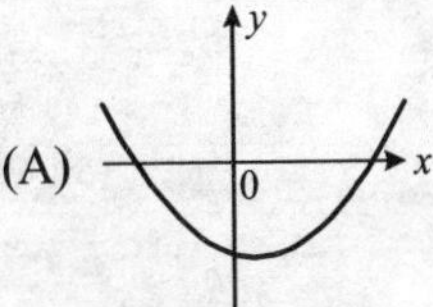

(B) 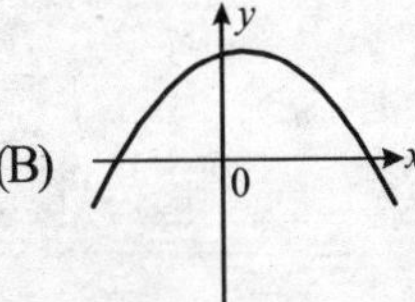

(C) 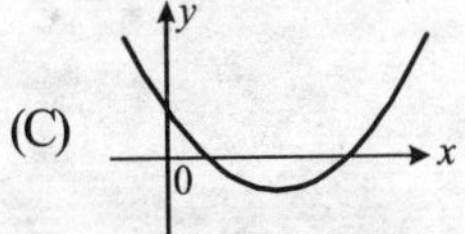

(D) 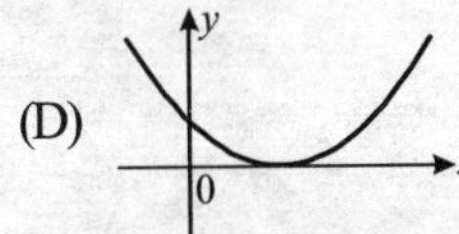

2-42 If the zeros of a quadratic polynomial are equal but opposite in sign then which of the following is correct :

(A) Constant term is zero
(B) Coefficient of x is positive
(C) Coefficient of x is negative
(D) Coefficient of x is zero

2-43 A non-zero constant polynomial has :

(A) Many roots (B) No root
(C) Only one root (D) None of these

2-44 Which of following statement is false :

(A) A polynomial of degree n has n roots
(B) Every real number is a root of zero polynomial
(C) If $f(a) = 0$, then $(x - a)$ is factor of $f(x)$
(D) $f(x) = \frac{a}{x} + b$ is linear polynomial.

2-45 Which of the following is a polynomial ?

(A) $x^2 - 5x + 6\sqrt{x} + 3$ (B) $\sqrt{x} + \frac{1}{\sqrt{x}}$
(C) $x^{3/2} - x + x^{1/2}$ (D) $x^3 - \sqrt{2}x + 4$

2-46 If α, β, γ are the zeros of a cubic polynomial and $\alpha + \beta + \gamma = 0$, $\alpha\beta + \beta\gamma + \gamma\alpha = 6$, $\alpha\beta\gamma = -20$, the cubic polynomial would be :

(A) $K(x^3 + 6x + 20)$ (B) $K(x^3 - 6x^2 + 20)$
(C) $K(x^3 - 6x + 20)$ (D) $K(x^3 + 6x - 20)$

2-47 If α and β are the zeroes of the polynomial $f(x) = x^2 - 5x + k$ such that $\alpha - \beta = 3$ then $k =$

(A) 4
(B) 6
(C) -4
(D) 3

2-48 If $x + y = a$ and $xy = b$ then the value of $\frac{1}{x^3} + \frac{1}{y^3}$ is :

(A) $\frac{a^3 - 3ab}{b^3}$
(B) $\frac{a^3 - 3a}{b^3}$
(C) $\frac{a^3 - 3}{b}$
(D) $\frac{a^3 - 3}{b^2}$

2-49 If x, y, z are positive real numbers and a, b, c are rational numbers, then the value of $\frac{1}{1 + x^{b-a} + x^{c-a}} + \frac{1}{1 + x^{a-b} + x^{c-b}} + \frac{1}{1 + x^{b-c} + x^{a-c}}$ is :

(A) -1
(B) 1
(C) 0
(D) None of these

2-50 If $2x^3 + 5x^2 - 4x - 6$ is divided by $2x + 1$, the remainder is :

(A) $-13/2$
(B) 3
(C) -3
(D) 6

* * * * *

PRACTICE EXERCISE - 2.2

2-1 The graph of $y = ax^2 + bx + c$ is given in figure-2.3. Then which is true :

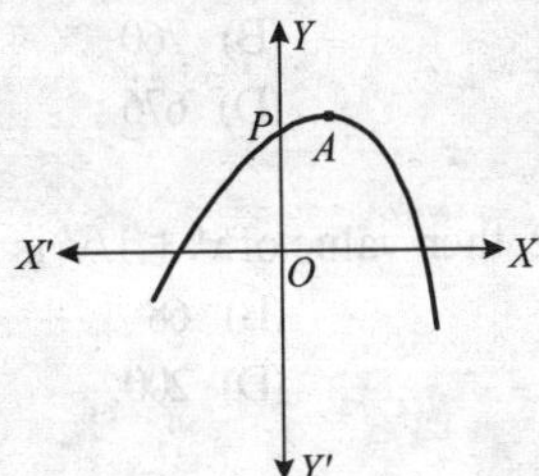

Figure 2.3

(A) $a<0, b>0, c<0$ (B) $a>0, b>0, c>0$
(C) $a<0, b<0, c<0$ (D) $a<0, b>0, c>0$

2-2 If $f(x) = ax^2 + bx + c$ has no real zeros and $a+b+c<0$, then :
(A) $c=0$ (B) $c>0$
(C) $c<0$ (D) None of these

2-3 In figure shows the graph of the polynomial $f(x) = ax^2 + bx + c$. Then :

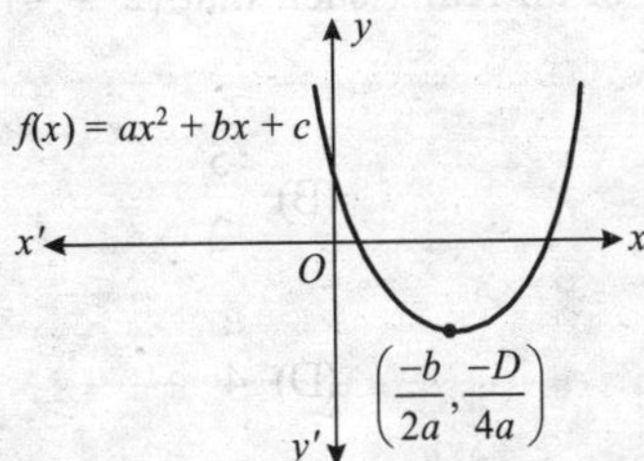

Figure 2.4

(A) $a>0, b>0$ and $c>0$ (B) $a>0, b<0$ and $c>0$
(C) $a>0, b<0$ and $c<0$ (D) $a>0, b>0$ and $c<0$

2-4 The value of a and b for which $x^4 + x^3 + 8x^2 + ax + b$ is divisible by $x^2 + 1$:
(A) $a=1, b=5$ (B) $a=1, b=-5$
(C) $a=1, b=7$ (D) None of these

2-5 If $3^x = 4^y = 12^z$, then the value of 'z' is :

(A) $\frac{xy}{x-y}$ (B) $\frac{xy}{x+y}$

(C) $\frac{y}{x+y}$ (D) $\frac{x}{x+y}$

2-6 If zero's of the polynomial $f(x) = x^3 - 3px^2 + qx - r$ are in A.P., then :
(A) $2p^3 = pq - r$ (B) $2p^3 = pq + r$
(C) $p^3 = pq - r$ (D) None of these

2-7 Which of the following is the graph of $p(x) = (x-2)^2 (x+2)$:

(A) 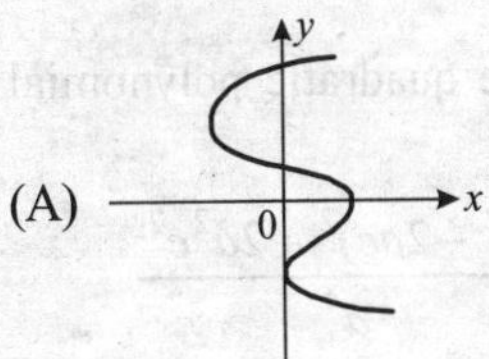

(B) 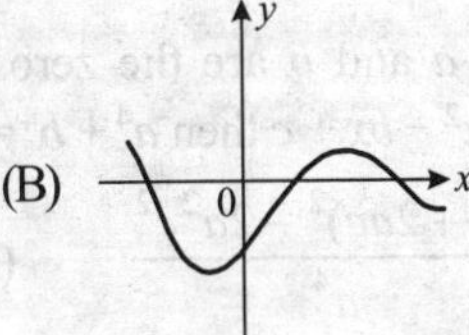

(C) 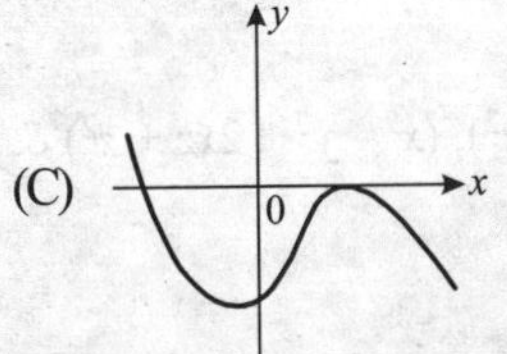

(D) 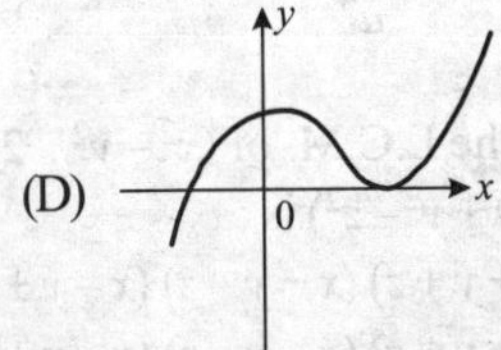

2-8 If $p(x) = x^3 + bx^2 + cx + 5$ has one zero $\sqrt{5}+2$ and b and c are rational numbers then find sum of other two zeros :
(A) $\sqrt{5}+7$ (B) $\sqrt{5}-7$
(C) $7+\sqrt{5}$ (D) $7-\sqrt{5}$

2-9 If α and β are the zeros of $p(x) = 3x^2 - 5x + b$ then find the polynomial whose zeros are $\frac{1}{\alpha}$ and $\frac{1}{\beta}$:
(A) $k[bx^2 + 5x + 3]$ (B) $k[bx^2 - 5x + 3]$
(C) $k[x^2 - 5x + 9]$ (D) $k[x^2 - x + 1]$

2-10 If α, β, γ are the zeroes of the polynomial $f(x) = ax^3 + bx^2 + cx + d$, then $\alpha^2 + \beta^2 + \gamma^2 =$

(A) $\frac{b^2 - ac}{a^2}$ (B) $\frac{b^2 - 2ac}{a}$

(C) $\frac{b^2 + 2ac}{b^2}$ (D) $\frac{b^2 - 2ac}{a^2}$

2-11 If $11^7 + 4^7$ is divided by 15 then the remainder is:
(A) 0 (B) 1
(C) 2 (D) −2

2-12 The factors of $(2x^2 - 3x - 2)(2x^2 - 3x) - 63$ are:
(A) $(x-3)(2x+3)(x-1)(x-7)$
(B) $(x+3)(2x-3)(x-1)(x-7)$
(C) $(x+3)(2x+3)(2x^2-3x+7)$
(D) $(x-3)(2x+3)(2x^2-3x+7)$

2-13 The number of values of the triplet (a, b, c) for which $a\cos^2 x + b\sin^2 x + c = 0$ is satisfied by all real x is :
(A) 0 (B) 2
(C) 3 (D) Infinite

2-14 If $x^2 + y^2 + z^2 = 4$, and $xy + yz + zx = k$ then :

(A) $k \geq -5/2$ (B) $k \leq -4$

(C) $k \geq -2$ (D) $k \geq -4$

2-15 If a and b are the zeros of the quadratic polynomial $f(x) = ax^2 + bx + c$ then $a^4 + b^4 =$

(A) $\dfrac{(b^2+2ac)^2 - 2a^2c^2}{a^4}$ (B) $\dfrac{(b^2-2ac)^2 + 2a^2c^2}{a^4}$

(C) $\dfrac{b^4 - 4ab^2c + 2a^2c^2}{a^4}$ (D) None of these

2-16 The L.C.M. of $(x^2 - y^2 - 2yz - z^2)$, $(x^2 - y^2 + 2xz + z^2)$ & $(x^2 - 2xy + y^2 - z^2)$ is :

(A) $(x+y+z)(x+y-z)(x-y+z)$

(B) $(x+y+z)(x-y-z)(x-y+z)$

(C) $(x+y+z)(x+y-z)(x-y-z)$

(D) None of these

2-17 Lowest value of $x^2 + 4x + 2$ is :

(A) 0 (B) -2

(C) 2 (D) 4

2-18 Maximum value of $2 - 4x - x^2$ is :

(A) 2 (B) 4

(C) 6 (D) 8

2-19 If $f(x) = ax^2 + bx + c$ has no real zeros and $a - b + c > 0$ then :

(A) $c = 0$ (B) $c > 0$

(C) $c < 0$ (D) None of these

2-20 If $(x^2 - 4)$ is a factor of $ax^4 + bx^3 + cx^2 + dx + e$ then $d =$

(A) $2b$ (B) $4b$

(C) $-4b$ (D) $-2b$

2-21 If $x + y + z = 0$ and $x^2 + y^2 + z^2 = 26$, find $x^4 + y^4 + z^4$:

(A) 174 (B) 260

(C) 338 (D) 676

2-22 If $x - 1/x = 2$, then value of $x^6 + 1/x^6$ is :

(A) 66 (B) 68

(C) 198 (D) 200

2-23 If $x > 0, y > 0$ and $z > 0$, and $12xyz = 108$, find the minimum value of $2x + 3y + 4z$:

(A) 12 (B) 18

(C) 24 (D) 27

2-24 If $(2x-1)(2x-2)(2x-3)(2x-4)(2x-5) > 0$, how many single-digit whole number values can x assume :

(A) 10 (B) 9

(C) 8 (D) 7

2-25 The sum of all real x such that $(2^x - 4)^3 + (4^x - 2)^3 = (4^x + 2^x - 6)^3$ is :

(A) 0 (B) $\dfrac{5}{2}$

(C) $\dfrac{7}{2}$ (D) 4

* * * * *

PRACTICE EXERCISE - 2.3

2-1 If α, β are the zeros of polynomial $f(x) = x^2 - p(x+1) - c$, then $(\alpha+1)(\beta+1) =$ **[NTSE-2014 (Stage-I) Rajasthan]**

(A) $c-1$ (B) $1-c$
(C) c (D) $1+c$

2-2 The graph of $y = p(x)$ is given below. The number of zeroes of polynomial $p(x)$, is : **[NTSE-2015 (Stage-I) Rajasthan]**

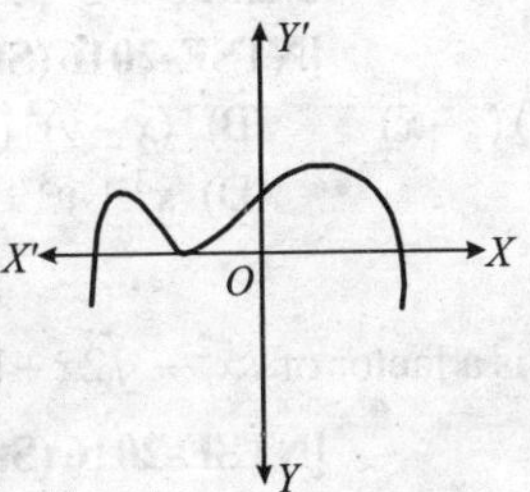

Figure 2.5

(A) 3 (B) 2
(C) 1 (D) 0

2-3 If the roots of the equation $2x^2 + ax + b = 0$ are reciprocals to each other, then the value of b is : **[NTSE-2015 (Stage-I) Rajasthan]**

(A) –1 (B) –2
(C) 2 (D) 1

2-4 The sum of the co-efficients $f(x)$, if $(16x^{16} - 11x + 2) f(x) = 2016. x^{2015}$ is... **[NTSE-2015 (Stage-I) Andhara Pradesh]**

(A) 143 (B) 288
(C) 146 (D) 165

2-5 If $x^2 + 2x + 5$ is a factor of $x^4 + Px^2 + Q$, then the value of $P + Q$ is : **[NTSE-2015 (Stage-I) Andhara Pradesh]**

(A) 18 (B) 25
(C) 31 (D) 28

2-6 The roots of $x^3 + 3x^2 + 4x - 11 = 0$ are a, b and c; and that the roots of $x^3 + rx^2 + sx + t = 0$ are $a + b, b + c$ and $c + a$, then the value of t is : **[NTSE-2015 (Stage-I) Andhara Pradesh]**

(A) 23 (B) 25
(C) 20 (D) 18

2-7 If a polynomial $p(x)$ is divided by $(mx + n)$, then the remainder is : **[NTSE-2015 (Stage-I) TN]**

(A) $P\left(\frac{m}{n}\right)$ (B) $P\left(\frac{-m}{n}\right)$

(C) $P\left(\frac{n}{m}\right)$ (D) $P\left(\frac{-n}{m}\right)$

2-8 On dividing $x^3 - 3x^2 + x + 2$ by a polynomial $g(x)$, the quotient and remainder were $(x-2)$ and $(-2x+4)$ respectively, then g(x) is : **[NTSE-2015 (Stage-I) TN]**

(A) $x^2 + x - 1$ (B) $x^2 - x + 1$
(C) $x^2 - x - 1$ (D) $x^2 + x + 1$

2-9 If one of the zeros of polynomial $a^2x^2 + x + b^2$ is -1 then : **[NTSE-2015 (Stage-I) TN]**

(A) $a^2 + b^2 = 0$ (B) $a^2 + b^2 - 1 = 0$
(C) $a^2 - b^2 + 1 = 0$ (D) $a^2 + b^2 = -1$

2-10 $a^2 - (b-c)^2$ is : **[NTSE-2015 (Stage-I) TN]**

(A) $(a+b-c)(a-b+c)$ (B) $(a-b-c)(a-b-c)$
(C) $(a-b+c)(a+b-c)$ (D) $(a+b+c)(a+b+c)$

2-11 If $x^2 + \frac{1}{x^2} = 23, x > 0$ then $x + \frac{1}{x}$ is : **[NTSE-2015 (Stage-I) TN]**

(A) 2 (B) 3
(C) 4 (D) 5

2-12 The factorization of
$2p(a-b) + 3q(5a-5b) + 4r(2b-2a)$ yields : **[NTSE-2015 (Stage-I) Chandigarh]**

(A) $(b-a)(2p+15q-8r)$ (B) $(a-b)(2p+15q-8r)$
(C) $(b-a)(2p-15q+8r)$ (D) $(a-b)(2p-15q+8r)$

2-13 If $x = \frac{(\sqrt{3}+1)}{2}$ then the value of $4x^3 + 2x^2 - 8x + 7$ is : **[NTSE-2015 (Stage-I) Chandigarh]**

(A) 8 (B) 10
(C) 15 (D) 14

2-14 If $x = 2 + 2^{1/3} + 2^{2/3}$ then $x^3 - 6x^2 + 6x =$ **[NTSE-2015 (Stage-I) Chandigarh]**

(A) 2 (B) 1
(C) 4 (D) 3

2-15 If $(x-4)$ is a factor of $5x^3 - 7x^2 - ax - 28$ then the value of a is : **[NTSE-2015 (Stage-I) Chandigarh]**

(A) 35 (B) 45
(C) 55 (D) 25

2-16 The coefficient of x^{49} in the product $(x-1)(x-3)(x-5)$ ... $(x-99)$ is : **[NTSE-2015 (Stage-I) Delhi]**

(A) 1 (B) –999
(C) –2990 (D) –2500

2-17 If $x = (5)^{1/3} + 2$, then value of $x^3 - 6x^2 + 12x - 10$ is : **[NTSE-2015 (Stage-I) Delhi]**

(A) 1 (B) -2
(C) -1 (D) 3

2-18 The HCF of expression $(x + 1)(x - 1)^2$ and $(x + 1)^2(x - 1)$ is : **[NTSE-2015 (Stage-I) UP]**

(A) $(x+1)(x-1)$ (B) $(x+1)^2$
(C) $(x-1)^2$ (D) $(x+1)^2(x-1)^2$

2-19 If $x = (3+\sqrt{8})$, then $\left(x^2 + \frac{1}{x^2}\right)$ will be : **[NTSE-2015 (Stage-I) UP]**

(A) 38 (B) 36
(C) 34 (D) 30

2-20 If $x - y = 5$, $xy = 24$ then the value of $x^2 + y^2$ will be : **[NTSE-2015 (Stage-I) UP]**

(A) 23 (B) 73
(C) 65 (D) 74

2-21 If $x - 2\sqrt{x} = 3$, then the value of x is : **[NTSE-2015 (Stage-I) West Bengal]**

(A) 1 (B) 3
(C) 9 (D) -1

2-22 The least value of $2x^2 - 4x + 3y^2 - 18y + 31$ is : **[NTSE-2015 (Stage-I) West Bengal]**

(A) 3 (B) -1
(C) 0 (D) 2

2-23 If $2r = h + \sqrt{r^2 + h^2}$, the value of $r : h$ is $(r, h \neq 0)$: **[NTSE-2015 (Stage-I) West Bengal]**

(A) 4 : 3 (B) 3 : 4
(C) 1 : 2 (D) 2 : 1

2-24 If $x = cy + bz$, $y = cx + az$, $z = bx + ay$, the value of $a^2 + b^2 + c^2 - 1$ is : **[NTSE-2015 (Stage-I) West Bengal]**

(A) abc (B) $-abc$
(C) $2abc$ (D) $-2abc$

2-25 When $10x^2 + x - 23$ is divided by $(2x + 3)$, the remainder is : **[NTSE-2015 (Stage-I) Chennai]**

(A) 1 (B) -2
(C) 2 (D) 0

2-26 The sum of $\frac{a^3}{b-a}$ and $\frac{b^3}{a-b}$ is : **[NTSE-2015 (Stage-I) Chennai]**

(A) $a^2 + ab + b^2$ (B) $-a^2 - ab - b^2$
(C) $a^2 - ab + b^2$ (D) $a^3 - b^3$

2-27 The degree of the polynomial $(x + 1)(x^2 - x - x^4 + 1)$ is : **[NTSE-2015 (Stage-I) Chennai]**

(A) 2 (B) 3
(C) 4 (D) 5

2-28 If HCF of $x^2 + 3x + 2$ and $x^2 + 5x + 6$ is $x + a$, then value of 'a' will be : **[NTSE-2015 (Stage-I) Chhatisgarh]**

(A) 1 (B) 2
(C) 3 (D) 6

2-29 If $a = x - y$, $b = y - z$ and $c = z - x$ then the value of $a^3 + b^3 + c^3$ is : **[NTSE-2016 (Stage-I) Rajasthan]**

(A) $3(x-y)(y-z)(z-x)$ (B) $(x-y)^3(y-z)^3(z-x)^3$
(C) $(x+y+z)^3$ (D) $x^3 + y^3 + z^3$

2-30 If $(x + \sqrt{2})$ is a factor of $kx^2 - \sqrt{2}x + 1$, then the value of k is : **[NTSE-2016 (Stage-I) Rajasthan]**

(A) $-\frac{3}{2}$ (B) $-\frac{2}{3}$
(C) $\frac{3}{2}$ (D) $\frac{2}{3}$

2-31 The graph below represents a polynomial $p(x)$. Which of these is the reminder, when $p(x)$ is divided by the polynomial $x^2 - 5x + 6$? **[NTSE-2016 (Stage-I) Telangana]**

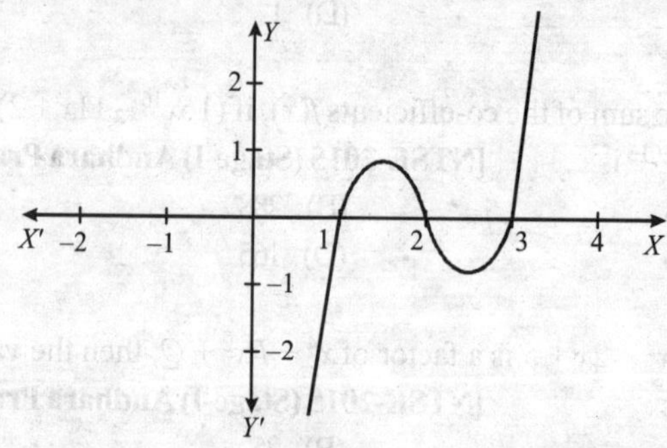

Figure 2.6

(A) 1 (B) 3
(C) $x - 1$ (D) 0

2-32 If $x + 3y - z = 4$, $3x + 3y + z = 12$, $(x + 3y)^2 - z^2 = 36$, then the value of $x = \ldots$ **[NTSE-2016 (Stage-I) Andhara Pradesh]**

(A) $\frac{3}{2}$ (B) $\frac{1}{3}$
(C) 3 (D) 5

2-33 Product of two roots $x^4 - 11x^3 + kx^2 + 269x - 2001$ is -69, then the value of $k = \ldots$ **[NTSE-2016 (Stage-I) Andhara Pradesh]**

(A) 5 (B) -7
(C) -10 (D) 8

2-34 If $p(x) = x^4 + ax^3 + bx^2 + cx + d$ $p(1) = p(2) = p(3) = 0$, then the value of $p(4) + p(0) = \ldots$

[NTSE-2016 (Stage-I) Andhara Pradesh]

(A) 10 (B) 24
(C) 25 (D) 12

2-35 If sin α and cos α are the roots of $ax^2 + bx + c = 0$, then $a^2 + 2ac = \ldots$ **[NTSE-2016 (Stage-I) Andhara Pradesh]**

(A) c^2 (B) $-2ab$
(C) b^2 (D) 0

2-36 The value of $\frac{(0.03)^2 - (0.01)^2}{0.03 - 0.01}$ is :

[NTSE-2016 (Stage-I) Bihar]

(A) 0.02 (B) 0.004
(C) 0.4 (D) 0.04

2-37 The simplified form of the expression given below is :

[NTSE-2016 (Stage-I) Delhi]

$$\frac{\dfrac{y^4 - x^4}{x(x+y)} - \dfrac{y^3}{x}}{y^2 - xy + x^2}$$

(A) 1 (B) 0
(C) −1 (D) 2

2-38 If $a = \frac{4xy}{x+y}$, then value of $\frac{a+2x}{a-2x} + \frac{a+2y}{a-2y}$ in most simplified form is : **[NTSE-2016 (Stage-I) Delhi]**

(A) 0 (B) 1
(C) −1 (D) 2

2-39 If one of the zeros of the cubic polynomial $x^3 + ax^2 + bx + c$ is −1, then the product of the other two zeros is :

[NTSE-2016 (Stage-I) Jharkhand]

(A) $a - b - 1$ (B) $b - a - 1$
(C) $1 - a + b$ (D) $1 + a - b$

2-40 If $xy + yz + zx = 0$,

then the value of $\left(\frac{1}{x^2 - yz} + \frac{1}{y^2 - zx} + \frac{1}{z^2 - xy}\right)$:

[NTSE-2016 (Stage-I) Jharkhand]

(A) 3 (B) 0
(C) 1 (D) $x + y + z$

2-41 If α, β and γ each is a zero of $x^3 - 6x^2 - x + 30$ and $\alpha \neq \beta \neq \gamma$, then what is the value of $5(\alpha\beta + \beta\gamma + \gamma\alpha)$?

[NTSE-2016 (Stage-I) Odisha]

(A) −1 (B) −5
(C) 1 (D) 5

2-42 The polynomials $(x^3 - 1)$ and $(x^2 + 1)$ are divided by $(x + 1)$ leave the remainder as R_1 and R_2. The true statement among the following is : **[NTSE-2016 (Stage-I) Karnatka]**

(A) $R_1 + R_2 = 0$ (B) $R_1 - R_2 = 0$
(C) $2R_1 + R_2 = 0$ (D) $R_1 - 2R_2 = 0$

2-43 If $a = \sqrt{5 + 2\sqrt{6}}$ then $\frac{1+a^4}{a^2} =$

[NTSE-2016 (Stage-I) Karnatka]

(A) $4\sqrt{6}$ (B) 10
(C) 5 (D) $2\sqrt{6}$

2-44 If one root of the equation $x^2 + ax + b = 0$ is $\frac{1}{3}$ times the other. Then the correct relation among the following is :

[NTSE-2016 (Stage-I) Karnatka]

(A) $3a^2 = 16b$ (B) $16a^2 = 3b$
(C) $3a = 16b^2$ (D) $16a = 3b^2$

2-45 If $a + b = 2$ and $\frac{1}{a} + \frac{1}{b} = 2$, then $a^3 + b^3$ will be :

[NTSE-2016 (Stage-I) Chhatisgarh]

(A) 1 (B) 2
(C) 3 (D) 4

2-46 If $a = \sqrt{6} + \sqrt{5}$; $b = \sqrt{6} - \sqrt{5}$, then find the value of $2a^2 - 5ab + 2b^2$: **[NTSE-2016 (Stage-I) Chhatisgarh]**

(A) 36 (B) 37
(C) 39 (D) 41

2-47 Out of group of Swans, $\frac{7}{2}$ times the square root of number of Swans are playing on the shore of the tank. Remaining two are quarreling in the water. Calculate the total number of Swans. Find the number of Swans playing on the shore of the tank :

[NTSE-2016 (Stage-I) Chhatisgarh]

(A) 14, 16 (B) 16, 12
(C) 14, 12 (D) 16, 14

2-48 If $\frac{x}{2y+z-x} = \frac{y}{2z+x-y} = \frac{z}{2x+y-z}$ and $x + y + z \neq 0$, then what is each ratio equal to :

[NTSE-2016 (Stage-I) Chhatisgarh]

(A) $\frac{1}{2}$ (B) $\frac{1}{3}$
(C) 2 (D) $\frac{2}{3}$

2-49 HCF and LCM of two polynomials are x and $(x^3 - 9x)$ respectively. If one polynomial is $(x^2 + 3x)$, then second will be : **[NTSE-2016 (Stage-I) Chhatisgarh]**

(A) $(x^2 + 3x)$ (B) $(x^2 - 9x)$
(C) $(x^2 + 9x)$ (D) $(x^2 - 3x)$

2-50 If $x^2 + xy + x = 12$ and $y^2 + xy + y = 18$, then the value of $x + y$ is : **[NTSE-2017 (Stage-I) Andhra Pradesh]**

(A) 5 or – 6 (B) 3 or 4
(C) 5 or 3 (D) 6 or – 3

2-51 If $x = \cfrac{1}{2 - \cfrac{1}{2 - \cfrac{1}{2 - x}}}$, $(x \neq 2)$, then the value of x is : **[NTSE-2017 (Stage-I) Andhra Pradesh]**

(A) 1 (B) 3
(C) 2 (D) 5

2-52 If α, β are roots of polynomial $3x^2 + 6x + k$ such that $\alpha^2 + \beta^2 + \alpha\beta = \frac{8}{3}$, then find the value of k : **[NTSE-2017 (Stage-I) Chandigarh]**

(A) – 8 (B) 8
(C) –4 (D) 4

2-53 If $x^2 - 5x + 1 = 0$ then the value of $x^5 + \frac{1}{x^5}$ is : **[NTSE-2017 (Stage-I) Chandigarh]**

(A) 2025 (B) 2725
(C) 225 (D) 2525

2-54 If one root of quadratic equation $(K + 1)x^2 - 5x + 2K = 0$ is reciprocal of other then value of K is : **[NTSE-2017 (Stage-I) Delhi]**

(A) 2 (B) 0
(C) – 1 (D) 1

2-55 If α, β are the roots of the equation $2x^2 - 5x + 16 = 0$ then the value of $\left(\frac{\alpha^2}{\beta}\right)^{\frac{1}{3}} + \left(\frac{\beta^2}{\alpha}\right)^{\frac{1}{3}}$ is : **[NTSE-2017 (Stage-I) Delhi]**

(A) $\frac{1}{4}$ (B) $\frac{5}{4}$
(C) $\frac{1}{3}$ (D) $\frac{5}{12}$

2-56 Value of $[(0.111)^3 + (0.222)^3 - (0.333)^3 + (0.333)^2(0.222)]^2$ will be : **[NTSE-2017 (Stage-I) Delhi]**

(A) 222 (B) 0
(C) 333 (D) 2

2-57 The product of $\left(a^{\frac{1}{16}} + a^{-\frac{1}{16}}\right)$, $\left(a^{\frac{1}{16}} - a^{-\frac{1}{16}}\right)$, $\left(a^{\frac{1}{8}} + a^{-\frac{1}{8}}\right)$ and $\left(a^{\frac{1}{4}} + a^{-\frac{1}{4}}\right)$ is : **[NTSE-2017 (Stage-I) Goa]**

(A) $\left(\frac{a^2 + 1}{a}\right)$ (B) $\left(\frac{a^2 - 1}{a}\right)$
(C) $\sqrt{\frac{a^4 - 1}{a^2}}$ (D) $\sqrt{\frac{(a-1)^2}{a}}$

2-58 Which one is the constant term of $4x^3 - 3x^2 + 2x - 5$: **[NTSE-2017 (Stage-I) Gujarat]**

(A) 4 (B) –5
(C) 2 (D) –3

2-59 The polynomial having 3 degree is known as —: **[NTSE-2017 (Stage-I) Gujarat]**

(A) Linear (B) Quadratic
(C) Polynomial (D) Trinomial (cubic)

2-60 Find the product of zeros of the quadratic polynomial $x^2 - 4x + 3$: **[NTSE-2017 (Stage-I) Gujarat]**

(A) 1 (B) 3
(C) 4 (D) – 4

2-61 If one zero of the quadratic polynomial $ax^2 + 15x + 6$ is reciprocal of the other, then the zeros of the polynomial are : **[NTSE-2017 (Stage-I) Haryana]**

(A) 2 and $\frac{1}{2}$ (B) –2 and $\frac{-1}{2}$
(C) 3 and $\frac{1}{3}$ (D) –3 and $\frac{-1}{3}$

2-62 If $(x + a)$ is the factor of the polynomials $(x^2 + px + q)$ and $(x^2 + mx + n)$ then the value of 'a' is : **[NTSE-2017 (Stage-I) Karnataka]**

(A) $\frac{n-q}{m-p}$ (B) $\frac{m-p}{n-q}$
(C) $\frac{q-n}{m-p}$ (D) $\frac{m-p}{q-n}$

2-63 Zeroes of the polynomial $x^3 - 4x^2 - 7x + 10$ are : **[NTSE-2017 (Stage-I) Madhya Pradesh]**

(A) 1, 5, –2 (B) 1, –5, 2
(C) –1, 5, 2 (D) 1, –5, –2

2-64 $(\sqrt[3]{3} + \sqrt[3]{2})(\sqrt[3]{9} + \sqrt[3]{4} - \sqrt[3]{6}) = ?$ **[NTSE-2017 (Stage-I) Maharashtra]**

(A) 5 (B) $\sqrt[9]{5}$

(C) $\sqrt[6]{5}$ (D) $\sqrt[3]{5}$

2-65 If the polynomial $x^3 + 2x^2 - \alpha x - 12$ is divided by $(x-4)$ the remainder is 52. Find the value of 'α' :

[NTSE-2017 (Stage-I) Maharashtra]

(A) $\frac{11}{2}$ (B) -5

(C) 8 (D) -8

2-66 If $p+q+r=0$ then the value $\frac{2p^2(q+r)+2q^2(p+r)+2r^2(p+q)}{pqr}$ will be :

[NTSE-2017 (Stage-I) Punjab]

(A) $3\,pqr$ (B) $\frac{1}{pqr}$

(C) 6 (D) -6

2-67 If $x = \frac{1}{\sqrt{3}-1}$ then find the value of $4x^2 + 2x^2 - 8x - 3$:

[NTSE-2017 (Stage-I) Punjab]

(A) 0 (B) 2

(C) -2 (D) $\sqrt{2}$

2-68 Find the solutions for 'x' in equation $\frac{1}{a+b+x} = \frac{1}{a} + \frac{1}{b} + \frac{1}{x}$ is: **[NTSE-2017 (Stage-I) Punjab]**

(A) $-a, b$ (B) $-a, -b$

(C) $a, -b$ (D) a, b

2-69 Value of $(x-y)^3 + (y-z)^3 + (z-x)^3$ is :

[NTSE-2017 (Stage-I) Rajasthan]

(A) $(x-y)3\,(y-z)^3\,(z-x)^3$ (B) $3(x-y)\,(y-z)\,(z-x)$

(C) $x^3 + y^3 + z^3 - 3xyz$ (D) $x^3 + y^3 + z^3 - 3xyz$

2-70 If a, b, c are all non-zero and $a+b+c=0$ then, the value of $\frac{a^2}{bc} + \frac{b^2}{ca} + \frac{c^2}{ab}$ is: **[NTSE-2017 (Stage-I) Tamilnadu]**

(A) 3 (B) abc

(C) $a^3 + b^3 + c^3$ (D) $a+b+c$

2-71 If $x = 2^{1/3} + 2^{2/3}$ then the value of $x^2 - 6x$ is :

[NTSE-2017 (Stage-I) Tamilnadu]

(A) 6 (B) 3

(C) 2 (D) -8

2-72 The expression $x^4 + 4$ can be factorised as :

[NTSE-2017 (Stage-I) Tamilnadu]

(A) $(x^2+2x+2)\,(x^2-2x+2)$

(B) $(x^2+2x+2)\,(x^2+2x-2)$

(C) $(x^2-2x-2)\,(x^2-2x+2)$

(D) $(x^2+2)\,(x^2-2)$

2-73 Factors of the polynomial $2y^4 + x^3 - 14x^2 - 19x - 2$ are :

[NTSE-2017 (Stage-I) Tamilnadu]

(A) $(x+1), (x-2), (x+3), (x-1)$

(B) $(x^2-1), (x-3), (x+1)$

(C) $(x+1), (x+2), (x-3), (2x+1)$

(D) $(x-1), (x-2), (x+3), (x-3)$

2-74 To make $(x^4 + 4y^4)$ perfect square we have to subtract :

[NTSE-2017 (Stage-I) Uttar Pradesh]

(A) $4xy$ (B) $2y^2x^2$

(C) $2yx$ (D) $4y^2x^2$

2-75 A polynomial in the following is :

[NTSE-2017 (Stage-I) Uttar Pradesh]

(A) $7x^2 - 5\sqrt{x} + \sqrt{5}$ (B) $t^3 - 2t + 1$

(C) $x^2 - \frac{1}{x^2}$ (D) $\sqrt{y} + 5y - 1$

2-76 The value of k for which $(x-1)$ is a factor of the polynomial $x^3 - kx^2 + 11x - 6$ is : **[NTSE-2017 (Stage-I) Uttar Pradesh]**

(A) -6 (B) 5

(C) 2 (D) 6

2-77 The factors of $\left[\frac{2}{x^4} = \frac{1}{x^2}\right]$ will be :

[NTSE-2017 (Stage-I) Uttrakhand]

(A) $\left(\frac{\sqrt{2}}{x^4}+\frac{1}{x}\right)\left(\frac{\sqrt{2}}{x^4}-\frac{1}{x}\right)$ (B) $\left(\frac{\sqrt{2}}{x^2}+\frac{1}{x}\right)\left(\frac{\sqrt{2}}{x^2}-\frac{1}{x}\right)$

(C) $\left(\frac{\sqrt{2}}{x}+\frac{1}{x}\right)\left(\frac{\sqrt{2}}{x}-\frac{1}{x}\right)$ (D) None of these

2-78 If $f(x) = 2x^3 - 3x + 4$, the value of $f(x) + f(-x)$ is : **[NTSE-2017 (Stage-I) West Bengal]**

(A) 4 (B) 6

(C) 0 (D) 8

2-79 If $\frac{x^2}{by+cz} = \frac{y^2}{cz+ax} = \frac{z^2}{ax+by} = 2$, the value of $\frac{c}{2c+z} + \frac{c}{2b+y} + \frac{c}{2a+x}$ is: **[NTSE-2017 (Stage-I) West Bengal]**

(A) 2 (B) $\frac{1}{2}$

(C) 4 (D) $\frac{1}{4}$

2-80 If $(x+2)$ and $(2x-1)$ are factors of $(2x^3+ax^2+bx+10)$, the value of (a^2+b^2) is : **[NTSE-2017 (Stage-I) West Bengal]**

(A) 338 (B) 218
(C) 74 (D) 198

2-81 If $a+b=2c$, the value of $\frac{a}{a-c}+\frac{b}{b-c}$ is : **[NTSE-2017 (Stage-I) West Bengal]**

(A) 0 (B) 1
(C) 2 (D) -1

2-82 What do we get on simplifying the expression $\frac{x}{x+1}+\frac{x+1}{x}+\frac{x}{x(x+1)}$? **[NTSE-2017 (Stage-I) Kerala]**

(A) $2+\frac{1}{x}$ (B) $\frac{1}{2}$
(C) $2x$ (D) $\frac{1}{2}x$

2-83 If a polynomial $x^4-4x^2+x^3+2x+1$ is divided by $x-1$, then remainder will be : **[NTSE-2018 (Stage-I) Rajasthan]**

(A) 0 (B) 1
(C) 9 (D) -1

2-84 If $x^2+4y^2+9y^2-4xy-12yz+6xz=0$
[NTSE-2018 (Stage-I) Rajasthan]

(A) $x=2y-3z$ (B) $x=y-3z$
(C) $2x=y-3z$ (D) $x=3y-2z$

2-85 If $a^{x-1}=bc$, $b^{y-1}=ca$, $c^{z-1}=ab$ than $xy+yz+zx$: **[NTSE-2018 (Stage-I) Andhra Pradesh]**

(A) xyz (B) 0
(C) 1 (D) $\frac{1}{x}+\frac{1}{y}+\frac{1}{z}$

2-86 One of the factor for $x^3-23x^2+142x-120$ is : **[NTSE-2018 (Stage-I) Andhra Pradesh]**

(A) $x-1$ (B) $x+10$
(C) $x-4$ (D) $x+12$

2-87 If the zero of the polynomial x^3-3x^2+x+1 are $(a-d)$, a and $(a+d)$ then $(a+d)$ is : **[NTSE-2018 (Stage-I) Bihar]**

(A) a rational number (B) an integer
(C) a natural number (D) an irrational number

2-88 If $x+y+z=0$ and $x \neq 0, y \neq 0, z \neq 0$, then find the value of $\frac{x^2}{yz}+\frac{y^2}{xz}+\frac{z^2}{xy}$: **[NTSE-2018 (Stage-I) Chandigarh]**

(A) 0 (B) 1
(C) 2 (D) 3

2-89 If $x+\frac{1}{x}=5$, then find the value of $x^9+\frac{1}{x^9}$
[NTSE-2018 (Stage-I) Chandigarh]

(A) 1330690 (B) 1310330
(C) 1330670 (D) 1310370

2-90 A polynomial Which divided by $x+2$, the quotient is $2x^2-3x+1$, and reminder is 5 :
[NTSE-2018 (Stage-I) Chhattisgarh]

(A) $2x^3+x^2-5x+7$ (B) $2x^3-x^2+5x+7$
(C) $2x^3+x^2+5x+7$ (D) $2x^3+x^2-5x-7$

2-91 If x^2-3x+2 is a factor of x^4-px^2+q, then the value of p and q respectively are : **[NTSE-2018 (Stage-I) Delhi]**

(A) $-5, 4$ (B) $-5, -5$
(C) $5, 4$ (D) $5, -4$

2-92 If α, β, γ are the roots of the equation $x^3+4x+1=0$, then $(\alpha+\beta)^{-1}+(\beta+\gamma)^{-1}+(\gamma+\alpha)^{-1}$ is equal to :
[NTSE-2018 (Stage-I) Delhi]

(A) 2 (B) 4
(C) 3 (D) 5

2-93 If one factor of the polynomial $x^3+4x^2-3x-18$ is $x+3$, then the other factor is : **[NTSE-2018 (Stage-I) Gujarat]**

(A) x^2+x (B) x^2+x+6
(C) x^2+x-6 (D) x^2-x+6

2-94 The sum of the zero of $3x^2+5x-2$ is ________ :
[NTSE-2018 (Stage-I) Gujarat]

(A) $\frac{3}{5}$ (B) $-\frac{3}{5}$
(C) $\frac{5}{3}$ (D) $-\frac{5}{3}$

2-95 If $\sqrt{3}$ and $-\sqrt{3}$ are the zeros of a polynomial $p(x)$, then is not the factor of the $p(x)$: **[NTSE-2018 (Stage-I) Gujarat]**

(A) $x+\sqrt{3}$ (B) $x-\sqrt{3}$
(C) x^2-3 (D) x^2+3

2-96 All the zeroes of the polynomial x^3+2x^2+a are also zeros of the polynomial $x^5-x^4-4x^3+3x^2+3x+b$. Then, the values of a and b are respectively : **[NTSE-2018 (Stage-I) Haryana]**

(A) -1 and 2 (B) -1 and -2
(C) 1 and -2 (D) 1 and 2

2-97 If p, q, r are the roots of the equation $x^3+5x^2-16x+48=0$ then value of the expression $p(qr+q+r)+qr$ is :
[NTSE-2018 (Stage-I) Himachal Pradesh]

(A) 13 (B) -32
(C) -64 (D) 32

2-98 If $a^2+b^2=234$ and $ab=108$, find the value of $\frac{a+b}{a-b}$:
[NTSE-2018 (Stage-I) Jharkhand]
(A) 10 (B) 8
(C) 5 (D) 4

2-99 If 1, m and n are zeroes of the polynomial $f(x)=2x^3+5x^2+6x+10$ then the value of $\frac{1}{l}+\frac{1}{m}+\frac{1}{n}$ is :
[NTSE-2018 (Stage-I) Karnataka]
(A) $-\frac{5}{2}$ (B) $-\frac{3}{5}$
(C) $-\frac{5}{3}$ (D) $-\frac{2}{5}$

2-100 Zero of polynomial $p(x)=2x+1$ is :
[NTSE-2018 (Stage-I) Madhya Prasesh]
(A) $-\frac{1}{2}$ (B) $\frac{1}{2}$
(C) 0 (D) ∞

2-101 Remainder on dividing polynomial $3x^2-x^3-3x+5$ by $x-1-x^2$ is :
[NTSE-2018 (Stage-I) Madhya Prasesh]
(A) 7 (B) 3
(C) 0 (D) $2x+5$

2-102 If $x^2+\frac{1}{x^2}=14$, then the value of $x^3+\frac{1}{x^3}$ is :
[NTSE-2018 (Stage-I) Tamil Nadu]
(A) 52 (B) 42
(C) 24 (D) 25

2-103 The polynomials ax^3+4x^2+3x-4 and x^3-4x+a leave the same remainder when divided by $x-3$, then the value of a is :
[NTSE-2018 (Stage-I) Tamil Nadu]
(A) –1 (B) –4
(C) 4 (D) 1

2-104 If the product of two zeroes of the polynomial $x^3-6x^2+11x-6$ is 2, then the third zero is :
[NTSE-2018 (Stage-I) Tamil Nadu]
(A) 1 (B) 2
(C) 3 (D) 4

2-105 Let x be real number such that $x^3+4x=8$, then the value of x^7+64x^2 is : **[NTSE-2018 (Stage-I) Telangana]**
(A) 136 (B) 146
(C) 128 (D) 156

2-106 If $P(x)=x^4+ax^4+bx^2+cx+d$, $a, b, c, d \in Z$ and $P(1)=P(2)=P(3)=0$, then the value of $P(4)+P(0)$ will be ... :
[NTSE-2018 (Stage-I) Telangana]
(A) –12 (B) 24
(C) 16 (D) 18

2-107 If $a+b+c=1$, $a^2+b^2+c^2=9$ and $a^3+b^3+c^3=1$, then the value of $\frac{1}{a}+\frac{1}{b}+\frac{1}{c}$ is : **[NTSE-2018 (Stage-I) Telangana]**
(A) 4 (B) $\frac{1}{2}$
(C) 1 (D) $\frac{1}{4}$

2-108 If $x+\frac{1}{x}=5$, then $\frac{2x}{3x^2-5x+3}$ is equal to :
[NTSE-2018 (Stage-I) Telangana]
(A) 5 (B) $\frac{1}{5}$
(C) 3 (D) $\frac{1}{3}$

2-109 When x^3+3x^2-kx+4 is divided by $x-2$ remainder is $2k$, then the value of k is : **[NTSE-2018 (Stage-I) Telangana]**
(A) 6 (B) –6
(C) 2 (D) –2

2-110 If $x=7-4\sqrt{3}$, the value of $x^2+\frac{1}{x^2}$ will be :
[NTSE-2018 (Stage-I) Telangana]
(A) 146 (B) 148
(C) 194 (D) 196

2-111 Find the zeroes of the polynomial $2x^3+5x^2-9x-18$ if it given that the product of its two zeroes is –3 :
[NTSE-2018 (Stage-I) Uttar Pradesh]
(A) $2, \frac{-3}{2}$ (B) $1, \frac{1}{3}$
(C) $3, -1$ (D) $3, -\frac{1}{3}$

2-112 Polynomial $x^4+x^3-2x^2+x+1$ divided by $x-1$, the remainder will be : **[NTSE-2018 (Stage-I) Uttarakhandh]**
(A) 2 (B) 1
(C) 0 (D) 3

2-113 If $x^2+\frac{1}{x^2}=83$ then the value of $x^3-\frac{1}{x^3}$ will be :
[NTSE-2018 (Stage-I) Uttarakhandh]
(A) 729 (B) 756
(C) 709 (D) None of these

2-114 In equation $4^{1+x} + 4^{1-x} = 10$, the value of x will be : **[NTSE-2018 (Stage-I) Uttarakhandh]**

(A) $\frac{1}{2}, -\frac{1}{2}$ (B) $-\frac{1}{2}, -\frac{1}{2}$

(C) $\frac{1}{2}, \frac{1}{2}$ (D) None of these

2-115 For the equation $|x|^2 + |x| - 6 = 0$, **[NTSE-2014 (Stage-II)]**

(A) There are four roots
(B) The sum of the roots is –1
(C) The product of the roots is – 4
(D) The product of the roots is – 6

2-116 If the value of a quadratic polynomial $p(x)$ is 0 only at $x = -1$ and $p(-2) = 2$, then the value of $p(3)$ is : **[NTSE-2015 (Stage-II)]**

(A) 18 (B) 9
(C) 6 (D) 3

2-117 When a polynomial $p(x)$ is divided by $x - 1$, the remainder is 3. When $p(x)$ is divided by $x - 3$, the remainder is 5. If $r(x)$ is the remainder when $p(x)$ is divided by $(x - 1)(x - 3)$, then the value of $r(-2)$ is : **[NTSE-2016 (Stage-II)]**

(A) –2 (B) –1
(C) 0 (D) 4

2-118 The value(s) of k for which $x^2 + 5kx + k^2 + 5$ is exactly divisible by $x + 2$ but not by $x + 3$ is (are) : **[NTSE-2016 (Stage-II)]**

(A) 1 (B) 5
(C) 1, 9 (D) 9

2-119 If the polynomial $x^4 - 6x^3 + 16x^2 - 25x + 10$ is divided by another polynomial $x^2 - 2x + k$, the remainder comes out to be $x + a$, then the value of a is : **[NTSE-2017 (Stage-II)]**

(A) – 1 (B) – 5
(C) 1 (D) 5

* * * * *

ANSWERS

PRACTICE EXERCISE-2.1

1	(A)	2	(B)	3	(D)
4	(A)	5	(A)	6	(A)
7	(B)	8	(D)	9	(A)
10	(D)	11	(B)	12	(D)
13	(A)	14	(B)	15	(B)
16	(B)	17	(D)	18	(D)
19	(A)	20	(A)	21	(C)
22	(D)	23	(B)	24	(B)
25	(A)	26	(C)	27	(B)
28	(C)	29	(D)	30	(C)
31	(B)	32	(C)	33	(A)
34	(B)	35	(B)	36	(B)
37	(D)	38	(A)	39	(B)
40	(D)	41	(A)	42	(D)
43	(B)	44	(D)	45	(D)
46	(A)	47	(A)	48	(A)
49	(B)	50	(C)		

PRACTICE EXERCISE-2.2

1	(D)	2	(C)	3	(B)
4	(C)	5	(B)	6	(A)
7	(D)	8	(D)	9	(A)
10	(D)	11	(A)	12	(D)
13	(D)	14	(C)	15	(C)
16	(B)	17	(B)	18	(C)
19	(A)	20	(C)	21	(C)
22	(C)	23	(B)	24	(D)
25	(C)				

PRACTICE EXERCISE-2.3

1	(B)	2	(A)	3	(C)
4	(B)	5	(C)	6	(A)
7	(D)	8	(B)	9	(B)
10	(C)	11	(D)	12	(B)
13	(B)	14	(A)	15	(B)
16	(D)	17	(D)	18	(A)
19	(C)	20	(B)	21	(C)
22	(D)	23	(A)	24	(D)
25	(B)	26	(B)	27	(D)
28	(B)	29	(A)	30	(A)
31	(D)	32	(A)	33	(C)
34	(B)	35	(C)	36	(D)
37	(C)	38	(D)	39	(C)
40	(B)	41	(B)	42	(A)
43	(B)	44	(A)	45	(B)
46	(C)	47	(D)	48	(A)
49	(D)	50	(A)	51	(A)
52	(D)	53	(D)	54	(D)
55	(B)	56	(B)	57	(D)
58	(B)	59	(D)	60	(B)
61	(B)	62	(A)	63	(A)
64	(A)	65	(C)	66	(D)
67	(A)	68	(B)	69	(B)
70	(A)	71	(A)	72	(A)
73	(C)	74	(D)	75	(B)
76	(D)	77	(B)	78	(D)
79	(B)	80	(A)	81	(C)
82	(A)	83	(B)	84	(A)
85	(A)	86	(A)	87	(D)
88	(D)	89	(C)	90	(A)
91	(C)	92	(B)	93	(C)
94	(D)	95	(D)	96	(B)
97	(B)	98	(C)	99	(B)
100	(A)	101	(B)	102	(A)
103	(A)	104	(C)	105	(C)
106	(B)	107	(C)	108	(B)
109	(A)	110	(C)	111	(A)
112	(A)	113	(B)	114	(A)
115	(C)	116	(A)	117	(C)
118	(D)	119	(B)		

Solutions of PRACTICE EXERCISE-2.1

Sol. 1 (A) Given

$$\frac{\frac{1}{x^{2007}}-\frac{1}{x^{2009}}}{\frac{1}{x^{2008}}-\frac{1}{x^{2010}}}=\frac{\frac{1}{x^{2007}}\left[1-\frac{1}{x^2}\right]}{\frac{1}{x^{2008}}\left[1-\frac{1}{x^2}\right]}$$

$$=x^{-2007+2008}=x$$

Hence Ans is (A)

Sol. 2 (B) Given

$$x+\frac{1}{x}=5,$$

Then $$\frac{x^4+1}{x^2}=x^2+\frac{1}{x^2}=\left(x+\frac{1}{x}\right)^2-2$$

$$=5^2-2=23$$

Hence Ans is (B)

Sol. 3 (D) I: x^4+x^2+1

$$=x^4+2x^2+1-x^2$$

$$=(x^2+1)^2-x^2$$

$$=(x^2+x+1)(x^2-x+1)$$

III: $x^4-2x^2+1=(x^2-1)^2$

So, option (I) and (III) are can be factorized with integral coefficient.

Hence Ans is (D)

Sol. 4 (A) Let

$$f(x)=x^3-6x^2-6x+1$$

Then $$f(-1)=-1-6+6+1=0$$

So, $x+1$ is one factor x^3-6x^2-6x+1

Hence Ans is (A)

Sol. 5 (A) Given

$$x = (2008)^{1004} + (2008)^{-1004}$$
$$y = (2008)^{1004} - (2008)^{-1004}$$
$$x + y = 2(2008)^{1004} \quad \ldots(1)$$
$$x - y = 2(2008)^{-1004} \quad \ldots(2)$$
$$(x+y)(x-y) = 2(2008)^{1004}\,2(2008)^{-1004}$$
$$= 4(2008)^{1004-1004}$$
$$= 4(2008)^0 = 4$$

Hence Ans is (A)

Sol. 6 (A) $\frac{a}{b} + \frac{b}{a} - ab$

$$= \frac{a^2+b^2-a^2b^2}{ab}$$
$$= \frac{a^2+b^2-(a-b)^2}{ab}$$
$$= \frac{a^2+b^2-a^2-b^2+2ab}{ab}$$
$$= \frac{2ab}{ab} = 2$$

Hence Ans is (A)

Sol. 7 (B) Let

$$a+1 = b+2 = c+3 = d+4$$
$$= a+b+c+d+5 = k \quad \ldots(1)$$
$$\Rightarrow (a+1)+(b+2)+(c+3)+(d+4)$$
$$= a+b+c+d+10 = 4K$$
$$= a+b+c+d+5+5 = 4K$$
$$\Rightarrow K+5 = 4K \quad [\text{from (1) } a+b+c+d+5 = k]$$
$$3K = 5$$
$$K = \frac{5}{3}$$
$$a+b+c+d+5 = K$$
$$a+b+c+d = K-5 = \frac{5}{3} - 5 = \frac{-10}{3}$$

Hence Ans is (B)

Sol. 8 (D)

$$\frac{(a-b)^2}{(b-c)(c-a)} + \frac{(b-c)^2}{(a-b)(c-a)} + \frac{(c-a)^2}{(a-b)(b-c)}$$

Taking LCM as $(a-b)(b-c)(c-a)$

$$\Rightarrow \frac{(a-b)^3+(b-c)^3+(c-a)^3}{(a-b)(b-c)(c-a)}$$

[Since $a-b+b-c+c-a = 0$, $(a-b)^3+(b-c)^3+(c-a)^3 = 3(a-b)(b-c)(c-a)$]

$$= \frac{3(a-b)(b-c)(c-a)}{(a-b)(b-c)(c-a)} = 3$$

Hence Ans is (D)

Sol. 9 (A) Given $(a^2+b^2)^3 = (a^3+b^3)^2$

$$\Rightarrow a^6+b^6+3a^2b^2(a^2+b^2) = a^6+b^6+2a^3b^3$$
$$\Rightarrow 3a^2b^2(a^2+b^2) = 2a^3b^3$$
$$\Rightarrow 3(a^2+b^2) = \frac{2a^3b^3}{a^2b^2}$$
$$\Rightarrow 3(a^2+b^2) = 2ab$$
$$\Rightarrow \frac{a^2+b^2}{ab} = \frac{2}{3}$$
$$\Rightarrow \frac{a^2}{ab} + \frac{b^2}{ab} = \frac{2}{3}$$
$$\Rightarrow \frac{a}{b} + \frac{b}{a} = \frac{2}{3}$$

Hence Ans is (A)

Sol. 10 (D) Given,

$$x = \sqrt{2+\sqrt{2}}$$
$$\Rightarrow x^2 = 2+\sqrt{2}$$
$$\Rightarrow x^4 = 4+2+4\sqrt{2} = 6+4\sqrt{2}$$
$$\Rightarrow \frac{1}{x^4} = \frac{1}{6+4\sqrt{2}} \times \frac{6-4\sqrt{2}}{6-4\sqrt{2}}$$
$$\Rightarrow \frac{1}{x^4} = \frac{6-4\sqrt{2}}{4}$$
$$\Rightarrow \frac{4}{x^4} = 6-4\sqrt{2}$$
$$\Rightarrow x^4 + \frac{4}{x^4} = 6+4\sqrt{2} + 6-4\sqrt{2} = 12$$

Hence Ans is (D)

Sol. 11 (B) $\frac{x^{-3}-y^{-3}}{x^{-3}y^{-1}+(xy)^{-2}+y^{-3}+x^{-1}}$

$$= \frac{\frac{1}{x^3}-\frac{1}{y^3}}{\frac{1}{x^3y}+\frac{1}{x^2y^2}+\frac{1}{xy^3}}$$

$$= \frac{\frac{y^3-x^3}{x^3y^3}}{\frac{y^2+xy+x^2}{x^3y^3}} = \frac{y^3-x^3}{y^2+xy+x^2}$$

$$= \frac{(y-x)(y^2+xy+x^2)}{y^2+xy+x^2} = y-x$$

Hence Ans is (B)

Sol. 12 (D) $\frac{(\sqrt{a}-\sqrt{b})^2+4\sqrt{ab}}{a-b} = \frac{5}{3}$

$$\Rightarrow \frac{a+b-2\sqrt{ab}+4\sqrt{ab}}{a-b} = \frac{5}{3}$$

$$\Rightarrow \frac{a+b+2\sqrt{ab}}{a-b} = \frac{5}{3}$$

$$\Rightarrow \frac{(\sqrt{a}+\sqrt{b})^2}{(\sqrt{a})^2-(\sqrt{b})^2} = \frac{5}{3}$$

$$\Rightarrow \frac{(\sqrt{a}+\sqrt{b})^2}{(\sqrt{a}-\sqrt{b})(\sqrt{a}+\sqrt{b})} = \frac{5}{3}$$

$$\Rightarrow \frac{\sqrt{a}+\sqrt{b}}{\sqrt{a}-\sqrt{b}} = \frac{5}{3}$$

Apply componendo & dividendo

$$\frac{2\sqrt{a}}{2\sqrt{b}} = \frac{8}{2}$$

$$\frac{\sqrt{a}}{\sqrt{b}} = \frac{4}{1}$$

$$\frac{a}{b} = \frac{16}{1}$$

Hence Ans is (D)

Sol. 13 (A)

$$\frac{1}{\dfrac{1}{\dfrac{1}{\frac{1}{x}+\frac{1}{2}}+\dfrac{1}{\frac{1}{x}+\frac{1}{2}}}+\dfrac{1}{\dfrac{1}{\frac{1}{x}+\frac{1}{2}}+\dfrac{1}{\frac{1}{x}+\frac{1}{2}}}} = \frac{x}{36}$$

$$= \frac{1}{\dfrac{1}{\dfrac{1}{\frac{2+x}{2x}}+\dfrac{1}{\frac{2+x}{2x}}}+\dfrac{1}{\dfrac{1}{\frac{2+x}{2x}}+\dfrac{1}{\frac{2+x}{2x}}}}$$

$$= \frac{1}{\dfrac{1}{\frac{2x}{2+x}+\frac{2x}{2+x}}+\dfrac{1}{\frac{2x}{2+x}+\frac{2x}{2+x}}}$$

$$= \frac{1}{\frac{2+x}{4x}+\frac{2+x}{4x}} = \frac{4x}{4+2x} = \frac{x}{36}$$

$$4\times 36 = 4+2x$$

$$144 = 4+2x$$

$$x = \frac{140}{2} = 70$$

Hence Ans is (A)

Sol. 14 (B) Given $P(x) = (x-1)^2+1$

The given expression is always positive so there exist no x for which expression is zero.

Hence Ans is (B)

Sol. 15 (B) Given

$ax^2+bx+c=0$ with roots $\alpha = 0$, $\beta = 0$

$$\alpha+\beta = 0$$

$$\frac{-b}{a} = 0 \Rightarrow b = 0$$

& $\alpha\beta = 0$

$$\frac{c}{a} = 0$$

$$c = 0$$

Hence Ans is (B)

Sol. 16 (B) $x^2-px-p-c=0$ with roots α, β

$$x^2-px-p-c = (x-\alpha)(x-\beta)$$

Replace x by -1, we get

$$1+p-p-c = (-1-\alpha)(-1-\beta)$$

$$1-c = (1+\alpha)(1+\beta)$$

Hence Ans is (B)

Sol. 17 (D) It's degree will be less than the divisor

Hence Ans is (D)

Sol. 18 (D) $f(x) = ax^2+bx+c$ with roots α, 2α

$$\Rightarrow 3\alpha = \frac{-b}{a}$$

$$\Rightarrow \alpha = \frac{-b}{3a}$$

& $2\alpha.\alpha = \frac{c}{a}$

$$\Rightarrow 2\alpha^2 = \frac{c}{a}$$

$$\Rightarrow 2\left(\frac{-b}{3a}\right)^2 = \frac{c}{a}$$

$\Rightarrow \quad \frac{2b^2}{9a^2} = \frac{c}{a}$

$\Rightarrow \quad 2b^2 = 9ac$

Hence Ans is (D)

Sol. 19 (A) Let us divide the given expression and find the remainder

$$\begin{array}{r|l} & 2x^2 - 2x \\ 2x^2 + x - 2 & 4x^4 - 2x^3 - 6x^2 + x - 5 \\ & -(4x^4 + 2x^3 - 4x^2) \\ \hline & -4x^3 - 2x^2 + x \\ & -(-4x^3 - 2x^2 + 4x) \\ \hline & 3x - 5 \end{array}$$

Hence Ans is (A)

Sol. 20 (A) Let the other root be 'α'

$f(x) \equiv x^2 - 2px + p$ with roots a and α

given one zero $= a$

So $\quad f(a) = 0$

$\Rightarrow \quad a^2 - 2ap + p = 0$

$p = \frac{a^2}{2a-1}$

Now $\quad a.\alpha = \frac{p}{1}$

$a.\alpha = \frac{a^2}{2a-1}$

$\alpha = \frac{a}{2a-1}$

Hence Ans is (A)

Sol. 21 (C) $lx^2 + mx + n$ with roots α and β

Let $\quad \alpha = 3x \;\&\; \beta = 4x$

$\alpha + \beta = -\frac{m}{l}$

$\Rightarrow \quad 7x = -\frac{m}{l}$

$\Rightarrow \quad x = -\frac{m}{7l}$ ...(1)

Also $\quad \alpha\beta = \frac{n}{l}$

$\Rightarrow \quad 12x^2 = \frac{n}{l}$

$\Rightarrow \quad 12 \times \frac{m^2}{49l^2} = \frac{n}{l}$ [From (1) $x = -\frac{m}{7l}$]

$12m^2 = 49\,ln$

Hence Ans is (C)

Sol. 22 (D) Given

$x^y = y^x$

$y = (x^y)^{1/x}$

$= x^{y/x}$ ...(1)

Now $\quad \left(\frac{x}{y}\right)^{x/y}$

From (1) $\quad y = x^{y/x}$

$\Rightarrow \quad \left(\frac{x}{x^{y/x}}\right)^{\frac{x}{y}}$

$\Rightarrow \quad \left[x^{\left(1-\frac{y}{x}\right)}\right]^{\frac{x}{y}} = x^{\frac{x-y}{x}.\frac{x}{y}}$

$= x^{\frac{x-y}{y}} = x^{\frac{x}{y}-1}$

Hence Ans is (D)

Sol. 23 (B) $2(a+b)^2 - a(a+b) - 5$

Let $x = a + b$

$\Rightarrow \quad 2x^2 - 9x - 5$

$\Rightarrow \quad x(2x+1) - 5(2x+1)$

$\Rightarrow \quad (2x+1)(x-5)$

$\Rightarrow \quad (2a+2b+1)(a+b-5)$

Hence Ans is (B)

Sol. 24 (B) Given

$a^x = b$ ...(1)

$b^y = c$ ...(2)

$c^z = a$ ...(3)

Consider $\quad c^z = a$

$\Rightarrow \quad (b^y)^z = a$ ... from (2)

$\Rightarrow \quad (b)^{yz} = a$

$\Rightarrow \quad (a^x)^{yz} = a$ ... from (1)

$\Rightarrow \quad (a)^{xyz} = a^1$

$\Rightarrow \quad xyz = 1$

Hence Ans is (B)

Sol. 25 (A) $2x^2 + 5x + k$ with roots α and β

$$\alpha+\beta=-\frac{5}{2}$$

$$\alpha\beta=\frac{k}{2}$$

Given $\quad \alpha^2+\beta^2+\alpha\beta=\dfrac{21}{4}$

$\Rightarrow \quad (\alpha+\beta)^2-\alpha\beta=\dfrac{21}{4}$

$\Rightarrow \quad \dfrac{25}{4}-\dfrac{k}{2}=\dfrac{21}{4}$

$\Rightarrow \quad \dfrac{k}{2}=1$

$\Rightarrow \quad k=2$

Hence Ans is (A)

Sol. 26 (C) Given

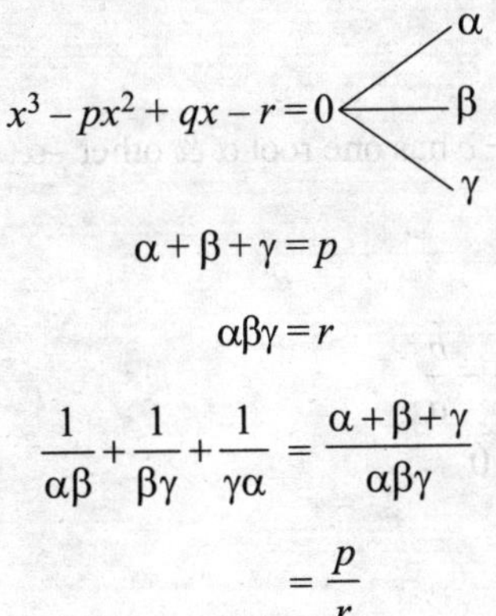

$x^3-px^2+qx-r=0$ with roots α, β, γ

$$\alpha+\beta+\gamma=p$$

$$\alpha\beta\gamma=r$$

$$\frac{1}{\alpha\beta}+\frac{1}{\beta\gamma}+\frac{1}{\gamma\alpha}=\frac{\alpha+\beta+\gamma}{\alpha\beta\gamma}$$

$$=\frac{p}{r}$$

Hence Ans is (C)

Sol. 27 (B) Given

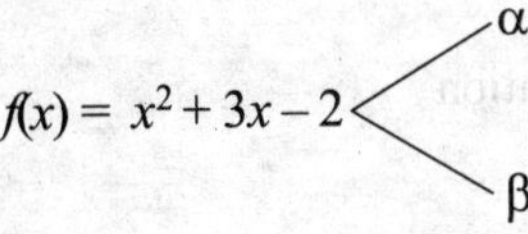

$f(x)=x^2+3x-2$ with roots α, β

Here $\quad \alpha+\beta=-3$

$\alpha\beta=-2$

Equation whose roots are given is

$(x^2-(\text{sum of roots})x+\text{product of root})$

$=x^2-(3\alpha+2\beta+2\alpha+3\beta)x+(3\alpha+2\beta)(3\beta+2\alpha)$

$=x^2-5(\alpha+\beta)x+[6(\alpha^2+\beta^2)+13\alpha\beta]$

$=x^2-5(\alpha+\beta)x+[6(\alpha^2+\beta^2+2\alpha\beta)+\alpha\beta]$

$=x^2+15x+[6(-3)^2-2]$

$=x^2+15x+52$

Hence Ans is (B)

Sol. 28 (C) Given ax^3+bx^2+cx+d with roots α, β, γ

$$\alpha+\beta+\gamma=\frac{-b}{a}$$

$$\alpha\beta+\beta\gamma+\gamma\alpha=\frac{c}{a}$$

$$\alpha\beta\gamma=\frac{-d}{a}$$

Then $\quad \dfrac{1}{\alpha}+\dfrac{1}{\beta}+\dfrac{1}{\gamma}=\dfrac{\alpha\beta+\beta\gamma+\gamma\alpha}{\alpha\beta\gamma}=\dfrac{c/a}{-d/a}$

$$=\frac{-c}{d}$$

Hence Ans is (C)

Sol. 29 (D) x^4+4x^2+5

Since the value of the given expression is always greater than zero, hence there is no value of x for which expression become zero therefore no real zero.

Hence Ans is (D)

Sol. 30 (C) Let $f(x)\equiv 2x^3+ax^2+3x-5$

& $\quad g(x)\equiv x^3+x^2-4x+a$ & divisor $(x-2)$

Since remainder in same

$\Rightarrow \quad f(2)=g(2)$

$\Rightarrow \quad 2\times 8+4a+3\times 2-5=8+4-4\times 2+a$

$\Rightarrow \quad 3a=4-17$

$\Rightarrow \quad a=\dfrac{-13}{3}$

Hence Ans is (C)

Sol. 31 (B) Let

$$f(x)\equiv px^3+x^2-2x+q$$

$f(-1)=f(1)=0 \quad$ [as $x+1$ & $x-1$ are factors]

$$-p+1+2+q=p+1-2+q$$

$$2p=4 \;\Rightarrow\; p=2$$

Now $\quad f(-1)=0$

$\Rightarrow \quad -p+3+q=0$

$\Rightarrow \quad -2+3+q=0$

$\Rightarrow \quad q=-1$

Hence Ans is (B)

Sol. 32 (C) Number of times graph cut x-axis $=4$

So 4 real zeros

Hence Ans is (C)

Sol. 33 (A) Only one time graph cut x-axis so real zero $=1$

Hence Ans is (A)

Sol. 34 (B) Given $a<0$

The graph will be an inverted cone

Hence Ans is (B)

Sol. 35 (B) Let the roots of the equation be $a-d$, a, $a+d$ as it is given there are in A.P.

$$x^3-12x^2+39x+k \quad \begin{cases} a-d=\alpha \\ a=\beta \\ a+d=\gamma \end{cases}$$

$\Rightarrow \quad \alpha+\beta+\gamma=12$

$\Rightarrow \quad 3a=12$

$\Rightarrow \quad a=4$

$\Rightarrow \quad \alpha\beta+\beta\gamma+\gamma\alpha=39$

$\Rightarrow \quad a(a-d)+a(a+d)+(a-d)(a+d)=39$

$\Rightarrow \quad a^2-ad+a^2+ad+a^2-d^2=39$

$\Rightarrow \quad 3a^2-d^2=39$

$\Rightarrow \quad 3\times 16-d^2=39$

$\Rightarrow \quad 48-39=d^2$

$\Rightarrow \quad d^2=9$

$\Rightarrow \quad d=\pm 3$

$\Rightarrow \quad \alpha\beta\gamma=-\dfrac{k}{1}$

$\Rightarrow \quad (a-d)\,a(a+d)=-\dfrac{k}{1}$

$\Rightarrow \quad (4-3)(4)(4+3)=-k$

$\Rightarrow \quad k=-28$

Hence Ans is (B)

Sol. 36 (B) Let the roots be α, β and γ

Given $\alpha+\beta+\gamma=3$

$\alpha\beta+\beta\gamma+\gamma\alpha=-1$

$\alpha\beta\gamma=-3$

The cubic polynomial formed will be

$\Rightarrow \quad k[x^3-(\alpha+\beta+\gamma)x^2+(\alpha\beta+\beta\gamma+\gamma\alpha)x-\alpha\beta\gamma]$

$\Rightarrow \quad k[x^3-3x^2-x+3]$

Hence Ans is (B)

Sol. 37 (D) All the Statement are true

Hence Ans is (D)

Sol. 38 (A) Let $f(x)\equiv x^3+3x^2-5x+4$

Remainder when $f(x)$ is divided by $x-1$

$\Rightarrow \quad f(1)=1+3.1-5.1+4=3$

Hence Ans is (A)

Sol. 39 (B) Consider $(a+b+c)^2\geq 0$

$a^2+b^2+c^2+2(ab+bc+ca)\geq 0$

$\Rightarrow \quad 2(ab+bc+ca)\geq -1$

As $a^2+b^2+c^2=1$ (given)

$\Rightarrow \quad ab+bc+ca\geq -\dfrac{1}{2}$

Hence Ans is (B)

Sol. 40 (D) Given $p(x)=(x+1)^2+2$

Since expression is always positive i.e. $P(x)>0$ for all $x\in R$

So it will not cut x-axis

Hence Ans is (D)

Sol. 41 (A) $p(x)=x^2+x-6=(x+3)(x-2)$

Since $a>0$ & there are two real zeroes

Hence Ans is (A)

Sol. 42 (D) Let ax^2+bx+c has one root α & other $-\alpha$

Then sum of roots $=-\dfrac{b}{a}$

$\alpha-\alpha=-\dfrac{b}{a}$

$\Rightarrow \quad b=0$

$\Rightarrow$ coefficient of x is zero

Hence Ans is (D)

Sol. 43 (B) By observation

Hence Ans is (B)

Sol. 44 (D) By observation

Hence Ans is (D)

Sol. 45 (D) By observation

Hence Ans is (D)

Sol. 46 (A) The cubic polynomials is formed as

$\Rightarrow \quad k[x^3-(\alpha+\beta+\gamma)x^2+(\alpha\beta+\beta\gamma+\gamma\alpha)x-\alpha\beta\gamma]$

$\Rightarrow \quad k[x^3-0x^2+6x+20]$

$\Rightarrow \quad k[x^3+6x+20]$

Hence Ans is (A)

Sol. 47 (A) Let

$$f(x)=(x^2-5x+k) \quad \begin{cases} \alpha \\ \beta \end{cases}$$

Here $\alpha+\beta=5$

$$\alpha - \beta = 3$$

$$2\alpha = 8$$

$\Rightarrow$ $\alpha = 4$ & $\beta = 1$

As $\alpha\beta = k$

$\Rightarrow$ $k = 4$

Hence Ans is (A)

Sol. 48 (A) Given $x + y = a$ & $xy = b$

$$\frac{1}{x^3}+\frac{1}{y^3} = \frac{x^3+y^3}{x^3y^3}$$

$$= \frac{(x+y)^3 - 3xy(x+y)}{x^3y^3} = \frac{a^3-3ab}{b^3}$$

Hence Ans is (A)

Sol. 49 (B) Consider $\dfrac{x^a}{x^a(1+x^{b-a}+x^{c-a})}$

$$+\frac{x^b}{x^b(1+x^{a-b}+x^{c-b})}+\frac{x^c}{x^c(1+x^{b-c}+x^{a-c})}$$

$$= \frac{x^a}{x^a+x^b+x^c}+\frac{x^b}{x^b+x^a+x^c}+\frac{x^c}{x^c+x^b+x^a}$$

$$\Rightarrow \frac{x^a+x^b+x^c}{x^a+x^b+x^c} = 1$$

Hence Ans is (B)

Sol. 50 (C) Let

$f(x) = 2x^3 + 5x^2 - 4x - 6$

and Divisor is $2x + 1$

$\Rightarrow$ Remainder is $f\left(-\dfrac{1}{2}\right)$

$$\Rightarrow 2\left(-\frac{1}{2}\right)^3 + 5\left(-\frac{1}{2}\right)^2 - 4\times\left(-\frac{1}{2}\right) - 6$$

$$\Rightarrow -\frac{2}{8}+\frac{5\times 2}{4\times 2}+\frac{4}{2}-6$$

$$\Rightarrow \frac{8}{8}+2-6 = -3$$

Hence Ans is (C)

Solutions of PRACTICE EXERCISE-2.2

Sol. 1 (D) By observation

$a < 0$ as graph is concave downward

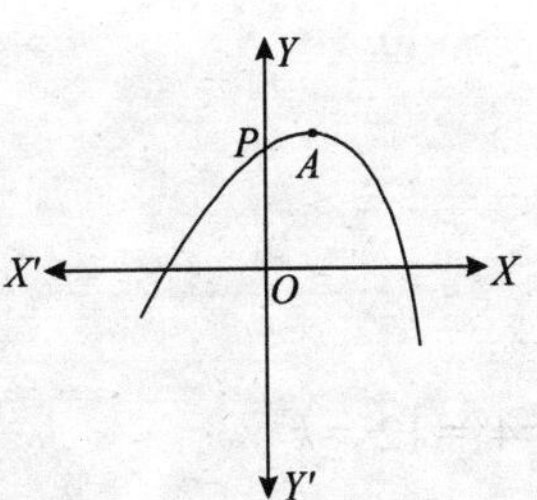

When $x = 0, y = c$

$\Rightarrow$ $c > 0$

and $\dfrac{-b}{2a} > 0$

$\Rightarrow$ $b > 0$

Hence Ans is (D)

Sol. 2 (C) Given $f(x) = ax^2 + bx + c$ has no real zero mean $D < 0$ and since

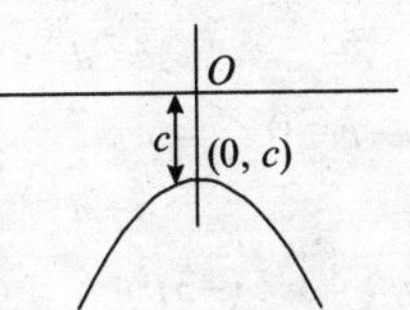

$a + b + c < 0$ mean $f(1) < 0$

So graph of $f(x)$ as shown in the figure

Has $f(0) = c < 0$

Hence Ans is (C)

Sol. 3 (B) By observation

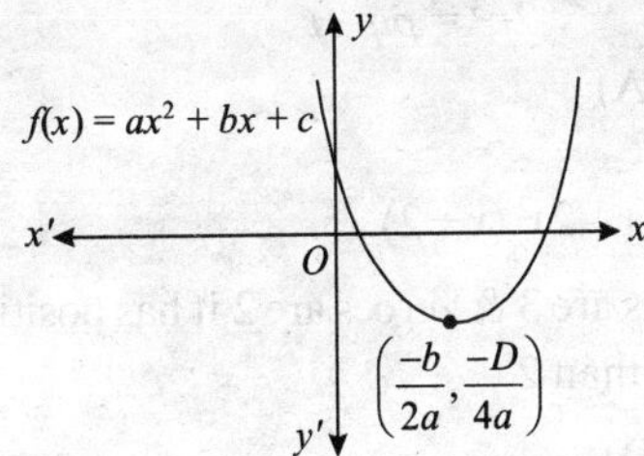

As $a > 0$

$c > 0$

$\Rightarrow$ $-\dfrac{b}{2a} > 0$

$\Rightarrow$ $b < 0$

Hence Ans is (B)

Sol. 4 (C) Replace x^2 by -1

Given $x^4 + x^3 + 8x^2 + ax + 5$ is divides by $x^2 + 1$

as $(x^2 + 1)$ is a factor

$\Rightarrow$ $1 - x - 8 + ax + b = 0$

$\Rightarrow$ $(a - 1)x + (b - 7) = 0$

Equating same coefficient both sides

We get

$a=1 \quad b=7$

Hence Ans is (C)

Sol. 5 (B) Given

$$3^x = 4^y = 12^z = k$$

$$3 = (k)^{1/x} \quad 4 = (k)^{1/y} \quad 12 = (k)^{1/z}$$

$$3 \times 4 = 12$$

$$(k)^{1/x}.\ (k)^{1/y} = (k)^{1/z}$$

$$\frac{1}{x}+\frac{1}{y} = \frac{1}{z}$$

$$z = \frac{xy}{x+y}$$

Hence Ans is (B)

Sol. 6 (A) Let $a-d$, a & $a+d$ are zeroes of the polynomial

$$x^3 - 3px^2 + 9x - r = 0 \begin{cases} a-d \\ a \\ a+d \end{cases}$$

$$\text{sum of roots} = -\frac{(-3p)}{1}$$

$$a-d+a+a+d = 3p$$

$$\Rightarrow \quad 3a = 3p$$

$$\Rightarrow \quad a = p$$

Now a satisfies given polynomial

$$p^3 - 3p.p^2 + qp - r = 0$$

$$2p^3 = pq - r$$

Hence Ans is (A)

Sol. 7 (D) In $(x-2)^2(x+2)$

total no. of roots are 3 & zeroes are 2 it has positive sign for the values of more than 2

Hence Ans is (D)

Sol. 8 (D) We know irrational roots occur always in conjugate pair

$\Rightarrow$ The other root is $2-\sqrt{5}$ let the third root be α

$$x^3 + bx^2 + cx + 5 \begin{cases} \sqrt{5}+2 \\ 2-\sqrt{5} \\ \alpha \end{cases}$$

$$\text{Product of all zeroes} = -\frac{5}{1}$$

$$(2+\sqrt{5})\ (2-\sqrt{5})\ .\alpha = -5$$

$$(4-5) \times \alpha = -5$$

$$\alpha = 5$$

Sum of $2-\sqrt{5}$ & $5 = 7-\sqrt{5}$

Hence Ans is (D)

Sol. 9 (A) $3x^2 - 5x + b \begin{cases} \alpha \\ \beta \end{cases}$

To get the equation whose roots are $\frac{1}{\alpha}$ & $\frac{1}{\beta}$ replace x by $\frac{1}{x}$

We get

$$\frac{3}{x^2} - \frac{5}{x} + b = 0$$

$$\Rightarrow \quad k[3 - 5x + bx^2] = 0$$

Hence Ans is (B)

Sol. 10 (D) Given

$$ax^3 + bx^2 + cx + d = 0 \begin{cases} \alpha \\ \beta \\ \gamma \end{cases}$$

$$\text{Here} \quad \alpha+\beta+\gamma = -\frac{b}{a}$$

$$\Rightarrow \quad \alpha\beta+\beta\gamma+\gamma\alpha = \frac{c}{a}$$

$$\Rightarrow \quad \alpha\beta\gamma = -\frac{d}{a}$$

Consider

$$\alpha^2+\beta^2+\gamma^2 = (\alpha+\beta+\gamma) - 2(\alpha\beta+\beta\gamma+\gamma\alpha)$$

$$= \frac{b^2}{a^2} - 2.\left(\frac{c}{a}\right)$$

$$= \frac{b^2 - 2ac}{a^2}$$

Hence Ans is (D)

Sol. 11 (A) $11^7 + 4^7$ is divisible by 15

So remainder = 0

as $x^n + a^n$ is divisible by $(x+a)$

if n is odd

Hence Ans is (A)

Sol. 12 (D) Let

$$f(x) = (2x^2 - 3x - 2)(2x^2 - 3x) - 63$$

Let $\quad 2x^2 - 3x = y$

$$\Rightarrow \quad f(x) = y.(y-2) - 63$$

$$= y^2 - 2y - 63$$

$$= (y+7)(y-9)$$

$$= (2x^2 - 3x + 7).(2x^2 - 3x - 9)$$

$$= (2x^2 - 3x + 7)(2x^2 + 3x - 6x - 9)$$

$$= (2x^2 - 3x + 7)(x-3)(2x+3)$$

Hence Ans is (D)

Sol. 13 (D) $a\cos^2 x + b\sin^2 x + c = 0$

$\Rightarrow \quad a(1-\sin^2 x) + b\sin^2 x + c = 0$

$\Rightarrow \quad (a+c) + (b-a)\sin^2 x = 0$

$\Rightarrow \quad \sin^2 x = \dfrac{(a+c)}{a-b}$

As $0 \le \sin^2 x \le 1$

So we can have infinite set of value of (a, b, c) which satisfies

Hence Ans is (D)

Sol. 14 (C) Consider

$$x^2 + y^2 + z^2 = 4, \quad \ldots(1)$$

and $\quad xy + yz + zx = k \quad \ldots(2)$

Consider $\quad (x+y+z)^2 \ge 0$

$x^2 + y^2 + z^2 + 2(xy + yz + zx) \ge 0$ from (1) & (2)

$$2k \ge -4$$

$$k \ge -2$$

Hence Ans is (C)

Sol. 15 (C) $ax^2 + bx + c = 0 \begin{cases} a \\ b \end{cases}$

$$a + b = -\frac{b}{a}$$

$$ab = \frac{c}{a}$$

$$a^4 + b^4 = (a^2 + b^2)^2 - 2a^2b^2$$

$$= [(a+b)^2 - 2ab]^2 - 2(ab)^2$$

$$= \left[\frac{b^2}{a^2} - \frac{2.c}{a}\right]^2 - 2\cdot\frac{c^2}{a^2}$$

$$= \frac{(b^2 - 2ac)^2}{(a^2)^2} - 2\frac{c^2}{a^2}$$

$$= \frac{b^4 + 2a^2c^2 - 4acb^2}{a^4}$$

Hence Ans is (C)

Sol. 16 (B) Let

$p(x) = (x^2 - y^2 - 2yz - z^2)$

$\Rightarrow \quad p(x) = [x^2 - (y+z)^2]$

$\Rightarrow \quad p(x) = (x+y+z)(x-y-z)$

Similarly

$q(x) = (x^2 + 2xz + z^2 - y^2)$

$= [(x+z)^2 - y^2]$

$q(x) = (x+z+y) \times (x+z-y)$

& $\quad r(x) = (x-y-z)(x-y+z)$

LCM of $p(x)$, $q(x)$ & $r(x)$

$$= (x+y+z)(x-y-z)(x+z-y)$$

Hence Ans is (B)

Sol. 17 (B) Let $E = x^2 + 4x + 2$

Try to make it a perfect square

$\Rightarrow \quad x^2 + 4x + 2 + 2 - 2$

$\Rightarrow \quad (x+2)^2 - 2$

lowest value is -2

Hence Ans is (B)

Sol. 18 (C) Let $E = 2 - 4x - x^2$

Try to make it a perfect square

$$E = 6 - 4 - 4x - x^2$$

$\Rightarrow \quad E = 6 - (x+2)^2$

$\Rightarrow \quad E = 6 - 4 - 4x - x^2$

$\Rightarrow \quad E = 6 - (x+2)^2$

Maximum value of $E = 6$

Hence Ans is (C)

Sol. 19 (A) $f(x) \equiv ax^2 + bx + c$ has no real zero means $D < 0$ so graph is either concave upward on concave downward.

But $f(-1) > 0$ means $a - b + c > 0$

$\Rightarrow$ 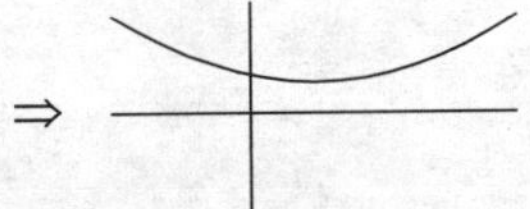

$\Rightarrow \quad c > 0$

Hence Ans is (B)

Sol. 20 (C) $ax^4 + bx^3 + cx^2 + dx + e$ has $x^2 - 4$ as a factor then replace x^2 by 4. we have

$$16a + 4bx + 4c + dx + e = 0$$

$\Rightarrow \quad 16a + 4c + e + x(d + 4b) = 0$

Comparing the coefficients

$\Rightarrow \quad 16a + 4c + e = 0$ & $d + 4b = 0$

$\Rightarrow \quad d = -4b$

Hence Ans is (C)

Sol. 21 (C) Given

$$x + y + z = 0$$

& $\quad x^2 + y^2 + z^2 = 26$

$$x^2 + y^2 + z^2 + 2(xy + yz + zx) = 0$$

$$xy + yz + zx = -13$$

Squaring again

$$x^2y^2+y^2z^2+z^2x^2+2xyz(x+y+z)=169$$

$$\Rightarrow \quad x^2y^2+y^2z^2+z^2x^2=169$$

Now $\quad x^2+y^2+z^2=26$

$$\Rightarrow \quad x^4+y^4+z^4+2(x^2y^2+y^2z^2+z^2x^2)=676$$

$$\Rightarrow \quad x^4+y^4+z^4=676-338$$

$$\Rightarrow \quad x^4+y^4+z^4=338$$

Hence Ans is (C)

Sol. 22 (C) $\quad x-\frac{1}{x}=2$

$$x^2+\frac{1}{x^2}-2=4$$

$$x^2+\frac{1}{x^2}=6$$

$$\left(x^2+\frac{1}{x^2}\right)^3=(6)^3$$

$$x^6+\frac{1}{x^6}+3\left(x^2+\frac{1}{x^2}\right)=216$$

$$x^6+\frac{1}{x^6}+3\times 6=216$$

$$x^6+\frac{1}{x^6}=216-18$$

Hence Ans is (C)

Sol. 23 (B) Given

$$12xyz=108$$

We know $\quad$ A.M. $\geq$ GM.

$$\Rightarrow \quad \frac{2x+3y+4z}{3}\geq\sqrt[3]{2x\cdot 3y\cdot 4z}$$

$$\Rightarrow \quad \frac{2x+3y+4z}{3}\geq\sqrt[3]{2.12xyz}$$

$$\Rightarrow \quad 2x+3y+4z\geq 1$$

$$\Rightarrow \quad 3\sqrt{2.108} \text{ [given } 12xyz=108]$$

$$\Rightarrow \quad \frac{2x+3y+4z}{3}\geq 3\sqrt{216}$$

$$\Rightarrow \quad 2x+3y+4z\geq 18$$

Hence Ans is (B)

Sol. 24 (D) $(2x-1)(2x-2)(2x-3)(2x-4)(2x-5)>0$

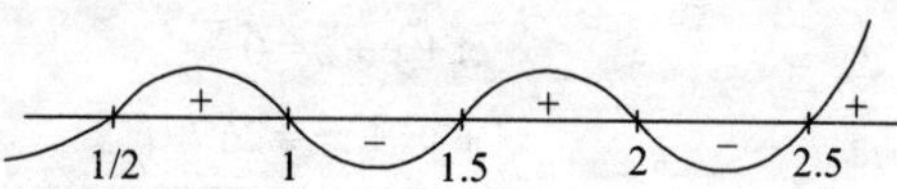

So there are 7 single digit value x can have for which expression has + *ve* sign

i.e. (3, 4, 5, 6, 7, 8, 9)

Hence Ans is (D)

Sol. 25 (C) Given $(2^x-4)^3+(4^x-2)^3=(4^x+2^x-6)^3$

Let $\quad 2^x-4=a$

and $\quad 4^x-2=b$

Now $\quad a^3+b^3=(a+b)^3$

$$\Rightarrow \quad a^3+b^3=a^3+b^3+3ab(a+b)$$

$$\Rightarrow \quad 3ab(a+b)=0$$

$$\Rightarrow \quad ab=0 \text{ or } a+b=0$$

$$\Rightarrow \quad 2^x-4+4^x-2=0$$

$$\Rightarrow \quad (2^x-4)(4^x-2)=0$$

Case-I: $(2^x-4)(4^x-2)=0$

$$\Rightarrow \quad 2^x=4 \text{ or } 4^x=2$$

$$\Rightarrow \quad 2^x=2^2 \text{ or } 2^{2x}=2^1$$

$$\Rightarrow \quad x=2 \text{ or } 2x=1$$

or $\quad x=\frac{1}{2}$

Case-II: $2^x+4^x-6=0$

$$2^x=y$$

$$y^2+y-6=0$$

$$(y+3)(y-2)=0$$

So $\quad y=-3$ or 2

$2^x=-3$ is not possible

$2^x=2,$

$$\Rightarrow \quad x=1$$

It's possible only

When $x=1$

So the sum of all real n is :

$$2+1+\frac{1}{2}=3\frac{1}{2}=\frac{7}{2}$$

Hence Ans is (C)

Solutions of PRACTICE EXERCISE-2.3

Sol. 1 (B) Given α, β are the roots of

$$f(x)=x^2-px-p-c$$

So $\quad$ sum of roots $=-\frac{b}{a}$

$$\Rightarrow \quad \alpha+\beta=p \qquad \ldots(1)$$

Now product of roots $=\frac{c}{a}$

$$\Rightarrow \quad \alpha.\beta=-p-c \qquad \ldots(2)$$

$\Rightarrow \quad (\alpha+1)(\beta+1) = \alpha\beta + (\alpha+\beta) + 1$

$\Rightarrow \quad (\alpha+1)(\beta+1) = (-p-c) + p + 1$

$\Rightarrow$ [from (1) & (2)]

$(\alpha+1)(\beta+1) = 1 - c$

Hence Ans is (B)

Sol. 2 (A) The graph cut or touch the x-axis at 3 distinct points

$\Rightarrow$ Number of zeros = 3

Hence Ans is (A)

Sol. 3 (C) Let roots are α and $\frac{1}{\alpha}$

So product of zeroes = $\frac{c}{a}$

Hence $\alpha \times \frac{1}{\alpha} = \frac{b}{2} \Rightarrow b = 2$

Hence Ans is (C)

Sol. 4 (B) Given

$(16x^{16} - 11x + 2)f(x) = 2016x^{2015}$

Replace $x = 1$ to get the sum of coefficient of $f(x)$

$(16 - 11 + 2)f(1) = 2016$

$f(1) = \frac{2016}{7}$

$f(1) = 288$

So sum of coefficient of $f(x) = 288$

Hence Ans is (B)

Sol. 5 (C) Given $x^2 + 2x + 5$ is a factor of $x^4 + Px^2 + Q$ then let $x^2 + ax + b$ be other factor of $x^4 + Px^2 + Q$

$\Rightarrow \quad (x^2 + 2x + 5)(x^2 + ax + b) = x^4 + Px^2 + Q$

$\Rightarrow \quad x^4 + ax^3 + bx^2 + 2x^3 + 2ax^2 + 2bx + 5x^2 + 5ax + 5b$

$= x^4 + Px^2 + Q$

$\Rightarrow \quad x^4 + x^3(a+2) + x^2(b + 2a + 5) + x(2b + 5a) + 5b$

$= x^4 + Px^2 + Q$

Equating same power on both sides.

$a + 2 = 0$

$2b + 5a = 0 \Rightarrow 2b = 10 \Rightarrow b = 5$

$\Rightarrow \quad P = b + 2a + 5 = 5 - 4 + 5 = 6$

$\Rightarrow \quad (a = -2, b = 5)$

$\Rightarrow \quad Q = 5b = 25$

$\Rightarrow \quad P + Q = 31$

Hence Ans is (C)

Sol. 6 (A) Given a, b, c are the roots of

$x^3 + 3x^2 + 4x - 11 = 0$

$\Rightarrow \quad a + b + c = -3 \quad \ldots(1)$

$\Rightarrow \quad ab + bc + ca = 4 \quad \ldots(2)$

$\Rightarrow \quad abc = 11 \quad \ldots(3)$

and also roots of $x^3 + rx^2 + sx + t = 0$

are $a + b, b + c$ & $c + a$

$\Rightarrow \quad t = -$ Product of all roots

$\Rightarrow \quad t = -(a+b)(b+c)(c+a)$

$\Rightarrow \quad t = -[-3-c][-3-a][-3-b]$

$\Rightarrow \quad t = (3+c)(3+a)(3+b)$

$\Rightarrow \quad t = 27 + 9(a+b+c) + 3(ab+bc+ca) + abc$

$\Rightarrow \quad t = 27 + 9 \times -3 + 3 \times 4 + 11$

[using equestion-(1), (2) & (3)]

$t = 27 - 27 + 12 + 11$

$t = 23$

Hence Ans is (A)

Sol. 7 (D) Critical point of linear divisor $mx + n$ is equal to

$= -\frac{n}{m}$

So remainder is the value of the function of the critical point of the divisor

$\Rightarrow$ Remainder $= P\left(\frac{-n}{m}\right)$

Hence Ans is (D)

Sol. 8 (B) Given

$P(x) \equiv x^3 - 3x^2 + x + 2$

& divisor $= g(x)$

quotient $= (x-2)$

remainder $= (-2x+4)$

We know that

Dividend = Divisor × Quotient + Remainder

$x^3 - 3x^2 + x + 2 = g(x) \times (x-2) + (-2x+4)$

$\Rightarrow \quad g(x) = \frac{x^3 - 3x^2 + x + 2 + 2x - 4}{(x-2)}$

$\Rightarrow \quad g(x) = \frac{x^3 - 3x^2 + 3x - 2}{(x-2)}$

$\Rightarrow \quad g(x) = \frac{x^3 - 2x^2 - x^2 + 2x + x - 2}{x-2}$

$\Rightarrow \quad g(x) = \frac{(x-2)[x^2 - x + 1]}{(x-2)}$

$\Rightarrow \quad g(x) = x^2 - x + 1$

Hence Ans is (B)

Sol. 9 (B) Given one zero of $a^2x^2 + x + b^2$ is -1.

So it will satisfies the equation

$$a^2(-1)^2 + (-1) + b^2 = 0$$

$$a^2 - 1 + b^2 = 0$$

$$a^2 + b^2 - 1 = 0$$

Hence Ans is (B)

Sol. 10 (C) Given $a^2 - (b-c)^2$

$$[a-(b-c)]\,[a+(b-c)]$$

$$(a-b+c)\,(a+b-c)$$

Hence Ans is (C)

Sol. 11 (D) Given

$$x^2 + \frac{1}{x^2} = 23$$

$$x^2 + \frac{1}{x^2} + 2 = 25$$

$$\left(x + \frac{1}{x}\right)^2 = 25$$

$$x + \frac{1}{x} = 5 \text{ as } x > 0$$

Hence Ans is (D)

Sol. 12 (B) Given

$$2p(a-b) + 3q(5a-5b) + 4r(2b-2a)$$

$$2p(a-b) + 3q(a-b)\times 5 + 4r \times 2(b-a)$$

$$(a-b)\,[2p + 15q - 8r]$$

Hence Ans is (B)

Sol. 13 (B) Given

$$x = \frac{\sqrt{3}+1}{2}$$

$$2x = \sqrt{3}+1$$

$$2x - 1 = \sqrt{3}$$

$$4x^2 + 1 - 4x = 3$$

$$4x^2 - 4x - 2 = 0$$

$$2x^2 - 2x - 1 = 0$$

Now we need to find the value of

$4x^3 + 2x^2 - 8x + 7$ when

$$x = \frac{\sqrt{3}+1}{2}$$

So $(2x^2 - 2x - 1)\overline{)4x^3 + 2x^2 - 8x + 7}$ (quotient $2x+3$)

$$4x^3 - 4x^2 - 2x$$

$$\overline{6x^2 - 6x + 7}$$

$$6x^2 - 6x - 3$$

$$\overline{10}$$

$$\Rightarrow 4x^3 + 2x^2 - 8x + 7 = (2x^2 - 2x - 1)(2x+3) + 10$$

So when $x = \dfrac{\sqrt{3}+1}{2}$

Hence Ans is (B)

Sol. 14 (A) Given

$$x = 2 + 2^{1/3} + 2^{2/3}$$

$$(x-2) = 2^{1/3} + 2^{2/3} \quad \ldots(1)$$

$$(x-2)^3 = (2^{1/3} + 2^{2/3})^3$$

$$x^3 - 8 - 3x - 2.(x-2) = (2^{1/3})^3 + (2^{2/3})^3 + 3.2^{2/3}.\,2^{1/3}.\,(2^{1/3} + 2^{2/3})$$

$$x^3 - 8 - 6x^2 + 12x = 2 + 4 + 6(x-2) \quad \text{Using (1)}$$

$$x^3 - 6x^2 - 6x = 2$$

Hence Ans is (A)

Sol. 15 (B) Given $(x-4)$ is a factor of

$5x^3 - 7x^2 - ax - 28$

$\Rightarrow$ $x = 4$ will satisfies the expression

$$\Rightarrow \quad 5(4)^3 - 7(4)^2 - a \times 4 - 28 = 0$$

$$\Rightarrow \quad 5 \times 64 - 7 \times 16 - 4a - 28 = 0$$

$$\Rightarrow \quad 320 - 112 - 28 = 4a$$

$$\Rightarrow \quad 180 = 4a$$

$$\Rightarrow \quad a = 45$$

Hence Ans is (B)

Sol. 16 (D) Coefficient of x^{49} in the product of $(x-1)(x-3)(x-5)\ldots(x-99)$

Will be ($-$ sum of roots of expression)

$$\Rightarrow \; -(1 + 3 + 5 + \ldots + 99)$$

$$\Rightarrow \; -2500$$

Hence Ans is (D)

Sol. 17 (D) If $\quad x = \sqrt[3]{5} + 2$

$$x - 2 = \sqrt[3]{5}$$

$$(x-2)^3 = (\sqrt[3]{5})^3$$

$$x^3 - 8 - 6x^2 + 12x = 5$$

$x^3 - 6x^2 + 12x - 10 = 3$

Hence Ans is (D)

Sol. 18 (A) Let

$$f(x) = (x+1)(x-1)^2$$

and $\quad g(x) = (x+1)^2(x-1)$

We know $\quad HCF = (x+1)(x-1)$

Hence Ans is (A)

Sol. 19 (C) Given $x = 3+\sqrt{8}$

$$\frac{1}{x} = 3-\sqrt{8}$$

$$x+\frac{1}{x} = 3+\sqrt{8}+3-\sqrt{8} = 6$$

$$x^2+\frac{1}{x^2}+2 = 36$$

$$x^2+\frac{1}{x^2} = 34$$

Hence Ans is (C)

Sol. 20 (B) Given $x-y=5, xy=24$

$$(x-y)^2 = 25$$

$\Rightarrow \quad x^2+y^2-2xy = 25$

$\Rightarrow \quad x^2+y^2 = 25+48$

$\Rightarrow \quad x^2+y^2 = 73$

Hence Ans is (B)

Sol. 21 (C) Given $x - 2\sqrt{x} = 3$

Let $\quad \sqrt{x} = y$

$$y^2-2y-3=0$$

$$y^2+y-3y-3=0$$

$$(y+1)(y-3)=0$$

$\Rightarrow \quad y \neq -1; y=3$

$\Rightarrow \quad \sqrt{x} = 3$

$\Rightarrow \quad x = 9$

Hence Ans is (C)

Sol. 22 (D) Let $E = 2x^2-4x+3y^2-18y+31$

$\Rightarrow \quad E = 2x^2-4x+2+3y^2-18y+27+2$

$\Rightarrow \quad E = 2(x-1)^2+3(y-3)^2+2$

Least value of the expression will be at

$x = 1$ & $y = 3$

$\Rightarrow \quad E_{\min} = 2$

Hence Ans is (D)

Sol. 23 (A) Given $2r = h+\sqrt{r^2+h^2}$

$\Rightarrow \quad (2r-h) = \sqrt{r^2+h^2}$

$\Rightarrow \quad (2r-h) = (\sqrt{r^2+h^2})^2$

$\Rightarrow \quad 4r^2+h^2-4rh = r^2+h^2$

$\Rightarrow \quad 3r^2 = 4rh$

$\Rightarrow \quad 3r = 4h$

$\Rightarrow \quad \frac{r}{h} = \frac{4}{3}$

Hence Ans is (A)

Sol. 24 (D) Given $x = cy+bz$ ...(1)

$y = cx+az$ ...(2)

$z = bx+ay$ ...(3)

$$y = c(cy+bz)+az$$

Using (1) in equation-(2)

$(1-c^2)y = (bc+a)z$ ...(4)

Using (1) in equation-(3)

$$z = b(cy+bz)+ay$$

$(1-b^2)z = (bc+a)\times y$ ...(5)

Using (5) in equation-(4)

$$(1-c^2)y = (bc+a)\cdot\frac{(bc+a)y}{(1-b^2)}$$

$$(1-c^2)(1-b^2) = (bc+a)^2$$

$$1-b^2-c^2+b^2c^2 = b^2c^2+a^2+2abc$$

$$a^2+b^2+c^2-1 = -2abc$$

Hence Ans is (D)

Sol. 25 (B) Given

$$P(x) \equiv 10x^2+x-23$$

divisor $= 2x+3$

$$\text{Remainder} \equiv P\left(\frac{-3}{2}\right)$$

$$= 10\cdot\left(\frac{-3}{2}\right)^2+\left(\frac{-3}{2}\right)-23$$

$$= 10\times\frac{9}{4}-\frac{3}{2}-23$$

$$= \frac{45}{2}-\frac{49}{2} = \frac{45-49}{2} = \frac{-4}{2}$$

$$= -2$$

Hence Ans is (B)

Sol. 26 (B) Consider $\frac{a^3}{b-a}+\frac{b^3}{a-b}$

$$= \frac{-a^3}{a-b} + \frac{b^3}{(a-b)}$$

$$= \frac{(b^3 - a^3)}{(a-b)}$$

$$= \frac{(b-a)(b^2+ab+a^2)}{(a-b)}$$

$$= -a^2 - ab - b^2$$

Hence Ans is (B)

Sol. 27 (D) $P(x) \equiv (x+1)(x^2 - x - x^4 + 1)$

Degree of the polynomial = 5

Hence Ans is (D)

Sol. 28 (B) Given

$$P_1(x) \equiv x^2 + 3x + 2 \equiv (x+2)(x+1)$$

$$P_2(x) \equiv x^2 + 5x + 6 \equiv (x+2)(x+3)$$

So HCF of $P_1(x)$ & $P_2(x) = (x+2)$

$\Rightarrow \quad a = 2$

Hence Ans is (B)

Sol. 29 (A) Since $a+b+c=0$

So $a^3 + b^3 + c^3 = 3abc$, then we have

$(x-y)^3 + (y-z)^3 + (z-x)^3 = 3(x-y)(y-z)(z-x)$

Hence Ans is (A)

Sol. 30 (A) Let $p(x) = kx^2 - \sqrt{2}x + 1$

and we have $(x+\sqrt{2})$ as a factor of $kx^2 - \sqrt{2}x + 1$

So $\quad p(-\sqrt{2}) = 0$

$$k(-\sqrt{2})^2 - \sqrt{2} \times (-\sqrt{2}) + 1 = 0$$

$$2k + 2 + 1 = 0$$

$$2k = -3$$

$$k = \frac{-3}{2}$$

Hence Ans is (A)

Sol. 31 (D) The given polynomial will be

$$p(x) \equiv (x-1)(x-2)(x-3)$$

Given divisor $(x^2 - 5x + 6)$ can be written as $(x-2)(x-3)$

So remainder will be zero if $p(x)$ is divided by divisor.

Hence Ans is (D)

Sol. 32 (A) $\quad x + 3y - z = 4 \quad \ldots(1)$

$$3x + 3y + z = 12 \quad \ldots(2)$$

$$(x+3y)^2 - z^2 = 36 \quad \ldots(3)$$

$$(x+3y+z)(x+3y-z) = 36$$

$$(x+3y+z)(4) = 36$$

$$x + 3y + z = 9 \quad \ldots(4)$$

$(2)-(4) \quad \Rightarrow \quad 2x = 3$

$$x = 3/2$$

Hence Ans is (A)

Sol. 33 (C) Given $x^4 - 11x^3 + kx^2 + 269x - 2001$

a, b, c, d, are roots

$a+b+c+d = 11$

$\Rightarrow \quad x + y = 11$

$ab + bc + cd + da + ac + bd = k$

$\Rightarrow \quad abc + bcd + cda + abd = -269$

$\Rightarrow \quad abcd = -2001$

$\Rightarrow \quad cd = -69 \quad \Rightarrow ab = 29$

$\Rightarrow \quad 29(c) + b(-69) + a(-69) + d(29) = -269$

$a + b = 6$

$c + d = 5$

$k = ab + bc + cd + da + ac + db$

$= 29 - 69 + (a+b)(c+d) = 29 - 69 + 30 = -10$

Hence Ans is (C)

Sol. 34 (B) Consider

$$p(x) = x^4 + ax^3 + bx^2 + cx + d$$

$$p(1) = p(2) = p(3) = 0$$

$$p(x) = (x-1)(x-2)(x-3)(x-a)$$

$$p(4) + p(0) = (4-1)(4-2)(4-3)(4-a)$$

$$+ (-1)(-2)(-3)(-a)$$

$$= 6(4-a) + 6a$$

$$= 24 - 6a + 6a$$

$$= 24$$

Hence Ans is (B)

Sol. 35 (C) Given $\sin\alpha + \cos\alpha = \frac{-b}{a} \quad \ldots(1)$

$$\sin\alpha \cdot \cos\alpha = \frac{c}{a}$$

Squaring equation-(1)

$$(\sin\alpha + \cos\alpha)^2 = \left(-\frac{b}{a}\right)^2$$

$$\Rightarrow \sin^2\alpha + \cos^2\alpha + 2\sin\alpha\cos\alpha = \frac{b^2}{a^2}$$

$$\Rightarrow \quad 1 + \frac{2c}{a} = \frac{b^2}{a^2}$$

$$\Rightarrow \quad a^2 + 2ac = b^2$$

Hence Ans is (C)

Sol. 36 (D) Given

$$\frac{(0.03)^2-(0.01)^2}{(0.03)-(0.01)}$$

$$=\frac{[(0.03)+(0.01)][(0.03)-(0.01)]}{[(0.03)-(0.01)]}$$

$$=0.04$$

Hence Ans is (D)

Sol. 37 (C) Consider $\dfrac{\dfrac{y^4-x^4}{x(x+y)}-\dfrac{y^3}{x}}{y^2-xy+x^2}$

$$=\frac{\dfrac{(y-x)(y+x)(y^2+x^2)}{x(x+y)}-\dfrac{y^3}{x}}{y^2-xy+x^2}$$

$$=\frac{(y-x)(y^2+x^2)-y^3}{x(x^2+y^2-xy)}$$

$$=\frac{y^3+x^2y-xy^2-x^3-y^3}{x(x^2-xy+y^2)}$$

$$=\frac{-x(x^2+y^2-xy)}{x(x^2-xy+y^2)}=-1$$

Hence Ans is (C)

Sol. 38 (D) Given $a=\dfrac{4xy}{x+y}$ ...(1)

$$\frac{a}{2x}=\frac{2y}{x+y}$$

Now applying componendo & & dividendo

$$\frac{a+2x}{a-2x}=\frac{2y+x+y}{2y-x-y}=\frac{3y+x}{y-x} \quad ...(2)$$

Similarly

$$\frac{a}{2y}=\frac{2x}{x+y}$$

$$\frac{a+2y}{a-2y}=\frac{3x+y}{x-y} \quad ...(3)$$

$$\Rightarrow \frac{a+2x}{a-2x}+\frac{a+2y}{a-2y}=\frac{3y+x}{y-x}+\frac{3x+y}{x-y}$$

$$\Rightarrow \frac{a+2x}{a-2x}+\frac{a+2y}{a-2y}=\frac{3y+x-3x-y}{y-x}=\frac{2y-2x}{y-x}$$

$$\Rightarrow \frac{a+2x}{a-2x}+\frac{a+2y}{a-2y}=\frac{2(y-x)}{y-x}=2$$

Hence Ans is (D)

Sol. 39 (C) Given x^3+ax^2+bx+c with roots $\alpha=-1$, β, γ

Now $\alpha\beta+\beta\gamma+\gamma\alpha=\dfrac{b}{1}$ ...(1)

& $\alpha+\beta+\gamma=-a$

$-1+\beta+\gamma=-a$

$\Rightarrow \beta+\gamma=1-a$ ...(2)

Now from (1)

$\alpha(\beta+\gamma)+\beta\gamma=b$

$-1(1-a)+\beta\gamma=b$ Using (2)

$\beta\gamma=1-a+b$

Hence Ans is (C)

Sol. 40 (B) Given

$$xy+yz+zx=0$$

$$xy+zx=-yz$$

$$x^2+xy+zx=x^2-yz$$

$$x(x+y+z)=x^2-yz$$

$$\Rightarrow \frac{1}{x(x+y+z)}=\frac{1}{x^2-yz} \quad ...(1)$$

Similarly

$$\frac{1}{y^2-zx}=\frac{1}{y(x+y+z)} \quad ...(2)$$

$$\frac{1}{z^2-xy}=\frac{1}{z(x+y+z)} \quad ...(3)$$

Adding (1), (2) & (3)

$$\frac{1}{x^2-yz}+\frac{1}{y^2-zx}+\frac{1}{z^2-xy}$$

$$=\frac{1}{(x+y+z)}\left|\frac{1}{x}+\frac{1}{y}+\frac{1}{z}\right|$$

$$=0$$

Hence Ans is (B)

Sol. 41 (B) From the given equations

$$\alpha\beta+\beta\gamma+\gamma\alpha=\frac{c}{a}=-1$$

Also $5(\alpha\beta+\beta\gamma+\gamma\alpha)=-5$

Hence Ans is (B)

Sol. 42 (A) Let

$f(x)=x^3-1$

& $g(x)=x^2+1$

divisor $=x+1$

$R_1=f(-1)$ & $R_2=f(-1)$

$R_1=-1-1$ & $R_2=+1+1$

$R_1=-2$ & $R_2=2$

So $R_1+R_2=0$

Hence Ans is (A)

Sol. 43 (B) Given $a=\sqrt{5+2\sqrt{6}}$

$$a=\sqrt{(\sqrt{2}+\sqrt{3})^2}$$

$$a=\sqrt{3}+\sqrt{2}$$

$$\Rightarrow \quad \frac{1}{a}=\frac{1}{\sqrt{3}+\sqrt{2}}=\sqrt{3}-\sqrt{2}$$

$$\frac{a^4+1}{a^2}=a^2+\frac{1}{a^2}$$

$$=\left(a+\frac{1}{a}\right)^2-2$$

$$=[\sqrt{3}+\sqrt{2}+\sqrt{3}-\sqrt{2}]^2-2$$

$$=12-2=10$$

Hence Ans is (B)

Sol. 44 (A) Given $x^2+ax+b=0$ with roots α and $\beta=\frac{1}{3}\alpha$

Sum of roots

$$\alpha+\beta=\frac{-a}{1}$$

$$\alpha+\frac{1}{3}\alpha=-a$$

$$\frac{4\alpha}{3}=-a$$

$$\alpha=\frac{-3a}{4}$$

Product of roots

$$\alpha\beta=b$$

$$\alpha\left(\frac{1}{3}\alpha\right)=b$$

$$\alpha^2=3b$$

$$\frac{9a^2}{16}=3b$$

$$9a^2=48b$$

$$3a^2=16b$$

Hence Ans is (A)

Sol. 45 (B) Given $a+b=2$

& $\quad \frac{1}{a}+\frac{1}{b}=2$

$$\frac{a+b}{ab}=2$$

$$\Rightarrow \quad ab=1$$

$$\Rightarrow \quad (a+b)=2$$

$$\Rightarrow \quad (a+b)^3=a^3+b^3+3ab(a+b)$$

$$\Rightarrow \quad a^3+b^3=(a+b)^3-3ab(a+b)$$

$$=(2)^3-3\times 1(2)$$

$$=8-6=2$$

Hence Ans is (B)

Sol. 46 (C) Given $a=\sqrt{6}+\sqrt{5}$, $b=\sqrt{6}-\sqrt{5}$

$$\Rightarrow \quad 2(a^2+b^2)=2.2(6+5)=4\times 11=44$$

Given $\quad 5ab=5.(1)=5$

$$\Rightarrow \quad 2(a^2+b^2)-5ab=44-5=39$$

Hence Ans is (C)

Sol. 47 (D) Let the total number of swan $=x$

Given

$$\frac{7}{2}\sqrt{x}+2=x$$

$$\Rightarrow \quad x-2=\frac{7\sqrt{x}}{2}$$

$$\Rightarrow \quad 2x-4=7\sqrt{x}$$

$$\Rightarrow \quad 4x^2-65x+16=0$$

$$\Rightarrow \quad x=16$$

Hence Ans is (D)

Sol. 48 (A) Let $\frac{x}{2y+z-x}=\frac{y}{2z+x-y}$

$$=\frac{2}{2x+y-2}=K$$

$$\Rightarrow \quad x=K(2y+z-x)$$

$$\Rightarrow \quad y=K(2z+x-y)$$

$$\Rightarrow \quad z=K(2x+y-z)$$

Add. $(x+y+z)=K(2x+2y+2z)$

$$K=\frac{1}{2}$$

Hence Ans is (A)

Sol. 49 (D) Given HCF $=x$

$$\text{LCM}=x^3-9x$$

$$P_1(x)=x^2+3x$$

$$P_1(x)\times P_2(x)=\text{HCF}\times\text{LCM}$$

$$(x^2+3x)\times P_2(x)=x\times(x^3-9x)$$

$$P_2(x)=\frac{x\times x(x^2-9)}{(x^2+3x)}$$

$$=\frac{x\times x(x-3)(x+3)}{x(x+3)}$$

$$=x^2-3x$$

Hence Ans is (D)

Sol. 50 (A) $x^2+xy+x=12 \quad \ldots(1)$

$y^2+xy+y=18 \quad \ldots(2)$

From (1) + (2) $(x+y)(x+y+1)=30$ let $x+y=t$ then $t(t+1)=30$

$\Rightarrow \quad t^2+t-30=0$

$\Rightarrow \quad (t-5)(t+6)=0$

Hence $x+y=5$ or $x+y=-6$

Hence Ans is (A)

Sol. 51 (A) $x=\dfrac{1}{2-\dfrac{1}{2-\dfrac{1}{2-x}}}$

$$x=\frac{1}{2-\dfrac{2-x}{3-2x}}$$

$\Rightarrow \quad x=\dfrac{3-2x}{4-3x}$

$\Rightarrow \quad x^2-2x+1=0$

Hence Ans is (A)

Sol. 52 (D) α, β are zeroes of $3x^2+6x+k$

Since $\quad \alpha+\beta=-\dfrac{6}{3}$

$$\alpha\beta=\frac{k}{3}$$

$$\alpha^2+\beta^2+\alpha\beta=\frac{8}{3}$$

$\Rightarrow \quad (\alpha+\beta)^2-\alpha\beta=\dfrac{8}{3}$

$\Rightarrow \quad (-2)^2-\dfrac{k}{3}=\dfrac{8}{3}$

$\Rightarrow \quad 4-\dfrac{k}{3}=\dfrac{8}{3}$

$\Rightarrow \quad \dfrac{k}{3}=\dfrac{4}{3}$

$\Rightarrow \quad k=4$

Hence Ans is (D)

Sol. 53 (D) $x^2-5x+1=0$

Dividing above equation by x

$$x-5+\frac{1}{x}=0$$

$\Rightarrow \quad x+\dfrac{1}{x}=5 \qquad \ldots(1)$

Squaring equation-(1)

$$x^2+\frac{1}{x^2}+2=25$$

$\Rightarrow \quad x^2+\dfrac{1}{x^2}=23 \qquad \ldots(2)$

Squaring equation-(2)

$$x^4+\frac{1}{x^4}+2=529$$

$$x^4+\frac{1}{x^4}=527 \qquad \ldots(3)$$

Cubing equation-(1)

$$x^3+\frac{1}{x^3}+3(x)\left(\frac{1}{x}\right)\left(x+\frac{1}{x}\right)=125$$

$\Rightarrow \quad x^3+\dfrac{1}{x^3}+3(5)=125$

$\Rightarrow \quad x^3+\dfrac{1}{x^3}=110 \qquad \ldots(4)$

Now $\left(x^4+\dfrac{1}{x^4}\right)\left(x+\dfrac{1}{x}\right)=\left(x^5+\dfrac{1}{x^5}\right)+\left(x^3+\dfrac{1}{x^3}\right)$

Substituting values from (1), (2), (3)

$$(527)(5)=\left(x^5+\frac{1}{x^5}\right)+110$$

$$2635-110=x^5+\frac{1}{x^5}$$

$$2525=x^5+\frac{1}{x^5}$$

Hence Ans is (D)

Sol. 54 (D) $\alpha\times\dfrac{1}{\alpha}=\dfrac{2K}{K+1}$

$$2K=K+1$$

$$K=1$$

Hence Ans is (D)

Sol. 55 (B) $2x^2-5x+16=0$

$$\alpha+\beta=\frac{5}{2}\alpha\beta=8$$

$$\left(\frac{\alpha^2}{\beta}\right)^{\frac{1}{3}}+\left(\frac{\beta^2}{\alpha}\right)^{\frac{1}{3}}$$

$\Rightarrow \quad \dfrac{\alpha^{\frac{2}{3}}}{\beta^{\frac{1}{3}}}+\dfrac{\beta^{\frac{2}{3}}}{\alpha^{\frac{1}{3}}}=\dfrac{\alpha+\beta}{(\alpha\beta)^{\frac{1}{3}}}$

$$=\frac{\frac{5}{2}}{(8)^{\frac{1}{3}}}=\frac{5}{2\times 2}=\frac{5}{4}$$

Hence Ans is (B)

Sol. 56 (B) $[(0.111)^3+(0.222)^3-(0.333)^3+(0.333)^2(0.222)^2]$

$a^3+b^3+c^3=3abc$ if $a+b+c=0$

Hence Ans is (B)

Sol. 57 (D) $\left(a^{\frac{1}{16}}+a^{-\frac{1}{16}}\right)\times\left(a^{\frac{1}{16}}-a^{-\frac{1}{16}}\right)\times\left(a^{\frac{1}{8}}+a^{-\frac{1}{8}}\right)\times\left(a^{\frac{1}{4}}+a^{-\frac{1}{4}}\right)$

$$=\left(a^{\frac{1}{8}}-a^{-\frac{1}{8}}\right)\left(a^{\frac{1}{8}}+a^{-\frac{1}{8}}\right)\left(a^{\frac{1}{4}}+a^{-\frac{1}{4}}\right)$$

$$=\left(a^{\frac{1}{4}}-a^{-\frac{1}{4}}\right)\left(a^{\frac{1}{4}}+a^{-\frac{1}{4}}\right)\left(a^{\frac{1}{2}}+a^{-\frac{1}{2}}\right)$$

$$\sqrt{a}-\frac{1}{\sqrt{a}}=\frac{a-1}{\sqrt{a}}$$

$$=\sqrt{\frac{(a-1)^2}{a}}$$

Hence Ans is (D)

Sol. 58 (B) (–5)

Sol. 59 (D) Trinomial (cubic)

Sol. 60 (B) Product $=\frac{c}{a}=\frac{3}{1}=3$

Sol. 61 (B) $ax^2+15x+6$

Let zeros are α & $\frac{1}{\alpha}$

$$\alpha\times\frac{1}{\alpha}=\frac{6}{a}\Rightarrow a=6$$

Now zeros of $6x^2+15x+6=0$

$$x=-2\ \frac{-1}{2}$$

Hence Ans is (B)

Sol. 62 (A) Given $(x+a)$ is a factor of x^2+px+q & x^2+mx+n

$$a^2-pa+q=a^2-ma+n$$

$$(m-p)\,a=n-q$$

$$a=\frac{n-q}{m-p}$$

Hence Ans is (A)

Sol. 63 (A) At $x=1, 5, -2$, value of the polynomial becomes.

Hence Ans is (A)

Sol. 64 (A) $\left(3^{\frac{1}{3}}+2^{\frac{1}{3}}\right)\left(9^{\frac{1}{3}}+4^{\frac{1}{3}}-6^{\frac{1}{3}}\right)$

$$=\left(3^{\frac{1}{3}}+2^{\frac{1}{3}}\right)\left(3^{\frac{2}{3}}-3^{\frac{1}{3}}\times2^{\frac{1}{3}}+2^{\frac{2}{3}}\right)=\left(2^{\frac{3}{3}}+3^{\frac{3}{3}}\right)$$

$$=3+2=5$$

Hence Ans is (A)

Sol. 65 (C) Since remainder is 52 therefore according to remainder theorem,

$$4^3+2(4)^2-\alpha(4)-12=52$$

$$64+32-4\alpha-12=52$$

$$\Rightarrow\ \alpha=8$$

Hence Ans is (C)

Sol. 66 (D) $p+q=-r$

$$\frac{2p^2(q+r)+2q^2(p+r)+2r^2(p+q)}{pqr}$$

$$\Rightarrow\ \frac{2p^3-2q^3-2r^3}{pqr}$$

$$\Rightarrow\ \frac{-2(p^3+q^3+r^3)}{pqr}$$

$$\Rightarrow\ \frac{-2(3pqr)}{pqr}=-6$$

Hence Ans is (D)

Sol. 67 (A) Consider $x=\frac{1}{\sqrt{3}-1}\times\frac{\sqrt{3}+1}{\sqrt{3}-1}=\frac{\sqrt{3}+1}{2}$

$$2x-1=\sqrt{3}$$

Squaring

$$4x^2-4x+1=3$$

$$2x^2-2x-1=0$$

$$4x^3+2x^2-8x-3$$

$$=4x^3-4x^2-2x+6x^2-6x-3$$

$$=2x\times0+3\times0=0$$

Hence Ans is (A)

Sol. 68 (B) Consider $\frac{1}{a+b+x}=\frac{1}{a}+\frac{1}{b}+\frac{1}{x}$

$$\frac{1}{a+b+x}-\frac{1}{x}=\frac{1}{a}+\frac{1}{b}$$

$$\frac{x-(a+b+x)}{(a+b+x)x}=\frac{1}{a}+\frac{1}{b}$$

$$\frac{-(a+b)}{x(a+b+x)}=\frac{a+b}{ab}$$

$$-ab=(a+b)x+x^2$$

$x^2+(a+b)x+ab=0$

$x=-a,-b$

Hence Ans is (B)

Sol. 69 (B) Given $a=x-y\,;b=y-z\,;c=z-x$

$a+b+c=x-y+y-z+z-x=0$

$\Rightarrow\; a^3+b^3+c^3=3abc$

$=3(x-y)(y-z)(z-x)$

Hence Ans is (B)

Sol. 70 (A) $a+b+c=0$

$$\frac{a^2}{bc}+\frac{b^2}{ac}+\frac{c^2}{ab}=\frac{a^3+b^3+c^3}{abc}=\frac{3abc}{abc}=3$$

Hence Ans is (A)

Sol. 71 (A) $x^3=\left(2^{1/3}+2^{2/3}\right)^3$

$=2+2^2+3.2^{1/2}.2^{1/3}\left(2^{1/3}+2^{2/3}\right)$

$=6+6x$

$x^3-6x=6$

Hence Ans is (A)

Sol. 72 (A) $x^4+4=(x^2)+2^2$

$=(x^2)+2^2+2.x^2.2-2.x^2.2$

$=(x^2+2)^2-(2x)^2$

$=(x^2+2+2x)(x^2+2-2x)$

Hence Ans is (A)

Sol. 73 (C) $f(1)\neq 0 \Rightarrow x-1$ is not a factor of $f(x)$. So, option (C)

Hence Ans is (C)

Sol. 74 (D) Given $x^4+4y^4-4x^2y^2=(x-2y^2)^2$

$\Rightarrow\; 4x^2y^2$ is subtracted to make it perfect square.

Hence Ans is (D)

Sol. 75 (B) Clearly t^3-2t+1

Hence Ans is (B)

Sol. 76 (D) If $(x-1)$ is a factor of $f(x)=x^3-kx^2+11x-6$ then, $f(1)=0$

$\Rightarrow\quad 1^3-k(1)^2+11(1)-6=0$

$\Rightarrow\quad k=6$

Hence Ans is (D)

Sol. 77 (B) Using identity $a^2-b^2=(a+b)(a-b)$

$$\left(\frac{\sqrt{2}}{x^2}\right)^2-\left(\frac{1}{x}\right)^2=\left(\frac{\sqrt{2}}{x^2}+\frac{1}{x}\right)\left(\frac{\sqrt{2}}{x^2}-\frac{1}{x}\right)$$

Hence Ans is (B)

Sol. 78 (D) Consider $f(x)+f(-x)$

$=2x^3-3x+4+(-2x^3+3x+4)$

$=8$

Hence Ans is (D)

Sol. 79 (B) $\dfrac{c}{2c+z}+\dfrac{b}{2b+y}+\dfrac{a}{2a+x}$

$$=\frac{cz}{2cz+z^2}+\frac{by}{2by+y^2}+\frac{ax}{2ax+x^2}$$

$$=\frac{cz}{2cz+2ax+2by}+\frac{by}{2by+2cz+2ax}+\frac{ax}{2ax+2by+2cz}$$

$$=\frac{ax+by+cz}{2(ax+by+cz)}=\frac{1}{2}$$

Hence Ans is (B)

Sol. 80 (A) Given $f(-2)=0$

$\Rightarrow\quad 2a-b=3$

$f\left(\frac{1}{2}\right)=0 \Rightarrow a+2b=-41$

$\Rightarrow\quad a=-7, b=-17$

and $\quad a^2+b^2=338$

Hence Ans is (A)

Sol. 81 (C) Given $a+b=2c$

$$\Rightarrow\quad \frac{a}{a-c}+\frac{b}{b-c}=\frac{a}{c-b}+\frac{b}{b-c}$$

$$=\frac{b-a}{b-c}=\frac{b-(2c-b)}{b-c}$$

$$=\frac{2(b-c)}{(b-c)}=2$$

Hence Ans is (C)

Sol. 82 (A) $\dfrac{x}{x+1}+\dfrac{x+1}{x}+\dfrac{x}{x(n+1)}$

$$=\frac{x^2+(x+1)^2+x}{x(x+1)}$$

$$=\frac{x^2+x^2+1+2x+x}{x(x+1)}$$

$$=\frac{2x^2+3x+1}{x(x+1)}$$

$$=\frac{2x^2+2x+x+1}{x(x+1)}$$

$$= \frac{2x(x+1)+1(x+1)}{(x+1)\cdot x}$$

$$= \frac{(2x+1)(x+1)}{(x+1)x}$$

$$= \frac{2x+1}{x}$$

$$= 2 + \frac{1}{x}$$

Hence Ans is (A)

Sol. 83 (B) Consider $P(x) = x^4 - 4x^2 + x^3 + 2x + 1$

Divided by $(x-1)$

Remainder $= P(1) = 1 - 4 + 1 + 2 + 1 = 1$

Hence Ans is (B)

Sol. 84 (A) Consider

$$x^2 + 4y^2 + 9z^2 - 4xy - 12yz + 6xz = 0$$

$$(x - 2y + 3z)^2 = 0$$

$$\Rightarrow \quad (x - 2y + 3z)^2 = 0$$

$$\Rightarrow \quad x = 2y - 3z$$

Hence Ans is (A)

Sol. 85 (A) Given $a^{x-1} = bc$

$\Rightarrow \quad a^x = abc$

$\Rightarrow \quad a = (abc)^{1/x}$ ...(1)

$b^{y-1} = ca \Rightarrow b^y = abc \Rightarrow b = (abc)^{1/y}$ ...(2)

$c^{z-1} = ab \Rightarrow c^x = abc \Rightarrow a = (abc)^{1/z}$ ...(3)

Multiplying equation-(1), (2) and (3) we get

$$abc = (abc)^{\frac{1}{x}+\frac{1}{y}+\frac{1}{z}}$$

$$\Rightarrow \quad 1 = \frac{1}{x} + \frac{1}{y} + \frac{1}{z}$$

$$\Rightarrow \quad xyz = xy + yz + zx$$

Hence Ans is (A)

Sol. 86 (A) Consider $x^3 - 23x^2 + 142x - 120$

$= x^2(x-1) - 22x(x-1) + 120(x-1)$

$= (x-1)(x^2 - 22x + 120)$

$\Rightarrow$ One of factor is $(x-1)$

Hence Ans is (A)

Sol. 87 (D) Given $P(x) = x^3 - 3x^2 + x + 1$

Zeros are $(a+d)$, a, $(a-d)$

Sum of zero $= a + d + a + a - d = -(-3)$

$$3a = 3$$

$$a = 1$$

Product of zero $= (a+d)(a)(a-d) = -1$

$$(a^2 - d^2)\,a = -1$$

$$(1 - d^2)(1) = -1 \qquad (\because a = 1)$$

$$2 = d^2$$

$$d = \pm\sqrt{2}$$

Hence Ans is (D)

Sol. 88 (D) Answer coming only if we take 2 as z

$$x + y + z = 0$$

$$\frac{x^2}{yz} + \frac{y^2}{xz} + \frac{z^2}{xy} = \frac{x^3 + y^3 + z^3}{xyz} = \frac{3xyz}{xyz} = 3$$

Hence Ans is (D)

Sol. 89 (C) $x + \frac{1}{x} = 5$

$$x^2 + \frac{1}{x^2} = 25 - 2$$

$$x^2 + \frac{1}{x^2} = 23$$

$$x^3 + \frac{1}{x^3} = \left(x + \frac{1}{x}\right)^3 - 3\left(x + \frac{1}{x}\right)$$

$$= 125 - 15 = 110$$

$$x^6 + \frac{1}{x^6} = (110)^2 - 2 = 12100 - 2 = 12098$$

$$\left(x^6 + \frac{1}{x^6}\right)\left(x^3 + \frac{1}{x^3}\right) = x^9 + x^3 + \frac{1}{x^3} + \frac{1}{x^9}$$

$$(12098)(110) = 110 + \left(x^9 + \frac{1}{x^9}\right) = 1330670$$

Hence Ans is (C)

Sol. 90 (A) Polynomial = (divisor × quotient) + Reminder

$= (x + 2) \times (2x^2 - 3x + 1) + 5$

$= x(2x^2 - 3x + 1) + 2(2x^2 - 3x + 1) + 5$

$= 2x^3 - 3x^2 + x + 4x^2 - 6x + 2 + 5$

$= 2x^3 + x^2 - 5x + 7$

Hence Ans is (A)

Sol. 91 (C) Since $x^2 - 3x + 2 = (x-1)(x-2)$

$f(x) = x^4 - px^2 + q$

$f(1) = 1 - p + q = 0$ ...(1)

$f(2) = 16 - 4p + q = 0$ ...(2)

Solving (1) and (2) $p = 5, q = 4$

Hence Ans is (C)

Sol. 92 (B) $\alpha + \beta + \gamma = 0$

$$\alpha\beta + \beta\gamma + \gamma\alpha = 4$$

$$\alpha\beta\gamma = -1$$

Now $(\alpha+\beta)^{-1}+(\beta+)^{-1}+(\gamma+\alpha)^{-1}$

$\Rightarrow (-\gamma)^{-1}+(-\alpha)^{-1}+(-\beta)^{-1}$

$\Rightarrow -\left[\frac{1}{\alpha}+\frac{1}{\beta}+\frac{1}{\gamma}\right]$

$\Rightarrow -\left[\frac{\alpha\beta+\beta\gamma+\gamma\alpha}{\alpha\beta\gamma}\right]=-\left[\frac{4}{-1}\right]=4$

Hence Ans is (B)

Sol. 93 (C)

$$\begin{array}{r|l} x+3 & x^3+4x^2-3x-18 \quad (x^2+x-6 \\ & x^3+3x^2 \\ & \underline{-\quad -} \\ & x^2-3x-18 \\ & x^2+3x \\ & \underline{-\quad -} \\ & -6x-18 \\ & -6x-18 \\ & \underline{+\quad +} \\ & 0 \end{array}$$

$\Rightarrow$ Other factor is (x^2+x-6)

Hence Ans is (C)

Sol. 94 (D) Sum of zero is given by $\frac{-b}{a}$

For given equation, sum of zeroes are $-\frac{5}{3}$

Hence Ans is (D)

Sol. 95 (D) If $\sqrt{3}$ and $-\sqrt{3}$ are zeros of polynomial $p(x)$ then its factors are $(x-\sqrt{3})$, $(x+\sqrt{3})$ and $(x-\sqrt{3})$, $(x+\sqrt{3})$.

Also $(x-\sqrt{3}), (x+\sqrt{3})=x^2-3$

So x^2+3 is not the factor of $p(x)$.

Hence Ans is (D)

Sol. 96 (B) According to the question

(x^3+2x^2+a) will completely divide

$x^5-x^4-4x^3+3x^2+3x+b$

$$\begin{array}{r|l} x^3+2x^2+a & x^5-x^4-4x^3+3x^2+3x+b \quad (x^2-3x+2 \\ & x^5+2x^4+ax^2 \\ & \underline{-\quad -\quad -} \\ & -3x^4-4x^3+(3-a)x^2+3x+b \\ & -3x^4-6x^3-3ax \\ & \underline{+\quad +\quad +} \\ & 2x^3+(3-a)x^2+(3a+3)x+b \\ & 2x^3+4x^2+2a \\ & \underline{-\quad -\quad -} \\ & -(a+1)x^2+(3a+3)x+b-2a \end{array}$$

Since, the remainder is zero, therefore,cofficient of each term will be zero

$\Rightarrow a+1=0 \quad \Rightarrow a=-1$

$b-2a=0 \quad \Rightarrow b=2a$

$\Rightarrow b=-2$

Hence Ans is (B)

Sol. 97 (B) Given $p+q+r=-5$

$pq+pr+rq=16$

$pqr=-48$

According to question

$pqr+pq+pr+qr$

$(-48)+(16)$

$=-32$

Hence Ans is (B)

Sol. 98 (C) Given $a^2+b^2=234$, $ab=108$

Now,

$(a+b)^2=a^2+b^2+2ab=234+216$

$(a+b)^2=450$

$\Rightarrow \quad a+b=\sqrt{450}$

Also $\quad (a-b)^2=a^2+b^2-2ab=234-216=18$

$\Rightarrow \quad a-b=\sqrt{18}$

Hence, $\quad \frac{a+b}{a-b}=\sqrt{\frac{450}{18}}$

$=\sqrt{25}=5$

Hence Ans is (C)

Sol. 99 (B) Given : $f(x)=2x^3+5x^2+6x+10$

$=\frac{1}{l}+\frac{1}{m}+\frac{1}{n}$

$=\frac{mn+\ln+\text{lm}}{lmn}$

$=\frac{\frac{6}{2}}{\frac{-10}{2}}$

$=\frac{-3}{5}$

Hence Ans is (B)

Sol. 100 (A) For zero of the polynomial, $2x+1=0$,

$x=-\frac{1}{2}$

Hence Ans is (A)

Sol. 101 (B)

$$\begin{array}{r} x-2 \\ -x^2+x-1\overline{)-x^3+3x^2-3x+5} \\ -x^3+x^2-x \\ \underline{+\quad -\quad +} \\ 2x^2-2x+5 \\ 2x^2-2x+2 \\ \underline{-\quad +\quad -} \\ +3 \end{array}$$

$\Rightarrow$ Remainder is 3

Hence Ans is (B)

Sol. 102 (A) Given $x^2+\dfrac{1}{x^2}=14$

$\Rightarrow \quad \left(x+\dfrac{1}{x}\right)^2=16$

$\Rightarrow \quad x+\dfrac{1}{x}=\pm 4$

Taking +4, $\quad x+\dfrac{1}{x}=4$

Cubing both sides

$$\left(x+\frac{1}{x}\right)^3=64$$

$\Rightarrow \ x^3+\dfrac{1}{x^3}+3\left(x+\dfrac{1}{x}\right)\cdot 1=64$

$\Rightarrow \ x^3+\dfrac{1}{x^3}=64-12=52$

Hence Ans is (A)

Sol. 103 (A) Given ax^3+4x^2+3x-4

According to question :

$$27a+36+9-4=27-12+a$$

$\Rightarrow \quad 26a=-26$

$$a=-1$$

Hence Ans is (A)

Sol. 104 (C) Given $x^3-6x^2+11x-6=0$

$$\alpha\beta\gamma=6$$

Given $\quad \alpha\beta=2$

$\Rightarrow \quad \gamma=3$

Hence Ans is (C)

Sol. 105 (C) $x^3=8-4x$

Squaring both sides

$$x^6=64+16x^2-64x$$

$$(x^6+64x=16x^2+64)\times x$$

$$x^7+64x^2=16x^3+64x$$

$$=16x(x^2+4)$$

$$=16\times 8 \text{ As}, x(x^2+4)=8$$

$$=128$$

Hence Ans is (C)

Sol. 106 (B) let $P(x)=(x-1)(x-2)(x-3)(x-\alpha)$

$$P(0)=6\alpha$$

$$P(4)=3\times 2\times 1\,(4-\alpha)$$

$\Rightarrow \quad P(4)=24-6\alpha$

$\Rightarrow \quad P(4)=24-P(0)$

$\Rightarrow \quad P(4)+P(0)=24$

Hence Ans is (B)

Sol. 107 (C) Consider $a^3+b^3+c^3-3abc$

$=(a+b+c)\,(a^2+b^2+c^2-ab-bc-ac)$ ...(1)

Squaring,

$$a+b+c=1$$

$$(a+b+c)=(1)^2$$

$$a^2+b^2+c^2+2\,(ab+bc+ac)=1$$

$$9+2(ab+bc+ac)=1$$

$$2\,(ab+bc+ac)=-8$$

$$ab+bc+ac=-4$$

Now from (1), $1-3abc=1\,(9+4)$

$$1-13=3abc$$

$$abc=\frac{-12}{3}=-4$$

So, $\dfrac{ab+bc+ac}{abc}=\dfrac{-4}{-4}=1$

Hence Ans is (C)

Sol. 108 (B) Given $x+\dfrac{1}{x}=5$

$$=\frac{\frac{2x}{x}}{\frac{3x^2-5x+3}{x}}=\frac{2}{3x+\frac{3}{x}-5}$$

$$=\frac{2}{3\left(x+\frac{1}{x}\right)-5}$$

$$=\frac{2}{3\times 5-5}$$

$$=\frac{2}{10}$$

$$=\frac{1}{5}$$

Hence Ans is (B)

Sol. 109 (A) $f(x) = x^3 + 3x^2 - kx + 4$

$$f(2) = 2k$$
$$(2)^3 + 3(2)^2 - 2k + 4 = 2k$$
$$8 + 12 + 4 = 4k$$
$$4k = 24$$
$$k = 6$$

Hence Ans is (A)

Sol. 110 (C) $x = 7 - 4\sqrt{3}$

$$\Rightarrow \quad \frac{1}{x} = \frac{1}{7-4\sqrt{3}} = 7 + 4\sqrt{3}$$
$$\Rightarrow \quad x^2 + \frac{1}{x^2} = \left(x + \frac{1}{x}\right)^2 - 2 \times x \times \frac{1}{x}$$
$$\Rightarrow \quad = (7 - 4\sqrt{3} + 7 + 4\sqrt{3})^2 - 2$$
$$\Rightarrow \quad = (14)^2 - 2$$
$$= 194$$

Hence Ans is (C)

Sol. 111 (A) Given $2x^3 + 5x^2 - 9x - 18 = P(x)$

For $x = 2$

$$P(2) = 2 \times 2^3 + 5 \times 2^2 - 9 \times 2 - 18$$
$$= 16 + 20 - 18 - 18$$
$$= 36 - 36$$
$$= 0$$

$\Rightarrow$ $x = 2$ is zero of polynomial $P(x)$

$\Rightarrow$ $x - 2$ is a factor

$$
\begin{array}{r|l}
 & 2x^2 + 9x + 9 \\
x-2 & 2x^3 + 5x^2 - 9x - 18 \\
 & 2x^3 - 4x^2 \\
 & - \quad + \\
 & 9x^2 - 9x - 18 \\
 & 9x^2 - 18x - 18 \\
 & - \quad + \\
 & 0
\end{array}
$$

$$\Rightarrow \quad P(x) = 2x^3 + 5x^2 - 9x - 18$$
$$= (x-2)(2x^2 + 9x + 9)$$
$$= (x-2)(2x^2 + 6x + 3x + 9)$$
$$= (x-2)(x+3)(2x+3)$$

Zero's are 2, -3 $\frac{-3}{2}$

Hence Ans is (A)

Sol. 112 (A) Consider $P(x) = x^4 + x^3 - 2x^2 + x + 1$

By remainder theorem,

If $p(x)$ is divided by $(x - a)$

then the remainder is $P(a)$

$\Rightarrow$ remainder

$$P(1) = 1^4 + 1^3 - 2 \times 1^2 + 1 + 1$$
$$P(1) = 1 + 1 - 2 + 1 + 1 = 2$$

Hence Ans is (A)

Sol. 113 (B) Consider $x^2 + \frac{1}{x^2} = 83$

$$x^2 + \frac{1}{x^2} - 2 = 83 - 2$$
$$\left(x - \frac{1}{x}\right)^2 = 81$$
$$\left(x - \frac{1}{x}\right) = 9$$

Cubing on both sides

$$\left(x - \frac{1}{x}\right)^3 = 9^3$$
$$x^3 - \frac{1}{x^3} - 3 \times x \times \frac{1}{x}\left(x - \frac{1}{x}\right) = 729$$
$$x^3 - \frac{1}{x^3} - 3 \times 9 = 729$$
$$x^3 - \frac{1}{x^3} = 729 + 27$$
$$x^3 - \frac{1}{x^3} = 756$$

Hence Ans is (B)

Sol. 114 (A) Given $4^{1+x} + 4^{1-x} = 10$

$$4 \times 4^x + 4 \times \frac{1}{4^x} = 10$$
$$a = 4^x$$
$$4a + \frac{4}{a} = 10$$
$$\frac{4a^2 + 4}{a} = 10$$
$$4a^2 - 10a + 4 = 0$$
$$4a^2 - 8a - 2a + 4 = 0$$
$$4a(a-2) - 2(a-2) = 0$$
$$(4a-2)(a-2) = 0$$
$$a = \frac{1}{2} \text{ or } a = 2$$
$$\Rightarrow \quad 4^x = \frac{1}{2} \text{ or } 4^x = 2$$
$$2^{2x} = 2^{-1} \text{ or } 2^{2x} = 2^1$$

$$x=-\frac{1}{2} \text{ or } 2x=1$$

$$x=\frac{1}{2}$$

Hence Ans is (A)

Sol. 115 (C) Given

$$|x|^2+|x|-6=0$$

$\Rightarrow \quad (|x|+3)(|x|-2)=0$

$\Rightarrow \quad |x|=-3 \quad \text{or} \quad |x|=2$

$\Rightarrow \quad |x|=-3$ is not possible

So $\quad |x|=2$

$\Rightarrow \quad x=2$ or -2

Hence Ans is (C)

Sol. 116 (A) Given $p(x)=k(x+1)^2 \quad \ldots(1)$

Given $\quad p(-2)=2$

$\Rightarrow \quad k(-2+1)^2=2$

$\Rightarrow \quad k=2$

$$p(x)=2(x+1)^2 \quad \text{[from (1)]}$$

Hence $\quad p(3)=2(2+1)^2=2\times 9=18$

Hence Ans is (A)

Sol. 117 (C) Consider

$$P(x)=(x-1)Q+3 \quad \ldots(1)$$

$$P(x)=(x-3)Q''+5 \quad \ldots(2)$$

$$P(x)=(x-1)(x-3)Q'''+ax+b \quad \ldots(3)$$

Where $\quad ax+b=r(x)$

For $x=1$, From equation-(1)

$$P(1)=(1-1)Q+3$$

$$P(1)=3$$

For $x=3$, From equation-(2)

$$P(3)=(3-3)Q''+5$$

$$P(3)=5$$

From equation-(3)

$$P(1)=(1-1)(1-3)Q'''+[a(1)+b]$$

$$3=a+b \quad \ldots(4)$$

$$P(3)=(3-1)(3-3)Q'''+[3a+b]$$

$$5=3a+b \quad \ldots(5)$$

Equation-(5) – Equaiton-(4)

$$2a=2 \Rightarrow a=1$$

Put $a=1$ in equation-(4)

$$3=1+b \Rightarrow b=2$$

According to question

$$r(x)=ax+b=1(x)+2=x+2$$

$$r(-2)=-2+2=0$$

Sol. 118 (D) Given $\quad P(x)=x^2+5kx+k^2+5$

It is divisibly by $(x+2)$ so

$$P(-2)=0$$

$$(-2)^2+5k(-2)+k^2+5=0$$

$$4-10k+k^2+5=0$$

$$k^2-10k+9=0$$

$$k^2-9k-k+9=0$$

$$(k-9)(k-1)=0 \Rightarrow k=9,1$$

and $P(-3)\neq 0$

$$(-3)^2+5k(-3)+k^2+5\neq 0$$

$$9-15k+k^2+5\neq 0$$

$$k^2-15k+14\neq 0$$

$$k^2-14k-k+14\neq 0$$

$$(k-14)(k-1)\neq 0$$

$$k\neq 14, \text{ and } k\neq 1$$

The only value of k is 9

Sol. 119 (B)

$$
\begin{array}{r|l}
 & x^2-4x+(8-k) \\
x^2-2x+k & x^4-6x^3+16x^2-25x+10 \\
 & x^4-2x^3+kx^2 \\
 & -\quad +\quad - \\ \hline
 & -4x^3+(16-k)x^2-25x+10 \\
 & -4x^3+8x^2-4kx \\
 & +\quad -\quad + \\ \hline
 & (8-k)x^2+(-25+4k)x+10 \\
 & (8-k)x^2-(16-2k)x+8k-k^2 \\
 & -\quad +\quad -\quad + \\ \hline
 & (-25+4k+16-2k)x+10-8k+k^2
\end{array}
$$

Remainder $=(-9+2k)x+10-8k+k^2$

$$-9+2k=1$$

$\Rightarrow \quad k=5$

$$a=10-8k+k^2$$

$$=10-40+25$$

$$=-5$$

Hence Ans is (B)

* * * * *

Linear Equation

3

- An equation which can be put in the form $ax + by + c = 0$, where a, b and c are real numbers and a and b are not both zero, is called a linear equation in two variables x and y.

- Every solution of the equation $ax + by + c = 0$ is a point on the line representing it. Or each solution (x, y), of a linear equation in two variables $ax + by + c = 0$, corresponds to a point on the line representing the equation and vice-versa.

- A linear equation in two variables has an infinite number of solutions.

- If we consider two equations of the form $a_1x + b_1y + c_1 = 0$, $a_2x + b_2y + c_2 = 0$, a pair of such equations is called a system of linear equations.

- We have three types of systems of two linear equations.

(i) **Independent System**, which has a unique solution. Such system is termed as a consistent system with unique solution.

(ii) **Inconsistent System**, which has no solution.

(iii) **Dependent System**, which represents a pair of equivalent equations and has an infinite number of solutions. Such system is also termed as a consistent system with infinite solutions.

- A pair of linear equations in two variables which has a common point, i.e., which has only one solution is called a consistent pair of linear equations.

- A pair of linear equations in two variables which has no solution, i.e., the lines are parallel to each other is called an inconsistent pair of linear equations.

- A pair of linear equations in two variables which are equivalent and has infinitely many solutions are called dependent pair of linear equations. Note that a dependent pair of linear equations is always consistent with infinite number of solutions.

- A pair of linear equations $a_1x + b_1y + c_1 = 0$ and $a_2x + b_2y + c_2 = 0$ represents

(i) intersecting lines, then $\frac{a_1}{a_2} \neq \frac{b_1}{b_2}$

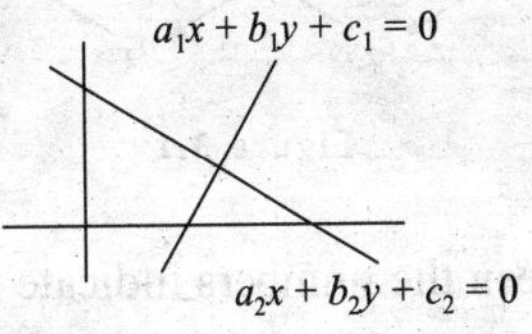

(ii) parallel lines, then $\frac{a_1}{a_2} = \frac{b_1}{b_2} \neq \frac{c_1}{c_2}$

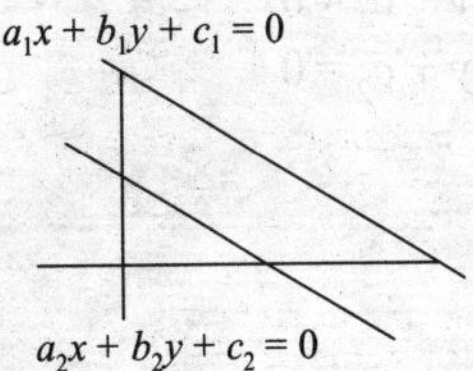

(iii) coincident lines, then $\frac{a_1}{a_2} = \frac{b_1}{b_2} = \frac{c_1}{c_2}$

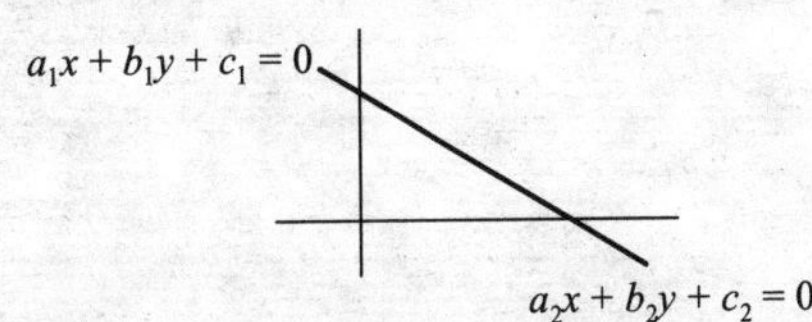

Converse of the above statement is also true.

- **Methods of Solving a Pair of Linear Equations**

1. **Graphical method :**
2. **Algebraic Methods :**

(a) **Substitution method :**

(b) **Elimination method :**

(c) **Cross multiplication method :**

(i) The system of two linear equations

$$a_1x + b_1y + c_1 = 0,$$
$$a_2x + b_2y + c_2 = 0,$$

where $\frac{a_1}{a_2} \neq \frac{b_1}{b_2}$ has a unique solution, given by

$$x = \frac{(b_1c_2 - b_2c_1)}{(a_1b_2 - a_2b_1)},$$

$$y = \frac{(c_1a_2 - c_2a_1)}{(a_1b_2 - a_2b_1)}$$

We generally write it as

$$\frac{x}{b_1c_2 - b_2c_1} = \frac{y}{c_1a_2 - c_2a_1} = \frac{1}{a_1b_2 - a_2b_1}$$

The following diagram will help to apply the cross-multiplication method directly.

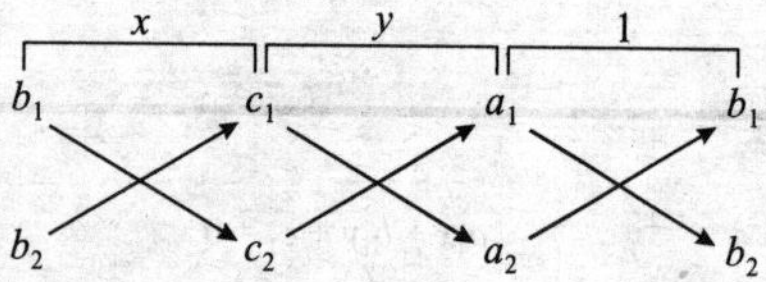

Figure 3.1

The arrows between the numbers indicate that they are to be multiplied. The products with upward arrows are to be subtracted from the products with downward arrows.

(ii) The system of equations

$$a_1x + b_1y + c_1 = 0 \quad \ldots(1)$$

$$a_2x + b_2y + c_2 = 0 \quad \ldots(2)$$

(a) Is consistent with unique solution, if $\frac{a_1}{a_2} \neq \frac{b_1}{b_2}$, i.e., lines represented by equations-(1) and (2) intersect at a point.

(b) Is inconsistent, if $\frac{a_1}{a_2} = \frac{b_1}{b_2} \neq \frac{c_1}{c_2}$ i.e., lines represented by equations-(1) and (2) are parallel and non coincident.

(c) Is consistent with infinitely many solutions, if

$$\frac{a_1}{a_2} = \frac{b_1}{b_2} = \frac{c_1}{c_2}$$

i.e., lines represented by equations (1) and (2) are coincident.

* * * * *

PRACTICE EXERCISE - 3.1

3-1 Number of equations needed to solve a problem in n variables is :
(A) 1 (B) n
(C) $2n$ (D) Can't be determined

3-2 An inconsistent system of two linear equations in two variables will have :
(A) One solution (B) Two solutions
(C) No solution (D) More than two solutions

3-3 $x+y=0$ and $2x+2y=0$ has :
(A) No solution (B) One solution
(C) Two solutions (D) More than two solutions

3-4 Solve $5x-2y=19$ and $3x+y=18$:
(A) $x=-2, y=-3$ (B) $x=5, y=1$
(C) $x=4, y=3$ (D) $x=5, y=3$

3-5 A man has some hens and cows. If the number of heads be 48 and number of feet equals 140, the number of hens will be :
(A) 22 (B) 23
(C) 24 (D) 26

3-6 The value of k for which the system of equations $8x+7y=0$ and $4x+ky=0$ has a non-zero solution, is :
(A) 0 (B) 3
(C) $\frac{7}{2}$ (D) $\frac{-7}{2}$

3-7 If $2x-3y=7$ and $(a+b)x-(a+b-3)y=4a+b$ represent coincident lines, then a and b satisfy the equation :
(A) $a+5b=0$ (B) $5a+b=0$
(C) $a-5b=0$ (D) $5a-b=0$

3-8 The solution of the system of the equation $\sqrt{2}x+\sqrt{5}y=0$ and $\sqrt{3}x-\sqrt{7}y=0$ is :
(A) $x=\sqrt{3}, y=\sqrt{5}$ (B) $x=\sqrt{2}, y=\sqrt{7}$
(C) $x=1, y=\sqrt{2}$ (D) $x=0, y=0$

3-9 A system of linear equations $a_1x+b_1y+c_1=0$, $a_2x+b_2y+c_2=0$ is inconsistent if the lines represented by the system are :
(A) Coincident (B) Non-parallel
(C) Parallel (D) None of these

3-10 The solution of $mx-ny=m^2+n^2, x+y=2m$ is :
(A) $x=m+n, y=m-n$
(B) $x=n+m, y=n-m$
(C) $x=m+2n, y=m-2n$
(D) $x=m+2n, y=2m-n$

3-11 If $3x+ay=4$ and $bx-3y=13$ passes through $(2,-1)$ then find $a+b$:
(A) 12 (B) 11
(C) 7 (D) 13

3-12 If $ax+by+21=0$ and $-2x-by=5a+2$ passes through $(-3,2)$ then find the value of a and b :
(A) 5, 2 (B) –5, 3
(C) $\frac{25}{4}, \frac{92}{16}$ (D) $\frac{25}{8}, \frac{-93}{16}$

3-13 Which of the following line is not parallel to $3x-5y=7$:
(A) $6x-10y=3$ (B) $-6x+10y-7=0$
(C) $5x-\frac{25}{3}y=1$ (D) $4x-7y=8$

3-14 If a line $3x-5y=b$ passes through the intersection point of $5x-4y=-2$ and $3x+4y=18$ then find value of b :
(A) 6 (B) 7
(C) 9 (D) -9

3-15 Find the value of K for which the following pair of equations has no solution :

$$(3k+1)x+11y-22=0;$$
$$x+(2k-1)y-47=0$$

(A) 3 (B) $\frac{3}{2}$
(C) $\frac{-4}{3}$ (D) Both (B) and (C)

3-16 3 chairs and 2 tables cost Rs 700 and 5 chairs and 3 tables cost Rs 1100. What is the cost of 2 chairs and 3 tables :
(A) Rs 300 (B) Rs 400
(C) Rs 500 (D) Rs 800

3-17 For what value of K, the system of equations $kx+3y=k-3$ and $12x+ky=k$ has infinitely many solutions.
(A) $K=-6$ (B) $K=3$
(C) $K=6$ (D) No value exists

3-18 The solution of the equations $x-y=0.9$ and $\frac{11}{2(x+y)}=1$ is :
(A) $x=3.2, y=2.3$ (B) $x=1, y=0.1$
(C) $x=2, y=1.1$ (D) None of these

3-19 Consider the equations $P: \frac{2}{x}+\frac{3}{y}=6$ and $Q: \frac{1}{x}+\frac{1}{2y}=2$.

Then, $x=\frac{2}{3}, y=1$ satisfy :

(A) P, not Q (B) Q, not P
(C) P and Q both (D) Neither P nor Q

3-20 The value of k for which the system of equations $x+2y-3=0$ and $5x+ky+7=0$ has no solution, is :

(A) 10 (B) 6
(C) 3 (D) 1

3-21 In a ΔABC, $\angle A = x°$, $\angle B = 3x°$, $\angle C = y°$. If $3y - 5x = 30°$ then the triangle is :

(A) Equilateral (B) Isosceles
(C) Right angled (D) None of these

3-22 A system of two simultaneous linear equations in two variables is inconsistent, if their graphs :

(A) Are parallel (B) Are coincident
(C) Intersect in one point (D) None of these

3-23 The equations $ax+b=0$ and $cx+d=0$ are consistent, if :

(A) $ad=bc$ (B) $ad+bc=0$
(C) $ab-cd=0$ (D) $ab+cd=0$

3-24 Find the value of x in terms of y in equation $\frac{2x-y-3}{3}=\frac{4x+y-3}{4}$:

(A) $\frac{-3+7y}{2}$ (B) $\frac{-3-7y}{2}$
(C) $\frac{7y-3}{4}$ (D) $\frac{-3-7y}{4}$

3-25 If the system of equations $ax+by=c$, $lx+my=n$ have a unique solution then :

(A) $am=bl$ (B) $ab=ml$
(C) $ab \neq ml$ (D) $am \neq bl$

3-26 The solution set of $2(ax - by) + a + 4b = 0$, $2(bx+ay)+b-4a=0$ is :

(A) $x=\frac{1}{2}, y=2$ (B) $x=-\frac{1}{2}, y=2$
(C) $x=\frac{-a}{2}, y=2b$ (D) None of these

3-27 The value of k for which the system of equations $x+2y=5$, $3x+ky+15=0$ has no solution is :

(A) 6 (B) -6
(C) $\frac{3}{2}$ (D) None of these

3-28 Find the value of k for which the system of equation have infinite solutions :

$$x+(k+1)y=5\,;\,(k+1)x+9y=8k-1$$

(A) $k=-4$ (B) $k=2$
(C) $k=-3$ (D) $k=3$

3-29 If a pair of linear equations has no solution then graphically :

(A) Lines will coincide
(B) Lines are parallel
(C) Lines intersect at one point
(D) None of these

3-30 If $2x-3y=7$ and $(a+b)x-(a+b-3)y=4a+b$ represent coincident lines, then a and b satisfy the equation :

(A) $a+5b=0$ (B) $5a+b=0$
(C) $a-5b=0$ (D) $5a-b=0$

3-31 37 pens and 53 pencils together cost Rs. 320, while 53 pens are 37 pencils together cost Rs. 400. The total cost of a pen and a pencil is :

(A) Rs. 8 (B) Rs. 6.50
(C) Rs. 5.50 (D) Rs. 7.50

3-32 The value of a for which following system of equations $2x + 3y = 7$ and $a(2x + y) + by = 28$ has infinite number of solutions, is :

(A) -4 (B) 3
(C) -3 (D) None of these

3-33 If $\frac{x+y}{11}=\frac{x+y}{2}$ and $\frac{x-y}{3}=\frac{x-y}{7}$ then find the value of x and y :

(A) $x=0\ y=3$ (B) $x=0\ y=-1$
(C) $x=0\ y=0$ (D) Can't be determined

3-34 The value of 'k' for which the system of equations $x+2y=5$, $3x+ky-15=0$ has no solution is :

(A) $k=6$ (B) $k \neq 6$
(C) A and B both (D) None of these

3-35 The solution of the system of equations $\frac{2x+5y}{xy}=6$ and $\frac{4x-5y}{xy}+3=0$ (where $x \neq 0, y \neq 0$) is :

(A) $x=1, y=2$ (B) $x=0, y=0$
(C) $x=-1, y=2$ (D) $x=1, y=-2$

3-36 For what values of a and b will the equations $2x+3y=7$, $(a-b)x+(a+b)y=(3a+b-2)$ represent coincident lines ?

(A) $a=-5, b=1$ (B) $a=5, b=1$
(C) $a=-5, b=-1$ (D) $a=5, b=-1$

3-37 For what value of k, the system of equations $kx - y = 2$, $6x - 2y = 3$ has infinitely many solutions ?

(A) $k = 3$ (B) $k \neq 4$

(C) $k = 6$ (D) Does not exist

3-38 For what value of k, the system of equations $x + 2y = 3, 5x + ky + 7 = 0$ has unique solution?

(A) $k = 10$

(B) All real values except 10

(C) All natural numbers except 10

(D) Does not exist

3-39 If $am \neq bl$, then the system of equations : $ax + by = c, lx + my = n$:

(A) Has a unique solution

(B) Has no solution

(C) Has infinitely many solutions

(D) May or may not have a solution

3-40 For what value of λ the following system of equations has no solutions $\lambda x + 3y = \lambda - 3, 12x + \lambda y = \lambda$:

(A) -6 (B) -3

(C) 3 (D) 6

3-41 Two candles of equal length start burning at the same instant. One of the candles bums in 5 hrs. and the other in 4 hrs. By the time one candle is 2 times the length of the other. The candles have already burnt for :

(A) $2\frac{1}{2}$ hrs. (B) $3\frac{1}{2}$ hrs.

(C) $3\frac{1}{9}$ hrs. (D) $3\frac{1}{3}$ hrs.

3-42 $\frac{x+y}{xy} = 2, \frac{x-y}{xy} = 6$:

(A) $-\frac{1}{2}, \frac{1}{4}$ (B) $\frac{1}{2}, -\frac{1}{4}$

(C) $\frac{1}{2}, -\frac{3}{2}$ (D) $-\frac{1}{4}, -\frac{3}{2}$

3-43 $\frac{1}{2x} - \frac{1}{y} = -1, \frac{1}{x} + \frac{1}{2y} = 8$:

(A) $\frac{2}{3}, \frac{2}{5}$ (B) $\frac{1}{4}, \frac{1}{5}$

(C) $\frac{1}{6}, \frac{1}{4}$ (D) $-\frac{1}{6}, -\frac{1}{4}$

3-44 $\frac{2x}{a} + \frac{y}{b} = 2, \frac{x}{a} - \frac{y}{b} = 4$:

(A) $\frac{2}{a}, \frac{2}{b}$ (B) $2a, -2b$

(C) $-2a, 2b$ (D) $\frac{a}{2}, -\frac{b}{2}$

3-45 For what value of k, the following equations have no solutions ?

$9x + 4y = 9$

$7x + ky = 5$

(A) 3 (B) 4.7

(C) 28/9 (D) 9/28

3-46 For what value of k, two lines $kx + 2y = 2$ and $3x + y = 1$ will be coincident ?

(A) 2 (B) 3

(C) 5 (D) 6

3-47 For what value of k, will the equations $2x + 3y - 5 = 0$, $6x + ky - 15 = 0$ have an infinite number of solutions ?

(A) 0 (B) 9

(C) 2 (D) 3

3-48 The total cost of 8 buckets and 5 mugs is Rs. 92 and the total cost of 5 buckets and 8 mugs is Rs. 77. Find the cost of 2 mugs and 3 buckets :

(A) Rs. 35 (B) Rs. 70

(C) Rs. 30 (D) Rs. 38

3-49 The sum of two numbers is 8. If their sum is four times their difference, find the numbers :

(A) 6, 2 (B) 7, 1

(C) 5, 3 (D) 6, 3

3-50 The numerator of a fraction is 4 less than its denominator. If the numerator is decreased by 2 and the denominator is increased by 1, then the denominator is eight times the numerator. Find the fraction :

(A) 3/7 (B) 4/8

(C) 2/7 (D) 3/8

* * * * *

PRACTICE EXERCISE - 3.2

3-1 If x and y are positive integers such that $(3x + 7y)$ is a multiple of 11, then which of the following will also be divisible by 11?

(A) $4x+6y$ (B) $x+y+4$
(C) $4x-9y$ (D) $9x+4y$

3-2 $y=\min\{(x+7),(5-x)\}$ if x belongs to real numbers, what is the maximum value of y?

(A) 4 (B) 6
(C) 8 (D) 7

3-3 Find the unique values of x and y.

I. $12x+18y=24$ II. $18x+27y=36$
III. $26x+39y=23$

Which of the following options is correct regarding the question?

(A) Unique values of x and y can be determined with the help of any two statements.
(B) Unique values of x and y can be determined with the help of statement I and either II or III.
(C) Unique values of x and y can be determined with the help of statement II and III together only.
(D) None of the statements gives the unique values for x and y.

3-4 How many ordered pairs (m, n) are possible such that the following system of equations has no solution for x and y, where m and n are positive integers.

$5x+my=17$
$nx+42y=13$

(A) 16
(B) 42
(C) 64
(D) In finitely many possible pairs

3-5 $4x+my=15$
$nx+3y=10$

is a system of linear equations in two variable where 'm' and 'n' are integers. Which of the following is false?

(A) There are many possible values of m and n for which the system of linear equations has unique solution.
(B) There are six pairs of (m, n) such that the system of equations has no solution for x and y.
(C) There is at least one pair (m, n) such that the system of equations has infinite solutions for x and y.
(D) None of these

3-6 Let $g(x)=\max(5-x, x+2)$. The smallest possible value of $g(x)$ is :

(A) 4 (B) 4.5
(C) 1.5 (D) None of these

3-7 **Statement-I :** $1990\text{m}-173\text{n}=11$ has no solution in integers for m and n.

Statement-II : $3x-12y=7$ has many solutions in integers for x and y.

Which of the following is true?

(A) Statement-I is correct and Statement-II is wrong
(B) Statement-I is wrong and statement-II is correct
(C) Statement-I and II both are correct
(D) Statement-I and II both are wrong

3-8 In drilling the world's deepest hole, it was found that the temperature 'T' in degrees Celsius, x km below the surface of the earth, was given by

$T=30+25(x-3), 3<x<15.$

At what depth will the temperature be between 200°C and 300°C?

(A) Between 6.8 to 10.8 (B) Between 9.8 to 13.8
(C) Between 8.2 to 10.8 (D) Between 10.8 to 13.8

Directions (Q. 3-9 to 3-10) In an examination, there are 100 questions divided into three groups A, B and C such that each group contains at least one question. Each question in group A carries 1 mark, each question in group B carries 2 marks, and each question in group C carries 3 marks. It is known that the questions in group A together carry at least 60% of the total marks.

3-9 If group B contains 23 questions, then how many questions are there in group C?

(A) 1 (B) 2
(C) 3 (D) Can't say

3-10 If group C contains 8 questions and group B carries at least 20% of the total marks, which of the following best describes the number of questions in group B?

(A) 11 or 12 (B) 12 or 13
(C) 13 or 14 (D) 14 or 15

3-11 Points A and B are 90 km apart from each other on a highway. A car starts from A and another from B at the same time. If they go in the same direction, they meet in 9 hours and if they go in opposite directions, they meet in 9/7 hours. Find their speed (in km/h) :

(A) 25, 45 (B) 20, 50
(C) 30, 40 (D) 35, 65

3-12 Priyanka has only 25 paise coins and 50 paise coins in her purse. If in all she has 40 coins totalling Rs. 12.75, how many coins of 25 paise does she have ?

(A) 30 (B) 29
(C) 32 (D) 26

3-13 Astha has pens and pencils which together are 40 in number. If she has 5 more pencils and 5 less pens, the number of pencils would have become 4 times the number of pens. Find the original number of pens with Astha :

(A) 11 (B) 12
(C) 13 (D) 14

3-14 A father is three times as old as his son. After twelve years, his age will be twice as that of the age of his son then, find their present ages in years :

(A) 10, 30 (B) 12, 36
(C) 6, 36 (D) 124, 24

3-15 Five years ago, *A* was three times as old as *B* and ten years later, *A* shell be twice as old as *B*. What are the present ages of *A* and *B* (in years) ?

(A) 45, 15 (B) 30, 40
(C) 50, 30 (D) 50, 20

3-16 Astha and Saumya each have certain number of oranges. Astha says to saumya, "If you give me 10 of your oranges, I will have twice the number of oranges left with you." Saumya replies, "If you give me 10 of you oranges, I will have the same number of oranges as left with you." Find the number of oranges with Astha and Saumya respectively.

(A) 60, 40 (B) 70, 50
(C) 60, 80 (D) 70, 90

3-17 Shubham travels 760 km to his home partly by train and partly by car. He takes 8 hours if he travels 160 km by train and the rest by car. He takes 12 minutes more if he travels 240 km by train and the rest by car. Find the speed of the train and the car respectively (in km/hr.) :

(A) 40, 80 (B) 60, 120
(C) 80, 100 (D) 100, 120

3-18 A person invested some amount at the rate of 12% p.a. simple interest and some other amount at the rate of 10% p.a. simple interest. He received yearly interest of Rs. 130. But if he had interchanged the amounts invested he would have received Rs. 4 more as interest. How much amount did he invest at 10% p.a. simple interest ?

(A) Rs. 700 (B) Rs. 500
(C) Rs. 800 (D) Rs. 400

3-19 The solution of the equations $\frac{3x-y+1}{3}=\frac{2x+y+2}{5}=\frac{3x+2y+1}{6}$ given by :

(A) $x=2, y=1$ (B) $x=1, y=1$
(C) $x=-1, y=-1$ (D) $x=1, y=2$

3-20 The course of an enemy submarine as plotted on a set of rectangular axes gives the equation $2x+3y=5$. On the same axes, the course of destroyer is indicated by $x-y=10$. The point (x, y) at which the submarine can be destroyed is :

(A) $(-3, 7)$ (B) $(7, -3)$
(C) $(-7, 3)$ (D) $(3, -7)$

3-21 Let *a*, *b*, *c* be the positive numbers. The following system of equations in *x*, *y* and *z*.

$$\frac{x^2}{a^2}+\frac{y^2}{b^2}-\frac{z^2}{c^2}=1$$

$$\frac{x^2}{a^2}-\frac{y^2}{b^2}+\frac{z^2}{c^2}=1$$

$$-\frac{x^2}{a^2}+\frac{y^2}{b^2}+\frac{z^2}{c^2}=1, \text{ has}$$

(A) No solution (B) Unique solution
(C) Infinitely many solutions (D) Finitely many solutions

3-22 It the system of equations, $x-ky-z=0$, $kx-y-z=0$, has a non zero solution, then the possible values of k are :

(A) $-1, 2$ (B) $1, 2$
(C) $0, 1$ (D) $-1, 1$

3-23 The system of equations $a_1x+b_1y=0$, $a_2x+b_2y=0$ will have a non trivial solution if :

(A) $a_1b_2-a_2b_1\neq 0$ (B) $a_1b_2-a_2b_1=0$
(C) $a_1b_2-a_2b_1<0$ (D) $a_1b_2-a_2b_1>0$

3-24 For a regular polygon, the sum of the interior angles is twice the sum of the exterior angles. Then the number of sides of the regular polygon is :

(A) 4 (B) 6
(C) 8 (D) 10

3-25 What is the minimum number of points that we need to draw the graph of $ax+by+c=0$:

(A) One (B) Two
(C) Three (D) More than three

* * * * *

PRACTICE EXERCISE - 3.3

3-1 Present ages of Anil and Sunil are in the ratio 4 : 5. Eight years from now the ratio of their ages will be 5 : 6. Find their present ages : **[NTSE-2012 (Stage-I) Rajasthan]**

(A) 16 Yrs., 20 Yrs. (B) 25 Yrs., 30 Yrs.
(C) 20 Yrs., 25 Yrs. (D) 32 Yrs., 40 Yrs.

3-2 For which values of 'a' and 'b' does the following pair of linear equations have an infinite number of solution :

$2x+3y=7, (a-b)x+(a+b)y=3a+b-2$

[NTSE-2013 (Stage-I) Rajasthan]

(A) $a=5, b=1$ (B) $a=4, b=2$
(C) $a=1, b=5$ (D) $a=2, b=4$

3-3 If the system of equations $kx + 3y - (k - 3) = 0$, $12x+ky-k=0$ has infinitely many solutions, then $k=$

[NTSE-2014 (Stage-I) Rajasthan]

(A) 6 (B) -6
(C) 0 (D) None of these

3-4 If the system of equations $3x+y=1$; $(2k-1)x+(k-1)y=(2k+1)$, has no solution, then the value of k is : **[NTSE-2015 (Stage-I) Rajasthan]**

(A) 2 (B) 3
(C) -2 (D) 1

3-5 In a two digit number, the ten's place digit is double that of unit's place digit. If we exchange the digits mutually then the number decreases by 18, then the number is :

[NTSE-2015 (Stage-I) MP]

(A) 24 (B) 36
(C) 39 (D) 42

3-6 The system of equations –

$x+2y=6, 3x+6y=18$ **[NTSE-2015 (Stage-I) MP]**

(A) Is inconsistent
(B) Has a unique solution
(C) Has an infinite number of solutions
(D) None of these

3-7 A fraction becomes $\frac{1}{3}$ when one is subtracted from the numerator and it becomes $\frac{1}{4}$ when 8 is added to the denominator, then the fraction is : **[NTSE-2015 (Stage-I) TN]**

(A) $\frac{5}{12}$ (B) $\frac{2}{11}$
(C) $\frac{9}{11}$ (D) $\frac{1}{7}$

3-8 Students of a class are made to stand in rows. If one student is extra in a row, there would be two rows less. If one student is less in a row there would be three rows more. The number of students in the class are : **[NTSE-2015 (Stage-I) Chandigarh]**

(A) 7 (B) 50
(C) 60 (D) 80

3-9 The equation of a line which passes through points $P(4, 0)$ and $Q(0, -3)$ will be : **[NTSE-2015 (Stage-I) UP]**

(A) $\frac{x}{4}+\frac{y}{3}=1$ (B) $\frac{x}{3}-\frac{y}{4}=7$
(C) $\frac{x}{4}-\frac{y}{3}=1$ (D) $\frac{x}{3}+\frac{y}{4}=7$

3-10 A boat takes 7 hours to travel 30 km upstream and 28 km downstream. It takes 5 hours to travel 21 km upstream and to return back. Find the speed of the boat in still water :

[NTSE-2015 (Stage-I) Maharashtra]

(A) 10 km/hr (B) 20 km/hr
(C) 14 km/hr (D) 6 km/hr

3-11 The cost of 20 guavas and 5 apples is same as that of 12 guavas and 7 apples then how many times the cost of an apple is to that of a guava? **[NTSE-2015 (Stage-I) Maharashtra]**

(A) Two times (B) Half times
(C) Four times (D) Five times

3-12 If $x+y=7$ and $3x-2y=11$. Then the value of x will be :

[NTSE-2015 (Stage-I) Chhatisgarh]

(A) 5 (B) 6
(C) 7 (D) 8

3-13 Sum of the digits of two digit number is 9. The number obtained by interchanging the digits is 18 more than twice the original number. The original number is :

[NTSE-2015 (Stage-I) Chennai]

(A) 72 (B) 27
(C) 36 (D) 63

3-14 In the equations $3x + 2y = 13xy$ and $4x - 5y = 2xy$, the values of x and y that satisfy the equations are :

[NTSE-2016 (Stage-I) Rajasthan]

(A) $(2,3)$ (B) $(3,2)$
(C) $\left(\frac{1}{2},\frac{1}{3}\right)$ (D) $\left(\frac{1}{3},\frac{1}{2}\right)$

3-15 Two numbers are in the ratio 3 : 4. If 5 is subtracted from each, then the ratio will be 2 : 3. What is the smallest number ? **[NTSE-2016 (Stage-I) Bihar]**

(A) 15 (B) 18
(C) 20 (D) 24

3-16 The present age difference between father and son is 14 years. The ratio of their age will be 4 : 3 after 11 years. How old is son now? **[NTSE-2016 (Stage-I) Bihar]**

(A) 24 yrs (B) 31 yrs
(C) 30 yrs (D) 28 yrs

3-17 The value of K if the linear equations $x + 2y = 3$ and $5x + ky + 7 = 0$ has unique solution is : **[NTSE-2016 (Stage-I) Chandigarh]**

(A) $K \neq 1$ (B) $K \neq 10$
(C) $K \neq 15$ (D) $K \neq 5$

3-18 If we divide a two digit number by the sum of its digits we get 4 as quotient and 3 as remainder. Now if we divide that two digit number by the product of its digits, we get 3 as quotient and 5 as remainder the two digit number is : **[NTSE-2016 (Stage-I) Delhi]**

(A) Even (B) Odd prime
(C) Odd composite (D) Odd

3-19 A boat goes 16 km upstream and 24 km downstream in 6 hours. Also it covers 12 km up stream and 36 km downstream in the same time. Find the speed of the boat in still water ? **[NTSE-2016 (Stage-I) Jharkhand]**

(A) 8 km/h (B) 4 km/h
(C) 2½ km/h (D) None of these

3-20 If $a + 8b = 14$ and $5a - 2b = 16$, then what is the mean of a and b? **[NTSE-2016 (Stage-I) Odisha]**

(A) 15 (B) 7.5
(C) 5 (D) 2.5

3-21 Two lines are to be parallel. The equation of one of the lines is $8x + 6y = 28$. The equation of the second line can be : **[NTSE-2016 (Stage-I) Karnatka]**

(A) $3x + 4y = 14$ (B) $6x + 8y = 28$
(C) $2y + x = 28$ (D) $3y + 4x = 14$

3-22 Ganesh has to pay Rs. 482 for 19 apples and 11 guavas. If he would have exchanged the number of apples and guavas purchased, then he would have paid Rs. 64 less. Find how much more amount he has to pay to purchase 1 apple than 1 guava? **[NTSE-2016 (Stage-I) Chhatisgarh]**

(A) Rs. 19 (B) Rs. 8
(C) Rs. 11 (D) Rs. 7

3-23 If a line passes through the intersection point of the graphs of the lines $x + 2y = 7$ and $x - y = 4$ and the origin, then find the equation of the line : **[NTSE-2016 (Stage-I) Chhatisgarh]**

(A) $y = 0.5x$ (B) $y = 5x$
(C) $y = 0.2x$ (D) $y = -2x$

3-24 If $217x + 131y = 913$ and $131x + 217y = 827$, then the value of $x + y$ is : **[NTSE-2017 (Stage-I) Andhra Pradesh]**

(A) 8 (B) 5
(C) 7 (D) 6

3-25 A fraction becomes $\frac{5}{7}$ if 2 is added to both its numerator and denominator. If 4 is added to numerator and 3 is added to denominator, the fraction becomes $\frac{7}{8}$. Find the original fraction : **[NTSE-2017 (Stage-I) Chandigarh]**

(A) $\frac{8}{11}$ (B) $\frac{3}{5}$
(C) $\frac{5}{11}$ (D) $\frac{7}{9}$

3-26 A 320 m long train moving at an average speed of 120 km/h crosses a platform in 24 seconds. A man crossed the same platform in 4 minutes. The speed of the man in m/s is : **[NTSE-2017 (Stage-I) Delhi]**

(A) 2.0 (B) 2.4
(C) 1.6 (D) 1.5

3-27 In a certain office, $\frac{1}{3}$ of the workers are women, $\frac{1}{2}$ of the same are married and $\frac{1}{3}$ of the married women have children. If $\frac{3}{4}$ of the men are married and $\frac{2}{3}$ of the married men have children, then what part of worker are without children ? **[NTSE-2017 (Stage-I) Delhi]**

(A) $5/18$ (B) $4/9$
(C) $11/18$ (D) $17/36$

3-28 The height of three towers are in the ratio of 5 : 6 : 7. If a spider takes 15 minutes to climb the smallest tower, how much time it will take to climb the highest one ? **[NTSE-2017 (Stage-I) Delhi]**

(A) 15 minutes (B) 18 minutes
(C) 21 minutes (D) 54 minutes

3-29 A train meets an accident after moving 30 km. Its speed then comes to four-fifth of the original one. Consequently runs 45 minutes late. If the accident takes place 18 km farther away it would have been 36 minutes late. The distance between the two stations is : **[NTSE-2017 (Stage-I) Goa]**

(A) 150 (B) 200
(C) 240 (D) 120

3-30 If $\frac{x+y}{xy}=2$ and $\frac{x-y}{xy}=6$ then y—: **[NTSE-2017 (Stage-I) Gujarat]**

(A) $\frac{1}{4}$ (B) $\frac{-1}{2}$
(C) $\frac{-1}{4}$ (D) $\frac{1}{3}$

3-31 The value of λ satisfying the relation $y=\lambda x+5$, where x and y are the solution of pair equations $x+2y=10$ and $3x+4y=360$ is : **[NTSE-2017 (Stage-I) Haryana]**

(A) $\frac{1}{4}$ (B) $\frac{-1}{4}$
(C) $\frac{1}{2}$ (D) $\frac{-1}{2}$

3-32 The ratio of income of two persons is 11 : 7 and the ratio of their expenditures is 9 : 5. If each of them manage to save Rs 400 per month then the sum of their monthly income is : **[NTSE-2017 (Stage-I) Karnataka]**

(A) Rs. 3,600 (B) Rs. 3,200
(C) Rs. 2,800 (D) Rs. 1,700

3-33 Which value of m, equation

$2x+my-4=0$
$3x-7y-10=0$

has no solution ? **[NTSE-2017 (Stage-I) Madhya Pradesh]**

(A) $\frac{2}{3}$ (B) $\frac{4}{10}$
(C) $-\frac{14}{3}$ (D) $\frac{14}{3}$

3-34 Five years ago age of Sunita was thrice the age of Vineeta. After 10 years Sunita's age will be twice the age of Vineeta, what is the present age of Sunita ? **[NTSE-2017 (Stage-I) Madhya Pradesh]**

(A) 50 years (B) 20 years
(C) 70 years (D) 30 years

3-35 A train travels some distance at a constant speed. If the speed of the train would have increased by 15 km/hr, then it would have required 2 hours less. But if the speed of the train would have decreased by 5 km/hr, then to cover the same distance it would have required 1 hour more. Find the distance covered by the train : **[NTSE-2017 (Stage-I) Maharashtra]**

(A) 120 km (B) 240 km
(C) 360 km (D) 400 km

3-36 If x men can do a piece of work in 8 days and $(x+4)$ men can do the same work in 6 days then x is equal to : **[NTSE-2017 (Stage-I) Punjab]**

(A) 10 (B) 6
(C) 12 (D) 24

3-37 8 men and 12 boys can finish a work in 10 days while 6 men and 8 boys can finish it in 14 days. Then the number of days taken by one man alone is : **[NTSE-2017 (Stage-I) Tamilnadu]**

(A) 240 (B) 200
(C) 140 (D) 280

3-38 There are two taps to fill a tank. If both are opened, the tank fills in 1 hour. If the smaller tap alone is opened, it takes 3 hours to fill the tank. How many hours will it take to fill the tank, if the larger tap alone is opened ? **[NTSE-2017 (Stage-I) Kerala]**

(A) 2 (B) $1\frac{1}{2}$
(C) $1\frac{1}{3}$ (D) $1\frac{1}{4}$

3-39 For which value of k, pair of equations $x+y-4=0$, $2x+ky-3=0$ has no solution : **[NTSE-2018 (Stage-I) Rajasthan]**

(A) 0 (B) 2
(C) 6 (D) 8

3-40 If $\frac{x+1}{2}+\frac{y-1}{3}=8$ and $\frac{x-1}{3}+\frac{y+1}{2}=9$, then $y=$ **[NTSE-2018 (Stage-I) Andhra Pradesh]**

(A) 7 (B) 12
(C) 13 (D) 8

3-41 $\frac{1}{2(3x+4y)}+\frac{12}{7(4x-3y)}=\frac{1}{2}\frac{7}{(3x+4y)}+\frac{4}{(4x-3y)}=2.$

Find the values of x and y if $3x+4y\neq O$, $4x-3y\neq 0$: **[NTSE-2018 (Stage-I) Chandigarh]**

(A) $x=\frac{444}{25}$, $y=\frac{16}{25}$ (B) $x=0, y=1$
(C) $x=\frac{16}{25}, y=\frac{256}{25}$ (D) $x=\frac{37}{25}, y=\frac{16}{25}$

3-42 A gardener wants to grow some plants in a garden. If 4 plants are grown extra in each row, the number of rows will reduce by 2. If 4 plants are grown less in each row, the number of rows increases by 4. Find the total number of plants grown :
[NTSE-2018 (Stage-I) Chandigarh]

(A) 90 (B) 100
(C) 108 (D) 96

3-43 A pair of equation $x = m$ and $y = n$ graphically represent lines which are_____: **[NTSE-2018 (Stage-I) Chandigarh]**

(A) Intersecting at (n, m) (B) Coincident
(C) Parallel (D) Intersecting at (m, n)

3-44 If there is no solution of linear equation system $kx - 5y = 2$ and $6x + 2y = 7$, then the value of k will be :
[NTSE-2018 (Stage-I) Chhattisgarh]

(A) –10 (B) –5
(C) –6 (D) –15

3-45 Equation $\frac{2}{3}x + \frac{3}{2}y = 5$ can be expressed in the standard form as_____: **[NTSE-2018 (Stage-I) Gujarat]**

(A) $2x + 3y - 5 = 0$ (B) $4x + 9y - 5 = 0$
(C) $4x + 9y + 30 = 0$ (D) $4x + 9y - 30 = 0$

3-46 A person can row a boat at 10 km/h in still water. He takes two and half hours to row from A to B and back. If the distance between A and B is 12 km, then the speed of the stream is :
[NTSE-2018 (Stage-I) Haryana]

(A) 3 km/h (B) $2\frac{1}{2}$ km/h
(C) 2 km/h (D) $1\frac{1}{2}$ km/h

3-47 Present age of a father is six times his son's age. After four years, the father will be four times his son's age. The present ages (in years) of father and son are respectively :
[NTSE-2018 (Stage-I) Haryana]

(A) 24 and 4 (B) 30 and 5
(C) 36 and 6 (D) 28 and 7

3-48 The equation $x - \frac{2}{x-1} = 1 - \frac{2}{x-1}$ has :
[NTSE-2018 (Stage-I) Himachal Pradesh]

(A) No roots (B) One roots
(C) Two equal roots (D) Infinite roots

3-49 A set of farmers can completely harvest a crop in 10 days. However 12 farmers fell ill and now the remaining can do this job in 15 days. Find the original no of farmers :
[NTSE-2018 (Stage-I) Himachal Pradesh]

(A) 40 farmer (B) 36 farmer
(C) 27 farmer (D) 25 farmer

3-50 The sum of the five consecutive number is equal to 170. What is the product of largest and the smallest of these numbers :
[NTSE-2018 (Stage-I) Jharkhand]

(A) 1512 (B) 1102
(C) 1152 (D) 1210

3-51 A man had 170 currency notes in all, some of which were of Rs.100 denominations and some of are Rs.50 denomination. The total amount of all these currency notes was Rs.10000. How much amount did he have in the denominations of Rs. 50 :
[NTSE-2018 (Stage-I) Jharkhand]

(A) Rs.4000 (B) Rs.9000
(C) Rs.7000 (D) Rs.6000

3-52 The difference between the ages of Sonu and Sneha is 12 years. If the ratio of their ages is 3 : 5 then the age of Sneha is :
[NTSE-2018 (Stage-I) Jharkhand]

(A) 32 yrs (B) 24 yrs
(C) 28 yrs (D) 30 yrs

3-53 In the class, the number of boys and girls are in the ratio of 4 : 5. If 10 more boys join the class, the ratio of number of boys and girls become 6 : 5. How many girls are there in the class : **[NTSE-2018 (Stage-I) Jharkhand]**

(A) 20 (B) 30
(C) 25 (D) None of these

3-54 The difference between the two adjacent angles of a parallelogram is 20º. What would be the ratio between the smaller and the longer angles of the parallelogram respectively :
[NTSE-2018 (Stage-I) Jharkhand]

(A) 4 : 5 (B) 4 : 7
(C) 3 : 5 (D) 5 : 6

3-55 If the graphs of $x - y = 2$ and $kx + y = 3$ (k is constant) intersect at a point in first quadrant then the value of k is :
[NTSE-2018 (Stage-I) Karnataka]

(A) Equal to (B) Greater than –1
(C) Less than $\frac{4}{3}$ (D) Between –1 and $\frac{4}{3}$

3-56 A rational number becomes $\frac{1}{3}$ on substracting 1 from its numerator and it becomes $\frac{1}{4}$ when 8 is added to its denominator, the rational number is :
[NTSE-2018 (Stage-I) Madhya Prasesh]

(A) $\frac{5}{12}$ (B) $\frac{1}{12}$
(C) $\frac{7}{12}$ (D) $\frac{3}{17}$

3-57 Which of the following two linear equations have only one unique solution $x = 2$ and $y = -3$:

[NTSE-2018 (Stage-I) Maharashtra]

(A) $x + y = 1; 2x - 3y = -5$
(B) $2x + 5y = -11; 4x + 10y = 22$
(C) $2x - y = 1; 3x + 2y = 0$
(D) $x - 4y - 14 = 0; 5x - y - 13 = 0$

3-58 The number formed when 5 is subtracted after multiplying by 8 to the sum of digit of a two digit number is equal to the number formed when 3 is added after multiplying by 16 to the difference of digits in a number. What is the number :

[NTSE-2018 (Stage-I) Maharashtra]

(A) 83 (B) 84
(C) 85 (D) 78

3-59 The graphs of the linear system $x + y = 1$; $2x + 2y = 2$ gives :

[NTSE-2018 (Stage-I) Tamil Nadu]

(A) No solution (B) Unique solution
(C) Infinitely many solution (D) Two solutions

3-60 If $x = a, y = b$ is the solution of the equation $x - y = 2$ and $x + y = 4$ then the values of a and b are respectively :

[NTSE-2018 (Stage-I) Uttar Pradesh]

(A) 3 and 5 (B) 3 and 1
(C) 5 and 3 (D) –3 and –1

3-61 Half of a herd of deer are grazing in the field and three fourths of the remaining are playing nearly. If the remaining 9 are drinking water from a pond, then the difference between the number of deer who are grazing and those who are playing is a multiple of :

[NTSE-2012 (Stage-II)]

(A) 4 (B) 6
(C) 8 (D) 9

3-62 If amongst two supplementary angles, the measure of smaller angle is four times its complement, then their difference is :

[NTSE-2012 (Stage-II)]

(A) 30° (B) 36°
(C) 43° (D) 45°

3-63 There are several human beings and several dogs in a room. One tenth of the humans have lost a leg. The total numbers of feet are 77. Then the number of dogs is :

[NTSE-2013 (Stage-II)]

(A) Not determinable due to insufficient data
(B) 4
(C) 5
(D) 6

3-64 Suppose you walk from home to the bus stand at 4 km/h and immediately return at x km/h. If the average speed is 6 km/h then x is :

[NTSE-2013 (Stage-II)]

(A) 8 km/h
(B) 10 km/h
(C) 12 km/h
(D) Cannot be determined unless the distance from home to bus stand is known.

3-65 The graphs of the equations $x - y = 2$ and $kx + y = 3$, where k is a constant, intersect at the point (x, y) in the first quadrant, if and only if k is :

[NTSE-2015 (Stage-II)]

(A) Equal to –1 (B) Greater than –1
(C) Less than $\frac{3}{2}$ (D) Lying between –1 and $\frac{3}{2}$

3-66 For what value of p, the following pair of linear equations in two variables will have infinitely many solutions ?

[NTSE-2016 (Stage-II)]

$$px + 3y - (p - 3) = 0$$
$$12x + py - p = 0$$

(A) 6 (B) –6
(C) 0 (D) 2

3-67 Cost of 2 apples, 3 bananas and one coconut is Rs. 26. Also the cost of 3 apples, 2 bananas and two coconuts is Rs. 35. Then the cost of 12 apples, 13 bananas and 7 coconuts is :

[NTSE-2016 (Stage-II)]

(A) Rs. 172 (B) Rs. 148
(C) Rs. 143 (D) Rs. 126

* * * * *

ANSWERS

PRACTICE EXERCISE-3.1

1 (B)	2 (C)	3 (D)
4 (D)	5 (D)	6 (C)
7 (C)	8 (D)	9 (C)
10 (A)	11 (C)	12 (D)
13 (D)	14 (D)	15 (D)
16 (D)	17 (C)	18 (A)
19 (C)	20 (A)	21 (C)
22 (A)	23 (A)	24 (D)
25 (D)	26 (B)	27 (A)
28 (B)	29 (B)	30 (C)
31 (A)	32 (D)	33 (C)
34 (D)	35 (A)	36 (B)
37 (D)	38 (B)	39 (A)
40 (A)	41 (D)	42 (A)
43 (C)	44 (B)	45 (C)
46 (D)	47 (B)	48 (A)
49 (C)	50 (A)	

PRACTICE EXERCISE-3.2

1 (C)	2 (B)	3 (D)
4 (A)	5 (C)	6 (D)
7 (D)	8 (B)	9 (A)
10 (C)	11 (C)	12 (B)
13 (C)	14 (B)	15 (D)
16 (B)	17 (C)	18 (A)
19 (B)	20 (B)	21 (D)
22 (D)	23 (B)	24 (B)
25 (B)		

PRACTICE EXERCISE-3.3

1 (D)	2 (A)	3 (A)
4 (A)	5 (D)	6 (C)
7 (A)	8 (C)	9 (C)
10 (A)	11 (C)	12 (A)
13 (B)	14 (C)	15 (A)
16 (B)	17 (B)	18 (B)
19 (A)	20 (D)	21 (D)
22 (B)	23 (C)	24 (B)
25 (B)	26 (A)	27 (C)
28 (C)	29 (A)	30 (A)
31 (D)	32 (A)	33 (C)
34 (A)	35 (C)	36 (C)
37 (C)	38 (B)	39 (B)
40 (C)	41 (D)	42 (D)
43 (D)	44 (D)	45 (D)
46 (C)	47 (C)	48 (A)
49 (B)	50 (C)	51 (C)
52 (D)	53 (C)	54 (A)
55 (D)	56 (A)	57 (D)
58 (A)	59 (C)	60 (B)
61 (D)	62 (B)	63 (C)
64 (C)	65 (D)	66 (A)
67 (B)		

Solutions of PRACTICE EXERCISE-3.1

Sol. 1 (B) 'n' equations needed to solve a problem in n variables
Hence Ans is (B)

Sol. 2 (C) An inconsistent system of two linear equations in two variables will have no solution
Hence Ans is (C)

Sol. 3 (D) $x+y=0$ ...(1)

$2x+2y=0$ ...(2)

These two lines are co-incident lines so they are having infinite solution
Hence Ans is (D)

Sol. 4 (D) $5x-2y=19$ ...(1)

$3x+y=18$ ...(2)

From (1) & (2) $x=5, y=3$
Hence Ans is (D)

Sol. 5 (D) Let number of hens $=x$
number of cows $=y$

$x+y=48$ ...(1)

$2x+4y=140$ ...(2)

From (1) & (2) $x=26$
Hence Ans is (D)

Sol. 6 (C) $8x+7y=0$ ...(1)

$4x+ky=0$ ...(2)

From (1) $x=\frac{-7y}{8}$

Putting this value of x in equation-(2)

$$4\left(\frac{-7y}{8}\right)+ky=0$$

$$\frac{-7}{2}y+ky=0$$

$$y\left[k-\frac{7}{2}\right]=0$$

Here $y\neq 0$

So, $k-\frac{7}{2}=0$

$$k=\frac{7}{2}$$

Hence Ans is (C)

Sol. 7 (C) $2x-3y=7$ ...(1)

$(a+b)x-(a+b-3)y=4a+b$ ...(2)

For co-incident line

$$\frac{2}{a+b}=\frac{-3}{-(a+b-3)}=\frac{7}{4a+b}$$

So, $$\frac{2}{a+b}=\frac{7}{4a+b}$$

$\Rightarrow$ $8a+2b=7a+7b$

$\Rightarrow$ $a-5b=0$

Hence Ans is (C)

Sol. 8 (D) $\sqrt{2}x+\sqrt{5}y=0$ ...(1)

$\sqrt{3}x-\sqrt{7}y=0$ ...(2)

From (1) & (2)

$x=0,$

$y=0$

Hence Ans is (D)

Sol. 9 (C) Given

$a_1x+b_1y+c_1=0$

$a_2x+b_2y+c_2=0$

These two equation will inconsistent when these two lines will be parallel

Hence Ans is (C)

Sol. 10 (A) $mx-ny=m^2+n^2$ ...(1)

$x+y=2m$ ...(2)

Multiply equation-(2) by n

$\Rightarrow$ $nx+ny=2mn$ ...(3)

Adding (1) & (3)

$mx-ny=m^2+n^2$

$nx+ny=2mn$

We get $x(m+n)=m^2+n^2+2mn$

$\Rightarrow$ $x(m+n)=(m+n)^2$

$\Rightarrow$ $x=m+n$

Putting the value of $x=m+n$ in equestion-(2)

We get $y=m-n$

Hence Ans is (A)

Sol. 11 (C) Both lines are passing (2, –1)

So, $3\times 2+a(-1)=4$

So, $a=2$

$2b-3(-1)=13$

$b=5$

So $a+b=2+5=7$

Hence Ans is (C)

Sol. 12 (D) $ax+by+21=0$ ...(1)

$-2x-by=5a+2$ ...(2)

these two lines passing through (–3, 2)

So from (1) $-3a+2b+21=0$ ...(3)

So from (2) $6-2b=5a+2$ ...(4)

Solving (3) & (4) $a=\frac{25}{8}, b=\frac{-93}{16}$

Hence Ans is (D)

Sol. 13 (D) If the two lines

$a_1x+b_1y=c_1$

& $a_2x+b_2y=c_2$

are parallel,

Then $$\frac{a_1}{a_2}=\frac{b_1}{b_2}$$

So check all the option, we find

$4x-7y=8$

Is not parallel to

$3x-5y=7$

Hence Ans is (D)

Sol. 14 (D) $5x-4y=-2$ ...(1)

$3x+4y=18$ ...(2)

Adding (1) & (2)

$8x=16$

$x=2$

Putting this value of x in (1)

$5\times 2-4y=-2$

$12=4y$

$y=3$

So, (2, 3) is the intersection point.

$3x-5y=b$

Is passing through (2, 3)

$3\times 2-5\times 3=b$

$b=-9$

Hence Ans is (D)

Sol. 15 (D) $(3k+1)x+11y-22=0$

$x+(2k-1)y-47=0$

For no solution

$$\frac{3k+1}{1}=\frac{11}{2k-1}\neq\frac{-22}{-47}$$

So, $$\frac{3k+1}{1}=\frac{11}{2k-1}$$

$\Rightarrow$ $(3k+1)(2k-1)=11$

On solving $k=\frac{3}{2}$ or $\frac{-4}{3}$

Hence Ans is (D)

Sol. 16 (D) Let the cost of a chair be $= x$

& the cost of a table be $= y$

It's given

$$3x + 2y = 700 \quad \dots(1)$$
$$5x + 3y = 1100 \quad \dots(2)$$

From (1) & (2)

$$x = 100, y = 200$$

So, $2x + 3y = 2 \times 100 + 3 \times 200$
$$= 800$$

Hence Ans is (D)

Sol. 17 (C) $kx + 3y = k - 3$
$$12x + ky = k$$

For infinitely having solution

$$\frac{k}{12} = \frac{3}{k} = \frac{k-3}{k}$$

On solving

$$k = 6$$

Hence Ans is (C)

Sol. 18 (A) Given

$$x - y = 0.9 = \frac{9}{10} \quad \dots(1)$$
$$\frac{11}{2(x+y)} = 1$$
$$\Rightarrow \quad x + y = \frac{11}{2} \quad \dots(2)$$

On solving we get

$$x = 3.2$$
$$y = 2.3$$

Hence Ans is (A)

Sol. 19 (C) $\frac{2}{x} + \frac{3}{y} = 6 \quad \dots(1)$

$$\frac{1}{x} + \frac{1}{2y} = 2 \quad \dots(2)$$

On solving (1) & (2), we get

$$x = \frac{2}{3}, y = 1$$

Hence they will satisfy by both the equations P and Q

Hence Ans is (C)

Sol. 20 (A) $x + 2y - 3 = 0$
$$5x + ky + 7 = 0$$

For no solution

$$\frac{1}{5} = \frac{2}{k} \neq \frac{-3}{7}$$

So, $k = 10$

Hence Ans is (A)

Sol. 21 (C) Given

$$\angle A = x^o$$
$$\angle B = 3x^o$$
$$\angle C = y^o$$

As we know, sum of three angles in a triangle = 180°

So $x^o + 3x^o + y^o = 180^o$

$$\Rightarrow \quad 4x + y = 180^o \quad \dots(1)$$

Given $3y - 5x = 30^o \quad \dots(2)$

From (1) & (2)

$$x = 30^o$$
$$y = 60^o$$

So, $3x^o = 90^o$

So triangle is right angled triangle

Hence Ans is (C)

Sol. 22 (A) A system of two simultaneous linear equations in two variables is inconsistent, if their graphs are parallel.

Hence Ans is (A)

Sol. 23 (A) Given

$$ax + b = 0$$
$$x = -\frac{b}{a}$$
$$cx + d = 0$$
$$\Rightarrow \quad x = -\frac{d}{c}$$

If these two are consistent, if

$$-\frac{b}{a} = -\frac{d}{c}$$
$$ad = bc$$

Hence Ans is (A)

Sol. 24 (D) $\frac{2x - y - 3}{3} = \frac{4x + y - 3}{4}$

On solving further we get

$$x = \frac{-3 - 7y}{4}$$

Hence Ans is (D)

Sol. 25 (D) Given

$$ax + by = c$$
$$lx + my = n$$

For unique solution

$$\frac{a}{l} \neq \frac{b}{m}$$
$$am \neq bl$$

Hence Ans is (D)

Sol. 26 (B) $2(ax-by)+a+4b=0$ ...(1)

$2(bx+ay)+b-4a=0$ ...(2)

From (1) & (2)

$$x=-\frac{1}{2}, y=2$$

Hence Ans is (B)

Sol. 27 (A) Given

$x+2y=5$ ...(1)

$3x+ky+15=0$ ...(2)

For no solution

$$\frac{1}{3}=\frac{2}{k}\neq\frac{5}{-15}$$

$\Rightarrow$ $k=6$

Hence Ans is (A)

Sol. 28 (B) Given

$x+(k+1)y=5$

$(k+1)x+9y=8k-1$

For infinite solution

$$\frac{1}{k+1}=\frac{k+1}{9}=\frac{5}{8k-1}$$

$$\Rightarrow \frac{1}{k+1}=\frac{x+1}{9}$$

$\Rightarrow$ $9=(k+1)^2$

$\Rightarrow$ $k^2+2k-8=0$

$\Rightarrow$ $(k+4)(k-2)=0$

$\Rightarrow$ $k=-4$

$\Rightarrow$ $k=2$

Check both the values

For equality

$$\frac{k+1}{9}=\frac{5}{8k-1}$$

Only $k=2$ satisfies

Hence Ans is (B)

Sol. 29 (B) If a pair of linear equations has no solution then graphically lines are parallel.

Hence Ans is (B)

Sol. 30 (C) $2x-3y=7$

$(a+b)x-(a+b-3)y=4a+b$

For coincident line

$$\frac{2}{a+b}=\frac{-3}{(a+b-3)}=\frac{7}{4a+b}$$

From this $a-5b=0$

Hence Ans is (C)

Sol. 31 (A) Let the cost of a pen is 'x' and the cost of a pencil is 'y'

Given $37x+53y=320$

$53x+37y=400$

From this $x=6.5,$

$y=1.5$

So, $x+y=6.5+1.5$

$=8$

Hence Ans is (A)

Sol. 32 (D) $2x+3y=7$ ...(1)

$a(2x+y)+by=28$ ...(2)

$$\frac{2}{2a}=\frac{3}{a+b}=\frac{7}{28}$$

From this $a=4$

Hence Ans is (D)

Sol. 33 (C) Given

$$\frac{x+y}{11}=\frac{x+y}{2}$$

On simplifying we get

$2x+2y=11x+11y$

$\Rightarrow$ $9x+9y=0$ ...(1)

$$\Rightarrow \frac{x-y}{3}=\frac{x-y}{7}$$

On simplifying we get

$7x-7y=3x-3y$

$\Rightarrow$ $4x-4y=0$ ...(2)

From (1) & (2)

We get $x=0,$

$y=0$

Hence Ans is (C)

Sol. 34 (D) Given

$x+2y=5$ ...(1)

$3x+ky-15=0$ ...(2)

For no solution

$$\frac{1}{3}=\frac{2}{k}\neq\frac{5}{15}$$

From this $k=6,$

But $\frac{2}{k}\neq\frac{5}{15}$

But here $\frac{2}{6}=\frac{5}{15}$

If $k=6$ these lines will be coincident

So, No value of k

Hence Ans is (D)

Sol. 35 (A) Given

$$\frac{2x+5y}{xy}=6$$

$$\Rightarrow \quad \frac{2}{y}+\frac{5}{x}=6 \quad \ldots(1)$$

$$\Rightarrow \quad \frac{4x-5y}{xy}+3=0$$

$$\Rightarrow \quad \frac{4}{y}-\frac{5}{x}=-3 \quad \ldots(2)$$

Let $\frac{1}{x}=a$ and $\frac{1}{y}=b$

then equation-(1) & (2) reduces, as

$$5a+2b=6 \quad \ldots(3)$$

$$-5a+4b=-3 \quad \ldots(4)$$

Adding (3) & (4) we get

$$6b=3$$

$$b=\frac{1}{2} \ \& \ a=1$$

Hence $x=1$,

$y=2$

Hence Ans is (A)

Sol. 36 (B) $2x+3y=7 \quad \ldots(1)$

$$(a-b)x+(a+b)y=3a+b-2$$

$$\frac{2}{a-b}=\frac{3}{a+b}=\frac{7}{3a+b-2}$$

From this $a=5$,

$b=1$

Hence Ans is (B)

Sol. 37 (D) Given

$$kx-y=2 \quad \ldots(1)$$

$$6x-2y=3 \quad \ldots(2)$$

For infinite solution $\frac{k}{6}=\frac{-1}{2}=\frac{2}{3}$

But $\frac{-1}{2}\neq\frac{2}{3}$

So infinitely many solution does not exist

Hence Ans is (D)

Sol. 38 (B) Given

$$x+2y=3$$

$$5x+ky+7=0$$

For unique solution $\frac{1}{5}\neq\frac{2}{k}$

$$\Rightarrow \quad k\neq 10$$

Hence Ans is (B)

Sol. 39 (A) Given

$$ax+by=c$$

$$lx+my=n$$

Given $am\neq bl$

$$\Rightarrow \quad \frac{a}{l}\neq\frac{b}{m}$$

So only unique solution

Hence Ans is (A)

Sol. 40 (A) Given

$$\lambda x+3y=\lambda-3$$

$$12x+\lambda y=\lambda$$

For no solution

$$\frac{\lambda}{12}=\frac{3}{\lambda}\neq\frac{\lambda-3}{\lambda}$$

$$\lambda=\pm 6$$

But $\lambda\neq 6$

As it does not satisfy

$$\frac{3}{6}\neq\frac{6-3}{6}$$

$$\frac{1}{2}\neq\frac{1}{2}$$

$$\Rightarrow \quad \lambda=-6$$

Hence Ans is (A)

Sol. 41 (D) Let the height be $=h$

I[st] candle $\rightarrow \frac{1}{5}$ part burnt in 1 hour

IInd candle $\rightarrow \frac{1}{4}$ part burnt in 1 hour

Let the time of burning be x hours

Now remaining height $\left(h-\frac{xh}{5}\right)$ and $\left(h-\frac{xh}{4}\right)$

According to the problem $\left(h-\frac{xh}{5}\right)=2\left(h-\frac{xh}{4}\right)$

$$\frac{5-x}{5}=\frac{4-x}{2}$$

$$\Rightarrow \quad 10-2x=20-5x$$

$$\Rightarrow \quad 3x=20-10$$

$$\Rightarrow \quad 3x=10$$

$$\Rightarrow \quad x=\frac{10}{3}$$

$$\Rightarrow \quad x=3\frac{1}{3}\text{ hrs}$$

Hence Ans is (D)

Sol. 42 (A) Given

$$\frac{x+y}{xy}=2$$

$\Rightarrow$ $$\frac{1}{x}+\frac{1}{y}=2 \quad \ldots(1)$$

and $$\frac{x-y}{xy}=6$$

$\Rightarrow$ $$\frac{1}{y}-\frac{1}{x}=6 \quad \ldots(2)$$

By adding equation-(1) and (2), we get

$$\frac{2}{y}=8$$

$\Rightarrow$ $$y=\frac{1}{4}$$

$\Rightarrow$ $$x=-\frac{1}{2}$$

or $$x=-\frac{1}{2}$$

and $$y=\frac{1}{4}$$

Aliter :

$$x+y=2xy$$

and $$x-y=6xy \quad \ldots(1)$$

$\Rightarrow$ $$3(x+y)=6xy$$

and $$x-y=6xy$$

$\Rightarrow$ $$3x+3y=x-y$$

$\Rightarrow$ $$2x=-4y$$

$\Rightarrow$ $$x=-2y$$

Substituting $x=-2y$. in the equation-(1), we get

$$-3y=6xy$$

$\Rightarrow$ $$x=-\frac{1}{2}$$

and $$y=\frac{1}{4}$$

Hence Ans is (A)

Sol. 43 (C) $\frac{1}{2x}-\frac{1}{y}-1$

and $$\frac{1}{x}+\frac{1}{2y}=8$$

$\Rightarrow$ $$\frac{1}{2x}-\frac{1}{y}=-1$$

and $$\frac{2}{x}+\frac{1}{y}=16$$

By adding these two equations, we get

$$\frac{5}{2x}=15$$

$\Rightarrow$ $$x=\frac{1}{6}$$

and $$y=\frac{1}{4}$$

Hence Ans is (C)

Sol. 44 (B) $\frac{2x}{a}+\frac{y}{b}=2 \quad \ldots(1)$

$$\frac{x}{a}-\frac{y}{b}=4 \quad \ldots(2)$$

Adding equation-(1) and (2), we get

$$\frac{3x}{a}=6$$

$\Rightarrow$ $$\frac{x}{a}=2$$

$\Rightarrow$ $$x=2a$$

Now put $x=2a$ in equation-(2)

$$\frac{y}{b}=-2$$

$$x=2a$$

and $$y=-2b$$

Hence Ans is (B)

Sol. 45 (C) For no solution

$$\frac{9}{7}=\frac{4}{k}\neq\frac{9}{5}$$

$\Rightarrow$ $$k=\frac{28}{9}$$

Hence Ans is (C)

Sol. 46 (D) Two linear equations will coincide if there are infinite number of solutions,

i.e., $$\frac{a_1}{a_2}=\frac{b_1}{b_2}=\frac{c_1}{c_2}$$

For $$a_1x+b_1y=c_1$$

and $$a_2x+b_2y=c_2$$

$\Rightarrow$ $$\frac{k}{3}=\frac{2}{1}=\frac{2}{1}$$

$\Rightarrow$ $$k=6$$

Hence Ans is (D)

Sol. 47 (B) For an infinite number of solutions

$$\frac{2}{6}=\frac{3}{k}=\frac{-5}{-15}$$

$\Rightarrow \quad k=9$

Hence Ans is (B)

Sol. 48 (A) Let the price of mug be M and the price of bucket be B

$$8B+5M=92 \quad \ldots(1)$$
$$5B+8M=77 \quad \ldots(2)$$

Multiply equation-(1) by 8 equation-(2) by 5, we get

$$\left.\begin{aligned}64B+40M&=736\\25B+40M&=385\end{aligned}\right\}$$

$$\begin{aligned}64B+40M&=736\\25B+40M&=385\\-\quad\ -\quad&\quad -\\\hline 39B\qquad\quad&=351\end{aligned}$$

$\Rightarrow \quad B=9$

$\Rightarrow \quad M=4$

$\Rightarrow \quad 2M+3B=35$

$\Rightarrow$ The required cost of 2 mugs and 3 buckets is Rs. 35

Hence Ans is (A)

Sol. 49 (C) Let the two numbers be x and y

Then $\quad x+y=8$

and $\quad (x+y)=4(x-y)$

$\Rightarrow \quad x-y=2$

Given $\quad x+y=8$

and $\quad x-y=2$

On solving $\quad 2x=10$

$\Rightarrow \quad x=5$

$\Rightarrow \quad y=3$

Hence Ans is (C)

Sol. 50 (A) Let numerator be x and denominator be y

Then $\quad x=y-4$

$$8(x-2)=(y+1)$$

The above equations can be written as

and $\quad y-x=4 \quad \ldots(1)$

$$y-8x=-17 \quad \ldots(2)$$

Equation-(1) equation-(2)

$$7x=21$$

$\Rightarrow \quad x=3$

$\Rightarrow \quad y=7$

$\Rightarrow$ the required fraction $=\dfrac{x}{y}=\dfrac{3}{7}$

Hence Ans is (A)

Solutions of PRACTICE EXERCISE-3.2

Sol. 1 (C) $3x+7y$ is divisible by 11. Find one particular solution of $3x+7y=11K$ (where K is any positive integer).

It is possible when $x=9$ and $y=4$ or multiple of that values

$3x+7y=55$, i.e. it is a multiple of 11.

Now, substitute these values of x and y in the answer options and check which of them is divisible by 11. From answer option (3)

$$4x-9y$$

$\Rightarrow \quad 4\times 9-9\times 4=36-36=0$

Hence Ans is (C)

Sol. 2 (B) $y=\min\{(x+7),(5-x)\}$

y is maximum i.e. minimum value of $(x+7)$ and $(5-x)$ where $x\in R$ have maximum value for the value of x for which

$$x+7=5-x$$

$\Rightarrow \quad x+x=5-7$

$\Rightarrow \quad 2x=-2$

$\Rightarrow \quad x=-1$

$\Rightarrow$ Maximum value of

$$y=\min((-1+7),(5-(-1)))$$
$$=\min\{6,6\}=6$$

Hence Ans is (B)

Sol. 3 (D) Equation I and II are identical because $1\times(1.5)=$ (II). Hence we can't find the unique values of x and y. Equation (II) and (III) satisfy the following condition

$$\frac{18}{26}=\frac{27}{39}\neq\frac{36}{23}$$

Hence (II) and (III) give no solution for x and y

Also, (I) and (III) satisfy the condition

$$\frac{12}{26}=\frac{18}{39}\neq\frac{24}{23}$$

Therefore (I) and (III) give no solution for x and y. Hence none of the equations gives unique solutions for x and y

Hence Ans is (D)

Sol. 4 (A) The system of equations has no solution for x and y if

$$\frac{5}{n}=\frac{m}{42}\neq\frac{17}{13}$$

It is equivalent to the following system of equations.

(i) $mn=210$

(ii) $17n\neq 65$

(iii) $13m\neq 42\times 17$

(ii) and (iii) hold for any integers m and n. Hence we have to find the integral solution of (i), i.e. $mn = 210$. In other words, "we have to find the number of ways in which 210 can be expressed as the product of two positive integers."

(See the method for solving such type of problems in the chapter **Number System.**)

$$210 = 2^1 \times 3^1 \times 5^1 \times 7^1$$

Required number of ways

$$= \frac{1}{2}\{(1+1)(1+1)(1+1)(1+1)\} = 8$$

There are 8 pairs of (m, n). But values of m and n may interchange their positions. Hence total no. of required pairs $= 2 \times 8 = 16$.

For example, $14 \times 15 = 210$

Hence, the system of equations $5x + 14y = 17$ and $15x + 42y = 13$ has no solution for x and y

$5x + 15y = 17$ and $14x + 42y = 13$ also have no solution for x and y

Hence Ans is (A)

Sol. 5 (C) The system of equations has a unique solution if $mn \neq 12$. (A) is true because there are many possible values of (m, n) such that $mn \neq 12$, i.e. there are many possible values of (m, n) such that the system of linear equations has unique solutions for x and y.

Now, system of equations has no solution if

$$\frac{4}{n} = \frac{m}{3} \neq \frac{15}{10}$$

i.e.. (a) $mn = 12$ (b) $10m \neq 45$ (c) $15n \neq 40$ (b) and (c) suggest that all positive integers (m, n) are possible.

Also, $12 = 2^2 \times 3$

$\Rightarrow$ Required number of ways in which 12 can be expressed as the product of two positive integers

$$= \frac{1}{2}\{(2+1)(1+1)\} = 3$$

$\Rightarrow$ Number of possible pairs of $(m, n) = 3 \times 2 = 6$

Hence (B) is true.

Again, $\frac{4}{n} = \frac{m}{3} = \frac{15}{10}$ is not possible for any $m, n \in$ set of integers. Hence there is no (m, n) such that the system of linear equations has infinite solutions for x and y.

Hence Ans is (C)

Sol. 6 (D) $g(x) = \max\{(5-x), (x+2)\}$

We have to find the smallest possible value of $g(x)$, i.e. we have to find the value of x for which maximum of $(5-x)$ and $(x+2)$ attains minimum values. The required value of x is the value for which

$$5 - x = x + 2$$

$$\Rightarrow \quad 5 - 2 = 2x$$

$$\Rightarrow \quad x = \frac{3}{2}$$

i.e. $\quad g(x) = 3.5$

Alternative Method :

(Quicker Method) Drawing the graph of $y_1 = 5 - x$ and $y_2 = x + 2$, we get

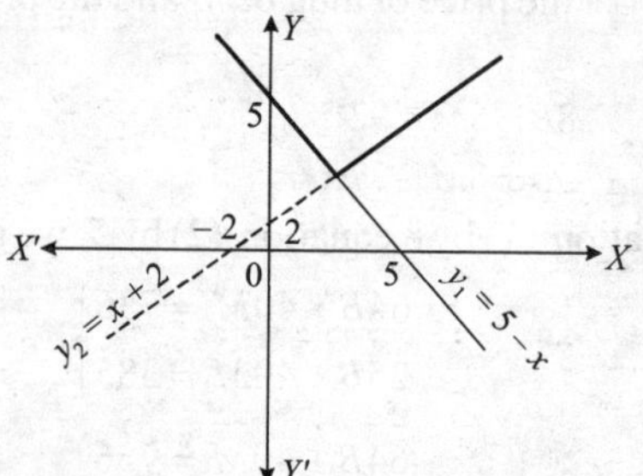

Darkened part of the graph shows

$\max(5-x, x+2)$ and it attains the smallest value at the point of intersection i.e. for $x = 1.5$.

$\Rightarrow$ Minimum possible value of

$$g(x) = \max(5-x, x+2)$$

$$= \max(5-1.5, 1.6+2)$$

Sol. 7 (D) Statement-I : The coefficients in the equation are large enough to make it difficult to find a particular solution. However, it is not hard to see that the numbers 1990 and 173 are relatively prime and this helps us reach the conclusion.

Hence we can find the solution of 1990 m-Hence statement I is wrong.

Statement-II : In the linear equation $3x - 12y = 7$; coefficients of x and y, i.e. 3 and 12, are not relatively prime. HCF of $(3, 12) = 3$. Also, constant 7 is not exactly divisible by 3.

Hence $3x - 12y = 7$ has no solution for x and y in integers.

Hence, statement II is wrong.

Hence Ans is (D)

Sol. 8 (B) It is given that

$$200 < T < 300$$

$$\Rightarrow \quad 200 < 30 + 28(x-3) < 300$$

$$\Rightarrow \quad \frac{200-30}{25} < x - 3 < \frac{300-30}{25}$$

$$\Rightarrow \quad 6.8 < x - 3 < 10.8$$

Between 9.8 km and 13.8 km

Hence Ans is (B)

Sol. 9 (A) Let groups A, B and C contain x, y and z questions.

According to question,

$$x, y, z \geq 1$$

$$x + y + z = 100$$

Also, $\quad x \geq 60\%$ of $(x + 2y + 3z)$

	A	B	C
Number of questions	$77-z$	23	z
Marks	$77-z$	46	$3z$

Also, $77 - z \geq 60\% \text{ of } (123 + 2z)$

$\Rightarrow \quad 385 - 5z \geq 369 + 6z$

$\Rightarrow \quad 385 - 369 \geq 6z + 5z$

$\Rightarrow \quad 16 \geq 11z$

$\Rightarrow \quad z = 1$

Hence Ans is (A)

Sol. 10 (C)

	A	B	C
Number of questions	$92-z$	z	8
Marks	$92-z$	$2z$	24

According to question,

$$2z \geq \frac{1}{5}(92 - z + 2z + 24)$$

$\Rightarrow \quad 10z \geq 116 + z$

$\Rightarrow \quad 9z \geq 116 \quad \ldots(1)$

Also, $92 - z \geq 60\% \text{ of } (116 + z)$

$\Rightarrow \quad 460 - 5z \geq 348 + 3z$

$\Rightarrow \quad 112 \geq 8z$

$\Rightarrow \quad z \leq 14 \quad \ldots(2)$

Combining-(1) and (2), we get

$$\frac{116}{9} \leq z \leq 14$$

$\Rightarrow \quad 13 \leq z \leq 14$

Hence Ans is (C)

Sol. 11 (C) Given Distance = 90 km

Let the speeds of car be x km/h and y km/h

Since Distance = Speed × Time

Relative speed when they are moving in opposite direction $= x + y$

So as per question

$$90 = (x + y) \times \frac{9}{7}$$

$\Rightarrow \quad x + y = 70$

Relative speed when they are moving in same direction is $= x - y$

So as per question

$$90 = (x - y) \times 9$$

$\Rightarrow \quad x - y = 10$

$\Rightarrow \quad x = 40$

and $\quad y = 30$

$\Rightarrow$ the required speed of cars

$= 40$ km/h and 30 km/h

Hence Ans is (C)

Sol. 12 (B) Let there be x coins of 25 paise denomination and y coins of 50 paise denomination, then

$$x + y = 40$$

$\Rightarrow \quad 25x + 25y = 1000 \quad \ldots(1)$

and $\quad 25x + 50y = 1275 \quad \ldots(2)$

Subtracting Equation-(1) from (2) we get

$$25y = 275$$

$\Rightarrow \quad y = 11$

$\Rightarrow \quad x = 29$

Hence Ans is (B)

Sol. 13 (C) Let there be x pencils and y pens, then

$$x + y = 40$$

$\Rightarrow \quad 4x + 4y = 160$

Given $\quad (x + 5) = 4(y - 5)$

$\Rightarrow \quad x - 4y = -25$

$\Rightarrow \quad 4x + 4y = 160 \quad \ldots(1)$

$\Rightarrow \quad x - 4y = -25 \quad \ldots(2)$

Equation-(1) + equation-(2)

$$5x = 135$$

$\Rightarrow \quad x = 27$

$\Rightarrow \quad y = 13$

Hence Ans is (C)

Sol. 14 (B) Let the present age of the son by 'x' years and the present age of his father be 'y' years.

Then $\quad y = 3x \quad \ldots(1)$

Again $\quad (y + 12) = 2(x + 12) \quad \ldots(2)$

Substituting $y = 3x$ in equastion-(2), we get

$$x = 12$$

$\Rightarrow \quad y = 36$

Hence Ans is (B)

Sol. 15 (D) Let the present age of A is x and the present age of B is y (in years)

Then, $\quad (x - 5) = 3(y - 5)$

$\Rightarrow \quad x - 3y = -10 \quad \ldots(1)$

Also $\quad (x + 10) = 2(y + 10)$

$\Rightarrow \quad x - 2y = 10 \quad \ldots(2)$

Subtracting equestion-(2) from equestion-(1), we get

$$-y = -20$$

$\Rightarrow \quad y = 20$

Also $\quad x = 50$

Hence Ans is (D)

Sol. 16 (B) Let Astha will have x number of oranges and Saumya will have y number of oranges. Then,

$$(x+10)=2(y-10)$$

$\Rightarrow$ $x-2y=-30$ ...(1)

and $(x-10)=(y+10)$

$\Rightarrow$ $x-y=20$ ...(2)

Subtracting equation-(2) from equation-(1), we get

$$-y=-50$$

$\Rightarrow$ $y=50$

$\Rightarrow$ $x=70$

Hence Ans is (D)

Sol. 17 (C) Total distance = 760 km.
Let the speed of car be x km/h and the speed of train be y km/h

We know Distance = Speed × Time

$\Rightarrow$ $\text{Time} = \dfrac{\text{distance}}{\text{speed}}$

$\Rightarrow$ $\dfrac{600}{x}+\dfrac{160}{y}=8$ ...(1)

and $\dfrac{520}{x}+\dfrac{240}{y}=8\dfrac{1}{5}$ ...(2)

$\Rightarrow$ equation-(1) can be written as

$600A+160B=8$ ...(3)

and equation-(2) can be written as

$520A+240B=\dfrac{41}{5}$ ...(4)

Where, $\dfrac{1}{x}=A$

and $\dfrac{1}{y}=B$

Solving equation-(3) and (4) we get

$$1800A+480B=24$$

$$1040A+480B=\frac{82}{5}$$

$$-\quad\quad-\quad\quad-$$

$$760A\quad=\frac{38}{5}$$

$\Rightarrow$ $A=\dfrac{1}{100}$

$\Rightarrow$ $x=100$ km/h

$\Rightarrow$ $B=\dfrac{1}{80}$

$\Rightarrow$ $y=80$ km/h

Hence Ans is (C)

Sol. 18 (A) Let he has invested Rs. x at 12% S.I. and Rs. y at 10% SI

We know $\left(SI=\dfrac{p\times r\times t}{100}\right)$

$$\frac{x\times 12\times 1}{100}+\frac{y\times 10\times 1}{100}=130$$

$\Rightarrow$ $12x+10y=13000$ ...(1)

$\Rightarrow$ $10x+12y=13400$ ...(2)

On solving we get

$$x=500$$

and $y=700$

Hence Ans is (A)

Sol. 19 (B) On solving

$$\frac{3x-y+1}{3}=\frac{2x+y+2}{5}$$

$\Rightarrow$ $5(3x-y+1)=3(2x+y+2)$

$\Rightarrow$ $9x-8y=1$ ...(1)

On solving

$\Rightarrow$ $\dfrac{2x+y+2}{5}=\dfrac{3x+2y+1}{6}$

$\Rightarrow$ $6(2x+y+2)=5(3x+2y+1)$

$\Rightarrow$ $3x+4y=7$ ...(2)

Multiplying (2) by 2 and adding to (1), we get

$$15x=15$$

or $x=1$

Putting $x=1$ in (1), we get

$$9\times 1-8y=1$$

$\Rightarrow$ $y=1$

Hence Ans is (B)

Sol. 20 (B) Submarine can be destroyed when it meets the destroyer. (To find the common point)

$\Rightarrow$ $2x+3y=5$ ...(1)

$x-y=10$ ...(2)

On solving (1) & (2), we get

$$x=7$$

and $y=-3$

So the required point is (7, – 3)

Hence Ans is (B)

Sol. 21 (D) $\dfrac{x^2}{a^2}+\dfrac{y^2}{b^2}-\dfrac{z^2}{c^2}=1$ ...(1)

$$\frac{x^2}{a^2}-\frac{y^2}{b^2}+\frac{z^2}{c^2}=1 \quad ...(2)$$

$$-\frac{x^2}{a^2}+\frac{y^2}{b^2}+\frac{z^2}{c^2}=1 \quad ...(3)$$

Adding equation-(1), (2) and (3), we have

$$\frac{x^2}{a^2}+\frac{y^2}{b^2}+\frac{z^2}{c^2}=3 \quad ...(4)$$

$$\Rightarrow \quad \frac{x^2}{a^2}=1 \Rightarrow x=\pm a$$

$$\frac{y^2}{b^2}=1 \Rightarrow y=\pm b$$

$$\frac{z^2}{c^2}=1 \Rightarrow z=\pm c$$

Hence Ans is (D)

Sol. 22 (D) As per the condition

$$\frac{a_1}{a_2}=\frac{b_1}{b_2}$$

$$\Rightarrow \quad \frac{1}{k}=\frac{k}{1}$$

$$\Rightarrow \quad k^2=1$$

$$\Rightarrow \quad k=\pm 1$$

Hence Ans is (D)

Sol. 23 (B) $a_1x+b_1y=0$

$a_2x+b_2y=0$

For non trivial solution

$$a_1b_2-a_2b_1=0$$

Hence Ans is (B)

Sol. 24 (B) Given

$$(2n-4)\times 90=2\times 360$$

$$\Rightarrow \quad 2n-4=8$$

$$\Rightarrow \quad 2n=12$$

$$\Rightarrow \quad n=6$$

Hence Ans is (B)

Sol. 25 (B) For any line, minimum two points are required to draw it

Hence Ans is (B)

Solutions of PRACTICE EXERCISE-3.3

Sol. 1 (D) Let the present ages of Anil and Sunil are $4x$ & $5x$ respectively, then as per questions, we have

$$\frac{4x+8}{5x+8}=\frac{5}{6}$$

$$24x+48=25x+40$$

$$8=x$$

32 years, 40 years

Hence Ans is (D)

Sol. 2 (A) Given $2x+3y=7$

$$(a-b)x+(a+b)y=3a+b-2$$

Condition for the system of to linear equation to have infinitely many solutions is

$$\frac{a_1}{a_2}=\frac{b_1}{b_2}=\frac{c_1}{c_2}$$

$$\frac{2}{a-b}=\frac{3}{a+b}=\frac{7}{3a+b-2}$$

So, $\frac{2}{a-b}=\frac{3}{a+b}$

$$\Rightarrow \quad a=5b \quad ...(1)$$

$$\Rightarrow \quad \frac{3}{a+b}=\frac{7}{3a+b-2}$$

$$\Rightarrow \quad a=2b+3 \quad ...(2)$$

On solving (1) & (2)

$$a=5, b=1$$

Hence Ans is (A)

Sol. 3 (A) Consider the given equation

$$kx+3y-(k-3)=0$$

$$12x+ky-k=0$$

Condition for the system of to linear equation to have infinitely many solutions is

$$\frac{a_1}{a_2}=\frac{b_1}{b_2}=\frac{c_1}{c_2}$$

$$\Rightarrow \quad \frac{k}{12}=\frac{3}{k}=\frac{-(k-3)}{-k}=\frac{k-3}{k}$$

$$\Rightarrow \quad k^2=36$$

$$\Rightarrow \quad k=\pm 6$$

$\Rightarrow$ $k=-6$ is not possible

So $k=6$

Hence Ans is (A)

Sol. 4 (A) Given $3x+y-1=0$

$$(2k-1)x+(k-1)y-(2k+1)=0$$

Condition for the system of linear equation to have no solution is

$$\frac{a_1}{a_2}=\frac{b_1}{b_2}\neq\frac{c_1}{c_2}$$

$$\Rightarrow \quad \frac{3}{2k-1}=\frac{1}{k-1}\neq\frac{-1}{-(2k+1)}$$

$$\Rightarrow \quad 3k-3=2k-1$$

$$k=2$$

Hence Ans is (A)

Sol. 5 (D) Let the two digit number be $10x+y$

given, $\quad x=2y \quad \ldots(1)$

If x and 'y' are exchanged then the number will be $10y+x$

Also given

$$(10x+y)-(10y+x)=18$$

$$\Rightarrow \quad 9x-9y=18$$

$$\Rightarrow \quad x-y=2 \quad \ldots(2)$$

Solving (1) & (2)

We get $\quad x=4, y=2$

$\Rightarrow$ the number is $(10\times 4)+2$

$$=42$$

Hence Ans is (D)

Sol. 6 (C) Given

$$x+2y=6$$

$$3x+6y=18$$

$$\frac{1}{3}=\frac{2}{6}=\frac{6}{18}$$

$$\Rightarrow \quad \frac{1}{3}=\frac{1}{3}=\frac{1}{3}$$

as $\quad \frac{a_1}{a_2}=\frac{b_1}{b_2}=\frac{c_1}{c_2}$

as $\quad \frac{a_1}{a_2}=\frac{b_1}{b_2}=\frac{c_1}{c_2}$

The system of equations has an infinite number of solutions.

Hence Ans is (C)

Sol. 7 (A) Let the fraction be $\frac{x}{y}$

Given $\quad \frac{x-1}{y}=\frac{1}{3} \quad \ldots(1)$

& $\quad \frac{x}{y+8}=\frac{1}{4} \quad \ldots(2)$

Solve (1) & (2)

But best method is to go by option in such question.

Hence Ans is (A)

Sol. 8 (C) Let x be the number of students in a row & y be the total number of rows.

Then total students $= xy$

Now as per question

$$xy=(x+1)(y-2)$$

$$\Rightarrow \quad xy=xy-2x+y-2$$

$$\Rightarrow \quad -2x+y=2 \quad \ldots(1)$$

$$\Rightarrow \quad xy=(x-1)(y+3)$$

$$\Rightarrow \quad xy=xy+3x-y-3$$

$$\Rightarrow \quad 3x-y=3 \quad \ldots(2)$$

Adding (1) & (2)

$$x=5$$

and $\quad y=12$

So number of students will be

$$xy=12\times 5=60$$

Hence Ans is (C)

Sol. 9 (C) Using intercept form

$$\frac{x}{a}+\frac{y}{b}=1$$

Here, $\quad a=4, b=-3$

$\Rightarrow$ Equation of line will be

$$\frac{x}{4}-\frac{y}{3}=1$$

Hence Ans is (C)

Sol. 10 (A) Let the speed of the boat be 'x' km/hr and the speed of the stream be 'y' km/hr

given $\quad \frac{30}{x-y}+\frac{28}{x+y}=7 \quad \ldots(1)$

$$\frac{21}{x-y}+\frac{21}{x+y}=5 \quad \ldots(2)$$

Let $\quad \frac{1}{x-y}=A \;\&\; \frac{1}{x+y}=B$

On substituting in equation-(1) & (2)

We get,

$$30A+28B=7 \quad \ldots(1)$$

$$21A+21B=5 \quad \ldots(2)$$

On solving we get

$$A=\frac{1}{6} \text{ and } B=\frac{1}{14}$$

On solving $\quad x-y=6$

$$x+y=14$$

$$2x=20$$

$$\Rightarrow \quad x=10$$

$\Rightarrow$ Speed of boat $= 10$ km/hr

Hence Ans is (A)

Sol. 11 **(C)** Let the cost of an Apple be 'A' and the cost of a Guava be 'G'

Given

$$20G+5A=12G+7A$$

$$\Rightarrow \quad 8G=2A$$

$$\Rightarrow \quad A=4G$$

$\Rightarrow$ Cost of an Apple is 4 time that of a guava

Hence Ans is (C)

Sol. 12 **(A)** Given $x+y=7$ ...(1)

& $3x-2y=11$ ...(2)

from (1) $y=7-x$ ...(3)

Using (3) in equation-(2), we get

$$3x-2(7-x)=11$$

$$\Rightarrow \quad 3x-14+2x=11$$

$$\Rightarrow \quad 5x=25$$

$$\Rightarrow \quad x=5$$

Hence Ans is (A)

Sol. 13 **(B)** Let the two digit number be $10x+y$

Given $x+y=9$ ...(1)

& $2(10x+y)+18=10y+x$

$\Rightarrow \quad 20x+2y+18=10y+x$

$\Rightarrow \quad 19x-8y=-18$ ...(2)

Using (1) in equation-(2), we get

$$19x-8(9-x)=-18$$

$$\Rightarrow \quad 19x-72+8x=-18$$

$$\Rightarrow \quad 27x=72-18=54$$

$$\boxed{x=2}$$

Using equation-(1)

$$y=2$$

So original number

$$10x+y=10\times2+7=27$$

Hence Ans is (B)

Sol. 14 **(C)** Dividing the given equations by 'xy'

We get $\dfrac{3x}{xy}+\dfrac{2y}{xy}=13$

$\Rightarrow \quad \dfrac{3}{y}+\dfrac{2}{x}=13$

Let $\dfrac{1}{y}=b$

and $\dfrac{1}{x}=a$

$3b+2a=13$ ...(1)

Similarly

$$\frac{4x}{xy}-\frac{5y}{xy}=2$$

$\Rightarrow \quad \dfrac{4}{y}-\dfrac{5}{x}=2$

$\Rightarrow \quad 4b-5a=2$ ...(2)

equation-(1) $\times$ 4 – equation-(2) $\times$ 3

$$12b+8a=52$$
$$12b-15a=6$$
$$\underline{\quad - \qquad - \quad}$$
$$23a=46$$

$$a=2$$

$\Rightarrow \quad b=3$ using (1)

$\Rightarrow \quad \dfrac{1}{x}=2$

So $x=\dfrac{1}{2}$

and $y=\dfrac{1}{3}$

Hence Ans is (C)

Sol. 15 **(A)** Let number be a & b

Given $a:b=3:4$

$\Rightarrow \quad a=3x$

and $b=4x$

Now $\dfrac{3x-5}{4x-5}=\dfrac{2}{3}$

$\Rightarrow \quad 9x-15=8x-10$

$$x=5$$

So $a=15$

and $b=20$

Hence Ans is (A)

Sol. 16 **(B)** Let the father present age be x

& the son present age by y

given $x-y=14$

their ages after 11 yr be $(x+11)$ & $(y+11)$ respectively

So as per question

$$\frac{x+11}{y+11}=\frac{4}{3}$$

$$\Rightarrow \quad 3x+33=4y+44$$

$$\Rightarrow \quad 3(y+14)+33=4y+44$$

$$\Rightarrow \quad 3y+42+33=4y+44$$

$$\Rightarrow \quad y=42+33-44=31 \text{ yr}$$

Hence Ans is (B)

Sol. 17 (B) Given,

$$x+2y=3$$
$$5x+ky=-7$$

Has a unique solution

$$\Rightarrow \quad \frac{a_1}{a_2} \neq \frac{b_1}{b_2}$$

$$\Rightarrow \quad \frac{1}{5} \neq \frac{2}{k}$$

$$\Rightarrow \quad k \neq 10$$

Hence Ans is (B)

Sol. 18 (B) Let the two digit number be $10x+y$ as per question 1st condition

$$10x+y=(x+y)\times 4+3 \quad \ldots(1)$$

& second condition

$$10x+y=xy.3+5 \quad \ldots(2)$$

$$\Rightarrow \quad 4x+4y+3=3xy+5$$

$$\Rightarrow \quad 4x+4y-3xy=2 \quad \ldots(3)$$

from (1) we have

$$6x-3y=3$$

$$\Rightarrow \quad 2x-y=1$$

$$\Rightarrow \quad y=2x-1 \quad \ldots(4)$$

Using (4) in equation-(3)

$$4x+4(2x-1)-3x(2x-1)=2$$

$$\Rightarrow \quad 4x+8x-4-6x^2+3x=2$$

$$\Rightarrow \quad 6x^2-15x+6=0$$

$$\Rightarrow \quad 2x^2-5x+2=0$$

$$\Rightarrow \quad 2x^2-4x-x+2=0$$

$$\Rightarrow \quad (2x-1)(x-2)=0$$

$$\Rightarrow \quad x=2$$

$$\& \quad y=3$$

hence the number is 23

Hence Ans is (B)

Sol. 19 (A) Let the speed of the boat be B km/H

& The speed of the river be R km/H

$$\text{Now} \quad \frac{16}{B-R}+\frac{24}{B+R}=6 \quad \ldots(1)$$

$$\frac{12}{B-R}+\frac{36}{B+R}=6 \quad \ldots(2)$$

(1)–(2)

$$\frac{4}{B-R}-\frac{12}{B+R}=0$$

$$\Rightarrow \quad \frac{1}{B-R}=\frac{3}{B+R}$$

$$\Rightarrow \quad 3B-3R=B+R$$

$$\Rightarrow \quad B=2R \quad \ldots(3)$$

Using (3) in (1)

$$\frac{16}{R}+\frac{24}{3R}=6$$

$$\Rightarrow \quad \frac{24}{R}=\frac{6}{1}$$

$$\Rightarrow \quad R=4$$

$$\Rightarrow \quad B=8 \text{ km/H}$$

Hence Ans is (A)

Sol. 20 (D) Given,

$$a+8b=14$$
$$5a-2b=16$$

$$\text{and} \quad 6a+6b=30$$

$$\Rightarrow \quad a+b=5$$

$$\Rightarrow \quad \text{mean}=\frac{a+b}{2}=2.5$$

Hence Ans is (D)

Sol. 21 (D) For parallel line ratio of coefficient are. Same

$$8x+6y=28$$

$$\& \quad 4x+3y=14$$

Since here the ratio are same so this satisfies.

Hence Ans is (D)

Sol. 22 (B) Let $x=$ price of one apple

$y=$ price of one guava

Given

$$19x+11y-482=0$$
$$11x+19y-418=0$$

by cross multiplication

$$\text{We get} \quad \frac{x}{-4598+9158}=\frac{y}{-5302+7942}=\frac{1}{361-121}$$

$$\Rightarrow \quad x=\frac{4560}{240}=19$$

$$\& \quad y=\frac{2640}{270}=11$$

$$\text{Hence} \quad x-y=8$$

Hence Ans is (B)

Sol. 23 (C) Consider the equation

$$x+2y=7$$
$$x-y=4$$

On solving we get

$$y=1$$

$$\Rightarrow \quad x=5$$

So equation of line passing through
(0, 0) & (5, 1)

is $(y-0)=\frac{(1-0)}{(5-0)}(x-0)$

$$x=5y$$

$$y=\frac{1}{5}x$$

$$y=0.2x$$

Hence Ans is (C)

Sol. 24 (B) Consider

$$217x+131y=913 \quad \ldots(1)$$

$$131x+217y=827 \quad \ldots(2)$$

(1) + (2)

$$x+y=5$$

Hence Ans is (B)

Sol. 25 (B) Let the original fraction be

$$\frac{x}{y}$$

$$\frac{x+2}{y+2}=\frac{5}{7}$$

$\Rightarrow$ $7x+14=5y+10$

$\Rightarrow$ $7x-5y+4=0 \quad \ldots(1)$

$$\frac{x+4}{y+3}=\frac{7}{8}$$

$$8x+32=7y+21$$

$$8x-7y+11=0 \quad \ldots(2)$$

Solving-(1) and (2) we get

$$x=3, y=5$$

Thus fraction is $\frac{3}{5}$

Hence Ans is (B)

Sol. 26 (A)

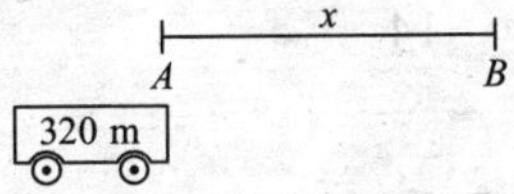

Speed of train = 120 km/hr = $120\times\frac{5}{80}=\frac{100}{3}$ m/s

$$\text{Time}=\frac{\text{Distance}}{\text{Speed}}$$

$$24=\frac{320+x}{\frac{100}{3}}$$

$$320+x=24\times\frac{100}{3}$$

$$x=480\,\text{m}$$

Speed of man = $\frac{480}{240}=2$ m/s

Hence Ans is (A)

Sol. 27 (C) Let total number of workers x

Women $\Rightarrow \frac{x}{3}$

Men $\Rightarrow \frac{2}{3}x$

Married women $\Rightarrow \frac{x}{6}$

Married men $\Rightarrow \frac{1}{2}x$

Married women with children $\Rightarrow \frac{x}{18}$

Married men with children $\Rightarrow \frac{x}{3}$

$\Rightarrow$ Total worker without children $=x-\left(\frac{x}{18}+\frac{x}{3}\right)$

Hence Ans is (C)

Sol. 28 (C) Given $H_1:H_2:H_3=5:6:7$

15 minutes to climb tower of height $5x$

$\Rightarrow$ 21 minutes to climb tower of height $7x$

Hence Ans is (C)

Sol. 29 (A) Let distance between two stations be x km original speed to y km/hr time at regular speed t/hr

$$\frac{30}{y}+\frac{x-30}{\frac{4}{5}y}=t+\frac{3}{4} \quad \ldots(1)$$

$$\frac{48}{y}+\frac{x-48}{\frac{4}{5}y}=t+\frac{3}{5} \quad \ldots(2)$$

Solving-(1) and (2) $x=120$ km

Hence Ans is (A)

Sol. 30 (A) Consider

$$\frac{x+y}{xy}=2,$$

$$\frac{x-y}{xy}=6$$

$$\frac{1}{y}+\frac{1}{x}=2 \quad \ldots(1)$$

$$\frac{1}{y}-\frac{1}{x}=6 \quad \ldots(2)$$

Adding (1) & (2)

$$2\left(\frac{1}{y}\right)=8$$

$\Rightarrow$ $\frac{1}{y}=4$

$\Rightarrow$ $y=\frac{1}{4}$

Hence Ans is (A)

Sol. 31 (D) Consider $y=\lambda x+5$

$x+2y=10$ ...(1)

$3x+4y=360$ ...(2)

Solving (1) & (2)

$2y=-330$

$y=-165$

$x-330=10$

$x=340$

$y=\lambda x+5$

$-165=\lambda(340)+5$

$-165-5=\lambda 340$

$-170=\lambda 340$

$\lambda=\frac{-1}{2}$

Hence Ans is (D)

Sol. 32 (A) Ratio of income = 11 : 7

$\Rightarrow$ $11x, 7x$

Ratio of expenditure = 9 : 5

$\Rightarrow$ $9y, 5y$

Solving,

$11x-9y=400$ ...(1)

$7x-5y=400$ ...(2)

$\Rightarrow$ (1) x 5 $\Rightarrow$ $55x-45y=2000$

(2) x 9 $\Rightarrow$ $63x-45y=3600$

$-8x=-1600$

$x=200$

Income = 2200 + 1400 = 3600

Hence Ans is (A)

Sol. 33 (C) For no solution

$$\frac{2}{3}=\frac{m}{-7}\neq\frac{-4}{-10}$$

$\Rightarrow$ $m=\frac{-14}{3}$

Hence Ans is (C)

Sol. 34 (A) Let present age of Sunita $=x$

and present age of Vineeta $=y$

According to question,

$x-5=3(y-5)$

$\Rightarrow$ $x+10=3y$ ...(1)

and $x+10=2(y+10)$

$\Rightarrow$ $3y=2(y+10)$

$\Rightarrow$ $y=20$

$\Rightarrow$ from (1), $x=50$ years

Hence Ans is (A)

Sol. 35 (C) Let speed of train be v and time taken by it be t,

$\Rightarrow$ Distance travelled = speed v time taken

$\Rightarrow$ $vt=(v+15)(t-2)=(v-5)(t+1)$

$\Rightarrow$ $vt=vt-2v+15t-30$

$\Rightarrow$ $15t=2v+30$ ...(1)

and $vt=vt+v-5t-5$

$\Rightarrow$ $v-5=5t$ ...(2)

Solving (1) and (2)

$v=45$ km/hr;

$t=8$ hours

$\Rightarrow$ Distance $=45\times 8=360$ km

Hence Ans is (C)

Sol. 36 (C) Total work $=8\times x=6(x+4)$

$4x=3(x+4)$

$x=12$

Hence Ans is (C)

Sol. 37 (C) $\frac{8}{x}+\frac{12}{y}=\frac{1}{10}$

$\frac{6}{x}+\frac{8}{y}=\frac{1}{14}$

Let $\frac{1}{x}=u$,

$\frac{1}{y}=v$

$8u+12v=\frac{1}{10}$

$6u+8v=\frac{1}{14}$

Solve $x=140$

Hence Ans is (C)

Sol. 38 (B) Let the larger pipe fill the cistern in x hour

As per condition

$$\frac{1}{x}+\frac{1}{3}=1$$

$$\frac{1}{x}=1-\frac{1}{3}=\frac{2}{3}$$

$$x=\frac{3}{2}=1\frac{1}{2}\text{ hour}$$

Hence Ans is (B)

Sol. 39 (B) For no solution,

$x+y-4, 2x+ky-3=0$

$$\frac{a_1}{a_2}=\frac{b_1}{b_2}\neq\frac{c_1}{c_2}$$

$$\frac{1}{2}=\frac{1}{k}\neq\frac{4}{3}$$

So, $k=2$

Hence Ans is (B)

Sol. 40 (C) $\frac{x+1}{2}+\frac{y-1}{3}=8$

$\Rightarrow\quad 3x+3+2y-2=48$

$\Rightarrow\quad 3x+2y=47 \quad\ldots(1)$

Also, $\frac{x-1}{3}+\frac{y+1}{2}=9$

$2x+3y=53 \quad\ldots(2)$

Adding equation-(1) and (2), we get

$5x+5y=100$

$\Rightarrow\quad x+y=20 \quad\ldots(3)$

Subtracting equation (2) from (1), we get

$x-y=-6 \quad\ldots(4)$

Now, from, equation (3) & (4), we get

$x+y=20$

$x-y=-6$

$-\ \ +\ \ +$

$2y=26$

$\Rightarrow y=13$

Hence Ans is (C)

Sol. 41 (D) Let $\frac{1}{3x+4y}=a\ \&\ \frac{1}{4x-3y}=b$

$\Rightarrow\quad \frac{a}{2}+\frac{12}{7}b=\frac{1}{2} \quad\ldots(1)$

$\Rightarrow\quad 7a+24b=7$

$7a+4b=2 \quad\ldots(2)$

$\Rightarrow\quad 7a+4b=2$, on solving we get

$20b=5$

$$b=\frac{1}{4}$$

Put in (2), we get

$7a+1=2$

$\Rightarrow\quad a=\frac{1}{7}$

$\Rightarrow\quad 3x+4y=7$

$\&\quad 4x-3y=4$

$\Rightarrow\quad 9x+12=21$

$16x-12y=16$

$25x=37$

$$x=\frac{37}{25}$$

$\Rightarrow\quad 4\left(\frac{37}{25}\right)-3y=4$

$\Rightarrow\quad 3y=\frac{148}{25}-4=\frac{48}{25},$

on solving we get

$$y=\frac{16}{25}$$

Hence Ans is (D)

Sol. 42 (D) Let no of row be 'r' and plants per row be 'x' per row

Now, if row reduced $\rightarrow r-2$ and plants increased to $(x+4)$

$(r-2)(x+4)=(r+4)(x-4)=x.r$

$xr+4r-2x-8=rx-4r+4x-16=xr$

$\Rightarrow\quad 4x-4r=16$

$\Rightarrow\quad x-r=4 \quad\ldots(1)$

Also $\Rightarrow\quad 2x-4r=-8$

$\Rightarrow\quad x-2r=-4 \quad\ldots(2)$

Subtract (2) from (1)

$\Rightarrow\quad r=8$

$\Rightarrow\quad x=12$

$\Rightarrow$ total plants $=96$

Hence Ans is (D)

Sol. 43 (D)

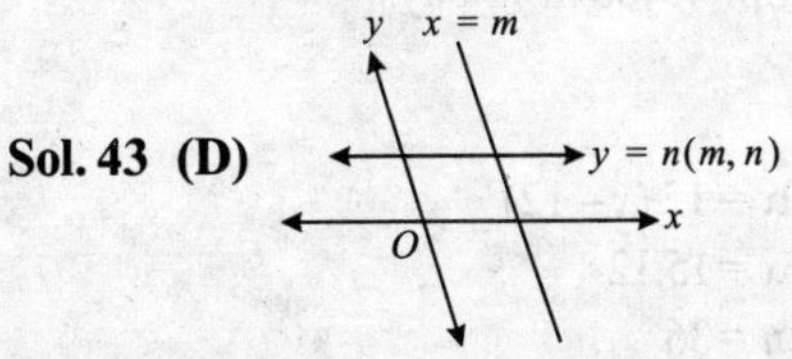

Hence Ans is (D)

Sol. 44 (D) The condition for no solution is

$$\frac{a_1}{a_2} = \frac{b_1}{b_2} \neq \frac{c_1}{c_2}$$

$\Rightarrow$ $$\frac{k}{6} = \frac{-5}{2}$$

$\Rightarrow$ $$k = -\frac{5\times 6}{2} = -15$$

Hence Ans is (D)

Sol. 45 (D) $\frac{2}{3}x + \frac{3}{2}y = 5,$

taking LCM, $\frac{4}{6}x + \frac{9}{6}y = 5$

$\Rightarrow$ $4x + 9y = 30$

$\Rightarrow$ $4x + 9y - 30 = 0$

Hence Ans is (D)

Sol. 46 (C) $x = 10$ km/h

Let speed of the stream $= y$ km/h

According to question

$$\frac{12}{(x+y)} + \frac{12}{(x-y)} = \frac{5}{2}$$

$\Rightarrow$ $y = 2$ km/h

Hence Ans is (C)

Sol. 47 (C) According to question

$f = 6s$ ...(1)

$f + 4 = 4(s + 4)$ ...(2)

From (1) & (2) $f = 36$ years & $s = 6$ years

Hence Ans is (C)

Sol. 48 (A) $x - \frac{2}{x-1} = 1 - \frac{2}{x-1}$

$x = 1$

But as $x - 1$ is in denominator

$\Rightarrow$ $x - 1 \neq 0$

$\Rightarrow$ $x \neq 0$

No solution

Hence Ans is (A)

Sol. 49 (B) Let x farmers complete job in 10 days

1 farmers in $10x$ days.

Now, $x - 12$ farmers complete job in 15 days

1 farmer in $15(x - 12)$

According to question

$10x = 15(x - 12)$

$5x = 15.12$

$n = 36$

Hence Ans is (B)

Sol. 50 (C) Let the numbers be $x - 2, x - 1, x, x + 1$ & $x + 2$

According to question

$x - 2 + x - 1 + x + x + 1 + x + 2 = 170$

$\Rightarrow$ $5x = 170$

$\Rightarrow$ $x = 34$

Numbers are 32, 33, 34, 35, 36.

Hence product of largest & smallest number will be $32 \times 36 = 1152$

Hence Ans is (C)

Sol. 51 (C) Let no. of

Rs. 100 notes $= x$

Let number of

Rs. 50 notes $= y$

$\Rightarrow$ $x + y = 170$ ...(1)

Also $100x + 50y = 10000$

$\Rightarrow$ $2x + y = 200$ ...(2)

Solving-(1) and (2), $x = 30$

and $y = 140$

$\Rightarrow$ Total amount of

Rs. $50 = 50 \times 140 = 7000$

Hence Ans is (C)

Sol. 52 (D) Let age of Sonu be $3x$

And let age of Sneha be $5x$

$\Rightarrow$ $5x - 3x = 2x = 12$

$\Rightarrow$ $x = 6$

Hence age of Sneha is 30 years

Hence Ans is (D)

Sol. 53 (C) Let total number of girls be $5x$ and total number of boys be $4x$

According to question

$$\frac{4x+10}{5x} = \frac{6}{5}$$

$\Rightarrow$ $20x + 50 = 30x$

$\Rightarrow$ $x = 5$

$\Rightarrow$ Total no of girls in the class = 25

Hence Ans is (C)

Sol. 54 (A) Let two adjacent angles be x° & $(x + 20)^\circ$

Then $\angle A + \angle B = 180^\circ$

$\Rightarrow$ $2x + 20 = 180^\circ$

$\Rightarrow$ $2x = 180^\circ - 20$

$x = 80^\circ$

$\angle A = 80^\circ, \angle B = 100^\circ, \angle C = 80^\circ, \angle D = 100^\circ$

Here required ratio $= \frac{80}{100} = \frac{4}{5}$

Hence Ans is (A)

Sol. 55 (D)

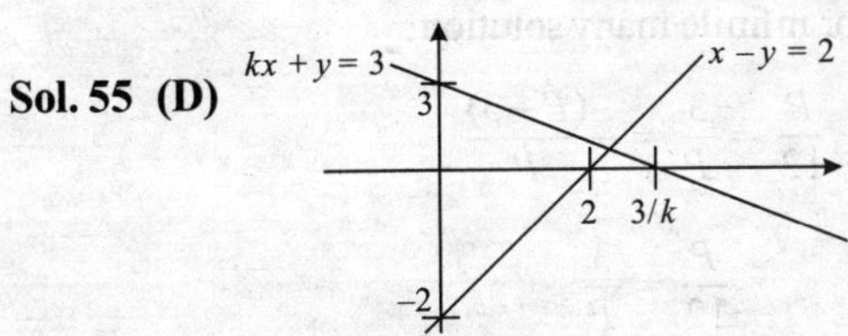

To intersect in 1st quadrant

If $K>0,$

$$\frac{3}{K}>2,$$

$$K<\frac{3}{2}$$

Also $(K+1)x=5$

$$x=\frac{5}{K+1},$$

$$y=\frac{5}{K+1}-2$$

$$\Rightarrow \frac{5-2K-2}{K+1}=\frac{3-2K}{K+1}$$

To be in 1st quad : $x>0, y>0$

$$\Rightarrow \frac{5}{K+1}>0$$

$$\Rightarrow K>-1$$

$$\frac{3-2K}{K+1}>0$$

$$\frac{2K-3}{K+1}<0$$

$$\Rightarrow K\in\left(-1\frac{3}{2}\right)$$

Hence Ans is (D)

Sol. 56 (A) Let the rational no. be $\frac{x}{y}$

Case I : $\frac{x-1}{y}=\frac{1}{3}$

$\Rightarrow y=3x-3$ ...(1)

Case II : $\frac{x}{y+8}=\frac{1}{4}$

$\Rightarrow 4x=y+8$ ...(2)

From (1) & (2)

$$4x=3x-3+8$$

$$\Rightarrow x=5$$

$$\Rightarrow y=3\times 5-3=12$$

$\Rightarrow$ rational number is $\frac{5}{12}$

Hence Ans is (A)

Sol. 57 (D) $x=2$

and $y=-3$

Putting in the option, we see

Hence Ans is (D)

Sol. 58 (A) Let the number $10x+y$

According to question,

$$8(x+y)-5=16(x-4y)+3$$

$$8x+8y-5=16x-16y+3$$

$$24y=8x+8$$

$\Rightarrow x+1=3y$ now go by the option

Hence Ans is (A)

Sol. 59 (C) Conceptual

Sol. 60 (B) If $x=a$ and $y=b$ then $a-b=2$ and $a+b=4$

On adding these equation

We get $2a=6$

Therefore $a=3$

and $b=1$

Hence Ans is (B)

Sol. 61 (D) Let the number of deers $=x$

Then as per question

$$\frac{1}{2}x+\frac{3}{4}\left(\frac{1}{2}x\right)+9=x$$

$$\Rightarrow 9=x-\frac{7}{8}x$$

$$\Rightarrow x=72$$

Hence Ans is (D)

Sol. 62 (B) Let the supplementary angle be x, $(180-x)$ then as per question

$$x=4(90-x)$$

$$\Rightarrow 5x=360$$

$$\Rightarrow x=72$$

So the supplement angle of 72 is 108

So the required answer is $108-72=36$

Hence Ans is (B)

Sol. 63 (C) Let the number of men $=x$

& number of dogs $=y$

Then as per question, we have number of legs

$$\frac{x}{10}\times 1+\frac{(9x)}{10}\times 2+y\times 4=77$$

$$\Rightarrow \frac{19x}{10}+4y=77$$

$$\Rightarrow \quad x = \frac{770 - 40y}{19}$$

For $\quad y = 5, x = 30$

So, number of dogs $= 5$

Hence Ans is (C)

Sol. 64 (C) Let S be the distance between home and bus stand then,

$$\text{Average speed} = \frac{\text{Total distance}}{\text{Total time}}$$

$$6 = \frac{2S}{\frac{S}{4} + \frac{S}{x}}$$

$$\Rightarrow \quad 3 = \frac{4x}{x+4}$$

$$\Rightarrow \quad 3x + 12 = 4x$$

$$\Rightarrow \quad x = 12 \text{ km/h}$$

Hence Ans is (C)

Sol. 65 (D) Given,

$$x - y - 2 = 0$$

$$\Rightarrow \quad x = y + 2$$

$$kx + y - 3 = 0$$

$$k(y+2) + y - 3 = 0$$

$$\Rightarrow \quad y = \frac{3-2k}{k+1} > 0$$

[Given point (x, y) lies in first quadrant]

$$\Rightarrow \quad \frac{2k-3}{k+1} < 0$$

$$\Rightarrow \quad -1 < k < \frac{3}{2}$$

Hence Ans is (D)

Sol. 66 (A) For infinite many solution

$$\frac{P}{12} = \frac{3}{P} = \frac{-(P-3)}{-P}$$

$$\Rightarrow \quad \frac{P}{12} = \frac{3}{P}$$

$$\Rightarrow \quad P^2 = 36$$

$$\Rightarrow \quad P = \pm 6 \qquad \ldots(1)$$

and from $\quad \frac{3}{P} = \frac{P-3}{P}$

$$\Rightarrow \quad 3P = P^2 - 3P$$

$$\Rightarrow \quad P^2 - 3P - 3P = 0$$

$$\Rightarrow \quad P^2 - 6P = 0$$

$$\Rightarrow \quad P(P-6) = 0$$

$$\Rightarrow \quad P = 0 \text{ or } P = 6 \qquad \ldots(2)$$

From (1) and (2)

$$P = 6$$

Sol. 67 (B) Let

A is apple

B is banana

C is coconut

Given $\quad 2A + 3B + 1C = 25 \qquad \ldots(1)$

$\quad 3A + 2B + 2C = 35 \qquad \ldots(2)$

Equation-(1) + Equation-(2)

$$= 5A + 5B + 3C = 61$$

$$= 10A + 10B + 6C = 122 \qquad \ldots(3)$$

Equation-(3) + Equation-(1)

$$12A + 13B + 7C = 148$$

* * * * *

Introduction To Trigonometry 4

"Trigonometry is a branch of mathematics used in fields such as astronomy, architecture, surveying, aviation and navigation. The term 'trigonometry' comes from two Greek words, trigonos and metron, meaning 'triangle measurement'."

- In trigonometry, we deal with relations between the sides and angles of a triangle.

- Ratios of the sides of a right angled triangle with respect to its acute angles, are called *trigonometric ratios of the angle*.

- For $\angle A$, AC is the base, BC the perpendicular and AB is the hypotenuse. For $\angle B$, BC is the base, AC the perpendicular and AB is the hypotenuse.

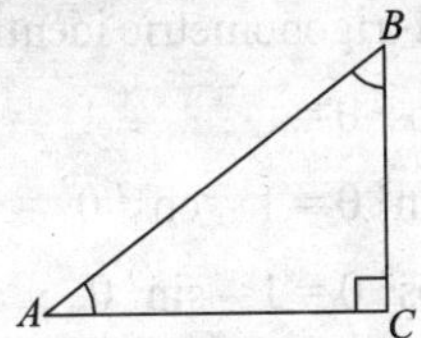

Figure 4.1

- **Six trigonometrical ratios :**

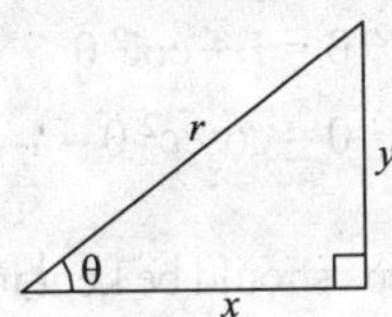

Figure 4.2

(i) Sine $\theta = \dfrac{\text{Perpendicular}}{\text{Hypotenuse}} = \dfrac{y}{r}$, Sine θ is written as sin θ.

(ii) Cosine $\theta = \dfrac{\text{Base}}{\text{Hypotenuse}} = \dfrac{x}{r}$, Cosine θ is written as cos θ.

(iii) Tangent $\theta = \dfrac{\text{Perpendicular}}{\text{Base}} = \dfrac{y}{x}$, Tangent θ is written as tan θ.

(iv) Cotangent $\theta = \dfrac{\text{Base}}{\text{Perpendicular}} = \dfrac{x}{y}$, Cotangent θ is written as cot θ.

(v) Secant $\theta = \dfrac{\text{Hypotenuse}}{\text{Base}} = \dfrac{r}{x}$, Secant θ is written as sec θ.

(vi) Cosecant $\theta = \dfrac{\text{Hypotenuse}}{\text{Perpendicular}} = \dfrac{r}{y}$, Cosecant θ is written as cosec θ.

- **Relations between trigonometric ratios :**

(a) Reciprocal relations

(i) $\text{cosec}\,\theta = \dfrac{1}{\sin\theta}$ or $\sin\theta = \dfrac{1}{\text{cosec}\,\theta}$

or $\sin\theta\,\text{cosec}\,\theta = 1$

(ii) $\sec\theta = \dfrac{1}{\cos\theta}$ or $\cos\theta = \dfrac{1}{\sec\theta}$ or $\cos\theta\sec\theta = 1$

(iii) $\cot\theta = \dfrac{1}{\tan\theta}$ or $\tan\theta = \dfrac{1}{\cot\theta}$ or $\tan\theta\cot\theta = 1$

(b) Quotient relations

(i) $\tan\theta = \dfrac{\sin\theta}{\cos\theta}$ (ii) $\cot\theta = \dfrac{\cos\theta}{\sin\theta}$

- sin A is a symbol which denotes the ratio $\dfrac{\text{perpendicular}}{\text{hypotenuse}}$.

It does not mean the product of sin and A i.e., $\sin A \neq \sin \times A$. In fact sin separated from A has no meaning. Similar interpretations follow for other trigonometric ratios.

- Table of values of various trigonometric ratios of 0°, 30°, 45°, 60° and 90°.

Angle θ / Ratio	0°	30°	45°	60°	90°
$\sin\theta$	0	$\frac{1}{2}$	$\frac{1}{\sqrt{2}}$	$\frac{\sqrt{3}}{2}$	1
$\cos\theta$	1	$\frac{\sqrt{3}}{2}$	$\frac{1}{\sqrt{2}}$	$\frac{1}{2}$	0
$\tan\theta$	0	$\frac{1}{\sqrt{3}}$	1	$\sqrt{3}$	Not defined
$\cot\theta$	Not defined	$\sqrt{3}$	1	$\frac{1}{\sqrt{3}}$	0
$\sec\theta$	1	$\frac{2}{\sqrt{3}}$	$\sqrt{2}$	2	Not defined
$\text{cosec}\,\theta$	Not defined	2	$\sqrt{2}$	$\frac{2}{\sqrt{3}}$	1

Students may find easier to memorize the first row (value of sine ratio) as

sin	0°	30°	45°	60°	90°
	$\sqrt{\frac{0}{4}}$	$\sqrt{\frac{1}{4}}$	$\sqrt{\frac{2}{4}}$	$\sqrt{\frac{3}{4}}$	$\sqrt{\frac{4}{4}}$
	$=0$	$=\frac{1}{2}$	$=\frac{1}{\sqrt{2}}$	$=\frac{\sqrt{3}}{2}$	$=1$

❍ Trigonometric ratios of complementary angles :

(i) $\sin(90° - \theta) = \cos\theta$, $\cos(90° - \theta) = \sin\theta$

(ii) $\tan(90° - \theta) = \cot\theta$, $\cot(90° - \theta) = \tan\theta$

(iii) $\sec(90° - \theta) = \text{cosec}\,\theta$, $\text{cosec}\,(90° - \theta) = \sec\theta$

Concept of sign of *T*-ratios in different quadrant angles

90°

II quadrant: only sine & cosec +ve	I quadrant: All +ve
III quadrant: only tan & cot +ve	IV quadrant: only cos & sec + ve

180° — 0°, 360°

270°

$\sin(-\theta) = -\sin\theta$	$\cos(-\theta) = \cos\theta$
$\tan(-\theta) = -\tan\theta$	$\sin(90° - \theta) = \cos\theta$
$\cos(90° - \theta) = \sin\theta$	$\tan(90° - \theta) = \cot\theta$
$\sin(90° + \theta) = \cos\theta$	$\cos(90° + \theta) = -\sin\theta$
$\tan(90° + \theta) = -\cot\theta$	$\sin(180° - \theta) = \sin\theta$
$\cos(180° - \theta) = -\cos\theta$	$\tan(180° - \theta) = -\tan\theta$
$\sin(180° + \theta) = -\sin\theta$	$\cos(180° + \theta) = -\cos\theta$
$\tan(180° + \theta) = \tan\theta$	$\sin(270° - \theta) = -\cos\theta$
$\cos(270° - \theta) = -\sin\theta$	$\tan(270° - \theta) = \cot\theta$
$\sin(270° + \theta) = -\cos\theta$	$\cos(270° + \theta) = \sin\theta$
$\tan(270° + \theta) = -\cot\theta$	$\sin(360° - \theta) = -\sin\theta$
$\cos(360° - \theta) = \cos\theta$	$\tan(360° - \theta) = -\tan\theta$
$\sin(360° + \theta) = \sin\theta$	$\cos(360° + \theta) = \cos\theta$
$\tan(360° + \theta) = \tan\theta$	

❍ Trigonometric Identities :

(a) An equation involving trigonometric ratios of an angle θ (say) is said to be a trigonometric identity, if it is satisfied for all values of θ for which the given trigonometric ratios are defined.

(b) Some important trigonometric identities :

(i) $\sin^2\theta + \cos^2\theta = 1$

or $\sin^2\theta = 1 - \cos^2\theta$

or $\cos^2\theta = 1 - \sin^2\theta$

(ii) $\sec^2\theta - \tan^2\theta = 1$

or $1 + \tan^2\theta = \sec^2\theta$

or $\tan^2\theta = \sec^2\theta - 1$

(iii) $\text{cosec}^2\theta - \cot^2\theta = 1$

or $\text{cosec}^2\theta = 1 + \cot^2\theta$

or $\cot^2\theta = \text{cosec}^2\theta - 1$

(c) The following steps should be kept in mind while proving trigonometric identities :

(i) Start with more complicated side of the identity and prove it equal to the other side.

(ii) If the identity contains sine, cosine and other trigonometric ratios, then express all the ratios in terms of sine and cosine.

(iii) If one side of an identity cannot be easily reduced to the other side value, then simplify both sides and prove them identically equal.

(iv) While proving identities, never transfer terms from one side to another.

❍ Trigonometric functions of sum or difference of two angles.

(i) $\sin(A \pm B) = \sin A \cos B \pm \cos A \sin B$

(ii) $\cos(A \pm B) = \cos A \cos \mp \sin A \sin B$

(iii) $\tan(A \pm B) = \dfrac{\tan A \pm \tan B}{1 \mp \tan A \tan B}$

❍ Sine Rule :

In a ΔABC if $AB = c$, $BC = a$ and $AC = b$, then by sine rule we have

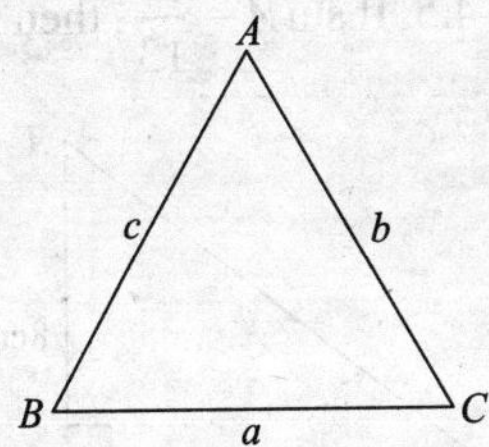

Figure 4.3

$$\frac{a}{\sin A} = \frac{b}{\sin B} = \frac{c}{\sin C}$$

❍ Cosine Rule :

In a ΔABC if $AB = c$, $BC = a$ and $AC = b$, then by sine rule we have

$$\cos A = \frac{b^2 + c^2 - a^2}{2bc}$$

$$\cos B = \frac{a^2 + c^2 - b^2}{2ac}$$

$$\cos C = \frac{a^2 + b^2 - c^2}{2ab}$$

* * * * *

PRACTICE EXERCISE - 4.1

4-1 If $\sec\theta - \tan\theta = p$, then $\cos\theta$ equals :

(A) $\frac{1}{p}$ (B) $1+\frac{1}{p^2}$

(C) $\frac{p}{\sqrt{1+p^2}}$ (D) $\frac{2p}{p^2+1}$

4-2 The value of $\sqrt{\frac{1-\cos\theta}{1+\cos\theta}}$ is :

(A) $\sec\theta + \tan\theta$ (B) $\sec\theta - \tan\theta$

(C) $\text{cosec}\theta - \cot\theta$ (D) $\text{cosec}\theta + \cot\theta$

4-3 The value of $\tan 1° \tan 2° \tan 3° \ldots \tan 89° =$

(A) 1 (B) 0

(C) -1 (D) None of these

4-4 If $\alpha + \beta = 90°$ and $\beta = 2\alpha$, then $\cos^2\alpha + \sin^2\beta$ equals :

(A) 1 (B) $\frac{3}{2}$

(C) 0 (D) 2

4-5 $1° =$

(A) $\frac{1}{180}$ radian (B) $\frac{180}{\pi}$ radian

(C) 1 radian (D) 0.0175 radian

4-6 In given figure-4.4, Find $\frac{\sin A + \sin B}{\cos A + \cos B}$:

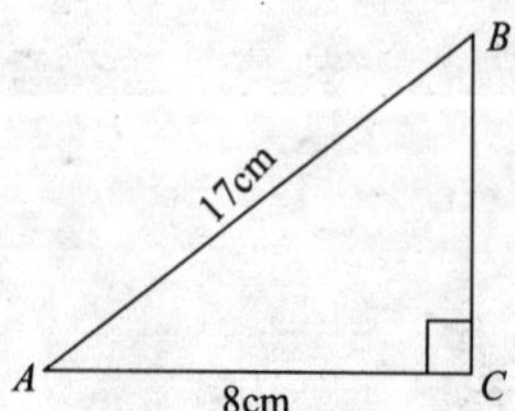

Figure 4.4

(A) $\frac{17}{8}$ cm (B) $\frac{17}{23}$ cm

(C) $\frac{23}{17}$ cm (D) 1 cm

4-7 In given figure-4.5, If $\sin A = \frac{8}{13}$, then find AB :

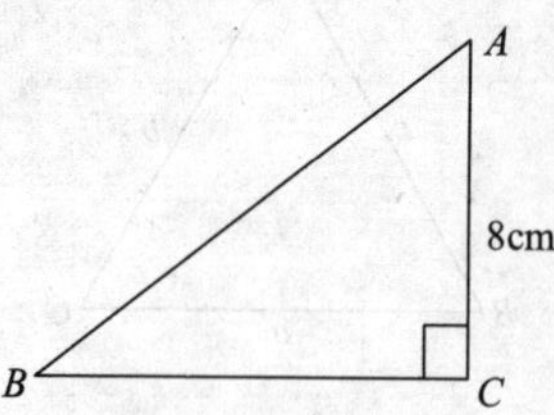

Figure 4.5

(A) $\frac{104\sqrt{105}}{110}$ (B) $\frac{104}{105}$

(C) $\frac{104}{\sqrt{105}}$ (D) 13 cm

4-8 $\sin^6 A + \cos^6 A + 3\sin^2 A\cos^2 A =$

(A) 0 (B) 1

(C) 2 (D) 3

4-9 The value of $\sin^2 5° + \sin^2 10° + \sin^2 15° + \ldots + \sin^2 85° + \sin^2 90°$ is :

(A) 7.5 (B) 8.5

(C) 9.5 (D) 10.5

4-10 The value of $(\cos^2\theta + \sec^2\theta)$ is always :

(A) Less than 1

(B) Equal to 1

(C) Greater than or equal to 2

(D) Greater than 1 but less than 2

4-11 If α and β are complementary angles $\left(0 < \alpha < \frac{\pi}{2}\right)$ and $\sin\alpha = \frac{1}{2}$, then the value of $(\cos\alpha\sin\beta - \sin\alpha\cos\beta)$ is :

(A) 0 (B) 1

(C) $\frac{1}{2}$ (D) 2

4-12 If $\text{cosec}\,\theta - \cot\theta = \frac{1}{2}$, $0 < \theta < \frac{\pi}{2}$, then $\cos\theta$ is equal to :

(A) $-\frac{3}{5}$ (B) $-\frac{5}{3}$

(C) $\frac{5}{3}$ (D) $\frac{3}{5}$

4-13 If $\operatorname{cosec} A + \cot A = \frac{11}{2}$, then $\tan A =$

(A) $\frac{21}{22}$ (B) $\frac{15}{16}$

(C) $\frac{44}{117}$ (D) $\frac{117}{43}$

4-14 Which of the following is true :

(A) $\sec\theta = \frac{1}{2}$ (B) $\operatorname{cosec}\theta = \frac{1}{\sqrt{3}}$

(C) $\sin\theta = \sqrt{3}$ (D) $\cos\theta = \frac{1}{5}$

4-15 Find the value of
$\sin^4\theta + \cos^4\theta + 2\sin^2\theta\cos^2\theta$

(A) 3 (B) 2
(C) –1 (D) 1

4-16 Which of the following gives the least value of A :
(A) $\cos 2A = \sin 3A$ (B) $\cos 3A = \sin 7A$
(C) $\tan A = \cot 3A$ (D) $\cot A = \tan 2A$

4-17 If $x = r\sin\theta\cos\phi$, $y = r\sin\theta\sin\phi$ and $z = r\cos\theta$, then $x^2 + y^2 + z^2$ is independent of :
(A) θ, ϕ (B) r, θ
(C) r, ϕ (D) r

4-18 Which is smaller, sin 66° or cos 66° ?
(A) sin 66° (B) cos 66°
(C) Both are equal (D) None of these

4-19 Which of the following relation is possible :

(A) $\sin\theta = \frac{5}{3}$ (B) $\tan\theta = 1002$

(C) $\cos\theta = \frac{1+p^2}{1-p^2}, (p \neq 1)$ (D) $\sec\theta = \frac{1}{2}$

4-20 If A, B and C are interior angles of a triangle ABC, then $\sin\left(\frac{B+C}{2}\right) =$

(A) $\sin\frac{A}{2}$ (B) $\cos\frac{A}{2}$

(C) $-\sin\frac{A}{2}$ (D) $-\cos\frac{A}{2}$

4-21 $\sec^4 A - \sec^2 A$ is equal to :
(A) $\tan^2 A - \tan^4 A$ (B) $\tan^4 A - \tan^2 A$
(C) $\tan^4 A + \tan^2 A$ (D) $-\tan^2 A - \tan^4 A$

4-22 $\frac{\sin\theta}{1-\cot\theta} + \frac{\cos\theta}{1-\tan\theta}$ is equal to :

(A) 0 (B) 1
(C) $\sin\theta + \cos\theta$ (D) $\sin\theta - \cos\theta$

4-23 $\frac{\cot\theta}{\cot\theta - \cot 3\theta} + \frac{\tan\theta}{\tan\theta - \tan 3\theta}$ is equal to :
(A) 0 (B) 1
(C) –1 (D) 2

4-24 In a ΔABC, $\angle C = 90°$, $AB = 29$cm, $BC = 21$ cm and $\angle ABC = \theta$ then $\cos^2\theta - \sin^2\theta =$

(A) $\frac{39}{841}$ (B) $\frac{40}{841}$

(C) $\frac{42}{841}$ (D) $\frac{41}{841}$

4-25 $2(\sin^6\theta + \cos^6\theta) - 3(\sin^4\theta + \cos^4\theta)$ is equal to :
(A) 0 (B) $\sin\theta + \cos\theta$
(C) –1 (D) None of these

4-26 If 'a' is the arithmetic mean of $\sin^2\theta$ and $\cos^2\phi$ & 'b' is the arithmetic mean of $\cos^2\theta$ and $\sin^2\phi$ then b equals :
(A) $1 - a$ (B) a
(C) 1 (D) $1 + a$

4-27 Which of the following is incorrect
(A) $\cos^4\theta - \sin^4\theta = \cos^2\theta - \sin^2\theta$
(B) $1 + \tan^2\theta = \sec^2\theta$
(C) $\sin 40° + \cos 50° = 2\sin 40°$
(D) $\sin^2\theta + \cos^2(-\theta) = -1$

4-28 If $7\sin\alpha = 24\cos\alpha$, $0 < \alpha < \frac{\pi}{2}$, the value of $14\tan\alpha - 75\cos\alpha - 7\sec\alpha$ is equal to :
(A) 1 (B) 2
(C) 3 (D) 4

4-29 If 5θ, 4θ are acute angles satisfying $\sin 5\theta = \cos 4\theta$, then $2\sin 3\theta - \sqrt{3}\tan 3\theta$ is equal to :
(A) 1 (B) 0
(C) –1 (D) $1 + \sqrt{3}$

4-30 The value of $\cos^2 17° - \sin^2 73°$ is :
(A) 1 (B) 0
(C) –1 (D) 2

4-31 If $\frac{x}{a}\cos\theta + \frac{y}{b}\sin\theta = 1$, $\frac{x}{a}\sin\theta - \frac{y}{b}\cos\theta = 1$, then which is true ?

(A) $x^2 + y^2 = a^2 + b^2$ (B) $\frac{x^2}{a^2} + \frac{y^2}{b^2} = 2$

(C) $a^2x^2 + b^2y^2 = 1$ (D) $x^2 - y^2 = a^2 - b^2$

4-32 The length of shadow of tower is $\sqrt{3}$ times that of its height, then angle of elevation of the sun is :

(A) 45° (B) 30°

(C) 60° (D) 90°

4-33 Which one is correct :

(A) $\text{cosec}^{-1}\,\theta = \sin\theta$ (B) $\text{cosec}\,\theta^{-1} = \sin\theta$

(C) $(\text{cosec}\,\theta)^{-1} = \sin\theta$ (D) $\sin^{-1}\theta = \text{cosec}\theta$

4-34 $3\cos^2 30° + \sec^2 30° + 2\cos 0° + 3\sin 90° - \tan^2 60° =$

(A) $\frac{65}{12}$ (B) $\frac{67}{12}$

(C) $\frac{69}{12}$ (D) $\frac{71}{12}$

4-35 $\sqrt{\frac{1-\cos^2\theta}{1+\cot^2\theta}} =$

(A) $\cos\theta$ (B) $\cos^2\theta$

(C) $\sin\theta$ (D) $\sin^2\theta$

4-36 If $\tan^2\theta = 1 - e^2$, then $\sec\theta + \tan^3\theta\,\text{cosec}\,\theta =$

(A) $(2 - e^2)^{1/2}$ (B) $(2 - e^2)^{3/2}$

(C) $2 - e^2$ (D) $(2 - e^2)^{5/2}$

4-37 $\tan 20° \tan 32° \tan 45° \tan 58° \tan 70° =$

(A) 0 (B) -1

(C) 1 (D) 2

4-38 If $\text{cosec}\theta - \sin\theta = x$ and $\sec\theta - \cos\theta = y$, then value of $x^2y^2(x^2 + y^2 + 3)$ will be :

(A) 1/2 (B) 1

(C) 1/3 (D) 2

4-39 The value of cos1° cos2° cos3°… cos179° is :

(A) $\frac{1}{\sqrt{2}}$ (B) 0

(C) 1 (D) None of these

4-40 In the given figure-4.6, AD is the tower, θ_1 and θ_2 are the angles of elevation. B and C are two consecutive milestones. If h be the height of tower then h equals :

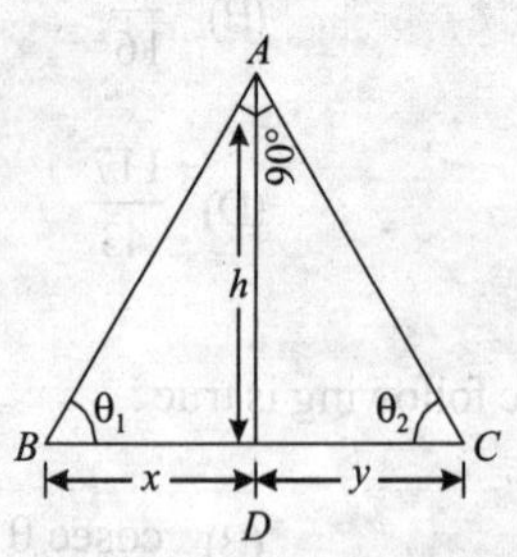

Figure 4.6

(A) $\sqrt{y(1-y)}$ (B) $\sqrt{x(1-x)}$

(C) $\sqrt{xy}$ (D) All of these

4-41 If $0 < \theta < 90°$, then $(\sin\theta + \cos\theta)$ is :

(A) Less than 1 (B) Equal to 1

(C) Greater than 1 (D) Greater then 2

4-42 The value of x satisfying the equation $\sin x + \frac{1}{\sin x} = \frac{7}{2\sqrt{3}}$ is :

(A) 10° (B) 30°

(C) 45° (D) 60°

4-43 If $\sin\theta - \cos\theta = 0$ and $0 < \theta \le \pi/2$, then θ is equal to :

(A) $\frac{\pi}{2}$ (B) $\frac{\pi}{4}$

(C) $\frac{\pi}{6}$ (D) 0

4-44 $\sin^6 A + \cos^6 A$ is equal to :

(A) $1 - 3\sin^2 A\cos^2 A$ (B) $1 - 3\sin A\cos A$

(C) $1 + 3\sin^2 A\cos^2 A$ (D) 1

4-45 If $\sec x = P$, $\text{cosec}\,x = Q$, then :

(A) $P^2 + Q^2 = PQ$ (B) $P^2 + Q^2 = P^2Q^2$

(C) $P^2 - Q^2 = P^2Q^2$ (D) $P^2 + Q^2 = -P^2Q^2$

4-46 Given that θ is acute and the $\sin\theta = \frac{3}{5}$. Let x, y be positive real numbers such that $3(x - y) = 1$, then one set of solutions for x and y expressed in terms of θ is given by :

(A) $x = \sec\theta, y = \text{cosec}\,\theta$ (B) $x = \cot\theta, y = \tan\theta$

(C) $x = \text{cosec}\,\theta, y = \cot\theta$ (D) $x = \sec\theta, y = \tan\theta$

4-47 In the third quadrant, the values of $\sin\theta$ and $\cos\theta$ are :

(A) Positive and negative respectively

(B) Negative and positive respectively

(C) Both positive

(D) Both negative

4-48 The value of $\frac{\cot 40°}{\tan 50°} - \frac{1}{2}\frac{\cos 35°}{\sin 55°}$ is :

(A) 1 (B) -1

(C) $\frac{1}{2}$ (D) $-\frac{1}{2}$

4-49 Maximum value of $(\cos\theta - \sin\theta)$ is :

(A) $\sqrt{2}$ (B) 1

(C) $\frac{1}{2}$ (D) $\frac{1}{\sqrt{2}}$

4-50 If $\tan\theta = \sqrt{2}$, then the value of θ is :

(A) Less than $\frac{\pi}{4}$ (B) Equal to $\frac{\pi}{4}$

(C) Between $\frac{\pi}{4}$ & $\frac{\pi}{3}$ (D) Greater than $\frac{\pi}{4}$

* * * * *

PRACTICE EXERCISE - 4.2

4-1 If $\tan\theta + \cot\theta = 2$, then the value of $\tan^6\theta + \cot^6\theta$ is :

(A) 4 (B) 64
(C) 256 (D) None of these

4-2 $\dfrac{\cot\theta}{\cot\theta - \cot 3\theta} + \dfrac{\tan\theta}{\tan\theta - \tan 3\theta}$ is equal to :

(A) 0 (B) 1
(C) –1 (D) 2

4-3 The value of $(1 + \tan\alpha \tan\beta)^2 + (\tan\alpha - \tan\beta)^2$ is :

(A) $\sec^2\alpha \sec^2\beta$ (B) $\tan^2\alpha + \tan^2\beta$
(C) $\cos^2\alpha \cos^2\beta$ (D) $\tan^2\alpha \tan^2\beta$

4-4 The greatest value of $\sin\theta \cos\theta$ is :

(A) 1 (B) $\dfrac{1}{2}$
(C) $\dfrac{1}{4}$ (D) 2

4-5 $\dfrac{\tan^2 A}{\cos^2 B} - \dfrac{\sec^2 A}{\cot^2 B}$ is equal to :

(A) $\cot^2 A - \cot^2 B$ (B) $\tan^2 A - \tan^2 B$
(C) $\dfrac{\tan^2 A}{\sec^2 B}$ (D) None of these

4-6 If $\sin\theta + \cos\theta = \sqrt{2}\sin(90° - \theta)$ then $\dfrac{1}{\sqrt{2}+1} =$

(A) $\cot\theta$ (B) $\dfrac{1}{\sqrt{2}-1}$
(C) $\tan\theta$ (D) None of these

4-7 If points $(\sin\theta, \sec\theta)$ $(\sin\theta - \cos\theta, \cos\theta)$ and $(-\cos\theta, \cos\theta - \sin\theta)$ are collinear where $0° < \theta < 90°$ then find the value of θ :

(A) 60° (B) 30°
(C) 45° (D) 90°

4-8 If $0 < \theta < \dfrac{\pi}{2}$, and if $\dfrac{y+1}{1-y} = \sqrt{\dfrac{1+\sin\theta}{1-\sin\theta}}$, then y is equal to :

(A) $\dfrac{\sin\theta}{1-\cos\theta}$ (B) $\dfrac{\sin\theta}{1+\cos\theta}$
(C) $\dfrac{1+\cos\theta}{\sin\theta}$ (D) $\dfrac{1+\cos\theta}{1-\cos\theta}$

4-9 If $a\cos A - b\sin A = c$, then $a\sin A + b\cos A$ is equal to :

(A) $\pm\sqrt{a^2+b^2-c^2}$ (B) $\pm\sqrt{b^2+c^2-a^2}$
(C) $\pm\sqrt{c^2+a^2-b^2}$ (D) $\pm\sqrt{a^2+b^2+c^2}$

4-10 If $\tan x = \dfrac{m}{m+1}$ and $\tan y = \dfrac{1}{(2m+1)}$, then $(x+y)$ is :

(A) $\dfrac{\pi}{6}$ (B) $\dfrac{\pi}{4}$
(C) $\dfrac{\pi}{3}$ (D) $\dfrac{\pi}{2}$

4-11 The maximum value of $(\sin x + \cos x)$ is :

(A) 2 (B) 1
(C) $\sqrt{2}$ (D) $\sqrt{3}$

4-12 The maximum and minimum values of $(1 + \cos 2x)$ are :

(A) – 1 and 1 (B) 1 & 2
(C) $-\dfrac{1}{2}$ & $\dfrac{1}{2}$ (D) 0 & 2

4-13 The value of $\left[\dfrac{1}{\sin 10°} - \dfrac{\sqrt{3}}{\cos 10°}\right]$ is :

(A) 1 (B) 2
(C) 3 (D) 4

4-14 If $\sin x + \sin y = a$ and $\cos x + \cos y = b$, then the value of $\sin(x+y)$ is :

(A) $\dfrac{2ab}{a^2-b^2}$ (B) $\dfrac{2ab}{a^2+b^2}$
(C) $2(a^2 - b^2)$ (D) $4ab$

4-15 Two persons are a metres apart and the height of one is double that of the other. If from the middle point of the line joining their feet, an observer finds the angular of elevation of their tops to be complementary, then the height of the shorter post is :

(A) $\dfrac{a}{4}$ (B) $\dfrac{a}{\sqrt{2}}$
(C) $a\sqrt{2}$ (D) $\dfrac{a}{2\sqrt{2}}$

4-16 A spherical balloon whose radius is r cm, subtends at an observer's eye an angle α, when an angular deviation of the centre is β. The height of the centre of the balloon is :

(A) r cosec $\alpha/2$ (B) r cosec $\alpha/2$ sin β
(C) r cosec α cosec β (D) None of these

4-17 From the top of a house 32m high, the angle of elevation of the top of a tower is 45°, and the angle of depression of the foot of the tower is 30°. The distance of the tower from the house is :

(A) $30\sqrt{3}\ m$ (B) $32\sqrt{3}\ m$
(C) $35\sqrt{3}\ m$ (D) None of these

4-18 Two stations due south of a leaning tower which leans towards the north are at distances a and b from its foot. It α, β be the elevations of the top of the tower from these stations, then $\cot\theta$ equals (where θ is its inclination to the horizontal) :

(A) $\dfrac{b\cot\beta - a\cot\alpha}{b-a}$ (B) $\dfrac{b\cot\alpha - a\cot\beta}{a-b}$
(C) $\dfrac{b\cot\alpha - a\cot\beta}{b-a}$ (D) None of these

4-19 If the angles A, B, C of a triangle ABC are in A.P such that $\sin(2A+B) = \dfrac{1}{2}$ then $\sin(B+2C) =$

(A) $-\dfrac{1}{2}$ (B) $\dfrac{1}{2}$
(C) $\dfrac{\sqrt{3}}{2}$ (D) $\dfrac{1}{\sqrt{2}}$

4-20 If $\tan\dfrac{\alpha}{2}$ and $\tan\dfrac{\beta}{2}$ are the roots of the equation $8x^2 - 25x + 15 = 0$ then $\cos(\alpha+\beta)$ is equal to :

(A) $-\dfrac{627}{725}$ (B) $\dfrac{627}{725}$
(C) -1 (D) None of these

4-21 If $|\tan A| < 1$ and $|A|$ is acute then $\dfrac{\sqrt{1+\sin 2A}+\sqrt{1-\sin 2A}}{\sqrt{1+\sin 2A}-\sqrt{1-\sin 2A}}$ is equal to :

(A) $\tan A$ (B) $-\tan A$
(C) $\cot A$ (D) $-\cot A$

4-22 The angle of elevation of an aeroplane from a point on the ground is 45°. After 15 second's flight, the elevation changes to 30°. If the aeroplane is flying at a height of 3000 m, the speed of the plane in km per hour is :

(A) 304.32 (B) 152.16
(C) 527 (D) 263.5

4-23 If D, G and R stand for degree, grade and radian respectively, then which one of the following is true:

(A) $\dfrac{D}{90} = \dfrac{G}{100} = \dfrac{R}{\pi}$ (B) $\dfrac{D}{100} = \dfrac{G}{90} = \dfrac{R}{\pi/2}$
(C) $\dfrac{D}{90} = \dfrac{G}{100} = \dfrac{2R}{\pi}$ (D) $\dfrac{2D}{90} = \dfrac{2G}{100} = \dfrac{R}{\pi}$

4-24 The value of $\dfrac{\cot\theta + \text{cosec}\theta - 1}{\cot\theta - \text{cosec}\theta + 1}$ on simplifying is equal to :

(A) $\dfrac{1+\sin\theta}{\cos\theta}$ (B) $\dfrac{1-\sin\theta}{\cos\theta}$
(C) $\dfrac{1-\cos\theta}{\sin\theta}$ (D) $\dfrac{1+\cos\theta}{\sin\theta}$

4-25 If $\sin\theta_1 + \sin\theta_2 + \sin\theta_3 = 3 (0 \le \theta_1, \theta_2, \theta_3 \le 90)$ then $\cos\theta_1 + \cos\theta_2 + \cos\theta_3 =$

(A) 3 (B) -3
(C) 1 (D) 0

* * * * *

PRACTICE EXERCISE - 4.3

4-1 If $\sin(A+B)=\dfrac{\sqrt{3}}{2}$, $\cos(A-B)=\dfrac{\sqrt{3}}{2}$ and $O<A+B\le 90°$, if $A>B$ then the value of A and B are :

[NTSE-2013 (Stage-I) Rajasthan]

(A) $A=45°, B=15°$ (B) $A=60°, B=30°$
(C) $A=0°, B=30°$ (D) $A=30°, B=0°$

4-2 If the Angle of elevation of sun increases from 0° to 90° then the change in the length of shadow of Tower will be :

[NTSE-2013 (Stage-I) Rajasthan]

(A) No change in length of shadow
(B) Length of shadow increase
(C) Length of shadow decreases
(D) Length of shadow will be zero

4-3 $(1+\tan\theta+\sec\theta)(1+\cot\theta-\operatorname{cosec}\theta)$ is equal to :

[NTSE-2014 (Stage-I) Rajasthan]

(A) 0 (B) 2
(C) 1 (D) –1

4-4 If $\sin\theta-\cos\theta=\sqrt{2}\sin(90°-\theta)$, then $\tan\theta=$

[NTSE-2014 (Stage-I) Rajasthan]

(A) $\sqrt{2}-1$ (B) $\sqrt{2}$
(C) $1-\sqrt{2}$ (D) $\sqrt{2}+1$

4-5 If $a\cos\theta-b\sin\theta=c$, then $a\sin\theta+b\cos\theta$ is equal to :

[NTSE-2014 (Stage-I) Rajasthan]

(A) $\pm\sqrt{a^2+b^2+c^2}$ (B) $\pm\sqrt{a^2+b^2-c^2}$
(C) $\pm\sqrt{c^2-a^2-b^2}$ (D) None of these

4-6 From the top of a 7 m high building, the angle of elevation of the top of a cable tower is 60° and the angle of depression of its foot is 45°. The height of the tower in metre is :

[NTSE-2014 (Stage-I) Rajasthan]

(A) $7(\sqrt{3}-1)$ (B) $7\sqrt{3}$
(C) $7+\sqrt{3}$ (D) $7(\sqrt{3}+1)$

4-7 $\tan 43°\tan 45°\tan 47°$ is equal to :

[NTSE-2015 (Stage-I) Rajasthan]

(A) $\sqrt{3}$ (B) $\dfrac{1}{\sqrt{3}}$
(C) 1 (D) 2

4-8 If $\sin(A+B)=\cos(A+B)$, then the value of $(A+B)$ is :

[NTSE-2015 (Stage-I) Rajasthan]

(A) $\dfrac{\pi}{4}$ (B) $\dfrac{\pi}{2}$
(C) $\dfrac{3\pi}{4}$ (D) $\dfrac{\pi}{8}$

4-9 If $\sin\theta+\sin^2\theta=1$, then the value of $\cos^2\theta+\cos^4\theta$ is :

[NTSE-2015 (Stage-I) Rajasthan]

(A) 3 (B) 2
(C) 1 (D) 0

4-10 The angle of elevation of the top of a building from the foot of tower is 30° and the angle of elevation of the top of the tower from the foot of the building is 60°. If the tower is 30 m high, then the height of the building is :

[NTSE-2015 (Stage-I) Rajasthan]

(A) 30m (B) 20m
(C) 15m (D) 10m

4-11 If $\sec x+\tan x=\dfrac{22}{7}$ and $\operatorname{cosec}x+\cot x=\dfrac{m}{n}$, where $\dfrac{m}{n}$ is in lowest terms, then the value of $m+n$ is :

[NTSE-2015 (Stage-I) Andhara Pradesh]

(A) 22 (B) 33
(C) 44 (D) 11

4-12 If $\sin\theta=\cos\theta$, then θ is : **[NTSE-2015 (Stage-I) TN]**

(A) 30° (B) 45°
(C) 60° (D) 90°

4-13 From an aeroplane vertically above a straight horizontal road, the angles of depression of two consecutive stones on opposite sides of the aeroplane are observed to be α and β. Then the height in metres of the aeroplane above the road is :

[NTSE-2015 (Stage-I) Chandigarh]

(A) $\dfrac{\tan\alpha\cdot\tan\beta}{\tan\beta+\tan\alpha}$ (B) $\dfrac{\cot\alpha\cdot\tan\beta}{\cot\beta+\cot\alpha}$

(C) $\dfrac{\tan\alpha\cdot\tan\beta}{\tan\beta-\tan\alpha}$ (D) $\dfrac{\cot\alpha\cdot\tan\beta}{\cot\beta-\cot\alpha}$

4-14 The value of $(1+\cot\theta-\operatorname{cosec}\theta).(1+\tan\theta+\sec\theta)$ is :

[NTSE-2015 (Stage-I) Chandigarh]

(A) –2 (B) 3
(C) 2 (D) 1

4-15 If $\tan\theta = \frac{4}{5}$ then the value of $\frac{5\sin\theta - 3\cos\theta}{5\sin\theta + 3\cos\theta}$ will be :

[NTSE-2015 (Stage-I) Chhatisgarh]

(A) $\frac{5}{7}$ (B) $\frac{4}{7}$

(C) $\frac{9}{7}$ (D) $\frac{1}{7}$

4-16 If $3\sin\theta + 4\cos\theta = 5$ then value of $4\sin\theta - 3\cos\theta$ is :

[NTSE-2015 (Stage-I) Delhi]

(A) 0 (B) 1

(C) −1 (D) 2

4-17 If $\frac{2\sin\alpha}{1+\sin\alpha+\cos\alpha} = \lambda$ then $\frac{1+\sin\alpha-\cos\alpha}{1+\sin\alpha}$ is equal to :

[NTSE-2015 (Stage-I) Delhi]

(A) $-\lambda$ (B) λ

(C) $\frac{1}{\lambda}$ (D) $1-\lambda$

4-18 The value of $\sin^2\theta + \frac{1}{(1+\tan^2\theta)}$ is :

[NTSE-2015 (Stage-I) UP]

(A) $\sin^2\theta$ (B) $\cos^2\theta$

(C) $\sec^2\theta$ (D) 1

4-19 If $\sec\theta + \tan\theta = P$ then the value of $\frac{P^2-1}{P^2+1}$:

[NTSE-2015 (Stage-I) UP]

(A) $\operatorname{cosec}\theta$ (B) $\cos\theta$

(C) $\frac{\tan\theta}{\sec\theta}$ (D) 1

4-20 If $\tan\theta = \frac{a}{b}$ then the value of $\frac{b\sin\theta - a\cos\theta}{b\sin\theta + a\cos\theta}$ is :

[NTSE-2015 (Stage-I) UP]

(A) 1 (B) $\frac{a^2-b^2}{a^2+b^2}$

(C) $\frac{b^2-a^2}{b^2+a^2}$ (D) 0

4-21 If $\sin\theta = \frac{4}{5}$, then value of $\cos 2\theta$ is :

[NTSE-2015 (Stage-I) UP]

(A) 8/5 (B) 3/5

(C) 7/35 (D) −7/25

4-22 Each exterior angle of a regular Polygon of m sides is :

[NTSE-2015 (Stage-I) UP]

(A) $\left(\frac{360}{m}\right)\pi$ degree (B) $\left(\frac{360}{m}\right)$ degree

(C) $\left(\frac{180}{m}\right)\pi^2$ degree (D) $\left(\frac{180}{m}\right)$ degree

4-23 $\frac{\sin^4\theta - \cos^4\theta}{1-\sin^2\theta}$ = how much :

[NTSE-2015 (Stage-I) Maharashtra]

(A) $1-\cot^2\theta$ (B) $1-\tan^2\theta$

(C) $\tan^2\theta - 1$ (D) $\cot^2\theta - 1$

4-24 If in a right angled triangle ABC, $\cos A = \frac{9}{41}$, then the value of $\cot A$ and $\operatorname{cosec} A$ will be : **[NTSE-2015 (Stage-I) MP]**

(A) $\frac{40}{9}, \frac{40}{41}$ (B) $\frac{9}{40}, \frac{41}{40}$

(C) $\frac{9}{41}, \frac{41}{9}$ (D) $\frac{9}{40}, \frac{40}{41}$

4-25 In ΔABC, if $\angle B = 90°$, $AB = 5$, $BC = 12$, then $\sin C = ...$

[NTSE-2015 (Stage-I) MP]

(A) $\frac{12}{13}$ (B) $\frac{5}{13}$

(C) $\frac{5}{12}$ (D) $\frac{13}{5}$

4-26 $(\sec\theta + \tan\theta)(1-\sin\theta) = ...$

[NTSE-2015 (Stage-I) MP]

(A) 0 (B) = 1

(C) $\cos\theta$ (D) $\sin\theta$

4-27 If $\tan\theta = \frac{1}{\sqrt{3}}$, then the value of $\frac{\operatorname{cosec}^2\theta - \sec^2\theta}{\operatorname{cosec}^2\theta + \sec^2\theta}$:

[NTSE-2015 (Stage-I) MP]

(A) $\sqrt{3}$ (B) 1/2

(C) $\frac{1}{\sqrt{2}}$ (D) $\sqrt{2}$

4-28 If in a right angled triangle ABC $\tan B = \sqrt{3}$, then value of $\sin B$ and $\cos B$ is : **[NTSE-2015 (Stage-I) MP]**

(A) 0, 1 (B) $\frac{1}{2}, \frac{\sqrt{3}}{2}$

(C) $\frac{1}{\sqrt{2}}, \frac{1}{\sqrt{2}}$ (D) $\frac{\sqrt{3}}{2}, \frac{1}{2}$

4-29 $\cos^4 x - \sin^4 x =$ **[NTSE-2015 (Stage-I) MP]**

(A) $2\sin^2 x - 1$ (B) $1 - 2\cos^2 x$

(C) $\sin^2 x - \cos^2 x$ (D) None of these

4-30 $\sqrt{\frac{1+\sin\theta}{1-\sin\theta}} + \sqrt{\frac{1-\sin\theta}{1+\sin\theta}}$: **[NTSE-2015 (Stage-I) MP]**

(A) $\frac{2}{\sin\theta}$ (B) $\frac{2}{\cos\theta}$

(C) $\frac{2}{\tan\theta}$ (D) $\frac{2}{\cot\theta}$

4-31 If $\sin(A+B) = 1$ and $\cos(A-B) = \frac{\sqrt{3}}{2}$, then the values of A and B are : **[NTSE-2015 (Stage-I) MP]**

(A) $45°, 45°$ (B) $30°, 45°$

(C) $60°, 30°$ (D) $0°, 90°$

4-32 If $\sin^2 A + \sin^4 A = 1$, the value of $\tan^2 A - \tan^4 A$ is : **[NTSE-2015 (Stage-I) West Bengal]**

(A) -1 (B) 1

(C) 0 (D) 2

4-33 If $ABCD$ is a cyclic quadrilateral, the value of $\tan\frac{A}{2}\tan\frac{C}{2} + \tan\frac{B}{2}\tan\frac{D}{2}$ is : **[NTSE-2015 (Stage-I) West Bengal]**

(A) 0 (B) 1

(C) -1 (D) 2

4-34 $\sqrt{1-\sin^2 A}\cdot\sqrt{\sec^2 A - 1}\cdot\sqrt{1+\cot^2 A}$: **[NTSE-2015 (Stage-I) Chennai]**

(A) 0 (B) 2

(C) 1 (D) -2

4-35 If $5x = \text{cosec}\,\theta$ and $\frac{5}{x} = \cot\theta$ then $5\left(x^2 - \frac{1}{x^2}\right) =$ **[NTSE-2015 (Stage-I) Chennai]**

(A) 25 (B) 1

(C) $\frac{1}{5}$ (D) -5

4-36 If $x = a\cos\theta$, $y = a\sin\theta$, then $x^2 + y^2 =$ **[NTSE-2015 (Stage-I) Chennai]**

(A) 1 (B) a

(C) a^2 (D) $a^2 + b^2$

4-37 If $\cot\theta = \frac{7}{8}$ then the value of $\frac{(1+\sin\theta)(1-\sin\theta)}{(1+\cos\theta)(1-\cos\theta)}$ is : **[NTSE-2015 (Stage-I) TN]**

(A) $\frac{64}{49}$ (B) $\frac{8}{7}$

(C) $\frac{7}{8}$ (D) $\frac{49}{64}$

4-38 Value of $\tan 25° \tan 35° \tan 45° \tan 55° \tan 65°$ is : **[NTSE-2016 (Stage-I) Rajasthan]**

(A) 0 (B) 1

(C) $\sqrt{2}$ (D) $\sqrt{3}$

4-39 The angles of elevation of the top of a tower from two points at a distance of 9m and 16m from the base of the tower and in the same straight line in the same direction with it are complementary. Then height of the tower is : **[NTSE-2016 (Stage-I) Rajasthan]**

(A) 12m (B) 15m

(C) 20m (D) 25m

4-40 If $\sin\theta = p$ and $\cos\theta = q$ then the value of $\frac{p-2p^3}{2q^3-q}$ is : **[NTSE-2016 (Stage-I) Rajasthan]**

(A) $\sec\theta$ (B) $\text{cosec}\,\theta$

(C) $\cot\theta$ (D) $\tan\theta$

4-41 In triangle ABC, $3\sin A + 4\cos B = 6$ and $4\sin B + 3\cos A = 1$, then $\angle C$ in degrees is : **[NTSE-2016 (Stage-I) Telangana]**

(A) 30 (B) 60

(C) 90 (D) 120

4-42 3 sides of triangle are consecutive integers and the largest angle is twice the smallest angle. The perimeter of triangle is : **[NTSE-2016 (Stage-I) Andhara Pradesh]**

(A) 15 units (B) 10 units

(C) 12 units (D) 16 units

4-43 If $x = a\sec\theta + b\tan\theta$ and $y = a\tan\theta - b\sec\theta$ then the value of $x^2 - y^2$ will be : **[NTSE-2016 (Stage-I) Chandigarh]**

(A) $a^2 - b^2$ (B) $a^2 + b^2$

(C) $a^2 + 1$ (D) $a^2 - 1$

4-44 If $A + B = 90°$ then $\frac{\tan A \times \tan B + \tan A \cot B}{\sin A \sec B} - \frac{\sin^2 A}{\cos^2 A}$: **[NTSE-2016 (Stage-I) Delhi]**

(A) $\cot^2 A$ (B) $\cot^2 B$

(C) $-\tan^2 A$ (D) $-\cot^2 A$

4-45 If $2^{\sin x+\cos y}=1$, $16^{\sin^2 x+\cos^2 y}=4$, then values of $\sin x$ and $\cos y$ respectively are : **[NTSE-2016 (Stage-I) Delhi]**

(A) $-\frac{1}{2},\frac{1}{2}$ (B) $\frac{1}{2},-\frac{1}{3}$

(C) $1,-1$ (D) $\frac{1}{\sqrt{2}},\frac{-1}{\sqrt{2}}$

4-46 If $\sin A+\sin^2 A=1$, then $\cos^2 A+\cos^4 A=\dots$ **[NTSE-2016 (Stage-I) Jharkhand]**

(A) ½ (B) 1

(C) 2 (D) 4

4-47 $\sqrt{\frac{\sec A-\tan A}{\sec A+\tan A}}=?$ **[NTSE-2016 (Stage-I) Jharkhand]**

(A) $\sec A-\tan A$ (B) $\sec A+\tan A$

(C) $\sec A \,.\, \tan A$ (D) None of these

4-48 If $\cos 9\alpha=\sin\alpha$ and $9\alpha<90°$, then the value of $\tan 5\alpha$? **[NTSE-2016 (Stage-I) Jharkhand]**

(A) $\frac{1}{\sqrt{3}}$ (B) $\sqrt{3}$

(C) 1 (D) 0

4-49 If $x=a\cos^3\theta$ and $y=b\sin^3\theta$ then $\left(\frac{x}{a}\right)^{2/3}+\left(\frac{y}{b}\right)^{2/3}=?$ **[NTSE-2016 (Stage-I) Jharkhand]**

(A) 2 (B) a

(C) b (D) 1

4-50 If $A+B+C=180°$ and $\cos B.\cos C=\cos A$, then what is the value of $\tan B.\tan C$? **[NTSE-2016 (Stage-I) Odisha]**

(A) -2 (B) -1

(C) 2 (D) 1

4-51 In ΔABC, $2(m\angle A+m\angle B)=3m\angle B=m\angle C$. If O is the circumcentre of ΔABC and the diameter of the circumcircle of ΔABC is 16 cm, what is the area of ΔOAB? **[NTSE-2016 (Stage-I) Odisha]**

(A) 8 sq. cm (B) $8\sqrt{3}$ sq. cm

(C) 16 sq. cm (D) $16\sqrt{3}$ sq. cm

4-52 If $\operatorname{cosec}\theta+\cot\theta=m$, then what is the value of $\sec\theta$? **[NTSE-2016 (Stage-I) Odisha]**

(A) m^2+1 (B) m^2-1

(C) $\frac{m^2-1}{m^2+1}$ (D) $\frac{m^2+1}{m^2-1}$

4-53 $\sin x=\frac{6\sin 30°-8\cos 60°+2\tan 45°}{2(\sin^2 30°+\cos^2 60°)}$, then x = how much? **[NTSE-2016 (Stage-I) Odisha]**

(A) 30° (B) 45°

(C) 60° (D) 90°

4-54 If $\sin x+\sin^2 x=1$ then the value of $\cos^{12}x+3\cos^{10}x+3\cos^8 x+\cos^6 x$ is : **[NTSE-2016 (Stage-I) Karnatka]**

(A) 0 (B) 1

(C) 2 (D) 3

4-55 There are two temples one on each bank of a rivers just opposite to each other. One temple is 40 m high. As observed from the top of this temple, the angle of depression of the top and foot of the other temple are 30° and 60° respectively. The width of river is : **[NTSE-2016 (Stage-I) Karnatka]**

(A) $\frac{40\sqrt{3}}{3}m$ (B) $\frac{40}{3}m$

(C) $\frac{120}{\sqrt{3}}m$ (D) $\frac{80}{\sqrt{3}}m$

4-56 If $\tan\theta+\cot\theta=3$ then $\tan^2\theta+\cot^2\theta=?$ **[NTSE-2016 (Stage-I) Chhatisgarh]**

(A) 7 (B) 9

(C) 11 (D) 27

4-57 If $\sin\theta-1=0$, then θ will be : **[NTSE-2016 (Stage-I) Chhatisgarh]**

(A) 0° (B) 90°

(C) 30° (D) 60°

4-58 Find the value of $\frac{\sin 48°+\cos 42°}{\cot 42°}-\frac{1}{\sec 48°}$: **[NTSE-2016 (Stage-I) Chhatisgarh]**

(A) cos 48° (B) sin 48°

(C) sec 48° (D) cot 42°

4-59 If $\tan\theta+\cot\theta=2$, then the value of $\tan^2\theta+\cot^2\theta$ is : **[NTSE-2017 (Stage-I) Andhra Pradesh]**

(A) 4 (B) 2

(C) $\frac{3}{2}$ (D) 5

4-60 If $\operatorname{cosec}\theta+\sin\theta=2$, then the value of $\operatorname{cosec}^{50}\theta+\sin^{50}\theta$ is … **[NTSE-2017 (Stage-I) Chandigarh]**

(A) 2 (B) 100

(C) 0 (D) 50

4-61 If cosec $4x = \sec 5x$, then the value of $\sin 3x + \cos 6x$ is : **[NTSE-2017 (Stage-I) Chandigarh]**

(A) 1 (B) 3

(C) 0 (D) –3

4-62 The length of shadow of a building, when the sun's altitude is 60º, is 20 m less than what it was when it was 45°. The height of the building is : **[NTSE-2017 (Stage-I) Chandigarh]**

(A) 54.48 m (B) 47.32 m

(C) 64.32 m (D) 57.48 m

4-63 If $5\tan\theta = 3$, then $\dfrac{5\sin\theta - 3\cos\theta}{5\sin\theta + 3\cos\theta} =$: **[NTSE-2017 (Stage-I) Delhi]**

(A) 0 (B) $\frac{5}{3}$

(C) $\frac{3}{5}$ (D) $\frac{4}{5}$

4-64 If $(\cos^2\phi)^2 + \dfrac{\tan^2\phi}{\sec^2\phi} = P$: **[NTSE-2017 (Stage-I) Goa]**

(A) $1 \le p \le 2$ (B) $\frac{1}{2} \le p \le 1$

(C) $\frac{3}{4} \le p \le 1$ (D) $\frac{3}{4} \le p \le \frac{13}{16}$

4-65 If $\tan\theta + \cot\theta = 3$ then $\dfrac{\sin^2\theta - \cos^2\theta}{\sin\theta\cos\theta}$: **[NTSE-2017 (Stage-I) Goa]**

(A) $\sqrt{3}$ (B) 4

(C) 7 (D) $\sqrt{5}$

4-66 If coses $\theta - \cot\theta = p$, then the value of $\dfrac{p^2-1}{p^2+1}$ is = : **[NTSE-2017 (Stage-I) Haryana]**

(A) $\cos\theta$ (B) $-\cos\theta$

(C) $\sin\theta$ (D) $-\sin\theta$

4-67 A peacock sitting on the top of a tree observes *n* serpent on the ground making an angle of depression 30º. If the peacock with a speed of 300 m per minute catches the serpent in 12 seconds, then the height of the tree is : **[NTSE-2017 (Stage-I) Haryana]**

(A) 30 m (B) $30\sqrt{3}$ m

(C) $\frac{30}{\sqrt{3}}$ m (D) 15 m

4-68 If $\cos\theta + \sin\theta = p$ and $\sec\theta + \text{cosec}\theta = V$, then the value of V is : **[NTSE-2017 (Stage-I) Haryana]**

(A) $\dfrac{p^2}{2p-1}$ (B) $\dfrac{2p-1}{.\,p^2}$

(C) $\dfrac{2p}{p^2-1}$ (D) $\dfrac{p^2-1}{2p}$

4-69 The value of $\cos^2 5° + \cos^2 10° + \cos^2 15° + \ldots + \cos^2 85° + \cos^2 90°$ is : **[NTSE-2017 (Stage-I) Karnataka]**

(A) $9\frac{1}{2}$ (B) 9

(C) $8\frac{1}{2}$ (D) 8

4-70 The angle of elevation of the top of a tower from two points at a distance of '*a*' and '*b*' (*a* > *b*) from its foot and in the same straight line from it are 30° and 60°. The height of the tower is : **[NTSE-2017 (Stage-I) Karnataka]**

(A) $a\sqrt{3}$ (B) $\dfrac{b}{\sqrt{3}}$

(C) $\sqrt{ab}$ (D) $\dfrac{1}{\sqrt{ab}}$

4-71 The Value of $\dfrac{\cos^2\theta + \tan^2\theta - 1}{\sin^2\theta}$ is : **[NTSE-2017 (Stage-I) Madhya Pradesh]**

(A) $\sin^2\theta$ (B) $\cos^2\theta$

(C) $\cot^2\theta$ (D) $\tan^2\theta$

4-72 Value of $\dfrac{\cos^2 20° + \cos^2 70°}{\sin^2 59° + \sin^2 31°}$ is : **[NTSE-2017 (Stage-I) Madhya Pradesh]**

(A) 0 (B) 1

(C) $\frac{1}{2}$ (D) –1

4-73 The angle of elevation of the sun when the length of the shadow of a tower is equal to its height is : **[NTSE-2017 (Stage-I) Madhya Pradesh]**

(A) 30º (B) 45º

(C) 60º (D) 90º

4-74 The value of $\sin\theta\,(\text{cosec}\theta - \sin\theta)$ is : **[NTSE-2017 (Stage-I) Madhya Pradesh]**

(A) $\sin^2\theta$ (B) $\tan^2\theta$

(C) $\cot^2\theta$ (D) $\cos^2\theta$

4-75 Value of $\left[\frac{\sin 49°}{\cos 41°}+\frac{\cos 41°}{\sin 49°}\right]^2$ is :

[NTSE-2017 (Stage-I) Madhya Pradesh]

(A) 2 (B) 4
(C) 1 (D) None of these

4-76 $\frac{\cos^2 30°+\cos 30°\sin 30°+\sin^2 30°}{\cos^3 30°-\sin^3 30°}=?$

[NTSE-2017 (Stage-I) Maharashtra]

(A) 1 (B) $\sqrt{3}+1$
(C) $\sqrt{3}-1$ (D) $\frac{1}{\sqrt{3}-1}$

4-77 If $\tan\theta=-1$ then find the value of $\frac{\sec\theta+\operatorname{cosec}\theta}{\cos\theta-\sin\theta}$

[NTSE-2017 (Stage-I) Maharashtra]

(A) 0 (B) 1
(C) $-\sqrt{2}$ (D) $\sqrt{2}$

4-78 From the top of a tower of h m high, the angles of depression of two objects, which are in line with the foot of the tower are α and β ($\beta>\alpha$). Find the distance between two objects : **[NTSE-2017 (Stage-I) Punjab]**

(A) $h(\tan\alpha-\tan\beta)$ (B) $h(\cot\alpha-\tan\beta)$
(C) $h(\cot\alpha-\cot\beta)$ (D) $h(\cot\alpha+\cot\beta)$

4-79 If $x^2+y^2+z^2=r^2$ where $x=r\sin A\cos B$, $y=r\sin A\sin B$ then z has one of the following values : **[NTSE-2017 (Stage-I) Punjab]**

(A) $r\sin B$ (B) $r\cos A$
(C) $r\tan A\cos B$ (D) $r\tan A\tan B$

4-80 The angles of elevation of the top of a 12 m high tower from two points in opposite directions with it are complementary. If distance of one point from its base is 16 m, then distance of second point from tower's base is :

[NTSE-2017 (Stage-I) Rajasthan]

(A) 24m (B) 9m
(C) 12m (D) 18m

4-81 If $m=\frac{\cos A}{\cos B}$ and $n=\frac{\cos A}{\sin B}$, then $(m^2+n^2)\cos^2 B$ is equal to : **[NTSE-2017 (Stage-I) Rajasthan]**

(A) m^2 (B) n^2
(C) m^2+n^2 (D) $m+n$

4-82 What is the radian value of angle 60°30′? **[NTSE-2017 (Stage-I) Rajasthan]**

(A) $\frac{\pi^c}{3}$ (B) $\frac{121}{360}\pi^c$
(C) $\frac{121\pi^c}{180}$ (D) $\frac{121}{540}\pi^c$

4-83 If $\tan\theta=\cot(30°+\theta)$, then $\theta=$: **[NTSE-2017 (Stage-I) Tamilnadu]**

(A) 45° (B) 30°
(C) 60° (D) 90°

4-84 Given $5\cos A-12\sin A=0$ evaluate $\frac{\sin A+\cos A}{2\cos A-\sin A}$:

[NTSE-2017 (Stage-I) Uttar Pradesh]

(A) $\frac{19}{17}$ (B) $\frac{17}{19}$
(C) $\frac{1}{2}$ (D) 1

4-85 The angle of elevation of a cloud from a point 100 metre above the surface of a lake is 30° and the angle of depression of its image in the lake is 60° then height of the cloud above the lake is : **[NTSE-2017 (Stage-I) Uttar Pradesh]**

(A) 100m (B) 50m
(C) 200m (D) 150m

4-86 If $\tan A=\cot B$ then the value of $(A+B)$ will be :

[NTSE-2017 (Stage-I) Uttrakhand]

(A) 90° (B) 45°
(C) 180° (D) None of these

4-87 If $\tan A=\sqrt{2}-1$ then the value of $\sin A.\cos A$ will be :

[NTSE-2017 (Stage-I) Uttrakhand]

(A) $\frac{\sqrt{2}-1}{4-2\sqrt{2}}$ (B) $\frac{\sqrt{3}+1}{3-2\sqrt{3}}$
(C) $\frac{\sqrt{2}+1}{4-2\sqrt{3}}$ (D) None of these

4-88 If two angles of a triangle are 87° 24′54″ and 32° 31′6″, the third angle is : **[NTSE-2017 (Stage-I) West Bengal]**

(A) $\frac{\pi}{6}$ (B) $\frac{\pi}{2}$
(C) $\frac{\pi}{3}$ (D) $\frac{\pi}{4}$

4-89 If $x\sin^3\alpha + y\cos^3\alpha = \sin\alpha\cos\alpha$ and $x\sin\alpha - y\cos\alpha = 0$, the value of $x^2 + y^2$ is : **[NTSE-2017 (Stage-I) West Bengal]**

(A) 0 (B) 1

(C) $\frac{1}{2}$ (D) $\frac{1}{3}$

4-90 If $\tan A = \sqrt{2} - 1$ where A is an acute angle thent the value of $\sin A.\cos A$ will be : **[NTSE-2018 (Stage-I) Rajasthan]**

(A) $2\sqrt{2}$ (B) $\sqrt{2}$

(C) $\frac{1}{2\sqrt{2}}$ (D) $\frac{3}{\sqrt{2}}$

4-91 The shadow of a tower, when the angle of elevation of the sun is 30º is to be 10 meter longer than when it was 60º. The height of the tower will be : **[NTSE-2018 (Stage-I) Rajasthan]**

(A) $5\sqrt{3}$ (B) $5(\sqrt{3}-1)$ m

(C) $5(\sqrt{3}+1)$ (D) $3\sqrt{5}$ m

4-92 If $\text{cosec}\theta - \sin\theta = 4$, then $\sin^2\theta + \text{cosec}^2\theta =$ **[NTSE-2018 (Stage-I) Andhra Pradesh]**

(A) 8 (B) 18

(C) 16 (D) 4

4-93 $3(\sin x - \cos x)^4 + 6(\sin x + \cos x)^2 + 4(\sin^6 x + \cos^6 x) =$ **[NTSE-2018 (Stage-I) Andhra Pradesh]**

(A) 14 (B) 13

(C) 7 (D) 9

4-94 If a flagstaff of 6 meters high placed on the top of a tower cast a shadow of $2\sqrt{3}$ metres along the ground then, the angle (in degrees) that the sun makes with the ground is : **[NTSE-2018 (Stage-I) Bihar]**

(A) 60º (B) 30º

(C) 45º (D) None of these

4-95 If $\cos\theta + \cos^2\theta = 1$ then $\sin^4\theta + \sin^2\theta =$ .... **[NTSE-2018 (Stage-I) Bihar]**

(A) 0 (B) 1

(C) $\frac{1}{2}$ (D) None of these

4-96 Solve :

$$\sqrt{\frac{1+\sin A}{1-\sin A}} + \sqrt{\frac{1-\sin A}{1+\sin A}} = ?$$

[NTSE-2018 (Stage-I) Chandigarh]

(A) cos 2A (B) 2 sec A

(C) 2 tan A (D) 2 sin A

4-97 If $x = 1 + \cos A$, $y = \text{cosec}^2 A$, $z = 1 - \cos A$, then the value of $(xy)\,z$ is _____ : **[NTSE-2018 (Stage-I) Chandigarh]**

(A) cosec$A$ (B) 1

(C) $1 - \text{cosec}^2 A$ (D) $\cos^2$

4-98 The value of $\frac{2\tan 30^\circ}{1+\tan^2 30^\circ}$ is : **[NTSE-2018 (Stage-I) Chhattisgarh]**

(A) sin 60º (B) cos 60º

(C) tan 60º (D) sin 30º

4-99 The angle of elevation of top a tower from a point on the ground is 30º. The point is 60 meter away from the foot of the tower. The height of tower will be : **[NTSE-2018 (Stage-I) Chhattisgarh]**

(A) $20\sqrt{3}$m (B) $30\sqrt{3}$m

(C) $60\sqrt{3}$m (D) $15\sqrt{3}$m

4-100 If $a\cos\theta - b\sin\theta = c$, then $a\sin\theta + b\cos\theta = ?$ **[NTSE-2018 (Stage-I) Delhi]**

(A) $\pm\sqrt{a^2+b^2+c^2}$ (B) $\pm\sqrt{a^2+b^2-c^2}$

(C) $\pm\sqrt{a^2-b^2+c^2}$ (D) $\pm\sqrt{a^2-b^2-c^2}$

4-101 If $\tan 5\theta.\tan 4\theta = 1$, then θ is _____ : **[NTSE-2018 (Stage-I) Gujarat]**

(A) 7 (B) 3

(C) 10 (D) 9

4-102 For right angle ΔABC, $\sin^2 A + \sin^2 B + \sin^2 C =$ _____ : **[NTSE-2018 (Stage-I) Gujarat]**

(A) 2 (B) 1

(C) 0 (D) –1

4-103 $\frac{\cos\theta - \sin\theta + 1}{\cos\theta + \sin\theta - 1}$ is equal to : **[NTSE-2018 (Stage-I) Haryana]**

(A) $\sec\theta + \tan\theta$ (B) $\sec\theta - \tan\theta$

(C) $\text{cosec}\theta - \cot\theta$ (D) $\text{cosec}\theta + \cot\theta$

4-104 From the top of a 60 m high tower, the angles of despression of the top and bottom of pillar are 30º and 60º respectively. Then the height of the pillar is : **[NTSE-2018 (Stage-I) Haryana]**

(A) 20m (B) $20\sqrt{3}$

(C) 40m (D) $40\sqrt{3}$

4-105 In $\Delta\angle ABC$, $\angle ABC = 90^\circ$ and $\angle BAC = 60^\circ$. If bisector of $\angle BAC$ meets BC at D, then $BD : DC$ is :

[NTSE-2018 (Stage-I) Haryana]

(A) $1:2$ (B) $1:\sqrt{3}$

(C) $1:\sqrt{2}$ (D) $1:1$

4-106 If x is real then which equation is not possible :

[NTSE-2018 (Stage-I) Himachal Pradesh]

(A) $\sin\theta = x + \frac{1}{x}$ (B) $\sin\theta = x^2 + \frac{1}{x^3}$

(C) $\sin\theta = x - \frac{1}{x}$ (D) $\tan\theta = x + \frac{1}{x}$

4-107 $\sec^2\theta - \tan^2\theta = 1$ is true when/for :

[NTSE-2018 (Stage-I) Himachal Pradesh]

(A) All value of θ

(B) θ lies in Ist or IVth quadrant only

(C) Not for all value of θ

(D) Always, if $\sec^2\theta - \tan^2\theta = 1$

4-108 The value of $\cos 15^\circ \cos 7\frac{1^\circ}{2} \sin 7\frac{1^\circ}{2}$ is :

[NTSE-2018 (Stage-I) Himachal Pradesh]

(A) $\frac{1}{2}$ (B) $\frac{1}{8}$

(C) $\frac{1}{4}$ (D) $\frac{1}{16}$

4-109 The angle of elevation of plane from a point on the ground is 60°. After 15 sec fight, the elevation changes to 30°. If the plane is flying at a height of $1500\sqrt{3}$ m then speed of the plane is : **[NTSE-2018 (Stage-I) Himachal Pradesh]**

(A) 200 km/h (B) 720 km/h

(C) 425 km/h (D) 600 km/h

4-110 If $(\sin\theta + \text{cosec}\theta)^2 + (\cos\theta + \sec\theta)^2 = \tan^2\theta + \cot^2\theta + k$ then the value of 'k' is : **[NTSE-2018 (Stage-I) Karnataka]**

(A) 9 (B) 7

(C) 4 (D) 3

4-111 If $(3\sin\theta) + (5\cos\theta) = 5$ then the value of $(5\sin\theta) - (3\cos\theta)$ is : **[NTSE-2018 (Stage-I) Karnataka]**

(A) ± 4 (B) ± 3

(C) ± 5 (D) ± 2

4-112 The string of a kite of length 100 m makes an angle of 60° with the horizontal, imagine that there is no slack in the string, the height of the kite from the ground is :

NTSE-2018 (Stage-I) Karnataka]

(A) $50\sqrt{3}$m (B) $100\sqrt{3}$m

(C) $50\sqrt{2}$m (D) 100m

4-113 The tip of a partially broken tree touches the ground at a point 10 m from foot of it and makes an angle of elevation of 30° from the ground. Then, the height of the tree is :

NTSE-2018 (Stage-I) Karnataka]

(A) $\frac{10}{\sqrt{3}}$m (B) $10\sqrt{3}$m

(C) $\frac{20}{\sqrt{3}}$m (D) $\frac{20}{\sqrt{3}}$m

4-114 Shape made by the bisectors of angles of a parallelogram is : **NTSE-2018 (Stage-I) Madhya Prasesh]**

(A) Rectangle (B) Square

(C) Circle (D) Straight line

4-115 Value of $\sec A\,(1 - \sin A)(\sec A + \tan A)$ is :

NTSE-2018 (Stage-I) Madhya Prasesh]

(A) 0 (B) 2

(C) 1 (D) ∞

4-116 Angle of elevation of a tower from a point at a distance of 15 meter from foot of the tower is 60°. Height of tower is :

NTSE-2018 (Stage-I) Madhya Prasesh]

(A) 15 meter (B) $\sqrt{3}$ meter

(C) $15\sqrt{3}$ meter (D) $\frac{15}{\sqrt{3}}$ meter

4-117 Observe the adjoing figure-4.7. From the given information the perimeter of the triangle is given below :

NTSE-2018 (Stage-I) Maharashtra]

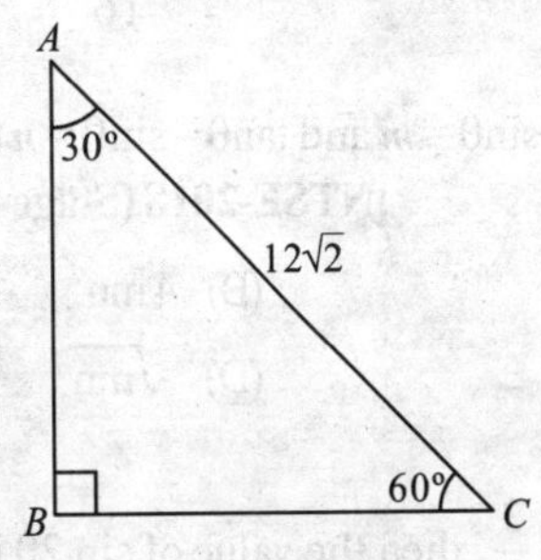

Figure 4.7

(a) $(18\sqrt{2} + 6\sqrt{6})$ (b) $(6\sqrt{3} + 12\sqrt{2})$

(c) $(18 + 6\sqrt{3})\sqrt{2}$ (d) $(18 + 6\sqrt{6})\sqrt{2}$

(A) a and b (B) a and c

(C) c and d (D) Only d

4-118 In ΔPQR $m\angle R = 90^\circ$, $m\angle P = 30^\circ$ $PQ = \sqrt{13}$ from the given information find the value of $\operatorname{cosec}60^\circ - \sec 60^\circ$:

[NTSE-2018 (Stage-I) Maharashtra]

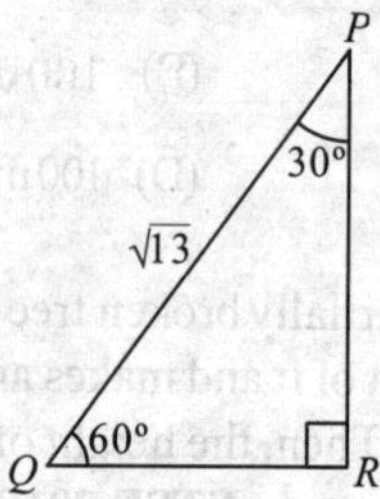

Figure 4.8

(A) 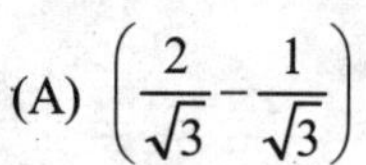 $\left(\frac{2}{\sqrt{3}}-\frac{1}{\sqrt{3}}\right)$
(B) $\left(\frac{\sqrt{13}}{2}-\frac{\sqrt{39}}{2}\right)$
(C) $\left(\frac{\sqrt{39}}{2}-\frac{\sqrt{13}}{2}\right)$
(D) $2\left(\frac{1}{\sqrt{3}}-1\right)$

4-119 If $\tan\theta = \frac{a}{x}$, then the value of $\frac{x}{\sqrt{a^2+x^2}}$ is :

[NTSE-2018 (Stage-I) Tamil Nadu]

(A) $\cos\theta$
(B) $\sin\theta$
(C) $\operatorname{coses}\theta$
(D) $\sec\theta$

4-120 In $\sin^3\theta + \cos^3\theta = 0$, then θ will be :

[NTSE-2018 (Stage-I) Telangana]

(A) 60º
(B) 45º
(C) 0
(D) –45º

4-121 If θ is in the first Quadrant and $\cos\theta = \frac{3}{5}$, then the value of $\frac{5\tan\theta - 4\operatorname{cos\,ec}\theta}{5\sec\theta - 4\cot\theta}$ will be : **[NTSE-2018 (Stage-I) Telangana]**

(A) $\frac{5}{16}$
(B) $\frac{5}{34}$
(C) $-\frac{5}{34}$
(D) $-\frac{5}{16}$

4-122 If $\tan\theta + \sin\theta = m$ and $\tan\theta - \sin\theta = n$ then find the value of $m^2 - n^2$: **[NTSE-2018 (Stage-I) Uttar Pradesh]**

(A) $4\sqrt{mn}$
(B) $4mn$
(C) $2\sqrt{mn}$
(D) $\sqrt{mn}$

4-123 If $\sin\theta = \frac{3}{5}$, then the value of $\sin 2\theta$ is :

[NTSE-2018 (Stage-I) Uttar Pradesh]

(A) $\frac{6}{5}$
(B) $\frac{4}{5}$
(C) $\frac{12}{25}$
(D) $\frac{24}{25}$

4-124 If $\sin\theta - \cos\theta = 0$, then the value of $\sin^4\theta + \cos^4\theta$ will be :

[NTSE-2018 (Stage-I) Uttarakhandh]

(A) 1
(B) $\frac{3}{4}$
(C) $\frac{1}{2}$
(D) $\frac{1}{4}$

4-125 If $\cos(\alpha+\beta) = 0$, then $\sin(\alpha-\beta)$ is equal to :

[NTSE-2018 (Stage-I) Uttarakhandh]

(A) $\cos\beta$
(B) $\cos 2\beta$
(C) $\sin\alpha$
(D) $\sin 2\alpha$

4-126 If $x = a\cos\theta$ and $y = b\sin\theta$ then the value of $(b^2x^2 + a^2y^2)$ will be : **[NTSE-2018 (Stage-I) Uttarakhandh]**

(A) $x^2 + y^2$
(B) $a^2 + b^2$
(C) a^2b^2
(D) ab

4-127 The value of $\tan 1^\circ \tan 2^\circ \tan 3^\circ \ldots \tan 89^\circ$ is :

[NTSE-2013 (Stage-II)]

(A) 0
(B) 1
(C) 2
(D) 3

4-128 If ϕ is an acute angle such that $\tan\phi = \frac{2}{3}$, then evaluate $\left(\frac{1+\tan\phi}{\sin\phi+\cos\phi}\right)\left(\frac{1-\cot\phi}{\sec\phi+\operatorname{cosec}\phi}\right)$: **[NTSE-2014 (Stage-II)]**

(A) $-\frac{1}{5}$
(B) $\frac{-4}{\sqrt{13}}$
(C) $\frac{1}{5}$
(D) $\frac{4}{\sqrt{13}}$

4-129 A person walks towards a tower. Initially when he starts, angle of elevation of the top of the tower is 30°. On travelling 20 metres towards the tower, the angle changes to 60°. How much more he has to travel to reach the tower ?

[NTSE-2015 (Stage-II)]

(A) $10\sqrt{3}$ metres
(B) 10 metres
(C) 20 metres
(D) $\frac{10}{\sqrt{3}}$ metres

4-130 If $\operatorname{cosec} x - \sin x = a$ and $\sec x - \cos x = b$, then :

[NTSE-2015 (Stage-II)]

(A) $(a^2b)^{2/3} + (ab^2)^{2/3} = 1$
(B) $(ab^2)^{2/3} + (a^2b^2)^{2/3} = 1$
(C) $a^2 + b^2 = 1$
(D) $b^2 - a^2 = 1$

4-131 If $\cos^4\theta + \sin^2\theta = m$, then : **[NTSE-2016 (Stage-II)]**

(A) $1 \le m \le 2$
(B) $\frac{1}{2} \le m \le 1$
(C) $\frac{3}{4} \le m \le 1$
(D) $\frac{3}{4} \le m \le \frac{13}{16}$

4-132 ABC is a field in the form of an equilateral triangle. Two vertical poles of heights 45m and 20m are erected at A and B respectively. The angles of elevation of the tops of the two poles from C are complementary to each other. There is a point D on AB such that from it, the angles of elevation of the tops of the two poles are equal. Then AD is equal to :

[NTSE-2016 (Stage-II)]

(A) $17\frac{5}{12}$m (B) $20\frac{10}{13}$m

(C) $20\frac{5}{13}$m (D) $17\frac{10}{12}$m

4-133 The value of $\cos x° - \sin x°$ $(0 \le x < 45)$ is :

[NTSE-2017 (Stage-II)]

(A) 0

(B) Positive

(C) Negative

(D) Sometimes negative and sometimes positive

4-134 A vertical pole of height 10 metres stands at one corner of a rectangular field. The angle of elevation of its top from the farthest corner is 30°, while that from another corner is 60°. The area (in m^2) of rectangular field is : **[NTSE-2017 (Stage-II)]**

(A) $\frac{200\sqrt{2}}{3}$ (B) $\frac{400}{\sqrt{3}}$

(C) $\frac{200\sqrt{2}}{\sqrt{3}}$ (D) $\frac{400\sqrt{2}}{\sqrt{3}}$

* * * * *

ANSWERS

PRACTICE EXERCISE-4.1

1 (D)	2 (C)	3 (A)
4 (A)	5 (D)	6 (D)
7 (C)	8 (B)	9 (C)
10 (C)	11 (C)	12 (D)
13 (C)	14 (D)	15 (D)
16 (B)	17 (A)	18 (B)
19 (B)	20 (B)	21 (C)
22 (C)	23 (B)	24 (D)
25 (C)	26 (A)	27 (D)
28 (B)	29 (B)	30 (B)
31 (B)	32 (B)	33 (C)
34 (B)	35 (D)	36 (B)
37 (C)	38 (B)	39 (B)
40 (D)	41 (C)	42 (D)
43 (B)	44 (A)	45 (B)
46 (C)	47 (D)	48 (C)
49 (A)	50 (C)	

PRACTICE EXERCISE-4.2

1 (D)	2 (B)	3 (A)
4 (B)	5 (B)	6 (C)
7 (C)	8 (B)	9 (A)
10 (B)	11 (C)	12 (D)
13 (D)	14 (B)	15 (D)
16 (B)	17 (B)	18 (C)
19 (A)	20 (A)	21 (C)
22 (C)	23 (C)	24 (D)
25 (D)		

PRACTICE EXERCISE-4.3

1 (A)	2 (C)	3 (B)
4 (D)	5 (B)	6 (D)
7 (C)	8 (A)	9 (C)
10 (D)	11 (C)	12 (B)
13 (A)	14 (C)	15 (D)
16 (A)	17 (B)	18 (D)
19 (C)	20 (D)	21 (D)
22 (B)	23 (C)	24 (B)
25 (B)	26 (C)	27 (B)
28 (D)	29 (D)	30 (B)
31 (C)	32 (A)	33 (D)
34 (C)	35 (C)	36 (C)
37 (D)	38 (B)	39 (A)
40 (D)	41 (A)	42 (A)
43 (A)	44 (B)	45 (A)
46 (B)	47 (A)	48 (C)
49 (D)	50 (C)	51 (D)
52 (D)	53 (D)	54 (B)
55 (C)	56 (A)	57 (B)
58 (A)	59 (B)	60 (A)
61 (A)	62 (B)	63 (A)
64 (C)	65 (D)	66 (B)
67 (A)	68 (C)	69 (C)
70 (C)	71 (D)	72 (B)
73 (B)	74 (D)	75 (B)
76 (B)	77 (A)	78 (C)
79 (B)	80 (B)	81 (B)
82 (B)	83 (B)	84 (B)
85 (C)	86 (A)	87 (A)
88 (C)	89 (B)	90 (C)
91 (A)	92 (B)	93 (B)
94 (A)	95 (B)	96 (B)
97 (B)	98 (A)	99 (A)
100 (B)	101 (C)	102 (A)
103 (D)	104 (C)	105 (A)
106 (A)	107 (A)	108 (B)
109 (B)	110 (B)	111 (B)
112 (A)	113 (B)	114 (A)
115 (C)	116 (C)	117 (B)
118 (D)	119 (A)	120 (D)
121 (A)	122 (A)	123 (D)
124 (C)	125 (B)	126 (C)
127 (B)	128 (A)	129 (B)
130 (A)	131 (C)	132 (B)
133 (B)	134 (A)	

Solutions of PRACTICE EXERCISE-4.1

Sol. 1 (D) Given

$$\sec\theta - \tan\theta = p \quad \ldots(1)$$

Then we have

$$\sec\theta + \tan\theta = \frac{1}{p} \quad \ldots(2)$$

As $\sec^2\theta - \tan^2\theta = 1$

Adding (1) & (2)

$$2\sec\theta = p + \frac{1}{p}$$

$$\Rightarrow \quad \sec\theta = \frac{p^2+1}{2p}$$

$$\Rightarrow \quad \cos\theta = \frac{2p}{p^2+1}$$

Hence Ans is (D)

Sol. 2 (C) Consider

$$\sqrt{\frac{1-\cos\theta}{1+\cos\theta}\times\frac{(1-\cos\theta)}{(1-\cos\theta)}} = \sqrt{\frac{(1-\cos\theta)^2}{1-\cos^2\theta}}$$

$$= \sqrt{\frac{(1-\cos\theta)^2}{\sin^2\theta}} = \frac{1-\cos\theta}{\sin\theta}$$

$$= \frac{1}{\sin\theta} - \frac{\cos\theta}{\sin\theta} = \operatorname{cosec}\theta - \cos\theta$$

Hence Ans is (C)

Sol. 3 (A) Given $\tan 1 . \tan 2 . \tan 3 \ldots\ldots \tan 89°$

$= \tan 1 \tan 2 \ldots\ldots \tan(90-2) \tan(90-1)$

$= \tan 1 \tan 2 \ldots\ldots \cot 2 . \cot 1$

$= (\tan 1 . \cot 1)(\tan 2 . \cot 2) \ldots \tan 45°$

$= 1$

Hence Ans is (A)

Sol. 4 (A) Given $\alpha + \beta = 90° \ \& \ \beta = 2\alpha$

$\Rightarrow \quad 3\alpha = 90$

$\Rightarrow \quad \alpha = 30$

$\Rightarrow \quad \beta = 60$

To find $\cos^2\alpha + \sin^2\beta = \cos^2 30 + \sin^2 60$

$$= \left(\frac{\sqrt{3}}{2}\right)^2 + \left(\frac{\sqrt{3}}{2}\right)^2 = \frac{6}{4} = \frac{3}{2}$$

Hence Ans is (B)

Sol. 5 (D) We know $1° = 0.0175$ radian

Hence Ans is (D)

Sol. 6 (D) By pythagoras theorem we have

$BC = 15$

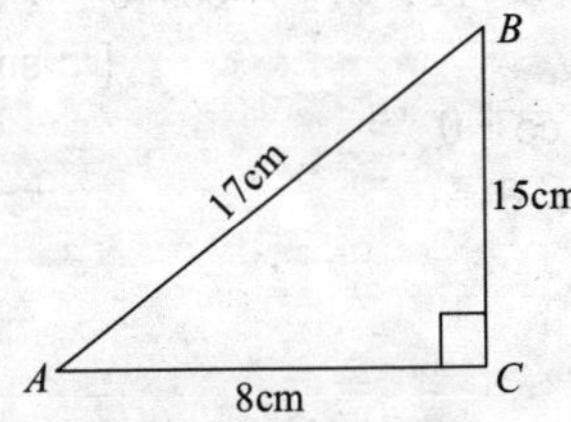

Now $\dfrac{\sin A + \sin B}{\cos A + \cos B} = \dfrac{\frac{15}{17} + \frac{8}{17}}{\frac{8}{17} + \frac{15}{17}} = 1$

Hence Ans is (D)

Sol. 7 (C) Given

$$\sin A = \frac{8}{13}$$

A

13x

8cm

B

8x

C

Then $\quad AC = \sqrt{169x^2 - 64x^2}$

$\Rightarrow \quad AC = \sqrt{105} \cdot x$

$\Rightarrow \quad 8 = x \cdot \sqrt{105}$

$\Rightarrow \quad x = \dfrac{8}{\sqrt{105}}$

$\Rightarrow \quad AB = 13x = \dfrac{13.8}{\sqrt{105}} = \dfrac{104}{\sqrt{105}}$

Hence Ans is (C)

Sol. 8 (B) Given

$\sin^6 A + \cos^6 A + 3\sin^2 A \cos^2 A$

$= \sin^6 A + \cos^6 A + 3\sin^2 A . \cos^2 A(\sin^2 A + \cos^2 A)$

$= (\sin^2 A + \cos^2 A)^3$

$= 1$

Hence Ans is (B)

Sol. 9 (C) Consider

$\sin^2 5° + \sin^2 10° + \sin^2 15° + \ldots + \sin^2 85° + \sin^2 90°$

$= \sin^2 5° + \sin^2 10 + \sin^2 15° + \ldots + \sin^2(90-5) + \sin^2 90°$

$= \sin^2 5° + \sin^2 10° + \sin^2 15° + \ldots + \cos^2 10° + \cos^2 5°$

$= (1 + \ldots 8 \text{ times}) + \sin^2 90° + \sin^2 45°$

$= 8 + 1 + \dfrac{1}{2}$

$\Rightarrow 9.5$

Hence Ans is (C)

Sol. 10 (C) Given expression

$\cos^2\theta + \sec^2\theta$

We know As $\quad AM \geq GM$

$\Rightarrow \quad \dfrac{\cos^2\theta + \sec^2\theta}{2} \geq \sqrt{\cos^2\theta + \sec^2\theta}$

$\Rightarrow \quad \cos^2\theta + \dfrac{1}{\cos^2\theta} \geq 2$

Hence Ans is (C)

Sol. 11 (C) Given

$\alpha + \beta = 90$

and $\quad \sin\alpha = \dfrac{1}{2}$

$\Rightarrow \quad \sin\alpha = \sin 30°$

$\alpha = 30°$

$\Rightarrow \quad \beta = 60°$

$\cos\alpha . \sin\beta - \sin\alpha . \cos\beta$

$\cos 30° \sin 60° - \sin 30° \cos 60°$

$$\frac{\sqrt{3}}{2} . \frac{\sqrt{3}}{2} - \frac{1}{2} . \frac{1}{2} = \frac{3}{4} - \frac{1}{4} = \frac{2}{4} = \frac{1}{2}$$

Hence Ans is (C)

Sol. 12 (D) Given

$$\operatorname{cosec}\theta - \cot\theta = \frac{1}{2} \quad \ldots(1)$$

Now $\quad \operatorname{cosec}\theta + \cot\theta = 2 \quad \ldots(2)$

As $(\operatorname{cosec}^2\theta - \cot^2\theta = 1)$

Adding (1) & (2)

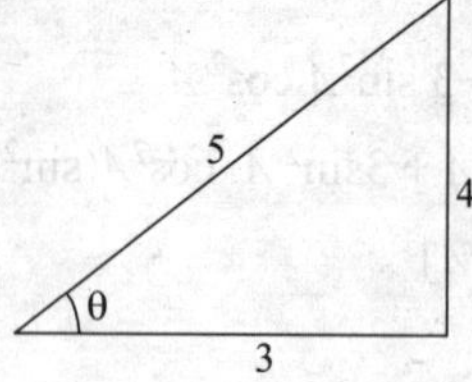

We get

$$2\operatorname{cosec}\theta = 2 + \frac{1}{2} = \frac{5}{2}$$

$$\Rightarrow \quad \operatorname{cosec}\theta = \frac{5}{4}$$

Then $\quad \cos\theta = \frac{3}{5}$

Hence Ans is (D)

Sol. 13 (C) $\operatorname{cosec} A + \cot A = \frac{11}{2} \quad \ldots(1)$

$$\Rightarrow \quad \operatorname{cosec} A - \cot A = \frac{2}{11} \quad \ldots(2)$$

As $\quad \operatorname{cosec}^2 A - \cot^2 A = 1$

Subtract (2) from equation-(1)

We get $\quad 2\cot A = \frac{11}{2} - \frac{2}{11}$

$$\Rightarrow \quad 2\cot A = \frac{121-4}{22} = \frac{117}{22}$$

$$\Rightarrow \quad \cot A = \frac{117}{44}$$

$$\Rightarrow \quad \tan A = \frac{44}{117}$$

Hence Ans is (C)

Sol. 14 (D) We know

$$-1 \le \sin\theta \le 1; -1 \le \cos\theta \le 1$$

$$\operatorname{cosec}\theta \ge 1 \text{ or } \operatorname{cosec}\theta \le 1; \sec\theta \ge 1$$

or $\quad \sec\theta \le -1$

$$-\infty < \tan\theta < \infty \;\&\; -\infty < \cot\theta < \infty$$

Hence Ans is (D)

Sol. 15 (D) $\sin^4\theta + \cos^4\theta + 2\sin^2\theta\cos^2\theta$

$\Rightarrow \quad (\sin^2\theta + \cos^2\theta)^2 = 1$

Hence Ans is (D)

Sol. 16 (B)

(A) $\quad \cos 2A = \sin 3A$

$\quad \cos 2A = \cos(90 - 3A)$

$\Rightarrow \quad 5A = 90$

$\Rightarrow \quad A = 18$

(B) $\quad \cos 3A = \sin 7A$

$\Rightarrow \quad \cos 3A = \cos(90 - 7A)$

$\Rightarrow \quad 10A = 90$

$\Rightarrow \quad A = 9$

(C) $\quad \cot 3A = \tan A$

$\Rightarrow \quad \cot 3A = \cot(90 - A)$

$\Rightarrow \quad 4A = 90$

$\Rightarrow \quad A = 22.5$

(D) $\quad \cot A = \tan 2A$

$\Rightarrow \quad \cot A = \cot(90 - 2A)$

$\Rightarrow \quad 3A = 90$

$\Rightarrow \quad A = 30$

Hence Ans is (B)

Sol. 17 (A) Given $x = r\sin\theta.\cos\phi\, y = r\sin\theta.\sin\phi$

$z = r\cos\theta$

then $x^2 + y^2 + z^2$

$\Rightarrow \quad r^2\sin^2\theta.\cos^2\phi + r^2\sin^2\theta.\sin^2\phi + r^2\cos^2\theta$

$\Rightarrow \quad r^2\sin^2\theta(\cos^2\phi + \sin^2\phi) + r^2\cos^2\theta$

$[\because \sin^2\theta + \cos^2\theta = 1]$

$\Rightarrow \quad r^2\sin^2\theta + r^2\cos^2\theta$

$\Rightarrow \quad r^2(\sin^2\theta + \cos^2\theta)$

$\Rightarrow \quad r^2$

Hence Ans is (A)

Sol. 18 (B) We know that the value of $\sin\theta$ increase from 0° to 90° and $\cos\theta$ decreases from 0° to 90°

$\Rightarrow \quad \cos 66° < \sin 66°$

Hence Ans is (B)

Sol. 19 (B) As we know

$$-\infty < \tan\theta < \infty$$

Where as

$$-1 \le \sin\theta \le 1;$$

$$-1 \le \cos\theta \le 1$$

& $\quad \sec\theta \ge 1 \text{ or } \sec\theta \le -1$

Hence Ans is (B)

Sol. 20 (B) Given $A + B + C = 180°$

then $\quad \sin\left(\frac{B+C}{2}\right) = \sin\left(\frac{180° - A}{2}\right)$

$$= \sin\left(90° - \frac{A}{2}\right)$$

$$= \cos\frac{A}{2}$$

Hence Ans is (B)

Sol. 21 (C) $\sec^4 A - \sec^2 A$

$\Rightarrow \sec^2 A(\sec^2 A - 1)$

$\Rightarrow (1+\tan^2 A)\tan^2 A$

$\Rightarrow \tan^2 A + \tan^4 A$

Hence Ans is (C)

Sol. 22 (C) $\dfrac{\sin\theta}{1-\cot\theta}+\dfrac{\cos\theta}{1-\tan\theta}$

$$\Rightarrow \frac{\sin\theta}{1-\frac{\cos\theta}{\sin\theta}}+\frac{\cos\theta}{1-\frac{\sin\theta}{\cos\theta}}$$

$$\Rightarrow \frac{\sin\theta\cdot\sin\theta}{\sin\theta-\cos\theta}-\frac{\cos^2\theta}{\sin\theta-\cos\theta}$$

$$\Rightarrow \frac{\sin^2\theta-\cos^2\theta}{\sin\theta-\cos\theta}$$

$$\Rightarrow \frac{(\sin\theta-\cos\theta)(\sin\theta+\cos\theta)}{(\sin\theta-\cos\theta)}$$

$\Rightarrow \sin\theta+\cos\theta$

Hence Ans is (C)

Sol. 23 (B) $\dfrac{\cot\theta}{\cot\theta-\cot 3\theta}+\dfrac{\tan\theta}{\tan\theta-\tan 3\theta}$

$$\Rightarrow \frac{\cot\theta}{\cot\theta-\cot 3\theta}+\frac{\frac{1}{\cot\theta}}{\frac{1}{\cot\theta}-\frac{1}{\cot 3\theta}}$$

$$\Rightarrow \frac{\cot\theta}{\cot\theta-\cot 3\theta}+\frac{\cot 3\theta}{\cot 3\theta-\cot\theta}$$

$$\Rightarrow \frac{\cot\theta}{\cot\theta-\cot 3\theta}-\frac{\cot 3\theta}{\cot\theta-\cot 3\theta}$$

Hence Ans is (B)

Sol. 24 (D) By pythagoras theorem

We have

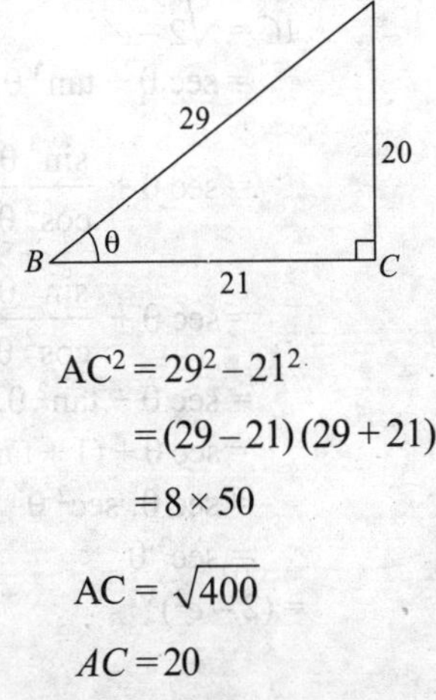

$$AC^2 = 29^2 - 21^2$$

$$=(29-21)(29+21)$$

$$=8\times 50$$

$$AC=\sqrt{400}$$

$$AC=20$$

To find value of

$$\cos^2\theta-\sin^2\theta=\frac{21^2}{29^2}-\frac{20^2}{29^2}$$

$$=\frac{441-400}{841}=\frac{41}{841}$$

Hence Ans is (D)

Sol. 25 (C) $2(\sin^6\theta+\cos^6\theta)-3(\sin^4\theta+\cos^4\theta)$

$= 2[(\sin^2\theta+\cos^2\theta)^3$

$-3\sin^2\theta.\cos^2\theta.(\sin^2\theta+\cos^2\theta)]$

$-3((\sin^2\theta+\cos^2\theta)^2-2\sin^2\theta.\cos^2\theta)$

$=2[1-3\sin^2\theta.\cos^2\theta]-3[1-2\sin^2\theta.\cos^2\theta]$

$=2-6\sin^2\theta.\cos^2\theta-3+6\sin^2\theta.\cos^2\theta$

$=-1$

Hence Ans is (C)

Sol. 26 (A) $a=\dfrac{\sin^2\theta+\cos^2\phi}{2}$

$\sin^2\theta+\cos^2\phi=2a$ ...(1)

& $\dfrac{\cos^2\theta+\sin^2\phi}{2}=b$

$\cos^2\theta+\sin^2\phi=2b$ ...(2)

Adding (1) & (2)

$2=2a+2b$

$\Rightarrow a+b=1$ $[\because \cos^2\theta+\sin^2\theta=1]$

$\Rightarrow b=1-a$

Hence Ans is (A)

Sol. 27 (D) By using identities

Hence Ans is (D)

Sol. 28 (B) $7\sin\alpha=24\cos\alpha$

$$\tan\alpha=\frac{24}{7}$$

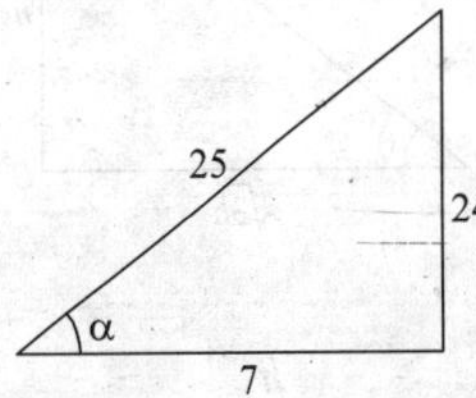

Consider $14\tan\alpha-75\cos\alpha-7\sec\alpha$

$$=14\times\frac{24}{7}-75\cdot\frac{7}{25}-7\cdot\frac{25}{7}$$

$$=48-21-25=2$$

Hence Ans is (B)

Sol. 29 (B) $\sin 5\theta = \cos 4\theta$

$\sin 5\theta = \sin (90 - 4\theta)$

$\Rightarrow \quad 9\theta = 90°$

$\Rightarrow \quad \theta = 10°$

Consider $\quad 2 \sin 3\theta - \sqrt{3} \tan 3\theta$

$= 2 \sin 3 \times 10° - \sqrt{3} . \tan 3 \times 10°$

$= 2 \sin 30° - \sqrt{3} . \tan 30°$

$= 2 \times \frac{1}{2} - \sqrt{3} \cdot \frac{1}{\sqrt{3}} = 0$

Hence Ans is (B)

Sol. 30 (B) Given $\cos^2 17° - \sin^2 73°$

$= \cos^2 17° - \sin^2 (90 - 17)$

$= \cos^2 17° - \cos^2 17° = 0$

Hence Ans is (B)

Sol. 31 (B) Given

$$\frac{x}{a} \cos\theta + \frac{y}{b} \sin\theta = 1 \quad \ldots(1)$$

$$\frac{x}{a} \sin\theta - \frac{y}{b} \cos\theta = 1 \quad \ldots(2)$$

Squaring (1) and (2) & then add

$$\frac{x^2}{a^2} (\cos^2\theta + \sin^2\theta) + \frac{y^2}{b^2} (\sin^2\theta + \cos^2\theta) = 2$$

$$\frac{x^2}{a^2} + \frac{y^2}{b^2} = 2$$

Hence Ans is (B)

Sol. 32 (B) Let AB = tower of height 'h' and BC be it's shadow

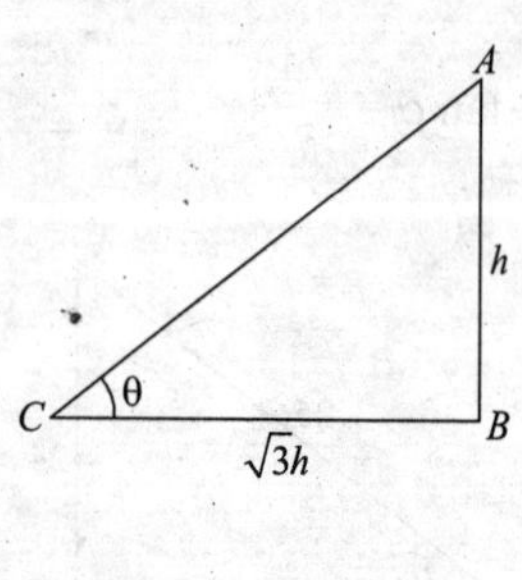

$$\tan\theta = \frac{h}{\sqrt{3}h}$$

$\Rightarrow \quad \tan\theta = \frac{1}{\sqrt{3}}$

$\Rightarrow \quad \theta = 30°$

Hence Ans is (B)

Sol. 33 (C) We have to check options In option (C)

$(\text{cosec } \theta)^{-1} = \sin\theta$

$$\frac{1}{\text{cosec } \theta} = \sin\theta$$

Hence Ans is (C)

Sol. 34 (B) Given

$3\cos^2 30° + \sec^2 30° + 2 \cos 0° + 3 \sin 90° - \tan^2 60°$

$= 3 \cdot \frac{3}{4} + \frac{4}{3} + 2 + 3 - 3$

$= \frac{9}{4} + \frac{4}{3} + 2 = \frac{27 + 16 + 24}{12} = \frac{67}{12}$

Hence Ans is (B)

Sol. 35 (D) $\sqrt{\frac{1 - \cos^2\theta}{1 + \cot^2\theta}}$

$= \sqrt{\frac{\sin^2\theta}{\text{cosec}^2\theta}}$

$= \sqrt{\sin^4\theta}$

$= \sin^2\theta$

Hence Ans is (D)

Sol. 36 (B) Given $\quad \tan^2\theta = 1 - e^2$

$\tan\theta = \sqrt{1 - e^2}$

By pythagoras theorem

$AC^2 = AB^2 + BC^2$

$= 1 - e^2 + 1$

$AC^2 = 2 - e^2$

$AC = \sqrt{2 - e^2}$

Consider

$= \sec\theta + \tan^3\theta . \text{cosec } \theta$

$= \sec\theta + \frac{\sin^3\theta}{\cos^3\theta} \cdot \frac{1}{\sin\theta}$

$= \sec\theta + \frac{\sin^2\theta}{\cos^2\theta} \cdot \frac{1}{\cos\theta}$

$= \sec\theta + \tan^2\theta . \sec\theta$

$= \sec\theta + (1 + \tan^2\theta)$

$= \sec\theta . \sec^2\theta$

$= \sec^3\theta$

$= (2 - e^2)^{3/2}$

Hence Ans is (B)

Sol. 37 (C) $\tan 20° \tan 32° \tan 45° \tan 58° \tan 70°$

$= \tan 20° \tan 32° \tan 45° \cot 32° \cot 70°$

$= (\tan 20° \cot 70°)(\tan 32° \cot 32°) \tan 45°$

As $\tan \theta \cot \theta = 1$

and $\tan 45° = 1$

$= 1 \times 1 \times 1$

$= 1$

Hence Ans is (C)

Sol. 38 (B) Given $\operatorname{cosec} \theta - \sin \theta = x$

$$x = \frac{1}{\sin \theta} - \sin \theta$$

$$x = \frac{1 - \sin^2 \theta}{\sin \theta}$$

$$x = \frac{\cos^2 \theta}{\sin \theta}$$

Similarly $y = \dfrac{\sin^2 \theta}{\cos \theta}$

Now $x^2y^2 (x^2 + y^2 + 3)$

$$\frac{\cos^4 \theta}{\sin^2 \theta} \cdot \frac{\sin^4 \theta}{\cos^2 \theta} \left(\frac{\cos^4 \theta}{\sin^2 \theta} + \frac{\sin^4 \theta}{\cos^2 \theta} + 3 \right)$$

$$= \cos^2 \theta . \sin^2 \theta \left(\frac{\cos^4 \theta}{\sin^2 \theta} + \frac{\sin^4 \theta}{\cos^2 \theta} + 3 \right)$$

$= (\cos^6 \theta + \sin^6 \theta + 3 \sin^2 \theta \cos^2 \theta)$

$= \cos^6 \theta + \sin^6 \theta + 3 \sin^2 \theta \cos^2 \theta (\sin^2\theta + \cos^2\theta)$

$= (\cos^2 \theta + \sin^2 \theta)^3 = 1$

Hence Ans is (B)

Sol. 39 (B) Consider $\cos 1° \cos 2° \cos 3° \ldots \cos 179° = 0$

As $\cos 90° = 0$

Hence Ans is (B)

Sol. 40 (D) Given

$\theta_1 + \theta_2 = 90°$

$x + y = 1$

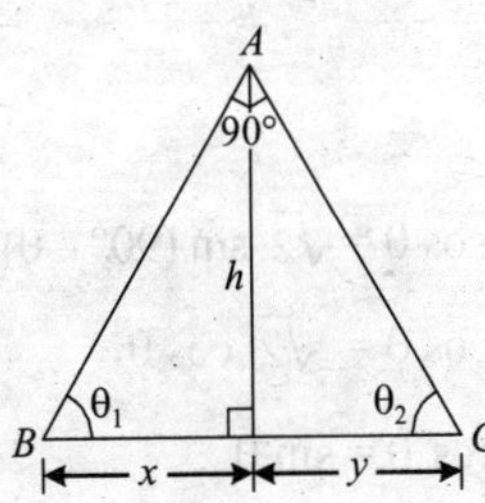

Then $\tan \theta_1 = \dfrac{h}{x}$ ...(1)

$\tan \theta_2 = \dfrac{h}{y}$

$\tan (90 - \theta_1) = \dfrac{h}{y}$

$\cot \theta_1 = \dfrac{h}{y}$ ...(2)

Multiply (1) and (2)

$$\tan \theta_1 . \cot \theta = \frac{h}{x} \cdot \frac{h}{y}$$

$$1 = \frac{h^2}{xy}$$

As $\tan \theta . \cot \theta = 1$

$h^2 = xy = h = \sqrt{xy}$

$\Rightarrow$ $h = \sqrt{x(1-x)} = \sqrt{y(1-y)}$

Hence Ans is (D)

Sol. 41 (C) Let $z = \sin \theta + \cos \theta$

$\Rightarrow$ $z^2 = 1 + \sin 2\theta$

Since $0 < \theta < 90°$

So $\sin 2\theta < 1$,

so that $z^2 < 2$,

Thus $z < \sqrt{2}$

i.e., z is greater than 1

Hence Ans is (C)

Sol. 42 (D) Go through options and verify

Hence Ans is (D)

Sol. 43 (B) $\sin \theta - \cos \theta = 0$

$\Rightarrow$ $\sin \theta = \cos \theta$

$\Rightarrow$ $\tan \theta = 1$

$\Rightarrow$ $\theta = \dfrac{\pi}{4}$

Hence Ans is (B)

Sol. 44 (A) $a^3 + b^3 = (a + b)^3 - 3ab(a + b)$

Let $a = \sin^2 \theta$,

$b = \cos^2 \theta$,

So that $a + b = \sin^2 \theta + \cos^2 \theta = 1$

$\Rightarrow$ $\sin^6 \theta + \cos^6 \theta = 1 - 3 \sin^2 \theta \cos^2 \theta$

Hence Ans is (A)

Sol. 45 (B) $\cos x = \dfrac{1}{P}$ and $\sin x = \dfrac{1}{Q}$

$1 = \cos^2 x + \sin^2 x$

$\Rightarrow$ $1 = \dfrac{1}{P^2} + \dfrac{1}{Q^2}$

$\Rightarrow$ $P^2 + Q^2 = P^2Q^2$

Hence Ans is (B)

Sol. 46 (C) Go through options and verify

Hint : $\sin\theta = \frac{3}{5}$ and $\text{cosec}\,\theta = \frac{5}{3}$

Hence Ans is (C)

Sol. 47 (D) By definition

Hence Ans is (D)

Sol. 48 (C) Given

$$\frac{\cot 40°}{\tan 50°} - \frac{1}{2}\frac{\cos 35°}{\sin 55°}$$

$$= \frac{\cot(90-50)}{\tan 50} - \frac{1}{2}\frac{\cos(90-55°)}{\sin 55°}$$

$$= \frac{\tan 50}{\tan 50} - \frac{1}{2}\frac{\sin 55°}{\sin 55°}$$

$$= 1 - \frac{1}{2}$$

$$= \frac{1}{2}$$

Hence Ans is (C)

Sol. 49 (A) $-\sqrt{a^2+b^2} \le a\cos\theta + b\sin\theta \le \sqrt{a^2+b^2}$

Here $-\sqrt{2} \le \cos\theta + \sin\theta \le \sqrt{2}$

Hence Ans is (A)

Sol. 50 (C) As we know

$$\tan\frac{\pi}{4} = 1$$

and $$\tan\frac{\pi}{3} = \sqrt{3}$$

By observation we can say

$$\tan\theta = \sqrt{2}$$

$$\Rightarrow \quad \frac{\pi}{4} < \theta < \frac{\pi}{3}$$

Hence Ans is (C)

Solutions of PRACTICE EXERCISE-4.2

Sol. 1 (D) Given $\tan\theta + \cot\theta = 2$

$$\Rightarrow \quad \tan\theta + \frac{1}{\tan\theta} = 2$$

$$\Rightarrow \quad \tan^2\theta + 1 = 2\tan\theta$$

$$\Rightarrow \quad (\tan\theta - 1)^2 = 0$$

$$\Rightarrow \quad \tan\theta = 1$$

$$\Rightarrow \quad \theta = 45°$$

$$\Rightarrow \quad \tan^6 45° + \cot^6 45° = 1 + 1 = 2$$

Hence Ans is (D)

Sol. 2 (B) Given $\dfrac{\cot\theta}{\cot\theta - \cot 3\theta} + \dfrac{\tan\theta}{\tan\theta - \tan 3\theta}$

$$= \frac{\cot\theta}{\cot\theta - \cot 3\theta} + \frac{\frac{1}{\cot\theta}}{\frac{\cot 3\theta - \cot\theta}{\cot\theta \cdot \cot 3\theta}}$$

$$= \frac{\cot\theta}{\cot\theta - \cot 3\theta} - \frac{\cot 3\theta}{\cot\theta - \cot 3\theta}$$

$$= 1$$

Hence Ans is (B)

Sol. 3 (A) Given $(1 + \tan\alpha\tan\beta)^2 + (\tan\alpha - \tan\beta)^2$

$= 1 + \tan^2\alpha.\ \tan^2\beta + 2\tan\alpha.\ \tan\beta + \tan^2\alpha$

$+ \tan^2\beta - 2\tan\alpha.\ \tan\beta$

$= (1 + \tan^2\alpha) + \tan^2\beta(1 + \tan^2\alpha)$

$= \sec^2\alpha.\ \sec^2\beta$

Hence Ans is (A)

Sol. 4 (B) Let

$E = \sin\theta\cos\theta$

$$\Rightarrow \quad E = \frac{1}{2}\,2\sin\theta.\cos\theta$$

$$\Rightarrow \quad E = \frac{1}{2}\sin 2\theta$$

Since $-1 \le \sin 2\theta \le 1$

So greatest value of $E = \sin$ of $\cos\theta$ is $\frac{1}{2}$.

Hence Ans is (B)

Sol. 5 (B) Given $\dfrac{\tan^2 A}{\cos^2 B} - \dfrac{\sec^2 A}{\cot^2 B}$

$= \tan^2 A.\ \sec^2 B - \sec^2 A.\ \tan^2 B$

$= \tan^2 A.(1 + \tan^2 B) - (1 + \tan^2 A).\ \tan^2 B$

$= \tan^2 A + \tan^2 A\ .\ \tan^2 B - \tan^2 B - \tan^2 A.\ \tan^2 B$

$= \tan^2 A - \tan^2 B$

Hence Ans is (B)

Sol. 6 (C) Given

$$\sin\theta + \cos\theta = \sqrt{2}\sin(90° - \theta)$$

$$\Rightarrow \quad \sin\theta + \cos\theta = \sqrt{2}\cos\theta$$

$$\Rightarrow \quad (\sqrt{2} - 1)\cos\theta = \sin\theta$$

$$\Rightarrow \quad \tan\theta = \sqrt{2} - 1$$

$$\Rightarrow \quad \tan\theta = \frac{1}{\sqrt{2} + 1}$$

Hence Ans is (C)

Sol. 7 (C) Let $A \equiv (\sin\theta, \sec\theta)$

$B \equiv (\sin\theta - \cos\theta, \cos\theta)$

$C \equiv (-\cos\theta, \cos\theta - \sin\theta)$

$ar \text{ of } \Delta ABC = 0$

$$\frac{1}{2}\begin{vmatrix} \sin\theta & \sec\theta \\ \sin\theta - \cos\theta & \cos\theta \\ -\cos\theta & \cos\theta - \sin\theta \\ -\sin\theta & \sec\theta \end{vmatrix} = 0$$

$$\frac{1}{2}[\sin\theta.\cos\theta - (\sin\theta - \cos\theta)^2 - \cos\theta.\sec\theta$$

$$(\sin\theta.\cos\theta - \sin^2\theta - \cos^2\theta + \tan\theta - 1)] = 0$$

$\Rightarrow$ $\sin\theta - \cos\theta - 1 + 2\sin\theta.\cos\theta - \cos\theta.\sec\theta$

$-\sin\theta \times \cos\theta + 1 - \tan\theta + 1 = 0$

$\Rightarrow$ $-1 + 2\sin\theta.\cos\theta - 1 + 1 - \tan\theta + 1 = 0$

$2\sin\theta.\cos\theta - \tan\theta = 0$

$\Rightarrow$ $\sin\theta\left[2\cos\theta - \frac{1}{\cos\theta}\right] = 0$

$\Rightarrow$ $\tan\theta\,(2\cos^2\theta - 1) = 0$

$\Rightarrow$ $\tan\theta = 0$

or $2\cos^2\theta - 1 = 0$

$\Rightarrow$ $\cos^2\theta = \frac{1}{2}$

$\theta = 0°$ or $\cos\theta = \frac{1}{\sqrt{2}}$

$\theta = 45°$

Hence Ans is (C)

Sol. 8 (B) $\frac{y+1}{1-y} = \sqrt{\frac{1+\sin\theta}{1-\sin\theta}}$

Multiply by $\sqrt{(1+\sin\theta)}$ in numerator & denominator of RHS

$$\frac{1+y}{1-y} = \frac{1+\sin\theta}{\cos\theta}$$

Apply compondo dividendo

We get $\frac{2}{2y} = \frac{1+\sin\theta+\cos\theta}{1+\sin\theta-\cos\theta}$

$$y = \frac{1+\sin\theta-\cos\theta}{1+\sin\theta+\cos\theta}$$

Divide each term by $\sin\theta$

$$y = \frac{\text{cosec}\,\theta - \cot\theta + 1}{\text{cosec}\,\theta + \cot\theta + 1}$$

$$= \frac{(\text{cosec}\,\theta - \cot\theta) + (\text{cosec}^2\theta - \cot^2\theta)}{\text{cosec}\,\theta + \cot\theta + 1}$$

$[\because \text{cosec}^2\theta - \cot^2\theta = 1]$

$$= \frac{(\text{cosec}\,\theta - \cot\theta) \times (1 + \text{cosec}\,\theta + \cot\theta)}{(\text{cosec}\,\theta + \cot\theta + 1)}$$

$$= \frac{1-\cos\theta}{\sin\theta} \times \frac{(1+\cos\theta)}{1+\cos\theta} = \frac{\sin\theta}{1+\cos\theta}$$

Hence Ans is (B)

Sol. 9 (A) $a\cos A - b\sin A = c$

Squaring

$\Rightarrow$ $a^2\cos^2 A + b^2\sin^2 A - 2ab\cos A\sin A = c^2$

$\Rightarrow$ $a^2(1 - \sin^2 A) + b^2(1 - \cos^2 A) - 2ab\cos A\sin A = c^2$

$\Rightarrow$ $a^2 + b^2 - c^2 = a^2\sin^2 A + b^2\cos^2 A + 2ab\cos A\sin A$

$\Rightarrow$ $(a\sin A + b\cos A)^2 = [a^2 + b^2 - c^2]$

$\Rightarrow$ $(a\sin A + b\cos A) = \pm\sqrt{a^2 + b^2 - c^2}$

Hence Ans is (A)

Sol. 10 (B) Given

$$\tan x = \frac{m}{m+1} \quad \text{and} \quad \tan y = \frac{1}{(2m+1)}$$

We know

$$\tan(x+y) = \frac{\tan x + \tan y}{1 - \tan x \cdot \tan y}$$

$$= \frac{\frac{m}{m+1} + \frac{1}{2m+1}}{1 - \frac{m}{m+1}\cdot\frac{1}{2m+1}}$$

$$= \frac{2m^2 + m + m + 1}{2m^2 + 2m + m + 1 - m}$$

$$= \frac{2m^2 + 2m + 1}{2m^2 + 2m + 1}$$

$\tan(x+y) = 1$

$\Rightarrow$ $\tan(x+y) = \tan 45$

$x + y = 45°$

Hence Ans is (B)

Sol. 11 (C) We have $\sin x + \cos x$

$$-\sqrt{a^2+b^2} \le a\sin x + b\cos x \le \sqrt{a^2+b^2}$$

$\Rightarrow$ $-\sqrt{2} \le \sin x + \cos x \le \sqrt{2}$

So maximum value is $\sqrt{2}$

Hence Ans is (C)

Sol. 12 (D) We know

$$-1 \le \cos 2x \le 1$$

$$-1 + 1 \le 1 + \cos 2x \le 1 + 1$$

$$0 \le 1 + \cos 2x \le 2$$

Hence Ans is (D)

Sol. 13 (D) Consider $\dfrac{1}{\sin 10^\circ} - \dfrac{\sqrt{3}}{\cos 10^\circ}$

$$= \frac{\cos 10^\circ - \sqrt{3}\sin 10^\circ}{\sin 10^\circ \cdot \cos 10^\circ}$$

$$= \frac{2\left[\frac{1}{2}\cos 10^\circ - \frac{\sqrt{3}}{2}\cdot \sin 10^\circ\right]}{\frac{1}{2}\sin 20^\circ}$$

$$= \frac{2\times 2[\sin 30^\circ \cos 10^\circ - \cos 30^\circ \sin 10^\circ]}{\sin 20^\circ}$$

$$= \frac{4\cdot \sin 20}{\sin 20} = 4$$

Hence Ans is (D)

Sol. 14 (B) Given

$$\sin x + \sin y = a$$

$$\Rightarrow \quad 2\sin\left(\frac{x+y}{2}\right)\cos\left(\frac{x-y}{2}\right) = a \quad \ldots(1)$$

$$\Rightarrow \quad \cos x + \cos y = b$$

$$\Rightarrow \quad 2\cos\frac{x+y}{2}\cos\left(\frac{x-y}{2}\right) = b \quad \ldots(2)$$

Divide (1) by (2)

$$\frac{2\sin\left(\frac{x+y}{2}\right)\cdot\cos\left(\frac{x-y}{2}\right)}{2\cos\left(\frac{x+y}{2}\right)\cdot\cos\left(\frac{x-y}{2}\right)} = \frac{a}{b}$$

$$\Rightarrow \quad \tan\frac{(x+y)}{2} = \frac{a}{b}$$

$$\Rightarrow \quad \sin(x+y) = \frac{2\tan\left(\frac{x+y}{2}\right)}{1+\tan^2\left(\frac{x+y}{2}\right)}$$

$$\Rightarrow \quad \sin(x+y) = \frac{2\frac{a}{b}}{1+\frac{a^2}{b^2}}$$

$$\sin(x+y) = \frac{2ab}{a^2+b^2}$$

Hence Ans is (B)

Sol. 15 (D) Let $AB = 2h$ & $DC = h$

$$BE = ED = \frac{a}{2}$$

$$\angle AED = \theta$$

Then $\angle CED = 90 - \theta$

$$\tan\theta = \frac{2h}{a/2} \quad \ldots(1)$$

& $$\tan(90-\theta) = \frac{h}{a/2} \quad \ldots(2)$$

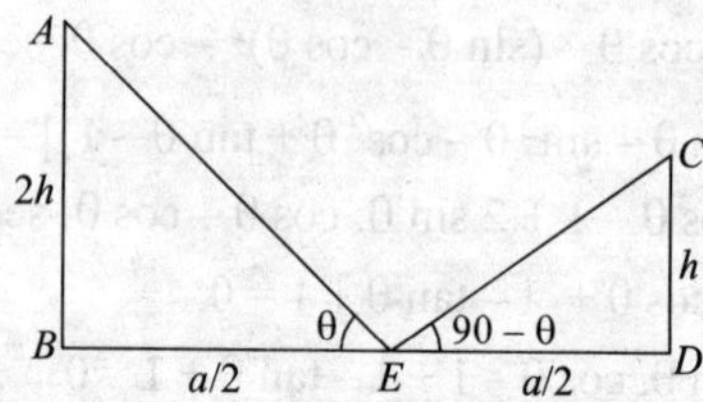

Multiply (1) × (2)

$$\tan\theta.\tan(90-\theta) = \frac{2h}{a/2}\cdot\frac{h}{a/2}$$

$$\Rightarrow \quad \tan\theta.\cot\theta = \frac{2h^2}{(a/2)^2}$$

$$\Rightarrow \quad 1 = \frac{2h^2}{(a/2)^2}$$

$$\Rightarrow \quad (a/2)^2 = 2h^2$$

$$\Rightarrow \quad h = \frac{a}{2\sqrt{2}}$$

Hence Ans is (D)

Sol. 16 (B) In ΔOCA

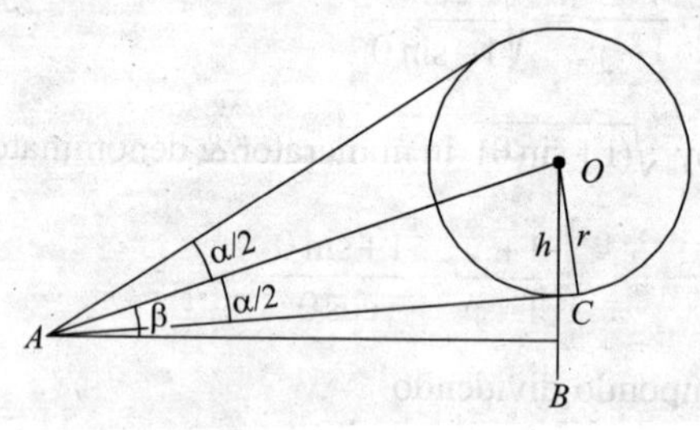

$$\frac{OC}{OA} = \sin\frac{\alpha}{2}$$

$$\frac{r}{OA} = \sin\frac{\alpha}{2}$$

$$OA = r\,\text{cosec}\,\frac{\alpha}{2}$$

In ΔOBA $\dfrac{OB}{OA} = \sin\beta$

$$OB = OA\sin\beta$$

$$= r\,\text{cosec}\,\frac{\alpha}{2}\sin\beta$$

Hence Ans is (B)

Sol. 17 (B) Let BC be a house & AD be a tower

Let $CD = EB = x$

Let the height of the tower be H

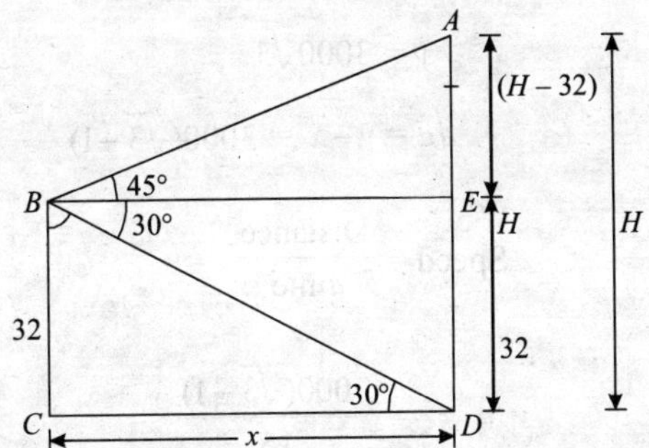

In ΔBCD

$$\tan 30 = \frac{32}{x}$$

$$x = 32\sqrt{3}$$

Hence Ans is (B)

Sol. 18 (C) In ΔAED

Let 'h' be the height of the tower

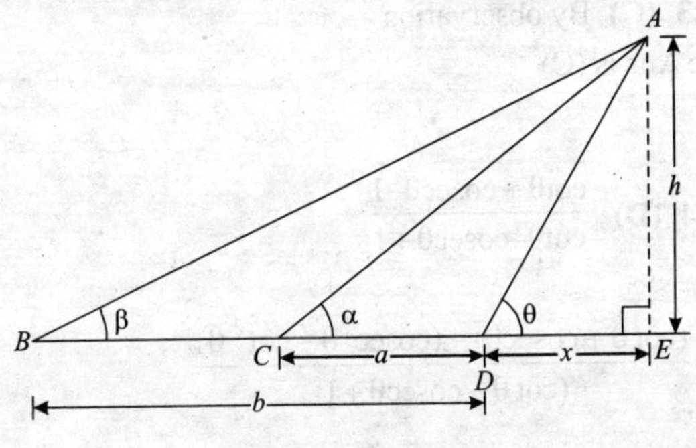

$$\cot\theta = \frac{x}{h} \quad \ldots(1)$$

In ΔAEC $$\cot\alpha = \frac{x+a}{h} \quad \ldots(2)$$

In ΔAEB $$\cot\beta = \frac{x+b}{h} \quad \ldots(3)$$

(3) – (2)

$$\cot\beta - \cot\alpha = \frac{b-a}{h}$$

$$h = \frac{(b-a)}{\cot\beta - \cot\alpha} \quad \ldots(4)$$

Dividing (2) by (3)

$$\frac{\cot\alpha}{\cot\beta} = \frac{x+a}{x+b}$$

$$x\cot\alpha + b\cot\alpha = x\cot\beta + a\cot\beta$$

$$x(\cot\beta - \cot\alpha) = b\cot\alpha - a\cot\beta$$

$$x = \frac{b\cot\alpha - a\cot\beta}{\cot\beta - \cot\alpha} \quad \ldots(5)$$

$$\cot\theta = \frac{x}{h} = \frac{\dfrac{b\cot\alpha - a\cot\beta}{(\cot\beta - \cot\alpha)}}{\dfrac{(b-a)}{(\cot\beta - \cot\alpha)}}$$

$$\cot\theta = \frac{b\cot\alpha - a\cot\beta}{(b-a)}$$

Hence Ans is (C)

Sol. 19 (A) Given A, B, C are in A.P.

$$2B = A + C$$

$$A + B + C = 180°$$

$$3B = 180°$$

$$B = 60°$$

& also given

$$\sin(2A + B) = \frac{1}{2}$$

$$2A + B = 30° \text{ or } 150$$

$$2A + 60 = 150$$

$$2A = 90$$

$$A = 45°$$

$$C = 75°$$

Now $$\sin(B + 2C) = \sin(60 + 150)$$

$$= \sin(210)$$

$$= \sin(180 + 30°)$$

$$= -\sin 30°$$

$$= -\frac{1}{2}$$

Hence Ans is (A)

Sol. 20 (A) Given $8x^2 - 25x + 15 = 0 \left\langle \begin{array}{l}\tan\frac{\alpha}{2} \\ \tan\frac{\beta}{2}\end{array}\right.$

$$\tan\frac{\alpha}{2} + \tan\frac{\beta}{2} = \frac{26}{8} = \frac{13}{4}$$

$$\tan\frac{\alpha}{2} \times \tan\frac{\beta}{2} = \frac{15}{8} = \frac{15}{8}$$

$$\tan\left(\frac{\alpha+\beta}{2}\right) = \frac{\tan\frac{\alpha}{2} + \tan\frac{\beta}{2}}{1 - \tan\frac{\alpha}{2}\cdot\tan\frac{\beta}{2}}$$

$$= \frac{13/4}{1 - \frac{15}{8}} = \frac{13/4}{-\frac{7}{8}}$$

$$= \frac{13}{4} \times \frac{-8}{7} = \frac{-26}{7}$$

$$\cos(\alpha+\beta) = \frac{1-\tan^2\frac{\alpha+\beta}{2}}{1+\tan^2\left(\frac{\alpha+\beta}{2}\right)}$$

$$= \frac{1-\frac{676}{49}}{1+\frac{676}{49}}$$

$$= \frac{49-676}{49+676} = \frac{-627}{725}$$

Hence Ans is (A)

Sol. 21 (C) $|\tan A| < 1; -1 < \tan A < 1$

$$-\frac{\pi}{4} < A < \frac{\pi}{4}; 0 < |A| < \frac{\pi}{4}$$

Now $\dfrac{\sqrt{1+\sin 2A}+\sqrt{1-\sin 2A}}{\sqrt{1+\sin 2A}-\sqrt{1-\sin 2A}}$

$$= \frac{\sqrt{\cos^2 A+\sin^2 A+2\sin A\cos A} + \sqrt{\cos^2 A+\sin^2 A-2\sin A\cos A}}{\sqrt{\cos^2 A+\sin^2 A+2\sin A\cos A} - \sqrt{\cos^2 A+\sin^2 A-2\sin A\cos A}}$$

$$= \frac{\sqrt{(\cos A+\sin A)^2}+\sqrt{(\cos A-\sin A)^2}}{\sqrt{(\cos A+\sin A)^2}-\sqrt{(\cos A-\sin A)^2}}$$

$$= \frac{\cos A+\sin A+\cos A-\sin A}{\cos A+\sin A-(\cos A-\sin A)}$$

$$= \frac{2\cos A}{2\sin A} = \cot A$$

Hence Ans is (C)

Sol. 22 (C) Let A & E be the position of the aeroplane

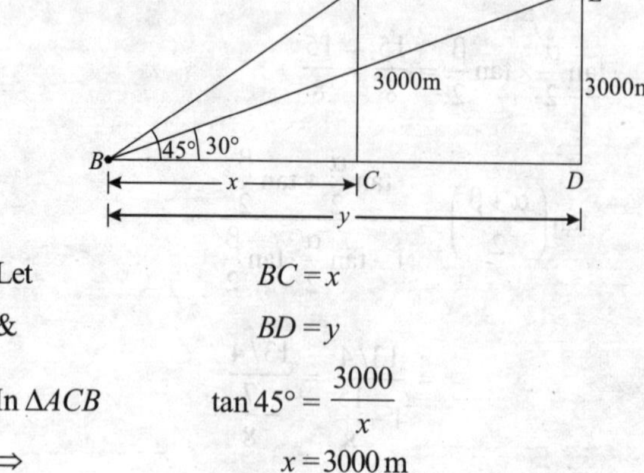

Let $BC = x$

& $BD = y$

In ΔACB $\tan 45° = \dfrac{3000}{x}$

$\Rightarrow$ $x = 3000\,\text{m}$

In ΔEDB $\tan 30° = \dfrac{3000}{y}$

$\Rightarrow$ $y = 3000\sqrt{3}$

$$AE = y - x = 3000(\sqrt{3}-1)$$

$$\text{Speed} = \frac{\text{Distance}}{\text{time}}$$

$$= \frac{3000(\sqrt{3}-1)}{15}$$

$$= 200(\sqrt{3}-1) \text{ m/s}$$

$$= 200(\sqrt{3}-1) \times \frac{18}{5} \text{ km/h}$$

$$= 40 \times 18(0.732) = 527$$

Hence Ans is (C)

Sol. 23 (C) By observation

Hence Ans is (C)

Sol. 24 (D) $\dfrac{\cot\theta+\text{cosec}\theta-1}{\cot\theta-\text{cosec}\theta+1}$

$$= \frac{(\cot\theta+\text{cosec}\theta)-(\text{cosec}^2\theta-\cot^2\theta)}{(\cot\theta-\text{cosec}\theta+1)}$$

$[\because \text{cosec}^2\theta - \cot^2\theta = 1]$

$$= \frac{(\cot\theta+\text{cosec}\theta)-(\text{cosec}\theta-\cot\theta)(\text{cosec}\theta+\cot\theta)}{(\cot\theta-\text{cosec}\theta+1)}$$

$$= \frac{(\cot\theta+\text{cosec}\theta)[1-\text{cosec}\theta+\cot\theta]}{(\cot\theta-\text{cosec}\theta+1)}$$

$$= \cot\theta + \text{cosec}\,\theta$$

$$= \frac{\cos\theta}{\sin\theta} + \frac{1}{\sin\theta} = \frac{1+\cos\theta}{\sin\theta}$$

Hence Ans is (D)

Sol. 25 (D) $\sin\theta_1 + \sin\theta_2 + \sin\theta_3 = 3$

$\Rightarrow$ $\theta_1 = \theta_2 = \theta_3 = 90°$

As $-1 \le \sin\theta \le 1$

Then $\cos\theta_1 + \cos\theta_2 + \cos\theta_3 = 0$

Hence Ans is (D)

Solutions of PRACTICE EXERCISE-4.3

Sol. 1 (A) We have,

$$\sin(A+B)=\frac{\sqrt{3}}{2}$$

$$\Rightarrow \quad \sin(A+B)=\sin 60^\circ$$

$$\Rightarrow \quad A+B=60^\circ \quad \ldots(1)$$

$$\cos(A-B)=\frac{\sqrt{3}}{2}$$

$$\Rightarrow \quad \cos(A-B)=\cos 30^\circ \quad \ldots(2)$$

$$\Rightarrow \quad A-B=30^\circ$$

On solving (1) & (2)

We get $\quad A=45^\circ, B=15^\circ$

Hence Ans is (A)

Sol. 2 (C) Length of shadow decreases as angle of elevation of sun increases 0° to 90°

Hence Ans is (C)

Sol. 3 (B) Consider

$$\left(1+\frac{\sin\theta}{\cos\theta}+\frac{1}{\cos\theta}\right)\left(1+\frac{\cos\theta}{\sin\theta}+\frac{1}{\sin\theta}\right)$$

$$=\left(\frac{\cos\theta+\sin\theta+1}{\cos\theta}\right)\left(\frac{\sin\theta+\cos\theta-1}{\sin\theta}\right)$$

$$=\frac{\cos^2\theta+\sin^2\theta+2\sin\theta\cdot\cos\theta-1}{\cos\theta\cdot\sin\theta}=2$$

Hence Ans is (B)

Sol. 4 (D) We have,

$$\sin\theta-\cos\theta=\sqrt{2}\sin(90-\theta)$$

$$\sin\theta-\cos\theta=\sqrt{2}\cos\theta$$

$$\sin\theta=(\sqrt{2}+1)\cos\theta$$

$$\tan\theta=\sqrt{2}+1$$

Hence Ans is (D)

Sol. 5 (B) Given $\quad a\cos\theta-b\sin\theta=c$

Let $\quad a\sin\theta+b\cos\theta=x$

Squaring and adding

$$a^2+b^2=c^2+x^2$$

$$x=\pm\sqrt{a^2+b^2-c^2}$$

Hence Ans is (B)

Sol. 6 (D)

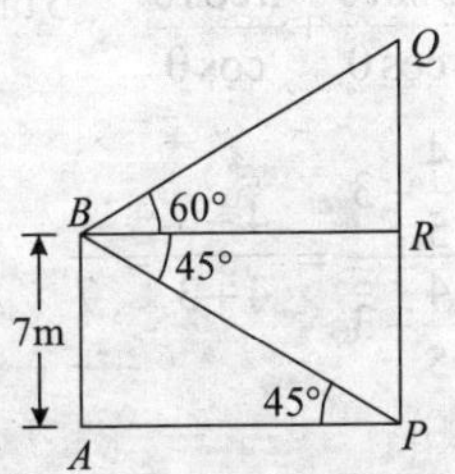

$$BR=AP=7$$

$$\tan 60^\circ=\frac{x}{7} \text{ where } x=QR$$

$$\sqrt{3}=\frac{x}{7} \Rightarrow 7\sqrt{3}=x$$

$$PQ=7\sqrt{3}+7=7(\sqrt{3}+1)$$

Hence Ans is (D)

Sol. 7 (C) Consider

$$\tan 43^\circ \tan 45^\circ \tan 47^\circ$$

$$=\tan 43^\circ\times 1\times\tan(90^\circ-43^\circ)$$

$$=\tan 43^\circ\times 1\times\cot 43^\circ$$

$$=1 \qquad (\because \tan\theta.\cot\theta=1)$$

Hence Ans is (C)

Sol. 8 (A) Given $\sin(A+B)=\cos(A+B)$

$$\cos\left(\frac{\pi}{2}-(A+B)\right)=\cos(A+B)$$

$$\Rightarrow \quad \frac{\pi}{2}-(A+B)=A+B$$

$$\Rightarrow \quad A+B=\frac{\pi}{4}$$

Hence Ans is (A)

Sol. 9 (C) Given

$$\sin\theta=1-\sin^2\theta$$

$$\Rightarrow \quad \sin\theta=\cos^2\theta \quad \ldots(1)$$

To final value of

$$\cos^2\theta+\cos^4\theta=\sin\theta+\sin^2\theta=1 \qquad [\text{from } \ldots(1)]$$

Hence Ans is (C)

Sol. 10 (D)

From figure we have,

$$\tan 60^\circ=\frac{30}{BC}$$

$$\Rightarrow \quad BC=\frac{30}{\sqrt{3}} \quad \ldots(1)$$

and $\quad \tan 30^\circ=\frac{AB}{BC}$

$$\Rightarrow \quad AB=BC\tan 30^\circ$$

$$\Rightarrow \quad AB=\frac{30}{\sqrt{3}}\times\frac{1}{\sqrt{3}}=10\text{m} \qquad (\text{using }(1))$$

Hence Ans is (D)

Sol. 11 (C) Given

$$\sec x + \tan x = \frac{22}{7}$$

Let $p = \frac{22}{7}$

So $\sec x + \tan x = p$ ...(1)

$\sec x - \tan x = \frac{1}{p}$ ...(2)

Subtract (2) from (1)

We get $2\tan x = p - \frac{1}{p}$

$\Rightarrow \quad 2\tan x = \frac{p^2-1}{p}$

$\Rightarrow \quad \tan x = \frac{p^2-1}{2p}$

We know $H^2 = (p^2-1) + 4p^2$

$\Rightarrow \quad H^2 = (p^2+1)^2$

$\Rightarrow \quad H^2 = (p^2+1)^2$

$\Rightarrow \quad H = (p^2+1)$

cosec x + cot x

$$\frac{(p^2+1)}{p^2-1} + \frac{2p}{p^2-1} = \frac{(p+1)^2}{p^2-1} = \frac{p+1}{p-1}$$

$$\Rightarrow \quad \operatorname{cosec} x + \cot x = \frac{p+1}{p-1} = \frac{\frac{22}{7}+1}{\frac{22}{7}-1} = \frac{29}{15}$$

$\Rightarrow \quad m = 29 \quad \& \quad n = 15$

$\Rightarrow \quad m + n = 29 + 15 = 44$

Hence Ans is (B)

Sol. 12 (B) Given

$\sin\theta = \cos\theta$

$\Rightarrow \quad \tan\theta = 1$

$\Rightarrow \quad \theta = 45°$

Hence Ans is (B)

Sol. 13 (A)

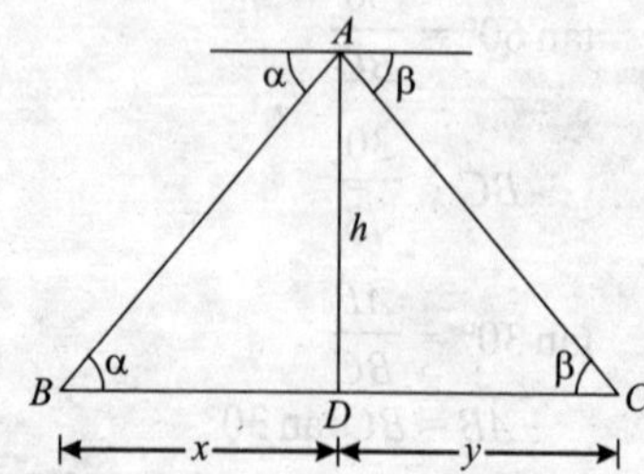

Given $x + y = 1$

Let h be the height of aeroplane above the ground then

In ΔABD

$$\tan\alpha = \frac{h}{x}$$

$\Rightarrow \quad x = h\cot\alpha$

Similarly ΔACD

$$\tan\beta = \frac{h}{y}$$

$\Rightarrow \quad y = h\cot\beta$

We have $x + y = 1$

$h\cot\alpha + h\cot\beta = 1$

$$\Rightarrow \quad h = \frac{1}{\cot\alpha + \cot\beta}$$

$$\Rightarrow \quad h = \frac{1}{\frac{1}{\tan\alpha} + \frac{1}{\tan\beta}}$$

$$= \frac{\tan\alpha \cdot \tan\beta}{\tan\alpha + \tan\beta}$$

Hence Ans is (A)

Sol. 14 (C) Given $(1 + \cot\theta - \operatorname{cosec}\theta)(1 + \tan\theta + \sec\theta)$

$\Rightarrow \quad 1 + \tan\theta + \sec\theta + \cot\theta + \cot\theta.\tan\theta$
$+ \cot\theta.\sec\theta - \operatorname{cosec}\theta - \operatorname{cosec}\theta.\tan\theta$
$- \operatorname{cosec}\theta.\sec\theta$

$$\Rightarrow \quad 1 + \frac{\sin\theta}{\cos\theta} + \frac{\cos\theta}{\sin\theta} + \frac{1}{\cos\theta} + \frac{\cos\theta}{\sin\theta}\cdot\frac{\sin\theta}{\cos\theta}$$

$$+ \frac{\cos\theta}{\sin\theta}\cdot\frac{1}{\cos\theta} - \frac{1}{\sin\theta} - \frac{1}{\sin\theta}\cdot\frac{\sin\theta}{\cos\theta} - \frac{1}{\sin\theta\cdot\cos\theta}$$

$$\Rightarrow \quad 1 + \frac{\sin^2\theta + \cos^2\theta}{\sin\theta\cos\theta} + \frac{1}{\cos\theta} + \frac{1}{1} + \frac{1}{\sin\theta}$$

$$- \frac{1}{\sin\theta} - \frac{1}{\cos\theta} - \frac{1}{\sin\theta\cdot\cos\theta}$$

$$\Rightarrow \quad 1 + \frac{1}{\sin\theta\cdot\cos\theta} + 1 - \frac{1}{\sin\theta\cdot\cos\theta} = 2$$

Hence Ans is (C)

Sol. 15 (D) Given, $\tan\theta = \frac{4}{5}$

To find

$$\frac{5\sin\theta - 3\cos\theta}{5\sin\theta + 3\cos\theta} = \frac{\frac{5\sin\theta}{\cos\theta} - \frac{3\cos\theta}{\cos\theta}}{\frac{5\sin\theta}{\cos\theta} + \frac{3\cos\theta}{\cos\theta}} = \frac{5\tan\theta - 3}{5\tan\theta + 3}$$

$$= \frac{5\cdot\frac{4}{5} - 3}{5\cdot\frac{4}{5} + 3} = \frac{4-3}{4+3} = \frac{1}{7}$$

Hence Ans is (D)

Sol. 16 (A) Given

$$3\sin\theta + 4\cos\theta = 5$$

Then $4\sin\theta - 3\cos\theta = ?$

We know if $a\cos\theta \pm b\sin\theta = c$

Then $b\cos\theta \mp a\sin\theta = \pm\sqrt{a^2+b^2-c^2}$

$\Rightarrow$ $4\sin\theta - 3\cos\theta = \pm\sqrt{3^2+4^2-5^2}$

$= 0$

Hence Ans is (A)

Sol. 17 (B) Given

$$\lambda = \frac{2\sin\alpha}{1+\sin\alpha+\cos\alpha} \times \frac{|(1+\sin\alpha)-\cos\alpha|}{|(1+\sin\alpha)-\cos\alpha|}$$

$$\Rightarrow \lambda = \frac{2\sin\alpha(1+\sin\alpha-\cos\alpha)}{(1+\sin\alpha)^2-\cos^2\alpha}$$

$$\Rightarrow \lambda = \frac{2\sin\alpha\cdot(1+\sin\alpha-\cos\alpha)}{(1+\sin\alpha)^2-(1-\sin^2\alpha)}$$

$$\Rightarrow \lambda = \frac{2\sin\alpha(1+\sin\alpha-\cos\alpha)}{(1+\sin\alpha)[1+\sin\alpha-1+\sin\alpha]}$$

$$\Rightarrow \lambda = \frac{(1+\sin\alpha-\cos\alpha)}{(1+\sin\alpha)}$$

Hence ans is (B)

Sol. 18 (D) Consider $\sin^2\theta + \dfrac{1}{1+\tan^2\theta}$

$$= \sin^2\theta + \frac{1}{\sec^2\theta} = \sin^2\theta + \cos^2\theta = 1$$

Hence Ans is (D)

Sol. 19 (C)

$$P^2 - 1 = \sec^2\theta + \tan^2\theta + 2\sec\theta\tan\theta - 1$$

$$P^2 = 2\tan^2\theta + 2\sec\theta + \tan\theta$$

$$P^2 = 2\tan\theta(\sec\theta + \tan\theta)$$

$$\Rightarrow \frac{P^2-1}{P^2+1} = \frac{2\tan\theta(\sec\theta+\tan\theta)}{2\sec\theta(\sec\theta+\tan\theta)} = \frac{\tan\theta}{\sec\theta} = \sin\theta$$

Hence Ans is (C)

Sol. 20 (D) Consider $\dfrac{b\sin\theta - a\cos\theta}{b\sin\theta + a\cos\theta}$

Dividing Nr. & Dr. $\cos\theta$

$$= \frac{b\tan\theta - a}{b\tan\theta + a} = \frac{b\times\frac{a}{b} - a}{b\times\frac{a}{b} + a} = \frac{0}{2a} = 0$$

Hence Ans is (D)

Sol. 21 (D) Given $\sin\theta = \dfrac{4}{5}$

$$\Rightarrow \sin^2\theta = \frac{16}{25}$$

We know $\cos 2\theta = 1 - 2\sin^2\theta$

$$= 1 - 2\times\frac{16}{25}$$

$$= \frac{-7}{25}$$

Hence Ans is (D)

Sol. 22 (B) Sum of exterior angles of regular polygon of m sides $= 360°$

$\Rightarrow$ Each exterior angle $= \left(\dfrac{360}{m}\right)^\circ$

Hence Ans is (B)

Sol. 23 (C) Consider

$$\frac{\sin^4\theta - \cos^4\theta}{1-\sin^2\theta}$$

$$= \frac{(\sin^2\theta+\cos^2\theta)(\sin^2\theta-\cos^2\theta)}{\cos^2\theta}$$

$$= \frac{\sin^2\theta}{\cos^2\theta} - \frac{\cos^2\theta}{\cos^2\theta} \qquad [\because \sin^2\theta + \cos^2\theta = 1]$$

$$= \tan^2\theta - 1$$

Hence Ans is (C)

Sol. 24 (B)

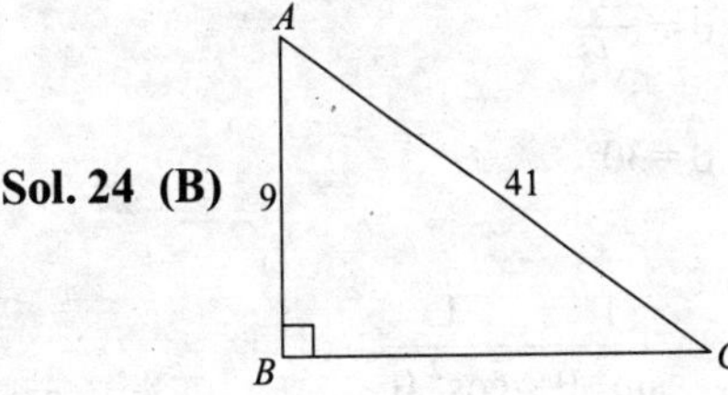

Given $\cos A = \dfrac{9}{41}$

In ΔABC

$$AC^2 = AB^2 + BC^2$$

$$(41)^2 = 9^2 + BC^2$$

$$\Rightarrow BC = 40$$

$$\Rightarrow \cot A = \frac{9}{40}$$

and $\operatorname{cosec} A = \dfrac{41}{40}$

Hence Ans is (B)

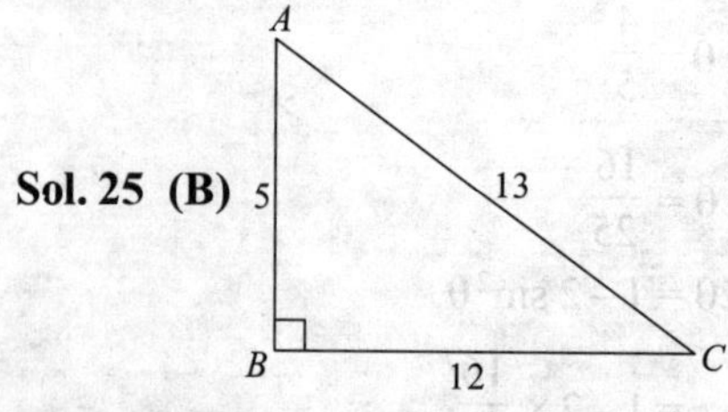

Sol. 25 (B)

In ΔABC

$$AC^2 = AB^2 + BC^2$$
$$AC^2 = 5^2 + 12^2$$
$$AC^2 = 169$$
$$\Rightarrow AC = 13$$
$$\Rightarrow \sin C = \frac{5}{13}$$

Hence Ans is (B)

Sol. 26 (C) Consider

$$(\sec\theta + \tan\theta)(1 - \sin\theta)$$
$$= \left(\frac{1+\sin\theta}{\cos\theta}\right)(1-\sin\theta)$$
$$= \frac{1-\sin^2\theta}{\cos\theta}$$
$$= \frac{\cos^2\theta}{\cos\theta}$$
$$= \cos\theta$$

Hence Ans is (C)

Sol. 27 (B) Given

$$\tan\theta = \frac{1}{\sqrt{3}}$$
$$\Rightarrow \theta = 30°$$

to find

$$\frac{\frac{1}{\sin^2\theta} - \frac{1}{\cos^2\theta}}{\frac{1}{\sin^2\theta} + \frac{1}{\cos^2\theta}}$$
$$= \frac{\cos^2\theta - \sin^2\theta}{\cos^2\theta + \sin^2\theta}$$
$$= \cos^2\theta - \sin^2\theta \qquad [\because \cos^2\theta + \sin^2\theta = 1]$$
$$= \cos^2 30° - \sin^2 30 \qquad [\theta = 30°]$$
$$= \left(\frac{\sqrt{3}}{2}\right)^2 - \left(\frac{1}{2}\right)^2 = \frac{3-1}{4} = \frac{1}{2}$$

Hence Ans is (B)

Sol. 28 (D)

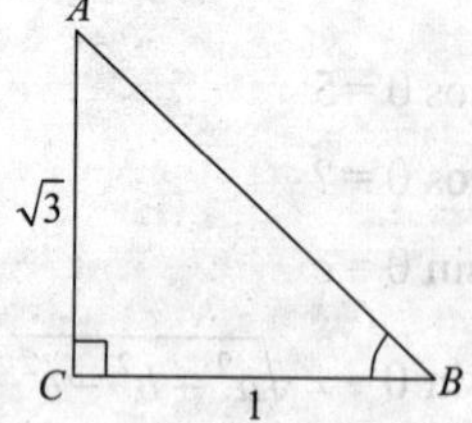

Given

$$\tan B = \sqrt{3}$$
$$\Rightarrow B = 60°$$
$$\Rightarrow \sin B = \sin 60° = \frac{\sqrt{3}}{2}$$
$$\cos B = \cos 60°$$
$$= \frac{1}{2}$$

Sol. 29 (D) Consider $\cos^4 x - \sin^4 x$

$$= (\cos^2 x + \sin^2 x)(\cos^2 x - \sin^2 x)$$
$$= 1.(\cos^2 x - \sin^2 x)$$
$$= (1 - \sin^2 x) - \sin^2 x$$
$$= 1 - 2\sin^2 x$$
$$= 2\cos^2 x - 1$$

Hence Ans is (D)

Sol. 30 (B) Consider

$$\sqrt{\frac{1+\sin\theta}{1-\sin\theta}} + \sqrt{\frac{1-\sin\theta}{1+\sin\theta}}$$
$$0 < \theta < 90°$$
$$= \frac{|1+\sin\theta| + |1-\sin\theta|}{\sqrt{1+\sin\theta}\sqrt{1-\sin\theta}}$$
$$= \frac{1+\sin\theta+1-\sin\theta}{\sqrt{1-\sin^2\theta}}$$
$$= \frac{2}{\cos\theta}$$

Hence Ans is (B)

Sol. 31 (C) Given

$$\sin(A+B) = 1$$

and
$$\cos(A-B) = \frac{\sqrt{3}}{2}$$
$$\Rightarrow A + B = 90° \qquad \ldots(1)$$
$$A - B = 30° \qquad \ldots(2)$$

Solving (1) & (2)

We get

$$A = 60°$$
$$B = 30°$$

Hence Ans is (C)

Sol. 32 (A) Given,

$$\sin^2 A + \sin^4 A = 1$$

$$\Rightarrow \quad \tan^4 A + \tan^2 A\,(\sec^2 A) = \sec^4 A$$

$$\Rightarrow \quad \tan^4 A + \tan^2 A\,(1 + \tan^2 A) = 1 + \tan^4 A + 2\tan^2 A$$

$$\Rightarrow \quad \tan^4 A + \tan^2 A = 1 + 2\tan^2 A$$

$$\Rightarrow \quad \tan^2 A - \tan^4 A = -1$$

Hence Ans is (A)

Sol. 33 (D) Given $ABCD$ is a cyclic quadrilateral

$$A + C = \pi$$

$$B + D = \pi$$

LHS

$$\tan\frac{A}{2}.\tan\frac{C}{2} + \tan\frac{B}{2}.\tan\frac{D}{2}$$

$$= \tan\left(\frac{\pi}{2} - \frac{C}{2}\right).\tan\frac{C}{2} + \tan\left(\frac{\pi}{2} - \frac{D}{2}\right)\cdot\tan\frac{D}{2}$$

$$= \cot\frac{C}{2}\cdot\tan\frac{C}{2} + \cot\frac{D}{2}\cdot\tan\frac{D}{2}$$

$$= 1 + 1 = 2$$

Hence Ans is (D)

Sol. 34 (C) Consider

$$\sqrt{1-\sin^2 A}\cdot\sqrt{\sec^2 A - 1}\cdot\sqrt{1+\cot^2 A}$$

$$= \sqrt{\cos^2 A}\cdot\sqrt{\tan^2 A}\cdot\sqrt{\operatorname{cosec}^2 A}$$

$$= \cos A\,.\,\tan A\,.\,\operatorname{cosec} A$$

$$= \cos A\,.\,\frac{\sin A}{\cos A}\cdot\frac{1}{\sin A}$$

$$= 1$$

Hence Ans is (C)

Sol. 35 (C) Consider

$$5x = \operatorname{cosec}\theta$$

$$\frac{5}{x} = \cot\theta$$

$$\operatorname{cosec}^2\theta - \cot^2\theta = 25x^2 - \frac{25}{x^2}$$

$$\Rightarrow \quad 1 = 25\left(x^2 - \frac{1}{x^2}\right)$$

$$\Rightarrow \quad 5\left(x^2 - \frac{1}{x^2}\right) = \frac{1}{5}$$

Hence Ans is (C)

Sol. 36 (C) Given,

$$x = a\cos\theta$$

$$y = a\sin\theta$$

$$x^2 + y^2 = a^2\cos^2\theta + a^2\sin^2\theta$$

$$= a^2(\cos^2\theta + \sin^2\theta)$$

$$= a^2$$

Hence Ans is (C)

Sol. 37 (D) Given,

$$\cot\theta = \frac{7}{8} \quad \& \quad \frac{(1+\sin\theta)(1-\sin\theta)}{(1+\cos\theta)(1-\cos\theta)}$$

$$\frac{1-\sin^2\theta}{1-\cos^2\theta} = \frac{\cos^2\theta}{\sin^2\theta}$$

$$= \cot^2\theta$$

$$= \left(\frac{7}{8}\right)^2 = \frac{49}{64}$$

Hence Ans is (D)

Sol. 38 (B) We have,

$$\tan 25°\tan 35°\tan 45°\tan 55°\tan 65°$$

$$= \tan(90°-65°)\tan(90°-55°)\tan 45°\tan 55°\tan 65°$$

$$= \cot 65°\cdot\cot 55\cdot 1\cdot\tan 55\cdot\tan 65 = 1$$

$$(\because\ \tan\theta\cdot\cot\theta = 1)$$

Hence Ans is (B)

Sol. 39 (A)

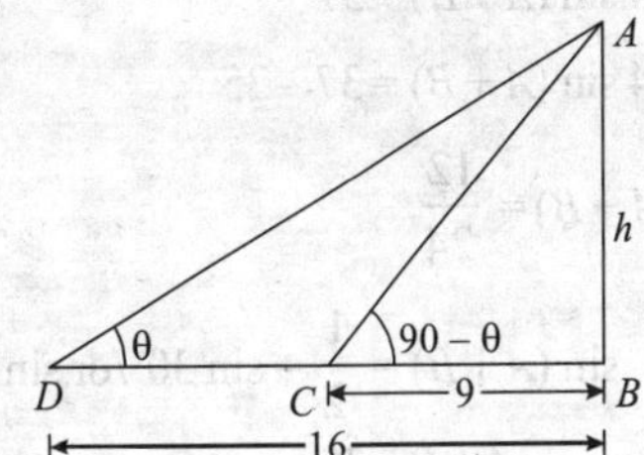

From figure we have

$$\tan\theta = \frac{h}{16} \quad \ldots(1)$$

$$\tan(90-\theta) = \frac{h}{9}$$

$$\cot\theta = \frac{h}{9} \quad \ldots(2)$$

Equation-(1) × equation-(2)

$$\tan\theta\cdot\cot\theta = \frac{h}{16}\cdot\frac{h}{9}$$

$$\Rightarrow \quad 1 = \frac{h^2}{16\times 9}$$

$$h^2 = 16\times 9$$

$$\Rightarrow \quad h = 4\times 3 = 12\text{ cm}$$

Hence Ans is (A)

Sol. 40 (D) Consider $\frac{\sin\theta - 2\sin^3\theta}{2\cos^3\theta - \cos\theta}$

$$= \frac{\sin\theta(1-2\sin^2\theta)}{\cos\theta(2\cos^2\theta - 1)}$$

$$= \frac{\tan\theta(1-2(1-\cos^2\theta))}{(2\cos^2\theta-1)}$$

$$(\because \sin^2\theta = 1-\cos^2\theta)$$

$$= \frac{\tan\theta(1+2\cos^2\theta-2)}{(2\cos^2\theta-1)}$$

$$= \frac{\tan\theta(2\cos^2\theta-1)}{(2\cos^2\theta-1)}$$

$$= \tan\theta$$

Hence Ans is (D)

Sol. 41 (A) Given,

$$3\sin A + 4\cos B = 6 \quad \ldots(1)$$

$$4\sin B + 3\cos A = 1 \quad \ldots(2)$$

squaring equation-(1) & equation-(2) & then adding

$$(3\sin A + 4\cos B)^2 + (4\sin B + 3\cos A)^2 = 6^2 + 1^2$$

$$\Rightarrow 9\sin^2 A + 16\cos^2 B + 24\sin A\cos B + 16\sin^2 B + 9\cos^2 A + 24\sin B.\cos A = 37$$

$$\Rightarrow 9(\sin^2 A + \cos^2 A) + 16(\cos^2 B + \sin^2 B) + 24(\sin A.\cos B + \cos A.\sin B) = 37$$

$$\Rightarrow 9 + 16 + 24\sin(A+B) = 37$$

$$24\sin(A+B) = 37 - 25$$

$$\Rightarrow \sin(A+B) = \frac{12}{24}$$

$$\Rightarrow \sin(A+B) = \frac{1}{2} = \sin 30°/\text{or } \sin 150$$

$$\Rightarrow A + B = 30$$

or $A + B = 150$

$$\angle C = 180 - (A+B)$$

$$= 180 - 30$$

$$= 150$$

$$\angle C = 180 - 150 = 30$$

Hence Ans is (A)

Sol. 42 (A) Let $a = x-1$,

$b = x$,

$c = x+1$

are the sides of the triangle

Given $\angle C = \angle 2A$

$$\sin C = \sin 2A$$

$$\Rightarrow \sin C = 2\sin A\cos A$$

$$\Rightarrow \frac{c}{2R} = \frac{2a}{2R}.\cos A$$

$$\Rightarrow \cos A = \frac{c}{2a}$$

$$\Rightarrow \frac{b^2+c^2-a^2}{2bc} = \frac{c}{2a}$$

$$\Rightarrow x = 5$$

$\Rightarrow$ sides are 4, 5, 6 perimeter is 15

Hence Ans is (A)

Sol. 43 (A) Given,

$$x = a\sec\theta + b\tan\theta$$

$$y = a\tan\theta - b\sec\theta$$

Consider

$$x^2 - y^2 = a^2(\sec^2 - \tan^2\theta) - b^2(\sec^2\theta - \tan^2\theta)$$

$$x^2 - y^2 = a^2 - b^2$$

Hence Ans is (A)

Sol. 44 (B) Given,

$$A + B = 90°$$

Consider

$$\frac{\tan A\cdot\tan(90-A) + \tan A\cot(90-A)}{\sin A\cdot\sec(90-A)} - \frac{\sin^2(90-A)}{\cos^2 A}$$

$$= \frac{\tan A\cdot\cot A + \tan A\cdot\tan A}{\sin A\cdot\operatorname{cosec} A} - \frac{\cos^2 A}{\cos^2 A}$$

$$= \frac{1+\tan^2 A}{1} - 1$$

$$= \tan^2 A$$

$$= \tan^2(90-B) = \cot^2 B$$

Hence Ans is (B)

Sol. 45 (A) Given

$$2^{\sin x + \cos y} = 1$$

$$\Rightarrow 2^{\sin x + \cos y} = 2^0$$

$$\Rightarrow \sin x + \cos y = 0$$

$$\Rightarrow \sin x = -\cos y \quad \ldots(1)$$

Also $16^{\sin^2 x + \cos^2 y} = 4$

$$\Rightarrow 2^{4\sin^2 x + 4\cos^2 y} = 2^2$$

$$\Rightarrow 4\sin^2 x + 4\cos^2 y = 2$$

$$\Rightarrow 2\sin^2 x + 2\cos^2 y = 1 \quad \ldots(2)$$

Using (1) in equation-(2)

$$2\cos^2 y + 2\cos^2 y = 1$$

$\Rightarrow \quad 4\cos^2 y = 1$

$\Rightarrow \quad \cos^2 y = \frac{1}{4}$

$\Rightarrow \quad \cos y = \pm\frac{1}{2}$

$\Rightarrow \quad \sin y = \frac{-1}{2}$

Hence Ans is (A)

Sol. 46 (B) Consider

$\sin A + \sin^2 A = 1$

$\sin A = \cos^2 A$

Now $\quad \cos^2 A + \cos^4 A$

$\sin A + \sin^2 A = 1$

Hence Ans is (B)

Sol. 47 (A) $\sqrt{\frac{\sec A - \tan A}{\sec A + \tan A} \times \frac{(\sec A - \tan A)}{\sec A - \tan A}}$

$= \sqrt{\frac{(\sec A - \tan A^2)}{\sec^2 A - \tan^2 A}}$

$= \sec A - \tan A$

Hence Ans is (A)

Sol. 48 (C) Given,

$\cos 9\alpha = \sin \alpha$

$\cos 9\alpha = \cos(90 - \alpha)$

$9\alpha = 90 - \alpha$

$\Rightarrow \quad 10\alpha = 90$

$\Rightarrow \quad \boxed{\alpha = 9}$

to find $\quad \tan 5\alpha = \tan 5 \times 9 = \tan 45$

$= 1$

Hence Ans is (C)

Sol. 49 (D) If $x = a\cos^3\theta$

$y = b\sin^3\theta$

$\Rightarrow \quad \frac{x}{a} = \cos^3\theta$

$\Rightarrow \quad \frac{y}{b} = \sin^3\theta$

$\Rightarrow \quad \left(\frac{x}{a}\right)^{2/3} = (\cos^3\theta)^{2/3}$

$\Rightarrow \quad \frac{y}{b} = (\sin^3\theta)^{2/3}$

$\Rightarrow \quad \left(\frac{x}{a}\right)^{2/3} + \left(\frac{y}{b}\right)^{2/3} = \cos^2\theta + \sin^2\theta = 1$

Hence Ans is (D)

Sol. 50 (C) Given

$A + B + C = 180$

$\cos B \cos C = \cos A \quad \ldots(1)$

$\Rightarrow \quad \cos(B + C) = -\cos A$

$\Rightarrow \quad \cos A - \sin B \sin C = -\cos A$

$\Rightarrow \quad \sin B \sin C = 2\cos A \quad \ldots(2)$

$\Rightarrow \quad (2)/(1) = \tan B \tan C = 2$

Hence Ans is (C)

Sol. 51 (D) From given relation,

$\angle A = 20°, \angle B = 40°, \angle C = 120°$

Area of $\Delta AOB \quad = \frac{1}{2}r^2 \sin 120 \quad (\because \angle AOB = 120)$

$= \frac{8^2}{2} \times \frac{\sqrt{3}}{2} = 16\sqrt{3}\ \text{cm}^2$

Hence Ans is (D)

Sol. 52 (D) Given,

$\operatorname{cosec}\theta + \cot\theta = m$

$\Rightarrow \quad \operatorname{cosec}\theta - \cot\theta = \frac{1}{m}$

$\Rightarrow \quad \sin\theta = \frac{2m}{m^2 + 1}$

$\Rightarrow \quad \cos\theta = \frac{m^2 - 1}{m^2 + 1}$

$\Rightarrow \quad \sec\theta = \frac{m^2 + 1}{m^2 - 1}$

Hence Ans is (D)

Sol. 53 (D) Given

$$\sin x = \frac{6\sin 30° - 8\cos 60° + 2\tan 45°}{2(\sin^2 30° + \cos^2 60°)}$$

$$= \frac{6 \times \frac{1}{2} - 8 \times \frac{1}{2} + 2.1}{2\left[\left(\frac{1}{2}\right)^2 + \left(\frac{1}{2}\right)^2\right]}$$

$$= \frac{3 - 4 + 2}{2\frac{1}{2}} = 1$$

$\sin x = 1$

$\Rightarrow \quad x = 90°$

Hence Ans is (D)

Sol. 54 (B) Given,

$$\sin x + \sin^2 x = 1$$

$\Rightarrow \quad \sin x = 1 - \sin^2 x$

$\Rightarrow \quad \sin x = \cos^2 x$

to find $\cos^{12}x + 3\cos^{10}x + 3\cos^8 x + \cos^6 x$

$$= \sin^6 x + 3\sin^5 x + 3\sin^4 x + \sin^3 x$$

$$= (\sin^2 x + \sin x)^3 = (1)^3$$

Hence Ans is (B)

Sol. 55 (C)

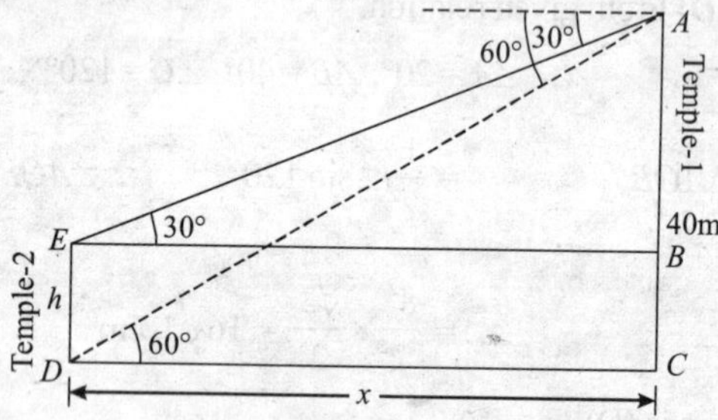

Let the height of temple-2 be 'h' & width be 'x'

$$\Delta ACD = \tan 60° = \frac{40}{x}$$

$\Rightarrow \quad x = 40\sqrt{3}$

$\Rightarrow \quad x = \dfrac{40 \cdot \sqrt{3} \times \sqrt{3}}{\sqrt{3}}$

$$= \frac{120}{\sqrt{3}}$$

Hence Ans is (C)

Sol. 56 (A) Given,

$$\tan\theta + \cot\theta = 3$$

$\Rightarrow \quad (\tan\theta + \cot\theta)^2 = (3)^2$

$\Rightarrow \quad \tan^2\theta + \cot^2\theta + 2\cot\theta.\tan\theta = 9$

$\Rightarrow \quad \tan^2\theta + \cot^2\theta = 9 - 2 = 7$

Hence Ans is (A)

Sol. 57 (B) $\sin\theta - 1 = 0$

$\Rightarrow \quad \sin\theta = 1$

$\Rightarrow \quad \sin\theta = \sin 90°$

$\Rightarrow \quad \theta = 90°$

Hence Ans is (B)

Sol. 58 (A) To find $\dfrac{\sin 48° + \cos 42°}{\cot 42°} - \dfrac{1}{\sec 48°}$

$$= \frac{\sin 48 + \sin 48}{\cot 42} - \cos 48$$

$$= 2\cos 48 - \cos 48$$

$$= \cos 48$$

Hence Ans is (A)

Sol. 59 (B) $\tan\theta + \cot\theta = 2$

$$\tan^2\theta + \cot^2\theta = (\tan\theta + \cot\theta)^2 - 2 = 2^2 - 2 = 2$$

Hence Ans is (B)

Sol. 60 (A) $\operatorname{cosec}\theta + \sin\theta = 2$

$\Rightarrow \quad \dfrac{1}{\sin\theta} + \sin\theta = 2$

$\Rightarrow \quad 1 + \sin^2\theta = 2\sin\theta$

$\Rightarrow \quad \sin^2\theta - 2\sin\theta + 1 = 0$

$\Rightarrow \quad (\sin\theta - 1)^2 = 0$

$\Rightarrow \quad \sin\theta = 1$

$\Rightarrow \quad \operatorname{cosec}\theta = 1$

$\Rightarrow \quad \operatorname{cosec}^{50}\theta + \sin^{50}\theta = 1 + 1$

$$\operatorname{cosec}^{50}\theta + \sin^{50}\theta = 2$$

Hence Ans is (A)

Sol. 61 (A) $\operatorname{cosec}4x = \sec 5x$

As cosec and sec are complementary trigonometric ratios

$\Rightarrow \quad \operatorname{cosec} 4x = \operatorname{cosec}(90° - 5x)$

$\Rightarrow \quad 4x = 90° - 5x$

$\Rightarrow \quad 9x = 90°$

$\Rightarrow \quad x = 10°$

Thus $\sin 3x + \cos 6x$

$$= \sin 30° + \cos 60°$$

$$= \frac{1}{2} + \frac{1}{2}$$

$$= 1$$

Hence Ans is (A)

Sol. 62 (B)

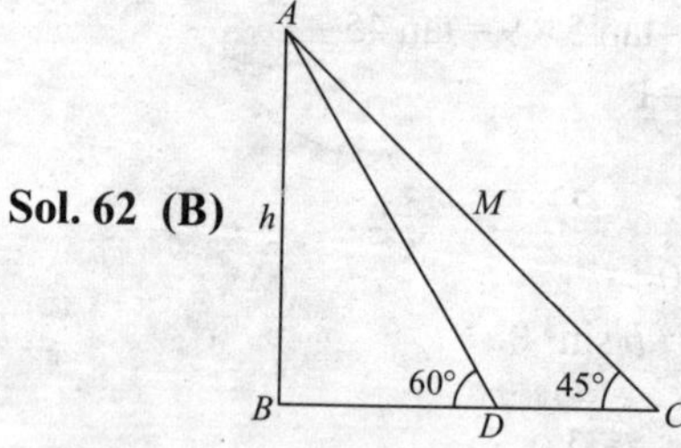

Let AB be the building of height h m

$$\tan 45° = \frac{AB}{BC}$$

$$1 = \frac{h}{BC}$$

$\Rightarrow \quad BC = hm$

Thus $\quad BD = (h - 20)$

$$\tan 60° = \frac{h}{h-20}$$

$$\sqrt{3}=\frac{h}{h-20}$$

$\Rightarrow \quad h\sqrt{3}-20\sqrt{3}=h$

$\Rightarrow \quad h(\sqrt{3}-1)=20\sqrt{3}$

$\Rightarrow \quad h=\frac{20\sqrt{3}}{\sqrt{3}-1}$

$\Rightarrow \quad h=\frac{20\sqrt{3}(\sqrt{3}+1)}{(\sqrt{3}-1)(\sqrt{3}+1)}$

$\Rightarrow \quad h=10\sqrt{3}(\sqrt{3}+1)$

$\Rightarrow \quad h=30+17.32$

$\Rightarrow$ Height of building is 47.32 m

Hence Ans is (B)

Sol. 63 (A) $\frac{5\tan\theta-3}{5\tan\theta+3}=\frac{5\left(\frac{3}{5}\right)-3}{5\left(\frac{3}{5}\right)+3}$

$$=\frac{0}{6}=0$$

Hence Ans is (A)

Sol. 64 (C) $(\cos^2\phi)^2+\sec^2\phi=P$

$\sin^4\phi-\sin^2\phi+1-P=0$

$$\left(\sin^2\phi-\frac{1}{2}\right)^2+\frac{3}{4}=P$$

Solving $\quad P\geq\frac{3}{4}$

Since $\sin^2\theta+\cos^2\theta\geq 1$

$\Rightarrow \quad \frac{3}{4}\leq P\leq 1$

Hence Ans is (C)

Sol. 65 (D) $\tan\theta+\frac{1}{\tan\theta}=3$

or $\quad x+\frac{1}{x}=3$

$$\frac{\sin^2\theta-\cos^2\theta}{\sin\theta\cos\theta}=\tan\theta-\frac{1}{\tan\theta}=x-\frac{1}{x}$$

$$\left(x-\frac{1}{x}\right)^2=\left(x-\frac{1}{x}\right)^2-4x\frac{1}{x}$$

Solving, $\quad x-\frac{1}{x}=\sqrt{5}$

Hence Ans is (D)

Sol. 66 (B) $\text{cosec}\theta-\cot\theta=p$

$$\text{cosec}\theta+\cot\theta=\frac{1}{p}$$

$$2\text{cosec}\theta=\frac{1+p^2}{p} \quad 2\cot\theta=\frac{1-p^2}{p}$$

$$\text{cosec}\theta=\frac{1+p^2}{2p} \quad \cot\theta=\frac{1-p^2}{2p}$$

$$\frac{p^2-1}{p^2+1}=-\cos\theta$$

Hence Ans is (B)

Sol. 67 (A) Speed = 300 m/minute

$$=\frac{300}{60}\text{ m/s}$$

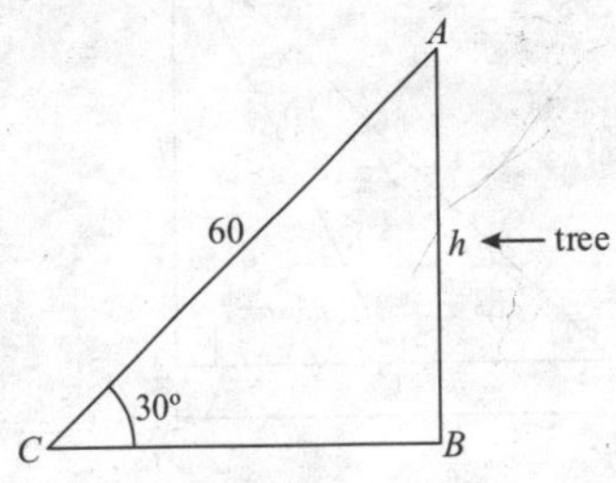

$$=5\text{ m/s}$$

Distance $\quad AC=12\times 5=60\text{ m}$

$$\frac{AB}{AC}=\sin 30°$$

$$h=AC\times\frac{1}{2}=30\text{ m}$$

Hence Ans is (A)

Sol. 68 (C) $\cos\theta+\sin\theta=p$ ...(1)

$\sec\theta+\text{cosec}\theta=V$

$$\frac{1}{\cos\theta}+\frac{1}{\sin\theta}=V$$

$$\frac{\sin\theta+\cos\theta}{\sin\theta\cos\theta}=V$$

$$\frac{p}{\sin\theta\cos\theta}=V \quad \text{...(2)}$$

by equation-(1)

$\sin^2\theta+\cos^2\theta+2\sin\theta\cos\theta=p^2$

$1+2\sin\theta\cos\theta=p^2$

$$\sin\theta\cos\theta=\frac{p^2-1}{2}$$

Putting sinθ cosθ in equation-(2)

$$V=\frac{p}{\frac{p^2-1}{2}}$$

$$V=\frac{2p}{p^2-1}$$

Hence Ans is (C)

Sol. 69 (C) $(\cos^2 5+\cos^2 85)+(\cos^2 10+\cos^2 80)+\ldots$ $(\cos^2 40+\cos^2 50)+\cos^2 45$

$$(1+1+\ldots+1)+\frac{1}{2}=8+\frac{1}{2}=8\frac{1}{2}$$

Hence Ans is (C)

Sol. 70 (C)

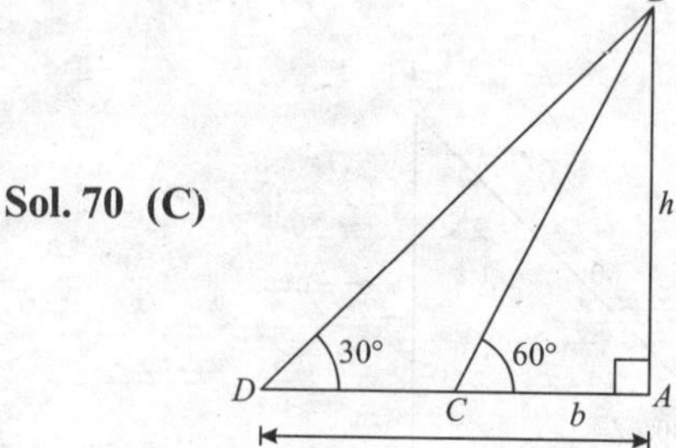

In ΔABC, $\tan 60° = \frac{h}{b}$

$$\frac{h}{b}=\sqrt{3} \Rightarrow h=\sqrt{3}\,b \qquad \ldots(1)$$

In ΔBAD, $\tan 30° = \frac{h}{a}$

$$\frac{h}{a}=\frac{1}{\sqrt{3}} \Rightarrow h=\frac{a}{\sqrt{3}} \qquad \ldots(2)$$

Multiplying (1) & (2)

We have $h^2=ab$

$\Rightarrow$ $h=\sqrt{ab}$

Hence Ans is (C)

Sol. 71 (D) $\frac{\tan^2\theta-\sin^2\theta}{\sin^2\theta}$

$$=\frac{\sin^2\theta}{\sin^2\theta}\left[\frac{1}{\cos^2\theta}-1\right]=\tan^2\theta$$

Hence Ans is (D)

Sol. 72 (B) $\frac{\sin^2 70°+\cos^2 70°}{\sin^2 59°+\cos^2 59°}=\frac{1}{1}=1$

Hence Ans is (B)

Sol. 73 (B) $\tan\theta=\frac{h}{b}$

$\Rightarrow$ $\tan\theta=1$ $[\because h=b]$

$\Rightarrow$ $\theta=45°$

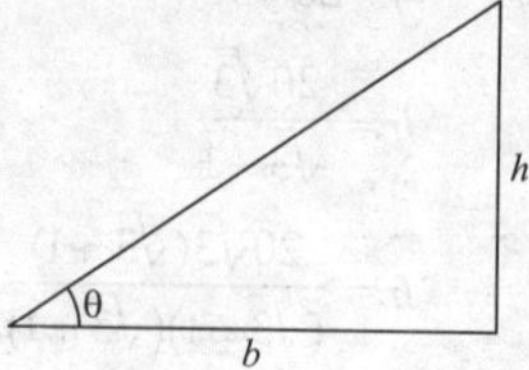

Hence Ans is (B)

Sol. 74 (D) $\sin\theta\left(\frac{1}{\sin\theta}-\sin\theta\right)$

$$=\sin\theta\times\frac{1-\sin^2\theta}{\sin 0}$$

$$=\cos^2\theta$$

Hence Ans is (D)

Sol. 75 (B) $[1+1]^2=4$

Hence Ans is (B)

Sol. 76 (B) $\frac{\cos^2 30°+\cos 30°\sin 30°+\sin^2 30°}{\cos^3 30°-\sin^3 30°}$

$$=\frac{(\cos^2 30°+\cos 30\sin 30+\sin^2 30°)}{(\cos 30-\sin 30)(\cos^2 30°+\cos 30.\sin 30+\sin^2 30)}$$

$$=\frac{1}{\cos 30°-\sin 30}=\frac{1}{\frac{\sqrt{3}}{2}-\frac{1}{2}}=\frac{2}{\sqrt{3}-1}$$

$$=\frac{2}{\sqrt{3}-1}\times\frac{\sqrt{3}+1}{\sqrt{3}+1}$$

$$=\frac{2(\sqrt{3}+1)}{(\sqrt{3})^2-(1)^2}$$

$$=(\sqrt{3}+1)$$

Hence Ans is (B)

Sol. 77 (A) Given that $\tan\theta=-1$, Now $\tan\theta$ is negative in 2nd & 4th quadrant

Hence if $\tan\theta=-1$ then there will be Two values of θ, which are $\theta=\frac{3\pi}{4}$ and $\theta=\left(2\pi-\frac{\pi}{4}\right)=\frac{7\pi}{4}$

Now at $\theta=\frac{3\pi}{4}$

$$= \frac{\sec\theta + \operatorname{cosec}\theta}{\cos\theta - \sin\theta}$$

$$= \frac{\sec\frac{3\pi}{4} + \operatorname{cosec}\frac{3\pi}{4}}{\cos\frac{3\pi}{4} - \sin\frac{3\pi}{4}}$$

$$= \frac{-\frac{1}{\sqrt{2}} + \frac{1}{\sqrt{2}}}{-\frac{1}{\sqrt{2}} - \frac{1}{\sqrt{2}}} = 0$$

Now, at $\theta = \frac{7\pi}{4}$ also value of $\sec\theta + \operatorname{cosec}\theta = 0$

Hence value of $\frac{\sec\theta + \operatorname{cosec}\theta}{\cos\theta - \sin\theta} = 0$

Hence Ans is (A)

Sol. 78 (C)

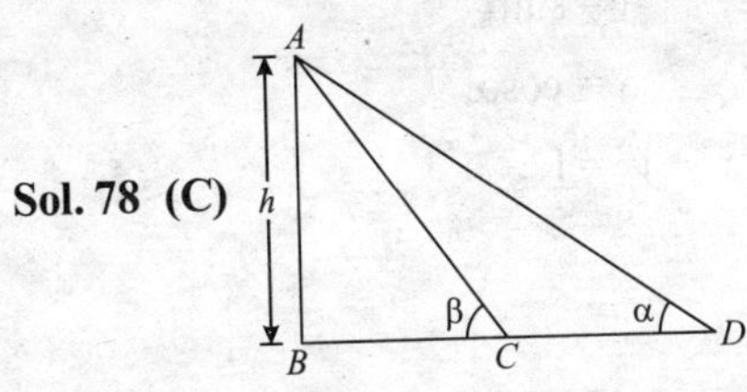

$$BC = h\cot\beta$$

$$BD = h\cot\alpha$$

Distance between objects $= h\cot\alpha - h\cot\beta$

$$= h(\cot\alpha - \cot\beta)$$

Hence Ans is (C)

Sol. 79 (B) $x^2 + y^2 + z^2 = r^2$

$$(r\sin A\cos B)^2 + (r\sin A\sin B)^2 + z^2 = r^2$$

$$r^2\sin^2 A\cos^2 B + r^2\sin^2 A\sin^2 B + z^2 = r^2$$

$$r^2\sin^2 A(\cos^2 B + \sin^2 B) + z^2 = r^2$$

$$z^2 = r^2 - r^2\sin^2 A = r^2\cos^2 A$$

$$z = r\cos A$$

Hence Ans is (B)

Sol. 80 (B)

$$\tan\theta = \frac{12}{16}$$

$$\cot\theta = \frac{12}{x}$$

$$x = 12\tan\theta$$

$$= 12 \times \frac{12}{16} = 9$$

Hence Ans is (B)

Sol. 81 (B) $m = \frac{\cos A}{\cos B}; n = \frac{\cos A}{\sin B}$

$$m^2 + n^2 = \left(\frac{\cos^2 A}{\cos^2 B} + \frac{\cos^2 A}{\sin^2 B}\right)\cos^2 B$$

$$= \cos^2 A\left[\frac{1}{\cos^2 B\sin^2 B}\right]\cos^2 B$$

$$= \frac{\cos^2 A}{\sin^2 B} = n^2$$

Hence Ans is (B)

Sol. 82 (B) Angle $= 60°30'$

$$180° \to \pi\,\text{radian}$$

$$\Rightarrow \quad 1° = \frac{\pi}{180}$$

$$\Rightarrow \quad \left(\frac{121}{2}\right)° = \frac{\pi}{180} \times \frac{121}{2} = \frac{121}{360}\pi^c$$

Hence Ans is (B)

Sol. 83 (B) $\cot(90 - \theta) = \cot(30 + \theta)$

$$90 - \theta = 30 + \theta$$

$$60 = 2\theta$$

$$\theta = 30°$$

Hence Ans is (B)

Sol. 84 (B) Given, $5\cos A - 12\sin A = 0$

$$\Rightarrow \quad 5\cos A = 12\sin A$$

$$\Rightarrow \quad \tan A = \frac{5}{12}$$

$$\Rightarrow \quad \frac{\sin A + \cos A}{2\cos A - \sin A} = \frac{\tan A + 1}{2 - \tan A}$$

(One dividing by $\cos A$)

$$\Rightarrow \quad \frac{17}{19}$$

Hence Ans is (B)

Sol. 85 (C)

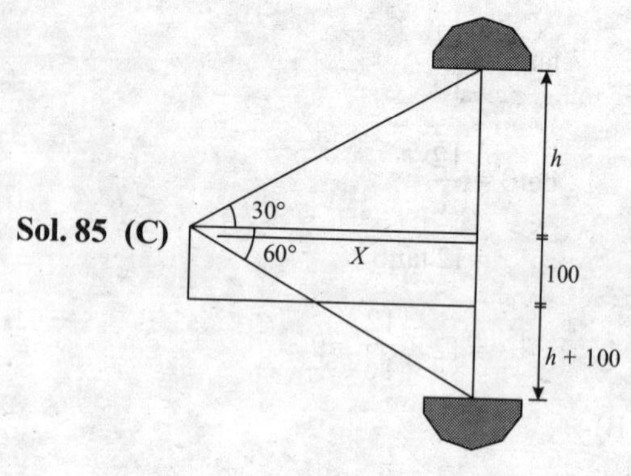

$$\tan 30° = \frac{h}{x}, x = \sqrt{3}\, h$$

$$\tan 60° = \frac{h+200}{x}$$

$\Rightarrow \quad \sqrt{3}\, x = h + 200$

$\Rightarrow \quad \sqrt{3}\,(\sqrt{3}\, h) = h + 200$

$\Rightarrow \quad 3h - h = 200$

$\Rightarrow \quad 2h = 200$

$\Rightarrow \quad h = 100\,\text{m}$

Height of cloud above lake $= h + 100 = 200$ m

Hence Ans is (C)

Sol. 86 (A) Given

$$\tan(A) = \cot(B)$$

$$\tan(A) = \tan\left(\frac{\pi}{2} - B\right)$$

Since $\quad \cot\theta = \tan\left(\frac{\pi}{2} - \theta\right)$

$\Rightarrow \quad A = \frac{\pi}{2} - B$

$$A + B = \frac{\pi}{2}$$

Hence Ans is (A)

Sol. 87 (A) $\tan A = \sqrt{2} - 1$

Value of $\sin A \cos A = ?$

Dividing and multiplying $(\sin A \cos A)$ by $\cos A$, we get

$$\left(\frac{\cos A}{\cos A}\right) \cdot \sin A \cdot \cos A$$

$$= \tan A \cdot \cos^2 A$$

$$= \frac{\tan A}{\sec^2 A} = \frac{\tan A}{1 + \tan^2 A}$$

$$= \frac{\sqrt{2}-1}{1+(\sqrt{2}-1)^2} = \frac{\sqrt{2}-1}{1+2+1-2\sqrt{2}}$$

$$= \frac{\sqrt{2}-1}{4-2\sqrt{2}}$$

Hence Ans is (A)

Sol. 88 (C) Third angle

$$x = 180° \,(87°24'54'' + 32°31'6'')$$

$$= 60°4'$$

$$= \frac{\pi}{3} \text{ (approx)}$$

Hence Ans is (C)

Sol. 89 (B) $\quad x\sin\alpha = y\cos\alpha$

$$y\cos\alpha.\sin^3\alpha + y\cos^3\alpha = \sin\alpha.\cos\alpha$$

$$y = \sin\alpha$$

$\Rightarrow \quad x = \cos\alpha$

$$x^2 + y^2 = 1$$

Hence Ans is (B)

Sol. 90 (C)

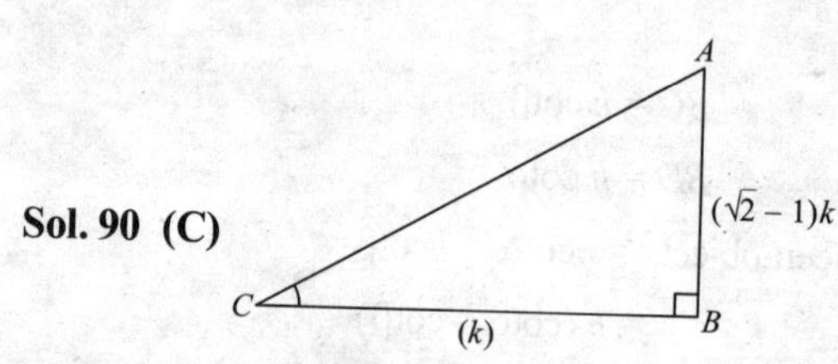

$$\tan A = \sqrt{2} - 1$$

$$AC = \sqrt{((\sqrt{2}-1)k)^2 + (k)^2}$$

$$\sin A \cos A = \frac{\sqrt{2}-1}{\sqrt{4-2\sqrt{2}}} \cdot \frac{1}{\sqrt{4-2\sqrt{2}}}$$

$$= \frac{1}{2\sqrt{2}}$$

Hence Ans is (C)

Sol. 91 (A)

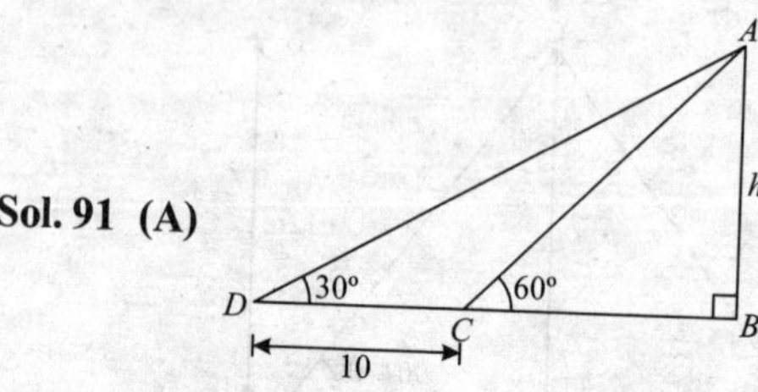

Let the height of tower AB be h

$\Rightarrow \qquad BC = \dfrac{h}{\sqrt{3}}$

$BD = h\sqrt{3}$

Given $\quad h\sqrt{3} - \dfrac{h}{\sqrt{3}} = 10$

$= \dfrac{3h-h}{\sqrt{3}} = 10$

$\Rightarrow \qquad 2h = 10\sqrt{3}$

$\Rightarrow \qquad h = 5\sqrt{3}$

Hence Ans is (A)

Sol. 92 (B) $\quad \text{cosec}\theta - \sin\theta = 4$

Squaring, we get

$\text{cosec}^2\theta + \sin^2\theta - 2\,\text{cosec}\theta.\sin\theta = 16$

$\Rightarrow \qquad \text{cosec}^2\theta + \sin^2\theta = 18$

Hence Ans is (B)

Sol. 93 (B) $3(\sin x - \cos x)^4 + 6(\sin x + \cos x)^2 + 4(\sin^6 x + \cos^6 x)$

$= 3(1 - 2\sin x\cos x)^2 + 6(1 + 2\sin x\cos x)$

$+ 4(\sin^2 x + \cos^2 x)(\sin^4 x + \cos^4 x - \sin^2 x\cos^2 x)$

$= 3(1 + 4\sin^2 x\cos^2 x - 4\sin x\cos x) + 6(1 + 2\sin x\cos x) + 4$

$[(\sin^2 x + \cos^2 x)^2 - 3\sin^2 x\cos^2 x]$

$= 3 + 12\sin^2 x\cos^2 x - 12\sin x\cos x + 6$

$+ 12\sin x\cos x + 4 - 12\sin^2 x\cos^2 x = 13$

Hence Ans is (B)

Sol. 94 (A) Given,

Height of tower = 6 m

Shadow of tower is = $2\sqrt{3}$

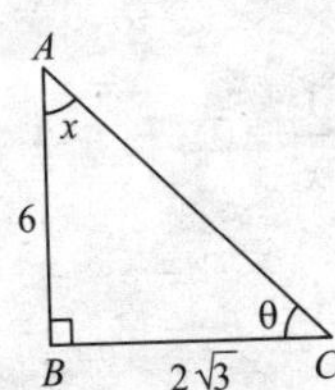

$\tan\theta = \dfrac{AB}{BC}$

$\tan\theta = \dfrac{6}{2\sqrt{3}}$

$\tan\theta = \sqrt{3}$

$\tan\theta = \tan 60^\circ$

$\theta = 60^\circ$

Hence Ans is (A)

Sol. 95 (B) If $\cos\theta + \cos^2\theta = 1$ then $\sin^4\theta + \sin^2\theta$

We can write

$\cos\theta = 1 - \cos^2\theta$

$\Rightarrow \qquad \cos\theta = \sin^2\theta$

$\Rightarrow \qquad \cos^2\theta = \sin^4\theta$

$1 - \sin^2\theta = \sin^4\theta$

$1 = \sin^2\theta + \sin^4\theta$

Hence Ans is (B)

Sol. 96 (B) $\sqrt{\dfrac{1+\sin A}{1-\sin A}} + \sqrt{\dfrac{1-\sin A}{1+\sin A}}$

$= \sqrt{\dfrac{(1+\sin A)(1+\sin A)}{(1-\sin A)(1-\sin A)}} + \sqrt{\dfrac{(1-\sin A)(1-\sin A)}{(1+\sin A)(1-\sin A)}}$

$= \dfrac{1+\sin A}{\cos A} + \dfrac{1-\sin A}{\cos A} = \dfrac{2}{\cos A} = 2\sec A$

Hence Ans is (B)

Sol. 97 (B) $\quad x = 1 + \cos A,$

$y = \text{cosec}^2 A,$

$z = 1 - \cos A,$

$x \cdot z = 1 - \cos^2 A = \sin^2 A = \dfrac{1}{y}$

$\Rightarrow \qquad xz = \dfrac{1}{y}$

$\Rightarrow \qquad xyz = 1$

Hence Ans is (B)

Sol. 98 (A) $\dfrac{2\tan 30^\circ}{1+\tan^2 30^\circ}$

$\dfrac{2\times\dfrac{1}{\sqrt{3}}}{1+\left(\dfrac{1}{\sqrt{3}}\right)^2} = \dfrac{\dfrac{2}{\sqrt{3}}}{1+\dfrac{1}{3}}$

$= \dfrac{2/\sqrt{3}}{4/3} = \dfrac{\sqrt{3}}{2} = \sin 60^\circ$

Hence Ans is (A)

Sol. 99 (A)

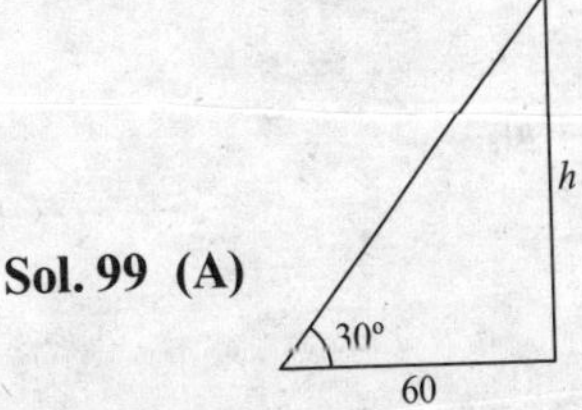

$$\tan 30^\circ = \frac{\text{height of tower(h)}}{60}$$

$$\Rightarrow \quad \frac{1}{\sqrt{3}} = \frac{h}{60}$$

$$\Rightarrow \quad h = \frac{60}{\sqrt{3}}$$

$$\Rightarrow \quad h = 20\sqrt{3}\text{m}$$

Hence Ans is (A)

Sol. 100 (B) $(a\cos\theta - b\sin\theta)^2 = (c)^2$

$$a^2\cos^2\theta + b^2\sin^2\theta - 2ab\sin\theta\cos\theta = c^2$$

$$a^2(1 - \sin^2\theta) + b^2(1 - \cos^2\theta) - 2ab\sin\theta\cos\theta = c^2$$

$$(a\sin\theta + b\cos\theta)^2 = a^2 + b^2 - c^2$$

$$a\sin\theta + b\cos\theta = \pm\sqrt{a^2 + b^2 - c^2}$$

Hence Ans is (B)

Sol. 101 (C) As,

$$\tan 5\theta \cdot \tan 4\theta = 1,$$

$$\tan 4\theta = \frac{1}{\tan 5\theta} = \cot 5\theta = \tan(90 - 5\theta)$$

$$\Rightarrow \quad 4\theta = 90 - 5\theta \text{ (Comparing both the sides)}$$

$$\Rightarrow \quad 9\theta = 90$$

$$\Rightarrow \quad \theta = 10$$

Hence Ans is (C)

Sol. 102 (A) $\sin^2 A + \sin^2 B + \sin^2 C$

$$= \sin^2 A + \sin^2 90 + \sin^2(90 - A)$$

$$= \sin^2 A + 1 + \cos^2 A = 1 + \sin^2 A + \cos^2 A$$

$$= 1 + 1 = 2 \qquad (\because \sin^2 A + \cos^2 A = 1)$$

Hence Ans is (A)

Sol. 103 (D) $\dfrac{\cos\theta - \sin\theta + 1}{\cos\theta + \sin\theta - 1} \quad \dfrac{\cot\theta - 1 + \text{cosec}\,\theta}{\cot\theta + 1 - \text{cosec}\,\theta}$

(dividing by $\sin\theta$)

$$\frac{\cot\theta + \text{cosec}\,\theta - (\text{cosec}\,\theta - \cot\theta)(\cot\theta + \text{cosec}\,\theta)}{(1 - \text{cosec}\,\theta + \cot\theta)}$$

$$= \cot\theta + \text{cosec}\,\theta$$

Hence Ans is (D)

Sol. 104 (C)

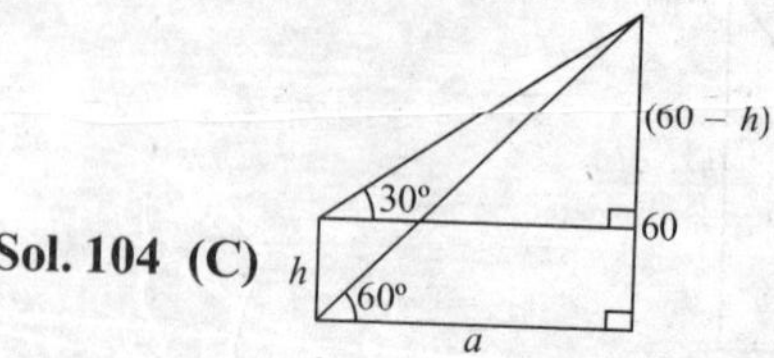

$$\frac{60 - h}{a} = \tan 30^\circ = \frac{1}{\sqrt{3}}$$

$$\frac{60}{a} = \tan 60^\circ = \sqrt{3}$$

$$\Rightarrow \quad \frac{60 - h}{60} = \frac{1}{3}$$

$$\Rightarrow \quad h = 40\,\text{m}$$

Hence Ans is (C)

Sol. 105 (A)

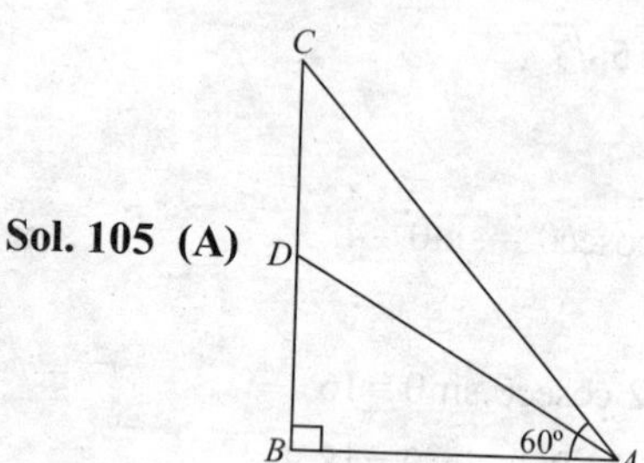

Let $\quad AB = a$

$$\Rightarrow \quad \frac{a}{AC} = \cos 60^\circ$$

$$\Rightarrow \quad AC = 2a$$

By angle bisector theorem of Δ

We have $\quad \dfrac{BD}{DC} = \dfrac{BA}{AC}$

$$\frac{BD}{DC} = \frac{a}{2a}$$

$$\frac{BD}{CD} = 1:2$$

Hence Ans is (A)

Sol. 106 (A) $-2 \le x + \dfrac{1}{x} \ge 2$

$\Rightarrow$ Not possible

Hence Ans is (A)

Sol. 107 (A) $\sec^2\theta - \tan^2\theta = 1$

Applicable for all value of θ

Hence Ans is (A)

Sol. 108 (B) $\cos 15^\circ \cos 7\dfrac{1^\circ}{2} \sin 7\dfrac{1^\circ}{2}$

$$= \frac{1}{2}[\cos 15^\circ \sin 15^\circ] \qquad \{\text{Using } \sin 2\theta = 2\sin\theta \times \cos\theta\}$$

$= \frac{1}{4}[\sin 30^\circ]$

$= \frac{1}{8}$

Hence Ans is (B)

Sol. 109 (B) 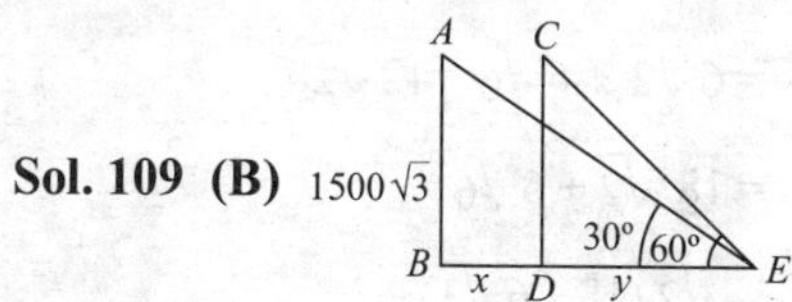

In ΔABE

$$\tan 30^\circ = \frac{1500\sqrt{3}}{x+y}$$

$$x+y = 4500 \qquad \ldots(1)$$

In ΔCDE

$$\tan 60^\circ = \frac{1500\sqrt{3}}{y}$$

$$y = 1500$$

From (1)

$$x = 3000\,\text{m}$$

$$\text{Speed} = \frac{3000}{15}\,\text{m/s}$$

$$= 200\,\text{m/s}$$

$$= \frac{200 \times 3600}{1000}$$

$$= 720\,\text{km/hr}$$

Hence Ans is (B)

Sol. 110 (B) $\sin^2\theta + \text{cosec}^2\theta + 2 + \cos^2\theta + \sec^2\theta + 2$

$$= \tan^2\theta + \cot^2\theta + K$$

$\Rightarrow \quad 1 + 1 + 2 + 2 = K$

$$K = 7$$

Hence Ans is (B)

Sol. 111 (B) Given,

$(3\sin\theta) + (5\cos\theta) = 5$

$(5\sin\theta) - (3\cos\theta) = K$

$\Rightarrow$ On squaring and adding;

We get $\quad 9 + 25 = 25 + K^2$

$\Rightarrow \quad K^2 = 9$

$\Rightarrow \quad K = \pm 3$

Hence Ans is (B)

Sol. 112 (A) 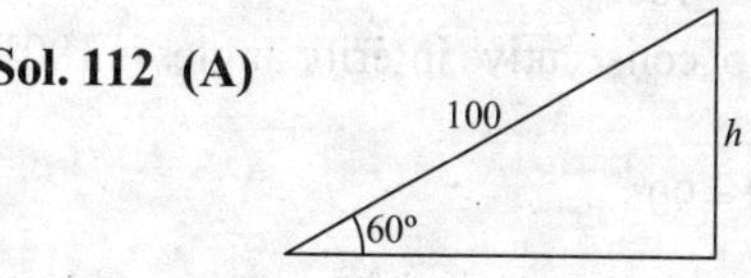

$$\sin 60 = \frac{h}{100}$$

$$h = 100 \sin 60$$

$$= 50\sqrt{3}\,\text{m}$$

Hence Ans is (A)

Sol. 113 (B) 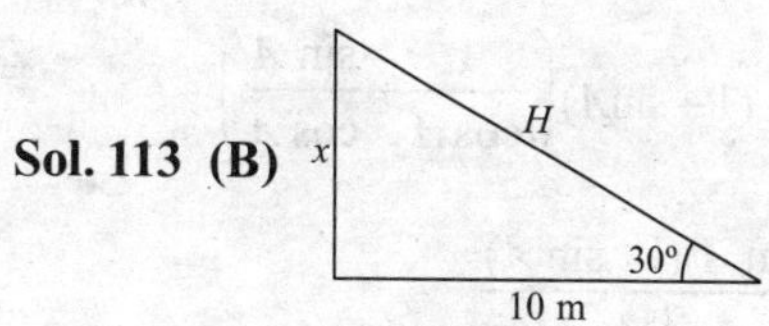

$$\tan 30 = \frac{x}{10}$$

$$x = 10 \times \frac{1}{\sqrt{3}}\,\text{m} = \frac{10}{\sqrt{3}}$$

$$\frac{10}{H} = \cos 30^\circ$$

$$\frac{10}{H} = \frac{\sqrt{3}}{2}$$

$$H = \frac{20}{\sqrt{3}}$$

So the height of the tree

$$= x + H = \frac{10}{\sqrt{3}} + \frac{20}{\sqrt{3}} = \frac{30}{\sqrt{3}}$$

$$= 10\sqrt{3}\,\text{m}$$

Hence Ans is (B)

Sol. 114 (A) 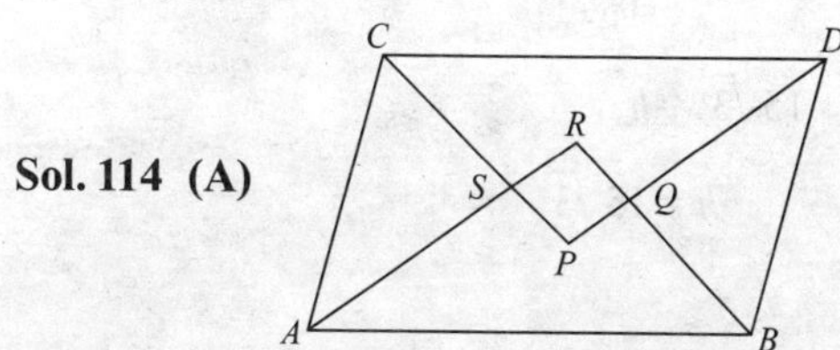

A parallelogram $ABCD$ in which bisecrtors of angles A, B, C, D intersect at P, Q, R, S to form a quadrilateral $PQRS$:

Since $ABCD$ is a parallelogram. Therefore,

$$AD \parallel BC$$

Now, $AD \parallel BC$ and transversal AB intersects them at A and B respectively. therefore,

$\angle A + \angle B = 180^\circ$

[$\because$ Sum of consecutive interior angles is 180°]

$\Rightarrow \quad \frac{1}{2}\angle A + \frac{1}{2}\angle B = 90^\circ$

Now by angle sum property by Δ

$\angle R = 90^\circ$

Similarly $\quad \angle S = \angle Q = 90^\circ$

Hence, *PQRS* is a rectangle.

Hence Ans is (A)

Sol. 115 (C) Sec A $(1 - \sin A)(\sec A + \tan A)$

$$= \frac{1}{\cos A}(1-\sin A)\left(\frac{1}{\cos A} + \frac{\sin A}{\cos A}\right)$$

$$= \frac{(1-\sin A)(1+\sin A)}{\cos^2 A}$$

$$= \frac{1-\sin^2 A}{\cos^2 A}$$

$$= \frac{\cos^2 A}{\cos^2 A}$$

$$= 1$$

Hence Ans is (C)

Sol. 116 (C)

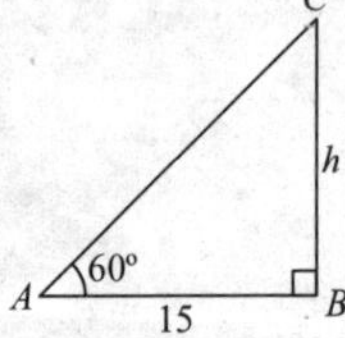

Let the height of tower is $BC = h\ m$

Now in right angle triangle ΔABC

$$\tan 60^\circ = \frac{BC}{AB}$$

$$\sqrt{3} = \frac{h}{15}$$

$$15\sqrt{3} = h$$

$$h = 15\sqrt{3}$$

Hence Ans is (C)

Sol. 117 (B) $\sin 60^\circ = \frac{AB}{12\sqrt{2}}$

$$AB = \frac{\sqrt{3}}{2} 12\sqrt{2}$$

$$= 6\sqrt{6}$$

$$\cos 60^\circ = \frac{BC}{12\sqrt{2}}$$

$$BC = 12\sqrt{2} \times \frac{1}{2}$$

$$= 6\sqrt{2}$$

$$\text{Perimeter} = AB + BC + AC$$

$$= 6\sqrt{2} + 6\sqrt{6} + 12\sqrt{2}$$

$$\Rightarrow \quad = 18\sqrt{2} + 6\sqrt{6}$$

$$\Rightarrow \quad = \sqrt{2}(18 + 6\sqrt{3})$$

Hence Ans is (B)

Sol. 118 (D) $\quad \angle R = 90^\circ$

$$\angle P = 30^\circ$$

$$PQ = \sqrt{13}$$

$$\frac{PR}{PQ} = \sin 60^\circ$$

$$PR = \sqrt{13} \times \frac{\sqrt{3}}{2} = \frac{\sqrt{39}}{2}$$

$$\frac{QR}{PQ} = \cos 60^\circ$$

$$QR = \frac{\sqrt{13}}{2}$$

coses 60° – sec60°

$$= \frac{\sqrt{13}}{\frac{\sqrt{39}}{2}} - \frac{\sqrt{13}}{\frac{\sqrt{13}}{2}}$$

$$= \frac{2}{\sqrt{3}} - 2$$

$$\Rightarrow \quad = 2\left(\frac{1}{\sqrt{3}} - 1\right)$$

$$\Rightarrow \quad = 2\left(\frac{1-\sqrt{3}}{\sqrt{3}}\right)$$

Hence Ans is (D)

Sol. 119 (A) Conceptual

Hence Ans is (A)

Sol. 120 (D) $\sin^3\theta + \cos^3\theta = (\sin\theta + \cos\theta)(\sin^2\theta + \cos^2\theta - \sin\theta\cos\theta) = 0$

$$\sin\theta + \cos\theta = 0$$

$$\sin\theta = -\cos\theta$$

$$\theta = -45^\circ$$

Hence Ans is (D)

Sol. 121 (A)

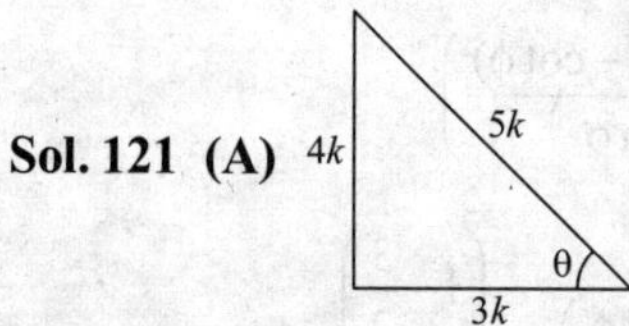

For a given triangle θ ∈ Quadrant 1

⇒ All trigonometric functions are positive

$$B = \sqrt{H^2 - P^2}$$

$$\Rightarrow \quad = \frac{5\tan\theta - 4\operatorname{cosec}\theta}{5\sec\theta - 4\cot\theta}$$

$$= \frac{5\left[\frac{4}{3}\right] - 4\left[\frac{5}{4}\right]}{5\left[\frac{5}{3}\right] - 4\left[\frac{3}{4}\right]}$$

$$\Rightarrow \quad = \frac{20}{3} - 5$$

$$= \frac{\frac{20}{3} - 5}{\frac{25}{3} - 3}$$

$$= \frac{\frac{5}{3}}{\frac{16}{3}}$$

$$= \frac{5}{16}$$

Hence Ans is (A)

Sol. 122 (A) When have,

$$\text{LHS} = m^2 - n^2$$

$$\Rightarrow \quad \text{LHS} = (\tan\theta + \sin\theta)^2 - (\tan\theta - \sin\theta)^2$$

$$\Rightarrow \quad \text{LHS} = 4\tan\theta\sin\theta$$

$$[\because\ (a+b)^2 - (a-b)^2 = 4ab]$$

And, $\quad \text{RHS} = 4\sqrt{nm}$

$$\Rightarrow \quad \text{RHS} = 4\sqrt{(\tan\theta + \sin\theta)(\tan\theta - \sin\theta)}$$

$$\Rightarrow \quad \text{RHS} = 4\sqrt{(\tan^2\theta - \sin^2\theta)}$$

$$\Rightarrow \quad \text{RHS} = 4\sqrt{\frac{\sin^2\theta}{\cos^2\theta} - \sin^2\theta}$$

$$\Rightarrow \quad \text{RHS} = 4\sqrt{\frac{\sin^2\theta - \sin^2\theta\cos^2\theta}{\cos^2\theta}}$$

$$\Rightarrow \quad \text{RHS} = 4\sqrt{\frac{\sin^2\theta(1-\cos^2\theta)}{\cos^2\theta}}$$

$$\Rightarrow \quad \text{RHS} = 4\sqrt{\frac{\sin^4\theta}{\cos^2\theta}}$$

$$= 4\frac{\sin^2\theta}{\cos\theta}$$

$$4\sin\theta\,\frac{\sin\theta}{\cos\theta} = 4\sin\theta\tan\theta.$$

Thus, we have

$$\text{LHS} = \text{RHS},$$

i.e., $\quad m^2 - n^2 = 4\sqrt{mn}$

Hence Ans is (A)

Sol. 123 (D)

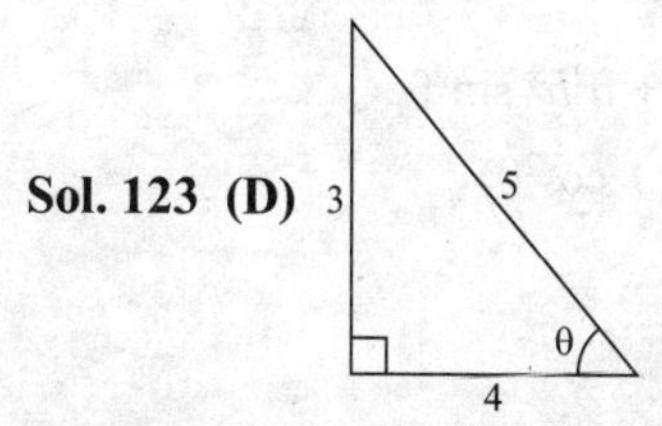

If $\quad \sin\theta = \frac{3}{5}\ \cos\theta = \frac{4}{5}$

using Pythagoras Theorem

Therefore $\quad \sin 2\theta = 2\sin\theta\cos\theta$

$$= 2 \times \frac{3}{5} \times \frac{4}{5} = \frac{24}{25}$$

Hence Ans is (D)

Sol. 124 (C) $\quad \sin\theta - \cos\theta = 0$

Squaring on both sides

$$(\sin\theta - \cos\theta) = 0^2$$

$$\sin^2\theta + \cos^2\theta - 2\sin\theta\cos\theta = 0$$

$$1 - 2\sin\theta\cos\theta = 0$$

$$1 = 2\sin\theta\cos\theta$$

$$\frac{1}{2} = \sin\theta\cos\theta \quad \ldots(1)$$

Now we know that

$$\sin^2\theta + \cos^2\theta = 1$$

Squaring on both sides

$$(\sin^2\theta + \cos^2\theta)^2 = 1^2$$

$$\sin^4\theta + \cos^4\theta + 2\sin^2\theta\cos^2\theta = 1 \quad \text{(using (i))}$$

$$\Rightarrow \quad \sin^4\theta + \cos^4\theta + 2 \times \left(\frac{1}{2}\right)^2 = 1$$

$$\sin^4\theta + \cos^4\theta = 1 - \frac{1}{2}$$

$$\sin^4\theta + \cos^4\theta = \frac{1}{2}$$

Hence Ans is (C)

Sol. 125 (B) $\cos(\alpha+\beta) = 0$

$$\alpha + \beta = 90^o$$
$$\alpha = 90^o - \beta$$
$$\sin(\alpha - \beta) = \sin(90^o - \beta - \beta)$$
$$= \sin(90^o - 2\beta) = \cos 2\beta$$

Hence Ans is (B)

Sol. 126 (C) $x = a\cos\theta$ & $y = b\sin\theta$

$$= b^2x^2 + a^2y^2$$
$$= b^2a^2\cos^2\theta + a^2b^2\sin^2\theta$$
$$= a^2b^2(\sin^2\theta + \cos^2\theta)$$
$$= a^2b^2$$

Hence Ans is (C)

Sol. 127 (B) Consider $\tan 1^\circ \tan 2^\circ \ldots \tan 89^\circ$

$= \tan 1^\circ \tan 2^\circ \ldots \tan(90^\circ - 2)\tan(90^\circ - 1)$

$= \tan 1^\circ \tan 2^\circ \ldots \cot 2^\circ \cot 1^\circ$

$= 1 \quad (\because \tan\theta \times \cot\theta = 1)$

Hence Ans is (B)

Sol. 128 (A) Given $\tan\phi = \dfrac{2}{3}$ ...(1)

to find $\left(\dfrac{1+\tan\phi}{\sin\phi+\cos\phi}\right)\left(\dfrac{1-\cot\phi}{\sec\phi+\operatorname{cosec}\phi}\right)$

$$= \left(\frac{1+\frac{\sin\phi}{\cos\phi}}{\sin\phi+\cos\phi}\right)\left(\frac{1-\cot\phi}{\frac{1}{\cos\phi}+\frac{1}{\sin\phi}}\right)$$

$$= \left(\frac{\frac{\cos\phi+\sin\phi}{\cos\phi}}{\sin\phi+\cos\phi}\right)\left(\frac{1-\cot\phi}{\frac{\cos\phi+\sin\phi}{\cos\phi\times\sin\phi}}\right)$$

$$= \left(\frac{1}{\cos\phi}\right)\left(\frac{\cos\phi\times\sin\phi\times(1-\cot\phi)}{\cos\phi+\sin\phi}\right)$$

$$= \left(\frac{(1-\cot\phi)}{\frac{\cos\phi+\sin\phi}{\sin\phi}}\right) = \left(\frac{1-\cot\phi}{1+\tan\phi}\right) = \frac{\left(1-\frac{3}{2}\right)}{\left(1+\frac{3}{2}\right)}$$

$$= \frac{\left(-\frac{1}{2}\right)}{\left(\frac{5}{3}\right)} = -\frac{1}{5}$$

Hence Ans is (A)

Sol. 129 (B)

From figure we have

$$\tan 30^\circ = \frac{h}{20+x}$$

$$\Rightarrow \quad h = (20+x) \times \tan 30^\circ$$

$$\Rightarrow \quad h = \frac{(20+x)}{\sqrt{3}} \quad \ldots(1)$$

and $$\tan 60^\circ = \frac{h}{x}$$

$$\Rightarrow \quad h = x\tan 60^\circ$$

$$\Rightarrow \quad h = \sqrt{3}x \quad \ldots(2)$$

From (1) & (2), we have

$$\frac{20+x}{\sqrt{3}} = \sqrt{3}x$$

$$\Rightarrow \quad 20 + x = 3x$$

$$\Rightarrow \quad x = 10\,\text{m}$$

Hence Ans is (B)

Sol. 130 (A) We have,

$$\operatorname{cosec} x - \sin x = a$$

and $$\sec x - \cos x = b$$

$$\Rightarrow \quad a = \frac{1}{\sin x} - \sin x$$

and $$b = \frac{1}{\cos x} - \cos x$$

$\Rightarrow \quad a = \dfrac{1-\sin^2 x}{\sin x}$

and $\quad b = \dfrac{1-\cos^2 x}{\cos x}$

$\Rightarrow \quad a = \dfrac{\cos^2 x}{\sin x}$

and $\quad b = \dfrac{\sin^2 x}{\cos x}$

$\Rightarrow \quad a = \cos x \cot x$

and $\quad b = \sin x \tan x$

consider $\quad a^2 b = \cos^2 x \cot^2 x \sin x \tan x = \cos^3 x$

consider $\quad ab^2 = \cos x \cot x \sin^2 x \tan^2 x = \sin^3 x$

$\Rightarrow \quad (a^2b)^{2/3} + (ab^2)^{2/3} = (\cos^3 x)^{2/3} + (\sin^3 x)^{2/3}$

$\Rightarrow \quad \cos^2 x + \sin^2 x = 1$

Hence Ans is (A)

Sol. 131 (C) $\quad m = \cos^4\theta + \sin^2\theta = m$

$= \left(\dfrac{\cos 2\theta + 1}{2}\right)^2 + \dfrac{1-\cos 2\theta}{2}$

$\Rightarrow \quad m = \dfrac{\cos^2 2\theta + 1 + 2\cos 2\theta}{4} + \dfrac{2-2\cos 2\theta}{4}$

$\Rightarrow \quad m = \dfrac{\cos^2 2\theta + 3}{4}$

$\Rightarrow \quad m = \dfrac{\dfrac{\cos 4\theta + 1}{2} + 3}{4}$

$\Rightarrow \quad m = \dfrac{\cos 4\theta + 7}{8}$

$\Rightarrow \quad m = \dfrac{1}{8}\ [\cos 4\theta + 7]\ [-1 \le \cos 4\theta \le 1]$

$\Rightarrow \quad \dfrac{3}{4} \le m \le 1$

Hence Ans is (C)

Sol. 132 (B) In ΔAFC $\tan\theta = \dfrac{AF}{AC} = \dfrac{45}{AC}$

In ΔBEC $\quad \tan(90-\theta) = \cot\theta = \dfrac{20}{CB}$

$AC = 45 \cot\theta$

$CB = 20 \tan\theta$

ABC is on equilateral Δ so,

$AC = CB$

$\Rightarrow \quad 45 \cot\theta = 20 \tan\theta$

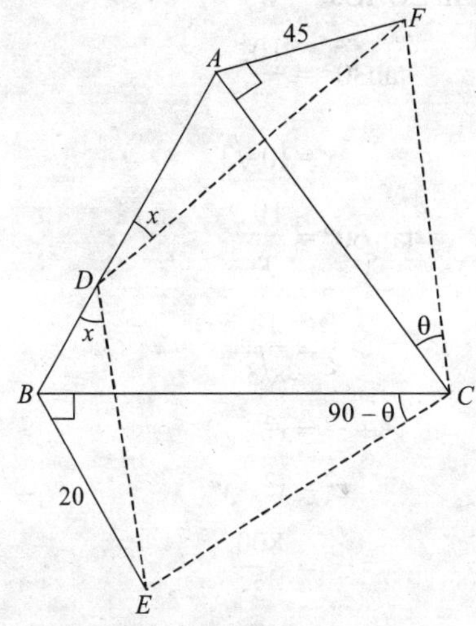

$\Rightarrow \quad \dfrac{45}{20} = \dfrac{\tan\theta}{\cot\theta}$

$\Rightarrow \quad \dfrac{9}{4} = \tan^2\theta$

$\Rightarrow \quad \tan\theta = \dfrac{3}{2} \quad \ldots(1)$

In ΔAFC $\quad \tan\theta = \dfrac{45}{AC} \quad \ldots(2)$

From Equation-(1) and Equation-(2)

$\dfrac{45}{AC} = \dfrac{3}{2}$

$\Rightarrow \quad AC = 30$

In ΔAFD, $\quad \tan x = \dfrac{45}{AD}$

In ΔBDE, $\quad \tan x = \dfrac{20}{BD}$

$\Rightarrow \quad \dfrac{45}{AD} = \dfrac{20}{BD}$

$\Rightarrow \quad \dfrac{AD}{BD} = \dfrac{45}{20} = \dfrac{9}{4}$

So, side $\quad AD = 30 \times \dfrac{9}{13}$

$\Rightarrow \quad \dfrac{270}{13} = 20\dfrac{10}{13}$ m

Hence Ans is (B)

Sol. 133 (B) $\quad 1 \ge \cos x^\circ > \dfrac{1}{\sqrt{2}}$,

Where $\quad 0 \le x < 45$

$0 \le \sin x^\circ < \dfrac{1}{\sqrt{2}}$,

Where $\quad 0 \le x < 45$

$\Rightarrow$ $\cos x^\circ - \sin x^\circ$ is always positive.

Hence Ans is (B)

Sol. 134 (A) In ΔOAC,

$$\tan 30° = \frac{10}{x}$$

$\Rightarrow$ $$x = 10\sqrt{3}$$

In ΔOCD, $$\tan 60° = \frac{10}{y}$$

$$y = \frac{10}{\sqrt{3}}$$

In ΔADC, $$y^2 + z^2 = x^2$$

$$z^2 = x^2 - y^2$$

$$z^2 = \frac{800}{3}$$

$$z = \frac{20\sqrt{2}}{\sqrt{3}}$$

$$\text{Required area} = yz = \frac{10}{\sqrt{3}} \times \frac{20\sqrt{2}}{\sqrt{3}} = \frac{200\sqrt{2}}{\sqrt{3}}$$

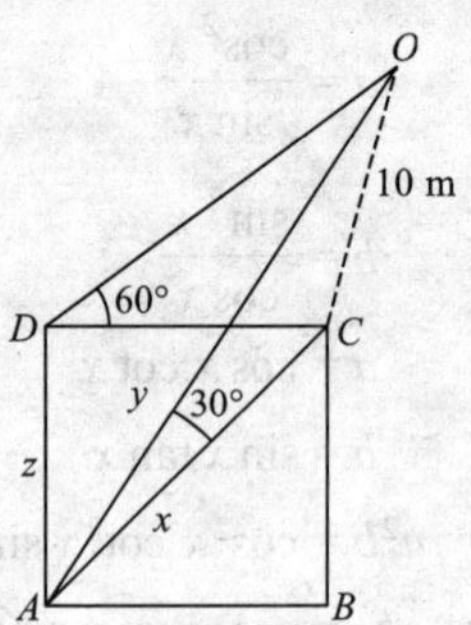

Hence Ans is (A)

* * * * *

Congruent Triangles & Similar Triangles 5

- Figures having the same shape and size are called congruent figures.

- Two circles of the same radii are congruent.

- Two squares of the same sides are congruent.

- If two triangles *ABC* and *DEF* are congruent under the correspondence $A \to D, B \to E$ and $C \to F$, then symbolically it is expressed as $\Delta ABC \cong \Delta DEF$.

- Two triangles are congruent, if two sides and the included angle of one triangle are equal to two sides and the included angle of the other triangle. It is called *SAS* congruence rule.

- Two triangles are congruent, if two angles and the included side of one triangle are equal to two angles and the included side of the other triangle. It is called *ASA* congruence rule.

- Two triangles are congruent, if any two pairs of angles and one pair of corresponding sides are equal. It is called *AAS* congruence rule.

- Angles opposite to equal sides of an isosceles triangle are equal.

- The sides opposite to equal angles of a triangle are equal.

- Each angle of an equilateral triangle is 60°.

- If three sides of one triangle are equal to the three sides of another triangle, then the two triangles are congruent. It is called *SSS* congruence rule.

- If in two right triangles, the hypotenuse and one side of one triangle are equal to the hypotenuse and one side of the other triangle, then the two triangles are congruent. It is called RHS congruence rule.

- If two sides of a triangle are unequal, the angle opposite to the longer side is larger.

- In any triangle, the side opposite to the larger angle is longer.

- The sum of any two sides of a triangle is greater than the third side

- Two figures having the same shape but not necessarily the same size are called similar figures.

- All the congruent figures are similar but the converse is not true.

- Two polygons of the same number of sides are similar, if (i) their corresponding angles are equal and (ii) their corresponding sides are in the same ratio (i.e., proportion).

The symbol ~ means "is similar to."

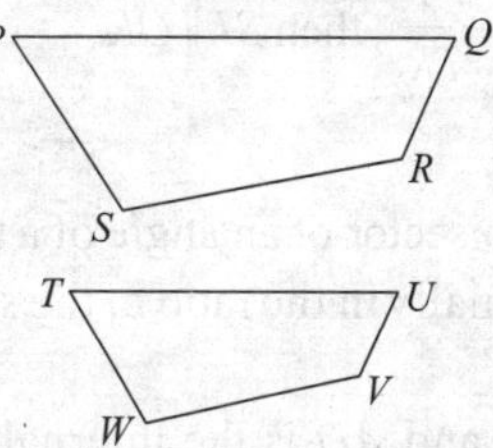

Figure 5.1

$PQRS \sim TUVW$

When you name similar figures, be sure to name corresponding vertices in the same order. For example, if $PQRS \sim TUVW$, then :

(i) $\angle P \cong \angle T, \angle Q \cong \angle U, \angle R \cong \angle V$ and $\angle S \cong \angle W$

(ii) $\dfrac{PQ}{TU} = \dfrac{QR}{UV} = \dfrac{RS}{VW} = \dfrac{SP}{WT}$

- Two triangles are similar, if

(i) Their corresponding angles are equal

(ii) Their corresponding sides are in the same ratio (or proportion).

- **Basic Proportionality Theorem (B.P.T.) (Thales Theorem) :**

In a triangle, a line drawn parallel to one side, to intersect the other sides in distinct points, divides the two sides in the same ratio.

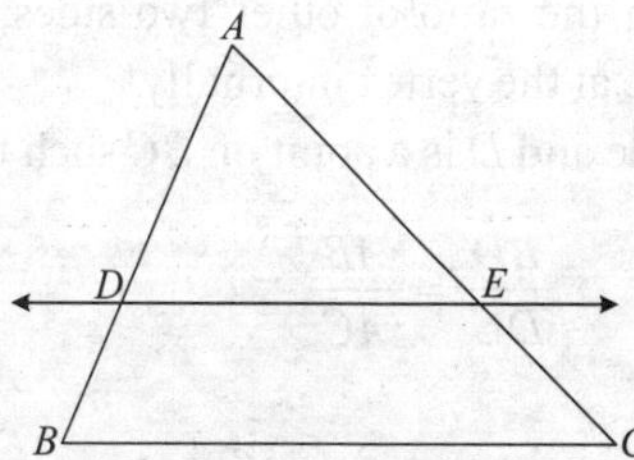

Figure 5.2

In ΔABC, if $DE \parallel BC$ then

(i) $\dfrac{AD}{DB} = \dfrac{AE}{EC}$ (ii) $\dfrac{AB}{AD} = \dfrac{AC}{AE}$

(iii) $\dfrac{AB}{DB} = \dfrac{AC}{EC}$

❍ **Converse of Basic Proportionality Theorem :**
If a line divides any two sides of a triangle in the same ratio, then the line is parallel to the third side.

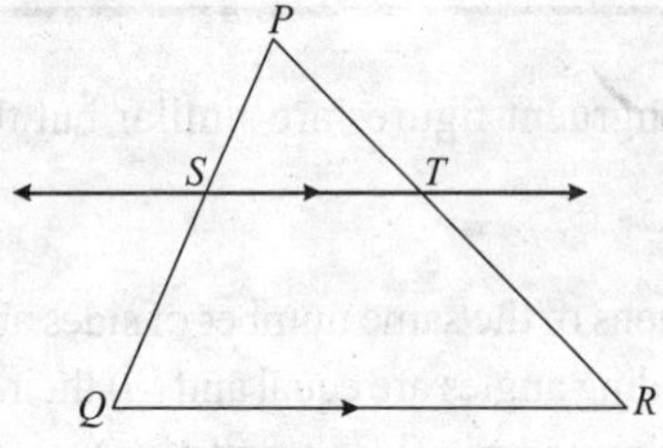

Figure 5.3

In ΔPQR, if $\dfrac{PS}{SQ} = \dfrac{PT}{TR}$, then $ST \parallel QR$.

❍ The internal bisector of an angle of a triangle divides the opposite side internally in the ratio of the sides containing the angle.
ABC is a triangle and AD is the internal bisector of $\angle BAC$ meeting BC at D [figure-5.4]

$\therefore \quad \angle BAD = \angle DAC.$

then $\quad \dfrac{BD}{DC} = \dfrac{AB}{AC}$

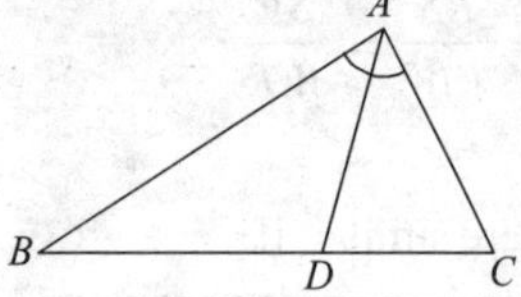

Figure 5.4

Converse of angle bisector theorem :
In a triangle ABC, if D is a point on BC such that $\dfrac{BD}{DC} = \dfrac{AB}{AC}$, then AD is the internal bisector of $\angle BAC$.

OR

If a line-segment through one vertex of a triangle divides the opposite side in the ratio of other two sides, then the line bisects the angle at the vertex internally.
ABC is a triangle and D is a point on BC such that

$$\frac{BD}{DC} = \frac{AB}{AC}$$

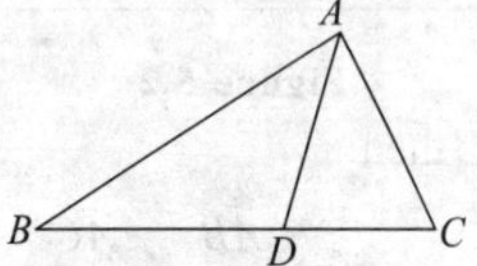

Figure 5.5

$\therefore \quad \angle BAD = \angle DAC$

❍ If in two triangles, corresponding angles are equal, then their corresponding sides are in the same ratio and hence the two triangles are similar (*AAA similarity criterion*).

❍ If in two triangles, two angles of one triangle are respectively equal to the two angles of the other triangle, then the two triangles are similar (*AA similarity criterion*).

❍ If in two triangles, corresponding sides are in the same ratio, then their corresponding angles are equal and hence the triangles are similar (*SSS similarity criterion*).

❍ If one angle of a triangle is equal to the one angle of another triangle and the sides including these angles are in the same ratio (proportional), then the triangles are similar (*SAS similarity criterion*).

❍ If a perpendicular is drawn from the vertex of the right angle of a right triangle to hypotenuse, then the triangles on both sides of the perpendicular are similar to the whole triangle and also to each other.

❍ The ratio of the areas of two similar triangles are equal to the ratio of the squares of any two corresponding sides. (dimension)

❍ The areas of two similar triangles are in the ratio of the squares of the corresponding altitudes.

❍ The areas of two similar triangles are in the ratio of the squares of the corresponding medians.

❍ If the areas of two similar triangles are equal, then the triangles are congruent, *i.e.*, equal and similar triangles are congruent.

❍ **The Pythagoras Theorem :**
In a right triangle, the square of the hypotenuse is equal to the sum of the squares of the other two sides. In figure-5.6, $\angle B = 90°$, so, $AC^2 = AB^2 + BC^2$.

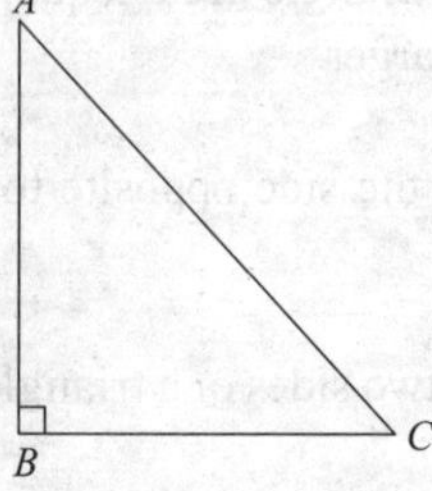

Figure 5.6

Converse of the Pythagoras Theorem

In a triangle, if the square of one side is equal to the sum of the squares of the other two sides, then the angle opposite to the first side is a right angle.

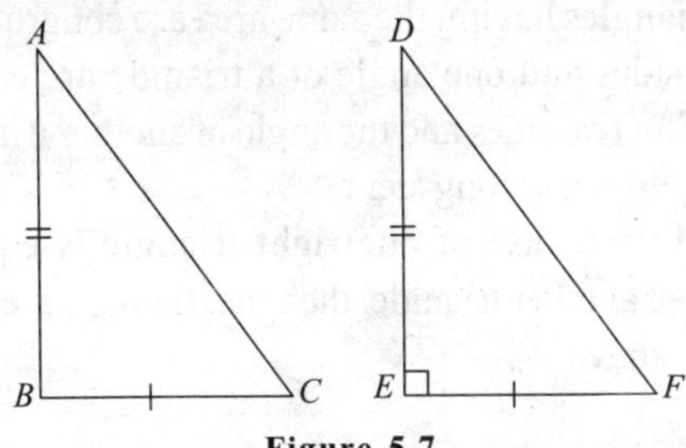

Figure 5.7

- In figure-5.8, ΔABC is an obtuse-angled triangle, where $\angle ABC$ is an obtuse angle. If AD is perpendicular to CB produced, then $AC^2 = AB^2 + BC^2 + 2BC.BD$ [Obtuse triangle property]

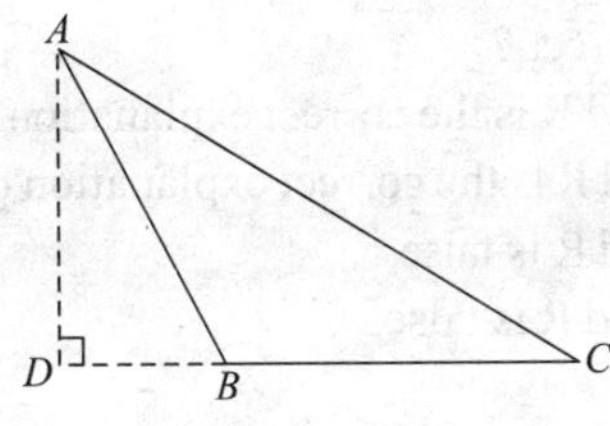

Figure 5.8

- In figure-5.9, $\angle ABC$ of ΔABC is acute and $AD \perp BC$. then $AC^2 = AB^2 + BC^2 - 2BC.\,BD$.

[Acute triangle property]

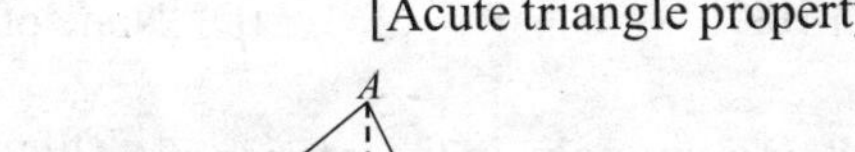
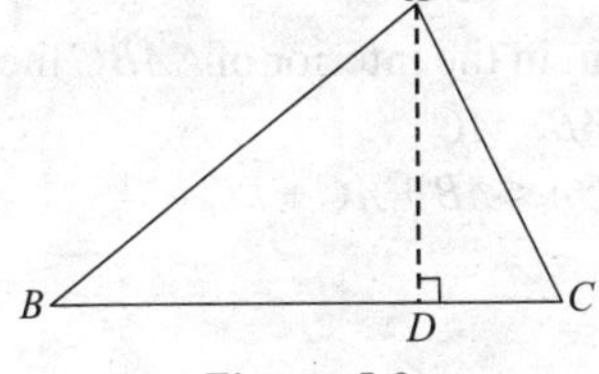

Figure 5.9

- If AD is a median of a triangle ABC, then $AB^2 + AC^2 = 2BD^2 + 2AD^2$

OR

In any triangle, the sum of the squares of any two sides is equal to twice the square of half the third side together with twice the square of the median which bisects the third side. [This result is known as Apollonius' theorem] ABC is a triangle and AD is a median of the triangle so that $BD = DC$. We assume that $AB > AC$. Then $AB^2 + AC^2 = 2BD^2 + 2AD^2$.

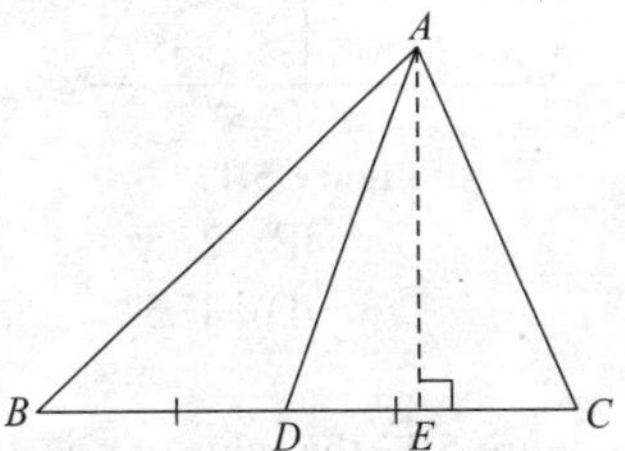

Figure 5.10

- Three times the sum of the squares of the sides of a triangle is equal to four times the sum of the squares of the medians of the triangle.

ABC is a triangle in which AD, BE and CF are the medians [Figure-5.11], then $3(AB^2 + BC^2 + CA^2) = 4(AD^2 + BE^2 + CF^2)$

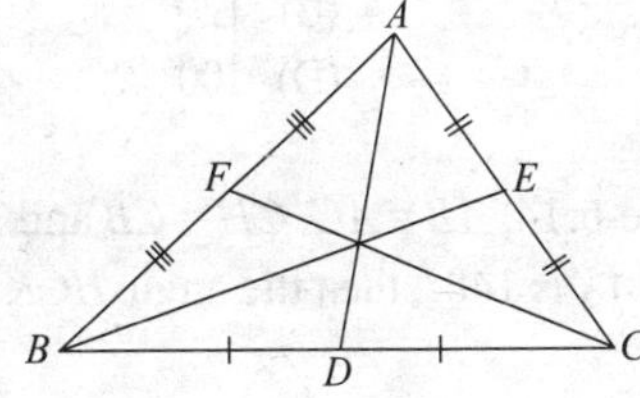

Figure 5.11

* * * * *

PRACTICE EXERCISE - 5.1

5-1 In the adjoining figure-5.12 $AM \perp BC$ and AN is the bisector of $\angle BAC$. If $\angle B = 70°$ and $\angle C = 35°$, then $\angle MAN$ is :

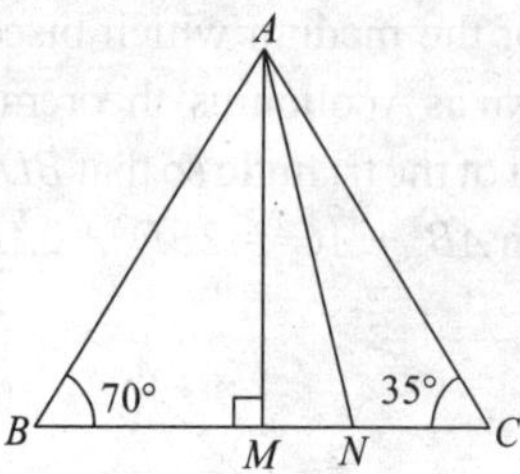

Figure 5.12

(A) 17.5° (B) 27.5°
(C) 37.5° (D) 47.5°

5-2 In the given figure-5.13 the value of x, if $AB \parallel CD$:

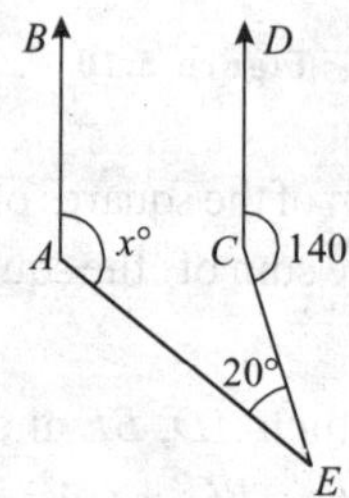

Figure 5.13

(A) 140° (B) 120°
(C) 110° (D) 100°

5-3 In the figure-5.14, $AB = AC$, $CH = CB$ and $HK \parallel BC$. If the exterior angle CAX is 140°, then the angle HCK is :

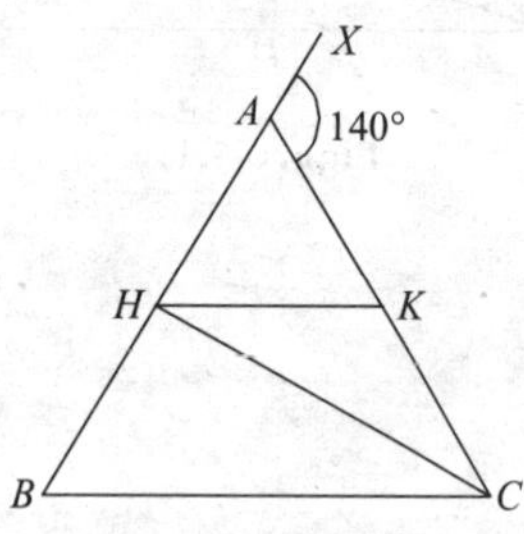

Figure 5.14

(A) 45° (B) 55°
(C) 50° (D) 30°

5-4 In the adjoining figure-5.15, the value of x is :

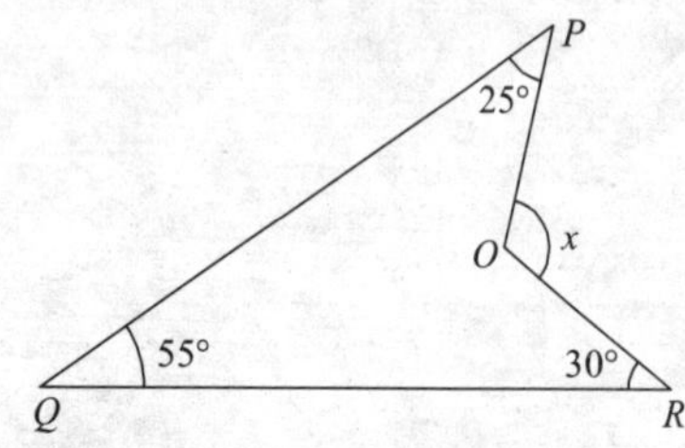

Figure 5.15

(A) 250° (B) 110°
(C) 120° (D) 80°

5-5 Which of the following statement(s) is/are false ?

(A) Two triangles having the same area are congruent
(B) If two sides and one angle of a triangle are equal to the corresponding two sides and the angle of another triangle, then the two triangles are congruent
(C) If the hypotenuse of one right triangle is equal to the hypotenuse of another triangle, then the triangles are congruent
(D) All the above

5-6 **A :** Two triangles are said to be congruent if two sides and an angle of one triangle are respectively equal to the two sides and an angle of the other.

R : Two triangles are congruent if two sides and the included angle of one triangle are equal to the corresponding two sides and the included angle of the other. Which of the following statements is correct ?

(A) A is false and R is the correct explanation of A
(B) A is true and R is the correct explanation of A
(C) A is true and R is false
(D) A is false and R is false

5-7 In a ΔABC, the internal bisectors of $\angle B$ and $\angle C$ meet at P and the external bisector of $\angle B$ and $\angle C$ meet at Q. Then $\angle BPC + \angle BQC =$

(A) 90° (B) $\angle A$
(C) 180° (D) None of these

5-8 D is any point in the interior of ΔABC then :

(A) $DB + DC < AB + AC$
(B) $DB + DC + DA < AB + AC + BC$
(C) A & B both
(D) None of these

5-9 $ABCD$ is quadrilateral in which diagonals AC and BD intersect at O then :

(A) $AB + BC + CD + DA > AC + BD$
(B) $AB + BC + CD + DA < 2(AC + BD)$
(C) A & B both
(D) None of these

5-10 In the given figure-5.16 PBC and PKH are straight lines. If $AH = AK$, $b = 70°$, $c = 40°$, the value of d is :

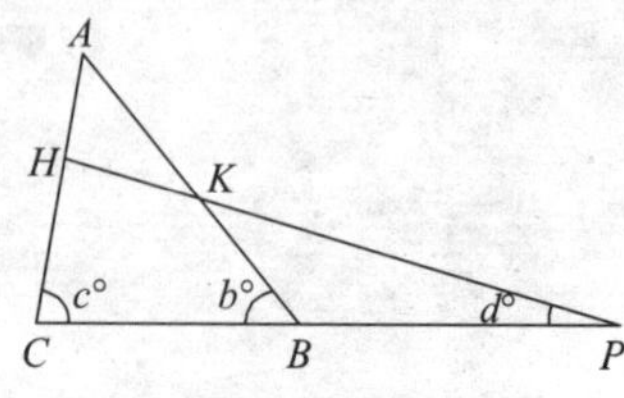

Figure 5.16

(A) 20° (B) 25°
(C) 15° (D) 35°

5-11 In a triangle ABC, if AB, BC and AC are the three sides of the triangle, then which of the statements is necessarily true ?

(A) $AB+BC<AC$ (B) $AB+BC>AC$
(C) $AB+BC=AC$ (D) $AB^2+BC^2=AC^2$

5-12 The sides of a triangle are 12 cm, 8 cm and 6 cm respectively, the triangle is :

(A) Actue (B) Obtuse
(C) Right (D) Can't be determined

5-13 If the sides of a triangle are produced then the sum of the exterior angles i.e.,

$\angle DAB+\angle EBC+\angle FCA$ is equal to :

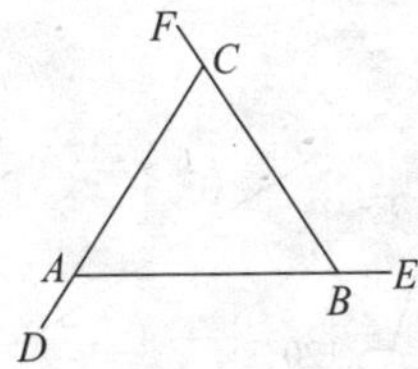

Figure 5.17

(A) 180° (B) 270°
(C) 360° (D) 240°

5-14 In the given figure-5.18 BC is produced to D and $\angle BAC=40°$ and $\angle ABC=70°$. Find the value of $\angle ACD$:

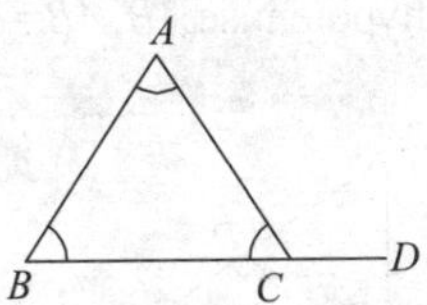

Figure 5.18

(A) 30° (B) 40°
(C) 70° (D) 110°

5-15 In a ΔABC, $\angle BAC>90°$, then $\angle ABC$ and $\angle ACB$ must be :

(A) Acute
(B) Obtuse
(C) One acute and one obtuse
(D) Can't be determined

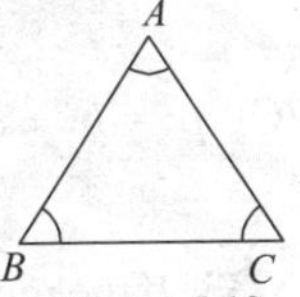

Figure 5.19

5-16 If the angles of a triangle are in the ratio 1 : 4 : 7, then the value of the largest angle is :

(A) 135° (B) 84°
(C) 105° (D) None of these

5-17 In the adjoining figure-5.20 $\angle B=70°$ and $\angle C=30°$. BO and CO are the angle bisectors of $\angle ABC$ and $\angle ACB$. Find the value of $\angle BOC$:

(A) 30°
(B) 40°
(C) 120°
(D) 130°

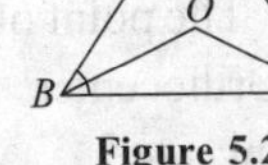

Figure 5.20

5-18 In the given diagram of ΔABC, $\angle B=80°$, $\angle C=30°$. BF and CF are the angle bisectors of $\angle CBD$ and $\angle BCE$ respectively. Find the value of $\angle BFC$:

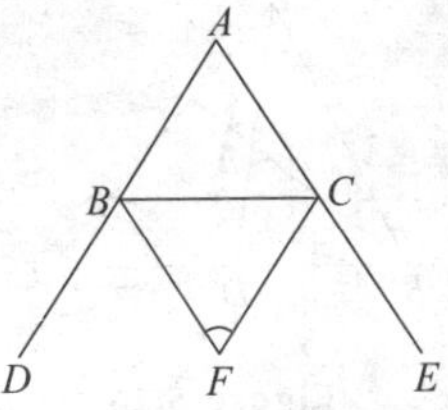

Figure 5.21

(A) 110° (B) 50°
(C) 125° (D) 55°

5-19 In an equilateral triangle, the incentre, circumcentre, orthocentre and centroid are :

(A) Concylic (B) Coincident
(C) Collinear (D) None of these

5-20 In the adjoining figure-5.22 D is the midpoint of BC of a ΔABC. DM and DN are the perpendicular on AB and AC respectively and $DM=DN$, then the ΔABC is :

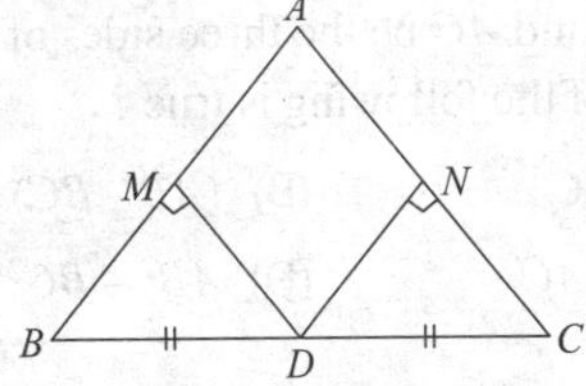

Figure 5.22

(A) Right angled (B) Isosceles
(C) Equilateral (D) Scalene

5-21 In the adjoining figure-5.23 of ΔABC, AD is the perpendicular bisector of side BC. The triangle ABC is :

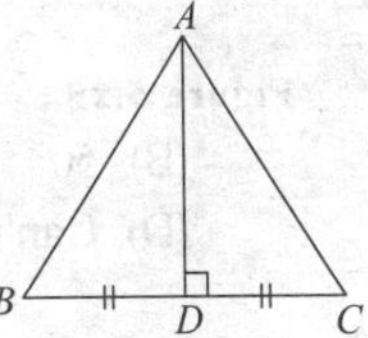

Figure 5.23

(A) Right angled (B) Isosceles
(C) Scalene (D) Equilateral

5-22 ΔABC is such that $AB=9$ cm, $BC=6$ cm, $AC=7.5$ cm. ΔDEF is similar to ΔABC. If $EF=12$ cm then DE is :

(A) 6 cm (B) 16 cm
(C) 18 cm (D) 15 cm

5-23 In ΔABC, $AB=5$cm, $AC=7$ cm. If AD is the angle bisector of $\angle A$. Then $BD:CD$ is :

(A) 25 : 49 (B) 49 : 25
(C) 6 : 1 (D) 5 : 7

5-24 In a ΔABC, D is the mid-point of BC and E is mid-point of AD, BF passes through E. What is the ratio of $AF : FC$?

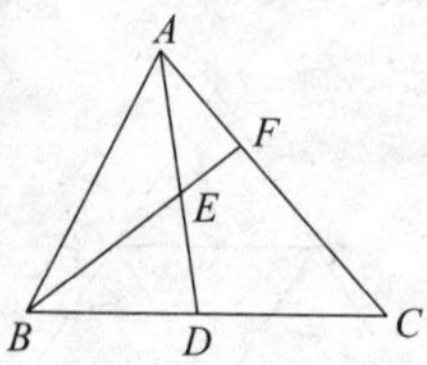

Figure 5.24

(A) 1 : 1 (B) 1 : 2
(C) 1 : 3 (D) 2 : 3

5-25 In a ΔABC, $AB = AC$ and $AD \perp BC$, then :
(A) $AB < AD$ (B) $AB > AD$
(C) $AB = AD$ (D) $AB \leq AD$

5-26 The difference between altitude and base of a right angled triangle is 17 cm and its hypotenuse is 25 cm. What is the sum of thc base and altitude of the triangle is :
(A) 24 cm (B) 31 cm
(C) 34 cm (D) Can't be determined

5-27 If AB, BC and AC be the three sides of a triangle ABC, then which one of the following is true ?
(A) $AB - BC = AC$ (B) $(AB - BC) > AC$
(C) $(AB - BC) < AC$ (D) $AB^2 - BC^2 = AC^2$

5-28 In the triangle ABC, side BC is produced to D. $\angle ACD = 100°$ if $BC = AC$, then $\angle ABC$ is :

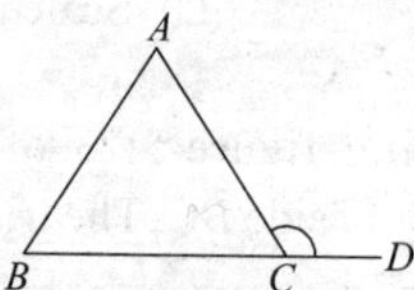

Figure 5.25

(A) 40° (B) 50°
(C) 80° (D) Can't be determined

5-29 In the adjoining figure-5.26 D, E and F are the mid-points of the sides BC, AC and AB respectively. ΔDEF is congruent to triangle :

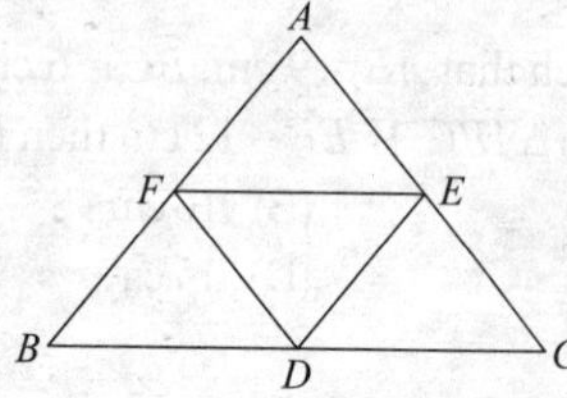

Figure 5.26

(A) ABC (B) AEF
(C) CDE, BFD (D) AFE, BFD and CDE

5-30 In the adjoining figure-5.27 $\angle BAC = 60°$ and $BC = a$, $AC = b$ and $AB = c$, then :

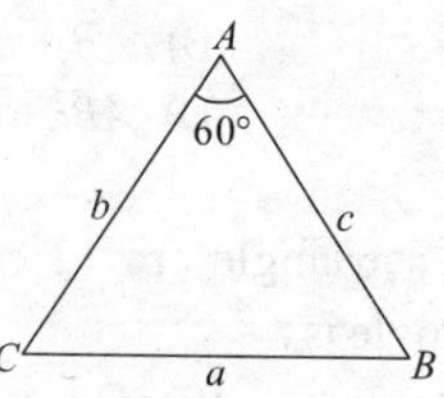

Figure 5.27

(A) $a^2 = b^2 + c^2$ (B) $a^2 = b^2 + c^2 - bc$
(C) $a^2 = b^2 + c^2 + bc$ (D) $a^2 = b^2 + 2bc$

5-31 In the adjoining figure-5.28 of ΔABC, $\angle BCA = 120°$ and $AB = c$, $BC = a$, $AC = b$ then :

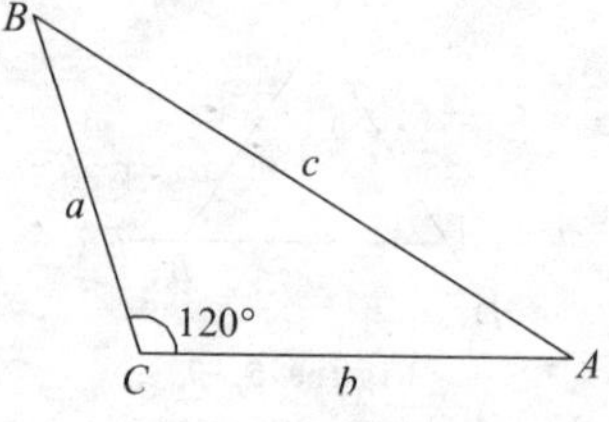

Figure 5.28

(A) $c^2 = a^2 + b^2 + ba$ (B) $c^2 = a^2 + b^2 - ba$
(C) $c^2 = a^2 + b^2 - 2ba$ (D) $c^2 = a^2 + b^2 + 2ab$

5-32 In a right angled ΔABC, $\angle C = 90°$ and CD is the perpendicular on the hypotenuse AB, $AB = c$, $BC = a$, $AC = b$ and $CD = p$, then :

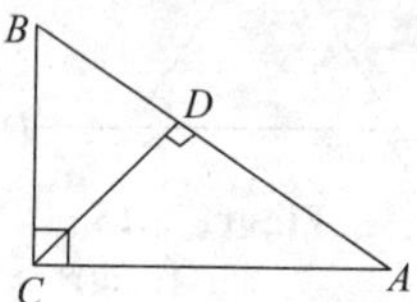

Figure 5.29

(A) $\dfrac{p}{a} = \dfrac{p}{b}$ (B) $\dfrac{1}{p^2} + \dfrac{1}{b^2} = \dfrac{1}{a^2}$

(C) $p^2 = b^2 + c^2$ (D) $\dfrac{1}{p^2} = \dfrac{1}{a^2} + \dfrac{1}{b^2}$

5-33 If the medians of a triangle are equal, then the triangle is :
(A) Right angled (B) Isoscels
(C) Equilateral (D) Scalene

5-34 The incenter of a triangle is determined by the:
(A) Medians (B) Angle bisector
(C) Perpendicular bisectors (D) Altitudes

5-35 The circumcenter of a triangle is determined by the :
(A) Altitudes (B) Median
(C) Perpendicular bisector (D) Angle bisectors

5-36 The point of intersection of the altitudes of a triangle is :
(A) Orthocenter (B) Centroid
(C) Incenter (D) Circumcenter

5-37 A triangle PQR is formed by joining the mid-point of the sides of a triangle ABC. 'O' is the circumcenter of ΔABC, then for ΔPQR, the point 'O' is :

(A) Incenter (B) Circumcenter
(C) Orthocenter (D) Centroid

5-38 If in a ΔABC, 'S' is the circumcenter then :

(A) S is equidistant from all the vertices of a triangle
(B) S is equidistant from all the sides of a triangle
(C) AS, BS and CS are the angular bisectors
(D) AS, BS and CS produced are the altitudes on the opposite sides

5-39 If AD, BE, CF are the altitudes of ΔABC whose orthocenter is H, then C is the orthocentre of :

(A) ΔABH (B) ΔBDH
(C) ΔABD (D) ΔBEA

5-40 In a right angled ΔABC, $\angle C = 90°$ and CD is the perpendicular on hypotenuse AB if $BC = 15$ cm and $AC = 20$ cm then CD is equal to :

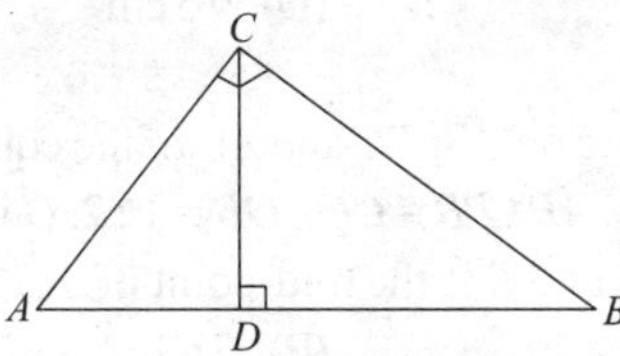

Figure 5.30

(A) 18 cm (B) 12 cm
(C) 17.5 cm (D) Can't be determined

5-41 In an equilateral ΔABC, if a, b and c denote the lengths of perpendicular from A, B and C respectively on the opposite sides, then :

(A) $a > b > c$ (B) $a > b < c$
(C) $a = b = c$ (D) $a = c \neq b$

5-42 What is the ratio of side and height of an equilateral triangle ?

(A) $2 : 1$ (B) $1 : 1$
(C) $2 : \sqrt{3}$ (D) $\sqrt{3} : 2$

5-43 The triangle is formed by joining the mid-points of the sides AB, BC and CA of ΔABC and the area of ΔPQR thus formed is 6 cm², then the area of ΔABC is :

(A) 36 cm² (B) 12 cm²
(C) 18 cm² (D) 24 cm²

5-44 One side other than the hypotenuse of right angle isosceles triangle is 6 cm. The length of the perpendicular on the hypotenuse from the opposite vertex is :

(A) 6 cm (B) $6\sqrt{2}$ cm
(C) 4 cm (D) $3\sqrt{2}$ cm

5-45 Any two of the four triangles formed by joining the mid-points of the sides of a given triangle are :

(A) Congruent
(B) Equal in area but not congruent
(C) Unequal in area and not congruent
(D) None of these

5-46 The internal bisectors of $\angle B$ and $\angle C$ of ΔABC meet at O. If $\angle A = 80°$ then $\angle BOC$ is :

(A) 50° (B) 160°
(C) 100° (D) 130°

5-47 The point in the plane of a triangle which is at equal perpendicular distance from the sides of the triangle is :

(A) Centroid (B) Incentre
(C) Circumcenre (D) Orthocentre

5-48 Incenter of a triangle lies in the interior of :

(A) A acute triangle only
(B) A right angled triangle only
(C) Any obtuse triangle only
(D) All of the above

5-49 In a triangle PQR, $PQ = 20$ cm and $PR = 6$ cm, the side QR is :

(A) Equal to 14cm (B) Less than 14cm
(C) Greater than 14cm (D) None of these

5-50 The four triangles formed by joining the pairs of mid-points of the sides of a given triangle are congruent if the given triangle is :

(A) An isosceles triangles (B) An equilateral triangle
(C) A right angled triangle (D) Of any shape

* * * * *

PRACTICE EXERCISE - 5.2

5-1 In the trapezium $PQRS$, PQ is parallel to RS and the ratio of the areas of the triangle POQ to triangle ROS is 225 : 900. Then SR = ?

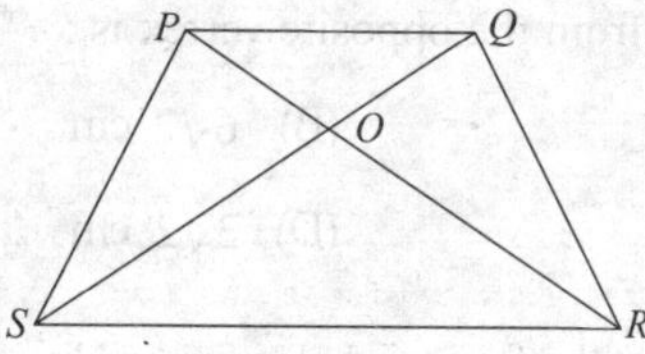

Figure 5.31

(A) $30\,PQ$ (B) $25\,PQ$

(C) $2\,PQ$ (D) PQ

5-2 In the following figure-5.32, $ABCD$ is a parallelogram, CB is extended to F and the line joining D and F intersect AB at E. Then,

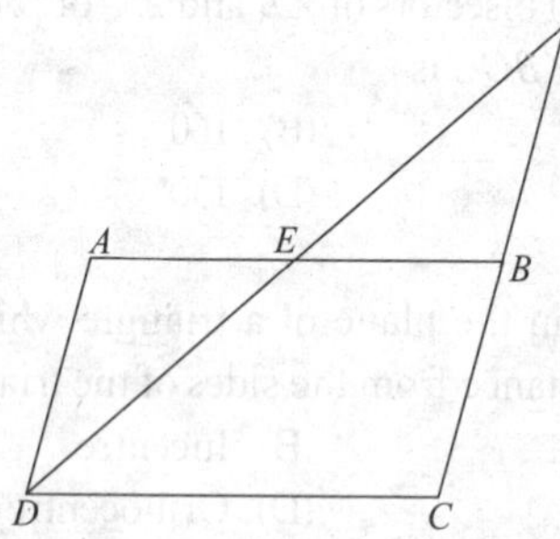

Figure 5.32

(A) $\frac{AD}{AE} = \frac{BF}{BE}$ (B) $\frac{AD}{AE} = \frac{CF}{CD}$

(C) $\frac{BF}{BE} = \frac{CF}{CD}$ (D) All of them are true

5-3

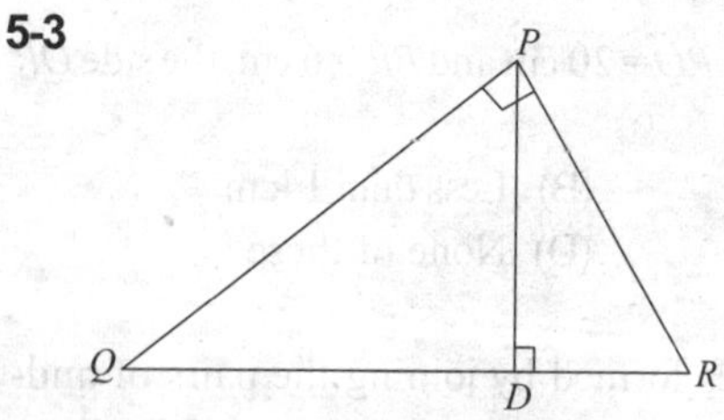

Figure 5.33

PQR is a right angled triangle, where $\angle P = 90°$. $\overline{PD}$ is perpendicular to $\overline{QR}$. $PQ : PR =$

(A) $QD : DR$ (B) $\sqrt{QD} : \sqrt{DR}$

(C) $QD^2 : RD^2$ (D) None of these

5-4 Diagonal AC of a rectangle $ABCD$ is produced to the point E such that $AC : CE = 2 : 1$. $AB = 8$ cm and $BC = 6$ cm. Find the length of DE.

(A) $2\sqrt{19}$ cm (B) 15 cm

(C) $3\sqrt{17}$ cm (D) 13 cm

5-5 In ΔPQR, $PQ = 6$ cm, $PR = 9$ cm and M is a point on QR such that it divides QR in the ratio 1 : 2. $PM \perp QR$. Find QR.

(A) $\sqrt{18}$ cm (B) $3\sqrt{12}$ cm

(C) $3\sqrt{15}$ cm (D) $\sqrt{20}$ cm

5-6 In the figure-5.34. below (not to scale), $ABCD$ is an isosceles trapezium. $AB \parallel CD$, a line drawn parallelogram to AB such that $AP : PD = BQ : QC = 1 : 2$. Given $AB = 9$ & $CD = 12$. Find PQ.

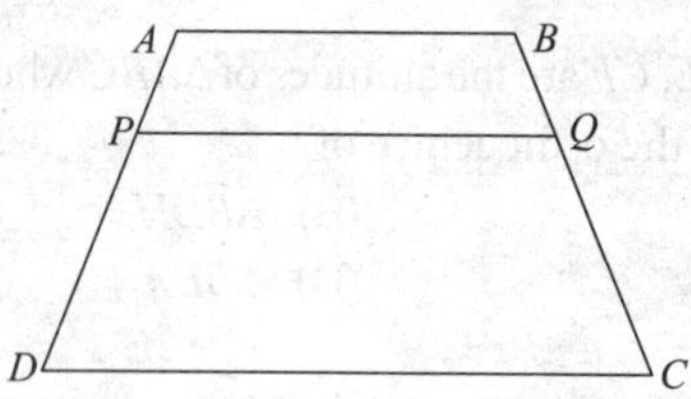

Figure 5.34

(A) 11 cm (B) 10.5 cm

(C) 10 cm (D) 9.5 cm

5-7 P, Q and R are on AB, BC and AC of the equilateral triangle ABC respectively. $AP : PB = CQ : QB = 1 : 2$. G is the centroid of the triangle PQB and R is the mid-point of AC. Find $BG : GR$.

(A) 1 : 2 (B) 2 : 3

(C) 3 : 4 (D) 4 : 5

5-8 In the figure-5.35 given below (not to scale), $AM : MC = 3 : 4$, $BP : PM = 3 : 2$ and $BN = 12$ cm. Find AN:

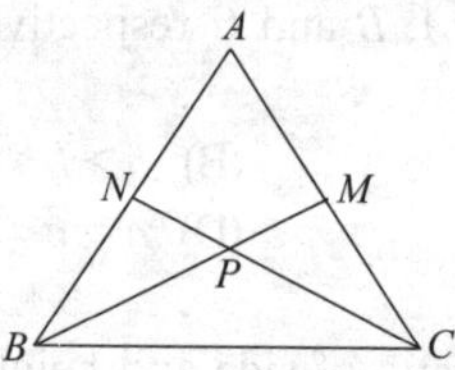

Figure 5.35

(A) 10 cm (B) 12 cm

(C) 14 cm (D) 16 cm

5-9 In the figure-5.36 below (not to scale), $\overline{AB} \perp \overline{CD}$ and AD is the bisector of $\angle BAE$. $AB = 3$ cm and $AC = 5$ cm. Find CD.

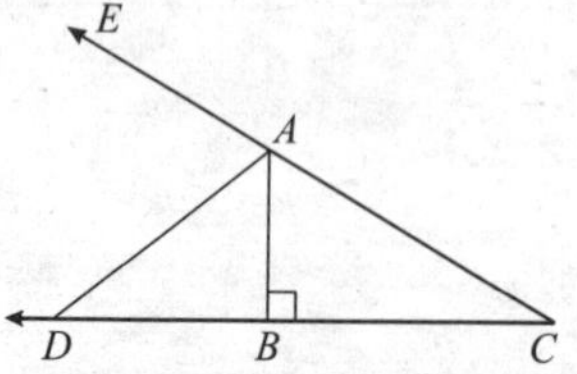

Figure 5.36

(A) 6 cm (B) 8 cm

(C) 10 cm (D) None of these

5-10 Two side of a triangle are 5 cm and 12 cm long. The measure of third side is an integer in cm. If the triangle is an obtuse triangle, then how many such triangles are possible ?

(A) 9 (B) 8
(C) 7 (D) 6

5-11 In a ΔPQR, M lies on PR and between P and R such that $QR = QM = PM$. If $\angle MQR = 40°$, then find $\angle P$:

(A) 35° (B) 25°
(C) 45° (D) 55°

5-12 In the following figure-5.37, E is an arbitrary point on side BC of ΔABC. ED is parallel to CA, and DF is parallel to AE. Which of the following is correct ?

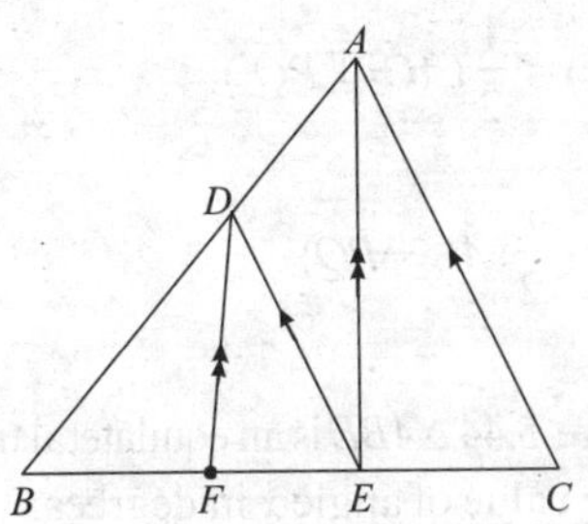

Figure 5.37

(A) $\dfrac{BF}{FE} = \dfrac{FD}{EA}$ (B) $\dfrac{BF}{FE} = \dfrac{AC}{DE}$

(C) $\dfrac{BE}{EC} = \dfrac{BF}{FE}$ (D) None of these

5-13 In the following figure-5.38, DE is parallel to AB, and EF is parallel to BD:

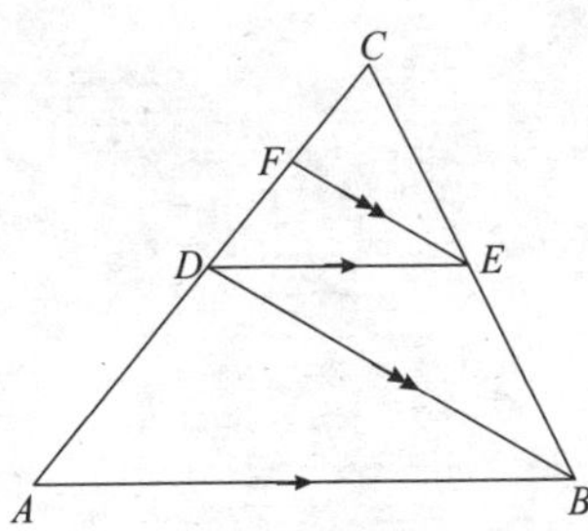

Figure 5.38

Which of the following is correct ?

(A) $2CD = CF + AC$ (B) $AC^2 - CF^2 = CD^2$

(C) $\dfrac{2}{CD} = \dfrac{1}{CF} + \dfrac{1}{AC}$ (D) $CD^2 = CD \times AC$

5-14 In the following figure-5.39, AD is the median through A, while DE and DF are the angle bisectors of $\angle ADB$ and $\angle ADC$ respectively :

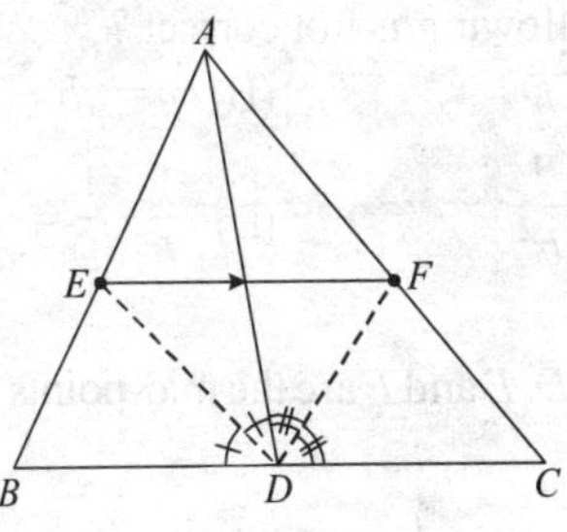

Figure 5.39

Which of the following is correct ?

(A) $EF \parallel BC$ in all cases
(B) $EF \parallel BC$ only if ΔABC is isosceles
(C) $EF \parallel BC$ only if ΔABC is acute-angled
(D) None of these

5-15 In the following figure-5.40, $AD : BD = 3 : 2$, and $DE \parallel AC$. The ratio of areas of trapezium $ADEC$ and ΔABC is :

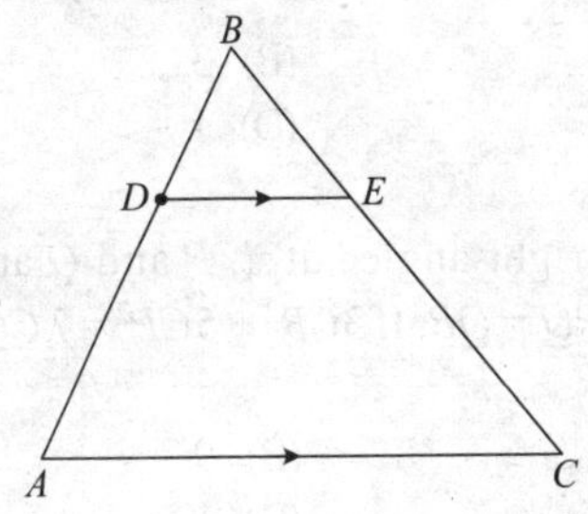

Figure 5.40

(A) 13 : 25 (B) 17 : 25
(C) 19 : 25 (D) 21 : 25

5-16 Consider the following figure-5.41. D is the mid-point of BC:

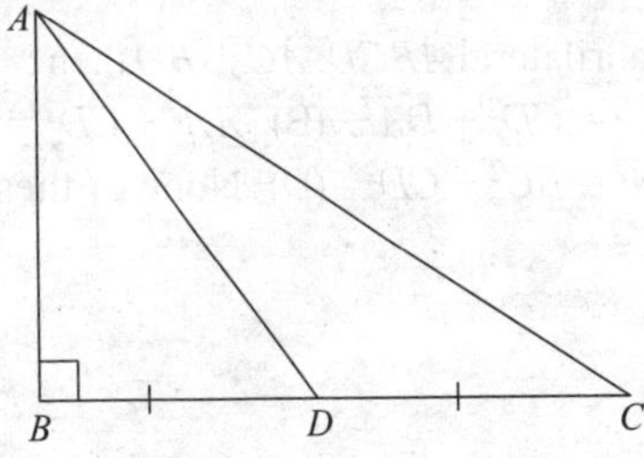

Figure 5.41

Which of the following relations is correct ?

(A) $AC^2 = 3AD^2 - AB^2$ (B) $AC^2 = 4AD^2 - 3AB^2$
(C) $AC^2 = 2AD^2 + AB^2$ (D) $AC^2 = AD^2 + 2AB^2$

5-17 Consider the following figure-5.42

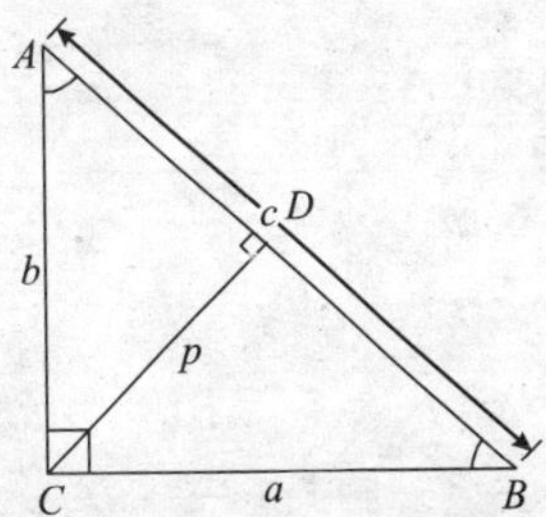

Figure 5.42

Which of the following is not correct ?

(A) $p^2 = AD \times CD$ (B) $cp = ab$

(C) $\frac{1}{p^2} = \frac{1}{a^2} + \frac{1}{b^2}$ (D) $\frac{1}{b} + \frac{1}{c} = \frac{1}{a} + \frac{1}{b}$

5-18 In $\Delta ABC, D, E$ and F are the mid-points of BC, CA and AB respectively :

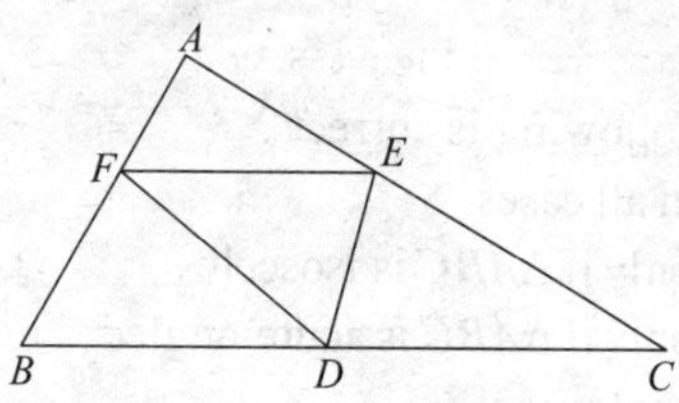

Figure 5.43

The value of $\frac{\text{area }(\Delta ABC)}{\text{area }(\Delta DEF)}$ is ______.

(A) 4 (B) 3
(C) 9 (D) 1

5-19 ΔABC is right-angled at A. P and Q are points on AB such that $AP = PQ = QB$. If $3CB^2 + 5CP^2 = \lambda CQ^2$ the value of λ is ______ :

(A) 8 (B) 9
(C) 6 (D) 1

5-20 In ΔABC, the angle bisector BE and CF of $\angle B$ and $\angle C$ respectively meet at I then :

(A) $AF \times CI = AC \times FI$ (B) $AF \times AC = FI \times IC$
(C) $AF \times FI = AC \times CI$ (D) None of these

5-21 In a quadrilateral $ABCD$, $AC \perp BD$ then :

(A) $AB^2 + BC^2 = CD^2 + DA^2$ (B) $AB^2 + CD^2 = BC^2 + DA^2$
(C) $AB^2 + DA^2 = BC^2 + CD^2$ (D) None of these

5-22 In a parallelogram $ABCD$, the side CD is bisected at P and BP meets AC at X. Find $AX : AC$:

(A) 2 : 3 (B) 3 : 2
(C) 5 : 2 (D) 3 : 5

5-23 O is orthocentre of a triangle PQR, which is formed by joining the mid-points of the sides of a ΔABC, O is :

(A) Orthocentre (B) Incentre
(C) Circumcentre (D) Centroid

5-24 In right angled ΔABC, $\angle B = 90°$, if P and Q are points on the sides AB and BC respectively, then :

(A) $AQ^2 + CP^2 = 2(AC^2 + PQ^2)$

(B) $AQ^2 + CP^2 = AC^2 + PQ^2$

(C) $(AQ^2 + CP^2) = \frac{1}{2}(AC^2 + PQ^2)$

(D) $(AQ + CP) = \frac{1}{2}(AC + PQ)$

5-25 In the figure-5.44 ΔABE is an equilateral triangle in a square $ABCD$. Find the value of angle x in degrees:

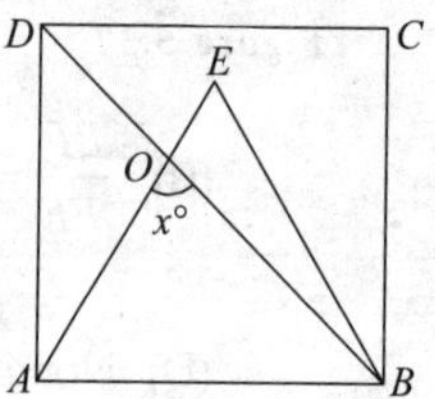

Figure 5.44

(A) 60° (B) 45°
(C) 75° (D) 90°

* * * * *

PRACTICE EXERCISE - 5.3

5-1 In a given figure-5.45 $PQ \parallel ST$, $\angle PQR = 110°$, $\angle RST = 130°$ then value of $\angle QRS$ is : **[NTSE-2013 (Stage-I) Rajasthan]**

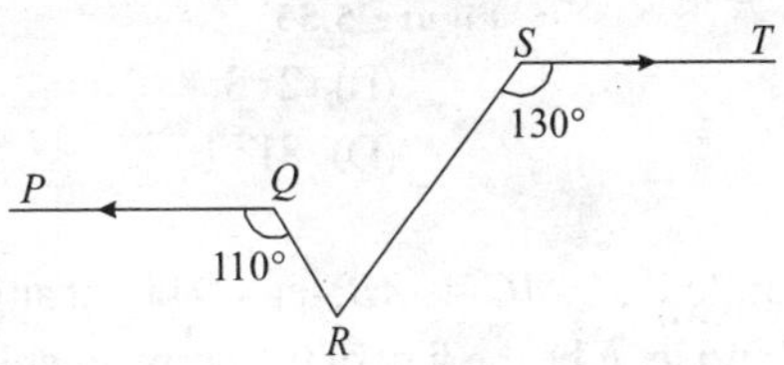

Figure 5.45

(A) 20° (B) 50°
(C) 60° (D) 70°

5-2 In a given figure-5.46 in trapazium $ABCD$ if $AB \parallel CD$ then value of x is : **[NTSE-2013 (Stage-I) Rajasthan]**

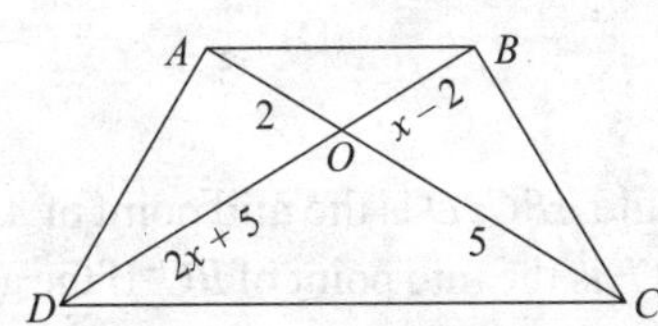

Figure 5.46

(A) $\frac{29}{8}$ (B) $\frac{8}{29}$
(C) 20 (D) $\frac{1}{20}$

5-3 If figure-5.47, if $QT \perp PR$, $\angle TQR = 40°$ and $\angle SPR = 30°$, then y is : **[NTSE-2014 (Stage-I) Rajasthan]**

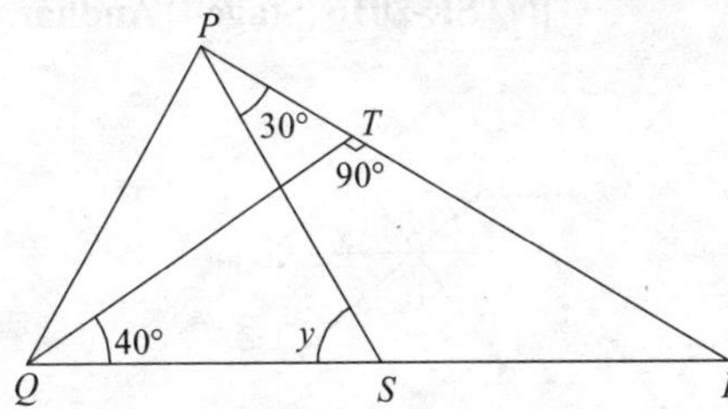

Figure 5.47

(A) 70° (B) 110°
(C) 90° (D) 80°

5-4 In ΔABC, $AB = 6\sqrt{3}$ cm, $AC = 12$ cm and $BC = 6$ cm. The angle B is : **[NTSE-2014 (Stage-I) Rajasthan]**

(A) 120° (B) 60°
(C) 90° (D) 45°

5-5 ABC and BDE are two equilateral triangles such that D is the mid-point of BC. Ratio of the areas of triangles ABC and BDE is : **[NTSE-2014 (Stage-I) Rajasthan]**

(A) 2 : 1 (B) 1 : 2
(C) 4 : 1 (D) 1 : 4

5-6 In the given figure-5.48, $\Delta ODC \sim \Delta OBA$, $\angle BOC = 115°$ and $\angle CDO = 80°$. Then $\angle OAB$ is equal to : **[NTSE-2015 (Stage-I) Rajasthan]**

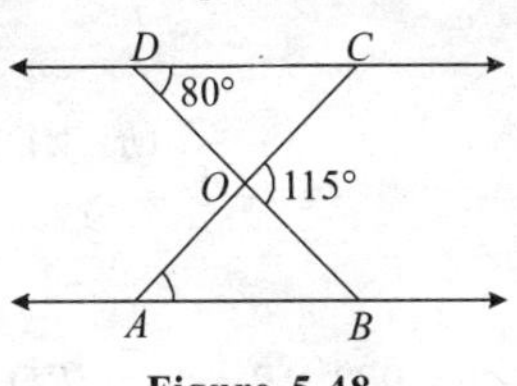

Figure 5.48

(A) 80° (B) 35°
(C) 45° (D) 65°

5-7 In the right-angled triangle shown in figure-5.49 $MB + MA = BC + AC$. If $BC = 8$ and $AC = 10$, then the value of MB is : **[NTSE-2015 (Stage-I) Andhara Pradesh]**

(A) $\frac{27}{15}$

(B) $\frac{40}{13}$

(C) 3

(D) $\frac{15}{7}$

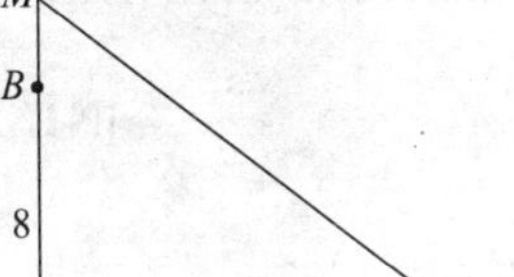

Figure 5.49

5-8 In ΔABC, if $DE \parallel BC$, $AD = 2$ cm, $DB = 3$ cm, $DE = 4$ cm, then the value of BC is : **[NTSE-2015 (Stage-I) TN]**

(A) 9 (B) 25
(C) 10 (D) 6

5-9 In a triangle ABC; OB and OC are the bisectors of $\angle ABC$ and $\angle ACB$ respectively. Then $\angle BOC$ is equal to : **[NTSE-2015 (Stage-I) Chandigarh]**

(A) $90° - \angle A/2$ (B) $90° - \angle A$
(C) $90° + \angle A/2$ (D) $180° - \angle A/2$

5-10 In given figure-5.50 measure of $\angle 1 + \angle 2 + \angle 3 + \angle 4 + \angle 5 + \angle 6$ is : **[NTSE-2015 (Stage-I) Delhi]**

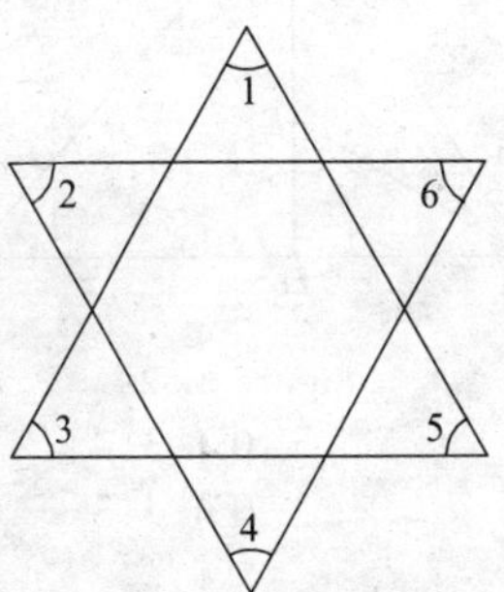

Figure 5.50

(A) 90° (B) 180°
(C) 270° (D) 360°

5-11 The base of a triangle is b and altitude is h. A rectangle of height x with the base of the rectangle on the base of triangle has its two vertices on other two sides of the triangle. The area of rectangle is : **[NTSE-2015 (Stage-I) Delhi]**

(A) $\frac{bx(h-x)}{h}$ (B) $\frac{hx}{b}(b-x)$

(C) $\frac{(b-x)}{h}$ (D) $\frac{(h-x)}{b}$

5-12 In ΔABC, $m\angle B = 90°$, $AB = 4\sqrt{5}$. $BD \perp AC$, $AD = 4$, then $ar(\Delta ABC) = ?$ **[NTSE-2015 (Stage-I) Maharashtra]**

(A) 96 sq. units (B) 80 sq. units

(C) 120 sq. units (D) 160 sq. units

5-13 In the following figure-5.51, $AB \parallel CD$. Diagonals AC and BD intersect at point O. If $AO : OC = 1 : 3$, then $\frac{ar(\Delta AOB)}{ar(\Delta ABD)} = ?$

[NTSE-2015 (Stage-I) Maharashtra]

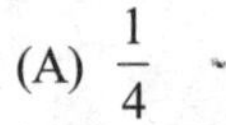
(A) $\frac{1}{4}$

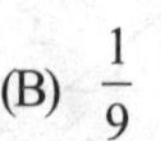
(B) $\frac{1}{9}$

(C) 16

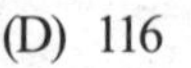
(D) 116

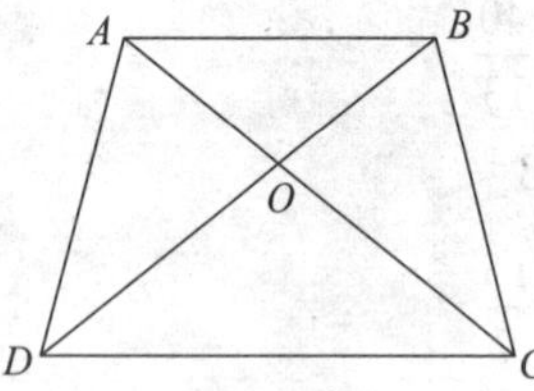

Figure 5.51

5-14 The vertical angles of two isosceles triangles are equal. If the ratio of the areas is 9 : 16, the ratio of the heights of the triangle is : **[NTSE-2015 (Stage-I) West Bengal]**

(A) 9 : 16 (B) 16 : 9

(C) 3 : 4 (D) 4 : 3

5-15 In the following figure-5.52 of triangle ABC, E is the midpoint of median AD. The ratio of areas of the triangles ABC and BED is : **[NTSE-2016 (Stage-I) Rajasthan]**

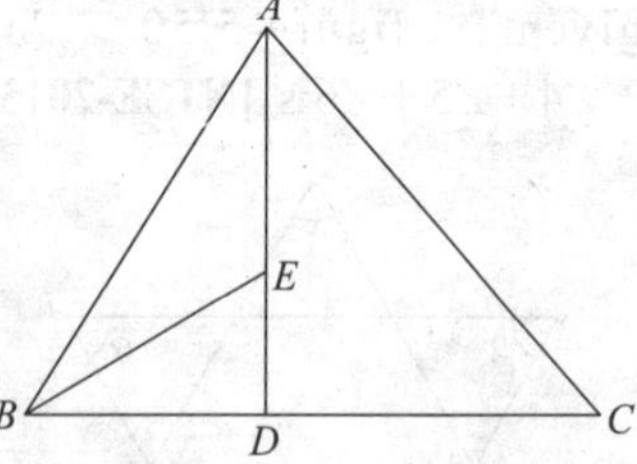

Figure 5.52

(A) 1 : 4 (B) 3 : 4

(C) 4 : 1 (D) 4 : 3

5-16 In the following figure-5.53 $\angle ACB = 90°$ and $CD \perp AB$. If $AD = 4$ cm and $BD = 9$ cm then the ratio $BC : AC$ is : **[NTSE-2016 (Stage-I) Rajasthan]**

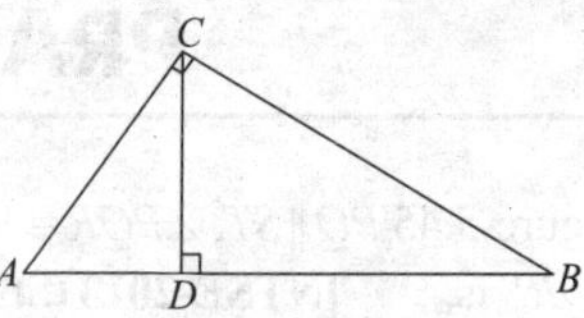

Figure 5.53

(A) 3 : 2 (B) 2 : 3

(C) 16 : 81 (D) 81 : 16

5-17 In triangle ABC, $AC = 3AB$, let AD bisect angle A with D lying on BC and let E be the foot of the perpendicular from C to AD. Then $\frac{\text{area of } \Delta ABD}{\text{area of } \Delta CDE} =$: **[NTSE-2016 (Stage-I) Andhara Pradesh]**

(A) 2 (B) $\frac{1}{3}$

(C) $\frac{1}{4}$ (D) $\frac{2}{3}$

5-18 In a triangle ABC, D is the mid point of AB, E is the mid point of DB and F is the mid point of BC. If the area of ΔABC is 96, then the area of ΔAEF is : **[NTSE-2016 (Stage-I) Andhara Pradesh]**

(A) 16 (B) 24

(C) 32 (D) 36

5-19 In the adjoining figure ABC is a triangle, P is an interior point in it. Three lines are drawn through the point P, parallel to three sides as shown in the figure-5.54. The triangle is divided into six parts. The areas of 3 smaller triangle are 4, 9 and 16 units, then the area of ΔABC is : **[NTSE-2016 (Stage-I) Andhara Pradesh]**

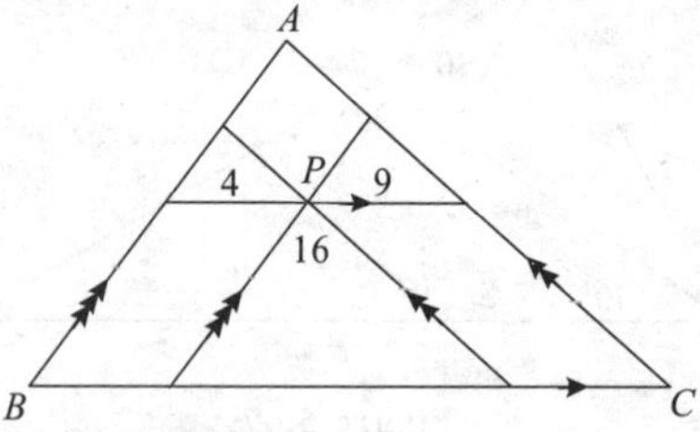

Figure 5.54

(A) 64 (B) 81

(C) 42 (D) 65

5-20 ABC is a right angle triangle, right angled at C. If p is the length of the perpendicular from C to AB, $AB = c$ and $BC = a$ and $AC = b$, then : **[NTSE-2016 (Stage-I) Chandigarh]**

(A) $\frac{1}{a^2} = \frac{1}{b^2} - \frac{1}{p^2}$ (B) $\frac{1}{p^2} = \frac{1}{a^2} - \frac{1}{b^2}$

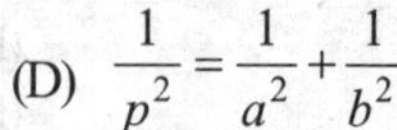

(C) $\frac{1}{b^2} = \frac{1}{p^2} - \frac{1}{a^2}$ (D) $\frac{1}{p^2} = \frac{1}{a^2} + \frac{1}{b^2}$

5-21 In a given figure-5.55, x in term of a, b and c is :

[NTSE-2016 (Stage-I) Chandigarh]

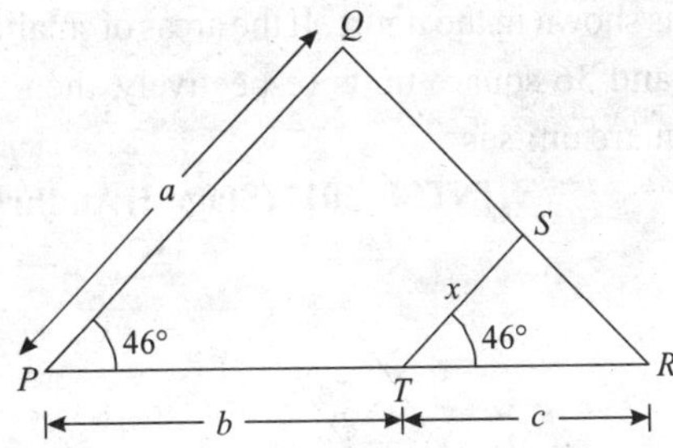

Figure 5.55

(A) $x = \frac{ac}{a+c}$ (B) $x = \frac{ab}{b+c}$

(C) $x = \frac{ac}{b+c}$ (D) $x = \frac{bc}{a+c}$

5-22 Two poles of height a meters and b meters are p meters apart. Height of the point intersection of the lines joining the top of each pole to the foot of the opposite pole is given by,

[NTSE-2016 (Stage-I) Chandigarh]

(A) $\frac{ab}{a+b}$ (B) $\frac{a+b}{ab}$

(C) $\frac{ab}{a-b}$ (D) $\frac{a-b}{ab}$

5-23 In ΔABC, $XY \parallel BC$ and XY divides the triangle into two parts of equal areas. The value of $\frac{AX}{BX}$ is :

[NTSE-2016 (Stage-I) Karnatka]

(A) $\sqrt{2}-1$ (B) $\frac{\sqrt{2}}{2}$

(C) $\frac{2}{\sqrt{2}}$ (D) $\sqrt{2}+1$

5-24 If the given figure-5.56, the angle bisector of $\angle B$ and $\angle C$ are BO and CO respectively. What is the value of x?

[NTSE-2016 (Stage-I) Chhatisgarh]

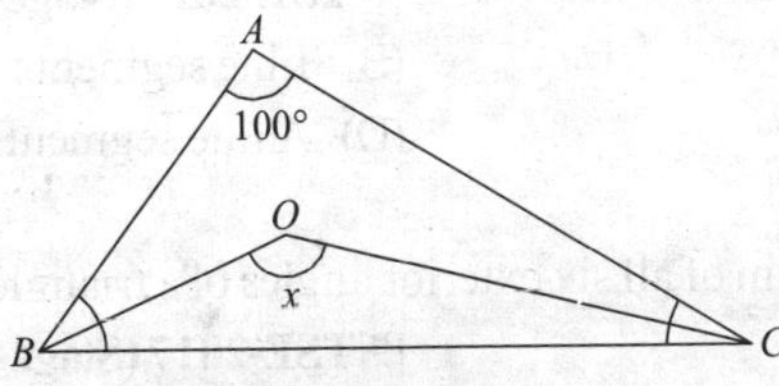

Figure 5.56

(A) 120° (B) 130°

(C) 140° (D) 150°

5-25 In the given figure-5.57 ΔABC, $m\angle B = 90°$, $BD \perp AC$, $AD = 4.5$, $AB = 7.5$, then find $ar(\Delta BDC) : ar(\Delta ABC)$:

[NTSE-2016 (Stage-I) Chhatisgarh]

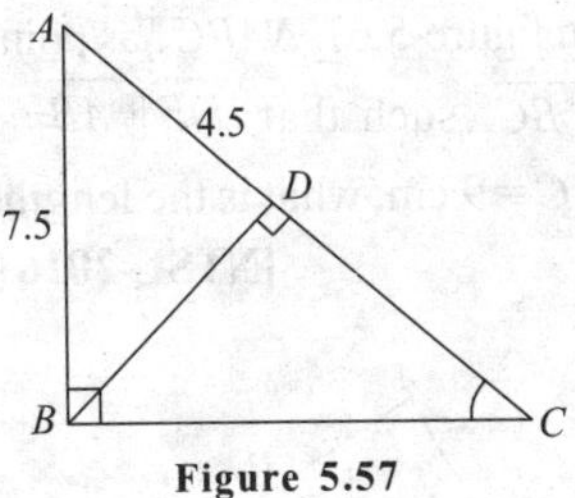

Figure 5.57

(A) 16 : 25 (B) 4 : 5

(C) 25 : 16 (D) 5 : 4

5-26 In the figure-5.58 ΔABC, $DE \parallel BC$, $A(\Delta ADE) = 48$ sq cm, $\frac{AD}{DB} = \frac{4}{5}$. Find the area of ΔBEC :

[NTSE-2016 (Stage-I) Chhatisgarh]

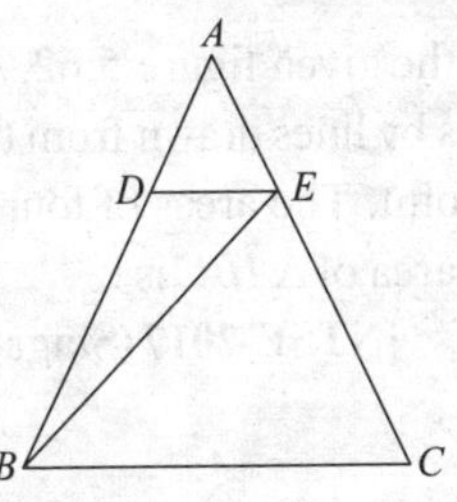

Figure 5.58

(A) 60 sq. cm (B) 95 sq. cm

(C) 108 sq. cm (D) 135 sq. cm

5-27 In the given figure-5.59, $AB \parallel DE$ and $BD \parallel EF$, then :

[NTSE-2016 (Stage-I) Jharkhand]

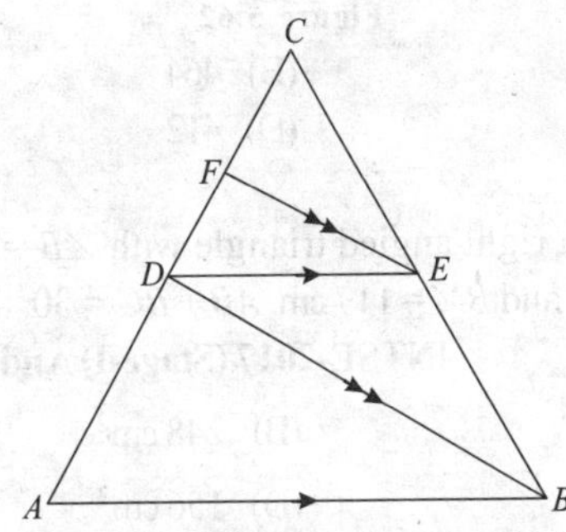

Figure 5.59

(A) $AD^2 = CF \times AC$ (B) $DC^2 = CF \times AC$

(C) $CE^2 = DE \times BF$ (D) $EF^2 = BD \cdot AB$

5-28 In the given figure-5.60, $DE \parallel BC$ and $AD : DB = 5 : 4$, find the ratio area (ΔDFE) : area (ΔCFB) :

[NTSE-2016 (Stage-I) Jharkhand]

(A) 5 : 9

(B) 4 : 9

(C) 25 : 81

(D) 81 : 25

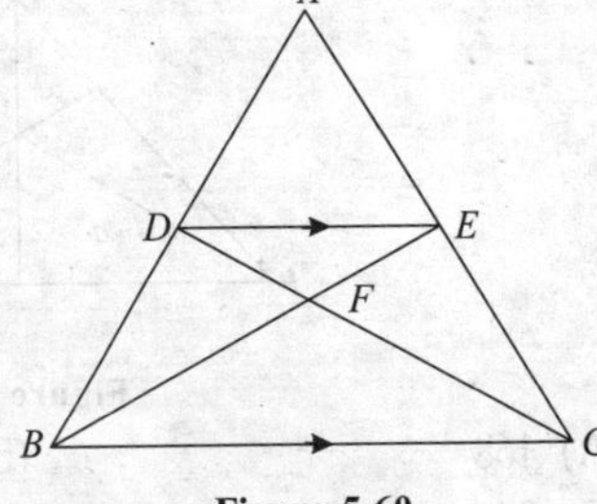

Figure 5.60

5-29 In the given figure-5.61, ΔABC has points D and F in $\overline{AC}$ and point E in $\overline{BC}$ such that $\overline{DE} \parallel \overline{AB}$ and $\overline{EF} \parallel \overline{BD}$. If $CF = 4$ cm and $AC = 9$ cm, what is the length of $\overline{DC}$?

[NTSE-2016 (Stage-I) Odisha]

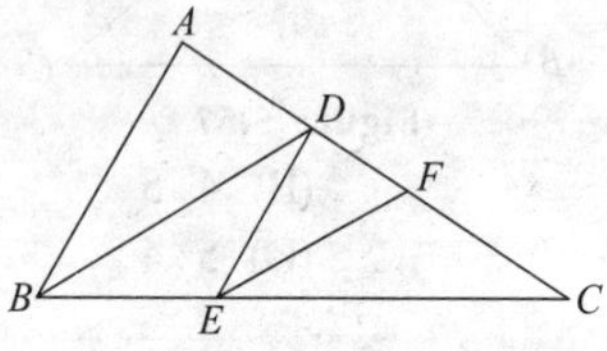

Figure 5.61

(A) 7 cm (B) 6 cm
(C) 5 cm (D) 4 cm

5-30 As shown in the given figure-5.62, ΔABC is divided into six smaller triangles by lines drawn from the vertices through a common interior point. The areas of four of 6 triangles are as indicated, then the area of ΔABC is :

[NTSE-2017 (Stage-I) Andhra Pradesh]

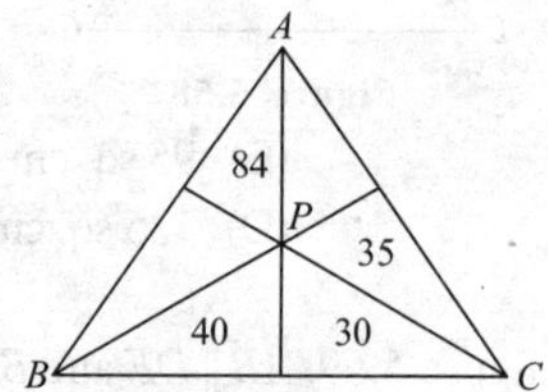

Figure 5.62

(A) 238 (B) 464
(C) 315 (D) 412

5-31 ABC is a right angled triangle with $\angle B = 90°$, M is the midpoint of AC and $BM = 117$ cm, $AB + BC = 30$, then the area of the triangle is : **[NTSE-2017 (Stage-I) Andhra Pradesh]**

(A) 108 cm^2 (B) 248 cm^2
(C) 316 cm^2 (D) 156 cm^2

5-32 Let p be an interior point of ΔABC, extend lines from the vertices through p to the opposite sides. Let a, b, c and d divides the lengths of the segments indicated in the figure-5.63. Find the product of abc, if $a + b + c = 43$ and $d = 3$:

[NTSE-2017 (Stage-I) Andhra Pradesh]

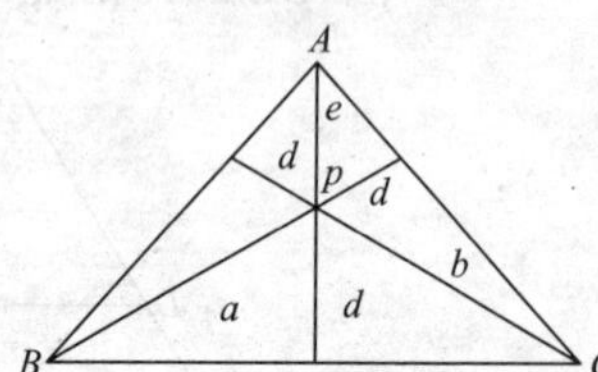

Figure 5.63

(A) 168 (B) 256
(C) 346 (D) 441

5-33 As shown in the figure-5.64 in ΔABC, p is an interior point. Through the point p, three lines are drawn parallel to three sides as shown in the figure. If the areas of smaller triangles are 16, 25 and 36 square units respectively, then the area of ΔABC in square units is :

[NTSE-2017 (Stage-I) Andhra Pradesh]

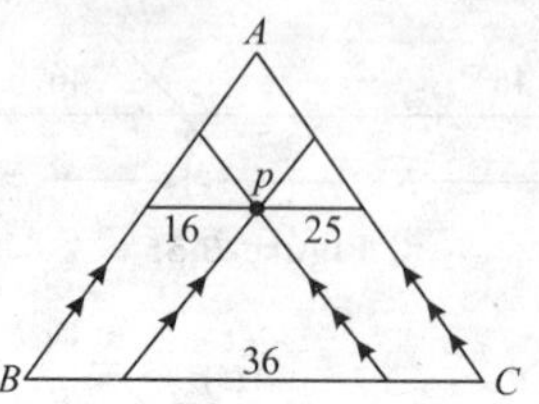

Figure 5.64

(A) 324 (B) 196
(C) 225 (D) 784

5-34 In an equilateral triangle ABC, the side BC is trisected at D, then $9AD^2$ is : **[NTSE-2017 (Stage-I) Andhra Pradesh]**

(A) $7AB^2$ (B) $8BC^2$
(C) $4AC^2$ (D) $\frac{3}{2}AB^2$

5-35 In ΔPQR, $PQ = PR$ and X is the midpoint of PQ. XY is parallel to QR and meets PR at point Y. What kind of triangle is PXY? **[NTSE-2017 (Stage-I) Chandigarh]**

(A) Isosceles (B) Scalene
(C) Equilateral (D) Right triangle

5-36 The Perimeter of a right isosceles triangle is $(2 + \sqrt{2})$ m. The length of its hypotenuse is ...

[NTSE-2017 (Stage-I) Chandigarh]

(A) 2m (B) 4m
(C) 6 (D) $\sqrt{2}$

5-37 An angle is the union set of— :

[NTSE-2017 (Stage-I) Gujarat]

(A) Lines (B) Line segments
(C) Rays (D) A line segment and ray

5-38 The sum of all six exterior angles of a triangle is — :

[NTSE-2017 (Stage-I) Gujarat]

(A) 180 (B) 360
(C) 720 (D) 90

5-39 In ΔABC, $\angle B$ is right angle. If $a = 16$ and $c = 12$ then $b =$:

[NTSE-2017 (Stage-I) Gujarat]

(A) 8 (B) 18
(C) 20 (D) 28

5-40 In a triangle ABC, points D is E are on sides AB and AC respectively such that $BCED$ is trapezium. If $AE : EC = 3 : 2$, then the ratio of area of ΔADE and trapezium $BCED$ is : **[NTSE-2017 (Stage-I) Haryana]**

(A) $9:16$ (B) $9:4$
(C) $9:25$ (D) $16:25$

5-41 ABC is a right angled triangle, right angled at B. If D and E are points on side AB such that $AD = DE = EB$, then the value of $\frac{AC^2 - EC^2}{DC^2 - BC^2}$ is : **[NTSE-2017 (Stage-I) Haryana]**

(A) $\frac{3}{1}$ (B) $\frac{5}{2}$
(C) $\frac{9}{4}$ (D) $\frac{2}{1}$

5-42 In ΔABC, the altitudes AL, BM and CN are intersect at 'O'. The value of $AN \times BL \times CM$ is same as : **[NTSE-2017 (Stage-I) Karnataka]**

(A) $BN \times LC \times AM$ (B) $AL \times CN \times BM$
(C) $OL \times OM \times ON$ (D) $OC \times OB \times OA$

5-43 In ΔABC, $AC = BC$ and $AD \perp BC$. The value of $AD^2 - BD^2$ is : **[NTSE-2017 (Stage-I) Karnataka]**

(A) $2BD \times CD$ (B) $2AC \times CD$
(C) $2(BD + CD)$ (D) $2(2AC + CD)$

5-44 In the adjacent figure-5.65 $PM \perp QS$. $RN \perp QS$. Diagonals QS and PR intersect at 'O' $ar(\Delta PMO)$; $ar(\Delta RNO) = 1 : 4$ then find. $ar(\Delta PQS) : ar(\Delta RQS)$: **[NTSE-2017 (Stage-I) Maharashtra]**

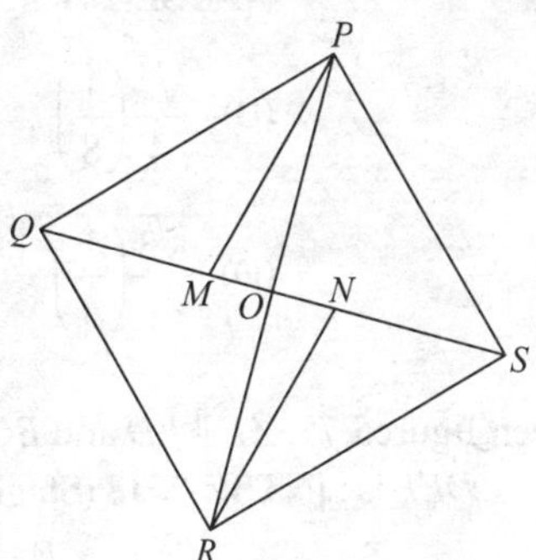

Figure 5.65

(A) $\frac{1}{16}$ (B) $\frac{1}{8}$
(C) $\frac{1}{4}$ (D) $\frac{1}{2}$

5-45 In the following figure-5.66 $QT \perp PR$ and $QS = PS$. If $\angle TQR = 40°$ and $\angle RPS = 20°$ then value of x is : **[NTSE-2017 (Stage-I) Rajasthan]**

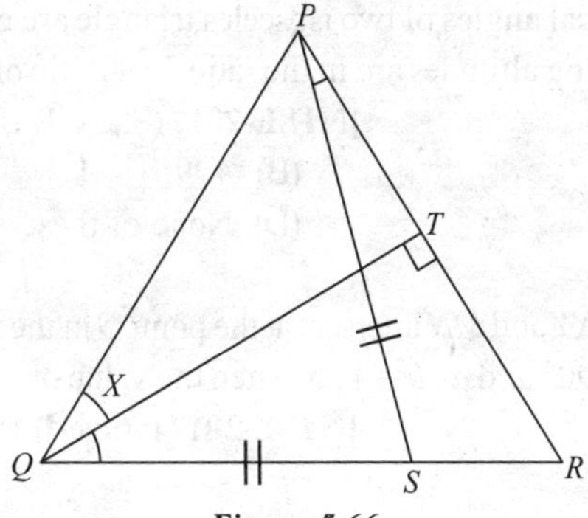

Figure 5.66

(A) 80° (B) 25°
(C) 15° (D) 35°

5-46 If ratio of height of two similar triangles is 4 : 9, then ratio between their areas is : **[NTSE-2017 (Stage-I) Rajasthan]**

(A) $2:3$ (B) $3:2$
(C) $81:16$ (D) $16:81$

5-47 In given ΔABC, AD and BE are medians of triangle which intersect each other at point G. If area of ΔBDG is 1 cm², then what is the area of $DCEG$? **[NTSE-2017 (Stage-I) Rajasthan]**

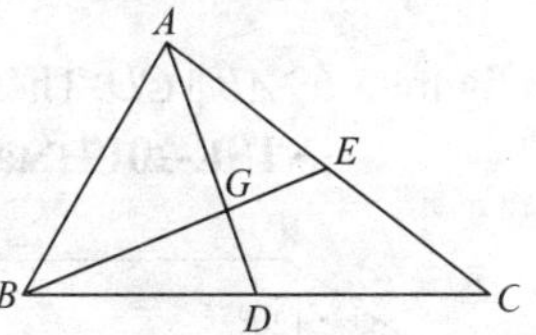

Figure 5.67

(A) 2 cm² (B) 3 cm²
(C) 4 cm² (D) 1 cm²

5-48 In ΔABC, if $2\angle A = 3\angle B = 6\angle C$ then the measures of $\angle A$, $\angle B$ and $\angle C$ are respectively : **[NTSE-2017 (Stage-I) Tamilnadu]**

(A) 30°, 60°, 90° (B) 90°, 60°, 30°
(C) 30°, 90°, 60° (D) 45°, 45°, 90°

5-49 In a right triangle ABC, $\angle B = 90°$, $AB = 9$ cm, $AC = 15$ cm and D, E are the midpoints of AB and AC respectively, then the area of ΔADE is : **[NTSE-2017 (Stage-I) Tamilnadu]**

(A) 12 cm² (B) 13.5 cm²
(C) 27 cm² (D) 24 cm²

5-50 If sides of two similar triangles are in the ratio 4 : 3, then the ratio of their areas is : **[NTSE-2017 (Stage-I) Tamilnadu]**

(A) $4:3$ (B) $3:4$
(C) $16:9$ (D) $9:16$

5-51 If an angle is five times its supplementary angle then the angle is : **[NTSE-2017 (Stage-I) Uttar Pradesh]**

(A) 75° (B) 150°
(C) 144° (D) 40°

5-52 Vertical angles of two isosceles triangle are equal. Their corresponding altitudes are in the ratio 4 : 9 Ratio of their areas will be : **[NTSE-2017 (Stage-I) Uttrakhand]**

(A) 16 : 81 (B) 4 : 9

(C) 2 : 3 (D) None of these

5-53 Line *XY* and *MN* intersect at the point *O* in the figure-5.68. If $\angle POY = 90°$ and $a : b = 4 : 5$. Then the value of *c* will be : **[NTSE-2017 (Stage-I) Uttrakhand]**

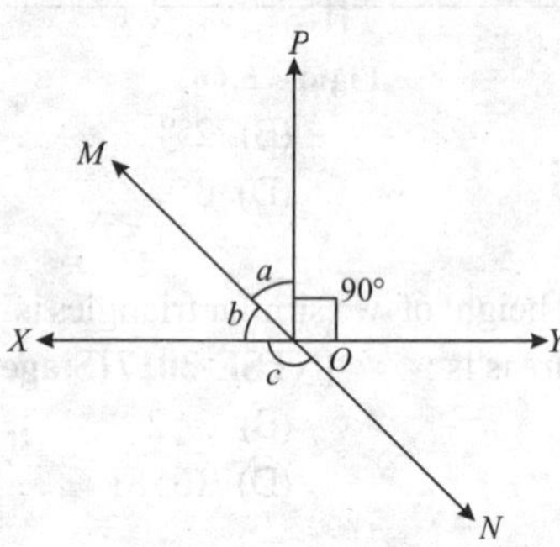

Figure 5.68

(A) 120° (B) 135°

(C) 125° (D) 130°

5-54 In the given figure-5.69 *AB* || *CD*. Then the value of *x*° is : **[NTSE-2017 (Stage-I) Uttrakhand]**

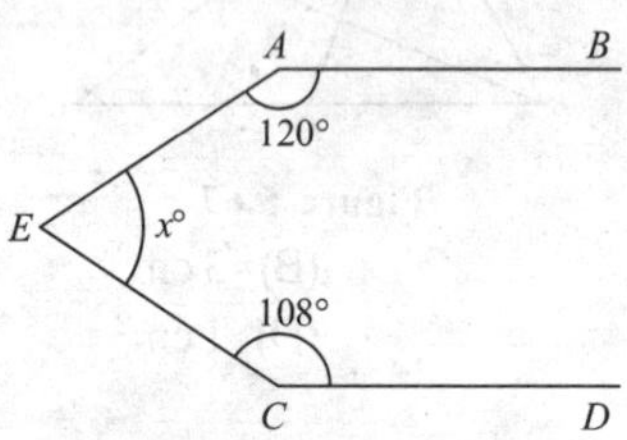

Figure 5.69

(A) 220° (B) 140°

(C) 150° (D) None of these

5-55 *ABC* is a right angled triangle and *AD* is perpendicular to the hypotenuse *BC*. If *AC* = 2 *AB*, then *BC* = : **[NTSE-2017 (Stage-I) West Bengal]**

(A) 5 *BD* (B) *BD*

(C) 5 *BD* (D) 4 *BD*

5-56 The figure-5.70 shows a right triangle and a square inside it.

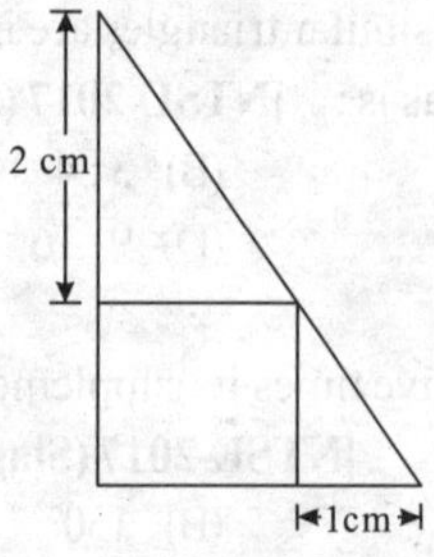

Figure 5.70

What is the length of aside of the squares ? **[NTSE-2017 (Stage-I) Kerala]**

(A) $\sqrt{3}$ (B) $\sqrt{2}$

(C) 2 (D) 1

5-57 In the figure-5.71, the bisector of an angle of the triangle cuts the opposite side into two parts.

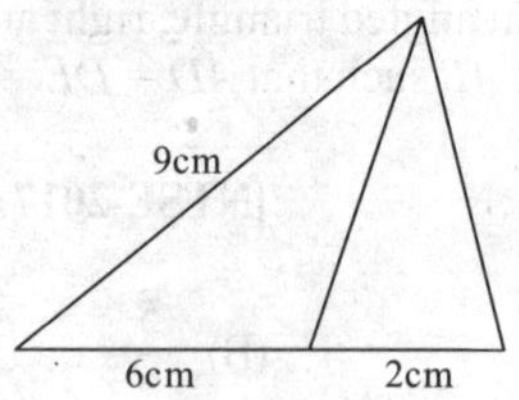

Figure 5.71

What is the length of the third side of the triangle in centimeters ? **[NTSE-2017 (Stage-I) Kerala]**

(A) 3 (B) 3.5

(C) 4 (D) 4.5

5-58 In the figure-5.72, each side of the largest triangle is 1 meter. By joining the midpoints of the sides of each triangle, an inner triangle is drawn.

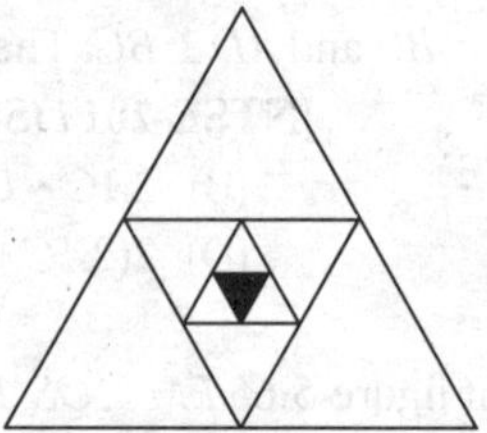

Figure 5.72

What is the area of the smallest triangle (in sq.m.)? **[NTSE-2017 (Stage-I) Kerala]**

(A) $\frac{\sqrt{3}}{2}\left(\frac{1}{16}\right)^2$ (B) $\frac{\sqrt{3}}{4}\left(\frac{1}{8}\right)^2$

(C) $\frac{\sqrt{3}}{4}\left(\frac{1}{2}\right)^2$ (D) $\frac{\sqrt{3}}{4}\left(\frac{1}{4}\right)^2$

5-59 In the given figure5.73, *AB* || *ED* and *BC* || *EF*, then the value of $\angle ABC + \angle DEF$ is : **[NTSE-2018 (Stage-I) Rajasthan]**

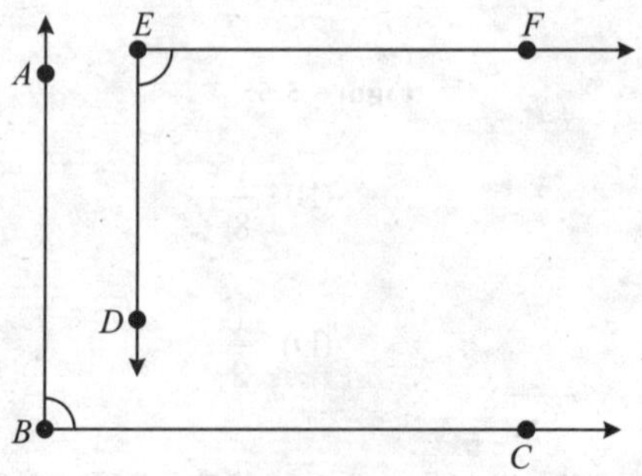

Figure 5.73

(A) 90° (B) 180°

(C) 120° (D) 360°

5-60 In the given figure-5.74, $AB = AC$, $\angle BAC = 40^\circ$, BE and CD are angle bisectors of $\angle B$ and $\angle C$ respectively. If $\angle DOE = x$, the value of x is : **[NTSE-2018 (Stage-I) Rajasthan]**

(A) 140º

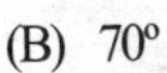

(B) 70º

(C) 110º

(D) 40º

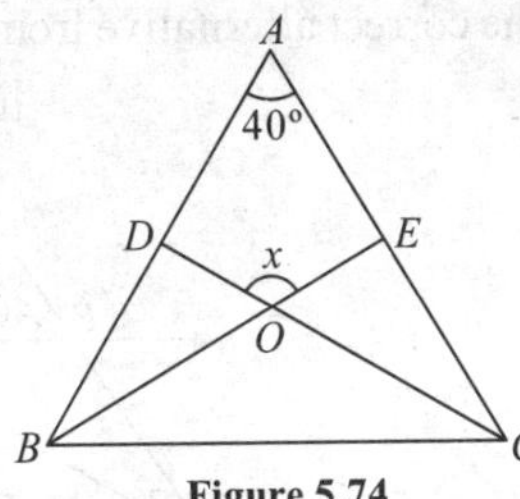

Figure 5.74

5-61 In ΔABC, D, E and F respectively mid points of the BC, CA and AB and P is a point on BC such that $AP \perp BC$. If $\angle DEF = 50^\circ$, then $\angle FPD =$

[NTSE-2018 (Stage-I) Andhra Pradesh]

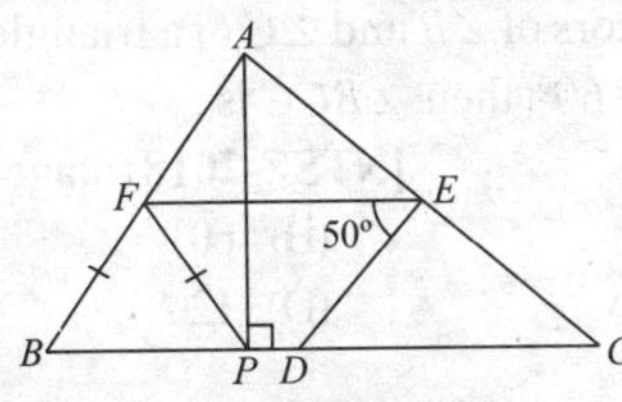

Figure 5.75

(A) 120º (B) 110º
(C) 135º (D) 130º

5-62 From the adjacent figure-5.76 ΔABC, $DE \,||\, BC$ and $\frac{AD}{DB} = \frac{3}{5}$, if $AC = 5.6$ then AE is :

[NTSE-2018 (Stage-I) Andhra Pradesh]

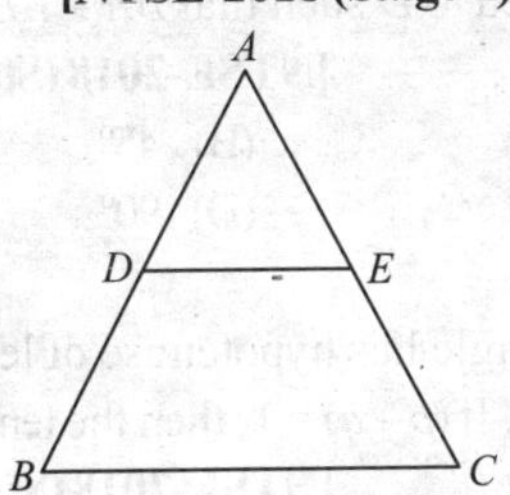

Figure 5.76

(A) 9 cm (B) 15 cm
(C) 6 cm (D) 2.1 cm

5-63 In $\Delta\ PQR$, $PX \perp QR$. Find the value of $PQ^2 + QR^2 - 2QR \cdot QX$: **[NTSE-2018 (Stage-I) Chandigarh]**

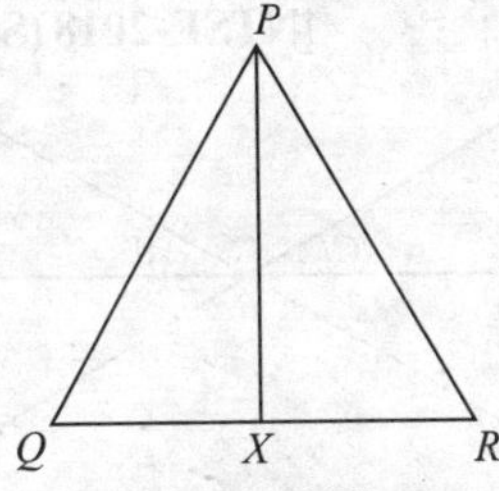

Figure 5.77

(A) PR^2 (B) $2PQ^2$
(C) $QR.QX^2$ (D) $2PR^2 + PQ^2$

5-64 In trapezium $PQRS$, $PQ \,\|\, RS$ and $PQ = 2RS$. If PR and QS intersect at point O, what will be the ratio of areas of ΔPOQ and ΔROS: **[NTSE-2018 (Stage-I) Chandigarh]**

(A) 1 : 1 (B) 2 : 1
(C) 4 : 1 (D) 1 : 2

5-65 If $\Delta\ ABC \sim \Delta DEF$ such that $DE = 3$ cm, $EF = 2$ cm, $DF = 2.5$ cm and $BC = 4$ cm. Then the perimeter of ΔABC will be : **[NTSE-2018 (Stage-I) Chhattisgarh]**

(A) 18 cm (B) 20 cm
(C) 12 cm (D) 15 cm

5-66 In the figure, $BC = CD = DE$ and P is mid point of CD. Then area of $\Delta\ APC$ is : **[NTSE-2018 (Stage-I) Delhi]**

(A) $\frac{1}{3} ar(\Delta\ ABC)$ (B) $\frac{1}{2} ar(\Delta\ ABD)$

(C) $\frac{1}{6} ar(\Delta\ ABC)$ (D) $\frac{1}{4} ar(\Delta\ ABD)$

5-67 If x, y, z are three positive number then the minimum value of $\frac{y+z}{x} + \frac{z+x}{y} + \frac{x+y}{z}$ is : **[NTSE-2018 (Stage-I) Delhi]**

(A) 1 (B) 2
(C) 3 (D) 6

5-68 The minimum value of the expression $\frac{3b+4c}{a} + \frac{4c+a}{3b} + \frac{a+3b}{4c}$, ($a,b,c$ are +ve) : **[NTSE-2018 (Stage-I) Delhi]**

(A) 1 (B) 4
(C) 6 (D) 8

5-69 $\overline{AD}$ and $\overline{BE}$ are the altitudes of ABC. If $AD = 6$ cm, $BC = 16$ cm, $BE = 8$ cm, then $CA =$ _____ cm.

[NTSE-2018 (Stage-I) Gujarat]

(A) 12 (B) 18
(C) 24 (D) 10

5-70 If the correspondence $ABC \leftrightarrow EFD$ is a similarity in ΔABC and ΔDEF, then following is not true :

[NTSE-2018 (Stage-I) Gujarat]

(A) $\frac{BC}{DF} = \frac{AC}{DE}$ (B) $\frac{AB}{DE} = \frac{BC}{DF}$

(C) $\frac{AB}{EF} = \frac{AC}{DE}$ (D) $\frac{BC}{DF} = \frac{AB}{EF}$

5-71 In ΔABC, $m\angle B = 90$, $AB = BC$. Then $AB : AC =$ _____ :

`[NTSE-2018 (Stage-I) Gujarat]

(A) 1 : 3 (B) 1 : 2
(C) 1 : $\sqrt{2}$ (D) $\sqrt{2}$: 1

5-72 ABC is a right angled triangle, right angled at $\angle B$. if side AB is divided into three equal parts by points D and E such that D is neaer to A, than $\frac{AC^2 - EC^2}{DC^2 - BC^2}$ is equal to :

[NTSE-2018 (Stage-I) Haryana]

(A) 3 (B) $2\frac{1}{2}$

(C) $2\frac{1}{4}$ (D) 2

5-73 ABC is a triangle in which $AB = 10$ cm, $AC = 24$ cm and $BC = 26$ cm. If AD is its median, then length of AD is :

[NTSE-2018 (Stage-I) Haryana]

(A) 12 cm (B) 12.5 cm

(C) 13 cm (D) 14.75 cm

5-74 In the given figure-5.78, AD is the bisector of $\angle BAC$. If $AB = 10$ cm, $AC = 6$cm, and $BC = 12$ cm, find B :

[NTSE-2018 (Stage-I) Jharkhand]

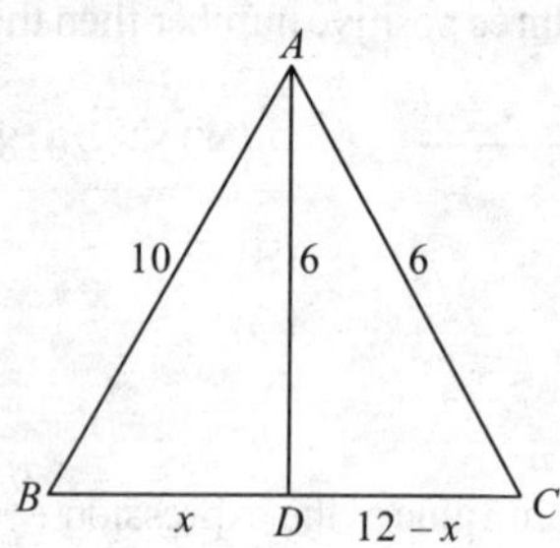

Figure 5.78

(A) 4.5 cm (B) 9 cm

(C) 7.5 cm (D) 3 cm

5-75 The perimeters of two similar triangles ΔABC and ΔDEF are 60 cm and 35 cm respectively. If $BC = 18$ cm then measure of EF is : **[NTSE-2018 (Stage-I) Karnataka]**

(A) 1.08 cm (B) 30 cm

(C) 10.8 cm (D) 8 cm

5-76 In the adjoining figure-5.79 ΔABC is a right angled triangle. Point D is the midpoint of hypotenuse AC. Segment $DE \perp$ side BC. $m\angle ABD = 70°$ then find $m\angle CDE - m\angle DBE =$:

[NTSE-2018 (Stage-I) Maharashtra]

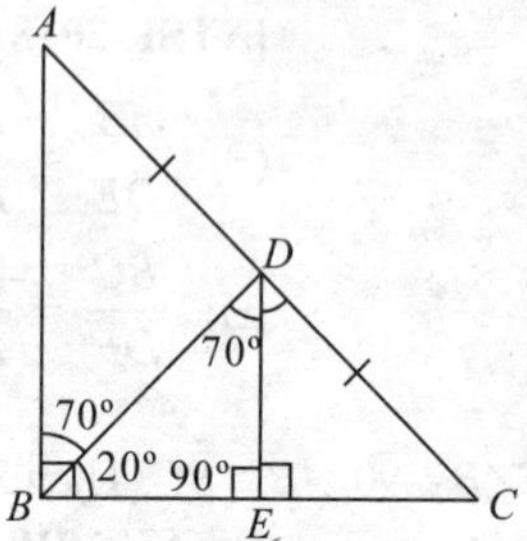

Figure 5.79

(A) 70° (B) 20°

(C) 50° (D) 30°

5-77 In the adjoing figure-5.80 ray BD bisects $\angle ABC$ of ΔABC seg $ED \parallel$ side BC $m\angle AED = 40°$ and $m\angle BDC = 110°$ then find the measurements of $\angle EDB$ and $\angle DCB$ respectively. Choose the correct alternative from the following :

[NTSE-2018 (Stage-I) Maharashtra]

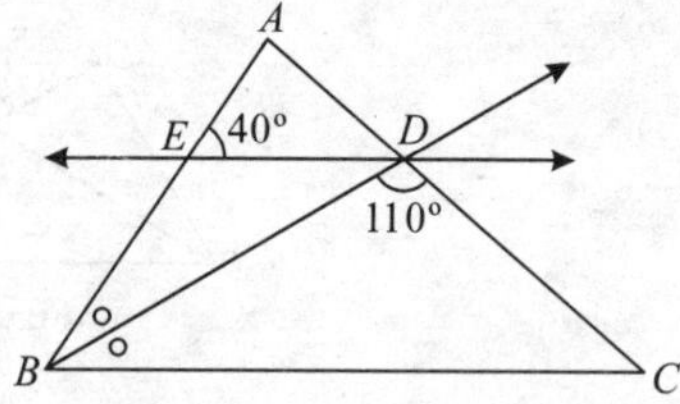

Figure 5.80

(A) 20° and 50° (B) 50° and 20°

(C) 40° and 50° (D) 40° and 70°

5-78 The bisectors of $\angle B$ and $\angle C$ of a triangle ABC meet at a point O. If $\angle A = 60°$, then $\angle BOC$ is :

[NTSE-2018 (Stage-I) Tamil Nadu]

(A) 30° (B) 60°

(C) 90° (D) 120°

5-79 The side BC of ΔABC is produced to a point D. The bisectors of $\angle ABC$ and $\angle ACD$ meet at point E. If $\angle BAC = 60°$, then $\angle BEC$ is : **[NTSE-2018 (Stage-I) Tamil Nadu]**

(A) 15° (B) 30°

(C) 60° (D) 120°

5-80 ΔABC is an isosceles triangle in which $AB = AC$. If the side BA is produced to D such that $BA = AD$, then $\angle BCD$ is :

[NTSE-2018 (Stage-I) Tamil Nadu]

(A) 30° (B) 45°

(C) 60° (D) 90°

5-81 A right triangle has hypotenuse of length p cm and one side of length q cm. If $(p - q) = 1$, then the length of third side is :

[NTSE-2018 (Stage-I) Tamil Nadu]

(A) $2q+1$ (B) $\sqrt{2q+1}$

(C) $2p+1$ (D) $\sqrt{2p+1}$

5-82 The value of angle B will be in the given figure-5.81, If $\angle A = 50°$, $\angle C = 60°$: **[NTSE-2018 (Stage-I) Telangana]**

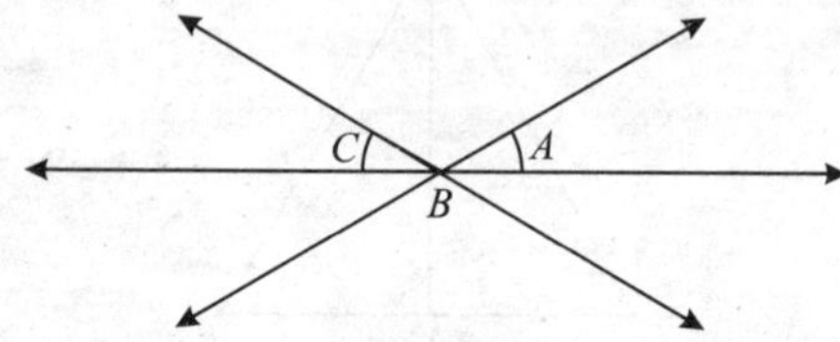

Figure 5.81

(A) 60° (B) 50°

(C) 70° (D) 80°

5-83 The edges of a plane surface are :
[NTSE-2018 (Stage-I) Uttar Pradesh]
(A) Lines (B) Points
(C) Angles (D) Planes

5-84 The area of two similar triangles ΔABC and ΔDEF are 48 cm^2 and 12 cm^2 respectively. If $EF = 3$ cm then BC is :
[NTSE-2018 (Stage-I) Uttar Pradesh]
(A) 6 cm (B) 4 cm
(C) 2 cm (D) 12 cm

5-85 In the given figure-5.82 if $PQ \parallel RS$, $\angle MXQ = 135°$ and $\angle MYR = 40°$ then value of $\angle XMY$ will be :
[NTSE-2018 (Stage-I) Uttarakhandh]

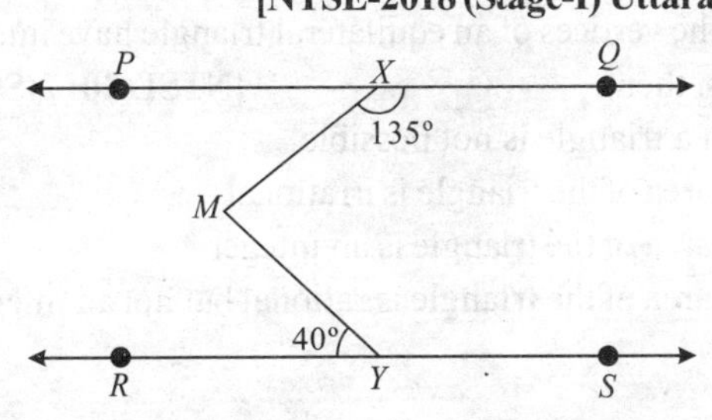

Figure 5.82

(A) 95° (B) 45°
(C) 140° (D) 85°

5-86 In the figure-5.83 if $QT \perp PR$ $\angle TQR = 40°$ and $\angle SPR = 30°$. Then the value of x and y will be :
[NTSE-2018 (Stage-I) Uttarakhandh]

(A) $x = 50°, y = 80°$

(B) $x = 80°, y = 50°$

(C) $x = 30°, y = 60°$

(D) $x = 60°, y = 30°$

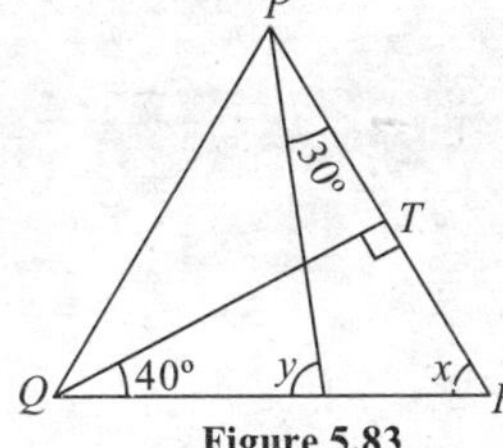

Figure 5.83

5-87 If angles of a triangle are in the ratio 2 : 4 : 9, then the difference of the two smaller exterior angles of the triangle is :
[NTSE-2012 (Stage-II)]
(A) 24° (B) 30°
(C) 44° (D) 60°

5-88 In the following figure-5.84, $\Delta ABD \cong \Delta ACD$. If $\angle BDC = 110°$ and $\angle DAC = 30°$, then the measure of angle $\angle DBA$ is :
[NTSE-2012 (Stage-II)]

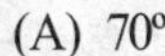

(A) 70°

(B) 40°

(C) 30°

(D) 25°

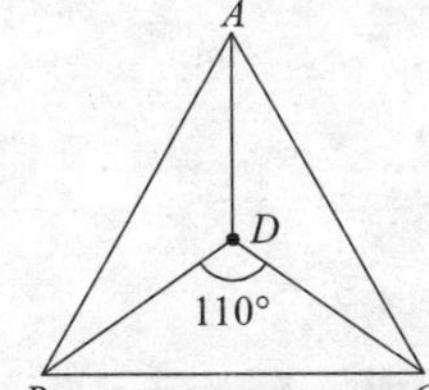

Figure 5.84

5-89 In a ΔABC, $AB = 4$ cm and $AC = 8$ cm. If M is the mid point of BC and $AM = 3$ cm, then length of BC, in cm, is :
[NTSE-2012 (Stage-II)]
(A) $2\sqrt{26}$ (B) $2\sqrt{31}$
(C) $\sqrt{31}$ (D) $\sqrt{26}$

5-90 A has a pair of triangles corresponding sides proportional, and B has a pair of pentagons with corresponding sides proportional,
$S_1 \equiv$ A's triangles must be similar
$S_2 \equiv$ B's pentagons must be similar
Which of the following statement is correct?
[NTSE-2013 (Stage-II)]
(A) S_1 is true but S_2 is not true
(B) S_2 is true, but S_1 is not ture
(C) Both S_1 and S_2 are true
(D) Neither S_1 nor S_2 is true

5-91 The sides of a triangle are of length 20, 21, and 29 units. The sum of the lengths of altitudes will be :
[NTSE-2014 (Stage-II)]
(A) $\dfrac{1609}{29}$ units (B) 49 units
(C) $\dfrac{1609}{21}$ units (D) 70 units

5-92 If P is a point inside the scalene triangle ABC such that ΔAPB, ΔBPC and ΔCPA have the same area, then P must be :
[NTSE-2014 (Stage-II)]
(A) In centre of ΔABC (B) Circumcentre of ΔABC
(C) Centroid of ΔABC (D) Orthocentre of ΔABC

5-93 In ΔABC, D is a point on BC such that $3BD = BC$. If each side of the triangle is 12cm, then AD equals :
[NTSE-2014 (Stage-II)]
(A) $4\sqrt{5}$ cm (B) $4\sqrt{6}$ cm
(C) $4\sqrt{7}$ cm (D) $4\sqrt{11}$ cm

5-94 In ΔABC, $\overline{XY}$ is parallel to $\overline{AC}$ and divides the triangle into the two parts of equal area. Then the $\dfrac{AX}{AB}$ equals :
[NTSE-2014 (Stage-II)]

(A) $\dfrac{\sqrt{2}+1}{2}$

(B) $\dfrac{2-\sqrt{2}}{2}$

(C) $\dfrac{2+\sqrt{2}}{2}$

(D) $\dfrac{\sqrt{2}-1}{2}$

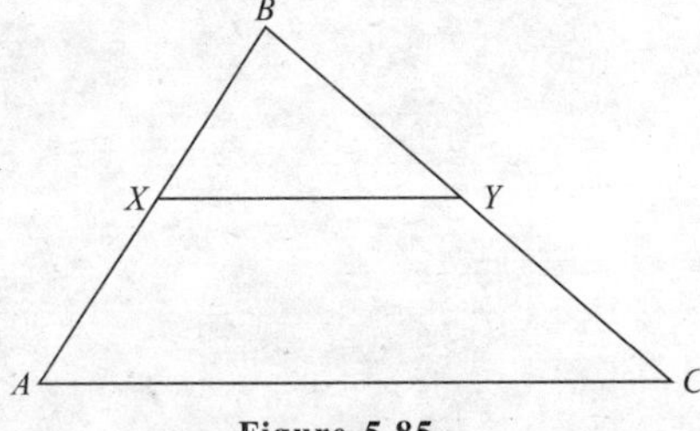

Figure 5.85

5-95 P is point in the interior of an equilateral triangle with side a units. If p_1, p_2 and p_3 are the distance of P from the three sides of the triangle, then $p_1 + p_2 + p_3$: **[NTSE-2014 (Stage-II)]**

(A) equals $\frac{2a}{3}$ units

(B) equals $\frac{a\sqrt{3}}{2}$ units

(C) is more than a units

(D) cannot be determined unless the location of P is specified

5-96 If in a triangle ABC, D is the mid-point of side BC, $\angle ADB = 45°$ and $\angle ACD = 30°$, then $\angle BAD$ and $\angle ABC$ are respectively equal to : **[NTSE-2015 (Stage-II)]**

(A) 15°, 105° (B) 30°, 105°

(C) 30°, 100° (D) 60°, 100°

5-97 Let l be the length of each equal side of an isosceles triangle. If the length of each equal side is doubled, keeping its height unchanged, then the difference of the squares of bases of the new triangle and the given triangle is : **[NTSE-2017 (Stage-II)]**

(A) 0 (B) $4l^2$

(C) $9l^2$ (D) $12l^2$

5-98 In ΔABC, $AB = AC$, P and Q are points on AC and AB respectively such that $BC = BP = PQ = AQ$. Then $\angle AQP$ is equal to (use $\pi = 180°$) : **[NTSE-2017 (Stage-II)]**

(A) $\frac{2\pi}{7}$ (B) $\frac{3\pi}{7}$

(C) $\frac{4\pi}{7}$ (D) $\frac{5\pi}{7}$

5-99 If the vertices of an equilateral triangle have integral co-ordinates, then : **[NTSE-2017 (Stage-II)]**

(A) Such a triangle is not possible

(B) The area of the triangle is irrational

(C) The area of the triangle is an integer

(D) The area of the triangle is rational but not an integer

* * * * *

ANSWERS

PRACTICE EXERCISE-5.1

1	(A)	**2**	(B)	**3**	(D)
4	(B)	**5**	(D)	**6**	(A)
7	(C)	**8**	(C)	**9**	(C)
10	(C)	**11**	(B)	**12**	(B)
13	(C)	**14**	(D)	**15**	(A)
16	(C)	**17**	(D)	**18**	(D)
19	(B)	**20**	(B)	**21**	(B)
22	(C)	**23**	(D)	**24**	(B)
25	(B)	**26**	(B)	**27**	(C)
28	(B)	**29**	(D)	**30**	(B)
31	(A)	**32**	(D)	**33**	(C)
34	(B)	**35**	(C)	**36**	(A)
37	(C)	**38**	(A)	**39**	(A)
40	(B)	**41**	(C)	**42**	(C)
43	(D)	**44**	(D)	**45**	(A)
46	(D)	**47**	(B)	**48**	(D)
49	(C)	**50**	(D)		

PRACTICE EXERCISE-5.2

1	(C)	**2**	(D)	**3**	(B)
4	(C)	**5**	(C)	**6**	(C)
7	(D)	**8**	(C)	**9**	(C)
10	(D)	**11**	(A)	**12**	(C)
13	(D)	**14**	(A)	**15**	(D)
16	(B)	**17**	(B)	**18**	(A)
19	(A)	**20**	(A)	**21**	(B)
22	(A)	**23**	(C)	**24**	(B)
25	(C)				

PRACTICE EXERCISE-5.3

1	(C)	**2**	(C)	**3**	(D)
4	(C)	**5**	(C)	**6**	(B)
7	(B)	**8**	(C)	**9**	(C)
10	(D)	**11**	(A)	**12**	(B)
13	(A)	**14**	(C)	**15**	(C)
16	(A)	**17**	(B)	**18**	(D)
19	(B)	**20**	(D)	**21**	(C)
22	(A)	**23**	(D)	**24**	(C)
25	(A)	**26**	(D)	**27**	(B)
28	(B)	**29**	(B)	**30**	(C)
31	(A)	**32**	(D)	**33**	(C)
34	(A)	**35**	(A)	**36**	(D)
37	(C)	**38**	(C)	**39**	(C)
40	(A)	**41**	(D)	**42**	(A)
43	(A)	**44**	(D)	**45**	(C)
46	(D)	**47**	(A)	**48**	(B)
49	(B)	**50**	(C)	**51**	(B)
52	(A)	**53**	(D)	**54**	(D)
55	(C)	**56**	(B)	**57**	(A)
58	(B)	**59**	(B)	**60**	(C)
61	(D)	**62**	(D)	**63**	(A)
64	(C)	**65**	(D)	**66**	(D)
67	(D)	**68**	(C)	**69**	(A)
70	(B)	**71**	(C)	**72**	(D)
73	(C)	**74**	(C)	**75**	(C)
76	(C)	**77**	(A)	**78**	(D)
79	(B)	**80**	(D)	**81**	(B)
82	(C)	**83**	(A)	**84**	(A)
85	(D)	**86**	(A)	**87**	(D)
88	(D)	**89**	(C)	**90**	(A)
91	(A)	**92**	(C)	**93**	(C)
94	(B)	**95**	(B)	**96**	(B)
97	(D)	**98**	(D)	**99**	(A)

Solutions of PRACTICE EXERCISE-5.1

Sol. 1 (A) Consider ΔAMC in the given figure

$\angle AMC = 90°$ [linear pair] ... (1)

In ΔAMC

$\angle MAC + \angle AMC + \angle ACM = 180°$

$\angle MAC + 90° + 35° = 180°$

[from (1) $\angle AMC = 90°$]

$\Rightarrow$ $\angle MAC = 180 - 125°$

$\angle MAC = 55°$ ...(2)

In ΔABC

$\angle A + \angle B + \angle C = 180°$

$\Rightarrow$ $\angle A + 70 + 35 = 180°$

$\Rightarrow$ $\angle A = 180 - 105$

$\Rightarrow$ $\angle A = 75°$ ...(3)

Given AN is the angle bisector

$\Rightarrow$ $\angle BAN + \angle NAC = 75°$ [from (3)]

$\Rightarrow$ $2\angle NAC = 75°$

$\Rightarrow$ $\angle NAC = \dfrac{75°}{2} = 37.5$ ...(4)

$\Rightarrow$ $\angle MAC = \angle MAN + \angle NAC$

$\Rightarrow$ $55° = \angle MAN + 37.5$

$\Rightarrow$ $\angle MAN = 55 - 37.5 = 17.5$

Hence Ans is (A)

Sol. 2 (B)

Join AC, As shown in the figure

Given $AB \parallel CD$

$\Rightarrow$ $\angle BAC = \angle DCT = \angle S$

[Corresponding angles are equal]

In ΔACE

TCE is an external angle of ΔACE

From the figure

$$\angle TCE = 140 - \angle S$$

Also $\angle CAE = x - \angle S$

We know

$$\angle TCE = \angle CAE + AEC$$

[Exterior angle is equal to the sum of interior alternate angles]

$$140 - \angle S = x - \angle S + 20°$$

$$x = 120°$$

Hence Ans is (B)

Sol. 3 (D)

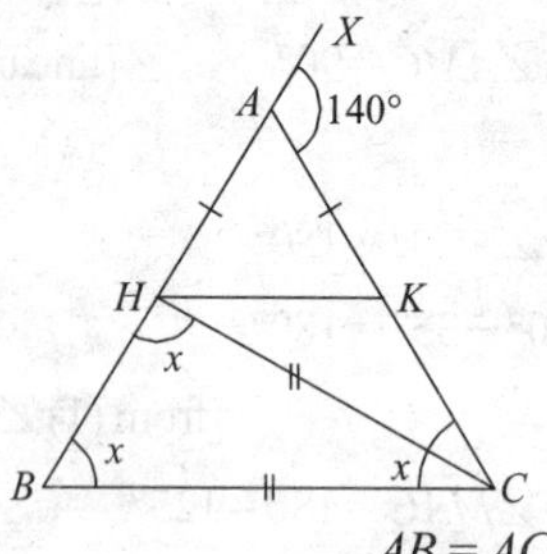

Given $AB = AC$

$\Rightarrow \quad \angle ABC = \angle ACB = x$

[Angles opposite to equal sides are equal]

Also given $CH = CB$

$\Rightarrow \quad \angle CHB = \angle ABC = x$

[Angles opposite to equal sides are equal]

Given XAC is the external angle of ΔABC

$\Rightarrow \quad \angle XAC = \angle ABC + \angle ACB$

$\Rightarrow \quad 140° = x + x$

$\Rightarrow \quad 2x = 140°$

$\Rightarrow \quad x = 70°$

In ΔHBC

$$\angle HBC + \angle HCB + \angle CHB = 180°$$

$\Rightarrow \quad x + \angle HCB + x = 180°$

$\Rightarrow \quad 70 + \angle HCB + 70 = 180°$

$\Rightarrow \quad \angle HCB = 180 - 140$

$\Rightarrow \quad \angle HCB = 40°$

We know

$$\angle ACB = \angle HCB + \angle HCK$$

$\Rightarrow \quad 70 = 40 + \angle HCK$

$\Rightarrow \quad \angle HCK = 30°$

Hence Ans is (D)

Sol. 4 (B)

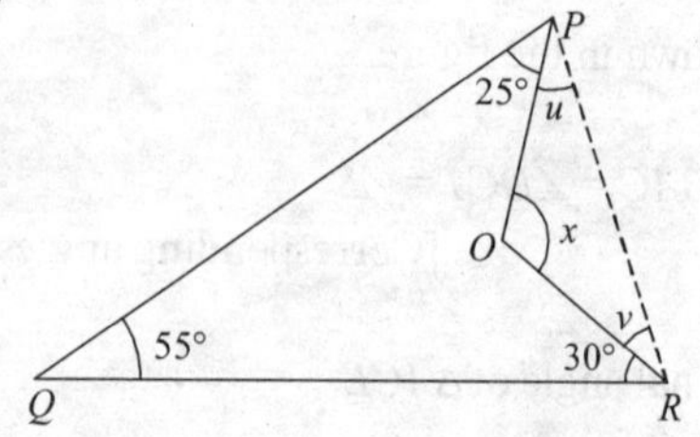

Join PR as shown in the figure,

Let $\angle OPR = u$

and $\angle PRO = v$

In ΔPQR

$$\angle PQR + \angle RPQ + \angle QRP = 180°$$

$\Rightarrow \quad 55° + (25° + u) + (30 + v) = 180°$

$\Rightarrow \quad 110 + u + v = 180°$

$\Rightarrow \quad u + v = 70° \quad \ldots(1)$

In ΔPOR

$$x + u + v = 180°$$

$\Rightarrow \quad x + 70° = 180°$ [From (1) $u + v = 70°$]

$\Rightarrow \quad x = 180 - 70$

$\Rightarrow \quad x = 110°$

Hence Ans is (B)

Sol. 5 (D) Geometric figures having the same area need not be congruent though congruent figures have equal area.

The angle must be included within the sides considered in the two triangles. Only then, the triangles are congruent.

Along with the hypotenuse and the right angle, the third side must also be correspondingly equal for the triangles to be congruent

Hence Ans is (D)

Sol. 6 (A) 'R' is the correct explantion

Hence Ans is (A)

Sol. 7 (C)

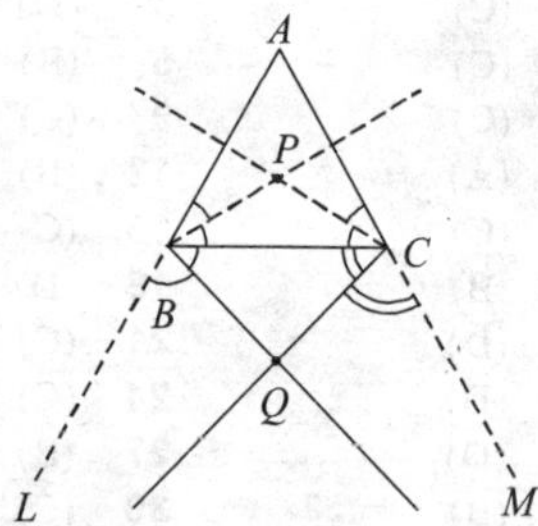

In ΔBPC

$$\angle PBC + \angle BCP + \angle CPB = 180°$$

$\Rightarrow \quad \dfrac{\angle B}{2} + \dfrac{\angle C}{2} + \angle CPB = 180°$

[given BP & PC are angle bisector]

$\Rightarrow \quad \angle CPB = 180 - \left(\dfrac{\angle B}{2} + \dfrac{\angle C}{2}\right)$

$$= 180 - \left(90 - \dfrac{\angle A}{2}\right)$$

[$\because$ $A + B + C = 180°$ also $\dfrac{A}{2} + \dfrac{B}{2} + \dfrac{C}{2} = 90°$]

$$= 90° + \dfrac{\angle A}{2} \quad \ldots(1)$$

In ΔBQC

$$\angle CBQ + \angle BQC + \angle QCB = 180°$$

$$\frac{180-B}{2} + \angle BQC + \frac{180-C}{2} = 180°$$

[given BQ & QC and external angle bisectors]

$$\Rightarrow \quad 90 - \frac{B}{2} + \angle BQC + 90 - \frac{C}{2} = 180°$$

$$\Rightarrow \quad \angle BQC = 180 - 90 - 90 + \frac{B}{2} + \frac{C}{2}$$

$$= 90 - \frac{A}{2} \quad \ldots(2)$$

$$\left[\text{as } A+B+C = 180°, \frac{A}{2}+\frac{B}{2}+\frac{C}{2} = 90°\right]$$

from (1) & (2)

$$\angle BPL + \angle BQC = 90° + \frac{A}{2} + 90° - \frac{A}{2}$$

$$= 180°$$

Hence Ans is (C)

Sol. 8 (C)

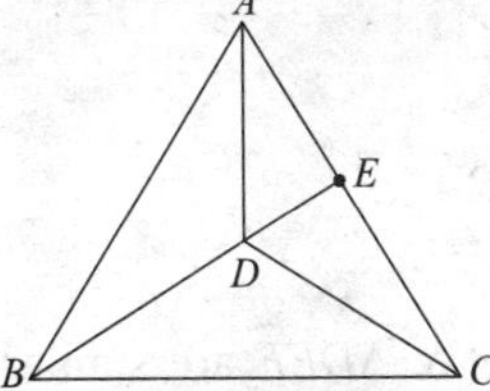

Extend BD to meet AC at E

Now by triangle inequality property we have

in ΔABE

$$AB + AE > BE > BD + DE \quad \ldots(1)$$

Similarly in ΔDEC

$$DE + EC > DC \quad \ldots(2)$$

Adding (1) & (2)

$$\Rightarrow \quad AB + AE + DE + EC > BD + DE + DC$$

$$AB + AC + DE > BD + DE + DC$$

$$AB + AC > BD + DC \quad \ldots(3)$$

Similarly

$$AB + BC > AD + DC \quad \ldots(4)$$

and

$$AC + BC > AD + BD \quad \ldots(5)$$

Adding (3), (4) & (5) we have

$$AB + BC + AC > AD + BD + DC$$

Hence Ans is (C)

Sol. 9 (C)

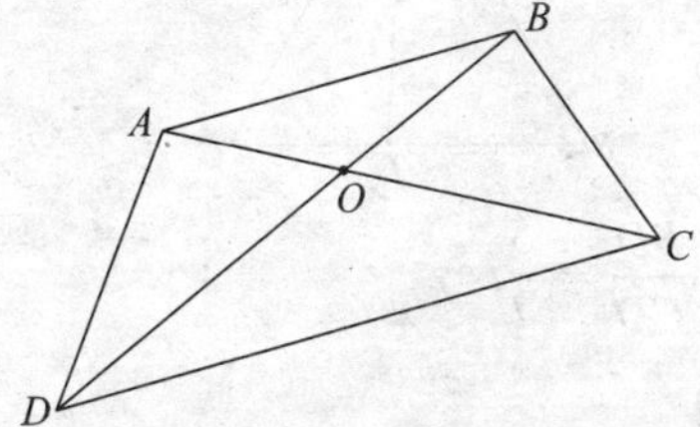

In ΔABC

$$AB + BC > AC$$

[sum of two sides is greater than the third side] ...(1)

In ΔBCD

$$BC + CD > BD \quad \ldots(2)$$

In ΔCDA

$$CD + DA > AC \quad \ldots(3)$$

In ΔDAB

$$AD + AB > BD \quad \ldots(4)$$

Adding (1), (2), (3) & (4)

We get

$$2(AB + BC + CD + DA) > 2(AC + BD)$$

$$\Rightarrow \quad AB + BC + CD + DA > AC + BD$$

We know difference of two sides is always less than the third side.

So in ΔAOB

$$AB - OB < OA \quad \ldots(5)$$

|||ly in ΔBOC

$$BC - OC < OB \quad \ldots(6)$$

In ΔDOC

$$CD - OC < OD \quad \ldots(7)$$

In ΔAOD

$$AD - OA < OD \quad \ldots(8)$$

Adding (5), (6), (7), (8)

We get

$$AB + BC + CD + AD - OB - OC - OC - OA < OA + OB + OD$$

$$\Rightarrow \quad AB + BC + CD + AD < 2OA + 2OB + 2OC + 2OD$$

$$< 2(OB + OD) + 2(OA + OC)$$

$$< 2(BD + AC)$$

Hence Ans is (C)

Sol. 10 (C)

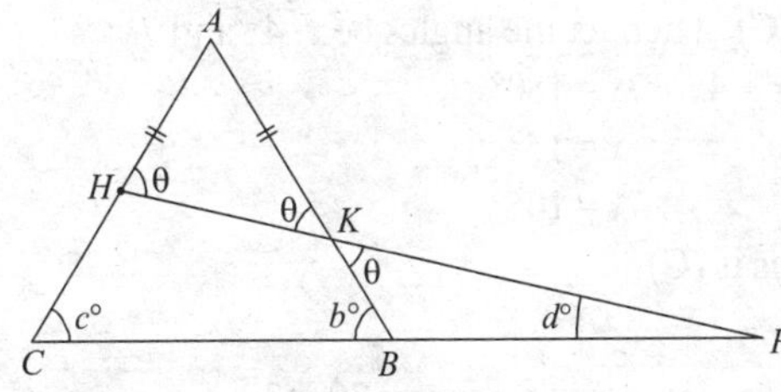

As shown in the figure,

$$AH = HK \quad \text{[given]}$$

Let $\angle AHK = \theta = \angle AKH$

[angles opposite to equal sides are equal]

In ΔABC

$$\angle A + \angle B + \angle C = 180°$$

$$\Rightarrow \quad \angle A + 70° + 40° = 180°$$

$$\Rightarrow \quad \angle A = 70°$$

In ΔAHK

$$\angle A + \angle H + \angle K = 180°$$

$$\Rightarrow \quad 70 + \theta + \theta = 180°$$

$\Rightarrow \quad 2\theta = 110°$

$\Rightarrow \quad \theta = 55°$

$\Rightarrow \quad \angle PKB = \theta$

[Vertically opposite angles are equal]

$\angle KBP = 180 - b$

$= 180 - 70 = 110$

In ΔKBP

$\angle KPB + \angle PBK + \angle PKB = 180°$

$d + 110° + 55° = 180°$

$d = 180° - (165°)$

$= 15°$

Hence Ans (C)

Sol. 11 (B) The sum of the smaller sides cannot be equal to or less than the largest side but sum of the two sides of a triangle is always greater than the third side

Hence Ans is (B)

Sol. 12 (B) We know $12^2 > 8^2 + 6^2$

$\Rightarrow$ obtuse triangle

Hence Ans is (B)

Sol. 13 (C) Sum of exterior angles = 360°

Hence Ans is (C)

Sol. 14 (D) $\angle ACD = \angle CBA + \angle BAC = 70° = 110°$

[exterior angle = sum of interior opposite angles]

Hence Ans is (D)

Sol. 15 (A) Given

$\Rightarrow \quad \angle BAC > 90°$

$\Rightarrow \quad \angle ABC + \angle ACB < 90°$

Hence Ans is (A)

Sol. 16 (C) Then let the angles be x, $4x$ and $7x$

$x + 4x + 7x = 180°$

$\Rightarrow \quad x = 15°$

$\Rightarrow \quad 7x = 105°$

Hence Ans is (C)

Sol. 17 (D) $\angle OBC + \angle OCB = \frac{70}{2} + \frac{30}{2} = 50°$

$\Rightarrow \quad \angle BOC = 180° - 50° = 130°$

Hence Ans is (D)

Sol. 18 (D) From the figure

$\angle BFC = 90° - \frac{1}{2}(\angle A)$

$= 90° - \frac{1}{2}[180° - (80° + 30°)] = 55°$

Hence Ans is (D)

Sol. 19 (B) The given all points are same in an equilateral triangle,

i.e. they are coincident

Hence Ans is (B)

Sol. 20 (B) In ΔBMD & ΔCND

We have $\quad \angle M = \angle N = 90°$

$DM = DN$ (given)

$BD = DC$ (given)

Hence $\quad \Delta BMD \cong \Delta DMC$ (by R.H.S.)

$\Rightarrow \quad \angle B = \angle C$ (c.p.c.t)

Hence Ans is (B)

Sol. 21 (B) In ΔADB & ΔADC

$\angle ADB = \angle ADC = 90°$ (given)

$AD = AD$ (common)

$BD = DC$ (given)

Hence $\quad \Delta ADB \cong \Delta ADC$

$\Rightarrow \quad \angle B = \angle C$

Hence Δ isosceles

Hence Ans is (B)

Sol. 22 (C) Given ΔABC & ΔDEF are similar so ratio of corresponding sides are equal

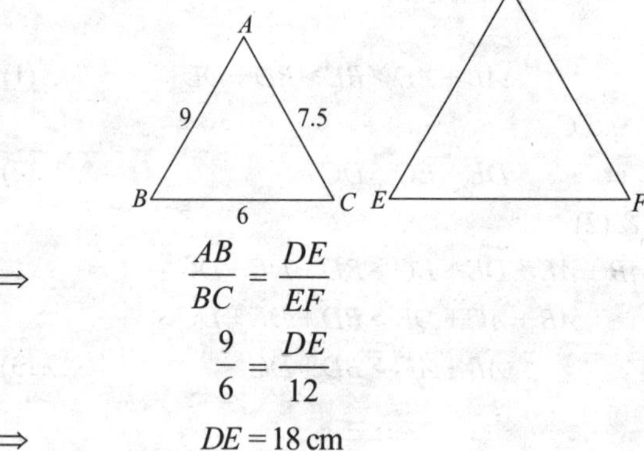

$\Rightarrow \quad \frac{AB}{BC} = \frac{DE}{EF}$

$\frac{9}{6} = \frac{DE}{12}$

$\Rightarrow \quad DE = 18$ cm

Hence Ans is (C)

Sol. 23 (D) Using angle bisector theorem in ΔABC

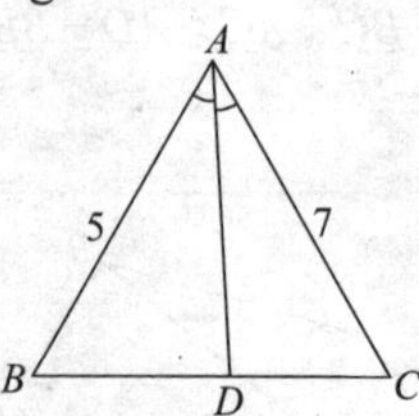

We have $\frac{AB}{AC} = \frac{BD}{CD} = \frac{5}{7}$

Hence Ans is (D)

Sol. 24 (B) Draw a line $DG \parallel$ to BE

Now apply converse of mid-point theorem in ΔADG

We have F is the mid-point of AG

$\Rightarrow \quad AF = FG \quad \ldots(1)$

Again apply converse of mid-point theorem in ΔBFC

We have

$FG = GC \quad \ldots(2)$

From (1) & (2) $AF = FG = GC$

Hence $AF : FC = 1:2$

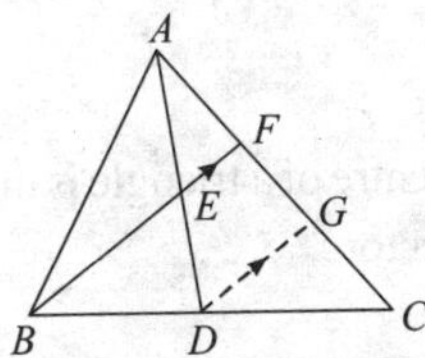

Apply mid-point theorem between ΔADG & ΔBCF

Hence Ans is (B)

Sol. 25 (B)

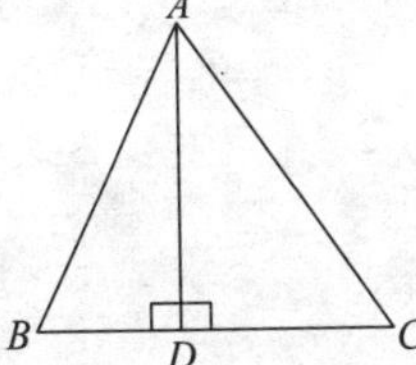

AB is hypotenuse and AD is perpendicular in ΔABD,

$\Rightarrow \quad AB > AD$

Hence Ans is (B)

Sol. 26 (B) Given, In ΔABC

$AC = 25$

$x^2 + (x-17)^2 = 25^2$ (Using Pythagorus theorem)

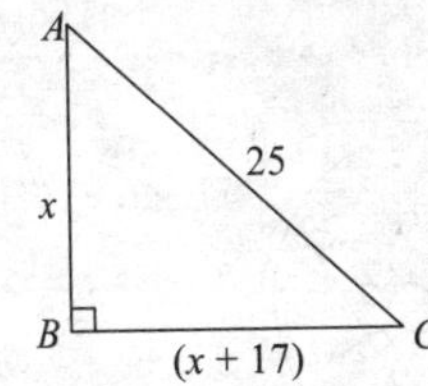

$\Rightarrow \quad x = 7$ cm

$\Rightarrow$ Altitude + Base $= 24 + 7 = 31$ cm

Hence Ans is (B)

Sol. 27 (C) Sum of the two sides of a triangle is greater than the third

Hence Ans is (C)

Sol. 28 (B) $\angle ACB = 180° - 100° = 80°$

and $\angle BAC + \angle ABC = 180° - 80° = 100°$

$\Rightarrow \quad \angle ABC = 50° \quad (\because \angle BAC = \angle ABC)$

Hence Ans is (B)

Sol. 29 (D) Given D, E & F are the mid-points of BC, AC & AB respectively

Hence by using mid-point theorem

We have $FE \parallel BC$ & $FE = 1/2\, BC$

$\Rightarrow \quad FE \parallel BD$ & $FE = BD$

Hence $FEDB$ is a parallelogram & DF is diagonal then by property of parallelogram

$\Delta BDF \cong \Delta DEF$

Similarly $\Delta DEC \cong \Delta DEF$

and $\Delta DEF \cong \Delta AEF$

Hence Ans is (D)

Sol. 30 (B) We know

$$\cos A = \frac{b^2 + c^2 - a^2}{2bc} \quad \text{(cosine rule)}$$

$$\frac{1}{2} = \frac{b^2 + c^2 - a^2}{2bc} \quad (\because \cos 60° = 1/2)$$

$$\Rightarrow \quad a^2 = b^2 + c^2 - bc$$

Hence Ans is (B)

Sol. 31 (A) Using cosine rule

In ΔABC

$$\cos C = \frac{a^2 + b^2 - c^2}{2ab}$$

$$-\frac{1}{2} = \frac{a^2 + b^2 - c^2}{2ab}$$

$$\Rightarrow \quad c^2 = a^2 + b^2 + ab$$

Hence Ans is (A)

Aliter :

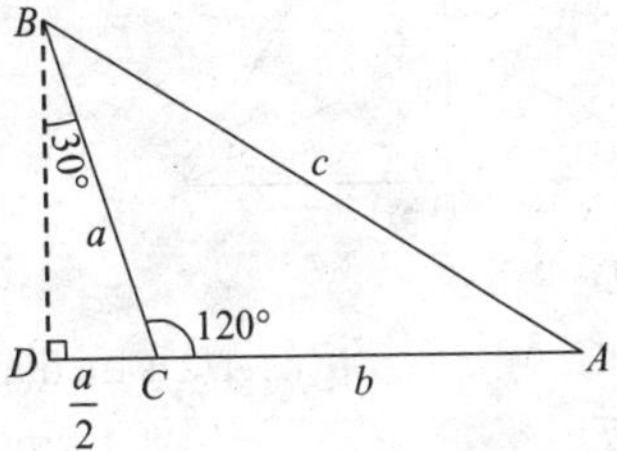

Construction : Extend AC to D and join BD such that ΔBDA is a right angled triangle

In ΔBDC

$$\sin 30° = \frac{DC}{BC}$$

$$\frac{1}{2} = \frac{DC}{a}$$

$$DC = \frac{a}{2}$$

In ΔBDA, $BD^2 = C^2 - \left(\dfrac{a}{2}+b\right)^2$ ...(1)

In ΔBDC, $BD^2 = a^2 - \left(\dfrac{a}{2}\right)^2$ ...(2)

(1) = (2)

$$\Rightarrow \quad c^2 - \left(\frac{a}{2}+b\right)^2 = a^2 - \left(\frac{a}{2}\right)^2$$

$$c^2 - \frac{a^2}{4} - b^2 - ab = \frac{3a^2}{4}$$

$$4c^2 - a^2 - 4b^2 - 4ab = 3a^2$$

$$4a^2 + 4b^2 + 4ab = 4c^2$$

$$\Rightarrow \quad c^2 = a^2 + b^2 + ab$$

Hence Ans is (A)

Sol. 32 (D)

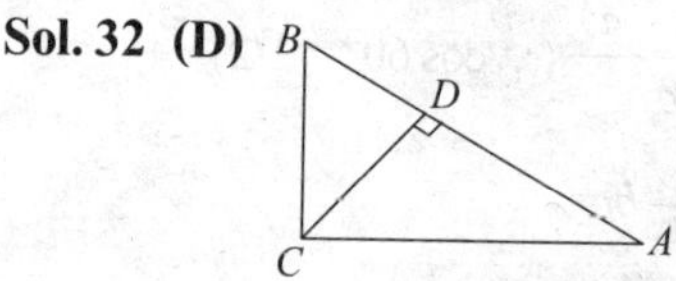

$\dfrac{1}{p^2} = \dfrac{1}{a^2} + \dfrac{1}{b^2}$ (Apply similarity b/w Δ BDC & ΔBCA also between ΔADC & ΔACB)

Hence Ans is (D)

Sol. 33 (C) G is the point of intersection of medians so it is known as centroid which divides the medians in the ratio 2 : 1 from vertex to base.

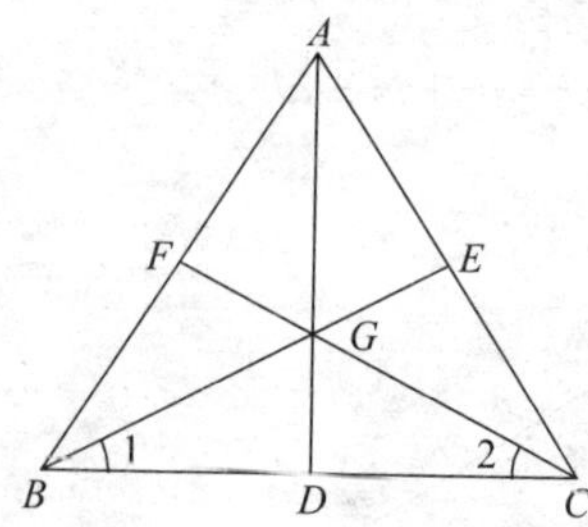

Now in ΔBGD & ΔCGD

$BD = DC$ (as AD is median to BC)

$GD = GD$ (common)

& $BG = GC$ (given $BE = CF$ then $\dfrac{2}{3}BE = \dfrac{2}{3}CF$)

$\Rightarrow$ $\Delta BGD \cong \Delta CGD$ (SSS)

Hence by c.p.c.t.

$\angle 1 = \angle 2$

Now in ΔBEC & ΔCFB

$\angle 1 = \angle 2$ (proved above)

$BC = BC$ (common)

$BE = CF$ (given)

$\Rightarrow$ $\Delta BEC \cong \Delta CFB$ (SAS)

Hence $\angle B = \angle C$

Similarly $\angle C = \angle A$

$\Rightarrow$ $\angle A = \angle B = \angle C$

Hence triangle is an equilateral triangle

Hence Ans is (C)

Sol. 34 (B) Incenter of a triangle is the point of intersection of angle bisectors.

Hence Ans is (B)

Sol. 35 (C) Circumcentre of a triangle is the point of intersection of perpendicular bisectors.

Hence Ans is (C)

Sol. 36 (A) Orthocentre of a triangle is the point of intersection of altitudes.

Hence Ans is (A)

Sol. 37 (C)

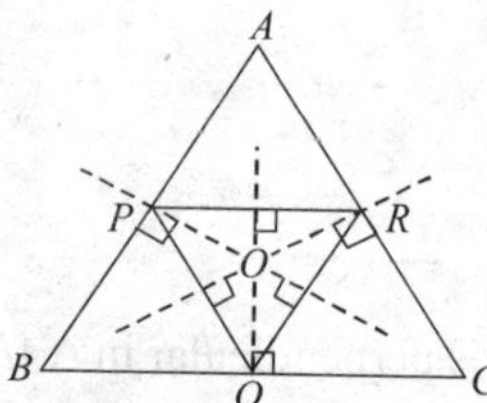

We know that circumcentre of any triangle is the point of intersection of perpendicular bisector & orthocenter of any triangle is the point of intersection of altitudes.

From the figure it is clear that perpendicular bisector of ΔABC become altitude of ΔPQR.

$\Rightarrow$ The point O is the orthocentre of ΔPQR

Hence Ans is (C)

Sol. 38 (A)

As we know that circumcentre ('S') of any triangle is the point of intersection of perpendicular bisector so it should be equidistant from the vertices A, B and C.

Hence Ans is (A)

Sol. 39 (A)

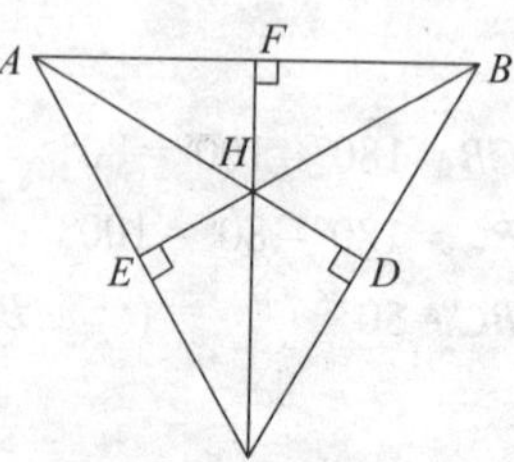

Orthocenter of an obtuse angle triangle lies outside the triangle

Hence Ans is (A)

Sol. 40 (B)

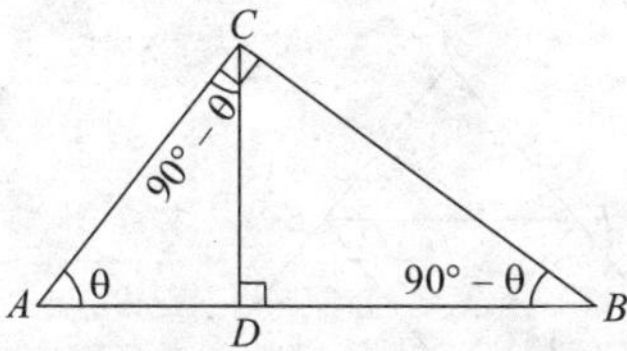

$\Delta ADC \sim \Delta ACB$ (by AA similarity)

Then the ratio of corresponding sides are proportional.
Hence

$$\frac{CD}{BC} = \frac{AC}{AB}$$

$$CD = \frac{AC \times BC}{AB}$$

Hence Ans is (B)

Sol. 41 (C)

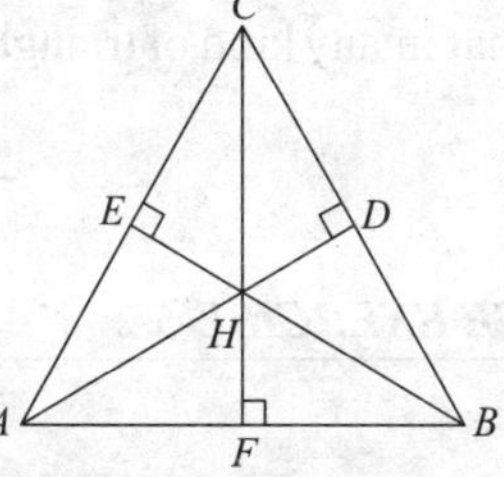

Consider ΔABD & ΔBAE

$AB = AB$ (common)

$\angle A = \angle B = 60°$

(as the triangle is equilateral)

$AE = BD$

(As $AC = BC$ being the sides of equilateral triangle so 1/2 of AC = 1/2 of BC)

Hence $\Delta ABD \cong \Delta BAE$ (by SAS)

So $BE = AD$ (by c.p.c.t)

Similarly we can prove that $BE = CF$

$\Rightarrow \quad AD = BE = CF$

Hence Ans is (C)

Sol. 42 (C) In ΔABC

$AB^2 = BD^2 + AD^2$ (Pythagoras theorem)

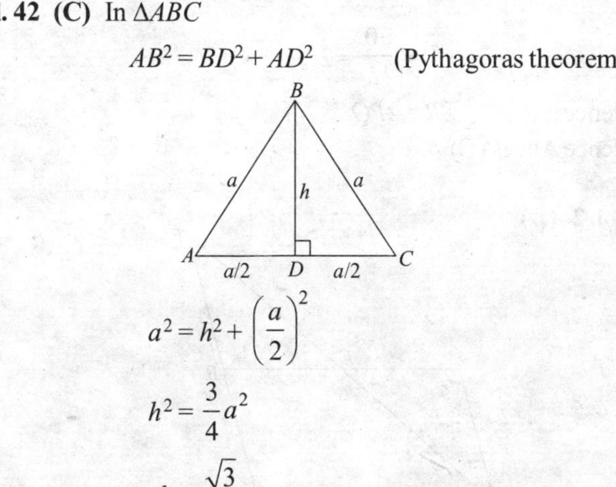

$$a^2 = h^2 + \left(\frac{a}{2}\right)^2$$

$$\Rightarrow \quad h^2 = \frac{3}{4}a^2$$

$$\Rightarrow \quad h = \frac{\sqrt{3}}{2}a$$

$$\Rightarrow \quad \frac{a}{h} = \frac{2}{\sqrt{3}}$$

Hence Ans is (C)

Sol. 43 (D) There are 4 congruent triangles. As by mid-point theorem we can prove that $PRQB$ is a parallelogram with PQ diagonal which divides the parallelogram into two equal triangles having same area.

Similarly parallelogram $PRCQ$ & parallelogram $ARQP$ has the same property.

Hence, $ar(\Delta ABC) = 6 \times 4 = 24$ cm^2

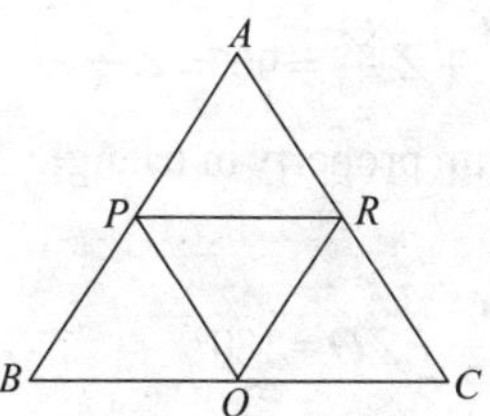

Hence Ans is (D)

Sol. 44 (D)

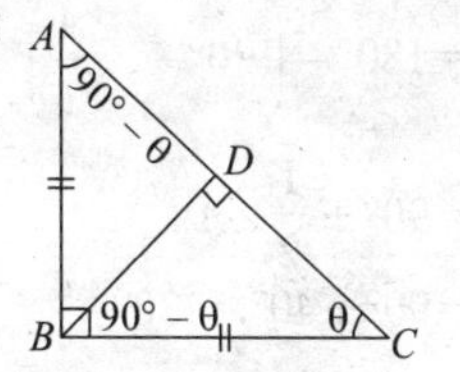

$\Delta BDC \sim \Delta ABC$ (by AA)

So $$\frac{BD}{AB} = \frac{BC}{AC}$$

$$BD = \frac{AB \times BC}{AC}$$

$$= \frac{6 \times 6}{6\sqrt{2}} = 3\sqrt{2} \text{ cm}$$

Hence Ans is (D)

Sol. 45 (A)

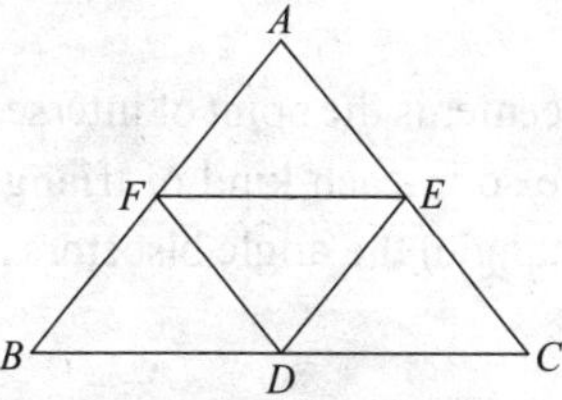

Given D, E & F are the mid-points of BC, AC & AB respectively

Hence by using mid-point theorem

We have FE parallelogram BC & $FE = 1/2\ BC$

$\Rightarrow$ FE parallelogram BD & $FE = BD$

Hence $FEDB$ parallelogram & DF is diagonal

Then by property of $||^r$ gm

$\Delta BDF \cong \Delta DEF$

Similarly $\Delta DEC \cong \Delta DEF$

and $\Delta DEF \cong \Delta AEF$

Hence Ans is (A)

Sol. 46 (D)

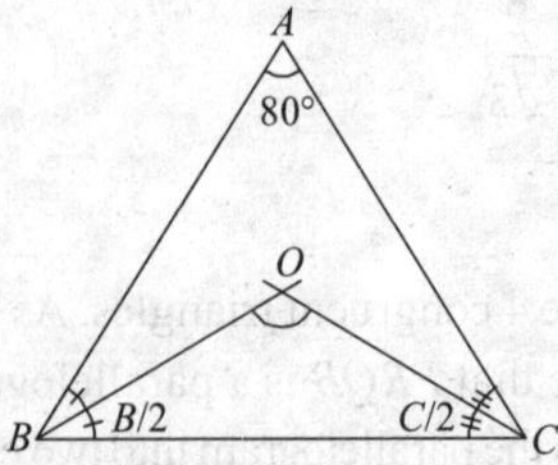

We know by angle sum property of a triangle

$$\angle A+\angle B+\angle C=180°$$

$$\angle\frac{A}{2}+\angle\frac{B}{2}+\angle\frac{C}{2}=90°$$

$$\angle\frac{B}{2}+\angle\frac{C}{2}=90°-\angle\frac{A}{2}$$

Now apply angle sum property in triangle ΔBOC

We have

$$\angle\frac{B}{2}+\angle\frac{C}{2}+\angle O=180°$$

$$\angle O=180°-\left(\angle\frac{B}{2}+\angle\frac{C}{2}\right)$$

$$\angle O=180°-\left(90°-\angle\frac{A}{2}\right)$$

$$\angle BOC=90°+\frac{1}{2}\angle A$$

$$=90°+40°=130°$$

Hence Ans is (D)

Sol. 47 (B)

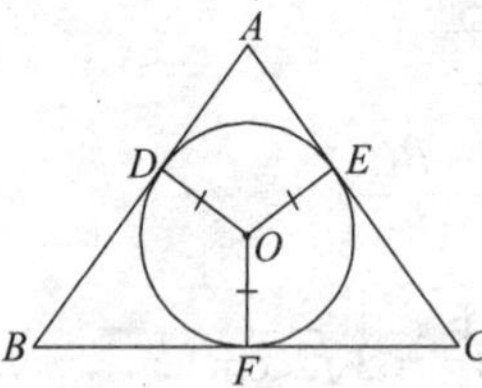

Given $OD=OE=OF$.

Now from figure it is clear that O is the in center of a triangle

Hence Ans is (B)

Sol. 48 (D) Since incenter is the point of intersection of angle bisectors of a triangle so in each kind of triangle (viz acute, obtuse, right angle triangle) the angle bisectors always lies in side the triangle

Hence Ans is (D)

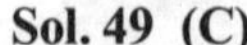

Sol. 49 (C)

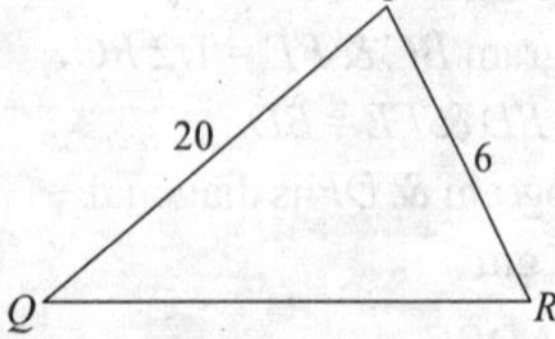

Side QR of a triangle will be more than the difference between other two sides and less than the sum of the other two sides.

$\Rightarrow$ $PQ-PR<QR<PQ+PR$

Hence Ans is (C)

Sol. 50 (D)

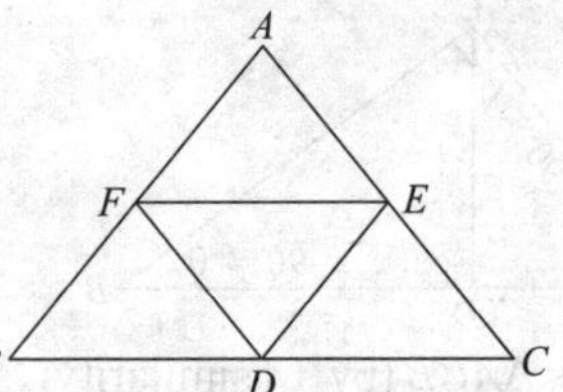

Given D, E & F are the mid-points of BC, AC & AB respectively

Hence by using mid-point theorem

We have FE parallelogram BC & $FE=1/2\ BC$

$\Rightarrow$ FE parallelogram BD & $FE=BD$

Hence $FEDB$ parallelogram & DF is diagonal

Then by property of parallelogram

$\Delta BDF\cong\Delta DEF$

Similarly $\Delta DEC\cong\Delta DEF$

and $\Delta DEF\cong\Delta AEF$

Therefore it is proved that in any kind of triangle this relation hold good

Hence Ans is (D)

Solutions of PRACTICE EXERCISE-5.2

Sol. 1 (C)

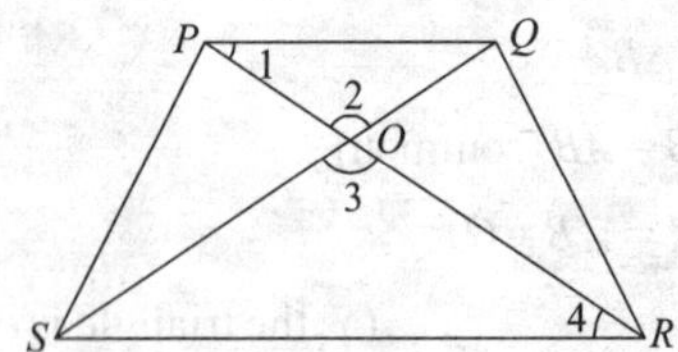

In ΔPOQ and ΔROS

$\angle 2=\angle 3$ (vertically opposite angle)

$\angle 1=\angle 4$ (alternate angle)

Hence $\Delta POQ\sim\Delta ROS$ (by AA)

So,

SR and PQ are proportional to the square roots of the areas of similar triangles SOR and POQ

$$\frac{SR}{PQ}=\sqrt{\frac{\text{area of }\Delta\ ROS}{\text{area of }\Delta\ POQ}}=\sqrt{\frac{900}{225}}$$

$$=\frac{30}{15}=2$$

Hence $SR=2PQ$

Hence Ans is (C)

Sol. 2 (D)

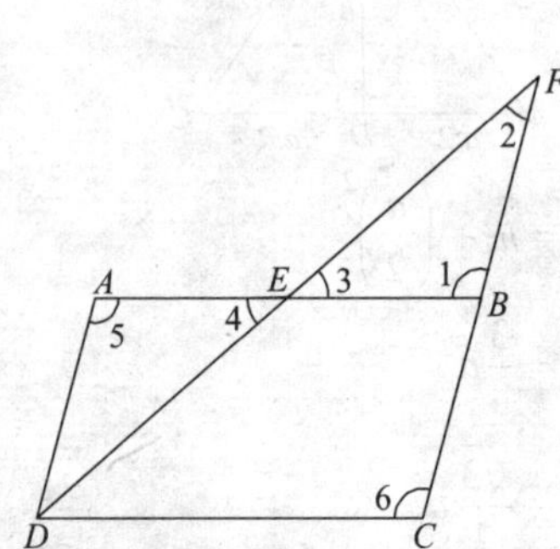

In ΔFEB and ΔFDC

$\angle 1 = \angle 6$ (corresponding angle)

$\angle 2 = \angle 2$ (common)

Hence $\Delta FEB \sim \Delta FDC\ (AA)$

So ratio of corresponding sides are equal

$$\frac{FB}{FC} = \frac{BE}{DC} \quad \ldots(1)$$

Now in ΔAED and ΔEFB

$\angle 4 = \angle 3$ (vertically opposite angle)

$\angle 5 = \angle 1$ (alternate angle)

Hence $\Delta AED \sim \Delta BEF$

So ratio of corresponding sides are equal

$$\frac{AD}{BF} = \frac{AE}{BE} = \frac{DE}{EF} \quad \ldots(2)$$

Hence using (1) & (2) all options are correct

Hence Ans is (D)

Sol. 3 (B)

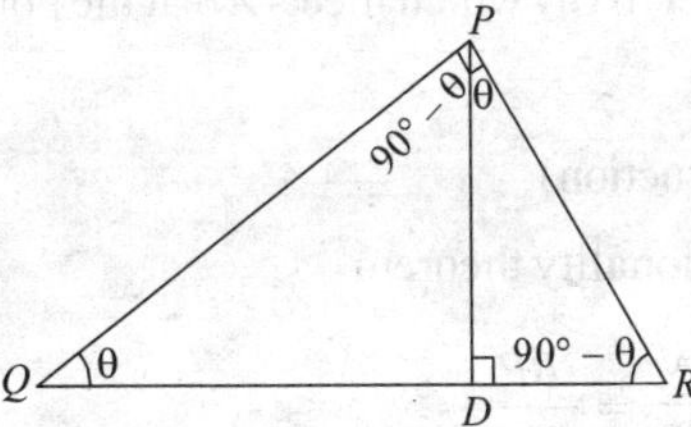

In ΔPDR & ΔQPR

$\angle P = \angle Q$ (each equal to $\theta°$)

$\angle D = \angle P$ (each 90°)

Hence $\Delta PDR \sim \Delta QPR$

So, corresponding sides of similar triangles are proportional.

$$\frac{PR}{QR} = \frac{DR}{PR} \quad \ldots(1)$$

Similarly considering ΔPQD & ΔDQP we have

$\angle P = \angle D$ (each 90°)

& $\angle Q = \angle Q$ (common)

Hence $\Delta PQD \sim \Delta DQP$

So, corresponding sides of similar triangles are proportional

$$\frac{PQ}{QR} = \frac{QD}{PQ} \quad \ldots(2)$$

Dividing (2) by (1)

$$\frac{PQ}{QR} \div \frac{PR}{QR} = \frac{QD}{PQ} \div \frac{DR}{PR}$$

$$\frac{PQ}{QR} \times \frac{QR}{PR} = \frac{QD}{PQ} \times \frac{PR}{DR}$$

$$\frac{PQ^2}{PR^2} = \frac{QD}{DR}$$

$$\frac{PQ}{PR} = \frac{\sqrt{QD}}{\sqrt{DR}}$$

Hence Ans is (B)

Sol. 4 (C)

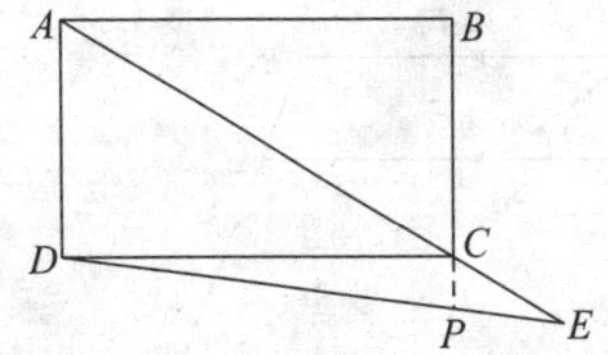

Given $AB = 8$ cm and $BC = 6$ cm

$\Rightarrow \quad AC = \sqrt{8^2 + 6^2} = 10$ cm

And also given

$AC : CE = 2 : 1$

Produce BC to meet DE at the point P

As CP is parallel to AD

$\Delta ECP \sim \Delta EAD$ – (1)

$\Rightarrow \quad \frac{CP}{AD} = \frac{CE}{AE};\ \frac{CP}{6} = \frac{1}{3}$

$\Rightarrow \quad CP = 2$ cm

ΔCPD is a right triangle

$\Rightarrow \quad DP = \sqrt{CD^2 + CP^2}$

$= \sqrt{68} = 2\sqrt{17}$ cm

But $PD = PE = 2 : 1$ (from (1))

$PE = \sqrt{17}$ cm

$\Rightarrow \quad DE = DP + PE$

$= 2\sqrt{17} + \sqrt{17}$

$= 3\sqrt{17}$ cm

Hence Ans is (C)

Sol. 5 (C)

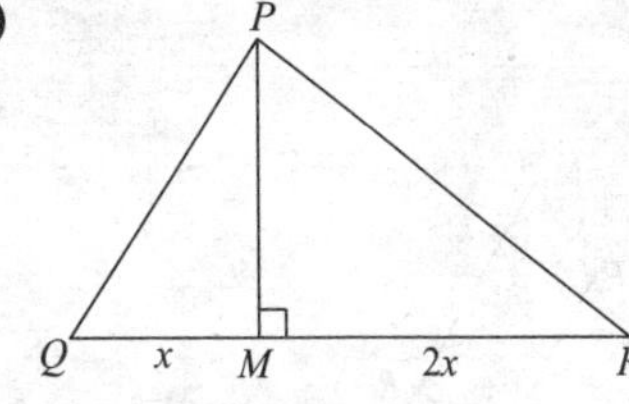

Given $PQ = 6$ cm, $PR = 9$ cm

and $QM : MR = x : 2x$

Let $QM = x$ and $MR = 2x$

As PM is perpendicular QR, ΔPMQ and ΔPMR are right triangles.

$\Rightarrow \quad (PM)^2 = (PQ)^2 - (QM)^2 \quad \ldots(1)$

$(PM)^2 = (PR)^2 - (MR)^2 \quad \ldots(2)$

From (1) and (2), we

$(PQ)^2 - (QM)^2 = (PR)^2 - (MR)^2$

$(6)^2 - (x)^2 = (9)^2 - (2x)^2$

$\Rightarrow \quad 3x^2 = 45$

$\Rightarrow \quad x^2 = 15$

$\Rightarrow \quad x = \sqrt{15}$ cm

$\Rightarrow \quad QR = 3\sqrt{15}$ cm

Hence Ans is (C)

Sol. 6 (C)

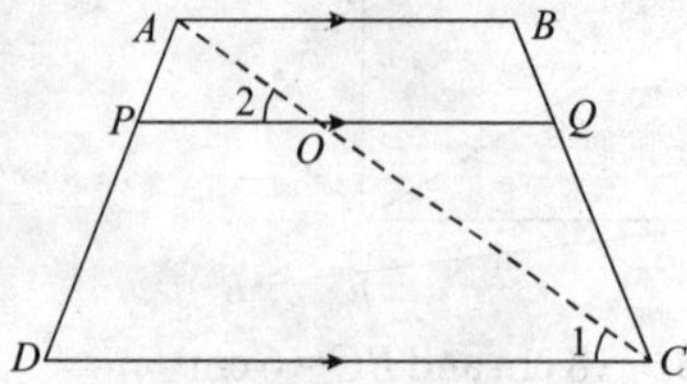

In ΔAPO & ΔADC given $PO \parallel DC$

So by basic proportionality theorem

We have $\frac{AP}{AD} = \frac{PO}{DC}$

$$\frac{1}{3} = \frac{OP}{12}$$

(given $AP : PD = 1 : 2$ and $CD = 12$)

So $OP = 4$

Similarly from ΔCQO & ΔCBA apply basic proportionality theorem, we have

$$\frac{CQ}{CB} = \frac{OQ}{AB}$$

$$\frac{2}{3} = \frac{OQ}{9}$$

Given $CQ : BQ = 2 : 1$ & $AB = 9$

So $OQ = 6$

Hence $PQ = PO + OQ = 4 + 6 = 10$

Hence Ans is (C)

Sol. 7 (D)

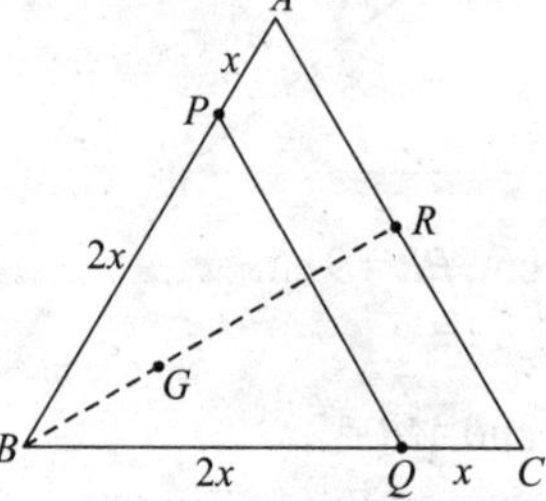

Let $AB = BC = AC = 3x$

$\Rightarrow$ $BP = BQ = PQ = 2x$

($\because AP : BP = CQ : BQ = 1 : 2$)

As ΔBPQ and ΔBAC are equilateral triangle, the centroid of ΔBPQ lies on BR (where BR is median drawn on to AC)

We know that centroid divides the median in the ratio 2 : 1

$\Rightarrow$ $BG = \frac{2}{3}\frac{[\sqrt{3}(2x)]}{2} = \frac{2\sqrt{3}x}{3}$

But $BR = \frac{\sqrt{3}(3x)}{2} = \frac{3\sqrt{3}x}{2}$

Now $GR = BR - BG$

$$= \frac{3\sqrt{3}x}{2} - \frac{2\sqrt{3}x}{3} = \frac{5\sqrt{3}x}{6}$$

Now $BG = GR = \frac{2\sqrt{3}x}{3} : \frac{5\sqrt{3}x}{6} = 4 : 5$

Hence Ans is (D)

Sol. 8 (C)

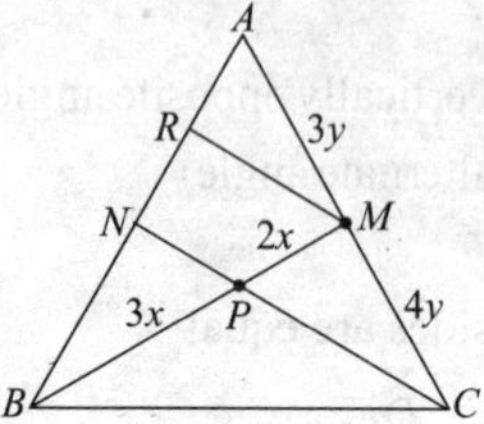

Given $AM : MC = 3 : 4$

$BP : PM = 3 : 2$

and $BN = 12$ cm

Draw MR parallel to CN which meets AB at the point R

Consider ΔBMR

$PN \parallel MR$ (Construction)

By basic proportionality theorem

$$\frac{BN}{NR} = \frac{BP}{PM}$$

$\Rightarrow$ $\frac{12}{NR} = \frac{3}{2}$

Consider ΔANC, $RM \parallel NC$ (By construction)

By BPT,

$$\frac{AR}{RN} = \frac{AM}{MC}$$

$\Rightarrow$ $\frac{AR}{8} = \frac{3}{4}$

$\Rightarrow$ $AR = 6$ cm

$\Rightarrow$ $AN = AR + RN$

$= 6 + 8 = 14$ cm

Hence Ans is (C)

Sol. 9 (C)

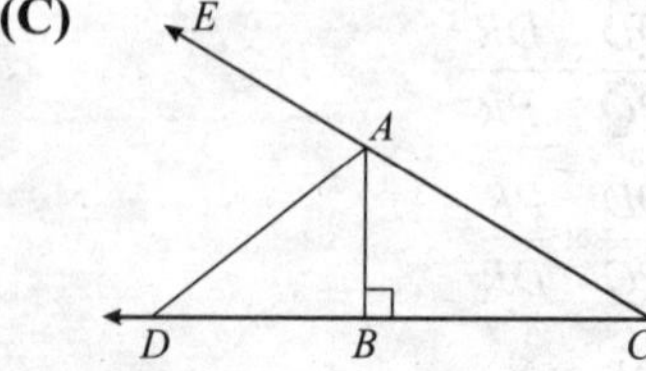

Let BD be x cm

Given $AB = 3$ cm,

$AC = 5$ cm and $\angle ABC = 90°$

$\Rightarrow$ $BC = 4$ cm

And also given, AD is the bisector of $\angle BAE$

$\Rightarrow$ By vertical angle bisector theorem.

$$\frac{AB}{AC} = \frac{BD}{CD}$$

$$\frac{3}{5} = \frac{x}{4+x}$$

$\Rightarrow$ $12 + 3x = 5x$

$\Rightarrow$ $x = 6\text{ cm}$

$\Rightarrow$ $CD = 4 + 6 = 10\text{ cm}$

Hence Ans is (C)

Sol. 10 (D) Two sides of a triangle 5 cm and 12 cm

Let $a = 5$ cm and $b = 12$ cm

Let the third side be x cm

$\Rightarrow$ $12 - 5 < x < 12 + 5$

$\Rightarrow$ $7 < x < 17$

$\Rightarrow$ Possible integer values for x are 8, 9, 10, 11, 12, 13, 14, 15 and 16

Case-(i)

If b is the longest side then

$$b^2 > a^2 + x^2$$

$\Rightarrow$ $12^2 > 5^2 + x^2$

$\Rightarrow$ $144 - 25 > x^2$

$\Rightarrow$ $x^2 < 119$

$\Rightarrow$ x can be 8, 9 or 10

Case-(ii)

If x is the longest side, then $x^2 > a^2 + b^2$

$\Rightarrow$ $x^2 > 5^2 + 12^2$

$\Rightarrow$ $x^2 > 169$

$\Rightarrow$ x can be 14, 15 or 16

$\Rightarrow$ Number of possible triangles = 6

(Since the measurement of third side is an integer in cm)

Hence Ans is (D)

Sol. 11 (A)

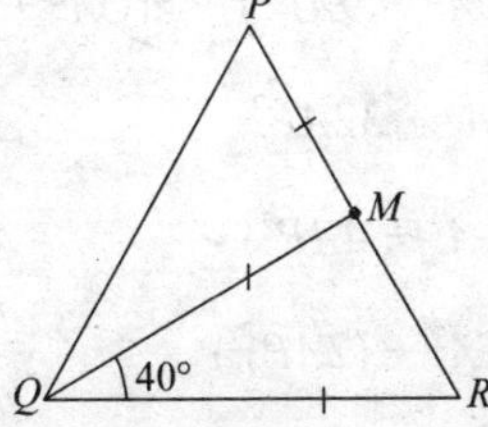

Given $\quad QR = QM = PM$

and $\quad \angle MQR = 40°$

In ΔQMR, $\quad QM = QR$

$\Rightarrow$ $\angle QRM = \angle QMR$

Now $\quad \angle QRM = \angle QMR$

$$= \frac{1}{2}(180° - 40°) = 70°$$

In ΔMPQ, $\quad PM = MQ$

$$\angle PQM = \angle MPQ - (1)$$

But $\quad \angle PQM + \angle MPQ = \angle QMR$

$$= 70° - (2)$$

From (1) and (2)

$$\angle MPQ = \frac{1}{2}(70°) = 35°$$

Hence Ans is (A)

Sol. 12 (C) Using the basic proportionality theorem in ΔBEA, we have

$$\frac{BF}{FE} = \frac{BD}{DA} \quad \dots (1)$$

Using the BPT in ΔBCA, we have

$$\frac{BD}{DA} = \frac{BE}{EC} \quad \dots (2)$$

From (1) and (2),

$$\frac{BF}{FE} = \frac{BE}{EC}$$

Hence Ans is (C)

Sol. 13 (D) Using the basic proportionality theorem in ΔCDB gives

$$\frac{CF}{FD} = \frac{CE}{EB} \quad \dots (1)$$

Using the basic proportionality theorem in ΔCAB gives

$$\frac{CD}{DA} = \frac{CE}{EB} \quad \dots (2)$$

from (1) & (2), we have

$$\frac{CF}{FD} = \frac{CD}{DA}$$

$\Rightarrow$ $$\frac{CF}{CF + FD} = \frac{CD}{CD + DA}$$

$\Rightarrow$ $$\frac{CF}{CD} = \frac{CD}{AC}$$

$\Rightarrow$ $CD^2 = CD \times AC$

Hence Ans is (D)

Sol. 14 (A) Using the angle bisector theorem in ΔADB, we have

$$\frac{AD}{DB} = \frac{AE}{EB} \quad \dots (1)$$

Similarly, in ΔADC, we have

$$\frac{AD}{DC} = \frac{AF}{FC} \quad \dots(2)$$

Using (1) and (2) and the fact that $DB = DC$, we have

$$\frac{AE}{EB} = \frac{AF}{FC}$$

Thus, $EF \parallel BC$, and this is true regardless of what kind of triangle ΔABC is

Hence Ans is (A)

Sol. 15 (D) We note that $\Delta BDE \sim \Delta BAC$, and thus

$$\frac{\text{area}(\Delta BDE)}{\text{area}(\Delta BAC)} = \frac{BD^2}{BA^2} = \frac{BD^2}{(BD+DA)^2}$$

$$\frac{1}{\left(1+\frac{DA}{BD}\right)^2} = \frac{1}{\left(1+\frac{3}{2}\right)^2} = \frac{4}{25}$$

Thus,

$$\frac{\text{area}(\text{trap } ADEC)}{\text{area}(\Delta ABC)} = 1 - \frac{\text{area}(\Delta BDE)}{\text{area}(\Delta BAC)}$$

$$= 1 - \frac{4}{25} = \frac{21}{25}$$

Hence Ans is (D)

Sol. 16 (B) We have (using the Pythagoras Theorem)

$$AC^2 = AB^2 + BC^2$$

$$= AB^2 + 4BD^2$$

$$= AB^2 + 4(AD^2 - AB^2)$$

$$= AB^2 + 4AD^2 - 4AB^2$$

$$= 4AD^2 - 3AB^2$$

Hence Ans is (B)

Sol. 17 (B)

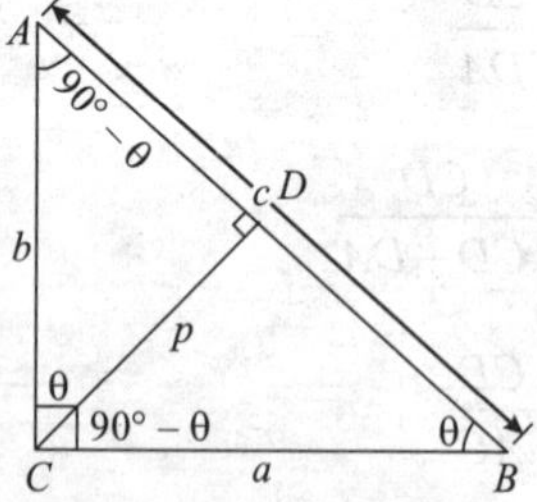

$\Delta ADC \sim \Delta ACB$

So $\quad \frac{AD}{b} = \frac{b}{c} = \frac{p}{a} \quad \dots(1)$

Similarly, $\quad \Delta BDC \sim \Delta BCA$

$$\frac{BD}{a} = \frac{a}{c} = \frac{p}{b} \quad \dots(2)$$

Thus, from (1), we have

$$cp = ab$$

$$\Rightarrow \quad c^2p^2 = a^2b^2$$

$$\Rightarrow \quad (a^2 + b^2)p^2 = a^2b^2$$

$$\Rightarrow \quad \frac{1}{a^2} + \frac{1}{b^2} = \frac{1}{p^2}$$

Also, from (1) & (2),

$$p^2 = AD \times CD$$

Hence Ans is (B)

Sol. 18 (A) It is easy to prove that $\Delta ABC \sim \Delta DEF$, and so

$$\frac{\text{area }(\Delta ABC)}{\text{area }(\Delta DEF)} = \left(\frac{AB}{DE}\right)^2 = 4$$

Hence Ans is (A)

Sol. 19 (A) Consider the following figure

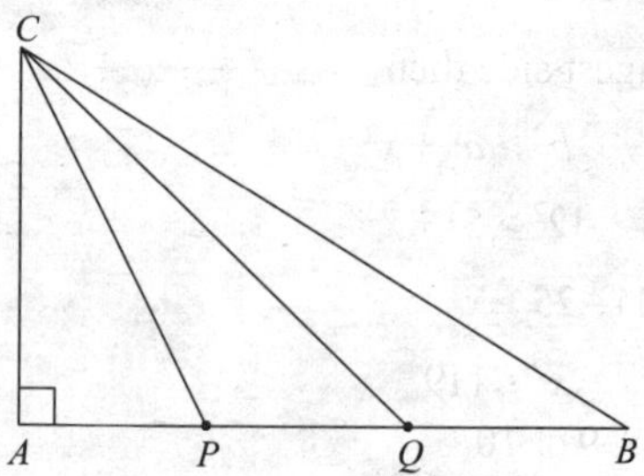

We have

$$CB^2 = CA^2 + BA^2$$

$$= CA^2 + 3(AP)^2$$

$$= CA^2 + 9AP^2$$

$$CP^2 = CA^2 + AP^2$$

Thus, $3CB^2 + 5CP^2$

$$= 3(CA^2 + 9AP^2) + 5(CA^2 + AP^2)$$

$$= 8CA^2 + 32AP^2$$

$$= 8(CA^2 + 4AP^2)$$

$$= 8(CA^2 + (2AP)^2)$$

$$= 8(CA^2 + AQ^2)$$

$$= 8CQ^2$$

This means that $\lambda = 8$

Hence Ans is (A)

Sol. 20 (A) Consider the following figure, where we have also drawn the angle bisector AD of $\angle A$, which will pass through I

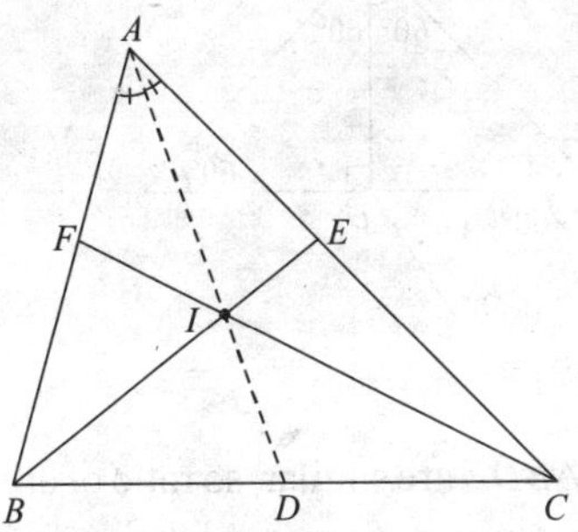

Applying the angle bisector theorem to $\angle AFC$, we have

$$\frac{AF}{AC} = \frac{FI}{CI}$$

$$\Rightarrow \quad \frac{AF}{FI} = \frac{AC}{CI}$$

Hence Ans is (A)

Sol. 21 (B) Consider the following figure, which shows AC and BD intersecting at E at right angles

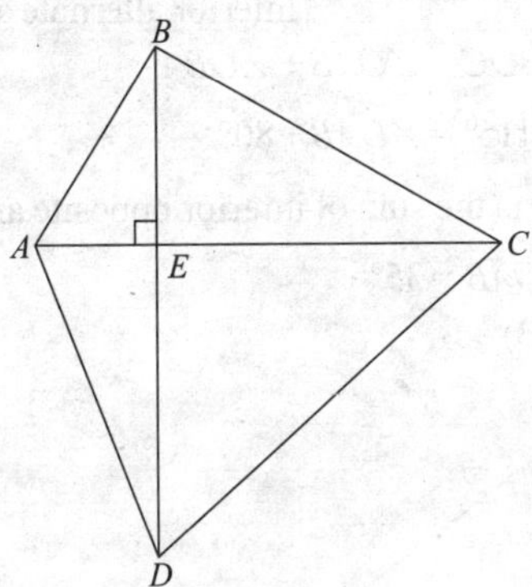

Using the Pythagoras Theorem, we have

$$AB^2 = AE^2 + BE^2$$

$$CD^2 = CE^2 + DE^2$$

$$\Rightarrow \quad AB^2 + CD^2 = AE^2 + BE^2 + CE^2 + DE^2$$

$$= (BE^2 + CE^2) + (AE^2 + DE^2)$$

$$= BC^2 + AD^2$$

Hence Ans is (B)

Sol. 22 (A) Consider the following figure

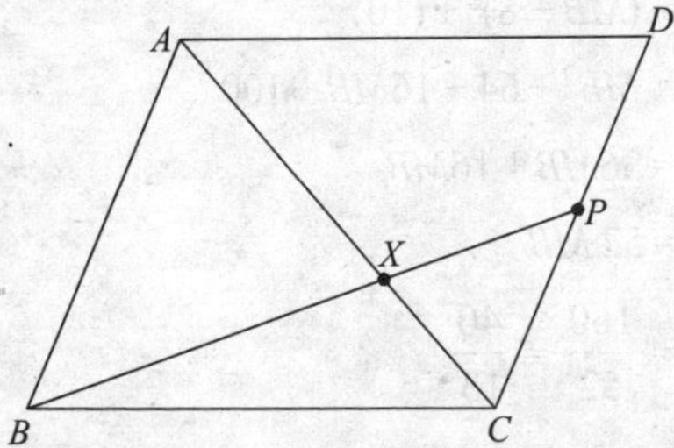

Clearly, $\Delta AXB \sim \Delta CXP$ by the AA criterion.

Thus,

$$\frac{AX}{XC} = \frac{AB}{PC} = \frac{2}{1}$$

$$\Rightarrow \quad \frac{AX}{AX + XC} = \frac{2}{2+1}$$

$$\Rightarrow \quad \frac{AX}{AC} = \frac{2}{3}$$

Hence Ans is (A)

Sol. 23 (C)

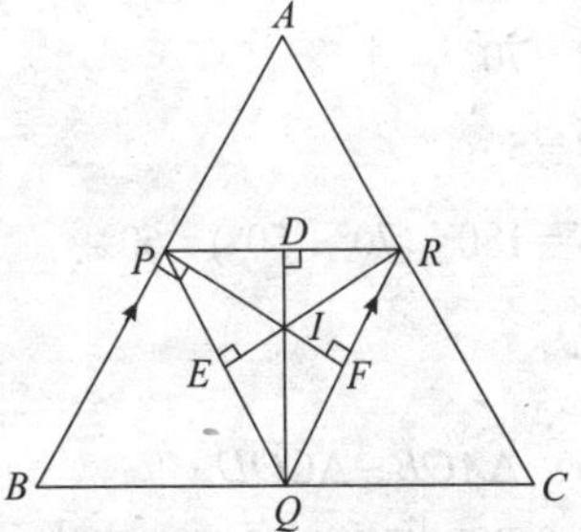

From the figure it is clear that I is the orthocenter of ΔPQR

$\because$ P, Q, R are respectively the mid-points of AB, BC & CA

hence $PQ \parallel AC$ (by mid-point theorm)

So I become the circumcenter for ΔABC

Hence Ans is (C)

Sol. 24 (B)

Apply pythagoras theorem in ΔPBQ, we have

$$PQ^2 = PB^2 + BQ^2 \quad \ldots(1)$$

again apply pythagoras theorem in ΔABC,

$$AC^2 = AB^2 + BC^2 \quad \ldots(2)$$

Adding (1) & (2),

$$PQ^2 + AC^2 = PB^2 + BQ^2 + AB^2 + BC^2$$

$$PQ^2 + AC^2 = (PB^2 + BC^2) + (BQ^2 + AB^2)$$

$$PQ^2 + AC^2 = PC^2 + AQ^2$$

Hence Ans is (B)

Sol. 25 (C) Given ΔFAB is an equilateral Δ

$$\Rightarrow \quad \angle EAB = \angle OAB = 60°$$

$$\angle ABD = 45° \quad \text{[as } ABCD \text{ is a square]}$$

In ΔAOB

$$\Rightarrow \quad \angle AOB = 180° - (60° + 45°) = 75°$$

Hence Ans is (C)

Solutions of PRACTICE EXERCISE-5.3

Sol. 1 (C)

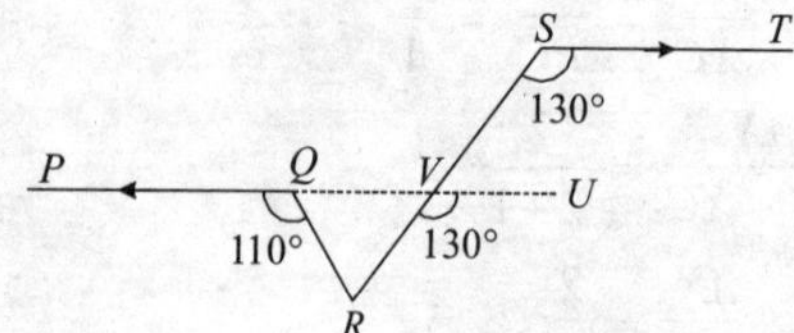

From the figure

$\angle RVU = \angle VST$ (corresponding angle)

$\angle VQR = 70°$

$\angle QVR = 50°$

So, $\angle QRS = 180 - (70° + 50°) = 60°$

Hence Ans is (C)

Sol. 2 (C) We know $\Delta AOB \sim \Delta COD$
so ratio of their corresponding sides are equal

$$\frac{AO}{OC} = \frac{OB}{OD} = \frac{AB}{CD}$$

$$\frac{2}{5} = \frac{x-2}{2x+5}$$

$$2(2x+5) = 5(x-2)$$

$$4x + 10 = 5x - 10$$

$$x = 20$$

Hence Ans is (C)

Sol. 3 (D) In triangle TQR,

$\angle TRQ = 50°$

$\Rightarrow$ In ΔPSR, $\angle PSQ = \angle y = \angle SPR + \angle PRS$

[Exterior angle is sum of interior opposite angle]

$= 30° + 50° = 80°$

Hence Ans is (D)

Sol. 4 (C)

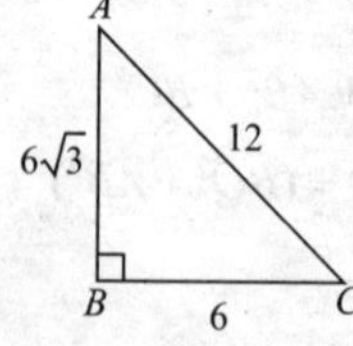

Here we have,

$$AB^2 + BC^2 = (6\sqrt{3})^2 + (6)^2$$

$$= 144 = 12^2 = AC^2$$

[by pythagoras theorem]

$\Rightarrow$ $\angle B = 90°$

Hence Ans is (C)

Sol. 5 (C)

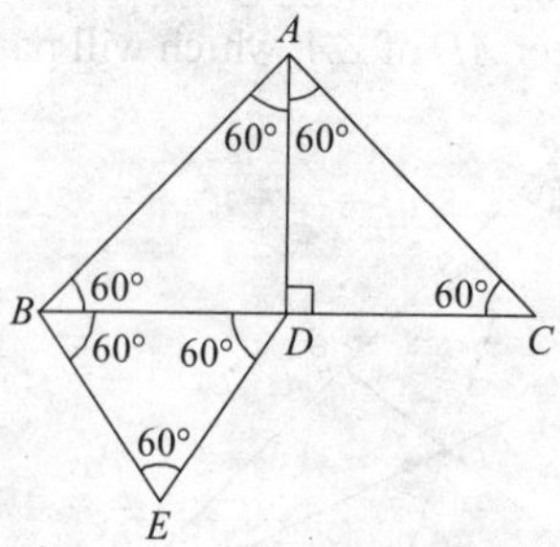

Here ΔABC & ΔBDE are similar, so ratio of area of two similar triangle is equal to ratio of square of their corresponding sides.

$$\frac{ar(\Delta ABC)}{ar(\Delta BDE)} = \left(\frac{BC}{BD}\right)^2 = \left(\frac{2BD}{BD}\right)^2$$

$$= \left(\frac{2}{1}\right)^2 = \frac{4}{1}$$

Hence Ans is (C)

Sol. 6 (B) From the figure

$\angle OBA = 80°$

[Interior alternate angle are equal]

$\Rightarrow$ $\angle BOC = \angle OAB + \angle OBA$

$\Rightarrow$ $115° = \angle OAB + 80°$

[Exterior angle is the sum of interior opposite angles]

$\Rightarrow$ $\angle OAB = 35°$

Hence Ans is (B)

Sol. 7 (B)

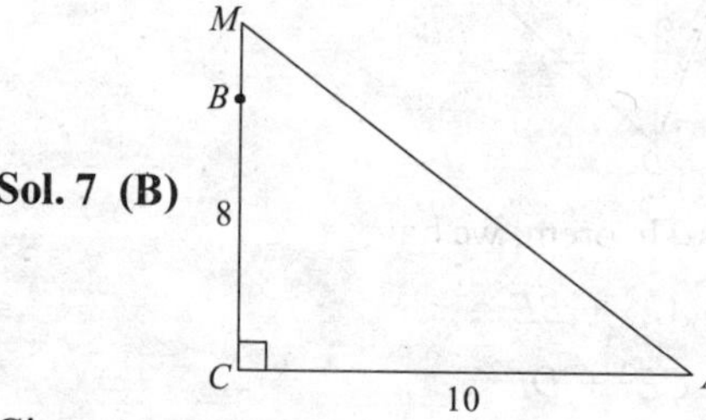

Given

$$MB + MA = BC + AC$$

$$= 8 + 10$$

$$MB + MA = 18 \quad \ldots(1)$$

Now apply pythagoras theorem is ΔMCA

$$MA^2 = MC^2 + AC^2$$

$$(18 - MB)^2 = (MB + 8)^2 + (10)^2$$

$$324 + MB^2 - 36MB = MB^2 + 64 + 16MB + 100$$

$$324 - 100 - 64 = 36MB + 16MB$$

$$160 = 52\,MB$$

$$MB = \frac{160}{52} = \frac{40}{13}$$

Hence Ans is (B)

Sol. 8 (C)

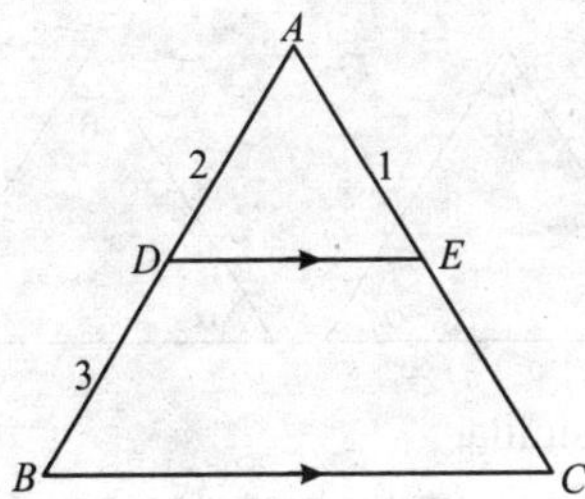

Here in the ΔABC

$DE \parallel BC$

$\Rightarrow \quad \Delta ADE \sim \Delta ABC$

$$\Rightarrow \quad \frac{AD}{AB} = \frac{DE}{BC}$$

$$\frac{2}{5} = \frac{4}{BC}$$

$$BC = 10$$

Hence Ans is (C)

Sol. 9 (C)

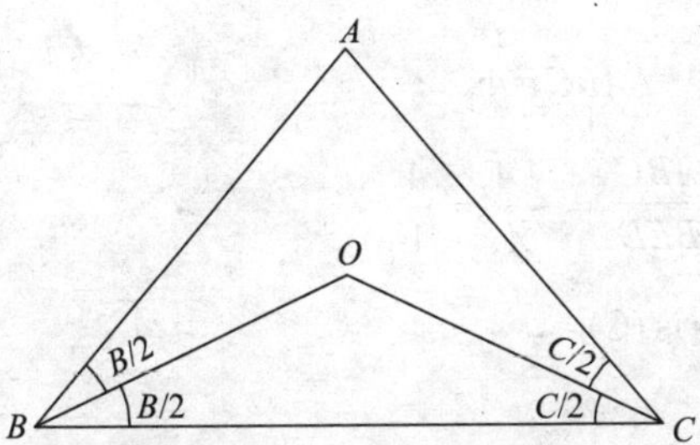

Given OB & OC are the bisector of $\angle B$ & $\angle C$ respectively
In ΔABC we have

$$\angle A + \angle B + \angle C = 180°$$

$$\frac{\angle A}{2} + \frac{\angle B}{2} + \frac{\angle C}{2} = 90°$$

$$\frac{\angle B}{2} + \frac{\angle C}{2} = 90 - \frac{\angle A}{2} \quad \ldots(1)$$

Now in ΔBOC

$$\frac{\angle B}{2} + \frac{\angle C}{2} + \angle O = 180°$$

$$\angle O = 180° - \left(\frac{\angle B}{2} + \frac{\angle C}{2}\right)$$

$$= 180 - \left(90 - \frac{\angle A}{2}\right) \quad \text{Using (1)}$$

$$\angle O = 90 + \frac{\angle A}{2}$$

Hence Ans is (C)

Sol. 10 (D) We know

Sum of all angle of Δ is equal to 180°

Here two triangle are there

So sum of all angle of hexagon means

$$\angle 1 + \angle 3 + \angle 5 + \angle 2 + \angle 4 + \angle 6$$

$$= 180 + 180$$

$$= 360$$

Hence Ans is (D)

Sol. 11 (A)

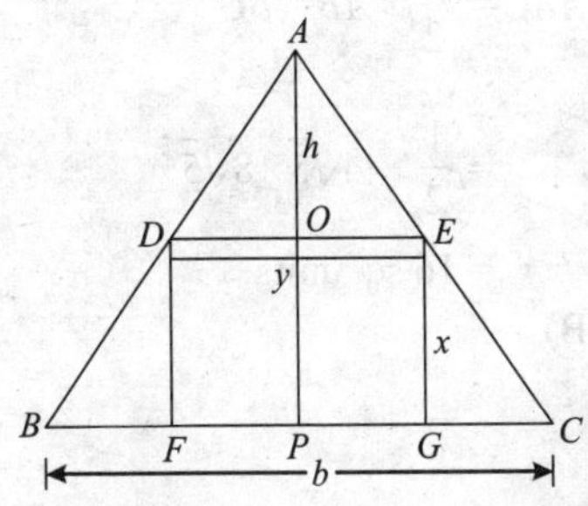

Let $\quad DE = y$

$$\Delta ADE \sim \Delta ABC$$

$$\Rightarrow \quad \frac{DE}{BC} = \frac{AO}{AP}$$

$$\Rightarrow \quad \frac{y}{b} = \frac{h-x}{h}$$

$$\Rightarrow \quad y = \frac{b}{h}(h-x)$$

Area of rectangle

$$= x \times y$$

$$= \frac{x \times b(h-x)}{h}$$

Hence Ans is (A)

Sol. 12 (B)

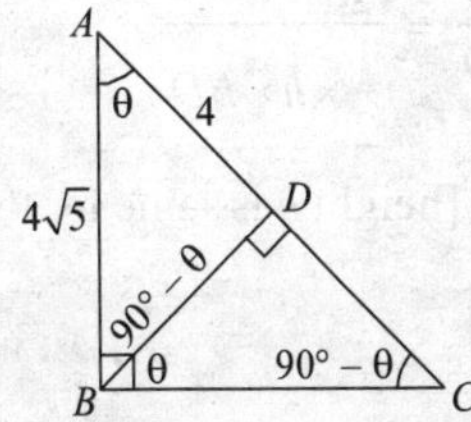

From the figure

$$\Delta ABC \sim \Delta ADB$$

$$\Rightarrow \quad \frac{AB}{AD} = \frac{BC}{BD} \quad \ldots(1)$$

In ΔABD

$$BD^2 = AB^2 - AD^2$$

$$= (4\sqrt{5})^2 - (4)^2$$
$$= 80 - 16$$
$$BD^2 = 64$$
$$\Rightarrow \quad BD = 8$$

From (1)

$$\frac{4\sqrt{5}}{4} = \frac{BC}{BD}$$
$$BC = 8\sqrt{5}$$

Area of $\Delta ABC = \frac{1}{2} \times AB \times BC$

$$= \frac{1}{2} \times 4\sqrt{5} \times 8\sqrt{5}$$
$$= 16 \text{ sq. units}$$

Hence Ans is (B)

Sol. 13 (A)

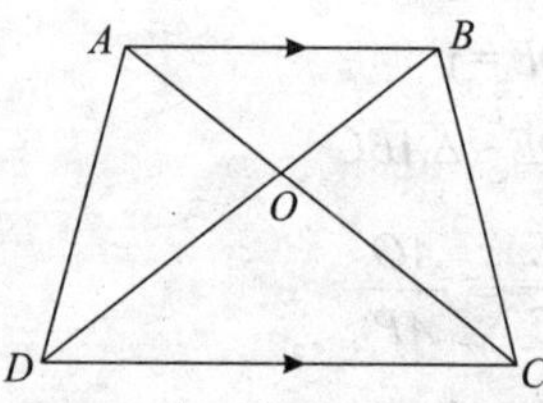

Given $AB \parallel CD$

From the figure

$$\Delta AOB \sim \Delta COD$$
$$\Rightarrow \quad \frac{AO}{OC} = \frac{OB}{OD} = \frac{AB}{CD}$$
$$\Rightarrow \quad \frac{1}{3} = \frac{OB}{OD} \qquad \left[\text{given } \frac{AO}{OC} = \frac{1}{3}\right]$$
$$\Rightarrow \quad OB = \frac{OD}{3}$$

To find

$$\frac{\text{Area of } \Delta AOB}{\text{Area of } \Delta ABD} = \frac{\frac{1}{2} \times h \times OB}{\frac{1}{2} \times h \times BD}$$

[height h is same for the both the triangle]

$$\Rightarrow \quad \frac{\frac{1}{2} \times h \times \frac{OD}{3}}{\frac{1}{2} \times h(OD + OB)}$$
$$\Rightarrow \quad \frac{\frac{1}{2} \times h \times \frac{OD}{3}}{\frac{1}{2} \times h \times \frac{4OD}{3}} = \frac{1}{4}$$

Hence Ans is (A)

Sol. 14 (C)

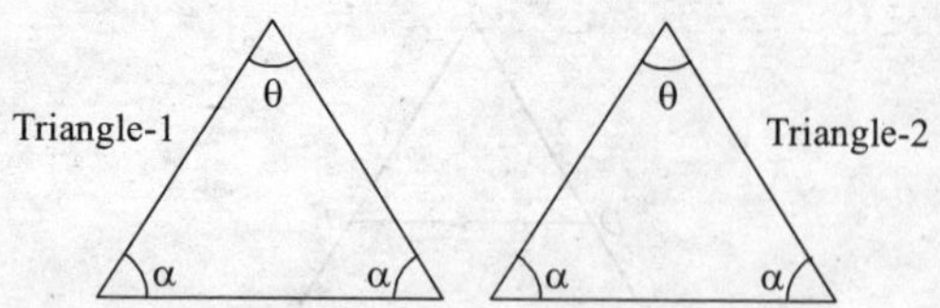

Both triangle are similar

So ratio of area of two similar triangle is equal to ratio of square of their corresponding height

$$\Rightarrow \quad \frac{h_1^2}{h_2^2} = \frac{9}{16} = \frac{h_1}{h_2} = \frac{3}{4}$$

Hence Ans is (C)

Sol. 15 (C) In ΔABD, BE is median

Median divides the triangle in to two parts having same area so

Let Area $\quad \Delta ABE = \Delta BED = A$

So area $\quad \Delta ABD = 2A$

$\Rightarrow$ Area $\quad \Delta ADC = 2A$

As AD is median

$\Rightarrow$ Area $\quad \Delta ABC = 4A$

Now $\quad \frac{ar\Delta ABC}{ar\Delta BED} = \frac{4A}{A} = \frac{4}{1}$

Hence Ans is (C)

Sol. 16 (A)

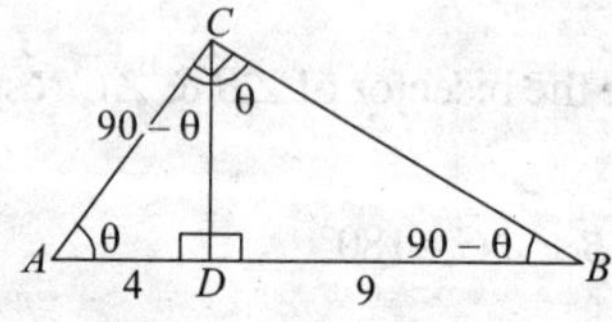

$$\Delta ADC \sim \Delta ACB \qquad \text{(by } AA \text{ similarity)}$$
$$\Rightarrow \quad \frac{AC}{13} = \frac{4}{AC}$$
$$\Rightarrow \quad AC^2 = 13 \times 4 \qquad \ldots(1)$$

Similarly $\quad \Delta BDC \sim \Delta BCA$

We have $\quad \frac{BC}{13} = \frac{9}{BC}$

$$\Rightarrow \quad BC^2 = 13 \times 9 \qquad \ldots(2)$$

Equation-(2) ÷ equation-(1)

$$\frac{BC}{AC} = \frac{3}{2}$$

Hence Ans is (A)

Sol. 17 (B)

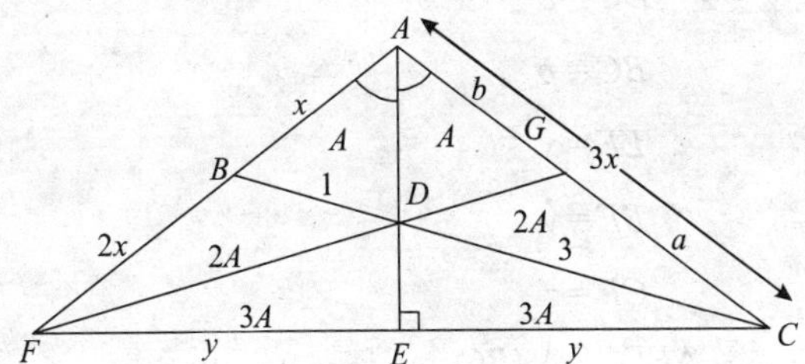

In ΔAFC

$$\frac{AB}{BF}\times\frac{FE}{EC}\times\frac{CG}{GA}=1$$

$$\frac{x}{2x}\times\frac{y}{y}\times\frac{a}{b}=1$$

$$\frac{a}{b}=\frac{2}{1}$$

Ceva divides the area of the triangle in the same ratio in which it divides opposite side

$$\frac{ar(\Delta ABD)}{ar(\Delta CDE)}=\frac{1}{3}$$

Hence Ans is (B)

Sol. 18 (D)

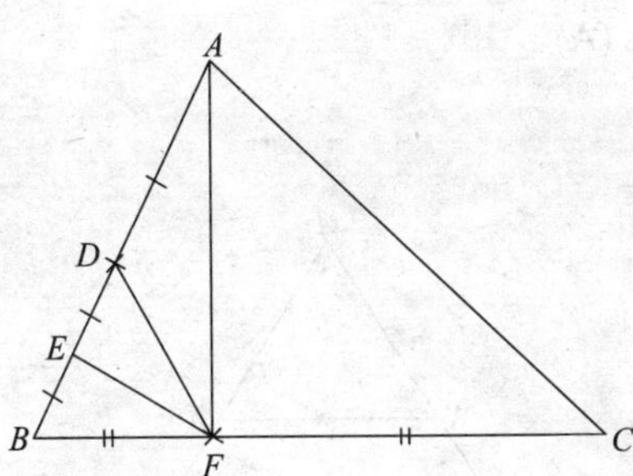

Given

$ar(\Delta ABC)=96$

$ar(\Delta ABF)=48$

$ar(\Delta ADF)=24,$

$ar(\Delta BDF)=24,$

$ar(\Delta EDF)=12,$

$ar(\Delta AEF)=(\Delta ADF)+ar(\Delta EDF)$

$=24+12=36$

Hence Ans is (D)

Sol. 19 (B)

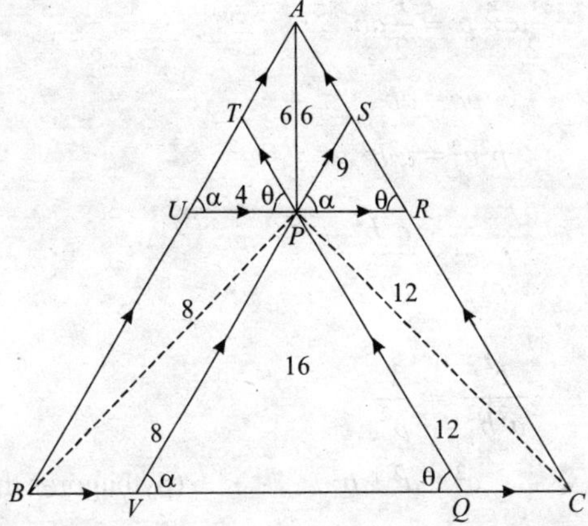

We know

Ratio of area of two similar triangle = ratio of square of their corresponding sides

$$\Delta TUP \sim \Delta PVQ$$

$$\frac{UP^2}{VQ^2}=\frac{ar\Delta TUP}{ar\Delta PVQ}=\frac{4}{16}$$

$$\Rightarrow \quad \frac{UP}{VQ}=\frac{2}{4}=\frac{1}{2}$$

$$\Rightarrow \quad \frac{BV}{VQ}=\frac{1}{2} \qquad (\text{As } UP=BV)$$

Now $\quad \Delta SPR \sim \Delta PVQ$

$$\frac{PR^2}{VQ^2}=\frac{ar\Delta SPR}{ar\Delta PVQ}=\frac{9}{16}$$

$$\Rightarrow \quad \frac{PR}{VQ}=\frac{3}{4}$$

$$\Rightarrow \quad \frac{QC}{VQ}=\frac{3}{4} \qquad (\text{As } PR=QC)$$

Similarly $\quad \dfrac{AT}{TU}=\dfrac{3}{2}$

Hence Ans is (B)

Sol. 20 (D)

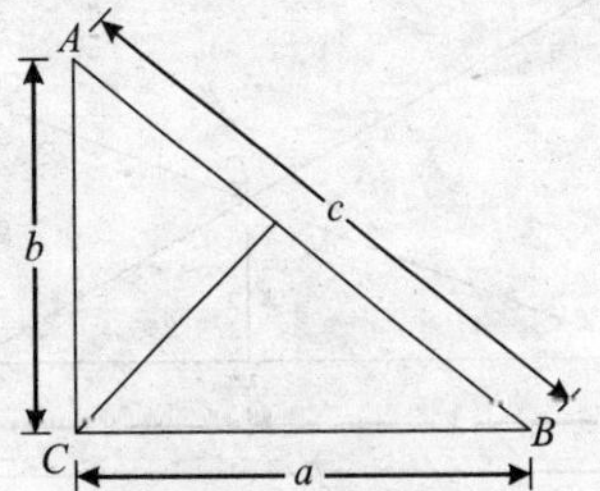

Here we have area of ΔABC

$$\frac{1}{2}c \times p = \frac{1}{2}ab$$

$$pc = ab$$

$$p^2c^2 = a^2b^2$$

$$c^2 = \frac{a^2b^2}{p^2}$$

$$\frac{c^2}{a^2b^2} = \frac{1}{p^2}$$

But $\quad c^2 = a^2 + b^2 \quad$ (pythagoras theorem)

$$\frac{a^2+b^2}{a^2b^2} = \frac{1}{p^2}$$

$$\Rightarrow \quad \frac{1}{b^2} + \frac{1}{a^2} = \frac{1}{p^2}$$

Hence Ans is (D)

Sol. 21 (C)

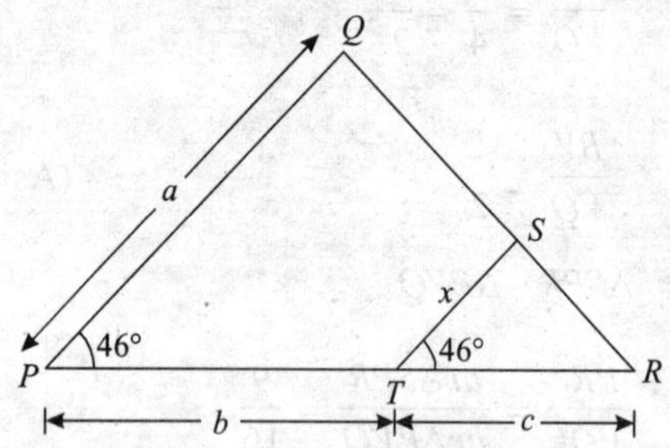

$\Delta STR \sim \Delta QPR \quad$ (by *AA* similarly)

$$\Rightarrow \quad \frac{RT}{RP} = \frac{ST}{PQ}$$

$$\frac{c}{b+c} = \frac{x}{a}$$

$$\Rightarrow \quad x = \frac{ac}{b+c}$$

Hence Ans is (C)

Sol. 22 (A)

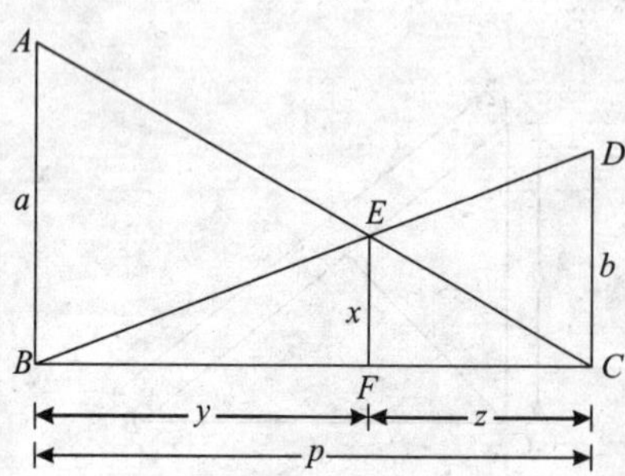

Here given $\quad AB = a;$

$DC = b$

& $\quad BC = p$

Let $\quad EF = x;$

$BF = y$

& $\quad CF = z$

Now $\quad \Delta EFC \sim \Delta ABC$

$$\frac{x}{a} = \frac{z}{y+z} \quad \ldots(1)$$

Similarly $\quad \Delta EFB \sim \Delta DCB$

$$\frac{x}{b} = \frac{y}{y+z} \quad \ldots(2)$$

Adding equation-(1) & (2)

$$\frac{x}{a} + \frac{y}{b} = 1$$

$$\Rightarrow \quad \frac{1}{x} = \frac{1}{a} + \frac{1}{b}$$

$$\Rightarrow \quad \frac{a+b}{ab}$$

$$\Rightarrow \quad x = \frac{ab}{a+b}$$

Hence Ans is (A)

Sol. 23 (D)

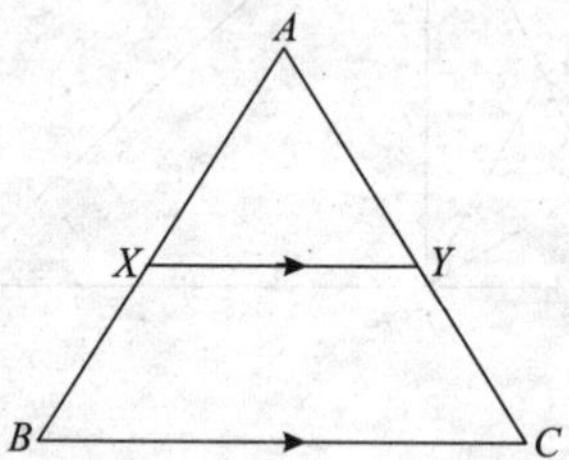

Given

$$ar\Delta AXY = arBXYC$$

Let $\quad ar\Delta AXY = A$

$$\Rightarrow \quad ar\Delta ABC = 2A$$

$$\frac{ar\Delta AXY}{ar\Delta ABC} = \frac{A}{2A} = \frac{AX^2}{AB^2}$$

$$\frac{AX^2}{AB^2} = \frac{1}{2}$$

$$\Rightarrow \quad \frac{AX}{AB} = \frac{1}{\sqrt{2}}$$

$$\frac{AB}{AX} = \frac{\sqrt{2}}{1}$$

$$\frac{AB - AX}{AX} = \frac{\sqrt{2}-1}{1}$$

$$\frac{BX}{AX} = \frac{\sqrt{2}-1}{1}$$

$$\Rightarrow \quad \frac{AX}{BX} = \frac{1}{\sqrt{2}-1} \times \frac{\sqrt{2}+1}{\sqrt{2}+1}$$

$$\frac{AX}{BX} = \frac{\sqrt{2}+1}{1}$$

Hence Ans is (D)

Sol. 24 (C)

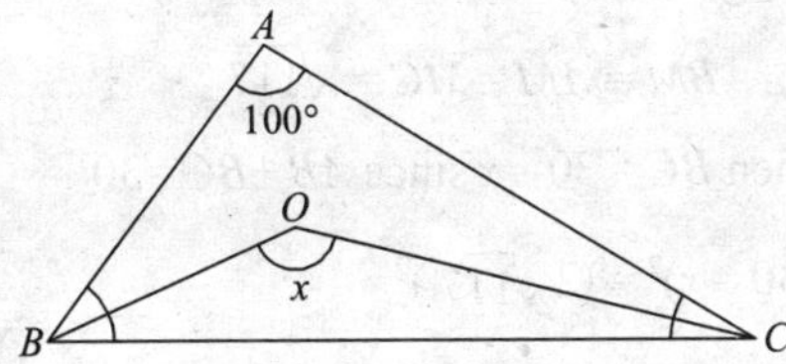

We know if OB & OC are angle bisector then

$$\angle O = 90 + \frac{1}{2}\angle A$$

$$= 90 + \frac{1}{2} \times 100 = 90 + 50 = 140$$

Hence Ans is (C)

Sol. 25 (A)

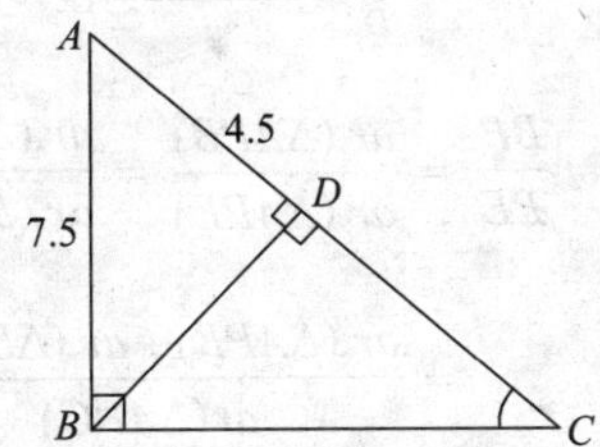

$$BD^2 = 7.5^2 - 4.5^2$$

$$= (7.5 - 4.5)(7.5 + 4.5)$$

$$BD^2 = 3 \times 12$$

Now $\Delta BDC \sim \Delta ABC$

$$\Rightarrow \quad \frac{A(\Delta BDC)}{A(\Delta ABC)} = \frac{BD^2}{AB^2} = \frac{3 \times 12 \times 100}{7.5 \times 7.5}$$

$$= \frac{16}{25}$$

Hence Ans is (A)

Sol. 26 (D)

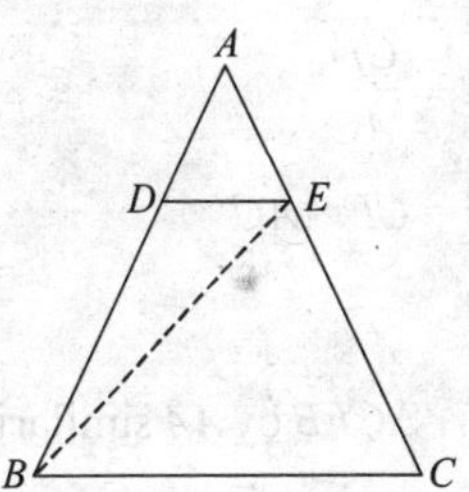

Given

$DE \parallel BC$

$\Rightarrow \quad \Delta ADE \sim \Delta ABC$

$$\frac{A(\Delta ADE)}{A(\Delta ABC)} = \frac{AD^2}{AB^2}$$

$$\frac{48}{A(\Delta ABC)} = \left(\frac{4}{9}\right)^2$$

$$\frac{48}{A(\Delta ABC)} = \frac{16}{81}$$

$$A(\Delta ABC) = 243$$

Now since $DE \parallel BC$

$$\Rightarrow \quad \frac{AD}{DB} = \frac{AE}{EC} = \frac{4}{5}$$

So $\quad ar\Delta BEC = \frac{5}{9} \times A(\Delta ABC)$

$$= \frac{5}{9} \times 243$$

$$= 135$$

Hence Ans is (D)

Sol. 27 (B)

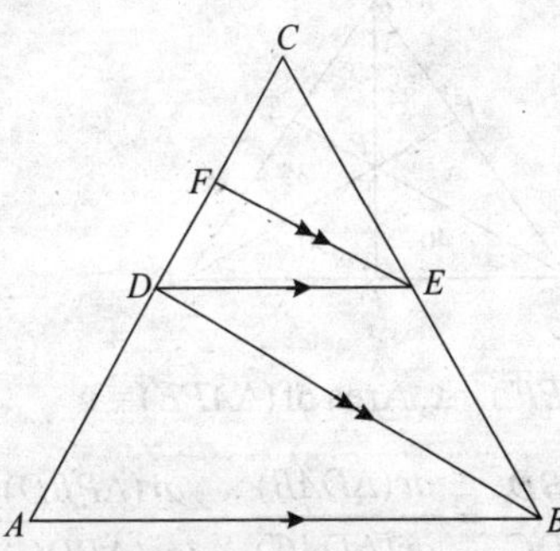

In ΔCDB by BPT the

$$\frac{CF}{CD} = \frac{CE}{BC} \quad \ldots(1)$$

& in ΔCAB apply BPT

$$\frac{CD}{AC} = \frac{CE}{CB} \quad \ldots(2)$$

Equating -(1) & (2)

$$\frac{CF}{CD} = \frac{CD}{AC}$$

$\Rightarrow$ $CD^2 = CF \times AC$

Hence Ans is (B)

Sol. 28 (B) $\Delta DFE \sim \Delta CFB$ by AA similarity

$$\Rightarrow \frac{DE}{BC} = \frac{AD}{AB} = \frac{5}{9}$$

So $$\frac{arDFE}{arCFB} = \left(\frac{5}{9}\right)^2 = \frac{25}{81}$$

Hence Ans is (B)

Sol. 29 (B)

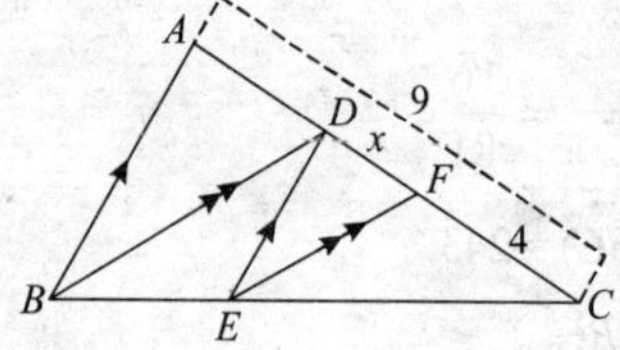

Given $\Delta CFE \sim \Delta CDB$

$$\Rightarrow \frac{EC}{BC} = \frac{4}{4+x} \quad \ldots(1)$$

Given, $\Delta CDE \sim \Delta CAB$

$$\frac{EC}{BC} = \frac{4+x}{9} \quad \ldots(2)$$

From (1) and (2), $4 + x = 6$

Hence Ans is (B)

Sol. 30 (C)

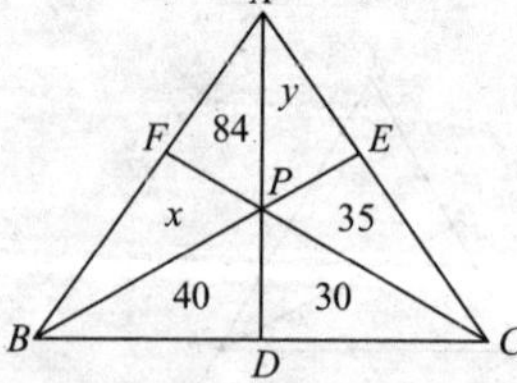

Let area of $(\Delta BPF) = x$, Area of $(\Delta APE) = y$

Then $$\frac{BD}{DC} = \frac{ar(\Delta DAB)}{ar(\Delta DAC)} = \frac{ar(\Delta PBD)}{ar(\Delta PDC)}$$

$$\Rightarrow \frac{84+x}{y+35} = \frac{40}{30}$$

$$\Rightarrow 3x - 4y = -112 \quad \ldots(1)$$

$$\frac{AE}{EC} = \frac{ar(\Delta APB)}{ar(\Delta BPC)} = \frac{ar(\Delta APE)}{ar(\Delta EPC)}$$

$$\Rightarrow \frac{84+x}{70} = \frac{y}{35}$$

$$\Rightarrow 2y - x = 84 \quad \ldots(2)$$

By solving (1) & (2) we get $x = 56$,

$y = 70$

Hence are $(\Delta ABC) = 84 + 56 + 40 + 30 + 35 + 70 = 315$

Hence Ans is (C)

Sol. 31 (A)

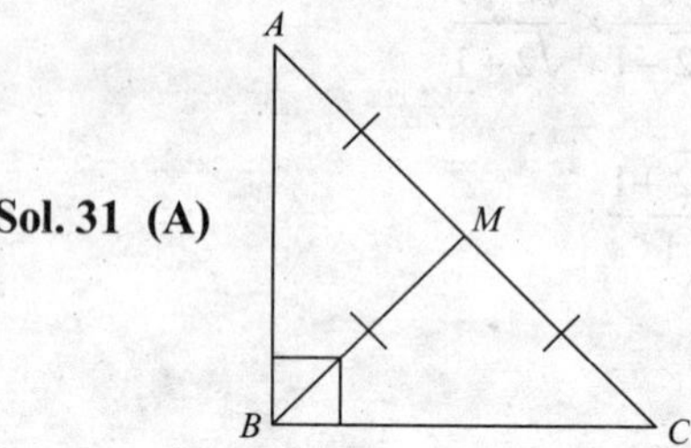

In a right triangle ABC,

$$BM = AM = MC = \sqrt{117}$$

Let $AB = x$ then $BC = 30 - x$ since $AB + BC = 30$

$$x^2 + (30 - x)^2 = (2\sqrt{117})^2$$

By solving $x = 12$ or 18

Hence area of $\Delta ABC = \frac{1}{2} \times 12 \times 18 = 108$ cm^2

Hence Ans is (A)

Sol. 32 (D)

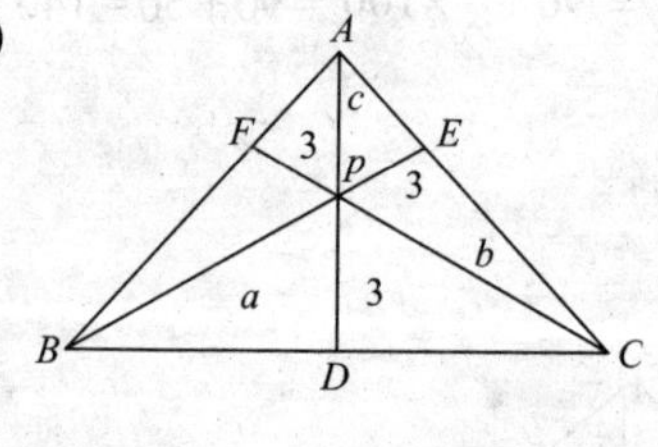

$$\frac{BP}{PE} = \frac{ar.(\Delta APB)}{ar.(\Delta APE)} = \frac{ar.(\Delta BPC)}{ar.(\Delta CPE)}$$

$$= \frac{ar.(\Delta APB) + ar.(\Delta BPC)}{ar(\Delta APC)}$$

$$\Rightarrow \frac{a}{3} = \frac{ar.(\Delta APB) + ar.(\Delta BPC)}{ar(\Delta APC)}$$

$$\Rightarrow \frac{a+3}{3} = \frac{ar.(\Delta ABC)}{ar.(\Delta APC)}$$

$$\Rightarrow \frac{ar.(\Delta APC)}{ar.(\Delta ABC)} = \frac{3}{a+3} \quad \ldots(1)$$

Similarly $$\frac{ar.(\Delta APB)}{ar.(\Delta ABC)} = \frac{3}{b+3} \quad \ldots(2)$$

$$\frac{a.(\Delta BPC)}{ar.(\Delta ABC)} = \frac{3}{c+3} \quad \dots(3)$$

Adding (1), (2) and (3)

$$\frac{a.(\Delta ABC)}{ar.(\Delta ABC)} = \frac{3}{a+3} + \frac{3}{b+3} + \frac{3}{c+3}$$

$$1 = \frac{3}{a+3} + \frac{3}{b+3} + \frac{3}{c+3}$$

$$(a+3)(b+3)(c+3) = 3\Sigma(a+3)(b+3)$$

After simplification

$\Rightarrow \quad abc = 441$

Hence Ans is (D)

Sol. 33 (C)

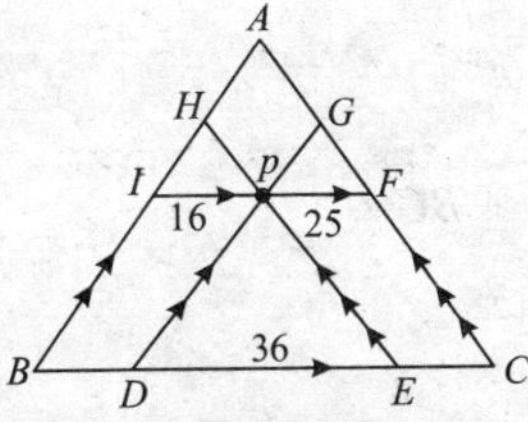

$$\Delta ABC \sim \Delta HIP \sim \Delta PDE \sim \Delta GPF$$

$$\frac{ar(\Delta HIP)}{ar(\Delta PDE)} = \left(\frac{IP}{DE}\right)^2$$

$$\Rightarrow \quad \sqrt{\frac{16}{36}} = \frac{IP}{DE}$$

$$IP = 4x,$$
$$DE = 6x$$

$$\frac{ar(\Delta PDE)}{ar(\Delta GPF)} = \left(\frac{DE}{PF}\right)^2 = \sqrt{\frac{36}{25}} = \frac{DE}{PF}$$

$$DE = 6x, PF = 5x$$

$$IP = BD, PF = EC$$

$$\Rightarrow \quad BC = BD + DE + EC = 15x$$

$$\Delta ABC \sim \Delta HIP$$

$$\Rightarrow \quad \frac{ar(\Delta ABC)}{ar(\Delta HIP)} = \left(\frac{BC}{IP}\right)^2$$

Area of $\Delta ABC = \left(\frac{15x}{4x}\right)^2 \times 16 = 225$

Hence Ans is (C)

Sol. 34 (A)

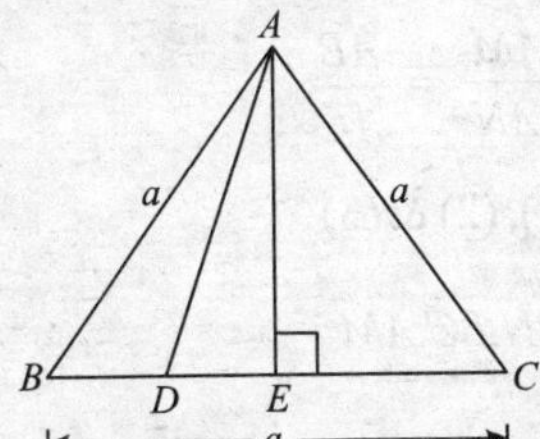

$$BD = \frac{a}{3},$$

$$EC = \frac{a}{2},$$

$$DE = a - \left(\frac{a}{3} + \frac{a}{2}\right) = \frac{a}{6}$$

$$AE = \frac{\sqrt{3}}{2}a$$

$$\frac{3}{4}a^2 + \frac{a^2}{36} = AD^2$$

Hence $\quad 9AD^2 = 7AB^2$

Hence Ans is (A)

Sol. 35 (A)

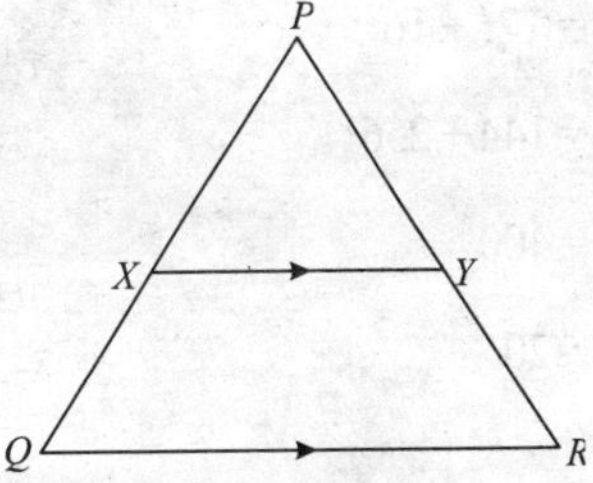

X is mid point of PQ and $XY \parallel QR$

$\Rightarrow \quad PY = YR$

[By converse of mid point theorem]

$$PQ = PR$$

$$\Rightarrow \quad \frac{1}{2}PQ = \frac{1}{2}PR$$

$$\Rightarrow \quad PX = PY$$

Thus ΔPXY is isosceles

Hence Ans is (A)

Sol. 36 (D)

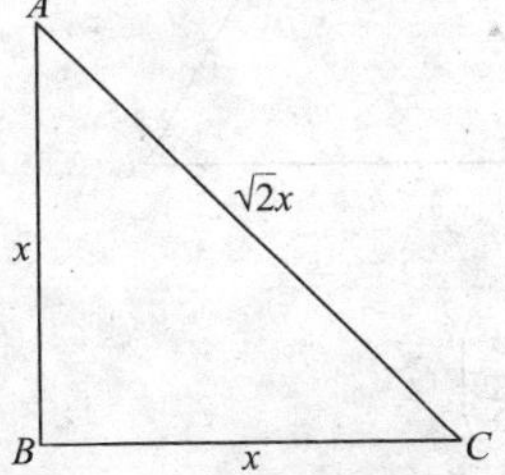

$$x + x + \sqrt{2}x = 2 + \sqrt{2}$$

$$\Rightarrow \quad 2x + \sqrt{2}x + 2 + \sqrt{2}$$

$$\Rightarrow \quad x(2+\sqrt{2}) = (2+\sqrt{2})$$

$$\Rightarrow \quad x = 1$$

Thus hypotenuse is $\sqrt{2}$ m

Hence Ans is (D)

Sol. 37 (C) Rays

Hence Ans is (C)

Sol. 38 (C) At each vertex we have two exterior angles

$360° + 360° = 720°$

Hence Ans is (C)

Sol. 39 (C) Using Pythagoras theorem

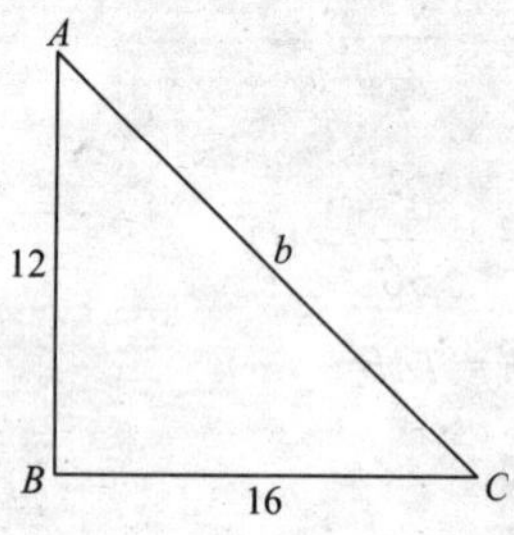

$$b^2 = 12^2 + 16^2$$
$$= 144 + 256$$
$$= 400$$
$$b = 20$$

Hence Ans is (C)

Sol. 40 (A) Since $BCED$ is a trapezium

Since $DE \parallel BC$

$\Rightarrow \quad \Delta ADE \sim \Delta ABC$

$$\frac{ar(ADE)}{ar(ABC)} = \frac{AE^2}{AC^2}$$

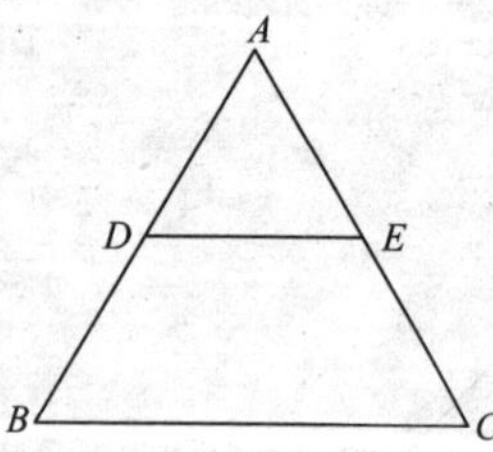

$$\frac{ar(ADE)}{ar(ABC)} = \left(\frac{3}{5}\right)^2$$

$\Rightarrow \quad ar(ADE) = 9k,$

$ar(ABC) = 25k,$

$ar(BCED) = 16k$

$$\Rightarrow \quad \frac{ar(ADE)}{ar(BCED)} = \frac{9k}{16k} = \frac{9}{16}$$

Hence Ans is (A)

Sol. 41 (D)

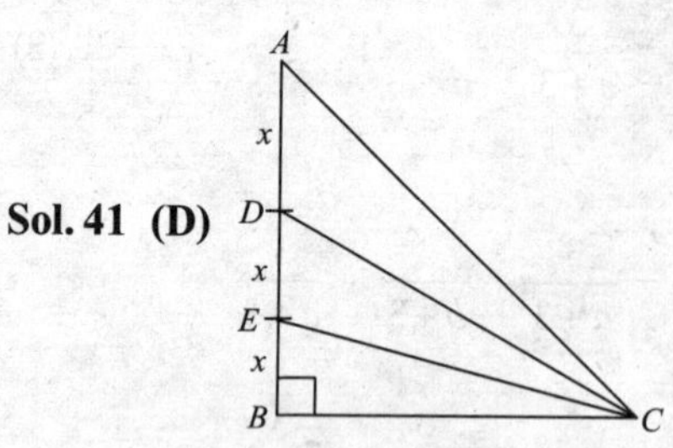

$$AC^2 = AB^2 + BC^2$$
$$= (3x)^2 + BC^2$$
$$AC^2 = 9x^2 + BC^2 \quad \ldots(1)$$
$$DC^2 = 4x^2 + BC^2$$
$$DC^2 - BC^2 = 4x^2 \quad \ldots(2)$$
$$EC^2 = x^2 + BC^2 \quad \ldots(3)$$
$$\Rightarrow \quad AC^2 - EC^2 = 8x^2 \quad \ldots(4)$$

$\Rightarrow$ by^2 (4) ÷ (2)

$$\frac{AC^2 - EC^2}{DC^2 - BC^2} = \frac{8x^2}{4x^2} = \frac{2}{1}$$

Hence Ans is (D)

Sol. 42 (A)

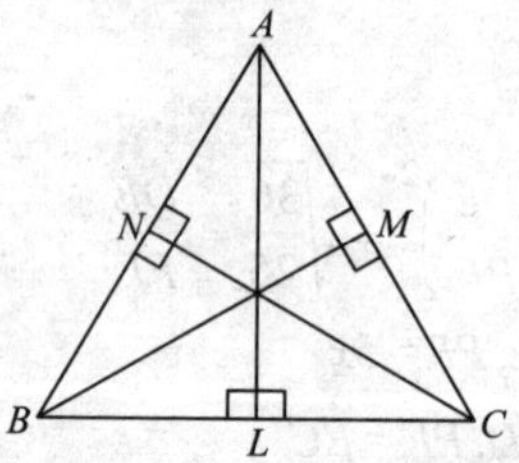

Clearly ΔALB is similar to ΔCNB ...(1)

$$\frac{AL}{CN} = \frac{BL}{BN} = \frac{AB}{BC}$$

Clearly ΔBMC is similar to ΔALC ...(2)

$$\frac{BM}{AL} = \frac{CM}{CL} = \frac{BC}{AC}$$

Clearly ΔBMA is similar to ΔCNA

$$\frac{BM}{CN} = \frac{AM}{AN} = \frac{AB}{AC} \quad \ldots(3)$$

multiplying equation-(1), (2) & (3)

$\Rightarrow \quad AN.BL.CM = BN.LC.AM$

Hence Ans is (A)

Sol. 43 (A)

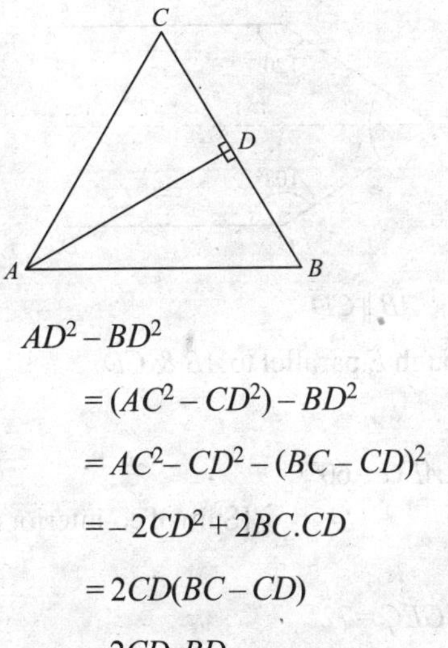

$AD^2 - BD^2$

$= (AC^2 - CD^2) - BD^2$

$= AC^2 - CD^2 - (BC - CD)^2$

$= -2CD^2 + 2BC.CD$

$= 2CD(BC - CD)$

$= 2CD.BD$

Hence Ans is (A)

Sol. 44 (D) $\frac{PM^2}{PN^2} = \frac{1}{4}$

$\Rightarrow \quad \frac{PM}{PN} = \frac{1}{2}$

$$\frac{ar(\Delta PQS)}{ar(\Delta RQS)} = \frac{\frac{1}{2} \times QS \times PM}{\frac{1}{2} \times QS \times PN} = \frac{PM}{PN} = \frac{1}{2}$$

Hence Ans is (D)

Sol. 45 (C)

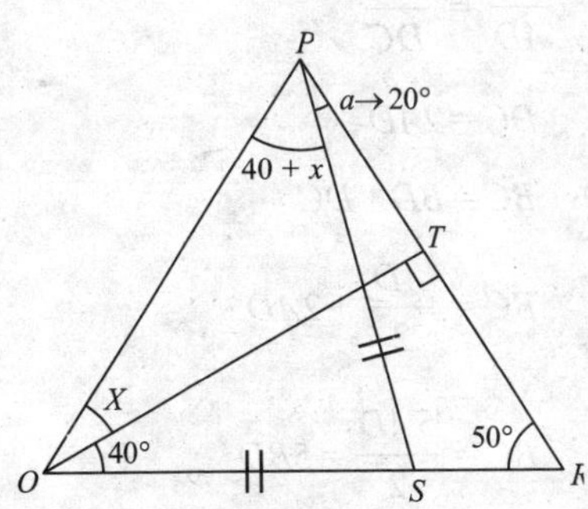

$40 + x + \alpha + x = 90°$, [Where $\alpha = 20°$]

$60 + 2x = 90°$

$\Rightarrow \quad x = 15°$

Hence Ans is (C)

Sol. 46 (D) Ratio of area of two similar triangle is equal to the ratio of square of their corresponding heights

Hence Ans is (D)

Sol. 47 (A)

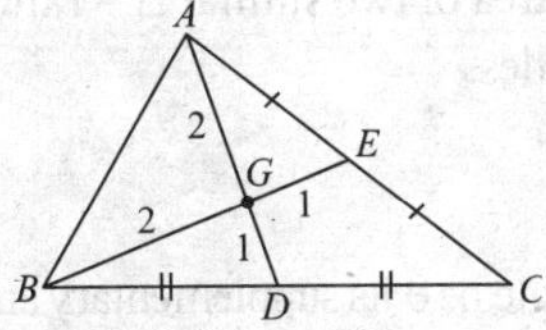

$$\frac{ar(BDG)}{ar(ABG)} = \frac{GD}{AG}$$

$$\frac{1}{ar(ABG)} = \frac{1}{2}$$

$\text{ar}(ABG) = 2 \text{ cm}^2$

$\text{ar}(ADC) = 3 \text{ cm}^2$

Also, $\Delta BGD \sim \Delta AGE\ (SAS)$

$\Rightarrow \quad \text{ar}(BGD) = \text{ar}(AGE)$

$\Rightarrow \quad \text{ar}(DCEG) = \text{ar}(ADC) - \text{ar}(AGE)$

$= 3 - 1 = 2 \text{ cm}^2$

Hence Ans is (A)

Sol. 48 (B) $2A = 3B = 6C = k$

$A = \frac{k}{2} \quad B = \frac{k}{3} \quad C = \frac{k}{6}$

$A + B + C = 180$

$\frac{k}{2} + \frac{k}{3} + \frac{k}{6} = 180 \mid A = 90°$,

$B = 60°$;

$C = 30°$

Hence Ans is (B)

Sol. 49 (B) $DE \parallel BC$,

by $\quad BPT\, DE = \frac{BC}{2}$

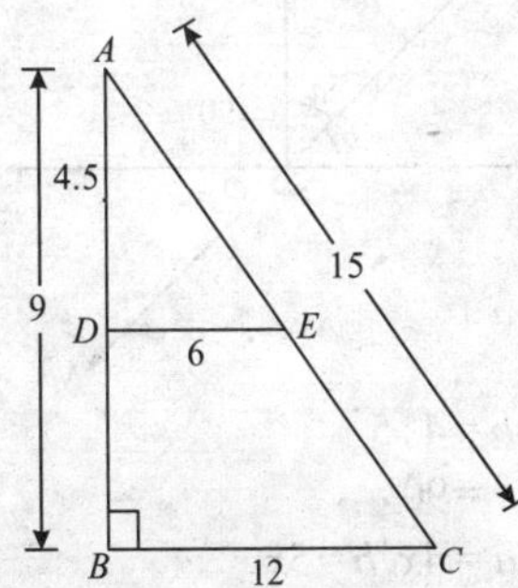

$$Ar(\Delta ADE) = \frac{1}{2} DE.AD$$

$= \frac{1}{2} \times 6 \times 4.5$

$= 13.5 \text{ cm}^2$

Hence Ans is (B)

Sol. 50 (C) Ratio of area of two similar Δ = ratio of square of their corresponding sides.

Hence Ans is (C)

Sol. 51 (B) Let the angle be θ its supplementary angle is $180-\theta$

According to Question

Angle = 5 (supplementary angle)

$\Rightarrow \quad \theta = 5(180-\theta)$

$\Rightarrow \quad 6\theta = 900$

$\Rightarrow \quad \theta = 150°$

Hence Ans is (B)

Sol. 52 (A)

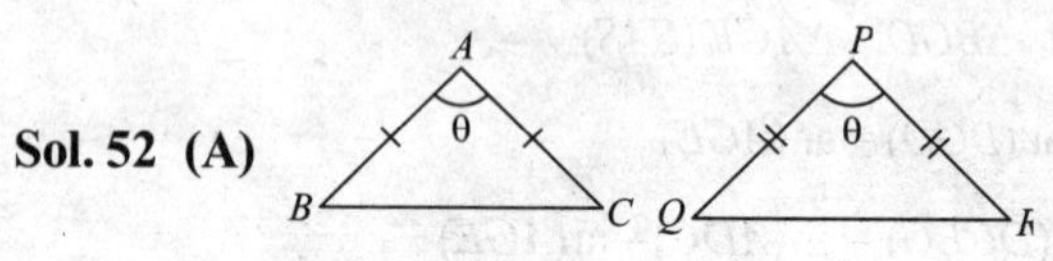

In ΔABC & ΔPQR

$$\frac{AB}{PQ} = \frac{AC}{PR} \quad [AB = AC \text{ and } PQ = PR]$$

$$\angle BAC = \angle QPR \quad \text{(Given)}$$

$\Rightarrow$ By *SAS* criteria

$$\Delta ABC \sim \Delta PQR$$

We know

Ratio of area of two similar Triangle

= (Ratio of square of their corresponding altitude)

$\Rightarrow$ Ratio of their areas $= \left(\frac{4}{9}\right)^2 = \frac{16}{81}$

Hence Ans is (A)

Sol. 53 (D)

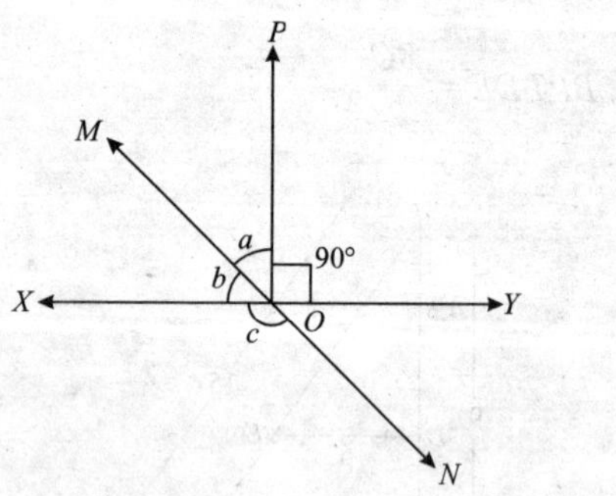

Given $\quad a : b = 4 : 5$

$a + b = 90°$

Let $\quad a = 4x, b = 5x$

$\Rightarrow \quad 9x = 90°$

$x = 10$

So, $\quad a = 40°$

$b = 50°$

$c = a + 90° \quad$ (vertically opposite angles)

$= 130°$

Hence Ans is (D)

Sol. 54 (D)

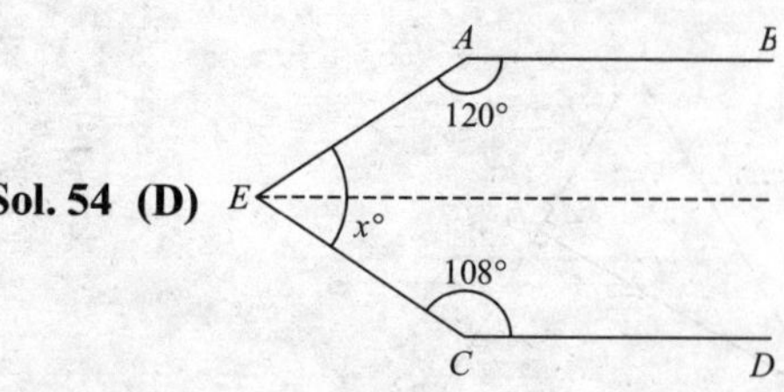

Given $\quad AB \parallel CD$

Draw line through E parallel to AB & CD

$AB \parallel EG$,

$\Rightarrow \quad \angle AEG = 60°$

[Sum of co-interior angle is 180°]

$CD \parallel EG$,

$\Rightarrow \quad \angle GEC = 72°$

[Sum of co-interior angle is 180°]

$\Rightarrow \quad x = 60° + 72°$

$= 132°$

Hence Ans is (D)

Sol. 55 (C) $\Delta ABC \sim \Delta DBA$

$$\Rightarrow \quad \frac{AB}{BD} = \frac{AC}{AD}$$

$$\Rightarrow \quad BD = \frac{AD}{2}$$

and $\quad \Delta ABC \sim \Delta DAC$

$$\frac{AB}{AD} = \frac{AC}{DC}$$

$$\frac{x}{AD} = \frac{2x}{DC}$$

$$DC = 2AD$$

$$\Rightarrow \quad BC = BD + DC$$

$$BC = \frac{AD}{2} + 2AD$$

$$\Rightarrow \quad BC = \frac{5AD}{2} = 5BD$$

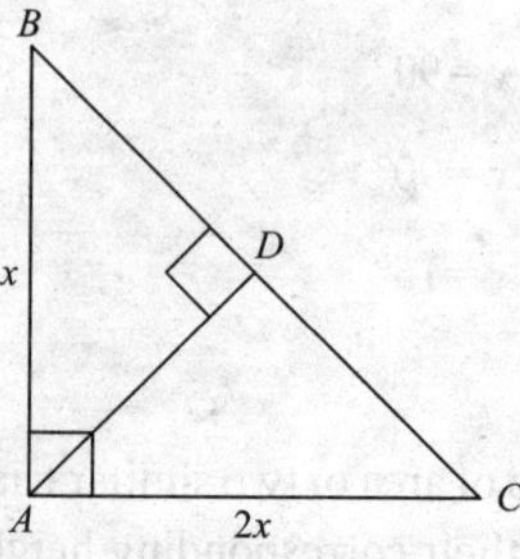

Hence Ans is (C)

Sol. 56 (B) Let the side of square be 'x'

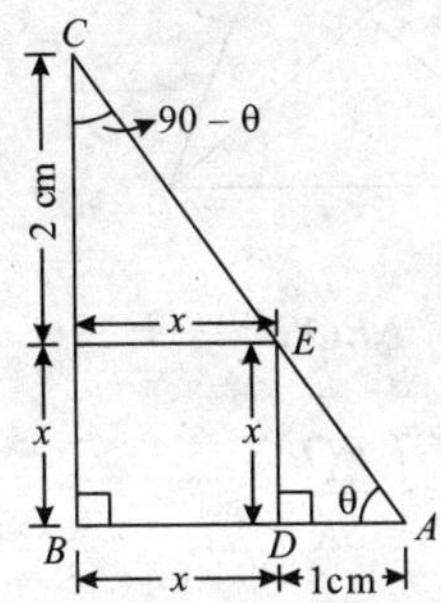

$\Delta ADE \sim \Delta ABC$

$$\frac{AD}{AB} = \frac{DE}{BC}$$

$$\frac{1}{x+1} = \frac{x}{x+2}$$

$$x+2 = x^2 + x$$

$$x^2 = 2$$

$$x = \sqrt{2}$$

Hence Ans is (B)

Sol. 57 (A)

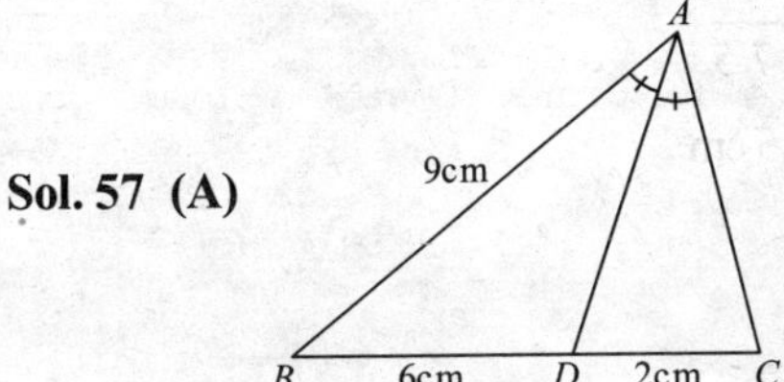

Given AD is the bisector of angle A so by angle bisector theorem

$$\frac{BA}{AC} = \frac{BD}{DC}$$

$$\frac{9}{AC} = \frac{6}{2}$$

$$AC = 3 \text{ cm}$$

Hence Ans is (A)

Sol. 58 (B)

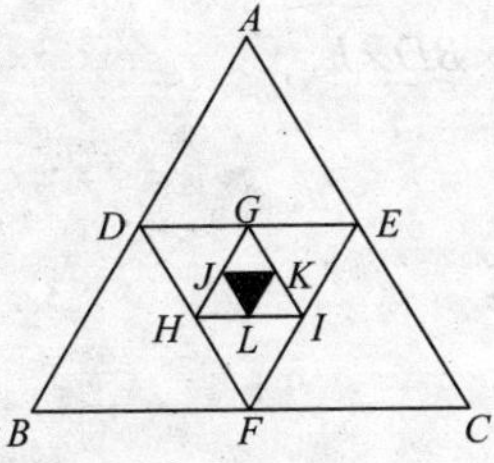

By mid point theorem we have

$$DE = \frac{1}{2}BC$$

& parallel to BC similarly

$$HI = \frac{1}{2}DE = \frac{1}{2}\left(\frac{1}{2}BC\right) = \frac{1}{4}BC$$

& $$JK = \frac{1}{2}HI = \frac{1}{2}\left(\frac{1}{4}BC\right) = \frac{1}{8}BC$$

$$JK = \frac{1}{8} \text{ as } BC = 1 \text{ given}$$

So area of equilateral

$$\Delta = \frac{\sqrt{3}}{4}\left(\frac{1}{8}\right)^2$$

Hence Ans is (B)

Sol. 59 (B) $\angle ABC + \angle EMC$

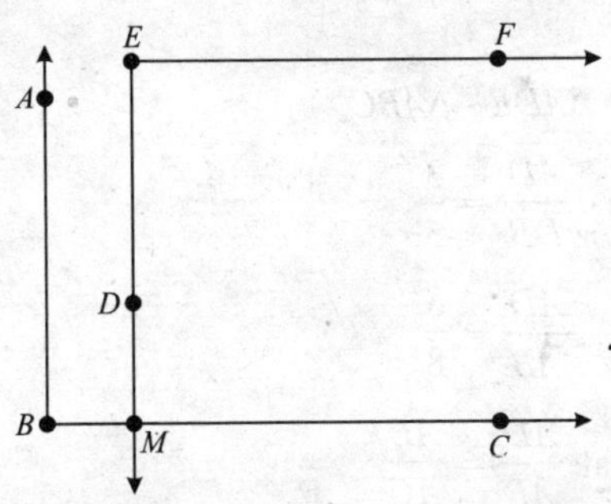

$$\angle DEF + \angle EMC = 180^\circ$$

(co-interior angles)

$\Rightarrow$ $$\angle DEF + \angle ABC = 180^\circ$$

As $\angle ABC = \angle DMC$ (Corresponding angles)

Hence Ans is (B)

Sol. 60 (C)

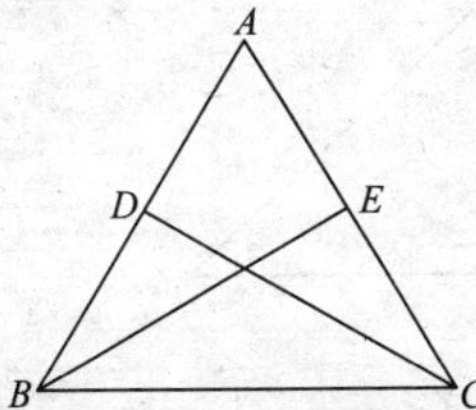

Given $AB = AC$

$\Rightarrow$ $\angle D = \angle C = 70^\circ$ ($\therefore BAC = 40^\circ$)

$\Rightarrow$ $$\angle DOE = \angle BOC = 90 + \frac{A}{2}$$

$$= 90 + 20$$
$$= 110^\circ$$

Hence Ans is (C)

Sol. 61 (D)

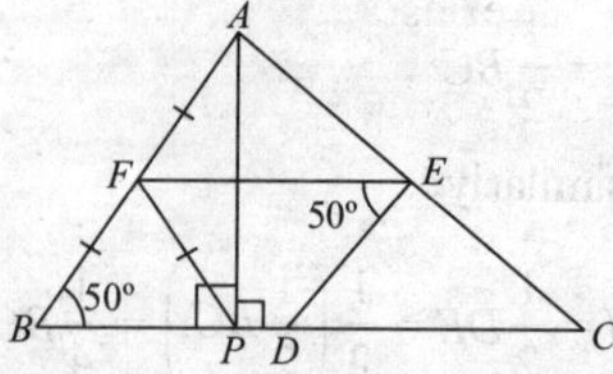

$$FE = \frac{1}{2}BC = BD \;\&\; FE \,||\, BD$$

($\because$ Mid point theorem)

$\Rightarrow$ BDEF is a Parallelogram

($\because$ One pair of opposite side are Parallel & equal)

$\Rightarrow \quad \angle FBP = \angle FED = 50^\circ$

$PF = BF$

(In a right angled triangle, median on hypotenuse is half of hypotenuse)

$\Rightarrow \quad \angle FPB = \angle FBP = 50^\circ$

$\Rightarrow \quad \angle FPD = 180^\circ - \angle FPB = 130^\circ$

Hence Ans is (D)

Sol. 62 (D) $\Delta ADE \sim \Delta ABC$ ($\because$ $DE \,||\, BC$)

Given $\dfrac{AD}{DB} = \dfrac{3}{5}$

$\Rightarrow \quad \dfrac{AD}{AB} = \dfrac{3}{8}$

We know that $\dfrac{AD}{AB} = \dfrac{AE}{AC}$

$\Rightarrow \quad \dfrac{3}{8} = \dfrac{AE}{5.6}$

$\Rightarrow \quad AE = \dfrac{5.6 \times 3}{8} = 2.1$ cm

Hence Ans is (D)

Sol. 63 (A)

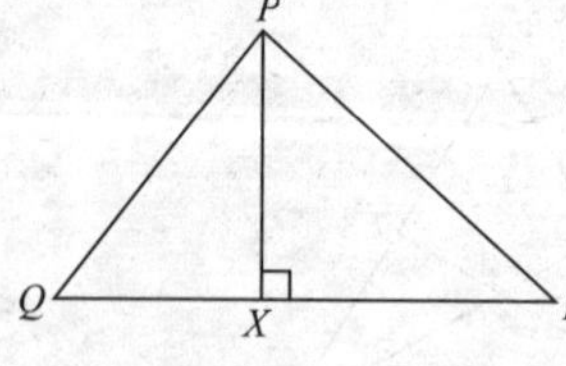

$PQ^2 + QR^2 - 2QR \cdot QX$

$= PQ^2 + (QX + XR)^2 - 2QR \cdot QX$

$= PQ^2 + QX^2 + XR^2 + 2QX \cdot XR - 2(QX + XR)QX$

$= PQ^2 + QX^2 + XR^2 + 2QX \cdot XR - 2QX^2 - 2XR \cdot QX$

$= PQ^2 - QX^2 + XR^2$

$= PX^2 + XR^2 = PR^2$ (Using pythagoras)

Hence Ans is (A)

Sol. 64 (C)

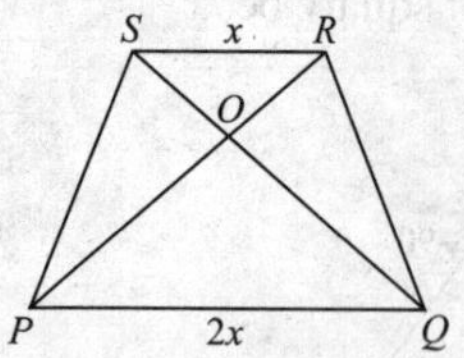

$\Delta POQ \sim \Delta ROS$

$$\frac{ar(POQ)}{ar(ROS)} = \left(\frac{PQ}{SR}\right)^2 \text{s}$$

$$= \left(\frac{2x}{x}\right)^2 = \frac{4}{1}$$

Hence Ans is (C)

Sol. 65 (D) $\dfrac{BC}{EF} = \dfrac{\text{perimeter of } \Delta ABC}{\text{perimeter of } \Delta DEF}$

$\Rightarrow \quad \dfrac{4}{2} = \dfrac{p}{DE + EF + DF}$

$\Rightarrow \quad 2 = \dfrac{p}{3 + 2 + 2.5}$

$\Rightarrow \quad 2 = \dfrac{p}{7.5}$

$\Rightarrow \quad p = 15$ cm

Hence Ans is (D)

Sol. 66 (D)

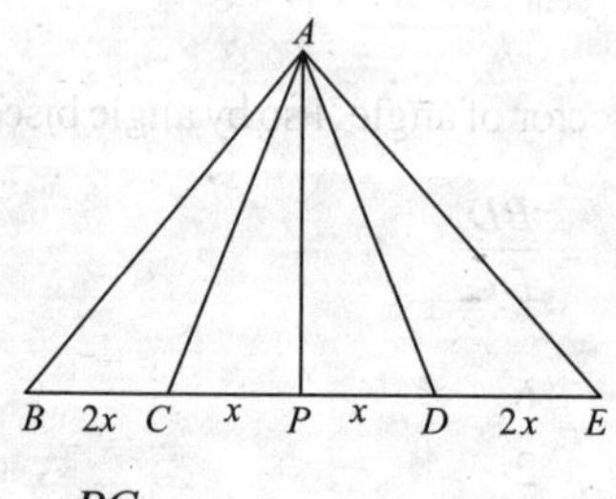

$PC = x$

and $BD = 4x$

Now $\dfrac{ar(\Delta APC)}{ar(\Delta ABD)} = \dfrac{\frac{1}{2} \times PC \times h}{\frac{1}{2} \times BD \times h}$

$$= \frac{x}{4x}$$

$$= \frac{1}{4}$$

Hence Ans is (D)

Sol. 67 (D) $\frac{y+z}{x}+\frac{z+x}{y}+\frac{x+y}{z}$

$\Rightarrow \quad \left(\frac{y}{x}+\frac{x}{y}\right)+\left(\frac{y}{z}+\frac{z}{y}\right)+\left(\frac{z}{x}+\frac{x}{z}\right)$

we know that by *AM-GM*

$$\left(a+\frac{1}{a}\right)\geq 2$$

Thus for minimum $2+2+2=6$

Hence Ans is (D)

Sol. 68 (C) $\frac{3b+4c}{a}+\frac{4c+a}{3b}+\frac{a+3b}{4c}$

$$\left(\frac{3b}{a}+\frac{a}{3b}\right)+\left(\frac{4c}{a}+\frac{a}{4c}\right)+\left(\frac{4c}{3b}+\frac{3b}{4c}\right)$$

We know that by AM-GM

$$\left(a+\frac{1}{a}\right)\geq 2$$

Thus for minimum $2+2+2=6$

Hence Ans is (C)

Sol. 69 (A) Area of $ABC=\frac{1}{2}\times$ Base $\times$ Height

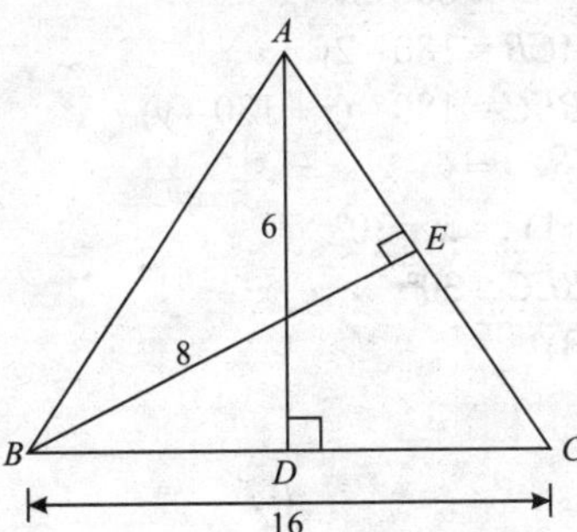

If BC is base then AD is height and if CA is base, BE is height. Equating area in both the ways we get

$$\frac{1}{2}\times BC\times AD=\frac{1}{2}\times CA\times BE$$

$\Rightarrow \quad 16\times 6=CA\times 8$

$\Rightarrow \quad CA=\frac{16\times 6}{8}$

$=12$ cm

Hence Ans is (A)

Sol. 70 (B) From Figure it is clear that (B) is not true.

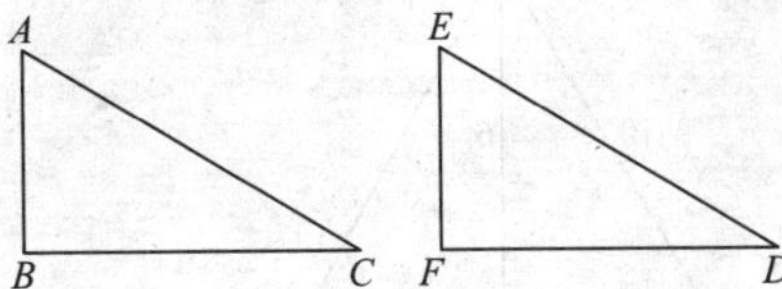

Hence Ans is (B)

Sol. 71 (C) If $AB=BC$

and $\angle B=90$,

Let $AB=BC=x$.

As per Pythagoras theorem,

$$AC^2=AB^2+BC^2=x^2+x^2=2x^2$$

$\Rightarrow \quad AC=\sqrt{2}$

$$AB:AC=x:\sqrt{2}x=1:\sqrt{2}$$

Hence Ans is (C)

Sol. 72 (D)

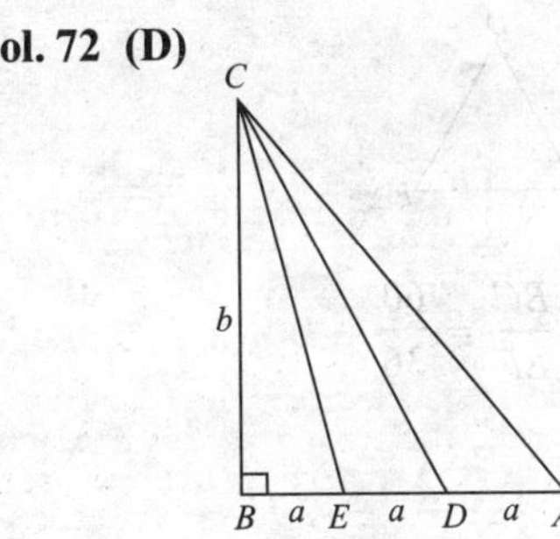

Let $AD=a$

and $BC=b$

$\Rightarrow \quad AC^2-EC^2=[b^2+(3a)^2]-(b^2+a^2)=8a^2$

$$DC^2-BC^2=(4a^2+b^2)-(b^2)=4a^2$$

$\Rightarrow \quad \frac{AC^2-EC^2}{DC^2-BC^2}=\frac{8a^2}{4a^2}=2$

Hence Ans is (D)

Sol. 73 (C)

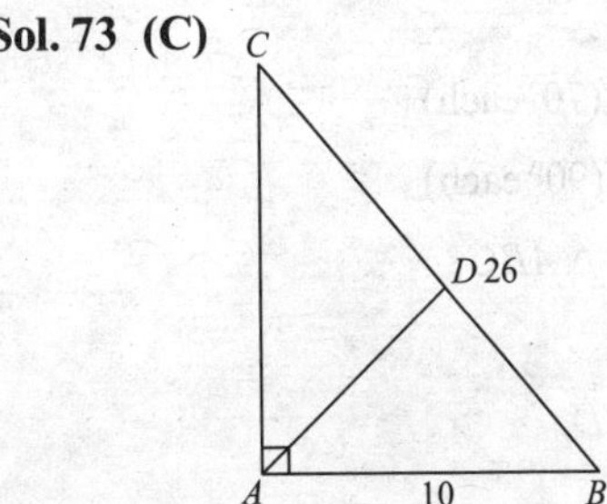

Since the sides (10, 24, 26) are Pythagorean triplet

$\Rightarrow$ Triangle ABC is a right angle triangle (angle $A=90°$)

Since, in a right angle triangle median is half of the hypotenuse

$\Rightarrow \quad AD=13$ cm

Hence Ans is (C)

Sol. 74 (C)

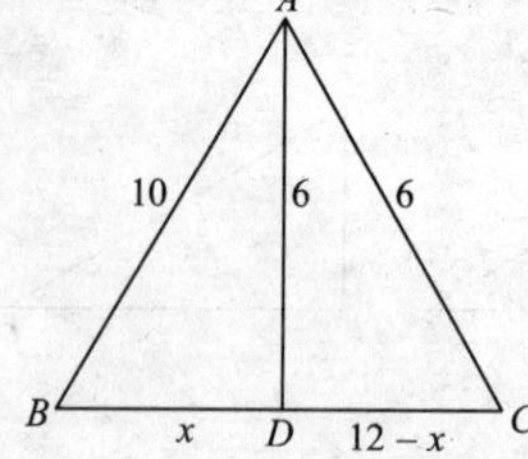

Since AD is internal angle bisector,

So, $\dfrac{BD}{DC} = \dfrac{AB}{AC}$

$\Rightarrow \dfrac{x}{12-x} = \dfrac{10}{6}$

$\Rightarrow 3x = 60 - 5x$

$\Rightarrow x = 7.5$ cm

Hence Ans is (C)

Sol. 75 (C)

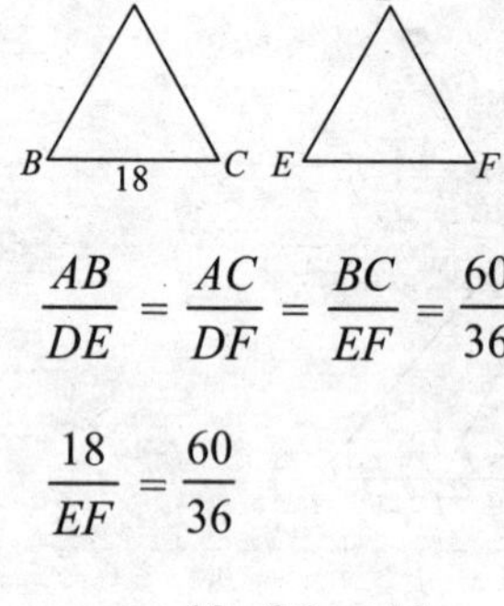

$$\frac{AB}{DE} = \frac{AC}{DF} = \frac{BC}{EF} = \frac{60}{36}$$

$$\frac{18}{EF} = \frac{60}{36}$$

$$EF = \frac{18 \times 36}{60} = \frac{54}{5}$$

$= 10.8$ cm

Hence Ans is (C)

Sol. 76 (C) Given

$AD = DC$

$DE \perp BC$

$\angle ABD = 70^\circ$

$\angle ABD = \angle BDE$ (70° each)

$\angle DEB = \angle ABC$ (90° each)

If D is the midpoint of AC of ΔABC

$\Rightarrow$ D is the circumcenter

$\Rightarrow AD = BD = CD$

$\Rightarrow \angle DCB = 20^\circ$

$\Rightarrow \angle CDE = 70^\circ$

$\Rightarrow \angle CDE - \angle DCB$

$= 70^\circ - 20^\circ$

$= 50$

Hence Ans is (C)

Sol. 77 (A) BD bisects $\angle ABC$

$ED \parallel BC$

$\angle ABC = 40^\circ$

$\angle BDC = 110^\circ$

$\angle EDB = ?$

$\angle DCB = ?$

$2x = 40^\circ$

$x = 20 \ \angle EDB = 20^\circ$

$\angle DCB = 180^\circ - (110 + 20) = 50^\circ$

Hence Ans is (A)

Sol. 78 (D)

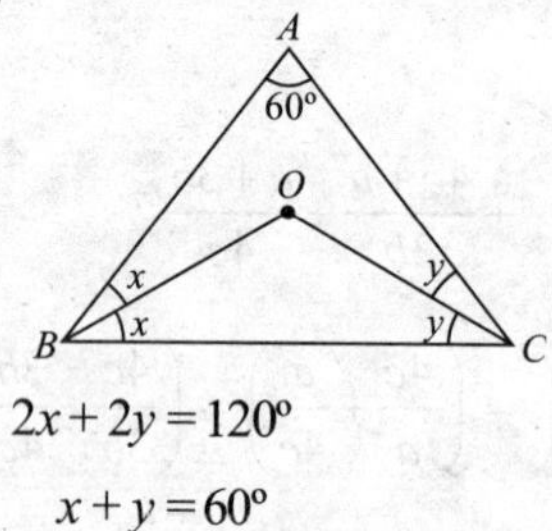

$2x + 2y = 120^\circ$

$x + y = 60^\circ$

$\Rightarrow \angle BOC = 120^\circ$

Hence Ans is (D)

Sol. 79 (B)

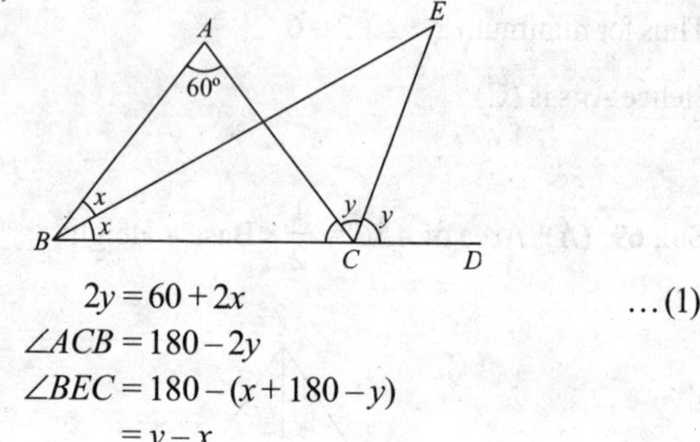

$2y = 60 + 2x$ ...(1)

$\angle ACB = 180 - 2y$

In ΔBEC, $\angle BEC = 180 - (x + 180 - y)$

$= y - x$

From equation-(1) $y - x = 30^\circ$

$\Rightarrow \angle BEC = 30^\circ$

Hence Ans is (B)

Sol. 80 (D)

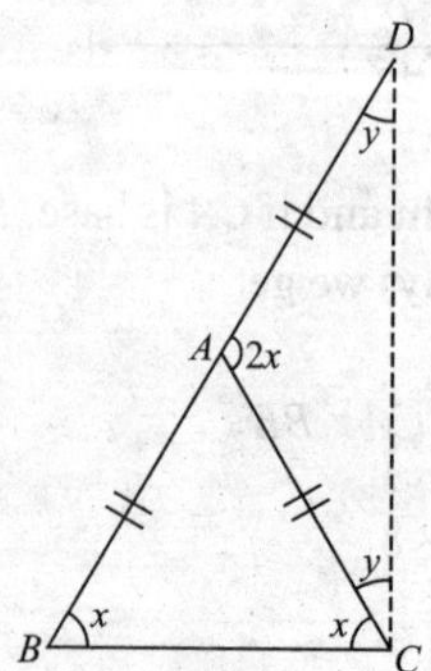

Now $2y + 2x = 18$

$\Rightarrow y + x = 90^\circ$

$\Rightarrow \angle BCD = 90^\circ$

Hence Ans is (D)

Sol. 81 (B)

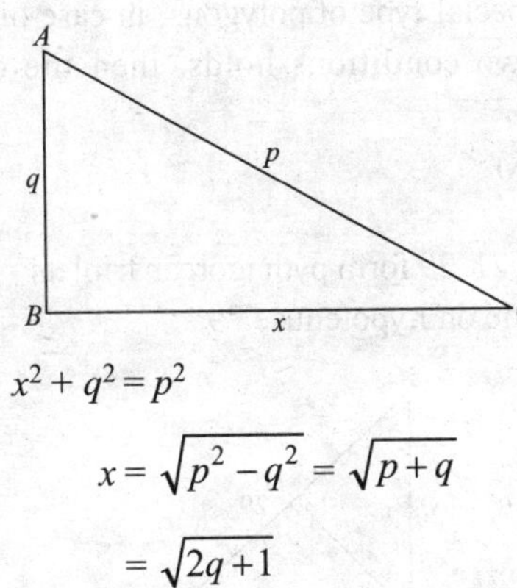

$$x^2 + q^2 = p^2$$

$$x = \sqrt{p^2 - q^2} = \sqrt{p+q}$$

$$= \sqrt{2q+1}$$

Hence Ans is (B)

Sol. 82 (C) $\angle A = x = 50^\circ$

$\angle C = x = 60^\circ$

$\angle B = 180^\circ - (60^\circ + 50^\circ)$

$= 180^\circ - 110^\circ$

$= 70^\circ$

Hence Ans is (D)

Sol. 83 (A) Edges of any face of finite area of 3-D figures are Line segment. If surface has infinite area then it edges should be called as lines.
Hence Ans is (A)

Sol. 84 (A) Since ΔABC and ΔDEF are similar

Therefore $\dfrac{\text{area of } \Delta ABC}{\text{area of } \Delta DEF} = \left(\dfrac{BC}{EF}\right)^2$

$$\frac{12}{48} = \frac{3^2}{EF^2}$$

$$EF^2 = \frac{48 \times 9}{12} = 36$$

Therefore $EF = 6$ cm

Hence Ans is (A)

Sol. 85 (D)

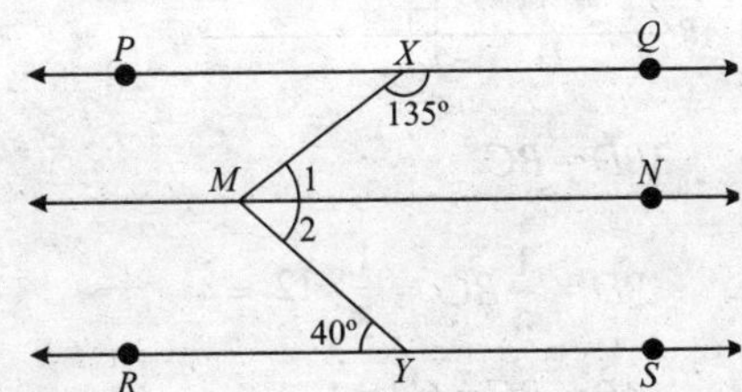

Draw $MN \parallel PR$

$\Rightarrow$ $MN \parallel PQ \parallel SR$

$\angle 1 + 135 = 180^\circ$ (Co-interior angles)

$\Rightarrow$ $\angle 1 = 45^\circ$

$\angle 2 = 40^\circ$ (Alternate interior angles)

$\Rightarrow$ $\angle XMY = 85^\circ$

Hence Ans is (D)

Sol. 86 (A) In ΔQTR

$x = 180^\circ - (90^\circ + 40^\circ)$ (Angle sum property)

$x = 50^\circ$

$y = 30 + x$ (Exterior angle property)

$y = 30 + 50 = 80^\circ$

Hence Ans is (A)

Sol. 87 (D)

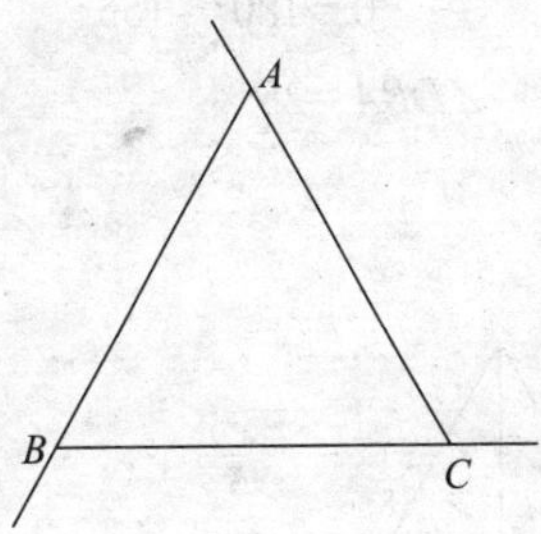

Let $\angle A = 2x$

$\angle B = 4x$

$\angle C = 9x$

We have by angle sum property of triangle

$\angle A + \angle B + \angle C = 180^\circ$

$2x + 4x + 9x = 180^\circ$

$x = 12$

So $\angle A = 2x = 24$

$\angle B = 4x = 48$

$\angle C = 9x = 108$

So ext. $\angle A = 180 - \angle A = 180 - 24 = 156$

ext. $\angle B = 180 - \angle B = 180 - 48 = 132$

ext. $\angle C = 180 - \angle C = 180 - 108 = 72$

Now required difference between two smaller exterior angle is

$132 - 72 = 60^\circ$

Hence Ans is (D)

Sol. 88 (D)

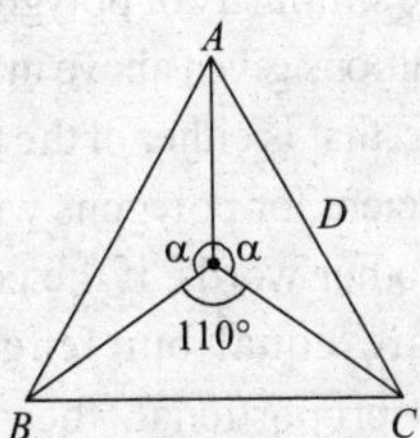

Given $\Delta ABD \cong \Delta ACD$

$\Rightarrow$ $\angle BDA = \angle CDA = \alpha$

& $\angle DBA = \theta$

Now $\alpha + \alpha + 110^\circ = 360^\circ$

$$2\alpha = 360^\circ - 110^\circ$$

$$2\alpha = 250^\circ$$

$$\alpha = 125^\circ$$

Now in ΔDBA

By angle sum property of Δ

We have

$$\angle DAB + \angle DBA + \angle BDA = 180^\circ$$

$$30 + \theta + \alpha = 180^\circ$$

$$30 + \theta + 125 = 180^\circ$$

$$\theta = 180^\circ - 155^\circ$$

$\Rightarrow$ $\angle DBA = 25^\circ$

Hence Ans is (D)

Sol. 89 (C)

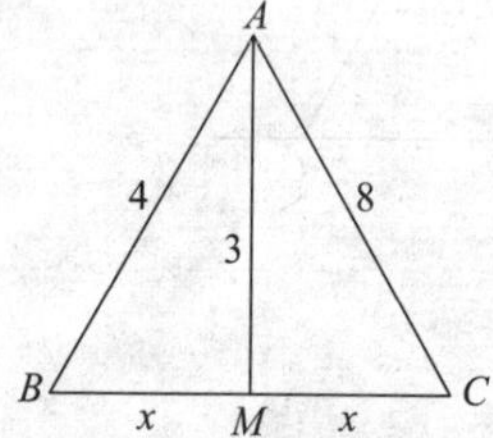

Given M is the mid point of BC Applying the apollonius theorem

$$AB^2 + AC^2 = 2(BM^2 + AM^2)$$

$$16 + 64 = 2(x^2 + 9)$$

$\Rightarrow$ $80 = 2(x^2 + 9)$

$$40 = x^2 + 9$$

$$x^2 = 31$$

$$x = \sqrt{31}$$

$$BC = 2x = 2\sqrt{31}$$

Hence Ans is (C)

Sol. 90 (A) SIMILAR POLYGONS

Definition-Two polygons are said to be similar to each other ,if

(A) Their corresponding angles are equal, and

(B) The lengths of their corresponding sides are proportional

It should be noted that for the similarity of polygons with more than three sides, the two conditions given above in the definition are independent of each other ,that is either of the two condition without the other is not sufficient for polygons with more than three sides to be similar. In other words, if the corresponding angles of two polygons are equal but lengths of their corresponding sides are not proportional, the polygon need not be similar. Similarly, if the corresponding angles of two polygons are not equal but lengths of their corresponding sides are proportional , the polygon need not be similar.

Triangles are special type of polygons, in case of triangles if either of the two conditions holds, then the other holds automatically

Hence Ans is (A)

Sol. 91 (A) 20, 21, 29 form pythagorean triplets

Length of altitude on hypotenuse 29

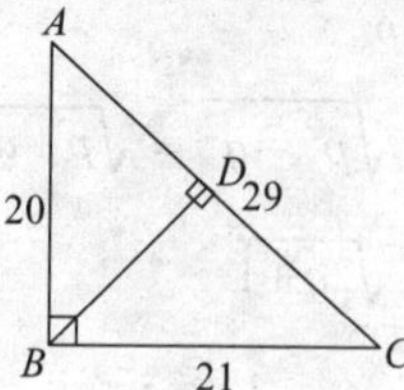

Area of ΔABC

$$\frac{1}{2} \times 20 \times 21 = \frac{1}{2} \times 29 \times AD$$

$\Rightarrow$ $AD = \dfrac{20 \times 21}{29}$

$\Rightarrow$ Sum of altitudes

$$20 + 21 + \frac{20 \times 21}{29} = \frac{1609}{29} \text{ units}$$

Hence Ans is (A)

Sol. 92 (C)

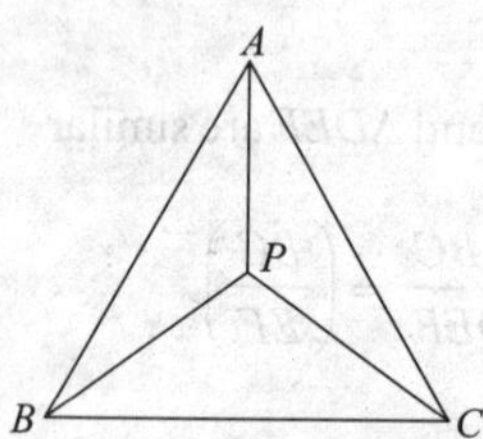

Centroid divides the triangle in three parts of equal area

Hence Ans is (C)

Sol. 93 (C)

We have $3BD = BC$

$\Rightarrow$ $BD = \dfrac{1}{3} BC = \dfrac{1}{3} \times 12 = 4$

Given that $AB = BC = CA = 12$

$\Rightarrow$ Triangle is equilateral

So height of equilateral triangle $= \dfrac{\sqrt{3}}{2} \times a$

$\Rightarrow \quad AE = \frac{\sqrt{3}}{2} \times 12 = 6\sqrt{3}$

We have $\quad BE = EC = 6$

& $\quad BD = 4$

$\Rightarrow \quad DE = 2$

Now in ΔAED, apply pythagoras theorem

$$AD^2 = AE^2 + DE^2$$

$$AD^2 = 2^2 + (6\sqrt{3})^2$$

$$= 4 + 108$$

$$= 112$$

$$= 4\sqrt{7}$$

Hence Ans is (C)

Sol. 94 (B) Given that

In $\Delta ABC, XY \parallel AC$

and $\quad ar[BXY] = ar[AXYC]$

$\Rightarrow \quad ar[BXY] = \frac{1}{2} ar[ABC] \quad \ldots(1)$

Since $\quad \Delta BXY \sim \Delta BAC$

So ratio of areas of two similar triangle is equal to ratio of square of their corresponding sides

$$\frac{ar\Delta BXY}{ar\Delta BAC} = \left(\frac{BX}{AB}\right)^2$$

$$\Rightarrow \quad \frac{1}{2} = \left(\frac{BX}{AB}\right)^2$$

$$\Rightarrow \quad \frac{1}{\sqrt{2}} = \frac{BX}{AB}$$

$$\Rightarrow \quad 1 - \frac{1}{\sqrt{2}} = 1 - \frac{BX}{AB}$$

$$\Rightarrow \quad \frac{\sqrt{2}-1}{\sqrt{2}} = \frac{AX}{AB}$$

$$\Rightarrow \quad \frac{2-\sqrt{2}}{2} = \frac{AX}{AB}$$

Hence Ans is (B)

Sol. 95 (B)

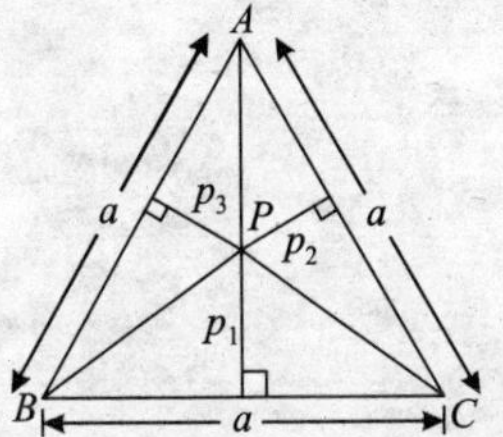

ar of ΔPBC + ar of ΔPAC + ar of ΔPAB = ar ΔABC

$$\frac{1}{2} \times p_1 \times a + \frac{1}{2} p_2 \times a + \frac{1}{2} \times p_3 \times a = \frac{\sqrt{3}}{4} a^2$$

$$\frac{1}{2} a (p_1 + p_2 + p_3) = \frac{\sqrt{3}}{4} \times a^2$$

$$p_1 + p_2 + p_3 = \frac{\sqrt{3}}{2} a$$

Hence Ans is (B)

Sol. 96 (B) According to question

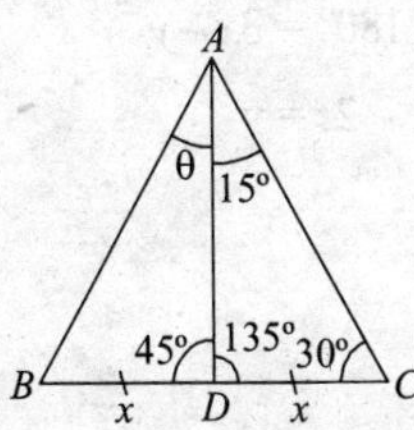

$\angle BAD + \angle ABC = 135°$

(Exterior angle is the sum of interior opposite angle)

Hence Ans is (B)

Sol. 97 (D) In ΔABC,

$$BC = 2\sqrt{l^2 - h^2}$$

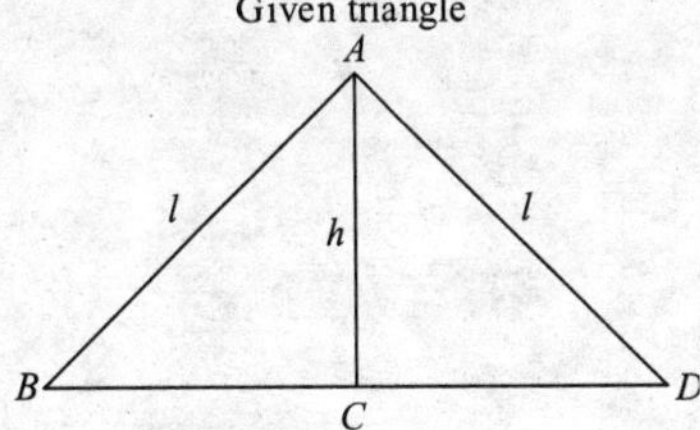

In ΔPQR,

$$QR = 2\sqrt{4l^2 - h^2}$$

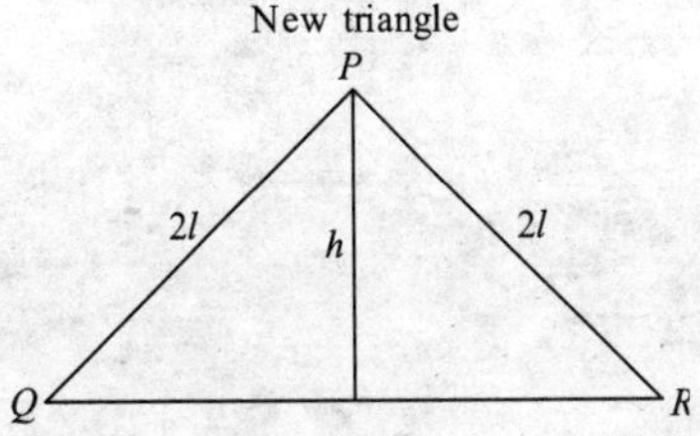

Now $\quad QR^2 - BC^2 = 4(4l^2 - h^2) - 4(l^2 - h^2)$

$$= 16l^2 - 4l^2$$

$$= 12l^2$$

Hence Ans is (D)

Sol. 98 (D)

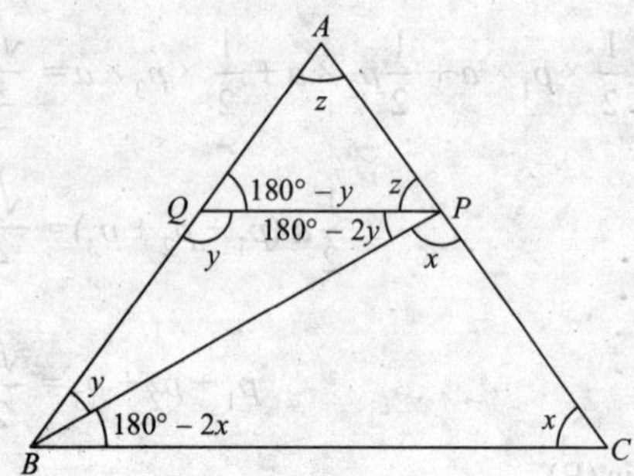

In ΔABC $\quad AB = AC$

$$y + 180° - 2x = x$$

$$\Rightarrow \quad 180° = 3x - y \quad \ldots(1)$$

In ΔAQP $\quad 2z = y \quad \ldots(2)$

Since APC is a straight line

$$\Rightarrow \quad z + x + 180° - 2y = 180°$$

$$\Rightarrow \quad 2x = 3y \quad \ldots(3)$$

From (1) and (3)

$$y = \frac{360°}{7}$$

$$\angle AQP = 180° - \frac{360°}{7}$$

$$= \frac{900°}{7} = \frac{5\pi}{7}$$

Hence Ans is (D)

Sol. 99 (A) Option (A) is correct

Hence Ans is (A)

* * * * *

Quadratic Equation Theory 6

The standard form of a quadratic equation is $ax^2 + bx + c = 0$ where a, b, c are real numbers ($a \neq 0$) and x is a variable.

6.1 Types of Quadratic Equations

A quadratic equation can be of the following types:

(i) $b = 0, c \neq 0$ i.e. of the type $ax^2 + c = 0$

(Pure quadratic equation)

(ii) $b \neq 0, c = 0$ i.e. of the type $ax^2 + bx = 0$

(iii) $b = 0, c = 0$ i.e. of the type $ax^2 = 0$

(iv) $b \neq 0, c \neq 0$ i.e. of the type $ax^2 + bx + c = 0$

(Mixed or complete quadratic equation)

6.2 Roots of Quadratic Equation

The values of the variable satisfying a given quadratic equation are called its roots i.e. $x = \alpha$ is called a root of a quadratic equation $ax^2 + bx + c = 0$ if $a\alpha^2 + b\alpha + c = 0$.

Note : A quadratic equation has maximum two roots.

Remarks

(i) A quadratic equation can not have more than two roots.

(ii) The roots of a quadratic equation generally denoted by α and β.

6.3 Relation Between Roots and Coefficients of a Quadratic Equation

Let α and β be the roots of the quadratic equation $ax^2 + bx + c = 0$, $a \neq 0$.

Then $$\alpha = \frac{-b + \sqrt{b^2 - 4ac}}{2a}$$

and $$\beta = \frac{-b - \sqrt{b^2 - 4ac}}{2a}$$

$\Rightarrow$ The sum of roots

$$\alpha + \beta = -\frac{b}{a} = -\frac{\text{Coeff. of } x}{\text{Coeff. of } x^2}$$

and product of roots

$$= \alpha . \beta = \frac{c}{a}$$

$$= \frac{\text{constant term}}{\text{coefficient of } x^2}$$

6.4 Methods of Solving a Quadratic Equation

We have three methods for solving a quadratic equation: These methods are as follow :

(i) Factorization method

(ii) By completing the square method

(iii) Formula method

6.5 Nature of the Roots of the Quadratic Equation

Let the quadratic equation be $ax^2 + bx + c = 0$, ...(1)

Where $a \neq 0$ and $a, b, c \in R$.

The roots of the given equation are given by

$$x = \frac{-b \pm \sqrt{D}}{2a},$$

Where $D = b^2 - 4ac$ is the discriminant.

i.e., if α and β are two roots of the quadratic equation-(1) Then,

$$\alpha = \frac{-b + \sqrt{D}}{2a}$$

and $$\beta = \frac{-b - \sqrt{D}}{2a}$$

Now, the following cases are possible.

Case-I : When $D > 0$, Roots are real and unequal (distinct).

The roots are given by

$$\alpha = \frac{-b + \sqrt{D}}{2a}$$

and $$\beta = \frac{-b - \sqrt{D}}{2a}$$

Case-II : When $D = 0$, Roots are real and equal and each root

$$\alpha = \frac{-b}{2a} = \beta$$

Case-III : When $D < 0$, No real roots exist. Both the roots are imaginary.

- If D is a perfect square then the roots are rational and in case it is not a perfect square then the roots are irrational.

- If $p + \sqrt{q}$ is one root of a quadratic equation, then the other must be the conjugate $p - \sqrt{q}$ and vice versa. (where p is rational and $\sqrt{q}$ is a surd).

- If $a = b = c = 0$, then equation becomes identity and has infinite roots.

- Quadratic equations $a_1x^2 + b_1x + c_1 = 0$ and $a_2x^2 + b_2x + c_2 = 0$ have both roots common when

$$\frac{a_1}{a_2} = \frac{b_1}{b_2} = \frac{c_1}{c_2}$$

- An identity is an expression which is true for all the values of the variable.

- A quadratic equation cannot have more than two real roots.

Graph of Quadratic equations $ax^2 + bx + c$

$a > 0 \cup$ Concave upward	$a < 0 \cap$ Concave downward
$D > 0$ Roots are real and distinct	$D > 0$ Roots are real and distinct
$D = 0$ Roots are real and equal	$D = 0$ Roots are real and equal
$D < 0$ Roots are imaginary In this kind of graph we do not have any maximum value of quadratic expression but we do have minimum value & it lies at $x = \frac{-b}{2a}$ & the value is $\frac{-D}{4a}$	$D < 0$ Roots are imaginary In this kind of graph we do not have any minimum value of quadratic expression but we do have maximum value & it lies at $x = \frac{-b}{2a}$ & the value is $\frac{-D}{4a}$

Sign convention for a,b,c,

- If graph is concave up ward then $a > 0$ and if graph if concave down ward then $a < 0$

- If graph cuts y-axis above origin then $c > 0$ and if it cuts below origin then $c < 0$

- For sign of b, we see that vertex lies in which quadrant then based on sign convention of cartesian system be get the sign of b.

* * * * *

PRACTICE EXERCISE - 6.1

6-1 If $ax^2+bx+c=0$ has equal roots then $c=$

(A) $\frac{-b}{2a}$ (B) $\frac{b}{2a}$

(C) $\frac{-b^2}{4a}$ (D) $\frac{b^2}{4a}$

6-2 If $x-\frac{1}{x-2}=2-\frac{1}{x-2}$ then x is equal to :

(A) 1 (B) 2

(C) 3 (D) None of these

6-3 The value of 'k' for which the roots of equation $(x-1)(x-5)+k=0$ differ by 2 is :

(A) 3 (B) 6

(C) -3 (D) 1/2

6-4 If the equation $ax^2-ax+1=0$ has two distinct roots, then which of the following could be the answer :

(A) $a=2$ (B) $a<2$

(C) $a>4$ (D) None of these

6-5 The condition for the roots of equation $x^2-lx+m=0$ to differ by one is :

(A) $l^2=4m+1$ (B) $l^2+m^2=1$

(C) $m^2=4l+1$ (D) $l=m+1$

6-6 If one root of a quadratic equation is $\frac{1}{\sqrt{4}-\sqrt{3}}$, then the quadratic equation can be :

(A) $x^2-2\sqrt{4}x+1=0$ (B) $x^2-\sqrt{4}x+1=0$

(C) $x^2+2\sqrt{4}x+1=0$ (D) $x^2-2\sqrt{3}x+1=0$

6-7 If $a = b = c$, then the roots of the equation $(x-a)(x-b)+(x-b)(x-c)+(x-c)(x-a)=0$ are :

(A) Only real (B) Imaginary

(C) Real and equal (D) Unequal

6-8 Find the number of zeros of $P(x)=(x+2)^2-3$

(A) 2 (B) 1

(C) 0 (D) 3

6-9 If one root of the equation $(k^2+1)x^2+13x+4k=0$ is reciprocal of the other then k has the value :

(A) $-2+\sqrt{3}$ (B) $2-\sqrt{3}$

(C) 1 (D) None of these

6-10 The values of α and β for which α, β are roots of $x^2-3\alpha x+\beta=0$ are :

(A) 1, 2 (B) 2, 1

(C) 1, 1 (D) $1, \frac{1}{2}$

6-11 If $x^2+3x+5=0$ and $ax^2+bx+2=0$ have a common root and $a, b \in R$, then minimum value of $a+b$ is equal to :

(A) 8 (B) $\frac{4}{5}$

(C) $\frac{8}{5}$ (D) None of these

6-12 For $a \neq b$, if the equations $x^2+ax+b=0$ and $x^2+bx+a=0$ has a common root, then value of $(a+b)$ is :

(A) -1 (B) 0

(C) 1 (D) 2

6-13 The set of values of p for which both roots of the equation $3x^2+2x+p(p-1)=0$ are positive is :

(A) $p \in \left(\frac{1}{3}, \frac{2}{3}\right)$ (B) $p \in \phi$

(C) $p \in (0, 1)$ (D) None of these

6-14 The polynomial x^2+4x+7 have :

(A) Two real zeros (B) One real zero

(C) No real zeros (D) None of these

6-15 Find the nature of roots of $(ax+b)^2+c^2=0$:

(A) Equal (B) Not real

(C) Rational (D) Irrational

6-16 If $(a-b)x^2+(b-c)x+(c-a)=0$ has equal roots, then roots are :

(A) 3, 3 (B) 2, 2

(C) 1, 1 (D) 4, 4

6-17 In equation $ax^2+bx+c=0$, if a & c are of opposite sign, then :

(A) Both roots are positive

(B) Both roots are negative

(C) Both roots are of opposite sign

(D) Can't say anything

6-18 If $x = \sqrt{7+4\sqrt{3}}$, then $x + \frac{1}{x} =$

(A) 4 (B) 6
(C) 3 (D) 2

6-19 The sides of a right-angled triangle (in cm) are $x-1$, x and $x+1$. Find x:

(A) 0 (B) 4
(C) 0, 4 (D) None of these

6-20 A two digit number is four times the sum and three times the product of its digits. Then the number is :

(A) 42 (B) 24
(C) 62 (D) 26

6-21 The roots of the equation $x^2 - x - a(a+1) = 0$ are :

(A) $a, a-1$ (B) $a+1, a$
(C) $a, 1-a$ (D) $-a, a+1$

6-22 If one root of $p(x) = ax^2 + bx + c$ is nth times of other then :

(A) $nb = ac(n+1)$ (B) $n^2b^2 = ac(n+1)^2$
(C) $nb^2 = ac(n+1)^2$ (D) $b = ac(n+1)^2$

6-23 If $\frac{x}{y} = \frac{3}{4}$ then the incorrect expression in the following is :

(A) $\frac{x+y}{y} = \frac{7}{4}$ (B) $\frac{y}{y-x} = \frac{4}{1}$
(C) $\frac{x+2y}{x} = \frac{11}{3}$ (D) $\frac{x}{2y} = -\frac{3}{8}$

6-24 If the roots of the equation $px^2 + 2qx + r = 0$ and $qx^2 - 2\sqrt{pr}\,x + q = 0$ be simultaneously real, then :

(A) $p = q$ (B) $q^2 = pr$
(C) $p^2 = qr$ (D) $r^2 = pq$

6-25 For what value of 'a' will the sum of squares of roots of the equation $x^2 - (a-2)x - a - 1 = 0$ have the least value :

(A) 0 (B) 1
(C) 2.5 (D) 6.4

6-26 The equation $ax^2 + bx + c = 0, a \neq 0$ has no real roots, if :

(A) $b^2 < 4ac$ (B) $b^2 > 4ac$
(C) $b^2 = 4ac$ (D) $b = 4ac$

6-27 The value of x satisfying the equation $x^2 + p^2 = (q-x)^2$ is:

(A) $\frac{q^2-p^2}{2}$ (B) $\frac{p^2-q^2}{2p}$
(C) $\frac{q^2-p^2}{2q}$ (D) $\frac{p^2-q^2}{2}$

6-28 How many values of x are there which satisfy the given equation :

$3^{2x} \times 2 - 5 \times 3^x - 3 = 0$

(A) 1 (B) 2
(C) 3 (D) 0

6-29 If α and β are roots of the equation $9x^2 - 14x - 8 = 0$ then find $\alpha - \beta$ if $\alpha > \beta$:

(A) 2 (B) $\frac{14}{9}$
(C) $\frac{-14}{9}$ (D) None of these

6-30 The equation $\sqrt{x+1} - \sqrt{x-1} = 1$ has :

(A) One real solution (B) Two real solutions
(C) No real solution (D) None of these

6-31 A quadratic equation always have :

(A) At least one real root (B) At most one real root
(C) Two real roots (D) None of these

6-32 The value of x which satisfy the equation $\frac{2}{x^2} - \frac{5}{x} + 2 = 0$ are :

(A) 2, 1 (B) $\frac{1}{2}, 3$
(C) $\frac{1}{2}, 2$ (D) $-\frac{1}{2}, -2$

6-33 If $x = \cfrac{1}{2 - \cfrac{1}{2 - \cfrac{1}{2-x}}}$, then $x =$

(A) 2 (B) -2
(C) -1 (D) 1

6-34 The perimeter of a rectangular field is 82 cm and its area is 400 cm^2 then its length is :

(A) 16 cm (B) 25 cm
(C) 25 or 16 cm (D) None of these

6-35 If $x = \sqrt{12 + \sqrt{12 + \sqrt{12 + \ldots\infty}}}$ then find x :

(A) 12 (B) 2
(C) 4 (D) 3

6-36 If α, β are the roots of the equation $x^2 - 3x + 2 = 0$, then the equation whose roots are $(\alpha + 1)$ and $(\beta + 1)$ is :

(A) $x^2 + 5x + 6 = 0$ (B) $x^2 - 5x - 6 = 0$
(C) $x^2 + 5x - 6 = 0$ (D) $x^2 - 5x + 6 = 0$

6-37 At how many points the curve of the function $f(x) = 4x^2 - 4x + 1$, intersect the x-axis :
(A) 1 (B) 2
(C) 0 (D) Can not be determined

6-38 If α, β are the roots of the equation $x^2 - 8x + p = 0$ and $\alpha^2 + \beta^2 = 40$, then p is equal to :
(A) 8 (B) 10
(C) 12 (D) 14

6-39 If three numbers are in ratio of 1 : 2 : 3 and half the sum is 18, then the ratio of squares of the number is :
(A) 6 : 12 : 13 (B) 1 : 2 : 4
(C) 36 : 144 : 324 (D) None of these

6-40 If r_1 and r_2 are the roots of $x^2 + bx + c = 0$ and $S_0 = r_1^0 + r_2^0$, $S_1 = r_1 + r_2$ and $S_2 = r_1^2 + r_2^2$, then the value of $S_2 + bS_1 + cS_0$ is :
(A) Depends on b only
(B) Depends on c only
(C) Depends on both b and c
(D) Does not dependent on b and c

6-41 A swimming pool is filled with three pipes with uniform flow. The first two pipes operating simultaneously, fill the pool in the sometime during which the pool is filled by the third pipe alone the second pipe fills the pool five hours faster than the first pipe and four hours slower than the third pipe the time required by each pipe to fill the pool separately :
(A) 10 h, 12 h, 6h (B) 15h, 10 h, 9h
(C) 15h, 10 h, 6h (D) None of these

6-42 If $\sin\theta$ and $\cos\theta$ are the roots of equation $ax^2 + bx + c = 0$, then :
(A) $b^2 + a^2 = 2ac$ (B) $b^2 - a^2 = 2ac$
(C) $b^2 - a^2 = ac$ (D) None of these

6-43 Two taps are running continuously to fill a tank. The 1st tap could have filled it in 5 hours by itself and the second one by itself could have filled it in 20 hours. But the operator failed to realise that there was leak in the tank from the beginning which caused a delay of one hour in the filling of the tank. Find the time in which the leak would empty a filled tank :
(A) 15 hours (B) 20 hours
(C) 25 hours (D) 40 hours

6-44 Rishikant, during his journey, travels for 20 minutes at a speed of 30 km/h, another 30 minutes at a speed of 50 km/h, and 1 hour at a speed of 50 km/h and 1 hour at a speed of 60 km/h. What is the average velocity? (approx)
(A) 51.18 km/h (B) 62 km/h
(C) 39 km/h (D) 48 km/h

6-45 If $\sqrt{2}$ and $-\sqrt{2}$ are two zeroes of $2x^4 - 3x^3 - 3x^2 + 6x - 2$ then other roots are :
(A) $1, -\frac{1}{2}$ (B) $-1, \frac{1}{2}$
(C) $1, \frac{1}{2}$ (D) $-1, -\frac{1}{2}$

6-46 If in applying the quadratic formula to a quadratic equation $f(x) = ax^2 + bx + c = 0$ it happens that $c = \frac{b^2}{4a}$, then the graph of $y = f(x)$ will certainly :
(A) Have a maximum
(B) Have a minimum
(C) Have a tangent parallel to the x-axis
(D) Have a tangent parallel to the y-axis

6-47 For what value of a, the equation $(a^2 - a - 2)x^2 + (a^2 - 4)x + a^2 - 3a + 2 = 0$ will have more than two solutions :
(A) $a = 2$ (B) $a = 1, 2$
(C) $a = 1$ (D) $a = 0$

6-48 If roots of
$$(a - 2b + c)x^2 + (b - 2c + a)x + (c - 2a + b) = 0$$
are equal, then :
(A) $a = b = c$ (B) $a = c$
(C) $a = 2b$ (D) $a = b$

6-49 Two trains leaves a railway station at the same time. The first train travels due west and the second train due north. The first train travels 5 km/hr faster than the second train. If after two hours, they air 50 km apart, find the average speed of each train : (in km / hr)
(A) 25, 15 (B) 15, 30
(C) 20, 15 (D) None of these

6-50 If $a + b + c = 0$ and equation $ax^2 + bx + c = 0$ has equal roots, then both roots are equal to :
(A) 0 (B) -1
(C) 1 (D) None of these

* * * * *

PRACTICE EXERCISE - 6.2

6-1 If $(x+a)^2+(y+b)^2=4(ax+by)$, where x, a, y, b are real, the value of $xy-ab$ is :
(A) a (B) 0
(C) b (D) None of these

6-2 If $x^2-x-1=0$, then the value of x^3-2x+1 is:
(A) 0 (B) 2
(C) $\frac{1+\sqrt{5}}{2}$ (D) $\frac{1-\sqrt{5}}{2}$

6-3 If a, b, c and d are natural numbers such that $a^5=b^6$, $c^3=d^4$, and $d-a=61$, then the smallest value of $c-b$ is :
(A) 61 (B) 122
(C) 239 (D) 593

6-4 The sum of real values of y satisfying the equations $x^2+x^2y^2+x^2y^4=525$ and $x+xy=xy^2=35$ is :
(A) 15 (B) 10
(C) 5/2 (D) 3/2

6-5 If $x+y+z=1$, then $1-3x^2-3y^2-3z^2+2x^3+2y^3+2z^3$ is equal to :
(A) $6xyz$ (B) $3xyz$
(C) $2xyz$ (D) xyz

6-6 If $(a-5)^2+(b-c)^2+(c-d)^2+(b+c+d-9)^2=0$, then the value of $(a+b+c)(b+c+d)$ is :
(A) 0 (B) 11
(C) 33 (D) 99

6-7 A cubic polynomial $p(x)$ is such that $p(1)=1, p(2)=2, p(3)=3$ and $p(4)=5$, then the value of $p(6)$ is :
(A) 16 (B) 13
(C) 10 (D) 7

6-8 If the zero of the polynomial $f(x)=k^2x^2-17x+k+2 (k>0)$ are reciprocal of each other, then the value of k is :
(A) 2 (B) -1
(C) -2 (D) 1

6-9 The sum of the reciprocals of the roots of the equation, $\frac{2009}{2010}x+1+\frac{1}{x}=0$, is:
(A) $-\frac{2010}{2009}$ (B) -1
(C) $\frac{2009}{2010}$ (D) 1

6-10 If α is a root, repeated twice, of the quadratic equation $(a-d)x^2+ax+(a+d)=0$ then $\frac{d^2}{a^2}$ has the value equal to :
(A) $\sin^2 90°$ (B) $\cos^2 60°$
(C) $\sin^2 45°$ (D) $\cos^2 30°$

6-11 If the sum of the roots of the equation $\frac{1}{x+a}+\frac{1}{x+b}=\frac{1}{c}$ is zero, then the product of roots is :
(A) $-(a^2+b^2)$ (B) a^2+b^2
(C) $\frac{a^2+b^2}{2}$ (D) $-\frac{a^2+b^2}{2}$

6-12 Product of real roots of equation $|x|^{6/5}-26|x|^{3/5}-27=0$ is :
(A) -3^{10} (B) -3^{12}
(C) $-3^{12/5}$ (D) $-3^{21/5}$

6-13 Number of roots of equation $(5+2\sqrt{6})^{x^2-3}+(5-2\sqrt{6})^{x^2-3}=10$ are:
(A) 4 (B) 3
(C) 2 (D) 1

6-14 The sum of the real roots of the equation $x^2+|x|-6=0$ is :
(A) 4 (B) 0
(C) -1 (D) None of these

6-15 If $-a+d$ and a are roots of $x^2+mx-15=0$, $-a$ and $a+d$ are roots of $x^2+nx-35=0$, then find $m+n$, given that $a>0$:
(A) 2 (B) 3
(C) 4 (D) -4

6-16 If one root of the equation $ax^2+bx+c=0$ be square of the other, then $3abc=$
(A) $b^3+a^2c+ac^2$ (B) $a^3+b^2c+bc^2$
(C) $c^3+ab^2+a^2b$ (D) None of these

6-17 If $ax^2+bx+c=0$ is an identity, then how many zeroes will be there :
(A) 0 (B) 2
(C) 1 (D) Infinite

6-18 The number of real values of x satisfying the equations $2\left(x^2+\frac{1}{x^2}\right)-9\left(x+\frac{1}{x}\right)+14=0$ is :
(A) 1 (B) 2
(C) 3 (D) 4

6-19 Number of real solutions of $(x-1)(x+1)(2x+1)(2x-3) = 15$ is :

(A) 0 (B) 2
(C) 3 (D) 4

6-20 The equation

$$\sqrt{x+1} - \sqrt{x-1} = \sqrt{4x-1}, (x \in R):$$

(A) No solution (B) One solution
(C) Two solution (D) More than two solutions

6-21 The sum of all the real roots of the equation $|x-2|^2 + |x-2| - 2 = 0$ is :

(A) 7 (B) 4
(C) 1 (D) None of these

6-22 The roots of equation $|x^2 - x - 6| = x + 2$ are :

(A) $-2, 1, 4$ (B) $0, 2, 4$
(C) $0, 1, 4$ (D) $-2, 2, 4$

6-23 The number of real roots of :

$$\left(\frac{x-1}{x+1}\right)^4 - 13\left(\frac{x-1}{x+1}\right)^2 + 36 = 0, x \neq -1 \text{ is}:$$

(A) 0 (B) 2
(C) 3 (D) 4

6-24 The number of negative roots of $9^{x+2} - 6(3^{x+1}) + 1 = 0$ is :

(A) 0 (B) 1
(C) 2 (D) 4

6-25 Find which of the following is true in reference to the graph of $p(x) = ax^2 + bx + c$:

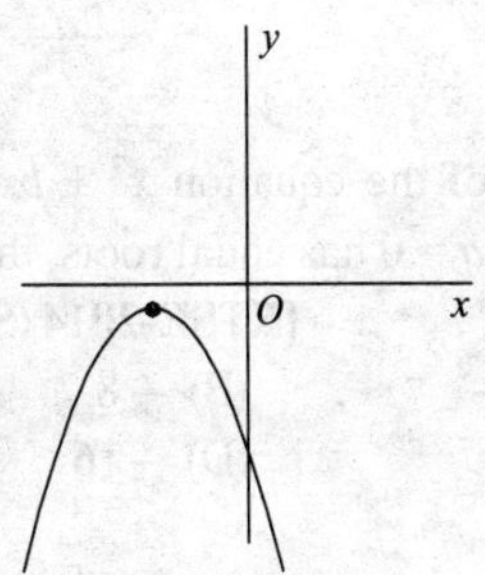

Figure 6.1

(A) $a<0, b<0, c<0$ (B) $a>0, b>0, c<0$
(C) $a>0, b>0, c<0$ (D) $a<0, b>0, c<0$

* * * * *

PRACTICE EXERCISE - 6.3

6-1 If $b^2 - 4ac \geq 0$ then the roots of quadratic equation $ax^2 + bx + c = 0$ is : **[NTSE-2013 (Stage-I) Rajasthan]**

(A) $\frac{b}{2a} \pm \frac{\sqrt{b^2 - 4ac}}{2a}$ (B) $-\frac{b}{2a} \pm \sqrt{\frac{b^2 - 4ac}{2a}}$

(C) $\frac{b}{2a} \pm \frac{\sqrt{b^2 + 4ac}}{2a}$ (D) $-\frac{b}{2a} \pm \frac{\sqrt{b^2 - 4ac}}{2a}$

6-2 If 2 is a root of the equation $x^2 + bx + 12 = 0$ and the equation $x^2 + bx + q = 0$ has equal roots, then q is equal to : **[NTSE-2014 (Stage-I) Rajasthan]**

(A) 8 (B) -8
(C) 16 (D) -16

6-3 The roots of the equation $3x^2 - 4\sqrt{3}x + 4 = 0$ are : **[NTSE-2015 (Stage-I) MP]**

(A) Real and unequal (B) Real and equal
(C) Imaginary (D) Real and Imaginary both

6-4 The difference of the squares of two numbers is 180. The square of the smaller number is 8 times the larger number. The two numbers are : **[NTSE-2015 (Stage-I) MP]**

(A) 32, 4 (B) 24, 8
(C) 16, 2 (D) 18, 12

6-5 The sum of squares of the two consecutive natural numbers is 421, the numbers are : **[NTSE-2015 (Stage-I) MP]**

(A) 14, 15 (B) 21, 22
(C) 9, 10 (D) 17, 18

6-6 Let $\alpha \neq \beta$, $\alpha^2 + 3 = 5\alpha$ and $\beta^2 = 5\beta - 3$. The quadratic equation whose roots are $\frac{\alpha}{\beta}$ and $\frac{\beta}{\alpha}$ will be : **[NTSE-2015 (Stage-I) Delhi]**

(A) $3x^2 - 19x + 3 = 0$ (B) $3x^2 + 19x + 3 = 0$
(C) $3x^2 - 19x - 3 = 0$ (D) $3x^2 - 3x + 1 = 0$

6-7 If roots of equation $2x^2 - 8x + c = 0$ are equal. Then the value of c will be : **[NTSE-2015 (Stage-I) UP]**

(A) 2 (B) 4
(C) 6 (D) 8

6-8 The difference between the two roots of a quadratic equation is 2 and the difference between the cubes of the roots is 98, then which of the following is that quadratic equation ? **[NTSE-2015 (Stage-I) Maharashtra]**

(A) $x^2 - 2x + 15 = 0$ (B) $x^2 + 2x - 15 = 0$
(C) $x^2 + 5x + 15 = 0$ (D) $x^2 - 5x - 15 = 0$

6-9 One of the root of a quadratic equation is $(3 - \sqrt{2})$, then which of the following is that equation : **[NTSE-2015 (Stage-I) Maharashtra]**

(A) $(x^2 - 6x - 7) = 0$ (B) $(x^2 + 6x - 7) = 0$
(C) $(x^2 + 6x + 7) = 0$ (D) $(x^2 - 6x + 7) = 0$

6-10 For what value of k, the equation $3x^2 + 2x + k = 0$ will have real roots : **[NTSE-2015 (Stage-I) MP]**

(A) $k \leq \frac{1}{3}$ (B) $k \geq \frac{1}{3}$
(C) $k = \frac{2}{3}$ only (D) None of the above

6-11 The product of Meera's age 5 years ago and her age 8 years later is 30. Her present age is : **[NTSE-2015 (Stage-I) MP]**

(A) 11 years (B) 9 years
(C) 7 years (D) 5 years

6-12 If α and β are the zeros of the polynomials $25x^2 - 16$, then $\alpha^2 + \beta^2$ is : **[NTSE-2015 (Stage-I) Chennai]**

(A) $\frac{32}{25}$ (B) $\frac{25}{32}$
(C) $\frac{25}{16}$ (D) $\frac{16}{25}$

6-13 If the roots of a quadratic equation $2x^2 + 3kx + 8 = 0$ are equal, the value of k is : **[NTSE-2016 (Stage-I) Rajasthan]**

(A) $\pm\frac{2}{3}$ (B) $\pm\frac{3}{2}$
(C) $\pm\frac{3}{8}$ (D) $\pm\frac{8}{3}$

6-14 If the roots of quadratic equation $x^2 + px + q = 0$ are tan 30° and tan 15° respectively, then the value of $2 + q - p = \ldots$ **[NTSE-2016 (Stage-I) Andhara Pradesh]**

(A) 3 (B) 4
(C) -1 (D) -2

6-15 If α and β be the zeroes of the polynomial $ax^2 + bx + c$, then the value of $\sqrt{\frac{\alpha}{\beta}} + \sqrt{\frac{\beta}{\alpha}}$ is : **[NTSE-2016 (Stage-I) Chandigarh]**

(A) b (B) $\frac{-b}{\sqrt{ac}}$
(C) $\frac{-b}{ac}$ (D) $\frac{1}{ac}$

6-16 If – 4 is a root of the quadratic equation $x^2 + px - 4 = 0$ and the quadratic equation $x^2 + px + k = 0$ has equal roots, find the value of k : **[NTSE-2016 (Stage-I) Chandigarh]**

(A) $\frac{3}{4}$ (B) $\frac{7}{4}$

(C) $\frac{2}{9}$ (D) $\frac{9}{4}$

6-17 The value of $\sqrt{6+\sqrt{6+\sqrt{6+\ldots}}}$ is : **[NTSE-2016 (Stage-I) Chandigarh]**

(A) 4 (B) 3

(C) – 4 (D) 3.5

6-18 If $x = 1$ a common root of the equations $ax^2 + ax + 3 = 0$ and $x^2 + x + b = 0$, then ab : **[NTSE-2016 (Stage-I) Chandigarh]**

(A) 3 (B) 3.5

(C) 6 (D) – 3

6-19 If $\frac{x^2 - bx}{ax - c} = \frac{m-1}{m+1}$, has roots which are numerically equal but of opposite signs, the value of m must be : **[NTSE-2016 (Stage-I) Delhi]**

(A) $(a - b).(a + b)$ (B) $(a + b)/(a - b)$

(C) c (D) $\frac{1}{c}$

6-20 In the figure-6.2 $\angle D = 90°$ $AB = 16$ cm, $BC = 12$ cm and $CA = 6$ cm, then CD is : **NTSE-2016 (Stage-I) Delhi]**

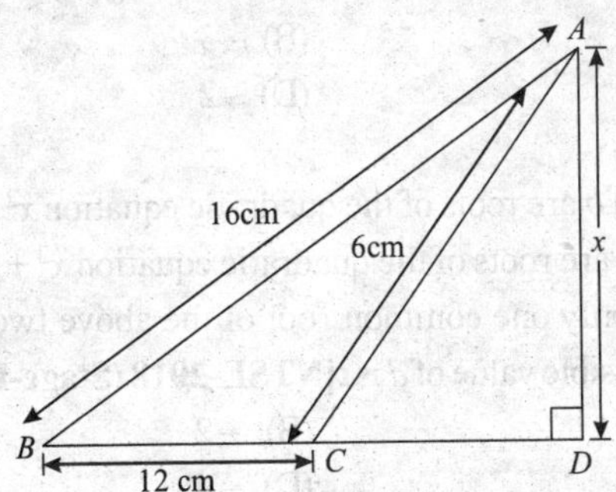

Figure 6.2

(A) $\frac{13}{6}$ cm (B) $\frac{17}{6}$ cm

(C) $\frac{19}{6}$ cm (D) $\frac{18}{5}$ cm

6-21 What is the solution of the equation $3 \times 5^{2x-1} - 2 \times 5^{x-1} = 0.2$? **[NTSE-2016 (Stage-I) Odisha]**

(A) $x = 5$ (B) $x = 1$

(C) $x = -1$ (D) $x = 0$

6-22 If α and β are the roots of the quadratic equation $4x^2 - 20x = p^2$, what is the difference between α and β ? **[NTSE-2016 (Stage-I) Odisha]**

(A) $\sqrt{25+p^2}$ (B) $\sqrt{25-p^2}$

(C) $5+p$ (D) $5-p$

6-23 The sum of squares of two successive natural numbers is 145. The numbers will be : **[NTSE-2016 (Stage-I) Chhatisgarh]**

(A) 6, 7 (B) 7, 8

(C) 8, 9 (D) 9, 10

6-24 Find the quadratic equation whose one root is $2+\sqrt{5}$: **[NTSE-2016 (Stage-I) Chhatisgarh]**

(A) $x^2 - 4x + 1 = 0$ (B) $x^2 - 4x - 1 = 0$

(C) $x^2 - 4x + 3 = 0$ (D) $x^2 - 4x - 3 = 0$

6-25 If quadratic equation $x^2 + px + k = 0$ has equal roots and –4 is a root of the quadratic equation $x^2 + px - 4 = 0$, then the value of k is : **[NTSE-2017 (Stage-I) Haryana]**

(A) $\frac{3}{2}$ (B) $\frac{-3}{2}$

(C) $\frac{-9}{4}$ (D) $\frac{9}{4}$

6-26 a and b are roots of a quadratic equation $x^2 + 5x + d = 0$, while a and c are the roots of the quadratic equation $x^2 + 6x + 2d = 0$. If there is only one common root in the two equations, then value of d is : **[NTSE-2017 (Stage-I) Haryana]**

(A) –2 (B) –4

(C) 2 (D) 4

6-27 If – 4 is a root of the quadratic equation $x^2 + px - 4 = 0$ and the equation $x^2 + px + m = 0$ has equal roots, then the value of "m" is : **[NTSE-2017 (Stage-I) Karnataka]**

(A) – 4 (B) $\frac{9}{4}$

(C) +4 (D) $\frac{-25}{4}$

6-28 A quadratic equation $ax^2 + bx + c = 0$ has no real roots, if : **[NTSE-2017 (Stage-I) Madhya Pradesh]**

(A) $b^2 = 4ac = 0$ (B) $b^2 > 4ac$

(C) $b^2 < 4ac$ (D) $b^2 + 4ac = 0$

6-29 Which of the following are the roots of the quadratic equation $x^2 + 2\sqrt{2}x - 60$? **[NTSE-2017 (Stage-I) Maharashtra]**

(A) $-3\sqrt{2}, \sqrt{2}$ (B) $3\sqrt{2}, -2\sqrt{2}$

(C) 3, 2 (D) $3, 2\sqrt{2}$

6-30 The number obtained by adding 12 to a natural number is 160 times of the multiplicative inverse of that natural number. Find the number : **[NTSE-2017 (Stage-I) Maharashtra]**

(A) 20 (B) 16
(C) 12 (D) 8

6-31 For which positive values of k and p, equations $2x^2 + px + 8 = 0$ and $p(x^2 + x) + k = 0$ have equal roots ? **[NTSE-2017 (Stage-I) Rajasthan]**

(A) $k=1, p=4$ (B) $k=2, p=8$
(C) $k=4, p=8$ (D) $k=2, p=4$

6-32 If α, β are zeros of polynomial $x^2 - p(x+1) - k$ such that $(\alpha+1)(\beta+1) = 6$, then value of k is : **[NTSE-2017 (Stage-I) Rajasthan]**

(A) 5 (B) -1
(C) -3 (D) -5

6-33 The number 50 is divided into two parts such that the sum of their reciprocals is $\frac{1}{12}$ then these parts are : **[NTSE-2017 (Stage-I) Uttar Pradesh]**

(A) 30 and 20 (B) 10 and 40
(C) 25 and 25 (D) 15 and 35

6-34 If $ax^2 + bx + c = a(x-p)^2$, the relation among a, b, and c is : **[NTSE-2017 (Stage-I) West Bengal]**

(A) $abc = 1$ (B) $2b = a + c$
(C) $b^2 = ac$ (D) $b^2 = 4ac$

6-35 The number of real roots of the quadratic equation $3x^2 + 4 = 0$ is : **[NTSE-2017 (Stage-I) West Bengal]**

(A) 0 (B) 2
(C) 1 (D) 4

6-36 If the roots of $(b-c)x^2 + (c-a)x + (a-b) = 0$ are real and equal, than which of the following is true : **[NTSE-2018 (Stage-I) Rajasthan]**

(A) $2b = a + c$ (B) $2a = b + c$
(C) $2c = a + b$ (D) $2b = a - c$

6-37 If the equation $(k + 3)x^2 - (5 - k)x + 1 = 0$ has distinct roots, the value of k will be : **[NTSE-2018 (Stage-I) Andhra Pradesh]**

(A) $k = 1$ or $k = 13$ (B) $k < 13$ or $k > 1$
(C) $k > 12$ or $k < 1$ (D) $k > 13$ or $k < 1$

6-38 If the roots of the equation $(b-c)x^2 + (c-a)x + (a-b) = 0$ are equal, then $\frac{a+c}{b} =$ **[NTSE-2018 (Stage-I) Andhra Pradesh]**

(A) 4 (B) 2
(C) 3 (D) 1

6-39 If the sum of the squares of the roots of quadratic polynomial $f(x) = x^2 - 8x + k$ is 40, then $k =$ **[NTSE-2018 (Stage-I) Andhra Pradesh]**

(A) 18 (B) 6
(C) 12 (D) 36

6-40 If the sum of the roots of the equation $x^2 - x = \lambda(2x - 1)$ is zero, then the value of λ : **[NTSE-2018 (Stage-I) Andhra Pradesh]**

(A) $\frac{1}{2}$ (B) $-\frac{1}{2}$
(C) 2 (D) -2

6-41 If the product of the roots of the equation $x^2 - 2\sqrt{2}\,kx + 2e^{2\log k} - 1 = 0$ is 31, then the roots of the equations are real for k equal to : **[NTSE-2018 (Stage-I) Bihar]**

(A) 4 (B) 3
(C) 2 (D) 1

6-42 A certain number of tennis balls were purchased for 450. Five more balls could have been purchased for the same amount if each ball was cheap by Rs.15. The number of balls purchased is... **[NTSE-2018 (Stage-I) Bihar]**

(A) 15 (B) 20
(C) 25 (D) 10

6-43 In a quadratic equaition $x^2 + ax + 3 = 0$, if one of the roots is 1, then other root will be : **[NTSE-2018 (Stage-I) Chhattisgarh]**

(A) 3 (B) -3
(C) 2 (D) -2

6-44 a and b are roots of the quadratic equation $x^2 + 5x + d = 0$ and a and c are roots of the quadratic equation $x^2 + 6x + 2d = 0$. If there is only one common root of the above two equations, then the possible value of d is : **[NTSE-2018 (Stage-I) Haryana]**

(A) 2 (B) -2
(C) 4 (D) -4

6-45 There are 15 APs whose comman differences are 1, 2, 3........, 15 respectively, the first term of each being 1. Then sum of their 15th terms is : **[NTSE-2018 (Stage-I) Haryana]**

(A) 1695 (B) 1792
(C) 1800 (D) 1924

6-46 If $2^{x-1} + 2^{x+1} = 2560$, find the value of x : **[NTSE-2018 (Stage-I) Jharkhand]**

(A) 10 (B) 12
(C) 9 (D) 8

6-47 If the roots of $x^2-px+q=0$ are two consecutive integers the value of p^2-4q is : **[NTSE-2018 (Stage-I) Karnataka]**

(A) 4 (B) 3
(C) 2 (D) 1

6-48 If $\alpha+\beta=-3$ and $\alpha\beta=-\frac{5}{2}$ then find the quadratic equation whose roots are α and β : **[NTSE-2018 (Stage-I) Maharashtra]**

(A) $2x^2-5x+6=0$ (B) $2x^2-6x+5=0$
(C) $2x^2+6x-5=0$ (D) $2x^2-6x+5=0$

6-49 If roots of the quadratic equation $3ax^2+2bx+c=0$ are in the ratio 2 : 3 then which of the following statement is true : **[NTSE-2018 (Stage-I) Maharashtra]**

(A) $8ac=25b$ (B) $8ac=9b^2$
(C) $8b^2=9ac$ (D) $8b^2=25ac$

6-50 If the roots of the equation $(a^2+b^2)x^2-2b(a+c)x+(b^2+c^2)=0$ are equal, then : **[NTSE-2018 (Stage-I) Tamil Nadu]**

(A) $2b=a+c$ (B) $b=\frac{2ac}{a+c}$
(C) $b^2=ac$ (D) $b=ac$

6-51 If $5^{x+1}+5^{2-x}=126$ then x is equal to : **[NTSE-2018 (Stage-I) Uttar Pradesh]**

(A) −2, −1 (B) 1, −2
(C) −1, 3 (D) 2, −1

6-52 If the roots of the equation $(a-b)x^2+(b-c)x+(c-a)=0$, are equal then the value of $b+c$ will be : **[NTSE-2018 (Stage-I) Uttarakhandh]**

(A) $6a$ (B) $-6a$
(C) $2a$ (D) $-2a$

6-53 $ax^2+bx+c=0$, where a, b, c are real, has real roots if : **[NTSE-2013 (Stage-II)]**

(A) a, b, c are integers (B) $b^2>3ac$
(C) $ac>0$ and b is zero (D) $c=0$

6-54 The minimum value of the polynomial $p(x)=3x^2-5x+2$ is : **[NTSE-2014 (Stage-II)]**

(A) $-\frac{1}{6}$ (B) $\frac{1}{6}$
(C) $\frac{1}{12}$ (D) $-\frac{1}{12}$

6-55 If α and β are the roots of the quadratic equation $x^2-6x-2=0$ and if $a_n=\alpha^n-\beta^n$, then the value of $\frac{a_{10}-2a_8}{2a_9}$ is : **[NTSE-2015 (Stage-II)]**

(A) 6.0 (B) 5.2
(C) 5.0 (D) 3.0

6-56 Two quadratic equations $x^2-bx+6=0$ and $x^2-6x+c=0$ have a common root. If the remaining roots of the first and second equations are positive integers and are in the ration 3 : 4 respectively, then the common root is : **[NTSE-2016 (Stage-II)]**

(A) 1 (B) 2
(C) 3 (D) 4

6-57 If the discriminants of two quadratic equations are equal and the equations have a common root 1, then the other roots : **[NTSE-2016 (Stage-II)]**

(A) are either equal or their sum is 2
(B) have to be always equal
(C) are either equal or their sum is 1
(D) have their sum equal to 1

6-58 If the quadratic equation $x^2+bx+72=0$ has two distinct integer roots, then the number of all possible value for b is : **[NTSE-2016 (Stage-II)]**

(A) 12 (B) 9
(C) 15 (D) 18

6-59 The values of k, so that the equations $2x^2+kx-5=0$ and $x^2-3x-4=0$ have one root in common, are : **[NTSE-2017 (Stage-II)]**

(A) $3, \frac{27}{2}$ (B) $9, \frac{27}{4}$
(C) $-3, \frac{27}{4}$ (D) $-3, \frac{4}{27}$

* * * * *

ANSWERS

PRACTICE EXERCISE-6.1

1	(D)	2	(D)	3	(A)
4	(C)	5	(A)	6	(A)
7	(C)	8	(A)	9	(B)
10	(A)	11	(C)	12	(A)
13	(B)	14	(C)	15	(B)
16	(C)	17	(C)	18	(A)
19	(B)	20	(B)	21	(D)
22	(C)	23	(D)	24	(B)
25	(B)	26	(A)	27	(C)
28	(A)	29	(D)	30	(A)
31	(D)	32	(C)	33	(D)
34	(C)	35	(C)	36	(D)
37	(A)	38	(C)	39	(C)
40	(D)	41	(C)	42	(B)
43	(B)	44	(B)	45	(C)
46	(C)	47	(A)	48	(A)
49	(C)	50	(C)		

PRACTICE EXERCISE-6.2

1	(B)	2	(B)	3	(D)
4	(C)	5	(A)	6	(D)
7	(A)	8	(B)	9	(B)
10	(D)	11	(D)	12	(A)
13	(A)	14	(B)	15	(D)
16	(A)	17	(D)	18	(C)
19	(B)	20	(A)	21	(B)
22	(D)	23	(D)	24	(B)
25	(D)				

PRACTICE EXERCISE-6.3

1	(D)	2	(C)	3	(D)
4	(B)	5	(A)	6	(C)
7	(D)	8	(D)	9	(D)
10	(A)	11	(C)	12	(A)
13	(D)	14	(A)	15	(B)
16	(D)	17	(B)	18	(A)
19	(A)	20	(C)	21	(D)
22	(A)	23	(C)	24	(B)
25	(D)	26	(D)	27	(B)
28	(C)	29	(A)	30	(D)
31	(B)	32	(D)	33	(A)
34	(D)	35	(A)	36	(A)
37	(D)	38	(B)	39	(C)
40	(B)	41	(A)	42	(D)
43	(A)	44	(C)	45	(A)
46	(A)	47	(D)	48	(C)
49	(D)	50	(C)	51	(D)
52	(C)	53	(D)	54	(D)
55	(D)	56	(B)	57	(A)
58	(A)	59	(C)		

Solutions of PRACTICE EXERCISE-6.1

Sol. 1 (D) Given $ax^2+bx+c=0 \begin{cases}\alpha\\ \alpha\end{cases}$

if equal roots are there then

$$D=0$$

$$\Rightarrow \quad b^2-4ac=0$$

$$c=\frac{b^2}{4a}$$

Hence Ans is (D)

Sol. 2 (D) Given $x-\dfrac{1}{x-2}=2-\dfrac{1}{x-2}$

above equation say $x \neq 2$

Hence Ans is (D)

Sol. 3 (A) Given $(x-1)(x-5)+k=0 \begin{cases}\alpha\\ \beta\end{cases}$

On simplifying we get

$$x^2-6x+(5+k)=0 \begin{cases}\alpha\\ \beta\end{cases}$$

given $\qquad \alpha-\beta=2 \qquad \ldots(1)$

& here $\qquad \alpha+\beta=6 \qquad \ldots(2)$

Solving (1) & (2) we get

$$2\alpha=8$$

$$\Rightarrow \quad \alpha=4$$

$$\& \quad \beta=2$$

also $\qquad \alpha\beta=\dfrac{5+k}{1}$

$$4\times 2=5+k$$

$$\Rightarrow \quad k=3$$

Hence Ans is (A)

Sol. 4 (C) Given,

$$D>0$$

$$\Rightarrow \quad b^2-4ac>0$$

$$\Rightarrow \quad (-a)^2-4.a.1>0$$

$$\Rightarrow \quad a^2-4a>0$$

$$\Rightarrow \quad a(a-4)>0$$

0 4

$$a<0$$

or $\qquad a>4$

Hence Ans is (C)

Sol. 5 (A) Given,

$$x^2 - lx + m = 0 \quad \alpha,\ \alpha + 1 = \beta$$

Sum of the roots

$$\alpha + \beta = -\frac{(-l)}{1}$$

$\Rightarrow$ $\alpha + \beta = l$

$\Rightarrow$ $2\alpha + 1 = l$

$\Rightarrow$ $\alpha = \left(\frac{l-1}{2}\right)$

Product of roots

$$\alpha\beta = m$$

$$\alpha(\alpha + 1) = m$$

$\Rightarrow$ $\frac{(l-1)}{2}\cdot\left(\frac{l-1}{2}+1\right) = m$

$\Rightarrow$ $\frac{(l-1)}{2}\cdot\frac{(l+1)}{2} = m$

$\Rightarrow$ $l^2 - 1 = 4m$

$\Rightarrow$ $l^2 = 1 + 4m$

Hence Ans is (A)

Sol. 6 (A) Given

$$\alpha = \frac{1}{\sqrt{4}-\sqrt{3}} \times \frac{\sqrt{4}+\sqrt{3}}{\sqrt{4}+\sqrt{3}}$$

$$\alpha = \sqrt{4} + \sqrt{3}$$

then $\beta = \sqrt{4} - \sqrt{3}$

[irrational roots always occur in conjugate pairs]

required equation will be

$$x^2 - (\alpha + \beta)x + \alpha\beta = 0$$

$\Rightarrow$ $x^2 - (\sqrt{4}+\sqrt{3}+\sqrt{4}-\sqrt{3})\,x + (\sqrt{4}+\sqrt{3})\,(\sqrt{4}-\sqrt{3}) = 0$

$\Rightarrow$ $x^2 - 2\cdot\sqrt{4}x + 1 = 0$

$\Rightarrow$ $x^2 - 4x + 1 = 0$

Hence Ans is (A)

Sol. 7 (C) Given $a = b = c$

$$(x-a)(x-b) + (x-b)(x-c) + (x-c)(x-a) = 0$$

$\Rightarrow$ $3x^2 - 2(a+b+c)x + ab + bc + ca = 0$

We know

$$D = B^2 - 4AC$$

$\Rightarrow$ $[-2(a+b+c)]^2 - 4.3.(ab+bc+ca)$

$\Rightarrow$ $4(a+b+c)^2 - 4.3(ab+bc+ca)$

$\Rightarrow$ $4[a^2+b^2+c^2-ab-bc-ca]$

$\Rightarrow$ $2[2a^2+2b^2+2c^2-2ab-2bc-2cc]$

$\Rightarrow$ $2[(a-b)^2+(b-c)^2+(c-a)^2]$

$\Rightarrow$ 0 [given $a = b = c$]

Since $D = 0$

roots are real & equal

Hence Ans is (C)

Sol. 8 (A) Given

$$P(x) = (x+2)^2 - 3$$

$$P(x) = 0$$

$$x^2 + 4x + 4 - 3 = 0$$

$$x^2 + 4x + 1 = 0$$

Now $D > 0$

So two real zeros

Hence Ans is (A)

Sol. 9 (B) $(k^2+1)x^2 + 13x + 4k = 0 \quad \alpha,\ \beta$

Given $\beta = \frac{1}{\alpha}$

$$\alpha\beta = \frac{4k}{k^2+1}$$

$$1 = \frac{4k}{k^2+1}$$

$$k^2 + 1 = 4k$$

$$k^2 - 4k + 1 = 0$$

$$k = -\frac{(-4) \pm \sqrt{(-4)^2 - 4\times 1|x|}}{2\times 1}$$

as $k = \frac{-b \pm \sqrt{b^2-4ac}}{2a}$

$$k = \frac{4 \pm \sqrt{16-4}}{2}$$

$$= \frac{4 \pm 2\sqrt{3}}{2}$$

$$= 2 \pm \sqrt{3}$$

Hence Ans is (B)

Sol. 10 (A) Given $x^2 - 3\alpha x + \beta = 0 \quad \alpha,\ \beta$

$$\alpha + \beta = 3\alpha$$

$$2\alpha = \beta$$

& $\alpha\beta = \frac{\beta}{1}$

$$\alpha\beta - \beta = 0$$

$\Rightarrow$ $\beta(\alpha - 1) = 0$

$\Rightarrow$ $\alpha - 1 = 0$

$\Rightarrow$ $\alpha = 1$ or $\beta = 0$

if $\alpha = 1$, then $\beta = 2$ or if $\beta = 0$ then $\alpha = 0$

Hence Ans is (A)

Sol. 11 (C) Consider,

$$x^2+3x+5=0 \quad \ldots(1)$$

and $$ax^2+bx+2=0 \quad \ldots(2)$$

Since discriminant of (1) is less than zero.

So roots are imaginary hence both roots will be in conjugate pair ⇒ (1) & (2) are identical.

$$\Rightarrow \quad \frac{1}{a}=\frac{3}{b}=\frac{5}{2}$$

$$\Rightarrow \quad a=\frac{2}{5}$$

& $$b=\frac{6}{5}$$

So $$a+b=\frac{8}{5}$$

Hence Ans is (C)

Sol. 12 (A) Given

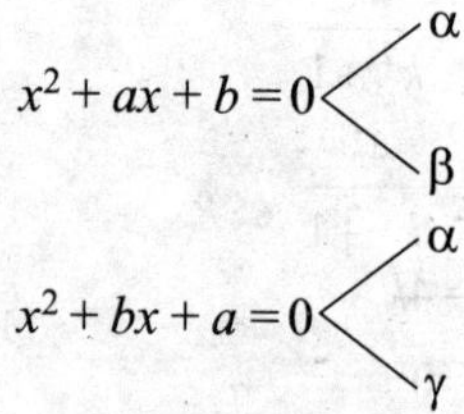

Let α be the common roots

$$\alpha^2+a\alpha+b=0 \quad \ldots(1)$$

$$\alpha^2+b\alpha+a=0 \quad \ldots(2)$$

Subtract

(2) from (1)

$$(a-b)\alpha+(b-a)=0$$

$$(a-b)\,\alpha=(a-b)$$

$$\alpha=1$$

So α satisfies (1) & (2)

hence $$1+a+b=0$$

$$a+b=-1$$

Hence Ans is (A)

Sol. 13 (B) Given

$$3x^2+2x+p(p-1)=0 \begin{cases}\alpha\\ \beta\end{cases}$$

Since $$\alpha \,\&\, \beta = \in R^+$$

$$\Rightarrow \quad \alpha+\beta \in R^+ \,\&\, \alpha\beta \in R^+$$

Here $$\alpha+\beta=-\frac{2}{3}$$

Hence Ans is (B)

Sol. 14 (C) Since

$$D=4^2-4\times 7\times 1$$

$$=16-28$$

$$=-12<0$$

So no real zero

Hence Ans is (C)

Sol. 15 (B) Given $(ax+b)^2+c^2=0$ the sum of two perfect square terms can never be zero. For any real value of 'x'

Hence Ans is (B)

Sol. 16 (C) Given $(a-b)x^2+(b-c)x+(c-a)=0$

Clearly $x=1$ satisfies the equation

Hence $x=1$ is a root of the equation, it's given roots are equal.

Hence Ans is (C)

Sol. 17 (C) Given $ax^2+bx+c=0 \begin{cases}\alpha\\ \beta\end{cases}$

$$\alpha\beta=\frac{c}{a}$$

$$\Rightarrow \quad \alpha\beta<0$$

as c & a are of opposite sign.

Hence α and β are also of opposite sign.

Hence Ans is (C)

Sol. 18 (A) If $$x=\sqrt{7+4\sqrt{3}}$$

$$x=\sqrt{7+2\sqrt{3\times 4}}$$

$$x=\sqrt{(\sqrt{4}+\sqrt{3})^2}$$

$$x=\sqrt{4}+\sqrt{3}$$

$$\frac{1}{x}=\frac{1}{\sqrt{4}+\sqrt{3}}=\sqrt{4}-\sqrt{3}$$

$$\Rightarrow \quad x+\frac{1}{x}=\sqrt{4}+\sqrt{3}+\sqrt{4}-\sqrt{3}$$

$$\Rightarrow \quad x+\frac{1}{x}=2\sqrt{4}$$

$$\Rightarrow \quad x+\frac{1}{x}=4$$

Hence Ans is (A)

Sol. 19 (B) Given $(x-1)$, x & $(x+1)$ are side of right angled Δ

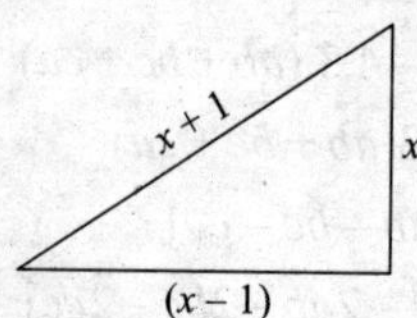

then apply pythagoras theorem

$$(x+1)^2 = x^2 + (x-1)^2$$
$\Rightarrow$ $x^2 + 1 + 2x = x^2 + x^2 + 1 - 2x$
$\Rightarrow$ $x^2 - 4x = 0$
$\Rightarrow$ $x(x-4) = 0$
$\Rightarrow$ $x \neq 0$
$\Rightarrow$ $x = 4$

Hence Ans is (B)

Sol. 20 (B) Let two digit also be $10x + y$

Given $10x + y = 4(x+y)$
$\Rightarrow$ $6x = 3y$
$\Rightarrow$ $y = 2x$ ...(1)

Also $10x + y = 3xy$
$\Rightarrow$ $10x + 2x = 3x.2x$ [from (1)]
$\Rightarrow$ $12x = 6x^2$
$\Rightarrow$ $6x^2 - 12x = 0$
$\Rightarrow$ $6x(x-2) = 0$
$x = 2$ as $x \neq 0$
$\Rightarrow$ $y = 4$

Number is
$$10x + y = 10 \times 2 + 4 = 24$$

Hence Ans is (B)

Sol. 21 (D) Apply quadratic formula.
$$x = \frac{-b \pm \sqrt{b^2 - 4ac}}{2a}$$
$\Rightarrow$ $x = 1 \pm \dfrac{\sqrt{1 + 4a(a+1)}}{2}$
$\Rightarrow$ $1 \pm 1 \pm \dfrac{\sqrt{1 + 4a^2 + 4a}}{2} = \dfrac{1 \pm (2a+1)}{2}$
$\Rightarrow$ $x = \dfrac{1 + 2a + 1}{2} = a + 1$
$\Rightarrow$ $x = \dfrac{1 - 2a - 1}{2}\; x = -a$

Hence Ans is (D)

Sol. 22 (C) Given
$$\alpha = n\beta$$
we know $\alpha + \beta = \dfrac{-b}{a}$
$\Rightarrow$ $\alpha + n\beta = -\dfrac{b}{a}$
$\Rightarrow$ $\beta(n+1) = \dfrac{-b}{a}$ ...(1)
$$\beta = \frac{-b}{a(n+1)}$$
$$\alpha\beta = c/a$$
$$n\beta^2 = \frac{c}{a}$$
$n \cdot \dfrac{b^2}{a^2(n+1)^2} = \dfrac{c}{a}$ [from (1)]
$$nb^2 = ac(n+1)^2$$

Hence Ans is (C)

Sol. 23 (D) Substitute the given value
$$\frac{x}{y} = \frac{3}{4}$$
in each option and check

Hence Ans is (D)

Sol. 24 (B) $px^2 + 2qx + r = 0$ ...(1)

& $qx^2 - 2\sqrt{pr}\,x + q = 0$ ...(2)

root are simultaneously real implied

$D \geq 0$ per both equation

$(2q)^2 - 4pr \geq 0$ for equation (1)

$(-2\sqrt{pr})^2 - 4q.q \geq 0$ for equation (2)

$\Rightarrow$ $4q^2 \geq 4pr$
$\Rightarrow$ $q^2 \geq pr$ for (1)
$4pr \geq 4q^2$
$\Rightarrow$ $pr \geq q^2$ for (2)
$\Rightarrow$ $q^2 = pr$

Hence Ans is (B)

Sol. 25 (B) $x^2 - (a-2)x - a - 1 = 0$ (roots α, β)

We know $\alpha + \beta = a - 2$
$\alpha\beta = -(a+1)$

for minimum value of
$$\alpha^2 + \beta^2 = (\alpha+\beta)^2 - 2\alpha\beta$$
$\Rightarrow$ $(a-2)^2 - 2.[-(a+1)]$
$\Rightarrow$ $a^2 + 4 - 4a + 2(a+1)$
$\Rightarrow$ $a^2 + 4 - 4a + 2a + 2$
$\Rightarrow$ $a^2 - 2a + 6$
$\Rightarrow$ $a^2 - 2a + 1 + 5$
$(a-1)^2 + 5$

for $a = 1$. $\alpha^2 + \beta^2 =$ will have min. value.

Hence Ans is (B)

Sol. 26 (A) Clearly discriminant is less than '0'

$\Rightarrow \quad b^2 - 4ac < 0$

$\Rightarrow \quad b^2 < 4ac$

Hence Ans is (A)

Sol. 27 (C) Given $x^2 + p^2 = (q - x)^2$

$$x^2 + p^2 = q^2 + x^2 - 2qx$$

$$\frac{p^2 - q^2}{-2q} = x$$

$$\Rightarrow \quad x = \frac{q^2 - p^2}{2q}$$

Hence Ans is (C)

Sol. 28 (A) $3^{2x} \times 2 - 5 \times 3^x - 3 = 0$

Let $3^x = y$

$$2y^2 - 5y - 3 = 0$$

$\Rightarrow \quad 2y^2 + y - 6y - 3 = 0$

$\Rightarrow \quad y(2y + 1) - 3(2y + 1) = 0$

$\Rightarrow \quad (y - 3)(2y - 3) = 0$

$\Rightarrow \quad y = 3$ or $y = \frac{3}{2}$

$\Rightarrow \quad 3^x = 3^1$ or $3^x \neq \frac{3}{2}$

$\Rightarrow \quad x = 1$

Hence Ans is (A)

Sol. 29 (D) Given $9x^2 - 14x - 8 = 0$ (roots α, β)

We know $\alpha + \beta = \frac{14}{9}$

$$\alpha\beta = -\frac{8}{9}$$

also $(\alpha - \beta)^2 = (\alpha + \beta)^2 - 4\alpha\beta$

$$= \left(\frac{14}{9}\right)^2 - 4 \cdot \left(\frac{-8}{9}\right)$$

$$= \frac{196}{81} + \frac{32}{9}$$

$$= \frac{196 + 288}{81} = \frac{484}{81}$$

$\Rightarrow \quad (\alpha - \beta)^2 = \frac{484}{81}$

$\Rightarrow \quad \alpha - \beta = \frac{22}{9}$

Hence Ans is (D)

Sol. 30 (A) Given,

$$\sqrt{x+1} - \sqrt{x-1} = 1$$

$$\sqrt{x+1} = 1 + \sqrt{x-1}$$

squaring both sides

$$x + 1 = 1 + x - 1 + 2\sqrt{x-1}$$

$$1 = 2\sqrt{x-1}$$

$$\sqrt{(x-1)} = \frac{1}{2}$$

Again squaring

$\Rightarrow \quad x - 1 = \frac{1}{4} \quad \Rightarrow \quad x = \frac{5}{4}$

Hence Ans is (A)

Sol. 31 (D) A quadratic equation can have imaginary roots also.

Hence Ans is (D)

Sol. 32 (C) Consider $\frac{2}{x^2} - \frac{5}{x} + 2 = 0$

Let $\frac{1}{x} = y$

$$2y^2 - 5y + 2 = 0$$

$\Rightarrow \quad 2y^2 - 4y - y + 2 = 0$

$\Rightarrow \quad (2y - 1)(y - 2) = 0$

$\Rightarrow \quad y = \frac{1}{2}$

$\Rightarrow \quad x = 2$ or $y = 2$

$\Rightarrow \quad x = \frac{1}{2}$

Hence Ans is (C)

Sol. 33 (D) Given, $x = \cfrac{1}{2 - \cfrac{1}{2 - \cfrac{1}{2 - x}}}$

$$x = \cfrac{1}{2 - \cfrac{1}{\cfrac{4 - 2x - 1}{2 - x}}}$$

$$= \cfrac{1}{2 - \cfrac{2 - x}{3 - 2x}}$$

$$x = \frac{3 - 2x}{6 - 4x - 2 + x}$$

$$x(4 - 3x) = 3 - 2x$$

$$3x^2 - 6x + 3 = 0$$

$$x^2 - 2x + 1 = 0$$

$\Rightarrow \quad (x - 1)^2 = 0$

$\Rightarrow \quad x = 1$

Hence Ans is (D)

Sol. 34 (C) Let l be the length & b be breadth of the rectangular field.

given $2(l+b)=82$

$\Rightarrow$ $l+b=41$ ...(1)

& $l.b=400$ ...(2)

$l(41-l)=400$ [using (1)]

$l^2-41l+400=0$

$(l-25)(l-16)=0$

$l=25, 16$

Hence Ans is (C)

Sol. 35 (C) Let $x=\sqrt{12+\sqrt{12+\sqrt{12+\ldots}}}$

$x=\sqrt{12+x}$

$x^2=12+x$

$x^2-x-12=0$

$(x+3)(x-4)=0$

$x=4$

Hence Ans is (C)

Sol. 36 (D) Given

$x^2-3x+2=0$ < α, β

$\Rightarrow$ $x=\alpha$

Now to make equation whose root is $\alpha+1$

$\Rightarrow$ $\alpha+1=x$

$\Rightarrow$ $\alpha=x-1$

Now replace x with $(x-1)$ in equation

$(x-1)^2-3(x-1)+2=0$

$x^2+1-2x-3x+3+2=0$

$x^2-5x+6=0$

Hence Ans is (D)

Sol. 37 (A) Given

$4x^2-4x+1$

$D\equiv b^2-4ac$

$(-4)^2-4\times 4=0$

Since $D=0$ so roots are equal.

Hence graph will touch at one point

Hence Ans is (A)

Sol. 38 (C) Given $x^2-8x+p=0$ < α, β

We know $\alpha+\beta=8$

and $\alpha\beta=p$

$\alpha^2+\beta^2=40$

$(\alpha+\beta)^2-2\alpha\beta=40$

$\Rightarrow$ $(8)^2-2p=40$

$\Rightarrow$ $64-40=2p$

$\Rightarrow$ $24=2p$

$\Rightarrow$ $p=12$

Hence Ans is (C)

Sol. 39 (C) Let number be x, $2x$ & $3x$

then sum is $6x$

given $\frac{1}{2}6x=18$

$x=6$

So number be 6, 12, 18

ratio of square is 36, 144, 324

Hence Ans is (C)

Sol. 40 (D) Given $S_0=r_1^0+r_2^0=2,$

$S_1=r_1+r_2=-b$

$S_2=r_1^2+r_2^2$

$=(r_1+r_2)^2-2r_1r_2$

$=(-b)^2-2c$

$=b^2-2c$

$S_2+bS_1+cS_0$

$=b^2-2c+b(-b)+c(2)$

$=b^2-2c-b^2+2c$

$=0$

So, it is independent of both b and c.

Hence Ans is (D)

Sol. 41 (C) Let the 2nd pipe filled in x h then the 1st pipe filled in $(x+5)h$ & the 3rd pipe filled in $(x-4)h$ as per question

$$\frac{1}{x}+\frac{1}{x+5}=\frac{1}{x-4}$$

$$\Rightarrow \quad \frac{2x+5}{x(x+5)}=\frac{1}{(x-4)}$$

$\Rightarrow$ $(2x+5)(x-4)=x^2+5x$

$\Rightarrow$ $2x^2-8x+5x-20=x^2+5x$

$\Rightarrow$ $x^2-8x-20=0$

$\Rightarrow$ $(x+2)(x-10)=0$

$\Rightarrow$ $x=10$

So first pipe will take $15h$ and third pipe with take $6h$.

Hence Ans is (C)

Sol. 42 (B) Given $ax^2+bx+c=0$ < $\sin\theta$, $\cos\theta$

$\sin\theta+\cos\theta=\frac{-b}{a}$ ...(1)

$\sin\theta.\cos\theta=\frac{c}{a}$ ...(2)

Squaring (1)

$$(\sin\theta + \cos\theta)^2 = \frac{b^2}{a^2}$$

$$\sin^2\theta + \cos^2\theta + 2\sin\theta\cdot\cos\theta = \frac{b^2}{a^2}$$

$$2\sin\theta\cdot\cos\theta = \frac{b^2}{a^2} - 1$$

$$\Rightarrow \quad \frac{2c}{a} = \frac{b^2 - a^2}{a^2}$$

$$\Rightarrow \quad b^2 - a^2 = 2ac$$

Hence Ans is (B)

Sol. 43 (B) Given 1st pipe alone fill the tank in $5H$ & 2nd pipe alone fill the tank in $20H$ then together they will fill the tank

$$= \frac{20\times 5}{20+5}$$

$$= 4H$$

Let leak empty the tank in xH
then tank will be filled in $5H$
then in one hour tank is going to be filled

$$\frac{1}{5} + \frac{1}{20} - \frac{1}{x} = \frac{1}{5}$$

$$\frac{1}{20} = \frac{1}{x}$$

$$\Rightarrow \quad x = 20H$$

Hence Ans is (B)

Sol. 44 (B) Average velocity $= \frac{\text{Total distance}}{\text{Total time}}$

$$\text{So total distance} = \frac{20}{60}\times 30 + \frac{30}{60}\times 50 + 1\times 50 + 1\times 60$$

$$10 + 25 + 50 + 60 = 145 \text{ km}$$

$$\text{Total time} = \frac{20}{60} + \frac{30}{60} + 1 + 1 = \frac{1}{3} + \frac{1}{2} + 2$$

$$= \frac{17}{6} \text{ hrs.}$$

$$\text{Average velocity} = \frac{145}{\frac{17}{6}} = \frac{145\times 6}{17}$$

$$= 51.18 \text{ km/h}$$

Hence Ans is (B)

Sol. 45 (C) Given $x = \sqrt{2}$ & $x = -\sqrt{2}$ are roots

$\Rightarrow$ $(x-\sqrt{2})$ & $(x+\sqrt{2})$ are factors

$\Rightarrow$ $(x-\sqrt{2})(x+\sqrt{2})$ is a factor of $f(x)$

$\Rightarrow$ (x^2-2) is a factor of $f(x)$

So $\quad 2x^2 - 3x + 1$

$$(x^2-2)\overline{)2x^4 - 3x^3 - 3x^2 + 6x - 2}$$

$$-(2x^4 + 0.x^3 - 4x^2)$$

$$-3x^3 + x^2 + 6x - 2$$

$$-(-3x^3 + 0x^2 + 6x)$$

$$x^2 - 2$$

$$-(x^2 - 2)$$

$$\times$$

$$\Rightarrow \quad 2x^4 - 3x^3 - 3x^2 + 6x - 2 = (x^2-2)(2x^2 - 3x + 1)$$

$$= (x^2-2)(2x^2 - 2x - x + 1)$$

$$= (x^2-2)(2x-1)(x-1)$$

So other roots arc $x = 1, \frac{1}{2}$

Hence Ans is (C)

Sol. 46 (C) If $\quad \frac{b^2}{4a} = c$

$$\Rightarrow \quad b^2 = 4ac$$

$$\Rightarrow \quad b^2 - 4ac = 0$$

$$\Rightarrow \quad D = 0$$

mean equation of has equal root mean graph touch x-axis at one point

Hence Ans is (C)

Sol. 47 (A) If a quadratic equation $ax^2 + bx + c = 0$ has more than two roots then it must be identity so

$$a = b = c = 0$$

So. $(a^2 - a - 2)x^2 + (a^2 - 4)x + (a^2 - 3a + 2) = 0$

$$(a+1)(a-2)x^2 + (a-2)(a+2)x + (a-2)(a-1) = 0$$

$\Rightarrow$ $a = 2$

Hence Ans is (A)

Sol. 48 (A) Given $(a-2b+c)x^2 + (b-2c+a)x + (c-2a+b) = 0$

Clearly $x = 1$ is a root of equation

$$a - 2b + c + b - 2c + a + c - 2a + b = 0$$

Since roots are equal, so other root = 1

So $\quad \alpha\beta = 1$

$$\Rightarrow \quad \frac{c-2a+b}{a-2b+c} = 1$$

$$\Rightarrow \quad c - 2a + b = a - 2b + c$$

$$\Rightarrow \quad 3b = 3a$$

$$\Rightarrow \quad a = b$$

Sum of roots = 2

$$\frac{b-2c+a}{a-2b+c} = 2$$

$$\Rightarrow \quad b - 2c + a = 2a - 4b + 2c$$

as $a=b$

$\Rightarrow \quad 2a-2c=2a-4a+2c$

$\Rightarrow \quad 4a=4c$

$\Rightarrow \quad a=c$

So $\quad a=b=c$

Hence Ans is (A)

Sol. 49 (C) Let the speed at 1st train be x km/h then 2nd train speed be $x-5$

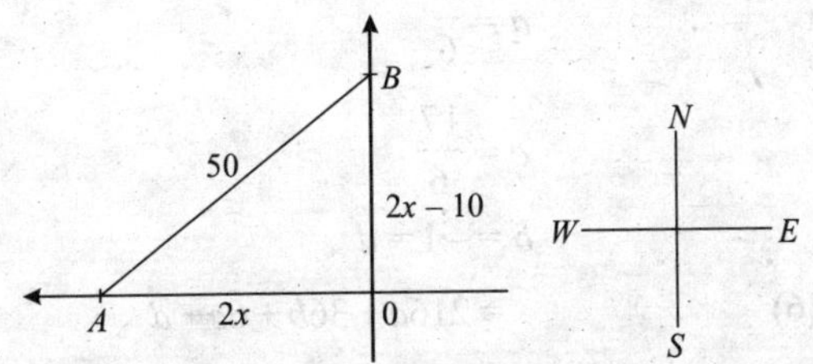

distance travelled by them in 2hours. is $2x$ & $(2x-10)$ respectively so

Apply pythagoras in ΔOAB

$$(2x)^2+(2x-10)^2=50^2$$

$\Rightarrow \quad 4x^2+4x^2+100-40x=2500$

$\Rightarrow \quad 8x^2-40x-2400=0$

$\Rightarrow \quad 2x^2-10x-600=0$

$\Rightarrow \quad x^2-5x-300=0$

$\Rightarrow \quad x^2+15x-20x-300=0$

$\Rightarrow \quad (x+15)(x-20)=0$

$\Rightarrow \quad x=20$

& then speed of 2nd train is

$$x-5=15.$$

Hence Ans is (C)

Sol. 50 (C) Clearly $x=1$ is a solution for the equation so both roots = 1

Hence Ans is (C)

Solutions of PRACTICE EXERCISE-6.2

Sol. 1 (B) Given

$$x^2+a^2+2ax+y^2+b^2+2by=4ax+4by$$

$$x^2+a^2-2ax+y^2+b^2-2by=0$$

$$(x-a)^2+(y-b)^2=0$$

As the sum of two perfect square can be zero only when both of them individually are zero.

$\Rightarrow$ when $\quad x-a=0$

& $\quad y-b=0$

$\Rightarrow \quad x=a \;\&\; y=b$

So $\quad xy-ab=ab-ab=0$

Hence Ans is (B)

Sol. 2 (B) Given $x^2-x-1=0 \quad \ldots(1)$

$$\begin{array}{r} x+1 \\ x^2-x-1 \overline{\big) \; x^3-2x+1 \;} \\ -(x^3-x^2-x) \\ \hline +x^2-x+1 \\ -(x^2-x-1) \\ \hline 2 \end{array}$$

So by fundamental theorem of division we have

Dividend = Divisor × Quotient + Remainder

$$x^3-2x+1=(x^2-x-1)\times(x+1)+2$$

Using (1) $\quad x^3-2x+1=2$

Hence Ans is (B)

Sol. 3 (D) Given, $\quad a^5=b^6$

$a=b^{6/5} \quad \ldots(1)$

Also given $\quad c^3=d^4$

Equation-(2) – equation-(1)

$d=c^{3/4} \quad \ldots(2)$

$$d-a=c^{3/4}-b^{6/5}=61$$

So $\quad c=5^4=625$

$$b=2^5=32$$

$$c-b=625-32=593$$

Hence Ans is (D)

Sol. 4 (C) Consider

$$x^2+x^2y^2+x^2y^4=525$$

$x^2(1+y^2+y^4)=525 \quad \ldots(1)$

$$x+xy+xy^2=35$$

$$x(1+y+y^2)=35$$

Square both side

$x^2(1+y+y^2)^2=(35)^2 \quad \ldots(2)$

Dividing (1) by (2)

$$\frac{1+y^2+y^4}{(1+y+y^2)^2}=\frac{525}{(35)^2}$$

$$\frac{1+y^2+y^4}{(1+y+y^2)^2}=\frac{3}{7}$$

$$\frac{(1+y+y^2)^2-2y(1+y+y^2)}{(1+y+y^2)^2}=\frac{3}{7}$$

$$1-\frac{2y}{1+y+y^2}=\frac{3}{7}$$

$$1-\frac{3}{7}=\frac{2y}{1+y+y^2}$$

$$\frac{2}{7}=\frac{y}{1+y+y^2}$$

On solving, we get $\quad 2y^2+5y+2=0$

so sum of the roots $=\frac{5}{2}$

Hence Ans is (C)

Sol. 5 (A) Given $x+y+z=1$

Now $1-3x^2-3y^2-3z^2+2x^3+2y^3+2z^3$

$$=1-3(x^2+y^2+z^2)+2(x^3+y^3+z^3)$$
$$=1-3(1-2xy-2yz-2zx)+$$
$$2\{(x+y+z)(x^2+y^2+z^2-xy-yz-zx)+3xyz\}$$
$$=1-3+6xy+6yz+6xz+2\{x^2+y^2+z^2-xy-yz-zx+3xyz\}$$
$$=1-3+2[x^2+y^2+z^2+2xy+2yz+2zx]+6xyz$$
$$=-2+2\{x+y+z\}^2+6xyz$$
$$=-2+2+6xyz$$
$$=6xyz$$

Hence Ans is (A)

Sol. 6 (D) Given

$$(a-5)^2+(b-c)^2+(c-d)^2+(b+c+d-9)=0$$

$\Rightarrow$ $a-5=0$ or $a=5$ ...(1)

$\Rightarrow$ $b-c=0$ or $b=c$

$\Rightarrow$ $c-d=0$ or $c=d$

$\Rightarrow$ $b+c+d-9=0$ ...(2)

Now $b=c=d$ ...(3)

So by (2) and (3)

$$3b=9$$
$$b=3$$

So $a=5, b=3, c=3$

and $d=3$

$$(5+3+3)(3+3+3)=9a$$

Hence Ans is (D)

Sol. 7 (A) Let the cubic polynomial be

$$ax^3+bx^2+cx+d=P(x)$$

$P(1)=a+b+c+d=1$ ...(1)

$P(2)=8a+4b+2c+d=2$ ...(2)

$P(3)=27a+9b+3c+d=3$ ...(3)

$P(4)=64a+16b+4c+d=5$ ...(4)

by equation-(1) and equation-(2)

$7a+3b+c=1$ ...(5)

Equation-(5) × 3 equation-(3)

$$-6a-d=0$$

$-6a=d$ ...(6)

Putting in equation (2) and (3)

$$2a+4b+2c=2$$

or $a+2b+c=1$ ...(7)

$$21a+9b+3c=3$$

or $7a+3b+c=1$ ...(8)

solving equation (8) and (7)

$$-6a=b$$

So $-6a=b=d$

Putting these values in (1) and (4)

$$-11a+c=1$$
$$-11a+c=1$$
$$-38a+4c=5$$

Solving these two

We get $a=\frac{1}{6}$

$$c=\frac{17}{6}$$

So $b=-1=d$

Now $P(6)$ $=216a+36b+6c+d$

$$=36-36+17-1$$
$$=16$$

Hence Ans is (A)

Sol. 8 (B) Given

$$k^2x^2-17x+k+2=0 \quad (\text{roots } \alpha,\ 1/\alpha)$$

$$\alpha\times\frac{1}{\alpha}=\frac{K+2}{K^2}$$

$\Rightarrow$ $1=\frac{K+2}{K^2}$

$\Rightarrow$ $K^2-K-2=0$

$\Rightarrow$ $(K-2)(K+1)=0$

$$K=2,-1$$

Hence Ans is (B)

Sol. 9 (B) Given $\frac{2009}{2010}x+1+\frac{1}{x}=0$

$$\frac{2009x^2+2010x+2010}{2010x}=0$$
$$2009x^2+2010x+2010=0$$
$$\alpha+\beta=\frac{-2010}{2009}$$
$$\alpha\beta=\frac{2010}{2009}$$
$$\frac{1}{\alpha}+\frac{1}{\beta}=\frac{\alpha+\beta}{\alpha\beta}=\frac{\frac{-2010}{2009}}{\frac{2010}{2009}}$$
$$=-1$$

Hence Ans is (B)

Sol. 10 (D) For repeated roots α.

We have discriminant = 0

$\Rightarrow \quad b^2 = 4ac$

$\Rightarrow \quad a^2 = 4 \times (a-d)(a+d)$

$\Rightarrow \quad a^2 = 4a^2 - 4d^2$

$\Rightarrow \quad 4d^2 = 3a^2$

$$\Rightarrow \quad \frac{d^2}{a^2} = \frac{3}{4} = \left(\frac{\sqrt{3}}{2}\right)^2 = \cos^2 30°$$

Hence Ans is (D)

Sol. 11 (D) Given $\quad \dfrac{1}{x+a} + \dfrac{1}{x+b} = \dfrac{1}{c}$

$$\frac{x+b+x+a}{(x+a)(x+b)} = \frac{1}{c}$$

$$\frac{|2x+(a+b)|}{x^2+(a+b)x+ab} = \frac{1}{c}$$

$$x^2+(a+b)x+ab = 2xc+(a+b)c$$

$$x^2+(a+b-2c)x+ab-ac-bc = 0 \left\langle \begin{matrix} \alpha \\ \beta \end{matrix} \right.$$

Some of roots = 0

$\alpha + \beta = 0$

$\Rightarrow \quad a+b-2c = 0$

$\Rightarrow \quad a+b = 2c$

$\Rightarrow \quad \alpha\beta = ab-(a+b)c$

$\Rightarrow \quad \alpha\beta = ab-2c^2 \qquad \ldots(1)$

Squaring (1)

$a^2+b^2+2ab = 4c^2$

$\Rightarrow \quad a^2+b^2 = 4c^2-2ab$

$$\Rightarrow \quad \frac{a^2+b^2}{2} = 2c^2-ab$$

$$\Rightarrow \quad -\frac{(a^2+b^2)}{2} = ab-2c^2$$

$$\Rightarrow \quad -\frac{(a^2+b^2)}{2} = \alpha\beta \qquad \text{[from (1)]}$$

Hence Ans is (D)

Sol. 12 (A) Consider

$|x|^{6/5} - 26|x|^{3/5} - 27 = 0$

Let $\quad |x|^{3/5} = y$

$y^2 - 26y - 27 = 0$

$\Rightarrow \quad y^2 + y - 27y - 27 = 0$

$\Rightarrow \quad (y+1)(y-27) = 0$

$\Rightarrow \quad y = -1; y = 27$

$\Rightarrow \quad |x|^{3/5} \neq -1$

So $\quad |x|^{3/5} = 27$

$\Rightarrow \quad |x| = (27)^{5/3} = 3^5$

$\Rightarrow \quad x = 3^5 \ \& -3^5$

$= -3^{10}$

So product of the roots $= -3^{10}$

Hence Ans is (A)

Sol. 13 (A) Let

$$(5+2\sqrt{6})^{x^2-3} = y$$

Then $\quad (5-2\sqrt{6})^{x^2-3} = \dfrac{1}{y}$

$$\Rightarrow \quad y + \frac{1}{y} = 10$$

$\Rightarrow \quad y^2 + 1 = 10y$

$\Rightarrow \quad y^2 - 10y + 1 = 0$

$$y = \frac{10 \pm \sqrt{10^2 - 4\times1\times1}}{2\times1}$$

$$= \frac{10 \pm \sqrt{96}}{2}$$

$y = 5 \pm 2\sqrt{6}$

$\Rightarrow \quad (5+2\sqrt{6})^{x^2-3} = (5 \pm 2\sqrt{6})$

$\Rightarrow \quad x^2 - 3 = 1$

or $\quad x^2 - 3 = -1$

$x^2 = 4$

or $\quad x^2 = 2$

$x = \pm 2$

$x = \pm\sqrt{2}$

Hence Ans is (A)

Sol. 14 (B) Given

$|x|^2 + |x| - 6 = 0$

$\Rightarrow \quad (|x|+2)(|x|-3) = 0$

Here $\quad |x| \neq 2$ so $|x| = 3$

$\Rightarrow \quad x = \pm 3$

Hence Ans is (B)

Sol. 15 (D) Given

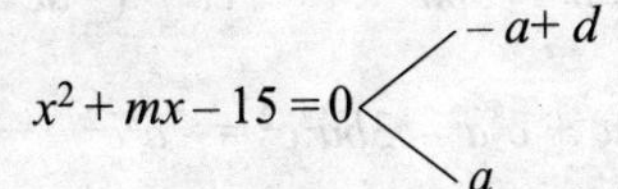

Sum of roots

$-a + a + d = -m$

$\Rightarrow \quad d = -m \qquad \ldots(A)$

Product of roots

$$(-a+d)a = -15$$

$$\Rightarrow \quad -a^2 + ad = -15 \quad \ldots(1)$$

Similarly $x^2 + nx - 35 = 0$ with roots $-a$ and $a+d$

$$-a + a + d = -n$$

$$\Rightarrow \quad d = -n \quad \ldots(B)$$

$$\Rightarrow \quad -a(a+d) = -35$$

$$\Rightarrow \quad -a^2 - ad = -35 \quad \ldots(2)$$

Adding (1) & (2)

$$-2a^2 = -50$$

$$\Rightarrow \quad a^2 = 25$$

$$\Rightarrow \quad a = 5$$

Using a in equation (1)

$$-25 + 5d = -15$$

$$\Rightarrow \quad 5d = -15 + 25$$

$$\Rightarrow \quad 5d = 10$$

$$\Rightarrow \quad d = 2$$

$$\Rightarrow \quad m = n = -d = -2$$

Using (A) & (B)

Hence $\quad m + n = -4$

Hence Ans is (D)

Sol. 16 (A) Given $\quad ax^2 + bx + c = 0$ with roots α and α^2

Sum of roots $\quad \alpha + \alpha^2 = -\dfrac{b}{a}$

& product of roots $\quad \alpha^3 = \dfrac{c}{a}$

$$\alpha = \left(\frac{c}{a}\right)^{1/3}$$

Since α is a root then it will satisfy.

$$a\alpha^2 + b\alpha + c = 0$$

$$a\left(\frac{c}{a}\right)^{2/3} + b\left(\frac{c}{a}\right)^{1/3} + c = 0$$

$$ac^{2/3} + b(ac)^{1/3} + ca^{2/3} = 0$$

$$b(ac)^{1/3} + ca^{2/3} = -ac^{2/3} \quad \ldots(1)$$

Cubing both sides,

$$b^3ac + c^3a^2 + 3b(ac)^{1/3}.\, ca^{2/3}\,[b(ac)^{1/3} + ca^{2/3}] = -a^3c^2$$

$$b^3ac + c^3a^2 + 3ba^{1/3}.\, c^{1/3}.\, ca^{2/3}\,(-ac^{2/3}) = -a^3c^2$$

Using (1)

$$b^3ac + c^3a^2 - 3ba^2c^2 = -a^3c^2$$

Divide by ac

$$b^3 + ac^2 - 3abc = -a^2c$$

$$3abc = b^3 + ac^2 + a^2c$$

Hence Ans is (A)

Sol. 17 (D) If $ax^2 + bx + c = 0$ is an identity then there will be infinite values of 'x' which will satisfy the equation.

Hence Ans is (D)

Sol. 18 (C) Given

$$2\left(x^2 + \frac{1}{x^2}\right) - 9\left(x + \frac{1}{x}\right) + 14 = 0$$

$$\Rightarrow \quad 2\left[\left(x + \frac{1}{x}\right)^2 - 2\right] - 9\left(x + \frac{1}{x}\right) + 14 = 0$$

Let $\quad x + \dfrac{1}{x} = y$

$$\Rightarrow \quad 2(y^2 - 2) - 9y + 14 = 0$$

$$\Rightarrow \quad 2y^2 - 4 - 9y + 14 = 0$$

$$\Rightarrow \quad 2y^2 - 9y + 10 = 0$$

$$\Rightarrow \quad 2y^2 - 4y - 5y + 10 = 0$$

$$\Rightarrow \quad 2y(y-2) - 5(y-2) = 0$$

$$\Rightarrow \quad (y-2)(2y-5) = 0$$

$$\Rightarrow \quad y = 2 \text{ or } y = \frac{5}{2}$$

When $\quad y = 2$

$$\Rightarrow \quad x + \frac{1}{x} = 2$$

$$\Rightarrow \quad x^2 - 2x + 1 = 0$$

$$\Rightarrow \quad (x-1)^2 = 0$$

$$\Rightarrow \quad x = 1$$

When $\quad y = \dfrac{5}{2}$

$$\Rightarrow \quad x + \frac{1}{x} = \frac{5}{2}$$

$$\Rightarrow \quad 2x^2 + 2 = 5x$$

$$\Rightarrow \quad 2x^2 - 5x + 2 = 0$$

$$\Rightarrow \quad (2x-1)(x-2) = 0$$

$$\Rightarrow \quad x = \frac{1}{2} \text{ or } x = 2$$

So three real solutions are there

Hence Ans is (C)

Sol. 19 (B) Given

$$(x-1)(2x+1)(x+1)(2x-3) = 15$$

$$(2x^2 - x - 1)(2x^2 - x - 3) = 15$$

Let $\quad 2x^2 - x = y$

$$\Rightarrow \quad (y-1)(y-3) = 15$$

$$\Rightarrow \quad y^2 - 4y + 3 = +15$$

$$\Rightarrow \quad y^2 - 4y - 12 = 0$$

$$\Rightarrow \quad (y+2)(y-6) = 0$$

$y=-2$ or $y=6$

$2x^2-x=-2$ $\quad$ $2x^2-x=6$

$2x^2-x+2=0$ $\quad$ $2x^2-x-6=0$

$D<0$ $\quad$ $D>0$

No real solution $\quad$ Two real solution

Hence Ans is (B)

Sol. 20 (A) Consider

$$\sqrt{x+1}-\sqrt{x-1}=\sqrt{4x-1}$$

Squaring both sides

$$\Rightarrow \quad (x+1)+(x-1)-2\sqrt{x^2-1}=4x-1$$

$$\Rightarrow \quad 2x-2\sqrt{x^2-1}=4x-1$$

$$\Rightarrow \quad -2\sqrt{x^2-1}=2x-1$$

Squaring again

$$\Rightarrow \quad 4(x^2-1)=(2x-1)^2$$

$$\Rightarrow \quad 4x^2-4=4x^2+1-4x$$

$$\Rightarrow \quad -5=-4x$$

$$\Rightarrow \quad x=\frac{5}{4}$$

Hence Ans is (A)

Sol. 21 (B) Given,

$$|x-2|^2+|x-2|-2=0$$

$$[|x-2|+2]\,[|x-2|-1]=0$$

$$|x-2|+2\neq 0$$

$$|x-2|=1$$

$$x-2=\pm 1$$

$$x=3 \text{ or } 1$$

So sum of roots $=4$

Hence Ans is (B)

Sol. 22 (D) Given

$$|x^2-x-6|=x+2$$

$$\Rightarrow \quad (x^2-x-6)=\pm(x+2)$$

$$\Rightarrow \quad x^2-x-6=x+2$$

$$\Rightarrow \quad x^2-2x-8=0$$

$$\Rightarrow \quad (x+2)(x-4)=0$$

$$\Rightarrow \quad x=-2,4$$

or

$$x^2-x-6=-x-2$$

$$\Rightarrow \quad x^2-4=0$$

$$\Rightarrow \quad x=\pm 2$$

So roots are $x=-2,4,2$

Hence Ans is (D)

Sol. 23 (D) Given $\left(\dfrac{x-1}{x+1}\right)^4-13\left(\dfrac{x-1}{x+1}\right)^2+36=0$

Let $\left(\dfrac{x-1}{x+1}\right)^2=y$

$$\Rightarrow \quad y^2-13y+36=0$$

$$\Rightarrow \quad (y-9)(y-4)=0$$

$$\Rightarrow \quad y=9$$

$$\Rightarrow \quad \left(\frac{x-1}{x+1}\right)^2=9$$

$$\Rightarrow \quad \frac{x-1}{x+1}=\pm 3$$

or $\quad y=4$

$$\left(\frac{x-1}{x+1}\right)^2=4$$

$$\frac{x-1}{x+1}=\pm 2$$

Hence 4 real roots are there

Hence Ans is (D)

Sol. 24 (B) $9^{x+2}-6(3^{x+1})+1=0$

$$81\cdot 9^x-18\cdot 3^x+1=0$$

Let $3^x=y$

$$\Rightarrow \quad 81y^2-18y+1=0$$

$$\Rightarrow \quad 81y^2-9y-9y+1=0$$

$$\Rightarrow \quad 9y(9y-1)-1(9y-1)=0$$

$$\Rightarrow \quad (9y-1)^2=0$$

$$\Rightarrow \quad 9y-1=0$$

$$\Rightarrow \quad y=\frac{1}{9}$$

$$\Rightarrow \quad 3^x=3^{-2}$$

$$\Rightarrow \quad x=-2$$

So only one root is negative

Hence Ans is (B)

Sol. 25 (D) By observation

Hence Ans is (D)

Solutions of PRACTICE EXERCISE-6.3

Sol. 1 (D) Given $ax^2+bx+c=0$

$$\text{then roots}=\frac{-b\pm\sqrt{b^2-4ac}}{2a}$$

$$=\frac{-b}{2a}\pm\frac{\sqrt{b^2-4ac}}{2a}$$

Hence Ans is (D)

Sol. 2 (C) Since 2 is a root of

$$x^2+bx+12=0$$

$\Rightarrow$ $4+2b+12$

$\Rightarrow$ $b=-8$

Now $x^2+bx+q=0$ become

$$x^2-8x+q=0$$

since roots of $x^2-8x+q=0$ are equal so discriminant D will be zero.

$$D=0$$

$\Rightarrow$ $b^2-4ac=0$

$\Rightarrow$ $64-4q=0$

$\Rightarrow$ $64=4q$

$\Rightarrow$ $q=16$

Hence Ans is (C)

Sol. 3 (D) If roots of a quadratic equation ax^2+bx+c are equal then discriminant

$$D=0$$

$\Rightarrow$ $b^2-4ac=0$

$\Rightarrow$ $9k^2-64=0$

$\Rightarrow$ $k=\pm\frac{8}{3}$

Hence Ans is (D)

Sol. 4 (B) Given,

$$3x^2-4\sqrt{3}x+4=0$$

Here $D=b^2-4ac$

$$=(-4\sqrt{3})^2-(4\times3\times4)$$

$$=48-48$$

$$=0$$

Since $D=0$

Roots are real and equal

Hence Ans is (B)

Sol. 5 (A) Let the two numbers be x and $x+1$

Given $x^2+(x+1)^2=421$

$\Rightarrow$ $x^2+x^2+1+2x=421$

$\Rightarrow$ $2x^2+2x-420=0$

$\Rightarrow$ $x^2+x-210=0$

$\Rightarrow$ $x^2+15x-14x-210=0$

$\Rightarrow$ $x(x+15)-14(x+15)=0$

$\Rightarrow$ $(x-14),(x+15)=0$

$\Rightarrow$ $x=14$, or $x=-15$

Since $x>0$

The other number is $x=15$

Hence Ans is (A)

Aliter : Also you can go by checking each option.

Sol. 6 (C) Given

$$\alpha^2=5\alpha-3$$

$$\beta^2=5\beta-3$$

Consider

$$\alpha^2-\beta^2=5(\alpha-\beta)$$

$$\alpha+\beta=5 \quad \ldots(1)$$

$$\alpha^2+\beta^2=5(\alpha+\beta)-6$$

$\Rightarrow$ $\alpha^2+\beta^2=25-6=19$ [using (1)] $\ldots(2)$

Also $\alpha+\beta=5$ on squaring

$$\alpha^2+\beta^2+2\alpha\beta=25 \quad \ldots(3)$$

Now using equation-(2) in equation-(3)

$$19+2\alpha\beta=25$$

$\Rightarrow$ $\alpha\beta=3$

Now equation whose roots are $\frac{\alpha}{13}$ & $\frac{\beta}{\alpha}$

$\Rightarrow$ $x^2-\left(\frac{\alpha}{\beta}+\frac{\beta}{\alpha}\right)x+\frac{\alpha}{\beta}\cdot\frac{\beta}{\alpha}=0$

$\Rightarrow$ $x^2-\frac{(\alpha^2+\beta^2)}{\alpha\beta}x+1=0$

$\Rightarrow$ $x^2-\frac{19}{3}x+1=0$

$\Rightarrow$ $3x^2-19x+3=0$

$\Rightarrow$ Hence Ans is (A)

Sol. 7 (D) Since roots of the equation are equal,

$\Rightarrow$ $b^2-4ac=0$

$\Rightarrow$ $(-8)^2-4\times2\times c=0$

$\Rightarrow$ $64-8c=0$

$\Rightarrow$ $c=8$

Hence Ans is (D)

Sol. 8 (D) Let the two roots of the quadratic equation be α and β

Given $\alpha-\beta=2 \quad \ldots(1)$

Also $\alpha^3-\beta^3=98$

$\Rightarrow$ $(\alpha-\beta)(\alpha^2+\beta^2+\alpha\beta)$

$\Rightarrow$ $2.(\alpha^2+\beta^2+\alpha\beta)=98$ [from (1)]

$\Rightarrow$ $\alpha^2+\beta^2+\alpha\beta=49 \quad \ldots(2)$

From (1)

$$\alpha=2+\beta$$

Substituting it in equation-(2)

We get

$$(2+\beta)^2+\beta^2+(2+\beta)\beta-49=0$$

$\Rightarrow$ $4+\beta^2+4\beta+\beta^2+2\beta+\beta^2-49=0$

$\Rightarrow$ $3\beta^2+6\beta-45=0$

$\Rightarrow$ $\beta^2+2\beta-15=0$

$\Rightarrow$ $x^2+2x-15=0$

Hence Ans is (D)

Sol. 9 (D) We know irrational roots always occur in conjugate pair

Here

One root $\alpha = 3-\sqrt{2}$

$\Rightarrow$ Therefore other root

$\beta = 3+\sqrt{2}$

Here quadratic equation will be

x^2 – (sum of roots) x + product of roots $=0$

$\Rightarrow \quad x^2-6x+7=0$

Hence Ans is (D)

Sol. 10 (A) Given

$3x^2+2x+k=0$

For real roots $D \geq 0$

$\Rightarrow \quad b^2-4ac \geq 0$

$\Rightarrow \quad 4-12k \geq 0$

$\Rightarrow \quad k \leq \frac{1}{3}$

Here Ans is (A)

Sol. 11 (C) Let Meera's present age be $= x$

Given

$(x-5)(x+8) = 30$

$\Rightarrow \quad x^2+8x-5x-40-30=0$

$\Rightarrow \quad x^2+3x-70=0$

$\Rightarrow \quad x^2+10x-7x-70=0$

$\Rightarrow \quad (x+10)(x-7)=0$

$\Rightarrow \quad x=7,-10$

$\Rightarrow \quad x=7$

Hence Ans is (C)

Sol. 12 (A) Given $25x^2-16=0 \begin{cases}\alpha \\ \beta\end{cases}$

$\Rightarrow \quad x^2 = \frac{16}{25}$

$\Rightarrow \quad x = \pm\frac{4}{5}$

$\alpha = \frac{4}{5} \quad \& \quad \beta = -\frac{4}{5}$

$\Rightarrow \quad \alpha^2+\beta^2 = (\alpha+\beta)^2-2\alpha\beta = (0)^2-2\cdot\frac{4}{5}\cdot\frac{-4}{5}$

$\Rightarrow \quad \alpha^2+\beta^2 = \frac{32}{25}$

Hence Ans is (A)

Sol. 13 (D) Let the two number be x and y

Given $x^2-y^2=180$ ...(1)

Let y' be the smaller number

Also $y^2 = 8x$

Substituting $y^2 = 8x$ in eq. (1)

We get $x^2-8x=180$

$\Rightarrow \quad x^2-8x-180=0$

$\Rightarrow \quad x^2-18x+10x-180=0$

$\Rightarrow \quad x(x-18)+10(x-10)=0$

$\Rightarrow \quad (x+10)(x-18)=0$

$x=-10; x=18$

So here $x=18$

$\Rightarrow \quad y^2 = 8\times 18$

$\Rightarrow \quad y^2=144$

$\Rightarrow \quad y=12$

$\Rightarrow$ The two number are 12 and 18

Hence Ans is (D)

Sol. 14 (A) Consider

$x^2+px+q=0$

Given $\alpha = \tan 30°, \beta = \tan 15°$

Here $\alpha+\beta = \tan 30° + \tan 15° = -p$

$\alpha\beta = \tan 30° \tan 15° = q$

Hence $\frac{\alpha+\beta}{1-\alpha\beta} = \frac{-p}{1-q}$

$\Rightarrow \quad \frac{\tan 30° + \tan 15°}{1-\tan 30° \tan 15°} = \frac{-q}{1-q}$

$\Rightarrow \quad \tan 45° = \frac{-p}{1-q}$

$\Rightarrow \quad 1-q=-p$

$\Rightarrow \quad q-p=1$

$\Rightarrow \quad 2+q-p=2+1=3$

Hence Ans is (A)

Sol. 15 (B) Given $\alpha\ \beta$ are the zeroes of ax^2+bx+c

$\Rightarrow \quad \alpha+\beta = \frac{-b}{a} \quad \& \quad \alpha.\beta = \frac{c}{a}$

Now $\sqrt{\frac{\alpha}{\beta}}+\sqrt{\frac{\beta}{\alpha}} = \frac{\alpha+\beta}{\sqrt{\alpha\beta}} = \frac{-b/a}{\sqrt{c/a}} = \frac{-b}{\sqrt{ac}}$

Hence Ans is (B)

Sol. 16 (D) Given -4 is a root of $x^2+px-4=0$

$\Rightarrow \quad (-4)^2+p(-4)-4=0$

$\Rightarrow \quad 4p=16-4$

$\Rightarrow \quad p=3$ ...(1)

Now $x^2+px+k=0$

Has equal roots

$\Rightarrow$ Discriminant $D \equiv b^2-4ac=0$

$\Rightarrow \quad p^2-4k=0$

$\Rightarrow \quad 9-4k=0$ Using (1)

$\Rightarrow \quad k=\frac{9}{4}$

Hence Ans is (D)

Sol. 17 (B) Let $\sqrt{6+\sqrt{6+\sqrt{6+...}}} = x$

On squaring $x^2 = 6+\sqrt{6+\sqrt{6+\sqrt{6+...}}}$

$\Rightarrow \quad x^2 = 6 + x$

$\Rightarrow \quad x^2 - x - 6 = 0$

$\Rightarrow \quad (x+2)(x-3) = 0$

$\Rightarrow \quad x = 3$

Hence Ans is (B)

Sol. 18 (A) Given $x = 1$ satisfies

$ax^2 + ax + 3 = 0$

& $\quad x^2 + x + b = 0$

$\Rightarrow \quad a + a + 3 = 0$

$\Rightarrow \quad 2a + 3 = 0$

$\Rightarrow \quad a = -\dfrac{3}{2}$

and $\quad 1 + b + 1 = 0$

$\Rightarrow \quad b = -2$

Hence Ans is (A)

Sol. 19 (A) Consider $\dfrac{x^2 - bx}{ax - c} = \dfrac{m-1}{m+1}$

$\Rightarrow \quad (m+1)x^2 - bx(m+1) = (m-1)ax - c(m-1)$

$\Rightarrow \quad (m+1)x^2 - x[b(m+1) + (m-1)a] + c(m-1) = 0$

Since roots are equal & opp. in sign so coefficient of x is zero

As sum of roots is equal to zero

$\Rightarrow \quad b(m+1) + (m-1)a = 0$

$\Rightarrow \quad bx + b + am - a = 0$

$\Rightarrow \quad m(a+b) = a - b$

$\Rightarrow \quad m = \dfrac{a-b}{a+b}$

Hence Ans is (A)

Sol. 20 (C) Let

$AD = x$

$AD^2 + CD^2 = 6^2$

$\Rightarrow \quad CD^2 = 36 - x^2$

$\Rightarrow \quad CD = \sqrt{36 - x^2}$

Now in ΔADB $\quad 16^2 = AD^2 + BD^2$

$\Rightarrow \quad 256 = x^2 + (\sqrt{36-x^2} + 12)^2$

$\Rightarrow \quad 256 = x^2 + 144 + 36 - x^2 + 2.12\sqrt{36-x^2}$

$\Rightarrow \quad 256 - 180 = 2 \times 12\sqrt{36-x^2}$

$\Rightarrow \quad \dfrac{76}{2 \times 12} = \sqrt{36-x^2}$

$\Rightarrow \quad \sqrt{36-x^2} = CD = \dfrac{19}{6}$

Hence Ans is (C)

Sol. 21 (D) Let $5^x = y$

$\dfrac{3}{5}y^2 - \dfrac{2y}{5} = \dfrac{1}{5}$

$\Rightarrow \quad 3y^2 - 2y - 1 = 0$

$\Rightarrow \quad 3y^2 + y - 3y - 1 = 0$

$\Rightarrow \quad (3y+1)(y-1) = 0$

$\Rightarrow \quad y = 1$ or $y \neq -\dfrac{1}{3}x$

$\Rightarrow \quad 5^x = 1 \Rightarrow x = 0.$

Hence Ans is (D)

Sol. 22 (A) Given $\alpha + \beta = 5$

and $\quad \alpha\beta = -\dfrac{p^2}{4}$

We know, $\quad (\alpha - \beta)^2 = (\alpha + \beta)^2 - 4\alpha\beta$

$\Rightarrow \quad \alpha - \beta = \sqrt{25 + p^2}$

Hence Ans is (A)

Sol. 23 (C) Consider

$n^2 + (n+1)^2 = 145$

$\Rightarrow \quad 2n^2 + 2n + 1 = 145$

$\Rightarrow \quad 2n^2 + 2n - 144 = 0$

$\Rightarrow \quad n^2 + n - 72 = 0$

$\Rightarrow \quad (n+9)(n-8) = 0$

$\Rightarrow \quad n = 8$

Hence Ans is (C)

Sol. 24 (B) Given one root is $2 + \sqrt{5}$

$\Rightarrow$ other roots is $2 - \sqrt{5}$

Hence, required equation

$x^2 - \{(2+\sqrt{5}) + (2-\sqrt{5})\}x + (2+\sqrt{5})(2-\sqrt{5}) = 0$

$\Rightarrow \quad x^2 - 4x - 1 = 0$

Hence Ans is (B)

Sol. 25 (D) $x^2 + px - 4 = 0$ has root -4

So $\quad (-4)^2 + p(-4) - 4 = 0$

$\Rightarrow \quad p = 3$

$x^2 + 3x + k = 0$ has equal roots

$D = 0$

$3^2 - 4k = 0$

$k = \dfrac{9}{4}$

Hence Ans is (D)

Sol. 26 (D) a & b are roots of equation

$x^2 + 5x + d = 0 \quad \text{...(1)}$

a & c are roots of equation

$x^2 + 6x + 2d = 0 \quad \text{...(2)}$

Common roots is given by

$$(x^2+6x+2d)-(x^2+5x+d)=0$$
$$x+d=0$$
$$x=-d$$

Putting $x=-d$ in equation-(1)

$$d^2-5d+d=0$$
$$d^2-4d=0$$
$$d(d-4)=0$$
$$d=0, d=4$$

Putting $x=-d$ in equation-(2)

$$d^2-6d+2d=0$$
$$d^2-4d=0$$
$$d=0, d=4$$
$$\Rightarrow \quad d=4 \text{ or } 0$$

(d cannot be 0 because both roots)

$\Rightarrow$ $d=4$ will become equal

Hence Ans is (D)

Sol. 27 (B) Given options are wrong

'– 4' is a root of equation

$$x^2+px-4=0$$
$$\Rightarrow \quad 16-4p-4=0$$
$$\Rightarrow \quad 4p=12$$
$$p=3$$

$x^2+3x+m=0$ has equal roots

$$\Rightarrow \quad b^2-4ac=0$$
$$9-4m=0$$
$$m=9/4$$

Hence Ans is (B)

Sol. 28 (C) $b^2-4ac<0$

$$\Rightarrow \quad b^2<4ac$$

Hence Ans is (C)

Sol. 29 (A) Consider $x^2+2\sqrt{2}x-6=0$

$$\Rightarrow x=\frac{-2\sqrt{2}\pm\sqrt{8-4\times1\times-6}}{2}=-3\sqrt{2}, \sqrt{2}$$

Hence Ans is (A)

Sol. 30 (D) Given $N+12=\dfrac{160}{N}$

$$\Rightarrow \quad N^2+12N-160=0$$
$$\Rightarrow \quad (N+20)(N-8)=0$$
$$\Rightarrow \quad N=-20, 8$$

Hence Ans is (D)

Sol. 31 (B) $2x^2+px+8=0$

$$D=0$$
$$p^2-4\times2\times8=0$$
$$p^2=8\times8$$
$$\Rightarrow \quad p=8$$
$$p(x^2+x)+k=0$$
$$\Rightarrow \quad 8x^2+8x+k=0$$
$$D=0$$
$$\Rightarrow \quad 64-4\times8\times k=0$$
$$\Rightarrow \quad k=\frac{8\times8}{4\times8}=2$$

Hence Ans is (B)

Sol. 32 (D) $x^2-p(x+1)-k=0$

$$x^2-px-p-k=0$$
$$x^2-px-(p+k)=0$$
$$\alpha+\beta=p$$
$$(\alpha+1)(\beta+1)=6$$
$$\alpha\beta+(\beta+\alpha)+1=6$$
$$-(p+k)+p+1=6$$
$$-k+1=6$$
$$\Rightarrow \quad k=-5$$

Hence Ans is (D)

Sol. 33 (A) Let the first part be x

Let the second part be $50-x$

$$\frac{1}{x}+\frac{1}{50-x}=\frac{1}{12}$$
$$\Rightarrow \quad \frac{50-x+x}{50x-x^2}=\frac{1}{12}$$
$$\Rightarrow \quad 600=50x-x^2$$
$$\Rightarrow \quad x^2-50x+600=0$$
$$\Rightarrow \quad x=30, 20$$

Hence Ans is (A)

Sol. 34 (D) $b^2=4ac$, since, repeated factors.

Hence Ans is (D)

Sol. 35 (A) $x^2=-\dfrac{4}{3}$,

$\Rightarrow x=\pm\sqrt{\dfrac{-4}{3}}$, which is imaginary.

Hence Ans is (A)

Sol. 36 (A) As sum of the coefficient zero.

So, one of the root is 1.

So, other root must be 1 as roots are equal.

So, $1 \times 1 = \dfrac{a-b}{b-c}$

$\Rightarrow \quad b - c = a - b$

$\Rightarrow \quad 2b = a + c$

Hence Ans is (A)

Sol. 37 (D) $(k+3)x^2 - (5-k)x + 1 = 0$

$D > 0 \quad (\because \text{roots are distinct})$

$\{-(5-k)\}^2 - 4(k+3)(1) > 0$

$25 + k^2 - 10k - 4k - 12 > 0$

$k^2 - 14k + 13 > 0$

$k^2 - 13k - k + 13 > 0$

$k(k-13) - 1(k-13) > 0$

$(k-1)(k-13) > 0$

+ (1) − (13) +

$\Rightarrow \quad k < 1 \ \& \ k > 13$

Hence Ans is (D)

Sol. 38 (B) $D = 0$

$(\because \text{roots are equal})$

$(c-a)^2 - 4(a-b)(b-c) = 0$

$c^2 + a^2 - 2ac - 4ab + 4ac + 4b^2 - 4bc = 0$

$a^2 + c^2 + (-2b)^2 + 2ac + 2a \times (-2b) + 2c(-2b) = 0$

$(a + c - 2b)^2 = 0$

$a + c = 2b$

$\Rightarrow \quad \dfrac{a+c}{b} = 2$

Alternate : As sum of coefficients is zero, $x = 1$ will be a root

Product of root $= 1 \times 1 = \dfrac{a-b}{b-c}$

$(\because \text{both roots are equal})$

$\Rightarrow \quad b - c = a - b$

$\Rightarrow \quad 2b = a + c$

$\Rightarrow \quad \dfrac{a+c}{b} = 2$

Hence Ans is (B)

Sol. 39 (C) $f(x) = x^2 - 8x + k$

Let the zeroes be α, β

$\alpha + \beta = 8$

$\alpha\beta = k$

Now $\alpha^2 + \beta^2 = 40$

$(\alpha + \beta)^2 - 2\alpha\beta = 40$

$(8)^2 - 2k = 40$

$64 - 40 = 2k$

$2k = 24$

$k = 12$

Hence Ans is (C)

Sol. 40 (B) Consider

$x^2 - x = \lambda(2x - 1)$

$x^2 - x(1 + 2\lambda) + \lambda = 0$

As, sum of roots is zero

$\Rightarrow \quad \dfrac{(1+2\lambda)}{1} = 0$

$\Rightarrow \quad \lambda = -\dfrac{1}{2}$

Hence Ans is (B)

Sol. 41 (A) Consider $x^2 - 2\sqrt{2}\,kx + 2e^{2\log k} - 1 = 0$

$x^2 - 2\sqrt{2}\,kx + 2k^2 - 1 = 0$

α, β are two zeros of equation

Product of zeros $(\alpha\beta) = 31$

$\Rightarrow \quad 2k^2 - 1 = 31$

$\Rightarrow \quad 2k^2 = 32$

$\Rightarrow \quad k^2 = 16$

$k = \pm 4$

But $k = -4$ is not possible

$k = 4$

Hence Ans is (A)

Sol. 42 (D) Let the number of balls purchased be x

ATQ, $\dfrac{450}{x} - \dfrac{450}{x+5} = 15$

$450\left(\dfrac{1}{x} - \dfrac{1}{x+5}\right) = 15$

$\dfrac{x + 5 - x}{x(x+5)} = \dfrac{15}{450}$

$\dfrac{5}{x^2 + 5x} = \dfrac{1}{30}$

$x_2 + 5x - 150 = 0$

$(x + 15)(x - 10) = 0$

$\Rightarrow \quad x - 10 = 0$

$\Rightarrow \quad x = 10$

Hence Ans is (D)

Sol. 43 (A) Given 1 is the solution of

$x^2 + ax + 3 = 0$

$\Rightarrow \quad (1)^2 + a(1) + 3 = 0$

$\Rightarrow \quad a = -4$

So, equation is $x^2 - 4x + 3 = 0$

$\Rightarrow \quad (x-3)(x-1) = 0$

$\Rightarrow \quad x - 3 = 0 \text{ or } x - 1 = 0$

$\Rightarrow \quad x = 3; x = 1$

So, other root will be 3

Hence Ans is (A)

Sol. 44 (C) According to be question

$$a^2 + 5a + d = 0 \quad \ldots(1)$$

$$a^2 + 6a + 2d = 0 \quad \ldots(2)$$

Subtracting (1) from (2)

$$a = -d$$

$\Rightarrow$ $(-d)^2 - 5d + d = 0$

$\Rightarrow$ $d = 4$

Hence Ans is (C)

Sol. 45 (A) Given

a_{15} of 1st $AP = 1 + 14 \times 1$

a_{15} of 2nd $AP = 1 + 14 \times 2$

$\vdots$

a_{15} of 15st $AP = 1 + 14 \times 15$

$\Rightarrow$ required Sum $= 1 \times 15 + 14\,(1 + 2 + 3 + \ldots + 15)$

$$15 + 14 \times \frac{15 \times 16}{2} = 1695$$

Hence Ans is (A)

Sol. 46 (A) Given $2^{x-1} + 2^{x+1} = 2560$

$\Rightarrow$ $\dfrac{2^x}{2} + 2^x \times 2 = 2560$

Let $2^x = m$

$\Rightarrow$ $\dfrac{m}{2} + 2m = 2560$

$\Rightarrow$ $5m = 2560 \times 2$

$\Rightarrow$ $m = 1024,$

Now $2^x = 1024 = 2^{10}$

$\Rightarrow$ $x = 10$

Hence Ans is (A)

Sol. 47 (D) $x^2 - px + q = 0$

Given $|\alpha - \beta| = 1$

$$\sqrt{(\alpha+\beta)^2 - 4\alpha\beta} = 1$$

$\Rightarrow$ $= \sqrt{p^2 - 4q}$

$$= p^2 - 4q = 1$$

Hence Ans is (D)

Sol. 48 (C) $\alpha + \beta = -3$

and $\alpha\beta = -\dfrac{5}{2}$

Roots are α, β

$\Rightarrow$ Equation will be

$$x^2 + 3x + \left(\frac{-5}{2}\right) = 0$$

$\Rightarrow$ $2x^2 + 6x - 5 = 0$

Hence Ans is (D)

Sol. 49 (D) $3ax^2 + 2bx + c = 0$

Roots are in ratio $= 3 : 2$

$\Rightarrow$ $\alpha : \beta = 3 : 2$

$\Rightarrow$ $\alpha = 3\lambda, \beta = 2\lambda$

$$\alpha + \beta = \frac{-2b}{3a} \quad \ldots(1)$$

$\Rightarrow$ $5\lambda = \dfrac{-2b}{3a}$

$\Rightarrow$ $\lambda = \dfrac{-2b}{15a}$

$$\alpha\beta = \frac{c}{3a} \quad \ldots(2)$$

$$6\lambda^2 = \frac{c}{3a}$$

$$6\left(\frac{2b}{15a}\right)^2 = \frac{c}{3a}$$

$\Rightarrow$ $8b^2 = 25ac$

Hence Ans is (D)

Sol. 50 (C) $(a^2 + b^2)x^2 - 2b\,(a + c)x + (b^2 + c^2) = 0$

$\Rightarrow$ $D = 0$

$\Rightarrow$ $4b^2(a + c)^2 = 4(a^2 + b^2)(b^2 + c^2)$

$\Rightarrow$ $b^2[a^2 + c^2 + 2ac] = a^2b^2 + a^2c^2 + b^4 + b^2c^2$

$\Rightarrow$ $2acb^2 = a^2c^2 + b^4$

$\Rightarrow$ $(b^2 - ac)^2 = 0$

$\Rightarrow$ $b^2 = ac$

Hence Ans is (C)

Sol. 51 (D) $5^{x+1} + 5^{2-x} = 126$

$$5 \times 5^x + \frac{5^2}{5^x} = 126$$

Let $5^x = y$ then $5y + \dfrac{25}{y} = 126$

$$5y^2 + 25 = 126y$$

$$5y^2 - 126y + 25 = 0$$

Solving this we get $(y - 25)(5y - 1) = 0$

Therefore $y = 25$ or $y = \dfrac{1}{5}$

If $y = 25$ then $5^x = 5^2$

Therefore $x = 2$

If $y = \dfrac{1}{5}$ then $5^x = 5^{-1}$

Therefore $x = -1$

So $x = 2$ or -1

Hence Ans is (D)

Sol. 52 (C) $(a-b)x^2+(b-c)x+(c-a)=0$

Since roots are equal

$\Rightarrow \quad d=0$

$\Rightarrow \quad (b-c)^2-4(a-b)(c-a)=0$

$\Rightarrow \quad b^2+c^2-2bc-4(ac-a^2-bc+ab)=0$

$\Rightarrow \quad b^2+c^2-2bc-4ac+4a^2+4bc-4ab)=0$

$\Rightarrow \quad (b+c-2a)^2=0$

$\Rightarrow \quad b+c-2a=0$

$\Rightarrow \quad b+c=2a$

Hence Ans is (C)

Sol. 53 (D) Given $ax^2+bx+c=0$

for real roots discriminant is always greater than or equal to zero.

$\Rightarrow \quad b^2-4ac\geq 0$

If $\quad c=0$

Then $\quad b^2\geq 0$

Which is always true

Hence Ans is (D)

Sol. 54 (D) Minimum value of a quadratic equation ax^2+bx+c is equal to $\dfrac{-D}{4a}$

$\Rightarrow \quad \text{Minimum value} = \dfrac{4ac-b^2}{4a}=\dfrac{4\times 3\times 2-5^2}{4\times 3}$

$= -\dfrac{1}{12}$

Hence Ans is (D)

Sol. 55 (D) Since roots $x^2-6x-2=0$ are α & β

$\Rightarrow \quad \alpha^2=6\alpha+2$ and $\beta^2=6\beta+2$

Given $\quad a_n=\alpha^n-\beta^n$

$\Rightarrow \quad a_{10}=\alpha^{10}-\beta^{10},\ a_8=\alpha^8-\beta^8,$

& $\quad a_9=\alpha^9-\beta^9$

Now $\quad \dfrac{a_{10}-2a_8}{2a_9}=\dfrac{(\alpha^{10}-\beta^{10})-2(\alpha^8-\beta^8)}{2(\alpha^9-\beta^9)}$

$\Rightarrow \quad \dfrac{\alpha^8(\alpha^2-2)+\beta^8(2-\beta^2)}{2(\alpha^9-\beta^9)}$

$\Rightarrow \quad \dfrac{\alpha^8(6\alpha+2-2)+\beta^8(2-6\beta-2)}{2(\alpha^9-\beta^9)}$

$\Rightarrow \quad \dfrac{6\alpha^9-6\beta^9}{2(\alpha^9-\beta^9)}\Rightarrow \dfrac{6}{2}=3$

Hence Ans is (D)

Sol. 56 (B) Given $x^2-bx+6=0$

Let roots are α and 3β

$x^2-6x+c=0$

Let roots are α and 4β

$\alpha+3\beta=b \qquad 3\alpha\beta=6 \Rightarrow \alpha\beta=2$

$\alpha+4\beta=6 \qquad 4\alpha\beta=c \Rightarrow c=8$

Now 2nd equation is $x^2-6x+8=0$

$\Rightarrow \quad (x-4)(x-2)=0$

$\Rightarrow$ root are 2 and 4

Because other roots are integer

So that $\quad 4b=4\Rightarrow \beta=1$

So, $\quad \alpha=2$

Hence Ans is (B)

Sol. 57 (A) Given

$(x-1)(x-\alpha)=0$ and $(x-1)(x-\beta)=0$

$x^2-x(\alpha+1)+\alpha=0$ and $x^2-x(\beta+1)+\beta=0$

Discriminants are equal so,

$(\alpha+1)^2-4\alpha=(\beta+1)^2-4\beta$

$(\alpha+1)^2-4\alpha=(\beta+1)^2-4\beta$

$(\alpha-1)^2=(\beta-1)^2$

$\alpha-1=\pm\beta-1$

$\alpha-1=\beta-1$ or $\alpha-1=\beta+1$

$\alpha=\beta$ or $\alpha+\beta=2$

Hence Ans is (A)

Sol. 58 (A) Let the root of the equation is α and β then $\alpha\beta=72$

α and β should be integer so

$1\times 72=72\,(-1)(-72)=72$

$2\times 36=72\,(-2)(-36)=72$

$3\times 24=72\,(-3)(-24)=72$

$4\times 18=72\,(-4)(-18)=72$

$6\times 12=72\,(-6)(-12)=72$

$8\times 9=72\,(-8)(-9)=72$

So total 12 pairs are possible.

Hence Ans is (A)

Sol. 59 (C) $x^2-3x-4=0 \qquad \ldots(1)$

$\Rightarrow$ 4 and -1 are the roots of equation-(1)

$2x^2+kx-5=0$

When $x=4$,

$2(4)^2+4k-5=0$

$\Rightarrow \quad k=-\dfrac{-27}{4}$

When $\quad x=-1$

$2(-1)^2-k-5=0$

$\Rightarrow \quad k=-3$

Hence Ans is (C)

* * * * *

Arithmetic Progression Theory

7

- Some numbers arranged in a definite order, according to a definite rule, are said to form a **sequence.**

- A sequence is called an **arithmetic progression** (AP), if the difference of any of its terms and the preceding term is always the same.
i.e., $t_{n+1} - t_n$ = constant

- The constant number is called the **common difference of the A.P.**

- If a is the first term and d the common difference of an AP, then the general form of the AP is $a, a + d, a + 2d, \ldots$

- Let a be the first term and d be the common difference of an AP, then, its nth term or general is given by
$t_n = a + (n - 1)d$

- If l is the last term of the AP, then n^{th} term from the end is the nth term of an AP, whose first term is l and common difference is $-d$.
$\Rightarrow$ n^{th} term from the end = Last term + $(n - 1)(-d)$
$\Rightarrow$ n^{th} term from the end = $l - (n - 1)d$

- If $a, b, c,$ are in AP, then
(i) $(a + k), (b + k), (c + k)$ are in AP.
(ii) $(a - k), (b - k), (c - k)$ are in AP.
(iii) $ak, bk, ck,$ are in AP.
(iv) $\frac{a}{k}, \frac{b}{k}, \frac{c}{k}$ are in AP $(k \neq 0)$

- Remember the following while working with consecutive terms in an AP.

(i) *Three consecutive terms in an AP.*
$a - d, a, a + d$
First term = $a - d$, common difference = d
Their sum = $a - d + a + a + d = 3a$

(ii) *Four consecutive terms in an AP.*
$a - 3d, a - d, a + d, a + 3d$
First term : $a - 3d$, common difference = $2d$
Their sum = $a - 3d + a - d + a + d + a + 3d = 4a$

(iii) *Five consecutive terms in an AP.*
$a - 2d, a - d, a, a + d, a + 2d$
First term = $a - 2d$, common difference = d

- The sum S_n up to n terms of an AP whose first term is a and common difference d is given by
$$S_n = \frac{n}{2}[2a + (n - 1)d]$$

- If the first term and the last term of an AP are t_1 and t_n, then
$$S_n = \frac{n}{2}(t_1 + t_n) = \frac{n}{2} \text{ (first term + last term)}$$
If $t_1 = a$, the first term and $t_n = l$, the last term, then
$$S_n = \frac{n}{2}(a + l)$$

- $S_n - S_{n-1} = t_n$

* * * * *

PRACTICE EXERCISE - 7.1

7-1 The mean of a, b, c is x. If $ab + bc + ca = 0$, then what is the mean of a^2, b^2 and c^2 :

(A) $\frac{x^3}{3}$ (B) x^2

(C) $3x^2$ (D) $9x^2$

7-2 Ajay started work in 1995 at an annual salary of Rs.5000 and received an increment of Rs.200 each year. In which year did his income reach Rs.7000 :

(A) 19th (B) 11th

(C) 12th (D) 15th

7-3 In an A.P. , the sum of first n terms is $\frac{3n^2}{2}+\frac{5n}{2}$. Find its 25th term :

(A) 74 (B) 75

(C) 76 (D) 77

7-4 The sum of "n" A.M.s inserted between "a" and "b" is :

(A) $(a+b)n$ (B) $\frac{n}{2}(a+b)$

(C) $\frac{n}{2}(b-a)$ (D) $2n(a+b)$

7-5 If a, b, c are in A.P. and $a - c = b$ then find the value of a in terms of b :

(A) $\frac{2b}{3}$ (B) $\frac{3b}{2}$

(C) $\frac{b}{2}$ (D) $\frac{b+2}{2}$

7-6 Which term of the sequence 17, 25, 33, 41… is just greater than 90 :

(A) 11 (B) 12

(C) 10 (D) 13

7-7 If a, A_1, A_2, b are in A.P. then find $\frac{A_1}{A_2}$:

(A) $\frac{2a+b}{a+b}$ (B) $\frac{2a+b}{a+2b}$

(C) $\frac{a+2b}{a+b}$ (D) $\frac{2a+3b}{a+b}$

7-8 Find the value of x and y if $x + 3, y + 7, x + y + 8, x + 3y + 20$ are in A.P. :

(A) $\frac{-5}{3}, \frac{-19}{3}$ (B) $\frac{5}{3}, \frac{19}{3}$

(C) $\frac{5}{3}, \frac{-19}{3}$ (D) $-\frac{5}{3}, \frac{19}{3}$

7-9 Which term of AP 19, $18\frac{1}{5}$, $17\frac{2}{5}$,…is the first negative term :

(A) 28th term (B) 25th term

(C) 30th term (D) 27th term

7-10 The 18th term of an AP exceeds its 12th term by 12. Find the common difference :

(A) 1 (B) 2

(C) –2 (D) –1

7-11 For what value of n, are the nth terms of two APs : 63, 65, 67 .... and 3, 10, 17, ... equal :

(A) 15 (B) 14

(C) 13 (D) 12

7-12 Find the sum of first 20 terms of the list of numbers whose nth term is given by $a_n = 3 + 2n$:

(A) 472 (B) 480

(C) 504 (D) None of these

7-13 The sum of 10 terms of the series $\sqrt{3}+\sqrt{12}+\sqrt{27}+\sqrt{48}+\ldots$ is :

(A) 55 (B) 66

(C) $45\sqrt{3}$ (D) $55\sqrt{3}$

7-14 The interior angles of a polygon are in A.P. If the smallest angle be 120° and the common difference be 5°, then the number of sides is :

(A) 9 (B) 16

(C) 8 (D) 6

7-15 If p^{th} term of an AP is $\frac{1}{q}$ and q^{th} term is $\frac{1}{p}$, then the sum of first pq terms is :

(A) pq (B) 0

(C) $pq+1$ (D) $\frac{1}{2}(pq+1)$

7-16 If sum of m terms of an AP is n and sum of n terms is m, then the sum of $(m+n)$ terms is :
(A) mn (B) 0
(C) $m+n$ (D) $-(m+n)$

7-17 The sum of all 2 digit numbers is :
(A) 4750 (B) 4895
(C) 4905 (D) 4680

7-18 If the sum of n terms of an A.P. is $2n^2+5n$, then its nth term is :
(A) $4n-3$ (B) $3n-4$
(C) $4n+3$ (D) $3n+4$

7-19 The sum of the first 100 positive integers exactly divisible by 7 is :
(A) 35350 (B) 35700
(C) 34650 (D) 1393

7-20 The sum of 20 terms of $\log 2+\log 4+\log 8+\ldots$ is :
(A) $20\log 2$ (B) Log 20
(C) $210\log 2$ (D) $\log 2$

7-21 If there are $(2n+1)$ terms in A.P. then the ratio of the sum of odd terms and the sum of even terms is :
(A) $n+1:n-1$ (B) $n+1:n^2$
(C) $n+1:n$ (D) None of these

7-22 Fourth term of an arithmetic progression is 8. What is the sum of the first 7 terms of the arithmetic progression :
(A) 7 (B) 64
(C) 56 (D) Can't be determined

7-23 The sum of integers from 1 to 100 that are divisible by 2 or 5 is :
(A) 3000 (B) 3050
(C) 4050 (D) None of these

7-24 If the sum of the series $54+51+48+\ldots$ is 513, then the number of terms are :
(A) 18 (B) 20
(C) 17 (D) None of these

7-25 Three terms are in A.P. if sum of these numbers be 6 and the product -90. Then numbers are :
(A) $-5, 2, 9$ (B) $8, 1, -5$
(C) Both A or B (D) $9, 6, -5$

7-26 There are four arithmetic means between 2 and -18. The means are :
(A) $-4, -7, -10, -13$ (B) $1, -4, -7, -10$
(C) $-2, -5, -9, -13$ (D) $-2, -6, -10, -14$

7-27 If a, x_1, x_2, b are in AP and $b, y_1, y_2\ c$ are also in AP then the value of $x_2+y_2-(x_1+y_1)$ is :
(A) $\frac{c-a}{2}$ (B) $\frac{c+a}{3}$
(C) $\frac{c-a}{3}$ (D) $\frac{c+2a}{3}$

7-28 If the ratio of the sum of n terms of two A.P.'s is $\frac{3n-1}{3n+1}$ then find the ratio of their fifth term :
(A) $\frac{14}{15}$ (B) $\frac{13}{14}$
(C) $\frac{16}{17}$ (D) $\frac{18}{19}$

7-29 The sum of money of A, B and C is Rs. 63. If C gives Rs. 6 to B and A each then their money form an AP Find B's original money :
(A) 10 (B) 15
(C) 38 (D) 13

7-30 If a, b, c are in A.P., then the straight line $ax+by+c=0$ will always pass through the point :
(A) $(-1,-2)$ (B) $(1,-2)$
(C) $(-1,2)$ (D) $(1,2)$

7-31 The maximum sum of the series $20+19\frac{1}{3}+18\frac{2}{3}+18+\ldots$ is :
(A) 930 (B) 290
(C) 320 (D) None of these

7-33 The 5th and 13th term of an A.P. are 5 and -3 respectively. The first term of the A.P. is :
(A) 1 (B) 9
(C) -15 (D) 2

7-34 A thief runs away from a police station with a uniform speed of 100 m/minute. After one minute a policeman runs behind the thief to catch him. He goes at a speed of 100 m/minute in first minute and increases his speed 10 m each succeeding minute. After how many minutes, the policeman will catch the thief :
(A) 1 minute (B) 10 minutes
(C) 4 minutes (D) 5 minutes

7-35 How many terms of the sequence 18, 16, 14, ... should be taken so that their sum is zero :
(A) 18 (B) 19
(C) 17 (D) None of these

7-36 Sum of first 22 terms of an A.P. in which $d = 22$ and $a_{22} = 149$ is :

(A) 1804 (B) -1804
(C) -1604 (D) -1704

7-37 Which term of the A.P. 15, 19, 23, … will be 20 more than its 13th term :

(A) 18 (B) 17
(C) 19 (D) None of these

7-38 If the arithmetic mean of a and b is $\frac{a^n + b^n}{a^{n-1} + b^{n-1}}$, then value of n is :

(A) -1 (B) 0
(C) 1 (D) None of these

7-39 The value of $\sum_{k=1}^{15} (2k-3)$ is :

(A) 390 (B) 195
(C) 210 (D) 426

7-40 If a clock strikes once at a one o'clock, twice at two o'clock and twelve times at 12 o'clock and again once at one o'clock and so on, how many times will the bell be struck in the course of 2 days:

(A) 156 (B) 312
(C) 78 (D) 288

7-41 In the arithmetic progression 5, 9, 13, 17, … upto 60 terms, and 2, 7, 12, 17, … upto 40 terms, find the number of identical terms in the two given series.

(A) 4 (B) 12
(C) 15 (D) 10

7-42 If $\frac{1}{b+c}, \frac{1}{c+a}, \frac{1}{a+b}$ are in AP, then :

(A) a, b, c are in AP (B) a^2, b^2, c^2 are in AP
(C) $\frac{1}{a}, \frac{1}{b}, \frac{1}{c}$ are in AP (D) None of these

7-43 The sum of the 3rd and the 15th elements of an arithmetic progression is equal to the sum of the 6th, 11th and 13th elements of the same progression. Then which element of the series should necessarily be equal to zero ?

(A) 1st (B) 9th
(C) 12th (D) None of these

7-44 The angles of a triangle are in AP, and the ratio of the greatest angle to the smallest is 3 : 1. Then the smallest angle is :

(A) 30° (B) 60°
(C) 45° (D) None of these

7-45 The least value of n for which the sum of the series $3 + 6 + 9 + \ldots +$ to n terms exceeds 1000 is :

(A) 24 (B) 25
(C) 26 (D) 27

7-46 The maximum value of the sum of the AP 30, 27, 24, 21, … is :

(A) 180 (B) 171
(C) 168 (D) 165

7-47 If S_n denotes the sum of n terms of an AP and $P^2S_p = PS_p{}^2$ for each natural number P, then S_n :

(A) Depends on d only (B) Is divisible by n^2
(C) Is divisible by $(n-1)$ (D) None of these

7-48 The 288th term of the series $a, b, b, c, c, c, d, d, d, d, e, e, e, e, e, f, f, f, f, f, f, \ldots$ is :

(A) u (B) v
(C) w (D) x

7-49 Find the sum of p terms of the series where n^{th} term is $\frac{n}{a} + b$:

(A) $\frac{P^2}{2a} + pb$ (B) $\frac{p(p+1)}{2a} + pb$
(C) $\frac{2p(p-1)}{a} + pb$ (D) None of these

7-50 A leaf is torn from a paperback novel. The sum of the numbers of the remaining pages is 15000. What are the page numbers on the torn leaf ?

(A) 112, 113 (B) 75, 76
(C) 25, 26 (D) Data inadequate

* * * * *

PRACTICE EXERCISE - 7.2

7-1 If $a_1, a_2, a_3, \ldots a_n$ be an AP of non zero terms, then $\frac{1}{a_1a_2}+\frac{1}{a_2a_3}+\ldots\frac{1}{a_{n-1}a_n}$ is :

(A) $\frac{1}{a_1a_n}$ (B) $\frac{n-1}{a_1a_n}$

(C) $\frac{a_1a_n}{n-1}$ (D) a_1a_n

7-2 If $\frac{b+c-a}{a}, \frac{c+a-b}{b}, \frac{a+b-c}{c}$ are in AP then which of the following is in A.P. :

(A) a, b, c (B) a^2, b^2, c^2

(C) $\frac{1}{a}, \frac{1}{b}, \frac{1}{c}$ (D) $a+b, b+c, c+a$

7-3 If the first, second and the last terms of an AP are a, b, c respectively, then the sum of AP is :

(A) $\frac{(a+b)(a+c-2b)}{2(b-a)}$ (B) $\frac{(b+c)(a+b-2c)}{2(b-a)}$

(C) $\frac{(a+c)(b+c-2a)}{2(b-a)}$ (D) None of these

7-4 If $a_1, a_2, a_3 \ldots a_n$ are in A.P. where $a_i > 0, i = 1, 2, 3 \ldots n$, then the value of $\frac{1}{\sqrt{a_1}+\sqrt{a_2}}+\frac{1}{\sqrt{a_2}+\sqrt{a_3}}+\ldots+\frac{1}{\sqrt{a_{n-1}}+\sqrt{a_n}}$ is :

(A) $\frac{1}{\sqrt{a_1}+\sqrt{a_n}}$ (B) $\frac{1}{\sqrt{a_1}-\sqrt{a_n}}$

(C) $\frac{n}{\sqrt{a_1}-\sqrt{a_n}}$ (D) $\frac{n-1}{\sqrt{a_1}+\sqrt{a_n}}$

7-5 The product of n positive numbers is unity, then their sum is :

(A) A positive integer (B) Divisible by n

(C) Equal to $n+\frac{1}{n}$ (D) Never less than n

7-6 If a, b, c are positive real numbers such that $a+b+c+d=2$, then $M=(a+b)(c+d)$ satisfies the relation :

(A) $0 \le M \le 1$ (B) $1 \le M \le 2$

(C) $2 \le M \le 3$ (D) $3 \le M \le 4$

7-7 If x, y, z are positive then the minimum value of $x^{\log y-\log z}+y^{\log z-\log x}+z^{\log x-\log y}$ is :

(A) 3 (B) 1

(C) 9 (D) 16

7-8 a, b, c are three positive numbers and abc^2 has the greatest value $\frac{1}{64}$. Then :

(A) $a=b=\frac{1}{2}, c=\frac{1}{4}$ (B) $a=b=\frac{1}{4}, c=\frac{1}{2}$

(C) $a=b=c=\frac{1}{3}$ (D) None of these

7-9 If $a>0, b>0, c>0$ and the minimum value of $a(b^2+c^2)+b(c^2+a^2)+c(a^2+b^2)$ is $\lambda\, abc$ then λ is :

(A) 2 (B) 1

(C) 6 (D) 3

7-10 If a, b, c, d are four positive real numbers such that $abcd=1$, then minimum value of $(1+a)(1+b)(1+c)(1+d)$ is :

(A) 16 (B) 32

(C) 8 (D) 4

7-11 The sum of n terms of three AP's are S_1, S_2 and S_3 respectively. The first term of each is unity and the common difference are 1, 2 and 3 respectively. Find which of the following relations is true :

(A) $S_1+S_2=S_3$ (B) $S_1+S_2+S_3=0$

(C) $S_1+S_3=2S_2$ (D) None of these

7-12 If a, b, c, d, e are in A.P., then the value of $a-4b+6c-4d+e$ equals :

(A) a (B) b

(C) c (D) None of these

7-13 If 9th term of an A.P. be zero then the ratio of its 29th and 19th term is

(A) 1 : 2 (B) 2 : 1

(C) 1 : 3 (D) 3 : 1

7-14 Three numbers x, y, z are such that $x^2+y^2=z^2$; If $z=m^2+n^2$ and $y=2mn$, then $\frac{1}{x}+\frac{1}{z}$ is equal to :

(A) $\frac{m^2}{m^2-n^2}$ (B) $\frac{n^2}{m^2-n^2}$

(C) $\frac{2m^2}{m^4-n^4}$ (D) $\frac{2n^2}{m^4-n^4}$

7-15 The last digit of $(1^3+2^3+3^3+\ldots 10^3)^3$ is :

(A) 2 (B) 8

(C) 5 (D) 0

7-16 If angles A, B, C of a ΔABC form an increasing AP, then $\sin B =$

(A) $\frac{1}{2}$ (B) $\frac{\sqrt{3}}{2}$

(C) 1 (D) $\frac{1}{\sqrt{2}}$

7-17 Find the sum of

$$\frac{1}{3\times 7}+\frac{1}{7\times 11}+\frac{1}{11\times 15}+\ldots+\frac{1}{99\times 103}$$

(A) $\frac{100}{309}$ (B) $\frac{101}{309}$

(C) $\frac{25}{309}$ (D) $\frac{105}{309}$

7-18 The sum of n terms of the series

$$\frac{1}{\sqrt{3}+\sqrt{5}}+\frac{1}{\sqrt{5}+\sqrt{7}}+\frac{1}{\sqrt{7}+\sqrt{9}}+\ldots \text{is}$$

(A) $\sqrt{2n+3}$ (B) $\frac{\sqrt{2n+3}}{2}$

(C) $\sqrt{2n+3}-\sqrt{3}$ (D) $\frac{\sqrt{2n+3}-\sqrt{3}}{2}$

7-19 The coefficient of x^{49} in the product $(x-1)(x-3)(x-5)(x-7)\ldots(x-99)$ is :

(A) -99^2 (B) 1

(C) -2500 (D) None of these

7-20 The sum of the series :

$$\frac{1}{\log_2 4}+\frac{1}{\log_4 4}+\frac{1}{\log_8 4}+\ldots+\frac{1}{\log_{2^n} 4} \text{ is:}$$

(A) $\frac{n(n+1)}{2}$ (B) $\frac{n(n+1)(2n+1)}{12}$

(C) $\frac{1}{n(n+1)}$ (D) $\frac{n(n+1)}{4}$

7-21 In the following two A.P.'s how many terms are identical?

2, 5, 8, 11... to 60 terms

3, 5, 7, 9, ... to 50 terms

(A) 16 (B) 17

(C) 18 (D) 20

7-22 The series of natural numbers are arranged as follow

1
2 3
4 5 6
7 8 9 10

The sum of the numbers in the nth row is :

(A) $\frac{n(n+1)}{2}$ (B) $\frac{n(n^2+1)}{2}$

(C) $\frac{n^2(n+1)}{2}$ (D) $\frac{n^2(n^2+1)}{2}$

7-23 If the roots of the equation $x^3-12x^2+39x-28=0$ are in AP, then their common difference will be :

(A) ± 1 (B) ± 2

(C) ± 3 (D) ± 4

7-24 Let S_n denote the sum of n terms of an A.P. whose first term is a. If the common difference d is given by $d = S_n - kS_{n-2}$, then $k =$

(A) 1 (B) 2

(C) 3 (D) None of these

7-25 The first and last term of an A.P. are a and l respectively. If S is the sum of all the terms of the A.P. and the common difference is given by :

$$\frac{l^2-a^2}{k-(l+a)} \text{ then } k=$$

(A) S (B) $2S$

(C) $3S$ (D) None of these

* * * * *

PRACTICE EXERCISE - 7.3

7-1 The sum of the third and seventh terms of an A.P. is 6 and their product is 8, then common difference is :

[NTSE-2013 (Stage-I) Rajasthan]

(A) ± 1 (B) ± 2

(C) $\pm\frac{1}{2}$ (D) $\pm\frac{1}{4}$

7-2 If 9, a, b, – 6 are in Arithmetic progression, then $a+b=$

[NTSE-2014 (Stage-I) Rajasthan]

(A) 1 (B) 5

(C) 15 (D) 3

7-3 The sum of eleven consecutive integers is 2002. What is the smallest of these integers?

[NTSE-2015 (Stage-I) Andhara Pradesh]

(A) 163 (B) 177

(C) 145 (D) 156

7-4 If the pth term of an A.P. is q and the qth term is p, then the nth term is : **[NTSE-2015 (Stage-I) Chandigarh]**

(A) $p+q-n$ (B) $p+q+n$

(C) $p-q-n$ (D) $q-p-n$

7-5 If $\frac{a^{n+1}+b^{n-1}}{a^n+b^n}$ is the arithmetic mean between a and b, then the value of n is : **[NTSE-2015 (Stage-I) Chandigarh]**

(A) 0 (B) 1

(C) – 1 (D) 2

7-6 In an A.P. the sum of 'n' terms is $5n^2 - 5n$. Find the 10th term of the A.P. : **[NTSE-2015 (Stage-I) Maharashtra]**

(A) 80 (B) 90

(C) 100 (D) 110

7-7 The total number of two digit numbers which are divisible by three will be : **[NTSE-2015 (Stage-I) Chhatisgarh]**

(A) 30 (B) 31

(C) 32 (D) 33

7-8 In the year 2013, Pravin saves Rs. 1 on the first day, Rs. 3 on the second day, Rs. 5 on the third day and so on. Find the total amount of his saving in that year :

[NTSE-2015 (Stage-I) Maharashtra]

(A) Rs. 133225 (B) Rs. 132225

(C) Rs. 123225 (D) Rs. 134225

7-9 Arithmetic mean of 20 observations is 15. If each observation is multiplied by $\frac{2}{3}$ then the arithmetic mean of them is : **[NTSE-2015 (Stage-I) Chennai]**

(A) 10 (B) 30

(C) 45 (D) 15

7-10 The first term of an A.P. is 5, the last term is 45 and the sum is 400. The fourth term of A.P. is :

[NTSE-2016 (Stage-I) Rajasthan]

(A) 13 (B) 11

(C) 15 (D) 14

7-11 In the five-sided star shown, the letters A, B, C, D and E are replaced by the numbers 3, 5, 6, 7 and 9 although not necessarily in that order. The sums of the numbers at the ends of the line segments $\overline{AB}$, $\overline{BC}$, $\overline{CD}$, $\overline{DE}$ and $\overline{EA}$ from an arithmetic sequence although not necessarily in that order. What is the middle term of the arithmetic sequence ?

[NTSE-2016 (Stage-I) Telangana]

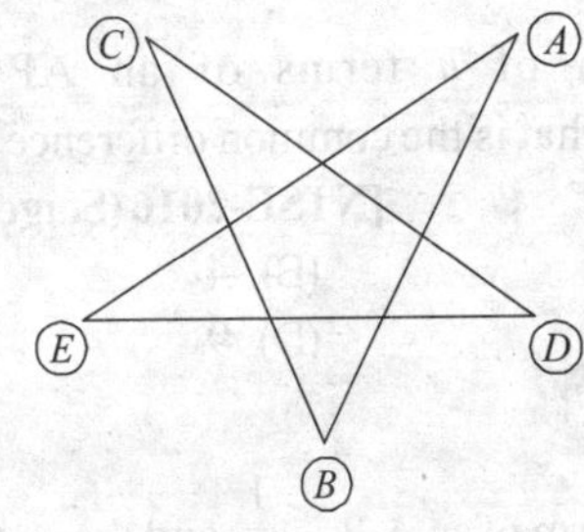

Figure 7.1

(A) 9 (B) 10

(C) 11 (D) 12

7-12 If a, b, c, d are positive real numbers such that a, b, c, d form an increasing arithmetic sequence and a, b, d form a geometric sequence, then $\frac{a}{d}$ is...

[NTSE-2016 (Stage-I) Telangana]

(A) $\frac{1}{12}$ (B) $\frac{1}{6}$

(C) $\frac{1}{4}$ (D) $\frac{1}{3}$

7-13 In an A.P., sum of first n terms is $\frac{3n^2}{2}+\frac{5n}{2}$. Find its 25th term : **[NTSE-2016 (Stage-I) Chandigarh]**

(A) 100 (B) 25

(C) 75 (D) 76

7-14 Sum of n terms of the series

$\sqrt{2}+\sqrt{8}+\sqrt{18}+\sqrt{32}+\ldots$ is :

[NTSE-2016 (Stage-I) Chandigarh]

(A) $\frac{n(n+1)}{2}$ (B) $2n(n+1)$

(C) $\frac{n(n+1)}{\sqrt{2}}$ (D) 1

7-15 Sum of first n odd natural numbers is :

[NTSE-2016 (Stage-I) Chandigarh]

(A) n^2 (B) $n+1$

(C) $2n+1$ (D) n

7-16 The value of the following expression is

$$\left[\frac{1}{(2^2-1)}\right]+\left[\frac{1}{(4^2-1)}\right]+\left[\frac{1}{(6^2-1)}\right]+\ldots+\left[\frac{1}{(20^2-1)}\right]$$ is :

[NTSE-2016 (Stage-I) Delhi]

(A) $\frac{10}{21}$ (B) $\frac{13}{27}$

(C) $\frac{15}{22}$ (D) $\frac{8}{33}$

7-17 The sum of n terms of an AP is given by ($Sn = 2n^2 + 3n$) what is the common difference of the A.P. :

[NTSE-2016 (Stage-I) Jharkhand]

(A) 3 (B) 4

(C) 5 (D) 9

7-18 If the mth term of an A.P. is $\frac{1}{n}$ and the nth term of it is $\frac{1}{m}$, then what is the mn^{th} term equal to ?

[NTSE-2016 (Stage-I) Odisha]

(A) 1 (B) 2

(C) $\frac{m}{n}$ (D) $\frac{n}{m}$

7-19 If the mth term of harmonic progression is "n" and n^{th} term is "m" then $(mn)^{th}$ term is :

[NTSE-2016 (Stage-I) Karnatka]

(A) mn (B) $\frac{1}{mn}$

(C) 1 (D) -1

7-20 If the sum of a progression.

$17+15+13+11+\ldots$ is 72.

Then number of terms in the progression will be :

[NTSE-2016 (Stage-I) Chhatisgarh]

(A) 6 (B) 7

(C) 8 (D) 9

7-21 $x_1, x_2, x_3, \ldots$, are in $A.P$ and If $x_1+x_7+x_{10}=-6$ and $x_3+x_8+x_{12}=-11$, then $x_3+x_8+x_{22}=?$

[NTSE-2017 (Stage-I) Andhra Pradesh]

(A) -21 (B) -15

(C) -18 (D) -31

7-22 If $\frac{2+5+8+\ldots n.\text{terms}}{7+11+15+\ldots n.\text{terms}}=\frac{23}{35}$ then n value is :

[NTSE-2017 (Stage-I) Andhra Pradesh]

(A) 17 (B) 15

(C) 18 (D) 23

7-23 The 7th term of an AP is 5 times the first term and its 9th term exceeds twice the 4th term by 1. The first term of the AP is …

[NTSE-2017 (Stage-I) Chandigarh]

(A) 151 (B) –39

(C) 3 (D) –124

7-24 If $\frac{a^{n+1}+b^{n+1}}{a^n+b^n}$ is the AM (arithmetic mean) between 'a' and 'b', then, find the value of n : **[NTSE-2017 (Stage-I) Delhi]**

(A) 1 (B) 3

(C) 2 (D) 0

7-25 If the sum of the first m terms of an AP is n and sum of its first n terms is m, then the sum of the its first $(m+n)$ terms is :

[NTSE-2017 (Stage-I) Haryana]

(A) $-(m+n)$ (B) $m+n$

(C) $-m+n$ (D) $m-n$

7-26 The lowest common multiple of two numbers is 14 times their greatest common divisor. The sum of LCM and GCD is 600. If one number is 80 then other number is :

[NTSE-2017 (Stage-I) Karnataka]

(A) 600 (B) 520

(C) 280 (D) 40

7-27 How many two-digit numbers are divisible by 2 :

[NTSE-2017 (Stage-I) Madhya Pradesh]

(A) 30 (B) 40

(C) 45 (D) 50

7-28 The sum of first 20 terms of AP : 8, 3, –2, … is :

[NTSE-2017 (Stage-I) Madhya Pradesh]

(A) -790 (B) -970

(C) -979 (D) -779

7-29 How many numbers between 10 to 300, when divided by 4, leave remainder 3 ? **[NTSE-2017 (Stage-I) Maharashtra]**

(A) 71 (B) 72

(C) 73 (D) 74

7-30 If pth term of an AP is q and qth term is p then mth term of this AP will be : **[NTSE-2017 (Stage-I) Punjab]**

(A) $p+q+m$ (B) $p+q-m$

(C) $p-q-m$ (D) $p-q+m$

7-31 Which term of $A.P.$ 20, $19\frac{1}{4}$, $18\frac{1}{2}$, ... is first negative term ? **[NTSE-2017 (Stage-I) Rajasthan]**

(A) 18th (B) 15th

(C) 28th (D) 27th

7-32 If the sum of n terms of an AP is $5n^2-3n$, then its 100th term is : **[NTSE-2017 (Stage-I) Tamilnadu]**

(A) 992 (B) 2

(C) 12 (D) $5n^2$

7-33 The 5th term of the arithmetic sequence is 5 and the sum of the first 5 terms is 55. What is its first term ? **[NTSE-2017 (Stage-I) Kerala]**

(A) 15 (B) 16

(C) 17 (D) 18

7-34 The sum of the first 11 terms and the sum of the first 17 terms of an arithmetic sequence are equal. What is the sum of the first 28 terms ? **[NTSE-2017 (Stage-I) Kerala]**

(A) 28 (B) 1

(C) –1 (D) 0

7-35 5th term of an $A.P.$ is 10 more than its 3rd term. What is the difference of its 9th and 6th terms : **[NTSE-2018 (Stage-I) Rajasthan]**

(A) 15 (B) 3

(C) 6 (D) 10

7-36 If a, b, c are in $A.P.$, then $ax+by+c=0$ will always pass through a fixed point whose co-ordinates are : **[NTSE-2018 (Stage-I) Andhra Pradesh]**

(A) $(-1,-2)$ (B) $(-1,2)$

(C) $(1,-2)$ (D) $(1,2)$

7-37 Four number in A. P. whose sum is 20 and the sum of whose squares is 120, then the numbers are : **[NTSE-2018 (Stage-I) Andhra Pradesh]**

(A) 8, 10, 12, 14 (B) 4, 6, 8, 10

(C) 6, 8, 10, 12 (D) 2, 4, 6, 8

7-38 If $S_n = nP+\frac{n}{2}(n-1)Q$, where S_n denotes the sum of the first n terms of an Arithmetic Progression (A.P), then the common difference is : **[NTSE-2018 (Stage-I) Bihar]**

(A) $P+Q$ (B) $2P+3Q$

(C) $2Q$ (D) Q

7-39 The first and last term of an arithmatic progression are 17 and 332 respectively and if common difference is 9, then the number of terms will be : **[NTSE-2018 (Stage-I) Chhattishgarh]**

(A) 34 (B) 35

(C) 36 (D) 37

7-40 If $x_1, x_2, x_3, ..., x_n$ are in $A.P.$, then the value of $\frac{1}{x_1x_2}+\frac{1}{x_2x_3}+\frac{1}{x_3x_4}+...+\frac{1}{x_{n-1}x_n}$ is : **[NTSE-2018 (Stage-I) Delhi]**

(A) $\frac{n-1}{x_1x_n}$ (B) $\frac{n-1}{x_2x_{n-1}}$

(C) $\frac{n}{x_1x_n}$ (D) $\frac{n+1}{x_1x_n}$

7-41 If $x^2+y^2+\frac{1}{x^2}+\frac{1}{y^2}=4$, then the value of x^2+y^2 is : **[NTSE-2018 (Stage-I) Delhi]**

(A) 2 (B) 4

(C) 8 (D) 16

7-42 If $a_1, a_2, a_3, ...a_n$ are in $A.P.$ and $a_1=0$, then the value of $\left(\frac{a_3}{a_2}+\frac{a_4}{a_3}+...+\frac{a_n}{a_{n-1}}\right)-a_2\left(\frac{1}{a_2}+\frac{1}{a_3}+...+\frac{1}{a_{n-2}}\right)$ is equal to : **[NTSE-2018 (Stage-I) Delhi]**

(A) $n+\frac{1}{n}$ (B) $n+\frac{1}{n-1}$

(C) $(n-1)+\frac{1}{(n-1)}$ (D) $(n-2)+\frac{1}{(n-2)}$

7-43 The mean of the data set comprising 16 observations is 16. If one of the observations with value 16 is deleted and three new observations 3, 4, 5 are added, then the new mean is : **[NTSE-2018 (Stage-I) Himachal Pradesh]**

(A) 17 (B) 15, 8

(C) 14 (D) 16, 8

7-44 If the sum of 'n' terms of an arithmetic progression is $S_n = 3n+2n^2$ then its common difference is : **[NTSE-2018 (Stage-I) Karnataka]**

(A) 9 (B) 6

(C) 4 (D) 3

7-45 How many numbers of two digits are divisible by 3 : **[NTSE-2018 (Stage-I) Madhya Prasesh]**

(A) 30 (B) 32

(C) 40 (D) 35

7-46 nth term of a list of numbers is given by $a_n = (3 + 2n)$. Sum of first 24 terms will be : **[NTSE-2018 (Stage-I) Madhya Prasesh]**

(A) 672 (B) 670
(C) 570 (D) 572

7-47 In Arithmetic Progression there are n terms (n is odd) and the middle term is m then what is $Sn = ?$ **[NTSE-2018 (Stage-I) Madhya Prasesh]**

(A) $mn/2$ (B) mn
(C) $2\,mn$ (D) mn^2

7-48 In an *A.P.*, the sum of m terms is equal to n and the sum of n terms is equal to m, then the sum of $(m + n)$ terms is : **[NTSE-2018 (Stage-I) Tamil Nadu]**

(A) $m + n$ (B) $-(m + n)$
(C) $(m - n)$ (D) $(n - m)$

7-49 The sum of the integers form 1 to 100 that are divisible by 2 or 5 is : **[NTSE-2018 (Stage-I) Telangana]**

(A) 2250 (B) 3050
(C) 3550 (D) 3600

7-50 How many numbers lie between 10 to 300 which when divided by 4 leave a remainder 3 : **[NTSE-2018 (Stage-I) Uttarakhandh]**

(A) 71 (B) 73
(C) 72 (D) 74

7-51 If a, b, c be the 4th, 7th and 10th term of an AP respectively, then the sum of the roots of the equation $ax^2 - 2bx + c = 0$: **[NTSE-2014 (Stage-II)]**

(A) is $-\dfrac{b}{a}$

(B) is $-\dfrac{2b}{a}$

(C) is $\dfrac{c+a}{a}$

(D) Cannot be determined unless some more information is given about the AP

7-52 If $S_1, S_2, S_3, \ldots, S_r$ are the sums of first n terms of r arithmetic progressions whose first terms are 1, 2, 3, … and whose common differences are 1, 3, 5, … respectively, then the value of $S_1 + S_2 + S_3 + \ldots + S_r$ is : **[NTSE-2015 (Stage-II)]**

(A) $\dfrac{(nr-1)(nr+1)}{2}$ (B) $\dfrac{(nr+1)nr}{2}$

(C) $\dfrac{(nr-1)nr}{2}$ (D) $\dfrac{n(nr+1)}{2}$

7-53 First term of an arithmetic progression is 2. If the sum of its first five terms is equal to one-fourth of the sum of the next five terms, then the sum of its first 30 terms is : **[NTSE-2016 (Stage-II)]**

(A) 2670 (B) 2610
(C) –2520 (D) –2550

7-54 The odd natural numbers have been divided in groups as (1, 3) ; (5, 7, 9, 11); (13, 15, 17, 19, 21, 23); … Then the sum of numbers in the 10th group is : **[NTSE-2017 (Stage-II)]**

(A) 4000 (B) 4003
(C) 4007 (D) 4008

* * * * *

ANSWERS

PRACTICE EXERCISE-7.1

1	(C)	2	(B)	3	(C)
4	(B)	5	(B)	6	(B)
7	(B)	8	(A)	9	(B)
10	(B)	11	(C)	12	(B)
13	(D)	14	(A)	15	(D)
16	(D)	17	(C)	18	(C)
19	(A)	20	(C)	21	(C)
22	(C)	23	(B)	24	(A)
25	(A)	26	(D)	27	(C)
28	(C)	29	(B)	30	(B)
31	(A)	32	(B)	33	(B)
34	(D)	35	(B)	36	(B)
37	(A)	38	(C)	39	(B)
40	(B)	41	(D)	42	(B)
43	(C)	44	(A)	45	(C)
46	(D)	47	(D)	48	(D)
49	(B)	50	(C)		

PRACTICE EXERCISE-7.2

1	(B)	2	(C)	3	(C)
4	(D)	5	(D)	6	(A)
7	(A)	8	(B)	9	(C)
10	(A)	11	(C)	12	(D)
13	(B)	14	(C)	15	(C)
16	(B)	17	(C)	18	(D)
19	(C)	20	(D)	21	(B)
22	(B)	23	(C)	24	(B)
25	(B)				

PRACTICE EXERCISE-7.3

1	(C)	2	(D)	3	(B)
4	(A)	5	(A)	6	(B)
7	(A)	8	(A)	9	(A)
10	(A)	11	(D)	12	(C)
13	(D)	14	(C)	15	(A)
16	(A)	17	(A)	18	(A)
19	(C)	20	(A)	21	(A)
22	(B)	23	(C)	24	(D)
25	(A)	26	(C)	27	(C)
28	(A)	29	(C)	30	(B)
31	(C)	32	(A)	33	(C)
34	(D)	35	(A)	36	(C)
37	(D)	38	(D)	39	(C)
40	(A)	41	(A)	42	(D)
43	(C)	44	(C)	45	(A)
46	(A)	47	(B)	48	(B)
49	(B)	50	(B)	51	(C)
52	(B)	53	(D)	54	(A)

Solutions of PRACTICE EXERCISE-7.1

Sol. 1 (C) Given

$$\frac{a+b+c}{3}=x$$

& $\quad ab+bc+ca=0$

$\Rightarrow \quad (a+b+c)=3x$

$\Rightarrow \quad (a+b+c)^2=9x^2$

$\Rightarrow \quad a^2+b^2+c^2+2(ab+bc+ca)=9x^2$

$\Rightarrow \quad a^2+b^2+c^2=9x^2$

$\Rightarrow \quad \dfrac{a^2+b^2+c^2}{3}=\dfrac{9x^2}{3}=3x^2$

Hence Ans is (C)

Sol. 2 (B) Given

$$a=5000\ d=200\ T_n=7000$$

$$T_n=a+(n-1)d$$

$\Rightarrow \quad 7000=5000+(n-1)\times 200$

$\Rightarrow \quad 2000=(n-1)\times 200$

$\Rightarrow \quad 10=(n-1)$

$\Rightarrow \quad n=11$

Hence Ans is (B)

Sol. 3 (C) Given

$$S_n=\frac{3n^2}{2}+\frac{5n}{2}$$

$$=\frac{3n^2+5n}{2}=\frac{n(3n+5)}{2}$$

Put $\quad n=1$

$$S_1=a=\frac{3}{2}+\frac{5}{2}=4=T_1$$

$$S_2=T_1+T_2=\frac{2\times(6+5)}{2}=11$$

$$T_2=S_2-S_1=7$$

So series in 4, 7, 10, …

$$T_{25}=a+24d=4+24\times 3$$

$$=76$$

Hence the Ans is (C)

Sol. 4 (B) Sum of first & last term in an AP is constant.

$$S_n=\frac{n}{2}(a+b)$$

Hence Ans is (B)

Sol. 5 (B) Given a, b, c are in A.P.

$$2b=a+c\ \ \&\ \ a-c=b$$

Add $\quad 3b=2a \Rightarrow a=\dfrac{3b}{2}$

Hence Ans is (B)

Sol. 6 (B) n^{th} term is greater than 90°

$$T_n \geq 90$$

$$\Rightarrow \quad a+(n-1)d \geq 90$$

$$\Rightarrow \quad 17+(n-1)\times 8 \geq 90$$

$$\Rightarrow \quad (n-1)\times 8 \geq 90-17$$

$$\Rightarrow \quad (n-1)\times 8 \geq 73$$

$$\Rightarrow \quad (n-1) \geq 9\frac{1}{8}$$

$$\Rightarrow \quad n \geq 10\frac{1}{8}$$

Hence $n = 11$

Hence Ans is (B)

Sol. 7 (B) Given a, A_1, A_2, b

Where A_1 & A_2 are two means

$$T_4 \equiv b = a+3d$$

$$d = \frac{b-a}{3}$$

$$\frac{A_1}{A_2} = \frac{T_2}{T_3} = \frac{a+d}{a+2d} = \frac{a+\frac{b-a}{3}}{a+\frac{2(b-a)}{3}}$$

$$= \frac{2a+b}{a+2b}$$

Hence Ans is (B)

Sol. 8 (A) Let the terms $T_1 : x+3$

$T_2 : y+7$

$T_3 : x+y+8$

$T_4 : x+3y+20$ are in A.P.

We know

$$T_2 - T_1 = T_3 - T_2$$

$$2T_2 = T_1 + T_3$$

$$2(y+7) = x+3+x+y+8$$

$$2y+14 = 2x+y+11$$

$$2x - y = 3 \qquad \ldots(1)$$

$$2T_3 = T_2 + T_4$$

$$2(x+y+8) = x+3y+20+y+7$$

$$2x+2y+16 = x+4y+27$$

$$x-2y = 11 \qquad \ldots(2)$$

Solving equation-(1) & (2)

We get $\quad 4x-2y = 6$

$\quad x-2y = 1$ (On subtraction)

$$-3x = 5$$

$$x = -\frac{5}{3}$$

Now using equation-(1)

$$y = 2x-3$$

$$= -\frac{10}{3} - 3$$

$$= -\frac{19}{3}$$

Hence Ans is (A)

Sol. 9 (B) Let n^{th} term be first negative term

$$T_n < 0$$

$$a+(n-1)d < 0$$

$$\Rightarrow \quad 19+(n-1)\times\frac{-4}{5} < 0$$

$$\Rightarrow \quad \frac{4}{5}(n-1) > 19$$

$$\Rightarrow \quad 4(n-1) > 95$$

$$\Rightarrow \quad (n-1) > \frac{95}{4}$$

$$\Rightarrow \quad n > \frac{95}{4}+1$$

$$\Rightarrow \quad n > \frac{99}{4}$$

$$n > 24\frac{3}{4}$$

Hence 25th term will be first negative

Hence Ans is (B)

Sol. 10 (B) Given

$$T_{18} = T_{12}+12$$

$$a+17d = a+11d+12$$

$$6d = 12$$

$$d = 2$$

Hence Ans is (B)

Sol. 11 (C) Given two AP's 63, 65, 67, … & 3, 10, 17, … also given n^{th} term of these two AP, are equal

$$\Rightarrow \quad T_n = T_n'$$

$$\Rightarrow \quad 63+(n-1)\times 2 = 3+(n-1)\times 7$$

$$\Rightarrow \quad 60 = (n-1)\times 7 - 2(n-1)$$

$$\Rightarrow \quad 60 = 5(n-1)$$

$$\Rightarrow \quad (n-1) = 12$$

$$\Rightarrow \quad n = 13$$

Hence Ans is (C)

Sol. 12 (B) Given

$$a_n = 3+2n$$
$$a_1 = 3+2 = 5$$
$$a_2 = 3+4 = 7$$
$$a_3 = 3+6 = 9$$

So, the A.P. is

5, 7, 9, ...

where $a = 5$

& $d = 2$

Now $S_n = \frac{n}{2}[2a+(n-1)d]$

$$S_{20} = \frac{20}{2}[2\times 5+19\times 2]$$
$$= 20 \quad [24]$$
$$= 480$$

Hence Ans is (B)

Sol. 13 (D) $\sqrt{3}+\sqrt{12}+\sqrt{27}+\sqrt{48}+\ldots$

$\sqrt{3} + 2\sqrt{3} + 3\sqrt{3} + 4\sqrt{3} + \ldots$

Here $a = \sqrt{3}\,;\, d = \sqrt{3}$

$$S_n = \frac{n}{2}[2a+(n-1)d]$$
$$S_{10} = \frac{10}{2}[2\times\sqrt{3}+(10-1)\times\sqrt{3}]$$
$$= 5\times 11\sqrt{3}$$
$$= 55\sqrt{3}$$

Hence Ans is (D)

Sol. 14 (A) Sum of all interior angles of polygon of n sides

$$= (n-2)\times 180$$

Now $S_n = (n-2)\times 180$

$$\Rightarrow \quad \frac{n}{2}[2\times 120+(n-1)\times 5] = (n-2)\times 180$$

as $a = 120$ & $d = 5$

$$n[240+5n-5] = (n-2)\times 360$$
$$\Rightarrow \quad 235n+5n^2 = 360n-720$$
$$\Rightarrow \quad 5n^2-125n+720 = 0$$
$$\Rightarrow \quad n^2-25n+144 = 0$$
$$\Rightarrow \quad (n-16)(n-9) = 0$$
$$\Rightarrow \quad n = 9, n = 16$$

if $n = 16$ then 16th angle $= 120+15+5$

$$= 195 > 180$$

which is not possible

$$\Rightarrow \quad n = 9$$

Hence Ans is (A)

Sol. 15 (D) Let a be the first term and d be the common difference

$$T_p = \frac{1}{q}$$
$$\Rightarrow \quad a+(p-1)d = \frac{1}{q} \quad \ldots(1)$$
$$T_q = \frac{1}{p}$$
$$a+(q-1)d = \frac{1}{p} \quad \ldots(2)$$

Subtract

$$(p-q)d = \frac{1}{q}-\frac{1}{p}$$
$$d = \frac{1}{pq}$$

Using d in equation-(1), we have

$$a = \frac{1}{pq}$$
$$S_{pq} = \frac{pq}{2}[2a+(pq-1)d]$$
$$= \frac{1}{2}(pq+1)$$

Hence Ans is (D)

Sol. 16 (D) Given

$$S_m = n$$

& $S_n = m$

$$\frac{m}{2}[2a+(m-1)d] = n \quad \ldots(1)$$
$$\frac{n}{2}[2a+(n-1)d] = m \quad \ldots(2)$$

Subtract (2) from equation-(1)

$$\frac{1}{2}[2a(m-n)+(m^2-m-n^2+n)] = n-m$$
$$\Rightarrow \quad \frac{1}{2}[(m-n)[2a+(m+n-1)d]] = -(m-n)$$
$$\Rightarrow \quad \frac{1}{2}|2a+(m+n-1)d| = -1$$
$$\Rightarrow \quad \frac{m+n}{2}[2a+(m+n-1)d] = -(m+n)$$
$$S_{m+n} = -(m+n)$$

Hence Ans is (D)

Sol. 17 (C) 10, 11, 12, … 99

$$a = 10 \quad d = 1 \quad P_n = 99$$

$$T_n = a + (n-1)d$$

$$99 = 10 + (n-1) \times 1$$

$$n = 90$$

$$S_n = \frac{n}{2}[a + l]$$

$$S_n = \frac{90}{2}[10 + 99]$$

$$= 45 \times 109$$

$$= 4905$$

Hence Ans is (C)

Sol. 18 (C) Given

$$S_n = 2n^2 + 5n$$

$$t_n = S_n - S_{n-1}$$

$$= 2n^2 + 5n - [2(n-1)^2 + 5(n-1)]$$

$$= 2[n^2 - (n-1)^2] + 5[n - (n-1)]$$

$$= 2(2n-1).1 + 5$$

$$= 4n - 2 + 5$$

$$= 4n + 3$$

Hence Ans is (C)

Sol. 19 (A) $a = 7$

$$d = 7$$

$$S_{100} = \frac{100}{2}[2 \times 7 + (100-1)7]$$

$$= 50[2 \times 7 + 99 \times 7]$$

$$= 50 \times 7 \times 101$$

Hence Ans is (A)

Sol. 20 (C) Given

$$\log 2 + \log 4 + \log 8 + \ldots$$

$$= \log 2 + \log 2^2 + \log 2^3 + \ldots$$

$$= \log 2 + 2\log 2 + 3\log 2 + \ldots$$

$$= \log 2(1 + 2 + 3 + \ldots + 20)$$

$$= \log 2\left[\frac{20}{2}(1 + 20)\right]$$

$$= 210 \log 2$$

Hence Ans is (C)

Sol. 21 (C) If there are $(2n+1)$ term then there are n even term & $(n+1)$ odd term

Sum of first $(n+1)$ odd from $= (n+1)^2$

& Sum of first n even term $= n(n+1)$

So ratio is $\dfrac{S_0}{Se} = \dfrac{(n+1)^2}{n(n+1)}$

$$= \frac{(n+1)}{n}$$

Hence Ans is (C)

Sol. 22 (C) Given

$$T_4 = 8$$

$$S_7 = ?$$

$$a + 3d = 8$$

$$S_7 = \frac{7}{2}[2a + 6d]$$

$$= 7 \times (a + 3d)$$

$$= 7 \times 8 = 56$$

Hence Ans is (C)

Sol. 23 (B) Given

1, 2, … 100

Sum of all numbers divisible by 2 or 5 = Sum of all numbers which are multiples of 2′

+ Sum of all number which are multiple of 5

– Sum of all number which are multiple of 10

$$\Rightarrow (2 + 4 + 6 \ldots + 100) + (5 + 10 + 15 + \ldots + 100) - (10 + 20 \ldots + 100)$$

$$\Rightarrow \frac{50}{2}(2 + 102) + \frac{20}{2}(5 + 100) - \frac{10}{2}[10 + 100]$$

Use $S_n = \frac{n}{2}[a + l] = 3050$

Hence Ans is (B)

Sol. 24 (A) Given

$$54 + 51 + 48 + \ldots = 513$$

$$S_n = 513$$

So, $\frac{n}{2}[2a + (n-1)d] = 513$

$$\Rightarrow \frac{n}{2}[2 \times 54 + (n-1) \times (-3)] = 513$$

$$\Rightarrow n[108 - 3n + 3] = 1026$$

$$\Rightarrow 111n - 3n^2 = 1026$$

$$\Rightarrow 3n^2 - 111n + 1026 = 0$$

$$\Rightarrow n^2 - 37n + 342 = 0$$

$$\Rightarrow (n-18)(n-19) = 0$$

$$n = 18$$

Hence Ans is (A)

Sol. 25 (A) Let the terms be

$a-d, a \& a+d$

given $a-d+a+a+d=6$

$$3a=6$$

$$a=2$$

$\Rightarrow$ $(a-d).a(a+d)=-90$

$\Rightarrow$ $2(2-d)(2+d)=-90$

$\Rightarrow$ $4-d^2=-45$

$\Rightarrow$ $d^2=49$

$\Rightarrow$ $d=\pm 7$

The term are

$(2-7)(2)(2+7)$

$\Rightarrow -5, 2, 9$

Hence Ans is (A)

Sol. 26 (D) Given $2\ A_1 A_2 A_3 A_4 - 18.$

$$T_1=2$$

$$T_6 \equiv -18=a+5d$$

$$-18=2+5d$$

$$5d=-20$$

$$d=-4$$

So $A_1=a+d=2-4=-2$

$$A_2=a+2d=2-8=-6$$

$$A_3=a+3d=2-12=-10$$

$$A_4=a+4d=2-16=-14$$

Hence Ans is (D)

Sol. 27 (C) Given

$a, x_1; x_2, b \& b, y_1, y_2, c$

$$T_4=b.\ T_1=a$$

$$a+3d=b$$

$$d=\frac{b-a}{3}$$

$$x_1=a+d$$

$$=a+\frac{b-a}{3}=\frac{b+2a}{3}$$

$$x_2=a+2d$$

$$=a+\frac{2(b-a)}{3}$$

$$x_2=\frac{2b+a}{3}$$

$$T_1=b\ \&\ T_4=c$$

$$T_4=c=b+3d$$

$$d_1=\frac{c-b}{3}$$

$$y_1=b+d_1=b+\frac{c-b}{3}$$

$$y_1=\frac{c+2b}{3}$$

$$y_2=b+2d_1=b+\frac{2(c-b)}{3}$$

$$y_2=\frac{2c+b}{3}$$

Now $x_2+y_2-(x_1+y_1)$

$$x_2-x_1+y_2-y_1$$

$$x_2-x_1+y_2-y_1$$

$$\frac{(2b+a)}{3}-\frac{(b+2a)}{3}+\frac{(2c+b)}{3}-\frac{(c+2b)}{3}$$

$$=\frac{2b+a-b-2a+2c+b-c-2b}{3}$$

$$=\frac{c-a}{3}$$

Hence Ans is (C)

Sol. 28 (C) Given $\frac{S_{n_1}}{S_{n_2}}=\frac{3n-1}{3n+1}$

$$\Rightarrow \frac{\frac{n}{2}[2a_1+(n-1)d_1]}{\frac{n}{2}[2a_2+(n-1)d_2]}=\frac{3n-1}{3n+1}$$

$$\Rightarrow \frac{[2a_1+(n-1)d_1]}{[2a_2+(n-1)d_2]}=\frac{3n-1}{3n+1} \quad \ldots(1)$$

To find

$$\frac{T_{n_1}}{T_{n_2}}=\frac{[a_1+(n-1)d_1]}{[a_2+(n-1)d_2]}$$

$$\frac{T_{n_1}}{T_{n_2}}=\frac{[2a_1+2(n-1)d_1]}{[2a_2+2(n-1)d_2]}$$

$\Rightarrow$ $2(n-1)=n'-1$

$\Rightarrow$ $n'=2n-1$

now replace n with $2n-1$ in equation-(1) both side we get

$$\frac{[2a_1+(2n-1-1)d_1]}{[2a_2+(2n-1-1)d_2]}=\frac{3(2n-1)-1}{3(2n-1)+1}$$

$$\Rightarrow \frac{T_{n_1}}{T_{n_2}}=\frac{6n-3-1}{6n-3+1}=\frac{6n-4}{6n-2}$$

$$\Rightarrow \frac{T_{n_1}}{T_{n_2}}=\frac{(3n-2)}{3n-1}$$

$$\Rightarrow \frac{T_5'}{T_5^2}=\frac{3\times 5-2}{3\times 5-1}=\frac{13}{14}$$

Hence Ans is (C)

Sol. 29 (B) Given

$$A+B+C=63$$

$$A+6, B+6, C-12$$

Given, $2(B+6)=A+6+C-12$

$$2B+12=A+C-6$$

$$2B+18=A+C \quad \ldots(1)$$

$$A+B+C=63$$

$$B+2B+18=63 \quad \text{[from (1)]}$$

$$3B=63-18$$

$$3B=45$$

$$B=15$$

Hence Ans is (B)

Sol. 30 (B) Given a, b, c are in A.P.

$\Rightarrow$ $2b=a+c$

$\Rightarrow$ $c=2b-a$

$$ax+by+2b-a$$

$\Rightarrow$ $a(x-1)+b(y+2)=0$

$\Rightarrow$ $x=1; y=-2$

Line will pass through $(1,-2)$.

Hence Ans is (B)

Sol. 31 (A) $20+19\frac{1}{3}+18\frac{1}{3}\ldots$

$$a=20$$

$$d=19\frac{1}{3}-20$$

$$d=-\frac{2}{3}$$

First –*ve* term $T_n<0$

$\Rightarrow$ $a+(n-1)d<0$

$\Rightarrow$ $20+(n-1)\left(-\frac{2}{3}\right)<0$

$\Rightarrow$ $2(n-1)>60$

$\Rightarrow$ $(n-1)>30$

$\Rightarrow$ $n>31$

$\Rightarrow$ $n=32$

So last positive term $=31$

$$T_{31}=a+30d=20+30\times\left(-\frac{2}{3}\right)$$

So sum of first 30 term

$$S_{30}=\frac{30}{2}[2\times 20+29\times -\frac{2}{3}]$$

$$=30[20-\frac{29}{3}]=310$$

Hence Ans is (A)

Sol. 32 (B) Given a, b, c, d are in A.P.

$\Rightarrow$ $2b=a+c \quad \ldots(1)$

$\Rightarrow$ $2c=b+d \quad \ldots(2)$

Also $2(2b-a)=b+d$ [from (1)]

$\Rightarrow$ $4b-2a=b+d$

$\Rightarrow$ $3b=2a+d$

Hence Ans is (B)

Sol. 33 (B) Given $T_5=5$

$$a+4d=5 \quad \ldots(1)$$

also $T_{13}=-3$

$$a+12d=-3 \quad \ldots(2)$$

Solving (1) & (2) we get,

$$8d=-8$$

$$d=-1$$

$$a=9$$

Hence Ans is (B)

Sol. 34 (D) Given $100+110+120+\ldots$

let after *t* min police catch thief then distance travelled by both will be equal.

$$100+110+120+\ldots t=100t+100$$

$\Rightarrow$ $\frac{t}{2}[2\times 100+(t-1)\times 10]=100t+100$

$\Rightarrow$ $100t+(t-1)t\times 5=100+100t$

$\Rightarrow$ $5t^2-5t=100$

$\Rightarrow$ $t^2-t-20=0$

$\Rightarrow$ $(t+4)(t-5)=0$

So $t=5, t=-4$ is rejected

Hence Ans is (D)

Sol. 35 (B) Let *n* term should be taken

So that $18+16+14+\ldots n$ terms $=0$

$$\frac{n}{2}[2\times 18+(n-1)\times(-2)]=0$$

$\Rightarrow$ $18+(n-1)(-1)=0$

$\Rightarrow$ $(n-1)=18$

$\Rightarrow$ $n=19$

Hence Ans is (B)

Sol. 36 (B) $a_{22}=149$

$\Rightarrow$ $a+(22-1)d=149$

$\Rightarrow$ $a+21\times 22=149$

$\Rightarrow$ $a=149-462$

$\Rightarrow$ $a=-313$

$$S_{22}=\frac{22}{2}[-313+149]$$

$$=11[-164]$$

$$=-1804$$

Hence Ans is (B)

Sol. 37 (A) Let T_n term be 20 more than T_{13}

$$T_n = 20 + T_{13}$$

$$\Rightarrow \quad 15 + (n-1) \times 4 = 20 + (15 + 12 \times 4)$$

$$\Rightarrow \quad 15 + 4n - 4 = 20 + 15 + 48$$

$$\Rightarrow \quad 4n = 24 + 48$$

$$\Rightarrow \quad n = 12 + 6$$

$$\Rightarrow \quad n = 18$$

Hence Ans is (A)

Sol. 38 (C) Given

$$\frac{a+b}{2} = \frac{a^n + b^n}{a^{n-1} + b^{n-1}}$$

$$a^n + ab^{n-1} + ba^{n-1} + b^n = 2a^n + 2b^n$$

$$a^n + b^n = ab^{n-1} + ba^{n-1}$$

$$a^n - ba^{n-1} = ab^{n-1} - b^n$$

$$a^{n-1}(a-b) = b^{n-1}(a-b)$$

$$a^{n-1} = b^{n-1}$$

$$\left(\frac{a}{b}\right)^{n-1} = 1$$

$$\Rightarrow \quad \left(\frac{a}{b}\right)^{n-1} = \left(\frac{a}{b}\right)^0$$

$$n - 1 = 0$$

$$n = 1$$

Hence Ans is (C)

Sol. 39 (B) Given

$$\sum_{k=1}^{15}(2k-3)$$

$$\Rightarrow \quad 2\sum_{k=1}^{15} k - 3\sum_{k=1}^{15} 1$$

$\Rightarrow$ $2(1+2+3+\ldots+15) - 3(1+1+\ldots 15 \text{ times})$

$\Rightarrow$ $2\frac{15}{2}(1+15) - 3 \times 15$

$\Rightarrow$ $(15 \times 16) - (3 \times 15)$

$\Rightarrow$ 195

Hence Ans is (B)

Sol. 40 (B) In 4 days, clock will strike in times

$(1+2+3+\ldots+12) \times 4$

$\Rightarrow$ $\frac{12}{2}(1+12) \times 4$

$\Rightarrow$ $6 \times 13 \times 4$

$\Rightarrow$ 312

Hence Ans is (B)

Sol. 41 (D) Let the mth term of the first Arithmetic Progression be expressed as

$$5 + (m-1)4 = 4m + 1$$

and the nth term of the second Arithmetic Progression be expressed as $2 + (n-1)5 = 2 + 5n - 5 = 5n - 3$

We have to find the number of identical terms, so,

$$4m + 1 = 5n - 3$$

$$\Rightarrow \quad 4m + 4 = 5n = k \text{ (say)}$$

$$\Rightarrow \quad \frac{m+1}{5} = \frac{n}{4} = k$$

$$\Rightarrow \quad m = 5k - 1$$

$$\text{and} \quad n = 4k$$

$$\Rightarrow \quad 5k - 1 \le 60$$

$$\text{and} \quad 4k \le 40$$

$$\Rightarrow \quad k \le 12\frac{1}{5}$$

$$\text{and} \quad k \le 10$$

$$\Rightarrow \quad k \le 10$$

$$\Rightarrow \quad k = 1, 2, 3, \ldots, 10.$$

Corresponding to each value of k, we get a pair of identical terms.

$\Rightarrow$ Number of identical terms = 10

Hence Ans is (D)

Sol. 42 (B) Since $\frac{1}{b+c}$, $\frac{1}{c+a}$ and $\frac{1}{a+b}$ are in AP

$$\Rightarrow \quad \frac{2}{c+a} = \frac{1}{b+c} + \frac{1}{a+b}$$

$$= \frac{a+b+b+c}{(a+b)(b+c)}$$

$$\Rightarrow \quad 2b^2 = a^2 + c^2$$

$\Rightarrow$ a^2, b^2, c^2 are in AP.

Hence Ans is (B)

Sol. 43 (C) Let the first term be a and common difference d.

As we know, n^{th} term of an AP $= a + (n-1)d$

According to the question,

$$3^{\text{rd}} \text{ term} + 15^{\text{th}} \text{ term} = 6^{\text{th}} \text{ term} + 11^{\text{th}} \text{ term} + 13^{\text{th}} \text{ term}$$

$$\Rightarrow \quad a + 2d + a + 14d = a + 5d + a + 10d + a + 12d$$

$$\Rightarrow \quad 2a + 16d = 3a + 27d$$

$$\Rightarrow \quad a = -11d.$$

Let the nth term be 0.

$$\Rightarrow \quad a + (n-1)d = 0$$

$$\Rightarrow \quad -11d + (n-1)d = 0$$

$$\Rightarrow \quad n = 12$$

Hence Ans is (C)

Sol. 44 (A) Let the angles be $(\alpha - d)$, (α) and $(\alpha + d)$ where d is the common difference and $(\alpha - d)$ is the smallest angle.

Now, $\alpha - d + \alpha + \alpha + d = 180°$

$\Rightarrow \quad 3\alpha = 180°$

$\Rightarrow \quad \alpha = 60°$

According to the question,

$$\frac{\alpha + d}{\alpha - d} = \frac{3}{1}$$

$$\Rightarrow \quad \frac{60 + d}{60 - d} = \frac{3}{1}$$

$\Rightarrow \quad 60 + d = 180 - 3d$

$\Rightarrow \quad d = 30°$

$\Rightarrow$ Smallest angle $= \alpha - d = 60° - 30° = 30°$

Hence Ans is (A)

Sol. 45 (C) Here $a = 3$ and $d = 3$. Therefore, the sum to n terms is given by

$$S_n = \frac{n}{2}\{2a + (n-1)d\}$$

$$= \frac{3n}{2}(n+1) = \frac{3n^2 + 3n}{2}$$

For $\quad S_n > 1000$

We have, $\quad \dfrac{3n^2 + 3n}{2} > 1000$

$\Rightarrow \quad 3n(n+1) > 2000$

$\Rightarrow \quad n(n+1) > 667.$

Thus the least value of n is 26

Hence Ans is (C)

Sol. 46 (D) Here $a = 30, d = -3$

Therefore, the sum of n terms is given by

$$S_n = \frac{n}{2}[2a + (n-1)d]$$

$$= \frac{n}{2}[(2)(30) + (n-1)(-3)]$$

$$= 30n - \frac{3}{2}n^2 + \frac{3}{2}n$$

$$= \frac{63n}{2} - \frac{3}{2}n^2$$

$$= \frac{1323}{8} - \frac{3}{2}\left(n - \frac{21}{2}\right)^2$$

S_n will be maximum when $\left(n - \dfrac{21}{2}\right)^2$ is the least.

Since n is a natural number, hence $\left(n - \dfrac{21}{2}\right)^2$ will be the least when $n = 10$ or $n = 11$.

Therefore, the maximum value of the sum is

$$S_{10} = S_{11} = \frac{1323}{8} - \frac{3}{8} = 165$$

Aliter : The maximum value of the sum of an AP is the sum of the series up to the term having positive value.

i.e. $\quad n^{th}$ term ≥ 0

$\Rightarrow \quad 30 + (n-1)(-3) \geq 0$

$\Rightarrow \quad 33 - 3n \geq 0$

$\Rightarrow \quad 3n - 33 \leq 0$

$\Rightarrow \quad 3n \leq 33$

$\Rightarrow \quad n \leq 11$

Maximum value $\quad = \dfrac{11}{2}[2 \times 30 + (11-1) \times (-3)]$

$$= \frac{11}{2}[60 - 30] = 165$$

Hence Ans is (D)

Sol. 47 (D) Since

$$P^2 S_P = P S_{P^2}$$

$$\Rightarrow \quad P^2 \times \frac{P}{2}[2a + (P-1)d]$$

$$= P \times \frac{P^2}{2}[2a + (P^2 - 1)d]$$

$\Rightarrow \quad (P-1)d = (P^2 - 1)d$

$\Rightarrow \quad (P^2 - P)d = 0$

Since this is true for all values of P, we get $d = 0$.

Thus, $\quad S_n = \dfrac{n}{2}[2a + (n-1)d] = na$

Hence Ans is (D)

Sol. 48 (D) a occurs once, b occurs twice, c occurs thrice, ... and so on.

Number of times the letters occur in alphabetical order is in AP

First, we find the how many terms sum to 288.

$$\Rightarrow \quad \frac{n}{2}[2 + (n-1)1] = 288$$

$$\Rightarrow \quad \frac{n(n+1)}{2} = 288$$

If $n = 23$, then $\quad \dfrac{n(n+1)}{2} = 276.$

It means that, 24th letter (i.e. x) in alphabetical order occurs exactly 24 times and first time it occurs at 277th place.

& hence 288th term $= x$.

Hence Ans is (D)

Sol. 49 (B) Given

$$n^{\text{th}}\text{ term} = \frac{n}{a} + b$$

$$1^{\text{st}}\text{ term} = \frac{1}{a} + b$$

$$2^{\text{nd}}\text{ term} = \frac{2}{a} + b$$

$$3^{\text{rd}}\text{ term} = \frac{3}{a} + b$$

$$\text{Common difference} = \left(\frac{2}{a}+b\right) - \left(\frac{1}{a}+b\right) = \frac{1}{a}$$

$$\text{Sum of } p \text{ terms} = \frac{p}{2}\left[2\left(\frac{1}{a}+b\right) + (p-1)\frac{1}{a}\right]$$

$$= \frac{p(p+1)}{2a} + pb$$

Hence Ans is (B)

Sol. 50 (C) Suppose there are n pages in the book. The sum of page numbers

$$= 1+2+3+\ldots+n = \frac{n(n+1)}{2}$$

Suppose that the torn pages bear the number k and $k+1$

Since the sum of the remaining pages is 15000

$$\Rightarrow \quad \frac{n(n+1)}{2} = 15000 + k + k + 1$$

Since $\quad k \geq 1,$

$$\frac{n(n+1)}{2} \geq 15000 + 1 + 2$$

$$\Rightarrow \quad n^2 + n \geq 30006$$

$$\Rightarrow \quad \left(n + \frac{1}{2}\right)^2 > (173)^2$$

$$\Rightarrow \quad n \geq 173$$

If $n = 173$, sum of all the page numbers up to 173

$= 15051$ and $15051 - 15000 = 51$

51 is sum of two consecutive page numbers of a single page i.e. 25, 26

Hence Ans is (C)

Solutions of PRACTICE EXERCISE-7.2

Sol. 1 (B) Consider $\frac{1}{a_1a_2} + \frac{1}{a_2a_3} + \ldots + \frac{1}{a_{n-1}a_n}$

$$\Rightarrow \frac{d}{d}\left[\frac{1}{a_1a_2} + \frac{1}{a_2a_3} + \ldots + \frac{1}{a_{n-1}a_n}\right]$$

$$\Rightarrow \frac{1}{d}\left[\frac{d}{a_1a_2} + \frac{d}{a_2a_3} + \ldots + \frac{d}{a_{n-1}a_n}\right]$$

$$\Rightarrow \frac{1}{d}\left[\frac{a_2-a_1}{a_1a_2} + \frac{a_3-a_2}{a_2a_3} + \ldots + \frac{a_n-a_{n-1}}{a_{n-1}a_n}\right]$$

$$\Rightarrow \frac{1}{d}\left[\frac{1}{a_1} - \frac{1}{a_2} + \frac{1}{a_2} - \frac{1}{a_3} + \ldots + \frac{1}{a_{n-1}} - \frac{1}{a_n}\right]$$

$$\Rightarrow \frac{1}{d}\left[\frac{1}{a_1} - \frac{1}{a_n}\right]$$

$$\Rightarrow \frac{1}{d}\cdot\frac{a_n - a_1}{a_1a_n} = \frac{(n-1)d}{da_1a_n}$$

$$= \frac{(n-1)}{a_1a_n}$$

Hence Ans is (B)

Sol. 2 (C) Given $\frac{b+c-a}{a}, \frac{c+a-b}{b}, \frac{a+b-c}{c}$ are in A.P.

$$\Rightarrow \frac{b+c-a}{a}+2, \frac{c+a-b}{b}+2, \frac{a+b-c}{c}+2 \text{ in A.P.}$$

$$\Rightarrow \frac{a+b+c}{a}, \frac{a+b+c}{b}, \frac{a+b+c}{c} \text{ are in A.P.}$$

$$\Rightarrow \frac{1}{a}, \frac{1}{b}, \frac{1}{c} \text{ are in A.P.}$$

Hence Ans is (C)

Sol. 3 (C) Given,

$$T_1 = a$$

$$T_2 = b$$

$$d = T_2 - T_1 = b - a$$

$$T_n = c$$

$$T_n = a + (n-1)(b-a) = c$$

$$(n-1) = \frac{c-a}{b-a}$$

$$n = \frac{c-a}{b-a} + 1$$

$$= \frac{c+b-2a}{b-a}$$

$$S_n = \frac{n}{2}[a+l] = \frac{(c+b-2a)}{2(b-a)}(a+c)$$

Hence Ans is (C)

Sol. 4 (D) Consider

$$\frac{1}{\sqrt{a_1}+\sqrt{a_2}} + \frac{1}{\sqrt{a_2}+\sqrt{a_3}} + \ldots + \frac{1}{\sqrt{a_{n-1}}+\sqrt{a_n}}$$

$$\Rightarrow \frac{\sqrt{a_2}-\sqrt{a_1}}{a_2-a_1} + \frac{\sqrt{a_3}-\sqrt{a_2}}{a_3-a_2} + \ldots \frac{\sqrt{a_n}-\sqrt{a_{n-1}}}{a_n-a_{n-1}}$$

$$\Rightarrow \frac{\sqrt{a_2}-\sqrt{a_1}+\sqrt{a_3}-\sqrt{a_2}\ldots\sqrt{a_n}-\sqrt{a_{n-1}}}{d}$$

$$\Rightarrow \frac{\sqrt{a_n}-\sqrt{a_1}}{d}$$

$$\Rightarrow \frac{a_n-a_1}{d(\sqrt{a_n}+\sqrt{a_1})}$$

$$\Rightarrow \frac{(n-1)d}{d(\sqrt{a_n}+\sqrt{a_1})}=\frac{(n-1)}{\sqrt{a_n}+\sqrt{a_1}}$$

Hence Ans is (D)

Sol. 5 (D) Given

$$a_1 . a_2 \ldots a_n = 1$$

We know $AM \geq GM$

$$\Rightarrow \frac{a_1+a_2+a_3+\ldots+a_n}{n} \geq \sqrt[n]{a_1 a_2 \ldots a_n}$$

$$\Rightarrow a_1+a_2+a_3+\ldots a_n \geq n$$

Hence Ans is (D)

Sol. 6 (A) We know

$$\text{AM} \geq \text{GM}$$

$$\frac{(a+b)+(c+d)}{2} \geq \sqrt[2]{(a+b)(c+d)}$$

$$\frac{2}{2} \geq \sqrt{(a+b)(c+d)}$$

$$M \leq 1$$

Since $a, b, c, d \in R^+$

Hence Ans is (A)

Sol. 7 (A) Since we know

$$AM \geq GM$$

$$\frac{x^{\log y - 1\log z}+y^{\log z-\log x}+z^{\log x-\log y}}{3}$$

$$\geq \sqrt{x^{\log y-\log z}\cdot y^{\log z-\log x}\cdot z^{\log x-\log y}}$$

$$\Rightarrow \frac{x^{\log y-\log z}+y^{\log z-\log x}+z^{\log x-\log y}}{3}$$

$$\geq \sqrt{\frac{x^{\log y}}{x^{\log z}}\cdot\frac{y^{\log z}}{y^{\log x}}\cdot\frac{z^{\log x}}{z^{\log y}}}$$

$$\Rightarrow \frac{x^{\log y-\log z}+y^{\log z-\log x}+z^{\log y}}{3} \geq 1$$

Hence Ans is (A)

Sol. 8 (B) We know

$$AM \geq GM$$

$$\Rightarrow \frac{a+b+c^2}{3} \geq \sqrt[3]{abc^2}$$

$$\Rightarrow \frac{a+b+c^2}{3} \geq \sqrt[3]{\frac{1}{64}}$$

$$\Rightarrow a+b+c^2 \geq \frac{3}{4}$$

Since product is constant sum will be minimum when all are equal

$$\Rightarrow a=b=c^2=k$$

$$3k=\frac{3}{4}$$

$$k=\frac{1}{4}$$

$$\Rightarrow a=b=c^2=\frac{1}{4}$$

$$\Rightarrow a=b=\frac{1}{4}$$

& $c^2=\frac{1}{4}$

$$\Rightarrow c=\frac{1}{2}$$

Hence Ans is (B)

Sol. 9 (C) To find the minimum value of

$$a(b^2+c^2)+b(c^2+a^2)+c(a^2+b^2)$$

We know $AM \geq GM$

$$\Rightarrow \frac{ab^2+ac^2+bc^2+ba^2+ca^2+cb^2}{6}$$

$$\geq \sqrt[6]{ab^2\cdot ac^2\cdot bc^2\cdot ba^2\cdot ca^2\cdot cb^2}$$

$$\Rightarrow \frac{ab^2+ac^2+bc^2+ba^2+ca^2+cb^2}{6} \geq \sqrt[6]{a^6\cdot b^6\cdot c^6}$$

$$\Rightarrow \frac{ab^2+ac^2+bc^2+ba^2+ca^2+cb^2}{6} \geq abc$$

$$ab^2+ac^2+bc^2+ba^2+ca^2+cb^2 \geq 6abc$$

$$\Rightarrow \lambda=6$$

Hence Ans is (C)

Sol. 10 (A) We know

$$\text{A.M.} \geq \text{GM.}$$

$$\frac{a+b+c+d}{4} \geq 4\sqrt{abcd}$$

$$\frac{a+b+c+d}{4} \geq 1$$

$$a+b+c+d \geq 4$$

Now sum will be minimum when all are equal

$$\Rightarrow a=b=c=d=k$$

$$4k=4$$

$$\Rightarrow k=1$$

$$\Rightarrow a=b=c=d=1$$

So $(1+a)(1+b)(1+c)(1+d)$

$$=16$$

Hence Ans is (A)

Sol. 11 (C) Given

$$a_1 = a_2 = a_3 = 1$$

$$d_1 = 1; \quad d_2 = 2; \quad d_3 = 3$$

$$S_1 \equiv \frac{n}{2}[2a_1 + (n-1)d_1]$$

$$S_1 = \frac{n}{2}[2\times 1 + (n-1)\times 1]$$

$$S_2 \equiv \frac{n}{2}[2\times 1 + (n-1)2]$$

$$S_3 = \frac{n}{2}[2\times 1 + (n-1)\times 3]$$

$$S_1 + S_3 = \frac{n}{2}[2\times(2\times 1) + (n-1)\times 4]$$

$$= \frac{n}{2}[2\times 1 + (n-1)\times 2]\times 2$$

$$= 2S_2$$

Hence Ans is (C)

Sol. 12 (D) Let common difference be x

then $\quad a = a$

$$b = a + x$$

$$c = a + 2x$$

$$d = a + 3x$$

$$e = a + 4x$$

To find the value of

$$a - 4b + 6c - 4d + e$$

$$= a - 4(a+x) + 6(a+2x) - 4(a+3x) + a + 4x$$

$$= a - 4a - 4x + 6a + 12x - 4a - 12x + a + 4x$$

$$= a - 4a - 4x + 6a + 12x - 4a - 12x + a + 4x$$

or consider a, b, c, d, e as 1, 2, 3, 4, 5 and then proceed

Hence Ans is (D)

Sol. 13 (B) Given

$$T_9 = 0$$

$$\Rightarrow \quad a + 8d = 0$$

Consider

$$\frac{T_{29}}{T_{19}} = \frac{a+28d}{a+18d} = \frac{-8d+28d}{-8d+18d}$$

$$\Rightarrow \quad \frac{20d}{10d} = \frac{2}{1}$$

Hence Ans is (B)

Sol. 14 (C) Given

$$x^2 = z^2 - y^2$$

$$= (z-y)(z+y)$$

$$x^2 = (m^2 + n^2 - 2mn)(m^2 + n^2 + 2mn)$$

$$x^2 = (m-n)^2(m+n)^2$$

$$x^2 = (m^2 - n^2)^2$$

$$x = m^2 - n^2$$

Now $\quad \frac{1}{x} + \frac{1}{z} = \frac{1}{m^2 - n^2} + \frac{1}{m^2 + n^2}$

$$\frac{1}{x} + \frac{1}{z} = \frac{2m^2}{m^4 - n^4}$$

Hence Ans is (C)

Sol. 15 (C) Given $(1^3 + 2^3 + 3^3 + \ldots 10^3)^3$

$$\Rightarrow \quad \left[\left[\frac{10(10+1)}{2}\right]^2\right]^3 \text{ as } \Sigma n^3 = \left(\frac{n(n+1)}{2}\right)^2$$

$\Rightarrow \quad (55)^6$

So last digit will be 5 only

Hence Ans is (C)

Sol. 16 (B) Given A, B, C and in AP

$$\Rightarrow \quad B - A = C - B$$

$$\Rightarrow \quad 2B = A + C \quad \ldots(1)$$

We know

$$A + B + C = 180$$

$$\Rightarrow \quad 3B = 180 \quad \text{[from (1)]}$$

$$\Rightarrow \quad B = 60°$$

$$\sin B = \sin 60° = \frac{\sqrt{3}}{2}$$

Hence Ans is (B)

Sol. 17 (C) Consider multiply both N^r & 0^r by 4

$$\left[\frac{1}{3\times 7} + \frac{1}{7\times 11} + \ldots \frac{1}{99+103}\right]$$

We get

$$\frac{1}{4}\left[\frac{4}{3\times 7} + \frac{4}{7\times 11} + \frac{4}{11\times 15} + \ldots + \frac{4}{99\times 103}\right]$$

$$= \frac{1}{4}\left[\frac{1}{3} - \frac{1}{7} + \frac{1}{7} - \frac{1}{11} + \frac{1}{11} - \frac{1}{15} + \ldots \frac{1}{99} - \frac{1}{103}\right]$$

$$= \frac{1}{4}\left[\frac{1}{3} - \frac{1}{103}\right] = \frac{100}{4\times 3\times 103} = \frac{25}{309}$$

Hence Ans is (C)

Sol. 18 (D) Consider $\frac{1}{\sqrt{3}+\sqrt{5}}+\frac{1}{\sqrt{5}+\sqrt{7}}+\ldots$

$$+\frac{1}{\sqrt{2n+1}+\sqrt{2n+3}}$$

$$=\frac{\sqrt{5}-\sqrt{3}}{2}+\frac{\sqrt{7}-\sqrt{5}}{2}+\ldots\frac{\sqrt{2n+3}-\sqrt{2n+1}}{2}$$

$$=\frac{\sqrt{5}-\sqrt{3}+\sqrt{7}-\sqrt{5}+\ldots\sqrt{2n+3}-\sqrt{2n+1}}{2}$$

$$=\frac{\sqrt{2n+3}-\sqrt{3}}{2}$$

Hence Ans is (D)

Sol. 19 (C) $(x-1)(x-3)\ldots(x-99)$

Coefficient at $x^{49}=-$(Sum of all roots)

$=-(1+3+5+\ldots+99)$

$=-2500$

Hence Ans is (C)

Sol. 20 (D) Given

$$\frac{1}{\log_2 4}+\frac{1}{\log_4 4}+\frac{1}{\log_8 4}+\ldots+\frac{1}{\log_{2^n} 4}$$

$$=\frac{\log 2}{\log 4}+\frac{\log 4}{\log 4}+\ldots\frac{\log 2^n}{\log 4}$$

$$=\frac{\log 2+2\log 2+3\log 3+\ldots n\log 2}{2\log 2}$$

$$=\frac{\log 2(1+2+3+\ldots+n)}{\log 2\times 2}=\frac{n(n+1)}{4}$$

Hence Ans is (D)

Sol. 21 (B) $2, 5, 8, 11, \ldots 179$

& $3, 5, 7, \ldots 101$

Common terms in the given series are

$5, 11, \ldots \leq 101$

$T_n \leq 101$

$\Rightarrow \quad 5+(n-1)\times 6 \leq 101$

$\Rightarrow \quad (n-1)\times 6 \leq 101-5$

$\Rightarrow \quad (n-1)\times 6 \leq 96$

$\Rightarrow \quad (n-1) \leq 16$

$\Rightarrow \quad n \leq 17$

$\Rightarrow \quad n = 17$

Hence Ans is (B)

Sol. 22 (B) Verify all the options

Hence Ans is (B)

Sol. 23 (C) Given, $x^3-12x^2+39x-28$ with roots $a-d$, a, $a+d$

Sum of roots $=-\frac{b}{a}$

$\Rightarrow \quad a-d+a+a+d=-\frac{(-12)}{1}$

$\Rightarrow \quad 3a=12$

$\Rightarrow \quad a=4$

Product of roots $-\frac{d}{a}$

$\Rightarrow \quad (a-d).a(a+d)=28$

$\Rightarrow \quad 4(4-d)(4+d)=28$

$\Rightarrow \quad 16-d^2=7$

$\Rightarrow \quad d^2=16-7$

$\Rightarrow \quad d^2=9$

$\Rightarrow \quad d=\pm 3$

Hence Ans is (C)

Sol. 24 (B) Let choose the value $n=3$ then question becomes

$d=S_3-kS_2+S_1$

$d=(a+a+d+a+2d)-k(a+a+d)+a$

$d=3a+3d-k(2a+d)+a$

$d=4a+3d-k(2a+d)$

$d=(4a-2ak)+3d-kd$

$d=a(4-2k)+d(3-k)$

Equating same coefficient on both sides.

$a(4-2k)=0$

$\Rightarrow \quad k=2$

or $\quad k=2$

Hence Ans is (B)

Sol. 25 (B) Given $\quad T_1=a$

$T_n=l$

$$d=\frac{l^2-a^2}{k-(l+a)}$$

$$S_n=\frac{n}{2}[a+l] \quad \ldots(1)$$

$T_n=a+(n-1)d$

$$l=a+(n-1)\times\frac{(l^2-a^2)}{k-(l+a)}$$

$$(l-a)=\frac{(n-1)(l-a)(l+a)}{k-(l+a)}$$

$k-(l+a)=n(l+a)-(l+a)$

$k=n(l+a)$

$k=2S$ Using (1)

Hence Ans is (B)

Solutions of PRACTICE EXERCISE-7.3

Sol. 1 (C) n^{th} term of an A.P. whose first term is 'a' and common difference is 'd' is given by

$$T_n = a + (n-1)d$$

given

$$T_3 + T_7 = 6$$
$$a + 2d + a + 6d = 6$$
$$2a + 8d = 6$$
$$a + 4d = 3 \quad \ldots(1)$$

Also given $T_3\, T_7 = 8$

$$(a+2d)(a+6d) = 8$$
$$(3-2d)(3+2d) = 8 \quad \text{using (1)}$$
$$9 - 4d^2 = 8$$
$$1 = 4d^2$$
$$d = \pm 1/2$$

Hence Ans is (C)

Sol. 2 (D) In an A.P. sum of first and last term is equal to sum of second and second last term and so on.

$$\Rightarrow \quad a + b = 9 - 6 = 3$$

Hence Ans is (D)

Sol. 3 (B) Let the first integer be n,

then $n + n + 1 + n + 2 \ldots + n + 10 = 2002$

$$\Rightarrow \quad 11n + (1 + 2 + \ldots + 10) = 2002$$
$$\Rightarrow \quad 11n + \frac{10 \times 11}{2} = 2002$$
$$\Rightarrow \quad 11n + 55 = 2002$$
$$\Rightarrow \quad n + 5 = 182$$
$$\Rightarrow \quad n = 177$$

Hence Ans is (B)

Sol. 4 (A) Let first term of an AP be A & common difference be D then given

$$T_p = q \;\&\; T_q = p$$
$$A + (p-1)D = q \quad \ldots(1)$$
$$A + (q-1)D = p \quad \ldots(2)$$

Equation-(1) – equation-(2)

$$(p-q)D = q - p$$
$$\Rightarrow \quad D = -1$$
$$\Rightarrow \quad A = p + q - 1$$

Using D is equation-(1)

So n^{th} term

$$T_n = A + (n-1)D$$
$$= p + q - 1 + (n-1) \times -1$$
$$= p + q - 1 - n + 1$$
$$= p + q - n$$

Hence Ans is (A)

Sol. 5 (A) Given $\dfrac{a^{n+1} + b^{n+1}}{a^n + b^n}$ is mean between a & b

$$\Rightarrow \quad \frac{a^{n+1} + b^{n+1}}{a^n + b^n} = \frac{a+b}{2}$$
$$\Rightarrow \quad 2a^{m+1} + 2b^{n+1} = a^{n+1} + ab^n + ba^n + b^{n+1}$$
$$\Rightarrow \quad a^{n+1} - ba^n + b^{n+1} - ab^n = 0$$
$$\Rightarrow \quad a^n(a-b) + b^n(b-a) = 0$$
$$\Rightarrow \quad (a-b)(a^n - b^n) = 0$$
$$\Rightarrow \quad (a-b) \neq 0$$
$$\Rightarrow \quad a^n - b^n = 0$$
$$\Rightarrow \quad \frac{a^n}{b^n} = 1$$
$$\Rightarrow \quad \left(\frac{a}{b}\right)^n = \left(\frac{a}{b}\right)^0$$
$$\Rightarrow \quad n = 0$$

Hence Ans is (A)

Sol. 6 (B) Given

$$S_n = 5n^2 - 5n$$

Here first term 'T_1' $= S_1$

$$S_1 = 5.(1)^2 - 5.1$$
$$= 5 - 5 = 0$$

Here sum of two terms T_1 & $T_2 = S_2$

$$S_2 = 5.(2)^2 - 5.2$$
$$= 20 - 10 = 10$$
$$T_1 + T_2 = 10$$
$$T_2 = 10 \text{ as } T_1 = 0$$

Here common difference

$$d = T_2 - T_1 = 10$$

So

$$T_{10} = a + 9d$$
$$= 0 + 9.(10)$$
$$= 90$$

Hence Ans is (B)

Sol. 7 (A) First two digit number divisible by 3 = 12 last two digit number divisible by 3 vs 99

So 12, 15, 18, … 99 is an A.P. whose first term $a = 12$ & common difference $d = 3$ last term = 99

So

$$T_n = 9 + (n-1)d$$
$$99 = 12 + (n-1) \times 3$$
$$99 - 12 = (n-1) \times 3$$
$$87 = (n-1) \times 3$$
$$(n-1) = \frac{87}{3} = 29$$
$$n = 30$$

Hence Ans is (A)

Sol. 8 (A) $1+3+5+\ldots$ to 365 terms

$$= \frac{365}{2}\{2+(364\times 2)\}$$

$$= \frac{365}{2}\{2+728\}$$

$$= \frac{365}{2}\times 730$$

$$= 365\times 365$$

$$= 133225$$

Hence Ans is (A)

Sol. 9 (A) If each observation is multiplied by a constant then mean is also multiplied by the same

$\Rightarrow$ $$\text{New mean} = \frac{2}{3}\text{old mean}$$

$$= \frac{2}{3}\times 15$$

$$= 10$$

Hence Ans is (A)

Sol. 10 (A) n^{th} term of an A.P. whose first term is 'a' and common difference is 'd' is given by

$$T_n = a+(n-1)d$$

$$40 = (n-1)d \quad \ldots(1)$$

(here $a=5$ & $T_n=45$)

Sum up to n terms of an A.P. whose first term is 'a' and common difference is 'd' is given by

$$S_n = \frac{n}{2}[2a+(n-1)d]$$

$$400 = \frac{n}{2}[2\times 5+40] \quad \text{(using (1))}$$

$$400 = \frac{n}{2}[50]$$

$\Rightarrow$ $$n = 16$$

Now $$T_n = a+(n-1)d$$

$$45 = 5+(16-1)\times d$$

$$\frac{40}{15} = d$$

$\Rightarrow$ $$d = \frac{8}{3}$$

$$T_4 = a+3d = 5+3\times\frac{8}{3} = 13$$

Hence Ans is (A)

Sol. 11 (D) Consider

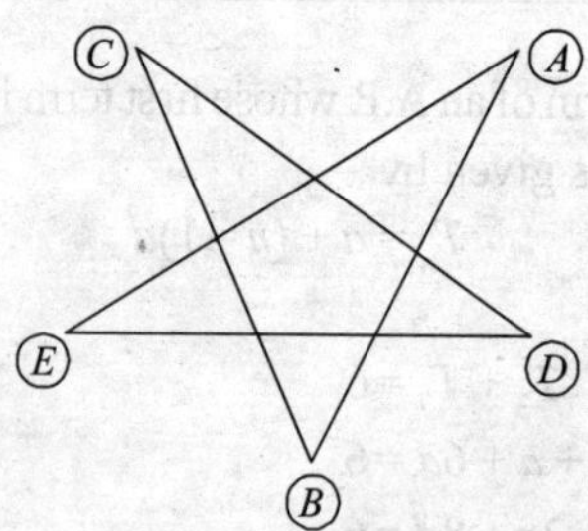

$$AB+BC+CD+DE+EA = 2(A+B+C+D+E)$$

The $(A+B+C+D+E)$. Will always be.

$$3+5+6+7+9 = 30$$

So the arithmetic sequence has the sum of $2\times 30 = 60$.
Since CD is the middle term it must be average of the five numbers, of $\frac{60}{5} = 12$

Hence Ans is (D)

Sol. 12 (C) Given a, b, c, d are in AP
Let common difference be 'x'
then $a, a+x, a+2x, a+3x$ are four terms of AP
Given a, b, d are in GP

$\Rightarrow$ $$b^2 = ad$$

$\Rightarrow$ $$(a+x)^2 = a(a+3x)$$

$\Rightarrow$ $$a^2+x^2+2ax = a^2+3ax$$

$\Rightarrow$ $$x^2-ax = 0$$

$\Rightarrow$ $$x(x-a) = 0$$

$\Rightarrow$ $$x = a$$

$\Rightarrow$ $$a = a \;\&\; d = a+3x = 4a$$

$\Rightarrow$ $$\frac{a}{d} = \frac{a}{4a} = \frac{1}{4}$$

Hence Ans is (C)

Sol. 13 (D) Given

$$S_n = \frac{3n^2}{2}+\frac{5n}{2}$$

$\Rightarrow$ $$S_n = \frac{3n^2+5n}{2} = \frac{n(3n+5)}{2}$$

$\Rightarrow$ $$S_1 = T_1 = \frac{1.(3\times 1+5)}{2} = \frac{8}{2} = 4$$

Now $$S_2 = T_1+T_2 = \frac{2\times(3\times 2+5)}{2} = 11$$

$\Rightarrow$ $$T_2 = S_2 - S_1 = 11-4 = 7$$

So A.P. will be 4, 7, 10, …
Hence 25th term of such AP

$$T_n = a+(n-1)d$$

$$T_{25} = 4+(25-1)\times 3$$

$$= 4+24\times 3$$

$$= 4+72 = 76$$

Hence Ans is (D)

Sol. 14 (C) Given $\sqrt{2}+\sqrt{8}+\sqrt{18}+\sqrt{32}\ \ldots$

$\Rightarrow\ \sqrt{2}+2\sqrt{2}+3\sqrt{2}+4\sqrt{2}\ \ldots$

$\Rightarrow\ \sqrt{2}\,(1+2+3+4+\ldots)$

$\Rightarrow\ \sqrt{2}\,\dfrac{n(n+1)}{2}$ (Sum upto n terms)

$\dfrac{n(n+1)}{\sqrt{2}}$

Hence Ans is (C)

Sol. 15 (A) Given $1+3+5+\ldots(2n-1)$

We have

$$S_n=\frac{n}{2}[2a+(n-1)\times d]$$

$$S_n=\frac{n}{2}[2\times 1+(n-1)2]$$

$$=\frac{n}{2}[2+2n-2]$$

$$=\frac{n}{2}\times 2n$$

$$=n^2$$

Hence Ans is (A)

Sol. 16 (A) Given

$$\frac{1}{(2^2-1)}+\frac{1}{4^2-1}+\frac{1}{6^2-1}+\ldots+\frac{1}{20^2-1}$$

$$=\frac{1}{(2-1)(2+1)}+\frac{1}{(4-1)(4+1)}+\frac{1}{(6-1)(6+1)}$$

$$+\ldots+\frac{1}{(20-1)(20+1)}$$

$$=\frac{1}{1.3}+\frac{1}{3.5}+\frac{1}{3.7}+\ldots\frac{1}{19.21}$$

$$=\frac{1}{2}\left[\frac{2}{1.3}+\frac{2}{3.5}+\frac{2}{5.7}+\ldots+\frac{2}{19.21}\right]$$

$$=\frac{1}{2}\left[\frac{1}{1}-\frac{1}{3}+\frac{1}{3}-\frac{1}{5}+\frac{1}{5}-\frac{1}{7}+\ldots\frac{1}{19}-\frac{1}{21}\right]$$

$$=\frac{1}{2}\left[1-\frac{1}{21}\right]=\frac{1}{2}\times\frac{20}{21}=\frac{10}{21}$$

Hence Ans is (A)

Sol. 17 (A) Given

$$Sn=2n^2+3n$$

$$S_1=T_1=2\times 1^2+3\times 1=5$$

$$S_2=T_1+T_2=2\times 2^2+3\times 2=14$$

$$S_3=T_1+T_2+T_3=2\times 3^2+3\times 3=27$$

$$T_2=S_2-S_1=14-5=9$$

$$T_3=S_3-S_2=27-14=13$$

So series is $T_1, T_2, T_3\ldots 5, 9, 13\ldots$

$$d=T_2-T_1=9-5=4$$

Hence Ans is (A)

Sol. 18 (A) Given

$$a+(m-1)d=\frac{1}{n}$$

$$a+(n-1)d=\frac{1}{m}$$

$$\Rightarrow\quad a=d=\frac{1}{mn}$$

Hence Ans is (A)

Sol. 19 (C) Let the first term be a & common difference be d. Since the reciprocal of harmonic term are is AP so.

$$T_m\equiv\frac{1}{a}+(m-1)\frac{1}{d}=\frac{1}{n}\qquad\ldots(1)$$

$$\&\quad T_n\equiv\frac{1}{a}+(n-1)\frac{1}{d}=\frac{1}{m}\qquad\ldots(2)$$

subtract

$$(m-n)\frac{1}{d}=\frac{(m-n)}{mn}$$

$$\frac{1}{d}=\frac{1}{mn}$$

& Using d in equation- (1)

$$\frac{1}{a}+(m-1)\frac{1}{mn}=\frac{1}{n}$$

$$\frac{1}{a}=\frac{1}{mn}$$

Now $$T_{mn}=\frac{1}{a}+(mn-1)\frac{1}{d}$$

$$=\frac{1}{mn}+(mn-1).\frac{1}{mn}$$

$$=1$$

Hence Ans is (C)

Sol. 20 (A) $17+15+13+11+\ldots=72$

Reverse A.P. $a=17; d=-2$

$$S_n \equiv \frac{n}{2}[2a+(n-1)d]=72$$

$$\frac{n}{2}[2\times 17+(n-1)\times(-2)]=72$$

$$n[17-n+1]=72$$

$$18n-n^2=72=0$$

$$n^2-18n+72=0$$

$$(n-12)(n-6)$$

$$n=6$$

Hence Ans is (A)

Sol. 21 (A) $x_1+x_7+x_{10}=-6$

$\Rightarrow$ $a+a+6d+a+9d=-6$

$\Rightarrow$ $a+5d=-2$ ...(1)

$x_3+x_8+x_{12}=-11$

$\Rightarrow$ $a+2d+a+7d+a+11d=-11$

$\Rightarrow$ $3a+20d=-11$ ...(2)

Solving (1) & (2) we get $a=3, d=-1$

$$x_3+x_8+x_{22}=a+2d+a+7d+a+21d$$

$$=3a+30d$$

$$x_3+x_8+x_{22}=-21 \text{ (Since } a=3, d=-1)$$

Hence Ans is (A)

Sol. 22 (B) 2, 5, 8 ... is in *AP* where $a_1=2, d_1=3$ & 7, 11, 15 ... is also in *AP* where $a_2=7, d_2=4$.

Since sum of *n*-terms in *AP* is

$$S_n=\frac{n}{2}[2a+(n-1)d]$$

$$\frac{2+5+8+\ldots n.\text{terms}}{7+11+15+\ldots n.\text{terms}}=\frac{23}{35}$$

$$\frac{\frac{n}{2}[2(2)+(n-1)3]}{\frac{n}{2}[2(7)+(n-1)4]}=\frac{23}{35}$$

$$\frac{3n+1}{4n+10}=\frac{23}{35}$$

$\Rightarrow$ $n=15$

Hence Ans is (B)

Sol. 23 (C) $A+(7-1)d=5A$

$\Rightarrow$ $A+6d=5A$

$\Rightarrow$ $4A-6d=0$

$\Rightarrow$ $2A=3d$ ...(1)

$$A+(9-1)d=2[A+(4-1)d]+1$$

$\Rightarrow$ $A+8d=2A+6d+1$

$\Rightarrow$ $A-2d+1=0$ ...(2)

Solving-(1) and (2) we get

$$d=2, A=3$$

$\Rightarrow$ First term = 3

Hence Ans is (C)

Sol. 24 (D) AM of *a* and *b* is

$$\frac{a+b}{2}=\frac{a^{n+1}+b^{n+1}}{a^n+b^n}$$

Which is at $n=0$

Hence Ans is (D)

Sol. 25 (A) $S_m=n$

$$\frac{m}{2}(2a+(m-1)d)=n$$

$\Rightarrow$ $2am+(m^2-m)d=2n$ ...(1)

Similarly

$2an+(n^2-n)d=2m$ ...(2)

(1) – (2)

$\Rightarrow$ $2a(m-n)+(m^2-m-n^2+n)d=-2(m-n)$

$\Rightarrow$ $2a(m-n)+[(m-n)(m+n)-(m-n)]$

$$d=-2(m-n)$$

$\Rightarrow$ $2a+(m+n-1)d=-2$

$$S_{m+n}=\frac{m+n}{2}[2a+(m+n-1)d]$$

$$=\frac{m+n}{2}\times(-2)$$

$$=-(m+n)$$

Hence Ans is (A)

Sol. 26 (C) $LCM=14\,GCD$

$LCM+GCD=600$

$\Rightarrow$ $15GCD=600$

$GCD=40$

$LCM=14.40=560$

$LCM\times GCD=a.b.$

$\Rightarrow$ $560\times 40=80\times b$

$b=280$

Hence Ans is (C)

Sol. 27 (C) 10, 12, 14, ..., 98

$2\times 5, 2\times 6, 2\times 7, \ldots 2\times 49$

$\Rightarrow$ Total number $=(49-5)+1=45$

Hence Ans is (C)

Sol. 28 (A) $\frac{20}{2}[2\times 8+19\times(-5)]=-790$

Hence Ans is (A)

Sol. 29 (C) Required numbers are 11, 15, 16 ... 299

$$a_n=11+(n-1)4=299$$

$$\Rightarrow \quad n=\frac{299-11}{4}+1=73$$

Hence Ans is (C)

Sol. 30 (B) $a+(p-1)d=q$ ...(1)

$a+(q-1)d=p$ ...(2)

(1) – (2)

$$(p-q)d=q-p$$

Hence $d=-1$

$$a+(p-1)(-1)=q$$

$$a=p+q-1$$

m^{th} term is $a+(m-1)d=(p+q-1)+-1\,(m-1)$

$$=p+q-m$$

Hence Ans is (B)

Sol. 31 (C) $20, 19\frac{1}{4}, 18\frac{1}{2}, \ldots$

$$T_n=20+(n-1)\left(-\frac{3}{4}\right)<0$$

or $80+3-3n<0$

$$\Rightarrow \quad n>\frac{83}{3}$$

$$\Rightarrow \quad n=28^{th}$$

Hence Ans is (C)

Sol. 32 (A) Let $S_n=5n^2-3n$

$$a_{100}=S_{100}-S_{99}$$

$$=[5(100)^2-3\times 99]-[5(99)^2-3(99)]$$

$$=5(100^2-99^2)-3(100-99)$$

$$=5\times 199-3$$

$$=992$$

Hence Ans is (A)

Sol. 33 (C) Given $T_5=5$ & $S_5=55$

let first term be 'a' & common difference be 'd'

$$a+(5-1)d=5$$

& $\frac{5}{2}[2a+(5-1)d]=55$

$a+4d=5$ ...(1)

& $2a+4d=22$ ...(2)

equation-(2) – equation-(1)

$$a=17$$

Hence Ans is (C)

Sol. 34 (D) Let the first term be 'a' & common difference be 'd'

given $S_{11}=S_{17}$

& $S_{28}=?$

$$\frac{11}{2}[2a+(11-1)d]=\frac{17}{2}[2a+(17-1)d]$$

$$22a+110d=34a+272d$$

$$12a+27d=0$$

$$2a+27d=0$$

So $S_{28}=\frac{28}{2}[2a+27d]$

$$=14\times 0=0$$

Hence Ans is (D)

Sol. 35 (A) Let an $A.P.$ whose first term is 'a', common difference 'd'

$$T_5=T_3+10$$

$$a+4d=a+2d+10$$

$$2d=10$$

$$d=5$$

$$T_9-T_6=(a+8d)-(a+5d)$$

$$=15$$

Hence Ans is (A)

Sol. 36 (C) $ax+by+c=0$ ...(1)

$$a, b, c\rightarrow A.P$$

$$\Rightarrow \quad a+c=2b$$

$\Rightarrow \quad a-2b+c=0$ ...(2)

Comparing-(1) and (2), we get

$$x=1, b=-2$$

Hence Ans is (C)

Sol. 37 (D) Let the number be

$$a-3d, a-d, a+d, a+3d$$

Now, $a-3d, a-d, a+d, a+3d=20$

$$4a=20$$

$$a=5$$

Also, $(a-3d)^2+(a-d)^2+(a+d)^2+(a+3d)^2=120$

$a^2+9d^2-6ad+a^2+d^2-2ad+a^2+d^2+2ad+a^2+9d^2+6ad=120$

$$4a^2 + 20d^2 = 120$$

$$a^2 + 5d = 30$$

Now, since $a = 5$

$$(5)^2 + 5d^2 = 30$$

$$25 + 5d^2 = 30$$

$$5d^2 = 5$$

$$d^2 = 1$$

$\Rightarrow$ $d = \pm 1$

Case I : If $d = 1$, then number are $5-3, 5-1, 5+1, 5+3$

$\Rightarrow$ 2, 4, 6, 8

Case II : If $d = -1$, then number are $5+3, 5+1, 5-1, 5-3$

$\Rightarrow$ 8, 6, 4, 2

Checking in option, we get 2, 4, 6, 8
Hence Ans is (D)

Sol. 38 (D) $S_n = nP + \frac{n}{2}(n-1)Q$

$$= nP + \frac{n^2Q}{2} - \frac{nQ}{2}$$

$$= n\left(P - \frac{Q}{2}\right) + \frac{n^2Q}{2}$$

Using $Sn = An^2 + Bn$

$$A = \frac{Q}{2}$$

$$B = P - \frac{Q}{2}$$

$\Rightarrow$ $d = 2A = 2 \times \frac{Q}{2} = Q$

$\Rightarrow$ $d = Q$

Hence Ans is (D)

Sol. 39 (C) $a = 17$

$$l = 332$$

$$d = 9$$

Taking 332 as nth term

$$a_n = a + (n-1)d$$

$\Rightarrow$ $332 = 17 + (n-1)9$

$\Rightarrow$ $332 - 17 = (n-1) \times 9$

$\Rightarrow$ $315 = (n-1)9$

$\Rightarrow$ $n = 36$

Hence Ans is (C)

Sol. 40 (A) $\frac{1}{x_1x_2} + \frac{1}{x_2x_3} + \frac{1}{x_3x_4} + \ldots + \frac{1}{x_{n-1}x_n}$

Let $x_2 - x_1 = d$

$\Rightarrow$ $\frac{1}{d}\left[\left(\frac{1}{x_1} - \frac{1}{x_2}\right) + \left(\frac{1}{x_2} - \frac{1}{x_3}\right) + \ldots + \left(\frac{1}{x_{n-1}} - \frac{1}{x_n}\right)\right]$

$\Rightarrow$ $\frac{1}{d}\left[\left(\frac{1}{x_1} - \frac{1}{x_n}\right)\right]$

$\Rightarrow$ $\frac{1}{d}\left(\frac{x_n - x_1}{x_1x_n}\right) = \frac{1}{d}\left(\frac{x_1 + (n-1)d - x_1}{x_1x_n}\right) = \frac{n-1}{x_1x_n}$

Hence Ans is (A)

Sol. 41 (A) We know $AM \geq GM$

$\Rightarrow$ $x^2 + \frac{1}{x^2} \geq 2$

Equality holds when $x^2 = \frac{1}{x^2}$

$\Rightarrow$ $x = \pm 1$

$\Rightarrow$ $y = \pm 1$

Thus, $x^2 + y^2 = 2$

Hence Ans is (A)

Sol. 42 (D) $a_1 = 0, a_2 = d, a_3 = 2d, a_4 = 3d, a_5 = 4d.$
Substituting 'n' as 5 in the above equation and verifying with the options we get the answer as option (D)
Hence Ans is (D)

Sol. 43 (C) $S = a_1 + a_2 + a_3 + \ldots\ldots + a_{16}$

$$\bar{x} = \frac{S}{n}$$

$$16 = \frac{S}{16}$$

$$S = 256$$

Let $a_{16} = 16$

$\Rightarrow$ $S - 16 = a_1 + a_2 + a_3 + \ldots. + a_{15}$

Three new observations are added.

$$S - 16 + 3 + 4 + 5 = a_1 + a_2 + a_3 + \ldots.. + a_{15} + 3 + 4 + 5$$

$\Rightarrow$ $\bar{x} = \frac{\text{Sum}}{\text{n}}$

$$\bar{x} = \frac{S-4}{18} = \frac{256-4}{18} = \bar{x} = 14$$

Hence Ans is (C)

Sol. 44 (C) $S_n = 3n + 2n^2$

$$T_1 = 5 = S_1$$

$$S_2 = 6 + 8 = 14$$

$\Rightarrow$ $T_2 = 9$

$$d = T_2 - T_1 = 9 - 5 = 4$$

Hence Ans is (C)

Sol. 45 (A) 12, 15, … 99

$$a = 12, d = 3$$
$$a_n = a + (n-1)d$$
$$\Rightarrow 99 = 12 + (n-1)3$$
$$\Rightarrow 87 = 3n - 3$$
$$\Rightarrow 3n = 90$$
$$\Rightarrow n = 30$$

Hence Ans is (A)

Sol. 46 (A) Given, $a_n = 3 + 2n$

Now,
$$a_1 = 5$$
$$a_2 = 3 + 2 \times 2 = 7$$
$$d = a_2 - a_1 = 7 - 5 = 2$$
$$d = 2$$
$$S_n = \frac{n}{2}[2a + (n-1)d]$$
$$S_{24} = \frac{24}{2}[2 \times 5 + 23 \times 2]$$
$$= 12[10 + 46]$$
$$= 12 \times 56$$
$$= 672$$

Hence Ans is (A)

Sol. 47 (B) Number of terms $= n$

Middle term $= m$

$S_n = ?$

Let there be n term $n =$ odd

$$\Rightarrow \text{Middle term} = \frac{n+1}{2}$$
$$\Rightarrow a_{\frac{n+1}{2}} = m = a + \left(\frac{n+1}{2} - 1\right)d$$
$$m = \frac{2a + (n-1)d}{2}$$
$$\Rightarrow S_n = \frac{n}{2} \times [2a + (n-1)d]$$
$$= \frac{n}{2} 2m \Rightarrow mn \Rightarrow S_n = mn$$

Hence Ans is (B)

Sol. 48 (B) Given $S_m = n$

$S_n = m$

$$\Rightarrow \frac{m}{2}[2a + (m-1)d] = n$$

Also: $\frac{n}{2}[2a + (n-1)d] = m$

$$2a + (m-1)d = \frac{2n}{m}$$
$$2a + (n-1)d = \frac{2m}{n}$$

Subtracting: $(m-n)d = \frac{2n}{m} - \frac{2m}{n}$

$$d(m-n) = 2\left[\frac{(n+m)(n-m)}{mn}\right]$$
$$d = \frac{-2(n+m)}{mn} \quad \ldots(1)$$

Also: $2a + (m-1)d = \frac{2n}{m}$

$$2a + (m-1)d + nd = \frac{2n}{m} + nd$$
$$= \frac{2n}{m} + n\left[\frac{-2(n+m)}{mn}\right] \quad \text{from (1)}$$
$$= -2$$

thus, sum of $m + n$ terms

$$= \left(\frac{m+n}{2}\right)[2a + (m+n-1)d]$$
$$= -(m+n)$$

Hence Ans is (B)

Sol. 49 (B) Divisible by 2

$$S_1 = 2 + 4 + 6 + 8 + \ldots + 100$$
$$= 2[1 + 2 + 3 + 4 + \ldots + 50]$$
$$= 2(50)\left(\frac{50+1}{2}\right)$$
$$= 50 \times 51 = 2550$$

Divisible by 5
$$S_2 = 5 + 10 + 15 + 20 + \ldots + 100$$
$$= 5[1 + 2 + 3 + 4 + \ldots + 20]$$
$$= 5 \times \frac{20 \times 21}{2}$$
$$= 50 \times 21 = 1050$$

Divisible by both 2 and 5 (i.e. 10)
$$S_3 = 10 + 20 + 30 + 40 + \ldots + 100$$
$$= 10[1 + 2 + 3 + 4 + \ldots + 10]$$
$$= 10 \times \frac{10 \times 11}{2} = 550$$
$$S = S_1 + S_2 - S_3$$
$$S = 2550 + 1050 - 550$$
$$S = 3050$$

Hence Ans is (B)

Sol. 50 (B) Numbers between 10 and 300 leaving remainder 3 when divided by 4 are 11, 15, 19 … 299

Which forms an *A.P.*

$$a = 11, d = 4, a_n = 299$$
$$a_n = a + (n-1)d$$
$$299 = 11 + (n-1)4$$
$$299 = -11 = 4(n-1)$$

$$\frac{288}{4} = (n-1)$$
$$72+1 = n$$
$$73 = n$$

Hence Ans is (B)

Sol. 51 (C) Let the first term be A, common difference $= d$ then n^{th} term of an A.P. is given by

$$T_n = A + (n-1)\,d$$

given $T_4 = a$

$\Rightarrow$ $A + 3d = a$ ...(1)

$T_7 = b$

$\Rightarrow$ $A + 6d = b$ ...(2)

$T_{10} = c$

$\Rightarrow$ $A + 9d = c$ ...(3)

Equation-(1) + equation-(3) = 2 equation-(2)

$\Rightarrow$ $c + a = 2b$ ...(4)

Now sum of the roots of quadratic equation $ax^2 + bx + c$ is given by

$$\alpha + \beta = -\frac{b}{a}$$

Hence sum of roots of

$$ax^2 - 2bx + c = \frac{2b}{a} = \frac{c+a}{a} \text{ (using (4))}$$

Hence Ans is (C)

Sol. 52 (B) $S_1 = 1 + 2 + 3 + \ldots n$ term n

$S_2 = 2 + 5 + 8 + \ldots n$ term $(n-1)$

$S_3 = 3 + 8 + 13 + \ldots n$ term

$S_r = r + (3r-1) + (5r-2) + \ldots n$ term

$$S_1 = \frac{n(n+1)}{2}$$

$$S_2 = \frac{n}{2}[2\times 2 + (n-1)3] = \frac{n}{2}[3n+1]$$

$$S_2 = \frac{n}{2}[2\times 3 + (n-1)5] = \frac{n}{2}[5n+1]$$

$$S_r = \frac{n}{2}[2r + (n-1)(2r-1)]$$

$$= \frac{n}{2}[2r + 2nr - n - 2r + 1]$$

$$= \frac{n}{2}[n(2r-1) + 1]$$

$$S_1 + S_2 + \ldots + Sr$$

$$= \frac{n}{2}[n + 3n + 5n + \ldots + n(2r-1) + r]$$

$$\Rightarrow \frac{n}{2}[n(1+3+5+\ldots+(2r-1)) + r]$$

$$\Rightarrow \frac{n}{2}\left[nr^2 + r\right] = \frac{nr}{2}(nr+1)$$

Hence Ans is (B)

Sol. 53 (D) First term $a = 2$

Common difference $= d$

Given, $S_5 = \frac{1}{4}(S_{10} - S_5)$

$\Rightarrow$ $4(S_5) = S_{10} - S_5$

$\Rightarrow$ $5(S_5) = S_{10}$

$\Rightarrow$ $5\left[\frac{5}{2}(2(2) + (5-1)d)\right] = \frac{10}{2}[2(2) + (10-1)d]$

$\Rightarrow$ $5\left[\frac{5}{2}(4+4d)\right] = 5[4+9d]$

$\Rightarrow$ $5(2+2d) = 4 + 9d$

$\Rightarrow$ $10 + 10d = 4 + 9d$

$\Rightarrow$ $d = -6$

So, $S_{30} = \frac{30}{2}[2a + (30-1)d]$

$= 15[2(2) + 29(-6)]$

$= 15(4 - 174)$

$= 15(-170)$

$= -2550$

Hence Ans is (D)

Sol. 54 (A) $(1, 3), (5, 7, 9, 11), (13, 15, 17, 19, 21, 23)$:

Number of terms in Group 1 = 2

Number of terms in Group 2 = 4

Number of terms in Group 10 = 20

Total number of terms before Group 10

$= 2 + 4 + 6 + \ldots + 18$

$= \frac{9}{2}(2 + 18)$

$= 90$

First term of 10th Group *i.e.*, 91st odd number

$= 1 + (90)2$

$= 181$

$\Rightarrow$ 181 is the first term of Group 10

$\Rightarrow$ Sum of terms in group 10

$= \frac{20}{2}(2 \times 181 + 19 \times 2)$

$= 4000$

Hence Ans is (A)

* * * * *

Probability

8

- The science which measures the degree of uncertainty is called **probability.**

- There are two types of approaches to the study of probability. These are experimental or empirical approach and theoretical approach.

- In the experimental approach to probability, we find the probability of the occurrence of an event by actually performing the experiment a number of times and record the happening of an event.

- In the theoretical approach to probability, we predict the results without actually performing the experiment.

- The observations of an experiment are called its **outcomes**.

- An experiment in which all possible outcomes are known and the exact outcome cannot be predicted in advance, is called a **random experiment**.

- The word **unbiased** means each outcome is equally likely to occur. For example, an unbiased die indicates that each of the outcomes 1, 2, 3, 4, 5 or 6 has equal chances to occur. We shall always assume that all the experiments have equally likely outcomes.

- The theoretical probability of an event E, written as $P(E)$ is defined as

$$P(E) = \frac{\text{Number of outcomes favourable to } E}{\text{Total number of all possible outcomes of the experiment}}$$

- An event having only one outcome of the experiment is called an **elementary** event.

- An event associated to a random experiment and obtained by combining two or more simple events associated to the same random experiment, is called a **compound event**.

OR

A **compound event** is an aggregate of some simple (elementary) event and is decomposable into simple events.

Ex. If we throw a die, then the event E of getting an odd number is a compound event because the event E contains three elements 1, 3 and 5, which is a compound of three simple events E_1, E_2 and E_3 containing 1, 3 and 5 respectively.

- The out comes of an experiment are said to be **equally likely** events if the chances of their happenings are neither less nor greater than other.

In other words, a given number of events are said to be equally likely if none of them is expected to occur in preference to the others.

Ex. In tossing a coin, getting head (H) and tail (T) are equally likely events.

- Two events are said to be **Mutually Exclusive** (or disjoint or incompatible) if the occurrence of one precludes (rules out) the simultaneous occurrence of the other. If A & B are two mutually exclusive events then

$$P(A \cap B) = 0$$

Consider, for example, choosing numbers at random from the set {3, 4, 5, 6, 7, 8, 9, 10, 11, 12}

If, Event A is the selection of a prime number, Event B is the selection of an odd number, Event C is the selection of an even number, then A and C are mutually exclusive as none of the numbers in this set is both prime and even. But A and B are not mutually exclusive as some numbers are both prime and odd (viz. 3, 5, 7, 11).

- Events $A, B, C\ldots N$ are said to be **Exhaustive Events** if no event outside this set can result as an outcome of an experiment. For example, if A & B are two events defined on a sample space S and A & B are exhaustive

$$\Rightarrow \quad A \cup B = S$$

$$\Rightarrow \quad P(A \cup B) = 1.$$

- The sum of the probabilities of all the elementary events of an experiment is 1.

In general for any event E

$$P(E) = 1 - P(\text{not } E) = 1 - P(\bar{E})$$

or $$P(\bar{E}) = 1 - P(E)$$

or $$P(E) + P(\bar{E}) = 1$$

Here the event $\bar{E}$, representing not E, is called the compliment of the event E.

- The probability of the event which is impossible to occur is 0. Such an event is called an **impossible event**.

- The probability of an event which is sure (or certain) to occur is 1. Such an event is called a **sure** or a **certain event**.

- For an event E, we have $0 \le P(E) \le 1$.

- $A \cup B = A + B = A$ or B denotes occurrence of at least A or B.

For 2 events A & B :

$$P(A \cup B) = P(A) + P(B) - P(A \cap B)$$

- If A & B are mutually exclusive then

$$P(A \cup B) = P(A) + P(B).$$

- A die is a well balanced cube with its six faces marked with numbers or dots 1 to 6. When we throw a die we are interested in the number that occurs on the top face.

- The pack or deck of playing cards consists of 52 cards, 26 of red colour and 26 of black colour. There are four suits each of 13 cards namely hearts (♥), spades (♠), diamonds (♦) and clubs (♣).

Each suit contains ace, king, queen, jack or knave, 10, 9, 8, 7, 6, 5, 4, 3, 2.

There are 4 aces, 4 kings, 4 queens, 4 jacks, 4 tens, and so on in a pack.

Kings, queens, and jacks are called face cards.

* * * * *

PRACTICE EXERCISE - 8.1

8-1 Find the probability of getting a head in a throw of a coin :

(A) $\frac{1}{2}$ (B) 1
(C) 2 (D) None of these

8-2 To 8-5 : Two fair coins are tossed simultaneously. Find the probability of...

8-2 Getting only one head :
(A) 1/2 (B) 1/3
(C) 2/3 (D) 3/4

8-3 Getting atleast one head :

(A) $\frac{1}{4}$ (B) $\frac{3}{4}$

(C) $\frac{1}{2}$ (D) $\frac{3}{8}$

8-4 Getting two heads :

(A) $\frac{2}{7}$ (B) $\frac{1}{4}$

(C) $\frac{1}{2}$ (D) $\frac{4}{5}$

8-5 Getting atleast two heads :

(A) $\frac{3}{4}$ (B) $\frac{1}{2}$

(C) $\frac{1}{4}$ (D) 1

8-6 To 8-12 : Three fair coins are tossed simultaneously. Find the probability of...

8-6 Getting one head :
(A) 0 (B) 3/4

(C) $\frac{5}{8}$ (D) $\frac{3}{8}$

8-7 Getting one tail :

(A) 1 (B) $\frac{1}{4}$

(C) $\frac{5}{8}$ (D) $\frac{3}{8}$

8-8 Getting atleast one head :

(A) $\frac{7}{8}$ (B) $\frac{1}{8}$

(C) $\frac{3}{4}$ (D) $\frac{1}{4}$

8-9 Getting two heads :

(A) $\frac{3}{5}$ (B) $\frac{3}{8}$

(C) $\frac{5}{8}$ (D) $\frac{2}{5}$

8-10 Getting atleast two heads :

(A) $\frac{3}{8}$ (B) $\frac{7}{8}$

(C) $\frac{1}{2}$ (D) $\frac{1}{4}$

8-11 Getting atleast one head and one tail :

(A) $\frac{2}{8}$ (B) $\frac{1}{2}$

(C) $\frac{3}{10}$ (D) $\frac{3}{4}$

8-12 Getting more heads than the number of tails :
(A) 2 (B) 7/8

(C) $\frac{5}{8}$ (D) $\frac{1}{2}$

8-13 To 8-18 : An unbiased die is rolled. Find the probability of...

8-13 Getting a number less than 7 but greater than zero :
(A) 0 (B) 3/4

(C) 1 (D) $\frac{7}{8}$

8-14 Getting a multiple of 3 :

(A) $\frac{1}{6}$ (B) $\frac{1}{3}$

(C) $\frac{5}{6}$ (D) None of these

8-15 Getting a prime number :

(A) $\frac{1}{2}$ (B) $\frac{3}{5}$

(C) $\frac{5}{7}$ (D) $\frac{5}{8}$

8-16 Getting an even number :

(A) $\frac{1}{2}$ (B) $\frac{4}{5}$

(C) $\frac{2}{8}$ (D) $\frac{3}{4}$

8-17 Getting exactly one head or two heads :

(A) $\frac{1}{4}$ (B) $\frac{3}{4}$

(C) $\frac{1}{2}$ (D) $\frac{3}{8}$

8-18 Getting no heads :

(A) 0 (B) 1

(C) $\frac{1}{8}$ (D) $\frac{7}{8}$

8-19 To 8-27 : Two unbiased diced are rolled simultaneously. Find the probability of...

8-19 Getting a total of 9 :

(A) $\frac{1}{3}$ (B) $\frac{1}{9}$

(C) $\frac{8}{9}$ (D) $\frac{9}{10}$

8-20 Getting a sum greater than 9 :

(A) $\frac{10}{11}$ (B) $\frac{5}{6}$

(C) $\frac{1}{6}$ (D) $\frac{8}{9}$

8-21 Getting a total of 9 or 11 :

(A) $\frac{2}{99}$ (B) $\frac{20}{99}$

(C) $\frac{1}{6}$ (D) $\frac{1}{10}$

8-22 Getting a doublet :

(A) 1/12 (B) 0

(C) 5/8 (D) 1/6

8-23 Getting a doublet of even numbers :

(A) 5/8 (B) 0

(C) 5/8 (D) 1/6

8-24 Getting a multiple of 2 on one die and a multiple of 3 on the other :

(A) $\frac{15}{36}$ (B) $\frac{25}{36}$

(C) $\frac{11}{36}$ (D) $\frac{5}{6}$

8-25 Getting the sum of numbers on the two faces divisible by 3 or 4 :

(A) $\frac{4}{9}$ (B) $\frac{1}{7}$

(C) $\frac{5}{9}$ (D) $\frac{7}{12}$

8-26 Getting the sum as a prime number :

(A) $\frac{3}{5}$ (B). $\frac{5}{12}$

(C) $\frac{1}{2}$ (D) $\frac{3}{4}$

8-27 Getting atleast one '5' :

(A) $\frac{3}{5}$ (B) $\frac{1}{5}$

(C) $\frac{5}{36}$ (D) $\frac{11}{36}$

8-28 To 8-35 : One card is drawn from a pack of 52 cards, each of the 52 cards being equally likely to be drawn find the probability such that ...

8-28 The card drawn is black :

(A) $\frac{1}{2}$ (B) $\frac{1}{4}$

(C) $\frac{8}{13}$ (D) Can't be determine

8-29 The card drawn is a queen :

(A) $\frac{1}{12}$ (B) $\frac{1}{13}$

(C) $\frac{1}{4}$ (D) $\frac{3}{4}$

8-30 The card drawn is black and a queen :

(A) $\frac{1}{13}$ (B) $\frac{1}{52}$

(C) $\frac{1}{26}$ (D) $\frac{5}{6}$

8-31 The card drawn is either black or a queen :

(A) $\frac{15}{26}$ (B) $\frac{13}{17}$

(C) $\frac{7}{13}$ (D) $\frac{15}{26}$

8-32 The card drawn is either king or a queen :

(A) $\frac{5}{26}$ (B) $\frac{1}{13}$

(C) $\frac{2}{13}$ (D) $\frac{12}{13}$

8-33 The card drawn is either a heart, a queen or a king :

(A) $\frac{17}{52}$ (B) $\frac{21}{52}$

(C) $\frac{19}{52}$ (D) $\frac{9}{26}$

8-34 The card drawn is neither a spade nor a king :

(A) 0 (B) $\frac{9}{13}$

(C) $\frac{1}{2}$ (D) $\frac{4}{13}$

8-35 The card drawn is neither an ace nor a king :

(A) $\frac{11}{13}$ (B) $\frac{1}{2}$

(C) $\frac{2}{13}$ (D) $\frac{11}{26}$

8-36 To 8-37 : If A & B be two mutually exclusive events in a sample space such that

$$P(A) = \frac{2}{5} \text{ \& } P(B) = \frac{1}{2} \text{ then...}$$

8-36 Find $P(\bar{A})$:

(A) $\frac{2}{5}$ (B) $\frac{3}{5}$

(C) $\frac{4}{5}$ (D) $\frac{6}{7}$

8-37 Find $P(\bar{B})$:

(A) $\frac{1}{4}$ (B) $\frac{3}{4}$

(C) $\frac{1}{2}$ (D) $\frac{4}{5}$

8-38 What is the probability that a number selected from the numbers 1, 2, 3, ... 20, is a prime number when each of the given numbers is equally likely to be selected ?

(A) 7/10 (B) 2/15

(C) 2/5 (D) 3/5

8-39 Find the probability that a leap year selected at random will contain 53 Sundays :

(A) $\frac{5}{7}$ (B) $\frac{3}{4}$

(C) $\frac{4}{7}$ (D) $\frac{2}{7}$

8-40 If there are two children in a family, find the probability that there is atleast one girl in the family :

(A) $\frac{1}{4}$ (B) $\frac{1}{2}$

(C) $\frac{3}{4}$ (D) None of these

8-41 To 8-44 : Four dice thrown simultaneously find the probability such that...

8-41 All of them show the same face :

(A) $\frac{1}{216}$ (B) $\frac{15}{16}$

(C) $\frac{15}{36}$ (D) $\frac{1}{2}$

8-42 All of them show the different face :

(A) $\frac{3}{28}$ (B) $\frac{5}{18}$

(C) $\frac{15}{36}$ (D) $\frac{11}{36}$

8-43 Two of them show the same face and remaining two show the different faces :

(A) $\frac{4}{9}$ (B) $\frac{5}{9}$

(C) $\frac{11}{18}$ (D) $\frac{7}{9}$

8-44 Atleast two of them show the same face :

(A) $\frac{37}{72}$ (B) $\frac{11}{36}$

(C) $\frac{47}{72}$ (D) $\frac{25}{36}$

8-45 The odds in favour of an event are 2 : 7. Find the probability of occurrence of this event :

(A) $\frac{2}{9}$ (B) $\frac{5}{12}$

(C) $\frac{7}{12}$ (D) $\frac{2}{5}$

8-46 To 8-50 : A bag contains 8 red and 4 green balls find the probability such that...

8-46 The ball drawn is red when one ball is selected at random :

(A) $\frac{2}{3}$ (B) $\frac{1}{3}$

(C) $\frac{1}{6}$ (D) $\frac{5}{6}$

8-47 All the 4 balls drawn are red when four balls are drawn at random :

(A) $\frac{17}{32}$ (B) $\frac{14}{99}$

(C) $\frac{7}{12}$ (D) None of these

8-48 All the 4 balls drawn are green when four balls are drawn at random :

(A) $\frac{1}{495}$ (B) $\frac{7}{99}$

(C) $\frac{5}{12}$ (D) $\frac{2}{3}$

8-49 Two balls are red and one ball is green when three balls are drawn at random :

(A) $\frac{56}{99}$ (B) $\frac{112}{495}$

(C) $\frac{78}{495}$ (D) None of these

8-50 Three balls are drawn and none of them is red :

(A) $\frac{68}{99}$ (B) $\frac{7}{99}$

(C) $\frac{4}{495}$ (D) None of these

* * * * *

PRACTICE EXERCISE - 8.2

8-1 Tickets are numbered from 1 to 18 are mixed up together and then 9 ticket is drawn at random. Find the probability that the ticket has a number, which is a multiple of 2 or 3 :

(A) $\frac{1}{3}$ (B) $\frac{3}{5}$

(C) $\frac{2}{3}$ (D) $\frac{5}{6}$

8-2 In a lottery of 100 tickets numbered 1 to 100, two tickets are drawn simultaneously. Find the probability that both the tickets drawn have prime numbers :

(A) $\frac{2}{33}$ (B) $\frac{7}{50}$

(C) $\frac{7}{20}$ (D) $\frac{5}{66}$

8-3 In the previous question, find the probability that none of the tickets drawn has a prime number :

(A) $\frac{29}{66}$ (B) $\frac{17}{33}$

(C) $\frac{37}{66}$ (D) $\frac{17}{50}$

8-4 The odds against of an event are 5 : 7, find the probability of occurrence of this event :

(A) $\frac{3}{8}$ (B) $\frac{7}{12}$

(C) $\frac{2}{7}$ (D) $\frac{5}{12}$

8-5 From a group of 3 men and 2 women, two persons are selected at random. Find the probability that atleast one woman is selected :

(A) $\frac{1}{5}$ (B) $\frac{7}{10}$

(C) $\frac{2}{5}$ (D) $\frac{5}{6}$

8-6 A box contains 5 defective and 15 non-defective bulbs. Two bulbs are chosen at random. Find the probability that both the bulbs are non-defective :

(A) $\frac{5}{19}$ (B) $\frac{3}{20}$

(C) $\frac{21}{38}$ (D) None of these

8-7 In the previous question, find the probability that atleast 3 bulbs are defective when 4 bulbs are selected at random :

(A) $\frac{32}{969}$ (B) $\frac{7}{20}$

(C) $\frac{1}{20}$ (D) None of these

8-8 The probability of occurrence of two events A and B are 1/4 and 1/2 respectively. The probability of their simultaneous occurrence is $\frac{7}{50}$. Find the probability that either A or B must occur :

(A) $\frac{61}{100}$ (B) $\frac{29}{100}$

(C) $\frac{39}{100}$ (D) $\frac{56}{99}$

8-9 In the previous question, find the probability that neither A nor B occurs :

(A) $\frac{25}{99}$ (B) $\frac{39}{100}$

(C) $\frac{61}{100}$ (D) $\frac{17}{100}$

8-10 If A and B be two events in a sample space such that $P(A)=\frac{3}{10}$ and $P(B)=\frac{1}{2}$ and $P(A\cap B)=\frac{1}{5}$. Find $P(A\cup B)$:

(A) $\frac{1}{5}$ (B) $\frac{2}{5}$

(C) $\frac{3}{5}$ (D) $\frac{4}{5}$

8-11 If A and B be two events in a sample space such that $P(A)=\frac{2}{5}$, $P(B)=\frac{1}{2}$ and $P(A\cup B)=\frac{3}{5}$, find $P(A\cap B)$:

(A) $\frac{3}{10}$ (B) $\frac{7}{10}$

(C) $\frac{4}{7}$ (D) $\frac{4}{15}$

8-12 From a well shuffled pack of 52 cards, three cards are drawn at random. Find the probability of drawing an ace, a king and a jack :

(A) $\frac{16}{5525}$ (B) $\frac{16}{625}$

(C) $\frac{16}{3125}$ (D) None of these

8-13 Four cards are drawn at random from a pack of 52 cards. Find the probability of getting all the four cards of same number :

(A) $\frac{17}{1665}$ (B) $\frac{1}{20825}$

(C) $\frac{7}{25850}$ (D) None of these

8-14 From a well shuffled pack of 52 playing cards, four cards are accidently dropped. Find the probability that one card is missing from each suit :

(A) $\frac{17}{20825}$ (B) $\frac{2197}{20825}$

(C) $\frac{197}{1665}$ (D) None of these

8-15 Four cards are drawn at random from a pack of 52 cards. Find the probability of getting all the four cards of different numbers :

(A) $\frac{141}{4165}$ (B) $\frac{117}{833}$

(C) $\frac{264}{4165}$ (D) None of these

8-16 Two dice are rolled one after another. The probability that the number on the first is smaller than that on the second is :

(A) $\frac{1}{2}$ (B) $\frac{7}{18}$

(C) $\frac{3}{4}$ (D) $\frac{5}{12}$

8-17 A number is selected at random from first thirty natural numbers. What is the chance that is a multiple of 3 or 13 :

(A) $\frac{17}{30}$ (B) $\frac{11}{30}$

(C) $\frac{2}{5}$ (D) $\frac{4}{5}$

8-18 A box contains 2 black, 4 white and 3 red balls. One ball is drawn at random from the box and kept aside. From the remaining balls in the box, another ball is drawn at random and kept aside with the first. This process is repeated till all the balls are drawn from the box. The probability that the balls drawn are in the sequence of 2 black, 4 white and 3 red is :

(A) $\frac{1}{1260}$ (B) $\frac{1}{7560}$

(C) $\frac{1}{126}$ (D) None of these

8-19 Three numbers are chosen from 1 to 30. The probability that they are not consecutive is :

(A) $\frac{144}{145}$ (B) $\frac{143}{145}$

(C) $\frac{142}{145}$ (D) None of these

8-20 A speaks truth in 60% cases and B speaks truth in 70% cases. The probability that they will say the same thing while describing a single event is :

(A) 0.56 (B) 0.54

(C) 0.38 (D) 0.94

8-21 Three integers are chosen at random from the first 20 integers. The probability that their product is even, is :

(A) $\frac{2}{19}$ (B) $\frac{3}{29}$

(C) $\frac{17}{19}$ (D) $\frac{4}{29}$

8-22 Three dice are thrown. The probability that the same number will appear on each of them is :

(A) $\frac{1}{6}$ (B) $\frac{1}{18}$

(C) $\frac{1}{36}$ (D) None of these

8-23 The probability that the 13th day of a randomly chosen month is a Friday, is :

(A) $\frac{1}{12}$ (B) $\frac{1}{7}$

(C) $\frac{1}{84}$ (D) None of these

8-24 Two coins and a dice are tossed. The probability that both coins fall heads and the dice shows a 3 or 6 is :

(A) $\frac{1}{8}$ (B) $\frac{1}{12}$

(C) $\frac{1}{16}$ (D) None of these

8-25 One hundred cards are numbered from 1 to 100. The probability that a randomly chosen card has a digit 5 is :

(A) $\frac{1}{100}$ (B) $\frac{9}{100}$

(C) $\frac{19}{100}$ (D) None of these

* * * * *

PRACTICE EXERCISE - 8.3

8-1 The author of the book "The Book on games of chance" based on probability theory : **[NTSE-2013 (Stage-I) Rajasthan]**

(A) J. Cardon (B) R.S. Woodwards
(C) P.S. Laplace (D) P.D. Pherma

8-2 A die is thrown twice. The probability that 5 will not come up either of the time is : **[NTSE-2014 (Stage-I) Rajasthan]**

(A) $\frac{35}{36}$ (B) $\frac{25}{36}$
(C) $\frac{1}{36}$ (D) $\frac{11}{36}$

8-3 A die is thrown twice. The probability of the sum being odd is : **[NTSE-2015 (Stage-I) Rajasthan]**

(A) $\frac{1}{2}$ (B) $\frac{1}{3}$
(C) $\frac{1}{4}$ (D) $\frac{1}{6}$

8-4 The probability that a leap year will have 53 Fridays or 53 Saturday is : **[NTSE-2015 (Stage-I) Tamilnadu]**

(A) $\frac{2}{7}$ (B) $\frac{1}{7}$
(C) $\frac{4}{7}$ (D) $\frac{3}{7}$

8-5 The probability of guessing the correct answer to a certain test question is $x/12$. If the probability of not guessing the correct answer is 2/3, then x is equal to : **[NTSE-2015 (Stage-I) Chandigarh]**

(A) 2 (B) 3
(C) 4 (D) 6

8-6 A bag contains five red balls and some blue balls. If the probability of drawing the blue ball is double that of red ball, then the number of blue balls in the bag is : **[NTSE-2015 (Stage-I) Chandigarh]**

(A) 19 (B) 20
(C) 10 (D) 25

8-7 Two coins are tossed simultaneously, the probability of getting at least one head is : **[NTSE-2015 (Stage-I) Maharashtra]**

(A) $\frac{3}{4}$ (B) $\frac{1}{2}$
(C) $\frac{2}{3}$ (D) $\frac{3}{5}$

8-8 A point is selected at random from the interior of a circle. The probability that the selected point is closer to the centre then the boundary of the circle is : **[NTSE-2015 (Stage-I) Delhi]**

(A) $\frac{1}{2}$ (B) $\frac{1}{3}$
(C) $\frac{1}{4}$ (D) $\frac{1}{5}$

8-9 From a pack of 52 playing cards, face club cards are removed. The remaining cards are well shuffled and a card is drawn at random. Find the probability that the card drawn is a heart card : **[NTSE-2015 (Stage-I) Maharashtra]**

(A) $\frac{1}{4}$ (B) $\frac{13}{49}$
(C) $\frac{3}{52}$ (D) $\frac{49}{52}$

8-10 One card is drawn at random from a deck of 52 cards. The probability of getting a face card is : **[NTSE-2015 (Stage-I) MP]**

(A) $\frac{3}{13}$ (B) $\frac{1}{26}$
(C) $\frac{3}{26}$ (D) $\frac{4}{13}$

8-11 The probability to select a prime number from the numbers 3, 4, 5, 6… 25 will be : **[NTSE-2015 (Stage-I) Chhatisgarh]**

(A) $\frac{7}{23}$ (B) $\frac{8}{23}$
(C) $\frac{9}{23}$ (D) $\frac{10}{23}$

8-12 There are 6 defective items in a sample of 20 items. One items is drawn at random. The probability that it is a non-defective item is : **[NTSE-2015 (Stage-I) Chennai]**

(A) $\frac{7}{10}$ (B) 0
(C) $\frac{3}{10}$ (D) $\frac{2}{3}$

8-13 Two coins are tossed once. The probability of getting at least one tail is : **[NTSE-2016 (Stage-I) Rajasthan]**

(A) $\frac{1}{2}$ (B) $\frac{1}{3}$
(C) $\frac{1}{4}$ (D) $\frac{3}{4}$

8-14 The probability that it will rain today is 0.84. What is the probability that it will not rain today?

[NTSE-2016 (Stage-I) Jharkhand]

(A) 2 (B) 1
(C) 0.16 (D) 0.61

8-15 A letter is chosen at random from the word MATHEMATICS. What is the probability that it will be a vowel?

[NTSE-2016 (Stage-I) Odisha]

(A) $\frac{1}{2}$ (B) $\frac{3}{8}$
(C) $\frac{3}{11}$ (D) $\frac{4}{11}$

8-16 Two coins are tossed simultaneously. What is the probability of having at least one head?

[NTSE-2016 (Stage-I) Chhatisgarh]

(A) $\frac{1}{4}$ (B) $\frac{2}{4}$
(C) $\frac{3}{4}$ (D) $\frac{4}{4}$

8-17 A coin and a die is tossed simultaneously. Find the probability of the event that 'tail' and a prime number turns up?

[NTSE-2016 (Stage-I) Chhatisgarh]

(A) $\frac{1}{2}$ (B) $\frac{1}{4}$
(C) $\frac{1}{3}$ (D) $\frac{2}{3}$

8-18 Two dice are thrown simultaneously. Find the probability of getting the sum prime number :

[NTSE-2016 (Stage-I) Chandigarh]

(A) 12/5 (B) 12/15
(C) 5/12 (D) 1

8-19 A bag contains 15 balls of which x are black and remaining are red. If the number of red balls are increased by 5, the probability of drawing the red balls doubles, then the probability of drawing red ball is: **[NTSE-2017 (Stage-I) Andhra Pradesh]**

(A) $\frac{1}{5}$ (B) $\frac{4}{5}$
(C) $\frac{3}{5}$ (D) $\frac{2}{5}$

8-20 Three fair dice are rolled, what is the probability that the three numbers that come up form the sides of a triangle ?

[NTSE-2017 (Stage-I) Goa]

(A) $\frac{1}{6}$ (B) $\frac{35}{216}$
(C) $\frac{37}{72}$ (D) $\frac{31}{36}$

8-21 Three fair dice are rolled, what is the probability that the three numbers that come up form the sides of a triangle ?

[NTSE-2017 (Stage-I) Goa]

(A) $\frac{1}{6}$ (B) $\frac{35}{216}$
(C) $\frac{37}{72}$ (D) $\frac{31}{36}$

8-22 A bag contains two coins. One of them is a regular coin whereas the other has tails on both sides. From this bag, a coin is picked at random and tossed. Then, the probability of getting a head is : **[NTSE-2017 (Stage-I) Haryana]**

(A) 0 (B) $\frac{1}{4}$
(C) $\frac{1}{2}$ (D) $\frac{3}{4}$

8-23 A box contains some black balls and 30 white balls. If the probability of drawing a black ball is two fifths of a white ball, then the number of black balls in the box is :

[NTSE-2017 (Stage-I) Karnataka]

(A) 6 (B) 12
(C) 18 (D) 30

8-24 Two coin are tossed simultaneously, then the probability of getting head on the coin and tail on another coin is :

[NTSE-2017 (Stage-I) Madhya Pradesh]

(A) 2 (B) 1/2
(C) 4 (D) 1/4

8-25 Sita and Gita are friends, what is the probability that both will have different birthdays (ignoring a leap year) :

[NTSE-2017 (Stage-I) Madhya Pradesh]

(A) $\frac{1}{365}$ (B) $\frac{1}{364}$
(C) $\frac{364}{365}$ (D) None of these

8-26 There are 50 cards marked with the numbers 1 to 50. One card is drawn at random. What is the probability that number on the card is a prime number ?

[NTSE-2017 (Stage-I) Maharashtra]

(A) $\frac{3}{10}$ (B) $\frac{1}{5}$
(C) $\frac{1}{4}$ (D) $\frac{2}{15}$

8-27 Two dice are thrown. Find the probability that sum of numbers of both up sides of both dice is a perfect square : **[NTSE-2017 (Stage-I) Punjab]**

(A) $\frac{1}{6}$ (B) $\frac{7}{36}$

(C) $\frac{5}{36}$ (D) 0

8-28 If a leap year is selected randomly, then what is the probability of having 53 Mondays in this year ? **[NTSE-2017 (Stage-I) Rajasthan]**

(A) $\frac{1}{7}$ (B) $\frac{2}{7}$

(C) $\frac{53}{366}$ (D) $\frac{52}{365}$

8-29 The probability that a leap year selected at random which contains 53 Sundays is : **[NTSE-2017 (Stage-I) Tamilnadu]**

(A) $\frac{2}{7}$ (B) $\frac{53}{366}$

(C) $\frac{53}{188}$ (D) $\frac{7}{53}$

8-30 Two dice marked with numbers 1 to 6 are rolled together. What is the probability of getting an odd numbers on one of these and a multiple of three on the other ? **[NTSE-2017 (Stage-I) Kerala]**

(A) $\frac{1}{6}$ (B) $\frac{1}{3}$

(C) $\frac{11}{36}$ (D) $\frac{13}{36}$

8-31 A dice is thrown once. If the probability of getting a number less than 4 is x and the probability of getting a number greater than 4 is y, then $x-y$ is : **[NTSE-2018 (Stage-I) Rajasthan]**

(A) $\frac{5}{6}$ (B) $\frac{1}{6}$

(C) $\frac{2}{3}$ (D) $\frac{1}{3}$

8-32 14 cards numbered 5, 6, 7, 8, 9, 10, 11, 12, 13, 14, 15, 16, 17, 18 are placed in a box and mixed thoroughly. If a card is drawn from the box, then probability that the number on the card divisible by 3 or 2 is : **[NTSE-2018 (Stage-I) Andhra Pradesh]**

(A) $\frac{12}{14}$ (B) $\frac{9}{14}$

(C) $\frac{4}{14}$ (D) $\frac{5}{14}$

8-33 A card selected at random from well - shuffled pack of 52 cards. The probability that the selected card is not an ace is ______ : **[NTSE-2018 (Stage-I) Gujarat]**

(A) $\frac{12}{13}$ (B) $\frac{4}{13}$

(C) $\frac{1}{13}$ (D) $\frac{13}{4}$

8-34 Two balanced dice are thrown once. The probability of getting sum of numbers is divisible by 5 is : **[NTSE-2018 (Stage-I) Gujatar]**

(A) $\frac{29}{36}$ (B) $\frac{5}{36}$

(C) $\frac{1}{6}$ (D) $\frac{7}{36}$

8-35 Two dice are thrown at the same time. The probability that, the sum of two numbers appearing on the top of the dice is greater than 6 but less than 9, is : **[NTSE-2018 (Stage-I) Haryana]**

(A) $\frac{11}{36}$ (B) $\frac{1}{3}$

(C) $\frac{5}{6}$ (D) $\frac{4}{9}$

8-36 Three squares of a chess board are selected at random. The probability of getting two squares of one colour and other of a different colour is : **[NTSE-2018 (Stage-I) Karnataka]**

(A) $\frac{16}{21}$ (B) $\frac{8}{21}$

(C) $\frac{3}{32}$ (D) $\frac{3}{8}$

8-37 A box contain 3 blue, 2 white and 4 red marbles. A marble is drawn randomly. Probability of getting white marble is : **[NTSE-2018 (Stage-I) Madhya Prasesh]**

(A) $\frac{3}{5}$ (B) $\frac{2}{6}$

(C) $\frac{2}{9}$ (D) $\frac{2}{5}$

8-38 What is the probability of having 53 Thursday in ordinary year (except leap year) : **[NTSE-2018 (Stage-I) Maharashtra]**

(A) 2/7 (B) 3/7

(C) 1/7 (D) 4/7

8-39 Two dice are rolled simultaneously, what is the probability of getting sum of the digit on the upper face as a prime number : **[NTSE-2018 (Stage-I) Maharashtra]**

(A) 5/36 (B) 5/12

(C) 5/18 (D) 11/36

8-40 A fair die is thrown once. The probability of getting neither a prime nor a composite number is : **[NTSE-2018 (Stage-I) Tamil Nadu]**

(A) 1 (B) 0

(C) $\frac{5}{6}$ (D) $\frac{1}{6}$

8-41 One integer is chosen out of 1, 2, 3,..., 100. What is the probability that it is neither divisible by 4 nor by 6 : **[NTSE-2013 (Stage-II)]**

(A) 0.59 (B) 0.67

(C) 0.41 (D) 0.33

8-42 In how may ways can you partition 6 into ordered summands? (For example, 3 can be partitioned in 3 ways as : $1+2,\ 2+1,\ 1+1+1$): **[NTSE-2014 (Stage-II)]**

(A) 27 (B) 29

(C) 31 (D) 33

8-43 Three dice are thrown simultaneously. The probability of getting a total of at least 5 of the numbers appearing on their tops is : **[NTSE-2015 (Stage-II)]**

(A) $\frac{5}{54}$ (B) $\frac{7}{54}$

(C) $\frac{49}{54}$ (D) $\frac{53}{54}$

8-44 A box contains four cards numbered as 1, 2, 3 and 4 and another box contains four cards numbered as 1, 4, 9 and 16. One card is drawn at random from each box. What is the probability of getting the product of the two numbers so obtained, more than 16 ? **[NTSE-2017 (Stage-II)]**

(A) $\frac{5}{8}$ (B) $\frac{1}{2}$

(C) $\frac{3}{8}$ (D) $\frac{1}{4}$

* * * * *

ANSWERS

PRACTICE EXERCISE-8.1

1	(A)	2	(A)	3	(B)
4	(B)	5	(C)	6	(D)
7	(D)	8	(A)	9	(B)
10	(C)	11	(D)	12	(D)
13	(C)	14	(B)	15	(A)
16	(A)	17	(B)	18	(C)
19	(B)	20	(C)	21	(C)
22	(D)	23	(B)	24	(C)
25	(C)	26	(B)	27	(D)
28	(A)	29	(B)	30	(C)
31	(C)	32	(C)	33	(C)
34	(B)	35	(A)	36	(B)
37	(C)	38	(C)	39	(D)
40	(C)	41	(A)	42	(B)
43	(B)	44	(C)	45	(A)
46	(A)	47	(B)	48	(A)
49	(B)	50	(C)		

PRACTICE EXERCISE-8.2

1	(C)	2	(A)	3	(C)
4	(B)	5	(B)	6	(C)
7	(A)	8	(A)	9	(B)
10	(C)	11	(A)	12	(A)
13	(B)	14	(B)	15	(C)
16	(D)	17	(C)	18	(A)
19	(A)	20	(B)	21	(C)
22	(C)	23	(C)	24	(B)
25	(C)				

PRACTICE EXERCISE-8.3

1	(A)	2	(B)	3	(A)
4	(A)	5	(C)	6	(C)
7	(A)	8	(C)	9	(B)
10	(A)	11	(B)	12	(A)
13	(D)	14	(C)	15	(D)
16	(C)	17	(B)	18	(C)
19	(A)	20	(B)	21	(B)
22	(B)	23	(B)	24	(C)
25	(C)	26	(A)	27	(B)
28	(B)	29	(A)	30	(C)
31	(B)	32	(B)	33	(A)
34	(D)	35	(A)	36	(A)
37	(C)	38	(C)	39	(B)
40.	(D)	41	(B)	42	(C)
43	(D)	44	(C)		

Solutions of PRACTICE EXERCISE-8.1

Sol. 1 (A) The sample space

$$S = \{H, T\}$$

$\Rightarrow \quad n(S) = 2$

Event of getting head $= \{H\}$

$\Rightarrow \quad n(E) = 1$

$\Rightarrow$ Probability of getting a head is given by

$$P(E) = \frac{\text{Favorable outcome}}{\text{Total number of outcomes}}$$

$$= \frac{n(6)}{n(s)} = \frac{1}{2}$$

Hence Ans is (A)

Sol. 2 (A) $S = \{HH, HT, TH, TT\} \Rightarrow n(S) = 4$

$$E = \{HT, TH\} \Rightarrow n(E) = 2$$

$$\Rightarrow \quad P(E) = \frac{n(E)}{n(S)} = \frac{2}{4} = \frac{1}{2}$$

Hence Ans is (A)

Sol. 3 (B) $S = \{HH, HT, TH, TT\} \Rightarrow n(S) = 4$

$$E = \{HH, HT, TH\}$$

$\Rightarrow \quad n(E) = 3$

$\Rightarrow \quad P(E) = \dfrac{3}{4}$

Hence Ans is (B)

Sol. 4 (B) $S = \{HH, HT, TH, TT\} \Rightarrow n(S) = 4$

$$E = \{HH\} \Rightarrow n(E) = 1$$

$\Rightarrow \quad P(E) = \dfrac{1}{4}$

Hence Ans is (B)

Sol. 5 (C) $S = \{HH, HT, TH, TT\} \Rightarrow n(S) = 4$

$$E = \{HH\}$$

$\Rightarrow \quad n(E) = 1$

$\Rightarrow \quad P(E) = \dfrac{1}{4}$

Hence Ans is (C)

Sol. 6 (D) $S = \{HHH, HHT, HTH, HTT, THH, THT, TTH, TTT\}$

$\Rightarrow \quad n(S) = 8$

$$E = \{HTT, THT, TTH\}$$

$\Rightarrow \quad n(E) = 3$

$$P(E) = \frac{3}{8}$$

Hence Ans is (D)

Sol. 7 (D) $S = \{HHH, HHT, HTH, HTT, THH, THT, TTH, TTT\}$

$\Rightarrow \quad n(S) = 8$

$E = \{HHT, HTH, THH\}$

$\Rightarrow \quad n(E) = 3$

$P(E) = \frac{3}{8}$

Hence Ans is (D)

Sol. 8 (A) $S = \{HHH, HHT, HTH, HTT, THH, THT, TTH, TTT\}$

$\Rightarrow \quad n(S) = 8$

$E = \{HHH, HHT, HTH, HTT, THH, THT, TTH\}$

$\Rightarrow \quad n(E) = 7$

$\Rightarrow \quad P(E) = \frac{7}{8}$

Hence Ans is (A)

Sol. 9 (B) $S = \{HHH, HHT, HTH, HTT, THH, THT, TTH, TTT\}$

$\Rightarrow \quad n(S) = 8$

$E = \{HHT, HTH, THH\}$

$\Rightarrow \quad P(E) = \frac{3}{8}$

Hence Ans is (B)

Sol. 10 (C) $S = \{HHH, HHT, HTH, HTT, THH, THT, TTH, TTT\}$

$\Rightarrow \quad n(S) = 8$

$E = \{HHH, HHT, HTH, THH\}$

$\Rightarrow \quad n(E) = 4$

$\Rightarrow \quad P(E) = \frac{4}{8} = \frac{1}{2}$

Hence Ans is (C)

Sol. 11 (D) $S = \{HHH, HHT, HTH, HTT, THH, THT, TTH, TTT\}$

$\Rightarrow \quad n(S) = 8$

$E = \{HHT, HTH, HTT, THH, THT, TTH\}$

$\Rightarrow \quad n(E) = 6$

$\Rightarrow \quad P(E) = \frac{6}{8} = \frac{3}{4}$

Hence Ans is (D)

Sol. 12 (D) $S = \{HHH, HHT, HTH, HTT, THH, THT, TTH, TTT\}$

$\Rightarrow \quad n(S) = 8$

$E = \{HHH, HHT, HTH, THH\}$

$\Rightarrow \quad n(E) = 4$

$\Rightarrow \quad P(E) = \frac{4}{8} = \frac{1}{2}$

Hence Ans is (D)

Sol. 13 (C) $S = \{1, 2, 3, 4, 5, 6\}$

$\Rightarrow \quad n(S) = 6$

$E = \{1, 2, 3, 4, 5, 6\}$

$\Rightarrow \quad n(E) = 6$

$\Rightarrow \quad P(E) = \frac{6}{6} = 1$

Hence Ans is (C)

Sol. 14 (B) $S = \{1, 2, 3, 4, 5, 6\}$

$\Rightarrow \quad n(S) = 6$

$E = \{3, 6\}$

$\Rightarrow \quad n(E) = 2$

$\Rightarrow \quad P(E) = \frac{2}{6} = \frac{1}{3}$

Hence Ans is (B)

Sol. 15 (A) $S = \{1, 2, 3, 4, 5, 6\}$

$\Rightarrow \quad n(S) = 6$

$E = \{2, 3, 5\}$

$\Rightarrow \quad n(E) = 3$

$\Rightarrow \quad P(E) = \frac{3}{6} = \frac{1}{2}$

Hence Ans is (A)

Sol. 16 (A) $S = \{1, 2, 3, 4, 5, 6\}$

$\Rightarrow \quad n(S) = 6$

$E = \{2, 4, 6\}$

$\Rightarrow \quad n(E) = 3$

$\Rightarrow \quad P(E) = \frac{3}{6} = \frac{1}{2}$

Hence Ans is (A)

Sol. 17 (B) $S = \{HHH, HHT, HTH, THH, TTH, THT, HTT, TTT\}$

$\Rightarrow \quad n(S) = 8$

$E = \{HHT, HTH, THH, TTH, THT, HTT\}$

$\Rightarrow \quad n(E) = 6$

$\Rightarrow \quad P(E) = \frac{6}{8} = \frac{3}{4}$

Hence Ans is (B)

Sol. 18 (C) $S = \{HHH, HHT, HTH, THH, TTH, THT, HTT, TTT\}$

$\Rightarrow \quad n(S) = 8$

$E = \{TTT\}$

$\Rightarrow \quad n(E) = 1$

$\Rightarrow \quad P(E) = \frac{1}{8}$

Hence Ans is (C)

Sol. 19 (B) $S = \{(1, 1), (1, 2), (1, 3), (1, 4), (1, 5), (1, 6), (2, 1), (2, 2), \ldots (6, 5), (6, 6)\}$

$\Rightarrow \quad n(S) = 6 \times 6 = 36$

$E = \{(6, 3), (5, 4), (4, 5), (3, 6)\}$

$n(E) = 4$

$\Rightarrow \quad P(E) = \frac{4}{36} = \frac{1}{9}$

Hence Ans is (B)

Sol. 20 (C) $S = \{(1, 1), (1, 2), (1, 3), (1, 4), (1, 5), (1, 6), (2, 1), (2, 2), \ldots (6, 5), (6, 6)\}$

$\Rightarrow \quad n(S) = 6 \times 6 = 36$

$E = \{(6, 4), (5, 5), (4, 6), (6, 5), (5, 6), (6, 6)\}$

$n(E) = 6$

$\Rightarrow \quad P(E) = \frac{6}{36} = \frac{1}{6}$

Hence Ans is (C)

Sol. 21 (C) $S = \{(1, 1), (1, 2), (1, 3), (1, 4), (1, 5), (1, 6), (2, 1), (2, 2), \ldots (6, 5), (6, 6)\}$

$\Rightarrow \quad n(S) = 6 \times 6 = 36$

$E = \{(6, 3), (5, 4), (4, 5), (3, 6), (6, 5), (5, 6)\}$

$\Rightarrow \quad n(E) = 6$

$\Rightarrow \quad P(E) = \frac{6}{36} = \frac{1}{6}$

Hence Ans is (C)

Sol. 22 (D) $S = \{(1, 1), (1, 2), (1, 3), (1, 4), (1, 5), (1, 6), (2, 1), (2, 2), \ldots (6, 5), (6, 6)\}$

$\Rightarrow \quad n(S) = 6 \times 6 = 36$

$E = \{(1, 1), (2, 2), (3, 3), (4, 4), (5, 5), (6, 6)\}$

$n(E) = 6$

$\Rightarrow \quad P(E) = \frac{6}{36} = \frac{1}{6}$

Hence Ans is (D)

Sol. 23 (B) $S = \{(1, 1), (1, 2), (1, 3), (1, 4), (1, 5), (1, 6), (2, 1), (2, 2), \ldots (6, 5), (6, 6)\}$

$\Rightarrow \quad n(S) = 6 \times 6 = 36$

$E = \{(2, 2), (4, 4), (6, 6)\}$

$\Rightarrow \quad n(E) = 3$

$\Rightarrow \quad P(E) = \frac{3}{36} = \frac{1}{12}$

Hence Ans is (B)

Sol. 24 (C) $S = \{(1, 1), (1, 2), (1, 3), (1, 4), (1, 5), (1, 6), (2, 1), (2, 2), \ldots (6, 5), (6, 6)\}$

$\Rightarrow \quad n(S) = 6 \times 6 = 36$

$E = \{(2, 3), (2, 6), (4, 3), (4, 6), (6, 3), (6, 6), (3, 2), (6, 2), (3, 4), (6, 4), (3, 6)\}$

$\Rightarrow \quad n(E) = 11$

$\Rightarrow \quad P(E) = \frac{11}{36}$

Hence Ans is (C)

Sol. 25 (C) $S = \{(1, 1), (1, 2), (1, 3), (1, 4), (1, 5), (1, 6), (2, 1), (2, 2), \ldots (6, 5), (6, 6)\}$

$\Rightarrow \quad n(S) = 6 \times 6 = 36$

$E = \{(1, 2), (1, 5), (2, 1), (2, 4), (3, 3), (3, 6), (4, 2), (4, 5), (5, 1), (5, 4), (6, 3), (6, 6), (1, 3), (2, 2), (2, 6), (3, 1), (3, 5), (4, 4), (5, 3), (6, 2)\}$

$\Rightarrow \quad n(E) = 20$

$\Rightarrow \quad P(E) = \frac{20}{36} = \frac{5}{9}$

Hence Ans is (C)

Sol. 26 (B) $S = \{(1, 1), (1, 2), (1, 3), (1, 4), (1, 5), (1, 6), (2, 1), (2, 2), \ldots (6, 5), (6, 6)\}$

$\Rightarrow \quad n(S) = 6 \times 6 = 36$

$E = \{(1, 1), (1, 2), (1, 4), (1, 6), (2, 1), (2, 3), (2, 5), (3, 2), (3, 4), (4, 1), (4, 3), (5, 2), (5, 6), (6, 1), (6, 5)\}$

$\Rightarrow \quad n(E) = 15$

$\Rightarrow \quad P(E) = \frac{15}{36} = \frac{5}{12}$

Hence Ans is (B)

Sol. 27 (D) $S = \{(1, 1), (1, 2), (1, 3), (1, 4), (1, 5), (1, 6), (2, 1), (2, 2), \ldots (6, 5), (6, 6)\}$

$\Rightarrow \quad n(S) = 6 \times 6 = 36$

$E = \{(1, 5), (2, 5), (3, 5), (4, 5), (5, 5), (6, 5), (5, 1), (5, 2), (5, 3), (5, 4), (5, 6)\}$

$\Rightarrow \quad n(E) = 11$

$\Rightarrow \quad P(E) = \frac{11}{36}$

Hence Ans is (D)

Sol. 28 (A) $S = \{52 \text{ cards}\}$

52 cards

(26) Red — Black (26)

Hearts (13), Diamonds (13), Spades (13), Clubs (13)

In each of the four suits there is one ace, one king, one queen and one jack (or knave) and rest 9 cards are numbered

$\Rightarrow \quad n(S) = 52$

$n(E) = 26$

$\Rightarrow \quad P(E) = \frac{26}{52} = \frac{1}{2}$

Hence Ans is (A)

Sol. 29 (B) $S = \{52 \text{ cards}\}$

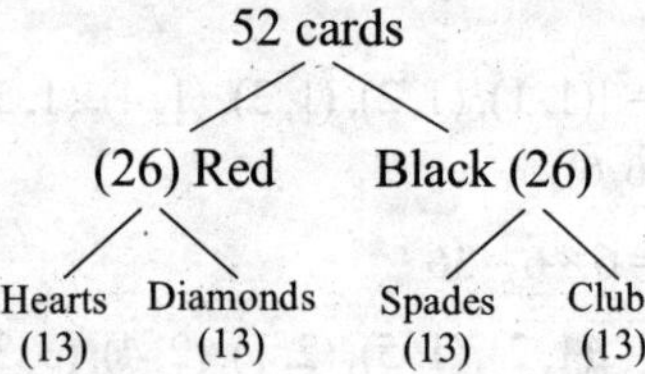

In each of the four suits there is one ace, one king, one queen and one jack (or knave) and rest 9 cards are numbered.

$n(S) = 52$

$n(E) = 4$

$\Rightarrow \quad P(E) = \frac{4}{52} = \frac{1}{13}$

Hence Ans is (B)

Sol. 30 (C) $S = \{52 \text{ cards}\}$

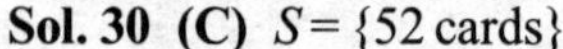

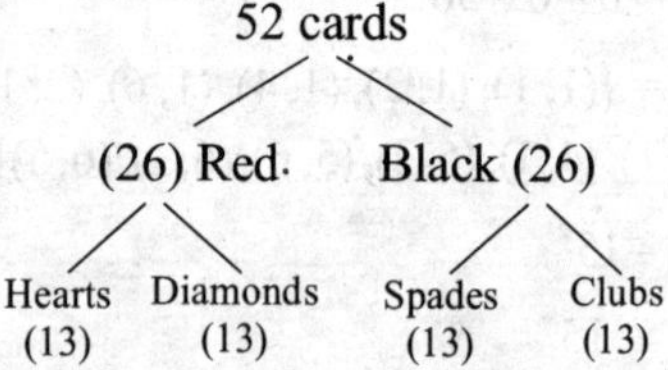

In each of the four suits there is one ace, one king, one queen and one jack (or knave) and rest 9 cards are numbered.

$n(S) = 52$

Since drawn card must be black & a queen so there are only two black queens.

Hence $\quad n(E) = 2$

$\Rightarrow \quad P(E) = \frac{2}{52} = \frac{1}{26}$

Hence Ans is (C)

Sol. 31 (C) $S = \{52 \text{ cards}\}$

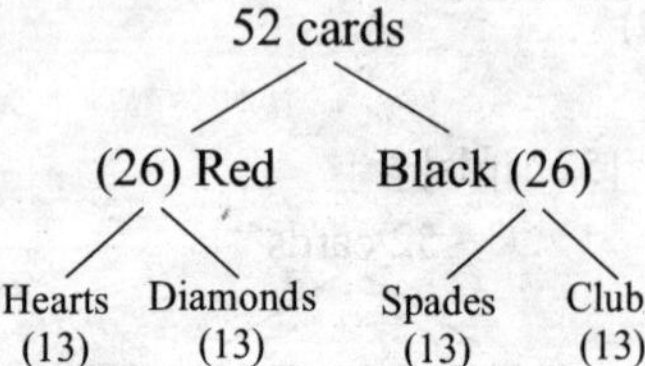

In each of the four suits there is one ace, one king, one queen and one jack (or knave) and rest 9 cards are numbered.

$n(S) = 52$

There are 26 black cards (including two queens). Besides it there are two more queens (in red colours)

Thus $\quad n(E) = 26 + 2 = 28$

$\Rightarrow \quad P(E) = \frac{28}{52} = \frac{7}{13}$

Hence Ans is (C)

Sol. 32 (C) $S = \{52 \text{ cards}\}$

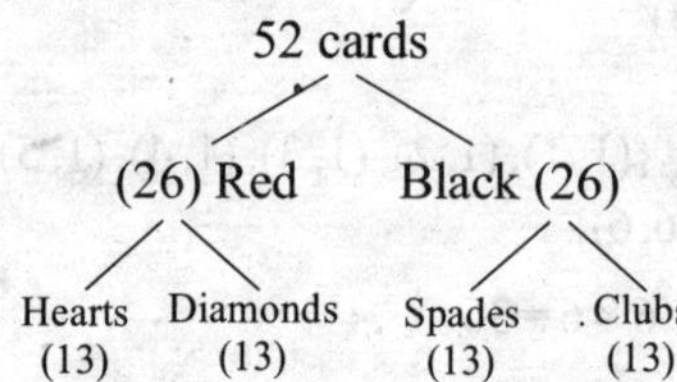

In each of the four suits there is one ace, one king, one queen and one jack (or knave) and rest 9 cards are numbered.

$n(S) = 52$

There are 4 kings and 4 queens

$E = K \cup Q$

$\Rightarrow \quad n(E) = 4 + 4 = 8$

$\Rightarrow \quad P(E) = \frac{8}{52} = \frac{2}{13}$

Hence Ans is (C)

Sol. 33 (C) $S = \{52 \text{ cards}\}$

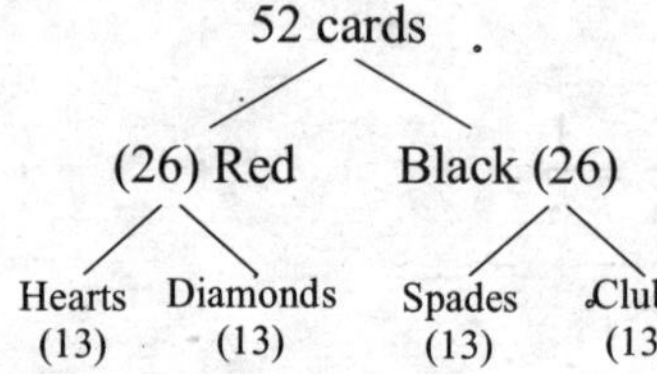

In each of the four suits there is one ace, one king, one queen and one jack (or knave) and rest 9 cards are numbered.

$n(S) = 52$

There are 13 hearts (including one queen and one king). Besides it there are 3 queens and 3 kings in remaining 3 suits each.

Thus $\quad n(E) = 13 + 3 + 3 = 19$

$\Rightarrow \quad P(E) = \frac{19}{52}$

Hence Ans is (C)

Sol. 34 (B) $S = \{52 \text{ cards}\}$

52 cards

(26) Red Black (26)

Hearts (13) Diamonds (13) Spades (13) Clubs (13)

In each of the four suits there is one ace, one king, one queen and one jack (or knave) and rest 9 cards are numbered.

$n(S) = 52$

There are 13 spades (including one king). Besides there are 3 more kings in remaining 3 suits).

Thus $n(E) = 13 + 3 = 16$

Hence $n(\bar{E}) = 52 - 16 = 36$

$\Rightarrow \quad P(\bar{E}) = \frac{36}{52} = \frac{9}{13}$

Hence Ans is (B)

Sol. 35 (A) $S = \{52 \text{ cards}\}$

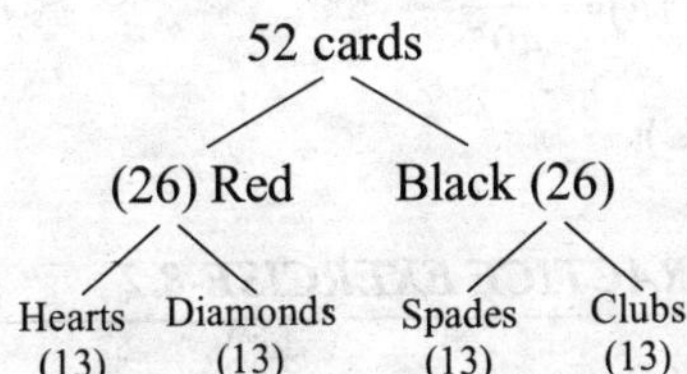

In each of the four suits there is one ace, one king, one queen and one jack (or knave) and rest 9 cards are numbered.

$n(S) = 52$

There are 4 aces and 4 kings

$\Rightarrow \quad n(E) = 4 + 4 = 8$

$\Rightarrow \quad n(\bar{E}) = 52 - 8 = 44$

$\Rightarrow \quad P(\bar{E}) = \frac{44}{52} = \frac{11}{13}$

Hence Ans is (A)

Sol. 36 (B) $P(\bar{A}) = 1 - P(A) = 1 - \frac{2}{5} = \frac{3}{5}$

Hence Ans is (B)

Sol. 37 (C) $P(\bar{B}) = 1 - P(B) = 1 - \frac{1}{2} = \frac{1}{2}$

Hence Ans is (C)

Sol. 38 (C) $E = \{2, 3, 5, 7, 11, 13, 17, 19\}$

$\Rightarrow \quad n(E) = 8$

$S = \{1, 2, 3, 4, \ldots 20\}$

$\Rightarrow \quad n(S) = 20$

$\Rightarrow \quad P(E) = \frac{n(E)}{n(S)} = \frac{8}{20} = \frac{2}{5}$

Hence Ans is (C)

Sol. 39 (D) A leap your has 366 days

$\Rightarrow \quad 366 = 7 \times 52 + 2$

It means a leap year has 52 full weeks and 2 more days. These 2 days can be :

(i) Sunday and Monday

(ii) Monday and Tuesday

(iii) Tuesday and Wednesday

(iv) Wednesday and Thursday

(v) Thursday and Friday

(vi) Friday and Saturday

(vii) Saturday and Sunday

Clearly atleast there are 52 Sundays.

Now, for having 53 Sundays in the year, one of the above 2 consecutive, days must be Sunday.

Thus, out of the above 7 possibilities, 2 possibilities are in favour [(i) and (vii)] of the event that one of the two days is a Sunday.

$\Rightarrow$ Required probability $= \frac{2}{7}$

Hence Ans is (D)

Sol. 40 (C) $S = \{GG, GB, BG, BB\}$

and $E = \{GG, GB, BG\}$

$\Rightarrow \quad P(E) = \frac{n(E)}{n(S)} = \frac{3}{4}$

Hence Ans is (C)

Sol. 41 (A) $n(S) = 6 \times 6 \times 6 \times 6 = 6^4$

$n(E) = 6$

Since $E = \{(1, 1, 1, 1), (2, 2, 2, 2), (3, 3, 3, 3) \ldots (6, 6, 6, 6)\}$

$\Rightarrow \quad P(E) = \frac{n(E)}{n(S)} = \frac{6}{6^4} = \frac{1}{6^3} = \frac{1}{216}$

Hence Ans is (A)

Sol. 42 (B) $n(S) = 6 \times 6 \times 6 \times 6 = 6^4$

$n(E) = {}^6C_1 \times {}^5C_1 \times {}^4C_1 \times {}^3C_1 = 360$

$\Rightarrow \quad P(E) = \frac{360}{6^4} = \frac{5}{18}$

Hence Ans is (B)

Sol. 43 (B) $n(S) = 6 \times 6 \times 6 \times 6 = 6^4$

Select a number which occurs on two dice out of six numbers (1, 2, 3, 4, 5, 6). This can be done in ${}^6C_1$, ways.

Now select two distinct number out of remaining 5 numbers which can be done in ${}^5C_2$ ways. Thus these 4 numbers can be arranged in $\frac{4!}{2!}$ ways.

So, the number of ways in which two dice show the same face and the remaining two show different faces is

$${}^6C_1 \times {}^5C_2 \times \frac{4!}{2!} = 720$$

$$\Rightarrow \quad n(E) = 720$$

$$\Rightarrow \quad P(E) = \frac{720}{6^4} = \frac{5}{9}$$

Hence Ans is (B)

Sol. 44 (C) $n(S) = 6 \times 6 \times 6 \times 6 = 6^4$

There are 3 possible cases

(i) 2 similar faces + 2 different faces

(ii) 3 similar faces + 1 different face

(iii) all 4 faces are similar

$\Rightarrow$ Required number of ways

$$= \left({}^6C_1 \times {}^5C_2 \times \frac{4!}{2!}\right) + \left({}^6C_1 \times {}^5C_1 \times \frac{4!}{3!}\right) + \left({}^6C_1 \times \frac{4!}{4!}\right)$$

$$= (6 \times 10 \times 12) + (6 \times 5 \times 4) + 6 = 846$$

$\Rightarrow$ $n(E) = 846$

and $n(S) = 6^4$

$$\Rightarrow \quad P(E) = \frac{846}{6^4} = \frac{47}{72}$$

Hence Ans is (C)

Sol. 45 (A) Total number of outcomes $= 2 + 7 = 9$

Favourable number of cases $= 2$

$$\Rightarrow \quad P(E) = \frac{2}{9}$$

Hence Ans is (A)

Sol. 46 (A) $n(S) = 8 + 4 = 12$

$$n(E) = 8$$

$$\Rightarrow \quad P(E) = \frac{8}{12} = \frac{2}{3}$$

Hence Ans is (A)

Sol. 47 (B) $n(S) = {}^{12}C_4 = 495$

$$n(E) = {}^8C_4 = 70$$

$$\Rightarrow \quad P(E) = \frac{70}{495} = \frac{14}{99}$$

Hence Ans is (B)

Sol. 48 (A) $n(S) = {}^{12}C_4 = 495$

$$n(E) = {}^4C_4 = 1$$

$$\Rightarrow \quad P(E) = \frac{1}{495}$$

Hence Ans is (A)

Sol. 49 (B) $n(S) = {}^{12}C_4 = 495$

$$n(E) = {}^8C_2 \times {}^4C_1 = 112$$

$$\Rightarrow \quad P(E) = \frac{112}{495}$$

Hence Ans is (B)

Sol. 50 (C) $n(S) = 495$

$$n(E) = {}^4C_3 = 4$$

$$\Rightarrow \quad P(E) = \frac{4}{495}$$

Hence Ans is (C)

Solutions of PRACTICE EXERCISE-8.2

Sol. 1 (C) $S = \{1, 2, 3, 4, \ldots, 18\}$

$\Rightarrow$ $n(S) = 18$

$$E_1 = \{2, 4, 6, 8, 10, 12, 14, 16, 18\}$$

$\Rightarrow$ $n(E_1) = 9$

$$E_2 = \{3, 6, 9, 12, 15, 18\}$$

$\Rightarrow$ $n(E_2) = 6$

$$(E_1 \cap E_2) = E_3 = \{6, 12, 18\}$$

$\Rightarrow$ $n(E_3) = 3$

$$\Rightarrow \quad E = E_1 \cup E_2 = E_1 + E_2 - E_3$$

$$n(E) = 9 + 6 - 3$$

where $E = \{2, 3, 4, 6, 8, 9, 10, 12, 14, 15, 16, 18\}$

$$\Rightarrow \quad P(E) = \frac{n(E)}{n(S)} = \frac{12}{18} = \frac{2}{3}$$

Hence Ans is (C)

Sol. 2 (A) $n(S) = {}^{100}C_2 = \frac{100 \times 99}{2} = 4950$

We know there are total 25 prime numbers upto 100

$$\Rightarrow \quad n(E) = {}^{25}C_2 = 300$$

$$\Rightarrow \quad P(E) = \frac{300}{4950} = \frac{2}{33}$$

Hence Ans is (A)

Sol. 3 (C) $n(S) = {}^{100}C_2 = 4950$

$$n(E) = {}^{75}C_2 = 2775 \; (100 - 25 = 75)$$

$$\Rightarrow \quad P(E) = \frac{2775}{4950} = \frac{37}{66}$$

Hence Ans is (C)

Sol. 4 (B) Total number of outcomes

$$=5+7=12$$

Number of cases against the occurrence of event

$$=5$$

$\Rightarrow$ Number of cases in favour of event

$$=12-5=7$$

$$\Rightarrow \quad P(E)=\frac{7}{12}$$

Hence Ans is (B)

Sol. 5 (B) $n(S)={}^5C_2=10$

$$n(E)=({}^2C_1\times{}^3C_1)+({}^2C_2)=7$$

$$\Rightarrow \quad P(E)=\frac{7}{10}$$

Hence Ans is (B)

Sol. 6 (C) $n(S)={}^{20}C_2=190$

$$n(E)={}^{15}C_2=105$$

$$\Rightarrow \quad P(E)=\frac{105}{190}=\frac{21}{38}$$

Hence Ans is (C)

Sol. 7 (A) $n(S)={}^{20}C_4=4845$

$$n(E)=({}^5C_3\times{}^{15}C_1)+({}^5C_4)=155$$

$$\Rightarrow \quad P(E)=\frac{155}{4845}=\frac{31}{969}$$

Hence Ans is (A)

Sol. 8 (A) $P(A)=\frac{1}{4}, P(B)=\frac{1}{2}$

and $\quad P(A\cap B)=\frac{7}{50}$

$\Rightarrow \quad P(A \text{ or } B)=P(A\cup B)$

$$=P(A)+P(B)-P(A\cap B)$$

$$=\frac{1}{4}+\frac{1}{2}-\frac{7}{50}=\frac{61}{100}$$

Hence Ans is (A)

Sol. 9 (B) P (neither A nor B) $=P(\bar{A}$ and $\bar{B})$

$$=P(\bar{A}\cap\bar{B})=P(\overline{A\cup B})=1-P(A\cup B)$$

$$=1-\frac{61}{100}=\frac{39}{100}$$

Hence Ans is (B)

Sol. 10 (C) $P(A\cup B)=P(A)+P(B)-P(A\cap B)$

$$=\frac{3}{10}+\frac{1}{2}-\frac{1}{5}=\frac{6}{10}=\frac{3}{5}$$

Hence Ans is (C)

Sol. 11 (A) $P(A\cup B)=P(A)+P(B)-P(A\cap B)$

$$\frac{3}{5}=\frac{2}{5}+\frac{1}{2}-P(A\cap B)$$

$$\Rightarrow \quad P(A\cap B)=\frac{3}{10}$$

Hence Ans is (A)

Sol. 12 (A) There are 4 aces, 4 kings and 4 jacks and their selection can be made in following ways:

$${}^{12}C_1\times{}^8C_1\times{}^4C_1=12\times8\times4$$

$$n(E)=12\times8\times4$$

Total selection can be made

$$={}^{52}C_3=52\times51\times50$$

$$P(E)=\frac{12\times8\times4}{52\times51\times50}=\frac{16}{5525}$$

Hence Ans is (A)

Sol. 13 (B) $E=\{(1,1,1,1),(2,2,2,2)\ldots(13,13,13,13)\}$

$$\Rightarrow \quad n(E)=13$$

and $\quad n(S)={}^{52}C_4=270725$

$$\Rightarrow \quad P(E)=\frac{n(E)}{n(S)}=\frac{13}{270725}=\frac{1}{20825}$$

Hence Ans is (B)

Sol. 14 (B) $n(E)={}^{13}C_1\times{}^{13}C_1\times{}^{13}C_1\times{}^{13}C_1=(13)^4$

$$n(S)={}^{52}C_4=270725$$

$$\Rightarrow \quad P(E)=\frac{n(E)}{n(S)}=\frac{(13)^4}{270725}=\frac{2197}{20825}$$

Hence Ans is (B)

Sol. 15 (C) $n(E)={}^{13}C_1\times{}^{12}C_1\times{}^{11}C_1\times{}^{10}C_1$

$$=13\times12\times11\times10$$

$$n(S)={}^{52}C_4=270725$$

$$\Rightarrow \quad P(E)=\frac{13\times12\times11\times10}{270725}=\frac{264}{4165}$$

Hence Ans is (C)

Sol. 16 (D) Consider two events:

$A_i \to$ getting number i on first dice

$B_i \to$ getting a number more than i on second dice

The required probability

$$= P(A_1 \cap B_1) + P(A_2 \cap B_2) + P(A_3 \cap B_3)$$

$$+ P(A_4 \cap B_4) + P(A_5 \cap B_5)$$

$$= \sum_{i=1}^{5} P(A_i \cap B_i) \sum_{i=1}^{5} P(A_i) P(B_i)$$

[$\because$ A_i, B_i are independent]

$$= \frac{1}{6}[P(B_1) + P(B_2) + \ldots + P(B_5)]$$

$$= \frac{1}{6}\left(\frac{5}{6} + \frac{4}{6} + \frac{3}{6} + \frac{2}{6} + \frac{1}{6}\right) = \frac{5}{12}$$

Note : You may consider this problem in the following ways:
When first dice shows 1, second may show 2, 3, 4, 5, 6 (ie 5 ways).
When first dice shows 2, second may show 3, 4, 5, 6 (ie 4 ways).
When first dice shows 3, ... 4, 5, 6 (ie 3 ways).

... ...

... ...

When first dice shows 5 ... ...
6 (ie 1 way).

$\Rightarrow$ Total favourable cases

$$= 1 + 2 + 3 + 4 + 5 = 15$$

$$\Rightarrow \text{ required probability} = \frac{15}{36} = \frac{5}{12}$$

Hence Ans is (D)

Sol. 17 (C) Multiples of '3' in

1 to 30 = 10

Multiple to 13 in 1 to 30 = 2(13, 26)

So $n(\in) = 10 + 2$

$n(s) = 30$

$$\text{Probability} = \frac{n(\in)}{n(s)}$$

$$= \frac{12}{30}$$

$$= \frac{2}{5}$$

Hence Ans is (C)

Sol. 18 (A) The required probability

$$= \frac{2}{9} \times \frac{1}{8} \times \frac{4}{7} \times \frac{3}{6} \times \frac{2}{5} \times \frac{1}{4} \times 1 \times 1 \times 1$$

$$= \frac{1}{1260}$$

Hence Ans is (A)

Sol. 19 (A) The total number of ways in which 3 numbers can be chosen out of 30 numbers

$$= {}^{30}C_3 = 4060$$

Three numbers are consecutive in 28 ways

$$\Rightarrow \text{ required probability} = 1 - \frac{28}{4060} = \frac{144}{145}$$

Hence Ans is (A)

Sol. 20 (B) Consider the following events:

$A_1 \to A$ speaks truth,

$A_2 \to B$ speaks truth.

Then, $P(A_1) = \frac{60}{100} = \frac{3}{5}$,

$P(A_2) = \frac{70}{100} = \frac{7}{10}$

For the required event either both of them should speak the truth or both of them should tell a lie.
Thus, the required probability

$$= P((A_1 \cap A_2) \cup (\bar{A}_1 \cap \bar{A}_2))$$

$$= P(A_1 \cap A_2) + P(\bar{A}_1 \cap \bar{A}_2)$$

$$= P(A_1) P(A_2) + P(\bar{A}_1) P(\bar{A}_2)$$

$$= \frac{3}{5} \times \frac{7}{10} + \left(1 - \frac{3}{5}\right)\left(1 - \frac{7}{10}\right) = 0.54$$

Hence Ans is (B)

Sol. 21 (C) The total number of ways in which three integers can be chosen from the first 20 is ${}^{20}C_3$.
The product of three integers will be even if at least one of the integers is even. Therefore, the required probability = 1 – Probability that none of the three integers is even (or all are odd).

$$= 1 - \frac{{}^{10}C_3}{{}^{20}C_3} = 1 - \frac{2}{19} = \frac{17}{19}$$

Hence Ans is (C)

Sol. 22 (C) Total number of ways in which the same number appears in all the three dies 6

$\Rightarrow \quad n(\in) = 6$

$[(1,1,1)(2,2,2)(3,3,3)(4,4,4)(5,5,5)(6,6,6)]$

Sample space

$n(S) = 6^3 = 216$

Therefore

$$\text{Probability} = \frac{n(\in)}{n(S)} = \frac{6}{6^3} = \frac{1}{6^2} = \frac{1}{36}$$

Hence Ans is (C)

Sol. 23 (C) Any month out of 12 months can be chosen with probability $= \frac{1}{12}$.

There are 7 possible ways in which the month can start and it will be a Friday on 13th day if the first day of the month is Sunday. Whose probability is $\frac{1}{7}$.

Hence, the required probability

$$= \frac{1}{12} \times \frac{1}{7} = \frac{1}{84}$$

Hence Ans is (C)

Sol. 24 (B) Consider the following events:

$A \rightarrow$ getting head on first coin.

$B \rightarrow$ getting head on second coin.

$C \rightarrow$ getting 3 or 6 on dice.

These three events are independent with respective probabilities.

$$P(A) = \frac{1}{2}, P(B) = \frac{1}{2}, P(C) = \frac{2}{6} = \frac{1}{3}$$

The required probability

$= P(A \cap B \cap C) = P(A)\,P(B)\,P(C)$

$$= \frac{1}{2} \times \frac{1}{2} \times \frac{1}{3} = \frac{1}{12}$$

Hence Ans is (B)

Sol. 25 (C) There are 10 number from 50 to 59 such that each has a digit 5 and there are 9 other numbers, 5, 15, 25, 35, 45, 65, 75, 85, 95, each containing at digit 5. Thus, the favourable number of cases is 19. The exhaustive number of cases is 100.

Hence, the required probability $= \frac{19}{100}$

Hence Ans is (C)

Solutions of PRACTICE EXERCISE-8.3

Sol. 1 (A) The book on games of chance is written by J. Cardon

Hence Ans is (A)

Sol. 2 (B) Required probability $= \frac{5}{6} \times \frac{5}{6} = \frac{25}{36}$

Hence Ans is (B)

Sol. 3 (A) Total number of outcomes when a die is thrown twice $= 6 \times 6 = 36$

Total number of favourable outcomes are given by

$(1,2), (2,1), (1,4), (2,3), (3,2), (4,1), (1,6), (2,5), (3,4), (4,3), (5,2), (6,1), (3,6), (4,5), (5,4), (6,3), (5,6), (6,5)$

Probability of sum being odd

$$= \frac{\text{Number of favourable outcome}}{\text{Total number of outcomes}}$$

i.e. $\quad P(\text{odd}) = \frac{18}{36} = \frac{1}{2}$

Hence Ans is (A)

Sol. 4 (A) A leap year has 52 week & 2 days total number of possibilities for two days are

D_1	D_2
Sunday	Monday
Monday	Tuesday
Tuesday	Wednesday
Wednesday	Thursday
Thursday	Friday
Friday	Saturday
Saturday	Sunday

Out of 7 possibilities 53 Friday will come in one case that is Thursday-Friday.

Similarly 53 Saturday will also come only in one case that is Saturday-Sunday

So the total Probability will be

$$\frac{1}{7} + \frac{1}{7} = \frac{2}{7}$$

Hence Ans is (A)

Sol. 5 (C) Given probability of guessing the correct answer

$$= \frac{x}{12}$$

So not guessing the answer

$$= 1 - \frac{x}{12}$$

Given not guessing the correct answer

$$= \frac{2}{3}$$

$$\Rightarrow \quad 1 - \frac{x}{12} = \frac{2}{3}$$

$$\frac{x}{12} = 1 - \frac{2}{3}$$

$$\frac{x}{12} = \frac{1}{3}$$

$$\Rightarrow \quad x = 4$$

Hence Ans is (C)

Sol. 6 (C) Let number of blue balls be x then total number of ball in the bag will be $5 + x$ given
Probability of drawing blue ball

= 2(Probability of drawing Red ball)

$$\frac{x}{5+x} = \frac{2\times 5}{5+x}$$

$$x^2 + 5x = 10 \times 5 + 10x$$

$$x^2 - 5x - 50 = 0$$

$$(x+5)(x-10) = 0$$

$$x = 10$$

Hence Ans is (C)

Sol. 7 (A) Sample space

$$= \{(H, T), (T, H), (H, H), (T, T)\}$$

$$\Rightarrow \quad n(S) = 4$$

Outcome of getting at least one head

$$= \{(H, T), (T, H), (H, H)\}$$

$$\Rightarrow \quad n(E) = 3$$

$$\Rightarrow \quad \text{Probability} = \frac{n(E)}{n(S)} = \frac{3}{4}$$

Hence Ans is (A)

Sol. 8 (C) Favourable outcome: the point should be nearer to the center than from the circumference it means the point could be anywhere within the radius $r/2$

$$= \pi(r/2)^2$$

Total possible outcome; the point could be any where within the radius r

$$= \pi r^2$$

Thus probability

$$= \frac{\pi(r/2)^2}{\pi r^2} = \frac{1}{4}$$

Hence Ans is (C)

Sol. 9 (B) Given, 3 face cards of club are removed therefore,

Now the cards left are

$$52 - 3 = 49$$

Number of heart cards = 13

$$\Rightarrow \quad \text{The probability of drawing a heart} = \frac{13}{49}$$

Hence Ans is (B)

Sol. 10 (A) There are 12 face cards in a deck of 52 cards

$\Rightarrow$ Probability of getting a face card

$$= \frac{12}{52}$$

$$= \frac{3}{13}$$

Hence Ans is (A)

Sol. 11 (B) Total cases $\equiv \{3, 4, 5, 6, \dots 25\} = 23$

Favorable cases $\equiv \{3, 5, 7, 11, 13, 17, 19, 23\} = 8$

$$\text{Probability} = \frac{8}{23}$$

Hence Ans is (B)

Sol. 12 (A) Total defective item = 6

Total item = 20

Non defective item = 20 – 6 = 14

Probability that a chosen is non defective

$$= \frac{\text{Favorable cases}}{\text{Total cases}}$$

$$= \frac{14}{20} = \frac{7}{10}$$

Hence Ans is (A)

Sol. 13 (D) Total number of elements when to coins are tossed once is given by

$$S \equiv \{HH, HT, TH, TT\}$$

Number of favourable cases is given by

$$E = \{HT, TH, TT\}$$

$$\text{Probability} = \frac{\text{Number of favourable outcome}}{\text{Total number of outcomes}}$$

$$P(E) = \frac{3}{4}$$

Hence Ans is (D)

Sol. 14 (C) Given probability that it will rain today $= 0.84$

So probability it will not rain

$$= 1 - 0.84 = .16$$

Hence Ans is (C)

Sol. 15 (D) $n(E) = 4$

$$n(S) = 11$$

$$P(E) = \frac{n(E)}{n(S)}$$

$$P(E) = \frac{4}{11}$$

Hence Ans is (D)

Sol. 16 (C) Total number of cases $= 4$

$\{HH, HT, TH, TT\}$

favourable number of cases $= 3$ $\{HH, HT, TH\}$

So probability $= \frac{3}{4}$

Hence Ans is (C)

Sol. 17 (B) $S = \{H, T\} \times \{1, 2, 3, 4, 5, 6\}$

$\Rightarrow \quad n(S) = 12$

$$nE = \{(T, 2), (T, 3), (T, 5)\}$$

$\Rightarrow \quad n(E) = 3$

$\Rightarrow \quad P(E) = \frac{3}{12} = \frac{1}{4}$

Hence Ans is (B)

Sol. 18 (C) When two dice thrown simultaneously total number of cases are 36.

The favorable case when sum on the dice appear is prime will be 2, 3, 5, 7, 11

So number of favorable cases will be

(1, 1), (1, 2), (2, 1), (1, 4), (2, 3), (3, 2), (4, 1), (1, 6) (2, 5), (3, 4), (4, 3), (5, 2), (6, 1) (5, 6), (6, 5)

So probability $= \frac{15}{36} = \frac{5}{12}$

Hence Ans is (C)

Sol. 19 (A) Given number of black balls $= x$ then

Number of red balls $= 15 - x$

Hence P (red ball) $= \frac{15 - x}{15}$

Given five more red balls added. Hence number of red balls $= 20 - x$

$\Rightarrow \quad P \text{(red ball)} = \frac{20 - x}{20}$

by given condition

$$\frac{20 - x}{20} = 2\left(\frac{15 - x}{15}\right)$$

by solving we get

$$x = 12$$

$\Rightarrow$ Number of red balls $= 15 - 12 = 3$ hence

$$P \text{(red ball)} = \frac{3}{15} = \frac{1}{5}$$

Hence Ans is (A)

Sol. 20 (B) To have the numbers as sides of triangle, sum of two sides be greater than third side. Number of equilateral triangles i.e., all three dices have same figure = 6 number of isosceles triangle = 15 i.e., two dices have same figure and third one is different but sum of two is greater then the figure of third dice.

Number of scalene triangle = total number of triangle number of combination on dice whose total of two dice is less than the third dice.

$$= {}^6C_3 - [4 + 2] = 14$$

Total triangles possible

$$= 6 + 15 + 14 = 35$$

Hence probability $= \frac{35}{216}$

Hence Ans is (B)

Sol. 21 (B) To have the numbers as sides of triangle, sum of two sides be greater than third side. Number of equilateral triangles i.e., all three dices have same figure = 6 number of isosceles triangle = 15 i.e., two dices have same figure and third one is different but sum of two is greater then the figure of third dice.

Number of scalene triangle = total number of triangle number of combination on dice whose total of two dice is less than the third dice.

$$= {}^6C_3 - [4+2] = 14$$

Total triangles possible

$$= 6+15+14 = 35$$

Hence probability $= \frac{35}{216}$

Hence Ans is (B)

Sol. 22 (B)

Coin-1 Coin-2

H T T T

$\Rightarrow \quad P(H) = \frac{1}{2} \times 0 + \frac{1}{2} \times \frac{1}{2} = \frac{1}{4}$

Hence Ans is (B)

Sol. 23 (B) Let number of balls be 'x'

$\Rightarrow \quad \frac{x}{x+30} = \frac{2}{5} \times \frac{30}{x+30}$

$\Rightarrow \quad x = 12$

Hence Ans is (B)

Sol. 24 (C) Total number of cases = 4

Favourable number of cases = 2

$\Rightarrow$ Required Probability $= \frac{2}{4} = \frac{1}{2}$

Hence Ans is (C)

Sol. 25 (C) Total number of cases = 365

Favourable number of cases = 364

$\Rightarrow$ Required Probability $= \frac{364}{365}$

Hence Ans is (C)

Sol. 26 (A) Sample space

$$S = \{1, 2, 3, \ldots, 50\}$$

$\Rightarrow \quad n(S) = 50$

Event

$$E = \{2, 3, 5, 7, 11, 13, 17, 19, 23, 29, 31, 37, 41, 43, 47\}$$

$\Rightarrow \quad n(E) = 15$

$\Rightarrow$ Probability $p(E) = \frac{n(E)}{n(S)} = \frac{15}{50} = \frac{3}{10}$

Hence Ans is (A)

Sol. 27 (B) Sum of numbers possible are 2,3,4, …, 12 perfect square are 4, 9

Cases for 4 $\rightarrow$ (1, 3), (3, 1), (2, 2)

Cases for 9 $\rightarrow$ (3, 6), (6, 3), (4, 5), (5, 4)

Total cases $\rightarrow$ 36

Hence probability $= \frac{7}{36}$

Hence Ans is (B)

Sol. 28 (B) Required probability $= \frac{2}{7}$

Hence Ans is (B)

Sol. 29 (A) A leap year has 2 odd days (S, M) (M, T) (T, W) (W, Th) (Th, F) (F, Sa), (Sa, S)

$$P(A) = \frac{n(A)}{n(S)} = \frac{2}{7}$$

Hence Ans is (A)

Sol. 30 (C) Total number of elements in sample space

$$n(s) = 36$$

Favourable number of cases

$n(E) = \{(1,3)(1,6)(3,3)(3,6)(5,3)(5,6)(3,1)(6,1)(6,3)$ $(3,5)(6,5)\}$

$$= 11$$

$$P(E) = \frac{n(E)}{n(S)} = \frac{11}{36}$$

Hence Ans is (C)

Sol. 31 (B) A dice is rolled once

$\Rightarrow$ Probability of getting number less than 4 is

$$\frac{3}{6} = \frac{1}{2}$$

$\Rightarrow$ Probability of getting number greater than 4 is

$$\frac{1}{3}$$

$\Rightarrow \quad \frac{1}{2} - \frac{1}{3} = \frac{1}{6}$

Hence Ans is (B)

Sol. 32 (B) 5, 6, 7, 8, 9, 10, 11, 12, 13, 14, 15, 16, 17, 18

Total numbers divisible by 2 or 3 = 9

$$P(E) = \frac{9}{14}$$

Hence Ans is (B)

Sol. 33 (A) There are 4 ace in a deck of 52 cards.

$$P\,(\text{Ace}) = \frac{4}{52} = \frac{1}{13}$$

$$P\,(\text{Not an Ace}) = 1 - \frac{1}{13} = \frac{12}{13}$$

Hence Ans is (A)

Sol. 34 (D) Both dice can have numbers 1 to 6 on each of them.

Sum can be any numbers form 2 to 12. Out of these 5 and 10 are divisible by 5.

Favorable cases :

(1, 4), (2, 3), (3, 2), (4, 1), (5, 5), (4, 6), (6, 4)

i.e. total 7 cases.

Total cases = 6 × 6 = 36 cases

$$\text{Probability} = \frac{7}{36}$$

Hence Ans is (D)

Sol. 35 (A) Sum = 7 or 8

7 = {(1, 6), (2, 5), (3, 4), (4, 3), (5, 2), (6, 1)}

= 6 ways

8 = {(2, 6), (3, 5), (4, 4), (5, 3), (6, 2)}

= 5 ways

$$\Rightarrow \text{Required probability} = \frac{11}{36}$$

Hence Ans is (A)

Sol. 36 (A) $\dfrac{{}^{32}C_2 \times {}^{32}C_1 \times 2}{{}^{64}C_3}$

(Two white + 1 black or Two black + 1 white)

$$= \frac{\frac{32 \times 31}{2} \times 32 \times 2}{\frac{64 \times 63 \times 62}{6}}$$

$$\Rightarrow \quad = \frac{32 \times 31 \times 32 \times 6}{64 \times 63 \times 62}$$

$$= \frac{48}{63}$$

$$= \frac{16}{21}$$

Hence Ans is (A)

Sol. 37 (C) Total marbles = 9

White marbles = 2

$$\text{Probability (white marbles)} = \frac{2}{9}$$

Hence Ans is (C)

Sol. 38 (C) Normal year has 52 weeks.

But number of day in an ordinary year = 365

⇒ 52 × 7 = 364 days are covered in 52 weeks

⇒ 1 remaining day can be Sun, Mon, Tue, Thus, Fri, Sat.

$$\Rightarrow P(\text{1 remaining day} = \text{Thursday}) = \frac{1}{7}$$

Hence Ans is (C)

Sol. 39 (B) 2 dies are rolled

Total sample space = 36

Sum as prime number =

2 - 1 ways

3 - 2 ways

5 - 4 ways 15 possible ways

7 - 6 ways

11 - 2 ways

⇒ P(Sum = prime) = 15/36 = 5/12

Hence Ans is (B)

Sol. 40 (D) $n(S) = \{1, 2, 3, 4, 5, 6\}$

$n(E) = \{1\}$

$P(E) = 1/6$

Hence Ans is (D)

Sol. 41 (B) Total number which are divisible by 4 and 6 between 1 and 100 will be 33

$$\text{So, Required probability} = \frac{100 - 33}{100} = .67$$

Hence Ans is (B)

Sol. 42 (C) 6 can be summed up by either 2 summands or 3 or 4 or 5 or 6 summands.

There are a total of 5 ordered summands when 6 is summed up by only 2 summands.

They are: {1, 5}, {2, 4}, {3, 3}, {4, 2}, {5, 1}

3 summands to get a 6 can be of three types :

{1, 1, 4} or {1, 2, 3} or {2, 2, 2}

$\{1, 1, 4\}$ can be arranged among each other in $\frac{3!}{2!} = 3$ ways

$\{1, 2, 3\}$ can be arranged among each other in ${}^3P_3 = 6$ ways

So, there area a total of $6 + 3 + 1 = 10$

ordered summands when 6 is obtained by 3 summands.

4 summands to obtain a 6 can be of two types :

$\{1, 1, 1, 3\}$ or $\{1, 1, 2, 2\}$

$\{1, 1, 1, 3\}$ can be arranged among each other in

$\frac{4!}{3!} = 4$ ways

$\{1, 1, 2, 2\}$ can be arranged among each other in $\frac{4!}{2! \times 2!} = 6$ ways

So, there area a total of $4 + 6 = 10$

ordered summands when 6 is obtained by 4 summands.

5 summands to obtain a 6 is of type $\{1, 1, 1, 1, 2\}$

It can be arranged among each other in $\frac{5!}{4!} = 5$ ways

So, there area a total of 5 ordered summands when 6 is obtained by 5 summands.

There is only 1 ordered summand to obtain a 6 using 6 summands and it is $\{1, 1, 1, 1, 1, 1\}$

Therefore, total number of ordered summands of 6 is

$= 5 + 10 + 10 + 5 + 1 = 31$

Hence Ans is (C)

Sol. 43 (D) Total number of cases when three dice thrown simultaneously

$= 6 \times 6 \times 6 = 216$

Favourable number of out come for sum = 3 is given by

(1, 1, 1)

and favourable number of out come for sum = 4 is given by

(1, 1, 2), (1, 2, 1), (2, 1, 1)

Hence favourable number of out come of getting a sum of atleast

$5 = 216 - 4 = 212$

Required probability $= \frac{212}{216} = \left(\frac{53}{54}\right)$

Hence Ans is (D)

Sol. 44 (C) Number of possible outcomes = 16

Number of favourable outcomes

$= \{(2, 9), (2, 16), (3, 9), (3, 16), (4, 9), (4, 16)\}$

$P(E) = \frac{6}{16} = \frac{3}{8}$

Hence Ans is (C)

* * * * *

Circle 9

Important terms, Definitions, and Results:

❍ The collection of all the points in a plane, which are at a fixed distance from a fixed point in the plane, is called a **circle**.

❍ The fixed point is called the **centre** of the circle and the fixed distance is called the **radius** of the circle.

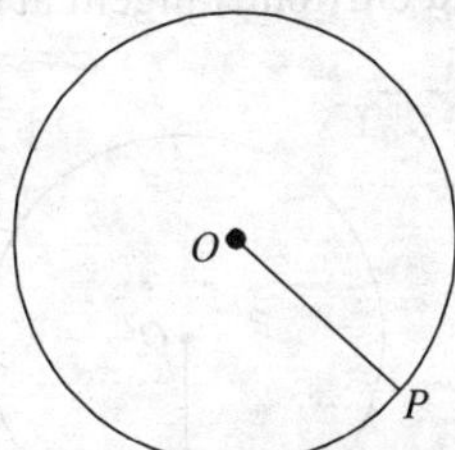

Figure 9.1

In the given figure-9.1, O is the centre and the length OP is the radius of the circle.

❍ A circle divides the plane on which it lies into three parts. They are : (i) inside the circle, which is also called the **interior** of the circle; (ii) the circle and (iii) outside the circle, which is also called the **exterior** of the circle. The circle and its interior make up the **circular region.**

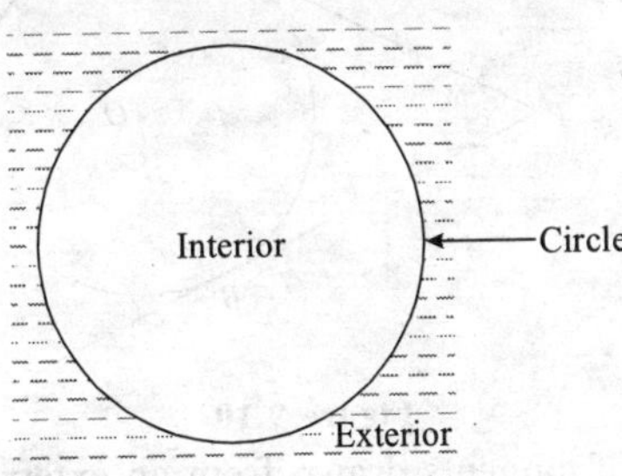

Figure 9.2

❍ A **chord** of a circle is a line segment joining any two points on the circle. In the given figure-9.3 PQ, RS and AOB are the chords of a circle.

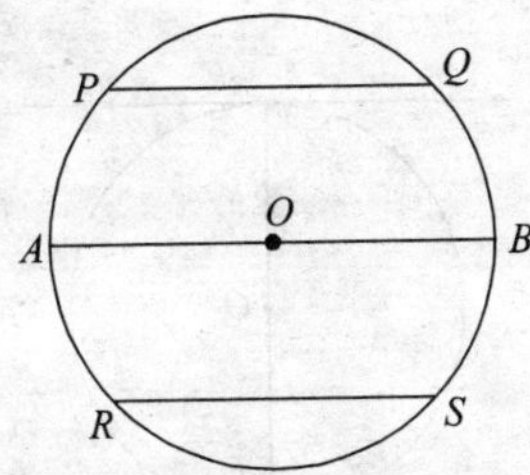

Figure 9.3

❍ A **diameter** is a chord of a circle passing through the centre of the circle. In the given figure, AOB is the diameter of the circle. A diameter is the longest chord of a circle.

Diameter = 2 × radius

❍ A piece of a circle between two points is called an **arc.** Look at the pieces of the circle between two points P and Q in the given figure-9.4. You find that there are two pieces, one longer and the other smaller. The longer one is called the **major *arc* PQ** and the shorter one is called the **minor *arc* PQ.**

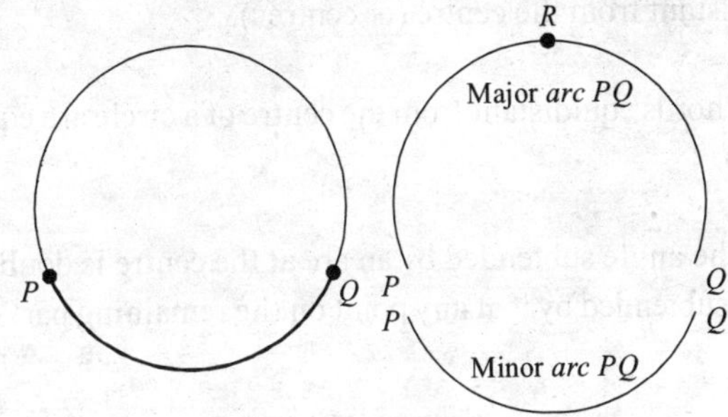

Figure 9.4

❍ The length of the complete circle is called its **circumference.** The region between a chord and either of its arcs is called a **segment** of the circular region or simply a **segment** of the circle. You will find that there are two types of segments also, which are the **major segment** and the **minor segment.**

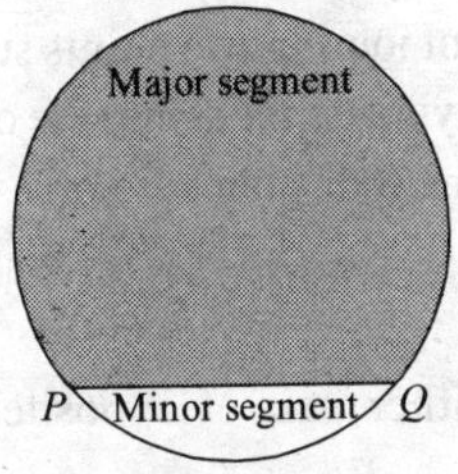

Figure 9.5

❍ The region between an arc and the two radii, joining the centre to the end points of the *arc* is called a **sector.** Like segments, you find that the minor *arc* corresponds to the **minor sector** and the major *arc* corresponds to the **major sector.**

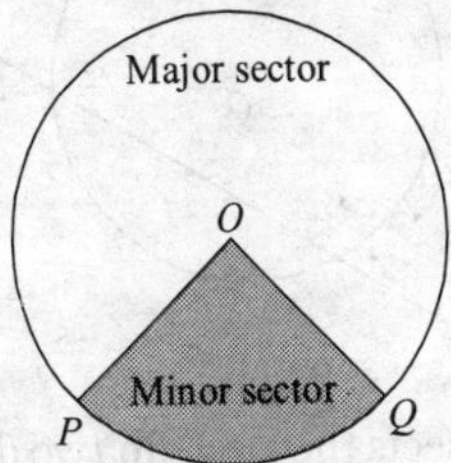

Figure 9.6

- Equal chords of a circle subtend equal angles at the centre.

- If the angles subtended by the chords of a circle at the centre are equal, then the chords are equal.

- The perpendicular from the centre of a circle to a chord bisects the chord.

- The line drawn through the centre of a circle to bisect a chord is perpendicular to the chord.

- There is one and only one circle passing through three given non-collinear points.

- Equal chords of a circle (or of congruent circles) are equidistant from the centre (or centres).

- Chords equidistant from the centre of a circle are equal in length.

- The angle subtended by an arc at the centre is double the angle subtended by it at any point on the remaining part of the circle.

- Angles in the same segment of a circle are equal.

- Points which lie on the same circle are called concyclic points.

- A quadrilateral is said to be a cyclic quadrilateral if there is a circle passing through all its four vertices.

- If a line segment joining two points subtends equal angles at two other points lying on the same side of the line containing the line segment, the four points lie on a circle (i.e., they are concyclic).

- The sum of either pair of opposite angles of a cyclic quadrilateral is 180°.

- If the sum of a pair of opposite angles of a quadrilateral is 180°, the quadrilateral is cyclic.

- 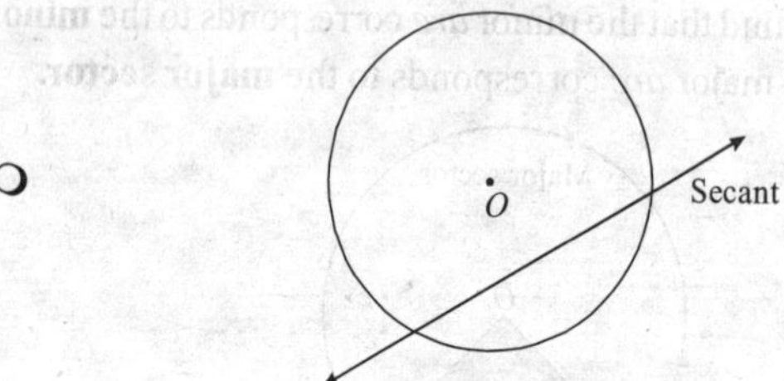

Figure 9.7

A line, which intersects the circle in two distinct points, is called a **secant.**

- 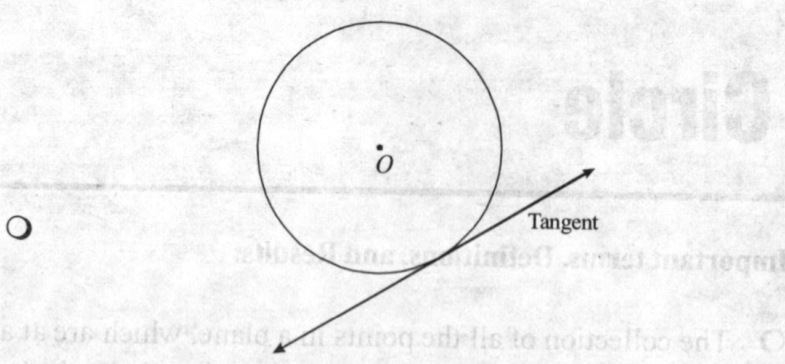

Figure 9.8

A line which has only one point common to the circle is called a **tangent** to the **circle.**

- There is one and only one tangent at a point of the circle.

- 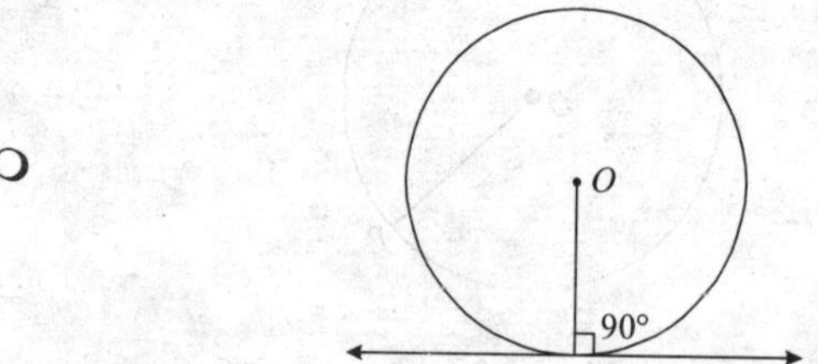

Figure 9.9

The tangent at any point of a circle is perpendicular to the radius through the point of contact.

- No tangent can be drawn from a point inside the circle.

- 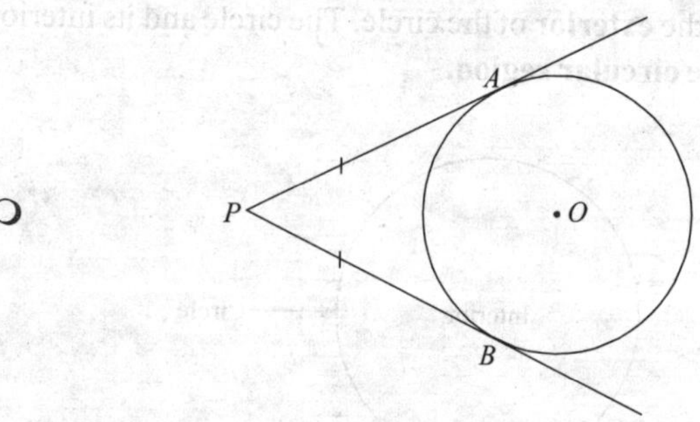

Figure 9.10

The lengths of tangents drawn from an external point to a circle are equal.

- The perpendicular at the point of contact to the tangent to a circle passes through the centre of the circle.

- Tangents drawn at the end points of a diameter of a circle are parallel.

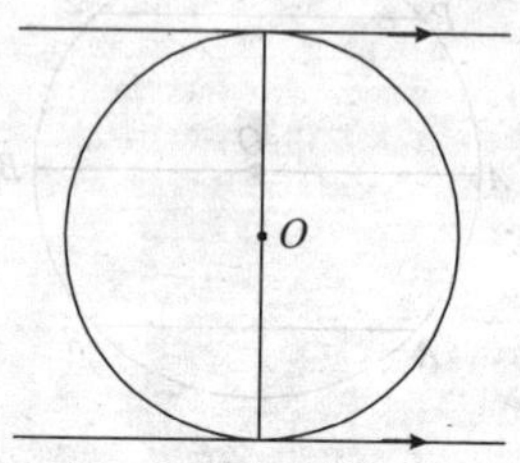

Figure 9.11

Common tangents of two circles

- Two common tangents can be drawn to intersecting circles.

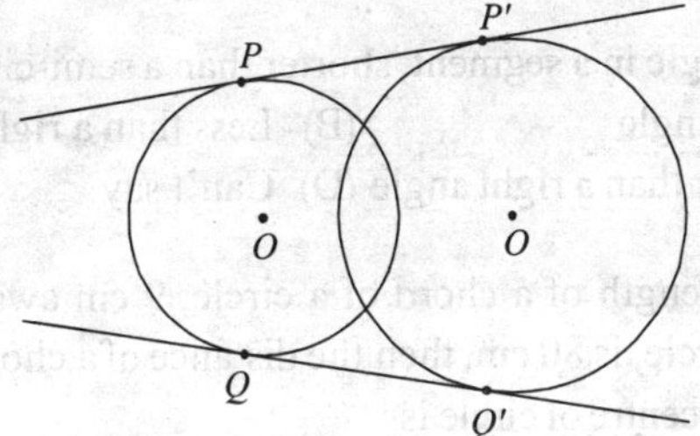

Figure 9.12

$PP' = QQ'$

- Three common tangents can be drawn to two circles which touch each other externally at a point.

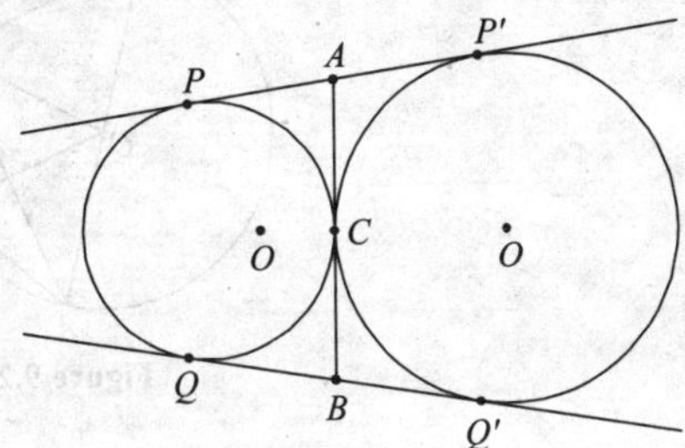

Figure 9.13

$PP' = QQ'$

AB is the bisector of *PP'* & *QQ'*

- One common tangent can be drawn of two circles which touch each other internally at a point.

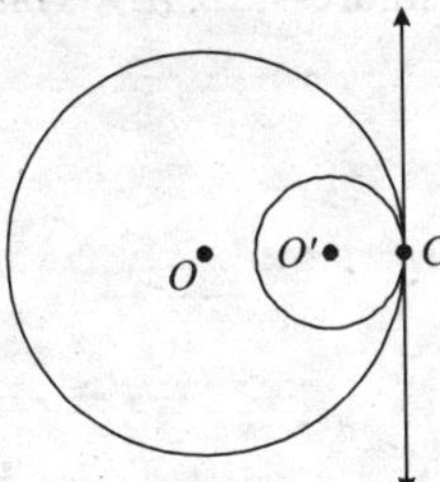

Figure 9.14

- No common tangent is drawn to two non-intersecting and non-touching circles

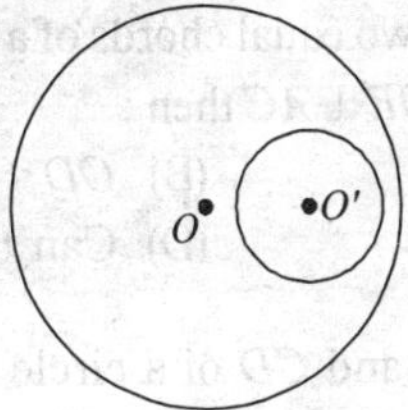

Figure 9.15

- Four common tangents can be drawn on two circles which are at a certain distance apart from each other.

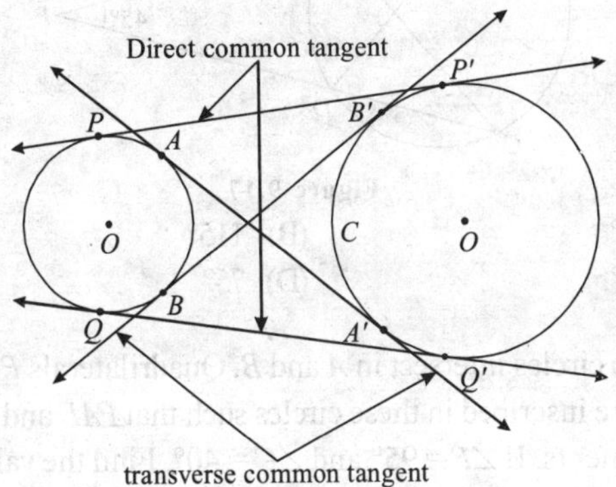

Figure 9.16

$PP' = QQ'$ and $AA' = BB'$.

* * * * *

PRACTICE EXERCISE - 9.1

9-1 AB and AC are two equal chords of a circle whose centre is O. If $OD \perp AB$ and $OE \perp AC$ then :

(A) $OD > OE$ (B) $OD < OE$
(C) $OD = OE$ (D) Can't say

9-2 Two chords AB and CD of a circle cut each other when produced outside the circle at P. AD and BC are joined. If $\angle PAD = 30°$ and $\angle CPA = 45°$, find $\angle CBP$:

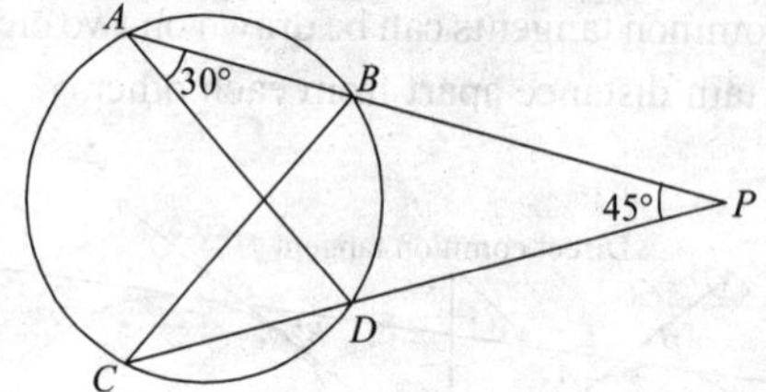

Figure 9.17

(A) 105° (B) 115°
(C) 135° (D) 75°

9-3 Two circles intersect in A and B. Quadrilaterals $PCBA$ and $ABDE$ are inscribed in these circles such that PAE and CBD are line segments. If $\angle P = 95°$ and $\angle C = 40°$. Find the value of Z:

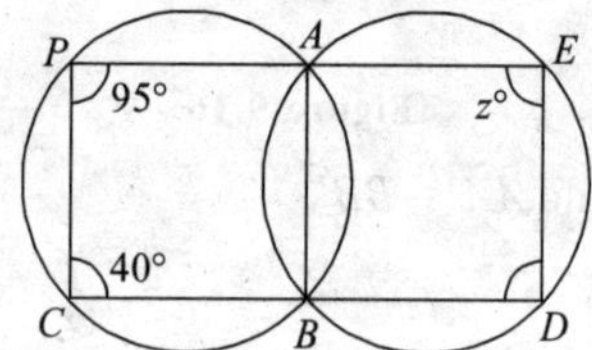

Figure 9.18

(A) 65° (B) 105°
(C) 95° (D) 85°

9-4 In the given figure-9.19 the value of $\angle PQS$ is equal to :

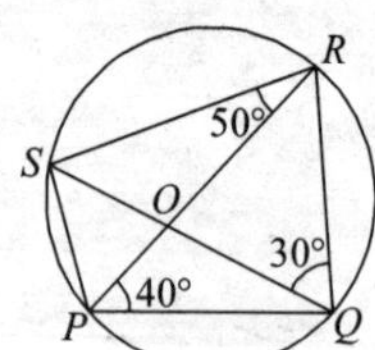

Figure 9.19

(A) 40° (B) 50°
(C) 30° (D) Can't be determined

9-5 In the figure-9.20 below, $RSTV$ is a square inscribed in a circle with centre O and radius r. The total area of shaded region is :

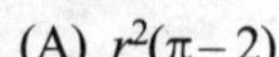
(A) $r^2(\pi - 2)$

(B) $2r(2 - \pi)$

(C) $\pi(r^2 - 2)$

(D) $\pi r^2 - 8r$

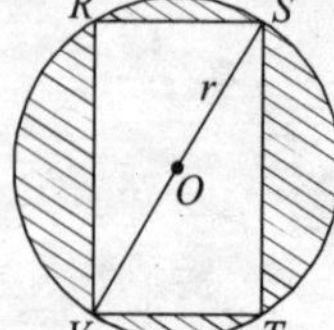

Figure 9.20

9-6 The angle in a segment, shorter than a semi-circle is :

(A) Right angle (B) Less than a right angle
(C) Greater than a right angle (D) Can't say

9-7 If the length of a chord of a circle, 9 cm away from the centre of circle, is 80 cm, then the distance of a chord of length 18 cm from centre of circle is :

(A) 40 cm (B) 17 cm
(C) 18 cm (D) 19 cm

9-8 In the given figure-9.21, O is centre, $\angle CAD = 35°$, then $\angle AEB =$

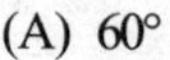
(A) 60°

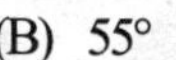
(B) 55°

(C) 70°

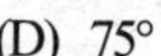
(D) 75°

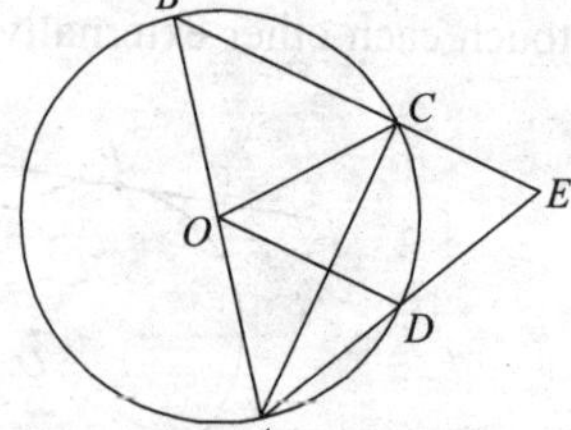

Figure 9.21

9-9 There are two concentric circles of radii 13 cm and 12 cm. Then the length of the chord of the outer circle which touches the inner circle is :

(A) 10 cm (B) 13 cm
(C) 12 cm (D) 12.5 cm

10-10 In the given figure-9.22, AD is bisector of $\angle BAC$ then $\angle ABC =$

(A) 55°

(B) 56°

(C) 57°

(D) 58°

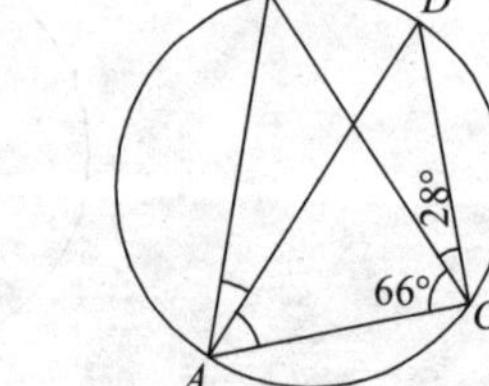

Figure 9.22

9-11 In the figure-9.23 given below O is the centre of the circle. Line AB intersects the circle only at point B, and line DC intersects the circle only at point C. If the circle has a radius of 2 cm. Then AC is :

(A) 4 cm

(B) $2 + \sqrt{2}$ cm

(C) $4 + \sqrt{2}$ cm

(D) $2 + 2\sqrt{2}$ cm

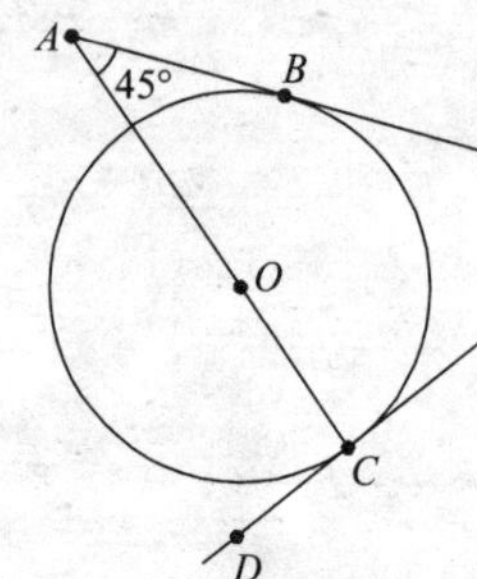

Figure 9.23

9-12 *PQ*, *PR* are tangents to a circle and *QS* is a diameter, then :

(A) $\angle QPR = \frac{1}{2}\angle RQS$ (B) $\angle QPR = 2\angle RQS$

(C) $\angle QPR = \angle RQS$ (D) None of these

9-13 In the following figure-9.24, *QS* is the diameter and *APT* the tangent at *P*. Then $\angle APQ$ is equal to :

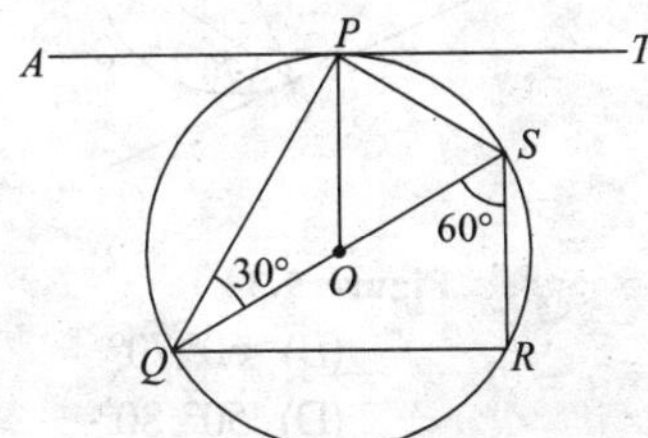

Figure 9.24

(A) 60° (B) 30°
(C) 40° (D) 50°

9-14 In the adjoining figure-9.25 *AOB* is a diameter, *MPQ* is a tangent at *P*, then the value of $\angle MPA$ is equal to :

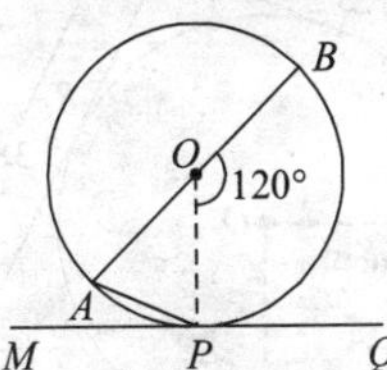

Figure 9.25

(A) 25° (B) 26°
(C) 27° (D) 30°

9-15 *PQRS* is a square. *SR* is a tangent (at point *S*) to the circle with centre *O* and *TR* = *OS*. Then, ratio of area of the square to the area of circle is :

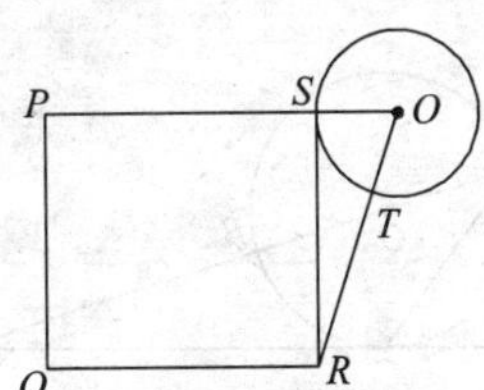

Figure 9.26

(A) $\frac{\pi}{3}$ (B) $\frac{11}{7}$

(C) $\frac{3}{\pi}$ (D) $\frac{7}{11}$

9-16 Two circles of radii *a* and *b* touch each other externally. If *ST* is their common tangent at *S* and *T*, then the value of ST^2 is equals to :

(A) $a - b$ (B) $(a - b)^2$
(C) $2ab$ (D) $4ab$

9-17 In the given figure-9.27, circle *AXB* passes through '*O*' the centre of circle *AYB*. *AX*, *BX* and *AY*, *BY* are tangents to the circles *AYB* and *AXB* respectively. The value of $y°$ is:

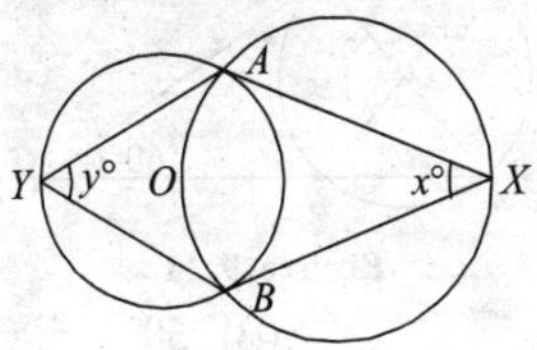

Figure 9.27

(A) $180° - x°$ (B) $180° - 2x°$

(C) $\frac{1}{2}(90° - x°)$ (D) $90° - \left(\frac{x°}{2}\right)$

9-18 In the figure-9.28 given below, $\angle QSR$ is equal to :

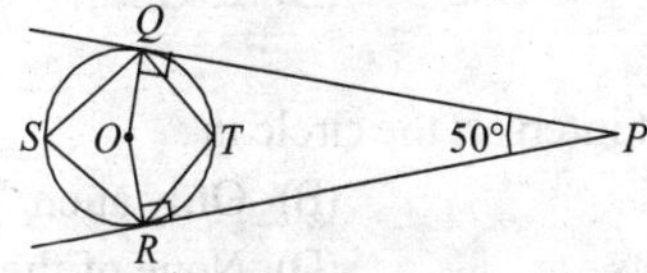

Figure 9.28

(A) 65° (B) 50°
(C) 70° (D) 75°

9-19 In the adjoining figure-9.29 (not drawn to scale), *A*, *B* and *C* are three points on a circle with centre *O*. The chord *BA* is extended to a point *T* such that *CT* becomes a tangent to the circle at point *C*. If $\angle ATC = 30°$ and $\angle ACT = 50°$, then find $\angle BOA$:

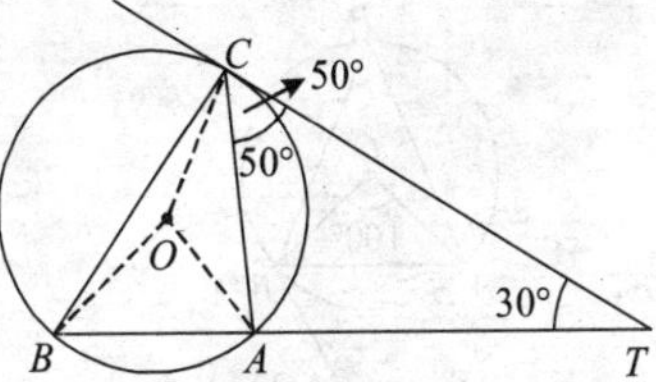

Figure 9.29

(A) 60° (B) 100°
(C) 50° (D) 120°

9-20 A circle is inscribed in a ΔABC having sides 8 cm, 10 cm and 12 cm as shown in figure-9.30. Find *AD* :

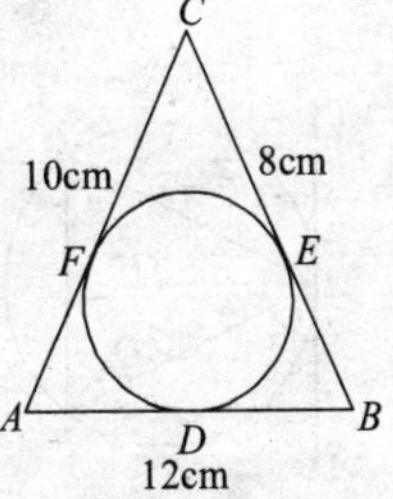

Figure 9.30

(A) 5 cm (B) 4 cm
(C) 6 cm (D) 7 cm

9-21 In the figure-9.31, if O is the centre of the circle, then $\angle DOB$ equals :

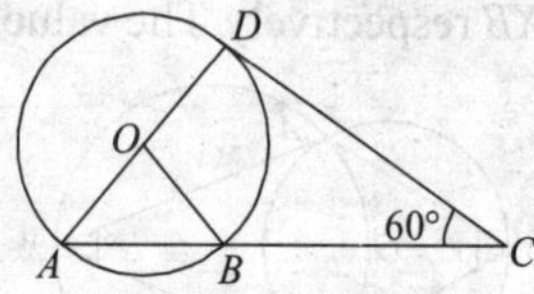

Figure 9.31

(A) 120° (B) 30°
(C) 90° (D) 60°

9-22 The length of the tangent from a point A at a circle of radius 3 cm, is 4 cm. The distance of A from the centre of the circle is :

(A) $\sqrt{7}$ cm (B) 7 cm
(C) 5 cm (D) 25 cm

9-23 A tangent intersect the circle in :
(A) Two points (B) Only at one point
(C) Three points (D) None of these

9-24 The incircle of ΔABC, touches the sides BC, CA and AB at D, E and F respectively then $AE + BF + CD =$
(A) $AB + BC + CA$ (B) $2(AB + BC + CA)$
(C) $\frac{1}{2}(AB + BC + CA)$ (D) None of these

9-25 In the given figure-9.32 find $\angle ABQ$:

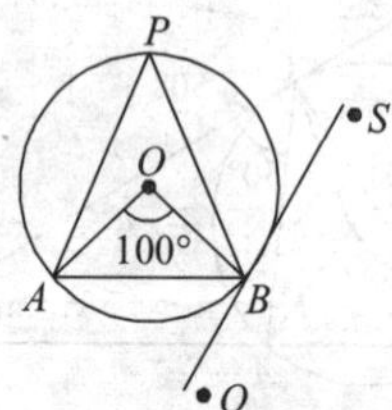

Figure 9.32

(A) 45° (B) 50°
(C) 65° (D) 75°

9-26 In the given figure-9.33, TAS is a tangent of the circle, with centre O, at the point A. If $\angle OBA = 32°$, find the values of x and y :

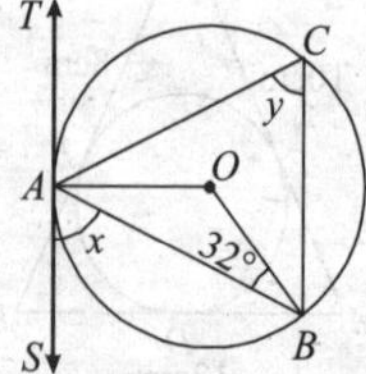

Figure 9.33

(A) $x = 56°, y = 58°$ (B) $x = 58°, y = 58°$
(C) $x = 56°, y = 56°$ (D) $x = 58°, y = 56°$

9-27 In the given figure-9.34, TBP and TCQ are tangents to the circle whose center is O. Also $\angle PBA = 60°$ and $\angle ACQ = 70°$. Determine $\angle BAC$ and $\angle BTC$:

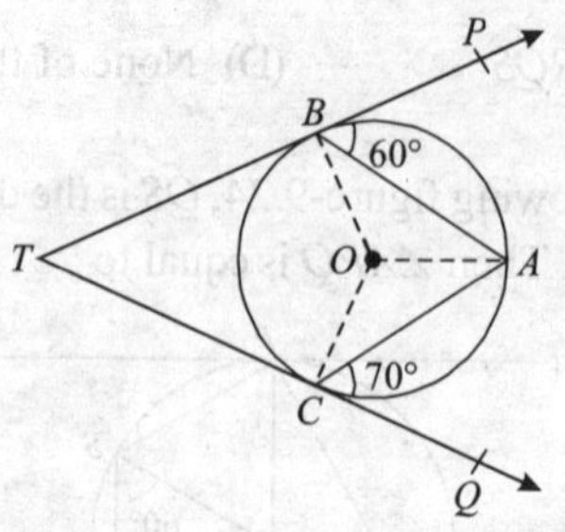

Figure 9.34

(A) 50°, 60° (B) 60°, 70°
(C) 50°, 70° (D) 50°, 80°

9-28 In the given figure-9.35, quadrilateral $ABCD$ is circumscribed touching the circle at P, Q, R, and S such that $\angle DAB = 90°$. If $CS = 27$ cm and $CB = 38$ cm and the radius of the circle is 10 cm, then find AB :

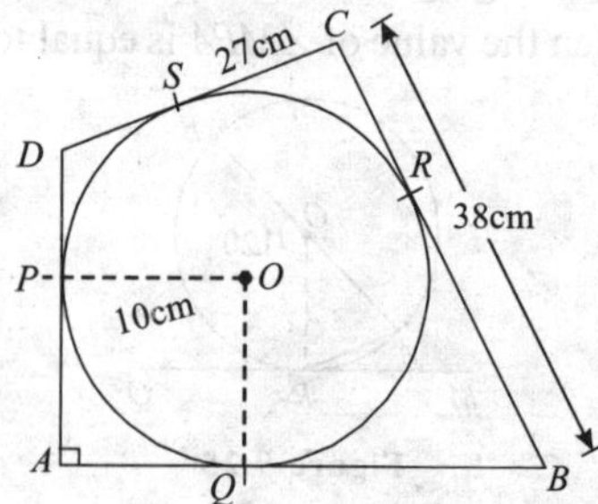

Figure 9.35

(A) 22 cm (B) 10 cm
(C) 21 cm (D) 20 cm

9-29 In the figure-9.36, if O is the centre of the circle, then $\angle BTC$ equals :

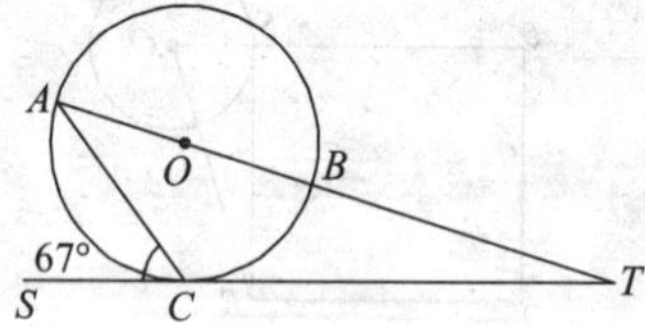

Figure 9.36

(A) 44° (B) 113°
(C) 23° (D) None of these

9-30 The length l of a tangent drawn from a point A to a circle is $\frac{4}{3}$ of the radius r. The shortest distance from A to the circle is :

(A) $\frac{1}{2}r$ (B) r

(C) $\frac{3}{4}r$ (D) $\frac{2}{3}r$

9-31 In figure-9.37, O is centre and $\angle ABD = 52°$ then $\angle AOC =$

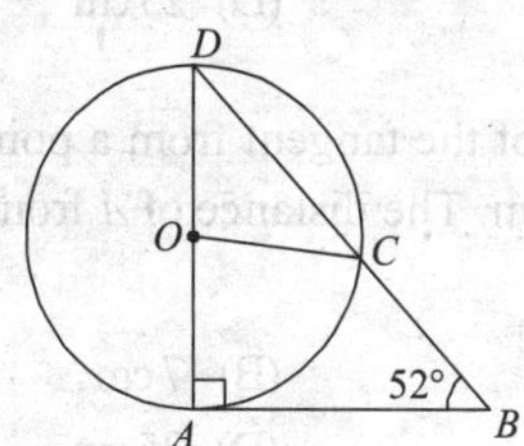

Figure 9.37

(A) 72° (B) 76°
(C) 78° (D) 82°

9-32 If tangents PA and PB from a point P to a circle with centre O are inclined to each other at an angle of 80° then $\angle POA$ is equal to :
(A) 50° (B) 60°
(C) 65° (D) 80°

9-33 Number of tangents that can be drawn from a point lies inside of a circle are :
(A) 0 (B) 1
(C) 2 (D) More than 2

9-34 Two perpendicular tangents are drawn from a point P to the circle then figure formed by these tangents and radius drawn on point of contact is :
(A) Rectangle (B) Square
(C) Rhombus (D) Trapezium

9-35 The tangents at the end points of a diameter of a circle :
(A) Intersect at a point
(B) Are parallel to each other
(C) Are perpendicular to each other
(D) Meeting at an angle of 45°

9-36 In the given figure-9.38, ABC is a right angled triangle with $AB = 6$ cm and $AC = 8$ cm. A circle with centre O has been inscribed inside the triangle. Calculate the value of r, the radius of the inscribed circle :

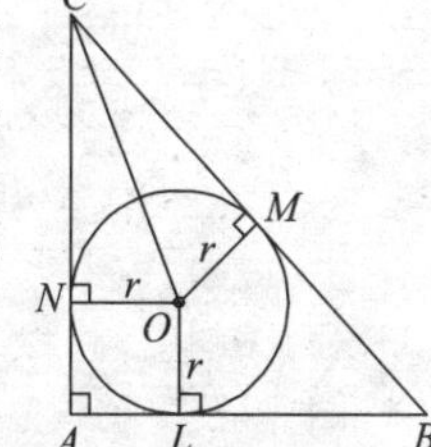

Figure 9.38

(A) 2 cm
(B) 1 cm
(C) 1.5 cm
(D) 2.5 cm

9-37 If ΔABC is circumscribed touching the circle at P, Q and R. If $AP = 4$ cm, $BP = 6$ cm and $AC = 12$ cm, and $BC = x$ cm. Find the value of x :
(A) 14 cm (B) 15 cm
(C) 16 cm (D) 13 cm

9-38 If three circles with centers A, B, C respectively touch each other externally. If $AB = 5$cm, $BC = 7$cm and $CA = 6$ cm. Then find the radius of the circle with centre A :
(A) 3 cm (B) 2 cm
(C) 2.5 cm (D) 3.5

9-39 In the adjoining figure-9.39, AOB is a chord of a circle ABC, T is a point on the tangent at A, the tangents at B meets AT produced to D. $\angle ATO = 55°$, $\angle BOT = 120°$, find $\angle BPT$:

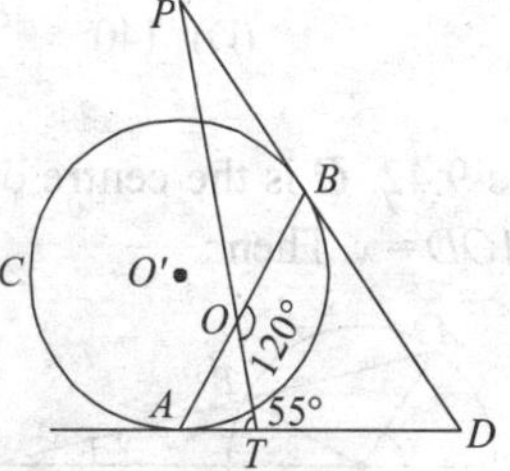

Figure 9.39

(A) 5° (B) 10°
(C) 12° (D) 15°

9-40 PT is a tangent to a circle drawn from an external point P and PBA is a secant. If $AP = 10$ cm, $BP = 8$ cm then $PT =$
(A) 3 cm (B) 4 cm
(C) 5 cm (D) $4\sqrt{5}$ cm

9-41 In the given figure-9.40 :

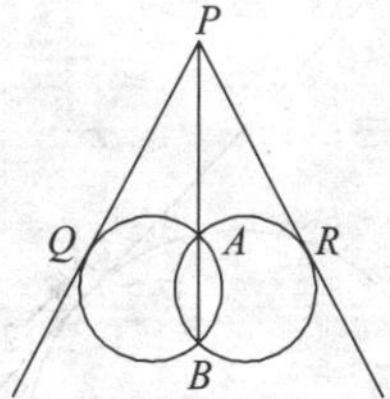

Figure 9.40

(A) $PQ = PR$ (B) $QR = AB$
(C) $BQ = BR$ (D) $AQ = AR$

9-42 Two circles touch each other externally at C and AB is a common tangent to the circles. Then, $\angle ACB =$
(A) 60° (B) 45°
(C) 30° (D) 90°

9-43 Two concentric circles are of radii 5cm and 3cm. Then the length of the chord of the larger circle which touches the smaller circle is :
(A) 4 cm (B) 8 cm
(C) 5 cm (D) 3 cm

9-44 How many circles can be drawn passing through three collinear points :
(A) Only one (B) Two
(C) Infinite (D) No Circle

9-45 In figure-9.41, O is centre then $\angle AOC$ is :

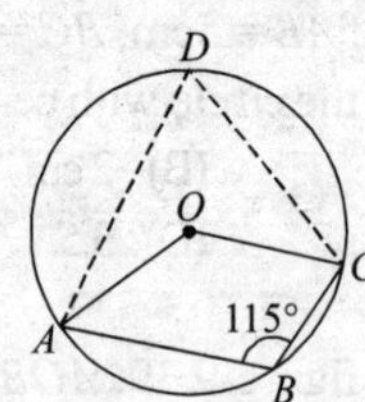

Figure 9.41

(A) 100° (B) 115°
(C) 130° (D) 140°

9-46 In the figure-9.42, O is the centre of circle, $BC = OB$, $\angle ACD = y$ and $\angle AOD = x$. Then :

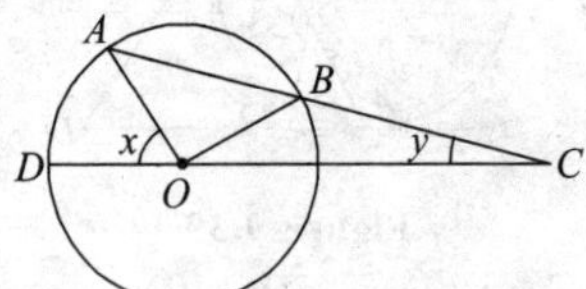

Figure 9.42

(A) $x = y$ (B) $x = 3y$
(C) $x = 4y$ (D) $x = 2y$

9-47 A circle is inscribed in a quadrilateral $PQRS$. If $QR = 30$ cm, $QA = 22$ cm, $RS = 30$ cm and $PS \perp SR$ then radius of circle is :

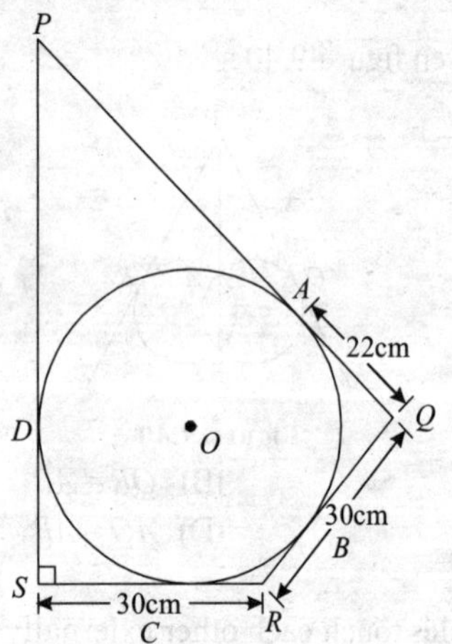

Figure 9.43

(A) 20 cm (B) 22 cm
(C) 24 cm (D) 25 cm

9-48 The length of the tangent from a point A at a circle of radius 3 cm, is 4 cm. The distance of A from the centre of the circle is :

(A) $\sqrt{7}$ cm (B) 7 cm
(C) 5 cm (D) 25 cm

9-49 In the given circle with centre O, $PT = 12$ cm, $PA = 3$ cm, $PC = 4$ cm, find $PB + PD$.

(A) 80 cm. (B) 84 cm.
(C) 90 cm. (D) None

9-50 What is the maximum number of common tangents that can be drawn to two circles which touches externally?

(A) 0 (B) 1
(C) 2 (D) 3

* * * * *

PRACTICE EXERCISE - 9.2

9-1 In the diagram the circle contains the vertices A, B, C of triangle ABC. Now $\angle ABC$ is 30° and the length of AC is 5. The diameter of the circle is :

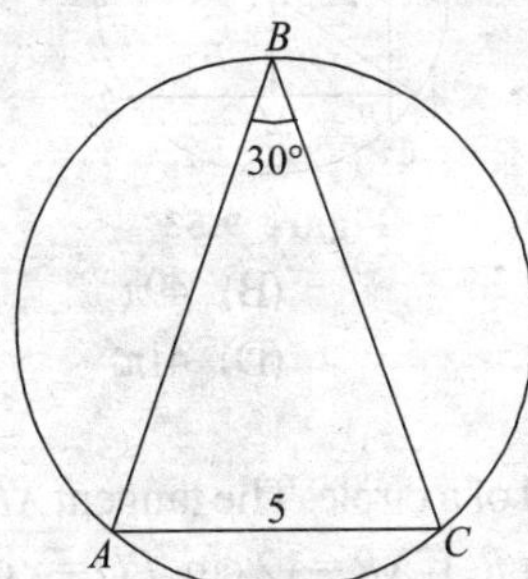

Figure 9.44

(A) $5\sqrt{3}$ (B) 8
(C) 10 (D) $5\sqrt{5}$

9-2 The three circles in the figure-9.45 centered at A, B and C are tangent to one another and have radii 7, 21 and 6 respectively. The area of the triangle ABC, is :

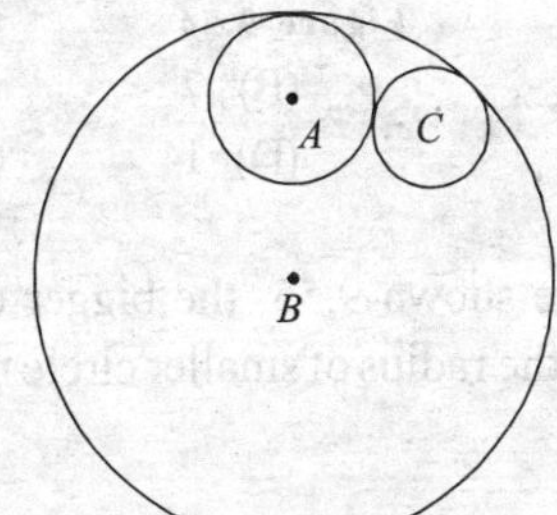

Figure 9.45

(A) 54 (B) 64
(C) 74 (D) 84

9-3 Triangle PAB is formed by three tangents to circle with centre O and $\angle APB = 40°$, then angle AOB is :

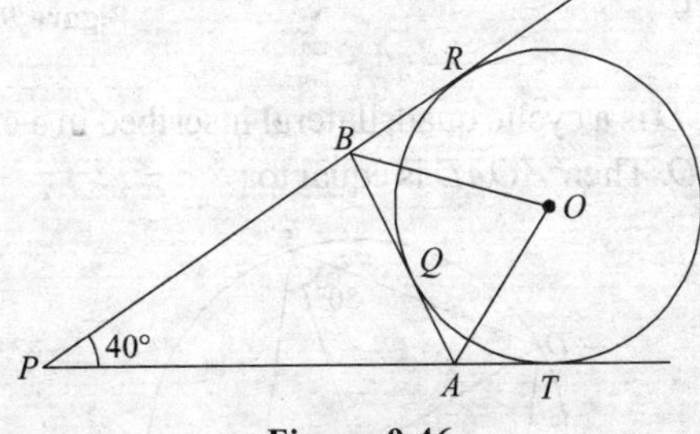

Figure 9.46

(A) 45° (B) 50°
(C) 60° (D) 70°

9-4 Which of the following shapes of equal perimeter, the one having the largest area is :
(A) Circle (B) Equilateral triangle
(C) Square (D) Regular pentagon

9-5 On a plane are two points A and B at a distance of 5 unit apart. The number of straight lines in this plane which are at distance of 2 units from A and 3 units from B, is :
(A) 1 (B) 2
(C) 3 (D) 4

9-6 In the circle shown $AB = 24$, and the perpendicular chord CD bisects AB. If DM is 4 times as long as CM then the length of BD, is :

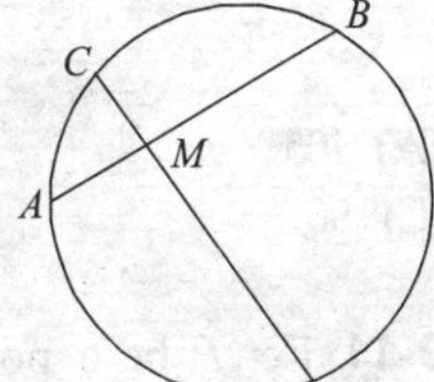

Figure 9.47

(A) $8\sqrt{5}$
(B) $12\sqrt{5}$
(C) $16\sqrt{5}$
(D) $20\sqrt{5}$

9-7 Let ΔXYZ be right angle triangle, with right angle at Z. Let A_x denotes the area of the circle with diameter YZ. Let A_y denote the area of the circle with diameter XZ and let A_z denotes the area of the circle diameter XY. Which of the following relation is true?
(A) $A_z = A_x + A_y$ (B) $A_z = A_x^2 + A_y^2$
(C) $A_z^2 = A_x^2 + A_y^2$ (D) $A_z^2 = A_x^2 - A_y^2$

9-8 In the figure-9.48, assume that the circle are mutually tangent and that the circle with centre at A has radius 1. The lines AB and AC are tangent to the circle at with centre 'O' at the points B and C respectively. If the area of the shaded region is $\pi/4$, the radius of the circle centered at O, is :

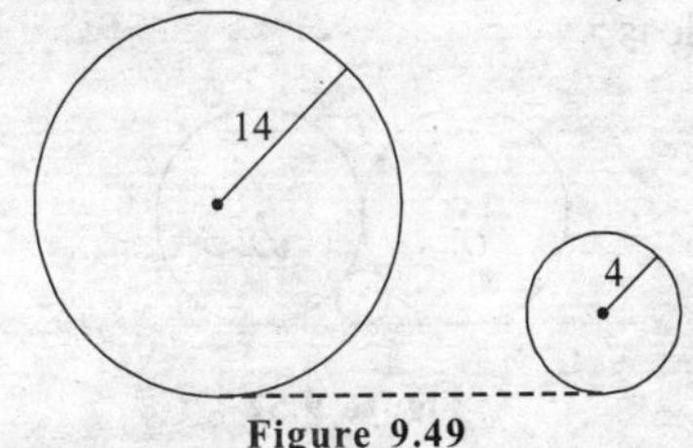

(A) $r = \sqrt{2} - 1$
(B) $r = 5$
(C) $r = 1 + \sqrt{2}$
(D) $2 + \sqrt{2}$

Figure 9.48

9-9 Two circles of radii 4 cm and 14 cm have a common external tangent of length 24 cm. The distance between the centres of these circles (in cm) is :

Figure 9.49

(A) 24 (B) 25
(C) 26 (D) 27

9-10 In a triangle ABC, $AB = 130$, $AC = 200$ and $BC = 260$. Point D is chosen on BC so that the circles inscribed in triangle ABD and ADC are tangent to AD at the same point. Length of BD is equal to :

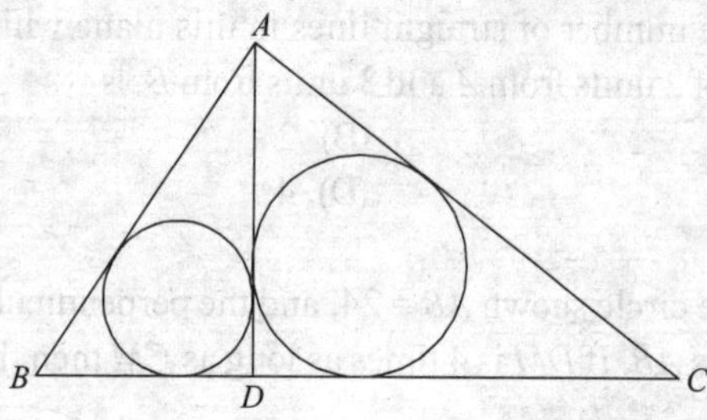

Figure 9.50

(A) 105 (B) 95
(C) 90 (D) 85

9-11 Let P be a point on the circumference of a circle. Perpendicular PA and PB are drawn to points A and B on two mutually perpendicular diameters. If $AB = 36$ cm, the diameter of the circle is :

(A) 16 cm (B) 24 cm
(C) 36 cm (D) 72 cm

9-12 Three circles are mutually tangent externally. Their centres form a triangle whose sides are of lengths 3, 4 and 5. The total area of the three circles (in square units), is :

(A) 9π (B) 16π
(C) 21π (D) 14π

9-13 The circle and the square have the same centre and the same area. If the circle has radius 1, the length of AB, is :

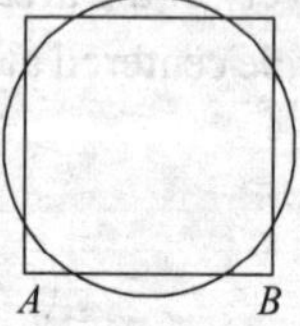

Figure 9.51

(A) $4-\pi$ (B) $4-2\sqrt{\pi}$
(C) $2-\sqrt{\pi}$ (D) $\sqrt{4-\pi}$

9-14 Circles with centre O. O' and P each tangent of the line L and also mutually tangent. If the radii of circle O and circle O' are equal and the radius of the circle P is 6, then the radius of the larger circle is :

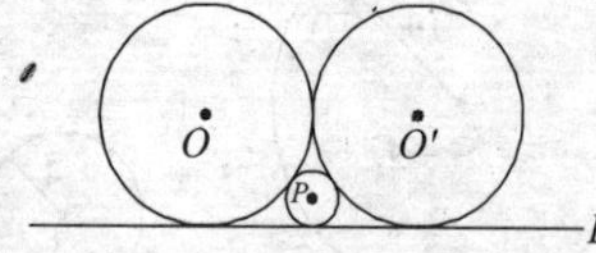

Figure 9.52

(A) 22 (B) 23
(C) 24 (D) 25

9-15 In the circle with centre 'O' as shown, chord AB and CD intersect at P and are perpendicular to each other. If $AP = 4$, $PB = 6$ and $PC = 2$, then the area of the circle is :

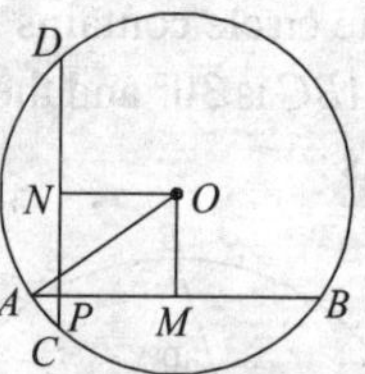

Figure 9.53

(A) 45π (B) 49π
(C) 50π (D) 41π

9-16 PQ is a chord of a circle. The tangent XR at X on the circle cuts PQ produced at R. If $XR = 12$ cm, $PQ = x$ cm. $QR = x-2$ cm, then x in cm is :

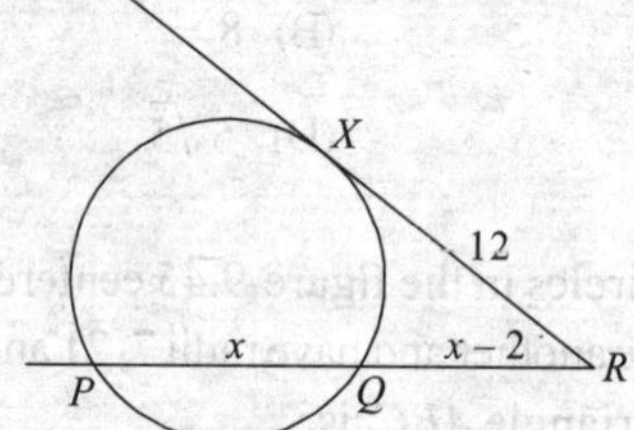

Figure 9.54

(A) 6 (B) 7
(C) 10 (D) 14

9-17 In the figure shown-9.55, the bigger circle has radius 1 unit. Therefore, the radius of smaller circle must be :

(A) $\sqrt{2}+1$

(B) $\frac{1}{2}$

(C) $\frac{1}{\sqrt{2}}$

(D) $\frac{1}{\sqrt{2}+1}$

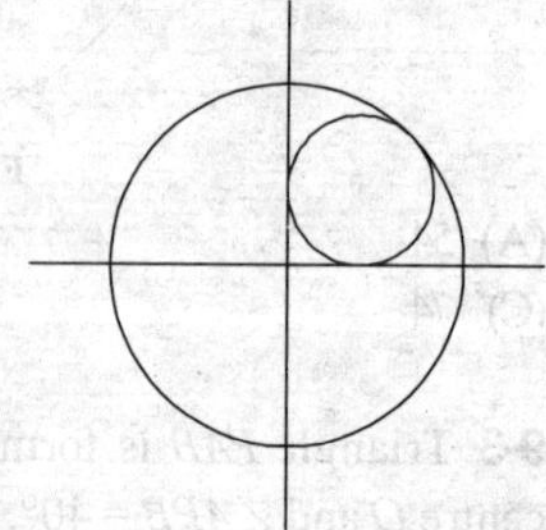

Figure 9.55

9-18 $ABCD$ is a cyclic quadrilateral inscribed in a circle with the centre O. Then $\angle OAD$ is equal to :

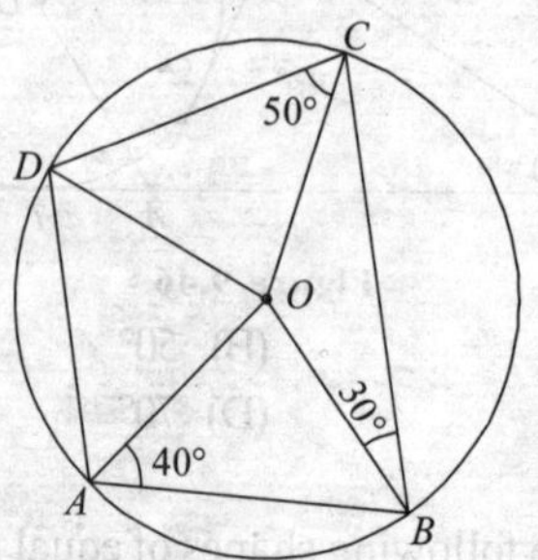

Figure 9.56

(A) 30° (B) 40°
(C) 50° (D) 60°

9-19 Point Q is the centre of a circle with a radius of 25 centimetres. A square is constructed with two vertices on the circle and the side joining the other two vertices containing the centre Q. The area of the square, in square centimetres, is :

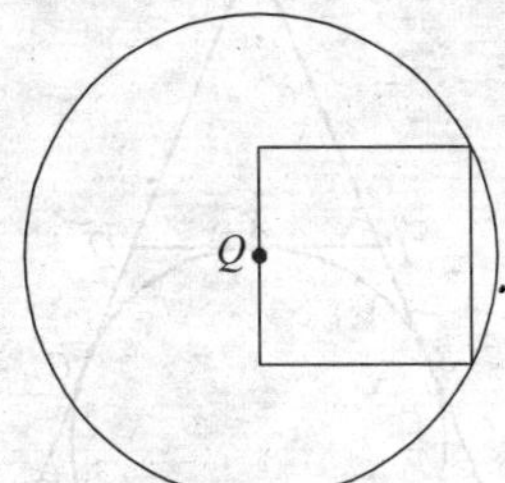

Figure 9.57

(A) 125 (B) $125\sqrt{5}$
(C) 500 (D) 250

9-20 In the diagram, the angle at A is 60° and the radius of the larger circle is 6. The radius of the smaller circle is :

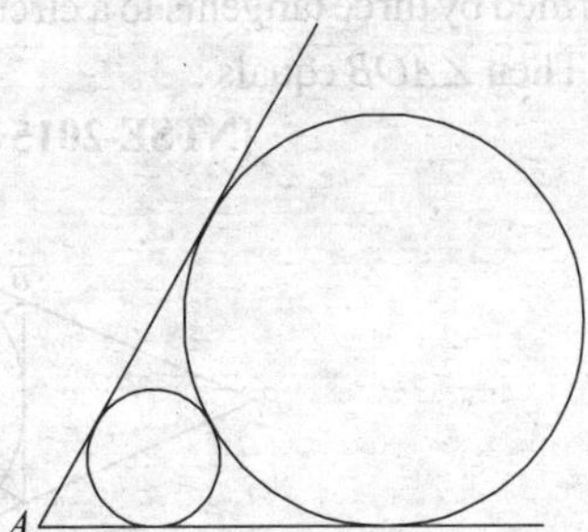

Figure 9.58

(A) 2 (B) 3
(C) $\frac{3}{2}$ (D) 4

9-21 In the given figure-9.59, $AB = 4$, $BC = 5$, $CD = 9$ and $DA = 4$, then find the area of shaded part :

(A) $36\pi - 14\sqrt{3}$
(B) $16\pi - 14\sqrt{3}$
(C) $\frac{61\pi - 42\sqrt{3}}{3}$
(D) $64\pi - 14\sqrt{3}$

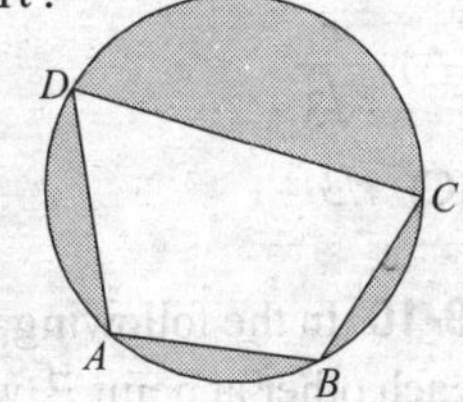

Figure 9.59

9-22 A triangle ABC is inscribed in a circle, and the bisectors of the angles meet the circumference at X, Y, Z. The angles of the triangle X, Y, Z are respectively :

(A) $90° - \frac{A}{2}, 90° - \frac{B}{2}, 90° - \frac{C}{2}$
(B) $90°, 60°, 30°$
(C) $\frac{A}{2}, \frac{B}{2}, \frac{C}{2}$
(D) $\frac{B}{2}, \frac{A}{2}, \frac{A}{2} - \frac{B}{2}$

9-23 A rectangle contains three circles, as in the diagram, all tangent to the rectangle and to each other. The height of the rectangle is 4. Determine the width of the rectangle.

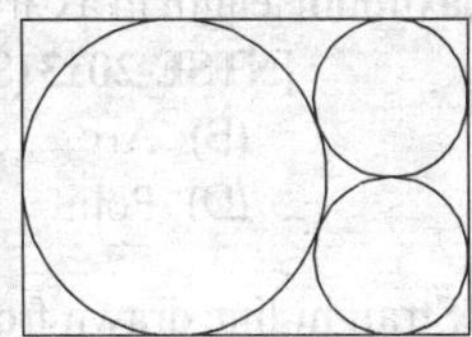

Figure 9.60

(A) $2+2\sqrt{2}$ (B) $3+2\sqrt{2}$
(C) $3-\sqrt{2}$ (D) $8-2\sqrt{2}$

9-24 A circle of radius 1 cm rolls around the inside of a regular hexagon with all sides of length 4 cm, so that the circle is always touching at least one of the hexagon walls. (See the diagram.) The distance measured in centimetres that the centre of the circle travels before the circle returns to where it began is :

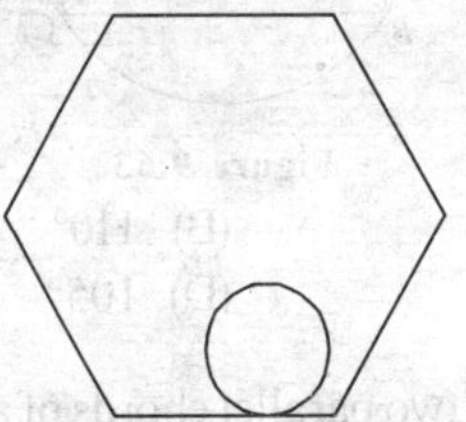

Figure 9.61

(A) $12\sqrt{3}$ (B) 18
(C) $42-12\sqrt{3}$ (D) $24-4\sqrt{3}$

9-25 Three congruent circles are tangent to one another as shown in figure-9.62. Circle A is tangent to both the x-axis and the y-axis. Circle B is tangent to the x-axis. The centre of circle A has coordinates (2, 2). What are the coordinates of the centres of circles B and C?

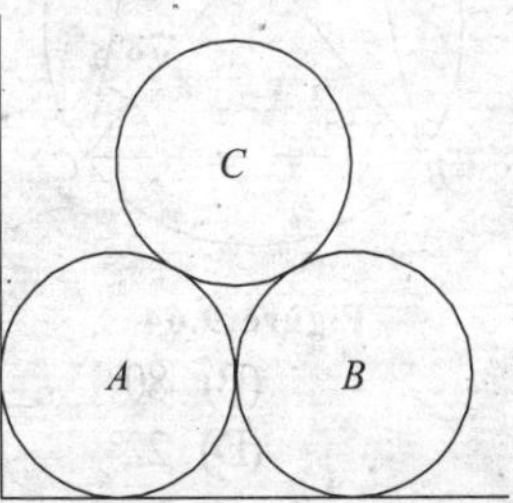

Figure 9.62

(A) (6, 2), (4, 6) respectively (B) (4, 6), (6, 2) respectively
(C) (2, 2), (2, 4) respectively (D) None of these

* * * * *

PRACTICE EXERCISE - 9.3

9-1 The Chord of maximum length in a Circle is called : **[NTSE-2013 (Stage-I) Rajasthan]**

(A) Radius (B) Arc
(C) Diameter (D) Point

9-2 The number of Straight line drawn from one point to any other point are : **[NTSE-2013 (Stage-I) Rajasthan]**

(A) 4 (B) 3
(C) 2 (D) 1

9-3 In figure-9.63, A, B, C and D are four points on a circle. AC and BD interest at a point E such that $\angle BEC = 125°$ and $\angle ECD = 30°$. Then $\angle BAC =$ **[NTSE-2014 (Stage-I) Rajasthan]**

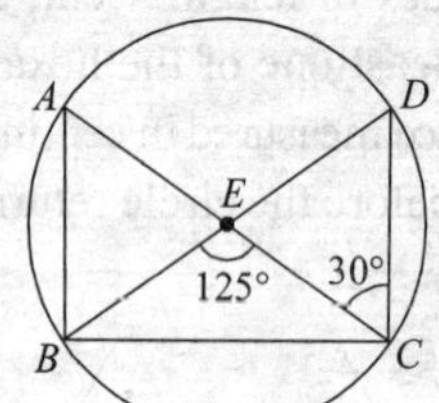

Figure 9.63

(A) 95° (B) 110°
(C) 85° (D) 105°

9-4 The lengths of two parallel chords of a circle are 6 cm and 8 cm. If the smaller chord is at distance 4 cm from the centre, then the distance of the other chord from the centre is : **[NTSE-2015 (Stage-I) Rajasthan]**

(A) 5 cm (B) 4 cm
(C) 3 cm (D) 2 cm

9-5 In the given figure-9.64, $\angle DBC = 22°$ and $\angle DCB = 78°$ then $\angle BAC$ is equal to : **[NTSE-2015 (Stage-I) Rajasthan]**

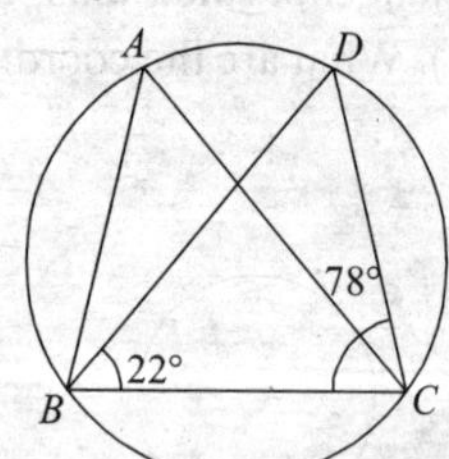

Figure 9.64

(A) 90° (B) 80°
(C) 78° (D) 22°

9-6 ABC is a right angled triangle, having the right angle at B, such that $BC = 6$ cm and $AB = 8$ cm. Then the radius of incircle is equal to : **[NTSE-2015 (Stage-I) Chandigarh]**

(A) 4 cm (B) 3 cm
(C) 2 cm (D) 1 cm

9-7 If AB, AC, PQ are tangents in the figure-9.65 and $AB = 5$cm then perimeter of ΔAPQ is : **[NTSE-2015 (Stage-I) Delhi]**

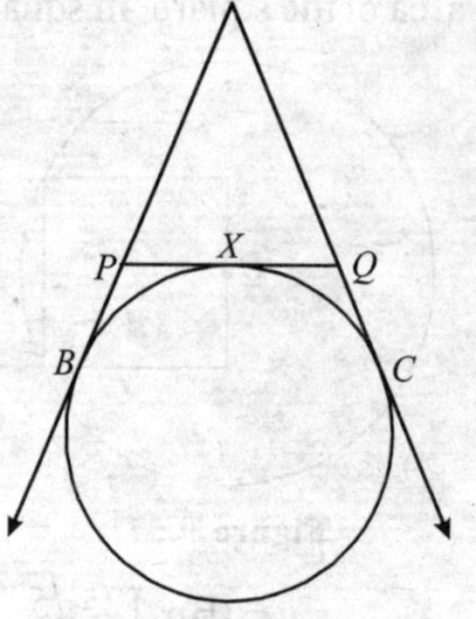

Figure 9.65

(A) 5 cm (B) 10 cm
(C) 12 cm (D) 15 cm

9-8 ΔPAB is formed by three tangents to a circle with centre O. If $\angle APB = 40°$. Then $\angle AOB$ equals : **[NTSE-2015 (Stage-I) Delhi]**

(A) 45°

(B) 55°

(C) 60°

(D) 70°

Figure 9.66

9-9 If two equal circles of radius r passes through centre of the other, then the length of their common chord is : **[NTSE-2015 (Stage-I) UP]**

(A) $\frac{r}{\sqrt{3}}$ (B) $r\sqrt{3}$
(C) $r/3$ (D) $r\sqrt{2}$

9-10 In the following figure-9.67 secants QS and TR intersect each other at point P, which is outside the circle. O is the point of intersection of Chords SR and TQ. If $OS = 5$ cm, $OT = 10$ cm, $TR = 12$ cm, $PR = 8$ cm, then find (PQ) : **[NTSE-2015 (Stage-I) Maharashtra]**

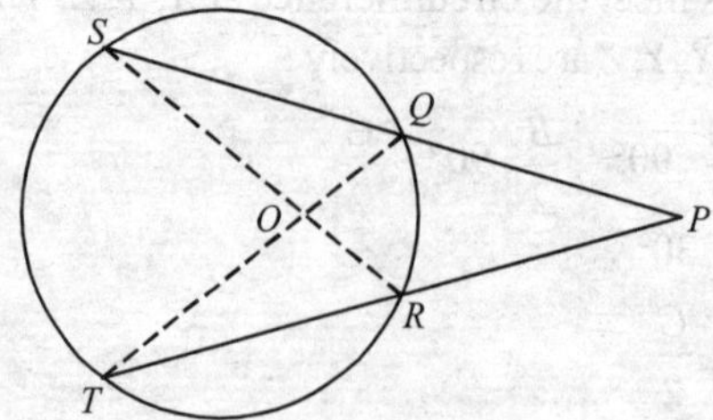

Figure 9.67

(A) 6 cm (B) 10 cm
(C) 12 cm (D) 16 cm

9-11 In the given figure-9.68 $PB = 24$ cm, $OP = 25$ cm, PA and PB are tangents of the circle. The length of PA and OB will be : **[NTSE-2015 (Stage-I) Chhatisgarh]**

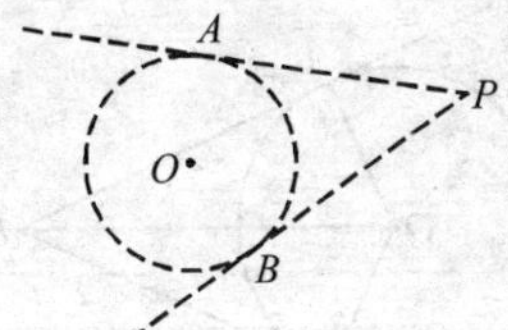

Figure 9.68

(A) 24 cm, 7 cm (B) 25 cm, 7 cm
(C) 24 cm, 13 cm (D) 25 cm, 12 cm

9-12 AB and CD are two chords of a circle which intersect each other externally at P. If $AB = 4$ cm, $BP = 5$ cm, $PD = 3$ cm, then the length of CD is : **[NTSE-2015 (Stage-I) Chennai]**

(A) 10 cm (B) 12 cm
(C) 8 cm (D) 11 cm

9-13 Equilateral triangle ABC is inscribed in a circle. If side of the triangle = 24 cm, then the radius is : **[NTSE-2015 (Stage-I) Chennai]**

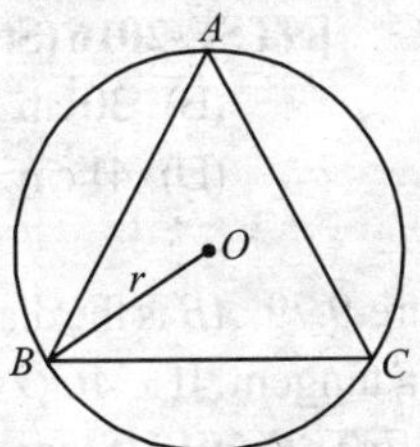

Figure 9.69

(A) $6\sqrt{3}$ cm (B) $12\sqrt{3}$ cm
(C) $8\sqrt{3}$ cm (D) 6 cm

9-14 If tangents PA and PB from a point P to a circle with centre O are inclined to each other at an angle of 110°, then then $\angle POA$ is equal to : **[NTSE-2016 (Stage-I) Rajasthan]**

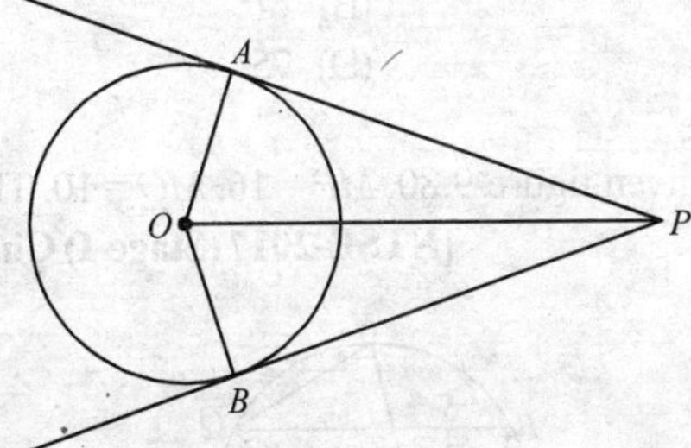

Figure 9.70

(A) 65° (B) 55°
(C) 45° (D) 35°

9-15 In the following figure-9.71 O is the centre of circle and $\angle ACB = x°$, $\angle OBA = y°$ then the value of $x° + y°$ is : **[NTSE-2016 (Stage-I) Rajasthan]**

(A) 90°

(B) 120°

(C) 150°

(D) 180°

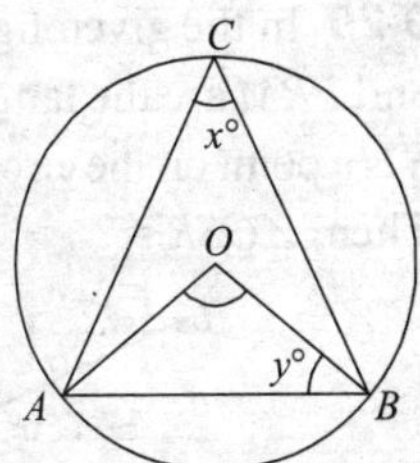

Figure 9.71

9-16 PAB, PCD are two secants. $AB = 9$ cm, $PC = 8$ cm and $CD = 10$ cm, then the length of tangent from P to the circle, will be : **[NTSE-2016 (Stage-I) Telangana]**

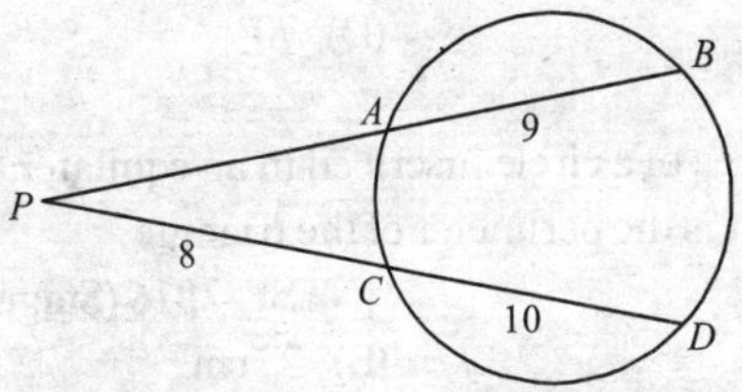

Figure 9.72

(A) 7 cm (B) 10 cm
(C) 14 cm (D) 12 cm

9-17 In the figure-9.73 O is the center of the circle, CAB is a secant, $CO = 41$ cm, $CA = 28$ cm and $OB = 15$. $OE \perp AB$, then AE = ... **[NTSE-2016 (Stage-I) Andhara Pradesh]**

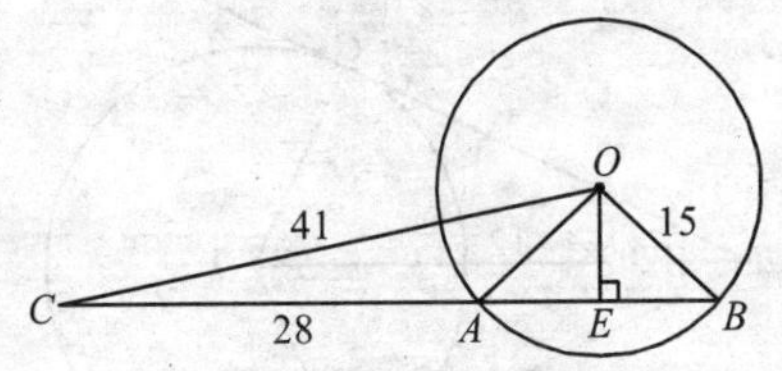

Figure 9.73

(A) 8 cm (B) 10 cm
(C) 12 cm (D) 15 cm

9-18 If tangents PA and PB drawn from a point P to a circle with centre O are inclined to each other at angle of 80°, then $\angle POA$ is equal to : **[NTSE-2016 (Stage-I) Chandigarh]**

(A) 50° (B) 60°
(C) 70° (D) 80°

9-19 In the diagram, PQ and QR are tangents to the circle centre O, at P and R respectively. Find the value of x : **[NTSE-2016 (Stage-I) Chandigarh]**

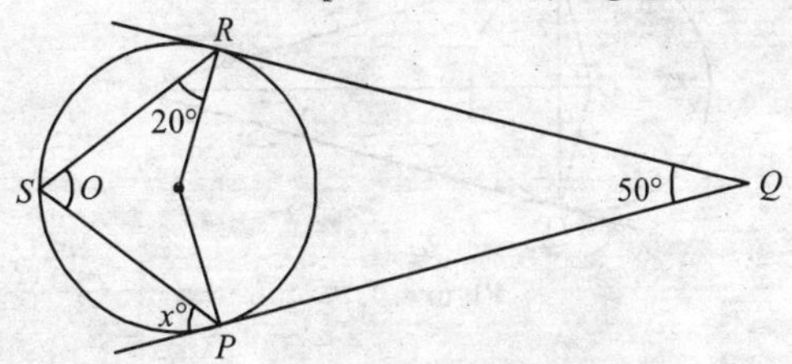

Figure 9.74

(A) 25 (B) 35
(C) 45 (D) 55

9-20 In the given figure-9.75, O is the centre of a circle. PQL and PRM are the tangents at the points Q & R respectively and S is a point on the circle such that $\angle SQL = 50°$ and $\angle SRM = 60°$. Then, $\angle QSR = ?$ **[NTSE-2016 (Stage-I) Jharkhand]**

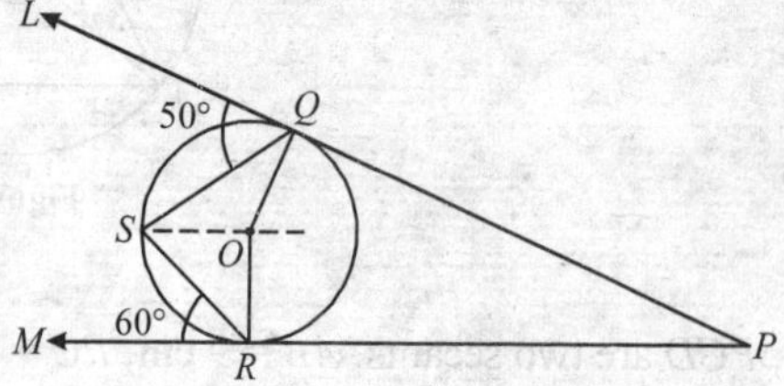

Figure 9.75

(A) 40° (B) 50°
(C) 60° (D) 70°

9-21 The area of a circle inscribed in an equilateral triangle is 48π sq. What is the perimeter of the triangle? **[NTSE-2016 (Stage-I) Odisha]**

(A) 24 cm (B) 27 cm
(C) 36 cm (D) 72 cm

9-22 Two tangent segments $\overline{BC}$ and $\overline{BD}$ are drawn to a circle with centre O. If $m\angle CBD = 120°$ and $OB = 12$ cm, then what is the length of $\overline{CD}$? **[NTSE-2016 (Stage-I) Odisha]**

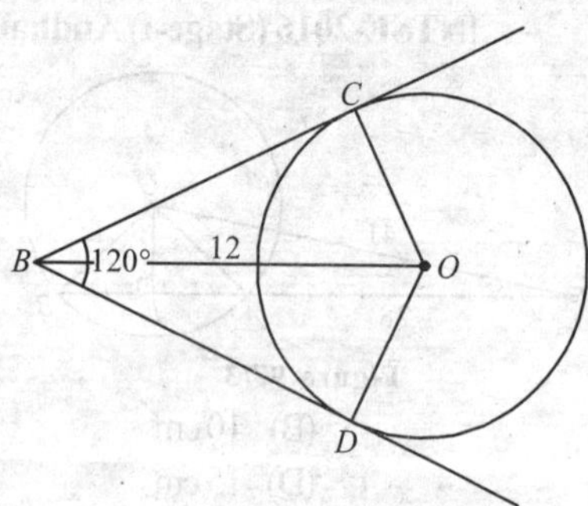

Figure 9.76

(A) $6\sqrt{3}$ cm (B) $12\sqrt{3}$ cm
(C) 6 cm (D) 12 cm

9-23 TP and TQ are tangents drawn to a circle with centre 'O' $\angle OPQ = 2a$, measure of $\angle PTO$ is : **[NTSE-2016 (Stage-I) Karnatka]**

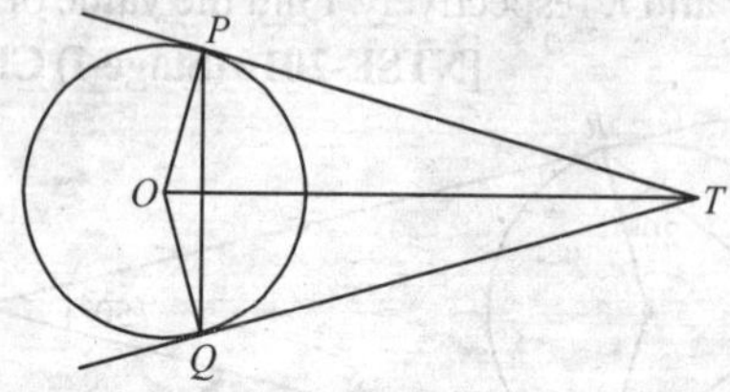

Figure 9.77

(A) $\frac{1}{2}a$ (B) a
(C) $2a$ (D) $4a$

9-24 In the given figure-9.78 O is the center of circle and PA, PB are its tangents. If $PA = 8$ cm. and $PO = 10$cm then what is the value of OB ? **[NTSE-2016 (Stage-I) Chhatisgarh]**

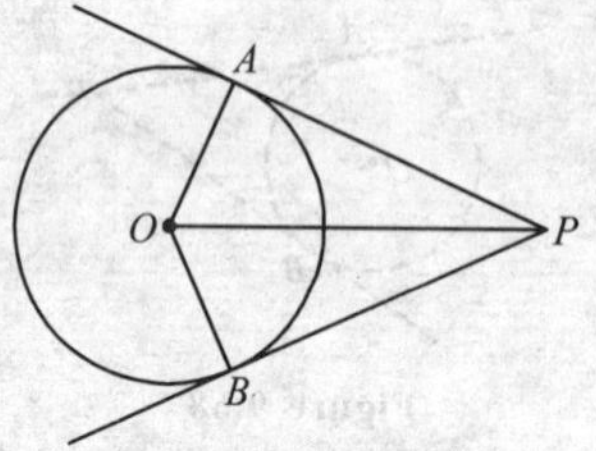

Figure 9.78

(A) 4 cm (B) 3 cm
(C) 5 cm (D) 6 cm

9-25 In ΔABC, $m\angle BAC = 140°$, 'P' is the centre of the circumcircle of ΔABC. Find $m\angle PBC$: **[NTSE-2016 (Stage-I) Chhatisgarh]**

(A) 40° (B) 50°
(C) 80° (D) 100°

9-26 The incircle of ΔABC touches the sides AB, BC and AC in the point P, Q and R respectively. If $AP = 7$ cm, $BC = 13$ cm, find the perimeter of ΔABC : **[NTSE-2016 (Stage-I) Chhatisgarh]**

(A) 27 cm (B) 30 cm
(C) 40 cm (D) 41 cm

9-27 In the given figure-9.79, AB is the diameter of a circle with O as center and AT is a tangent. If $\angle AOQ = 58°$, then the value of $\angle ATQ$ is : **[NTSE-2017 (Stage-I) Andhra Pradesh]**

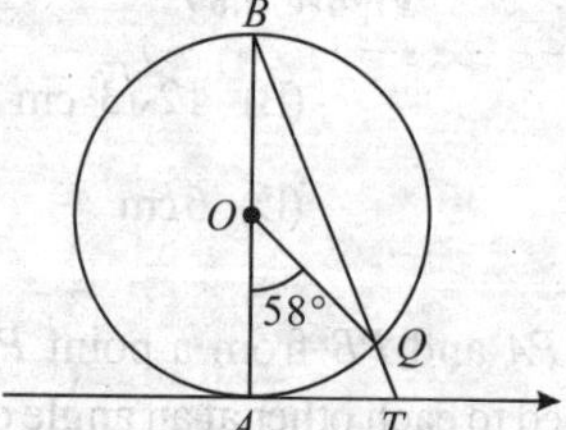

Figure 9.79

(A) 52° (B) 61°
(C) 46° (D) 75°

9-28 In the given figure-9.80, $MP = 16$, $MQ = 10$. The value of $MO \times MS$ is ... **[NTSE-2017 (Stage-I) Chandigarh]**

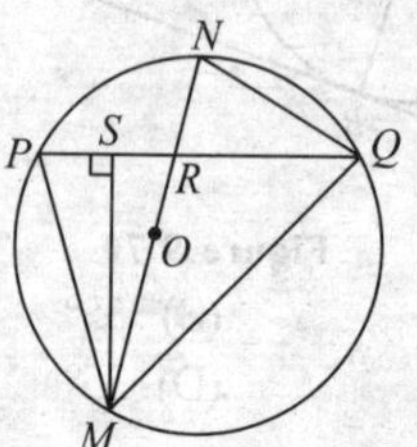

Figure 9.80

(A) 160 (B) 100
(C) 120 (D) 80

9-29 In the given figures-9.81, the value of $\angle PXR$ is : **[NTSE-2017 (Stage-I) Chandigarh]**

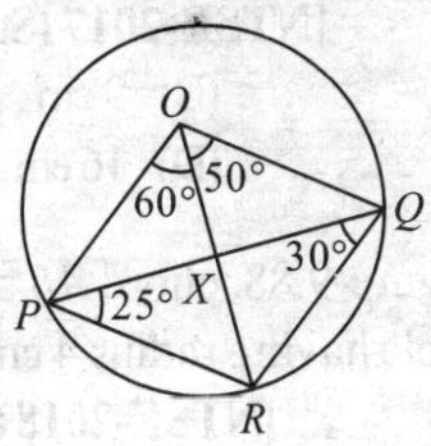

Figure 9.81

(A) 85° (B) 100°
(C) 95° (D) 120°

9-30 a, b and c are the sides of a right angled triangle and a circle of radius r touches the sides of the triangle. If c is the hypotenuse of the triangle, then the value of r is : **[NTSE-2017 (Stage-I) Haryana]**

(A) $\frac{a+b+c}{2}$ (B) $\frac{a+b-c}{3}$
(C) $\frac{a+b+c}{3}$ (D) $\frac{a+b-c}{2}$

9-31 Angles A, B, C and D of a cyclic quadrilateral $ABCD$ are in the ratio 3 : 3 : 2 : 2 respectively. If $AB = 5$ cm, $BC = 3.5$ cm and $CD = 8$ cm, then the length of AD is : **[NTSE-2017 (Stage-I) Haryana]**

(A) 5 cm (B) 3.5 cm
(C) 8 cm (D) 4 cm

9-32 In the given figure-9.82, PM is a tangent to the circle and $PA = AM$ then, **[NTSE-2017 (Stage-I) Karnataka]**

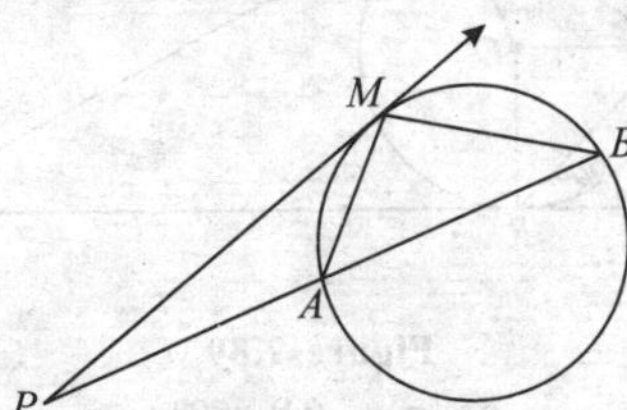

Figure 9.82

(a) ΔPMB is isosceles (b) $PA \times PB = MB^2$
(A) (a) is true, but (b) is false (B) (b) is true, but (a) is false
(C) Both (a) and (b) are false (D) Both (a) and (b) are true

9-33 Length of Chord which is at a distance of 3 cm from the centre of circle of radius 5 cm is : **[NTSE-2017 (Stage-I) Madhya Pradesh]**

(A) 4 cm (B) 6 cm
(C) 8 cm (D) 10 cm

9-34 The sum of pair of opposite angles of a cyclic quadrilateral is : **[NTSE-2017 (Stage-I) Madhya Pradesh]**

(A) 90° (B) 180°
(C) 270° (D) 360°

9-35 In the adjoining figure-9.83 'O' is the center of the circle $AB = BC$, $m\angle AOD = x$ and $m\angle ACB = y$ then find $\frac{x}{y}$: **[NTSE-2017 (Stage-I) Maharashtra]**

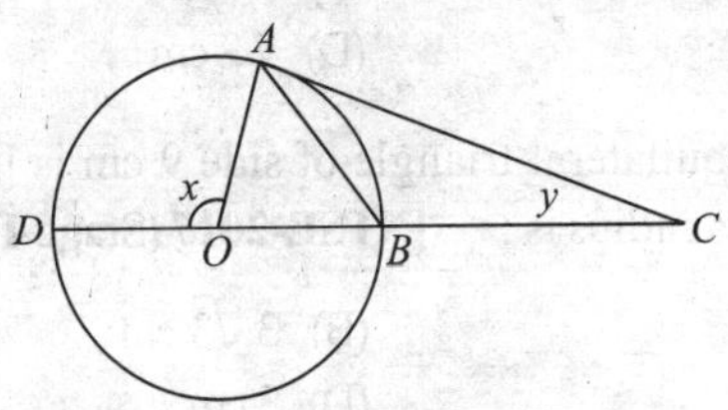

Figure 9.83

(A) $\frac{1}{2}$ (B) 2
(C) 4 (D) $\frac{1}{4}$

9-36 In the adjoining figure-9.84 if $AB = 16$ and $CD = 40$ then find the ratio of $ar(\Delta OCD)$: $ar(\Delta OAB)$: **[NTSE-2017 (Stage-I) Maharashtra]**

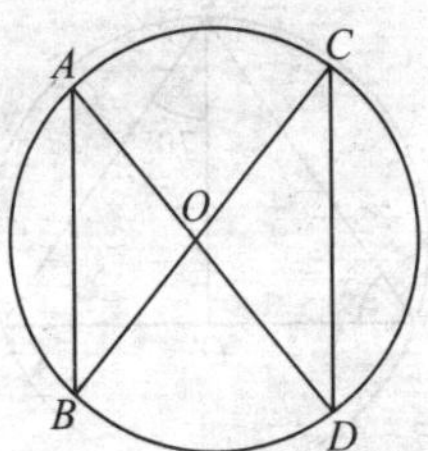

Figure 9.84

(A) $\frac{5}{2}$ (B) $\frac{2}{9}$
(C) $\frac{25}{4}$ (D) $\frac{4}{25}$

9-37 If the distance between the points $(4, q)$ and $(1, 0)$ is 5 units then the value of q is : **[NTSE-2017 (Stage-I) Punjab]**

(A) 4 (B) –4
(C) ±4 (D) 0

9-38 In the given figure-9.85 $ABCD$ is a cyclic quadrilateral. If $\angle BAC = 60°$, $\angle BCA = 20°$ then find the value of $\angle ADC$: **[NTSE-2017 (Stage-I) Punjab]**

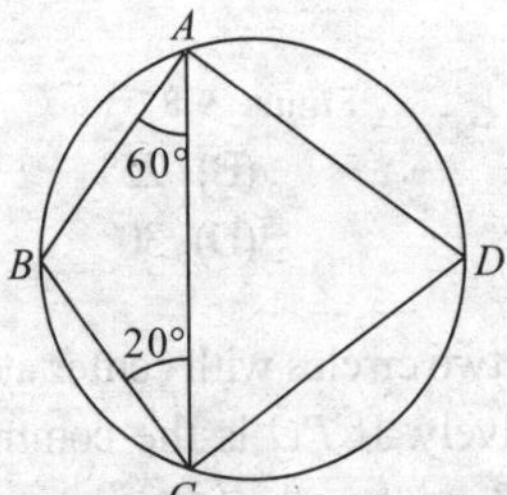

Figure 9.85

(A) 15° (B) 50°
(C) 80° (D) 40°

9-39 In a circle of 10 cm radius, two chords $AB = AC = 12$ cm, then the length of the chord BC is : **[NTSE-2017 (Stage-I) Rajasthan]**

(A) 12 cm (B) 9.6 cm
(C) 19.2 cm (D) 7.2 cm

9-40 If an equilateral triangle of side 9 cm is inscribed in a circle, then its radius is : **[NTSE-2017 (Stage-I) Tamilnadu]**

(A) $4.5\sqrt{3}$ (B) $3\sqrt{3}$ cm
(C) 6 cm (D) 3 cm

9-41 $ABCD$ is a cyclic quadrilateral such that AB is a diameter of the circle circumscribing it and $\angle ADC = 140°$, then $\angle BAC$ is : **[NTSE-2017 (Stage-I) Tamilnadu**

(A) 80° (B) 50°
(C) 40° (D) 30°

9-42 If in the given figure-9.86 O is the centre of the circle, then the value of x is : **[NTSE-2017 (Stage-I) Uttar Pradesh]**

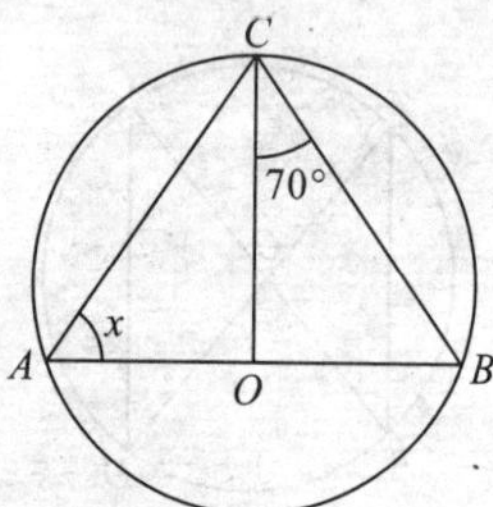

Figure 9.86

(A) 90° (B) 50°
(C) 20° (D) 40°

9-43 In the given figure-9.87 the value of $x° + y°$ will be : **[NTSE-2017 (Stage-I) Uttrakhand]**

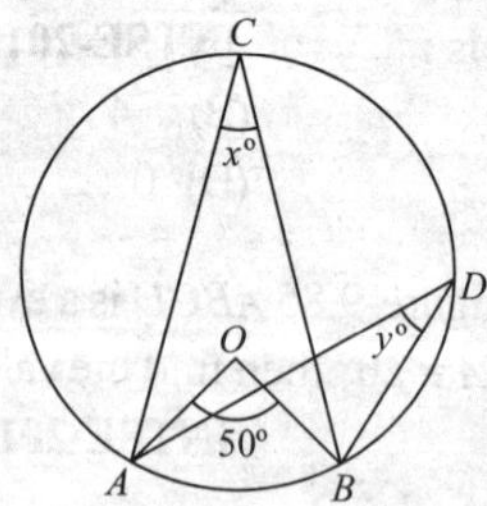

Figure 9.87

(A) 60° (B) 25°
(C) 50° (D) 30°

9-44 The radii of two circles with center at A and B are 11 cm and 6 cm respectively. If PQ is the common tangent of the circles and $AB = 13$ cm, length of PQ is : **[NTSE-2017 (Stage-I) West Bengal]**

(A) 13 cm (B) 12 cm
(C) 17 cm (D) 8.5 cm

9-45 The chords PQ and RS of a circle are extended to meet at the point O. If $PQ = 6$ cm, $OQ = 8$ cm, $OS = 7$ cm, then $RS =$: **[NTSE-2017 (Stage-I) West Bengal]**

(A) 12 cm (B) 9 cm
(C) 10 cm (D) 16 cm

9-46 In the given figure-9.88, chord AB subtends an angle 90° at center O of the circle having radius 4 cm. Area of the shaded region will be : **[NTSE-2018 (Stage-I) Rajasthan]**

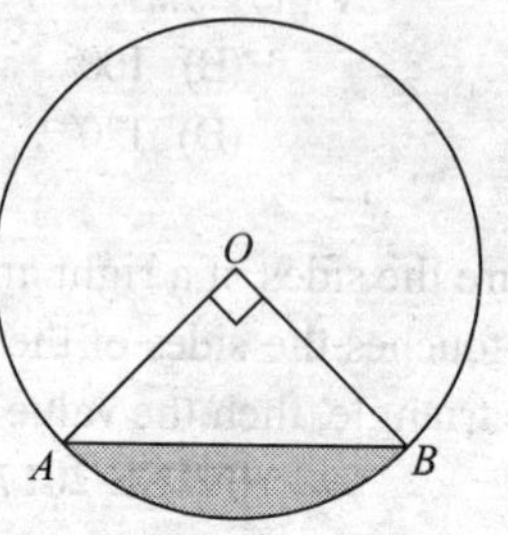

Figure 9.88

(A) $(4\pi - 2)$ cm^2 (B) $4(\pi - 2)$ cm^2
(C) $(\pi - 8)$ cm^2 (D) $(\pi - 2)$ cm^2

9-47 In the adjoining figure-9.89, O is the centre of a circle; PQL and PRM are the tangents at the points Q and R respectively and S is a point on the circle such that $\angle SQL = 50°$ and $\angle SRM = 60°$ then the value of $\angle QSR$ is : **[NTSE-2018 (Stage-I) Bihar]**

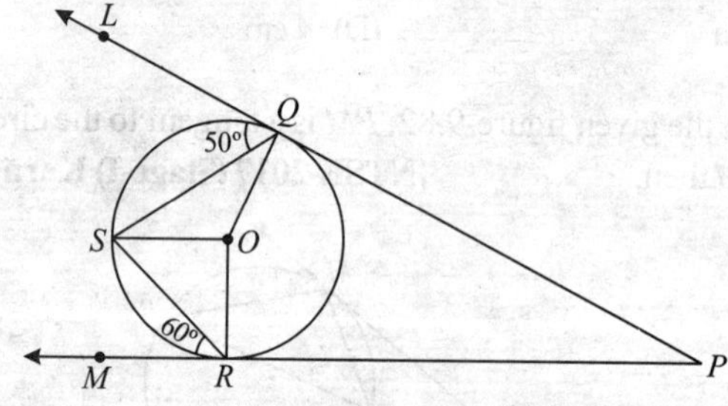

Figure 9.89

(A) 40° (B) 50°
(C) 60° (D) 70°

9-48 O is the center of a circle and $\angle XOY = 100°$. Find the measure of $\angle XZP$: **[NTSE-2018 (Stage-I) Chandigarh]**

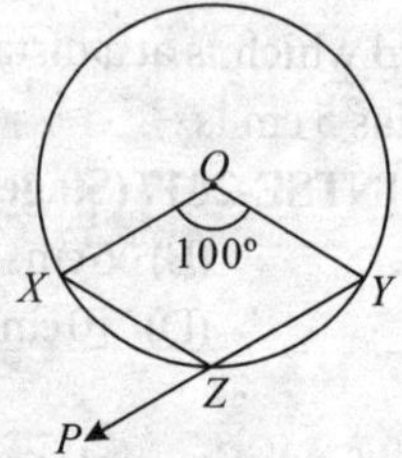

Figure 9.90

(A) 50° (B) 100°
(C) 150° (D) 80°

9-49 In the given figure-9.91, a circle is centered at O. APB is a tangent at a point P, if $\angle QPB = 50^\circ$, then the measurement of $\angle POQ$ will be : **[NTSE-2018 (Stage-I) Chhattisgarh]**

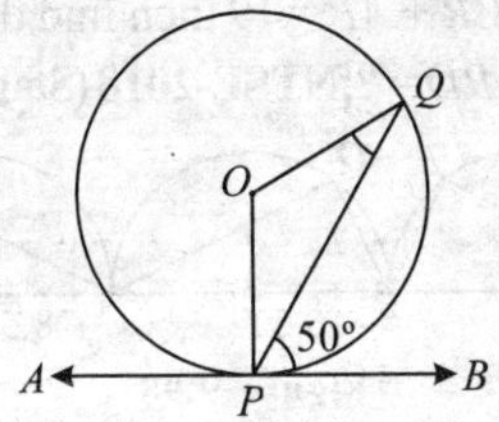

Figure 9.91

(A) 100° (B) 120°
(C) 140° (D) 150°

9-50 In a right angled triangle ABC, $AB = 3$ cm, $BC = 4$ cm and $\angle B = 90^\circ$. A circumcircle is constructed. Radius of circumcircle will be : **[NTSE-2018 (Stage-I) Chhattisgarh]**

(A) 3 cm (B) 4 cm
(C) 5 cm (D) 2.5 cm

9-51 In the given figure-9.92 O is the center of circle. If $AC = 8$cm, $BC = 6$cm. Then the area of the shaded part will be ($\pi = 3.14$) **[NTSE-2018 (Stage-I) Chhattisgarh]**

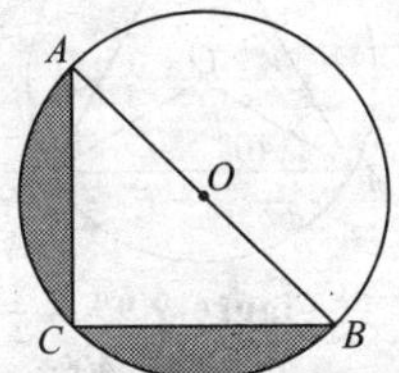

Figure 9.92

(A) 24 cm^2 (B) 78.50 cm^2
(C) 39.25 cm^2 (D) 15.25 cm^2

9-52 A chord of length 24 cm is situated 5 cm from the center of a circle. The diameter of the circle will be : **[NTSE-2018 (Stage-I) Chhattisgarh]**

(A) 24 cm (B) 29 cm
(C) 26 cm (D) 13 cm

9-53 There circles touch each other externally and all the three touch a line. If two of them are equal and radius of third circle is 4 cm, then radius of equal circles is : **[NTSE-2018 (Stage-I) Delhi]**

(A) 12 cm (B) 8 cm
(C) 16 cm (D) 20 cm

9-54 $PQRS$ is a square of side 6 cm each and T is mid point of QR. What is the radius of circle inscibed in ΔTSR : **[NTSE-2018 (Stage-I) Delhi]**

(A) $\dfrac{3}{3-\sqrt{5}}$ (B) $\dfrac{6}{3+\sqrt{5}}$
(C) $\dfrac{2}{3+\sqrt{5}}$ (D) $3+\sqrt{5}$

9-55 A chord of $\odot(O, 5)$ touches $\odot(O, 3)$. Therefore, the length of the chord = ____ : **[NTSE-2018 (Stage-I) Gujarat]**

(A) 8 (B) 10
(C) 7 (D) 6

9-56 In figure-9.93, PQ is a chord of a circle with center O PT is its tangent at P. If $\angle QPT = 60^\circ$, then $\angle PRQ$ is : **[NTSE-2018 (Stage-I) Haryana]**

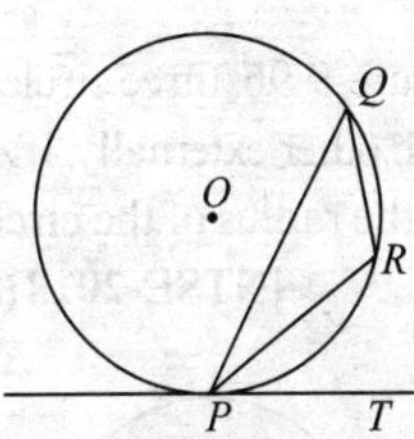

Figure 9.93

(A) 105° (B) 115°
(C) 120° (D) 130°

9-57 In the figure-9.94, points P, Q, R and S lie on a circle. Then the value of x and y are respectively : **[NTSE-2018 (Stage-I) Haryana]**

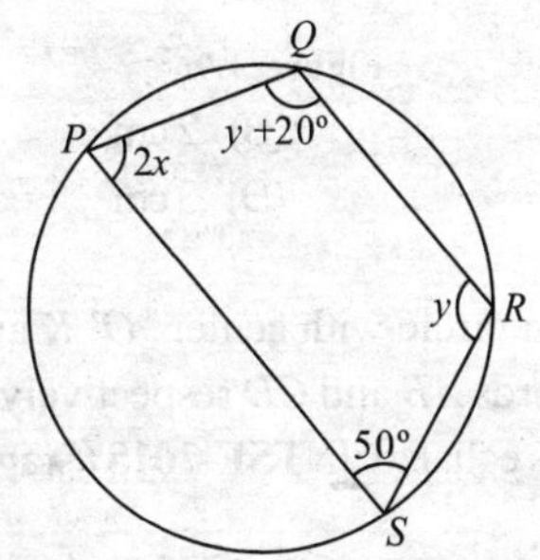

Figure 9.94

(A) 40° and 100° (B) 35° and 110°
(C) 50° and 80° (D) 30° and 120°

9-58 In the figure-9.95 below, area of triangle ΔOAB is 72 sq. units and area of triangle ΔODC is 288 sq. Then length of BC and AD are : **[NTSE-2018 (Stage-I) Himachal Pradesh]**

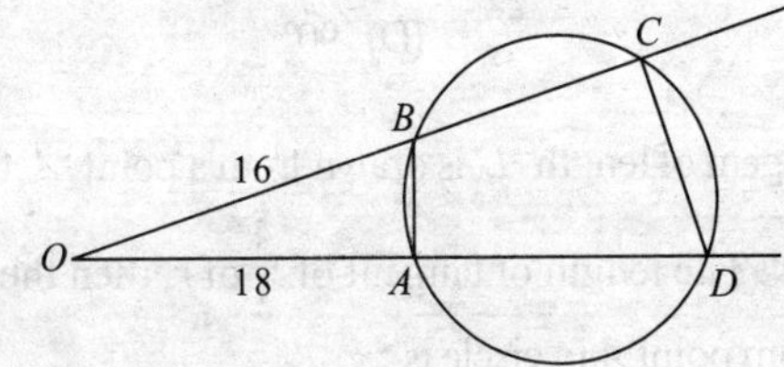

Figure 9.95

(A) $BC = 15$ $AD = 16$
(B) $BC = 22$ $AD = 12$
(C) $BC = 18$ $AD = 16$
(D) $BC = 20$ $AD = 14$

9-59 PQ is a chord of length 8cm of a circle of radius 5 cm. The tangent at P & Q interest at a point T. Find the length TP.
[NTSE-2018 (Stage-I) Himachal Pradesh]

(A) $\frac{10}{3}$ cm (B) $\frac{20}{3}$ cm
(C) 10 cm (D) $\frac{40}{3}$ cm

9-60 In the given figure-9.96, three circles with centers A, B, C respectively touch each other externally. If $AB = 5$ cm, $BC = 7$ cm and $CA = 6$ cm, then the radius of the circle with A :
[NTSE-2018 (Stage-I) Jharkhand]

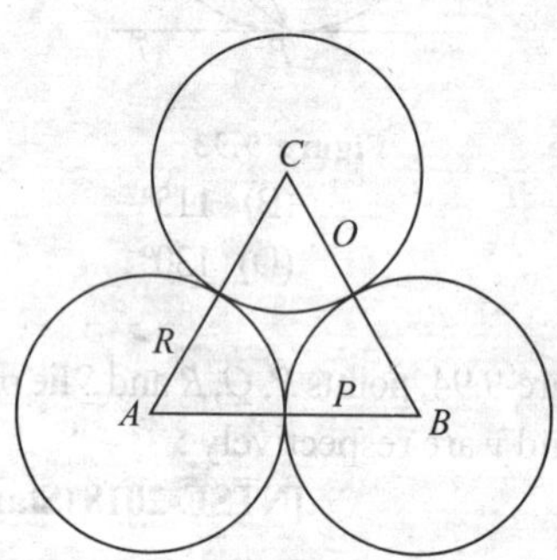

Figure 9.96

(A) 1.5 cm (B) 2 cm
(C) 2.5 cm (D) 3 cm

9-61 In the given circle with center 'O' K and L are the mid point of equal chords AB and CD respectively. $OLK = 25°$ then the value of LKB is equal to : **[NTSE-2018 (Stage-I) Karnataka]**

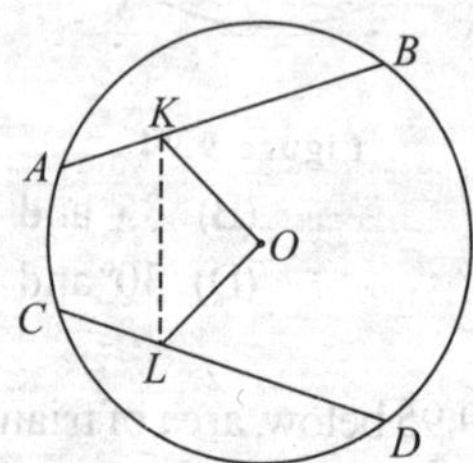

Figure 9.97

(A) 125° (B) 115°
(C) 105° (D) 90°

9-62 A tangent of length 'L' is drawn from a point 'A' to a circle of radius 'r'. The length of tangent of $\frac{4}{3}$ of r, then the shortest distance from point A to circle is :
[NTSE-2018 (Stage-I) Karnataka]

(A) $\frac{r}{2}$ (B) $\frac{2r}{3}$
(C) $\frac{L}{2}$ (D) $\frac{2L}{2}$

9-63 In the figure-9.98, semi-circles are drawn whose center are X, Y, Z respectively. Points (X, Y, Z) are collinear points $(X- Y- Z)$ $AX = 2.5$, $BY = 6.5$, $CZ = 8.5$ and $AP + QC = 16$, $QC + CR = 27$ and $CR + AP = 19$ then find the value of $AP + PB + BQ + QC + CR + RD = ?$ **[NTSE-2018 (Stage-I) Maharashtra]**

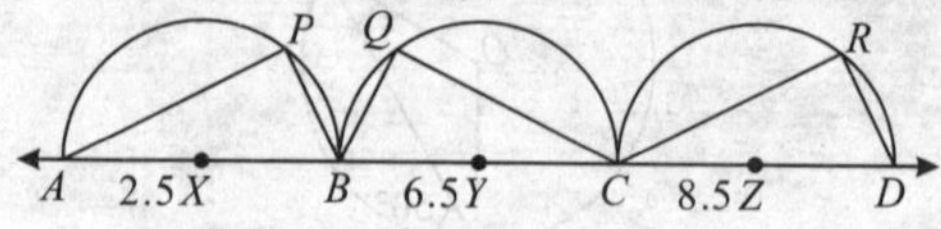

Figure 9.98

(A) 37 (B) 41
(C) 53 (D) 47

9-64 The points A, B and C be on a circle in such a way that $\angle ABC = 52°$ and $\angle ACB = 78°$. The measure of the angle subtended at the center by the arc BC will be :
[NTSE-2018 (Stage-I) Telangana]

(A) 26° (B) 50°
(C) 100° (D) 115°

9-65 If figure-9.99 if $\angle OAB = 40°$ then $\angle ACB$ is equal to :
[NTSE-2018 (Stage-I) Uttarakhandh]

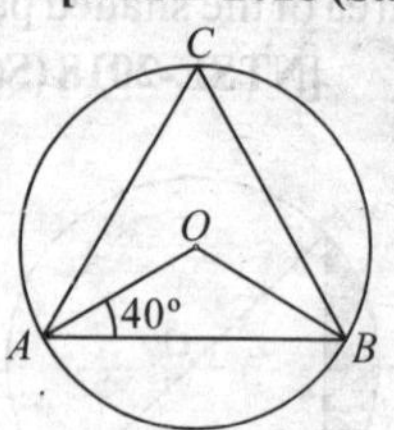

Figure 9.99

(A) 50° (B) 40°
(C) 60° (D) 70°

9-66 Let C and A be the circumference and the area of a circle respectively. If $x\,C$ is the circumference of another circle whose area is $2A$, then x equals : **[NTSE-2012 (Stage-II)]**

(A) $2\sqrt{2}$ (B) 2
(C) $\sqrt{2}$ (D) $\frac{1}{2}$

9-67 C_1 and C_2 are two circles in a plane. If N is the total number of common tangents, then which of the following is wrong ? **[NTSE-2014 (Stage-II)]**

(A) $N = 2$ when C_1 and C_2 intersect but do not touch
(B) $N = 4$ when C_1 and C_2 are disjoint
(C) When C_1 and C_2 touch then N must be 3
(D) N can never be more than 4

9-68 In ΔABC, angle B is obtuse. The smallest circle which covers the triangle is the : **[NTSE-2014 (Stage-II)]**

(A) Circumcircle
(B) Circle with AB as diameter
(C) Circle with BC as diameter
(D) Circle with AC as diameter

9-69 ABC is a triangle in which $AB = 4$ cm, $BC = 5$ cm and $AC = 6$ cm. A circle is drawn to touch side BC at P, side AB extended at Q and side AC extended at R. The, AQ equals : **[NTSE-2015 (Stage-II)]**

(A) 7.0 cm (B) 7.5 cm
(C) 6.5 cm (D) 15.0 cm

9-70 Two circles with centres P and R touch each other externally at O. A line passing through O cuts the circles at T and S respectively. Then : **[NTSE-2015 (Stage-II)]**

(A) PT and RS are of equal length
(B) PT and RS are perpendicular to each other
(C) PT and RS are intersecting
(D) PT and RS are parallel

9-71 Three circles with radii R_1, R_2 and r touch each other externally as shown in the adjoining figure-9.100. If PQ is their common tangent and $R_1 > R_2$, then which of the following relations is correct ? **[NTSE-2015 (Stage-II)]**

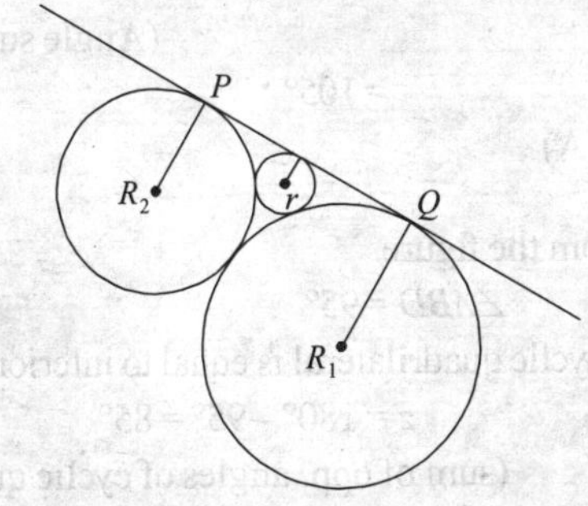

Figure 9.100

(A) $R_1 - R_2 = r$ (B) $R_1 + R_2 = 2r$

(C) $\frac{1}{R_1} + \frac{1}{R_2} = \frac{1}{r}$ (D) $\frac{1}{\sqrt{R_1}} + \frac{1}{\sqrt{R_2}} = \frac{1}{\sqrt{r}}$

9-72 Three circular wires are attached in series such that, if one wire is rotated, other two also get rotated. If the diameter of a wire is 4/5 times that of immediate left wire and the left most wire rotates at the speed of 32 revolutions per minute, then the number of revolutions made by right most wire per minute will be : **[NTSE-2016 (Stage-II)]**

(A) 40 (B) 49
(C) 50 (D) 60

9-73 A circle C is drawn inside a squar S so that the four sides of S are tangents to C. An equilateral triangle T is drawn indide C with its vertices on C. If the area of S is k times the are of T, then the value of k is : **[NTSE-2016 (Stage-II)]**

(A) $\frac{16}{3\sqrt{3}}$ (B) $\frac{16}{\sqrt{3}}$

(C) $\frac{32}{3\sqrt{3}}$ (D) $\frac{32}{\sqrt{3}}$

9-74 Let AP be a diameter of a circle of radius r and PT be the tangent to the circle at the point P such that the line AT intersects the circle at B. If $PT = 8$ units and $BT = 4$ units, then r is equal to : **[NTSE-2016 (Stage-II)]**

(A) $4\sqrt{3}$ units (B) 4 units

(C) $\frac{4}{\sqrt{3}}$ units (D) $2\sqrt{3}$ units

9-75 In the adjoining figure-9.101, ABC is a triangle in which $\angle B = 90°$ and its in circle C_1 has radius 3. A circle C_2 of radius 1 touches sides AC, BC and the circle C_1. Then length AB is equal to : **[NTSE-2017 (Stage-II)]**

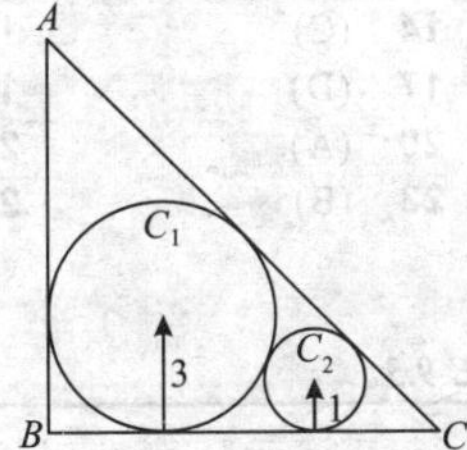

Figure 9.101

(A) $3 + 6\sqrt{3}$ (B) $10 + 3\sqrt{2}$

(C) $10 + 2\sqrt{3}$ (D) $9 + 3\sqrt{3}$

9-76 A line from one vertex A of an equilateral ΔABC meets the opposite side BC in P and the circumcircle of ΔABC in Q. If $BQ = 4$ cm and $CQ = 3$ cm, then PQ is equal to : **[NTSE-2017 (Stage-II)]**

(A) 7 cm (B) $\frac{4}{3}$ cm

(C) $\frac{12}{7}$ cm (D) 2 cm

* * * * *

ANSWERS

PRACTICE EXERCISE-9.1

1	(C)	2	(A)	3	(D)
4	(B)	5	(A)	6	(C)
7	(A)	8	(B)	9	(A)
10	(D)	11	(D)	12	(B)
13	(A)	14	(D)	15	(C)
16	(D)	17	(D)	18	(A)
19	(B)	20	(D)	21	(D)
22	(C)	23	(B)	24	(C)
25	(B)	26	(B)	27	(D)
28	(C)	29	(A)	30	(D)
31	(B)	32	(A)	33	(A)
34	(B)	35	(B)	36	(A)
37	(A)	38	(B)	39	(A)
40	(D)	41	(A)	42	(D)
43	(B)	44	(D)	45	(C)
46	(B)	47	(B)	48	(C)
49	(B)	50	(D)		

PRACTICE EXERCISE-9.2

1	(C)	2	(D)	3	(D)
4	(A)	5	(C)	6	(B)
7	(A)	8	(C)	9	(C)
10	(B)	11	(D)	12	(D)
13	(D)	14	(C)	15	(C)
16	(C)	17	(D)	18	(D)
19	(C)	20	(A)	21	(C)
22	(A)	23	(B)	24	(D)
25	(D)				

PRACTICE EXERCISE-9.3

1	(C)	2	(D)	3	(A)
4	(C)	5	(B)	6	(C)
7	(B)	8	(D)	9	(B)
10	(B)	11	(A)	12	(B)
13	(C)	14	(D)	15	(A)
16	(D)	17	(C)	18	(A)
19	(C)	20	(D)	21	(D)
22	(A)	23	(D)	24	(D)
25	(B)	26	(C)	27	(B)
28	(D)	29	(C)	30	(D)
31	(B)	32	(D)	33	(C)
34	(B)	35	(C)	36	(C)
37	(C)	38	(C)	39	(C)
40	(B)	41	(B)	42	(C)
43	(C)	44	(B)	45	(B)
46	(B)	47	(D)	48	(A)
49	(A)	50	(D)	51	(D)
52	(C)	53	(C)	54	(B)
55	(A)	56	(C)	57	(B)
58	(D)	59	(B)	60	(B)
61	(B)	62	(B)	63	(D)
64	(C)	65	(A)	66	(A)
67	(C)	68	(A)	69	(B)
70	(D)	71	(D)	72	(C)
73	(A)	74	(A)	75	(D)
76	(C)				

Solutions of PRACTICE EXERCISE-9.1

Sol. 1 (C) Consider

C, E, O, A, D, B

$$OD = OE$$

(as equal chords are equidistant from the centre of circle)

Hence Ans is (C)

Sol. 2 (A) From the figure

$$\angle BCD = 30^\circ$$

(Angles in the same segment)

$$\angle CBP = 180^\circ - 75^\circ$$

(Angle sum property)

$$= 105^\circ$$

Hence Ans is (A)

Sol. 3 (D) From the figure

$$\angle ABD = 95^\circ$$

(Ext. angle of cyclic quadrilateral is equal to interior opp. angle)

$$z = 180^\circ - 95^\circ = 85^\circ$$

(sum of opp. angles of cyclic quad is 180°)

Hence Ans is (D)

Sol. 4 (B) From the figure

$$\angle PQS = \angle PRS = 50^\circ$$

(angle in same segment)

Hence Ans is (B)

Sol. 5 (A) In the given figure

Diagonal of square $= 2r$

i.e. side of square $= \sqrt{2}r$

area of square $= 2r^2$

area of circle $= \pi r^2$

i.e. area of shaded region $= \pi r^2 - 2r^2 = r^2(\pi - 2)$

Hence Ans is (A)

Sol. 6 (C)

C, 90°, E, F, A, B

Clearly $\angle ECF > 90^\circ$

Hence Ans is (C)

Sol. 7 (A) Given

$OL = 9$ cm, $AB = 80$ cm

$LB = 40$ cm

$OB^2 = OL^2 + LB^2 = 81 + 1600$

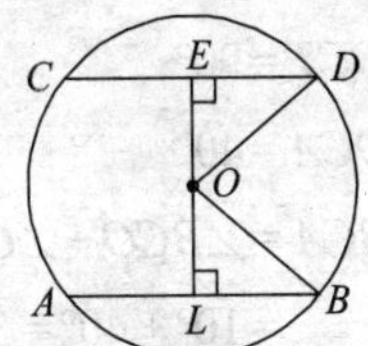

$OB^2 = 1681$

$OB = 41$ cm (Radius)

$CD = 18$ cm

$ED = 9$ cm,

$OD = OB = \text{Radius} = 41$ cm

$OE = 40$ cm

(By pythagoras theorem in ΔOED)

Hence Ans is (A)

Sol. 8 (B) In the given figure

$\Delta BCA = 90^\circ$ (Angle in semicircle)

$\angle CAD = 35^\circ$

In ΔCAE

$90^\circ + 35^\circ + \angle AEB = 180^\circ$

$\angle AEB = 55^\circ$

Hence Ans is (B)

Sol. 9 (A) Given

$OA = 13$ cm, $OC = 12$ cm

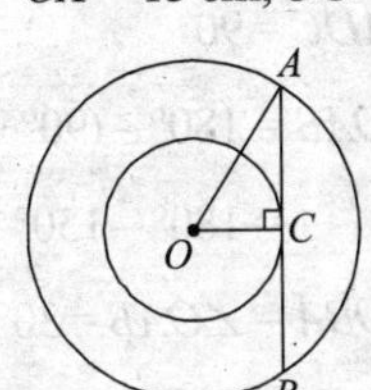

$AC^2 = OA^2 - OC^2 = 169 - 144 = 25$

i.e. $AC = 5$ cm

$AB = 2 \times 5 = 10$ cm

Hence Ans is (A)

Sol. 10 (D) In the given figure

$\angle BCD = 28^\circ = \angle BAD$

(Angle in the same segment)

$\angle BAC = 56^\circ$ [given AD is the angle bisector of BAC]

By angle sum property in ΔABC

$\angle ABC + \angle BAC + \angle ACB = 180^\circ$

$\angle ABC + 56^\circ + 66^\circ = 180^\circ$

$\angle ABC = 180^\circ - 122^\circ = 58^\circ$

Hence Ans is (D)

Sol. 11 (D) Given

Radius of circle = 2 cm

Join O to B point.

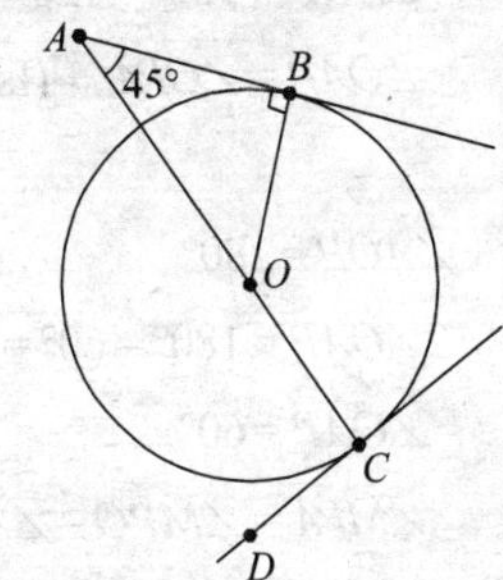

OB is Perpendicular to AB.

$\angle OAB = 45^\circ$

$\angle OBA = 90^\circ$

So, $\angle AOB = 45^\circ$

$AB = OB = 2$

ΔOBA is right angled triangle

$OA = 2\sqrt{2}$

$AC = OC + OA = (2 + 2\sqrt{2})$cm

Hence Ans is (D)

Sol. 12 (B) Let, O be the centre of circle

$\angle QPR = \alpha$

$\angle QOR = (180^\circ - \alpha)$

$\angle SOR = \alpha$ [QS is the diameter]

$\angle SQR = \dfrac{\angle SOR}{2} = \left(\dfrac{\alpha}{2}\right)$

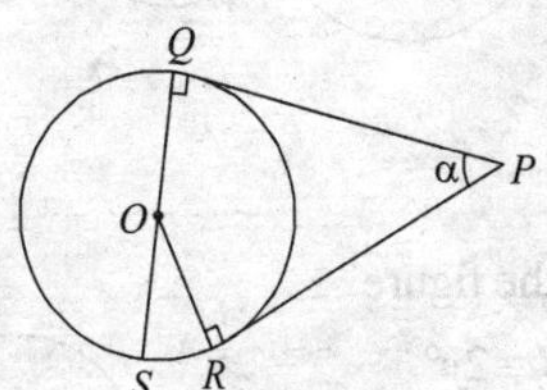

$\angle SQR = \dfrac{1}{2}\angle QPR$

$\angle QPR = 2\angle SQR$

Hence Ans is (B)

Sol. 13 (A) In ΔPOQ,

$OP = OQ$ (Radius of circle)

$\angle OQP = \angle OPQ = 30^\circ$

$\angle APO = 90^\circ$

$\angle APQ = \angle APO - \angle OPQ$

$= 90^\circ - 30^\circ = 60^\circ$

Hence Ans is (A)

Sol. 14 (D) In the given figure

$$\angle AOP + \angle BOP = 180^\circ$$

$$\angle AOP = 180^\circ - 120^\circ = 60^\circ$$

$$\angle OAP = \angle OPA \quad \text{(Isosceles Triangle)}$$

In ΔAOP

$$\angle OAP + \angle OPA + \angle AOP = 180^\circ$$

$$2\angle OAP = 180^\circ - 60^\circ = 120^\circ$$

$$\angle OAP = 60^\circ$$

$$\angle MPA = \angle MPO - \angle APO$$

$$= 90^\circ - 60^\circ = 30^\circ$$

Hence Ans is (D)

Sol. 15 (C) Let the radius of circle be r

$$SO = OT = TR$$

$$SR = \sqrt{RO^2 - OS^2}$$

$$= \sqrt{4r^2 - r^2} = \sqrt{3}r$$

$$\frac{\text{Area of square}}{\text{Area of circle}} = \frac{\sqrt{3}r \cdot \sqrt{3}r}{\pi r^2} = \left(\frac{3}{\pi}\right)$$

Hence Ans is (C)

Sol. 16 (D) From the figure

$$ST^2 = (a+b)^2 - (a-b)^2 = 4ab$$

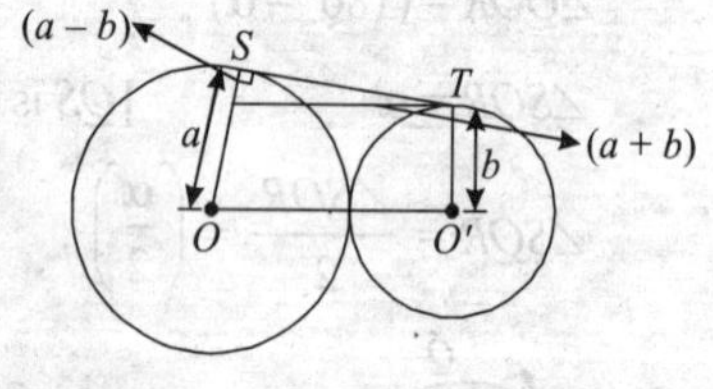

Hence Ans is (D)

Sol. 17 (D) In the figure

$$\angle AOB = 2y^\circ$$

$$x^\circ + 2y^\circ = 180^\circ$$

$$y^\circ = 90^\circ - \frac{x^\circ}{2}$$

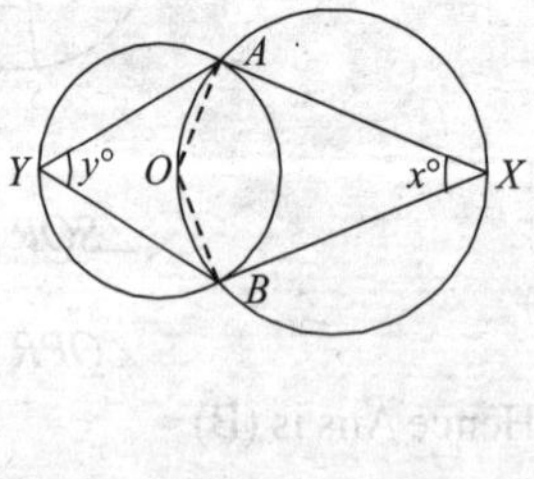

Hence Ans is (D)

Sol. 18 (A) In the figure

$$\angle QOR = 360^\circ - (90^\circ + 90^\circ + 50^\circ) = 130^\circ$$

$$\angle QSR = \frac{1}{2}\angle QOR$$

$$= \frac{1}{2} \times 130^\circ = 65^\circ$$

Hence Ans is (A)

Sol. 19 (B) From the figure

$$\angle CAB = 80^\circ$$

So $\angle BOC = 160^\circ$

and $\angle OBC = \angle OCB = 10^\circ$

$$\angle OCT = 90^\circ \quad [OC \perp CT]$$

$\Rightarrow$ $\angle OCA = 40^\circ$

$$\angle BCA = \angle BCO + \angle OCA$$

$$= 10^\circ + 40^\circ = 50^\circ$$

and $\angle BOA = 2\angle BCA = 100^\circ$

Hence Ans is (B)

Sol. 20 (D) Given

$$AB = 12 \text{ cm}$$

$$BC = 8 \text{ cm}$$

$$AC = 10 \text{ cm}$$

We know $AD = AF = x$,

[length of tangent are equals]

Similarly $BD = BE = y,\ CF = CE = z$

$$x + y = 12,$$

$$y + z = 8,\ z + x = 10$$

$\Rightarrow$ $x + y + z = 15$

on Solving $x = 7$

Hence Ans is (D)

Sol. 21 (D) From the figure

$$\angle ADC = 90^\circ \quad [OD \perp CD]$$

$$\angle OAB = 180^\circ - (90^\circ + 60^\circ)$$

$$= 180^\circ - 150^\circ = 30^\circ$$

$$\angle OBA = \angle OAB = 30^\circ$$

$$\angle DOB = \angle OBA + \angle OAB$$

[Exterior angle of a triangle is equal to sum of alternate interior angles]

$$= 30^\circ + 30^\circ = 60^\circ$$

Hence Ans is (D)

Sol. 22 (C) Using pythagoras theorem in ΔATO

$$AO^2 = AT^2 + TO^2$$

$$AO^2 = 4^2 + 3^2 = 25$$

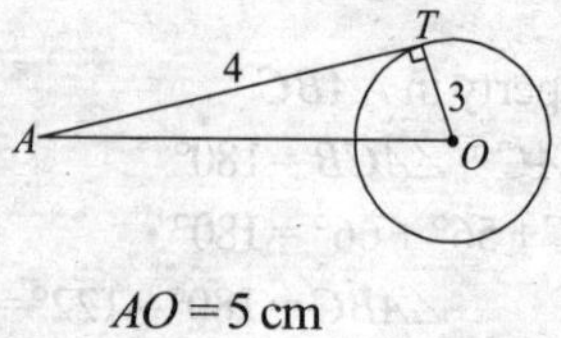

$$AO = 5 \text{ cm}$$

Hence Ans is (C)

Sol. 23 (B) Tangent touches the circle only at one point.
Hence Ans is (B)

Sol. 24 (C) Here $AE = AF = x$,
[length of tangents from the same point are equal]

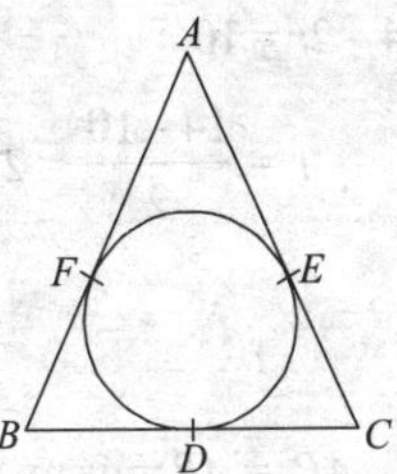

Similarly get

$$BF = BD = y$$
$$CE = CD = z$$

On adding, we get

$$AE + AF + BF + BD + CE + CD$$
$$= 2x + 2y + 2z$$
$$AB + BC + CA = 2(AE + BF + CD)$$
$$AE + BF + CD = \frac{1}{2}(AB + BC + CA)$$

Hence Ans is (C)

Sol. 25 (B) We know

$$\angle OBQ = 90°, \qquad [OB \perp SQ]$$
$$\angle OBA = \angle OAB = 40° \qquad [\because OA = OB]$$
$$\Rightarrow \quad \angle ABQ = 90° - 40° = 50°$$

Hence Ans is (B)

Sol. 26 (B) We know

$$\angle OAS = 90°, \qquad [OA \perp TS]$$
$$\angle OAB = 32° \qquad [\text{given}]$$
$$x = 90° - 32° = 58°$$
$$\angle AOB = 180° - 2 \times 32°$$
$$= 180° - 64° = 116°$$
$$y = \frac{1}{2}\angle AOB$$
$$= \frac{1}{2} \times 116° = 58°$$

Hence Ans is (B)

Sol. 27 (D) We know

$$\angle OCQ = \angle OBP = 90°$$
$$[OC \perp TQ \text{ and } OS \perp TP]$$

from the figure

$$\angle OCA = \angle OAC = 90° - 70° = 20°$$
$$\angle OBA = \angle BAO = 90° - 60° = 30°$$

also $\quad \angle BAC = \angle OAC + \angle BAO$

$\Rightarrow \quad \angle BAC = 20° + 30° = 50°$

$\Rightarrow \quad \angle BOC = 2 \times \angle BAC = 100°$

[angle subtended at the center is twice the angle subtended at circumference]

$\Rightarrow \quad \angle BTC = 180° - 100° = 80°$

Hence Ans is (D)

Sol. 28 (C) Given $AQOP$ is a square

$$AQ = 10 \text{ cm}$$
$$CR = CS = 27 \text{ cm}$$

[length of tangents from the sume point are equal]

$$BR = BC - CR = 38 - 27$$

$\Rightarrow \quad BR = 11$ cm

We know $\quad BQ = BR = 11$ cm

$$AB = AQ + BQ = 10 + 11 = 21 \text{ cm}$$

Hence Ans is (C)

Sol. 29 (A)

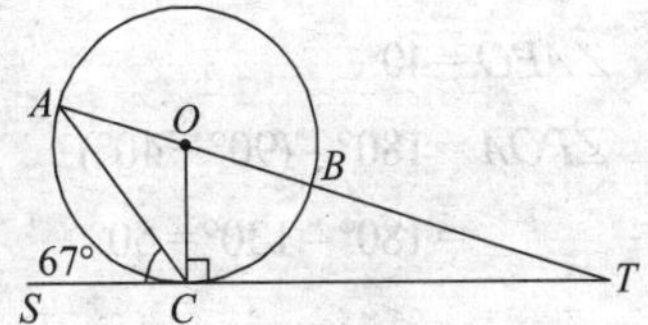

Join OC,

$$\angle OCS = 90°$$
$$\angle OCA = 90° - 67°$$
$$\angle OCA = 23°$$
$$\angle OCA = \angle OAC = 23°$$
$$\angle ACS = \angle CAT + \angle ATC$$
$$67° = 23° + \angle BTC$$
$$\angle BTC = 67° - 23°$$
$$\angle BTC = 44°$$

Hence Ans is (A)

Sol. 30 (D) Using phythagoras theorem in ΔATP

$$AO^2 = AT^2 + TO^2$$
$$\Rightarrow \quad AO^2 = \left(\frac{4}{3}r\right)^2 + r^2$$
$$\Rightarrow \quad AO^2 = \frac{16r^2 + 9r^2}{9} \Rightarrow \frac{25r^2}{9}$$
$$\Rightarrow \quad AO = \frac{5r}{3}$$

Shortest distance

$$AP = AO - OP = \frac{5r}{3} - r$$
$$AP = \frac{2r}{3}$$

Hence Ans is (D)

Sol. 31 (B) In ΔDAB

$$\angle ADB = 180° - (90° + 52°)$$
$$= 180° - 142° = 38°$$

We know

$$\angle AOC = 2 \times \angle ADB$$

[angle subtended at the centre is equal to twice the angle subtended at circumference]

$$= 2 \times 38° = 76°$$

Hence Ans is (B)

Sol. 32 (A)

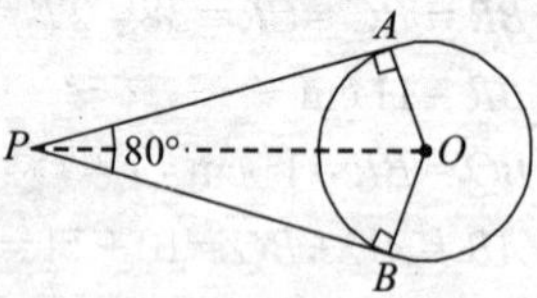

We know $[OA \perp AP]$

$$\angle PAO = 90°,$$
$$\angle APO = 40°$$
$$\Rightarrow \quad \angle POA = 180° - (90° + 40°)$$
$$= 180° - 130° = 50°$$

Hence Ans is (A)

Sol. 33 (A) No tangent can be drawn
Hence Ans is (A)

Sol. 34 (B) *PAOB* will be rectangle or square
But $AO = BO$

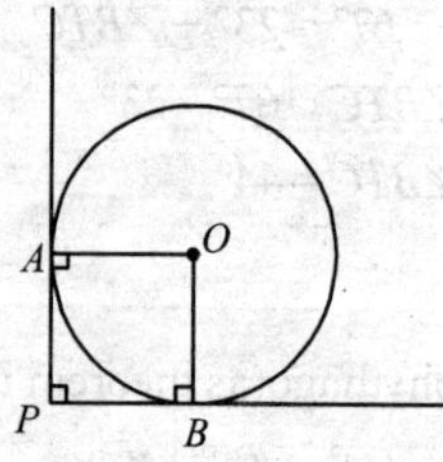

i.e. *PAOB* is a square
Hence Ans is (B)

Sol. 35 (B)

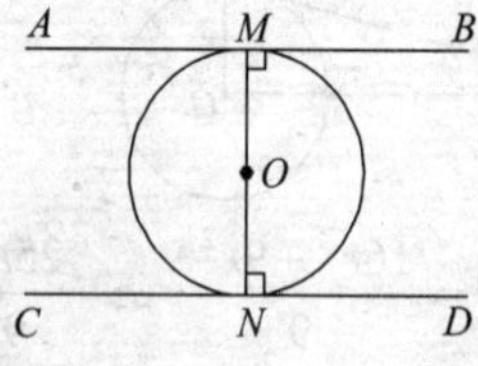

From the figure $AB \parallel CD$
Hence Ans is (B)

Sol. 36 (A) We know

$AL = AN = r$ [radii are equal]

$LB = MB = 6 - r$ [tangente are equal]

Also $CN = CM = 8 - r$ [tangente are equal]

From the figure

$$BC = CM + MB = 6 - r + 8 - r$$
$$\Rightarrow \quad BC = 14 - 2r$$
$$\Rightarrow \quad BC = 10$$
$$14 - 2r = 10$$
$$r = \frac{14 - 10}{2} = 2 \text{ cm}$$

Hence Ans is (A)

Sol. 37 (A) Given

Also $AP = AR = 4$ cm

[tangent are equal from same point]

$BP = BQ = 6$ cm

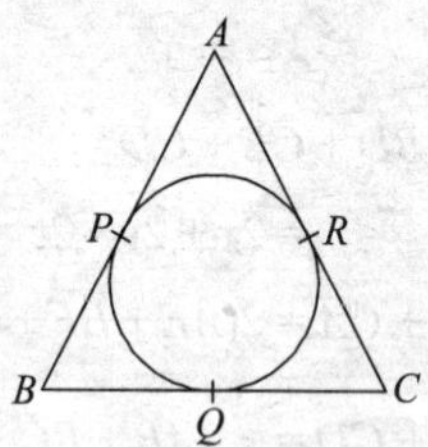

From the figure

$$CR = AC - AR = 12 - 4 = 8 \text{ cm}$$
$$BC = BQ + CQ$$
$$= 6 + CR = 6 + 8 = 14 \text{ cm}$$

Hence Ans is (A)

Sol. 38 (B) We know

$AP = AR = x,$ [length of tangent]

$BP = BQ = y,$ [Similarly are equals]

$CQ = CR = z$

Also $AB = x + y = 5$ ...(1)

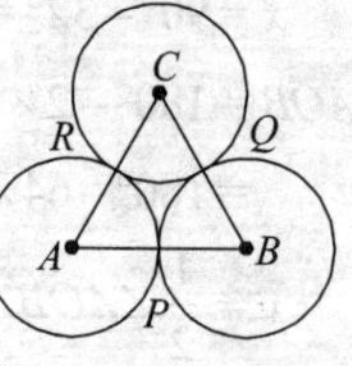

$BC = y + z = 7$ ...(2)

$CA = z + x = 6$ ...(3)

Adding (1) and (3)

$$2x + y + z = 11$$

from (2)

$$2x + 7 = 11$$
$$2x = 4$$
$$x = 2$$

radius of the circle with centre $A = 2$ cm
Hence Ans is (B)

Sol. 39 **(A)** Let O' is a centre of a circle

$$\angle OAT = 120° - 55° = 65°$$

[Exterior angle of a triangle is equal to sum of interior alternate angles]

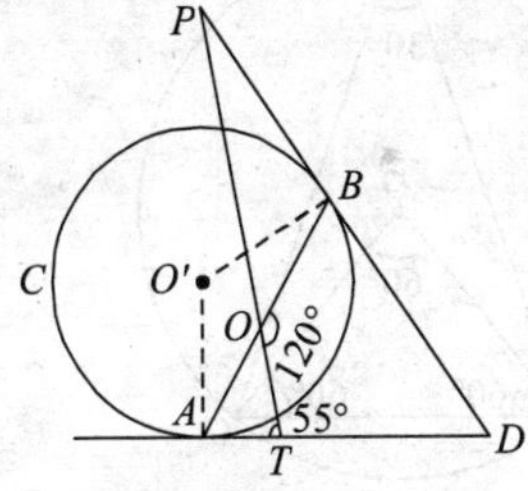

$$\angle O'AT = 90° \quad [O'A \perp AT]$$

Also $\angle O'AB = 90° - 65° = 25°$

$$\angle O'BA = \angle O'AB = 25°$$

$\Rightarrow$ $\angle AO'B = 180° - 2 \times 25° = 130°$

$$= 180 - (25 + 25)$$

$\Rightarrow$ $\angle BDA = 180° - 130° = 50°$

$$\angle BPT = 55° - 50° = 5°$$

Hence Ans is (A)

Sol. 40 **(D)** Here

$$PT^2 = PA \times PB$$

$$PT^2 = 10 \times 8$$

$$PT^2 = 80$$

$$PT = \sqrt{16 \times 5} = 4\sqrt{5}\text{cm}$$

Hence Ans is (D)

Sol. 41 **(A)** Here

$$PQ = PA \times PB \quad \dots(1)$$

(Tangent secant theorem)

Also $PR = PA \times PB \quad \dots(2)$

(Tangent secant theorem)

$\Rightarrow$ $PQ = PR$ (using equation-(1) & (2))

Hence Ans is (A)

Sol. 42 **(D)** From the figure

$$\alpha + \theta + \alpha + \theta = 180°$$

$$2(\alpha + \theta) = 180°$$

$$\alpha + \theta = 90°$$

$\Rightarrow$ $\angle ACB = 90°$

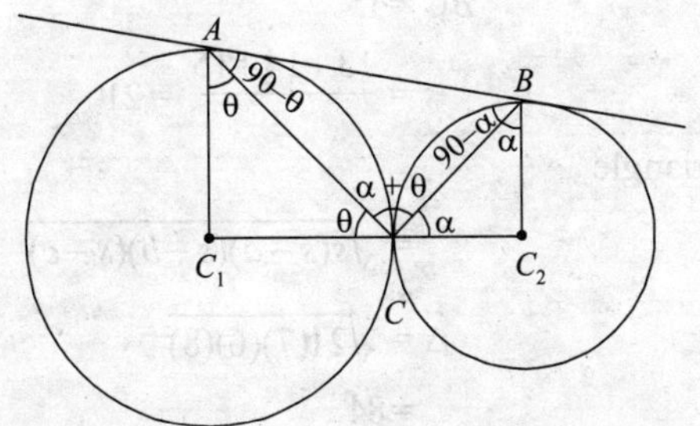

Hence Ans is (D)

Sol. 43 **(B)** In ΔACO

$$\angle ACO = 90° \quad [OC \perp AC]$$

Given $OA = 5$ cm

Also $OC = 3$ cm

In ΔAOC,

$$AC = \sqrt{AO^2 - OC^2}$$

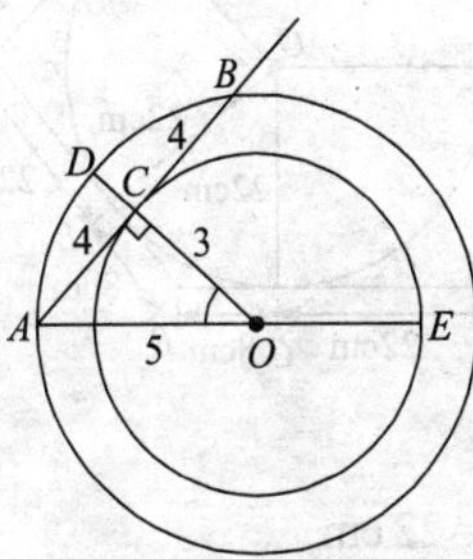

$$= \sqrt{5^2 - 3^2} = 4\text{ cm}$$

$\Rightarrow$ $AB = 2 \times AC = 8$ cm

Hence Ans is (B)

Sol. 44 **(D)** No circle can be drawn.

Hence Ans is (D)

Sol. 45 **(C)** Take a point 'D'

on the circumference join AD & CD

Now $ABCD$ is a cyclic quadrilateral

$\Rightarrow$ $\angle ADC = 180° - 115°$

$$= 60°$$

$$AOC = 2\angle ADC$$

[angle subtended at the circle is twice the angle subtended at any point are circumference]

$$= 2 \times 6\text{J}$$

$$= 130$$

$$\angle AOC = (180° - 115°) \times 2 = 65° \times 2 = 130°$$

Hence Ans is (C)

Sol. 46 **(B)** Given

$$OB = BC$$

$$OA = OB \quad \text{(Radii of same circle)}$$

Let $\angle OAB = \angle ABO = z$

$\Rightarrow$ $z = 2y$

$$180 - 2z + x + y = 180$$

$$x + y = 2z$$

$$x + y = 4y$$

$\Rightarrow$ $x = 3y$

Hence Ans is (B)

Sol. 47 (B)

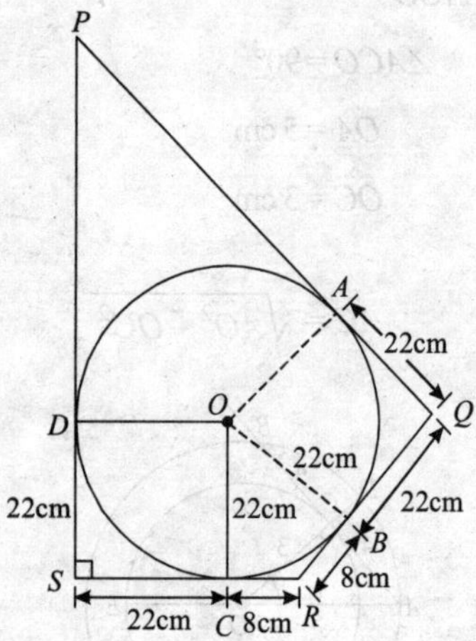

From the figure

So required radius = 22 cm

Hence Ans is (B)

Sol. 48 (C) In ΔAOB

$$OA = \sqrt{OB^2 + AB^2}$$

$$= \sqrt{3^2 + 4^2}$$

$$= \sqrt{25}$$

$$= 5 \text{ cm}$$

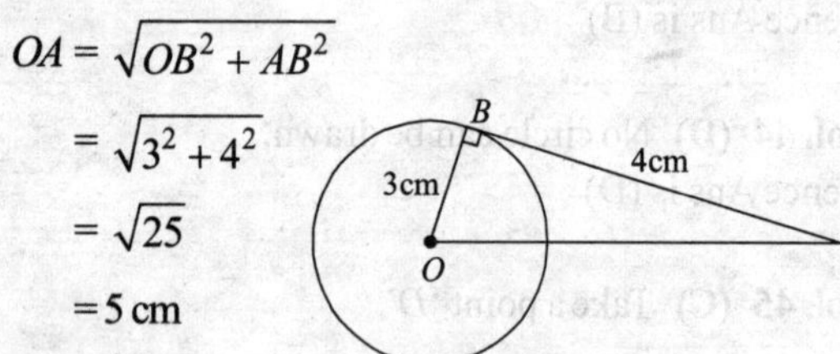

Hence Ans is (C)

Sol. 49 (B) We know

$$PA \cdot PB = PC \cdot PD = PT^2$$

$$\Rightarrow \quad PA \cdot PB = 144$$

$$\Rightarrow \quad 3 \cdot PB = 144$$

$$\Rightarrow \quad PB = 48 \text{ cm}$$

$$PC \cdot PD = 144$$

$$\Rightarrow \quad PD = 36 \text{ cm}$$

$$\Rightarrow \quad PB + PD = 84 \text{ cm}$$

Hence Ans is (B)

Sol. 50 (D)

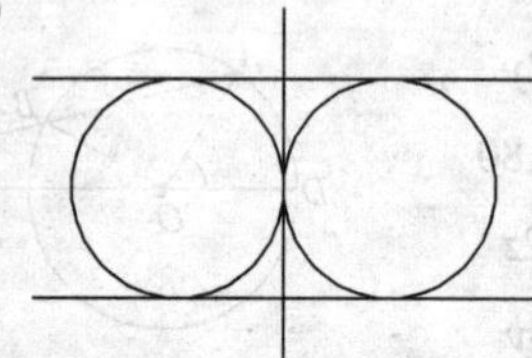

Number of tangents drawn = 3

Hence Ans is (D)

Solutions of PRACTICE EXERCISE-9.2

Sol. 1 (C)

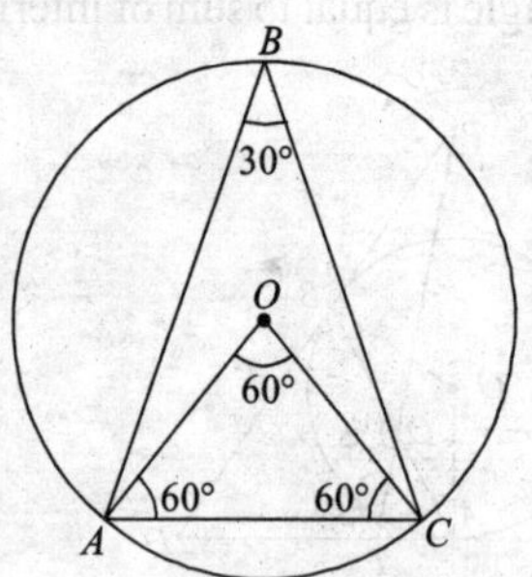

In the figure

$$\angle ABC = 30^\circ$$

$$\Rightarrow \quad \angle AOC = 60^\circ$$

[Angle subtended by arc at the centre is double the angle made by arc in the alternate segment]

In ΔAOC

$$OA = OC = \text{radius}$$

$\Rightarrow$ ΔAOC is an equilateral triangle

So, Diameter of the circle

$$= 2(AC) = 2(5) = 10$$

Hence Ans is (C)

Sol. 2 (D) From the figure

$$BD = BA + AD$$

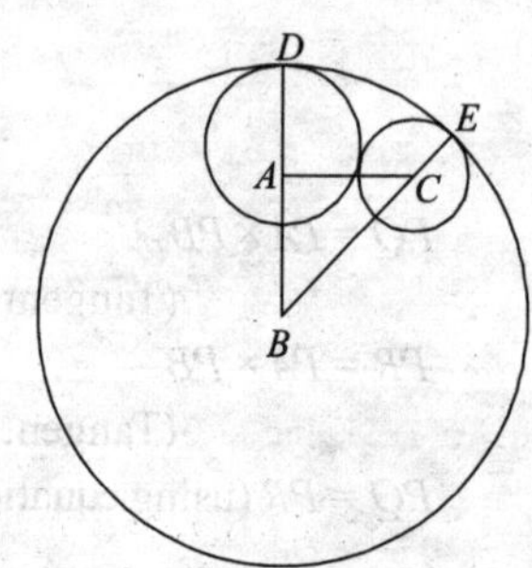

$$\Rightarrow \quad 21 = BA + 7$$

$$\Rightarrow \quad BA = 14$$

Also $\quad BE = BC + CE$

$$\Rightarrow \quad 21 = BC + 6$$

$$\Rightarrow \quad BC = 15$$

$$s = \frac{13 + 14 + 15}{2} = 21$$

Area of triangle

$$= \sqrt{s(s-a)(s-b)(s-c)}$$

$$\Delta = \sqrt{21(7)(6)(8)}$$

$$= 84$$

Hence Ans is (D)

Sol. 3 (D)

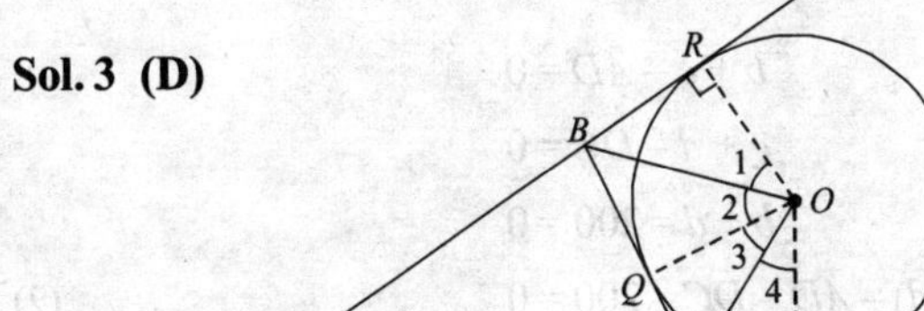

In quadrilateral $ORPT$

$$\angle ROT = 180° - 40° = 140°$$

$$[\because \angle ORP = 90° \text{ and } \angle OTP = 90°]$$

We can say

$$\Delta ROB \cong \Delta QOB$$

$$\Rightarrow \quad \angle 1 \cong \angle 2 \qquad \text{[c.p.c.t.]...(1)}$$

Similarly $\quad \Delta QOA \cong \Delta TOA$

$$\Rightarrow \quad \angle 3 = \angle 4 \qquad \text{[c.p.c.t.]...(2)}$$

$$\angle 2 + \angle 3 = \frac{1}{2}(\angle 1 + \angle 2 + \angle 3 + \angle 4)$$

[from (1) & (2)]

$$= \frac{1}{2}(140°) = 70°$$

Hence Ans is (D)

Sol. 4 (A) For the given perimeter the figure having maximum number of sides having maximum area.

So circle containing infinite number of sides so it is having maximum area

Hence Ans is (A)

Sol. 5 (C) Draw two circles of radius 2, 3 units taking centre A, B respectively.

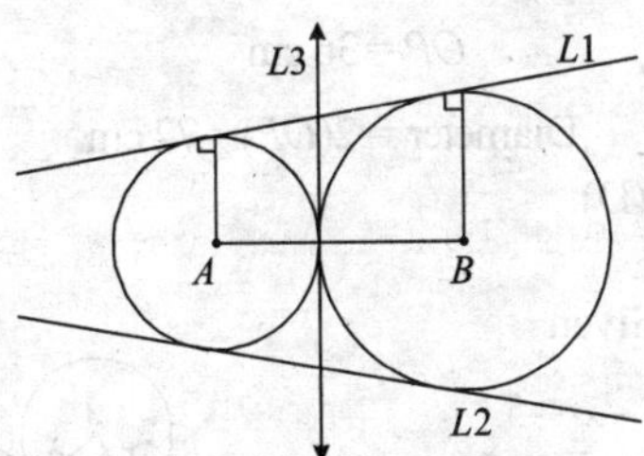

Three straight lines $L1$, $L2$ & $L3$ can be drawn as shown in figure, which are at the distance 2 unit from A and 3 unit from B

Hence Ans is (C)

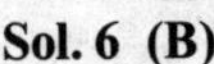

Sol. 6 (B)

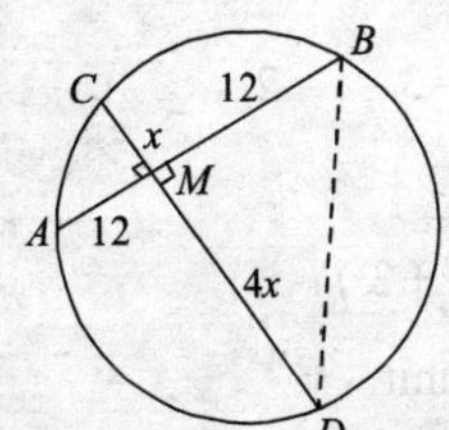

We know, $\quad MA \times MB = MC \times MD$

$$\Rightarrow \quad 12 \times 12 = x \times 4x$$

$$\Rightarrow \quad 144 = 4x^2$$

$$x = 6$$

$$MD = 4x = 24$$

$$BD = \sqrt{12^2 + 24^2}$$

$$= \sqrt{144 + 576}$$

$$= \sqrt{720}$$

$$= 12\sqrt{5}$$

Hence Ans is (B)

Sol. 7 (A)

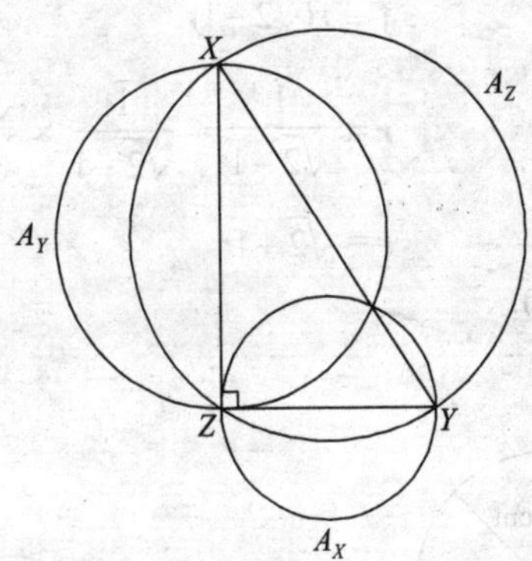

From the figure, In triangle XYZ

$$XY^2 = XZ^2 + YZ^2$$

Divide by 4 and multiply by π on both sides

$$\Rightarrow \quad \pi\left(\frac{XY}{2}\right)^2 = \pi\left(\frac{XZ}{2}\right)^2 + \pi\left(\frac{YZ}{2}\right)^2$$

$$A_z = A_x + A_y$$

Hence Ans is (A)

Sol. 8 (C)

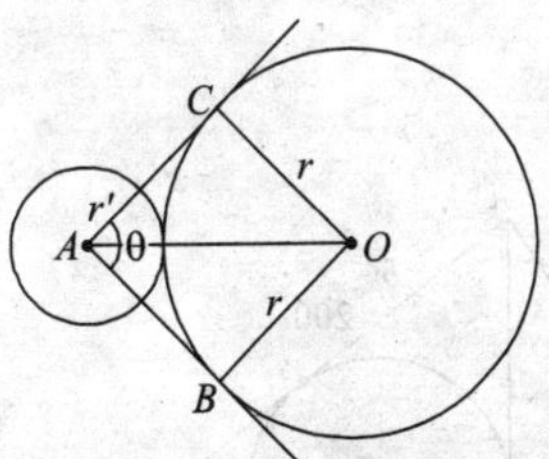

Given area of the shaded region $= \dfrac{\pi}{4}$

$$\Rightarrow \quad \frac{\theta}{360°} \times \pi(r')^2 = \frac{\pi}{4}$$

$$\Rightarrow \quad \frac{\theta}{360°} \times \pi(1)^2 = \frac{\pi}{4}$$

$$\theta = 90°$$

from the figure

$$\Delta CAO \cong \Delta BAO$$

$$\Rightarrow \quad \angle CAO = \angle BAO$$

$$\angle CAO = \angle BAO = \frac{1}{2}\theta = 45°$$

In ΔCAO

$$\sin 45° = \frac{r}{r+1}$$

$$\frac{1}{\sqrt{2}} = \frac{r}{r+1}$$

$$r+1 = \sqrt{2}r$$

$$1 = \sqrt{2}r - r$$

$$1 = r(\sqrt{2}-1)$$

$$r = \frac{1}{\sqrt{2}-1} = \frac{1}{\sqrt{2}-1} \times \frac{\sqrt{2}+1}{\sqrt{2}+1}$$

$$\Rightarrow \quad r = \sqrt{2}+1$$

Hence Ans is (C)

Sol. 9 (C)

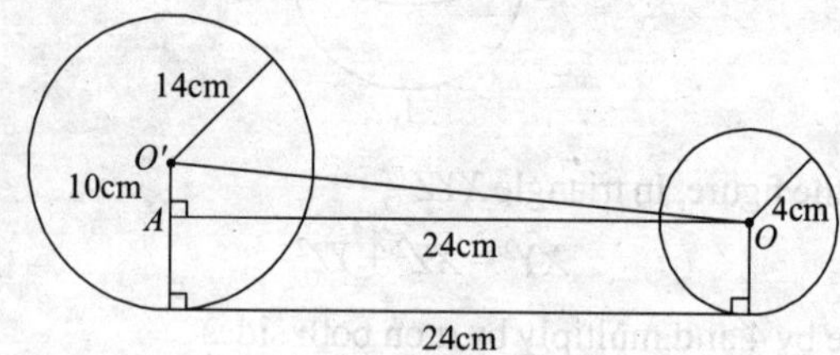

In $\Delta O'OA$

$$(OO')^2 = AO^2 + AO^2$$

$$= 24^2 + 10^2$$

$$= 576 + 100 = 676$$

$$OO' = 26 \text{ cm}$$

Hence Ans is (C)

Sol. 10 (B)

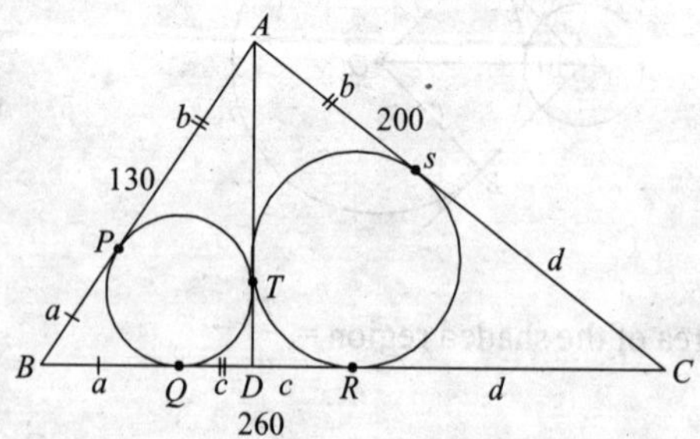

In ΔABD

$$a + b - 130 = 0$$

$$a + c - BD = 0$$

$$b + c - AD = 0$$

$$2(a+b+c) - 130 - BD - AD = 0 \quad \ldots(1)$$

In ΔADC

$$b + c - AD = 0$$

$$c + d - DC = 0$$

$$b + d - 200 = 0$$

$$2(b+c+d) - AD - DC - 200 = 0 \quad \ldots(2)$$

Compare (1) & (2)

$$2(a+b+c) - 130 - BD - AD$$

$$= 2(b+c+d) - AD - DC - 200$$

$$2a - 130 - BD = 2d - DC - 200$$

$$2a - 130 - a - c = 2d - c - d - 200$$

$$a - 130 = d - 200$$

$$d - a = 70$$

In ΔABC

$$a + 2c + d = 260$$

$$2a + 2c + d - a = 260$$

$$2(a+c) + 70 = 260$$

$$2BD = 190$$

$$BD = 95$$

Hence Ans is (B)

Sol. 11 (D)

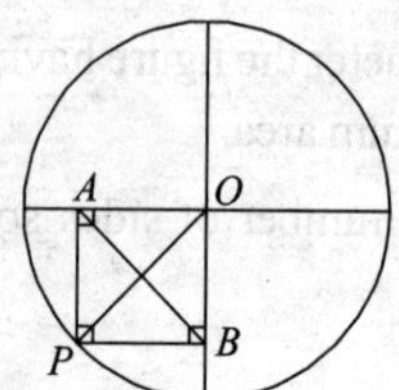

From the figure

$OAPB$ will be recangle.

$\Rightarrow$ Diagonal $\quad OP = AB$

So, $\quad OP = 36$ cm

$\Rightarrow \quad$ Diameter $= 2(OP) = 72$ cm

Hence Ans is (D)

Sol. 12 (D) Given

$$3 - x + 4 - x = 5$$

$$7 - 2x = 5$$

$$2x = 2$$

$$x = 1$$

So, radius of three circles be

$$x = 1, 3 - x = 3 - 1 = 2$$

and $\quad 4 - x = 4 - 1 = 3.$

Total area is $\quad = \pi(1^2 + 2^2 + 3^2)$

$$= 14\pi \text{ sq. unit}$$

Hence Ans is (D)

Sol. 13 (D)

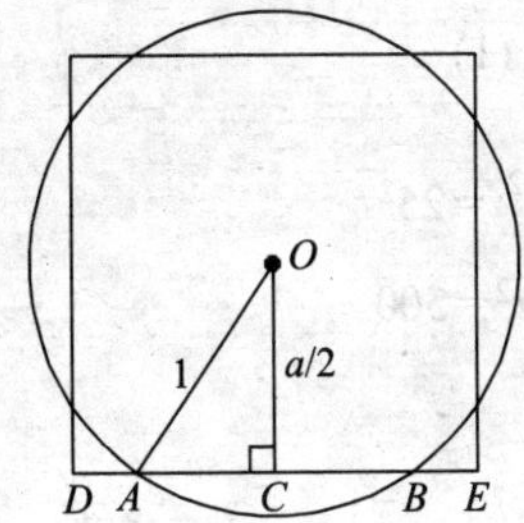

Let r and a be the radius of circle and side of square respectively. given

$$\pi r^2 = a^2$$

$$\Rightarrow \quad a^2 = \pi \qquad (\because r = 1)$$

In ΔOAC

$$OA^2 = AC^2 + OC^2$$

$$\Rightarrow \quad 1 = AC^2 + \left(\frac{a}{2}\right)^2$$

We know $AC = \sqrt{1 - \frac{a^2}{4}}$

$$AB = 2AC$$

$$= 2\sqrt{1 - \frac{a^2}{4}}$$

$$= \sqrt{1 - \frac{\pi}{4}} = \sqrt{4 - \pi} \qquad [\because a^2 = \pi]$$

$$= \sqrt{4 - \pi}$$

Hence Ans is (D)

Sol. 14 (C)

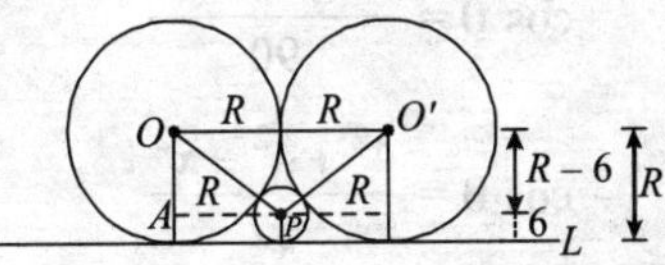

From the figure

$$OP = R + 6, OA = R - 6$$

and $AP = R$

In ΔOAP

$$OP^2 = OA^2 + AP^2$$

$$\Rightarrow \quad (R + 6)^2 = (R - 6)^2 + R^2$$

$$R^2 + 12R + 36 = R^2 - 12R + 36 + R^2$$

$$24R = R^2$$

So, $R = 24$ unit

Hence Ans is (C)

Sol. 15 (C) Given

$$AP + PB = 4 + 6$$

$$AB = 10 \qquad \ldots(1)$$

We know

and $AP \times BP = PC \times PD$

$$\Rightarrow \quad PD = \frac{4 \times 6}{2}$$

$$\Rightarrow \quad PD = 12$$

and $DC = PC + PD$

$$\Rightarrow \quad DC = 12 + 2$$

$$\Rightarrow \quad CD = 14 \qquad \ldots(2)$$

Now, $NC = \frac{1}{2} \times CD$

Now $NC = \frac{1}{2} \times 14 = 7$

Area $NP = NC - PC = 7 - 2 = 5$

So, $NP = OM = 5$

and $AM = \frac{1}{2} \times AB = \frac{1}{2} \times 10 = 5$

In ΔAMO

$$AO^2 = AM^2 + OM^2$$

$$\Rightarrow \quad r^2 = 5^2 + 5^2$$

$$\Rightarrow \quad r^2 = 50$$

So, area of the circle $= \pi r^2 = 50\pi$

Hence Ans is (C)

Sol. 16 (C) From the given figure

We know that

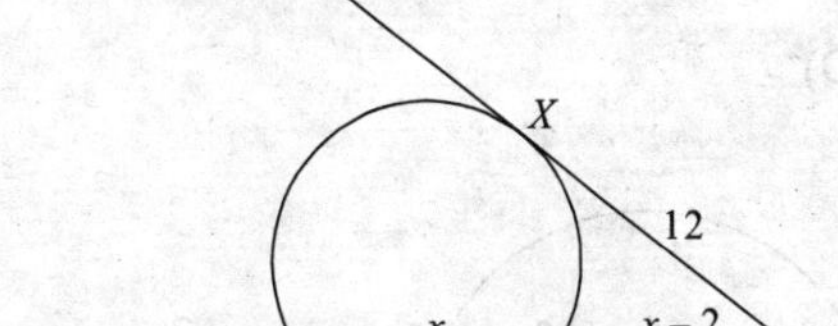

$$PR \times RQ = RX^2$$

$$\Rightarrow \quad (2x - 2) \times (x - 2) = 12^2$$

$$\Rightarrow \quad (x - 1)(x - 2) = 72$$

$$\Rightarrow \quad x^2 - 3x - 70 = 0$$

$$\Rightarrow \quad x^2 - 10x + 7x - 70 = 0$$

$$\Rightarrow \quad x(x - 10) + 7(x - 10) = 0$$

$$\Rightarrow \quad (x + 7)(x - 10) = 0$$

$$\Rightarrow \quad x = -7$$

Not possible,

So $x = 10$

Hence Ans is (C)

Sol. 17 (D) Consider the first quadrant the figure will be as below

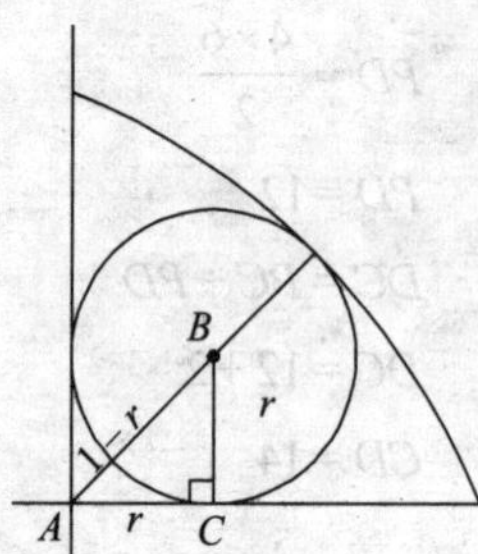

In ΔABC

$$AB^2 = BC^2 + AC^2$$
$$(1-r)^2 = r^2 + r^2$$
$$(1-r)^2 = 2r^2$$
$$\Rightarrow \quad 1 - r = \sqrt{2}r$$
$$1 = r(\sqrt{2}+1)$$
$$r = \frac{1}{\sqrt{2}+1}$$

Hence Ans is (D)

Sol. 18 (D) In ΔBOC

$$\angle OBC = \angle OCB \qquad [OB = OC]$$
$$\Rightarrow \quad \angle OCB = 30^\circ$$
$$\angle BCD + \angle BAD = 180^\circ$$

[Opposite angles of a cyclic quadrilateral are supplementary]

$$\Rightarrow \quad 50^\circ + 30^\circ + 40^\circ + \angle AOD = 180^\circ$$
$$\Rightarrow \quad \angle OAD = 60^\circ$$

Hence Ans is (D)

Sol. 19 (C)

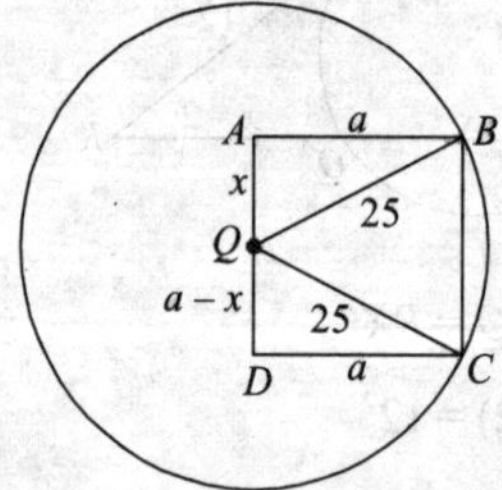

In ΔQAB

$$x^2 + a^2 = 25^2 \qquad \ldots(1)$$

In ΔQDC

$$(a-x)^2 + a^2 = 25^2 \qquad \ldots(2)$$

Substract (1) from (2)

$$(a-x)^2 - x^2 = 0$$
$$a - x = x$$
$$a = 2x$$
$$x = \frac{a}{2}$$

Using $x = \frac{a}{2}$ in equation (1)

$$\frac{a^2}{4} + a^2 = 25^2$$
$$a^2 = 500$$

Hence Ans is (C)

Sol. 20 (A) In ΔOBA

$$\frac{r}{OA} = \sin 30^\circ$$
$$OA = 2r$$

In $\Delta O'AC$

$$\frac{O'C}{O'A} = \sin 30^\circ$$

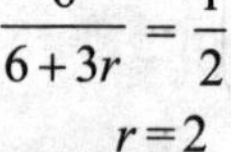

$$\frac{6}{6+3r} = \frac{1}{2}$$
$$r = 2$$

Hence Ans is (A)

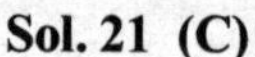

Sol. 21 (C)

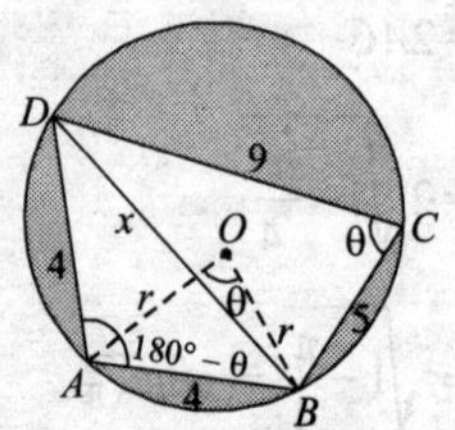

Let $\qquad BD = x$

Apply cosine rule in ΔBCD & ΔABD

$$\cos\theta = \frac{9^2 + 5^2 - x^2}{90} \qquad \ldots(1)$$
$$-\cos\theta = \frac{4^2 + 4^2 - x^2}{32} \qquad \ldots(2)$$

Add (1) & (2)

$$0 = \frac{106 - x^2}{90} + \frac{32 - x^2}{32}$$
$$0 = 106 \times 16 - 16x^2 + 45 \times 32 - 45x^2$$
$$61x^2 = 16[106 + 90]$$
$$x^2 = \frac{16 \times 196}{61}$$

Using (2)

$$-\cos\theta = \frac{32 - x^2}{32}$$
$$\cos\theta = \frac{x^2 - 32}{32} = \frac{x^2}{32} - 1$$
$$\cos\theta = \frac{16 \times 196}{61 \times 32} - 1 \qquad \ldots(3)$$

In ΔOAB

Apply cosine rule

$$\cos\theta = \frac{r^2 + r^2 - 16}{2r^2}$$

Using (3)

$$\frac{16\times 196}{61\times 32} - 1 = \frac{r^2 + r^2 - 16}{2r^2}$$

$$r^2 = \frac{61}{3}$$

Area of circle $= \pi r^2 = \dfrac{61\pi}{3}$

Area of cyclic quad $\sqrt{(s-a)(s-b)(s-c)(s-d)}$

$$s = \frac{a+b+c+d}{2}$$

$$= (14\sqrt{3})$$

Shaded area = Area of circle – Area of cyclic quad.

$$= \frac{61\pi - 42\sqrt{3}}{3}$$

Hence Ans is (C)

Sol. 22 (A)

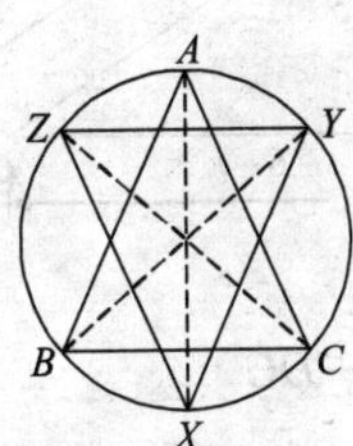

From the figure

$$\angle YXA = \angle YBA = \frac{B}{2}$$

(angle in same segment)

also $\angle ZXA = \angle ZCA = \dfrac{C}{2}$

(angle in same segment)

also $\angle ZXY = \angle YXA + \angle ZXA = \dfrac{B}{2} + \dfrac{C}{2}$

$$\angle X = 90° - \frac{A}{2}$$

Similarly $\angle Y = 90° - \dfrac{B}{2}, \angle Z = 90° - \dfrac{C}{2}$

Hence Ans is (A)

Sol. 23 (B)

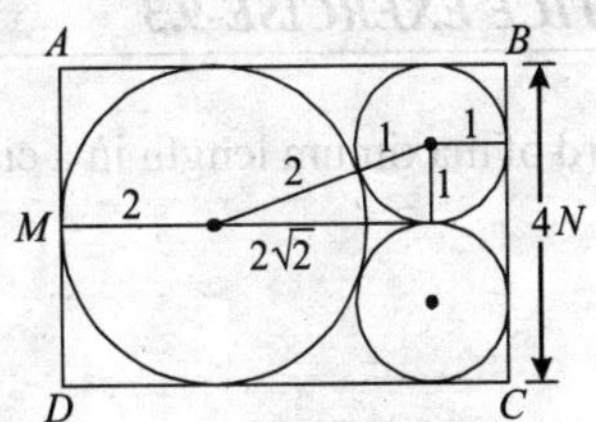

From the figure,

$$MN = 2 + 2\sqrt{2} + 1 = 3 + 2\sqrt{2}$$

Hence Ans is (B)

Sol. 24 (D) In $\Delta OA'B'$

$$\tan 30° = \frac{A'B'}{OB'} = \frac{2}{OB'}$$

$$OB' = 2\sqrt{3}$$

$$OB = OB' - 1$$

$$= (2\sqrt{3} - 1)$$

Now ΔOAB

$$\tan 30° = \frac{AB}{OB}$$

$$OB = \sqrt{3}AB$$

$$(2\sqrt{3} - 1) = \sqrt{3}AB$$

$$AB = \left(\frac{2}{1} - \frac{1}{\sqrt{3}}\right)$$

Length of similar hexagon

$$2AB = \left(4 - \frac{2}{\sqrt{3}}\right)$$

So distance travelled by the center

$$12AB = 24 - 4\sqrt{3}$$

Hence Ans is (D)

Sol. 25 (D)

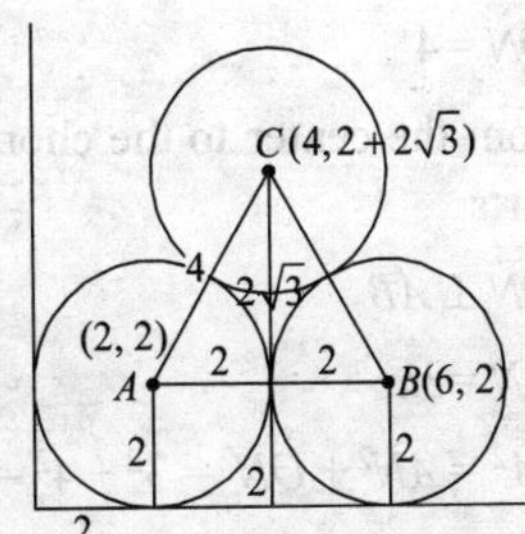

From the figure,

co-ordinates of B is (6, 2) and co-ordinates of C is $(9, 2 + 2\sqrt{3})$

Hence Ans is (D)

Solutions of PRACTICE EXERCISE-9.3

Sol. 1 (C) The chord of maximum length in a circle is called diameter

Hence Ans is (C)

Sol. 2 (D) The number of straight line drawn from one point to any other point are equal to one

Hence Ans is (D)

Sol. 3 (A) From the figure

$$\angle ABD = \angle ACD = 30°$$

(angle in a same segment)

$$\angle AEB + \angle BEC = 180° \text{ (linear pair)}$$

$$\angle AEB + 125° = 180°$$

$$\Rightarrow \quad \angle AEB = 180° - 125° = 55°$$

Now in ΔAEB, we have

$$\angle ABE + \angle AEB + \angle BAE = 180°$$

$$30° + 55° + \angle BAE = 180°$$

$$\Rightarrow \quad \angle BAE = 180° - 85° = 95°$$

$$\angle BAC = 95°$$

Hence Ans is (A)

Sol. 4 (C)

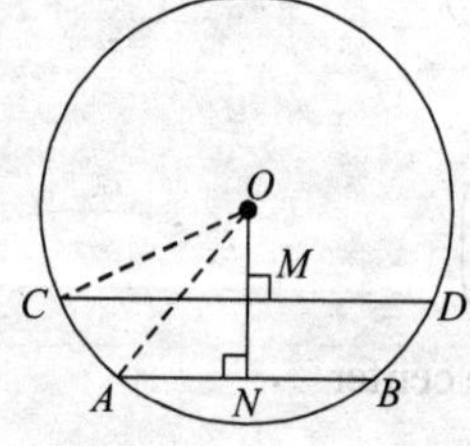

given

$$AB = 6$$

$$CD = 8$$

$$ON = 4$$

Perpendicular drawn from the center to the chord bisect the chord in to two equal parts

Since $\quad ON \perp AB$

$\Rightarrow \quad AN = 3\text{m}$

$$OA^2 = AN^2 + ON^2 = 3^2 + 4^2 = 5^2$$

$\Rightarrow \quad OA = 5$

Now $\quad OC^2 = OM^2 + CM^2$

$\Rightarrow \quad 5^2 = OM^2 + 4^2$

$\Rightarrow \quad OM = 3\text{ cm}$

Hence Ans is (C)

Sol. 5 (B)

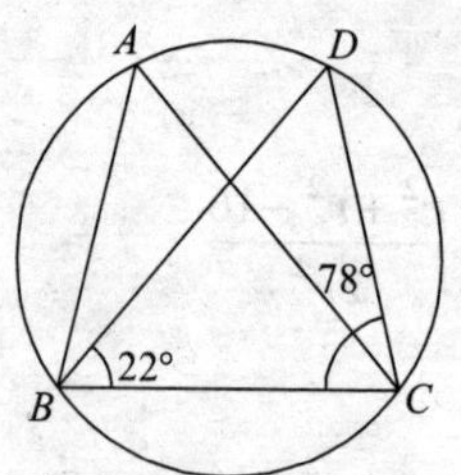

given

$$\angle DBC = 22°$$

$$\angle DCB = 78°$$

In ΔDBC, we have

$$\angle DBC + \angle DCB + \angle BDC = 180°$$

$$22° + 78° + \angle BDC = 180°$$

$$\Rightarrow \quad \angle BDC = 180° - 100° = 80°$$

$$\angle BDC = \angle BAC = 80°$$

[Angle in the same segment are equal]

Hence Ans is (B)

Sol. 6 (C)

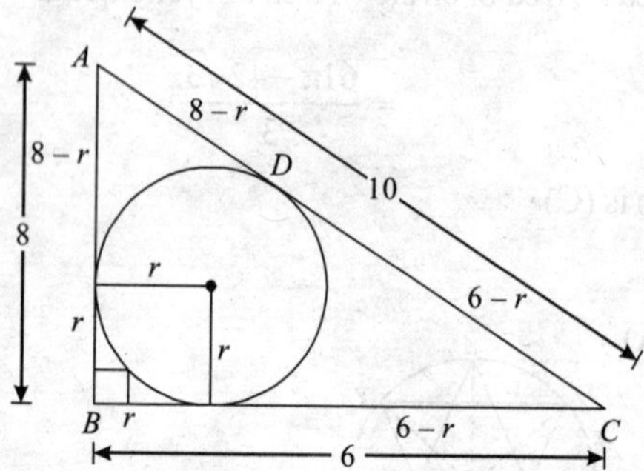

From the figure it is clear

$$AC = AD + DC$$

$$10 = 8 - r + 6 - r \text{ (by tangent theorem)}$$

$$2r = 4$$

$$r = 2$$

Hence Ans is (C)

Sol. 7 (B) We know

$$AP + PQ + AQ = \text{Perimeter of } \Delta APQ$$

$$AP + PX + XQ + AQ = \text{Perimeter of } \Delta APQ$$

(tangents drawn from an external point are equal)

$$AP + PB + QC + AQ = \text{Perimeter of } \Delta APQ$$

(tangents drawn from an external point are equal)

$$AB + AC = \text{Perimeter of } \Delta APQ$$

$\Rightarrow$ Perimeter of

$$\Delta APQ = 2AB = 2 \times 5 = 10$$

Hence Ans is (B)

Sol. 8 (D)

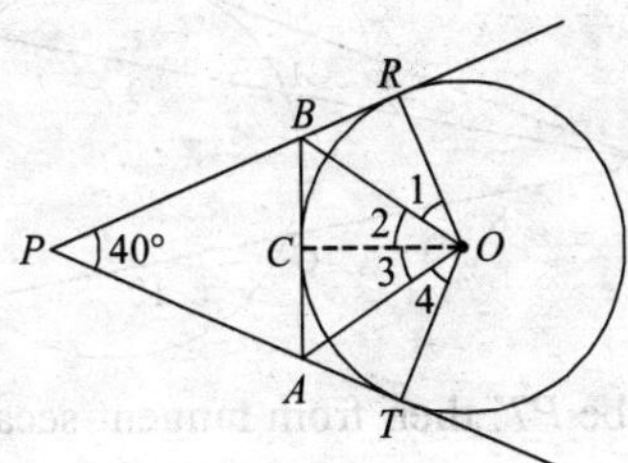

Given $\angle APB = 40°$

$\Rightarrow \angle TOR = 180 - 40$

$= 140$

But $\angle 1 = \angle 2$ as $\Delta BOR \cong \Delta BOC$

& $\angle 3 = \angle 4$ as $\Delta COA \cong \Delta AOT$

$\Rightarrow 2\angle 2 + 2\angle 3 = 140$

$\Rightarrow \angle 2 + \angle 3 = 70$

Hence Ans is (D)

Sol. 9 (B)

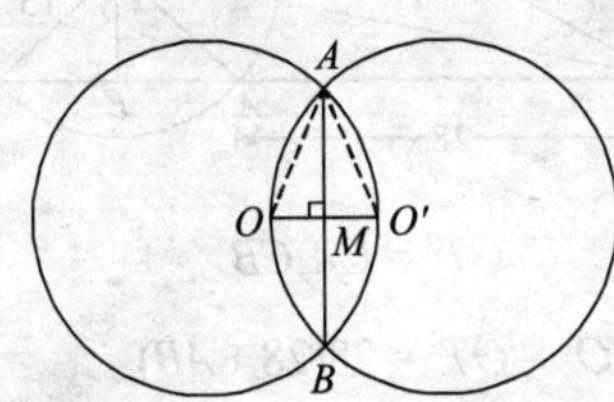

In right angled ΔAMO

$$OM^2 + AM^2 = r^2 \quad \ldots(1)$$

In right angled $\Delta AMO'$

$$(MO')^2 + AM^2 = r^2 \quad \ldots(2)$$

$(\because OA = O'A \text{ given})$

From (1) and (2)

$$OM = O'M = \frac{r}{2}$$

$$\Rightarrow \frac{r^2}{4} + AM^2 = r^2 \quad \text{from (1)}$$

$$\Rightarrow AM^2 = \frac{3}{4}r^2$$

$$\Rightarrow AM = \frac{\sqrt{3}}{2}r$$

$$\Rightarrow AB = \sqrt{3}r$$

Alternate solution

Since $\Delta OAO'$ is an equilateral triangle

$$\Rightarrow AM = \frac{r\sqrt{3}}{2}$$

$$\Rightarrow AB = 2AM = r\sqrt{3}$$

Hence Ans is (B)

Sol. 10 (B) In given the figure

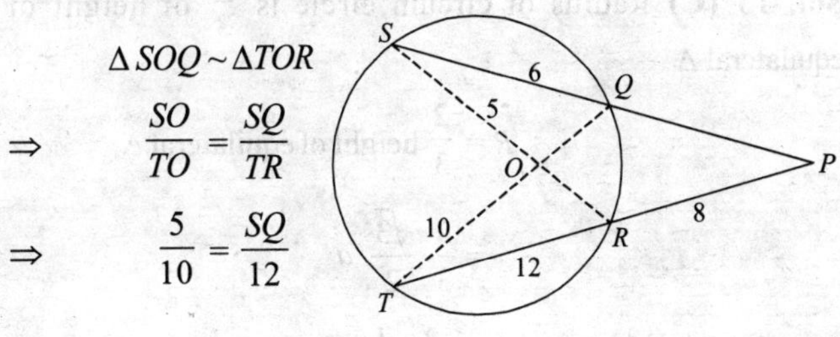

$\Delta SOQ \sim \Delta TOR$

$$\Rightarrow \frac{SO}{TO} = \frac{SQ}{TR}$$

$$\Rightarrow \frac{5}{10} = \frac{SQ}{12}$$

$$\Rightarrow SQ = 6 \quad \ldots(1)$$

We know,

$$PS \times PQ = PT \times PR$$

Let $PQ = x$

$\Rightarrow (SQ + PQ) \times PQ = PT \times PR$

$\Rightarrow (6 + x) \times x = (8 + 12) \times 8$

$\Rightarrow 6x + x^2 = 160$

$\Rightarrow x^2 + 6x - 160 = 0$

$\Rightarrow (x + 16)(x - 10) = 0$

$\Rightarrow x = 10$

$\Rightarrow PQ = 10$

Hence Ans is (B)

Sol. 11 (A)

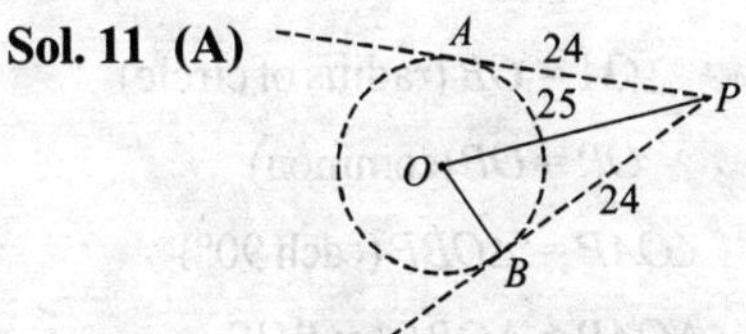

Tangent drawn from an external point are equal in length

$\Rightarrow PA = PB = 24$ cm

Now in right angle ΔOBP apply pythagoras

$$OP^2 = OB^2 + PB^2$$

$$(25)^2 = OB^2 + (24)^2$$

$$OB^2 = (25)^2 - (24)^2$$

$$= (25 - 24)(25 + 24)$$

$$OB^2 = 1 \times 49$$

$$OB = 7 \text{ cm}$$

Hence Ans is (A)

Sol. 12 (B)

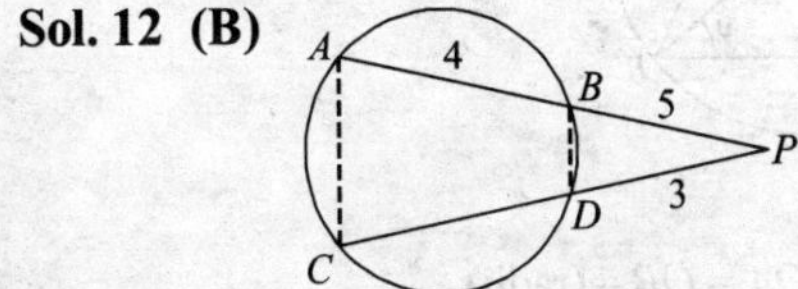

We know

$$PA \times PB = PC \times PO$$

$$9 \times 5 = PC \times 3$$

$\Rightarrow PC = 15$

$\Rightarrow CD = PC - PD = 15 - 3 = 12$

Hence Ans is (B)

Sol. 13 (C) Radius of circum circle is $\frac{2}{3}$ of height of equilateral Δ

$$R = \frac{2}{3} \text{ height of equilateral } \Delta$$

$$= \frac{2}{3} \cdot \frac{\sqrt{3}}{2} \cdot a$$

$$= \frac{2}{\sqrt{3}} \cdot \frac{1}{2} \cdot 24$$

$$R = 8\sqrt{3}$$

Hence Ans is (C)

Sol. 14 (D)

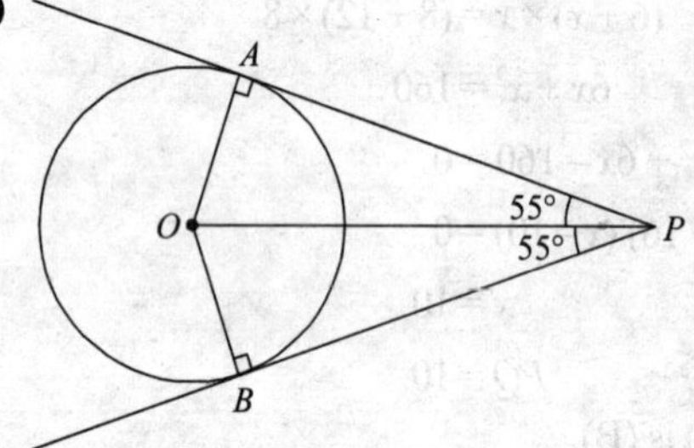

In ΔOAP & ΔOBP

$$OA = OB \text{ (radius of circle)}$$

$$OP = OP \text{ (common)}$$

$$\angle OAP = \angle OBP \text{ (each } 90°)$$

$\Rightarrow$ $\Delta OAP \cong \Delta OBP$ by RHS,

therefore $\angle OPA = \angle OPB = 55°$

so by angle sum property of triangle in ΔOAP we have

$$\angle OAP + \angle POA + \angle OPA = 180°$$

$$90° + \angle POA + 55° = 180°$$

$\Rightarrow$ $\angle POA = 180° - 145° = 35°$

Hence Ans is (D)

Sol. 15 (A)

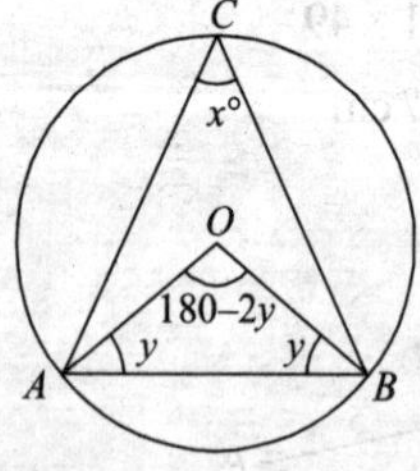

ΔOAB is isocesles

as $OA = OB = $ (radii)

$\Rightarrow$ $\angle O = 180 - 2y$

$$\angle O = 2\angle C$$

$$180 - 2y = 2x$$

$$x + y = 90$$

Hence Ans is (A)

Sol. 16 (D)

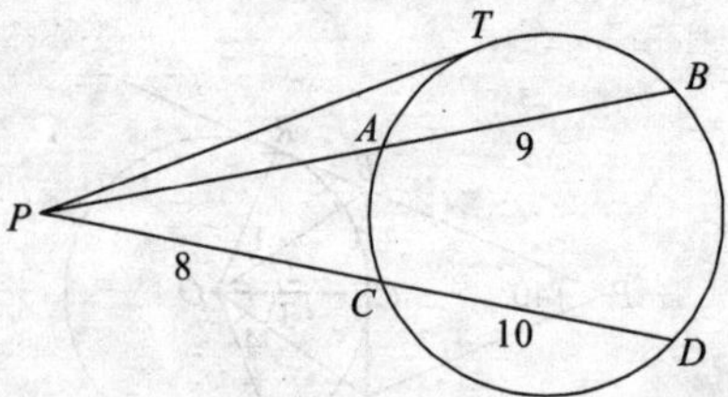

Let the tangent be PT. then from tangent secant theorem we have

$$PT^2 = PC \times PD$$

$$PT^2 = 8 \times 18$$

$$PT = \sqrt{144}$$

$$PT = 12$$

Hence Ans is (D)

Sol. 17 (C)

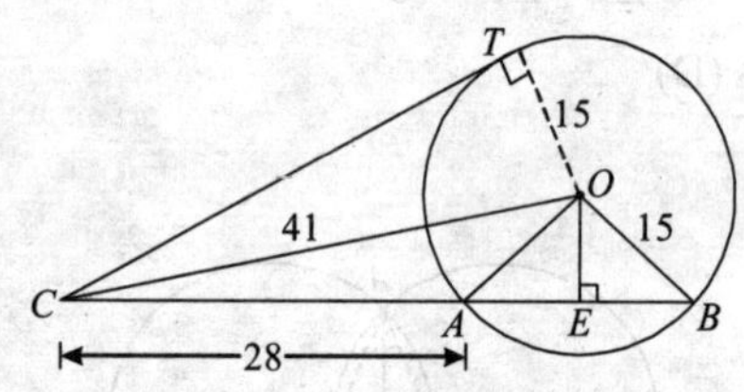

$$CT^2 = CA.CB$$

$$CO^2 - OT^2 = 28(28 + AB)$$

$$41^2 - 15^2 = 28(28 + AB)$$

$$AB = 24$$

$$AE = 12$$

Hence Ans is (C)

Sol. 18 (A)

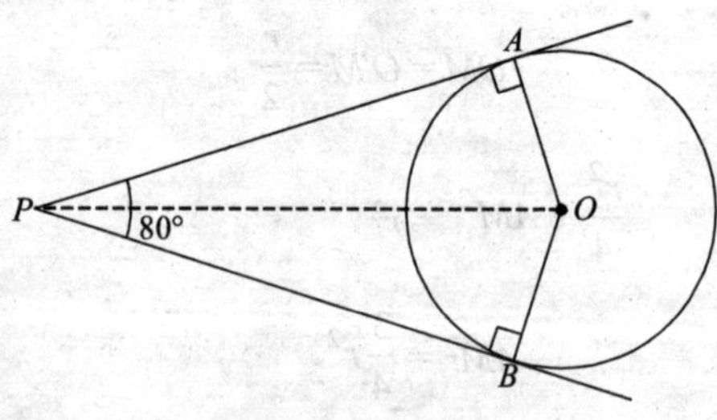

$$\Delta POA \cong \Delta POB$$

as $PA = PB$

(tangent from an external point are equal)

$OA = OB$ (radius)

$OP = OP$ (common)

$\Rightarrow$ $\angle APO = \angle BOP = 40$

$\Rightarrow$ $\angle AOP = 90 - 40 = 50$

Hence Ans is (A)

Sol. 19 (C)

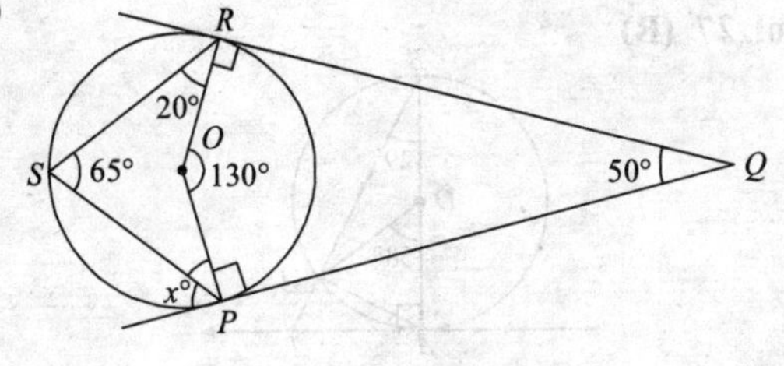

$$OR = OS$$

$\Rightarrow$ $\angle SRO = \angle OSR = 20°$

$\angle POR = 180° - 50 = 130$

(as $\angle Q + \angle POR = 180°$)

$\angle PSR = \frac{1}{2}\angle POR = \frac{1}{2} \times 130 = 65$

$\Rightarrow$ $\angle OSP = 65 - 20 = 45 = \angle SPO$

$\Rightarrow$ $x + \angle SPO + \angle OPQ = 180$

$x + 45 + 90 = 180$

$x = 180 - 135$

$= 45$

Hence Ans is (C)

Sol. 20 (D)

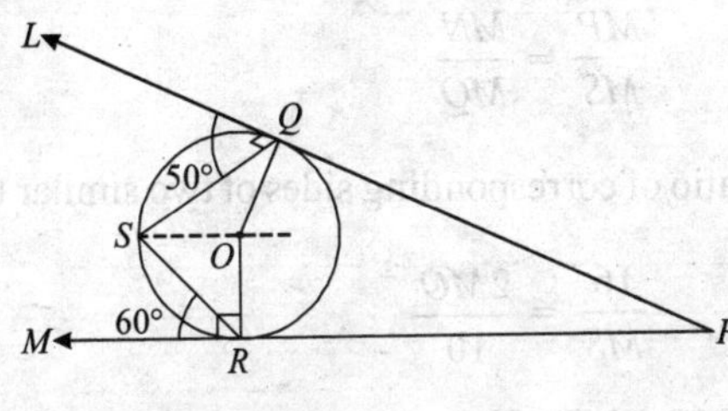

$OQ \perp PL$

$\Rightarrow$ $\angle SQO = 90 - 50 = 40 = \angle OSQ$

OR I PM

$\Rightarrow$ $\angle ORS = 90 - 60 = 30 = \angle OSR$

$\Rightarrow$ $\angle QSR = \angle OSQ + \angle OSR$

$= 40 + 30 = 70$

Hence Ans is (D)

Sol. 21 (D)

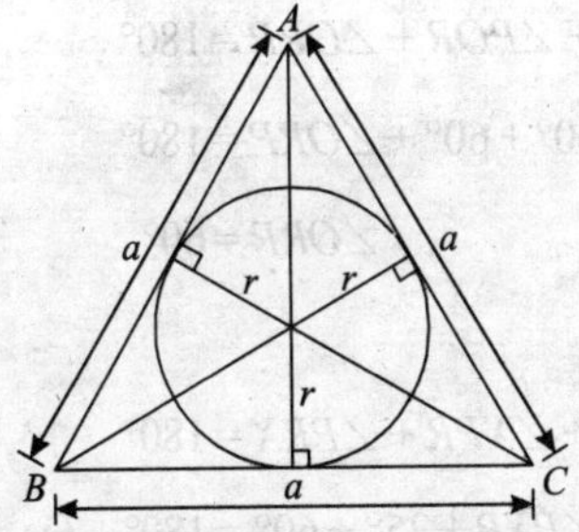

Let r be the radius of the in circle

given $\pi r^2 = 48\pi$

$\Rightarrow$ $r = 4\sqrt{3}$

Here $ar \text{ of } \Delta ABC = \frac{\sqrt{3}}{4}a^2$

$$\frac{1}{2}r(a + a + a) = \frac{\sqrt{3}}{4}a^2$$

$$\frac{4\sqrt{3}}{2}(3a) = \frac{\sqrt{3}}{4}a^2$$

$$a = 24$$

$\Rightarrow$ Perimeter $= 3a = 3 \times 24 = 72.$

Hence Ans is (D)

Sol. 22 (A)

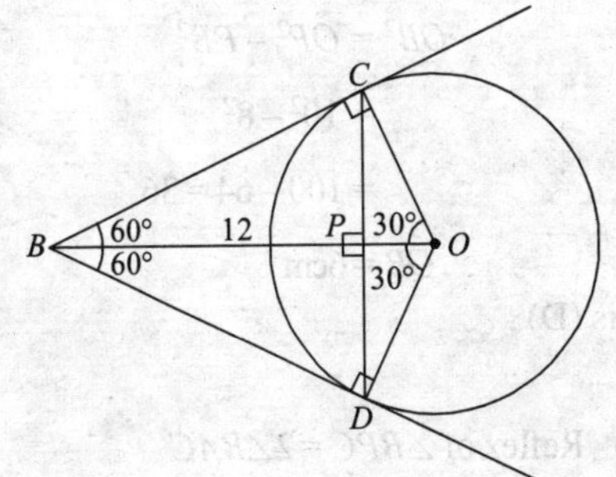

ΔOCB

$$\frac{OC}{OB} = \sin 60°$$

$$\frac{OC}{12} = \frac{\sqrt{3}}{2}$$

$$OC = 6\sqrt{3}$$

ΔOCB

$$\frac{CP}{OC} = \sin 30°$$

$$CP = OC \sin 30°$$

$$CP = 6\sqrt{3} \cdot \frac{1}{2}$$

$$CP = 3\sqrt{3}$$

$\Rightarrow$ $CD = 2CP$

$= 6\sqrt{3}$

Hence Ans is (A)

Sol. 23 (D)

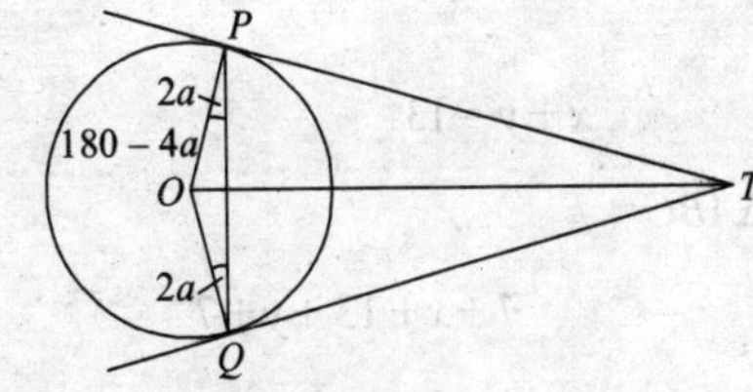

By angle sum property

$\angle POQ = 180 - 4a$

& Since $POQT$ is cyclic

So $\angle PTQ = 4a$

Hence Ans is (D)

Sol. 24 (D)

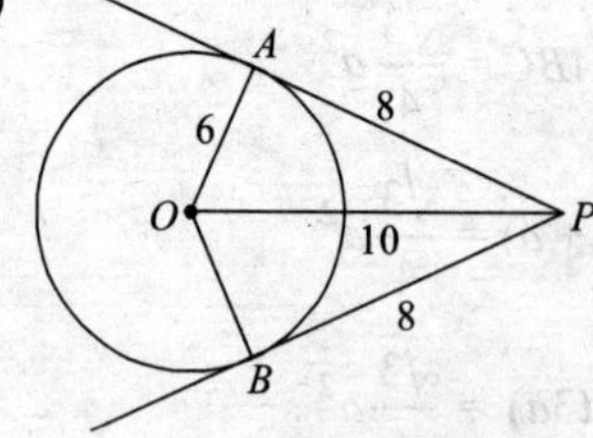

If $PA = 8$ cm

$\Rightarrow$ $PB = 8$cm

as tangent drawn from an external point are equal

Now apply pythagoras theorem in ΔOBP.

$$OB^2 = OP^2 - PB^2$$

$$= 10^2 - 8^2$$

$$= 100 - 64 = 36$$

$\Rightarrow$ $OB = 6$cm

Hence Ans is (D)

Sol. 25 (B) Reflex of $\angle BPC = 2\angle BAC$

$\Rightarrow$ Reflex of $\angle BPC = 280$

$$\angle BPC = 360 - 280$$

$$= 80$$

$\Rightarrow$ In ΔBPC

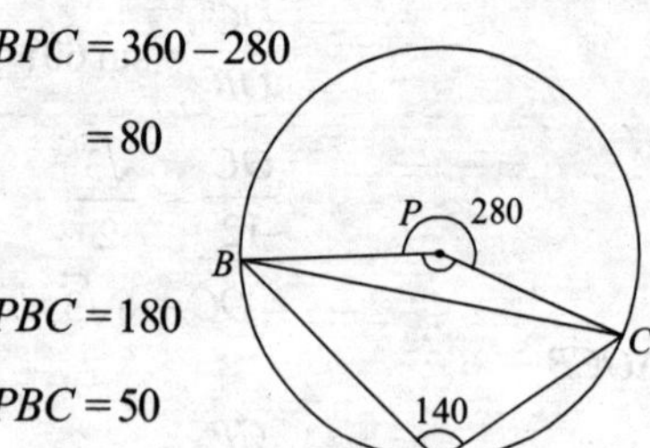

$$\angle BPC + 2\angle PBC = 180$$

$\Rightarrow$ $\angle PBC = 50$

As ΔBPC is isosceles Δ.

Hence Ans is (B)

Sol. 26 (C)

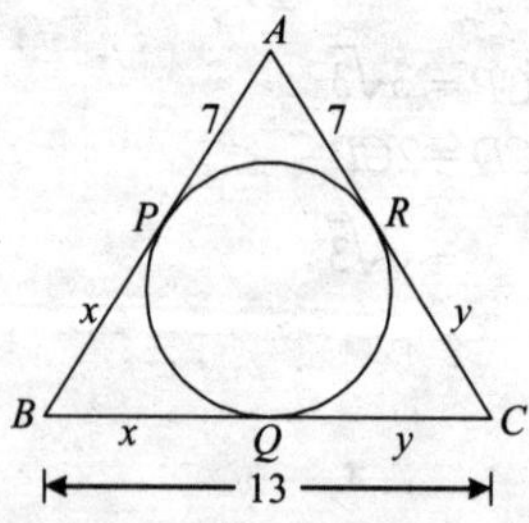

Given

$$x + y = 13$$

Perimeter of ΔABC

$$7 + x + 13 + y + 7$$

$$14 + 13 + (x + y)$$

$$14 + 13 + 13$$

$$14 + 26 = 40 \text{ cm}$$

Hence Ans is (C)

Sol. 27 (B)

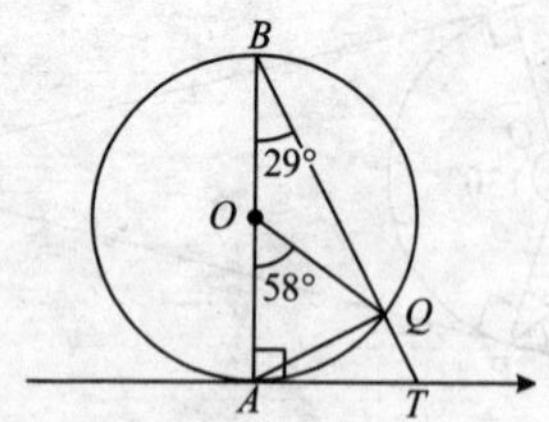

Join AQ then $\angle AOQ = 2\angle ABQ$

then $\angle ABQ = 29°$

Since $OQ \perp AT$

$\Rightarrow$ $\angle OAT = 90°$

Hence $\angle ATQ = 90° - 29° = 61°$

Hence Ans is (B)

Sol. 28 (D) In ΔMPS and ΔMNQ

$\angle MSP = \angle MQN$ (90° each)

$\angle MPS = \angle MNQ$ (angles in same segment)

Thus $\Delta MPS \sim \Delta MNQ$ (by AA similarity)

$$\Rightarrow \quad \frac{MP}{MS} = \frac{MN}{MQ}$$

(Ratio of corresponding sides of two similar triangles)

$$\Rightarrow \quad \frac{16}{MS} = \frac{2MO}{10}$$

$\Rightarrow$ $MO \times MS = 80$

Hence Ans is (D)

Sol. 29 (C) $\angle POQ = 110°$

$\angle OPQ = \angle OQP$ ($\because OP = OQ$, radii)

$\angle OPQ + \angle OQP = 70°$ (angle sum property)

$\Rightarrow$ $\angle OPQ = 35°$

In ΔOPR

$$\angle OPR + \angle POR + \angle ORP = 180°$$

$$60° + 60° + \angle ORP = 180°$$

$\Rightarrow$ $\angle ORP = 60°$

In ΔPXR

$$\angle PXR + \angle XPR + \angle PRX = 180°$$

$\Rightarrow$ $\angle PXR + 25° + 60° = 180°$ ($\because \angle PRX = \angle ORP$)

$\Rightarrow$ $\angle PXR = 95°$

Hence Ans is (C)

Sol. 30 (D) *OFCD* is a square

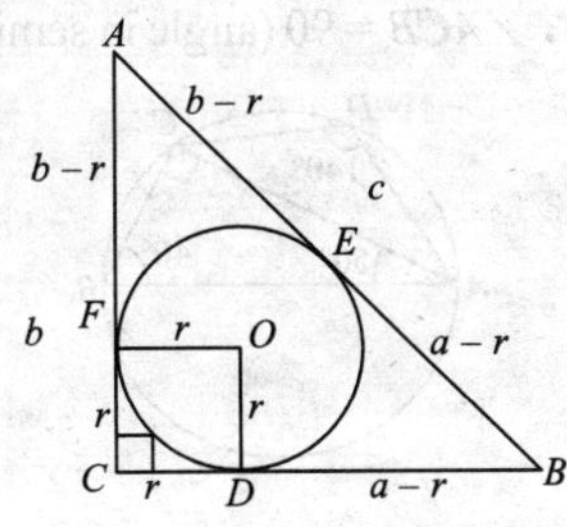

$$FC = CD = r$$
$$AF = AE = b - r$$
$$BD = BE = a - r$$
$$AB = c = AE + BE$$
$$c = b - r + a - r$$
$$2r = a + b - c$$
$$r = \frac{a+b-c}{2}$$

Hence Ans is (D)

Sol. 31 (B) Let the angle of quadrilateral *ABCD* be $3x, 3x, 2x, 2x$ respectively

$\Rightarrow$ $3x + 3x + 2x + 2 = 360°$

$$10x = 360$$
$$x = 36°$$
$$\angle A = 108°$$
$$\angle B = 108°$$
$$\angle C = 72°$$
$$\angle D = 72°$$

Which is an isosceles trapezium with $AB \parallel CD$

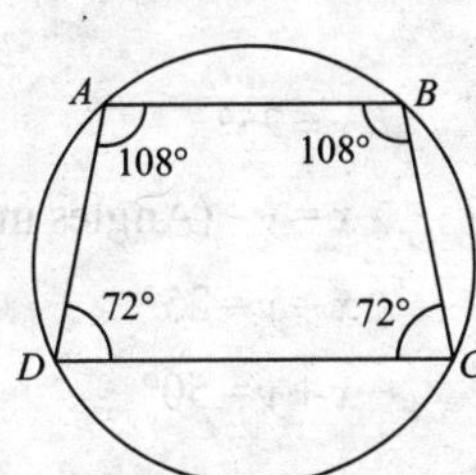

$\Rightarrow$ $AD = BC$

$\Rightarrow$ $AD = BC = 3.5$ cm

Hence Ans is (B)

Sol. 32 (D) In ΔAPM, $PA = AM$

$\Rightarrow$ $\angle APM = \angle PMA$

By alternate segment theorem

$$\angle AMP = \angle MBP$$

In ΔPMB, $\angle BPM = \angle PBM$

$\Rightarrow$ $PM = MB$

ΔPMB is an isosceles triangle

By Tangent secant theorem

$$AP.BP = PM^2$$
$$AP.BP = MB^2$$

Both (a) and (b) are true

Hence Ans is (D)

Sol. 33 (C)

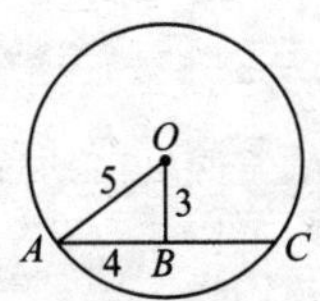

In ΔAOB

by Pythagoras theorem

$$AB = 4$$

$\Rightarrow$ $AC = 2AB$

$\Rightarrow$ $AC = 8$

Hence Ans is (C)

Sol. 34 (B) As per theoritical concept

Sol. 35 (C) In ΔAOB,

$$\angle ABO = \angle BAO = z$$
$$2z + 180 - x = 180 \Rightarrow z = \frac{x}{2}$$
$$\Delta ABC, \angle BAC = \angle BCA = y$$
$$y + 180 - \frac{x}{2} + y = 180 \Rightarrow 2y = \frac{x}{2}$$

$\Rightarrow$ $\frac{x}{y} = 4$

Hence Ans is (C)

Sol. 36 (C)

A diagram shows a circle with points A, C, O, B, D and angles x at B and D.

$\angle AOB = \angle COD$ (vertically opposite angles)

$\angle ABO = \angle CDO$ (angles in same segment)

$\Rightarrow$ $\Delta AOB \sim \Delta COD$ (by *AA*)

$$\Rightarrow \frac{ar(\Delta COD)}{ar(\Delta AOB)} = \frac{CD^2}{AB^2} = \left(\frac{40}{16}\right)^2 = \left(\frac{5}{2}\right)^2 = \frac{25}{4}$$

Hence Ans is (C)

Sol. 37 (C) Using distance formula

$$(4-1)^2+(q-0)^2=5^2$$
$$3^2+q^2=5^2$$
$$q^2=16$$
$$q=\pm 4$$

Hence Ans is (C)

Sol. 38 (C)

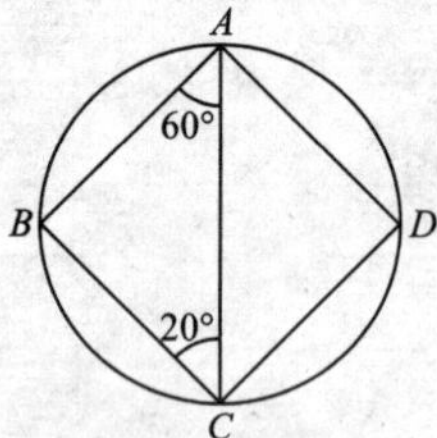

From triangle ABC

$$\angle B=100°$$
$$\angle B+\angle D=180°$$

Hence $\angle D=80°$

Hence Ans is (C)

Sol. 39 (C) $(10-x)^2+y^2=12^2$ ...(1)

$$x^2+y^2=10^2 \quad ...(2)$$
$$x=2.8\text{ cm};$$
$$y=9.6\text{ cm}$$
$$BC=2y=19.2\text{ cm}$$

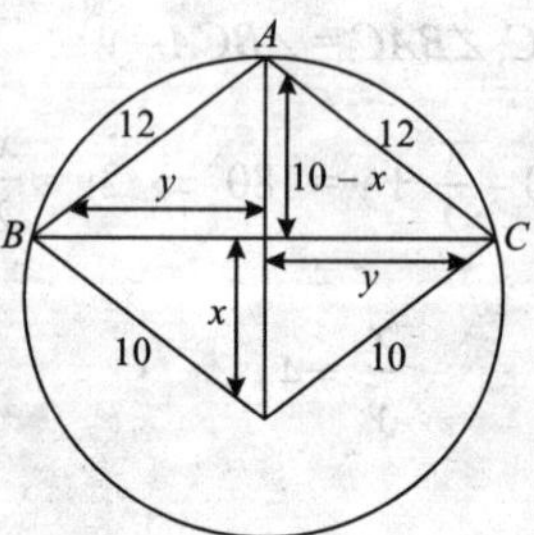

Hence Ans is (C)

Sol. 40 (B)

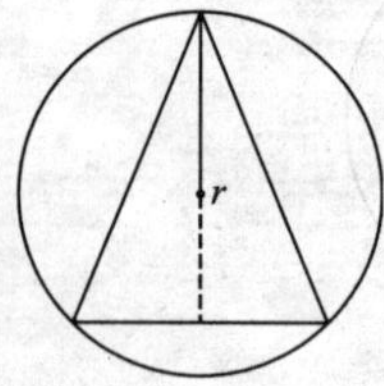

$$r=\frac{\sqrt{3}}{2}\text{ height of equilateral }\Delta$$

$$r=\frac{2}{3}\times\frac{\sqrt{3}}{2}\times 9$$
$$=3\sqrt{3}$$

Hence Ans is (B)

Sol. 41 (B) $\angle ABC=180-140=40$ (opposite angles)

$\angle ACB=90$ (angle in semi circle)

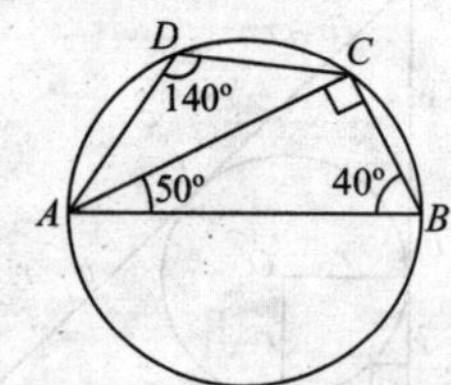

In ΔACB,

$$\angle CAB+90+40=180$$
$$\angle CAB=50°$$

Hence Ans is (B)

Sol. 42 (C) $\angle ACB=90°$

$\Rightarrow$ $\angle ACO=20°$

$OA=OC$

$\Rightarrow$ $\angle OAC=20°$

Hence Ans is (C)

Sol. 43 (C)

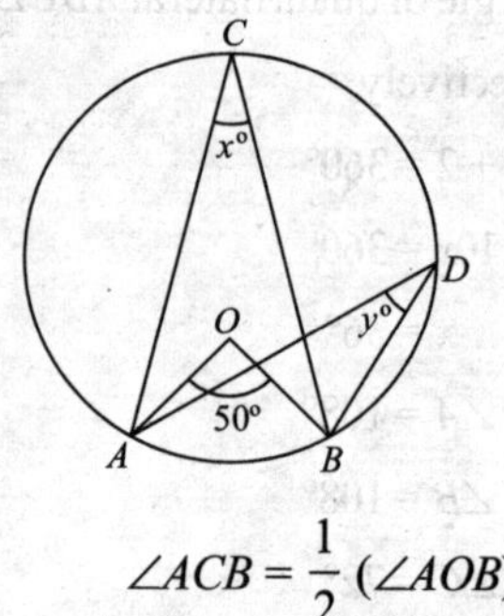

$$\angle ACB=\frac{1}{2}(\angle AOB)$$

[angle subtended by an arc at centre is double of the angle subtended by the arc at any other point on the remaining part of the circle]

$\Rightarrow$ $x=25°$

$x=y$ (Angles in the same segment)

$$x=y=25°$$
$$x+y=50°$$

Hence Ans is (C)

Sol. 44 (B) $AB^2=PQ_2+(r_1-r_2)^2$

$$169=PQ^2+25$$
$$PQ=12\text{ cm}$$

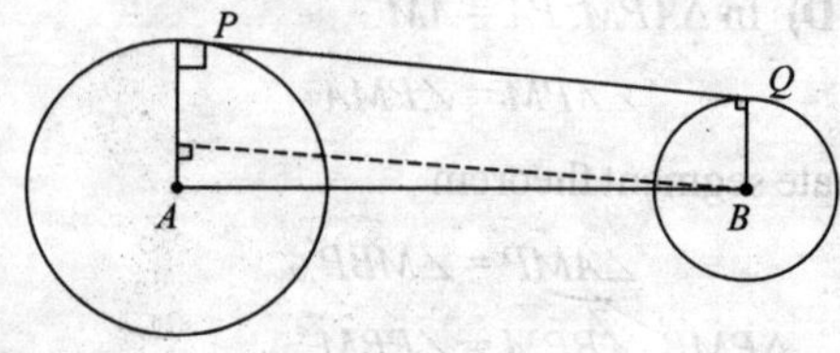

Hence Ans is (B)

Sol. 45 (B) We know

$$OQ \times OP = OS \times OR$$
$$8 \times 14 = 7 \times OR$$
$$OR = 16\text{ cm}$$
$$\Rightarrow \quad RS = 9\text{ cm}$$

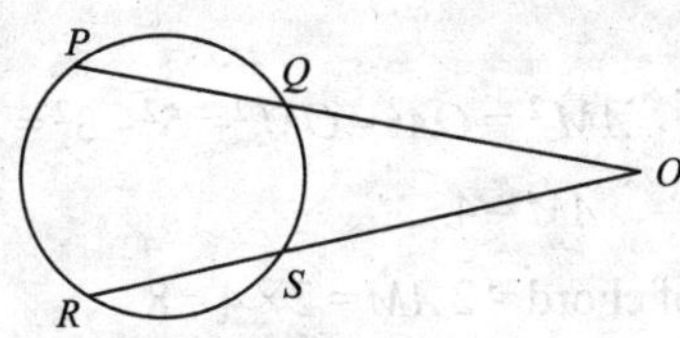

Hence Ans is (B)

Sol. 46 (B) Area of shaded region

$$= \frac{1}{4}\pi(4)^2 - \frac{1}{2} \times 4 \times 4 \times \sin 90^\circ$$
$$= \frac{1}{4}(\pi \times 16) - 8$$
$$= 4\pi - 8 = 4(\pi - 2)$$

Hence Ans is (B)

Sol. 47 (D)

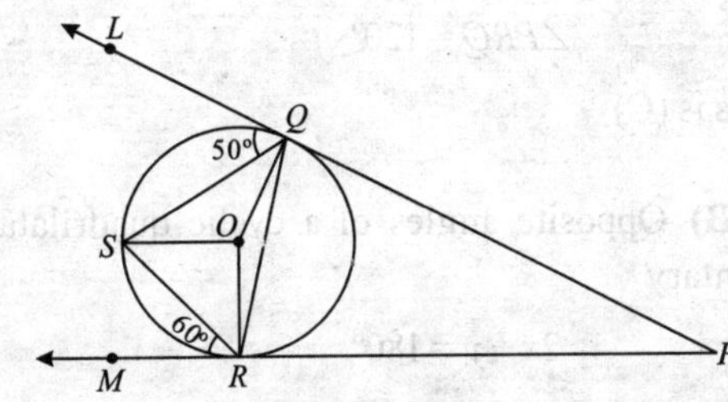

Join QR

$$\angle SRM = \angle SQR = 60^\circ$$

[Alternate segment theorem]

and $\angle SQL = \angle SRQ = 50^\circ$

[$\because$ Alternate segment theorem]

Now, in ΔSQR

$$\angle S + \angle Q + \angle R = 180^\circ$$
$$\angle S + 60^\circ + 50^\circ = 180^\circ$$
$$\angle S = 180^\circ - 110^\circ$$
$$\angle QSR = 70^\circ$$

Hence Ans is (D)

Sol. 48 (A)

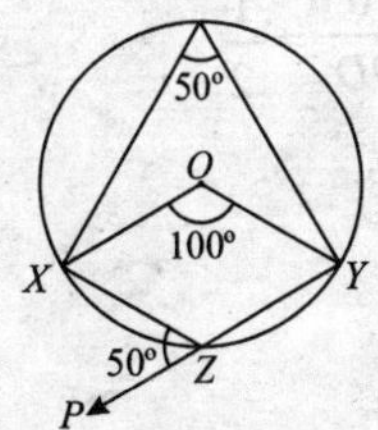

Hence Ans is (A)

Sol. 49 (A) $OP \perp AB$ ($\because$ radius is always perpendicular to tangent)

$$\Rightarrow \quad \angle OPB = 90^\circ$$
$$\Rightarrow \quad \angle OPQ + \angle QPB = 90^\circ$$
$$\Rightarrow \quad \angle OPQ + 50^\circ = 90^\circ$$
$$\Rightarrow \quad \angle OPQ = 40^\circ \qquad \ldots(1)$$

Now, In ΔOPQ,

$$OP = OQ = r$$
$$\Rightarrow \quad \angle OPQ = \angle OQP = 40^\circ \text{ (From-(1))}$$
$$\Rightarrow \quad \angle POQ = 180^\circ - 80^\circ$$
$$= 100^\circ$$

Hence Ans is (A)

Sol. 50 (D)

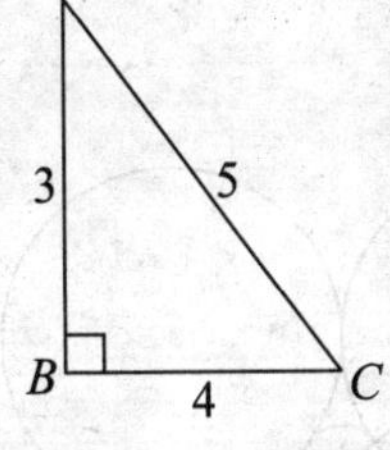

ΔABC is right angle triangle

$\Rightarrow$ AC is diameter

($\because$ diameter subtends 90° at any point of circle)

Now, appling pythagoras theorem in ΔABC

$$AC^2 = AB^2 + BC^2$$
$$= 3^2 + 4^2$$
$$= 9 + 16$$
$$= 25$$
$$\Rightarrow \quad AC = 5\text{ cm}$$
$$\Rightarrow \quad \text{radius} = 2.5\text{ cm}$$

Hence Ans is (D)

Sol. 51 (D) Area of semicircle – area of ΔABC

$$= \frac{\pi r^2}{2} - \frac{1}{2} \times b \times h$$
$$= \frac{3.14 \times 5^2}{2} - \frac{1}{2} \times 6 \times 8$$
$$= 39.25 - 24$$
$$= 15.25\text{ cm}^2$$

Hence Ans is (D)

Sol. 52 (C) Length of chord

$$AB = 24\text{ cm}$$

$$\Rightarrow \quad MB = \frac{1}{2}AB$$

$$= \frac{1}{2} \times 24$$

$$= 12\text{ cm}$$

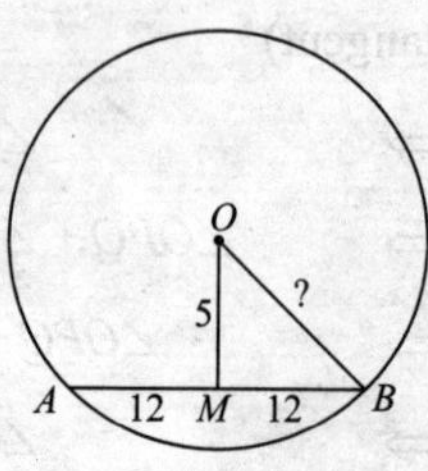

radius = OB

Now, ΔOMB is right angled triangle

$$\Rightarrow \quad OB^2 = OM^2 + MB^2$$

$$= 5^2 + 12^2$$

$$= 25 + 144$$

$$= 169$$

$$OB^2 = 13^2$$

$$\Rightarrow \quad OB = 13\text{ cm}$$

Hence Ans is (C)

Sol. 53 (C)

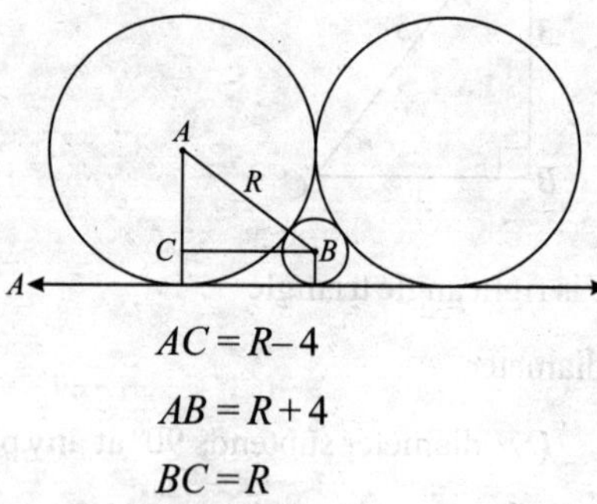

$$AC = R - 4$$

$$AB = R + 4$$

$$BC = R$$

ABC is a right angled triangle

Applying Pythagoras theorem, we get $R = 16$ cm

Hence Ans is (C)

Sol. 54 (B)

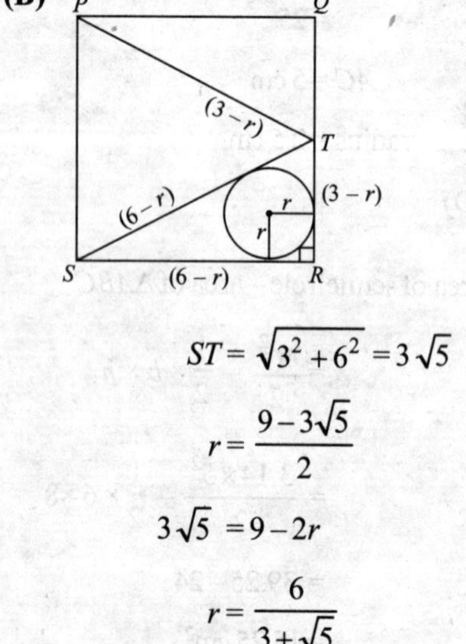

$$ST = \sqrt{3^2 + 6^2} = 3\sqrt{5}$$

$$r = \frac{9 - 3\sqrt{5}}{2}$$

$$3\sqrt{5} = 9 - 2r$$

$$r = \frac{6}{3 + \sqrt{5}}$$

Hence Ans is (B)

Sol. 55 (A)

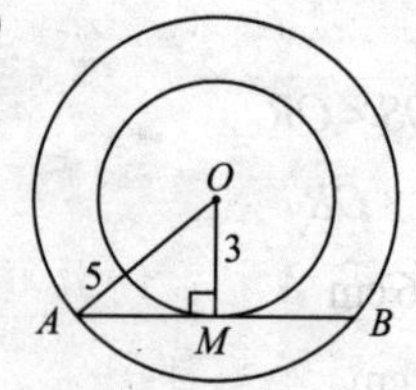

From figure,

$$AM^2 = OA^2 - OM^2 = 5^2 - 3^2 = 25 - 9 = 16$$

$$\Rightarrow \quad AM = 4.$$

Length of chord = $2\,AM = 2 \times 4 = 8$

Hence Ans is (A)

Sol. 56 (C)

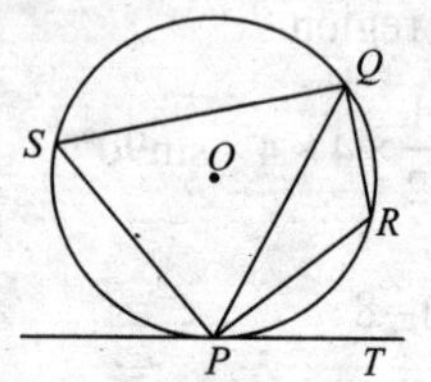

$\angle PSQ = 60^\circ$ (Alternate segment Theorem)

$\because$ $PRQS$ is cyclic quad

$$\Rightarrow \quad \angle S + \angle R = 180^\circ$$

$$\Rightarrow \quad \angle PRQ = 120^\circ$$

Hence Ans is (C)

Sol. 57 (B) Opposite angles of a cyclic quadrilatarial are supplementary

$$\Rightarrow \quad 2x + y = 180^\circ$$

$$y + 20 + 50^\circ = 180^\circ$$

$$\Rightarrow \quad y = 110^\circ$$

$$x = 35^\circ$$

Hence Ans is (B)

Sol. 58 (D) $\Delta OAB \sim \Delta OCD$

Also, $\dfrac{ar\Delta OAB}{ar\Delta OCD} = \dfrac{72}{288} = \dfrac{1}{4}$

$$\Rightarrow \quad \frac{1}{4} = \left(\frac{OA}{OC}\right)^2 = \left(\frac{OB}{OD}\right)^2$$

$$\Rightarrow \quad \frac{OA}{OC} = \frac{OB}{OD} = \frac{1}{2}$$

$$\Rightarrow \quad \frac{18}{OC} = \frac{16}{OD} = \frac{1}{2}$$

$$\Rightarrow \quad OC = 36,$$

$$OD = 32$$

$$\Rightarrow \quad BC = 20,$$

$$AD = 14$$

Hence Ans is (D)

Sol. 59 (B)

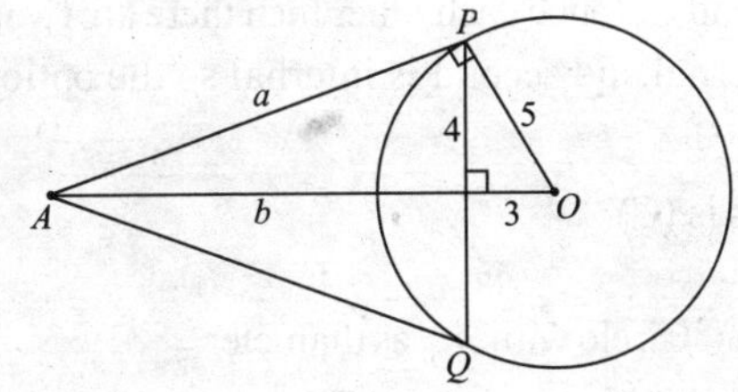

Let $PT = a, MT = b$

In ΔOPM

$$5^2 = OM^2 + PM^2$$

$$\Rightarrow \quad 25 = OM^2 + 4^2$$

$$\Rightarrow \quad OM = 3\text{cm}$$

Now, In ΔOPT

$$5^2 + a^2 = (b+3)^2 \quad \ldots(1)$$

Also, In ΔPMT

$$a^2 = b^2 + 4^2 \quad \ldots(2)$$

Putting in equation-(1), we get

$$25 + b^2 + 16 = b^2 + 6b + 9$$

$$\Rightarrow \quad a^2 = \left(\frac{16}{3}\right)^2 + 16$$

$$\Rightarrow \quad a^2 = \frac{256}{9} + 16$$

$$\Rightarrow \quad a^2 = \frac{400}{9}$$

$$\Rightarrow \quad a = \frac{20}{3}\text{ cm}$$

Hence Ans is (B)

Sol. 60 (B) Let radius of circle with center A be r,

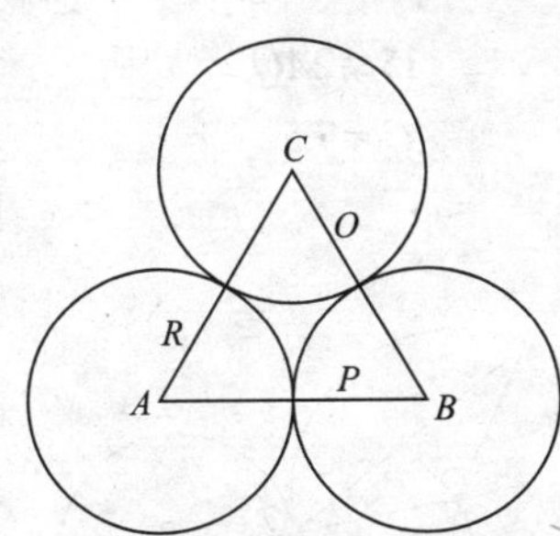

Then $PB = BQ = 5 - r$

& $RC = CQ = 6 - r$

Now, $CB = CQ + QB$

$$\Rightarrow \quad 7 = 5 - r + 6 - r$$

$$\Rightarrow \quad 2r = 4$$

$$\Rightarrow \quad r = 2\text{ cm}$$

Hence Ans is (B)

Sol. 61 (B)

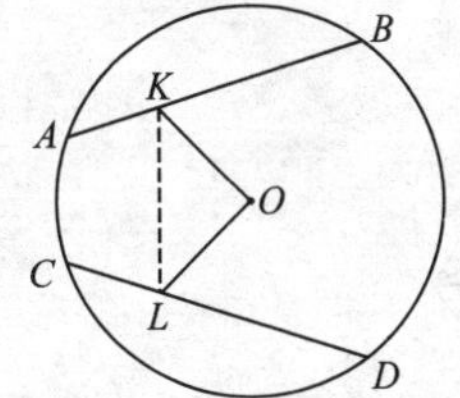

$$\angle LKB = 90 + 25 = 115^\circ$$

Hence Ans is (B)

Sol. 62 (B)

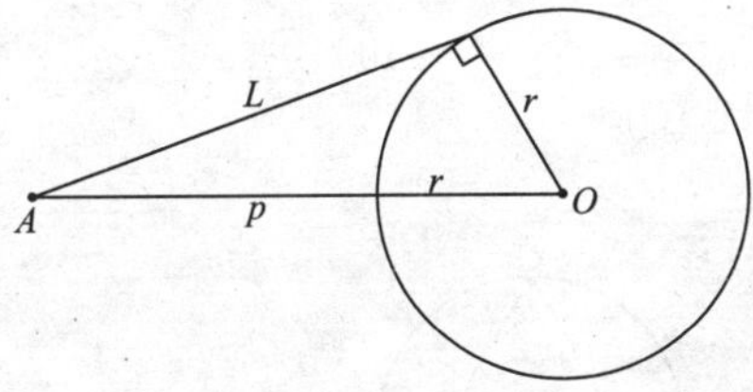

$$L = \frac{4}{3}r$$

$$AO = \sqrt{L^2 + r^2}$$

$$\Rightarrow \quad \sqrt{\frac{16}{9}r^2 + r^2} = \frac{5r}{3}$$

Thus; $AP = \frac{5r}{3} - r = \frac{2r}{3}$

Hence Ans is (B)

Sol. 63 (D)

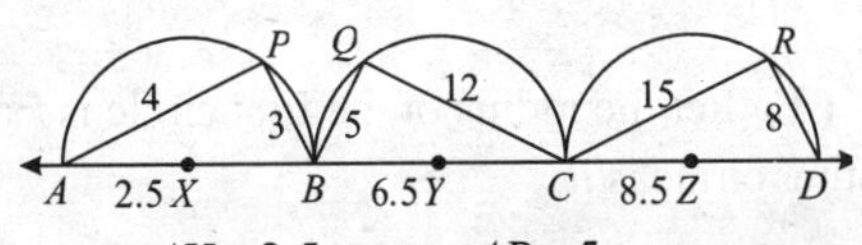

$AX = 2.5 \Rightarrow AB = 5$

$BY = 6.5 \Rightarrow BC = 13$ Hypotenuse

$CZ = 8.5 \Rightarrow CD = 17$

$$AP + QC = 16 \quad \ldots(1)$$

$$QC + CR = 27 \quad \ldots(2)$$

$$CR + AP = 19 \quad \ldots(3)$$

Adding (1) + (2) + (3)

$$2(AP + QC + CR) = 62$$

$$(AP + QC + CR) = 31 \quad \ldots(4)$$

Using (1) and (4) we have

$$CR = 15$$

Similarly using (2) and (4)

$$AP = 4$$

and using (3) and (4)

$$QC = 12$$

$\Rightarrow \quad CR = 15, AP = 4, BP = 3, QB = 5, QC = 12, RD = 8$

$$\Rightarrow \quad AP + PB + BQ + QC + CR + RD$$

$$= 15 + 8 + 12 + 5 + 3 + 4$$

$$= 47$$

Hence Ans is (D)

Sol. 64 (C)

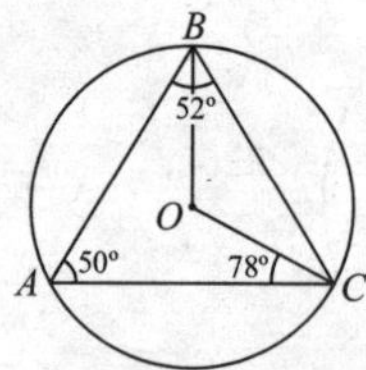

$$\angle A = 180° - [52° + 78°]$$
$$= 50°$$
$$\Rightarrow \quad \angle BOC = 2\angle A$$
$$= 100°$$

Hence Ans is (C)

Sol. 65 (A)

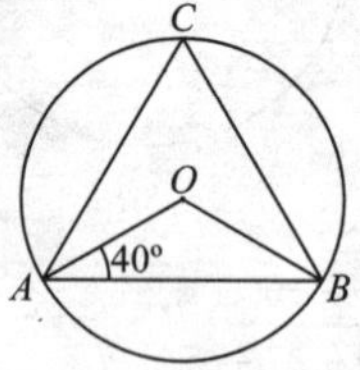

$$OA = OB \text{ (radius)}$$
$$\Rightarrow \quad \angle AOB = 40°$$
$$\Rightarrow \quad \angle AOB = 180° - 80° = 100°$$
$$\Rightarrow \quad \angle ACB = \frac{1}{2} \times \angle AOB = \frac{1}{2} \times 100° = 50°$$

Hence Ans is (A)

Sol. 66 (A) Let the radius of the first circle is r and radius of the another circle is R.

Area of another cirlce $= 2A$

$$\pi R^2 = 2A$$
$$\pi R^2 = 2 \times \pi r^2$$
$$R^2 = 2 \times r^2$$
$$R = \sqrt{2}r$$

Given circumference of another circle $= xC$

$$2\pi R = x \times 2\pi r$$
$$R = x \times r$$
$$\sqrt{2}r = x \times r$$
$$\Rightarrow \quad x = \sqrt{2}$$

Hence Ans is (A)

Sol. 67 (C)

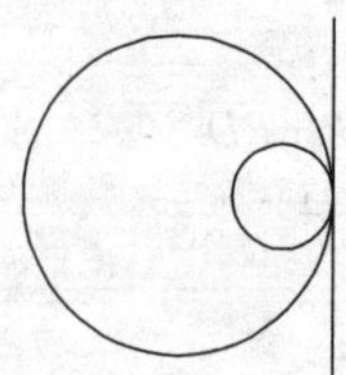

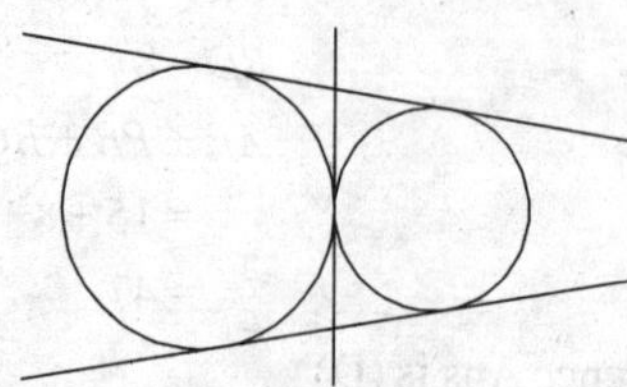

When C_1 and C_2 touch each other then there are two possiblities, one is external and second is internal so the option (C) is not always true

Hence Ans is (C)

Sol. 68 (A) Circle with AC as diameter

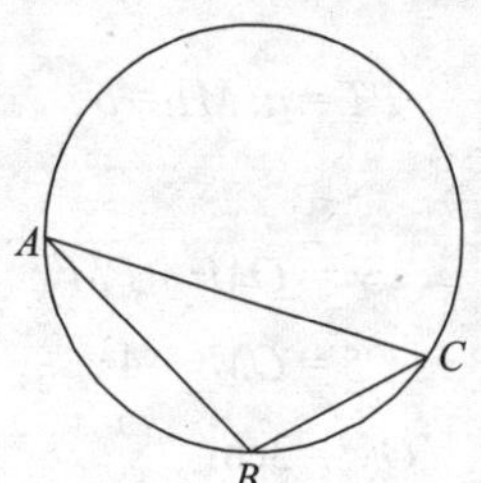

Hence Ans is (A)

Sol. 69 (B)

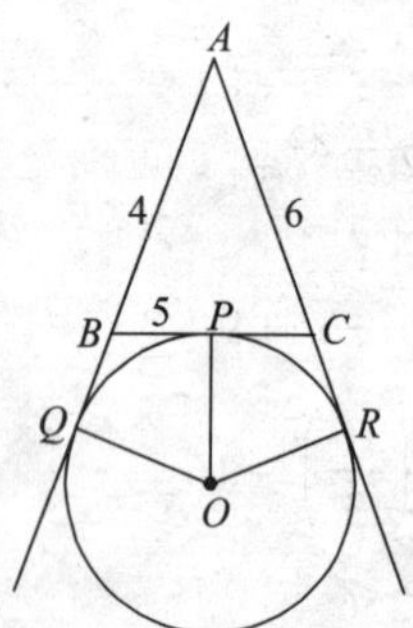

Tangents drawn from an external to a circle are equal in length

$\Rightarrow \{BQ = BP \text{ And } PC = CR \text{ \& also } AQ = AR\}$ ...(1)

Perimeter of ΔABC

$$= AB + BC + CA$$
$$= AB + BP + PC + CA$$
$$= AB + BQ + CR + AC \quad \text{(using (1))}$$
$$= AQ + AR$$
$$= 4 + 5 + 6 = 2AQ \quad \text{(using (1))}$$
$$15 = 2AQ$$
$$AQ = 7.5$$

Hence Ans is (B)

Sol. 70 (D)

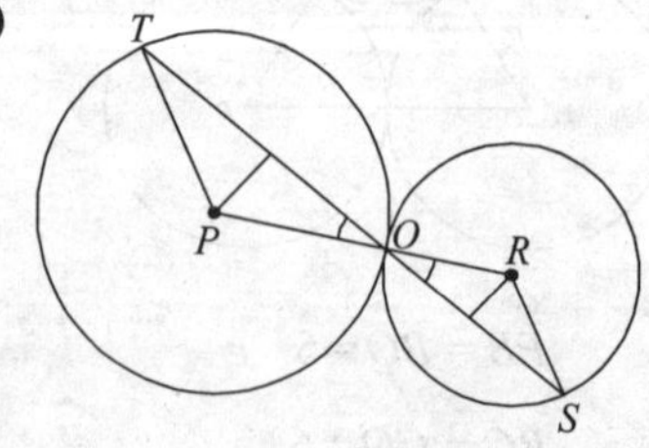

$$\angle ROS = \angle POT \text{(vertically opposite angle)}$$

and $\quad \angle ROS = \angle RSO \; (OR = RS)$

Also $\quad \angle POT = \angle PTO \; (PO = PT)$

So $\quad \angle PTO = \angle OSR$

But these are alternate angles

Hence $PT \parallel RS$

Hence Ans is (D)

Sol. 71 (D)

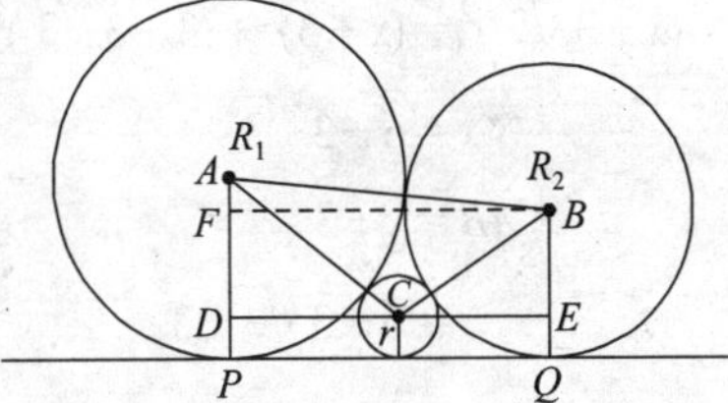

In ΔADC apply pythagoras theorem, we have

$$DC = \sqrt{(r+R_1)^2 - (R_1 - r)^2}$$

$$= \sqrt{4rR_1}$$

$$= 2\sqrt{rR_1}$$

Similarly from ΔBCE we have

$$CE = \sqrt{4rR_2} = 2\sqrt{rR_2}$$

Now in ΔABF

$$AB^2 - AF^2 = BF^2$$

$$(R_1 + R_2)^2 - (R_1 - R_2)^2 = BF^2$$

$$4R_1 \cdot R_2 = BF^2$$

$$BF = 2\sqrt{R_1 \cdot R_2}$$

Now, $BF = DE$

$$2\sqrt{R_1 \cdot R_2} = 2\sqrt{r}(\sqrt{R_1} + \sqrt{R_2})$$

$$\frac{1}{\sqrt{R_1}} + \frac{1}{\sqrt{R_2}} = \frac{1}{\sqrt{r}}$$

Hence Ans is (D)

Sol. 72 (C)

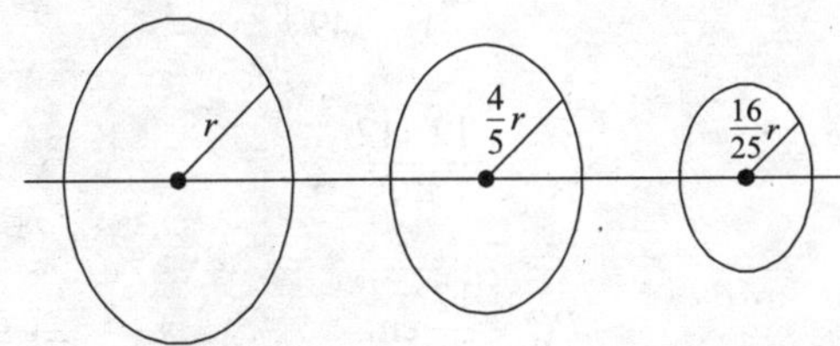

Distance covered in 32 revolution by

First ring $= 32 \times 2\pi r$

Number of turns by last ring is x

$$x = \frac{32 \times 2\pi r}{2\pi \times \frac{16}{25} \times r}$$

$$x = 50$$

Hence Ans is (C)

Sol. 73 (A) Let side of square is x

Area of square $= x^2$

$$\text{Area of circle} = \pi\left(\frac{x}{2}\right)^2$$

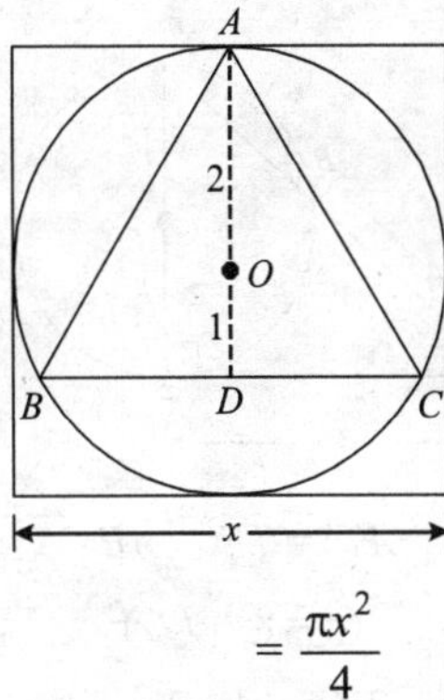

$$= \frac{\pi x^2}{4}$$

$$\text{Distance } AO = \frac{x}{2}$$

$$\text{Distance } AD = \frac{x}{2} + \frac{x}{4} = \frac{3x}{4}$$

$$\text{Height of equilateral triangle} = \frac{3x}{4}$$

In equilateral Δ,

$$\text{Height} = \frac{\sqrt{3}}{2} \times \text{side}$$

$$\frac{3x}{4} = \frac{\sqrt{3}}{2} \times \text{side}$$

$$\text{side} = \frac{\sqrt{3}x}{2}$$

$$\text{Area of equilateral triangle} = \frac{\sqrt{3}}{4}\left(\frac{\sqrt{3}x}{2}\right)^2$$

$$= \frac{\sqrt{3}}{4}\left(\frac{3x^2}{4}\right) = \frac{3\sqrt{3}x^2}{16}$$

According to equation

$$x^2 = K\frac{3\sqrt{3}x^2}{16}$$

$$\Rightarrow \quad K = \frac{16}{3\sqrt{3}}$$

Hence Ans is (A)

Sol. 74 (A) According to theorem

$$TP^2 = TB \times TA$$

$$8^2 = 4 \times TA$$

$$64 = 4 \times TA$$

$$TA = 16$$

So, $BA = 12$

Apply phythagorus theorem in ΔATP

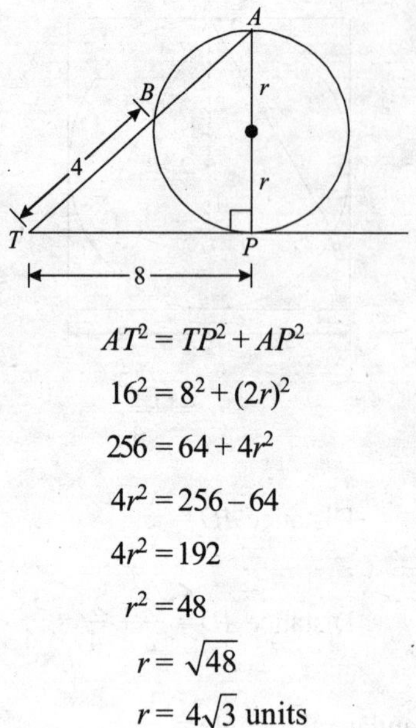

$$AT^2 = TP^2 + AP^2$$
$$16^2 = 8^2 + (2r)^2$$
$$256 = 64 + 4r^2$$
$$4r^2 = 256 - 64$$
$$4r^2 = 192$$
$$r^2 = 48$$
$$r = \sqrt{48}$$
$$r = 4\sqrt{3} \text{ units}$$

Hence Ans is (A)

Sol. 75 (D)

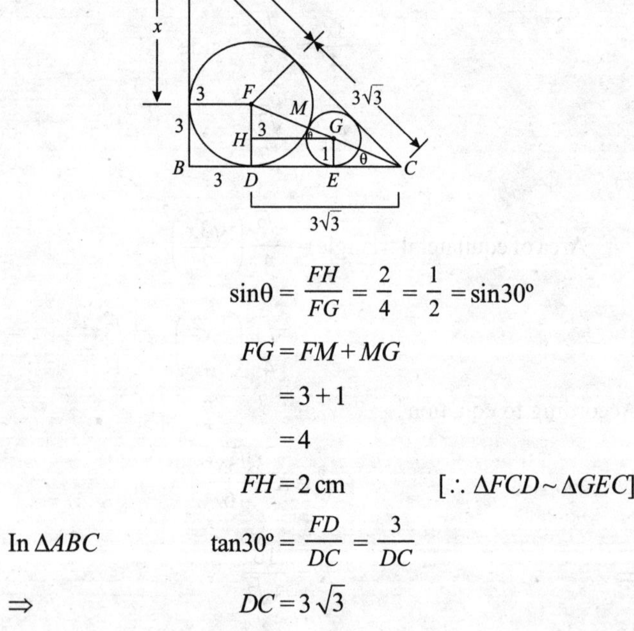

$$\sin\theta = \frac{FH}{FG} = \frac{2}{4} = \frac{1}{2} = \sin 30°$$
$$FG = FM + MG$$
$$= 3 + 1$$
$$= 4$$
$$FH = 2 \text{ cm} \qquad [\therefore \Delta FCD \sim \Delta GEC]$$

In ΔABC $\quad \tan 30° = \frac{FD}{DC} = \frac{3}{DC}$

$\Rightarrow \quad DC = 3\sqrt{3}$

$$(x + 3\sqrt{3})^2 = (x+3)^2 + (3 + 3\sqrt{3})^2$$

$\Rightarrow \quad x = 6 + 3\sqrt{3}$

$$AB = x + 3$$
$$= 6 + 3\sqrt{3} + 3$$
$$= 9 + 3\sqrt{3}$$

Hence Ans is (D)

Sol. 76 (C)

PQ is a bisector of $\angle BQC$

$$\cos 120° = \frac{4^2 + 3^2 - BC^2}{2 \times 4 \times 3}$$
$$BC^2 = 37$$
$$BC = \sqrt{37} \qquad \ldots(1)$$

We know that

$$PQ^2 = BQ \times QC - BP \times PC$$
$$= 4 \times 3 - 4k \times 3k$$
$$= 12(1 - k^2)$$
$$= 12\left(1 - \frac{37}{49}\right)$$
$$= \frac{12 \times 12}{49}$$
$$PQ = \frac{12}{7} \text{ cm}$$

Hence Ans is (C)

* * * * *

Co-ordinate Geometry 10

❍ In the rectangular coordinate system, two number lines are drawn at right angles to each other. The point of intersection of these two number lines is called the **origin** whose coordinates are taken as (0, 0). The horizontal number line is known as the x-axis and the vertical one as the y-axis.

❍ Position of a point on the plane is shown by on ordered pair (p, q), where p is called the *x-coordinate* or *abscissa* and q is known as *y-coordinate* or *ordinate* of the point.

❍ The coordinate plane is divided into four **quadrants**.

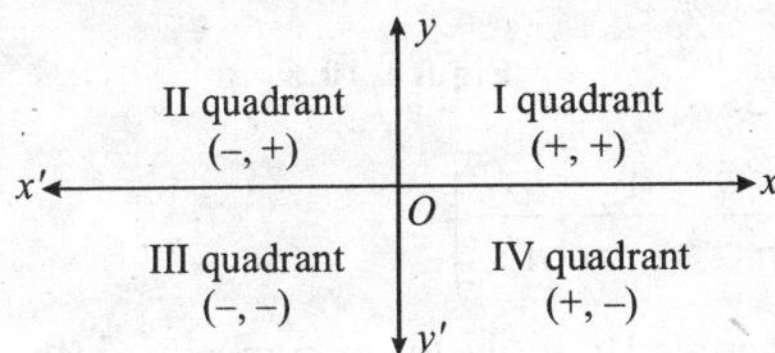

Figure 10.1

❍ The abscissa of a point is its perpendicular distance from y-axis.

❍ The ordinate of a point is its perpendicular distance from x-axis.

❍ The abscissa of every point situated on the right side of y-axis is **positive** and the abscissa of every point situated on the left side of y-axis is **negative**.

❍ The ordinate of every point situated above x-axis is **positive** and that of every point below x-axis is **negative.**

❍ The abscissa of every point on y-axis is zero.

❍ The ordinate of every point on x-axis is zero.

❍ The distance between any two points $P(x_1, y_1)$ and $Q(x_2, y_2)$ is given by

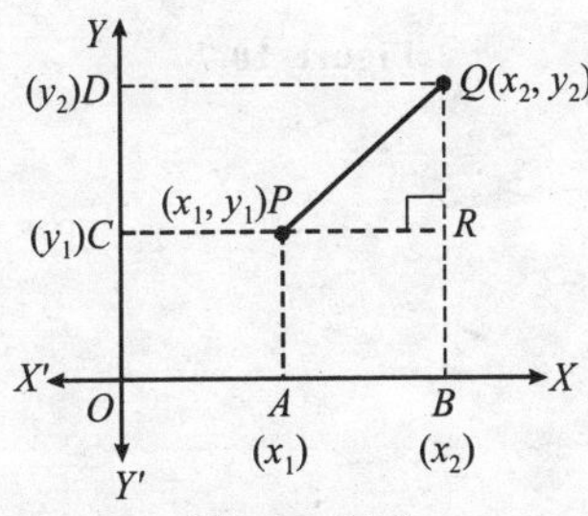

Figure 10.2

$$PQ = \sqrt{(x_2 - x_1)^2 + (y_2 - y_1)^2}$$

or $PQ = \sqrt{(x_1 - x_2)^2 + (y_1 - y_2)^2}$

$$\Rightarrow PQ = \sqrt{\begin{pmatrix}\text{Difference}\\ \text{of abscissa}\end{pmatrix}^2 + \begin{pmatrix}\text{Difference}\\ \text{of ordinates}\end{pmatrix}^2}$$

❍ If $O(0, 0)$ is the origin and $P(x, y)$ is any point, then from the above formula, we have :

$$OP = \sqrt{(x-0)^2 + (y-0)^2} = \sqrt{x^2 + y^2}$$

❍ In order to prove that a given figure is a :

(i) **Square**, prove that four sides are equal and the diagonals are equal.

(ii) **Rhombus**, prove that the four sides are equal.

(iii) **Rectangle**, prove the opposite sides are equal and the diagonals are also equal.

(iv) **Parallelogram**, prove that the opposite sides are equal.

(v) **Parallelogram but not a rectangle**, prove that its opposite sides are equal but diagonals are not equal.

❍ Three points A, B and C are said to be collinear, if they lie on the same straight line.

❍ For three points to be *collinear,* the sum of the distances between two pairs of points is equal to the third pair of points.

❍ Three points will make :

(i) **A scalene triangle**, if no two sides of the triangle are equal.

(ii) **An isosceles triangle**, if any two sides are equal.

(iii) **An equilateral triangle**, if all the three sides are equal.

(iv) **A right triangle**, if sum of the squares of any two sides is equal to the square of the third side.

❍ The coordinates of the point $P(x, y)$ which divides the line segment joining $A(x_1, y_1)$ and $B(x_2, y_2)$. Internally in the ratio $m : n$ are

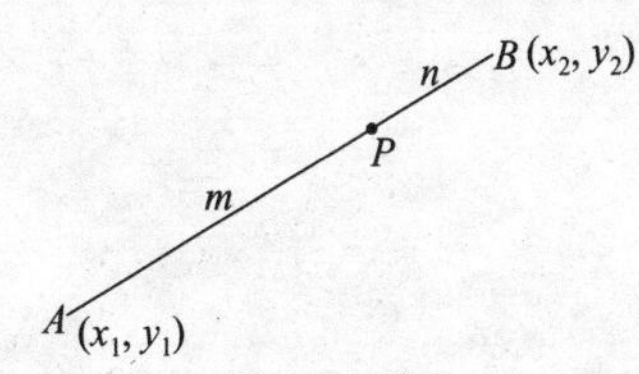

Figure 10.3

$$x = \frac{mx_2 + nx_1}{m+n}, y = \frac{my_2 + ny_1}{m+n}$$

❍ The coordinates of the mid-point M of a line segment AB with end points $A(x_1, y_1)$ and $B(x_2, y_2)$

$$\left[\frac{x_1+x_2}{2}, \frac{y_1+y_2}{2}\right]$$

❍ The point of intersection of the medians of a triangle is called its *centroid*.

❍ The coordinates of the centroid of the triangle whose vertices are (x_1, y_1), (x_2, y_2) and (x_3, y_3) are given

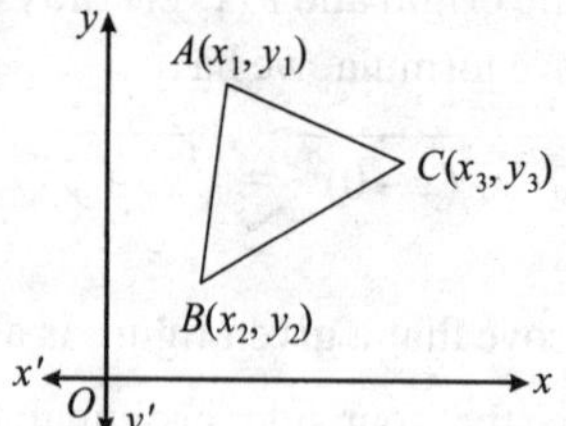

Figure 10.4

$$\left[\frac{x_1+x_2+x_3}{3}, \frac{y_1+y_2+y_3}{3}\right]$$

❍ The area of a ΔABC with vertices $A(x_1, y_1)$, $B(x_2, y_2)$ and $C(x_3, y_3)$ is given by:

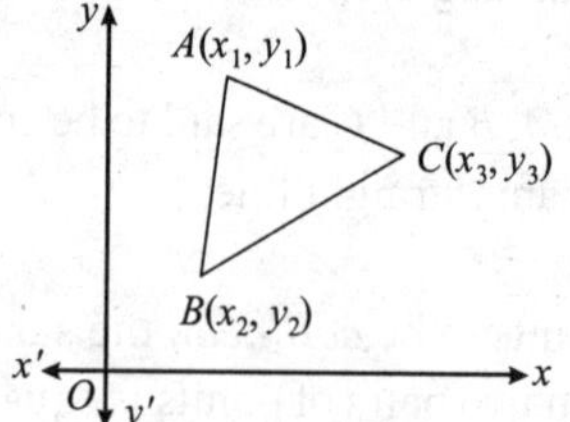

Figure 10.5

are (ΔABC)

$$= \left|\frac{1}{2}\{x_1(y_2-y_3)+x_2(y_3-y_1)+x_3(y_1-y_2)\}\right|$$

Since area of a triangle cannot be negative, we consider the absolute or numerical value of the area.

❍ Three given points $A(x_1, y_1)$, $B(x_2, y_2)$ and $C(x_3, y_3)$, are collinear if

$$\left|\frac{1}{2}\{x_1(y_2-y_3)+x_2(y_3-y_1)+x_3(y_1-y_2)\}\right| = 0$$

$$|\{x_1(y_2-y_3)+x_2(y_3-y_1)+x_3(y_1-y_2)\}| = 0$$

❍ The point of intersection of perpendicular bisectors of the sides of the triangle is called circumcentre and the point of intersection of altitudes of a triangle is called orthocentre.

❍ The co-ordinates of the point which divides the line segment joining the points (x_1, y_1) and (x_2, y_2) externally in the ratio $m : n$ are

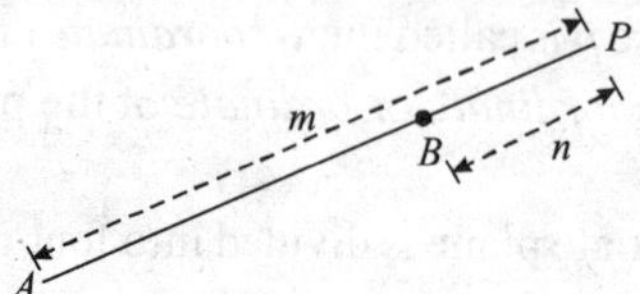

Figure 10.6

$$\left[\frac{mx_2-nx_1}{m-n}, \frac{my_2-ny_1}{m-n}\right]$$

❍ In a right angled triangle, the circumcentre is the mid point of hypotenuse and the orthocentre is the point where right angle is formed.

❍ In an equilateral triangle, the centroid, incentre, orthocentre and circumcentre coincide.

❍ The point of intersection of internal bisectors of the angles of the triangle is called incentre. The co-ordinates of the incentre of the triangle ABC whose co-ordinates $A(x_1, y_1)$, $B(x_2, y_2)$ and $C(x_3, y_2)$, and $BC = a$, $AC = b$ and $AB = c$, are

$$\left[\frac{ax_1+bx_2+cx_3}{a+b+c}, \frac{ay_1+by_2+cy_3}{a+b+c}\right]$$

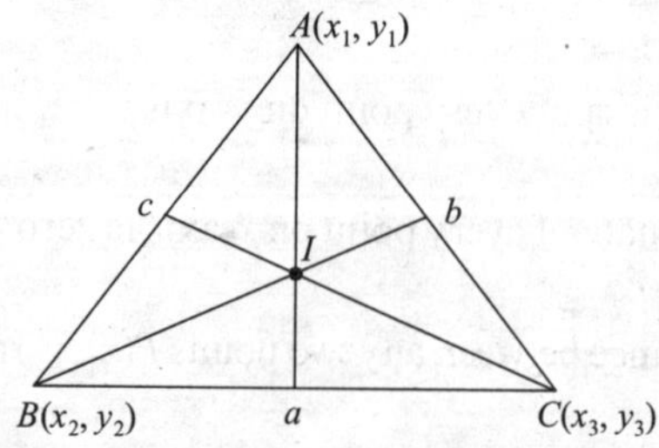

Figure 10.7

* * * * *

PRACTICE EXERCISE - 10.1

10-1 If two vertices of an equilateral triangle be (0, 0), $(3, \sqrt{3})$, find the third vertex :

(A) $(2\sqrt{3}, 0)$ (B) $(0, 2\sqrt{3})$
(C) $(3, -\sqrt{3})$ (D) Both (B) and (C)

10-2 Find the value of a if a line $3x + 4y = a$ passes through the point of intersection of line $3x - 5y = 1$ and line $5x + 2y = 12$:

(A) –6 (B) 8
(C) 10 (D) 12

10-3 Which of the following line is not parallel to $3x - 5y = 7$:

(A) $6x - 10y = 3$ (B) $-6x + 10y - 7 = 0$
(C) $5x - \frac{25}{3}y = 1$ (D) $4x - 7y = 8$

10-4 Find the number of points of intersection lines $-3x + 4y = 0$, $4x - 5y = 1$ and $2x + 3y = 17$:

(A) 0 (B) 3
(C) 2 (D) 1

10-5 Find the length of the line segment made on line $9x + 12y = 108$ by both the axes :

(A) 9 units (B) 15 units
(C) 12 units (D) 98 units

10-6 In what ratio does the x-axis divide the line segment joining the points (–3, 0) and (3, 0) :

(A) 3 : 1 (B) 1 : 2
(C) 2 : 1 (D) 1 : 1

10-7 The vertices of a triangle are (3, –1), (–3, –1) and (6, 2) then coordinates of its centroid is :

(A) (0, 2) (B) (2, 0)
(C) (2, 4) (D) (4, 2)

10-8 If points $(a, 0)$, $(0, b)$ and (1, 1) are collinear, then $\frac{1}{a} + \frac{1}{b} =$

(A) 1 (B) 2
(C) 0 (D) –1

10-9 The points (0, 8), (1, 8) and (1, – 9/8) are the vertices of :

(A) An equilateral triangle (B) The collinear points
(C) An isosceles triangle (D) A right-angled triangle

10-10 If the points (–2, –1), (1, 0), $(x, 3)$ and $(1, y)$ form a parallelogram, find the value of $x^2 - y$:

(A) 12 (B) 14
(C) 13 (D) 15

10-11 The points (a, a) $(-a, -a)$ and $(-\sqrt{3}\,a, \sqrt{3}\,a)$ form the vertices of an :

(A) Scalene triangle
(B) Right angled triangle
(C) Isosceles right angled triangle
(D) Equilateral triangle

10-12 The ratio in which the line segment joining (3, 4) and (–1, 2) is divided by the y-axis is :

(A) 1 : 2 (B) 1 : 3
(C) 3 : 2 (D) None of these

10-13 The slope of any line parallel to X-axis is :

(A) 0 (B) 1
(C) –1 (D) Not defined

10-14 The distance between the points $(\cos\theta, \sin\theta)$ and $(\sin\theta, -\cos\theta)$ is :

(A) $\sqrt{3}$ (B) $\sqrt{2}$
(C) 2 (D) 1

10-15 Find the centroid of triangle whose vertices are (0, 0), (0, 1) & (2, 0) :

(A) $\left(\frac{2}{3}, \frac{1}{3}\right)$ (B) (0, 0)
(C) (1, 5) (D) None of these

10-16 If the distance between $A(x, y)$ and $B(3, 2)$ is $\sqrt{2}$ find the value of x and y. If $2x + y = 7$:

(A) (2, 3) (B) $\left(\frac{16}{5}, \frac{3}{5}\right)$
(C) Both (A) and (B) (D) None of these

10-17 Find the area bounded by lines $x + y = 2$ and $x - y = 2$ and y-axis :

(A) 4 square units
(B) $\frac{2304 \times 10^{-2}}{2.4^2}$ square units
(C) $(3 \div 3 \div 3 + 3 - 3 \times 2 + 7 - \frac{1}{3})$ square units
(D) All of these

10-18 The distance between the points $(a\cos\theta + b\sin\theta, 0)$ and $(0, a\sin\theta - b\cos\theta)$ is :

(A) $a^2 + b^2$ (B) $a + b$
(C) $a^2 - b^2$ (D) $\sqrt{a^2 + b^2}$

10-19 The equation of the straight line which passes through the point $A(-4, 3)$ and $B(9, 5)$ is :

(A) $9x-20y-96=0$ (B) $9x+20y+96=0$

(C) $9x-20y+96=0$ (D) None of these

10-20 Area of triangle enclose between the coordinate axes with vertices (2, 0) and (0, 3) is :

(A) 4 sq. units (B) 5 sq. units

(C) 10 sq. units (D) None of these

10-21 If (x, y) be on the line joining the two points $(1, -3)$ and $(-4, 2)$. Which one is true ?

(A) $2x-3y-11=0$ (B) $x+2y=0$

(C) $x+y+2=0$ (D) $2x+y+3=0$

10-22 The centre of the circle passing through the points (5, 7), (6, 6) and (2, –2) is :

(A) (2,–3) (B) (2,–1)

(C) (2, 3) (D) None of these

10-23 The distance between the points (a cos 25°, 0) and (0, a cos 65°) is :

(A) a (B) $2a$

(C) $3a$ (D) $5a$

10-24 The orthocentre of the triangle formed by the lines $xy=0$ and $x+y=1$ is :

(A) (0, 0) (B) (0, 1)

(C) (1, 0) (D) (1, 1)

10-25 Find the orthocentre of the triangle formed by $O(0, 0)$, $A(1, 0)$ and $B(0, 1)$ where orthocentre is the point of intersection of altitudes drawn from vertices on opposite sides :

(A) $\left(\frac{1}{2}, \frac{1}{2}\right)$ (B) $\left(\frac{1}{3}, \frac{1}{3}\right)$

(C) 0, 0 (D) $\left(\frac{1}{4}, \frac{1}{4}\right)$

10-26 If the sum of intercepts made by $3x+4y=a$ on axes is 7, then find the value of a, $a>0$:

(A) 12 (B) 16

(C) 7 (D) 6

10-27 In what ratio does the x-axis divides the line segment joining the points $(-3, 4)$ and $(a, -5)$:

(A) 3 : 5 (B) 2 : 5

(C) 3 : 2 (D) 4 : 5

10-28 The points (0, 0), (–5, 0) and (4, 0) are :

(A) Collinear (B) On the x-axis

(C) On the y-axis (D) Both A and B

10-29 The line joining the points (2, 1) and (5, –8) is trisected at the points P and Q. If point P lies on the line $2x-y+K=0$ then find the value of K :

(A) $K=4$ (B) $K=8$

(C) $K=-8$ (D) $K=-4$

10-30 If $P(2, -1)$, $Q(3, 4)$, $R(-2, 3)$ and $S(-3, -2)$ be four points in a plane, then $PQRS$ is a :

(A) Rhombus (B) Rectangle

(C) Square (D) Parallelogram

10-31 If $A(-2, -1)$, $B(a, 0)$, $C(4, b)$ and $D(1, 2)$ are the vertices of a parallelogram, then $(a, b)=$

(A) (1, 3) (B) (3, 1)

(C) (5, 3) (D) (3, 5)

10-32 If three points (0, 0), $(3, \sqrt{3})$ and $(3, \lambda)$ form an equilateral triangle, then λ is equal to :

(A) 2 (B) –3

(C) – 4 (D) None of these

10-33 If (2, 1), (4, 5), (–1, –3) are the mid points of the sides of a triangle, then the coordinates of its vertices are :

(A) (–3, –7) (17, 9) (1, 1) (B) (–3, 7) (7, 9) (–1, –1)

(C) (–3, –7) (7, 9) (1, 1) (D) None of these

10-34 The mid point of the line segment joining $(2a, 4)$ and $(-2, 3b)$ is $(1, 2a+1)$ then the values of a and b are given by :

(A) $a=2, b=-2$ (B) $a=b=2$

(C) $a=1=b$ (D) $a=-2, b=2$

10-35 The mid point of the line segment AB shown in the figure-10.8 is (4, – 3). Then the coordinates of A and B are :

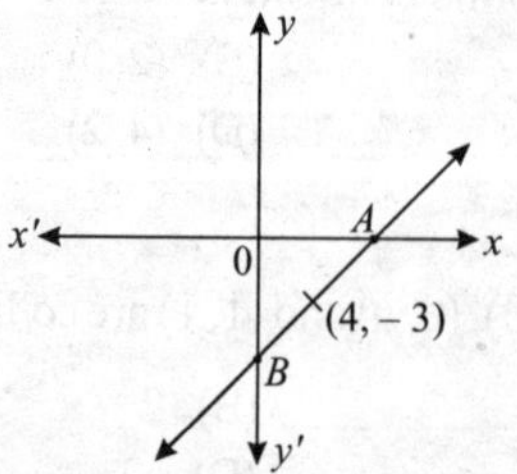

Figure 10.8

(A) (8, 0) and (0, – 6) (B) (0, 8) and (0, – 6)

(C) (8, 0) and (– 6, 0) (D) None of these

10-36 The ratio in which (4, 5) divides the line joining (2, 3) and (7, 8) is :

(A) 2 : 3 (B) – 2 : 3

(C) 3 : 1 (D) 2 : – 3

10-37 The orthocentre of ΔABC is B and the circumcentre is $S(a, b)$. If A is the origin then the co-ordinate of C are :

(A) $(2a, 2b)$ (B) $\left(\frac{a}{2}, \frac{b}{2}\right)$

(C) $(\sqrt{a^2+b^2}, 0)$ (D) None

10-38 Find the area bounded by line $3x + 4y = 12$ and both axes :

(A) 6 cm^2 (B) 16 cm^2
(C) 8 cm^2 (D) 9 cm^2

10-39 The area of triangle formed by $(a, b+c)$, $(b, c+a)$ and $(c, a+b)$ is :

(A) $(a+b+c)$ (B) abc
(C) $(a+b+c)^2$ (D) 0

10-40 If $A(x, y)$, $B(2, 3)$ and $C(-3, -4)$ are collinear then :

(A) $5x-7y=100$ (B) $7x-3y=1$
(C) $7x-5y-1=0$ (D) $7x-5y+1=0$

10-41 If (α, β, γ) are real roots of the equation $x^3 - 3px^2 + 3qx - 1 = 0$, then the centroid of the triangle with vertices $\left(\alpha, \frac{1}{\alpha}\right)$, $\left(\beta, \frac{1}{\beta}\right)$ and $\left(\gamma, \frac{1}{\gamma}\right)$ is at the point :

(A) (p, q) (B) $\left(\frac{p}{3}, \frac{q}{3}\right)$

(C) $(p+q, p-q)$ (D) $(3p, 3q)$

10-42 In triangle ABC, the coordinates of A and B are respectively $(2, 3)$ and $(8, 10)$. It is known that C also has integer coordinates. The minimum possible area of ABC is :

(A) 0 (B) $\frac{1}{2}$

(C) 1 (D) $\frac{3}{2}$

10-43 Let A, B, C, D be collinear points in that order. Suppose $AB : CD = 3 : 2$ and $BC : AD = 1 : 5$. Then $AC : BD$ is :

(A) $1:1$ (B) $11:10$
(C) $16:11$ (D) $17:13$

10-44 Three points A, B and C have coordinates $(a, b+c)$, $(b, c+a)$ and $(c, a+b)$ respectively. The area of the triangle ABC will be :

(A) $a^2+b^2+c^2$ (B) $(a^2+b^2+c^2)/2$
(C) $(a^2+b^2+c^2)/4$ (D) Zero

10-45 The incentre of the triangle with vertices $(1, \sqrt{3})$, $(0, 0)$ and $(2, 0)$ is :

(A) $\left(1, \frac{\sqrt{3}}{2}\right)$ (B) $\left(\frac{2}{3}, \frac{1}{\sqrt{3}}\right)$

(C) $\left(\frac{2}{3}, \frac{\sqrt{3}}{2}\right)$ (D) $\left(1, \frac{1}{\sqrt{3}}\right)$

10-46 The area bounded by the curves $y=|x|-1$ and $y=-|x|+1$ is :

(A) 1 (B) 2
(C) $2\sqrt{2}$ (D) 4

10-47 A line L is perpendicular to the line $5x-y=1$ and the area of the triangle formed by the line L and coordinate axes is 5. The equation of the line L is :

(A) $x+5y=5$ (B) $x+5y=\pm 5\sqrt{2}$
(C) $x-5y=5$ (D) $x-5y=5\sqrt{2}$

10-48 The area of triangle formed by the lines $x=0$, $y=0$ and $\frac{x}{a}+\frac{y}{b}=1$, is :

(A) ab (B) $\frac{ab}{2}$

(C) $2ab$ (D) $\frac{ab}{3}$

10-49 If the centroid and circumcentre of a triangle are $(3, 3)$ and $(6, 2)$ respectively, then the orthocentre is :

(A) $(-3, 5)$ (B) $(-3, 1)$
(C) $(3, -1)$ (D) $(9, 5)$

10-50 The points which trisect the line segment joining the points $(0, 0)$ and $(9, 12)$ are :

(A) $(3, 4)$ (B) $(8, 6)$
(C) $(6, 8)$ (D) $(4, 0)$

* * * * *

PRACTICE EXERCISE - 10.2

10-1 The mid point of the base of a triangle is equidistant from all the vertices. The triangle is :

(A) Equilateral (B) Right angled
(C) Isosceles (D) Ordinary

10-2 The locus of the centres of all circles of given radius 'r', in the same plane and passing through a fixed point is :

(A) A point (B) A straight Line
(C) A pair of straight lines (D) A circle

10-3 In the graph, co-ordinates of the point P are :

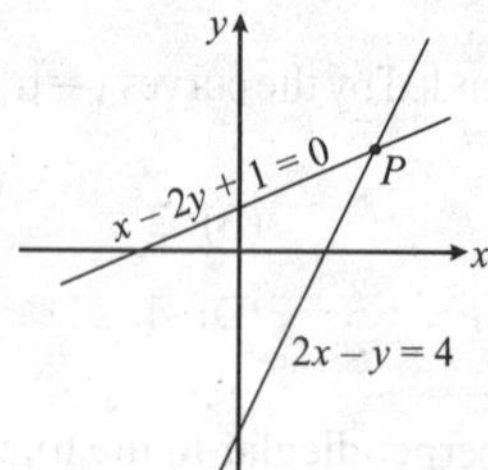

Figure 10.9

(A) (4, 4) (B) (5, 3)
(C) (3, 2) (D) (2, 3)

10-4 In the following diagram $ABCD$ is a square and E, F, G and H are mid-points of the sides, then which of the following is incorrect :

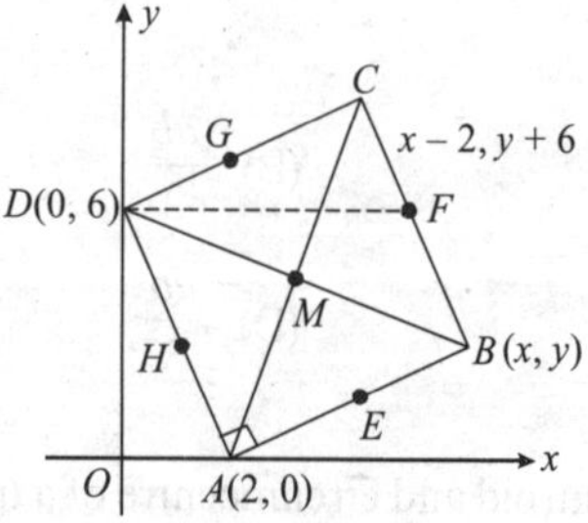

Figure 10.10

(A) Point E is (5, 1) (B) Point G is (3, 7)
(C) Point F is (7, 6) (D) Area of ΔHME is 5 sq. units

10-5 Find the area of the triangle whose vertices are $(a, b+c)$, $(a, b-c)$ and $(-a, c)$:

(A) $2ac$ (B) $2bc$
(C) $b(a+c)$ (D) $c(a-b)$

10-6 The orthocentre of the triangle ABC is 'B' and the circumcentre is 'S' (a, b). If A is the origin then the co-ordinates of C are :

(A) $(2a, 2b)$ (B) $\left(\frac{a}{2}, \frac{b}{2}\right)$
(C) $(\sqrt{a^2+b^2}, 0)$ (D) None

10-7 The in centre of the triangle formed by (0, 0), (5, 12), (16, 12) is :

(A) (7, 9) (B) (9, 7)
(C) (−9, 7) (D) (−7, 9)

10-8 If a vector, the circumcentre and the centroid of a triangle are (0, 0), (3, 4) and (6, 8) respectively, then the triangle must be :

(A) A right angled triangle
(B) An equilateral triangle
(C) An isosceles triangle
(D) A right angled isosceles triangle

10-9 If the middle points of the sides of a triangle be (− 2, 3), (4, − 3) and (4, 5), then centroid of triangle is :

(A) $\left(\frac{5}{3}, 2\right)$ (B) $\left(\frac{5}{6}, 1\right)$
(C) $\left(1, \frac{5}{6}\right)$ (D) $\left(2, \frac{5}{3}\right)$

10-10 If (1, 4) is the centroid of a triangle and the co-ordinates of its any two vertices are (4, − 8) and (− 9, 7). Then the are of the triangle is :

(A) $\frac{333}{2}$ sq. units (B) 166 sq. units
(C) 140 sq. units (D) $\frac{633}{2}$ sq. units

10-11 If the centroid of the triangle formed by the points (a, b), (b, c) and (c, a) is at the origin, then $a^3 + b^3 + c^3 =$

(A) abc (B) $a+b+c$
(C) $3abc$ (D) 0

10-12 Consider the triangle OAB in the xy-plane where $O = (0, 0)$, $A = (6, 0)$, $B = (\sqrt{2}, 3)$. A square $PQRS$ is inscribed in the square with P, Q on OA, R on AB and S on BO. Then the side of the square equals :

(A) $3/\sqrt{2}$ (B) $\frac{9}{4}$
(C) $\frac{3}{2}\sqrt{\frac{5}{2}}$ (D) 2

10-13 If the co-ordinates of two points A and B are (3, 4) and (5, − 2) respectively, then the co-ordinates of any point P if $PA = PB$ and Area of $\Delta PAB = 10$ is :

(A) (7, 2) or (1, 0) (B) (− 7, 2) or (3, 0)
(C) (7, − 2) or (5, 0) (D) (7, − 2) or (− 1, 0)

10-14 If $A(2, 2)$, $B(-4, -4)$, $C(5, -8)$ are the vertices of any triangle, the length of median passing through C will be :

(A) $\sqrt{65}$ (B) $\sqrt{117}$
(C) $\sqrt{85}$ (D) $\sqrt{113}$

10-15 If A & B are the points $(-3, 4)$ and $(2, 1)$, then the co-ordinates of the point C on AB produced such that $AC = 2BC$ are :

(A) $(2, 4)$ (B) $(3, 7)$
(C) $(7, -2)$ (D) $\left(-\frac{1}{2}, \frac{5}{2}\right)$

Directions : (10-16 to 10-17) Refer to the data below and answer the questions that follow.

A special fully automatic car is designed by the Indian scientist in the Hindustan Automobiles Ltd. The car follows only the following instructions.

$G_1(x)$: The car shall move forward to x metres.
$G_2(x)$: The car shall turn in right direction and move x metres
$G_3(x)$: The car shall turn in left direction and move x metres.
$G_4(x)$: The car shall move backward y metres.

10-16 The car is given instruction $G_1(100)$, $G_3(50)$, $G_4(10)$. Assume that car was initially at origin. Find the shortest distance of the car from the original position :

(A) $10\sqrt{115}$ (B) $10\sqrt{116}$
(C) $8\sqrt{116}$ (D) $5\sqrt{116}$

10-17 The car is given instruction $G_2(50)$, $G_3(30)$ and $G_4(20)$. Find the shortest distance of the car from the original position. Assume that car was initially at origin and facing $-ve$ x-axis :

(A) $10\sqrt{25}$ (B) $10\sqrt{26}$
(C) $10\sqrt{30}$ (D) $10\sqrt{15}$

10-18 Let A, B and C be three points whose coordinates are $(2, 3)$, $(3, b)$ and $(5, 7)$ respectively :

Column-I	Column-II
(1) If area of ΔABC is $\frac{1}{2}$ unit, then positive value of b is	(p) 6
(2) If A, B and C are collinear, then value of $3b$ is	(q) 5
(3) If A, B and C are collinear and B divides AC in the ratio $\lambda : 1$, then value of $4(\lambda + 1)$ is	(r) 4
(4) If $b = 4$, then the length of the longest side of ΔPQR is	(s) 13

(A) $1 \to r;\ 2 \to s;\ 3 \to p;\ 4 \to q$
(B) $1 \to p;\ 2 \to q;\ 3 \to r;\ 4 \to s$
(C) $1 \to r;\ 2 \to p;\ 3 \to q;\ 4 \to s$
(D) $1 \to q;\ 2 \to s;\ 3 \to r;\ 4 \to p$

10-19 If two vertices of an equilateral triangle have integral coordinates then the third vertex will have :

(A) Integral coordinates
(B) Coordinates which are rational
(C) At least one coordinate irrational
(D) Coordinates which are irrational

10-20 In the $\angle ABC$, the coordinates of B are $(0, 0)$, $AB = 2$, $\angle ABC = \frac{\pi}{3}$ and the middle point of BC has the coordinates $(2, 0)$. The centroid of the triangle is :

(A) $\left(\frac{1}{2}, \frac{\sqrt{3}}{2}\right)$ (B) $\left(\frac{5}{3}, \frac{1}{\sqrt{3}}\right)$
(C) $\left(\frac{4+\sqrt{3}}{3}, \frac{1}{3}\right)$ (D) None of these

10-21 The area of the pentagon whose vertices are $(4, 1)$, $(3, 6)$, $(-5, 1)$, $(-3, -3)$ and $(-3, 0)$ is :

(A) 30 unit^2 (B) 60 unit^2
(C) 120 unit^2 (D) None of these

10-22 ABC is an equilateral triangle such that the vertices B and C lie on two parallel lines at a distance 6. If A lies between the parallel lines at a distance 4 from one of them then the length of a side of the equilateral triangle is :

(A) 8 (B) $\sqrt{\frac{88}{3}}$
(C) $\frac{4\sqrt{7}}{\sqrt{3}}$ (D) None of these

10-23 The image of the point $(3, 8)$ in the line $x + 3y = 7$ is :

(A) $(1, 4)$ (B) $(4, 1)$
(C) $(-1, -4)$ (D) $(-4, -1)$

10-24 The area enclosed by $2|x| + 3|y| \le 6$ is :

(A) 3 sq. units (B) 12 sq. units
(C) 9 sq. units (D) 24 sq. units

10-25 Consider a triangle drawn on the X-Y plane with its three vertices at $(41, 0)$, $(0, 41)$ and $(0, 0)$, each vertex being represented by its (X, Y) coordinates. The number of points with integer coordinates inside the triangle (excluding all the points on the boundary) is :

(A) 780 (B) 800
(C) 820 (D) 741

* * * * *

PRACTICE EXERCISE - 10.3

10-1 If points $(x, 0)$, $(0, y)$ and $(1, 1)$ are collinear then the relation is : **[NTSE-2013 (Stage-I) Rajasthan]**
(A) $x+y=1$ (B) $x+y=xy$
(C) $x+y+1=0$ (D) $x+y+xy=0$

10-2 Graph drawn from the equation $y=x^2-3x-4$ will be : **[NTSE-2013 (Stage-I) Rajasthan]**
(A) Circle (B) Parabola
(C) Straight line (D) Hyperbola

10-3 The area of a triangle is 5 square units. Two of its vertices are $(2, 1)$ and $(3, -2)$. The third vertex lies on $y=x+3$. The third vertex is : **[NTSE-2014 (Stage-I) Rajasthan]**
(A) $\left(\frac{7}{2},\frac{3}{2}\right)$ (B) $\left(-\frac{3}{2},\frac{3}{2}\right)$
(C) $\left(-\frac{3}{2},\frac{13}{2}\right)$ (D) $\left(\frac{7}{2},\frac{5}{2}\right)$

10-4 The centre of a circle passing through the points $(7, -5)$, $(3, -7)$ and $(3, 3)$ is : **[NTSE-2015 (Stage-I) Rajasthan]**
(A) $(5, 6)$ (B) $(5, -1)$
(C) $(3, 2)$ (D) $(3, -2)$

10-5 If the distance between the points $(4, p)$ and $(1, 0)$ is 5, then the value of p is : **[NTSE-2015 (Stage-I) Chandigarh]**
(A) 4 (B) ± 4
(C) -4 (D) 0

10-6 If the vertices of a triangle ABC are $(0, 6)$, $(-5, 3)$ and $(3, 1)$ respectively. Then triangle is : **[NTSE-2015 (Stage-I) MP]**
(A) Isosceles (B) Equilateral
(C) Right angled (D) None of these

10-7 y-axis divides the line joining the points $P(-4, 2)$ and $Q(8, 3)$ in the ratio : **[NTSE-2015 (Stage-I) MP]**
(A) $3:1$ (B) $1:3$
(C) $2:1$ (D) $1:2$

10-8 Which point on x-axis is equidistant from the point $A(7, 6)$ and $B(-3, 4)$? **[NTSE-2015 (Stage-I) MP]**
(A) $(0, 4)$ (B) $(-4, 0)$
(C) $(3, 0)$ (D) $(0, 3)$

10-9 The point $A(0, 6)$, $B(-5, 3)$ and $C(3, 1)$ are the vertices of a triangle which is : **[NTSE-2015 (Stage-I) MP]**
(A) Isosceles (B) Equilateral
(C) Rightangled (D) None of these

10-10 The x-axis divides the line joining $A(2, -3)$ and $B(7, 4)$ in the ratio : **[NTSE-2015 (Stage-I) MP]**
(A) $1.5:2$ (B) $2:3$
(C) $3:2$ (D) $1:2$

10-11 Point on the X axis which is equidistant from the point $(0, 0)$ and $(2, 0)$ is : **[NTSE-2015 (Stage-I) Chhatisgarh]**
(A) $(0, 1)$ (B) $(1, 1)$
(C) $(1, 0)$ (D) $(0, 2)$

10-12 'O' is any point inside the rectangle $PQRS$, then : **[NTSE-2015 (Stage-I) West Bengal]**
(A) $OP^2+OR^2=OQ^2+OS^2$ (B) $OP^2+OQ^2=OR^2+OS^2$
(C) $OP^2+OS^2=OQ^2+QR^2$ (D) None of the above

10-13 For which value, point $A(a, b)$ lies in the quadrant III : **[NTSE-2015 (Stage-I) Chennai]**
(A) $a>0, b<0$ (B) $a<0, b<0$
(C) $a>0, b>0$ (D) $a<0, b>0$

10-14 The second and fourth terms of geometric sequence are 2 and 6. Which of the following is a possible first term ? **[NTSE-2016 (Stage-I) Telangana]**
(A) $-\sqrt{3}$ (B) $-\frac{2\sqrt{3}}{3}$
(C) $-\frac{\sqrt{3}}{3}$ (D) $\sqrt{3}$

10-15 The join of $A(-5, -3)$ and $B(4, 6)$ intersects the X-axis at D and the Y-axis at C respectively. AM, BN are perpendiculars on the X-axis. Find area ΔAMD : area ΔDCO : **[NTSE-2016 (Stage-I) Telangana]**

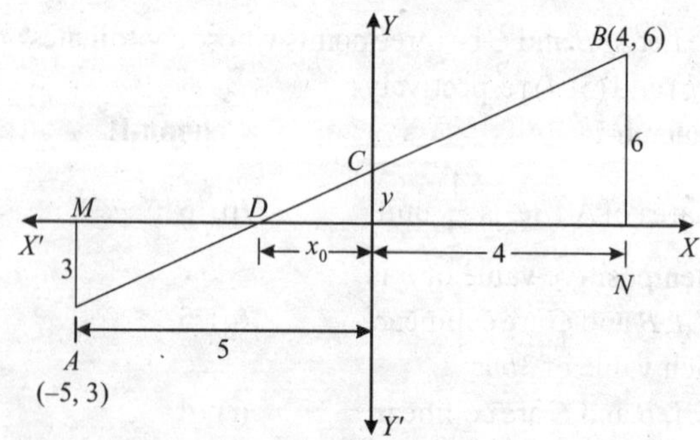

Figure 10.11

(A) $2:3$ (B) $9:4$
(C) $4:9$ (D) $3:2$

10-16 Which point in the y-axis is equidistant from the points $(3, -2)$ and $(4, 4)$? **[NTSE-2016 (Stage-I) Odisha]**
(A) $(0, 2)$ (B) $(0, -2)$
(C) $(0, 3)$ (D) $(0, -3)$

10-17 What is the distance between the points (3, – 6) and (–2, 6) : **[NTSE-2016 (Stage-I) Chhatisgarh]**

(A) 12 unit (B) 13 unit
(C) 14 unit (D) 15 unit

10-18 If the co-ordinates of the midpoints of the sides of a triangle are (1, 1), (2, –3) and (3, 4), then the centroid of the triangle is : **[NTSE-2017 (Stage-I) Andhra Pradesh]**

(A) $\left(3,\frac{1}{3}\right)$ (B) $\left(1,\frac{2}{3}\right)$

(C) (3, 1) (D) $\left(2,\frac{2}{3}\right)$

10-19 If two vertices of an equilateral triangle be (0, 0) and $(3, \sqrt{3})$, then the third vertex is .... : **[NTSE-2017 (Stage-I) Andhra Pradesh]**

(A) $(1, 3\sqrt{3})$ (B) $(0, 2\sqrt{3})$

(C) $(3, \sqrt{3})$ (D) $(1, \sqrt{3})$

10-20 Find the centre of circle passing through the points (1, 4) (–2, 6) and (3, 7) : **[NTSE-2017 (Stage-I) Chandigarh]**

(A) (1, 1) (B) (0, 0)

(C) $\left(\frac{1}{2},\frac{7}{2}\right)$ (D) $\left(\frac{1}{2},\frac{13}{2}\right)$

10-21 The two vertices of a triangle are (4, – 2) and (2, – 6). If centroid of a triangle is (0, 1) then third vertex of triangle will be : **[NTSE-2017 (Stage-I) Delhi]**

(A) (–6, 11) (B) (11, –6)
(C) (6, – 11) (D) (6, 11)

10-22 If $P(1, 2)$ and $Q(2, -1)$ and ΔPQR is an equilateral triangle then co-ordinates of : **[NTSE-2017 (Stage-I) Goa]**

(A) R cannot lie in the first quadrant
(B) R cannot lie in the second quadrant
(C) R is at the origin
(D) R lies in the third quadrant

10-23 Point (4, 0) lies on—:

(A) $\overline{XO}$ (B) $\overline{YO}$

(C) $\overline{OX}$ (D) $\overline{OY}$

10-24 Line $y = 4$ —: **[NTSE-2017 (Stage-I) Gujarat]**

(A) Parallel to Y-Axis (B) Intersecting both axes
(C) Parallel to X-Axis (D) Passes through origin

10-25 If P-Q-R, Then — is the opposite ray of $\overline{QR}$: **[NTSE-2017 (Stage-I) Gujarat]**

(A) $\overline{PQ}$ (B) $\overline{QP}$

(C) $\overline{RQ}$ (D) $\overline{PR}$

10-26 The area of a triangle with vertices $(p, 2 - 2p)$, $(-4 - p, 6 - 2p)$ and $(1 - p, 2p)$ is 70sq, units. Then, the numbers of possible integral values of p is : **[NTSE-2017 (Stage-I) Haryana]**

(A) 0 (B) 1
(C) 2 (D) 3

10-27 The condition of points $(a, 0)$, $(0, b)$ and (1, 1) lie on straight line will be : **[NTSE-2017 (Stage-I) Karnataka]**

(A) $ab = 1$ (B) $\frac{a+b}{ab} = 1$

(C) $a - b = 1$ (D) $\frac{ab}{a-b} = 1$

10-28 If a point $p\left(\frac{23}{5},\frac{33}{5}\right)$, divides line AB joining two points $A(3, 5)$ and $B(x, y)$ is internally in ratio of 2 : 3, then the values of x and y will be : **[NTSE-2017 (Stage-I) Rajasthan]**

(A) $x = 4, y = 7$ (B) $x = 5, y = 9$
(C) $x = 7, y = 9$ (D) $x = 7, y = 8$

10-29 By joining the points (5, 5), (– 5, 5) to the origin in the Cartesian plane, then the type of triangle formed is : **[NTSE-2017 (Stage-I) Tamilnadu]**

(A) Right angled triangle (B) Acute triangle
(C) Equilateral triangle (D) None of these

10-30 If the graph of the equation $4x + 3y = 12$ cuts the coordinate axes at A and B then the length of AB is : **[NTSE-2017 (Stage-I) Tamilnadu]**

(A) 4 units (B) 3 units
(C) 5 units (D) 2 units

10-31 If points (1, 2), (3, 5) and $(0, b)$ are co-linear then value of b is : **[NTSE-2017 (Stage-I) Uttar Pradesh]**

(A) $\frac{1}{2}$ (B) $\frac{7}{2}$

(C) 2 (D) – 1

10-32 If the points A (6, 1), B (8, 2), C (9, 4) and D (P, 3) are the vertices of a parallelogram then the value of P will be : **[NTSE-2017 (Stage-I) Uttrakhand]**

(A) 4 (B) 5
(C) 6 (D) 7

10-33 The sum of distances from x-axis and y-axis measured from the point (3, 5) will be : **[NTSE-2018 (Stage-I) Rajasthan]**

(A) –1 (B) 0
(C) 2 (D) 8

10-34 If $x < 1, y < -1$, then $(x-1, y-3)$ lies in : **[NTSE-2018 (Stage-I) Andhra Pradesh]**

(A) Q_3 (B) Q_4
(C) Q_2 (D) Q_1

10-35 If $(a, 0)$, $(0, b)$ and $(1, 1)$ are collinear then $\frac{1}{a}+\frac{1}{b}=$ **[NTSE-2018 (Stage-I) Andhra Pradesh]**

(A) 2 (B) 1
(C) 3 (D) 4

10-36 A and B are fixed point. The vertex C of ΔABC move such that $\cot A + \cot B$ = constant. The locus of C is : **[NTSE-2018 (Stage-I) Bihar]**

(A) A straight line perpendicular to AB
(B) A straight line parallel to AB
(C) Inclined at an angle $(A - B)$ to AB
(D) None of these

10-37 Find the value of m-n in the rectangles $PQRS$: **[NTSE-2018 (Stage-I) Chandigarh]**

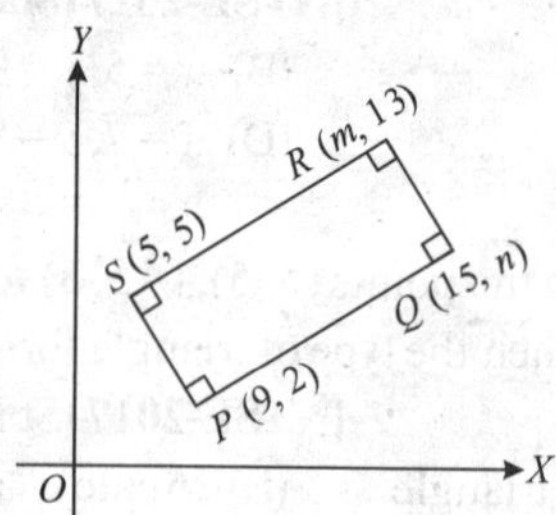

Figure 10.12

(A) 4 (B) –2
(C) –1 (D) 1

10-38 The Points $P(0, 4)$, $Q(-3, 1)$, $R(0, -2)$ and $S(3, 1)$ are the vertices of a : **[NTSE-2018 (Stage-I) Chandigarh]**

(A) Parallerogram (B) Square
(C) Kite (D) Rhombus

10-39 If point (0, 2) is equidistant from $(3, k)$ and $(k, 5)$, then the value of k will be : **[NTSE-2018 (Stage-I) Chhattisgarh]**

(A) 1 (B) –1
(C) 2 (D) –2

10-40 The foot of the perpendicular from $P(-3, 2)$ to the Y- axis is M. co-ordinates of M are ______: **[NTSE-2018 (Stage-I) Gujarat]**

(A) (3, 0) (B) (0, 2)
(C) $\left(\frac{3}{2}, -1\right)$ (D) (–3, 2)

10-41 The line segment joining the points $A(2, 2)$ and $B(-7, 4)$ is trisected at the point P and Q (P is nearer to A). If coordinates of P and Q are $(a, 0)$ and $(-4, b)$ respectively, then the values of a and b are respectively : **[NTSE-2018 (Stage-I) Haryana]**

(A) 1 and 2 (B) –1 and 2
(C) 1 and –2 (D) –1 and –2

10-42 A momento is made as shown in the figure-10.13. Its base $PBCQ$ is silver plated from the front side. The silver plated area is (use $\pi = \frac{22}{7}$): **[NTSE-2018 (Stage-I) Haryana]**

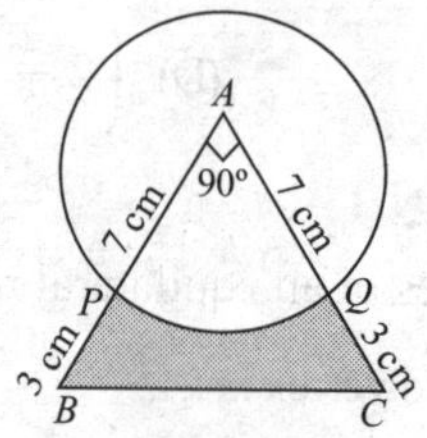

Figure 10.13

(A) 11 cm^2 (B) 11.5 cm^2
(C) 12.5 cm^2 (D) 13 cm^2

10-43 The centroid of a triangle is (2, 4) and circumcenter is (1, 7) then find the orthocenter : **[NTSE-2018 (Stage-I) Himachal Pradesh]**

(A) 3, 1 (B) 4, –2
(C) –2, 4 (D) –8, 4

10-44 Point $R(h, k)$ divides line segment AB between axes in the ratio 1 : 2 where A lies on X-axis. Find equation of line : **[NTSE-2018 (Stage-I) Himachal Pradesh]**

(A) $2hx + ky = 3hk$ (B) $2hx + hy = 3hk$
(C) $kx + hy = 2hk$ (D) $3kx + hy = 2h/k$

10-45 The value of 'C' if $\left(\frac{C}{2}, 14\right)$ is the mid point of the line joining the points (–3, 8) and (–15, 20) is : **[NTSE-2018 (Stage-I) Karnataka]**

(A) 2 (B) –9
(C) –18 (D) –15

10-46 If the line segment joining (2, 3) and (–1, 2) is divided internally in the ratio 3 : 4 by the line graph of the equation $x + 2y = k$ then the value of 'k' is : **[NTSE-2018 (Stage-I) Karnataka]**

(A) $\frac{5}{7}$ (B) $\frac{31}{7}$
(C) $\frac{36}{7}$ (D) $\frac{41}{7}$

10-47 Number of straight lines passing through the point (1, 2) is : **[NTSE-2018 (Stage-I) Madhya Prasesh]**

(A) 1 (B) 2

(C) 3 (D) ∞

10-48 Hero's formula for the Area of triangle is : **[NTSE-2018 (Stage-I) Madhya Prasesh]**

(A) $\frac{1}{2}$(Base × Height) (B) $\sqrt{s(s-a)(s-b)(s-c)}$

(C) $\frac{a+b+c}{2}$ (D) $\sqrt{s.b.c}$

10-49 Co-ordinates of a point on y-axis which is equidistant from the point (6, 5) and (–4, 3) are : **[NTSE-2018 (Stage-I) Madhya Prasesh]**

(A) (9, 0) (B) (0, 9)

(C) (3, 2) (D) (0, 0)

10-50 Two vertices of a triangle are (–1, 4) and (5, 2) if the centroid (0, –3) find the third vertex : **[NTSE-2018 (Stage-I) Uttar Pradesh]**

(A) (1, 4) (B) (4, 15)

(C) (–1, –4) (D) (–4, –15)

10-51 If $A(0, -1)$, $B(2, 1)$ and $C(0, 3)$ are the vertices of ΔABC then length of median drawn from a A will be : **[NTSE-2018 (Stage-I) Uttarakhandh]**

(A) 10 (B) $\sqrt{10}$

(C) $\sqrt{5}$ (D) None of these

10-52 The quadrilateral in a plane formed by joining the points (2, 3), (4, 6), (6, 3) and (4, 0) is a : **[NTSE-2012 (Stage-II)]**

(A) Square (B) Rectangle

(C) Rhombus

(D) Trapezium whose opposite angles are unequal

10-53 If the line segment joining (2, 3) and (–1, 2) is divided internally in the ratio 3 : 4 by the graph of the equation $x + 2y = k$, the value of k is : **[NTSE-2015 (Stage-II)]**

(A) $\frac{5}{7}$ (B) $\frac{31}{7}$

(C) $\frac{36}{7}$ (D) $\frac{41}{7}$

10-54 The centre of the circle passing through the pints (6, – 6), (3, – 7) and (3, 3) is : **[NTSE-2015 (Stage-II)]**

(A) (3, 2) (B) (–3, –2)

(C) (3, –2) (D) (–3, 2)

10-55 Let ABC be an equilateral triangle. If the co-ordinates of A are (1, 2) and co-ordinates of B are (2, –1), then : **[NTSE-2016 (Stage-II)]**

(A) C cannot lie in the first quadrant

(B) C cannot lie in the second quadrant

(C) C is the origin

(D) C cannot lie in the third quadrant

10-56 A line l passing through the origin makes an angle θ with positive direction of x-axis such that $\sin\theta = \frac{3}{5}$. The co-ordinates of the point, which lies in the fourth quadrant at a unit distance from the origin and on perpendicular to l, are : **[NTSE-2016 (Stage-II)]**

(A) $\left(\frac{3}{5}, -\frac{4}{5}\right)$ (B) $\left(\frac{4}{5}, -\frac{3}{5}\right)$

(C) (3, –4) (D) (4, –3)

* * * * *

ANSWERS

PRACTICE EXERCISE-10.1

1	(D)	2	(C)	3	(D)
4	(D)	5	(B)	6	(D)
7	(B)	8	(A)	9	(D)
10	(B)	11	(D)	12	(B)
13	(A)	14	(B)	15	(A)
16	(C)	17	(A)	18	(D)
19	(D)	20	(D)	21	(C)
22	(C)	23	(A)	24	(A)
25	(C)	26	(A)	27	(D)
28	(D)	29	(C)	30	(A)
31	(A)	32	(D)	33	(C)
34	(B)	35	(A)	36	(A)
37	(A)	38	(A)	39	(D)
40	(D)	41	(A)	42	(A)
43	(D)	44	(D)	45	(D)
46	(B)	47	(B)	48	(A)
49	(A)	50	(C)		

PRACTICE EXERCISE-10.2

1	(B)	2	(D)	3	(C)
4	(C)	5	(A)	6	(A)
7	(A)	8	(C)	9	(D)
10	(A)	11	(C)	12	(D)
13	(A)	14	(C)	15	(C)
16	(B)	17	(B)	18	(A)
19	(C)	20	(B)	21	(A)
22	(C)	23	(C)	24	(B)
25	(A)				

PRACTICE EXERCISE-10.3

1	(B)	2	(B)	3	(B)
4	(D)	5	(B)	6	(A)
7	(D)	8	(C)	9	(A)
10	(A)	11	(C)	12	(A)
13	(B)	14	(B)	15	(B)
16	(A)	17	(B)	18	(D)
19	(B)	20	(D)	21	(A)
22	(B)	23	(C)	24	(C)
25	(B)	26	(B)	27	(B)
28	(C)	29	(A)	30	(C)
31	(A)	32	(D)	33	(D)
34	(A)	35	(B)	36	(B)
37	(D)	38	(B)	39	(A)
40	(B)	41	(B)	42	(B)
43	(B)	44	(B)	45	(C)
46	(D)	47	(D)	48	(B)
49	(B)	50	(D)	51	(B)
52	(C)	53	(D)	54	(C)
55	(B)	56	(A)		

Solutions of PRACTICE EXERCISE-10.1

Sol. 1 (D) ΔACD and ΔABC are equilateral triangles.

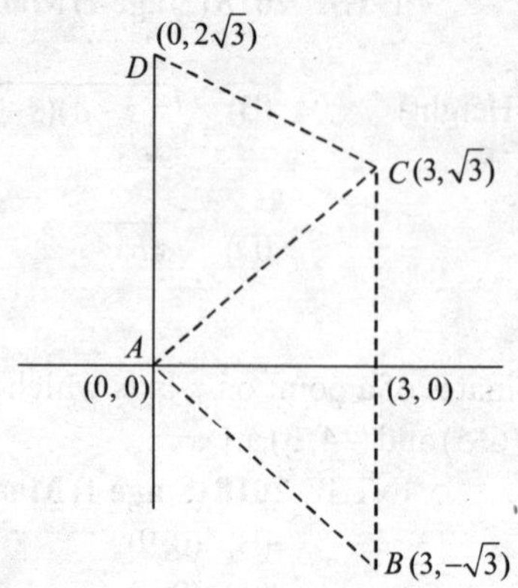

Hence Ans is (D)

Aliter : Let the co-ordinates of third vertex be (x, y)

Since it is an equilateral triangle all the three sides are equal

$$\Rightarrow \quad x^2 (x-0)^2 + (y-0)^2 = (x-3)^2 + (y-\sqrt{3})^2$$

$$= (y+\sqrt{3})^2$$

$$\Rightarrow \quad x^2 + y^2 = (x-3) + (y-\sqrt{3})^2 = 12$$

On solving this will get the values of x and y or we can go by substituting values from the options

Hence Ans is (D)

Sol. 2 (C) Given $3x - 5y = 1$ ...(1)

$5x + 2y = 12$ ...(2)

point of intersection of (1) and (2) is (2, 1)

the line $3x + 4y = a$

passes through (2, 1)

hence $3(2) + 4(1) = a$

$\Rightarrow \quad a = 10$

Hence Ans is (C)

Sol. 3 (D) $4x - 7y = 8$ is not parallel to $3x - 5y = 7$ because for these equations $\frac{a_1}{a_2} \neq \frac{b_1}{b_2}$ which is the condition for unique solution

Hence Ans is (D)

Sol. 4 (D) Intersection of $-3x + 4y = 0$ and $4x - 5y = 1$ is (4, 3) and $2x + 3y = 17$ passes through this point. So point of intersection is one only

Hence Ans is (D)

Sol. 5 (B) $9x+12y=108$

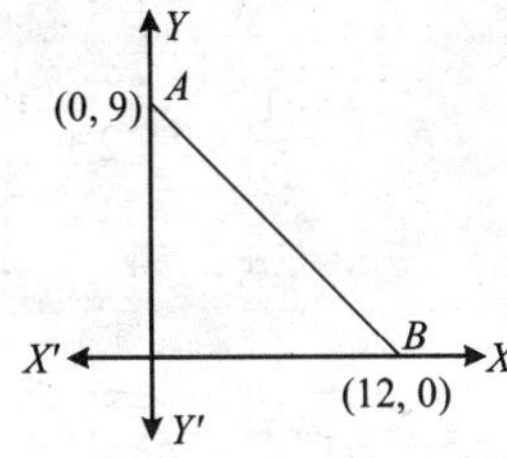

$$\frac{x}{12}+\frac{y}{9}=1$$

$$AB=\sqrt{9^2+12^2}=15$$

Hence Ans is (B)

Sol. 6 (D) 1 : 1 because origin is the mid point of the line segment

Hence Ans is (D)

Sol. 7 (B) Co-ordinate of centroid are

$$x=\frac{x_1+x_2+x_3}{3},$$

$$y=\frac{y_1+y_2+y_3}{3}$$

$$\Rightarrow \quad x=\frac{3-3+6}{3}=2$$

$$\Rightarrow \quad y=\frac{-1-1+2}{3}=0$$

Hence Ans is (B)

Sol. 8 (A) Given

$A(a, 0), B(0, b)$ & $C(1, 1)$ are collinear

$\Rightarrow$ area of $\Delta ABC=0$

$$\Rightarrow \quad \frac{1}{2}[x_1(y_2-y_3)+x_2(y_3-y_1)+x_3(y_1-y_2)]=0$$

$$\Rightarrow \quad \frac{1}{2}[a(b-1)+0(1-0)+1(0-b)]=0$$

$$\Rightarrow \quad ab-a-b=0$$

$$\Rightarrow \quad a+b=ab$$

$$\Rightarrow \quad \frac{1}{a}+\frac{1}{b}=1$$

Hence Ans is (A)

Sol. 9 (D) Let $A(0,8)$, $B(1,8)$ and $C(1,-9/8)$

then $AB=\sqrt{1}=1,\ BC=\left(\frac{73}{8}\right),$

$$AC=\sqrt{1+\frac{73^2}{64}}=\frac{\sqrt{64+73^2}}{8}$$

$$\Rightarrow \quad AC^2=AB^2+BC^2$$

$\Rightarrow$ ΔABC is a right angle triangle

Hence Ans is (D)

Sol. 10 (B) $A(-2,-1)$, $B(1,0)$, $C(x,3)$ & $D(1,y)$ form a parallelogram

$\Rightarrow$ Mid point of diagonal

$$AC=\left(\frac{x-2}{2},1\right)$$

& mid point of diagonal

$$BD=\left(1,\frac{y}{2}\right)$$

$$\Rightarrow \quad \frac{x-2}{2}=1 \ \& \ \frac{y}{2}=1$$

$$\Rightarrow \quad x=4,$$

$$y=2$$

$$\Rightarrow \quad x^2-y=16-2=14$$

Hence Ans is (B)

Sol. 11 (D) Given

points $A(a,a), B(-a,-a), C(-\sqrt{3}a,\sqrt{3}a)$

$$AB=\sqrt{4a^2+4a^2}=2a\sqrt{2},$$

$$BC=2a\sqrt{2},$$

$$CA=2a\sqrt{2}$$

as $AB=BC=CA$

$\Rightarrow$ ΔABC is an equilateral triangle.

Hence Ans is (D)

Sol. 12 (B) Let y-axis divides them in $m:n$, x-coordinate of y-axis will be zero.

so, $$\frac{3n+m(-1)}{m+n}=0$$

so, $$\frac{m}{n}=\frac{1}{3}$$

Hence Ans is (B)

Sol. 13 (A) Slope of x-axis is zero.

$\Rightarrow$ Slopes of two parallel lines are same

$\Rightarrow$ Slope of a line parallel to x-axis is also 'zero'.

Hence Ans is (A)

Sol. 14 (B) Let the given point be P ($\cos\theta$, $\sin\theta$), Q ($\sin\theta$, $-\cos\theta$)

Distance

$$PQ = \sqrt{(\cos\theta - \sin\theta)^2 + (\sin\theta + \cos\theta)^2}$$

$$PQ = \sqrt{2+0} = \sqrt{2}$$

Hence Ans is (B)

Sol. 15 (A) Centroid

$$= \left(\frac{0+0+2}{3}, \frac{0+1+0}{3}\right) = \left(\frac{2}{3}, \frac{1}{3}\right)$$

Hence Ans is (A)

Sol. 16 (C) Given distance

$$AB = \sqrt{2}$$

$$\Rightarrow \quad \sqrt{(x-3)^2 + (y-2)^2} = \sqrt{2}$$

(using distance formula)

$$\Rightarrow \quad (x-3)^2 + (y-2)^2 = 2$$

$$\Rightarrow \quad x^2 + 9 - 6x + y^2 - 4y + 11 = 0$$

$$\Rightarrow \quad x^2 + y^2 - 6x - 4y + 11 = 0$$

Also $$2x + y = 7$$

$$\Rightarrow \quad y = 7 - 2x$$

$$\Rightarrow \quad x^2 + (7-2x)^2 - 6x - 4(7-2x) + 11 = 0$$

$$\Rightarrow \quad 5x^2 - 26x + 32 = 0$$

$$\Rightarrow \quad x = \frac{26 \pm 6}{10} = \frac{32}{10}, 2$$

or $$x = \frac{16}{5}, 2$$

$$\Rightarrow \quad y = 3, \frac{3}{5}$$

$\Rightarrow$ The two possible ordered pairs of (x, y) are $\left(\frac{16}{5}, \frac{3}{5}\right)$

& $(2, 3)$

Hence Ans is (C)

Sol. 17 (A)

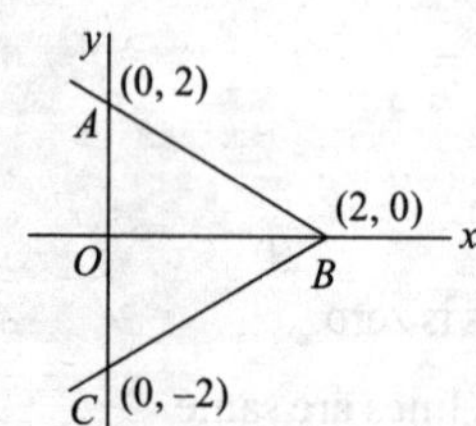

Area bounded by lines $x + y = 2$

& $x - y = 2$ and y-axis will be area of ΔABC

$\Rightarrow$ Area of the ΔABC = Area of ΔAOB + Angle of ΔBOC

$$= \frac{1}{2} \times 2 \times 2 + \frac{1}{2} \times 2 \times 2$$

$$= 2 + 2 = 4$$

Hence Ans is (A)

Sol. 18 (D) Distance

$$= \sqrt{(a\cos\theta + b\sin\theta - 0)^2 + (a\sin\theta - b\cos\theta)^2}$$

$$= \sqrt{a^2 + b^2}$$

Hence Ans is (D)

Sol. 19 (D) $A(-4, 3)$ —— $B(9, 5)$

Equation of line is given by

$$y - y_1 = \frac{y_2 - y_1}{x_2 - x_1}(x - x_1)$$

$$\Rightarrow \quad y - 3 = \frac{5-3}{9+4}(x - (-4))$$

$$\Rightarrow \quad y - 3 = \frac{2}{13}(x+4)$$

$$\Rightarrow \quad 13y - 39 = 2x + 8$$

$$\Rightarrow \quad 13y - 2x - 47 = 0$$

Hence Ans is (D)

Sol. 20 (D) Area of triangle

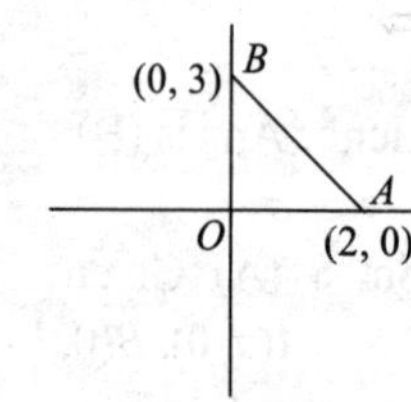

$$= \frac{1}{2} \times 2 \times 3$$

$$= \frac{6}{2} = 3 \text{ units}$$

Hence Ans is (D)

Sol. 21 (C) $A(1, -3)$ —— (x, y) —— $B(-4, 2)$

Equation of line AB is

$$y - y_1 = \frac{y_2 - y_1}{x_2 - x_1}(x - x_1)$$

$$\Rightarrow \quad y - 2 = \frac{2-(-3)}{-4-1}(x-(-4))$$

$$\Rightarrow \quad y - 2 = \frac{5}{-5}(x+4)$$

$$\Rightarrow \quad y + x + 4 - 2 = 0$$

$$\Rightarrow \quad y + x + 2 = 0$$

(x, y) lies on it

so $\Rightarrow \quad x + y + 2 = 0$

Hence Ans is (C)

Sol. 22 (C) Let the co-ordinates of centre 'O' be (x, y) we know

$$OA^2 = OB^2 = OC^2$$

$$(x-5)^2 + (y-7)^2 = (x-6)^2 + (y-6)^2$$

$$= (x-2)^2 + (y-(-2))^2$$

On solving we get $x = 2$

$y = 3$

$\Rightarrow \quad (x, y) = (2, 3)$

Hence Ans is (C)

Sol. 23 (A) Distance $= \sqrt{(x_2 - x_1)^2 + (y_2 - y_1)^2}$

Here distance

$$= \sqrt{(a\cos 25^\circ - 0)^2 + (0 - a\cos 65^\circ)^2}$$

$$= \sqrt{a^2\cos^2 25 + a^2\cos^2 65}$$

$$= \sqrt{a^2\cos^2 25 + a^2\sin^2 25}$$

$$= a$$

Hence Ans is (A)

Sol. 24 (A) Given a triangle is formed by line $xy = 0$

$\Rightarrow \quad x = 0$

and $\quad y = 0$

& the line $\quad x + y = 1$

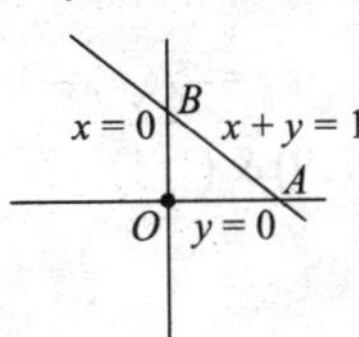

From the figure

OAB is right angled triangle

So orthocentre $= (0, 0)$

Hence Ans is (A)

Sol. 25 (C) Plot the given points. OAB is a right angled triangle right angle at $(0, 0)$

So, O will be orthocentre = (meeting point of altitudes)

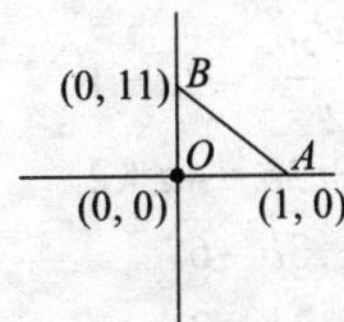

Hence Ans is (C)

Sol. 26 (A) $\quad 3x + 4y = a$

$\Rightarrow \quad \dfrac{x}{\frac{a}{3}} + \dfrac{y}{\frac{a}{4}} = 1$

$\Rightarrow \quad x \text{ intercept} = \dfrac{a}{3}$

$\Rightarrow \quad y \text{ intercept} = \dfrac{a}{4}$

Given, $\quad \dfrac{a}{3} + \dfrac{a}{4} = 7$

$\Rightarrow \quad \dfrac{7a}{12} = 7$

$\Rightarrow \quad a = 12$

Hence Ans is (A)

Sol. 27 (D) Let P & Q be the points $(-3, 4)$ & $(a, -5)$ respectively. Which divides PQ in the ratio $\lambda : 1$

Let co-ordinates of $R(x, 0)$, (A point on x-axis

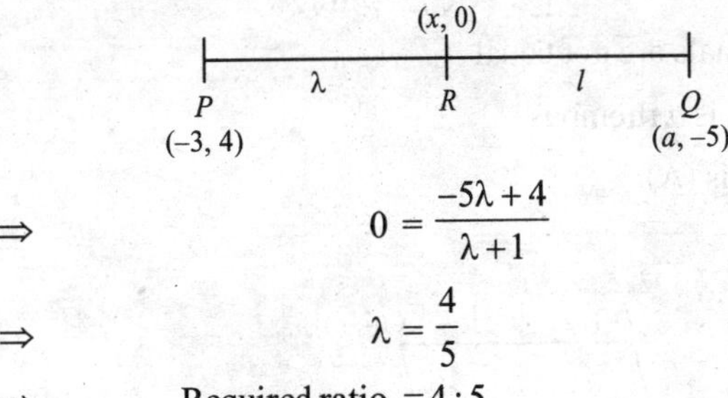

$\Rightarrow \quad 0 = \dfrac{-5\lambda + 4}{\lambda + 1}$

$\Rightarrow \quad \lambda = \dfrac{4}{5}$

$\Rightarrow \quad$ Required ratio $= 4 : 5$

Hence Ans is (D)

Sol. 28 (D) All the three given points lie on x-axis Therefore they are collinear

Hence Ans is (D)

Sol. 29 (C) The line segment joining $A(2, 1)$ & $B(5, -8)$ is trisected at P & Q as shown in the figure

$\Rightarrow \quad P$ divides AB in ratio $1 : 2$

Let co-ordinate of P be (x, y), using section formula

$$x = \frac{1\times 5 + 2\times 2}{1+2} = \frac{9}{3} = 3$$

$$y = \frac{1\times -8 + 2\times 1}{3}$$

$$= -2$$

$\Rightarrow \quad P(x, y) \equiv (3, -2)$ [from section formula]

Given $P(3, -2)$ lies on the line:

$2x - y + k = 0$

$\Rightarrow \quad 2\times 3 - (-2) + k = 0$

$k = -8$

Hence Ans is (C)

Sol. 30 **(A)** Given $P(2,-1)$, $Q(3,4)$, $R(-2,3)$ & $S(-3,-2)$

Now $PQ = \sqrt{1+25} = \sqrt{26}$

$RS = \sqrt{1+25} = \sqrt{26}$

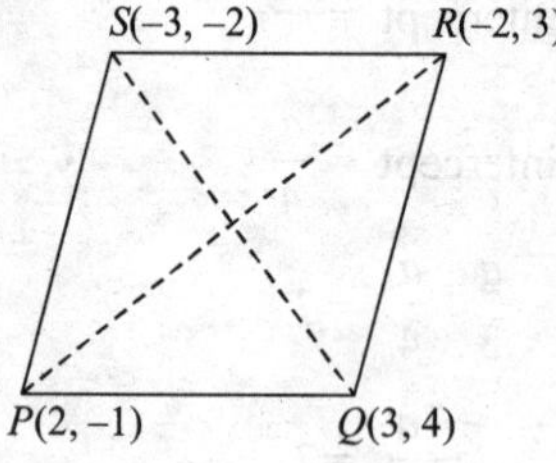

$QR = \sqrt{26}$

$SP = \sqrt{25+1} = \sqrt{26}$

$\Rightarrow$ All sides are equal

Diagonals $PR = \sqrt{32} = 4\sqrt{2}$

& $QS = \sqrt{72} = 6\sqrt{2}$

$\Rightarrow$ diagonals are not equal

$\Rightarrow$ *PQRS* is a rhombus

Hence Ans is (A)

Sol. 31 **(A)**

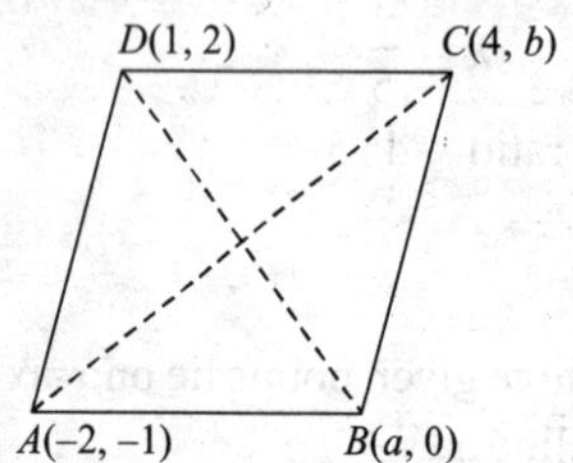

We know in a parallelogram, diagonals bisect each other

$\Rightarrow \quad \frac{a+1}{2} = \frac{-2+4}{2}$

So, $a = 1$

Also $\frac{-1+b}{2} = \frac{2+0}{2}$

So, $b = 3$

Hence Ans is (A)

Sol. 32 **(D)** Given $(0, 0)$ $(3, \sqrt{3})$ and $(3, \lambda)$ form an equilateral triangle

$\Rightarrow$ Sides will be equal

$\Rightarrow \quad \sqrt{9+3} = \sqrt{9+\lambda^2}$

$\Rightarrow \quad 12 = 9 + \lambda^2$

$\Rightarrow \quad \lambda^2 = 3$

$\Rightarrow \quad \lambda = \pm\sqrt{3}$

But $\lambda \neq +\sqrt{3}$

[the two points will coincide]

So, $\lambda = -\sqrt{3}$

Hence Ans is (D)

Sol. 33 **(C)**

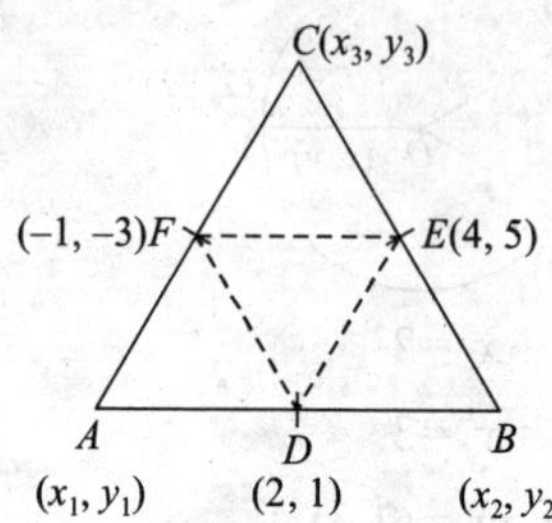

Let $A \equiv (x_1, y_1), B \equiv (x_2, y_2)$

and $C \equiv (x_3, y_3)$

$\because$ $D(2, 1)$ divides AB in ratio $1:1$.

$\Rightarrow \quad 2 = \frac{x_2 + x_1}{2}$

$\Rightarrow \quad x_1 + x_2 = 4 \quad \ldots(1)$

& $\quad 1 = \frac{y_2 + y_1}{2}$

$\Rightarrow \quad y_1 + y_2 = 2 \quad \ldots(2)$

Similarly $x_2 + x_3 = 8 \quad \ldots(3)$

$y_2 + y_3 = 10 \quad \ldots(4)$

$x_1 + x_3 = -2 \quad \ldots(5)$

$y_1 + y_3 = -6 \quad \ldots(6)$

Now solving (1), (3) & (5) we get :

$x_1 = -3, x_2 = 7; x_3 = 1$

& Solving (2), (4) & (6)

We get : $y_1 = -7; y_2 = 9; y_3 = 1$

Vertices are : $(-3, -7)$, $(7, 9)$ & $(1, 1)$

Hence Ans is (C)

Sol. 34 **(B)**

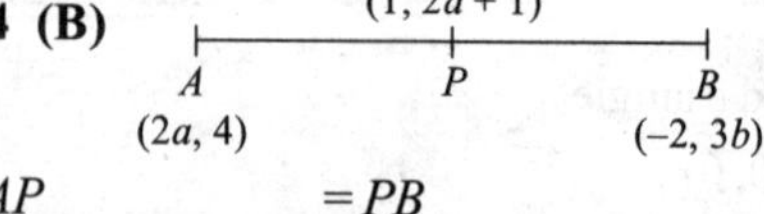

Since $AP = PB$

$\Rightarrow \quad \frac{-2+2a}{2} = 1$

$\Rightarrow \quad -2 + 2a = 2$

$\Rightarrow \quad 2a = 4$

$\Rightarrow \quad a = 2,$

$\frac{4+3b}{2} = 2a + 1$

$\Rightarrow \quad 4 + 3b = 4a + 2$

$\Rightarrow \quad 3b = 6$

$\Rightarrow \quad b = 2$

Hence Ans is (B)

Sol. 35 (A) Let $A \equiv (x, 0)$

& $B = (0, y)$

Given $(4, -3)$ is the mid point of AB

$\Rightarrow \quad 4 = x/2$

$\Rightarrow \quad x = 8$

& $\quad y/2 = -3$

$\Rightarrow \quad y = -6$

$\Rightarrow \quad A \equiv (8, 0)$

& $\quad B \equiv (0, -6)$

Hence Ans is (A)

Sol. 36 (A) Let $P(2, 3)$ & $Q(7, 8)$ is divided by $R(4, 5)$ in ratio $m : n$

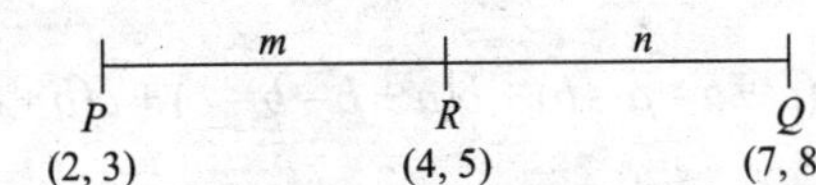

$$\Rightarrow \quad \frac{2n + 7m}{m + n} = 4$$

$$\Rightarrow \quad 2n + 7m = 4m + 4n$$

$$\Rightarrow \quad 2n - 3m = 0$$

$$\Rightarrow \quad \frac{m}{n} = \frac{2}{3}$$

$$\& \quad \frac{3n + 8m}{m + n} = 5$$

$$\Rightarrow \quad 3n + 8m = 5m + 5n$$

$$\Rightarrow \quad 2n - 3m = 0$$

$$\Rightarrow \quad \frac{m}{n} = \frac{2}{3}$$

$\Rightarrow$ Required ratio is 2 : 3

Hence Ans is (A)

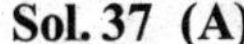

Sol. 37 (A)

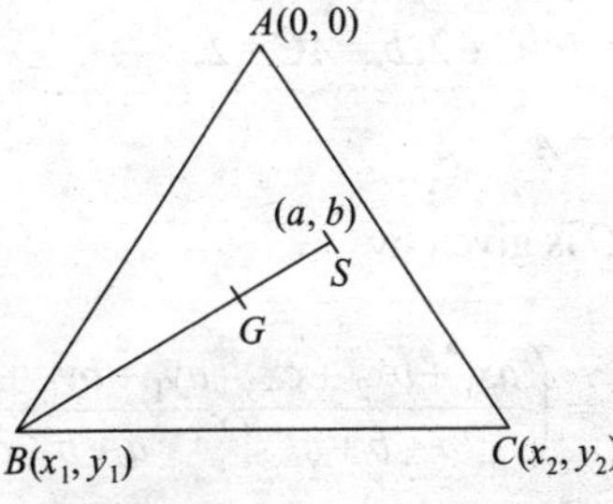

Centroid of ΔABC is given by

$$\left(\frac{x_1 + x_2}{3}, \frac{y_1 + y_2}{3}\right)$$

Now G divides BS in the ratio 2 : 1

$$\Rightarrow \quad \frac{x_1 + x_2}{3} = \frac{2a + x_1}{3}$$

$$\Rightarrow \quad x_2 = 2a$$

$$\& \quad \frac{y_1 + y_2}{3} = \frac{2b + y_1}{3}$$

$$\Rightarrow \quad y_2 = 2b$$

So co-ordinate of C are $(2a, 2b)$

Hence Ans is (A)

Sol. 38 (A) $3x + 4y = 12$ intersects the x-axis at $(4, 0)$

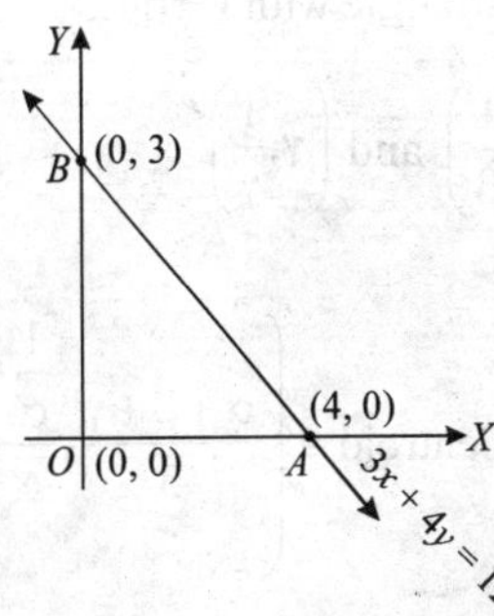

& the y-axis at $(0, 3)$

Now required area = area of ΔOAB

$$= \frac{1}{2} \times 4 \times 3$$

$$= 6 \text{ cm}^2$$

Hence Ans is (A)

Sol. 39 (D) Area of triangle formed by $(a, b + c)$, $(b, c + a)$ & $(c, a + b)$ is

$$= \frac{1}{2}[a(c + a - a - b)(b + c)(b - c) + (b)(a + b) - (c + a)c]$$

$$= \frac{1}{2}[a(c - b) - (b^2 - c^2) + ab + b^2 + - ac - c^2]$$

$$= \frac{1}{2}[ac - ab - b^2 + c^2 + ab + b^2 - ac - c^2]$$

$$= \frac{1}{2}[0] = 0 \text{ sq. units.}$$

Hence Ans is (D)

Sol. 40 (D) Area of

$$\Delta ABC = 0$$

$$\Rightarrow \quad \frac{1}{2}[x(3 + 4) + 2(-4 - y) - 3(y - 3)] = 0$$

$$\Rightarrow \quad 7x - 8 - 2y - 3y + 9 = 0$$

$$\Rightarrow \quad 7x - 5y + 1 = 0$$

Hence Ans is (D)

Sol. 41 (A) Given,

$$x^3 - 3px^2 + 3qx - 1 = 0 \quad \begin{cases} \alpha \\ \beta \\ \gamma \end{cases}$$

So, we have

$$\alpha + \beta + \gamma = 3p \qquad \dots(1)$$

$$\alpha\beta + \beta\gamma + \gamma\alpha = 3q \qquad \dots(2)$$

$$\alpha\beta\gamma = 1 \qquad \dots(3)$$

To find centroid of triangle with vertices

$$\left(\alpha, \frac{1}{\alpha}\right), \left(\beta, \frac{1}{\beta}\right) \text{ and } \left(\gamma, \frac{1}{\gamma}\right)$$

$$\text{Centroid} \equiv \left(\frac{\alpha+\beta+\gamma}{3}, \frac{\frac{1}{\alpha}+\frac{1}{\beta}+\frac{1}{\gamma}}{3}\right)$$

$$\equiv \left(\frac{\alpha+\beta+\gamma}{3}, \frac{\alpha\beta+\beta\gamma+\gamma\alpha}{3\alpha\beta\gamma}\right)$$

$$\equiv \left(\frac{3p}{3}, \frac{3q}{3}\right) \qquad \text{[from eq. 1, 2, 3]}$$

$$\equiv (p, q)$$

Hence Ans is (A)

Sol. 42 (A)

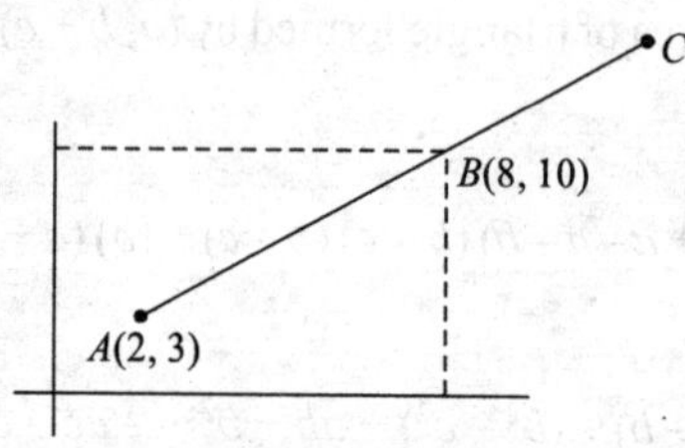

For minimum area

There are many integer point which can lie on line AB.

Therefore, minimum area can be zero.

Hence Ans is (A)

Sol. 43 (D)

Given
$$\frac{AC}{BD} = \frac{3x+y}{2x+y}$$

But
$$3x + y + 2x = 5y$$
$$5x = 4y$$
$$\frac{5x}{4} = y$$

$$\Rightarrow \quad \frac{AC}{BD} = \frac{3x+5x/4}{2x+5x/4} = \frac{17x}{13x} = \frac{17}{13}$$

$$\Rightarrow \quad AC = BD = 17:13$$

Hence Ans is (D)

Sol. 44 (D)

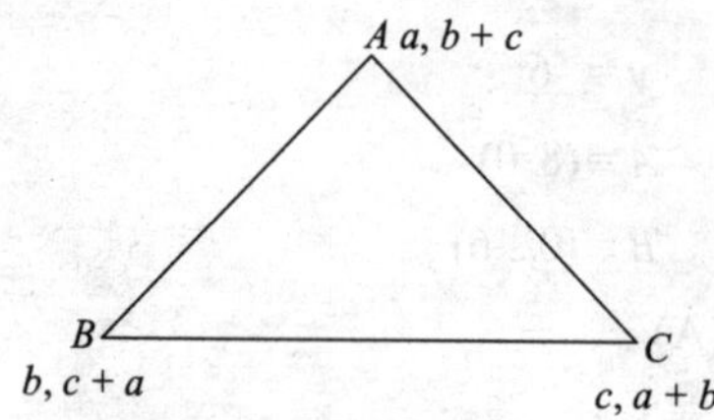

Area of ΔABC

$$= \frac{1}{2}[a(c+a-a-b) + b(a+b-b-c) + c(b+c-c-a)]$$

$$= \frac{1}{2}[a(c-b) + b(a-c) + c(b-a)]$$

$$= \frac{1}{2}[ac - ab + ba - bc + cb - ca] = 0$$

Hence Ans is (D)

Sol. 45 (D)

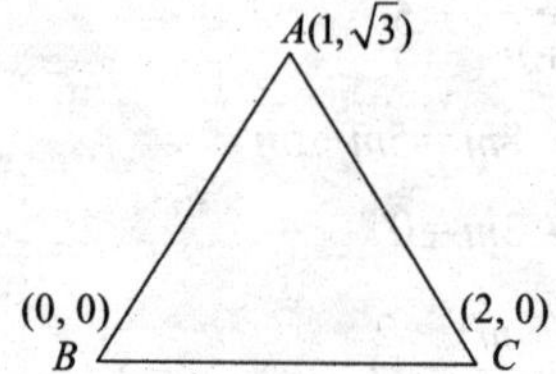

We know incenter of triangle

$$\equiv \left(\frac{ax_1+bx_2+cx_3}{a+b+c}, \frac{ay_1+by_2+cy_3}{a+b+c}\right)$$

Here $\quad a = BC = 2, b = AC = 2,$

$\quad c = AB = 2$

Incentre of ΔABC is given by

$$= \left(\frac{ax_1+bx_2+cx_3}{a+b+c}, \frac{ay_1+by_2+cy_3}{a+b+c}\right)$$

$$= \left(\frac{2+0+4}{2+2+2}, \frac{2\sqrt{3}+0+0}{2+2+2}\right)$$

$$= \left(1, \frac{1}{\sqrt{3}}\right)$$

Hence Ans is (D)

Sol. 46 (B) $y = |x| - 1$

For $x > 0$

$y = x - 1$

$\Rightarrow \quad x - y = 1$

For $x < 0$

$y = -x - 1$

$\Rightarrow \quad x + y = -1$

$y = -|x| + 1$

For $x > 0$

$y = -x + 1$

$\Rightarrow \quad x + y = 1$

For $x < 0$

$y = x + 1$

$\Rightarrow \quad x - y = -1$

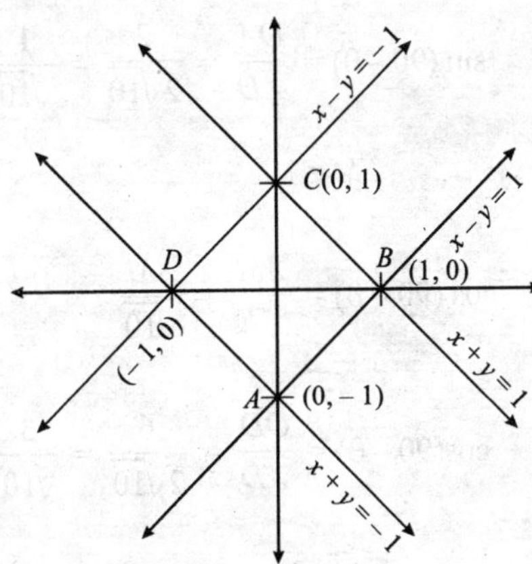

Area of curve $= \frac{1}{2} AC \times BD = \frac{1}{2} \times 2 \times 2$

$= 2$ sq. unit

Hence Ans is (B)

Sol. 47 (B)

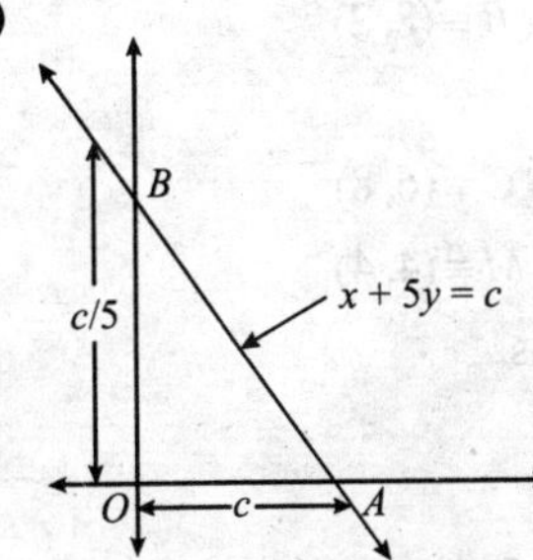

Equation of line L will b $x + 5y = c$

(given line L is perpendicular to line $5x - y = 1$)

$$\frac{x}{c} + \frac{y}{c/5} = 1$$

Given, Area of $\Delta OAB = 5$

$\Rightarrow \quad \frac{1}{2} \times OA \times OB = 4$

$\Rightarrow \quad \frac{1}{2} \times c \times \frac{c}{5} = 5$

$\Rightarrow \quad c^2 = 50$

$\Rightarrow \quad c = \pm 5\sqrt{2}$

Hence Ans is (B)

Sol. 48 (A)

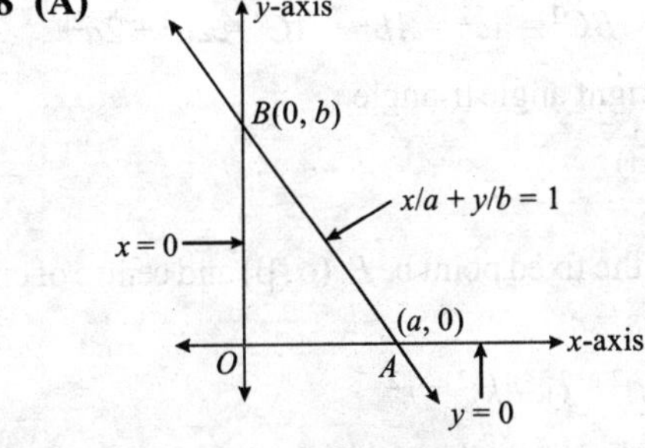

Area of $\Delta OAB = \frac{1}{2} \times OA \times OB = \frac{1}{2} ab$

Hence Ans is (A)

Sol. 49 (A) Circumcentre O, Centriod G and orthocentre O' of triangle ABC are collinear such that G divides $O'O$ i the ratio 2 : 1

(x, y) 2 1 (6, 2)
O' G(3, 3) O

$\Rightarrow \quad 3 = \frac{12 + x}{3}$

$\Rightarrow \quad x = -3$

And $\quad 3 = \frac{4 + y}{3}$

$\Rightarrow \quad y = 5$

So, orthocentre is $(-3, 5)$

Hence Ans is (A)

Sol. 50 (C) (0, 0) A C D B (9, 12)

C divides AB in the ratio 1 : 2.

$\Rightarrow$ Co-ordinates of $C\left(\frac{9+0}{1+2}, \frac{12+0}{2+1}\right) = C(3, 4)$

D divides AB in the ratio of 2 : 1.

$\Rightarrow$ Co-ordinates of $D\left(\frac{18+0}{2+1}, \frac{24+0}{2+1}\right) = D(6, 8)$

$\Rightarrow$ Trisection points are (3, 4) and (6, 8)

Hence Ans is (C)

Solutions of PRACTICE EXERCISE-10.2

Sol. 1 (B) Here $AD = BD = DC = a$

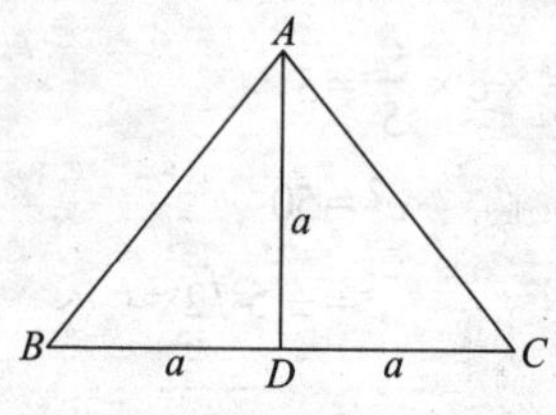

$\Rightarrow \quad AB = AC = \sqrt{2}a$

So $\quad BC^2 = 4a^2 = AB^2 + AC^2 = 2a^2 + 2a^2$

$\Rightarrow \quad \Delta ABC$ is right angle triangle

Hence Ans is (B)

Sol. 2 (D) Let the fixed point be $P.(\alpha, \beta)$ and centre of circle is (h, k) and radius $= r$

then $\quad (x-h)^2 + (y-k)^2 = r^2$

Since every circle passes through the point P so

$$(\alpha - h)^2 + (\beta + k)^2 = r^2$$

$\Rightarrow \quad (h-\alpha)^2 + (k-\beta)^2 = r^2$

$\Rightarrow \quad (x-a)^2 + (y-\beta)^2 = r^2$

Which is circle

Hence Ans is (D)

Sol. 3 (C) We have to find the point of intersection of two given lines

$$\left.\begin{aligned} x - 2y + 1 &= 0 \\ 2x - y &= 4 \end{aligned}\right\}$$

On solving

$$\begin{aligned} x - 2y &= -1 \\ 4x - 2y &= 8 \\ \hline -3x &= -9 \end{aligned}$$

$\Rightarrow \quad y = 6 - 4 = 2$

$\quad x = 3$

$\Rightarrow \quad P(x, y) = (3, 2)$

Hence Ans is (C)

Sol. 4 (C)

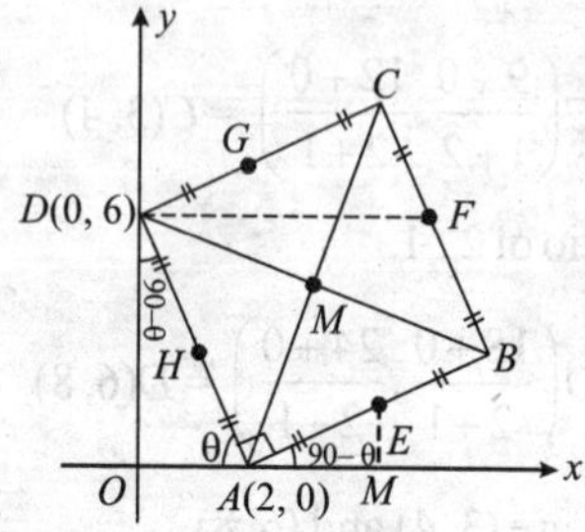

In ΔOAD

$$AD^2 = A^2 + OD^2$$
$$= 4 + 36$$
$$AD^2 = 40$$

$\Rightarrow \quad AD = 2\sqrt{10} \quad$ (side of the square)

To find co-ordinate of E

Draw $EM \perp x$-axis

where $\quad EM = b, AM = a$

Co-ordinates of $\quad E \equiv (2 + a, b)$

To find a and b

In ΔEAM

$$\sin(90-\theta) = \frac{EM}{AE} = \frac{EM}{\sqrt{10}}$$

$$\left[\because AE = \frac{1}{2}AB\right] \quad \ldots(1)$$

In ΔOAD

$$\sin(90-\theta) = \frac{OA}{AD} = \frac{2}{2\sqrt{10}} = \frac{1}{\sqrt{10}} \quad \ldots(2)$$

$(1) = (2)$

$\Rightarrow \quad EM = 1$

In ΔEAM

$$\cos(90-\theta) = \frac{AM}{AE} = \frac{AM}{\sqrt{10}} \quad \ldots(3)$$

In ΔAOD

$$\cos(90-\theta) = \frac{OD}{AD} = \frac{6}{2\sqrt{10}} = \frac{3}{\sqrt{10}} \quad \ldots(4)$$

$(3) = (4)$

$\Rightarrow \quad AM = 3$

$\Rightarrow \quad$ Co-ordinate of

$$E \equiv (2+3, 1)$$
$$\equiv (5, 1)$$

'E' is the midpoint of B

$\Rightarrow \quad$ Co-ordinate of

$$B \equiv (8, 2)$$

Similarly co-ordinates of

$$C \equiv (6, 8)$$

Co-ordinate of $\quad M \equiv (4, 4)$

Now check all the options.

Hence Ans is (C)

Sol. 5 (A) Area of triangle whose vertices are $(a, b+c)$, $(a, b-c)$ and $(-a, c)$

$$A = \frac{1}{2}|a(b-c-c) + a(c-b-c) + (-a)(b+c-b+c)|$$

$$A = \frac{1}{2}|ab - 2ac - ab - 2ac| = 2ac$$

Hence Ans is (A)

Sol. 6 (A)

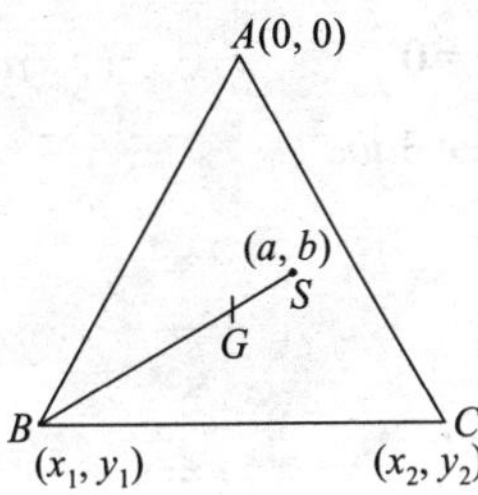

Centroid of ΔABC is $G\left(\frac{x_1+x_2}{3}, \frac{y_1+y_2}{3}\right)$

Now, G divides BS in the ratio 2 : 1

$\Rightarrow \quad \frac{x_1+x_2}{3} = \frac{2a+x_1}{3}$

$\Rightarrow \quad x_2 = 2a$

And $\quad \frac{y_1+y_2}{3} = \frac{2b+y_1}{3}$

$\Rightarrow \quad y_2 = 2b$

Hence Ans is (A)

Sol. 7 (A)

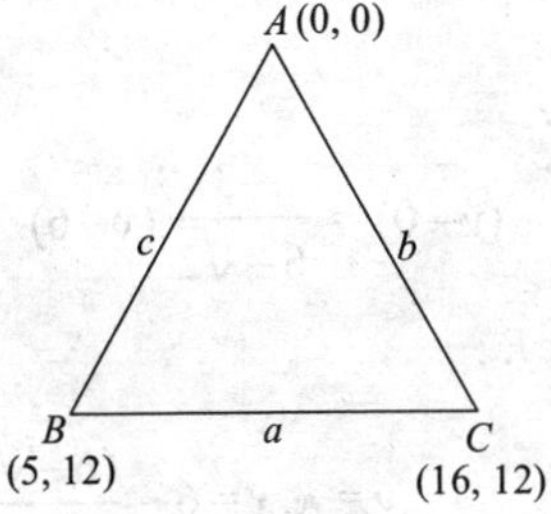

$$a = BC = \sqrt{(16-5)^2+(12-12)^2} = 11$$

$$b = AC = \sqrt{(16-0)^2+(12-0)^2} = 20$$

$$c = AB = \sqrt{(5-0)^2+(12-0)^2} = 13$$

So, co-ordinates of incentre are

$$\left(\frac{ax_1+bx_2+cx_3}{a+b+c}, \frac{ay_1+by_2+cy_3}{a+b+c}\right)$$

$$= \left(\frac{11\times 0+20\times 5+13\times 16}{11+20+13}, \frac{11\times 0+20\times 12+13\times 12}{11+20+13}\right)$$

$$= \left(\frac{308}{44}, \frac{396}{44}\right) = (7, 9)$$

Hence Ans is (A)

Sol. 8 (C) Here, a vertex (0, 0), circumcentre $C(3, 4)$ and centroid $G(6, 8)$ are collinear which impulse circumcentre C and the centroid G are on the median which is also the perpendicular bisector of the side. Therefore the Δ must be isosceles

Hence Ans is (C)

Sol. 9 (D) Let the vertices of triangle be

$A(x_1, y_1), B(x_2, y_2)$

and $C(x_3, y_3)$.

Given : D (mid point of AB)

$\Rightarrow \quad \frac{x_1+x_2}{2} = -2$

$\Rightarrow \quad x_1+x_2 = -4 \quad \ldots(1)$

And $\quad \frac{y_1+y_2}{2} = 3$

$\Rightarrow \quad y_1+y_2 = 6 \quad \ldots(2)$

E(mid point of AC)

$\Rightarrow \quad \frac{x_1+x_3}{2} = 4$

$\Rightarrow \quad x_1+x_3 = 8 \quad \ldots(3)$

And $\quad \frac{y_1+y_3}{2} = -3$

$\Rightarrow \quad y_1+y_3 = -6 \quad \ldots(4)$

F(mid point of BC)

$\Rightarrow \quad \frac{x_2+x_3}{2} = 4$

$\Rightarrow \quad x_2+x_3 = 8 \quad \ldots(5)$

And $\quad \frac{y_2+y_3}{2} = 5$

$\Rightarrow \quad y_2+y_3 = 10 \quad \ldots(6)$

Adding equation (1), (3) and (5)

$$2(x_1+x_2+x_3) = 12$$

$\Rightarrow \quad x_1+x_2+x_3 = 6$

Adding equation (2) (4) and (6)

$$2(y_1+y_2+y_3) = 10$$

$\Rightarrow \quad y_1+y_2+y_3 = 5$

So, Centroid $\left(\frac{x_1+x_2+x_3}{3}, \frac{y_1+y_2+y_3}{3}\right)$

$\Rightarrow \quad$ Centroid $\left(\frac{6}{3}, \frac{5}{3}\right)$ or $\left(2, \frac{5}{3}\right)$

Hence Ans is (D)

Sol. 10 (A)

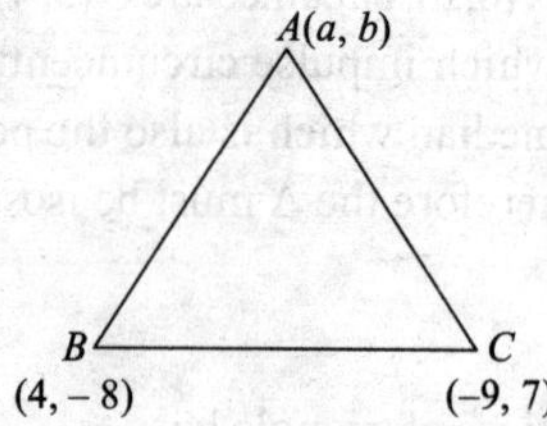

Let the third vertex of the Δ be (a, b) we know co-ordinates of centroid

$$G \equiv \left(\frac{x_1 + x_2 + x_3}{3}, \frac{y_1 + y_2 + y_3}{3}\right)$$

Given centroid ≡ (1, 4)

$$\Rightarrow \quad 1 = \frac{a+4-9}{3}$$

$$\Rightarrow \quad a = 3+5$$

$$= 8$$

$$4 = \frac{b-8+7}{3}$$

$$\Rightarrow \quad 12 = b-1$$

$$\Rightarrow \quad b = 13$$

$$\Rightarrow \quad (a, b) \equiv (8, 13)$$

Area of

$$\Delta = \left|\frac{1}{2}[x_1(y_2 - y_3) + x_2(y_3 - y_1) + x_3(y_1 + y_2)]\right|$$

$$= \left|\frac{1}{2}[8(-8-7) + 4(7-13) - 9(13+8)]\right|$$

$$= \left|\frac{1}{2}[8(-15) + 4(-6) - 9(21)]\right|$$

$$= \left|\frac{1}{2}[-120-24-189]\right|$$

$$= \left|\frac{1}{2}(-333)\right|$$

$$= \frac{333}{2} \text{ sq. unit}$$

Hence Ans is (A)

Sol. 11 (C) Vertices of triangle are $A(a, b)$, $B(b, c)$ and $C(c, a)$. Given that centroid is at origin.

So, $$\frac{a+b+c}{3} = 0$$

$$\Rightarrow \quad a+b+c = 0$$

$$a^3 + b^3 + c^3 - 3abc = (a+b+c)(a^2 + b^2 + c^2 - ab - bc - ca)$$

$$\Rightarrow \quad a^3 + b^3 + c^3 - 3abc = 0 \qquad (\because\ a+b+c=0)$$

$$\Rightarrow \quad a^3 + b^3 + c^3 = 3abc$$

Hence Ans is (C)

Sol. 12 (D)

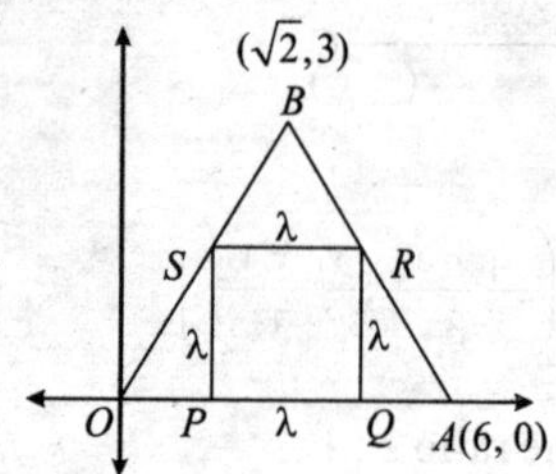

Equation of OB:

$$(y-0) = \frac{3}{\sqrt{2}}(x-0)$$

For the coordinates of point S:

$$y = \lambda, x = \frac{\sqrt{2}}{3}\lambda$$

Coordinate $S\left(\frac{\sqrt{2}}{3}\lambda, \lambda\right)$

Equation AB:

$$(y-0) = \frac{-3}{6-\sqrt{2}}(x-6)$$

For coordinates of point R:

$$y = \lambda, x = 6 - \frac{(6-\sqrt{2})\lambda}{3}$$

Now, $$RS = \lambda$$

$$6 - \frac{(6-\sqrt{2})\lambda}{3} - \frac{\sqrt{2}\lambda}{3} = \lambda$$

$$6 - \frac{6\lambda}{3} + \frac{\sqrt{2}}{3}\lambda - \frac{\sqrt{2}\lambda}{3} = \lambda$$

$$6 = 3\lambda$$

$$\lambda = 2$$

So, the side of the square is 2 unit

Hence Ans is (D)

Sol. 13 (A) Let P is (x, y)

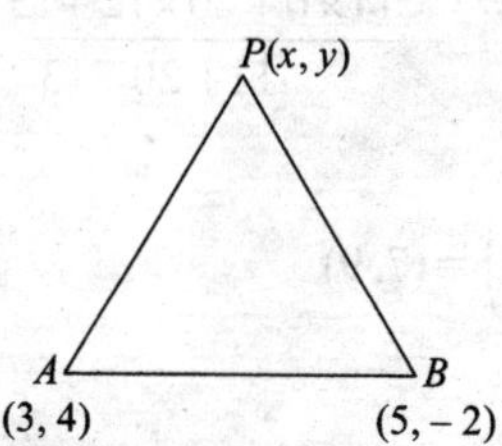

or, $PA^2 = PB^2$

$$(x-3)^2+(y-4)^2=(x-5)^2+(y+2)^2$$

$\Rightarrow$ $x^2-6x+9+y^2-8y+16=x^2-10x+25+y^2+4y+4$

$\Rightarrow$ $4x-12y=4$

$\Rightarrow$ $x-3y=1$ ...(1)

Also Area of $\Delta PAB = 10$

$\Rightarrow$ $\frac{1}{2}|x(6)+3(-2-y)+5(y-4)|=10$

$\Rightarrow$ $|6x-6-3y+5y-20|=20$

$\Rightarrow$ $6x+2y-26=\pm 20$

$\Rightarrow$ $6x+2y=46$ ...(2)

or, $6x+2y=6$ ...(3)

Solving equation-(1) and (2) $x=7, y=2$ and solving equation-(1) and (3) $x=1, y=0$.

So, the co-ordinates of P are (7, 2) or (1, 0)

Hence Ans is (A)

Sol. 14 (C)

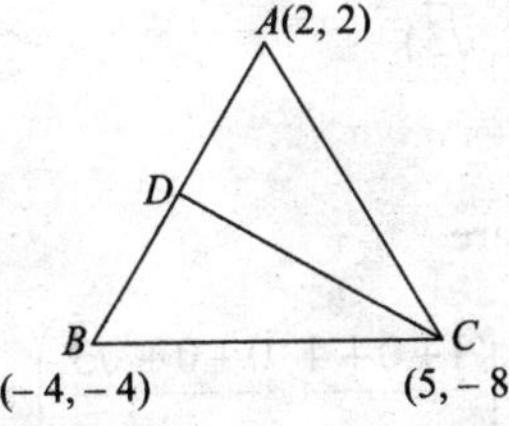

D(Mid point of AB)

$$=\left(\frac{2-4}{2},\frac{2-4}{2}\right)=(-1,-1)$$

Length of Median

$$CD=\sqrt{(5+1)^2+(-8+1)^2}$$

$$=\sqrt{36+49}=\sqrt{85}$$

Hence Ans is (C)

Sol. 15 (C) Given:

$$AC=2BC$$

(– 3, 4) A   (2, 1) B   (x, y) C

or, $\frac{AC}{BC}=2$

$$\frac{AB}{BC}+1=2$$

$$\frac{AB}{BC}=\frac{1}{1}$$

So, B is the mid point of AC

$\Rightarrow$ $2=\frac{-3+x}{2}$

$\Rightarrow$ $-3+x=4$

$\Rightarrow$ $x=7$

And $\frac{4+y}{2}=1$

$\Rightarrow$ $4+y=2$

$\Rightarrow$ $y=-2$

So, the point C are (7, – 2)

Hence Ans is (C)

Sol. 16 (B)

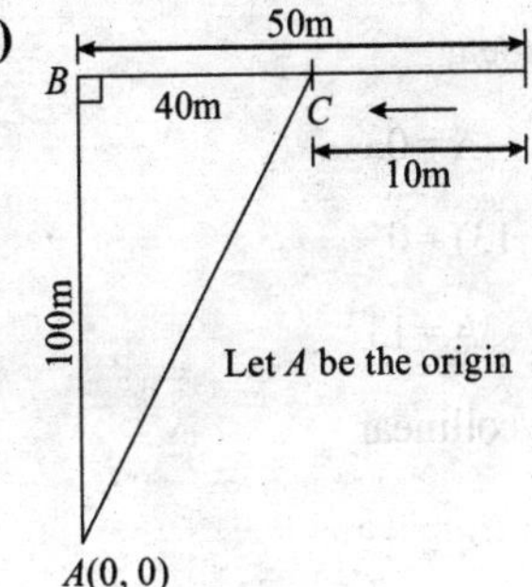

As ABC is a right Δ

$\Rightarrow$ $(AB)^2+(BC)^2=(AC)^2$

$$(AC)^2=(100)^2+(40)^2$$

$$=10000+1600=11600$$

$$AC=\sqrt{116\times 100}=10\sqrt{116}$$

Hence Ans is (B)

Sol. 17 (B)

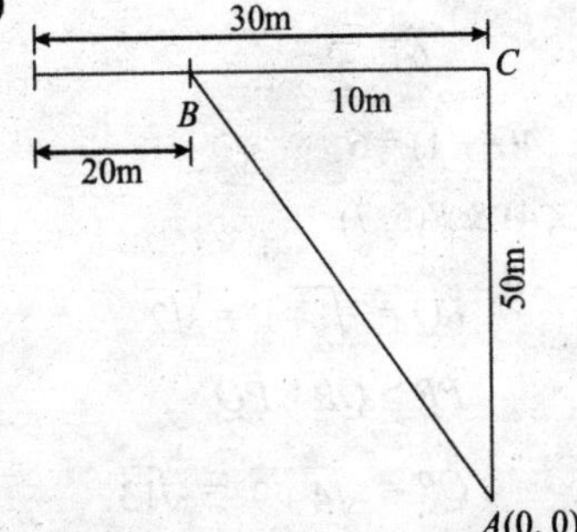

In ΔABC

$$(AC)^2+(BC)^2=(AB)^2$$

$$(50)^2+(10)^2=(AB)^2$$

$$2500+100=(AB)^2$$

$$AB=\sqrt{26\times 100}=10\sqrt{26}$$

Hence Ans is (B)

Sol. 18 (A) Area of ΔABC is

$$D = \pm\frac{1}{2}\begin{vmatrix} 2 & 3 & 1 \\ 3 & b & 1 \\ 5 & 7 & 1 \end{vmatrix} = \pm\frac{1}{2}(-3b+13)$$

(A) given $D = \frac{1}{2}$

$\Rightarrow$ $\frac{1}{2}(-3b+13) = \pm\frac{1}{2}$

$\Rightarrow$ $-3b+13 = \pm 1$

$\Rightarrow$ $b = 4 \;\&\; \frac{14}{3}$

(B) If A, B, C are Collinear

$\Rightarrow$ $\Delta = 0$

$\Rightarrow$ $(-3b+13) = 0$

$\Rightarrow$ $3b = 13$

(C) Given A, B, C are collinear

$\Rightarrow$ $b = \frac{13}{3}$

also B divides AC in the ratio $\lambda : 1$

$\Rightarrow$ $(3, b) = \left(\frac{5\lambda+2}{\lambda+1}, \frac{7\lambda+3}{\lambda+1}\right)$

$\Rightarrow$ $\frac{5\lambda+2}{\lambda+1} = 3$

& $\frac{7\lambda+3}{\lambda+1} = \frac{13}{3}\left(b = \frac{13}{3}\right)$

$\Rightarrow$ $\lambda = \frac{1}{2}$

Hence $4(\lambda+1) = 6$

(D) If $P(2, 3), Q(3, 4) \;\&\; R(5, 7)$

$\Rightarrow$ $PQ = \sqrt{1+1} = \sqrt{2}$

$\Rightarrow$ $PR > QR > PQ$

$QR = \sqrt{4+9} = \sqrt{13}$

$PR = \sqrt{9+16} = 5$

Hence Ans is (A)

Sol. 19 (C) If none of the coordinates are irrational then

$$\Delta = \frac{1}{2}\begin{vmatrix} x_1 & y_1 & 1 \\ x_2 & y_2 & 1 \\ x_3 & y_3 & 1 \end{vmatrix} = \frac{1}{2} \times \text{rational} = \text{rational}$$

But the area of an equilateral triangle

$$= \frac{\sqrt{3}}{4} \times (\text{side})^2 = \frac{\sqrt{3}}{4} \times \text{rational} = \text{irrational.}$$

So, both the coordinates of the third vertex cannot be rational

Hence Ans is (C)

Sol. 20 (B)

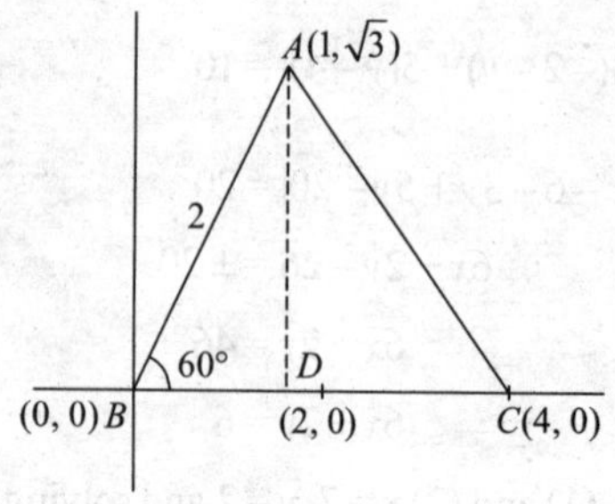

In ΔABC, as shown in the figure

$$AD = 2\sin 60^\circ$$

$$= 2 \times \frac{\sqrt{3}}{2} = \sqrt{3}$$

$\Rightarrow$ co-ordinate of $A\,(1, \sqrt{3})$

co-ordinate of $C(4, 0)$

co-ordinate of centroid are

$$G \equiv \left(\frac{1+0+4}{3}, \frac{0+0+\sqrt{3}}{3}\right) = \left(\frac{5}{3}, \frac{1}{\sqrt{3}}\right)$$

Hence Ans is (B)

Sol. 21 (A) As the points are in order, the area

$$= \left|\frac{1}{2}\left\{\begin{vmatrix} 4 & 1 \\ 3 & 6 \end{vmatrix} + \begin{vmatrix} 3 & 6 \\ -5 & 1 \end{vmatrix} + \begin{vmatrix} -5 & 1 \\ -3 & -3 \end{vmatrix} + \begin{vmatrix} -3 & -3 \\ -3 & 0 \end{vmatrix} + \begin{vmatrix} -3 & 0 \\ 4 & 1 \end{vmatrix}\right\}\right| = 30 \text{ unit}^2$$

Hence Ans is (A)

Sol. 22 (C) From the choice of the axes,

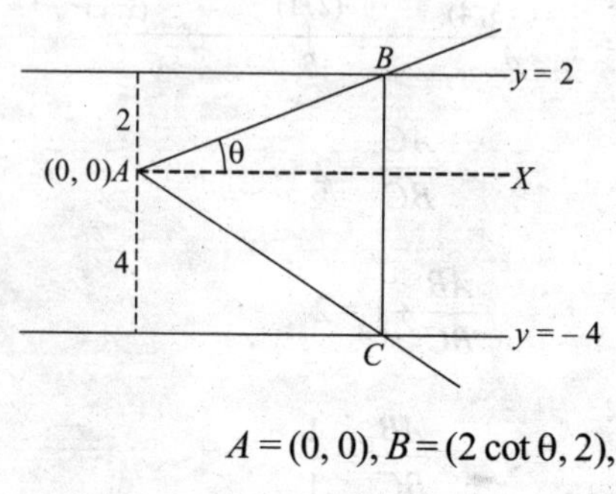

$$A = (0, 0), B = (2\cot\theta, 2),$$

$$C = (4\cot(60^\circ - \theta), -4)$$

(side of the equilateral triangle)^2

$$= 4\cot^2\theta + 4 = 16\cot^2(60° - \theta) + 16$$

$\Rightarrow$ $4\ \text{cosec}\ \theta^2 = 16\ \text{cosec}^2(60° - \theta)$

$\Rightarrow$ $\text{cosec}\ \theta = 2\ \text{cosec}\ (60° - \theta)$

or, $2\sin\theta = \sin(60° - \theta)$

$\Rightarrow$ $2\sin\theta = \frac{\sqrt{3}}{2}\cos\theta - \frac{1}{2}\sin\theta$

or, $5\sin\theta = \sqrt{3}\cos\theta$

$\Rightarrow$ $\tan\theta = \frac{\sqrt{3}}{5}$

$\Rightarrow$ the required length

$$= 2\ \text{cosec}\ \theta = 2 \times \frac{\sqrt{25+3}}{\sqrt{3}} = \frac{2\sqrt{28}}{\sqrt{3}} = \frac{4\sqrt{7}}{\sqrt{3}}$$

Hence Ans is (C)

Sol. 23 (C) Let $Q(x_1, y_1)$ be the image of the point $P(3, 8)$ in the line $x + 3y = 7$. Then, PQ is perpendicular to the given line.

So, $m_1 \times m_2 = -1$

$\Rightarrow$ $\frac{y_1 - 8}{x_1 - 3} \times -\frac{1}{3} = -1$

$\Rightarrow$ $3x_1 - y_1 = 1$ ...(1)

Also, $\left(\frac{x_1+3}{2}, \frac{y_1+8}{2}\right)$, lies on $x + 3y = 7$.

$\Rightarrow$ $x_1 + 3 + 3y_1 + 24 = 14$

$\Rightarrow$ $x_1 + 3y_1 + 13 = 0$ ...(2)

Solving (1) and (2), we get

$$x_1 = -1, y_1 = -4.$$

Hence, the required point is $(-1, -4)$

Hence Ans is (C)

Sol. 24 (B) We have, $2|x| + 3|y| \le 6$. This is equivalent to the following system of in equations:

$2x + 3y \le 6$, when $x \ge 0, y \ge 0$

$2x - 3y \le 6$, when $x \ge 0, y \le 0$

$-2x + 3y \le 6$, when $x \le 0, y \ge 0$

and $-2x - 3y \le 6$, when $x \le 0, y \le 0$

These in equations form a rhombus having its diagonals of lengths 6 and 4 units, along the coordinate axes.

So, required area $= \frac{1}{2}(6 \times 4) = 12$ sq. units

Hence Ans is (B)

Sol. 25 (A)

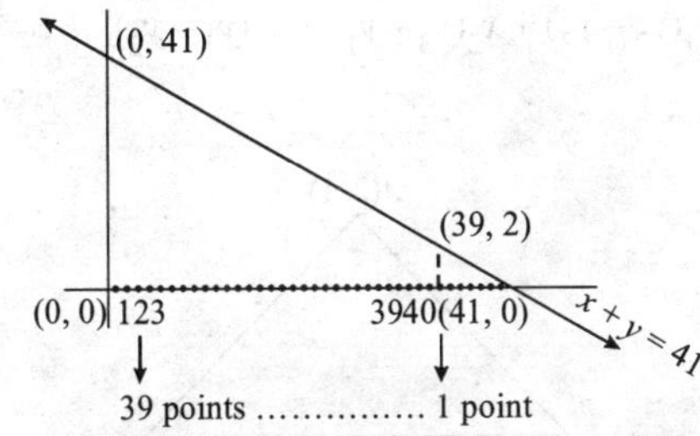

The equation of the straight line passing through the point (0, 41) and (41, 0) is $x + y = 41$.

So we need to find out all the possible integer combination in such a way that $x > 0, y > 0$ and $x + y < 41$

Let $x + y = 40$ then $x = 1, 2, \ldots 39$ and $y = 39, 38, \ldots, 1$ there are 39 combination.

Let $x + y = 39$ then $x = 1, 2, \ldots 38$ and $y = 38, 37 \ldots 1$

As there are 38 combination.

Let $x + y = 2$ then $x = 1$ & $y = 1$

So the is 1 combination

Therefore then are total

$1 + 2 + 3 \ldots + 39$ combination

It's an AP with $a = 1, d = 1$

$$\text{Sum} = \frac{39 \times 40}{2} = 780$$

Hence Ans is (A)

Solutions of PRACTICE EXERCISE-10.3

Sol. 1 (B)

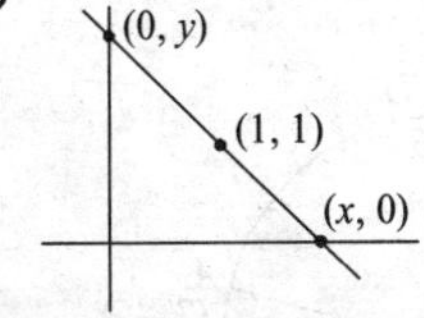

Equation of line passing through (0, y) and (x, 0) will be

$\frac{X}{x} + \frac{Y}{y} = 1$ it passes (1, 1) so

$$\frac{1}{x} + \frac{1}{y} = 1$$

$\Rightarrow$ $x + y = xy$

Hence Ans is (B)

Sol. 2 (B) Given $y = x^2 - 3x - 4$

Graph will be parabola

Hence Ans is (B)

Sol. 3 (B) Area of triangle whose vertices given by $A(x_1, y_1)$, $B(x_2, y_2)$ & $C(x_3, y_3)$ is given by

$$= \frac{1}{2}|x_1(y_2 - y_3) + x_2(y_3 - y_1) + x_3(y_1 - y_2)|$$

Here we have

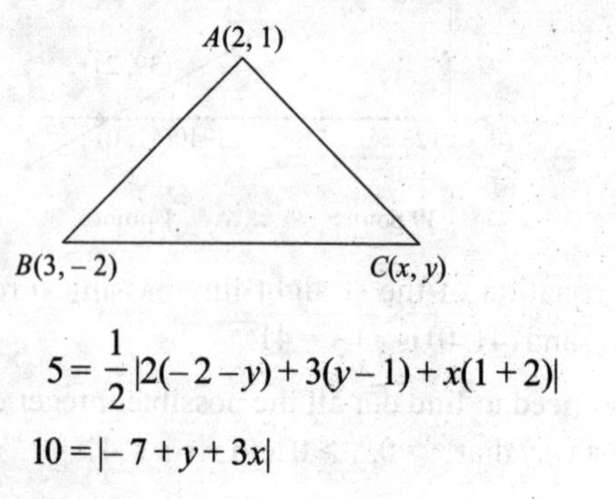

$$5 = \frac{1}{2}|2(-2 - y) + 3(y - 1) + x(1 + 2)|$$

$$10 = |-7 + y + 3x|$$

$\Rightarrow$ either $+10 = -7 + y + 3x$ ...(1)

or $-10 = -7 + y + 3x$ ...(2)

Since third vertex C lies on $y = x + 3$

so $y = x + 3$ ...(3)

on solving (2) and (3)

$$x = -\frac{3}{2}, y = \frac{3}{2}$$

on solving (1) and (3)

$$x = \frac{7}{2}, y = \frac{13}{2}$$

Hence Ans is (B)

Sol. 4 (D) We know that the distance between two points $A(x_1, y_1)$ & $B(x_2, y_2)$ is given by

$$= \sqrt{(x_2 - x_1)^2 + (y_2 - y_1)^2}$$

$A(7, -5)$, $B(3, -7)$ and $C(3, 3)$

Let the centre $O(x, y)$

$\Rightarrow$ $OA = OB = OC$ (radius of circle)

$\Rightarrow$ $OA = OB$

$\Rightarrow$ $(x - 7)^2 + (y + 5)^2 = (x - 3)^2 + (y + 7)^2$

$\Rightarrow$ $(x - 7)^2 - (x - 3)^2 = (y + 7)^2 - (y + 5)^2$

$\Rightarrow$ $(2x - 10)(-4) = (2y + 12) \times 2$

$\Rightarrow$ $-2x + 10 = y + 6$

$\Rightarrow$ $2x + y - 4 = 0$ ...(1)

$OB = OC$

$\Rightarrow$ $(x - 3)^2 + (y + 7)^2 = (x - 3)^2 + (y - 3)^2$

$\Rightarrow$ $(y + 7)^2 = (y - 3)^2$

$\Rightarrow$ $y^2 + 14y + 49 = y^2 - 6y + 9$

$\Rightarrow$ $20y = -40$

$\Rightarrow$ $y = -2$

Putting $y = -2$ in (1)

$\Rightarrow$ $x = 3$

i.e. $O(3, -2)$

Hence Ans is (D)

Sol. 5 (B) Let $A \equiv (4.p)$

& $B \equiv (1, 0)$

given $AB = 5$

$\Rightarrow$ $AB \equiv \sqrt{(4-1)^2 + (p-0)^2} = 5$

$3^2 + p^2 = 25$

$p^2 = 25 - 9 = 16$

$p = \pm 4$

Hence Ans is (B)

Sol. 6 (A)

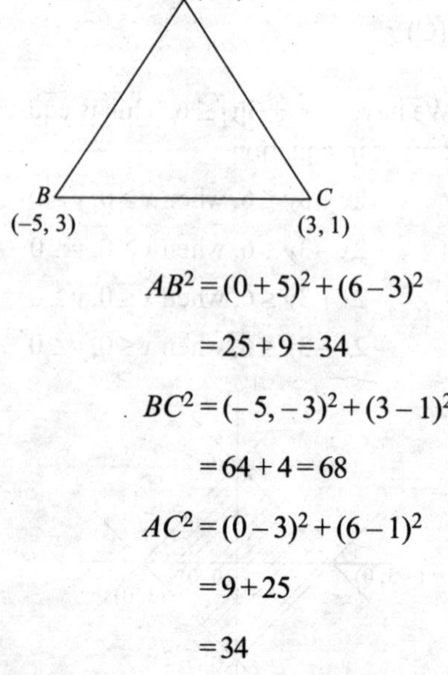

$AB^2 = (0 + 5)^2 + (6 - 3)^2$

$= 25 + 9 = 34$

$BC^2 = (-5, -3)^2 + (3 - 1)^2$

$= 64 + 4 = 68$

$AC^2 = (0 - 3)^2 + (6 - 1)^2$

$= 9 + 25$

$= 34$

Hence Ans is (A)

Sol. 7 (D)

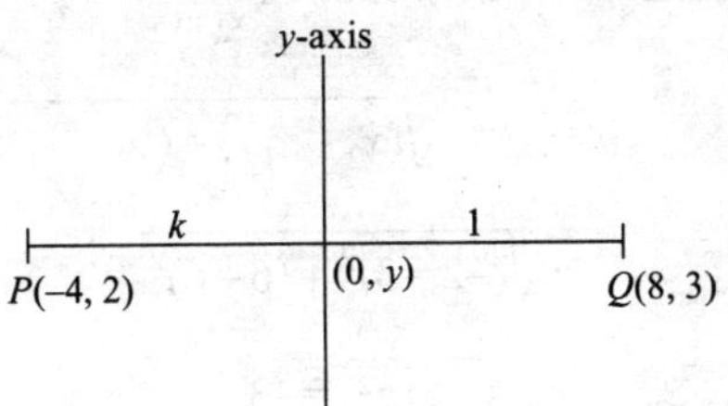

Let the ratio be $k:1$

$\Rightarrow \quad 0=\frac{8k-4}{k+1}$

$\Rightarrow \quad 8k=4$

$\Rightarrow \quad k=\frac{1}{2}$

Hence Ans is (D)

Sol. 8 (C) Let the point be $P(a, 0)$ given $A(7, 6)$ and $B(-3, 4)$ are equidistant from P

$\Rightarrow \quad PA=PB$

$\Rightarrow \quad PA^2=PB^2$

$\Rightarrow \quad (7-a)^2+6^2=(-3,-a)^2+4^2$

$\Rightarrow \quad 49+a^2-14a+36=9+a^2+6a+16$

$\Rightarrow \quad 85-25=20a$

$\Rightarrow \quad 20a=60$

$\Rightarrow \quad a=3$

$\Rightarrow \quad P\equiv(3,0)$

Hence Ans is (C)

Sol. 9 (A)

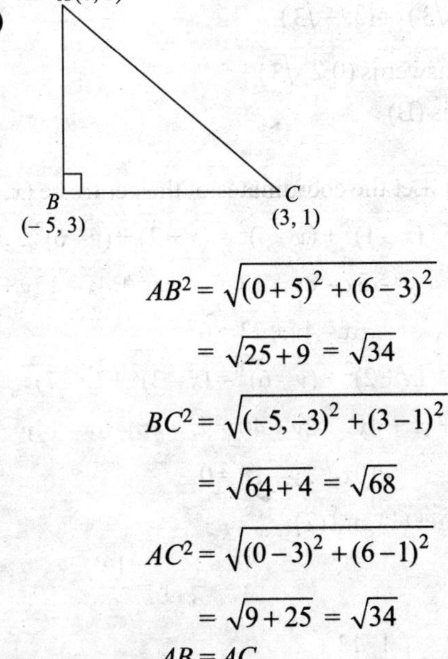

$$AB^2=\sqrt{(0+5)^2+(6-3)^2}$$

$$=\sqrt{25+9}=\sqrt{34}$$

$$BC^2=\sqrt{(-5,-3)^2+(3-1)^2}$$

$$=\sqrt{64+4}=\sqrt{68}$$

$$AC^2=\sqrt{(0-3)^2+(6-1)^2}$$

$$=\sqrt{9+25}=\sqrt{34}$$

Since $\quad AB=AC$

ΔABC is an isosceles Δ

Hence Ans is (A)

Sol. 10 (A)

k $P(a, 0)$ 1

$A(2, -3)$ $B(7, 4)$

$x_1 \; y_1$ $x_2 \; y_2$

Let the point $P(a, 0)$ divides the line AB in the ratio $k:1$

$$P\equiv\left(\frac{kx_2+x_1}{k+1}, \frac{ky_2+y_1}{k+1}\right)$$

Here $\quad \frac{ky_2+y_1}{k+1}=0$

$\Rightarrow \quad \frac{k4-3}{k+1}=0$

$\Rightarrow \quad 4k=3$

$\Rightarrow \quad k=\frac{3}{4}$

Hence Ans is (A)

Sol. 11 (C) Let $A(x, 0)$ be a point on x-axis

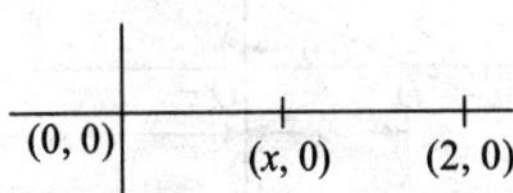

clearly it will be the mid point of the given points as ordinate of both point is zero so no need to apply distance formula.

So $\quad (1, 0)$ is the ans

Hence Ans is (C)

Sol. 12 (A)

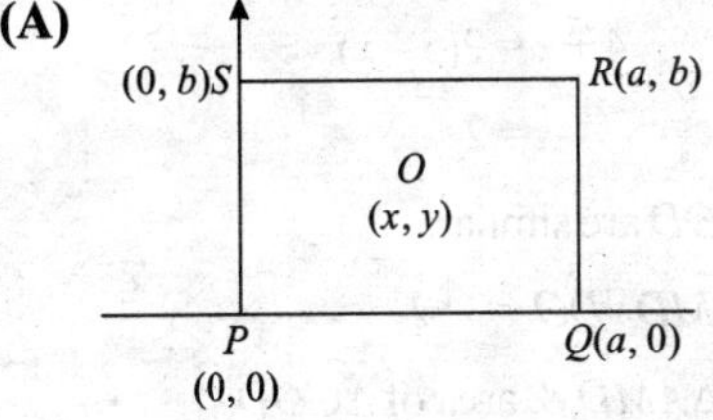

$$OP^2=x^2+y^2$$

$$OR^2=(x-a)^2+(y-b)^2$$

$$OQ^2=(x-a)^2+y^2$$

$$OS^2=(x^2)+(y-b)^2$$

$\Rightarrow \quad OP^2+OR^2=OQ^2+OS^2$

Hence Ans is (A)

Sol. 13 (B) In IIIrd quadrant both the x and y co-ordinates are negative.

Hence Ans is (B)

Sol. 14 (B) Let the first term be 'a' & common ratio be 'r', then n^{th} term of the GP is given by

$$T_n = ar^{n-1}$$

$\Rightarrow$ $T_2 = ar = 2$ ...(1)

$T_4 = ar^3 = 6$ ...(2)

Equation-(2) ÷ equation-(1)

$$r^2 = 3$$

$\Rightarrow$ $r = \pm\sqrt{3}$

$\Rightarrow$ $a = \frac{2}{r} = \pm\frac{2}{\sqrt{3}}$

$\Rightarrow$ $a = \frac{2\sqrt{3}}{\pm 3}$

Hence Ans is (B)

Sol. 15 (B)

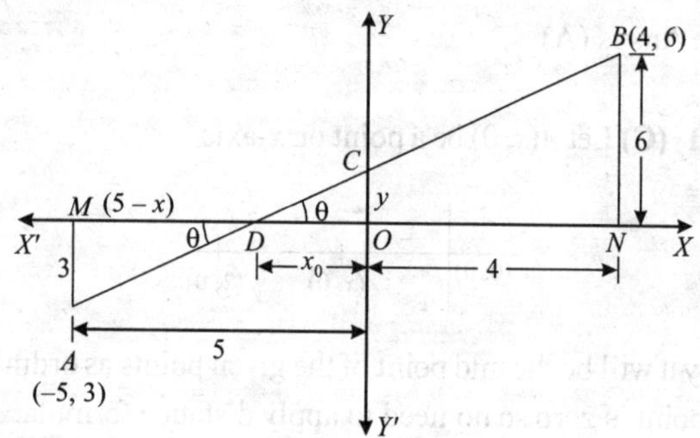

In $\Delta AMD, \Delta CDO$ & ΔBDN
we have

$$\tan\theta = \frac{3}{5-x} = \frac{y}{x} = \frac{6}{4+x}$$

$\Rightarrow$ $4 + x = 2(5 - x)$

$\Rightarrow$ $x = 2$

Now ΔAMD & ΔCOD are similar.

& $MD : DO = 3 : 2$

So ratio of area of ΔAMD & area of ΔCOD.

$$= MD^2 : DO^2$$
$$= 3^2 : 2^2 = 9 : 4$$

Hence Ans is (B)

Sol. 16 (A) $A(3, -2), B(4, 5)$

Let $C(0, y)$. be a point equidistant from A & B

$\Rightarrow$ $AC = BC$

$$\sqrt{(0-3)^2 + (y+2)^2} = \sqrt{(0-4)^2 + (y-5)^2}$$

$\Rightarrow$ $9 + y^2 + 4 + 4y = 16 + y^2 + 25 - 10y$

$\Rightarrow$ $y = 2$

$\Rightarrow$ $C(0, 2)$

Hence Ans is (A)

Sol. 17 (B) Let $A \equiv (\underset{x_1}{3}, \underset{y_1}{6})$ & $B \equiv (\underset{x_2}{-2}, \underset{y_2}{6})$

$$d = AB = \sqrt{(x_2 - x_1)^2 + (y_2 - y_1)^2}$$
$$= \sqrt{(-2, -3)^2 + (6+6)^2}$$
$$= \sqrt{5^2 + 12^2} = 13$$

Hence Ans is (B)

Sol. 18 (D)

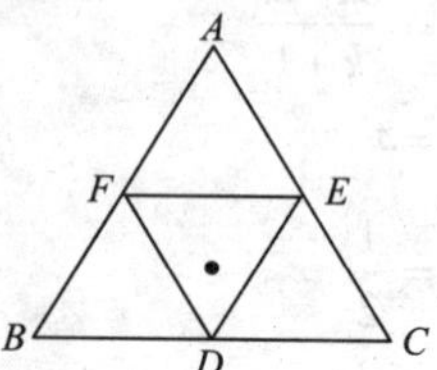

in $\Delta ABC, D, E, F$ are midpoints of sides BC, CA, AB

Hence centroid of ΔABC = centroid of ΔDEF

$$= \left(\frac{1+2+3}{3}, \frac{1-3+4}{3}\right)$$
$$= \left(2, \frac{2}{3}\right)$$

Hence Ans is (D)

Sol. 19 (B) $(x_1, y_1), (x_2, y_2)$ are two vertices of an equilateral triangle then its third vertex is

$$\left(\frac{x_1 + x_2 \pm \sqrt{3}(y_1 - y_2)}{2}, \frac{y_1 + y_2 + \sqrt{3}(x_1 - x_2)}{2}\right)$$

by substituting $(x_1, y_1) = (0, 0), (x_2, y_2) = (3, \sqrt{3})$ we get third vertex $(0, 2\sqrt{3})$ or $(3, -\sqrt{3})$

hence the answer is $(0, 2\sqrt{3})$

Hence Ans is (B)

Sol. 20 (D) Let the coordinates of the centre be (x, y)

Thus $(x-1)^2 + (y-4)^2 = (x+2) + (y-6)^2$

$\Rightarrow$ $x^2 + y^2 - 2x - 8y + 17 = x^2 + y^2 + 4x - 12y + 40$

$\Rightarrow$ $6x - 4y + 23 = 0$ ...(1)

Also $(x+2)^2 + (y-6)^2 = (x-3)^2 + (y-7)^2$

$\Rightarrow$ $x^2 + y^2 + 4x - 12y + 40 = x^2 + y^2 - 6x - 14y + 58$

$\Rightarrow$ $10x + 2y - 18 = 0$ ...(2)

Solving we get (1) and (2)

$$x = \frac{1}{2}, y = \frac{13}{2}$$

Thus centre is $\left(\frac{1}{2}, \frac{13}{2}\right)$

Hence Ans is (D)

Sol. 21 (A) $x = \frac{x_1 + x_2 + x_3}{3}$

$$y = \frac{y_1 + y_2 + y_3}{3}$$

$$0 = \frac{4 + 2 + x_3}{3}$$

$$1 = \frac{-2 - 6 + y_3}{3}$$

$$x_3 = -6$$

$$y_3 = 11$$

(−6, 11)

Hence Ans is (A)

Sol. 22 (B) Since the third vertex will lie on the perpendicular bisector of PQ as ΔPQR is an equilateral triangle and it does not passes through second quadrant.

Hence Ans is (B)

Sol. 23 (C) (4, 0) lies on X axis

Hence Ans is (C)

Sol. 24 (C) $y = c$ is a line parallel to X-axis

Hence Ans is (C)

Sol. 25 (B) $\overline{QP}$

Sol. 26 (B)

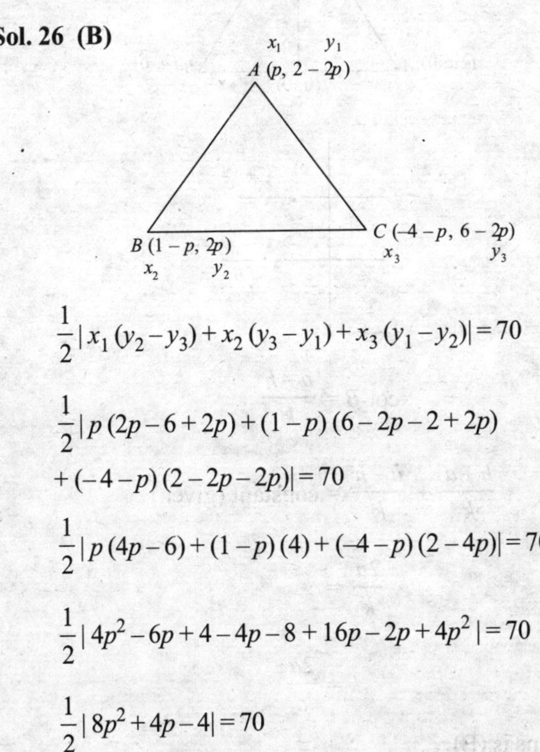

$$\frac{1}{2}|x_1(y_2 - y_3) + x_2(y_3 - y_1) + x_3(y_1 - y_2)| = 70$$

$$\frac{1}{2}|p(2p - 6 + 2p) + (1 - p)(6 - 2p - 2 + 2p) + (-4 - p)(2 - 2p - 2p)| = 70$$

$$\frac{1}{2}|p(4p - 6) + (1 - p)(4) + (-4 - p)(2 - 4p)| = 70$$

$$\frac{1}{2}|4p^2 - 6p + 4 - 4p - 8 + 16p - 2p + 4p^2| = 70$$

$$\frac{1}{2}|8p^2 + 4p - 4| = 70$$

$$|4p^2 + 2p - 2| = 70$$

$$|2p^2 + p - 1| = 35$$

$$2p^2 + p - 1 = 35$$

or $\quad 2p^2 + p - 1 = -35$

$$2p^2 + p - 36 = 0$$

or $\quad 2p^2 + p + 34 = 0$

$$2p^2 + 9p - 8p - 36 = 0$$

or $\quad D = 1 - 4(2)(34)$

$$p(2p + 9) - 4(2p + 9) = 0$$

$$D = -271$$

$$(2p + 9)(p - 4) = 0$$

or $\quad$ No real roots

$$p = -\frac{9}{2}$$

or $\quad p = 4$

No. of Integral values of $p = 1$

Hence Ans is (B)

Sol. 27 (B) $A(a, 0), B(0, b), C(1, 1)$ lie on a straight line slope of

$$\overrightarrow{AB} = \text{slope of } \overrightarrow{BC}$$

$$\frac{b - 0}{0 - a} = \frac{1 - b}{1 - 0}$$

$$\frac{b}{a} = \frac{1 - b}{1}$$

$$\Rightarrow \quad b = a - ab$$

$$\Rightarrow \quad a + b = ab$$

$$\Rightarrow \quad \frac{a + b}{ab} = 1$$

Hence Ans is (B)

Sol. 28 (C)

A (3, 5) —2— P $\left(\frac{23}{5}, \frac{33}{5}\right)$ —3— C (x, y)

$$\frac{23}{5} = \frac{3 \times 3 + 2 \times x}{5}$$

or $\quad 23 - 9 = 2x$

$$x = \frac{14}{2} = 7$$

$$\frac{33}{5} = \frac{3 \times 5 + 2y}{5}$$

or $\quad 33 - 15 = 2y$

or $\quad \frac{18}{2} = y$

$$y = 9$$

Hence Ans is (C)

Sol. 29 (A)

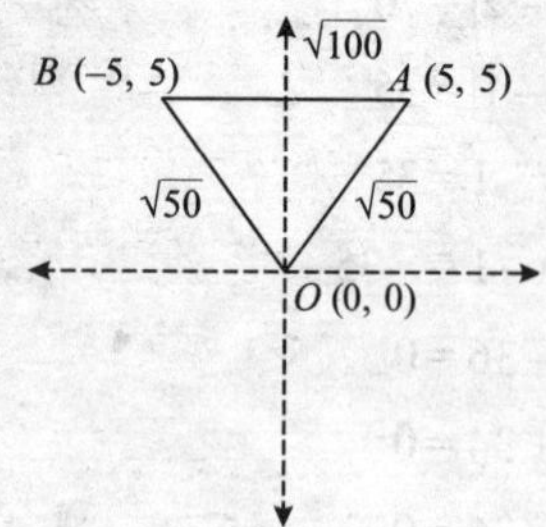

Hence Ans is (A)

Sol. 30 (C)

$$4(0)+3y=12$$
$$4x+3(0)=12$$
$$y=4$$
$$x=3$$
$$A(0,4)$$
$$B(3,0)$$
$$AB=5$$

Hence Ans is (C)

Sol. 31 (A) $A(1,2), B(3,5)$ and $C(0,b)$ are collinear then

Slope of AB = Slope of BC

$$\frac{5-2}{3-1}=\frac{b-5}{0-3}$$

$$\Rightarrow \quad \frac{3}{2}=\frac{b-5}{-3}$$

$$\Rightarrow \quad \frac{-9}{2}+5=b$$

$$\Rightarrow \quad b=\frac{1}{2}$$

Hence Ans is (A)

Sol. 32 (D)

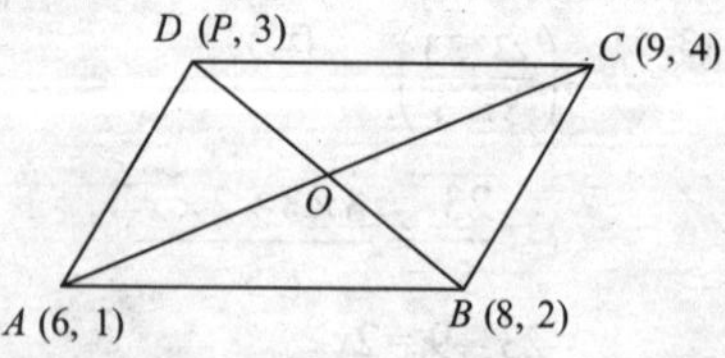

Diagonals of Parallelogram bisect each other coordinates of 'O' are $=\left(\frac{15}{2},\frac{5}{2}\right)$ (Using mid point formulae) O is also mid point of BD

$$\Rightarrow \quad \frac{8+P}{2}=\frac{15}{2}$$

$$P=7$$

Hence Ans is (D)

Sol. 33 (D) Distance from x axis is $=5$

Distance from y axis is $=3$

$\Rightarrow \quad$ Sum $=5+3=8$

Hence Ans is (D)

Sol. 34 (A)

$$x<1 \Rightarrow x-1<0$$
$$y<-1 \Rightarrow y-3<0$$

$\Rightarrow \quad$ 3rd quadrant

Hence Ans is (A)

Sol. 35 (B) $(a,0), (0,b), (1,1)$

Area of triangle $=0$

($\because$ points are collinear)

$$\Rightarrow \quad a(b-1)+0(1-0)+1(a-b)=0$$

$$\Rightarrow \quad ab-a-b=0$$

$$\Rightarrow \quad ab=a+b$$

$$\Rightarrow \quad 1=\frac{1}{a}+\frac{1}{b}$$

Hence Ans is (B)

Sol. 36 (B) Let the coordinate of $C\,(h,k)$

$$\cot A=\frac{h+a}{k}$$

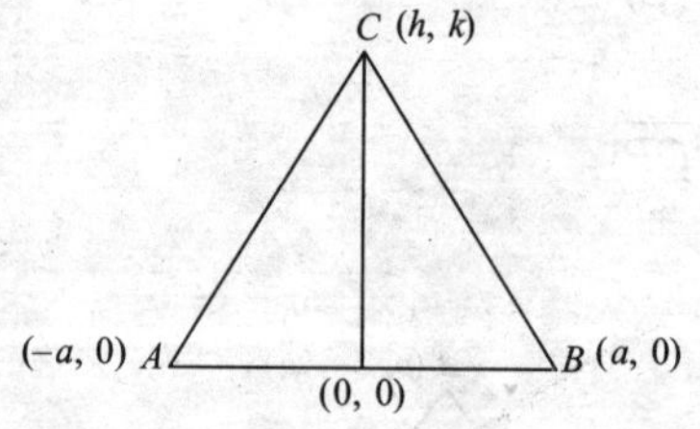

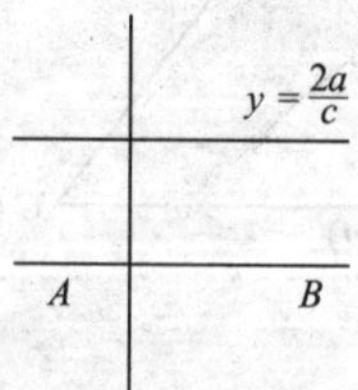

$$\cot B=\frac{a-h}{k}$$

$$\frac{h+a}{k}+\frac{a-h}{k}=\text{constant (given)}$$

$$\frac{2a}{k}=c$$

$$k=\frac{2a}{c}$$

Hence Ans is (B)

Sol. 37 (D)

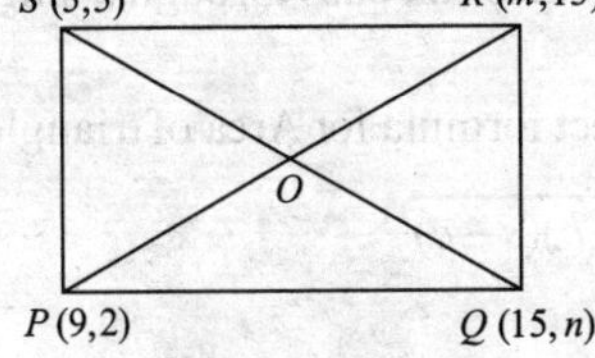

Mid points of $SQ = \left(10, \dfrac{5+n}{2}\right)$

Mid points of $PR = \left(\dfrac{m+9}{2}, \dfrac{15}{2}\right)$

$$10 = \frac{m+9}{2}$$

$$\frac{5+n}{2} = \frac{15}{2},$$

$$n = 10$$

$$m = 11$$

$$m - n = 11 - 10 = 1$$

Hence Ans is (D)

Sol. 38 (B) Mid point of $SQ = (0, 1)$

Mid point of $RP = (0, 1)$

S(3, 1) R(0, –2)

P(0, 4) Q(–3, 1)

$$PS = \sqrt{3^2 + 3^2} = 3\sqrt{2}$$

$$PQ = \sqrt{3^2 + 3^2} = 3\sqrt{2}$$

$$PR = \sqrt{6^2} = 6$$

$$SQ = \sqrt{6^2} = 6$$

$\Rightarrow$ $PQRS$ is a square

Hence Ans is (B)

Sol. 39 (A)

$A\,(3, k)$

$B\,(k, 5)$

$C\,(0, 2)$

$$AC^2 = BC^2$$

$$(3-0)^2 + (k-2)^2 = (k-0)^2 + (5-2)^2$$

$$\Rightarrow \quad 9 + k^2 - 4k + 4 = k^2 + 9$$

$$\Rightarrow \quad k = 1$$

Hence Ans is (A)

Sol. 40 (B)

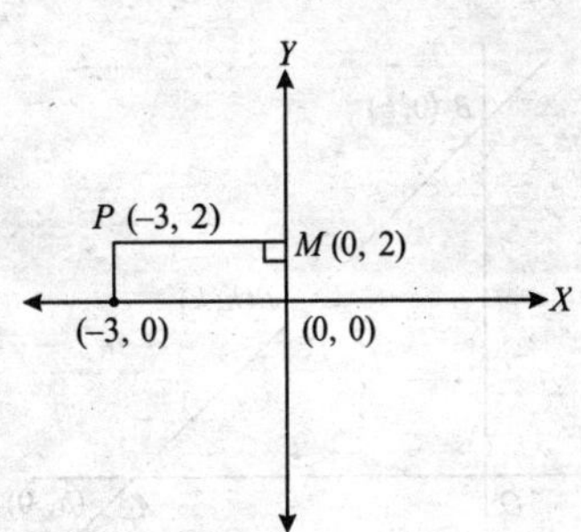

From figure it is clear that coordinates of M are $(0, 2)$

Hence Ans is (B)

Sol. 41 (B) $A(2, -2)$ $P(a, 0)$ $Q(-4, b)$ $B(-7, 4)$

$$a = \frac{a}{2a} = -1$$

$$b = \frac{2\times 4 + 1\times -2}{3} = 2$$

$$\Rightarrow \quad a = -1$$

and $\quad b = 2$

Hence Ans is (B)

Sol. 42 (B) Area of the shaded region

$= \text{area of } \Delta ABC - \text{area of sector}$

$$= \frac{1}{2} \times 10 \times 10 - \frac{90^\circ}{360^\circ} \times \frac{22}{7} \times 7 \times 7 = 11.5 \text{ cm}^2$$

Hence Ans is (B)

Sol. 43 (B) O (x, y) —2— G (2, 4) —1— C (1, 7)

Let orthocenter be (x, y)

$$\frac{2+x}{3} = 2$$

$$\Rightarrow \quad 2 + x = 6$$

$$\Rightarrow \quad x = 4$$

$$\frac{14+y}{3} = 4$$

$$\Rightarrow \quad 14 + y = 12$$

$$\Rightarrow \quad y = -2$$

$(4, -2)$

Hence Ans is (B)

Sol. 44 (B)

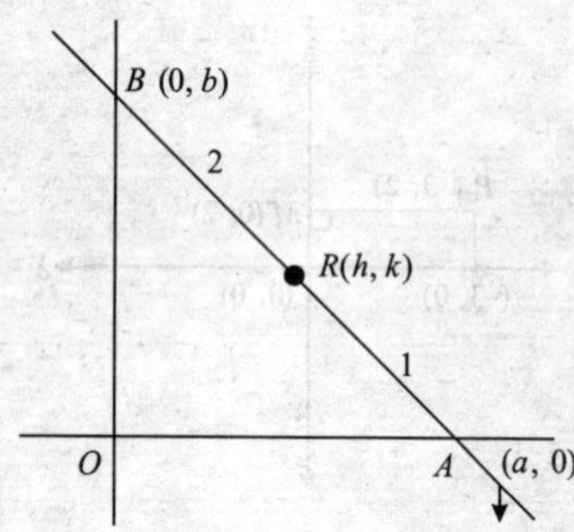

$$\Rightarrow \quad R \equiv \left(\frac{2a+0}{3}, \frac{0+b}{3}\right)$$

$$\Rightarrow \quad R \equiv \left(\frac{2a}{3}, \frac{b}{3}\right) = (h, k)$$

$$\Rightarrow \quad a = \frac{3h}{2}, b = 3k$$

So, slope intercept form of a line

$$\Rightarrow \quad \frac{x}{a} + \frac{y}{b} = 1$$

$$\Rightarrow \quad \frac{x}{\frac{3h}{2}} + \frac{y}{3k} = 1$$

$$\Rightarrow \quad 2kx + hy = 3hk$$

Hence Ans is (B)

Sol. 45 (C) $\frac{C}{2} = -9$

$C = -18$

Hence Ans is (C)

Sol. 46 (D) (2, 3) —3— P —4— (−1, 2)

$$P = \left(\frac{-3+8}{7}, \frac{6+12}{7}\right)$$

$$= \left(\frac{5}{7}, \frac{18}{7}\right)$$

Now, $\frac{5}{7} + 2\left(\frac{18}{7}\right) = K$

$$\Rightarrow \quad K = \frac{41}{7}$$

Hence Ans is (D)

Sol. 47 (D) Infinite lines can pass through a single point.

Sol. 48 (B) It is direct formula for Area of triangle

$$= \sqrt{s(s-a)(s-b)(s-c)}$$

Hence Ans is (B)

Sol. 49 (B) Let point on y axis be $P(0, y)$, it is equidistance from point A (6, 5) and point B (–4, 3) are equal

$$\Rightarrow \quad PA^2 = PB^2$$

$$(0-6)^2 + (5-y)^2 = (-4-0)^2 + (3-y)^2$$

$$36 + 25 + y^2 - 10y = 16 + 9 + y^2 - 6y$$

$$\Rightarrow \quad 36 + 25 - 25 = 4y$$

$$\Rightarrow \quad y = \frac{36}{4} = 9$$

$\Rightarrow$ Point (0, 9)

Hence Ans is (B)

Sol. 50 (D) $\frac{x_1 + x_2 + x_3}{3} = 0$

and $\frac{y_1 + y_2 + y_3}{3} = -3$

$$\frac{-1+5+x_3}{3} = 0$$

and $\frac{4+2+y_3}{3} = -3$

$$x_3 = -4$$

and $y_3 = -15$

Hence Ans is (D)

Sol. 51 (B)

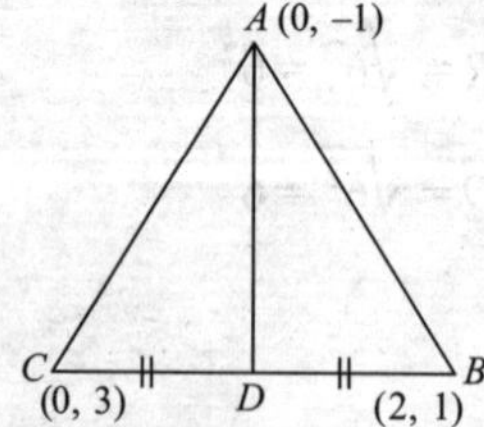

Let D be the mid-point of BC

$\Rightarrow$ Co-ordinate of $D = \left(\frac{0+2}{2}, \frac{3+1}{2}\right) = (1, 2)$

Now, length of $AD = \sqrt{(1-0)^2 + (2+1)^2}$

$$= \sqrt{1+9}$$

$$= \sqrt{10}$$

Hence Ans is (B)

Sol. 52 (C) We know the distance between two points $A(x_1, y_1)$ & $B(x_2, y_2)$ is given by

$$d=\sqrt{(x_2-x_1)^2+(y_2-y_1)^2} \quad \ldots(1)$$

D (4, 0) C (6, 3)

A (2, 3) B (4, 6)

Using equation-(1) we have,

$$AB=\sqrt{(2-4)^2+(3-6)^2}=\sqrt{(-2)^2+(-3)^2}$$

$$=\sqrt{4+9}=\sqrt{13}$$

$$BC=\sqrt{(4-6)^2+(6-3)^2}=\sqrt{(-2)^2+3^2}$$

$$=\sqrt{4+9}=\sqrt{13}$$

$$CD=\sqrt{(6-4)^2+(3-0)^2}=\sqrt{2^2+3^2}$$

$$=\sqrt{4+9}=\sqrt{13}$$

$$DA=\sqrt{(4-2)^2+(0-3)^2}=\sqrt{2^2+3^2}$$

$$=\sqrt{4+9}=\sqrt{13}$$

$$AC=\sqrt{(2-6)^2+(3-3)^2}=\sqrt{(-4)^2+(0)^2}$$

$$=\sqrt{16}$$

$$BD=\sqrt{(4-4)^2+(6-0)^2}=\sqrt{0^2+6^2}$$

$$=\sqrt{36}$$

Since $AB=BC=CD=DA=\sqrt{13}$

and $AC\neq BD$

Therefore it is a Rhombus

Hence Ans is (C)

Sol. 53 (D) The co-ordinate of a point (x, y) which divides the point $A(x_1, y_1)$ & $B(x_2, y_2)$ internally in the ratio in $m:n$ in given by

A (x_1, y_1) — m — P (x, y) — n — B (x_2, y_2)

$$x=\frac{mx_2+nx_1}{m+n} \quad \ldots(1)$$

& $$y=\frac{my_2+ny_1}{m+n} \quad \ldots(2)$$

Now as per question, we have

A (2, 3) x_1, y_1 — m = 3 — P (x, y) — n = 4 — B (–1, 2) x_2, y_2

Then $$x=\frac{3(-1)+4(2)}{3+4} \quad \text{(Using (1))}$$

$$=\frac{-3+8}{7}=\frac{5}{7}$$

$$y=\frac{3\times2+4\times3}{3+4} \quad \text{(Using (2))}$$

$$=\frac{6+12}{7}=\frac{18}{7}$$

Now this point lies on $x+2y=k$ so it will satisfy the given line

Hence $$\frac{5}{7}+\frac{2\times18}{7}=k$$

$$\Rightarrow \quad k=\frac{5+36}{7}=\frac{41}{7}$$

Hence Ans is (D)

Sol. 54 (C) We know the distance between two points $A(x_1, y_1)$ & $B(x_2, y_2)$ is given by

$$=\sqrt{(x_2-x_1)^2+(y_2-y_1)^2}$$

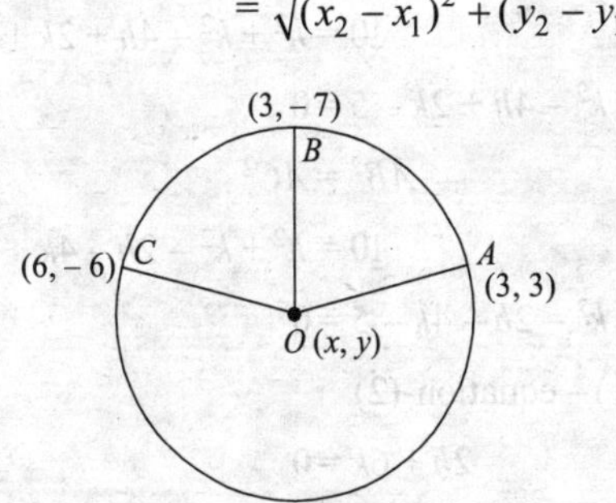

Let the center of the circle be given by

$$O\equiv(x, y)$$

$$OA=OB \quad \text{(radius of the circle)}$$

$$(x-3)^2+(y-3)^2=(x-3)^2+(y+7)^2$$

$$\Rightarrow \quad (y-3)^2=(y+7)^2$$

$$\Rightarrow \quad (y-3)^2-(y+7)^2=0$$

$$\Rightarrow \quad [(y-3)+(y+7)]\,[(y-3)-(y+7)]=0$$

$$\Rightarrow \quad 2y+4=0$$

$$y=-2$$

$$OB=OC \quad \text{(radius of the circle)}$$

$$\Rightarrow \quad (x-3)^2+(y+7)^2=(x-6)^2+(y+6)^2$$

$$\Rightarrow \quad x^2-6x+9+(-2+7)^2=x^2-12x+36+(-2+6)^2$$

(Use $y=-2$)

$\Rightarrow \quad x^2-6x+9+25=x^2-12x+36+16$

$\Rightarrow \quad 6x=52-34$

$\Rightarrow \quad x=3$

Required centre = (3, –2)

Hence Ans is (C)

Sol. 55 (B) Let the coordinate of $C(h, k)$

$$AB=\sqrt{(1-2)^2+(2+1)^2}$$

$$=\sqrt{1+9}=\sqrt{10}$$

$$BC=\sqrt{(2-h)^2+(-1-k)^2}$$

$$=\sqrt{4+h^2-4h+1+k^2+2k}$$

$$=\sqrt{h^2+k^2-4h+2k+5}$$

$$AC=\sqrt{(1-h)^2+(2-k)^2}$$

$$=\sqrt{1+h^2-2h+4+k^2-4k}$$

$$=\sqrt{h^2+k^2-2h-4k+5}$$

ABC is an equilateral triangle so

$$AB=BC$$

$$AB^2=BC^2$$

$$10=h^2+k^2-4h+2k+5$$

$$h^2+k^2-4h+2k-5=0 \quad \ldots(1)$$

and

$$AB^2=AC^2$$

$$10=h^2+k^2-2h-4k+5$$

$$h^2+k^2-2h-4k-5=0 \quad \ldots(2)$$

equation-(1) – equation-(2)

$$-2h+6k=0$$

$\Rightarrow \quad h=3k$

So, both h and k are either positive or negative or origin

If C is origin then

$$AB=\sqrt{10},$$

$$BC=\sqrt{(2-0)^2+(-1-0)^2}$$

$$=\sqrt{4+1}=5$$

$AB \neq BC$, so C is not origin

So C cannot lie in second quadrant.

Hence Ans is (B)

Sol. 56 (A)

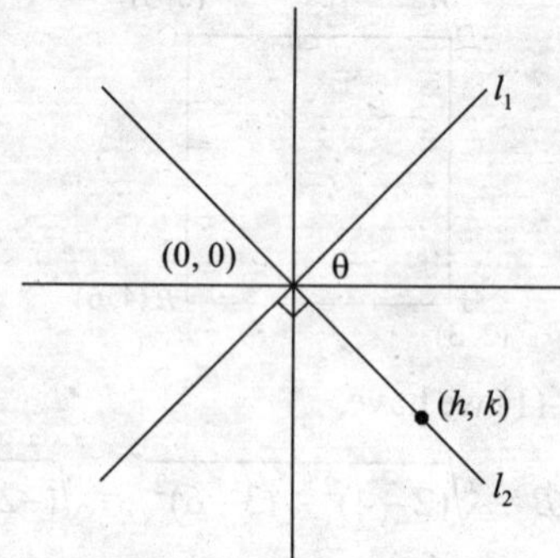

Given $\quad \sin\theta=\dfrac{3}{5}$

$\Rightarrow \quad \tan\theta=\dfrac{3}{4}$

Also given $\quad h^2+k^2=1 \quad \ldots(1)$

Slope of l_1 × Slope of $l_2=-1$

$$\frac{3}{4}\times\frac{k}{h}=-1$$

$$3k=-4h \quad \ldots(2)$$

from (2) and (1)

$$h^2+\frac{16h^2}{9}=1$$

$$\frac{25h^2}{9}=1$$

$$h=\pm\frac{3}{5}$$

$$k=\frac{-4}{3}\left(\pm\frac{3}{5}\right)=\mp\frac{4}{5}$$

in fourth quadrant

$$(h,k)=\left(\frac{3}{5},\frac{-4}{5}\right)$$

Hence Ans is (A)

* * * * *

Mensurations 11

- Perimeter (circumference) of a circle with diameter $d(d=2r$, where r is the radius) is given by $C=\pi d=2\pi r$.

- Perimeter of semicircle with radius $r=2r+\pi r=r(\pi+2)$

- Area of a circle with radius r is given by $A=\pi r^2$.

- Area of a semicircle of radius r

$$A=\frac{\pi r^2}{2}$$

- Area of a ring whose outer and inner radii are R and r respectively $=\pi(R^2-r^2)=\pi(R+r)(R-r)$

- If two circles touch internally, then the distance between their centres is equal to the difference of their radii.

- If two circles touch externally, then the distance between their centres is equal the sum of their radii.

- The distance moved by a rotating wheel in one revolution is equal to the circumference of the wheel.

- The number of revolutions completed by a rotating wheel in one minute $=\dfrac{\text{Distance moved in one minute}}{\text{Circumference of the wheel}}$

- Length of an arc which subtends an angle of $\theta°$ at the centre $=\dfrac{2\pi r\theta°}{360°}=\dfrac{\pi r\theta°}{180°}$

- Sector of a circle is a region enclosed by an arc of a circle and its two bounding radii.

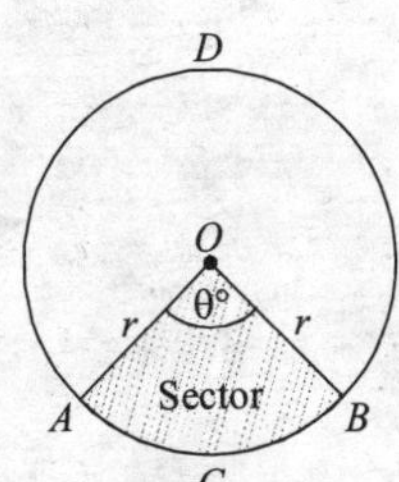

Figure 11.1

(i) Area of sector $OACBO=\dfrac{\pi r^2\theta°}{360°}$

(ii) Perimeter of sector $OACBO=2r+\dfrac{2\pi r\theta°}{360°}$

- **Minor sector :**

A sector of a circle is called a **minor sector** if the **minor arc** of the circle is a part of its boundary. In the above figure **minor sector** is *OACB*.

- **Major sector :**

A sector of a circle is called a **major sector,** if the **major arc** of the circle is a part of its boundary. In the above figure-11.1, *OADB* is the major sector.

- The sum of the arcs of major and minor sectors of a circle is equal to the circumference of the circle.

- The sum of the areas of major and minor sectors of a circle is equal to the area of the circle.

- The area of a sector is given by $A=\dfrac{1}{2}lr$, where $l=\left(\dfrac{\theta r}{180°}\times\pi\right)$

- Angle described by minute hand in 60 minutes $=360°$.

$\therefore$ angle described by minute hand in one minute

$$=\left(\frac{360}{60}\right)^{\circ}=6°.$$

Thus, the minute hand rotates through an angle of 6° in one minute.

- Angle described by hour hand in 12 hours $=360°$.

$\therefore$ angle described by hour hand in 1 hour

$$=\left(\frac{360}{12}\right)^{\circ}=30°.$$

Angle described by hour hand in one minute

$$=\left(\frac{30}{60}\right)^{\circ}=\frac{1}{2}^{\circ}$$

Thus, hour hand rotates through $\dfrac{1}{2}^{\circ}$ in 1 minute.

- A segment of a circle is the region bounded by an arc and a chord, including the arc and the chord.

- **Minor segment :**
If the boundary of a segment is a minor arc of a circle, then the corresponding segment is called a minor segment. In the figure-11.2, segment *PQR* (the area which is shaded) is a minor segment.

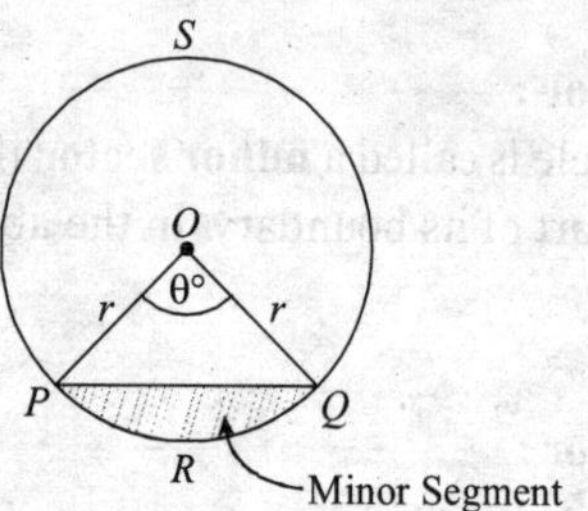

Figure 11.2

- **Major segment :**
A segment corresponding a major arc of a circle is known as the major segment. In the figure-11.2 above, segment *PQSP* is a major segment.

- Area of minor segment $PRQS = \frac{\pi r^2 \theta°}{360} - \frac{1}{2} r^2 \sin\theta$

- Area of major segment $PSQ = \pi r^2$ – area of minor segment *PRQ*.

Solid figures and their related formula

Formulae ↓	Cuboid	Cube	Right circular cylinder	Right circular cone	Sphere	Hemi-sphere
Name of the shapes of solids with figures→	h, b, l	a, a, a	h, r	h, l, r	r	r, r
Lateral surface or curved surface area	$2h(l+b)$	$4a^2$	$2\pi rh$	πrl	–	$2\pi r^2$
Total surface area	$2(lb+bh+hl)$	$6a^2$	$2\pi r(r+h)$	$\pi r(l+r)$	$4\pi r^2$	$3\pi r^2$
Volume	lbh	a^3	$\pi r^2 h$	$\frac{1}{3}\pi r^2 h$	$\frac{4}{3}\pi r^3$	$\frac{2}{3}\pi r^3$
Explanation of letters used	l = length b = breadth h = height	a = edge of the cube	r = radius of the base h = height	r = radius of the base h = height l = slant height	r = radius	r = radius

* * * * *

PRACTICE EXERCISE - 11.1

11-1 In the figure-11.3, the area of the shaded part is :

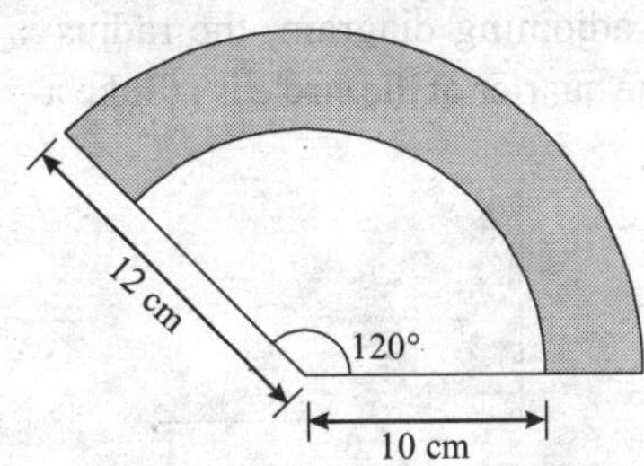

Figure 11.3

(A) 20π sq. cm (B) 44 sq. cm

(C) 44π sq. cm (D) $\frac{44\pi}{3}$ sq. cm

11-2 If the altitude of an equilateral triangle is $\sqrt{6}$ cm, its area in sq. cm is :

(A) $2\sqrt{2}$ (B) $2\sqrt{3}$

(C) $3\sqrt{3}$ (D) $6\sqrt{2}$

11-3 A sphere of radius r m can just be fitted into a cylindrical jar whose diameter and height are each $2r$ m. The empty space between them is :

(A) $\frac{1}{3}\pi r^3$ cu. m (B) $\frac{2}{3}\pi r^3$ cu. m

(C) $\frac{4}{3}\pi r^3$ cu. m (D) $\frac{5}{3}\pi r^3$ cu. m

11-4 A cylinder and a cone have the same height. If the ratio of their base radii is 1 : 2, then the ratio of their volumes is :

(A) 3 : 4 (B) 4 : 5

(C) 1 : 2 (D) 1 : 4

11-5 If the height and radius of a right circular cone are tripled, then the ratio of the new volume of the cone to that of the original cone is :

(A) 3 : 1 (B) 9 : 1

(C) 27 : 1 (D) 3π : 1

11-6 The diameter of a right circular cone is increased by 10% and its altitude is decreased by 10%. The percentage increase in its volume is :

(A) 3.9% (B) 5.9%

(C) 8.9% (D) 10%

11-7 The volume of a cone is 30 cu. cm. There is a second cone one-third as tall as the first one but its diameter is twice as long as that of the first one. The volume of the second cone is :

(A) 20 cu. cm (B) 30 cu. cm

(C) 40 cu. cm (D) 45 cu. cm

11-8 If the height and diameter of a cylinder are doubled, the new volume of the cylinder will be :

(A) 2 times the original volume

(B) 2π times the original volume

(C) 4 times the original volume

(D) 8 times the original volume

11-9 Let S_1 and S_2 be the total surface area of a sphere and the curved surface of the circumscribed cylinder. In terms of S_2, S_1 will be equal to :

(A) S_2 (B) $2S_2$

(C) $S_2/2$ (D) $2/3\ S_2$

11-10 AOB is a sector of a circle with radius 6 cm, $\angle AOB = 60°$. This sector is bent to form a cone, with AO touching BO. The base radius of the cone is :

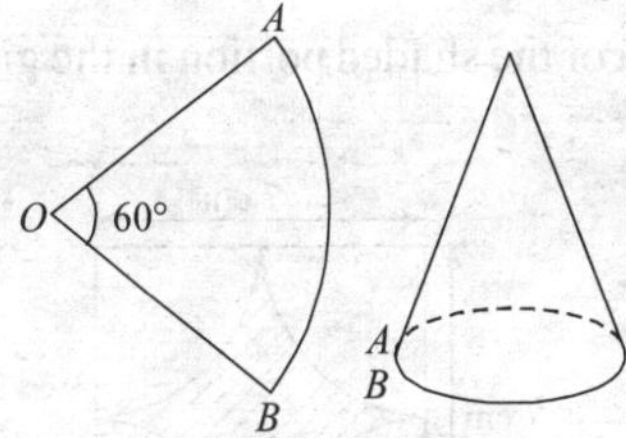

Figure 11.4

(A) 1 cm (B) 2 cm

(C) 2π cm (D) 6 cm

11-11 A cone and a hemisphere have the same base radius and the same volume. The ratio of their height and radius is :

(A) 2 : 1 (B) 2 : 3

(C) 2 : 5 (D) 3 : 4

11-12 Two similar regular polygons have perimeters p and $2p$. The ratio of their areas is :

(A) 1 : 2 (B) 1 : 3

(C) 2 : 3 (D) 1 : 4

11-13 If the circumference and the area of a circle are numerically equal, then what is the numerical value of the diameter ?

(A) 4 (B) 2

(C) 6 (D) 8

11-14 The volume of a cube is numerically equal to the sum of its edges. What is its total surface area in square units ?

(A) $6\sqrt{5}$ (B) $18\sqrt{3}$
(C) 36 (D) 72

11-15 What is the volume of the greatest right circular cone, which can be cut from a cube of edge 3 cm ?

(A) $\frac{7}{4}\pi$ cu. cm (B) $\frac{1}{4}\pi$ cu. cm
(C) $\frac{9}{4}\pi$ cu. cm (D) $\frac{1}{3}\pi$ cu. cm

11-16 What is the total area of the shaded portion if side of the square is $2a$?

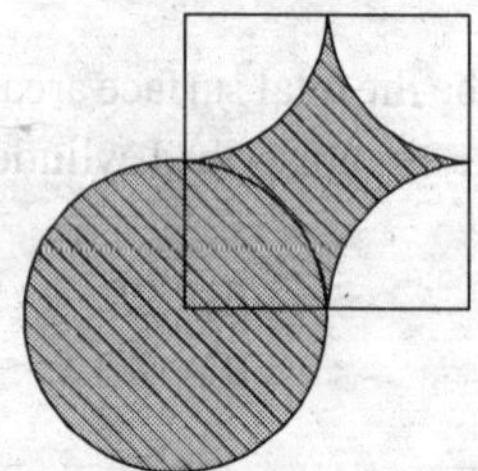

Figure 11.5

(A) $6a^2$ (B) $3a^2$
(C) $4a^2$ (D) $8a^2$

11-17 The area of the shaded portion in the given figure-11.6 is :

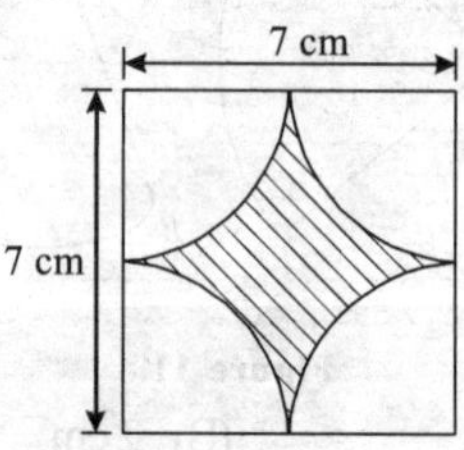

Figure 11.6

(A) 17.5 sq. cm (B) 10.5 sq. cm
(C) 8.5 sq. cm (D) 12.5^2 sq. cm

11-18 The volume of a wall, 5 times as high as it is broad and 8 times long as it is high is 18225 cu. *m*. The breadth of the wall is :

(A) 9/2 m (B) 9/4 m
(C) 9/8 m (D) 9m

11-19 In the figure-11.7 below, the rectangle at the corner measures 10 cm × 20 cm. The corner *A* of the rectangle is also a point on the circumference of the circle. What is the radius (in cm) of the circle ?

(A) 10 cm
(B) 20 cm
(C) 50 cm
(D) None of the above

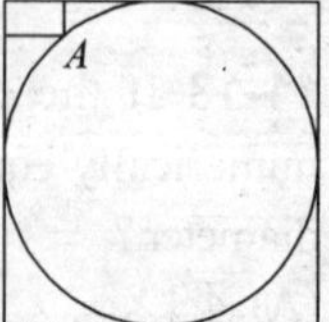

Figure 11.7

11-20 The perimeter of a semi-circular plate of radius 3.85 cm is (Take π to be 22/7) :

(A) 19.8 cm (B) 17.8 cm
(C) 18.8 cm (D) 20.8 cm

11-21 In the adjoining diagram, the radius is 3.5 cm. The perimeter of the quarter of the circle is : (Take $\pi = 22/7$)

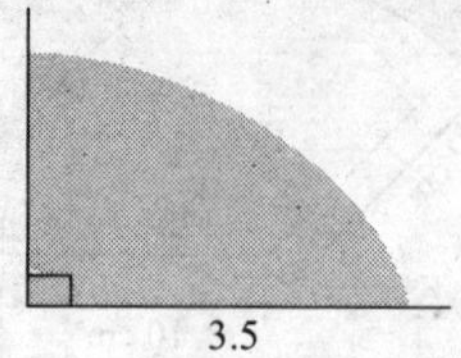

Figure 11.8

(A) 14 cm (B) 10.5 cm
(C) 12.5 cm (D) 17.5 cm

11-22 In the given diagram, *ABCDEF* is a running track, which has two parallel straight lines $AB = DE = 100$ m and two semi-circular ends, each of radii 7m. The distance travelled in one round of this field is :

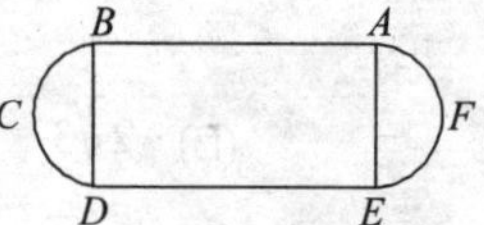

Figure 11.9

(A) 240m (B) 244m
(C) 254m (D) 264m

11-23 The total surface area of a cuboid *x* cm by *y* cm by *z* cm is :

(A) xyz cm² (B) $(xy + yz + zx)$ cm²
(C) $2(xy + yz + zx)$ cm² (D) $2(x^2 + y^2 + z^2)$ cm²

11-24 Four lead spheres each of radius *r*, are melted and recast into one large sphere. The ratio of the surface area of the new sphere to that of the four original spheres is :

(A) $\sqrt[3]{4} : 1$ (B) $1 : \sqrt[3]{4}$
(C) $\sqrt[3]{2} : 1$ (D) $1 : \sqrt[3]{2}$

11-25 In the given figure-11.10, the circle circumscribes the small square and touches all sides of the larger square. The ratio of the areas of the two squares is :

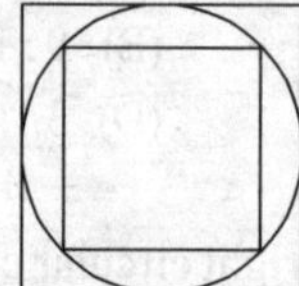

Figure 11.10

(A) $1 : \sqrt{2}$ (B) $1 : 2$
(C) $1 : \pi$ (D) $2 : \pi$

11-26 In the given figure-11.11, *ABCD* is a square inscribed in a circle. *WXYZ* is the largest square that can be inscribed in the semi-circle. The ratio of the areas of the two squares is :

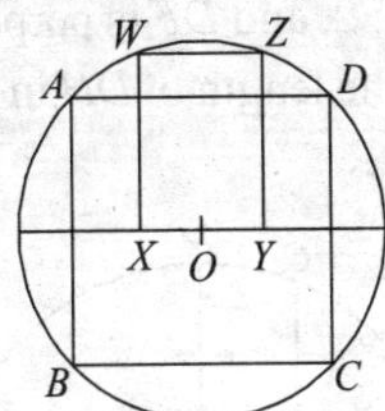

Figure 11.11

(A) 1 : 2 (B) 2 : 5

(C) $2\sqrt{2}:5$ (D) 1 : 3

11-27 In the given figure-11.12, a solid consists of a cone and a hemisphere with a common radius 6 cm. If the height of the cone is 10 cm, then the volume of the whole solid is :

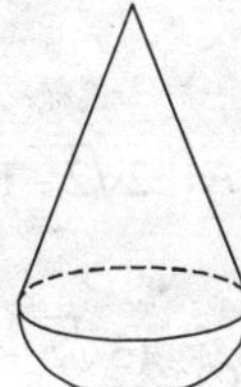

Figure 11.12

(A) 246 π cu, cm

(B) 264 π cu. cm

(C) 288 π cu. cm

(D) 528 π cu. cm

11-28 A ten rupee note measures 5 inches by 2 inches. A packet of 100 notes is ½ inch thick. What is the maximum money in ten rupee notes that can be laid flat in a box of size 15 inches × 8 inches × 3 inches ?

(A) Rs. 60000 (B) Rs. 48000

(C) Rs. 72000 (D) Rs. 42000

11-29 Height of a solid cylinder is 10 cm and diameter is 8 cm. Two equal conical holes have been made from its both ends. If the diameter of the hole is 6 cm and height is 4 cm, then the volume of the remaining solid is :

(A) 136 π cu. cm (B) 146 π cu. cm

(C) 152 π cu. cm (D) 112 π cu. cm

11-30 How many solid spheres of radii 6 cm can be made from a cylinder of base radius 4 cm and length 90 cm ?

(A) 6 (B) 5

(C) 4 (D) 7

11-31 A cone, a hemisphere and a cylinder stand on equal bases and have the same height. The ratio of their volumes is :

(A) 2 : 3 : 4 (B) 1 : 3 : 2

(C) 1 : 2 : 3 (D) 4 : 3 : 1

11-32 The cost of building a 5 m wide road at the cost of Rs. 20 per sq. *m* around a 80 m wide rectangular field is Rs. 38000. What is the length of the field ?

(A) 120m (B) 110m

(C) 90m (D) 100m

11-33 The volume of a hemisphere of diameter 21 cm is :

(A) 2425.5 cu. cm (B) 2835.5 cu. cm

(C) 2445.5 cu. cm (D) 2018.5 cu. cm

11-34 The length of the body diagonal of a cube, each of whose sides measures 4 cm is :

(A) 4.2 cm (B) 6.928 cm

(C) 7.2 cm (D) 6.248 cm

11-35 The area of the shaded region in the figure-11.13 (curves are parts of equal circles) is :

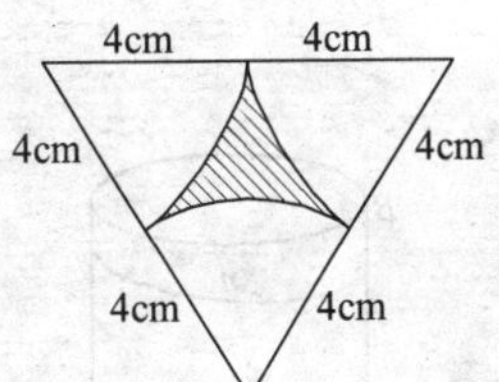

Figure 11.13

(A) 2.00 sq. cm (B) 2.33 sq. cm

(C) 2.58 sq. cm (D) 3.50 sq. cm

11-36 A model of a house is made on a scale of 1 : 100. If the height of the model is 12 cm, the area of the floor is 120 sq. cm and the capacity of the house is 700 cu. cm. Then the actual height, actual floor area and actual capacity of the house (in metres) will be :

(A) 12, 120, 700 (B) 12, 12, 70

(C) 120, 1200, 7000 (D) 12, 160, 720

11-37 A spherical ball 3 inches in diameter is melted and recast into three spherical balls. The diameters of two of them are 1.5 inches and 2 inches respectively. What is the diameter of the third ?

(A) 1 inch (B) 1.5 inches

(C) 2.5 inches (D) 2 inches

11-38 Given that the radius of a circle is *r* and *ABCD* is a square. The area of the shaded portion is :

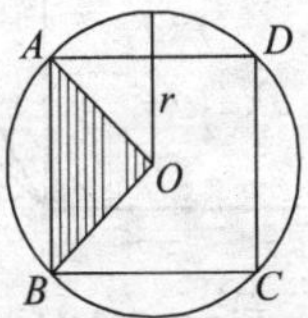

Figure 11.14

(A) $r^2\sqrt{2}$ (B) $(1/2)r^2$

(C) $r/\sqrt{2}$ (D) None of these

11-39 How many times will the wheel of a car rotate in a journey of 88 km if it is known that the diameter of the wheel is 56 cm ?

(A) 4000 (B) 30000

(C) 50000 (D) 60000

Direction (Q. 11-40 to 11-42) : Answer the questions on the basis of the information given below:

Consider a cylinder of height h cm and radius $r = \frac{2}{\pi}$ cm as shown in the figure (not drawn to scale). A string of a certain length, when wound on its cylindrical surface, starting at point a and ending at point B, gives a maximum of n turns (in other words, the string's length is the minimum length required to wind n turns).

11-40 What is the vertical spacing in cm between consecutive turns?

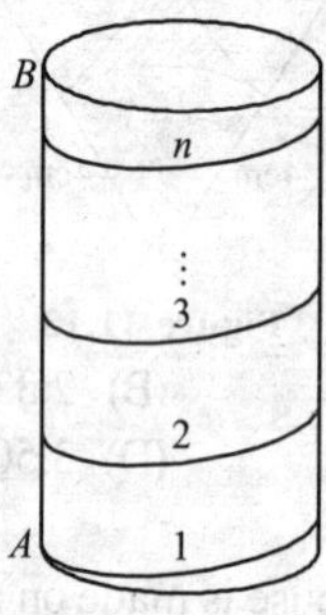

Figure 11.15

(A) h/n

(B) $h/\sqrt{n}$

(C) h/n^2

(D) Cannot be determined with the given in formation

11-41 The same string, when wound on the exterior four walls of a cube of side n cm, starting at point C and ending at point D, can give exactly one turn (see figure-11.16, not drawn to scale). The length of the string, in cm is :

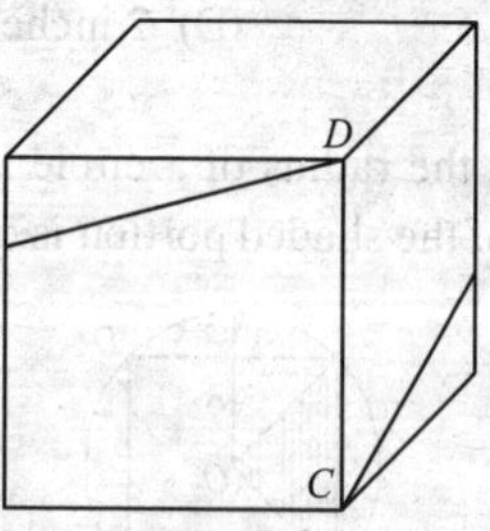

Figure 11.16

(A) $\sqrt{2n}$ (B) $\sqrt{17n}$

(C) n (D) $\sqrt{13n}$

11-42 In the setup of the previous two questions, how is h related on n?

(A) $h = \sqrt{2n}$ (B) $h = \sqrt{17n}$

(C) $h = n$ (D) $h = \sqrt{13n}$

11-43 In the following figure-11.17, the diameter of the circle is 3 cm. AB and MN are two diameters such that MN is perpendicular to AB. In addition, CG is perpendicular to AB such that $AE : EB = 1 : 2$, and DF is perpendicular to MN such that $NL : LM = 1 : 2$. The length of DH in cm is :

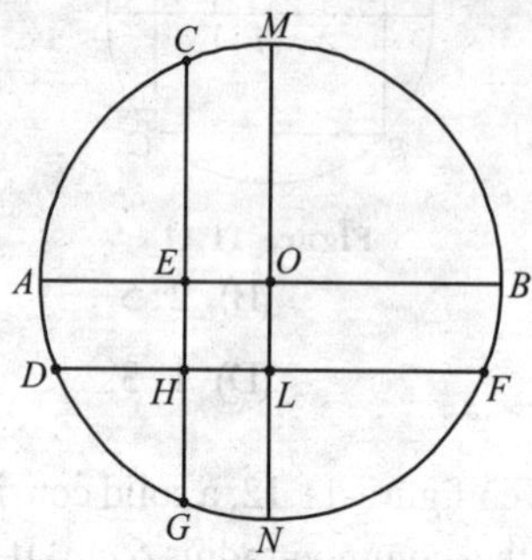

Figure 11.17

(A) $2\sqrt{2}-1$ (B) $\frac{(2\sqrt{2}-1)}{2}$

(C) $\frac{(3\sqrt{2}-1)}{2}$ (D) $\frac{(2\sqrt{2}-1)}{3}$

Direction (Q. 11-44 to 11-48): The volume of a cuboid is 2520 cm^3. There are also all other cuboids which occupy the same space, but length, breadth and height are of integral units. We have to place the cuboids in a cubical box of side 37 cm.

11-44 Find the number of different possible cuboids which have height 7 cm and volume 2520 cm^3 :

(A) 18 (B) 6

(C) 24 (D) 12

11-45 Find the (approx) length (in cm) of the biggest possible length of rod which can be placed in any one of the possible cuboids :

(A) 2520 (B) 1260

(C) 398 (D) None of these

11-46 Find the (approx) length (in cm) of the smallest possible length of rod which can be placed corner to corner diagonally in any one of the possible cuboids :

(A) 31 (B) 29

(C) 23 (D) 27

11-47 The height of the cuboid is 5 cm. Then find the number of all possible cuboids which can't be placed in the given cubical box?

(A) 7 (B) 8

(C) 9 (D) 14

11-48 If N_1 denotes the number of cuboids of height 8 cm which can be placed in the cubical box, N_2 denotes the number of cuboids of height 9 cm which can be placed in the cubical box, N_3 denotes the number of cuboids of height 6 cm which can be placed in the cubical box, then which of the following is true?

(A) $N_1 < N_2 < N_3$ (B) $N_1 < N_3 < N_2$

(C) $N_2 < N_1 < N_3$ (D) None of these

11-49 Sheets of paper in one pile is shown in the figure-11.18. If the height of the pile is known, what else must you know in order to calculate the thickness of one sheet ?

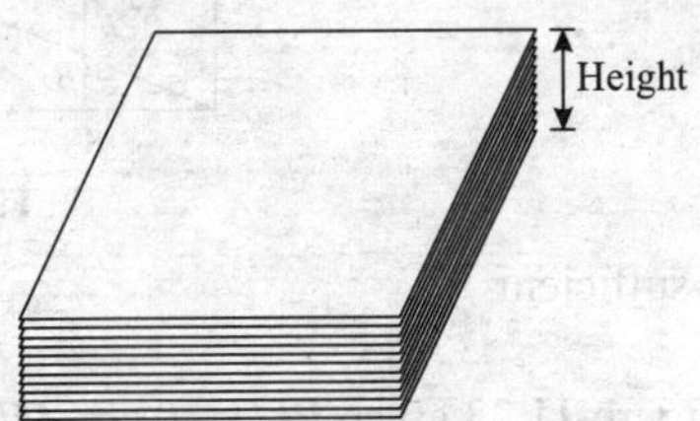

Figure 11.18

(A) Length of a sheet

(B) Area of a sheet

(C) Weight of the pile

(D) Number of sheets in the pile

11-50 A cube of edge 20 cm is completely immersed in a rectangular vessel containing water. If the dimensions of the base of the vessel are 20 cm by 40cm, then the rise in its water level will be :

(A) 2 cm (B) 8 cm

(C) 10 cm (D) 14 cm

* * * * *

PRACTICE EXERCISE - 11.2

11-1 *ABCD* is a rectangle, *P* lies on *AD* and *Q* and *AB*. The triangles *PAQ*, *QBC* and *PCD* all have the same area, and $BQ = 2$. The length of *AQ*, is :

(A) $3+\sqrt{5}$ (B) $2\sqrt{3}$

(C) $\sqrt{5}+1$ (D) Not uniquely determined

11-2 Points *M* and *N* are the midpoints of sides *PA* and *PB* of ΔPAB. As *P* moves along a line that is parallel to side *AB*, which one of the four quantities listed below will change ?

(A) The length of the segment *MN*

(B) The perimeter of ΔPAB

(C) The area of ΔPAB

(D) The area of trapezium *ABNM*

11-3 In this figure-11.19, *AOB* is a quarter circle of radius 10 and *PQRO* is a rectangle of perimeter 26. The perimeter of the shaded region is :

(A) $13+5\pi$

(B) $17+5\pi$

(C) $7+10\pi$

(D) $7+5\pi$

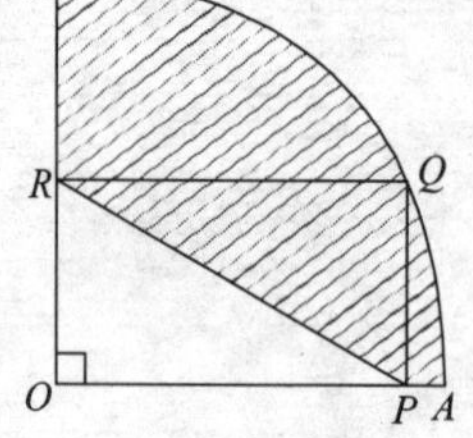

Figure 11.19

11-4 Each of the congruent circles shown is externally tangent to other circles and/or to the side(s) of the rectangle as shown in figure-11.20. If each circle has circumference 16π, then the length of a diagonal of the rectangle, is :

(A) 80

(B) 40

(C) 20

(D) 15

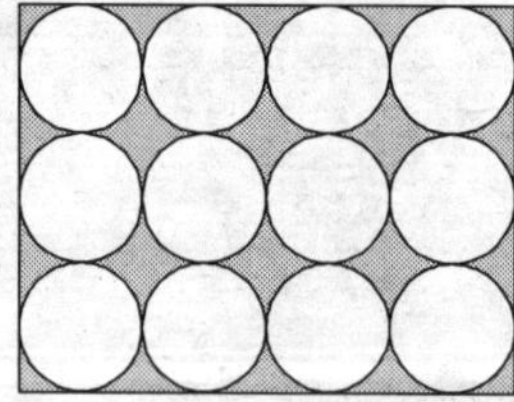

Figure 11.20

11-5 *ABCD* is a rectangle and lines *DX*, *DY* and *XY* are drawn as shown in figure-11.21. Area of ΔAXD is 5, Area of ΔBXY is 4 and area of ΔCYD is 3. If the area of ΔDXY can be expressed as $\sqrt{x}$ where $x \in N$ then *x* is equal to :

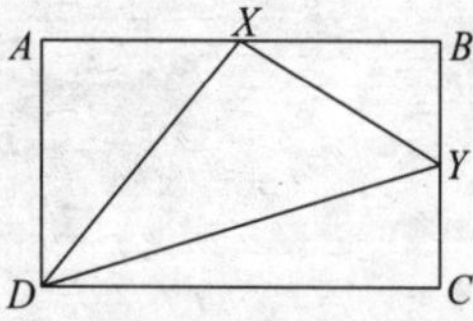

Figure 11.21

(A) 72 (B) 75

(C) 84 (D) 96

11-6 Given an isosceles trapezium *ABCD* in order with $AB = 6$, $CD = 12$ and area 36 sq. units. Length of the side *BC* is :

(A) 6 (B) 5

(C) 4.5 (D) 5.5

11-7 Three squares have the dimensions indicated in the diagram. The area of the quadrilateral *ABCD*, is :

(A) $\frac{21}{4}$

(B) $\frac{15}{4}$

(C) $\frac{42}{4}$

(D) Data not sufficient

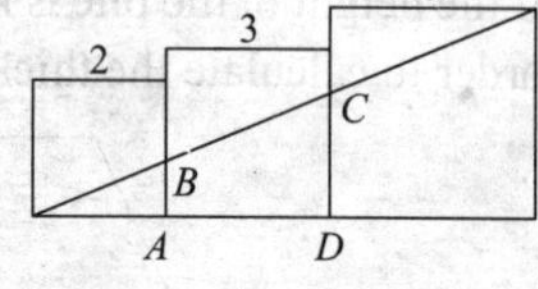

Figure 11.22

11-8 In the figure-11.23 given $PM = 10$ cm, $MN = 15$ cm and $PN = 17$ cm. Also $QM = QX$ and $XR = RN$. Perimeter of the ΔPQR, is :

(A) 32

(B) 27

(C) 25

(D) 21

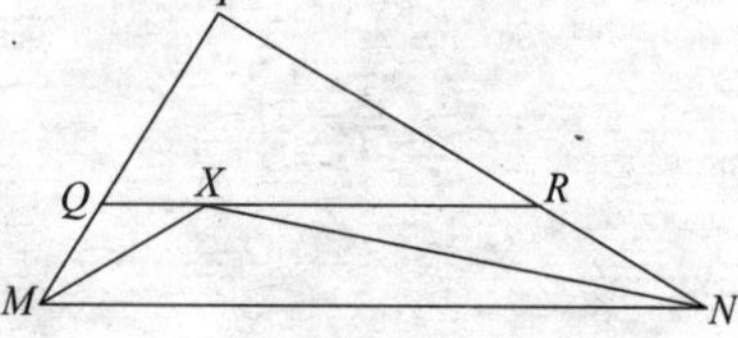

Figure 11.23

11-9 Two circles I and II are externally tangent. A tangent to the circle I passes through the centre of the circle II. The distance from the point of tangency to the centre of the circle II is three times the radius of the circle II. The ratio of the circumference of the circle I to the circumference of the circle II :

(A) 2 (B) 3

(C) 4 (D) 16

11-10 The side lengths of trapezium are $\sqrt[4]{3}$, $\sqrt[4]{3}$, $\sqrt[4]{3}$ and $2 \times \sqrt[4]{3}$. Its area is the ratio of two relatively prime positive integers, *m* and *n*. The value of $(m+n)$ is equal to :

(A) 5 (B) 7

(C) 9 (D) 13

11-11 In the figure-11.24 *C* is a right angle, $DE \perp AB$, $AE = 6$, $EB = 7$ and $BC = 5$. The area of the quadrilateral *EBCD* is :

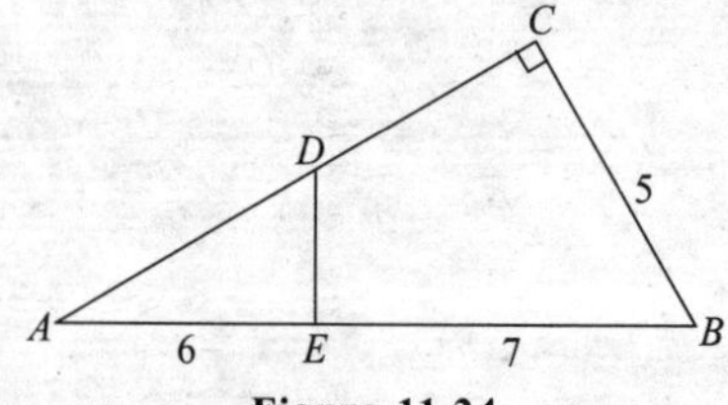

Figure 11.24

(A) 27.5 (B) 25

(C) 22.5 (D) 20

11-12 In the given figure-11.25, the diameter of the biggest semi-circle is 56 cm and the radius of the smallest circle is 7 cms. The area of the shaded portion is :

(A) 482 cm^2

(B) 462 cm^2

(C) 654 cm^2

(D) 804 cm^2

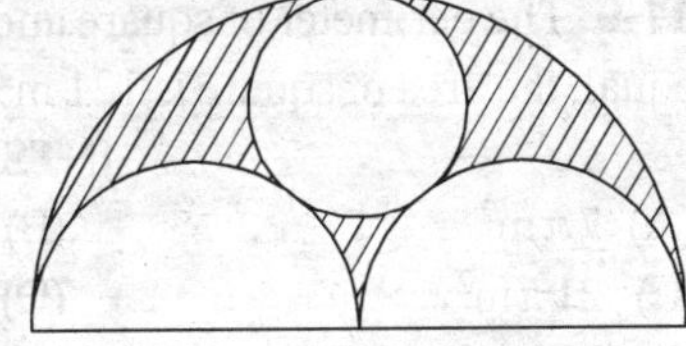

Figure 11.25

11-13 In the following figure-11.26, if O is the centre of the circle and radius $OA = 14$ cm, then the area of the shaded portion is :

(A) 98 cm^2

(B) 154 cm^2

(C) 56 cm^2

(D) None of these

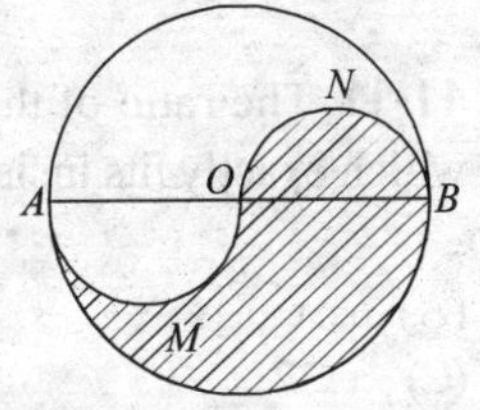

Figure 11.26

11-14 The perimeters of a regular hexagon & a square are equal. The ratio of the area of the square to the area of the hexagon is :

(A) $3:\sqrt{2}$ (B) $2:3\sqrt{3}$

(C) $1:\sqrt{3}$ (D) $3:2\sqrt{3}$

11-15 The lengths, breadth and height of a room are in the ratio 3 : 2 : 1. If the breadth and height are halved while the length is doubled, then the total area of the four walls of the room will :

(A) Remain the same (B) Decrease by 30%

(C) Decrease by 15% (D) Decrease by 18.75%

11-16 If the radius of a right circular cylinder is increased by 50% and height is decreased by 20% then the percentage change in volume of cylinder is :

(A) 40% (B) 50%

(C) 60% (D) 80%

11-17 If the surface area of cube A is 64% of the surface area of cube B, then the volume of cube A is 'k' percent of the volume of cube B. The value of 'k' is :

(A) 0.64 (B) 0.512

(C) 51.2 (D) 64

11-18 A reservoir is in the shape of a frustum of a right circular cone. It is 8 m across at the top and 4 m across at the bottom. If it is 6m deep its capacity is :

(A) 176 m^3 (B) 196 m^3

(C) 200 m^3 (D) 110 m^3

11-19 A right circular cone is cut off at the middle of its height and parallel to the base. Call the smaller cone so formed as A and the remaining part as B, then :

(A) Vol. A < Vol. B (B) Vol. A = Vol. B

(C) Vol. A > Vol. B (D) Vol. A = $\frac{1}{2}$ (Vol. B)

11-20 Water flows at the rate of 10 m per min. from a cylindrical pipe 5 mm in diameter. How long will it take to fill up a conical vessel whose diameter at the base is 40 cm and depth 24 cm.?

(A) 48 min. 15 sec (B) 51 min. 12 sec

(C) 52 min. 1 sec (D) 55 min

11-21 Two steel sheets each of length a_1 and breadth a_2 are used to prepare the surface of two right circular cylinders-one having volume V_1 and height a_2 and the other having volume V_2 and height a_1. Then :

(A) $V_1 = V_2$ (B) $a_1V_1 = a_2V_2$

(C) $a_2V_1 = a_1V_2$ (D) $\frac{V_1^2}{a_1} = \frac{V_2^2}{a_2}$

11-22 Let $P(4, k)$ be any point on the line $y = 6 - x$. If the vertical segment PQ is rotated about y-axis, the volume of the resulting cylinder is :

(A) 32π

(B) 16π

(C) $\frac{32}{3}\pi$

(D) 8π

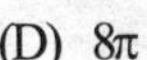

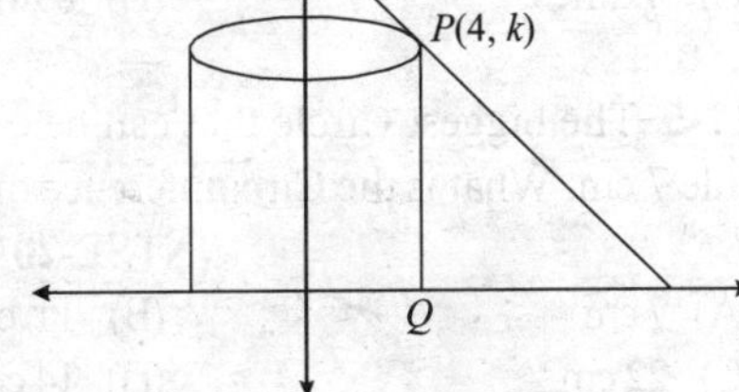

Figure 11.27

11-23 The surface water in a swimming pool forms a rectangle of length 40 m and breadth 15 m. The depth of water increases uniformly from 1.2 m at one end to 2.4 m at the other end. The volume (in m^3) of water in the pool is :

(A) 1080 (B) 720

(C) 600 (D) 540

11-24 If a right circular cone, with slant height l, and a right circular cylinder have the same radius r, same total surface area and height h and h' respectively, then $\sqrt{\frac{l-r}{l+r}} =$

(A) h/h' (B) $2h/h'$

(C) $h/2h'$ (D) $2h'/h$

11-25 A right triangle has angles which measure 30, 60 and 90 degrees. If the perimeter of this triangle is $15+5\sqrt{3}$ then the length of the hypotenuse of this triangle, is :

(A) 5 (B) 7.5

(C) 10 (D) 12.5

* * * * *

PRACTICE EXERCISE - 11.3

11-1 The area of a trapezium shaped field is 960 m^2, the distance between two Parallel sides is 30m and one of the Parallel side is 20 m, find the length of other Parallel side :

[NTSE-2012 (Stage-I) Rajasthan]

(A) 44 m (B) 22 m
(C) 88 m (D) 11 m

11-2 The floor of a building consists of 1500 rhombus shaped tiles and each of its diagonals are 45 cm and 30 cm in length. Find the total cost of Polishing the floor, if the cost per m^2 is Rs. 4/- :

[NTSE-2012 (Stage-I) Rajasthan]

(A) Rs. 610/- (B) Rs. 810/-
(C) Rs. 405/- (D) Rs. 450/-

11-3 Find the volume of a Cube whose surface area is 600 cm^2 :

[NTSE-2012 (Stage-I) Rajasthan]

(A) 900 cm^3 (B) 1000 cm^3
(C) 1500 cm^3 (D) 810 cm^3

11-4 If each edge of a Cube is doubled. How many times its volume will be? **[NTSE-2012 (Stage-I) Rajasthan]**

(A) 3 times (B) 6 times
(C) 4 times (D) 8 times

11-5 The biggest Circle that can be cut off from a Square of side 7 cm. What is the Circumference of this circle :

[NTSE-2012 (Stage-I) Rajasthan]

(A) 7 cm (B) 11 cm
(C) 22 cm (D) 14 cm

11-6 Solid shapes are called :

[NTSE-2012 (Stage-I) Rajasthan]

(A) One dimensional (B) Two dimensional
(C) Three dimensional (D) All the above

11-7 Curved surface of right circular cylinder is 4.4 m^2, radius of base is 0.7 m. then the height is : (Take $\pi = \frac{22}{7}$)

[NTSE-2013 (Stage-I) Rajasthan]

(A) 1 m (B) 2 m
(C) 3 m (D) 4 m

11-8 A drinking glass is in the shape of a frustum of a cone of height 14 cm. The diameter of its two circular ends are 4 cm and 2 cm then the capacity of glass is :

[NTSE-2013 (Stage-I) Rajasthan]

(A) $102\frac{2}{3}$ cm^3 (B) $102\frac{1}{3}$ cm^3
(C) $101\frac{2}{3}$ cm^3 (D) $101\frac{1}{3}$ cm^3

11-9 The perimeter of square and circumference of Circle are equal, the area of square is 121 m^2 then the area of Circle is :

[NTSE-2013 (Stage-I) Rajasthan]

(A) $7\pi m^2$ (B) $14\pi m^2$
(C) $21\pi m^2$ (D) $49\pi m^2$

11-10 Area of triangle *ABC* whose sides are 24 m. 40 m and 32 m is : **[NTSE-2013 (Stage-I) Rajasthan]**

(A) 96 m^2 (B) 384 m^2
(C) 43 m^2 (D) 192 m^2

11-11 The ratio of the volume of a cube to that of a sphere which exactly fits inside the cube is :

[NTSE-2014 (Stage-I) Rajasthan]

(A) $6:\pi$ (B) $\pi:6$
(C) $\pi:12$ (D) $12:\pi$

11-12 If the diameter of a sphere is decreased by 25%, by what per cent does its curved surface area decrease ?

[NTSE-2014 (Stage-I) Rajasthan]

(A) 43.75% (B) 21.88%
(C) 50% (D) 25%

11-13 In figure-11.28, *ABC* is a quadrant of a circle of radius 14 cm and a semicircle is drawn with *BC* as diameter. The area of the shaded region is : **[NTSE-2014 (Stage-I) Rajasthan]**

(A) 98 cm^2

(B) 154 cm^2

(C) 56 cm^2

(D) None of these

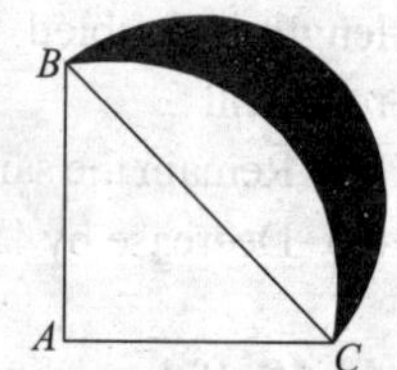

Figure 11.28

11-14 In the figure-11.29 given below, *ABC* is an equilateral triangle. *D, E, F, G, h* and *I* are the trisector points of the sides as shown. If the side of the triangle *ABC* is 6 cm, then the area of the regular hexagon *DEFGHI* is :

[NTSE-2015 (Stage-I) Rajasthan]

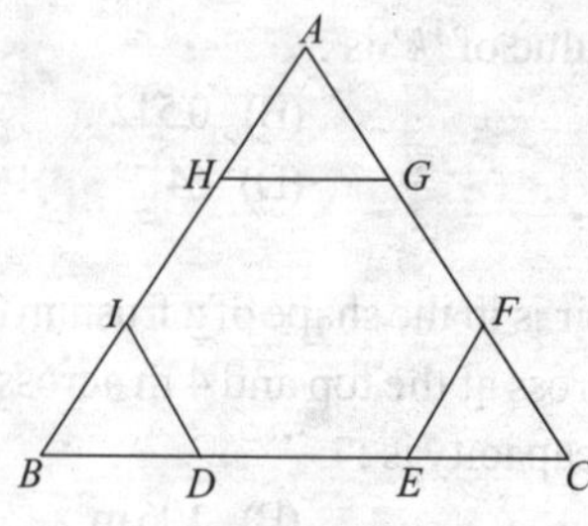

Figure 11.29

(A) $3\sqrt{3}$ cm^2 (B) $4\sqrt{3}$ cm^2
(C) $5\sqrt{3}$ cm^2 (D) $6\sqrt{3}$ cm^2

11-15 In the given figure-11.30, ABC is an equilateral triangle whose side is $2\sqrt{3}$ cm. A circle is drawn which passes through the midpoints D, E and F of its sides. The area of the shaded region is : **[NTSE-2015 (Stage-I) Rajasthan]**

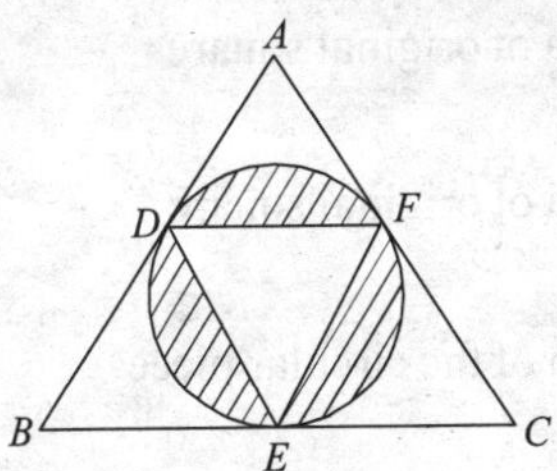

Figure 11.30

(A) $\frac{1}{4}(4\pi - 3\sqrt{3})$ cm^2 (B) $\frac{1}{4}(2\pi - \sqrt{3})$ cm^2

(C) $\frac{1}{4}(\pi - 3\sqrt{3})$ cm^2 (D) $\frac{1}{4}(3\pi - \sqrt{3})$ cm^2

11-16 If a cylinder of radius 3 cm and height of 10 cm is melted and recast into the shapes of small spheres of diameter 1 cm, then the number of spheres so formed is : **[NTSE-2015 (Stage-I) Rajasthan]**

(A) 135 (B) 270

(C) 540 (D) 1080

11-17 If the heights and radii of a cone and a hemisphere are same then the ratio of their volumes is : **[NTSE-2015 (Stage-I) Rajasthan]**

(A) 1 : 2 (B) 2 : 3

(C) 1 : 3 (D) 1 : 1

11-18 Three squares have the dimension indicated in the diameter. What is the area of shaded Quadrilateral? **[NTSE-2015 (Stage-I) Andhara Pradesh]**

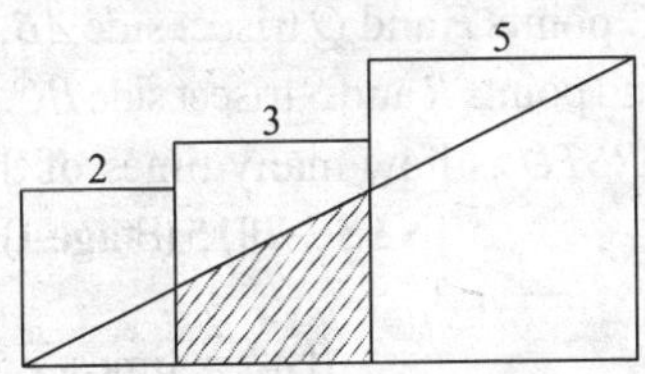

Figure 11.31

(A) 4.5 (B) $\frac{16}{7}$

(C) $\frac{21}{4}$ (D) 3.6

11-19 The height of an isosceles triangle is 6 cm, the perimeter of the triangle is 36 cm. Then the area of the triangle (in cm^2) is : **[NTSE-2015 (Stage-I) Andhara Pradesh]**

(A) 36 (B) 48

(C) 52 (D) 64

11-20 A regular hexagon overlap is formed by placing two congruent equilateral triangles on the top of each other. If the area of each triangle is 27 cm^2, then the area of the hexagon is : **[NTSE-2015 (Stage-I) Andhara Pradesh]**

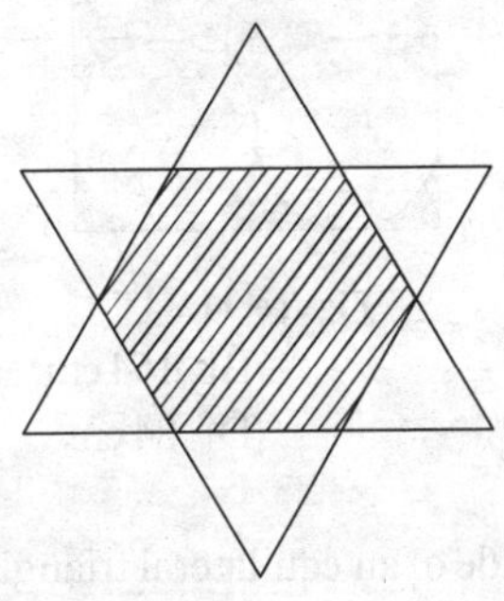

Figure 11.32

(A) 20 cm^2 (B) 18 cm^2

(C) 16 cm^2 (D) 15 cm^2

11-21 The lengths of the diagonals of a rhombus are 24 cm and 10 cm, then the side of the rhombus is__ cm : **[NTSE-2015 (Stage-I) Tamilnadu]**

(A) 26 (B) 13

(C) 169 (D) 240

11-22 The sides of a triangle are 11 m, 60 m, and 61 m. The length of altitude on the smallest side is : **[NTSE-2015 (Stage-I) Chandigarh]**

(A) 11 m (B) 66 m

(C) 60 m (D) 50 m

11-23 The volume (in cm^3) of the largest right circular cone that can be cut off from a cube of edge 4.2 cm is : **[NTSE-2015 (Stage-I) Chandigarh]**

(A) 9.7 (B) 77.6

(C) 58.2 (D) 19.4

11-24 In a given figure-11.33, if $AD = 7\sqrt{3}$; $\angle B = 30°$, $\angle ADC = 90°$, and $\angle C = 60°$, then BC equal to : **[NTSE-2015 (Stage-I) Chandigarh]**

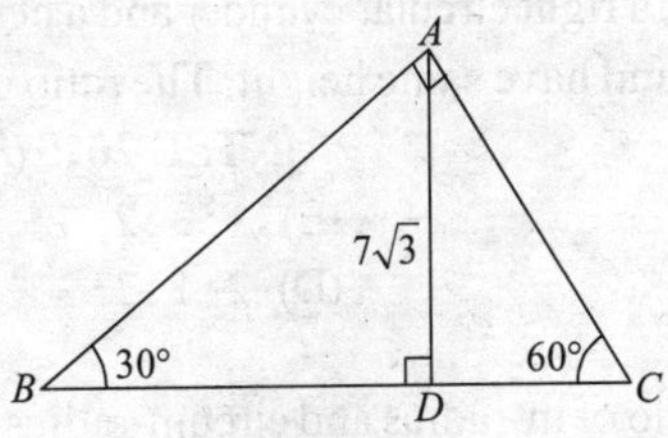

Figure 11.33

(A) 14 m (B) 27 m

(C) 29 m (D) 28 m

11-25 The area of the shaded portion where $ABCD$ is a square of side 14 cm is : **[NTSE-2015 (Stage-I) Chandigarh]**

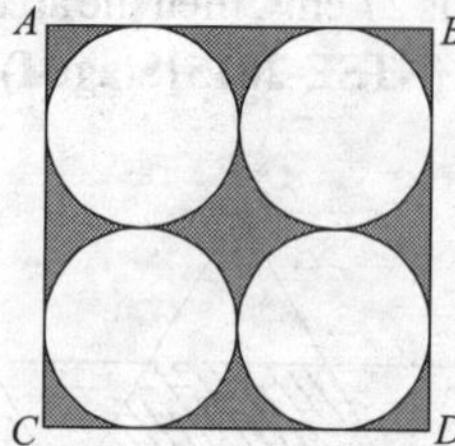

Figure 11.34

(A) 21 cm^2 (B) 154 cm^2
(C) 42 cm^2 (D) 84 cm^2

11-26 If the altitude of an equilateral triangle is x cm, then the area is equal to : **[NTSE-2015 (Stage-I) Chandigarh]**

(A) x^2 cm^2 (B) $(\sqrt{3}x^2/2)$ cm^2
(C) $(x^2/\sqrt{3})$ cm^2 (D) $(x^2/2)$ cm^2

11-27 The volume of a cube is 2744 cm^3. Its surface area is : **[NTSE-2015 (Stage-I) MP]**

(A) 196 cm^2 (B) 1176 cm^2
(C) 784 cm^2 (D) 588 cm^2

11-28 The height of an equilateral triangle is $\sqrt{6}$ cm. Its area is : **[NTSE-2015 (Stage-I) MP]**

(A) $2\sqrt{2}$ cm^2 (B) $6\sqrt{2}$ cm^2
(C) $2\sqrt{3}$ cm^2 (D) $3\sqrt{3}$ cm^2

11-29 The perimeter of a rectangular field is 82 meters and area is 400 meter^2? Then the breadth of the field is : **[NTSE-2015 (Stage-I) MP]**

(A) 9 meter (B) 12 meter
(C) 16 meter (D) 25 meter

11-30 If r is the radius of the base of a cylinder and h is the height of cylinder, then total surface are will be : **[NTSE-2015 (Stage-I) MP]**

(A) $2\pi rh$ (B) $2\pi rh + 2\pi r^2$
(C) $\pi r^2 h$ (D) None of these

11-31 A cone, a right circular cylinder and a hemisphere stand on equal base and have same height. The ratio of their volume is : **[NTSE-2015 (Stage-I) Delhi]**

(A) 1 : 2 : 3 (B) 1 : 3 : 2
(C) 2 : 3 : 1 (D) 2 : 1 : 3

11-32 The ratio of in-radius and circum-radius of a square is : **[NTSE-2015 (Stage-I) Delhi]**

(A) 1 : 2 (B) $1 : \sqrt{2}$
(C) 1 : 3 (D) $1 : \sqrt{3}$

11-33 A circular piece of metal of maximum area is cut out from a square piece and then a square piece of maximum area is cut out of the circular piece. The total area of wasted metal is : **[NTSE-2015 (Stage-I) Delhi]**

(A) $\frac{1}{4}$ of the area of original square

(B) $\frac{1}{2}$ of the area of original square

(C) $\frac{1}{2}$ of the area of the circular piece

(D) $\frac{1}{4}$ of the area of the circular piece

11-34 A cuboid of unit length, unit breadth and of height 10 units is cut into 10 cubical pieces of edge of 1 unit length each. The total surface area of these ten cubes will be : **[NTSE-2015 (Stage-I) Delhi]**

(A) 20 sq. units (B) 40 sq. units
(C) 42 sq. units (D) 60 sq. units

11-35 The radius of a sphere is r and radius of base of a cylinder is r and height is $2r$. The ratio of their volumes will be : **[NTSE-2015 (Stage-I) UP]**

(A) 2 : 3 (B) 3 : 4
(C) 4 : 3 (D) 3 : 2

11-36 In two spheres, the radius of first is half of the second. Then what will be volume of second in comparison of first : **[NTSE-2015 (Stage-I) UP]**

(A) 2 times (B) 4 times
(C) 8 times (D) $\frac{22}{7}$ times

11-37 In ΔABC points P and Q trisect side AB. Points T and U trisect side AC and points R and S trisect side BC. Then perimeter of hexagon $PQRSTU$ is how many times of the perimeter of ΔABC? **[NTSE-2015 (Stage-I) Maharashtra]**

(A) $\frac{1}{3}$ times (B) $\frac{2}{3}$ times
(C) $\frac{1}{6}$ times (D) $\frac{1}{2}$ times

11-38 The radius of a cylindrical vessel is 7 cm and its height is 12 cm $\frac{2}{3}$ of the vessel is filled with water. A sphere having radius 6 cm is dropped into the water. Find the volume of the water that will come out of the vessel : **[NTSE-2015 (Stage-I) Maharashtra]**

(A) 196 π cm^3 (B) 92 π cm^3
(C) 288 π cm^3 (D) 588 π cm^3

11-39 Radius of circle with centre 'O' is $4\sqrt{5}$ cm 'AB' is the diameter of the circle. $AE \parallel BC$, $BC = 8$ cm. Line EC is tangent at point D. Find the length of DE :

[NTSE-2015 (Stage-I) Maharashtra]

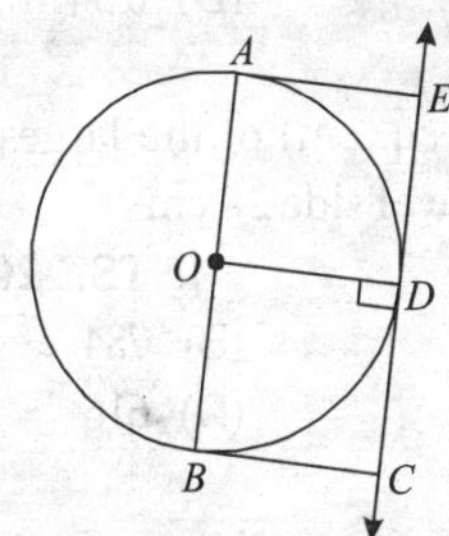

Figure 11.35

(A) $4\sqrt{5}$ cm (B) $6\sqrt{5}$ cm
(C) 8 cm (D) 10 cm

11-40 The area of right angled triangle is 96 sq. mtr. If base is three times the altitude, the length of base is :

[NTSE-2015 (Stage-I) MP]

(A) 24 mtr (B) 20 mtr
(C) 18 mtr (D) 15 mtr

11-41 The perimeter of the rectangular field is 206 meter. What will be its area if its length is 23 meter more than its breadth?

[NTSE-2015 (Stage-I) MP]

(A) 1520 meter^2 (B) 2420 meter^2
(C) 2480 meter^2 (D) 2520 meter^2

11-42 The total surface area of a cube is 864 cm^2. Its volume is :

[NTSE-2015 (Stage-I) MP]

(A) 3456 cm^3 (B) 432 cm^3
(C) 1728 cm^3 (D) 3466 cm^3

11-43 The length of the longest pole that can be kept in a room of size 12 m × 9 m × 8 m is :

[NTSE-2015 (Stage-I) MP]

(A) 29 m (B) 17 m
(C) 21 m (D) 19 m

11-44 The height of a cylinder is 14 cm and its curved surface area is 264 cm^2, the volume of cylinder is :

[NTSE-2015 (Stage-I) MP]

(A) 308 cm^3 (B) 396 cm^3
(C) 1232 cm^3 (D) 1848 cm^3

11-45 Radii of three solid spheres are 3 cm, 4 cm and 5 cm respectively. They are melted and converted in to a bigger solid sphere. The radius of the new sphere will be :

[NTSE-2015 (Stage-I) Chhatisgarh]

(A) 12 cm (B) 9 cm
(C) 8 cm (D) 6 cm

11-46 The perimeter of a right angled triangle is 24 cm. If the hypotenuse is 10 cm. Then area of this triangle will be :

[NTSE-2015 (Stage-I) Chhatisgarh]

(A) 20 cm^2 (B) 22 cm^2
(C) 24 cm^2 (D) 26 cm^2

11-47 The square of side 4 cm is inscribed in the circle. The area of the circle will be : **[NTSE-2015 (Stage-I) Chhatisgarh]**

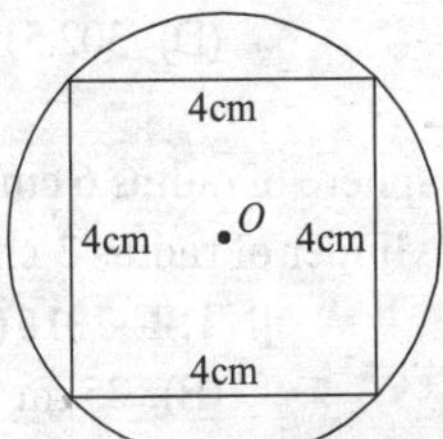

Figure 11.36

(A) 2π cm^2 (B) 8π cm^2
(C) 4π cm^2 (D) π cm^2

11-48 The length, breadth and height of a solid rectangular parallelopiped made of copper are 11 cm, 9 cm and 6 cm respectively. How many coins of radius 1.5 cm having thickness 0.25 cm can be produced by melting it ?

[NTSE-2015 (Stage-I) West Bengal]

(A) 168 (B) 170
(C) 336 (D) 340

11-49 If the perimeter of protractor is 72 cm, then it's radius is $\left(\text{take } \pi = \frac{22}{7}\right)$:

[NTSE-2015 (Stage-I) Chennai]

(A) 7 cm (B) 21 cm
(C) 14 cm (D) 3.5 cm

11-50 Two right circular cones have same radii. Ratio of their slant height is 4 : 3, then the ratio of their curved surface areas is :

[NTSE-2015 (Stage-I) Chennai]

(A) 16 : 9 (B) 2 : 3
(C) 4 : 3 (D) 3 : 4

11-51 The radii of two concentric circles are 7 cm and 14 cm are respectively. The area between the two sectors of the circles whose central angle 60° is :

[NTSE-2015 (Stage-I) Chennai]

(A) 154 sq. cm (B) 77 sq. cm
(C) 308 sq. cm (D) 98 sq. cm

11-52 Segment of a quadrant of a circle has area equal to :

[NTSE-2015 (Stage-I) Chennai]

(A) $\frac{r^2}{2}\left(\frac{\pi}{2}-1\right)$ sq. units (B) $\left(\frac{\pi}{4}+1\right)r^2$ sq. units

(C) $\left(1-\frac{\pi}{4}\right)\frac{r^2}{2}$ sq. units (D) $\left(\frac{\pi}{4}r^2-1\right)$ sq. units

11-53 A cow is tied with a rope of length 12 m at a corner of rectangular field of dimensions 25 m × 45 m. If the length of the rope is increased to 23 m, then the additional grassy area in which the cow can graze is (take $\pi = \frac{22}{7}$):

[NTSE-2016 (Stage-I) Rajasthan]

(A) $300.5 m^2$ (B) $312.5 m^2$
(C) $315.5 m^2$ (D) $302.5 m^2$

11-54 If a metallic sphere of radius 6 cm is melted and recast into the shape of a cylinder of radius 3 cm, then the height of the cylinder is : **[NTSE-2016 (Stage-I) Rajasthan]**

(A) 30 cm (B) 25 cm
(C) 35 cm (D) 32 cm

11-55 If in a right angled triangle the hypotenuse is to be 1 cm longer than the base and 2 cm longer than the altitude, then the perimeter of the triangle is : **[NTSE-2016 (Stage-I) Rajasthan]**

(A) 24 cm (B) 20 cm
(C) 12 cm (D) 10 cm

11-56 In the quadrilateral $ABCD$, $\angle A = \angle C = 90°$, $AE = 5$ cm, $BE = 12$ cm and $AC = 21$ cm. If $DF = x$, then the value of $x = ...$

[NTSE-2016 (Stage-I) Andhara Pradesh]

(A) $4\frac{3}{5}$ cm

(B) $5\frac{1}{4}$ cm

(C) $6\frac{2}{3}$ cm

(D) 7 cm

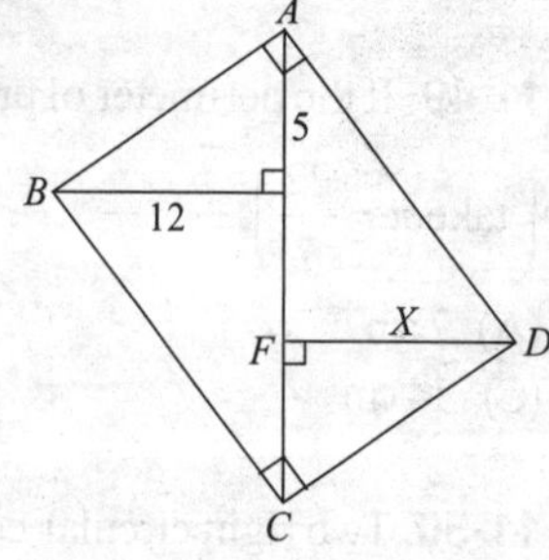

Figure 11.37

11-57 In the figure-11.38 'O' is the in-center of ΔABC where $AB = 3$ cm. $BC = 4$ cm and $AC = 5$ cm. Area of $\Delta ABC = rs$. Where r is the in-radius and s is the semiperimeter, then the value of $OC =$ **[NTSE-2016 (Stage-I) Andhara Pradesh]**

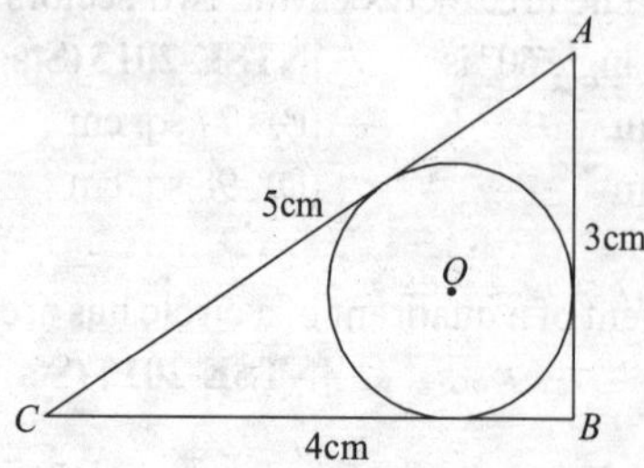

Figure 11.38

(A) $\sqrt{10}$ cm (B) 8 cm
(C) $\sqrt{5}$ cm (D) $2\sqrt{2}$ cm

11-58 The wheel of a motor car makes 1000 revolutions is moving 440 m. The diameter of the wheel is :

[NTSE-2016 (Stage-I) Bihar]

(A) 0.44 m (B) 0.14 m
(C) 0.24 m (D) 0.34 m

11-59 The area (in sq. cm) of the largest circle that can be drawn inside a square of side 28 cm :

[NTSE-2016 (Stage-I) Bihar]

(A) 17248 (B) 784
(C) 8624 (D) 616

11-60 If the volume of two cubes are in the ratio 27 : 64, then the ratio of their total surface area is :

[NTSE-2016 (Stage-I) Bihar]

(A) 27 : 64 (B) 3 : 4
(C) 9 : 16 (D) 3 : 8

11-61 If h be the height and α the Semi-vertical angle of a right circular cone, then its volume is given by :

[NTSE-2016 (Stage-I) Chandigarh]

(A) $\frac{1}{3}\pi h^3 \tan^2 \alpha$ (B) $\frac{1}{3}\pi h^2 \tan^2 \alpha$
(C) $\frac{1}{3}\pi h^2 \tan^3 \alpha$ (D) $\frac{1}{3}\pi h^3 \tan^3 \alpha$

11-62 A circle with radius 2 unit is placed against a right angle. Another smaller circle is also placed as shown in figure-11.39. What is the radius of the smaller circle ?

[NTSE-2016 (Stage-I) Chandigarh]

(A) $3 - 2\sqrt{2}$

(B) $4 - 2\sqrt{2}$

(C) $7 - 4\sqrt{2}$

(D) $6 - 4\sqrt{2}$

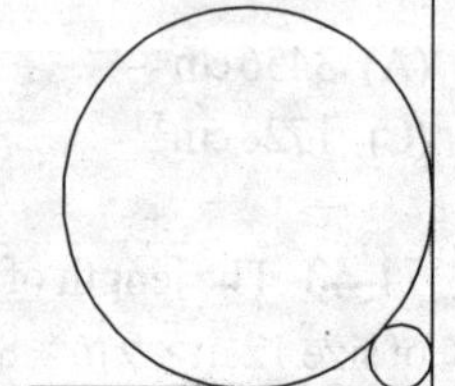
Figure 11.39

11-63 ΔABC is an equilateral triangle, we have $BD = EG = DF = DE = EC$, then the ratio of the area of the shaded portion to area of ΔABC is :

[NTSE-2016 (Stage-I) Delhi]

(A) $\frac{4}{11}$

(B) $\frac{7}{9}$

(C) $\frac{5}{12}$

(D) $\frac{6}{7}$

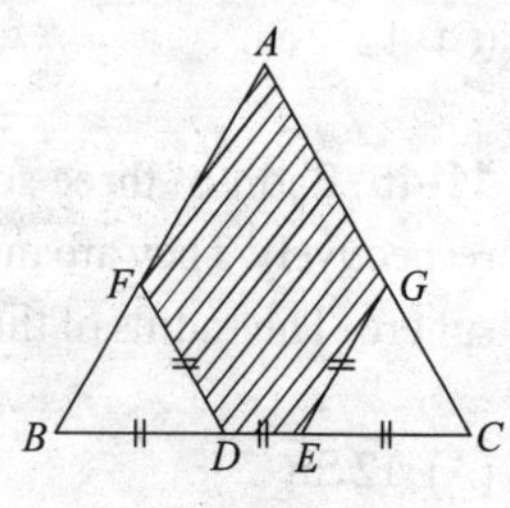

Figure 11.40

11-64 The volume and whole surface area of a cylindrical solid of radius 'r' units are v and s respectively. If the height of cylinder is 1 unit then $\frac{v}{s}$ is equal to : **[NTSE-2016 (Stage-I) Delhi]**

(A) $\frac{1}{2}\left(1-\frac{1}{r+1}\right)$ (B) $\frac{1}{2}\left(1+\frac{1}{r+1}\right)$

(C) $\frac{1}{2}\left(1-\frac{1}{r}\right)$ (D) $\frac{1}{2}\left(1+\frac{1}{r}\right)$

11-65 If the height of right circular cylinder is increased by 10% while the radius of bases is decreased by 10% then curved surface area of cylinder : **[NTSE-2016 (Stage-I) Delhi]**

(A) Remains same (B) Decreases by 1%
(C) Increases by 1% (D) Increases by 0.1%

11-66 In the given figure-11.41, ΔABC is a right-angled triangle semicircles are drawn on AB, AC and BC as diameters. It is given that $AB = 3$ cm and $AC = 4$ cm. Find the Area of shaded region : **[NTSE-2016 (Stage-I) Jharkhand]**

(A) 12 cm^2

(B) 6 cm^2

(C) 9 cm^2

(D) 15 cm^2

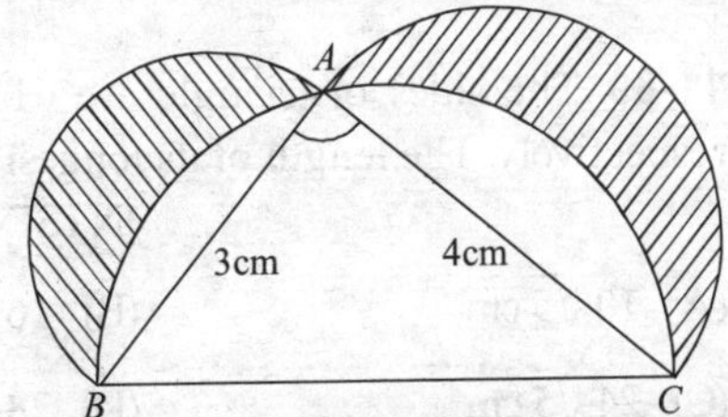

Figure 11.41

11-67 Water flows through a circular pipe whose internal diameter is 2 cm, at the rate of 0.7 m/s into a cylindrical tank, the radius of whose base is 40 cm. How much will the level of water rise in the tank in half an hour?
[NTSE-2016 (Stage-I) Jharkhand]

(A) 75 cm (B) 75.25 cm
(C) 78 cm (D) 78.75 cm

11-68 If points $A(a, 0)$, $B(0, b)$ and $C(1, 1)$ are collinear, then $\frac{1}{a}+\frac{1}{b}=?$ **[NTSE-2016 (Stage-I) Jharkhand]**

(A) 0 (B) 1

(C) 2 (D) $\frac{1}{2}$

11-69 The sum of the lengths of all the edges of a cube is 6 cm. What is the volume of the cube in cubic cm ?
[NTSE-2016 (Stage-I) Odisha]

(A) $\frac{1}{8}$ (B) $\frac{1}{6}$

(C) $\frac{1}{4}$ (D) $\frac{1}{2}$

11-70 In the given figure-11.42, if $AD \perp BC$, $AC = 4$, $BD = 2$, $AB = a$ and $CD = b$ then $a^2 + b^2 =$
[NTSE-2016 (Stage-I) Karnatka]

(A) 6

(B) 8

(C) 12

(D) 20

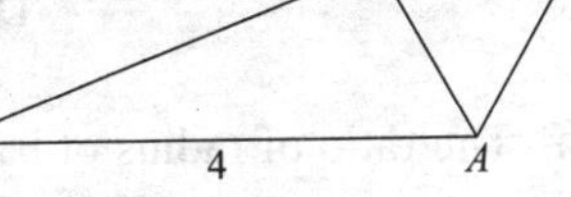

Figure 11.42

11-71 The area of the triangle formed by the points $(a, b+c)$, $(b, c+a)$ and $(c, a+b)$ is : **[NTSE-2016 (Stage-I) Karnatka]**

(A) 0 (B) 1

(C) $\frac{abc}{2}$ (D) $\frac{a+b+c}{2}$

11-72 The diameter of a metal ball is 3.5 cm. If the density of the metal is 9.8 g/cm^2 then mass of the ball is :
[NTSE-2016 (Stage-I) Karnatka]

(A) 200 g (B) 220 g
(C) 1600 g (D) 1760 g

11-73 A wheel rotates 100 times to cover a distance of 88 meters. What is its diameter ? **[NTSE-2016 (Stage-I) Chhatisgarh]**

(A) 7 cm (B) 14 cm
(C) 28 cm (D) 10 cm

11-74 Three cubes of edges of 3 cm, 4 cm, and 5 cm respectively are melted to form a bigger cube. The edge of the bigger cube will be : **[NTSE-2016 (Stage-I) Chhatisgarh]**

(A) 12 cm (B) 8 cm
(C) 7 cm (D) 6 cm

11-75 A roller of diameter 1.4 m and length 1.4 m is used to press the ground having area 3080 sq. m. Find the number of revolutions that the roller will make to press the ground :
[NTSE-2016 (Stage-I) Chhatisgarh]

(A) 700 (B) 500
(C) 1000 (D) 800

11-76 If the ratio of the radii of the circular ends of a conical bucket whose height is 60 cm is 2 : 1 and addition of the areas is 770 sq. cm. Find the capacity of the bucket in litres :
[NTSE-2016 (Stage-I) Chhatisgarh]

(A) 21.56 litres (B) 215.6 litres
(C) 21.560 litres (D) 2156 litres

11-77 The radii of two cylinders are in the ratio 2 : 3 and their heights are in the ratio 5: 3, then the ratio of their volumes is :
[NTSE-2017 (Stage-I) Andhra Pradesh]

(A) 15:16 (B) 14:17
(C) 20:27 (D) 4:9

11-78 If the area of three adjacent faces of a cuboid are x, y and z respectively, then the volume of a cuboid is : **[NTSE-2017 (Stage-I) Andhra Pradesh]**

(A) $\sqrt{xyz}$ (B) $x+y+z$
(C) $x^2 yz$ (D) $xy+z$

11-79 The ratio of radius of base to the height of the right circular cylinder is 1 : 2. If its volume is 2156 cm^3, then its total surface area is ... **[NTSE-2017 (Stage-I) Chandigarh]**

(A) 1024 cm^2 (B) 924 cm^2
(C) 874 cm^2 (D) 1204 cm^2

11-80 If radius of a right circular cylinder is increased by 10% and height is decreased by 10%, its volume will : **[NTSE-2017 (Stage-I) Chandigarh]**

(A) Increase by 9.8% (B) Decrease by 9.8%
(C) Increase by 8.9% (D) Decrease by 8.9%

11-81 A regular polygon is drawn with 35 diagonals. Its interior angle will be : **[NTSE-2017 (Stage-I) Delhi]**

(A) 154° (B) 164°
(C) 144° (D) None of these

11-82 What will be the ratio of volume of cube is to volume of sphere inscribed in the cube ? **[NTSE-2017 (Stage-I) Delhi]**

(A) $3:\pi$ (B) $6:\pi$
(C) 6 : 5 (D) $2:\pi$

11-83 The length of diagonals of three cubes A, B and C are given as $\sqrt{108}$ cm $\sqrt{192}$ cm and $\sqrt{300}$ cm respectively. A person desires to form a new cube by melting these cubes. What can be the length of the largest rod that can be placed in the new cube formed ? **[NTSE-2017 (Stage-I) Goa]**

(A) $11\sqrt{2}$ (B) $12\sqrt{3}$
(C) $13\sqrt{5}$ (D) $14\sqrt{6}$

11-84 In the given figure-11.43 a bigger circle is inscribed in a square with perimeter 4 units. A smaller circle touch the bigger circle at one point and the square at two points. What is the radius of the smaller circle ? **[NTSE-2017 (Stage-I) Goa]**

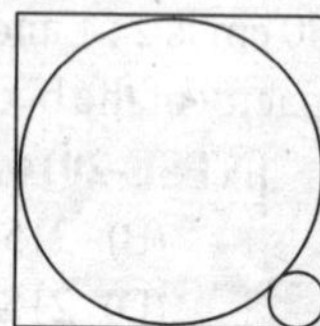

Figure 11.43

(A) $\frac{3-2\sqrt{2}}{2}$ (B) $\frac{\sqrt{2}-1}{1+2\sqrt{2}}$
(C) $\frac{\sqrt{2}-1}{2}$ (D) $\frac{3-2\sqrt{2}}{1+6\sqrt{2}}$

11-85 The length of minor arc $\overset{\frown}{AB}$ of $\odot(P, 7)$ is 14. Find the length of major arc $\overset{\frown}{AB}$: **[NTSE-2017 (Stage-I) Gujarat]**

(A) 18 (B) 21
(C) 28 (D) 30

11-86 The length of the edge of a equilateral triangle is 8 cm. Then semi circumference of such triangle is : **[NTSE-2017 (Stage-I) Gujarat]**

(A) 4 (B) 24
(C) 12 (D) 36

11-87 The formula of lateral surface area of cylinder is —: **[NTSE-2017 (Stage-I) Gujarat]**

(A) $A=2\pi rh$ (B) $A=2\pi r$
(C) $A=\pi r^2$ (D) $A=2\pi r^2 h$

11-88 Three spheres of radii 6 cm, x cm and y cm are melted to form a single sphere of radius 12 cm. If xy is equal to 80, then the value of $x+y$ is : **[NTSE-2017 (Stage-I) Haryana]**

(A) 21 (B) 18
(C) 24 (D) 42

11-89 The sides of triangle are 61 cm, 54 cm and 35 cm respectively. The length of its longest altitude is : **[NTSE-2017 (Stage-I) Haryana]**

(A) $10\sqrt{5}$ cm (B) $16\sqrt{5}$ cm
(C) $24\sqrt{5}$ cm (D) $28\sqrt{5}$ cm

11-90 The area of two concentric circles are 1386 cm^2 and 962.5 cm^2. The width of the ring is : **[NTSE-2017 (Stage-I) Karnataka]**

(A) 4.2 cm (B) 3.8 cm
(C) 3.5 cm (D) 2.8 cm

11-91 On increasing the radius of the base and height of a cone each by 20%, then the percentage increase in the volume will be : **[NTSE-2017 (Stage-I) Karnataka]**

(A) 20% (B) 40.8%
(C) 60% (D) 72.8%

11-92 The height of a hollow cylinder is 14 cm. If external diameter is 16 cm and total curved surface area of the hollow cylinder is 1320 sq. cm., then its internal diameter is : **[NTSE-2017 (Stage-I) Madhya Pradesh]**

(A) 14 cm (B) 16 cm
(C) 6 cm (D) 8 cm

11-93 How many spheres of iron having radius 1 cm can be made by melting a sphere of iron having 8 cm radius ? **[NTSE-2017 (Stage-I) Madhya Pradesh]**

(A) 64 (B) 128
(C) 356 (D) 512

11-94 The diameter of a cycle wheel is 1.6 m. The wheel revolves 21 times in one minutes, then how much distance will the cycle cover in one hour :

[NTSE-2017 (Stage-I) Madhya Pradesh]

(A) 3.636 km (B) 6.336 km
(C) 6.633 km (D) 2.640 km

11-95 Find the ratio of the volume to total surface area of a sphere of radius $\sqrt{7}$ cm : **[NTSE-2017 (Stage-I) Maharashtra]**

(A) $\frac{\sqrt{7}}{3}$ (B) $\frac{7}{3}$
(C) $\frac{7\sqrt{7}}{3}$ (D) $\frac{\sqrt{7}}{\sqrt{3}}$

11-96 The diameter of the base of a cylindrical metal block is 6.6 cm and its height is 0.4 m, How many discs of diameter 2.2 cm and height 0.2 cm can be cut from this metal block ?

[NTSE-2017 (Stage-I) Maharashtra]

(A) 180 (B) 600
(C) 1200 (D) 1800

11-97 The longest side of a triangle is 20 cm. and other side is 10 cm. The area of the triangle is 80 cm^2. Find the length of the remaining side of the triangle :

[NTSE-2017 (Stage-I) Maharashtra]

(A) $2\sqrt{65}$ (B) $5\sqrt{10}$
(C) $10\sqrt{3}$ (D) 15

11-98 A circle is inscribed in a square of side 2.5 cm. Another circle is circumscribing this square. The ratio of areas of outer circle and inner circle is : **[NTSE-2017 (Stage-I) Punjab]**

(A) $1 : \sqrt{2}$ (B) $\sqrt{2} : 1$
(C) 2 : 1 (D) $\sqrt{3} : 1$

11-99 How many revolutions will a circular wheel of radius r units will make to cover a distance of 100 times its diameter ?

[NTSE-2017 (Stage-I) Punjab]

(A) $\frac{100}{\pi}$ (B) 100π
(C) $\frac{\pi}{100}$ (D) $\frac{50}{\pi}$

11-100 The area of an equilateral triangle is $49\sqrt{3}$ cm^2. Taking each vertex as centre, circles are described with radius equal to half the length of the side of the triangle. Find the area of the part of the triangle which is not included in these circles

($\sqrt{3} = 1.77, \pi = \frac{22}{7}$) : **[NTSE-2017 (Stage-I) Punjab]**

(A) 84 cm^2 (B) 77.7 cm^2
(C) 7.77 cm^2 (D) 70.7 cm^2

11-101 One litre of water weights 1 kg. How many cubic millimeter of water weigh 0.1 gm ?

[NTSE-2017 (Stage-I) Punjab]

(A) 100 (B) 10
(C) 1 (D) 0.1

11-102 A copper wire when bent in the form of a square encloses and area of 484 cm^2. If the same wire is bent in the form of circle, the area enclosed by it is : **[NTSE-2017 (Stage-I) Punjab]**

(A) 210 cm^2 (B) 616 cm^2
(C) 512 cm^2 (D) 54 cm^2

11-103 Find the area of shaded region, where side of square $ABCD$ is 10 cm and two arcs drawn from two opposite vertices of the square : **[NTSE-2017 (Stage-I) Rajasthan]**

(A) $\frac{200}{7}$ sq. unit

(B) $\frac{400}{7}$ sq. unit

(C) $\frac{600}{7}$ sq. unit

(D) $\frac{100}{7}$ sq. unit

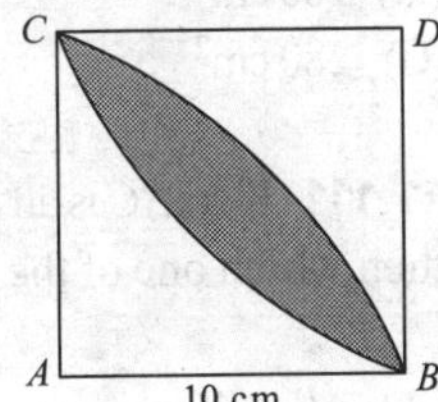

Figure 11.44

11-104 Find the capacity of a glass which is in the shape of frustum of height 14 cm and diameters of both circular ends are 4 cm and 2 cm : **[NTSE-2017 (Stage-I) Rajasthan]**

(A) $\frac{308}{3}$ cm^3 (B) $\frac{298}{21}$ cm^3
(C) 112 cm^2 (D) $\frac{298}{21}$ cm^2

11-105 If the length of circumference of a circle is 60 cm more than its diameter, then length of its circumference is :

[NTSE-2017 (Stage-I) Rajasthan]

(A) 14π cm (B) 28π cm
(C) 35π cm (D) 42π cm

11-106 The diameter of a sphere is decreased by 25%. By what per cent does its curved surface area decrease ?

[NTSE-2017 (Stage-I) Rajasthan]

(A) 25% (B) 56.25%
(C) 4375% (D) 6225%

11-107 The areas of three adjacent faces of a cuboid are p, q and r. If its volume is v, then the square of its volume is :

[NTSE-2017 (Stage-I) Tamilnadu]

(A) $\sqrt{pqr}$ (B) pqr
(C) $(pqr)^2$ (D) $\frac{pqr}{8}$

11-108 The perimeter of a right angled triangle is 24 cm. If its hypotenuse is 10 cm then area of this triangle is : **[NTSE-2017 (Stage-I) Uttar Pradesh]**

(A) 24 cm^2 (B) 10 cm^2
(C) 12 cm^2 (D) 48 cm^2

11-109 If the radii of a cone and a cylinder are in the ratio 2 : 3 and their heights are in the ratio 4 : 3 then the ratio of their volumes will be : **[NTSE-2017 (Stage-I) Uttar Pradesh]**

(A) 16 : 27 (B) 16 : 81
(C) 16 : 9 (D) 27 : 16

11-110 A rectangular piece of paper of length 20 cm and breadth 14 cm is folded about its breadth the curved surface area of the cylinder so formed is : **[NTSE-2017 (Stage-I) Uttar Pradesh]**

(A) 180 cm^2 (B) 200 cm^2
(C) 280 cm^2 (D) 190 cm^2

11-111 If ΔABC is an obtuse angled triangle in which $\angle C = 110°$ then which one of the following is true : **[NTSE-2017 (Stage-I) Uttar Pradesh]**

(A) $AB = AC$ (B) $AB < AC$
(C) $AB > AC$ (D) $AB < BC$

11-112 A cuboidal Vessel is 22 meter long and 10 meter wide. How high must it be made to hold 440 cubic meters of water : **[NTSE-2017 (Stage-I) Uttrakhand]**

(A) 4 meter (B) 2 meter
(C) 8 meter (D) 6 meter

11-113 If the diameter of a sphere is decreased by 25% then the curved surface area will be decreased by : **[NTSE-2017 (Stage-I) Uttrakhand]**

(A) $\frac{5\pi r^2}{4}$ (B) $\frac{2\pi r^2}{4}$
(C) $\frac{\pi r^2}{4}$ (D) $\frac{7\pi r^2}{4}$

11-114 The curved surface area of a right circular cylinder and that of a sphere are equal. If their radii are equal, the ratio of their volume is : **[NTSE-2017 (Stage-I) West Bengal]**

(A) 3 : 2 (B) 2 : 3
(C) 3 : 4 (D) 4 : 3

11-115 The sum of the length, breadth and height of a rectangular parallelepiped is 15 cm and its whole surface area is 264 sq. cm. The area of the square whose sides are equal to the length of the diagonal of this parallelepiped is : **[NTSE-2017 (Stage-I) West Bengal]**

(A) 256 sq. cm (B) 361 sq. cm
(C) 225 sq. cm (D) 324 sq. cm

11-116 A square is drawn with vertices on a circle. The area of the square is 4 square centimeters. What is the area of the circle (in sq.cm.) ? **[NTSE-2017 (Stage-I) Kerala]**

(A) π (B) $\sqrt{2}\pi$
(C) 2π (D) 4π

11-117 How many cubic centimetres make 100 kilolitre : **[NTSE-2018 (Stage-I) Rajasthan]**

(A) 10^{10} (B) 10^5
(C) 10^8 (D) 10^6

11-118 A cube of edge 1 cm is cut from a corner of a solid cube of edge 5 cm. What is the total surface area of the solid remained : **[NTSE-2018 (Stage-I) Rajasthan]**

(A) 150 cm^2 (B) 149 cm^2
(C) 151 cm^2 (D) 147 cm^2

11-119 The volume of regular cylindrical wire of diameter 2 mm is 99 cubic cm, then the length of wire in meter : **[NTSE-2018 (Stage-I) Andhra Pradesh]**

(A) 53.1 (B) 31.5
(C) 35.1 (D) 51.3

11-120 The radius of cone and cylinder are in the ratio 2 : 3 and their heights are in the ratio 3 : 2, then their volumes are in the ratio : **[NTSE-2018 (Stage-I) Andhra Pradesh]**

(A) 3 : 2 (B) 2 : 9
(C) 9 : 2 (D) 2 : 3

11-121 Three horses are tethered with 7 with meter long ropes at the three corner of a triangular field having sides 20 m, 34 m and 42 m. The area of the plot which can be grazed by horses is : **[NTSE-2018 (Stage-I) Bihar]**

(A) 50 m^2 (B) 77 m^2
(C) 82 m^2 (D) 90 m^2

11-122 A right circular cone is 8.4 cm high and the radius of its base is 2.1 cm. The cone is melted and recast into a sphere. Find the radius of the sphere : **[NTSE-2018 (Stage-I) Bihar]**

(A) 2.1 cm (B) 4.2 cm
(C) 5.3 cm (D) 6.4 cm

11-123 The internal and external diameters of a hollow hemispherical vessel are 24 cm and 25 cm respectively. If the cost for painting 1 cm^2 of the surface area is Rs.0.05 then the total cost of painting the vessel all over is : **[NTSE-2018 (Stage-I) Bihar]**

(A) Rs. 90.05 (B) Rs. 96.28
(C) Rs. 95.20 (D) Rs.96.29

11-124 If each edge of *a* cube is increased by 50% then the percentage increase in its surface area is : **[NTSE-2018 (Stage-I) Bihar]**

(A) 50% (B) 125%
(C) 130% (D) 140%

11-125 In the adjoining figure-11.45 *ABCPA* is a quadrant of a circle of radius 14 cm. With *AC* as diameter, a semicircle is drawn. The area of the shaded region is : **[NTSE-2018 (Stage-I) Bihar]**

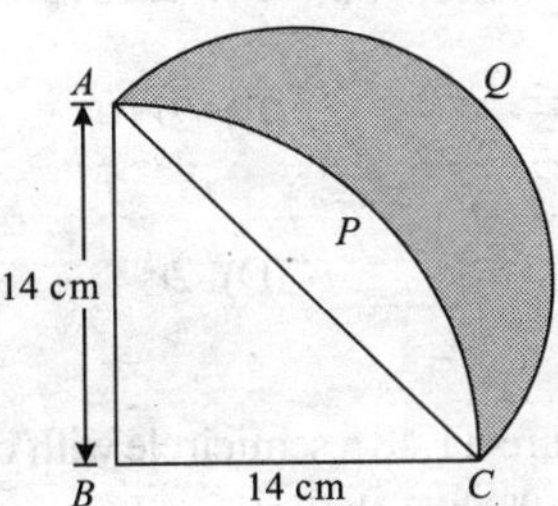

Figure 11.45

(A) 35 cm^2 (B) 64 cm^2
(C) 98 cm^2 (D) 132 cm^2

11-126 The sum of all sides of a cube is 9 cm. The volume of the cube is______: **[NTSE-2018 (Stage-I) Chandigarh]**

(A) $\frac{3}{4}cm^3$ (B) $\frac{81}{108}cm^3$

(C) $\frac{27}{64}cm^3$ (D) $\frac{27}{32}cm^3$

11-127 What will be the area of largest triangle that can be inscribed in a semicircle of radius $\frac{'r'}{16}$

[NTSE-2018 (Stage-I) Chandigarh]

(A) $16r^2$ (B) $\frac{r^2}{16}$

(C) $\frac{r^2}{32}$ (D) $\frac{r^2}{256}$

11-128 From a face of a cubical wooden block, a hemispherical depression is cut out in such a way that the diameter of hemisphere is half the edge '*l*'of the cube. What will be the surface area of remaining solid : **[NTSE-2018 (Stage-I) Chandigarh]**

(A) $\frac{l^2(l^2+4)}{2}$ (B) $64l^2$

(C) $\frac{1}{4}l^2(\pi+24)$ (D) $\frac{1}{16}l^2(\pi+96)$

11-129 Maximum length of the pole which can be put in the room whose length, breadth and height are 10 m, 10 m and 5 m respectively : **[NTSE-2018 (Stage-I) Chhattisgarh]**

(A) 25 m (B) 20 m
(C) 15 m (D) 10 m

11-130 A right angled triangle with sides 3 cm, 4 cm, and 5 cm is rotated about the side of 3 cm as the axis to form a cone. The volume of the cone that is formed by the traingle will be :
[NTSE-2018 (Stage-I) Chhattisgarh]

(A) $12\pi\, cm^3$ (B) $15\pi\, cm^3$
(C) $16\pi\, cm^3$ (D) $20\pi\, cm^3$

11-131 A square is inscribed in a circle of radius '*a*'. another circle is inscribed in that square and again a square is inscribed in this circle. This side of this square is :
[NTSE-2018 (Stage-I) Delhi]

(A) $2a$ (B) $\frac{a}{2}$

(C) $\frac{a}{\sqrt{2}}$ (D) a

11-132 If the height of right circular cylinder is increased is increased by 10% while radius of base is decreased by 10% then curved surface area of cylinder :
[NTSE-2018 (Stage-I) Delhi]

(A) Remains same (B) Decreases by 1%
(C) Increases by 1 % (D) Increases by 0.1%

11-133 In the given figure-11.46, the centre of the circle is *A* and *ABCDEF* is a regular hexagon of side 6 cm. The approximate area of segment *BPF* is : [Take $\pi = 3.14$]
[NTSE-2018 (Stage-I) Delhi]

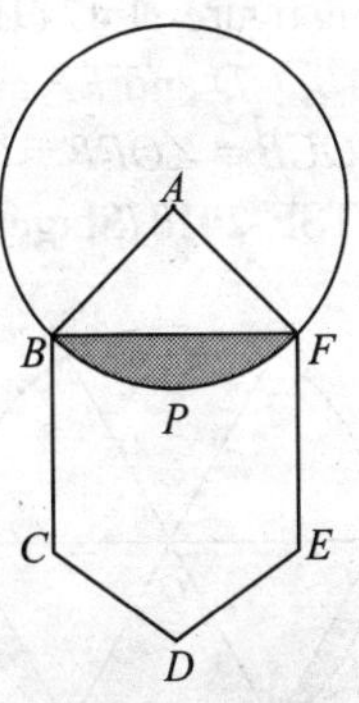

Figure 11.46

(A) 25 cm^2 (B) 22 cm^2
(C) 32 cm^2 (D) 30 cm^2

11-134 The volume of cube is numerically equal to sum of the length of its edges. The total surface area of cube in square units is : **[NTSE-2018 (Stage-I) Delhi]**

(A) 12 (B) 36
(C) 72 (D) 144

11-135 The diagonal of square is $5\sqrt{2}$. The length of the side of the square is : **[NTSE-2018 (Stage-I) Gujarat]**

(A) 10 (B) 5

(C) $3\sqrt{2}$ (D) $2\sqrt{2}$

11-136 A bucket is in the form of a frustum of a cone and it can holds 28.49 litres of water. The radii, of the top and bottom of the bucket are 28 cm and 21 cm respectively. Then slant height of the bucket is : [Use = $\frac{22}{7}$] **[NTSE-2018 (Stage-I) Haryana]**

(A) 15 cm (B) $\sqrt{246}$ cm

(C) $\sqrt{253}$ cm (D) $\sqrt{274}$ cm

11-137 Sum of the length of all edges of a cube is x metres. If the surface area of the cube is x sq. meters; then its volume (in cubic meters) is : **[NTSE-2018 (Stage-I) Haryana]**

(A) x^3 (B) 8

(C) x (D) 2

11-138 The ratio of volume of a cube to that of a sphere which exactly fits inside the cube is : **[NTSE-2018 (Stage-I) Himachal Pradesh]**

(A) $\pi : 6$ (B) $\pi : 12$

(C) $12 : \pi$ (D) $6 : \pi$

11-139 What is the length of the longest rod which can be placed in a cube of total surface area of 216 cm^3 : **[NTSE-2018 (Stage-I) Himachal Pradesh]**

(A) $\sqrt{18}$ cm (B) $6\sqrt{3}$ cm

(C) $6\sqrt{2}$ cm (D) $3\sqrt{6}$ cm

11-140 In the adjoining figure-11.47 O is the center of the circle with radius r where AB, CD and EF are the diameters of the circle and $\angle OAF = \angle OCB = \angle OEF = 60°$. What is the area of the shaded region : **[NTSE-2018 (Stage-I) Himachal Pradesh]**

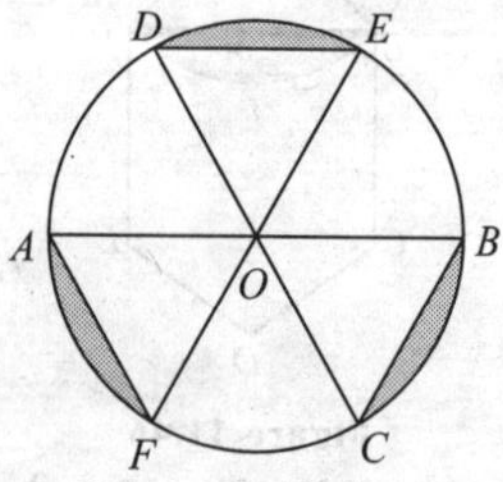

Figure 11.47

(A) $\frac{r^2}{2}\left(\pi - \frac{3\sqrt{3}}{2}\right)$ (B) $\frac{r^2}{2}\left(\pi - \frac{3\sqrt{3}}{4}\right)$

(C) $\frac{r^2}{3}\left(\pi - \frac{2\sqrt{3}}{3}\right)$ (D) Data insufficient

11-141 The capacity of two pots are 240 litre and 112 litre respectively. Find the capacity of a container which can exactly measure the contents of the two pots : **[NTSE-2018 (Stage-I) Jharkhand]**

(A) 9000 cc (B) 12000 cc

(C) 16000 cc (D) 8000 cc

11-142 The curved surface area of a right circular cylinder of base radius r is obtained by multiplying its volume by : **[NTSE-2018 (Stage-I) Jharkhand]**

(A) $\frac{2}{r^2}$ (B) $2r^2$

(C) $\frac{2}{r}$ (D) $2r$

11-143 In the figure-11.48 a semicircle with center 'O; is drawn on AB. If $ABP = 60°$ then the ratio of larger to smaller shaded region is : **[NTSE-2018 (Stage-I) Karnataka]**

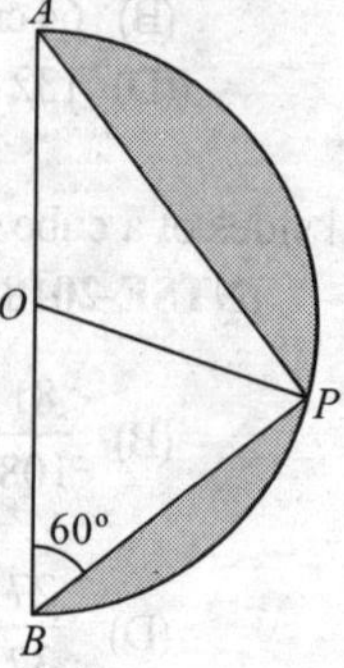

Figure 11.48

(A) $\frac{4\pi - 2\sqrt{3}}{2\pi - 2\sqrt{3}}$ (B) $\frac{4\pi - 3\sqrt{3}}{3\pi - 3\sqrt{3}}$

(C) $\frac{4\pi - 3\sqrt{3}}{2\pi - 3\sqrt{3}}$ (D) $\frac{2\pi - 2\sqrt{3}}{\pi - 2\sqrt{3}}$

11-144 The volume of a bucket of height 82.1 cm obtained by attaching hemispherical knob on one side of a cylinder of height 80 cm is: **[NTSE-2018 (Stage-I) Karnataka]**

(A) 1.1 Lt (B) 1.0 Lt

(C) 1.2 Lt (D) 1.4 Lt

11-145 A conical vessel of radius of radius 6 cm and height 8 cm is completely filled with water. A metal sphere is lowered into the water. The size of the sphere is such that when it touches the inner surface, it just gets immersed. Then, the fraction of water that overflows from the conical vessel is : **[NTSE-2018 (Stage-I) Karnataka]**

(A) $\frac{3}{8}$ (B) $\frac{5}{8}$

(C) $\frac{7}{8}$ (D) $\frac{5}{16}$

11-146 If side of each cube is 3 cm. Volume of given figure-11.49 is : **[NTSE-2018 (Stage-I) Madhya Prasesh]**

(A) 3 cm^3

(B) 27 cm^3

(C) 15 cm^3

(D) 405 cm^3

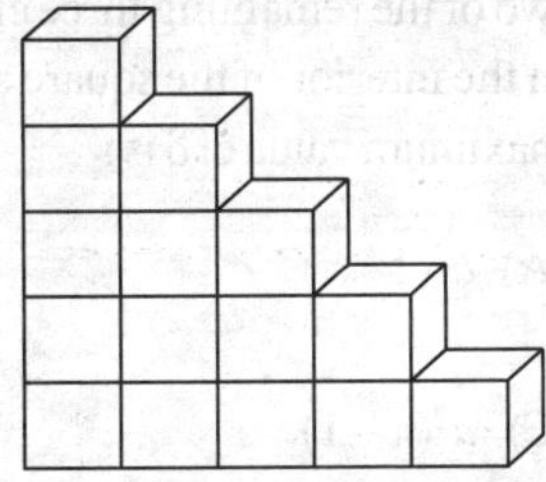

Figure 11.49

11-147 Length of Minute hand of a clock is 14 cm. Area formed by this hand in 5 minutes is :

[NTSE-2018 (Stage-I) Madhya Prasesh]

(A) $\frac{154}{3}$ (B) 154

(C) $\frac{215}{3}$ (D) $\frac{205}{3}$

11-148 The longest pole that can be kept in a room of dimensions 5m × 4m × 2m is :

[NTSE-2018 (Stage-I) Tamil Nadu]

(A) $9\sqrt{5}$ m (B) $6\sqrt{5}$ m

(C) $3\sqrt{5}$ m (D) $5\sqrt{3}$ m

11-149 If the volume of a sphere is equal to its surface area, then the circumference of a cross sectional circle whose centre coincides with the sphere is :

[NTSE-2018 (Stage-I) Tamil Nadu]

(A) 2π (B) 4π

(C) 6π (D) 8π

11-150 A circle is inscribed in a triangle *ABC* with right angle at *A*. The length of the sides containing the right angle are 6 cm and 8 cm respectively. The radius of the circle is :

[NTSE-2018 (Stage-I) Tamil Nadu]

(A) 2 cm (B) 6 cm

(C) 8 cm (D) 10 cm

11-151 If every side of a triangle is doubled, then increase in the area of the triangle is : **[NTSE-2018 (Stage-I) Telangana]**

(A) $100\sqrt{2}$ (B) 200 %

(C) 300 % (D) 400 %

11-152 The measures of the perpendiculars drawn from a point situated inside an equilateral triangles are 6 cm, 8 cm and 10 cm. The area of the triangle will be : **[NTSE-2018 (Stage-I) Telangana]**

(A) $256\sqrt{3}$ (B) $192\sqrt{3}$

(C) $64\sqrt{3}$ (D) $3\sqrt{3}$

11-153 If each exterior angle of a regular polygon is 18° find the number of sides of the polygon :

[NTSE-2018 (Stage-I) Uttar Pradesh]

(A) 10 (B) 15

(C) 20 (D) 8

11-154 The ratio of incomes of two persons *A* and *B* is 9 : 4 and the ratio of their expenditure is 3 : 1. If each of them manages to save Rs. 1000, then the income of *B* is :

[NTSE-2018 (Stage-I) Uttar Pradesh]

(A) 3000 (B) 4000

(C) 9000 (D) 8000/3

11-155 The sum of area of two squares is 468 cm^2. If the sum of their perimeters is 120 cm, then the difference of their side is :

[NTSE-2018 (Stage-I) Uttar Pradesh]

(A) 1.5 cm (B) 2 cm

(C) 4 cm (D) 6 cm

11-156 The radii of a right circular cone and a right circular cylinder are in the ratio 4 : 3 and their heights are in the ratio 2 : 3. The ratio of their volumes is :

[NTSE-2018 (Stage-I) Uttar Pradesh]

(A) 32 : 27 (B) 32 : 9

(C) 32 : 81 (D) 27 : 32

11-157 The dimensions of a cuboid are in the ratio of 1 : 2 : 3 and its total surface area is 88 m^2 then the dimensions will be :

[NTSE-2018 (Stage-I) Uttarakhandh]

(A) 1 m, 2 m and 3 m (B) 1 m, 4 m and 6 m

(C) 2 m, 4 m and 6 m (D) 1 m, 4 m and 9 m

11-158 The diameter of 120 cm long roller is 84 cm. If it takes 500 revolutions to level a playground, find the cost of levelling it at the rate of Rs.5 per square meter :

[NTSE-2018 (Stage-I) Uttarakhandh]

(A) 1584 (B) 7920

(C) 3500 (D) None of these

11-159 In the following figure-11.50 each quadrilateral is a square. The value of surface area of following figure will be :

[NTSE-2018 (Stage-I) Uttarakhandh]

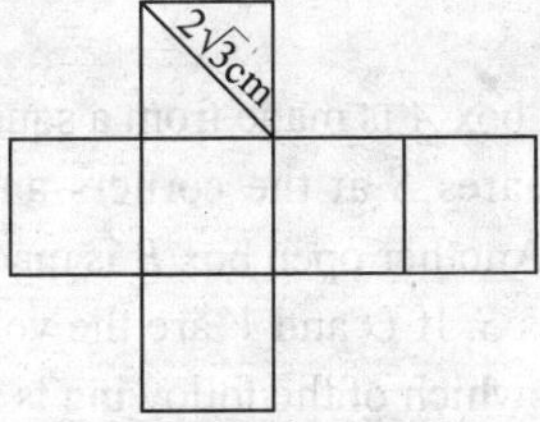

Figure 11.50

(A) $4\sqrt{3}$ cm^2 (B) $24\sqrt{3}$ cm^2

(C) 36 cm^2 (D) $8\sqrt{3}$ cm^2

11-160 If x denotes an angle between any two lines of symmetry of a regular hexagon, then the minimum value of x is : **[NTSE-2012 (Stage-II)]**

(A) 30º (B) 45º
(C) 60º (D) 90º

11-161 The area (in cm²) of the largest triangle that can be inscribed in a semicircle of radius r cm is : **[NTSE-2012 (Stage-II)]**

(A) $\frac{1}{3}\pi r^2$ (B) $2r^2$
(C) r^2 (D) $\frac{1}{2}\pi r^2$

11-162 If an angle of a regular polygon is 165º, then the number of sides of the polygon is : **[NTSE-2012 (Stage-II)]**

(A) 30 (B) 24
(C) 18 (D) 15

11-163 A solid metal sphere of surface area S_1 is melted and recast into a number of smaller spheres. S_2 is the sum of the surface areas of all the smaller spheres. Then : **[NTSE-2013 (Stage-II)]**

(A) $S_1 > S_2$
(B) $S_2 > S_1$
(C) $S_1 = S_2$
(D) $S_1 = S_2$ only if all the smaller spheres of equal radii

11-164 All the arcs in the following diagram are semi-circles. This diagram shows two paths connecting A to B. Path I is the single large semi-circle and Path II consists of the chain of small semi-circles : **[NTSE-2013 (Stage-II)]**

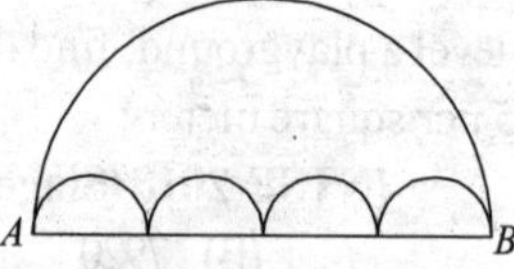

Figure 11.51

(A) Path I is longer than path II
(B) Path I of the same length of Path II
(C) Path I is shorter than Path II
(D) Path I is of the same length as Path II. Only if the number of semi circles is not more than 4

11-165 An open box A is made from a square piece of tin by cutting equal squares S at the corners and folding up the remaining flaps. Another open box B is made similarly using one of the squares S. If U and V are the volumes of A and B respectively, then which of the following is not possible ? **[NTSE-2013 (Stage-II)]**

(A) $U > V$ (B) $V > U$
(C) $U = V$
(D) Minimum value of $U >$ maximum value of V

11-166 $ABCD$ is a square with side a. With centres A, B, C and D four circles are drawn such that each circle touches externally two of the remaining three circles. Let δ be the area of the region in the interior of the square and exterior of the circles. Then the maximum value of δ is : **[NTSE-2013 (Stage-II)]**

(A) $a^2(1-\pi)$ (B) $a^2\left(\frac{4-\pi}{4}\right)$
(C) $a^2(\pi-1)$ (D) $\frac{\pi a^2}{4}$

11-167 ΔABC is an equilateral triangle of side $2\sqrt{3}$ cms. P is any point in the interior of ΔABC. If x, y, z are the distances of P from the sides of the triangle, then $x + y + z =$ **NTSE-2013 (Stage-II)]**

(A) $2+\sqrt{3}$ cms (B) 5 cms
(C) 3 cms (D) 4 cms

11-168 An open box is made from a square lamina of side 12 cm, by cutting equal squares at the corners and folding up the remaining flaps. The volume of this box cannot be : **[NTSE-2013 (Stage-II)]**

(A) 115 c.c. (B) 120 c.c.
(C) 125 c.c. (D) 130 c.c.

11-169 $PQRS$ is the smallest square whose vertices are on the respective sides of the square $ABCD$. The ratio of the area of □$PQRS$ to □$ABCD$ is : **[NTSE-2014 (Stage-II)]**

(A) 1 : 2 (B) $1 : \sqrt{2}$
(C) 1 : 3 (D) 2 : 3

11-170 In the figure-11.52, a semi-circle with centre O is drawn on AB. The ratio of the larger shaded area to the smaller shaded area is : **[NTSE-2014 (Stage-II)]**

(A) $\frac{4\pi-2\sqrt{3}}{2\pi-2\sqrt{3}}$

(B) $\frac{4\pi-3\sqrt{3}}{3\pi-3\sqrt{3}}$

(C) $\frac{4\pi-3\sqrt{3}}{2\pi-3\sqrt{3}}$

(D) $\frac{3\pi-2\sqrt{3}}{2\pi-2\sqrt{3}}$

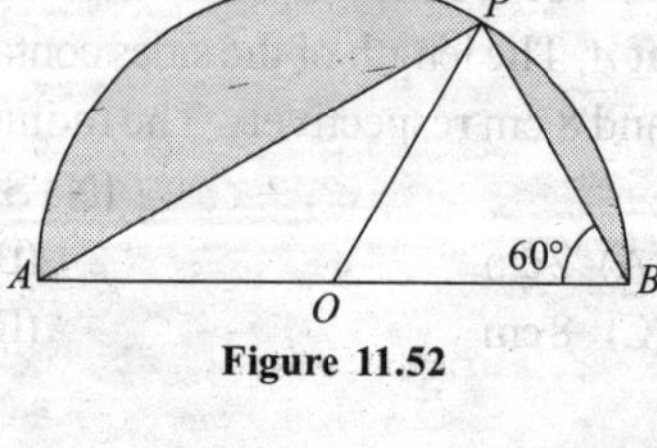

Figure 11.52

11-171 If Anish is moving along the boundary of a triangular field of sides 35 m, 53 m and 66 m and you are moving along the boundary of a circular field whose area is double the area of the triangular field, then the radius of the circular field is :

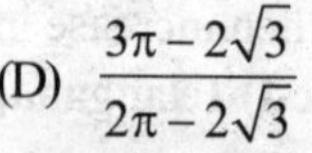
(Take $\pi = \frac{22}{7}$) **[NTSE-2015 (Stage-II)]**

(A) $14\sqrt{3}$ m (B) $3\sqrt{14}$ m
(C) $28\sqrt{3}$ m (D) $7\sqrt{3}$ m

11-172 A circular metallic sheet is divided into two parts in such a way that each part can be folded in to a cone. If the ratio of their curved surface areas is 1 : 2, then the ratio of their volumes is : **[NTSE-2015 (Stage-II)]**

(A) 1:8 (B) $1:\sqrt{6}$

(C) $1:\sqrt{10}$ (D) 2:3

11-173 A solid metallic block of volume one cubic metre is melted and recast into the form of a rectangular bar of length 9 metres having a square base. If the weight of the block is 90 kg and a biggest cube is cut off from the bar, then the weight of the cube is : **[NTSE-2015 (Stage-II)]**

(A) $6\frac{1}{3}$ kg (B) $5\frac{2}{3}$ kg

(C) $4\frac{2}{3}$ kg (D) $3\frac{1}{3}$ kg

11-174 If the area of a square inscribed in a semicircle is 2 cm^2, then the area of the square inscribed in a full circle of the same radius is : **[NTSE-2016 (Stage-II)]**

(A) 5 cm^2 (B) 10 cm^2

(C) $5\sqrt{2}$ cm^2 (D) 25 cm^2

11-175 Shyam wants to make a solid brick shape structure from 400 wooden cubes of unit volume each. If the sides of the solid brick have the ratio 1 : 2 : 3, then the maximum number of cubes, which can be used, will be : **[NTSE-2016 (Stage-II)]**

(A) 400 (B) 288

(C) 300 (D) 384

11-176 A circle is inscribed in a square and the square is circumscribed by another circle. What is the ratio of the areas of the inner circle to the outer circle ? **[NTSE-2017 (Stage-II)]**

(A) 1:2 (B) $1:\sqrt{2}$

(C) $\sqrt{2}:4$ (D) $1:\sqrt{3}$

11-177 The surface of water in a swimming pool, when it is full of water, is rectangular with length and breadth 36 m and 10.5 m respectively. The depth of water increases uniformly from 1 m at one end to 1.75 m at the other end. The water in the pool is emptied by a cylindrical pipe of radius 7 cm at the rate of 5 km/h.

The time (in hours) to empty water in the pool is (take $\pi = \frac{22}{7}$) **[NTSE-2017 (Stage-II)]**

(A) $6\frac{1}{4}$ (B) $\frac{1}{2}$

(C) $6\frac{3}{4}$ (D) $6\frac{4}{5}$

11-178 There is a right circular cone of height h and vertical angle 60°. A sphere when placed inside the cone, it touches the curved surface and the base of the cone. The volume of sphere is : **[NTSE-2017 (Stage-II)]**

(A) $\frac{4}{3}\pi h^3$ (B) $\frac{4}{9}\pi h^3$

(C) $\frac{4}{27}\pi h^3$ (D) $\frac{4}{81}\pi h^3$

11-179 A sealed bottle containing some water is made up of two cylinders A and B of radius 1.5 cm and 3 cm respectively, as shown in the figure-11.53. When the bottle is placed right up on a table, the height of water in it is 15 cm, but when placed upside down, the height of water is 24 cm. The height of the bottle is : **[NTSE-2017 (Stage-II)]**

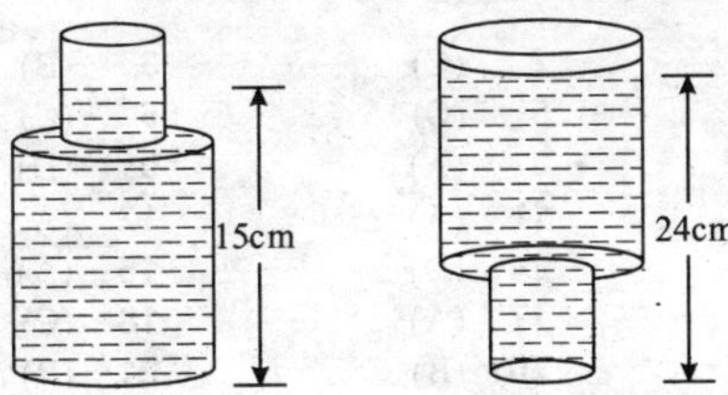

Figure 11.53

(A) 25 cm (B) 26 cm

(C) 27 cm (D) 28 cm

* * * * *

ANSWERS

PRACTICE EXERCISE-11.1

1	(D)	**2**	(B)	**3**	(B)
4	(A)	**5**	(C)	**6**	(C)
7	(C)	**8**	(D)	**9**	(A)
10	(A)	**11**	(A)	**12**	(D)
13	(A)	**14**	(D)	**15**	(C)
16	(C)	**17**	(B)	**18**	(A)
19	(C)	**20**	(A)	**21**	(C)
22	(B)	**23**	(C)	**24**	(B)
25	(B)	**26**	(B)	**27**	(B)
28	(C)	**29**	(A)	**30**	(B)
31	(C)	**32**	(D)	**33**	(A)
34	(B)	**35**	(C)	**36**	(A)
37	(C)	**38**	(B)	**39**	(C)
40	(A)	**41**	(B)	**42**	(C)
43	(B)	**44**	(D)	**45**	(A)
46	(C)	**47**	(C)	**48**	(A)
49	(D)	**50**	(C)		

PRACTICE EXERCISE-11.2

1	(C)	**2**	(B)	**3**	(B)
4	(A)	**5**	(C)	**6**	(B)
7	(A)	**8**	(B)	**9**	(C)
10	(D)	**11**	(C)	**12**	(B)
13	(A)	**14**	(D)	**15**	(B)
16	(D)	**17**	(C)	**18**	(A)
19	(A)	**20**	(B)	**21**	(C)
22	(A)	**23**	(A)	**24**	(D)
25	(C)				

PRACTICE EXERCISE-11.3

1	(A)	**2**	(C)	**3**	(B)
4	(D)	**5**	(C)	**6**	(C)
7	(A)	**8**	(A)	**9**	(D)
10	(B)	**11**	(A)	**12**	(A)
13	(A)	**14**	(D)	**15**	(A)
16	(C)	**17**	(A)	**18**	(C)
19	(B)	**20**	(B)	**21**	(B)
22	(C)	**23**	(D)	**24**	(D)
25	(C)	**26**	(C)	**27**	(B)
28	(C)	**29**	(C)	**30**	(B)
31	(B)	**32**	(B)	**33**	(B)
34	(D)	**35**	(A)	**36**	(C)
37	(B)	**38**	(B)	**39**	(A)
40	(A)	**41**	(D)	**42**	(C)
43	(B)	**44**	(B)	**45**	(D)
46	(C)	**47**	(B)	**48**	(C)
49	(A)	**50**	(C)	**51**	(B)
52	(A)	**53**	(D)	**54**	(D)
55	(C)	**56**	(C)	**57**	(A)
58	(B)	**59**	(D)	**60**	(C)
61	(A)	**62**	(D)	**63**	(B)
64	(A)	**65**	(B)	**66**	(B)
67	(D)	**68**	(B)	**69**	(A)
70	(D)	**71**	(A)	**72**	(B)
73	(C)	**74**	(D)	**75**	(B)
76	(A)	**77**	(C)	**78**	(A)
79	(B)	**80**	(C)	**81**	(C)
82	(B)	**83**	(B)	**84**	(A)
85	(D)	**86**	(C)	**87**	(A)
88	(B)	**89**	(C)	**90**	(C)
91	(D)	**92**	(A)	**93**	(D)
94	(B)	**95**	(A)	**96**	(D)
97	(A)	**98**	(C)	**99**	(A)
100	(C)	**101**	(A)	**102**	(B)
103	(B)	**104**	(A)	**105**	(B)
106	(C)	**107**	(B)	**108**	(A)
109	(B)	**110**	(C)	**111**	(C)
112	(B)	**113**	(D)	**114**	(A)
115	(B)	**116**	(C)	**117**	(C)
118	(A)	**119**	(B)	**120**	(B)
121	(B)	**122**	(A)	**123**	(D)
124	(B)	**125**	(C)	**126**	(C)
127	(D)	**128**	(D)	**129**	(C)
130	(C)	**131**	(D)	**132**	(B)
133	(B)	**134**	(C)	**135**	(B)
136	(D)	**137**	(B)	**138**	(D)
139	(B)	**140**	(A)	**141**	(C)
142	(C)	**143**	(C)	**144**	(A)
145	(A)	**146**	(D)	**147**	(A)
148	(C)	**149**	(C)	**150**	(A)
151	(C)	**152**	(B)	**153**	(C)
154	(D)	**155**	(D)	**156**	(C)
157	(C)	**158**	(B)	**159**	(C)
160	(A)	**161**	(C)	**162**	(B)
163	(B)	**164**	(B)	**165**	(D)
166	(B)	**167**	(C)	**168**	(D)
169	(A)	**170**	(C)	**171**	(A)
172	(C)	**173**	(D)	**174**	(A)
175	(D)	**176**	(A)	**177**	(C)
178	(D)	**179**	(C)		

Solutions of PRACTICE EXERCISE-11.1

Sol. 1 (D) The required area

$$= \pi\frac{120}{360}(12)^2 - \pi\frac{120}{360}(10)^2 \text{ sq. cm}$$

$$= \frac{1}{3}\pi(12^2 - 10^2) \text{ sq. cm}$$

$$= \frac{44\pi}{3} \text{ sq. cm}$$

Hence Ans is (D)

Sol. 2 (B) We know altitude of an equilateral triangle

$$= \frac{\sqrt{3}}{2}a$$

$$\Rightarrow \quad \frac{\sqrt{3}}{2}a = \sqrt{6}$$

$$\Rightarrow \quad a = 2\sqrt{2}$$

$$\Rightarrow \quad \text{Area} = \frac{\sqrt{3}}{4}(2\sqrt{2})^2 = 2\sqrt{3}$$

Hence Ans is (B)

Sol. 3 (B) Volume of cylinder

$= \pi r^2 h = \pi(r)^2(2r)$

$= 2\pi r^3$ cu. m

Volume of sphere $= \frac{4}{3}\pi r^3$ cu. m.

$\Rightarrow$ The empty space $= 2\pi r^3 - \frac{4}{3}\pi r^3$

$= \frac{2}{3}\pi r^3$ cu. m

Hence Ans is (B)

Sol. 4 (A) Let r be the base radius of the cylinder and h be their height. Then,

$$\frac{\text{Volume of cylinder}}{\text{Volume of cone}} = \frac{\pi r^2 h}{\frac{1}{3}\pi(2r)^2 h} = \frac{3}{4}$$

Hence Ans is (A)

Sol. 5 (C) $\frac{\text{New volume}}{\text{Orignal volume}} = \frac{\frac{1}{3}\pi(3r)^2(3h)}{\frac{1}{3}\pi r^2 h}$

$= \frac{27}{1} = 27:1$

Hence Ans is (C)

Sol. 6 (C) The original volume

$= \frac{1}{3}\pi\left(\frac{1}{2}d\right)^2 h = \frac{\pi}{12}d^2 h$

The new volume $= \frac{1}{3}\pi\left[\left(\frac{1}{2}1.1d\right)^2(0.9)h\right]$

$= \frac{\pi}{12}(1.089d^2 h)$

$\Rightarrow$ The increase percentage

$= \frac{1.089d^2h - d^2h}{d^2h} \times 100$

$= 8.9\%$

Hence Ans is (C)

Sol. 7 (C) Let V cu. be the volume of the second cone.

$$\frac{V}{30} = \frac{\frac{1}{3}\pi(2r)^2\left(\frac{1}{3}h\right)}{\frac{1}{3}\pi(r)^2 h} = \frac{4}{3}$$

$\Rightarrow$ $V = \frac{4}{3} \times 30$ cu. cm

$= 40$ cu. cm

Hence Ans is (C)

Sol. 8 (D) Let V and V_1 be the original volume and the new volume respectively

$$\frac{V_1}{V} = \frac{\pi(2r)^2(2h)}{\pi r^2 h} = 8$$

$\Rightarrow$ $V_1 = 8V$

Hence Ans is (D)

Sol. 9 (A) $S_1 = 4\pi r^2$,

$S_2 = 2\pi r \times 2r = 4\pi r^2$

[$\because$ height of the cylinder, in this case, becomes twice the radius of the sphere]

Hence Ans is (A)

Sol. 10 (A) Let r cm be the base radius of the cone.

Length of $arc\ AB = \frac{60}{360} \times [2\pi(6)]$ cm

$= 2\pi$

$\Rightarrow$ $2\pi = 2\pi r$

$\Rightarrow$ $r = 1$ cm

Hence Ans is (A)

Sol. 11 (A) Let r be the radius and h be the height of the cone given volume of hemisphere = volume of cone

$\Rightarrow$ $\frac{2}{3}\pi r^3 = \frac{1}{3}\pi r^2 h$

$2r = h$

$\Rightarrow$ $\frac{h}{r} = \frac{2}{1}$

Hence Ans is (A)

Sol. 12 (D) Ratio of areas $= \left(\frac{p}{2p}\right)^2 = \frac{1}{4} = 1:4$

Hence Ans is (D)

Sol. 13 (A) If the circumference and the area of a circle are numerically equal,

then $\pi r^2 = 2\pi r$

$\Rightarrow$ $r = 2$

$\Rightarrow$ $d = 4$

Hence Ans is (A)

Sol. 14 (D) Let the length of the edge be 'a'

Volume of cube $= a^3$ units

Given $(a)^3 = 12 \times a$

$\Rightarrow$ $a^2 = 12$

$\Rightarrow$ Surface area $= 6 \times a^2 = 6 \times 12$

$= 72$ sq. units

Hence Ans is (D)

Sol. 15 (C) The circular base of the cone will be a circle in the square base

radius of the circle = 3/2 cm

Height of the cone = 3 cm.

Volume of the cone = $1/3\pi \times 9/4 \times 3$

$= 9/4\ \pi$ cu. cm

Hence Ans is (C)

Sol. 16 (C) Area of the shaded portion = Area of the square + Area of the three sectors outside the square – Area of the 3 sectors in the square not shaded

$= (2a)^2 + 3 \times 1/4 \times \pi \times 2a/2 \times 2a/2$

$- 3 \times 1/4 \times \pi \times 2a/2 \times 2a/2$

$= 4a^2 + 3\pi a^2/4 - 3\pi a^2/4$

$= 4a^2$ sq. units

Hence Ans is (C)

Sol. 17 (B) Area of four sectors

$= 4 \times \theta/360 \times \pi r^2$

$= 4 \times 90/360 \times 22/7 \times 3.5 \times 3.5$

$= 11 \times 3.5 = 38.5$ sq. cm

Area of the square $= 7 \times 7 = 49$ sq. cm

$\Rightarrow$ Area of the shaded portion = area of square – area of four sectors

$= 49 - 38.5 = 10.5$ sq. cm

Hence Ans is (B)

Sol. 18 (A) Let the breadth be B. Height $= 5B$

Length $= 8H = 8 \times 5B = 40B$

Volume $= 40B \times 5B \times B = 200\,B^3$

$\Rightarrow \quad 200\,B^3 = 18225$

$\Rightarrow \quad B^3 = 18225/200$

$\Rightarrow \quad B = 9/2$ m

Hence Ans is (A)

Sol. 19 (C)

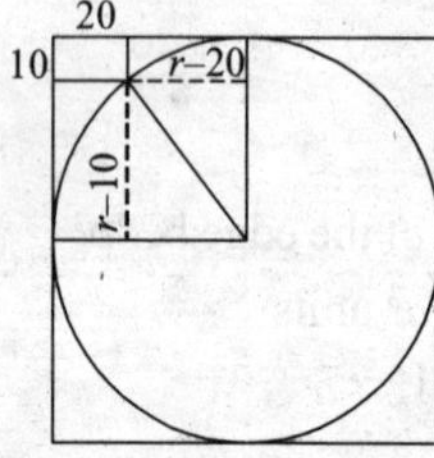

Let the radius be r. Thus we have

$(r-10)^2 + (r-20)^2 = r^2$

i.e., $\quad r^2 - 60r + 500 = 0$

$\Rightarrow \quad (r-50)(r-10) = 0$

$\Rightarrow \quad r = 10$ or 50

The radius of the circle should be 50 cm

Hence Ans is (C)

Sol. 20 (A) Perimeter of a semi-circular plate

$= \frac{1}{2} \times 2\pi r + 2r$

$= \pi r + 2r = r(\pi + 2) = 3.85 \times 36/7 = 19.8$ cm

Hence Ans is (A)

Sol. 21 (C) Perimeter of a quarter of a circle

$= 2r + \frac{1}{4} \times 2\pi r$

$= 2 \times 3.5 + \frac{1}{4} \times 2 \times \left(\frac{22}{7}\right) \times 3.5$

$= 12.5$ cm

Hence Ans is (C)

Sol. 22 (B) Distance covered in one round

= circumference of circle + two parallel sides

$= (22/7 \times 14 + 2 \times 100)\,m = 44 + 200 = 244$ m

Hence Ans is (B)

Sol. 23 (C) We know the total surface area of a cuboid

$= 2(xy + yz + zx)$

Hence Ans is (C)

Sol. 24 (B) Let R be the radius of the new sphere.

Given $\quad 4\left(\frac{4}{3}\pi r^3\right) = \frac{4}{3}\pi R^3,$

$\Rightarrow \quad R^3 = 4r^3,$

$\Rightarrow \quad R = \sqrt[3]{4}r$

Surface area of the new sphere

$= 4\pi(\sqrt[3]{4}r)^2$

$= 4\pi(4^{2/3}\,r^2)$

Surface area of the 4 original spheres

$= 4(4\pi r^2)$

$\Rightarrow \quad$ The required ratio $= \dfrac{4\pi\left(4^{\frac{2}{3}} r^2\right)}{4(4\pi r^2)}$

$= \dfrac{4^{\frac{2}{3}}}{4} = \dfrac{1}{4^{\frac{1}{3}}} = 1 : \sqrt[3]{4}$

Hence Ans is (B)

Sol. 25 (B) Change the diagram as shown below.
Let the side of the smaller square be 1 unit

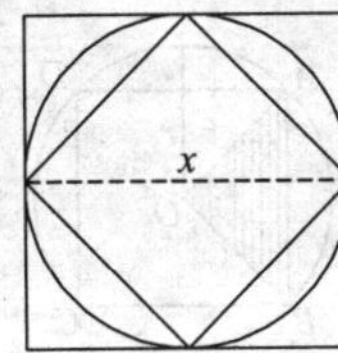

Then $x = \sqrt{2}$ units

Ratio of the areas $= (1)^2 : (\sqrt{2})^2 = 1 : 2$

Hence Ans is (B)

Sol. 26 (B) Join ZO and DO. Let $OY = 1$, then $YZ = 2$ units

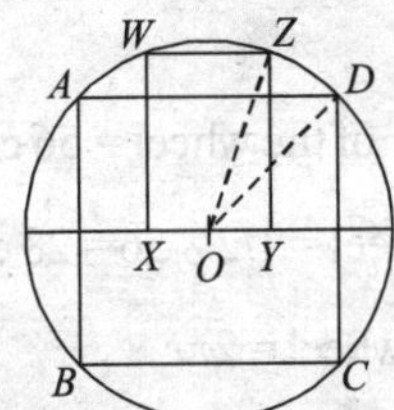

$OZ = \sqrt{1^2 + 2^2}$ units

$= \sqrt{5}$ units

$\Rightarrow$ Diagonal of $ABCD = 2\sqrt{5}$ units

Diagonal of $WXYZ = \sqrt{2^2 + 2^2} = 2\sqrt{2}$

$\Rightarrow$ The required ratio $= (2\sqrt{2})^2 : (2\sqrt{5})^2$

$= 2 : 5$

Hence Ans is (B)

Sol. 27 (B) Volume of solid = volume of cone + volume of hemisphere

$$= \frac{1}{3}\pi(6)^2(10) + \frac{2}{3}\pi(6)^3 \text{ cu.cm}$$

Hence Ans is (B)

Sol. 28 (C) Volume of box $= 15 \times 8 \times 3 = 360$ cu. inches

Volume of a packet of 100 notes

$= 5 \times 2 \times 1/2 = 5$ cu. inches.

$\Rightarrow$ Number of packets $= 360/5 = 72$

$\Rightarrow$ Value of the packet $= 72 \times 1000 =$ Rs. 72000

Hence Ans is (C)

Sol. 29 (A) Volume of the cylinder

$= \pi \times 4^2 \times 10 = 160\pi$ cu. cm

Volume of one cone $= 1/3\pi \times 3^2 \times 4 = 12\pi$ cu. cm

Volume of the remaining part

$= 160\pi - 2 \times 12\pi$ cu. cm

$= 136\pi$ cu. cm

Hence Ans is (A)

Sol. 30 (B) Volume of one sphere

$= 4/3\pi r^3 = 4/3\pi \times 6^3$

$= 288\pi$ cu. cm.

Volume of the cylinder $= \pi r^2 h = \pi \times 4^2 \times 90$

$= 1440\pi$ cu. cm

$\Rightarrow$ Required number of sphere = Volume of the cylinder/Volume of one sphere

$= 1440\pi/288\pi = 5$

Hence Ans is (B)

Sol. 31 (C) Consider ratio of volumes Volume of cone: volume of hemisphere : volume of cylinder

$\Rightarrow$ $1/3\ \pi r^2 h : 1/2 \times 4/3\pi r^3 : \pi r^2 h$

[$h = r$, because height of the hemisphere = height of the cone = height of the cylinder]

$\Rightarrow$ $1/3\pi r^3 : 2/3\pi r^3 : \pi r^3$

$\Rightarrow$ $1 : 2 : 3$

Hence Ans is (C)

Sol. 32 (D) Let the length of the field be x.
Area of the path $= 90(x + 10) - 80x = 38000/20$.

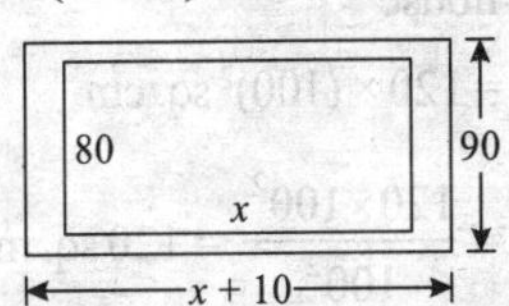

i.e. $10x + 900 = 1900$,

$\Rightarrow$ $x = 100$

Hence Ans is (D)

Sol. 33 (A) Volume $= \frac{2}{3}\pi r^3$

$$= \left(\frac{2}{3} \times \frac{22}{7} \times \frac{21}{2} \times \frac{21}{2} \times \frac{21}{2}\right)$$

$= 2425.5$ cu. cm

Hence Ans is (A)

Sol. 34 (B)

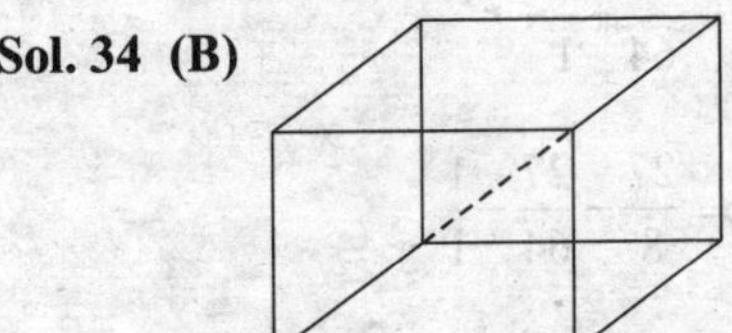

Diagonal $= \sqrt{3} \times a$ (where a is side of the cube)

$= (\sqrt{3} \times 4)$ cm $= (1.732 \times 4)$ cm $= 6.928$ cm

Hence Ans is (B)

Sol. 35 (C) Area of each cut out part is equal

$$= \frac{60}{360} \times \pi r^2 = \frac{1}{6} \times 3.14 \times 16 = 8.37 \text{ sq. cm}$$

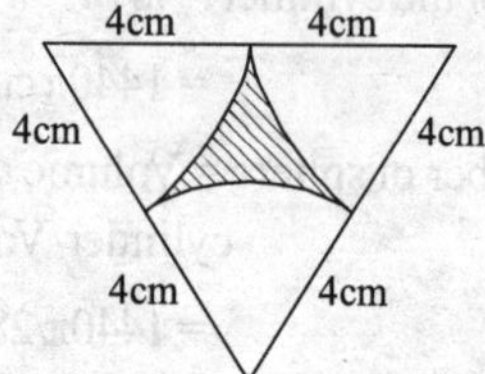

Area of equilateral

$$\Delta = \sqrt{3}/4\, a^2 = \sqrt{3}/4 \times 8^2$$

$$= 16\sqrt{3} \text{ sq. cm}$$

$$\text{Required area} = 16\sqrt{3} - 3(8.37)$$

$$= 27.71 - 25.13 = 2.58 \text{ sq. cm}$$

Hence Ans is (C)

Sol. 36 (A) Scale = 1 : 100.

Actual height of the house

$$= 12 \text{ cm} \times 100 = 1200 \text{ cm} = 12 \text{ m}$$

Actual area of the house

$$= 120 \times (100)^2 \text{ sq. cm}$$

$$= \frac{120 \times 100^2}{100^2} = 120 \text{ sq. m}$$

Actual volume of the house

$$= \frac{700 \times 100^3}{100^3}$$

$$= 700 \text{ cu. m}$$

Hence Ans is (A)

Sol. 37 (C) Let the radius of the third ball be r.
Since volume of bigger ball = volume of all three balls.

$$\Rightarrow \quad \frac{4}{3}\pi \times \left(\frac{3}{2}\right)^3 = \frac{4}{3}\pi \times \left(\frac{3}{4}\right)^3 + \frac{4}{3}\pi \times (1)^3 + \frac{4}{3}\pi \times (r)^3$$

$$\Rightarrow \quad \frac{27}{8} = \frac{27}{64} + \frac{1}{1} + r^3$$

$$\Rightarrow \quad r^3 = \frac{27}{8} - \frac{27}{64} - \frac{1}{1}$$

$$\Rightarrow \quad r^3 = \frac{216 - 27 - 64}{64} = \frac{125}{64}$$

$$\Rightarrow \quad r = d = \frac{5}{2} \text{ Inches}$$

Hence Ans is (C)

Sol. 38 (B) Let O be the centre of the circle. Consider the right-angled triangle AOB

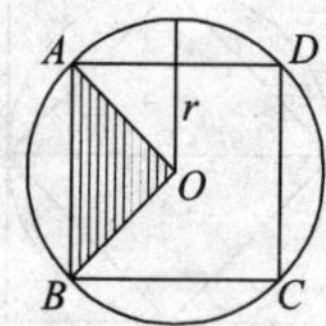

$$OA = r,$$

$$OB = r$$

$$\text{Area of } \Delta AOB = 1/2 \times \text{base} \times \text{height}$$

$$= 1/2 r^2$$

Hence Ans is (B)

Sol. 39 (C) Diameter of the wheel = 56 cm

$\Rightarrow$ Radius of the wheel = 1/2 × 56 = 28 cm

Circumference of the wheel = $2\pi r$

$$= 2 \times 22/7 \times 28 \text{ cm} = 176 \text{ cm}$$

$\Rightarrow$ Distance covered by the wheel in one revolution = 176 cm

Now $\quad 88 \text{ km} = 88 \times 1000 \times 100 \text{ cm}$

Hence the number of times the wheel will rotate

$$= \frac{88 \times 1000 \times 100}{176} = 50000$$

Hence Ans is (C)

Sol. 40 (A) A string of a certain length, when wound on a cylindrical surface, gives a maximum of n turns. It means that every turn in equidistant, starting from 1 to n.

$\Rightarrow$ Vertical distance between two consecutive turns

$$= \frac{\text{height of cylinder}}{\text{number of turns}} = \frac{h}{n}$$

Hence Ans is (A)

Sol. 41 (B) Opening up the four vertical sides of the cube of side n,

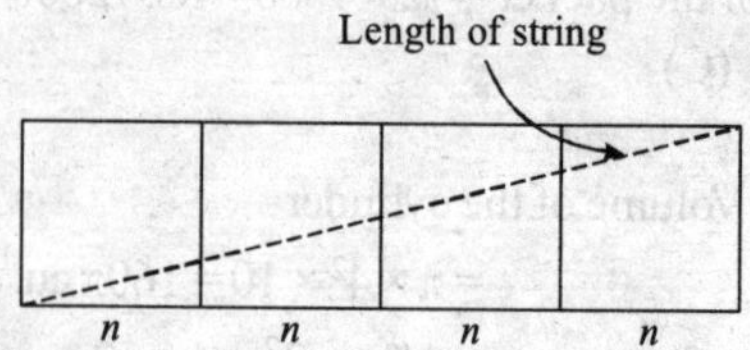

$$\text{Length of string} = \sqrt{(4n)^2 + (n)^2}$$

$$= \sqrt{17} \times n$$

Hence Ans is (B)

Sol. 42 (C) With the help of the string, we wind on the curved surface of the cylinder n times, thus reaching height h of the cylinder. Opening up the cylinder, we get that a length of $\sqrt{17}n$ of string reaches height h after winding the cylinder's circumference n times. Cylindrical circumference = n times the circumference of cross-sectional area

$$= n \times 2 \times \pi \times \frac{2}{\pi} = 4n$$

For the sake of simplicity, we can represent the relationship as below:

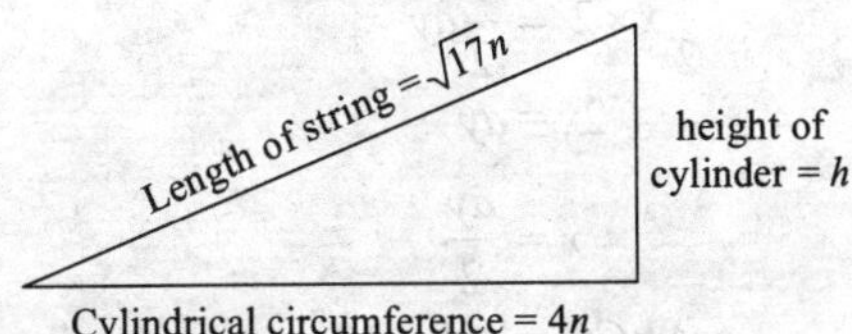

From the above figure,

$$(4n)^2 + (h)^2 = (\sqrt{17}n)^2$$

$\Rightarrow$ $h = n$

Hence Ans is (C)

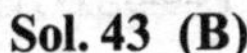

Sol. 43 (B)

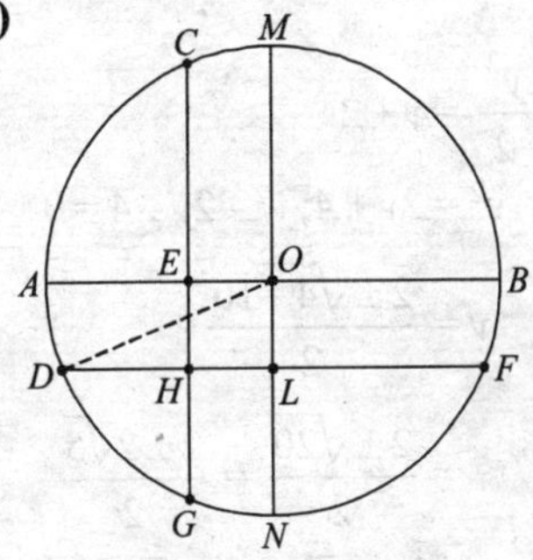

Join point O and point D.

Given $NL : LM = 1:2$

$\Rightarrow$ $NL = 1$ cm

and, $GL = ON - NL = 1.5\text{ cm} - 1\text{ cm}$

$= 0.5$ cm

With the same logic,

$HL = 0.5$ cm

$$DL = \sqrt{OD^2 - OL^2}$$

$$= \sqrt{(1.5)^2 - (0.5)^2}$$

$$= \sqrt{2.25 - 0.25} = \sqrt{2}$$

$\Rightarrow$ $DH = DL - HL$

$$= \sqrt{2} - 0.5 = \sqrt{2} - \frac{1}{2}$$

$$= \frac{2\sqrt{2} - 1}{2}\text{ cm}$$

Hence Ans is (B)

Sol. 44 (D) Height of the cuboid is 7 cm. Then area of the corresponding rectangular cross-section

$$= \frac{2520}{7} = 360\text{ cm}$$

Also, the sides of the cuboid are of integral unit. Therefore number of different possible rectangles whose sides are of integral unit is equal to the number of cuboids (height of cuboid is fixed).

Now, we have to find in how many ways we can express 360 as the product of two positive integers.

$$360 = 2 \times 2 \times 2 \times 3 \times 3 \times 5 = 2^3 \times 3^2 \times 5^1$$

Therefore required number of ways

$$= \frac{1}{2}(3+1)(2+1) + (1+1) = 12$$

Therefore, the number of possible cuboids = 12

Hence Ans is (D)

Sol. 45 (A) $2520 = 2^3 \times 3^2 \times 5^1 \times 7^1$

2520 can be expressed as the product of three positive integers ($l \times b \times h$) in many possible ways.

Also, we have to find the biggest possible length which can be put inside the cuboid of given volume, is maximum value of $l^2 + b^2 + h^2$.

It means that, we have to find the value of l, b and h such that $l \times b \times h = 2520$ and $l^2 + b^2 + h^2$ is maximum.

By trial and error method, $l^2 + b^2 + h^2$ is maximum when $l = 1$, $b = 1$ and $h = 2520$.

$$\Rightarrow D = \sqrt{1^2 + 1^2 + 2520^2} = \sqrt{1 + 1 + 6350400}$$

$$= \sqrt{6350402} \approx 2520\text{ units}$$

(slightly greater than 2520 units)

Hence Ans is (A)

Sol. 46 (C) In the above solution, we have to find the least possible value of $l^2 + b^2 + h^2$

$$2520 = 2^3 + 3^2 \times 5^1 \times 7^1$$

For the least value of $l^2 + b^2 + h^2$, l, b and h must be balanced, ie they should be near to each other.

Now, by trial and error method, the possible triplets are (8, 15, 21), (8, 9, 35), (12, 14, 15), … and so on ($l^2 + b^2 + h^2$) is minimum when difference among values are least. So the smallest possible rod

$$= \sqrt{12^2 + 14^2 + 15^2} = 23.77 \approx 23$$

Hence Ans is (C)

Sol. 47 (C) The height of the cuboid is 5 cm. The area of the corresponding rectangular cross-section

$$= \frac{2520}{5} = 504 \text{ cm}^2$$

and $504 = 2 \times 2 \times 2 \times 3 \times 3 \times 7 = 2^3 \times 3^2 \times 7$

504 can be expressed as the product of two positive integers in $\frac{1}{2}(3+1)(2+1)(1+1) = 12$ ways

We can put the resulting cuboid in the cubical box (37 cm × 37 cm × 37 cm), if both the factors of 504 are less than 37 cm. Out of 12 ways, only 3 ways ie (18 × 28), (21 × 24) and (36 × 14) have both factors less than 37 cm.

Therefore required number of cuboids which can't be put inside the cubical box = 12 – 3 = 9

Hence Ans is (C)

Sol. 48 (A) If height of the cuboid is 8 cm then the area of the corresponding rectangle = 315

And $315 = 5 \times 3 \times 3 \times 7 = 3^2 \times 5^1 \times 7$

315 can be expressed as the product of two positive integers in $\frac{1}{2}(2+1)(1+1)(1+1) = 6$ ways

Possible factors of 315 in which both the factors are less than 30 cm are (9 × 35) and (15 × 21)

$\Rightarrow \quad N_1 = 2$

Similarly, N_2 = possible factors of $\frac{2520}{9}$, ie 280, in which both the factors are less than 36

= {ie (8 × 35), (14 × 20) and (28 × 10)}

Similarly, N_3 = Possible factors of $\frac{2520}{6}$, ie 420, in which both the factors are less than 36

= 4{ie (12 × 35), (14 × 30), (21 × 20) and (15 × 28)}

Out of 12 ways of expressing 420 as the product of two positive integers only 4 ways are applicable.

$\Rightarrow N_1 < N_2 < N_3$

Hence Ans is (A)

Sol. 49 (D) As height of the pile is given, once we know the number of sheets, the thickness of one sheet can be calculated.

Hence Ans is (D)

Sol. 50 (C) Let rise in water level = h cm

then volume of water level rise = volume of the cube immersed

$\Rightarrow \quad 20 \times 40 \times h = 20 \times 20 \times 20$

$\Rightarrow \quad h = 10$ cm

Hence Ans is (C)

Solutions of PRACTICE EXERCISE-11.2

Sol. 1 (C)

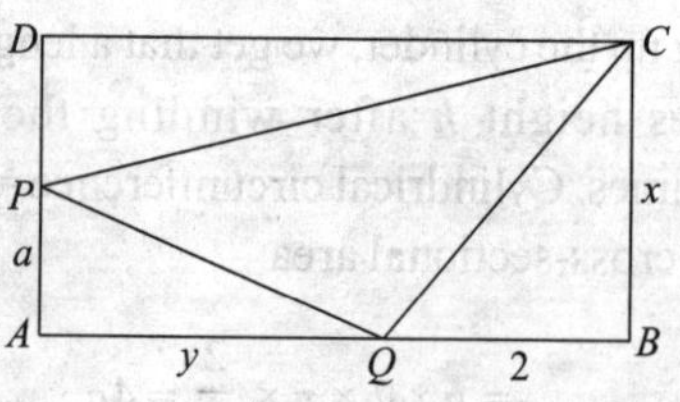

Let $AQ = y$

$ar\Delta BCQ = ar\Delta APQ$

$$\frac{1}{2}x \times 2 = \frac{1}{2}ay$$

$$2x = ay$$

$$x = \frac{ay}{2} \quad \ldots(1)$$

$ar\Delta BCQ = ar\Delta PDC$

$$\frac{1}{2} \times 2 \times x = \frac{1}{2}(x-a)(y+2)$$

$$2x = xy + 2x - ay - 2a$$

$$xy = ay + 2a$$

$$\frac{ay}{2} \times y = ay + 2a \quad \text{[Using (1)]}$$

$$\frac{y^2}{2} = y + 2$$

$$y^2 = 2y + 4; y^2 - 2y - 4 = 0$$

$$y = \frac{2 \pm \sqrt{4+16}}{2}$$

$$= \frac{2 \pm \sqrt{20}}{2} = \frac{2 \pm 2\sqrt{5}}{2}$$

Since $= 1 \pm \sqrt{5} = 1 \pm \sqrt{5}$

Hence Ans is (C)

Sol. 2 (B)

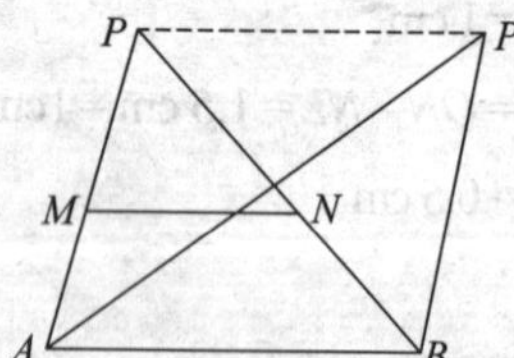

As P moves parallel to AB, only the perimeter of ΔPAB is changing and all the remaining option remains unchanged. Because.

→ (A) As AB remain same so length of line segment

$$MN = \frac{1}{2}AB$$

is also remains same

→ (C) As the P move parallel to AB. So its height remain same so area ΔPAB also remain same.

→ (D) As AB, MN remain same

⇒ area of trapezium $ABMN$ remain same

Hence Ans is (B)

Sol. 3 (B)

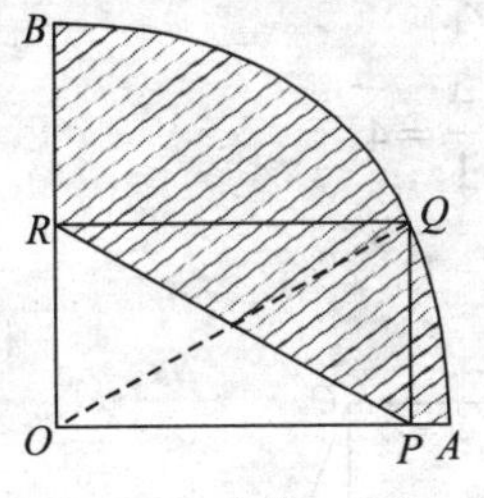

$$RP = OQ = r = 10$$

perimeter of

$$OPQR = 26$$
$$2(l+b) = 26$$
$$l+b = 13$$

Perimeter of shaded protion

$$= PA + \widehat{AQB} + BR + RP$$
$$= r - l + \frac{2\pi r}{4} + r - b + r$$
$$= 3r - (l+b) + \frac{\pi r}{2}$$
$$= 3 \times 10 - 13 + \frac{\pi \times 10}{2}$$
$$= 30 - 13 + 5\pi = 17 + 5\pi$$

Hence Ans is (B)

Sol. 4 (A)

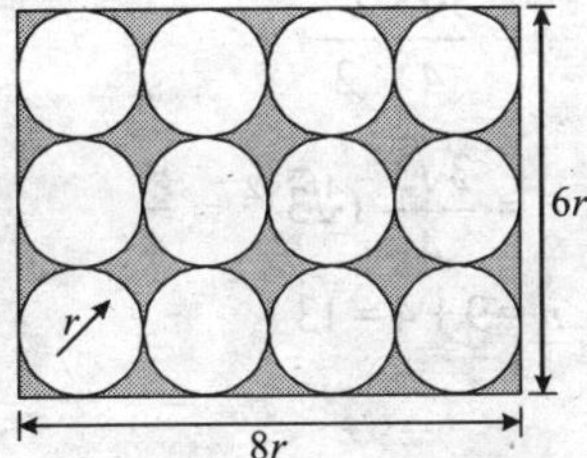

$$\text{diagonal} = \sqrt{(8r)^2 + (6r)^2} = 10r$$
$$2\pi r = 16\pi$$
$$r = 8$$
$$\text{diagonal} = 10 \times 8 = 80$$

Hence Ans is (A)

Sol. 5 (C)

Given $\quad ay = 10$

& $\quad xb = 6$

$$(x-a)(y-b) = 8$$
$$xy - ay - bx + ab = 8$$
$$xy - 10 - 6 + ab = 8$$
$$xy + ab = 24$$

$$xy - 12 = 12 - ab \quad \ldots(1)$$
$$xy + ab = 24$$
$$\frac{10}{a} \times \frac{6}{b} + ab = 24$$
$$a^2b^2 - 24ab + 60 = 0$$
$$ab = \frac{24 \pm \sqrt{576 - 240}}{2}$$
$$= \frac{24 \pm 2\sqrt{84}}{2}$$
$$= 12 - \sqrt{84}$$
$$12 - ab = \sqrt{84} \quad \ldots(2)$$

By compairing (1) & (2)

$$ab = \sqrt{84}$$
$$\Rightarrow \quad \sqrt{x} = \sqrt{84}$$
$$\Rightarrow \quad x = 84$$

Hence Ans is (C)

Sol. 6 (B)

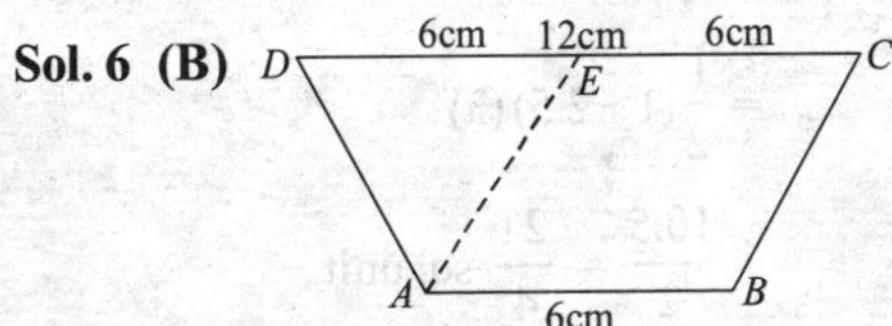

Construction: $AE \parallel BC$

So, $\quad AE = BC = AD$

or, $\quad DE = AB = 6$ unit

Area of trapezium

$$= \frac{1}{2}h(a+b) = 36$$
$$\frac{1}{2}h(6+12) = 36$$
$$h \times 9 = 36$$
$$h = 4\text{ cm}$$

If $\quad AE = a = AD$

$$\text{Area of } \Delta AED = \frac{1}{2} \times 6 \times 4$$
$$= \sqrt{(a+3)(a+3-a)(a+3-a)(a+3-6)}$$
$$12 = 3\sqrt{(a+3)(a-3)}$$
$$a^2 - 9 = 16$$
$$a^2 = 25$$
$$a = 5$$

So, $\quad BC = 5\text{cm}$

Hence Ans is (B)

Sol. 7 (A) Given

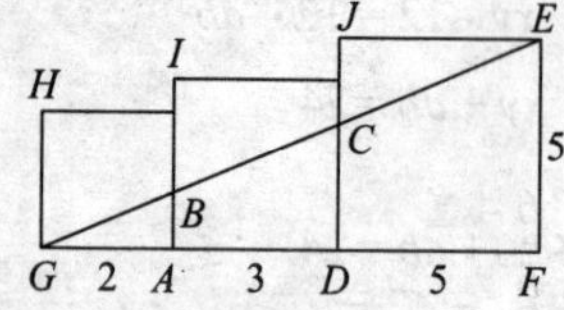

$$\Delta GCD \sim \Delta GEF$$

$$\frac{CD}{EF} = \frac{GD}{GF}$$

$$\frac{CD}{5} = \frac{5}{10}$$

$$CD = 2.5$$

$$\Delta GBA \sim \Delta GCD$$

$$\frac{AB}{CD} = \frac{GA}{GD}$$

$$\frac{AB}{2.5} = \frac{2}{5}$$

$$AB = 1$$

Area of the trapezium $ABCD$

$$= \frac{1}{2}(AB + CD)(AD)$$

$$= \frac{1}{2}(1 + 2.5)(3)$$

$$= \frac{10.5}{2} = \frac{21}{4} \text{ sq. unit}$$

Hence Ans is (A)

Sol. 8 (B) Perimeter of the ΔPQR

$$= PQ + QR + PR$$

$$= PQ + QX + XR + PR$$

$$= PQ + QM + PR + RN$$

$$[QM = QX \;\&\; XR = RN]$$

$$= PM + PN = 10 + 17 = 27 \text{ cm}$$

Hence Ans is (B)

Sol. 9 (C)

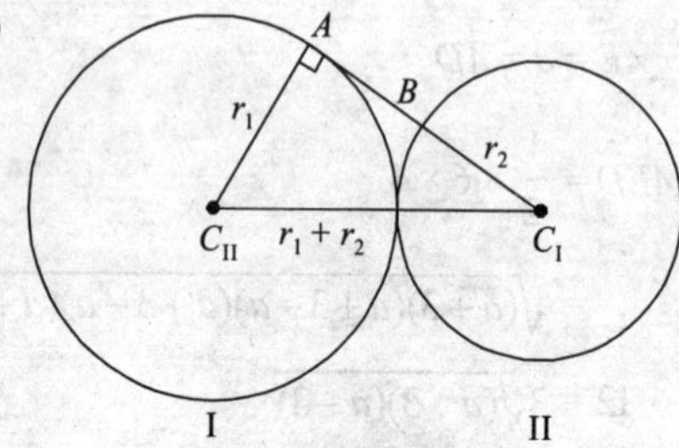

Now In $\Delta AC_I C_{II}$ we have

$$(C_I C_{II})^2 = (AC_I)^2 + (AC_{II})^2$$

$$\Rightarrow \quad (r_1 + r_2)^2 = r_1^2 + (3r_2)^2$$

$$\Rightarrow \quad r_1^2 + r_2^2 + 2r_1 r_2 = r_1^2 + 9r_2^2$$

$$\Rightarrow \quad 8r_2^2 = 2r_1 r_2$$

$$\Rightarrow \quad 4r_2 = r_1$$

$$\Rightarrow \quad \frac{r_1}{r_2} = \frac{4}{1} = 4$$

Hence Ans is (C)

Sol. 10 (D)

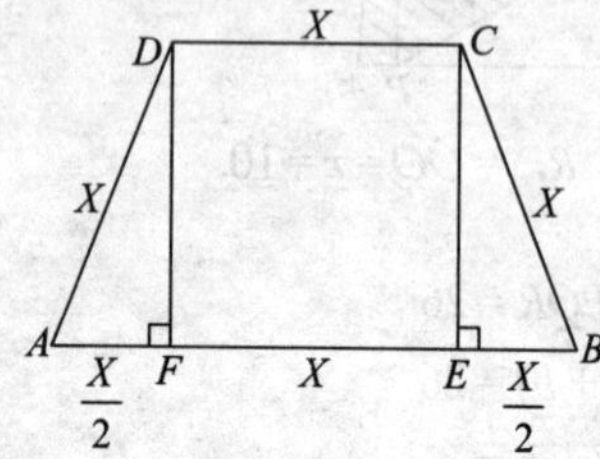

Given sides length of trapezium $= 4\sqrt{3}$

Let $4\sqrt{3} = x$

from the figure

$$DF = \sqrt{AD^2 - AF^2}$$

$$= \sqrt{x^2 - \frac{x^2}{4}} = \frac{\sqrt{3}x}{2}$$

Area of trapezium $= \frac{1}{2}$ (sum of parallel sides) $\times$ distance between them

$$\Rightarrow \quad = \frac{1}{2}(3x)\frac{\sqrt{3}x}{2}$$

$$\Rightarrow \quad = \frac{3\sqrt{3}}{4}\frac{x^2}{2}$$

$$\Rightarrow \quad = \frac{3\sqrt{3}}{4}(\sqrt[4]{3})^2 = \frac{9}{4}$$

$$\Rightarrow \quad m + n = 9 + 4 = 13$$

Hence Ans is (D)

Sol. 11 (C)

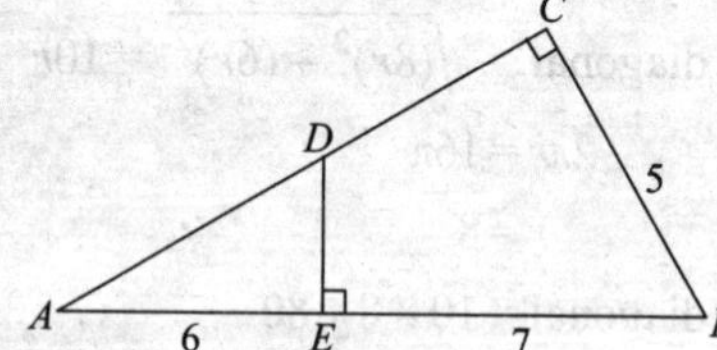

In ΔABC

$$AC = \sqrt{13^2 - 5^2} = 12$$

$$\Delta AED \sim \Delta ACB \quad \text{(By } AA\text{)}$$

$$\frac{AE}{AC} = \frac{ED}{CB}$$

$$\frac{6}{12} = \frac{ED}{5}$$

$$ED = 2.5$$

area of quadrilateral $EBCD$ = area ΔABC – areaΔAED

$$= \frac{1}{2} \times 5 \times 12 - \frac{1}{2} \times 6 \times 2.5$$

$$= 30 - 7.5 = 22.5$$

Hence Ans is (C)

Sol. 12 (B) Required area $= \left(\frac{1}{2}\times\frac{22}{7}\times 28\times 28\right)$

$$-\left[\left(2\times\frac{1}{2}\times\frac{22}{7}\times 14\times 14\right)+\left(\frac{22}{7}\times 7\times 7\right)\right]$$

$= 462\text{ cm}^2$

Hence Ans is (B)

Sol. 13 (A) From the figure, Area of segment *AMO*

= Area of segment *ONB*

⇒ We can say. Area of shaded portion = Area of semicircle with diameter *AB*.

Area of shaded portion is given by

$$= \frac{\pi(14)^2}{2} = \frac{196\pi}{2} = 98\pi\text{ cm}^2$$

Hence Ans is (A)

Sol. 14 (D) Let the side of the hexagon be a and of square be *b* then It's given

$$6a = 4b$$

$$\frac{a}{b} = \frac{2}{3}$$

$$\Rightarrow \quad \frac{b}{a} = \frac{3}{2}$$

then ratio of areas of square & hexagon

$$= \frac{b^2}{6\times\frac{\sqrt{3}}{4}\times a^2}$$

$$= \frac{3}{2\sqrt{3}}$$

Hence Ans is (D)

Sol. 15 (B) Let

$$l = 3x,\ b = 2x \text{ and } h = x$$

Now, Lateral Surface Area

$$= 2(3x+2x)x$$

$$= 10x^2$$

$$l = 6x,\ b = x,\ h = \frac{x}{2}$$

New Lateral Surface Area

$$= 2\left(\frac{x}{2}\right)(6x+x) = 7x^2$$

Decrease in Lateral Surface Area

$$= 10x^2 - 7x^2 = 3x^2$$

Decrease $\% = \frac{3x^2}{10x^2}\times 100 = 30\%$

Hence Ans is (B)

Sol. 16 (D) Let radius = r and height = h

New radius $= r + \frac{r}{2} = \frac{3}{2}r$

New height $= h - \frac{20h}{100} = \frac{4h}{5}$

Volume of original cylinder

$$(V_1) = \pi r^2 h$$

Volume of new cylinder

$$(V_2) = \pi\left(\frac{3}{2}r\right)^2 \times \left(\frac{4h}{5}\right)$$

$$= \pi\times\frac{9}{4}r^2\times\frac{4h}{5} = \frac{9}{5}\pi r^2 h$$

Percentage change in Volume

$$= \frac{V_2 - V_1}{V_1}\times 100$$

$$= \frac{\frac{9}{5}\pi r^2 h - \pi r^2 h}{\pi r^2 h}\times 100$$

$$= \frac{\pi r^2 h\left[\frac{9}{5}-1\right]}{\pi r^2 h}\times 100$$

$$= \frac{9-5}{5}\times 100$$

$$= 80\%$$

Hence Ans is (D)

Sol. 17 (C)

Cube-B	**Cube- A**
Assume surface area of Cube-B with side 'a'= 100	Given surface area of Cube-A with side 'a' is 64% of cube-B
⇒ $6a^2 = 100$	⇒ $6(a')^2 = 64$
⇒ $a = \frac{10}{\sqrt{6}}$	$a' = \frac{8}{\sqrt{6}}$
& $v = \left(\frac{10}{\sqrt{6}}\right)^3$	$v' = \frac{512}{6\sqrt{6}}$
$= \frac{1000}{6\sqrt{6}}$	

given $\quad v' = k\%$ of v

$$\frac{512}{6\sqrt{6}} = \frac{k}{100}\times\frac{1000}{6\sqrt{6}}$$

$$\Rightarrow \quad k = 51.2\%$$

Hence Ans is (C)

Sol. 18 (A) $R = 4\text{ m} \,\&\, r = 2\text{ m} \,\&\, h = 6\text{ m}$

$$\Rightarrow \quad \text{Capacity} = \frac{\pi h}{3}(R^2 + r^2 + Rr)$$

$$= \frac{22}{7} \times \frac{1}{3} \times 6\,(16 + 4 + 8)$$

$$= 176\text{ m}^3$$

Hence Ans is (A)

Sol. 19 (A) Let radius of cone $= R$ & its height $= H$.

$$\text{Its volume} = \frac{1}{3}\pi R^2 H$$

Radius of $A = (R/2)$ & Height of $A = (H/2)$

$$\Rightarrow \quad \text{Volume of } A = \frac{1}{3}\pi\left(\frac{R}{2}\right)^2\left(\frac{H}{2}\right)$$

$$= \frac{1}{24}\pi R^2 H$$

$$\Rightarrow \quad \text{Volume of } B = \frac{1}{3}\pi R^2 H - \frac{1}{24}\pi R^2 H$$

$$= \frac{7}{24}\pi R^2 H$$

$$\Rightarrow \quad \text{Vol. } A < \text{Vol. } B$$

Hence Ans is (A)

Sol. 20 (B) Volume flown $= \frac{1}{3}\pi \times (20)^2 \times 24 = 3200\pi$

$$\text{Volume flown in 1 min.} = \left(\pi \times \frac{2.5}{10} \times \frac{2.5}{10} \times 1000\right)$$

$$= 62.5\pi$$

$$\Rightarrow \quad \text{Time Taken} = \frac{3200\pi}{62.5\pi} = 51 \text{ min. } 12 \text{ sec}$$

Hence Ans is (B)

Sol. 21 (C) V_1 $\qquad$ V_2

$2\pi r_1 = a_1$ $\qquad$ $2\pi r_2 = a_2$

$h_1 = a$ $\qquad$ $h_2 = a_1$

$$\frac{v_1}{v_2} = \frac{\pi r_1^2 h_1}{\pi r_2^2 h_2}$$

$$= \left(\frac{r_1}{r_2}\right)^2 \times \frac{h_1}{h_2}$$

$$= \frac{v_1}{v_2} = \left(\frac{a_1}{a_2}\right)^2 \times \frac{a_2}{a_1}$$

$$= \frac{v_1}{v_2} = \frac{a_1}{a_2}$$

$$v_1 a_2 = v_2 a_1$$

Hence Ans is (C)

Sol. 22 (A) As $(4, k)$ lies on line

$$y = 6 - x$$

$$\Rightarrow \quad k = 6 - 4 = 2$$

$P(4, 2)$

$$r = 4$$
$$h = 2$$
$$V = \pi r^2 h$$
$$= 32\pi$$

Hence Ans is (A)

Sol. 23 (A)

2.4m, 1.2m, 15m

Area of cross section

$$= \frac{1}{2} \times 15 \times [1.2 + 2.4]$$

$$= 27\text{ m}^2$$

$$\text{volume} = \text{area} \times \text{height}$$

$$= 27\text{ m}^2 \times 40\text{ m}$$

$$= 1080\text{ m}^3$$

Hence Ans is (A)

Sol. 24 (D) Given

$$S_{\text{cone.}} = S_{\text{cylinder}}$$

$$\pi rl + \pi r^2 = 2\pi rh' + 2\pi r^2$$

$$l + r = 2h' + 2r$$

$$l^2 = r^2 + h^2$$

$$l^2 - r^2 = h^2$$

Now $\sqrt{\dfrac{(l-r)}{(l+r)}}$

$$= \sqrt{\frac{(l-r)^2}{l^2 - r^2}}$$

$$= \sqrt{\frac{(2h')^2}{h^2}}$$

$$= \frac{2h'}{h}$$

Hence Ans is (D)

Sol. 25 (C)

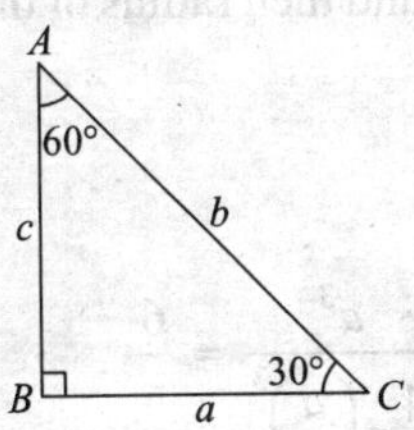

Given that $a+b+c=15+5\sqrt{3}$ ...(1)

Now, from sine rule

$$\frac{\sin 60°}{a}=\frac{\sin 30°}{c}=\frac{\sin 90°}{b}$$

$$=x(\text{say})$$

$$\Rightarrow \quad a=\frac{\sqrt{3}}{2x},$$

$$b=\frac{1}{x}$$

& $$c=\frac{1}{2x}$$

Now, $$a+b+c=\frac{\sqrt{3}}{2x}+\frac{1}{x}+\frac{1}{2x}$$

$$\Rightarrow \quad 15+5\sqrt{3}=\frac{\sqrt{3}+2+1}{2x}$$

$$\Rightarrow \quad x=\frac{1}{10}$$

So, the hypotenuse is

$$b=10$$

Hence Ans is (C)

Solutions of PRACTICE EXERCISE-11.3

Sol. 1 (A)

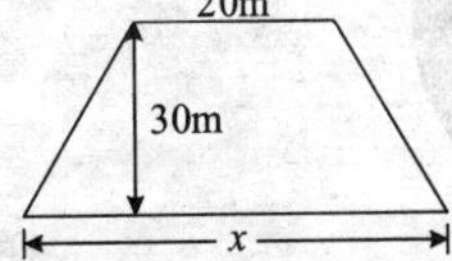

Let the other parallel side is 'x' then Area of trapezium = $\frac{1}{2}$(sum of parallel sides) × distance between parallel sides

$$960=\frac{1}{2}(20+x)\times 30$$

$$\frac{960\times 2}{30}-20=x$$

$$x=64-20=44\text{ m}$$

Hence Ans is (A)

Sol. 2 (C) Area of rhombus = $\frac{1}{2}$ product of diagonals

$$\text{Area of one tile}=\frac{1}{2}\times 45\times 30=675\text{ cm}^2$$

$$\text{total Area of 1500 tiles}=1500\times 675$$

$$=1012500\text{ cm}^2$$

$$=101.25\text{ m}^2$$

$$\text{Total cost}=101.25\times 4=405\text{ Rs}$$

Hence Ans is (C)

Sol. 3 (B) Let side of cube = a

$$6a^2=600$$

$$a=10$$

$$\text{Volume of cube}=a^3=(10)^3=1000\text{ cm}^3$$

Hence Ans is (B)

Sol. 4 (D) Let side of a cube = a

then volume = a^3

New side of a cube = $2a$

then new volume = $(2a)^3=8a^3$

Hence Ans is (D)

Sol. 5 (C)

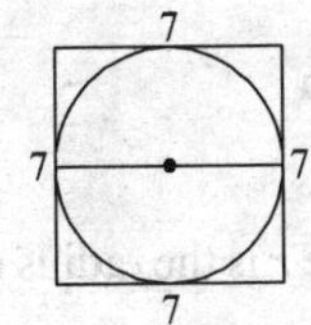

$$2r=7$$

$$r=\frac{7}{2}\text{ cm}$$

$$C=2\pi r=2\times\frac{22}{7}\times\frac{7}{2}$$

$$=22\text{ cm}$$

Hence Ans is (C)

Sol. 6 (C) Solid shapes are three-dimensional figures.

Hence Ans is (C)

Sol. 7 (A) Curved surface area of cylinder = $2\pi rh$

Given $2\pi rh=4.4$

$$2\times\frac{22}{7}\times(.7)h=4.4$$

$$h=1\text{ m}$$

Hence Ans is (A)

Sol. 8 (A) Volume of the frustum whose base radii is r & R and whose height is h is given by

$$V = \frac{1}{3}\pi[R^2 + r^2 + Rr] \times h$$

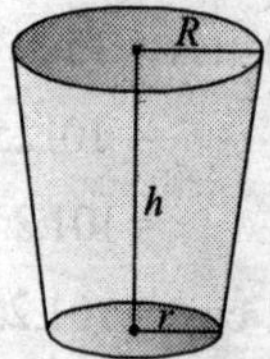

Capacity of glass

$$= \frac{1}{3}\pi(1^2 + 2^2 + 1 \times 2) \times 14$$

$$= \frac{1}{3} \times \frac{22}{7}[7] \times 14$$

$$= \frac{308}{3}$$

$$= 102\frac{2}{3}\text{ cm}^3$$

Hence Ans is (A)

Sol. 9 (D) Area of square = 121 m^2

So, side = 11 m

Perimeter of square = 44 m

So, circumference of circle = 44 cm

$2\pi r = 44$

(where r is the radius of a circle)

$r = 7$ m

area of circle $= \pi r^2 = \pi \times 7 \times 7 = 49\pi$

Hence Ans is (D)

Sol. 10 (B) Here ΔABC will be Right angled triangle because

$$40^2 = 24^2 + 32^2$$

$$\text{Area} = \frac{1}{2} \times 24 \times 32 = 384\text{ m}^2$$

Hence Ans is (B)

Sol. 11 (A)

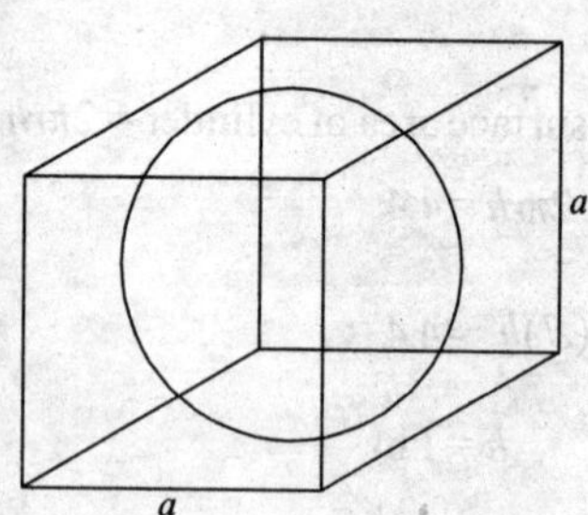

Let the side of the cube be a and then radius of the sphere will be $\frac{a}{2}$

$$\frac{\text{Volume of cube}}{\text{Volume of sphere}} = \frac{a^3}{\frac{4}{3}\pi\left(\frac{a}{2}\right)^3} = \frac{6}{\pi}$$

Hence Ans is (A)

Sol. 12 (A) Let the radius of the sphere be r

Curved Surface Area of sphere $= 4\pi r^2$

New radius will be $r - 25\%\, r = \frac{3}{4}r$

new Curved Surface Area

$$= 4\pi\left(\frac{3r}{4}\right)^2$$

$$= 4\pi r^2 \times \frac{9}{16}$$

$$\%\text{ decrease is} = \frac{\text{Old Area} - \text{New Area}}{\text{Old Area}}$$

$$\%\text{ decrease} = \frac{4\pi r^2\left(1 - \frac{9}{16}\right)}{4\pi r^2} \times 100$$

$$= \frac{700}{16} = 43.75\%$$

Hence Ans is (A)

Sol. 13 (A)

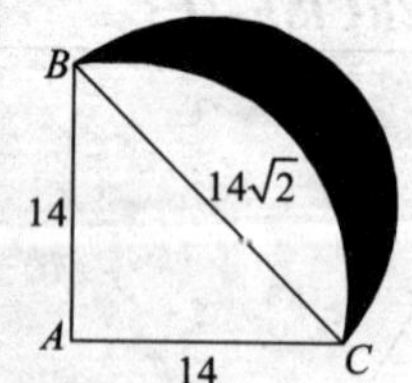

Area of shaded region

= Area of semi-circle with BC as diameter – [Area of quadrant of radius AB – ar ΔABC]

$$= \frac{1}{2} \times \frac{22}{7}(7\sqrt{2})^2$$

$$- \left[\frac{1}{4} \times \frac{22}{7}(14)^2 - \frac{1}{2} \times 14 \times 14\right]$$

$$= 98\text{ m}^2$$

Hence Ans is (C)

Sol. 14 (D) Since $IDEFGH$ is a regular hexagon so it has 6 equilateral triangle in side it

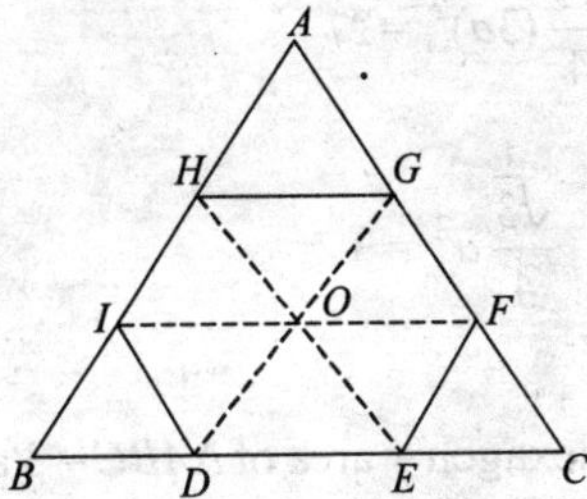

Area of regular hexagon $= 6 \times$ area of equilateral triangle

We have $DE = \frac{1}{3} BC = \frac{1}{3} \times 6 = 2$

So area of hexagon will be $6 \times \frac{\sqrt{3}}{4} \times a^2$

$$= 6 \times \frac{\sqrt{3}}{4} \times 2^2 = 6\sqrt{3}$$

Hence Ans is (D)

Sol. 15 (A) Radius of the inscribed circle

$$r = \frac{\Delta}{s}$$

$\Rightarrow$ $$r = \frac{\frac{\sqrt{3}}{4} \times (2\sqrt{3})^2}{3\sqrt{3}} = 1$$

As D, E, F are the mid-points of the repective sides so ΔDEF will also be equilateral triangle

As ABC is an equilateral triangle

$$DF = \frac{1}{2} BC = \frac{1}{2} \times 2\sqrt{3} = \sqrt{3}$$

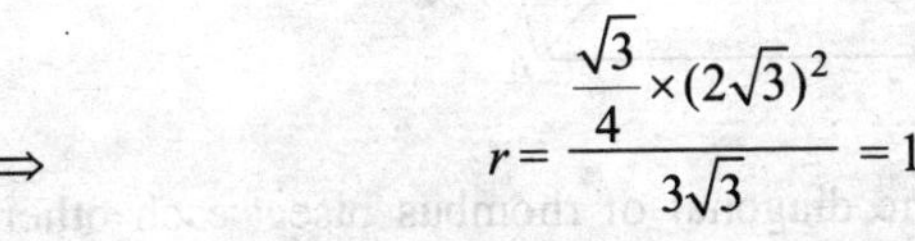

$\Rightarrow$ Shaded area = area of circle – area of equilateral triangle of sides DF

$$= \pi r^2 - \frac{\sqrt{3}}{4} DF^2$$

$\Rightarrow$ $$\pi - \frac{\sqrt{3}}{4} \times (\sqrt{3})^2 = \pi - \frac{3\sqrt{3}}{4}$$

Hence Ans is (A)

Sol. 16 (C) Let the radius of the cylinder be r and height be h also the radius of each sphere be R

Volume a cylinder $= n \times$ volume of each sphere

$$\pi r^2 h = n \times \frac{4}{3} \pi R^3$$

$\Rightarrow$ $$3^2 \times 10 = n \times \frac{4}{3}\left(\frac{1}{2}\right)^3$$

$\Rightarrow$ $$90 = n \times \frac{4}{3} \times \frac{1}{8}$$

$\Rightarrow$ $$n = 540$$

Hence Ans is (C)

Sol. 17 (A)

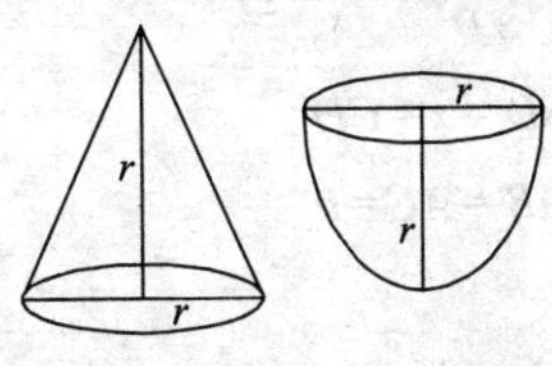

$$\frac{\text{volume}_{\text{cone}}}{\text{volume}_{\text{hemisphere}}} = \frac{\frac{1}{3}\pi r^3}{\frac{2}{3}\pi r^3} = \frac{1}{2}$$

Hence Ans is (A)

Sol. 18 (C)

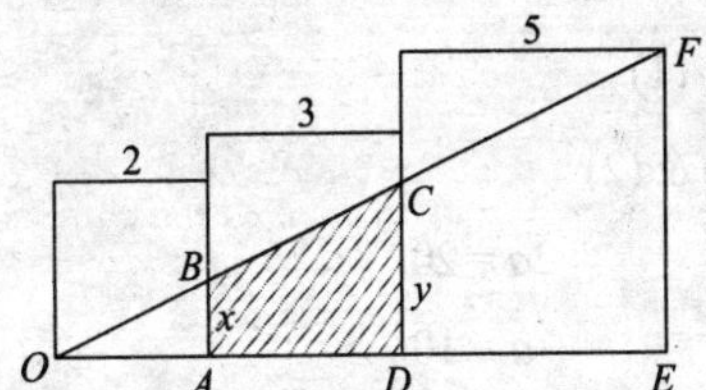

Given three square of dimension 2, 3 & 5 respectively let $AB = x$ & $CD = y$

$$\Delta OAB \sim \Delta OEF \text{ (AA similarly)}$$

$\Rightarrow$ $$\frac{OA}{OE} = \frac{AB}{EF}$$

$\Rightarrow$ $$\frac{2}{10} = \frac{x}{5}$$

$\Rightarrow$ $$x = 1$$

Similarly $\Delta OCD \sim \Delta OEF$

$\Rightarrow$ $$\frac{OD}{OE} = \frac{CD}{EF}$$

$\Rightarrow$ $$\frac{5}{10} = \frac{y}{5}$$

$\Rightarrow$ $$y = \frac{5}{2}$$

Now area of $ABCD$ = area of ΔODC – area of ΔOAB

$$= \frac{1}{2} \times 5 \times y - \frac{1}{2} \times 2 \times x$$

$$= \frac{1}{2} \times 5 \times \frac{5}{2} - \frac{1}{2} \times 2 \times 1$$

$$= \frac{25}{4} - 1 \Rightarrow \frac{21}{4}$$

Hence Ans is (C)

Sol. 19 (B)

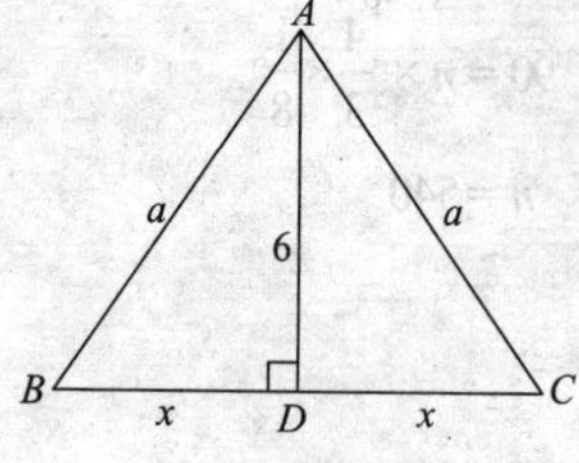

Let $BD = x = CD$

& $AB = AC = a$

Given

$$2a + 2x = 36$$

$$a + x = 18 \quad \ldots(1)$$

Also $a^2 = 6^2 + x^2$

$\Rightarrow$ $(a^2 - x^2) = 36$

$$(a - x)(a + x) = 36$$

$$a - x = 2$$

Using equation-(1)

Now adding (1) & (2)

$$2a = 20$$

$\Rightarrow$ $a = 10$

& from (1) $x = 8$

Now area of $\Delta ABC = \frac{1}{2} \times \text{Base} \times \text{height}$

$$= \frac{1}{2} \times 2x \times 6$$

$$= \frac{1}{2} \times 2 \times 8 \times 6$$

$$= 48$$

Hence Ans is (B)

Sol. 20 (B)

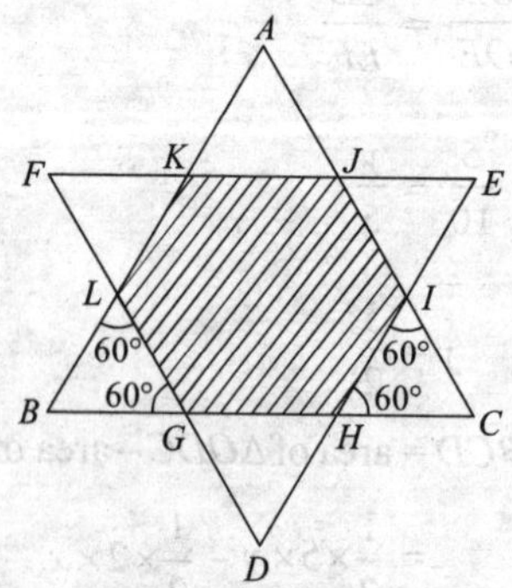

Given

$$ar\Delta ABC = 27$$

$$\Delta BLG \cong \Delta DGH \cong \Delta HIC$$

So let $BG = GH = HC = a$

So $BC = 3a$

Given area of $\Delta ABC = 27$

$$\frac{\sqrt{3}}{4}(3a)^2 = 27$$

$\Rightarrow$ $$\frac{\sqrt{3}}{4}a^2 = 3 \quad \ldots(1)$$

Now

area of hexagon = area of ΔABC – 3 area of ΔBLG

$$= \frac{\sqrt{3}}{4}(3a)^2 - 3\frac{\sqrt{3}}{4}a^2$$

$$= 27 - 3 \times 3$$

$$= 27 - 9$$

$$= 18$$

Hence Ans is (B)

Sol. 21 (B)

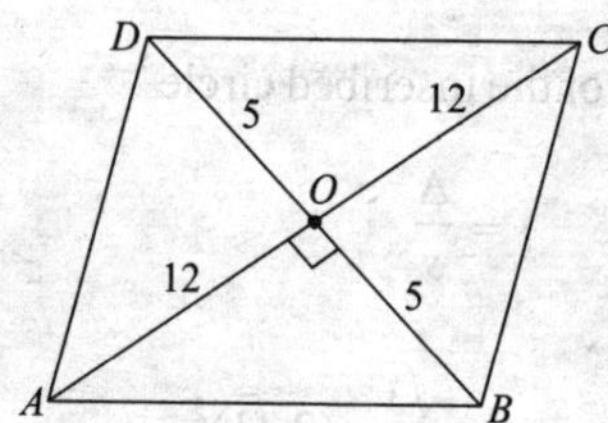

We know that the diagonal of rhombus bisect each other perpendicularly

$\Rightarrow$ $OA^2 + OB^2 = AB^2$

$$12^2 + 5^2 = AB^2$$

$$144 + 25 = AB^2$$

$\Rightarrow$ $AB^2 = 169$

$$AB = 13$$

Hence Ans is (B)

Sol. 22 (C)

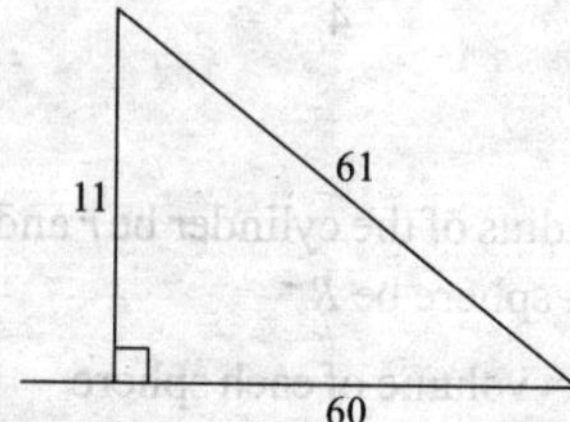

Here 11, 60 & 61 are the sides of right angle triangle.
So altitude on the smallest side will be having length of 60 m

Hence Ans is (C)

Sol. 23 (D) Largest cone which can be cut from cube will be having diameter & height equal to the edge of a cube

$\Rightarrow \quad 2r = 4.2$

& $\quad h = 4.2$

So volume of cone

$$= \frac{1}{3}\pi r^2 h$$

$$= \frac{1}{3} \times \frac{22}{7} \times 2.1 \times 2.1 \times 4.2$$

$$= 2.2 \times 2.1 \times 4.2$$

$$= 19.4 \text{ cm}^3$$

Hence Ans is (D)

Sol. 24 (D)

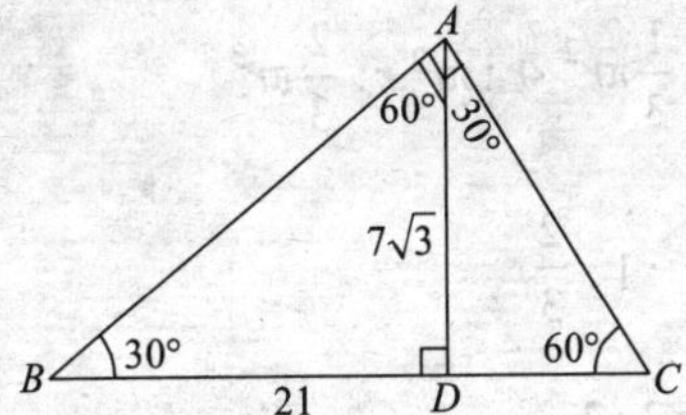

Given

$$AD = 7\sqrt{3}$$

$$\angle B = 30°$$

$$\angle ADC = 90°$$

& $\quad \angle C = 60°$

In ΔABD

$$\tan B = \frac{AD}{BD}$$

$$\tan 30° = \frac{7\sqrt{3}}{BD}$$

$$\frac{1}{\sqrt{3}} = \frac{7\sqrt{3}}{BD}$$

$$BD = 21$$

& In ΔADC

$$\tan 60° = \frac{AD}{DC}$$

$$\sqrt{3} = \frac{7\sqrt{3}}{DC}$$

$$DC = 7$$

So $\quad BC = BD + DC = 21 + 7 = 28$ cm

Hence Ans is (D)

Sol. 25 (C) Area of shaded region

= Area of square – 4 Area of circle

here side of square = $4r$

$\Rightarrow \quad 4r = 14$

$\Rightarrow \quad r = \frac{14}{4} = \frac{7}{2}$

$\Rightarrow$ Area of shaded region

$$= 14 \times 14 - 4 \cdot \frac{22}{7} \times \left(\frac{7}{2}\right)^2$$

$$= 196 - 4 \times \frac{22}{7} \times \frac{7}{2} \times \frac{7}{2}$$

$$= 196 - 154$$

$$= 42 \text{ cm}^2$$

Hence Ans is (C)

Sol. 26 (C) Given altitude of an equilateral $\Delta = x$

Let the side be a' of an equilateral Δ then altitude will be $\frac{\sqrt{3}}{2}a$

Here $\quad \frac{\sqrt{3}}{2}a = x$

$\Rightarrow \quad a = \frac{2x}{\sqrt{3}}$

So area of equilateral Δ

$$= \frac{\sqrt{3}}{4}(a)^2$$

$$= \frac{\sqrt{3}}{4} \times \left(\frac{2x}{\sqrt{3}}\right)^2$$

$$= \frac{\sqrt{3}}{4} \times \frac{4x^2}{3}$$

$$= \frac{x^2}{\sqrt{3}}$$

Hence Ans is (C)

Sol. 27 (B) Given,

Volume of a cube = 2744 cm^3

$\Rightarrow$ Let the side of the cube be 'a'

$\Rightarrow \quad a^3 = 2744$

$\Rightarrow \quad a = 14$

Surface area of the cube = $6a^2$

$$= 6 \times (14)^2$$

$$= 6 \times 196$$

$$= 1176 \text{ cm}^2$$

Hence Ans is (B)

Sol. 28 (C)

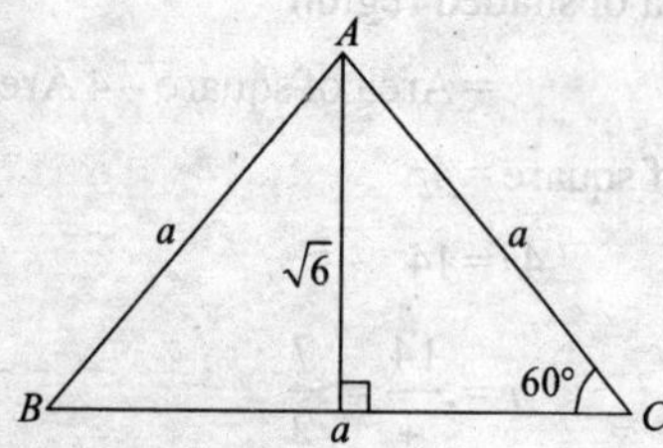

Let 'a' be the side of the equilateral triangle

We know in equilateral triangle

$$h = \frac{\sqrt{3}}{2}a$$

Here $$\sqrt{6} = \frac{\sqrt{3}}{2}a$$

$$\Rightarrow \quad a = 2\sqrt{2}$$

$$\Rightarrow \quad \text{Area} = \frac{\sqrt{3}}{4}a^2$$

$$= \frac{\sqrt{3}}{4} \times 8$$

$$= 2\sqrt{3} \text{ cm}^2$$

Hence Ans is (C)

Sol. 29 (C) Given

Perimeter of a rectangular field = 82 m

$$\Rightarrow \quad 2(l+b) = 82$$

$$l + b = 41 \quad \dots(1)$$

Also given

$$\text{Area} = 400\, m^2$$

$$l.b = 400 \quad \dots(2)$$

Solving (1) & (2)

We get

$$l = 25, b = 16$$

Hence Ans is (C)

Sol. 30 (B)

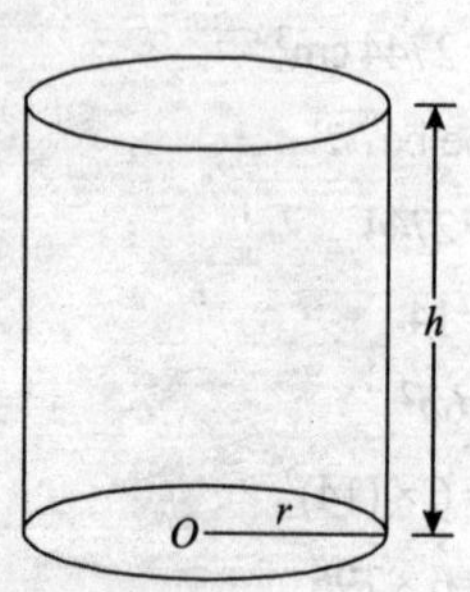

Total surface are = $2\pi rh + 2\pi r^2$

Hence Ans is (B)

Sol. 31 (B)

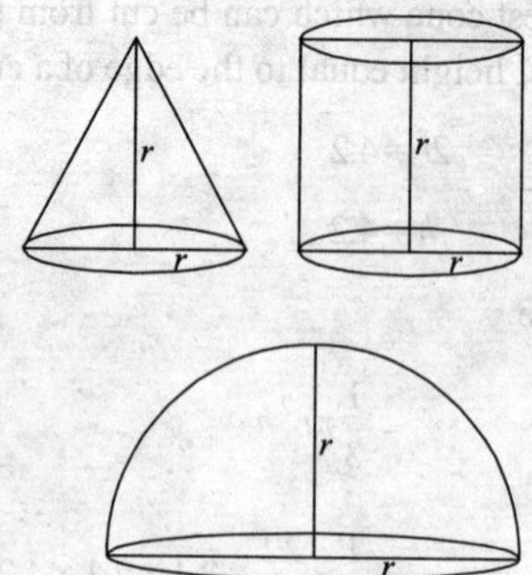

Given they have equal base ⇒ radius are same

& height of cone & cylinder = r

So ratio of volume of one : cylinder : sphere

$$= \frac{1}{3}\pi r^2 h : \pi r^2 h : \frac{2}{3}\pi r^3$$

$$= \frac{1}{3}\pi r^2 \cdot r : \pi r^2 . r : \frac{2}{3}\pi r^3$$

$$\frac{1}{3} : 1 : \frac{2}{3}$$

$$\Rightarrow \quad 1 : 3 : 2$$

Hence Ans is (B)

Sol. 32 (B)

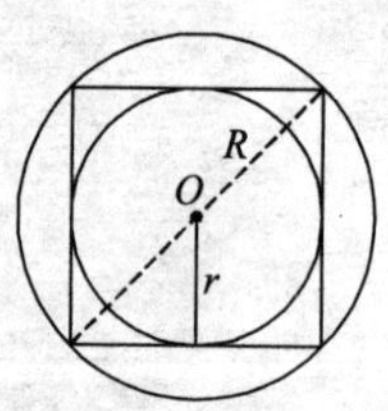

Let the side of square be 'a' circum radius of square

$$= \frac{1}{2} \text{ diagonal of square}$$

$$= \frac{1}{2}a\sqrt{2} = \frac{1}{\sqrt{2}}a$$

& in radius of square

$$= \frac{1}{2} \text{ side of square}$$

$$= \frac{1}{2}a$$

$$\text{So ratio} = \frac{\frac{1}{2}a}{\frac{1}{\sqrt{2}}a} = \frac{1}{\sqrt{2}}$$

Hence Ans is (B)

Sol. 33 (B)

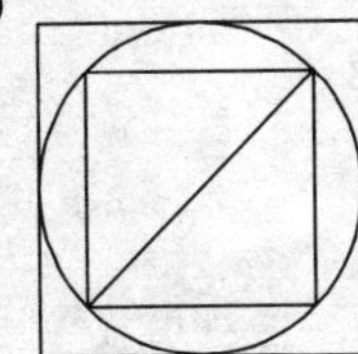

Let the side of square be 14 then incircle radius will be 7

& square diagonal which is inside the circle will be 14

Now area of big square = 196

Area of incircle = $\pi.7^2 = \frac{22}{7}\times 7\times 7 = 154$

So wasted area will be 196 – 154 = 42

Now are of inside sq. = $\frac{1}{2}196 = 98$

again wasted area = 154 – 98 = 56

Total wasted area = 56 + 42 = 98

Hence Ans is (B)

Sol. 34 (D) $l = 1; b = 1; h = 1$

Total surface of one cube

$= 6\times 1^2$

$= 6$

So total surface area of 10 cube.

= 10 × 6 = 60 sq. unit

Hence Ans is (D)

Sol. 35 (A) $\frac{\text{Volume of sphere}}{\text{Volume of cylinder}} = \frac{\frac{4}{3}\pi r^3}{\pi r^2 h} = \frac{\frac{4}{3}\pi r^3}{2\pi r^3}$

$= \frac{2}{3}$

$= 2:3$

Hence Ans is (A)

Sol. 36 (C) Let

$R_1 = r$

$R_2 = 2r$

$$\frac{V_2}{V_1} = \frac{\frac{4}{3}\pi R_2^3}{\frac{4}{3}\pi R_1^3} = \left(\frac{2r}{r}\right)^3 = 8$$

$\Rightarrow \quad V_2 = 8V_1$

Hence Ans is (C)

Sol. 37 (B)

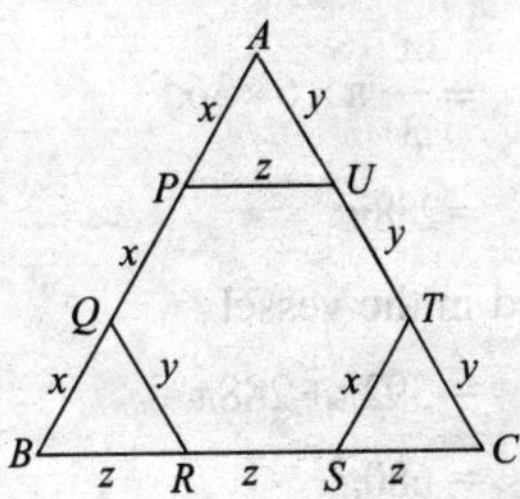

Given P and Q trisects the side AB

$\Rightarrow \quad BQ = QP = AP = x \quad \ldots(1)$

Similarly U and T trisects the side AC

$\Rightarrow \quad AU = UT = TC = y \quad \ldots(2)$

also R and S trisects the side BC

$\Rightarrow \quad BR = RS = SC = z \quad \ldots(3)$

Perimeter of ΔABC

$= AB + BC + AC$

$= 3x + 3y + 3z$

[from (1), (2) & (3)]

Perimeter of hexagon

$PQRSTU = 2x + 2y + 2z$

$$\Rightarrow \quad \frac{\text{Perimeter of Hexagon}}{\text{Perimeter of triangle}} = \frac{2(x+y+z)}{3(x+y+z)}$$

$= \frac{1}{3}$

Hence Ans is (A)

Sol. 38 (B)

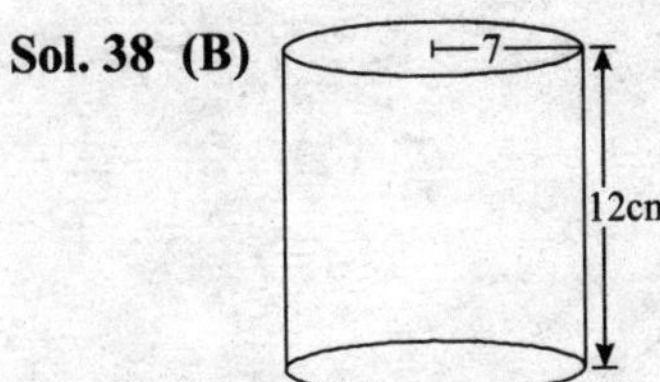

Volume of a cylinder = $\pi r^2 h$

here volume = $\pi \times (7)^2 \times 12$

$V = 588\pi$

Here cylinder is filled only $\frac{2}{3}^{rd}$

$\Rightarrow \quad \frac{2}{3}V$

$\Rightarrow \quad \frac{2}{3}\times 588\,\pi = 392\pi$

Volume of a sphere = $\frac{4}{3}\pi r^3$

Here $\quad r = 6$

$V = \frac{4}{3}\pi \times 6^3$

$= \frac{4}{3} \cdot \pi \times 6 \times 36$

$= 288\pi$

When sphere is dropped in the vessel

total volume $= 392\pi + 288\pi$

$= 680\pi$

Water spelled out $= 680\pi - 588\pi$

$= 92\pi$

Hence Ans is (B)

Sol. 39 (A)

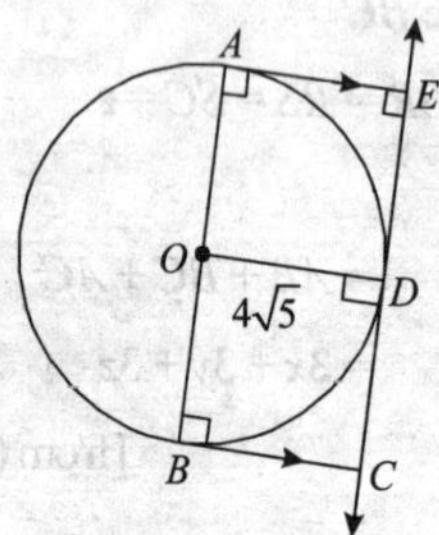

Given $OD = 4\sqrt{5}$ cm (radius)

From the figure it is clear man *OAED* is a require

$\Rightarrow$ all the sides are equal

$\Rightarrow$ $ED = OD = 4\sqrt{5}$ cm

Hence Ans is (A)

Sol. 40 (A)

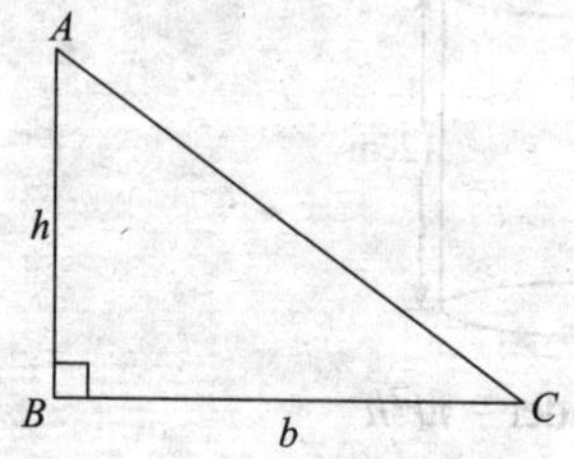

Given $b = 3h$

Also given Area $= 96m^2$

$\Rightarrow \frac{1}{2} \times b \times h = 96$

$\frac{1}{2} \times b \times \frac{b}{3} = 96$

$b^2 = 96 \times 6$

$b^2 = 576$

$b = 24$

Hence Ans is (A)

Sol. 41 (D) Given

$l = 23 + b$ ...(1)

Also given perimeter = 206 m

$\Rightarrow 2(l + b) = 206$

$\Rightarrow l + b = 103$ ...(2)

Solving (1) & (2)

$l = 63; b = 40$

Area $= l \times b$

$= 63 \times 40$

$= 2520m^2$

Hence Ans is (D)

Sol. 42 (C) Given,

Total surface area of a cube = 864 cm^2

$\Rightarrow 6a^2 = 864$

[where 'a' is the side of the cube]

$\Rightarrow a^2 = 144$

$\Rightarrow a = 12$

Volume of a cube $= a^3$

$\Rightarrow V = 12^3$

$= 1728$ cm^3

Hence Ans is (C)

Sol. 43 (B) The length of the longest pole that can be kept in a room is the length of the diagonal of that room.

here, diagonal

$= \sqrt{(12)^2 + (9)^2 + (8)^2}$

$= \sqrt{289}$

$d = 17$

Hence Ans is (B)

Sol. 44 (B) Curved surface area of a cylinder $2\pi rh$

given

$2\pi rh = 264$

$\Rightarrow 2\pi r \times 14 = 264$

$\Rightarrow 2\frac{22}{7} \times r \times 14 = 264$

$\Rightarrow r = \frac{264}{88} = 3$

Volume of cylinder $= \pi r^2 h$

$= \frac{22}{7} \times 3^2 \times 14$

$= 22 \times 9 \times 2$

$= 396$ cm^3

Hence Ans is (B)

Sol. 45 (D)

$$v_1 + v_2 + v_3 = V$$

$$\frac{4}{3}\pi r_1^3 + \frac{4}{3}\pi r_2^3 + \frac{4}{3}\pi r_3^3 = \frac{4}{3}\pi r^3$$

$$r_1^3 + r_2^3 + r_3^3 = r^3$$

$$3^3 + 4^3 + 5^5 = r^3$$

$$27 + 64 + 125 = r^3$$

$\Rightarrow$ $r^3 = 216$

$\Rightarrow$ $r^3 = 6^3$

$\Rightarrow$ $r = 6$ cm

Hence Ans is (D)

Sol. 46 (C)

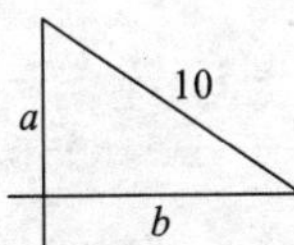

Given

$$a + b + 10 = 24$$

$$a + b = 14$$

We know smallest pythagorean triplet is (3, 4, 5) multiplied it by 2 we get (6, 8, 10)

Which satisfies our all condition, so sides of the right angle triangle are 6, 8 & 10

So area $= \frac{1}{2} \times ab = \frac{1}{2} \times 6 \times 8$

$= 24$ cm^2

Hence Ans is (C)

Sol. 47 (B)

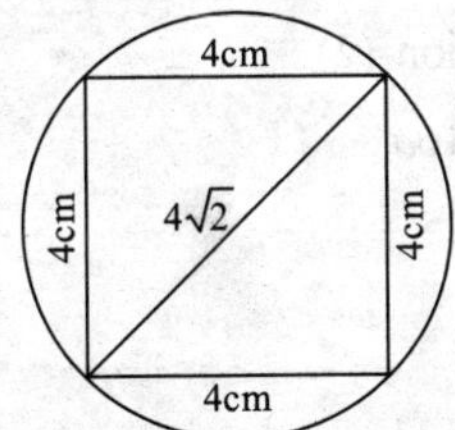

Diagonal of a square = diameter of circle

$\Rightarrow$ $2r = 4\sqrt{2}$

$\Rightarrow$ $r = 2\sqrt{2}$

So area of circle

$= \pi r^2$

$= \pi(2\sqrt{2})^2$

$= 8\pi$ cm^2

Hence Ans is (B)

Sol. 48 (C) Volume of parallelpiped = number of coins × volume of a coin

$\Rightarrow$ $11 \times 9 \times 6 = n \times \pi \times 1.5^2 \times 0.25$

$\Rightarrow$ $11 \times 9 \times 6 = \frac{22}{7} \times \frac{1.5}{10} \times \frac{1.5}{10} \times \frac{.25}{100} \times n$

$\Rightarrow$ $n = 336$

Hence Ans is (C)

Sol. 49 (A) Perimeter of protactor is 72

Let r be the radius of protactor

then perimeter $= 2r + \pi r$

$\Rightarrow$ $2r + \pi r = 72$

$\Rightarrow$ $r[2 + \pi] = 72$

$\Rightarrow$ $r\left[2 + \frac{22}{7}\right] = 36$

$\Rightarrow$ $r = \frac{36 \times 7}{36} = 7$

Hence Ans is (A)

Sol. 50 (C)

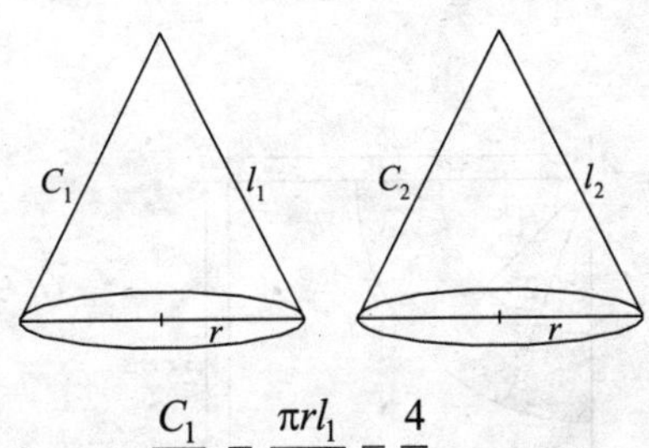

$$\frac{C_1}{C_2} = \frac{\pi r l_1}{\pi r l_2} = \frac{4}{3}$$

Hence Ans is (C)

Sol. 51 (B) Given

$\theta = 60°$

$R = 14$

$r = 7$

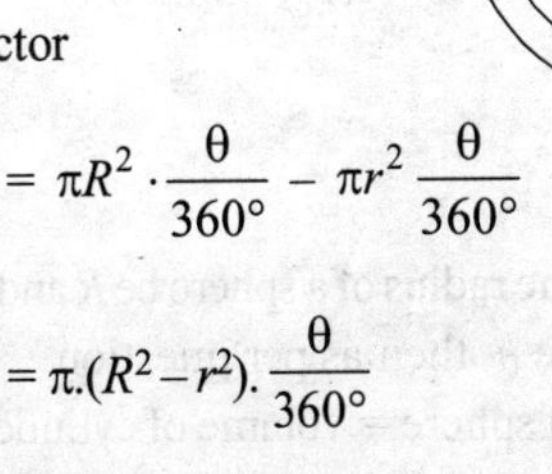

Area between sector

$$= \pi R^2 \cdot \frac{\theta}{360°} - \pi r^2 \frac{\theta}{360°}$$

$$= \pi.(R^2 - r^2).\frac{\theta}{360°}$$

$$= \frac{22}{7} \times (14^2 - 7^2) \cdot \frac{60}{360°}$$

$$= \frac{22}{7} \times 21 \times 7 \times \frac{1}{6}$$

$= 77$ sq. cm

Hence Ans is (B)

Sol. 52 (A)

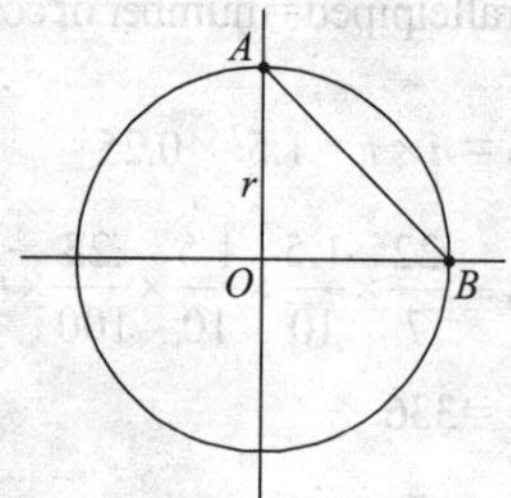

Let r be the radius of circle

$$ar(\Delta AOB) = \frac{1}{2}r \times r = \frac{1}{2}r^2$$

$$\text{Area of quadrant} = \frac{1}{4}\pi r^2$$

$$\text{Area of segment} = \frac{1}{4}\pi r^2 - \frac{1}{2}r^2$$

$$= \frac{r^2}{2}\left[\frac{\pi}{2} - 1\right] \text{ sq. unit}$$

Hence Ans is (A)

Sol. 53 (D)

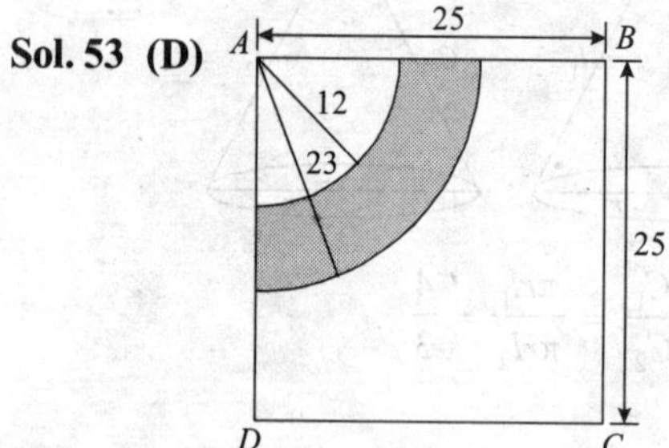

Let the cow be tied at 'A'

Additional grassy area will be the shaded area which form quadrant of a circle

$$\text{Shaded area} = \frac{1}{4} \times \pi(23^2 - 12^2) = 302.5\text{m}^2$$

Hence Ans is (D)

Sol. 54 (D) Let the radius of a sphere be R and radius of cylinder be r and height be h, then as per question

Volume of sphere = Volume of cylinder

$$\frac{4}{3}\pi R^3 = \pi r^2 h,$$

$$\frac{4}{3}\pi \times 6^3 = \pi \times 3^2 \times h$$

Hence $\quad 32 \text{ cm} = h$

Hence Ans is (D)

Sol. 55 (C)

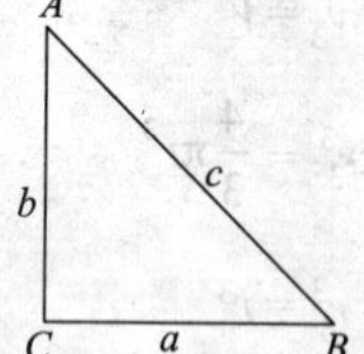

Let the base be 'a' hypotenuse be c and altitude be b.

Given $\quad c = a + 1 = b + 2$

$$a = b + 1$$

$$c^2 = b^2 + a^2 \text{ (by pythagoras theorem)}$$

$$(b+2)^2 = b^2 + (b+1)^2$$

$$\Rightarrow \quad b^2 - 2b - 3 = 0$$

$$(b = 3) \text{ as } (b \neq -1)$$

$$\Rightarrow \quad c = 5, a = 4$$

So perimeter

$$a + b + c = 12$$

Hence Ans is (C)

Sol. 56 (C) $\quad EF = a, FC = 16 - a$

$$\Delta AEB \sim \Delta DFA$$

$$\Delta BEC \sim \Delta CFD$$

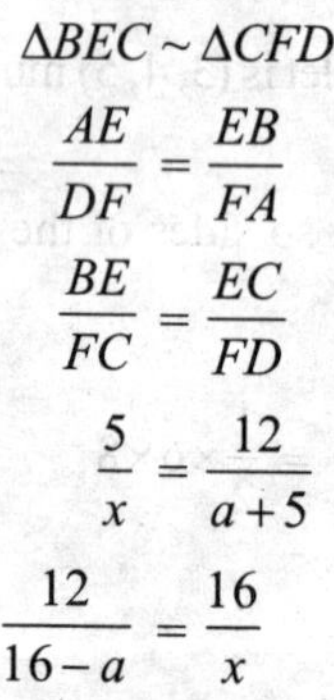

$$\frac{AE}{DF} = \frac{EB}{FA}$$

$$\frac{BE}{FC} = \frac{EC}{FD}$$

$$\frac{5}{x} = \frac{12}{a+5}$$

$$\frac{12}{16-a} = \frac{16}{x}$$

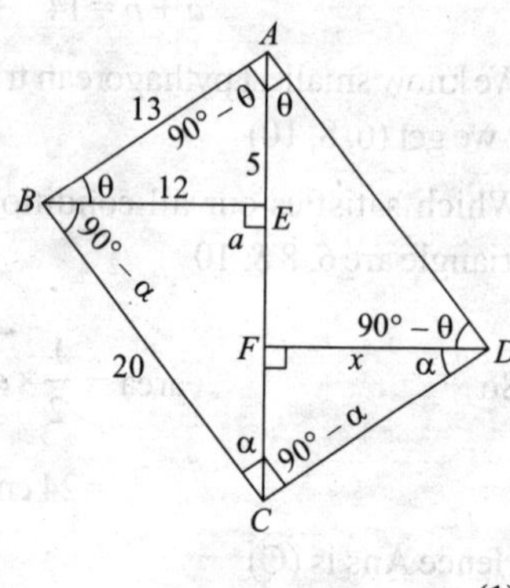

$$5a + 25 = 12x \quad \text{... (1)}$$

$$12x = 256 - 16a \quad \text{... (2)}$$

Using equation-(1) in equation-(2)

$$5a + 25 = 256 - 16a$$

$$\Rightarrow \quad 21a = 256 - 25$$

$$\Rightarrow \quad 21a = 231$$

$$\Rightarrow \quad a = \frac{231}{21} = 11$$

Using a in equation-(1)

$$5 \times 11 + 25 = 12x$$

$$\Rightarrow \quad 55 + 25 = 12x$$

$$\Rightarrow \quad 80 = 12x$$

$$\Rightarrow \quad x = \frac{80}{12}$$

$$\Rightarrow \quad x = \frac{20}{3} = 6\frac{2}{3}$$

Hence Ans is (C)

Sol. 57 (A)

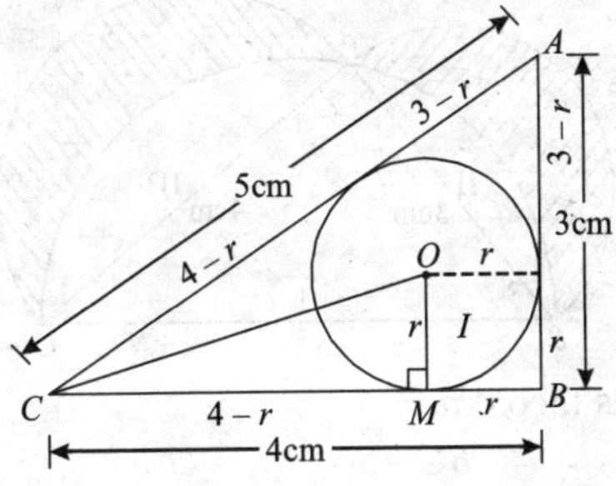

$$5 = 3 - r + 4 - r$$

$$\Rightarrow \quad r = 1$$

$$s = \frac{a+b+c}{2} = \frac{4+3+5}{2} = 6$$

$$\Delta = r \times s$$

$$\Delta = 1 \times 6 = 6$$

$$OC^2 = OM^2 + CM^2 = 1^2 + 3^2$$

$$OC = \sqrt{10}$$

Hence Ans is (A)

Sol. 58 (B) In one revolution it will cover distance equal to its circumference $2\pi r$.

Where r is radius of wheel.

So in 1000 revolution

$$1000 \times 2\pi r = 440$$

$$1000 \times 2 \times \frac{22}{7} \times r = 440$$

$$2r = \frac{14}{100}$$

$$2r = 0.14 \text{ m}$$

Hence Ans is (B)

Sol. 59 (D)

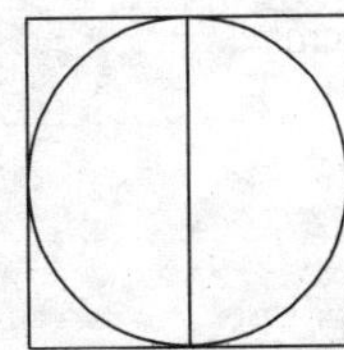

Diameter of circle will be equal to the length of side of square

$$\Rightarrow \quad 2r = 28$$

$$\Rightarrow \quad r = 14$$

So area of circle $= \pi r^2$

$$= \frac{22}{7} \times 14 \times 14 = 44 \times 14$$

$$= 616 \text{ cm}^2$$

Hence Ans is (D)

Sol. 60 (C) Let the side of first cube be a_1
& the side of second cube be a_2

$$\frac{V_1}{V_2} = \left(\frac{a_1}{a_2}\right)^3 = \frac{27}{64}$$

$$\Rightarrow \quad \frac{a_1}{a_2} = \frac{3}{4}$$

Ration of total surface area of cube

$$\frac{c_1}{c_2} = \frac{6a_1^2}{6a_2^2} = \left(\frac{a_1}{a_2}\right)^2 = \frac{9}{16}$$

Hence Ans is (C)

Sol. 61 (A)

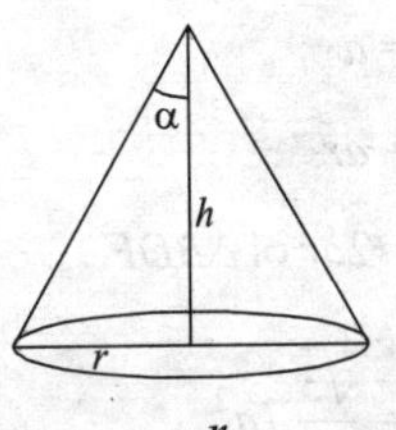

$$\frac{r}{h} = \tan\alpha$$

$$r = h\tan\alpha$$

So volume of cone

$$= \frac{1}{3}\pi r^2 h$$

$$= \frac{1}{3}\pi \cdot (h\tan\alpha)^2 h$$

$$= \frac{1}{3}\pi h^3 \tan^2\alpha$$

Hence Ans is (A)

Sol. 62 (D)

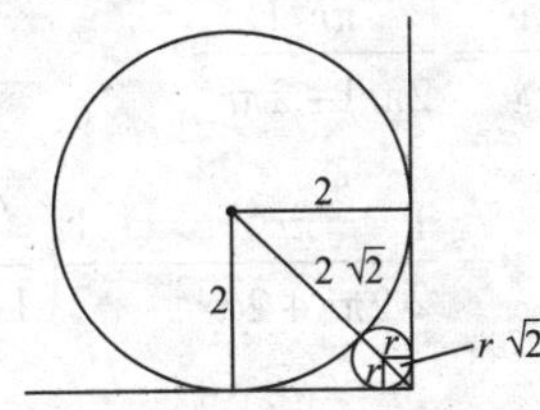

Let the radius of small circle be r then from the figure it is clear

$$2\sqrt{2} = 2 + r + r\sqrt{2}$$

$$r(1+\sqrt{2}) = 2\sqrt{2} - 2$$

$$r = \frac{2(\sqrt{2}-1)}{(\sqrt{2}+1)} \times \frac{(\sqrt{2}-1)}{(\sqrt{2}-1)}$$

$$= 2(\sqrt{2}-1)^2$$

$$= 2(2+1-2\sqrt{2})$$

$$= 6 - 4\sqrt{2}$$

Hence Ans is (D)

Sol. 63 (B)

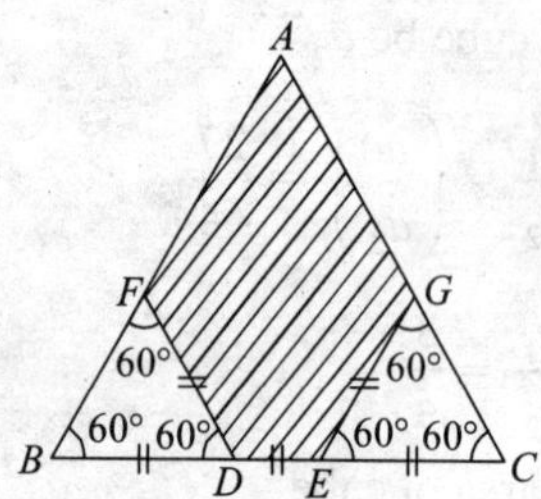

Given ΔABC is an equilateral Δ

Let $BC = 3a$

& Since $BD = DF$

$\Rightarrow$ ΔBDF is also an equilateral with

$BD = a$

$\Rightarrow$ Shaded region = ar of $\Delta ABC - 2ar$ of ΔBDF

$$\frac{\sqrt{3}}{4}(3a)^2 - 2\cdot\frac{\sqrt{3}}{4}a^2 = \frac{\sqrt{3}}{4}7a^2$$

Now
$$\frac{ar \text{ Shaded region}}{ar \text{ of } \Delta ABC} = \frac{\frac{\sqrt{3}}{4}.7a^2}{\frac{\sqrt{3}}{4}.9a^2} = \frac{7}{9}$$

Hence Ans is (B)

Sol. 64 (A) We know

$$v = \pi r^2 h$$

$$s = 2\pi rh + 2\pi r^2$$

$$\frac{v}{s} = \frac{\pi r^2 1}{2\pi r1 + 2\pi r^2}$$

$$= \frac{1}{2}\frac{\pi r^2}{2\pi r + 2\pi r^2} = \frac{1}{2}\left(\frac{r}{1+r}\right)$$

$$= \frac{1}{2}\left[1 - \frac{1}{r+1}\right]$$

Hence Ans is (A)

Sol. 65 (B) Given

$$h_1 = 1.1h$$

$$r_1 = 0.9r$$

Curved surface area

$$= 2\pi rh = 2\pi\, 1.1\, h \times 0.9r$$

$$= 0.99\,(2\pi rh)$$

Hence Ans is (B)

Sol. 66 (B)

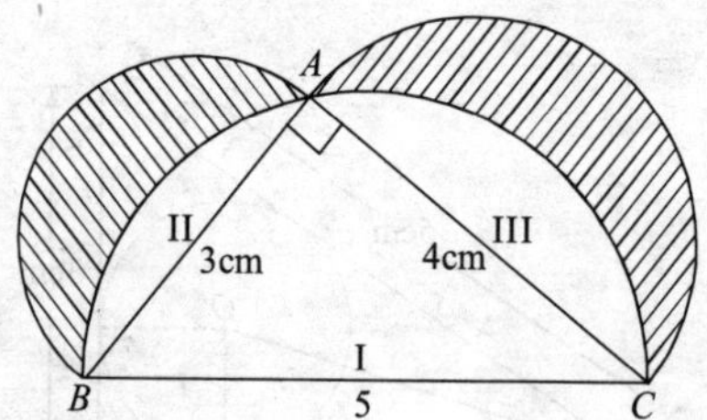

By pythagoras theorem

$$BC = 5$$

$$ar \text{ of } I = \frac{1}{2} \times 3 \times 4 = 6 \text{ cm}^2$$

ar of semicircle with 5 as diameter

$$= \frac{1}{2}\pi\cdot\left(\frac{5}{2}\right)^2 = \frac{25}{8}\pi$$

$$ar\,(\text{II} + \text{III}) = \frac{25}{8}\pi - \frac{1}{2}\times 3 \times 4 = \left(\frac{25}{8}\pi - 6\right)$$

ar of shaded region = *ar* of semicircle with 3 as diameter + *ar* of semicircle. 4 as diameter (II + III)

$$= \frac{1}{2}\pi\cdot\left(\frac{3}{2}\right)^2 + \frac{1}{2}\pi\left(\frac{4}{2}\right)^2 - \left(\frac{1}{2}\pi\left(\frac{5}{2}\right)^2 - 6\right) = 6$$

Hence Ans is (B)

Sol. 67 (D) Volume of water per sec

$$= 0.7 \times 100 \times \pi.1^2 = 70\,\pi \text{ cm}^3$$

Volume of water in half an hour

$$= 70\pi \times 1800 \text{ cm}^3$$

(as half an hour = 60 × 30 = 1800 sec.)

Let h be the height of cylinder

$\Rightarrow$ $\pi R^2 h = 70\pi \times 1800$

$\Rightarrow$ $\pi \times 40 \times 40 \times h = 70\pi \times 1800$

$\Rightarrow$ $h = \frac{630}{8}$

$= 78.75$ cm

Hence Ans is (D)

Sol. 68 (B)

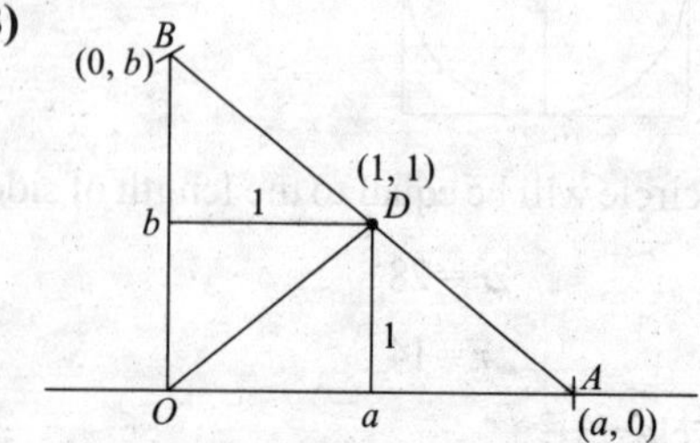

$$ar \text{ of } \Delta ABO = ar \text{ of } \Delta OAD + ar \text{ of } \Delta OBD$$

$$\frac{1}{2}ab = \frac{1}{2}a \times 1 + \frac{1}{2}\times b \times 1$$

$$ab = a + b$$

Hence Ans is (B)

Sol. 69 **(A)** Given length of each edge $= \frac{1}{2}$

$\Rightarrow \quad v = \frac{1}{8}\ \text{cm}^3$

Hence Ans is (A)

Sol. 70 **(D)**

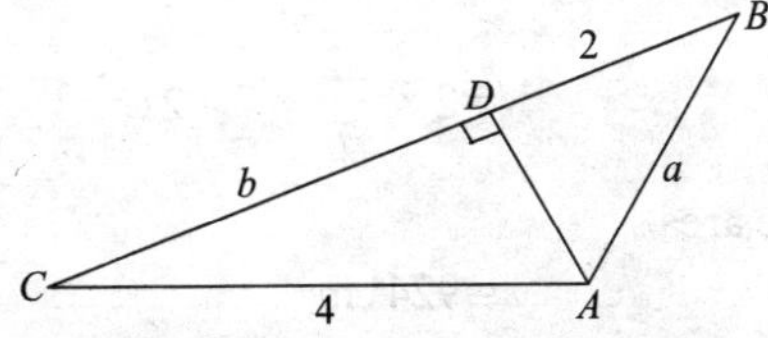

We know

$$AD^2 + b^2 = 4^2 \quad \ldots(1)$$
$$AD^2 + 2^2 = a^2 \quad \ldots(2)$$

(1) – (2)

$$b^2 - 2^2 = 4^2 - a^2$$
$$a^2 + b^2 = 4^2 + 2^2 = 20$$

Hence Ans is (D)

Sol. 71 **(A)**

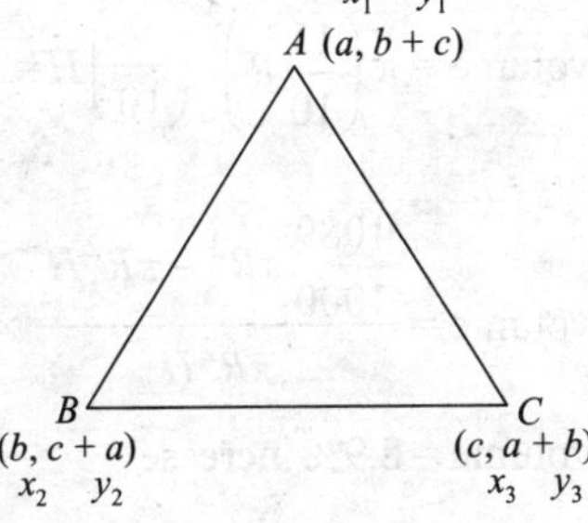

ar of ΔABC

$$= \frac{1}{2}[(x_1 y_2 + x_2 y_3 + x_3 y_1) - (y_1 x_2 + y_2 x_3 + y_3 x_1)]$$
$$= \frac{1}{2}[\{a(c+a) + b(a+b) + c(b+c)\}$$
$$- \{(b+c)\,b + (c+a)\,c + (a+b)a\}]$$
$$= \frac{1}{2}[ac + a^2 + ab + b^2 + bc + c^2 - b^2 - bc - c^2 - ac - a^2 - ba]$$
$$= 0$$

Hence Ans is (A)

Sol. 72 **(B)** Given $\quad 2r = 3.5$ cm

$$\rho = 9.89/\text{cm}^2$$

mass = volume × density

$$= \frac{4}{3}\pi r^3 \times 9.8$$
$$= \frac{4}{3} \times \frac{22}{7} \times \frac{3.5}{2} \times \frac{3.5}{2} \times \frac{3.5}{2} \times 9.8$$
$$= 220\ \text{g}$$

Hence Ans is (B)

Sol. 73 **(C)** In one rotation it covers a distance equal to its circumference $= 2\pi r$

So this implies

$$100 \times 2\pi r = 88$$
$$100 \times \frac{22}{7} \times 2r = 88$$
$$2r = \frac{7}{25} m$$
$$= \frac{7}{25} \times 100\ \text{cm}$$
$$= 28\ \text{cm}$$

Hence Ans is (C)

Sol. 74 **(D)** $\quad v_1 + v_2 + v_3 = V$

$$\Rightarrow \quad a_1^3 + a_2^3 + a_3^3 = a^3$$
$$\Rightarrow \quad 3^3 + 4^3 + 5^3 = a^3$$
$$\Rightarrow \quad 27 + 64 + 125 = a^3$$
$$\Rightarrow \quad a^3 = 216 = 6^3$$
$$a = 6$$

Hence Ans is (D)

Sol. 75 **(B)** In one revolution it will cover the area equal to is curved surface area

Let n revolution be there

$$n \times 2\pi rh = 3080$$
$$n \times 2 \times \frac{22}{7} \times 0.7 \times 14 = 3080$$
$$n = 500$$

Hence Ans is (B)

Sol. 76 **(A)** Let radii of each end be R & r respectively

$$\pi R^2 + \pi r^2 = 770$$
$$\frac{22}{7}[(2x)^2 + x^2] = 770$$

given $\quad R : r = 2 : 1$

$$\frac{22}{7} \times 5x^2 = 770$$
$$x^2 = 49$$
$$R = 2x = 14$$
$$r = 7$$

Volume of bucket

$$v = \frac{1}{3}\pi[R^2 + r^2 + R \times r].h$$

$$= \frac{1}{3}\cdot\frac{22}{7}[(R+r)^2 - R.r] \times 60$$

$$= \frac{1}{3}\cdot\frac{22}{7}[(14+7)^2 - 14\times 7]\times 60$$

$$= \frac{1}{3}\times\frac{22}{7}\times[(21)^2 - 98]\times 60$$

$$= \frac{1}{3}\times\frac{22}{7}\times(441-98)\times 60$$

$$= \frac{1}{3}\times\frac{22}{7}\times 343\times 60$$

$$= 21560 \text{ cm}^3$$

$$= 21.56l$$

Hence Ans is (A)

Sol. 77 (C) Let r_1, r_2, radii and h_1, h_2 heights of given cylinders

Given $r_1 : r_2 = 2:3,$

$h_1 : h_2 = 5:3$

Let $r_1 = 2x, r_2 = 3x, h_1 = 5y, h_2 = 3y$

Hence ratio of volumes

$$= \pi r_1^2 h_1 : \pi r_2^2 h_2$$

$$= (2x)^2.\ 5y : (3x)^2.\ 3y = 20:27$$

Hence Ans is (C)

Sol. 78 (A) Let l, b, h are length, breadth, height of Cuboid given

$$lb = x, bh = y, lh = z$$

then $(lbh)^2 = xyz$

$\Rightarrow$ $lbh = \sqrt{xyz}$

Hence volume $= \sqrt{xyz}$

Hence Ans is (A)

Sol. 79 (B) Let radius be r cm and height be h cm

$\Rightarrow$ $r : h = 1:2$

$\pi r^2 h = 2156$

$\Rightarrow$ $\pi r^2(2r) = 2156$

$\Rightarrow$ $\frac{22}{7}\times 2r^3 = 2156$

$\Rightarrow$ $r^3 = \frac{2156}{22\times 2}\times 7$

$\Rightarrow$ $r^3 = 7\times 7\times 7$

$\Rightarrow$ $r = 7,$

$\Rightarrow$ $h = 14$

Total surface area

$$= 2\pi r(r+h)$$

Total surface area

$$= 2\times\frac{22}{7}\times 7(7+14)$$

Total surface area

$$= 2\times\frac{22}{7}\times 7\times 21$$

Total surface area

$$= 924 \text{ cm}^2$$

Hence Ans is (B)

Sol. 80 (C) Let initially radius be R and height be H

$\Rightarrow$ Initial volume $= \pi R^2 H$

New radius $= R + 10\%$ of $R = \frac{11}{10}R$

New height $= H - 10\%$ of $H = \frac{9}{10}H$

New volume $= \pi\left(\frac{11}{10}R\right)^2\left(\frac{9}{10}\right)H = \left(\frac{1089}{1000}\right)\pi R^2 H$

% change in volume $= \dfrac{\frac{1089}{1000}\pi R^2 - \pi R^2 H}{\pi R^2 H}\times 100\%$

% change in volume = 8.9% increase

Hence Ans is (C)

Sol. 81 (C) $\frac{x(x-3)}{2} = 35$

$$x^2 - 3x - 70 = 0$$

$$x^3 - 10x + 7x - 70 = 0$$

$$(x-10)(x+7) = 0$$

$$x = 10$$

Each interior angle $= \frac{(x-2)180}{x} = \frac{8\times 180}{10} = 144°$

Hence Ans is (C)

Sol. 82 (B) $\dfrac{\text{Volume of cube}}{\text{Volume of sphere}} = \dfrac{a^3}{\frac{4}{3}\times\pi\left(\frac{a}{2}\right)^3}$

$$= \frac{a^3\times 24}{4\pi a^3} = \frac{6}{\pi}$$

Hence Ans is (B)

Sol. 83 (B) $\sqrt{3}\, l_1 = \sqrt{108}$

$\Rightarrow$ $l_1 = 6;\ V_1 = l_1^3 = 216$

$\sqrt{3}\, l_2 = \sqrt{192}$

$\Rightarrow$ $l_2 = 8;\ V_2 = l_2^3 = 512$

$\sqrt{3}\, l_3 = \sqrt{300}$

$\Rightarrow$ $l_3 = 10;\ V_3 = l_3^3 = 1000$

$V_{\text{Total}} = 1728 = 3L^3$

$\Rightarrow$ $L = 12$ cm

Diagonal $= \sqrt{3}\, L = 12\sqrt{3}$ cm

Hence Ans is (B)

Sol. 84 (A) $R + r + r\sqrt{2} = R\sqrt{2}$

$$r(\sqrt{2}+1) = R(\sqrt{2}-1)$$

$$r = \frac{1}{2}(\sqrt{2}-1)^2$$

$$= \frac{3-2\sqrt{2}}{2}$$

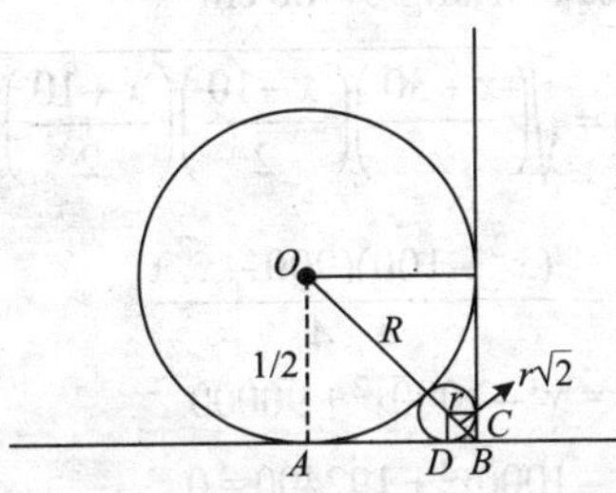

In ΔOAB; $OA^2 + AB^2 = OB^2$

$$\left(\frac{1}{2}\right)^2 + \left(\frac{1}{2}\right)^2 = OB^2$$

$\Rightarrow$ $OB^2 = \dfrac{1}{2}$

i.e., $OB = \dfrac{1}{\sqrt{2}}$

Hence, $\dfrac{1}{2} + r + \sqrt{2}\, r = \dfrac{1}{\sqrt{2}}$

Solving $r = \dfrac{\sqrt{2}-1}{2(\sqrt{2}+1)}$

or, $r = \dfrac{3-2\sqrt{2}}{2}$

Hence Ans is (A)

Sol. 85 (D) Length of major $arc = 2\pi r - 14$

$$= 2 \times \frac{22}{7} \times 7 - 14$$

$$= 44 - 14 = 30$$

Hence Ans is (D)

Sol. 86 (C) $s = \dfrac{a+b+c}{2} = \dfrac{8+8+8}{2} = 12$

Hence Ans is (C)

Sol. 87 (A) $2\pi rh$

Hence Ans is (A)

Sol. 88 (B) $\dfrac{4}{3}\pi 6^3 + \dfrac{4}{3}\pi x^3 + \dfrac{4}{3}\pi y^3 = \dfrac{4}{3}\pi [12]^3$

$$6^3 + x^3 + y^3 = 12^3$$

$$x^3 + y^3 = 12^3 - 6^3$$

$$(x+y)(x^2+y^2-xy) = 1728 - 216$$

$$(x+y)[(x+y)^2 - 3xy] = 1512$$

$$(x+y)[(x+y)^2 - 3 \times 80] = 1512$$

$$(x+y)[(x+y)^2 - 240] = 1512$$

Let $x + y = \lambda$

$$\lambda^3 - 240\lambda - 1512 = 0$$

$$\lambda = 18$$

Hence Ans is (B)

Sol. 89 (C)

A
61
54
B
M
35
C

Longest altitude must be along smallest side

$\Rightarrow$ $\dfrac{1}{2} AM \times BC = \sqrt{s(s-a)(s-b)(s-c)}$

$$s = \frac{61+35+54}{2}$$

$$s = \frac{150}{2} = 75$$

$$\frac{1}{2} AM \times 35 = \sqrt{75(75-35)(75-54)(75-61)}$$

$$= \sqrt{75 \times 40 \times 21 \times 14}$$

$$= \sqrt{25 \times 3 \times 2 \times 2 \times 2 \times 5 \times 3 \times 7 \times 2 \times 7}$$

$$\frac{1}{2} AM \times 35 = 7 \times 2 \times 2 \times 3 \times 5\sqrt{5}$$

$$AM = 24\sqrt{5}$$

Hence Ans is (C)

Sol. 90 (C)

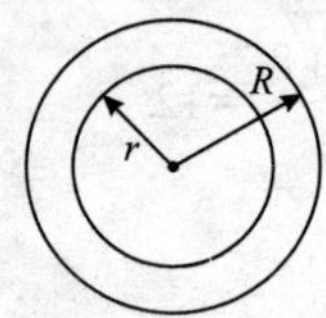

$\pi R^2 = 1386$

$\Rightarrow \quad R = 21$

$\pi r^2 = 962.5$

$w = R - r = 21 - 17.5 = 3.5$ cm

Hence Ans is (C)

Sol. 91 (D) Option 4

Volume of cone, $V = \frac{1}{3}\pi r^2 h$

New volume of cone $= \frac{1}{3}\pi\left(\frac{6}{5}r\right)^2\left(\frac{6h}{5}\right)$

$= \frac{1}{3}\pi\left(\frac{36}{25}r^2\right)\left(\frac{6h}{5}\right)$

$= \left(\frac{216}{125}\right)\frac{1}{3}\pi r^2 h$

$= (1.728)\left(\frac{1}{3}\pi r^2 h\right)$

$\%$ Increase in volume $= \frac{\text{New volume-old volume}}{\text{old volume}}$

$= \frac{1.728V - V}{V} \times 100 = 72.8\%$

Hence Ans is (D)

Sol. 92 (A) $h = 14$ cm

$R = 8$ cm

$T.C.S.A. = 2\pi h(R + r)$

$\Rightarrow \quad r = 7$

$\Rightarrow$ Diameter $= 2r = 14$ cm

Hence Ans is (A)

Sol. 93 (D) $\frac{4}{3}\pi \times 1^3 \times n = \frac{4}{3}\pi \times 8^3$

$\Rightarrow \quad n = 512$

Hence Ans is (D)

Sol. 94 (B) Distance covered in one revolution $= 2\pi r$.
Distance covered in 60 min

$= 60 \times 21 \times 2 \times \frac{22}{7} \times 0.8$

$= 6.336$ km

Hence Ans is (B)

Sol. 95 (A) Given that the radius of sphere $= \sqrt{7}$ cm
Now, According to question

$$\frac{(\text{Volume of Sphere})}{(\text{Total surface Area of Sphere})} = \frac{\frac{4}{3}\pi r^3}{4\pi r^2}$$

$$= \frac{r}{3} = \frac{\sqrt{7}}{3}$$

Hence Ans is (A)

Sol. 96 (D) Number of discs $= \frac{\pi r_1^2 h_1}{\pi r_2^2 h_2}$

$= \frac{\pi \times (3.3)^2 \times 40}{\pi \times (1.1)^2 \times 0.2} = 9 \times \frac{40}{0.2}$

$= 9 \times 200$

$= 1800$

Hence Ans is (D)

Sol. 97 (A) Area of triangle $= 80$ cm^2

$$80 = \sqrt{\left(\frac{x+30}{2}\right)\left(\frac{x-10}{2}\right)\left(\frac{x+10}{2}\right)\left(\frac{30-x}{2}\right)}$$

$$80^2 = \frac{(x^2 - 100)(900 - x^2)}{4 \times 4}$$

$80^2 \times 16 = x^4 - 1000x^2 + 90000$

$x^4 - 1000x^2 + 192400 = 0$

$x = 2\sqrt{65}$

Hence Ans is (A)

Sol. 98 (C)

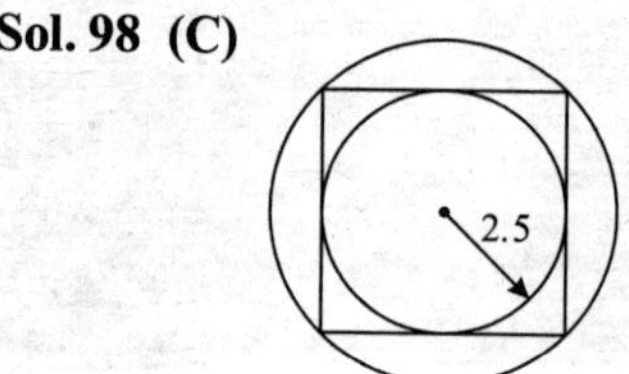

Diameter of inner circle = side of square radius of inner circle

$(r_1) = \frac{2.5}{2}$

Diameter of outer circle = diagonal of square radius of outer circle

$(r_2) = \frac{2.5 \times \sqrt{2}}{2}$

Hence ratio $= \frac{\pi r_2^2}{\pi r_1^2} = \frac{\pi\left(\frac{2.5 \times \sqrt{2}}{2}\right)^2}{\pi\left(\frac{2.5}{2}\right)^2} = 2 : 1$

Hence Ans is (C)

Sol. 99 (A) Distance covered in 1 revolution = $2\pi r$ let number of revolutions be k

Distance covered in k revolutions = $2\pi rk$

Distance covered in 100 times diameter = $100 \times 2r$

Hence $2\pi rk = 100 \times 2r$

$$k = \frac{100}{\pi}$$

Hence Ans is (A)

Sol. 100 (C)

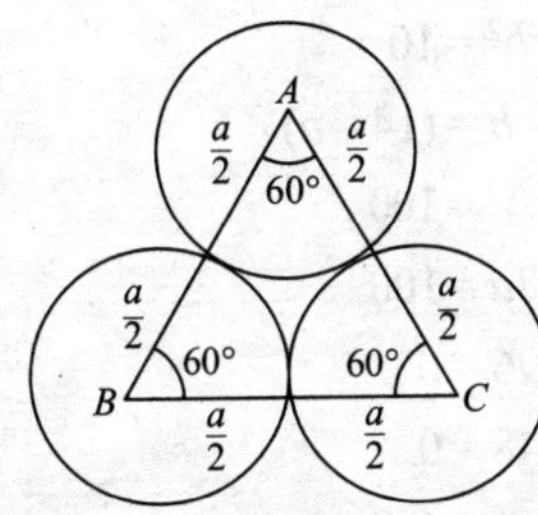

Area of equilateral triangle = $\frac{\sqrt{3}}{4}a^2$

$$\frac{\sqrt{3}}{4}a^2 = 49\sqrt{3}$$

$$a = 14 \text{ cm}$$

radius of circles = 7 cm

area of each sector

$$= \pi r^2 \times \frac{60°}{360°} = \pi \times 7^2 \times \frac{1}{6}$$

$$= \frac{22}{7} \times 7^2 \times \frac{1}{6}$$

$$= \frac{11 \times 7}{3} = \frac{77}{3}$$

Area of all 3 circular sectors

$$= 3 \times \frac{77}{3} = 77$$

Shaded area $= 49\sqrt{3} - 77$

$= 49 \times 1.73 - 77 = 7.77 \text{ cm}^2$

Hence Ans is (C)

Sol. 101 (A) 1 litre water = 1000 cm^3

1 kg water = 1000 cm^3

1 gm water = 1 cm^3

0.1 gm water = 0.1 cm^3

$= 0.1 \times 10^3 \text{ mm}^3$

$= 100 \text{ mm}^3$

Hence Ans is (A)

Sol. 102 (B) Let side of square = a

$$a^2 = 484$$

$$a = 22 \text{ cm}$$

Hence length of wire

$$= 4 \times 22 = 88 \text{ cm}$$

Perimeter of circle

$$= 2\pi r$$

$$2\pi r = 88$$

$$2 \times \frac{22}{7} r = 88$$

$$r = 14 \text{ cm}$$

$\Rightarrow$ $A = \pi r^2$

$$= \frac{22}{7} \times 14 \times 14$$

$$= 616 \text{ cm}^2$$

Hence Ans is (B)

Sol. 103 (B)

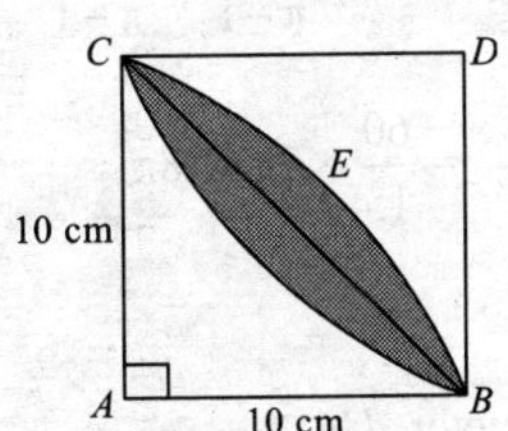

$AC = AB = r$ (say)

Area of shaded portion

$$= 2 \times ar(\text{segment } BECB)$$

$$= 2\left(\frac{1}{4}\pi r^2 - \frac{1}{2} \times 10 \times 10\right)$$

$$= \left(\frac{1}{2} \times \frac{22}{7} \times 100 - 100\right)$$

$$= 100 \times \frac{4}{7}$$

$$= \frac{400}{7} \text{ cm}^2$$

Hence Ans is (B)

Sol. 104 (A) $r_1 = 1$ cm; $r_2 = 2$ cm, $h = 14$ cm

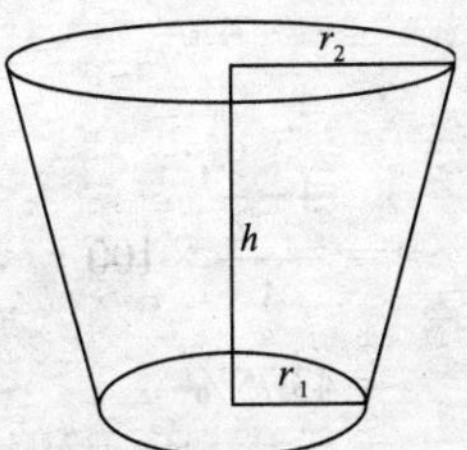

$\Rightarrow$ Capacity = Volume

$$= \frac{\pi h}{3}[r_1^2 + r_2^2 + r_1 r_2]$$

$$\frac{22}{7} \times \frac{14}{3}[1+4+1\times 2]$$

$$= \frac{44}{3}[7] = \frac{308}{3}\text{ cm}^2$$

Hence Ans is (A)

Sol. 105 (B) Circumference = $60 + 2r$

$$2\pi r = 60 + 2r$$

$$\Rightarrow \quad 2\pi r - 2r = 60$$

$$\Rightarrow \quad 2r(\pi - 1) = 60$$

$$r = \frac{30}{\pi - 1}$$

$$\Rightarrow \quad 2\pi r = 2\pi \times \frac{30}{\pi - 1} = \frac{60\pi}{\pi - 1}$$

$$= \frac{60}{15} \times 7\pi = 28\pi$$

Hence Ans is (B)

Sol. 106 (C) New diameter, d'

$$d' = d - \frac{25}{100} \times d$$

Original diameter = d

Original radius = r

Original curved surface area (CSA) = $4\pi r^2$

New radius, $r' = \frac{3}{4}r$

New $(CSA)' = 4\pi r'^2$

$$= 4\pi\left(\frac{3}{4}r\right)^2 = \frac{9\pi r^2}{4}$$

$$\Rightarrow \quad \%\text{age decrease} = \frac{CSA - (CSA)'}{CSA} \times 100$$

$$= \frac{4\pi r^2 - \frac{9}{4}\pi r^2}{4\pi r^2} \times 1N$$

$$= \frac{4 - \frac{9}{4}}{4} \times 100$$

$$= 43.75\%$$

Hence Ans is (C)

Sol. 107 (B) Given

$$lb = p;\ bh = q;\ hl = r$$

$$(lbh)^2 = pqr$$

Hence Ans is (B)

Sol. 108 (A) Given

$$a + b + c = 24$$

Here c = hypotenuse

$$c = 10$$

$$a + b = 14$$

and $$a^2 + b^2 = 10^2$$

$$b = (14 - a)$$

$$a^2 + (14 - a)^2 = 100$$

$$a^2 + 196 + a^2 - 28a = 100$$

$$2a^2 - 28a + 96 = 0$$

$$a - 14a + 48 = 0$$

$$a = 6, 8$$

If $a = 6$, then $b = 8$

$\Rightarrow$ Area of Triangle = $\frac{1}{2} \times 6 \times 8 = 24\text{ cm}^2$

Hence Ans is (A)

Sol. 109 (B) Let radii of cone be $2x$

Let radii of cylinder be $3x$

Let height of cone be $4y$

Let height of cylinder be $3y$

$$\text{Required Ratio} = \frac{\text{Volume of Cone}}{\text{Volume of Cylinder}}$$

$$= \frac{\frac{1}{3}\pi(2x)^2 4y}{\pi(3x)^2 3y} = \frac{\frac{1}{3}\times 4x^2 \times 4y}{9x^2 . 3y} = \frac{16}{81}$$

Hence Ans is (B)

Sol. 110 (C) Folded about breadth then $h = 14$ cm

$$2\pi r = 20\text{ cm}$$

$$CSA = 2\pi rh = 20 \times 14\text{ cm}^2 = 280\text{ cm}^2$$

Hence Ans is (C)

Sol. 111 (C) $AB > AC$

Hence Ans is (C)

Sol. 112 (B) Length of cuboidal vessel = 22 m

Width = 10 m

Let Height = x m

Volume = 440 m^3

$$V = lbh$$

$$440 = 22 \times 10 \times (x)$$

$$x = 2\text{ meter}$$

Hence Ans is (B)

Sol. 113 (D) Diameter is decreased by 25%

So radius also decreased by 25%

So radius becomes $0.75\,r$

Initial curved surface area $= 4\pi r^2$

Final curved surface area $= 4\pi(0.75r)^2$

$= 2.25\pi r^2$

So curved surface area will be decreased by

$4\pi r^2 - 2.25\pi r^2$

$= 1.75\pi r^2$

$= \frac{7}{4}\pi r^2$

Hence Ans is (D)

Sol. 114 (A) $2\pi rh = 4\pi r^2$

$\Rightarrow h = 2r$

$$\frac{\text{Vol. of cylinder}}{\text{Vol. of sphere}} = \frac{\pi r^2 h}{\frac{4}{3}\pi r^3} = \frac{\pi r^2(2r)}{\frac{4}{3}\pi r^3} = \frac{3}{2}$$

Hence Ans is (A)

Sol. 115 (B) $l + b + h = 25$

$2(lb + bh + lh) = 264$

$l + b + h = 25$

$\Rightarrow (l + b + h)^2 = 25^2$

$\Rightarrow l^2 + b^2 + h^2 + 2(lb + bh + lh) = 625$

$\Rightarrow l^2 + b^2 + h^2 + 264 = 625$

$\Rightarrow l^2 + b^2 + h^2 = 361$

Length of diagonal $= (\sqrt{l^2 + b^2 + h^2}) = \sqrt{361}$

$\Rightarrow$ Area $= (\sqrt{l^2 + b^2 + h^2})^2$

$= l^2 + b^2 + h^2 = 361$

Hence Ans is (B)

Sol. 116 (C) Let r be the radius of circle & a be side of square then

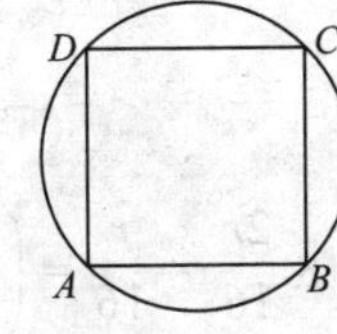

$a\sqrt{2} = 2r$ ...(1)

Given $a^2 = 4$

$\Rightarrow a = 2$

Using-(1) $2r = 2\sqrt{2}$

$r = \sqrt{2}$

Area of circle $\pi r^2 = \pi(\sqrt{2})^2 = 2\pi$

Hence Ans is (C)

Sol. 117 (C) $100\,\text{kl} = 100 \times 1000 \times 1000\,\text{cm}^3$

$= 10^8\,\text{cm}^3$

Hence Ans is (C)

Sol. 118 (A) Total surface area of the remaining solid is

$6 \times 5^2 - 3 \times 1^2 + 3 \times 1^2 = 150$

Hence Ans is (A)

Sol. 119 (B) Volume $= \pi r^2 h$

$\Rightarrow 99 = \frac{22}{7}\left(\frac{1}{10}\right)^2 h$

$\Rightarrow \frac{99 \times 100 \times 7}{22} = h$

$\Rightarrow h = \frac{900 \times 7}{2} = 31.5\,\text{m}$

Hence Ans is (B)

Sol. 120 (B) Let radius of cone $= 2x$, and that of cylinder $= 3x$

Also, height of the cone $= 3y$, and that of the cylinder $= 2y$

$$\frac{\text{volume of cone}}{\text{volume of cylinder}} = \frac{\frac{1}{3}\pi(2x)^2(3y)}{\pi(3x)^2(2y)} = \frac{\frac{1}{3}(12)}{(18)} = \frac{2}{9}$$

Hence Ans is (B)

Sol. 121 (B) The area of the field grazed by 3 horses = 3 sectors of a circle

radius $(r) = 7$ cm

Let the three angles be $\theta_1, \theta_2, \theta_3$

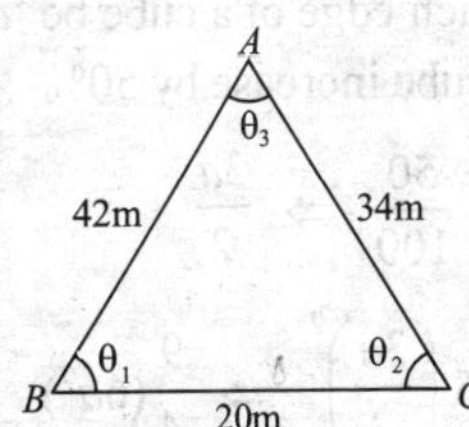

Now, $\frac{\pi r^2\theta_1}{360^\circ} + \frac{\pi r^2\theta_2}{360^\circ} + \frac{\pi r^2\theta_3}{360^\circ}$

$\Rightarrow \frac{\pi}{360^\circ} 7 \times 7(\theta_1 + \theta_2 + \theta_3)$ [by angle sum property]

$\Rightarrow \frac{22}{7} \times \frac{7 \times 7}{360^\circ} \times 180^\circ = 77\,\text{m}^2$

Hence Ans is (B)

Sol. 122 (A) Given, height of cone $(h) = 8.4$ cm

radius $(r) = 2.1$ cm

Let the radius of sphere be $= R$ cm

Volume of cone = volume of sphere

$$\frac{1}{3}\pi r^2 h = \frac{4}{3}\pi R^3$$

$$(2.1)^2 \times 8.4 = 4R^3$$

$$(2.1)^2 \times 2.1 \times 4 = 4R^3$$

$$\Rightarrow \quad R^3 = (2.1)^3$$

$$R = 2.1 \text{ cm}$$

Hence Ans is (A)

Sol. 123 (D) Let the external radius and internal radius are R and r. Total surface area area to be painted = External curved surface area + internal surface area + area of ring

$$2\pi R^2 + 2\pi r^2 + \pi R^2 - \pi r^2$$

$$\Rightarrow \pi(3R^2 + r^2)$$

$$\Rightarrow \frac{22}{7}(3 \times 12.5 \times 12.5 + 12 \times 12)$$

$$\Rightarrow \frac{22}{7}(468.75 + 144)$$

$$\Rightarrow \frac{22}{7} \times 612.75$$

$$\Rightarrow 1925.78 \text{ cm}^2$$

Rate of painting = 5 Paisa/cm^2

$$\text{Rs.}\frac{1925.78 \times 5}{100} = \text{Rs. } 96.29$$

Hence Ans is (D)

Sol. 124 (B) Let each edge of a cube be 'a' then area of cube $= 6a^2$ each edge of cube increase by 50%

New edge $= a + a \times \frac{50}{100} \Rightarrow \frac{3a}{2}$

New area of cube $= 6\left(\frac{3a}{2}\right)^2 \Rightarrow \frac{9}{4}(6a^2)$

then, the area increased (percentage)

$$= \frac{\frac{9}{4}(6a^2) - 6a^2}{6a^2} \times 100$$

$$= \left(\frac{9}{4} - 1\right) \times 100$$

$$\Rightarrow \frac{5}{4} \times 100 = 125\%$$

Hence Ans is (B)

Sol. 125 (C) AC is a diameter

$$\Rightarrow \quad AC^2 = AB^2 + BC^2$$

$$AC^2 = (14)^2 + (14)^2$$

$$AC^2 = 2(196)$$

$$AC = 14\sqrt{2} \text{ cm}$$

Then, radius $(r) = 7\sqrt{2}$ cm

Area of shaded region

= area of semicircle AQC

– (area of quad. $ABCP$ – area of ΔABC)

$$= \frac{1}{2} \times \frac{22}{7} \times 7\sqrt{2} \times 7\sqrt{2}$$

$$-\left(\frac{1}{4} \times \frac{22}{7} \times 14 \times 14 - \frac{1}{2} \times 14 \times 14\right)$$

$$= 154 - (154 - 98) = 98 \text{ cm}$$

Hence Ans is (C)

Sol. 126 (C) $12a = 9$

$$a = \frac{3}{4}$$

$$V = \left(\frac{3}{4}\right)^3$$

$$= \frac{27}{64}$$

Hence Ans is (C)

Sol. 127 (D) Area $= \frac{1}{2} \times \frac{2r}{16} \times \frac{r}{16} = \left(\frac{r}{16}\right)^2 = \frac{r^2}{256}$

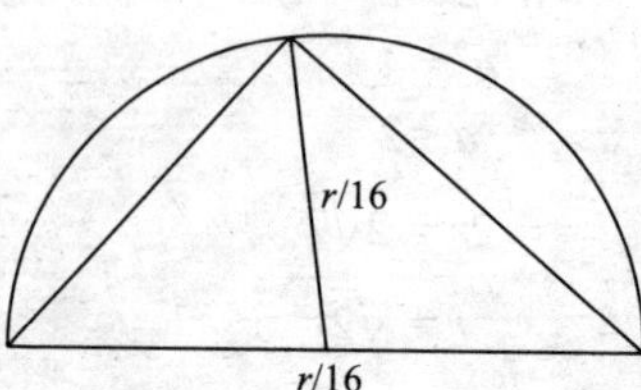

Hence Ans is (D)

Sol. 128 (D) (Bonus) l is mentioned in options but not given in the question statement.

If we take l as edge of cube then solution will be

Required surface area

= Area of 5 faces of cube + Region I + Area of hemisphere.

$$= 5 \times (4r)^2 + [(4r)^2 - \pi r^2] + 2\pi(r)^2$$

$$= 80r^2 + 16r^2 - \pi r^2 + 2\pi r^2$$

$$= 96r^2 + \pi r^2$$

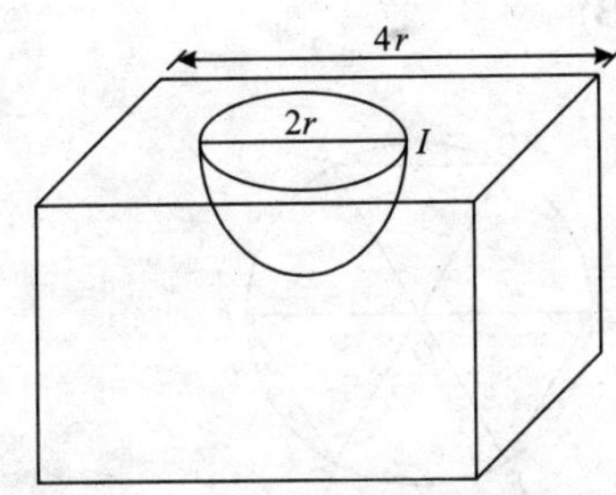

Let $l = 4r, r = l/4$

$$96 \times \frac{l^2}{16} + \pi \times \frac{l^2}{16} = \frac{l^2}{16}[\pi + 96]$$

Hence Ans is (D)

Sol. 129 (C) Maximum length of pole

= diagonal of the room

$$= \sqrt{l^2 + b^2 + h^2}$$

$$= \sqrt{10^2 + 10^2 + 5^2}$$

$$= \sqrt{225}$$

$$= 15 \text{ m}$$

Hence Ans is (C)

Sol. 130 (C) $h = 3$ cm

$r = 4$ cm

$$l^2 = r^2 + h^2$$

$$= 4^2 + 3^2$$

$$= 16 + 9$$

$$= 25$$

$\Rightarrow$ $l = 5$ cm

Volume of cone $= \dfrac{\pi r^2 h}{3}$

$$= \frac{\pi 4^2 \times 3}{3}$$

$$= 16\pi \text{ cm}^3$$

Hence Ans is (C)

Sol. 131 (D) Radius of (C_1) is $r_1 = a$

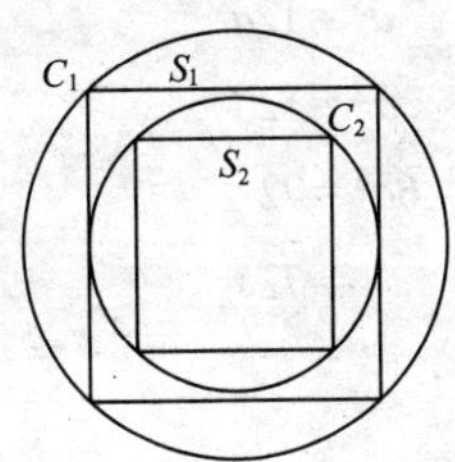

$$S_1\sqrt{2} = 2a$$

$$\Rightarrow \quad S_1 = a\sqrt{2}$$

$$2r_2 = a\sqrt{2}$$

$$r_2 = \frac{a}{\sqrt{2}}$$

$$2r_2 = a\sqrt{2}$$

$$a\sqrt{2} = S_2\sqrt{2}$$

$$a = S_2$$

Hence Ans is (D)

Sol. 132 (B) Let the height of the cylinder be h units and the radius of the base be r units.

The curved surface area of the cylinder with height h and radius $r = 2\pi rh$ sq units.

The new height $= \dfrac{110}{100}h$

New radius $= \dfrac{90}{100}r$

Hence new surface area $= 2\pi \times \dfrac{110}{100}h \times \dfrac{90}{100}r$

$$= \left(\frac{99}{100}\right) 2\pi rh \text{ sq. units}$$

Therefore the surface area has decreased by 1%.

Hence Ans is (B)

Sol. 133 (B) Area of the segment = Area of sector ABF − Area ΔABF

$$= \frac{\pi \times 6^2 \times 120^\circ}{360^\circ} - \frac{1}{2} \times AB \times AF \times \sin 120^\circ$$

$$= 12\pi - \frac{1}{2} \times 6 \times 6 \times \frac{\sqrt{3}}{2}$$

$$= 12 \times 3.14 - 9\sqrt{3}$$

$$= 22.092 \text{ sq. cm}$$

Hence Ans is (B)

Sol. 134 (C) Let edge of cube is 'a'

Thus, $a^3 = 12a$

$a^2 = 12$

$6a^2 = 72$

Total surface area $= 72$

Hence Ans is (C)

Sol. 135 (B) Diagonal of square having side = a is given by $a\sqrt{2}$

As $a\sqrt{2} = 5\sqrt{2}, a = 5$

Hence Ans is (B)

Sol. 136 (D) According to the question

$$V = \frac{\pi}{3}(r_1^2 + r_2^2 + r_1 r_2)\,h = 28.49 \times 1000$$

$\Rightarrow$ $h = 15$ cm

$l^2 = h^2 + (r_1 - r_2)^2$

$\Rightarrow$ $l = \sqrt{274}$ cm

Hence Ans is (D)

Sol. 137 (B) According to the question

$12a = x$

and $6a^2 = x$

$\Rightarrow$ $6a^2 = 12a$

$\Rightarrow$ $a = 2$

$\Rightarrow$ $V = 8$

Hence Ans is (B)

Sol. 138 (D) Volume of cube = a^3

Now, diameter of sphere = a

$\Rightarrow$ radius $= \frac{a}{2}$

$\Rightarrow$ volume of sphere $= \frac{4}{3}\pi\left(\frac{a}{2}\right)^3$

$$= \frac{4}{3}\pi\left(\frac{a^3}{8}\right)$$

$$= \frac{\pi a^3}{6}$$

$$\Rightarrow \frac{\text{Volume of cube}}{\text{Volume of sphere}} = \frac{a^3}{\frac{\pi}{6}a^3} = \frac{6}{\pi}$$

Hence Ans is (D)

Sol. 139 (B) Total surface area of cube

$= 216$ cm^3

$6a^2 = 216$

$a^2 = \frac{216}{6} = 36$

$\Rightarrow$ $a = 6$ cm

Length of longest rod

$= a\sqrt{3} = 6\sqrt{3}$ cm

Hence Ans is (B)

Sol. 140 (A)

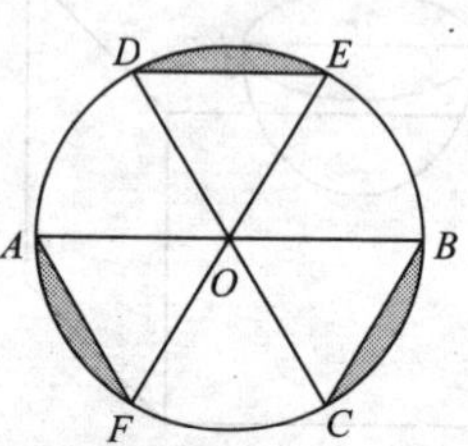

All 3Δ's AOF, BOC & DOE

Form an equilateral Δ

So, area of shaded region

$= 3$[area of sector – ar. of Δ]

$$= 3\left[\frac{60}{360} \times \pi r^2 - \frac{1}{2}r^2 \sin 60^\circ\right]$$

$$= 3\left[\frac{1}{6} \times \pi r^2 - \frac{1}{2}r^2 \times \frac{\sqrt{3}}{2}\right]$$

$$= \frac{\pi r^2}{2} - \frac{3\sqrt{3}r^2}{4}$$

$$= \frac{r^2}{2}\left[\pi - \frac{3\sqrt{3}}{2}\right]$$

Hence Ans is (A)

Sol. 141 (C) Clearly the required capacity

$=$ HCF (112, 240)

$= 16$ litre

$= 16 \times 1000$ cc

$= 16000$ cc

Hence Ans is (C)

Sol. 142 (C) Curved surface area $= 2\pi rh$,

volume $= \pi r^2 h$

$$\frac{\text{CSA}}{\text{Volume}} = \frac{2\pi rh}{\pi r^2 h} = \frac{2}{r}$$

Hence Ans is (C)

Sol. 143 (C)

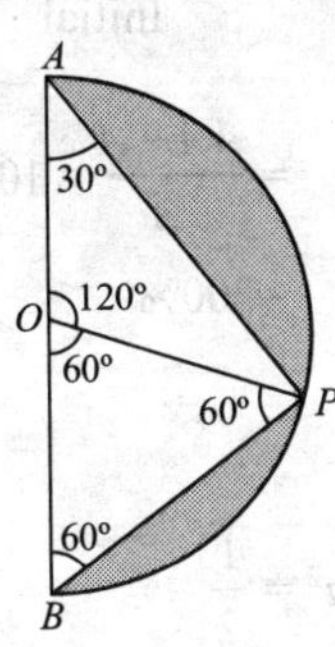

$$\frac{A_L}{A_S} = \frac{\frac{1}{3}\times \pi r^2 - \frac{1}{2}r^2 \sin 120^\circ}{\frac{1}{6}\pi r^2 - \frac{1}{2}r^2 \sin 60^\circ}$$

$$\Rightarrow \quad \frac{\frac{1}{3}\pi - \frac{1}{2}\frac{\sqrt{3}}{2}}{\frac{1}{6}\pi - \frac{1}{2}\frac{\sqrt{3}}{2}}$$

$$\Rightarrow \quad \frac{2(4\pi - 3\sqrt{3})}{4\pi - 6\sqrt{3}}$$

$$\Rightarrow \quad \frac{4\pi - 3\sqrt{3}}{2\pi - 3\sqrt{3}}$$

Hence Ans is (C)

Sol. 144 (A)

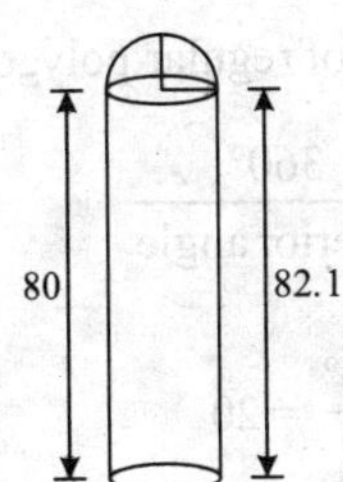

$r = 2.1$ cm

$$v = \pi r^2 h + \frac{2}{3}\pi r^3$$

$$= \pi\left[4.41\times 80 + \frac{2}{3}\times 9.261\right]$$

$$= \pi[352.8 + 6.174]$$

$= 1128.204$ cm^3

$= 1.12$ L

Hence Ans is (A)

Sol. 145 (A)

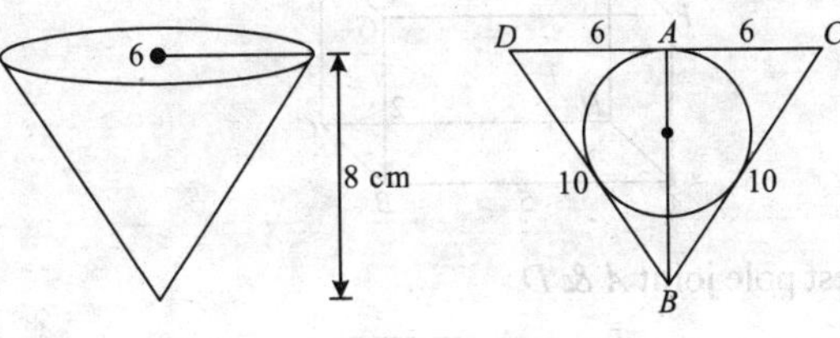

$AB = 8$

Area of $\quad \Delta BCD = \frac{1}{2}\times 12\times 8$

Semiperimeter of

$\Delta BCD = 16$

Radius of sphere

$$= \frac{48}{16} = 3$$

Thus fraction of volume :

$$\frac{\frac{4}{3}\pi r^3}{\frac{1}{3}\pi(6^2)8}$$

$$= \frac{4\times 27}{36\times 8}$$

$$= \frac{3}{8}$$

Hence Ans is (A)

Sol. 146 (D) Each side of cube is 3 cm

$\Rightarrow$ Volume of one cube = (side)^3

$\Rightarrow \quad (3)^3 = 27$ cm^3

These are 15 cube

$\Rightarrow \quad 27\times 15 = 405$ cm^3

Hence Ans is (D)

Sol. 147 (A) Angle made by minute hand in one minute is 6°

$\Rightarrow$ in 5 minutes it is 30°. It forms a sector in 5 minutes

$$= \frac{30}{360}\times\pi\times(14)^2$$

$$= \frac{1}{12}\times\frac{22}{7}\times 14\times 14$$

$$= \frac{154}{3}$$

Hence Ans is (A)

Sol. 148 (C)

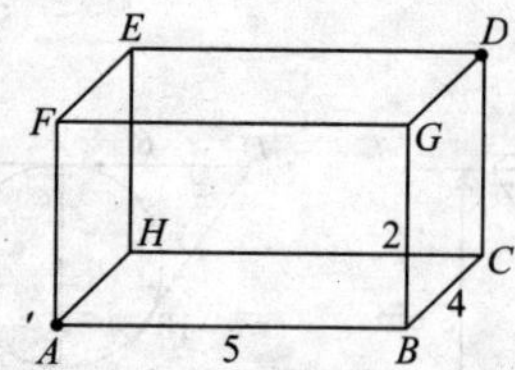

Longest pole joint A & D

$$AC = \sqrt{25+16}$$

$$= \sqrt{41}$$

$$AD = \sqrt{41+4}$$

$$= \sqrt{45}$$

$$= 3\sqrt{5}\text{ m}$$

Hence Ans is (C)

Sol. 149 (C) Given

$$\frac{4}{3}\pi R^3 = 4\pi R^2$$

$$R = 3$$

Circumference $= 2\pi R = 6\pi$

Hence Ans is (C)

Sol. 150 (A)

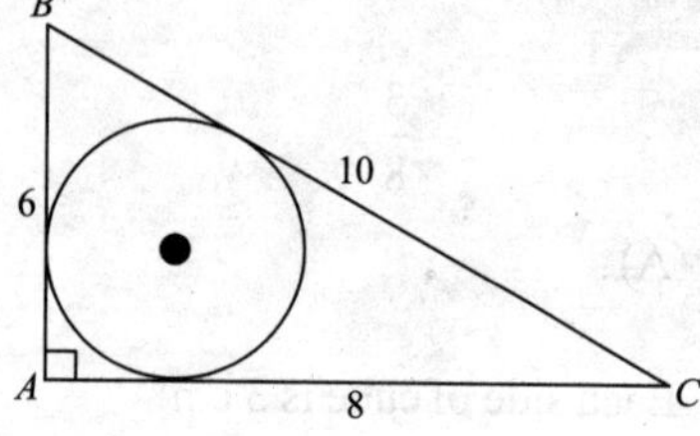

$$\text{Area of } \Delta = \frac{1}{2} \times 6 \times 8$$

$$= 24$$

Semi perimeter = 12

$$r = \frac{\Delta}{s} = \frac{24}{12} = 2\text{ cm}$$

Hence Ans is (A)

Sol. 151 (C)

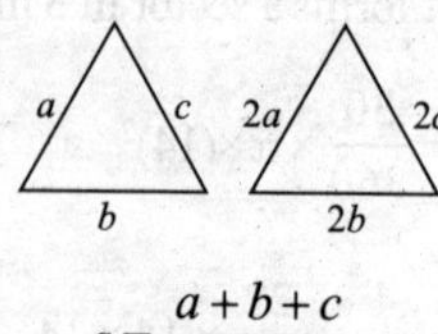

$$s = \frac{a+b+c}{2}$$

Initial area $= \sqrt{s(s-a)(s-b)(s-c)} = A$

New Area → $s_1 = 2s$

$$= \sqrt{2s(2s-2a)(2s-2b)(2s-2c)} = 4A$$

$$\text{Increase in Area} = \frac{\text{final} - \text{Initial}}{\text{Initial}} \times 100$$

$$= \frac{4A - A}{A} \times 100$$

$$= 300\%$$

Hence Ans is (C)

Sol. 152 (B) $\frac{\sqrt{3}}{4}a^2 = \frac{1}{2}$ $[6a + 8a + 10a]$

$$\frac{\sqrt{3}}{4}a^2 = \frac{1}{2} \times 24a$$

$$\frac{\sqrt{3}}{4}a = 12\text{ cm}$$

$$a = \frac{48}{\sqrt{3}} \times \frac{\sqrt{3}}{\sqrt{3}}\text{ cm}$$

$$= 16\sqrt{3}$$

$$\text{Area} = \frac{\sqrt{3}}{4} \times (\text{side})^2$$

$$= \frac{\sqrt{3}}{4} \times 16\sqrt{3} \times 16\sqrt{3}\text{ cm}^2$$

$$= 192\sqrt{3}\text{ cm}^2$$

Hence Ans is (B)

Sol. 153 (C) Number of sides of regular polygon are

$$= \frac{360^\circ}{\text{exterior angle}}$$

$$= \frac{360^\circ}{18^\circ} = 20$$

Hence Ans is (C)

Sol. 154 (D) Let the income of A and B be $9x$ and $4x$

Let the expenditure of A and B be $3y$ and $1y$

Therefore $9x - 3y = 1000,$

and $4x - y = 1000$

on solving these equation we get $x = \frac{2000}{3}$

Therefore income of $B = 4x = \frac{8000}{3}$

Hence Ans is (D)

Sol. 155 (D) let sides of squares are 'a' cm and 'b' cm

then $4a+4b=120$

and $a^2+b^2=468$

then $a+b=30$

$(a+b)^2=a^2+b^2+2ab$

$30^2=468+2ab$

Therefore $ab=216$

$(a-b)^2=(a+b)^2-4ab$

$(a-b)^2=900-864=36$

$a-b=6$

Hence Ans is (D)

Sol. 156 (C) Let radius and height of cone be 'r' and 'h'
Let radius and height of cylinder be 'R' and 'H'

Since $r:R=4:3$

and $h:H=2:3$

$$\frac{\text{Volume of Cone}}{\text{Volume of Cylinder}}=\frac{\frac{1}{3}\pi r^2 h}{\pi R^2 H}$$

$$=\frac{1}{3}\times\left(\frac{r}{R}\right)^2\times\frac{h}{H}$$

$$=\frac{1}{3}\times\left(\frac{4}{3}\right)^2\times\frac{2}{3}=\frac{32}{81}$$

$$\frac{\text{Volume of Cone}}{\text{Volume of Cylinder}}=\frac{32}{81}$$

$=32:81$

Hence Ans is (C)

Sol. 157 (C) $l:b:h=1:2:3$

Let $l=x, b=2x, h=3x$

Total surface area = 88 m^2

$2(lb+bh+hl)=88$

$2(x\times 2x+2x\times 3x+3x\times x)=88$

$2(2x^2+6x^2+3x^2)=88$

$2\times 11x^2=88$

$x^2=4$

$x=2$

$\Rightarrow$ $l=2$ m, $b=4$ m, $h=6$ m

Hence Ans is (C)

Sol. 158 (B) $h=120$ cm,

$2r=84$ cm

$h=120$ cm,

$r=42$ cm

Curved surface Area $=2\pi rh$

$$=2\times\frac{22}{7}\times 42\times 120=31680\text{ cm}^2$$

Area covered in 500 revolutions

$=500\times 31680$ cm^2

$=15840000$ cm^2

$=1584$ m^2

$\Rightarrow$ Cost of levelling

$=5\times 1584$

$=7920$

Hence Ans is (B)

Sol. 159 (C) $S\sqrt{2}=2\sqrt{3}$

$$S=\frac{2\sqrt{3}}{\sqrt{2}}$$

$$6S^2=6\times 4\times\frac{3}{2}$$

$=36$ cm^2

Hence Ans is (C)

Sol. 160 (A)

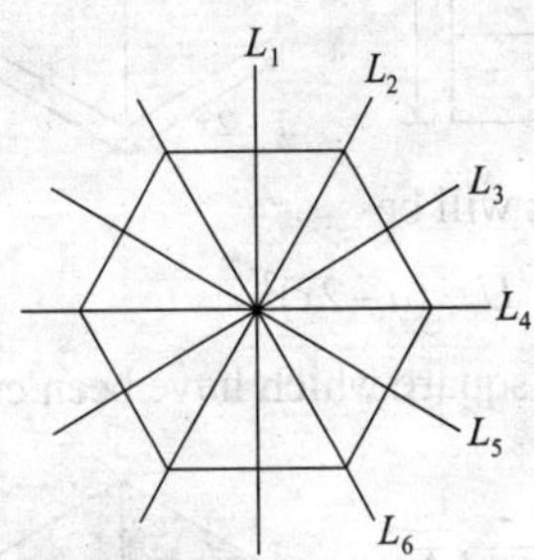

Minimum angle between any two lines of symmetry = 30°.

Hence Ans is (A)

Sol. 161 (C)

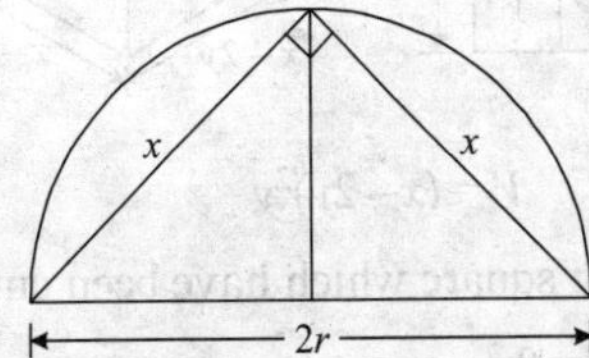

Largest triangle that can be inscribed in a semicircle will be an isosceles triangle so area of triangle will be $\frac{1}{2}$ base × height

$$=\frac{1}{2}2r\times r=r^2$$

Hence Ans is (C)

Sol. 162 (B) Each exterior angle of a regular polygon of side

$$n = \frac{360°}{n} \quad \ldots(1)$$

Given interior angle = 165°

so exterior angle will be

$$180° - 165° = 15°$$

Using equation-(1) we have $15° = \frac{360°}{n}$

$\Rightarrow \quad n = 24$

Hence Ans is (B)

Sol. 163 (B) Total surface area of all spheres always increases when *a* solid metal sphere is melted and recast into number of smaller spheres

Hence Ans is (B)

Sol. 164 (B) Path I is of same lengths as path II. It will be independent of no of semi circles or consider the length *AB* as 16 cm and verify the answer.

Hence Ans is (B)

Sol. 165 (D) Let the side of tin = *a*

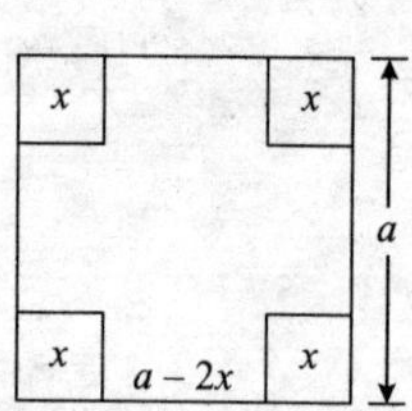

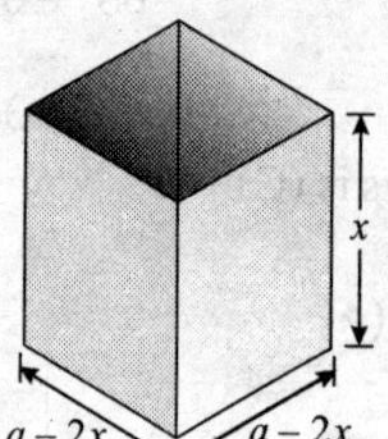

So volume of open box will be

$$U = (a - 2x)^2 x$$

Where *x* is the side of square which have been cut-off

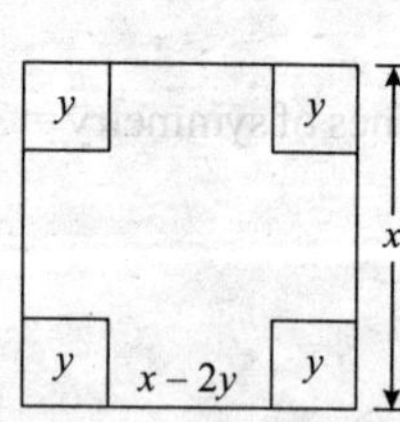

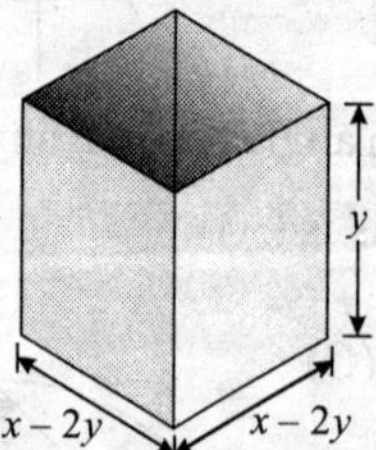

Similarly $\quad V = (x - 2y)^2 y$

where *y* is the side of square which have been cut-off

Minimum value of $U = 0$

Minimum value of $V = 0$

So, $U > V$ and $V > U$ and $U = V$ are possible

But minimum value of $U = 0$

It cannot be greater than maximum value of V

Hence Ans is (D)

Sol. 166 (B)

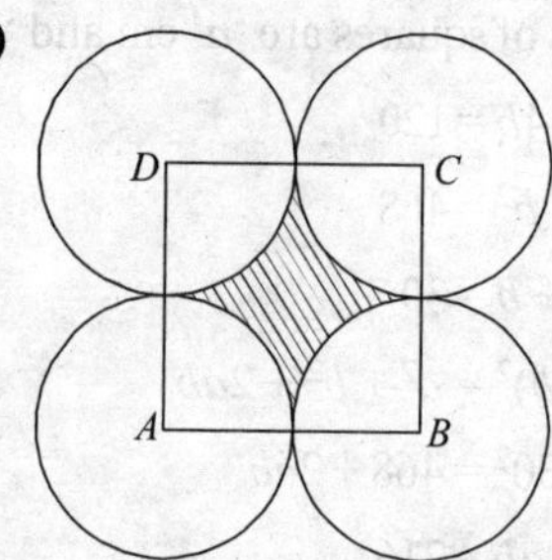

Area of shaded region = area of square of side $AB - 4 \times$ area of quadrant whose radius is half of $\frac{1}{2}AB$

$$\Rightarrow \quad a^2 - \frac{\pi a^2}{4}$$

$$= a^2\left[1 - \frac{\pi}{4}\right]$$

$$= a^2\left[\frac{4-\pi}{4}\right]$$

Hence Ans is (B)

Sol. 167 (C)

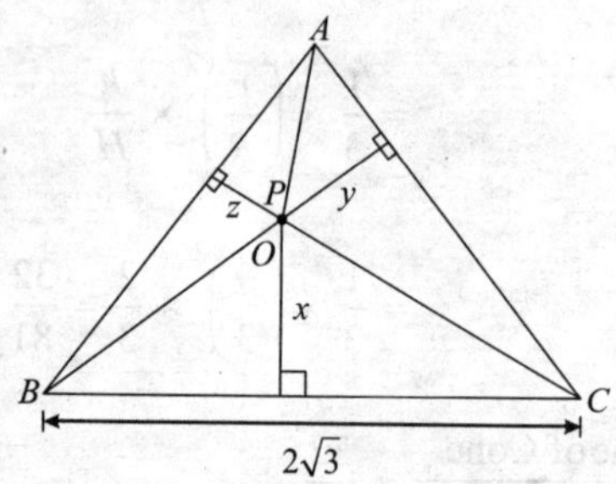

$$ar(\Delta ABC) = ar\,\Delta AOB + ar\Delta AOC + ar\,\Delta BOC$$

$$\frac{\sqrt{3}(2\sqrt{3})^2}{4} = \frac{1}{2}x \cdot 2\sqrt{3} + \frac{1}{2}y \cdot 2\sqrt{3} + \frac{1}{2} + z \cdot 2\sqrt{3}$$

$$\frac{12\sqrt{3}}{4} = \frac{1}{2}2\sqrt{3}\,[x+y+z]$$

$$3\sqrt{3} = \sqrt{3}\,[x+y+z]$$

$$3 = x+y+z$$

Hence Ans is (C)

Sol. 168 (D)

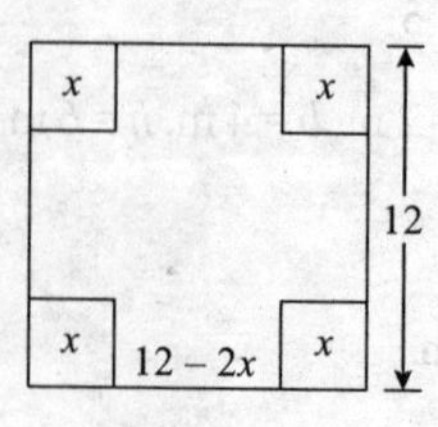

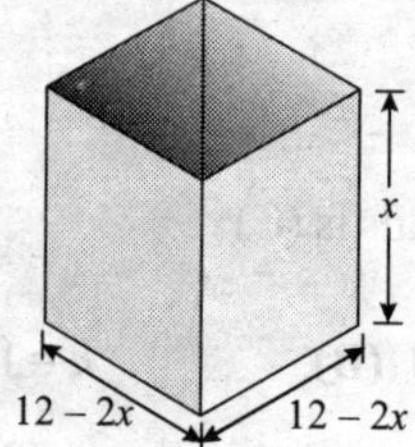

Let the sides of the square cut-off from the square lamina be x

Volume of box

$$V=(12-2x)^2 x$$
$$V=(144+4x^2-48x)x$$
$$V=4x^3-48x^2+144x$$

for maximum value

$$\frac{dv}{dx}=0$$
$$\frac{d(4x^3-48x^2+144x)}{dx}=0$$
$$12x^2-96x+144=0$$
$$x^2-8x+12=0$$
$$\Rightarrow \quad x=2 \text{ or } 6$$
$$\frac{d^2v}{dx^2}=24x-96$$
$$x\neq 6$$

So $\quad x=2$

For $\quad x=2$

$$V=(12-2\times 2)^2\times 2$$
$$V_{max}=128$$

So $\quad V\neq 130 \text{ c.c}$

Hence Ans is (D)

Sol. 169 (A) Let the side of the square be a

The smallest square so formed is a square formed by joining the midpoints of the side of the bigger square.

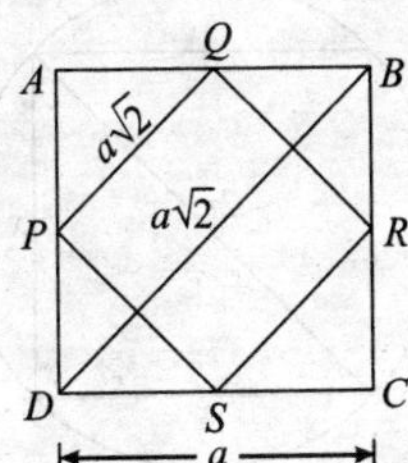

$$\frac{ar\ PQRS}{ar\ ABCD}=\left(\frac{a/\sqrt{2}}{a}\right)^2=\frac{1}{2}$$

Hence Ans is (A)

Sol. 170 (C) Let $\angle AOP=\theta_1=120°$

and $\quad \angle BOP=\theta_2=60°$

$$\frac{\text{Area larger segment}}{\text{Area smaller segment}}=\frac{\frac{\theta_1}{360}\pi r^2-\frac{1}{2}r^2\sin\theta_1}{\frac{\theta_2}{360}\pi r^2-\frac{1}{2}r^2\sin\theta_2}$$

$$=\frac{\frac{1}{3}\pi r^2-\frac{1}{2}r^2\sin 120°}{\frac{1}{6}\pi r^2-\frac{1}{2}r^2\sin 60°}$$

$$=\frac{r^2\left(\frac{\pi}{3}-\frac{\sqrt{3}}{4}\right)}{r^2\left(\frac{\pi}{6}-\frac{\sqrt{3}}{4}\right)}=\frac{4\pi-3\sqrt{3}}{2\pi-3\sqrt{3}}$$

Hence Ans is (C)

Sol. 171 (A) Semiperimeter of the triangle is given by

$$s=\frac{35+53+66}{2}=77$$

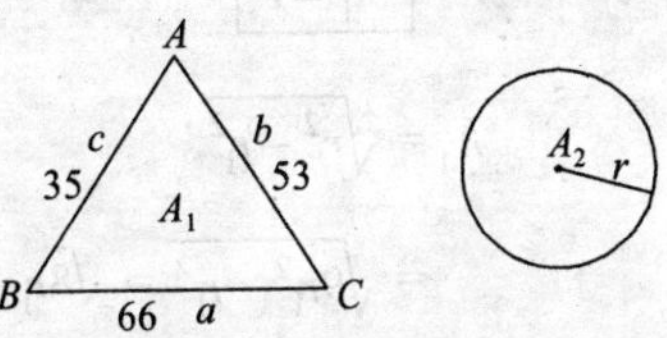

Using heron's formula we have

$$A_1=\sqrt{s(s-a)(s-b)(s-c)}$$
$$=\sqrt{77(77-35)(77-66)(77-53)}$$
$$A_1=\sqrt{77\times 42\times 11\times 24}$$
$$=\sqrt{7\times 11\times 7\times 6\times 11\times 6\times 4}$$
$$A_1=7\times 11\times 6\times 2$$
$$A_1=924\text{ m}^2$$
$$A_2=2A_1 \text{ (given)}$$
$$A_2=2\times 924=1848\text{ m}^2$$
$$1848=\frac{22}{7}\times r^2$$
$$r^2=\frac{1848\times 7}{22}=588$$
$$r=14\sqrt{3}\text{ m}$$

Hence Ans is (A)

Sol. 172 (C) Let radius of circle is r

i.e. slant height of both cone is r

Let radius of cone are r_1 and r_2

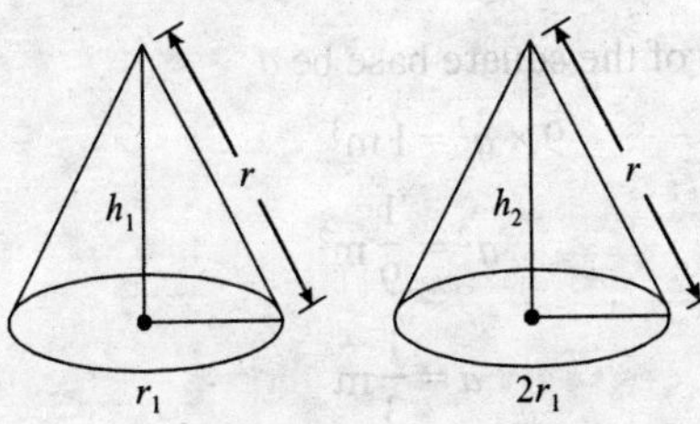

as per question ratio of curved surface area = 1 : 2

$$\frac{\pi r_1 l_1}{\pi r_2 l_2} = \frac{1}{2}$$

$$\frac{\pi r_1 r}{\pi r_2 r} = \frac{1}{2}$$

$$\Rightarrow \quad 2r_1 = r_2$$

$$C_1 = 2\pi r_1,$$

$$C_2 = 2\pi r_2 = 4\pi r_1$$

$$C_1 + C_2 = 2\pi r$$

$$2\pi r_1 + 4\pi r_1 = 2\pi r$$

$$6\pi r_1 = 2\pi r$$

$$\boxed{3r_1 = r}$$

$$h_1 = \sqrt{r^2 - r_1^2}$$

$$= \sqrt{9r_1^2 - r_1^2} = \sqrt{8}r_1$$

$$\& \quad h_2 = \sqrt{r^2 - 4r_1^2}$$

$$\sqrt{9r_1^2 - 4r_1^2} = \sqrt{5}r_1$$

$$\frac{v_1}{v_2} = \frac{\frac{1}{3}\pi r_1^2 h_1}{\frac{1}{3}\pi r_2^2 h_2} \Rightarrow \left(\frac{r_1}{r_2}\right)^2 \times \left(\frac{h_1}{h_2}\right)$$

$$= \frac{1}{4} \times \frac{\sqrt{8}r_1}{\sqrt{5}r_1}$$

$$= \frac{2\sqrt{2}}{4\sqrt{5}}$$

$$= \frac{1}{\sqrt{10}}$$

$$v_1 : v_2 = 1 : \sqrt{10}$$

Hence Ans is (C)

Sol. 173 (D) Volume of solid block = 1 m^3

Volume of rectangular bar = 1m^3

$\Rightarrow$ Area of base × height = 1m^3

Let the side of the square base be a

$$\Rightarrow \quad 9 \times a^2 = 1 \text{ m}^3$$

$$\Rightarrow \quad a^2 = \frac{1}{9} \text{ m}^2$$

$$\Rightarrow \quad a = \frac{1}{3} \text{ m}$$

Weight of largest cube = volume × density

$$= \left(\frac{1}{3}\right)^3 \times 90$$

$$= \frac{90}{27} \text{ kg} = 3\frac{1}{3} \text{ kg}$$

Hence Ans is (D)

Sol. 174 (A) Let the radius of circle is r

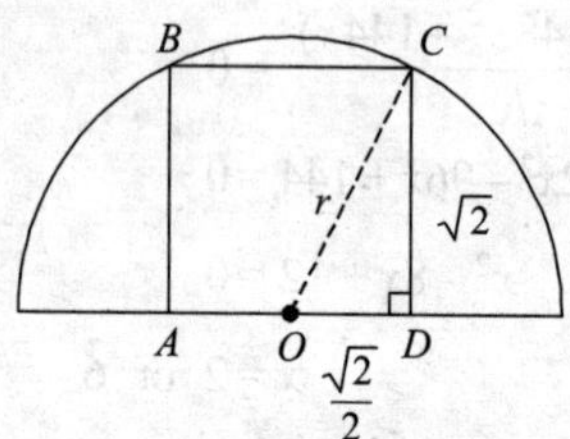

If area of square is 2, then its side is $\sqrt{2}$

Apply phythagorous is ΔCOD

$$r^2 = (\sqrt{2})^2 + \left(\frac{\sqrt{2}}{2}\right)^2$$

$$r^2 = 2 + \frac{1}{2}$$

$$r = \sqrt{\frac{5}{2}}$$

Now, let the side of square is x

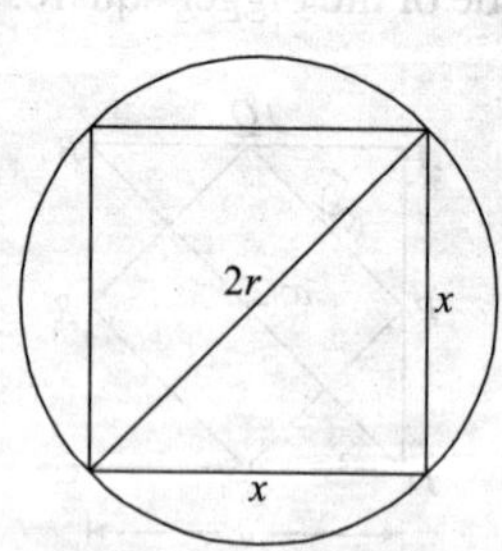

So, $$(2r)^2 = x^2 + x^2$$

$$\Rightarrow \quad 4r^2 = 2x^2$$

$$\Rightarrow \quad 4\left(\frac{\sqrt{5}}{\sqrt{2}}\right)^2 = 2x^2$$

$$\Rightarrow \quad 4 \times \frac{5}{2} = 2x^2$$

$$\Rightarrow \quad x^2 = 5$$

Hence Ans is (A)

Sol. 175 (D) Volume $= x \times 2x \times 3x = 6x^3$

Total number of cube are $= \dfrac{6x^3}{1} = 6x^3$

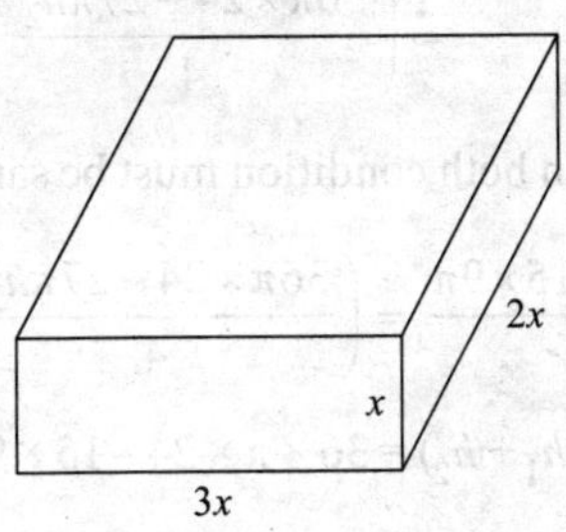

$$6x^3 \le 400$$

$$x^3 \le \frac{200}{3}$$

$$x^3 \le 66.66$$

So that $x^3 = 64$

$\Rightarrow$ $x = 4$

Total cubes are $= 6 \times (4)^3 = 6 \times 64 = 384$

Sol. 176 (A)

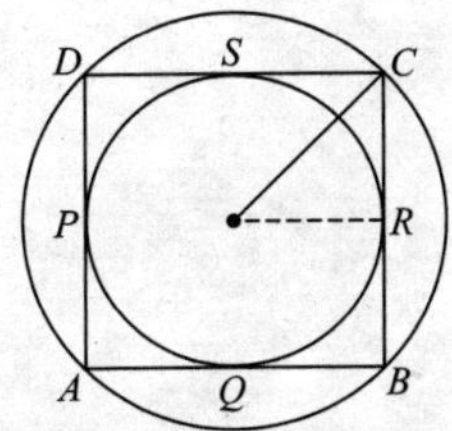

Radius of inner circle $= \dfrac{a}{2}$

[where a is the length of side of square]

Radius of outer circle $= \dfrac{a}{\sqrt{2}}$

$\Rightarrow$ Ratio of area of inner circle to outer circle

$$= \pi\left(\frac{a}{2}\right)^2 : \pi\left(\frac{a}{\sqrt{2}}\right)^2 = 1:2$$

Hence Ans is (A)

Sol. 177 (C)

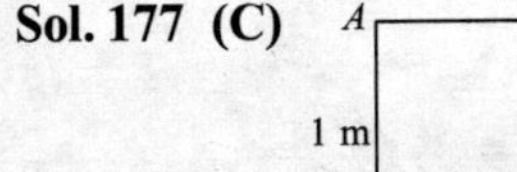

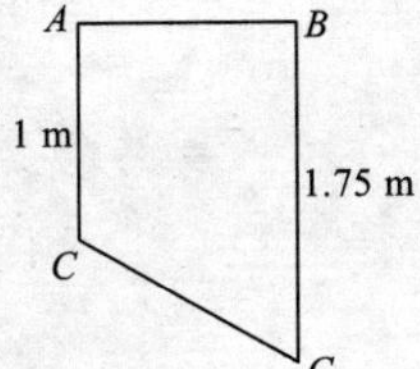

Volume of water in tank $= \left(36 \times 10.5 \times 1 + 36 \times 10.5 \times \dfrac{3}{4}\right) \times \dfrac{1}{2}$

$$= \frac{10.5 \times 99}{2} m^2$$

Volume of water flows through pipe in one hour

$$= \pi \times \left(\frac{7}{100}\right)^2 \times 5000 \text{ m}^3$$

Let time to empty water in pool is t hr

$$\Rightarrow \quad \pi \times \left(\frac{7}{100}\right)^2 \times 5000 \times t = \frac{10.5 \times 99}{2}$$

$$t = 6\frac{3}{4} \text{ hr}$$

Hence Ans is (C)

Sol. 178 (D)

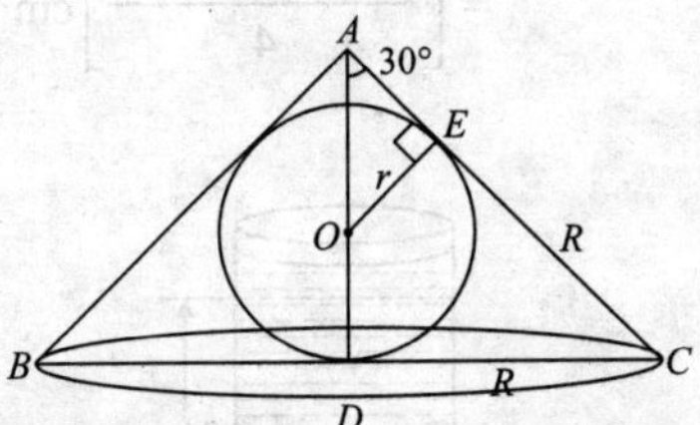

In ΔABD

$$\tan 30° = \frac{R}{h} \ (AD = h)$$

$$R = \frac{h}{\sqrt{3}}$$

In ΔADC $\quad AC^2 = h^2 + \left(\dfrac{h}{\sqrt{3}}\right)^2$

$$= \frac{4h^2}{3}$$

$$AC = \frac{2h}{\sqrt{3}}$$

$$CE = R = \frac{h}{\sqrt{3}}$$

$$\Rightarrow \quad AE = AC - CE$$

$$= \frac{h}{\sqrt{3}}$$

Now in ΔAOE $\quad \tan 30° = \dfrac{r}{AE}$

$$r = AE \times \frac{1}{\sqrt{3}} = \frac{h}{3}$$

$\Rightarrow$ Volume of sphere $= \dfrac{4}{3}\pi r^3 = \dfrac{4}{3}\pi\left(\dfrac{h}{3}\right)^3$

$$= \frac{4}{81}\pi h^3$$

Hence Ans is (D)

Sol. 179 (C) Condition (1)

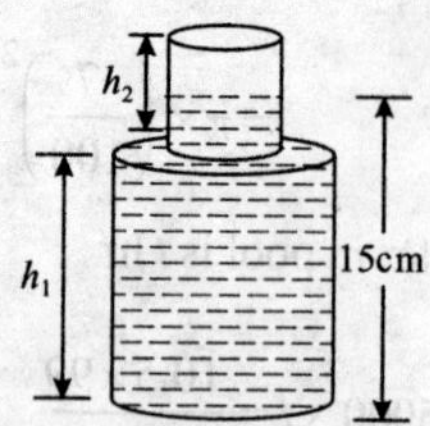

Let the height of cylinder having radius 3 cm and 1.5 cm are h_1 and h_2 respectively

$\Rightarrow$ Volume of water in condition (1)

$$\pi \times (3^2)h_1 + \pi(1.5)^2(15 - h_1)$$

$$= \left[\frac{27\pi h_1 + 15 \times 9\pi}{4}\right] \text{cm}^3$$

Condition (2)

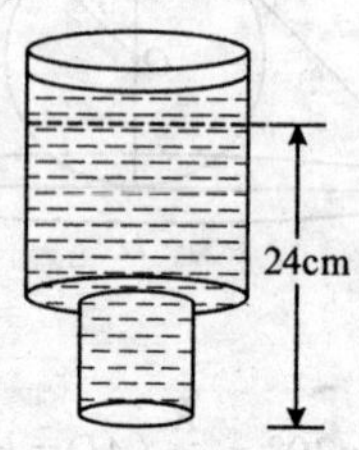

Volume of water in condition (2)

$$= \pi(1.5)^2 h_2 + (24 - h_2)9\pi$$

$$= \left(\frac{36\pi \times 24 - 27\pi h_2}{4}\right) \text{cm}^3$$

Volume of water in both condition must be same

$$\Rightarrow \quad \frac{27\pi h_1 + 15 \times 9\pi}{4} = \left(\frac{36\pi \times 24 - 27\pi h_2}{4}\right)$$

$$27\pi(h_1 + h_2) = 36 \times \pi \times 24 - 15 \times 9\pi$$

$$(h_1 + h_2) = \frac{9\pi \times 81}{27\pi}$$

$$\Rightarrow \quad h_1 + h_2 = 27 \text{ cm}$$

Hence Ans is (C)

* * * * *

Quadrilateral & Area of Parallelogram 12

❍ Sum of the angles of a quadrilateral is 360°.

❍ A diagonal of a parallelogram divides it into two congruent triangles.

❍ In a parallelogram,

(i) Opposite sides are equal

(ii) Opposite angles are equal

(iii) Diagonals bisect each other

❍ A quadrilateral is a parallelogram, if

(i) Opposite sides are equal or

(ii) Opposite angles are equal or

(iii) Diagonals bisect each other or

(iv) A pair of opposite sides is equal and parallel

❍ Diagonals of a rectangle bisect each other and are equal and vice-versa.

❍ Diagonals of a rhombus bisect each other at right angles and vice-versa.

❍ Diagonals of a square bisect each other at right angles and are equal, and vice-versa.

❍ The line segment joining the mid-points of any two sides of a triangle is parallel to the third side and is half of it.

❍ A line through the mid-point of a side of a triangle parallel to another side bisects the third side.

❍ The quadrilateral formed by joining the mid-points of the sides of a quadrilateral, in order, is a parallelogram.

❍ If two figures *A* and *B* are congruent, they must have equal areas.

Or, if *A* and *B* are congruent figures, then $ar(A) = ar(B)$

❍ Parallelograms on the same base and between the same parallels are equal in area.

❍ Area of a parallelogram is the product of its any side and the corresponding altitude.

❍ Parallelograms on the same base and having equal areas lie between the same parallels.

❍ If a parallelogram and a triangle are on the same base and between the same parallels, then area of the triangle, is half the area of the parallelogram.

❍ Two triangles on the same base and between the same parallels are equal in area.

❍ Two triangles having the same base and equal areas lie between the same parallels.

❍ Area of a triangle is half the product of its base and the corresponding altitude (or height).

❍ A median of a triangle divides it into two triangles of equal areas.

* * * * *

PRACTICE EXERCISE - 12.1

12-1 In the given figure-12.1, $ABCD$ is a parallelogram. The value of $AC^2 - 2AC.BD + BD^2$ is :

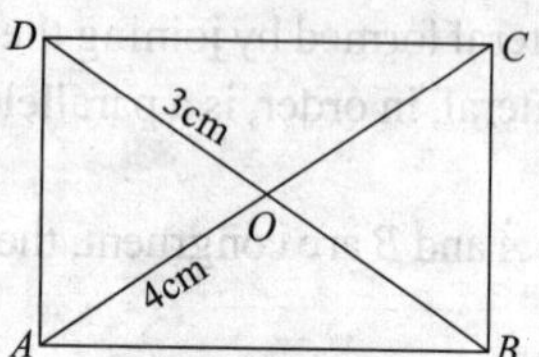

Figure 12.1

(A) 4 cm (B) 1 cm
(C) 8 cm (D) None of these

12-2 In the given figure-12.2. $ABCD$ is a quadrilateral in which P, Q, R and S are the points on sides AB, BC, CD and DA. The value of $\angle 1 + \angle 2 + \angle 3 + \angle 4 + \angle 5 + \angle 6 + \angle 7 + \angle 8$ is :

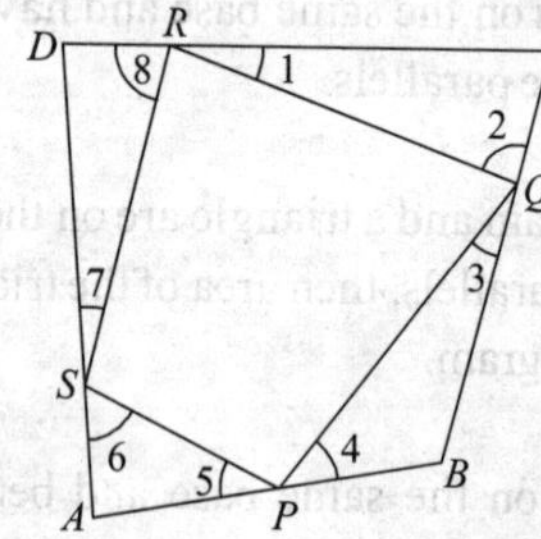

Figure 12.2

(A) 360º (B) 540º
(C) 180º (D) None of these

12-3 Taking any side of a rhombus as diameter a circle is drawn. The circle always passes through the point of intersection of the two diagonals. Which one is the correct option :

(A) It is always true (B) It is continually true
(C) It is never true (D) It cannot be determined

12-4 A quadrilateral has :

(A) 2 pairs of adjacent angles (B) 2 pairs of adjacent sides
(C) 4 pairs of adjacent angles (D) None of these

12-5 In the figure-12.3 given below, $PQRS$ is a rhombus, SQ and PR are the diagonals of the rhombus intersecting at O. If angle $OPQ = 35°$, then find the value of $\angle ORS + \angle OQP$:

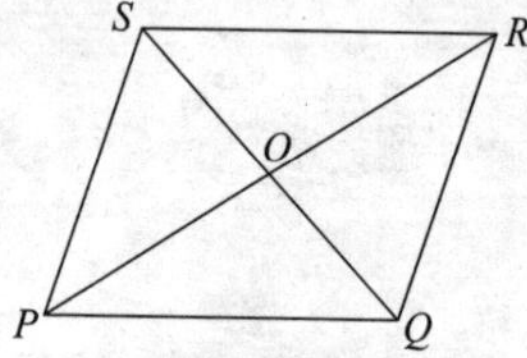

Figure 12.3

(A) 90º (B) 180º
(C) 135º (D) 45º

12-6 In the given figure-12.4, $L_1 \parallel L_2$, find the measure of $\alpha + \beta$:

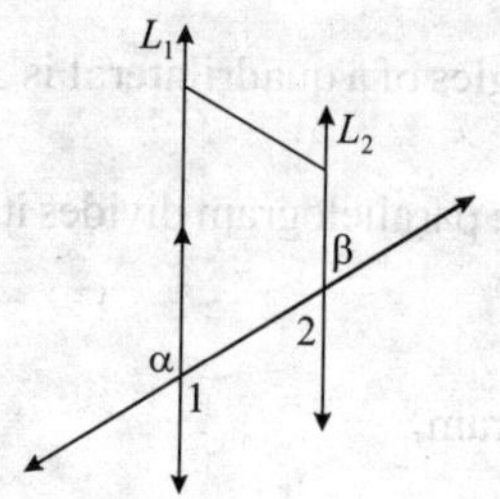

Figure 12.4

(A) 90º (B) 180º
(C) 45º (D) None of these

12-7 $ABCD$ is a quadrilateral such that all its four vertices are concyclic. The quadrilateral must be a :

(A) Square (B) A parallelogram
(C) A rectangle (D) Both 'A' and 'C'

12-8 In the given figure-12.5 $ABCD$ is a rhombus. The side AB is produced on both sides to points E and F such that $EA = AB = BF$. Find the value of $(y - x)$ if $xy = 1800$:

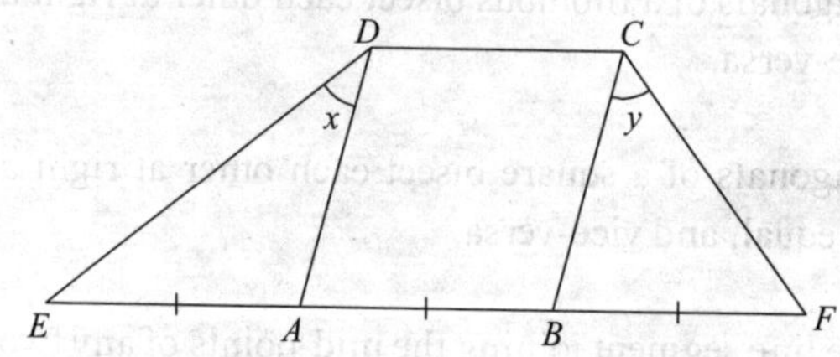

Figure 12.5

(A) 15º (B) 30º
(C) 50º (D) None of these

12-9 In the given figure-12.6, $ABCD$ is a parallelogram. $DN \perp AC$ and $BM \perp AC$ are drawn. The length of MN is 2.5 cm. What type of quadrilateral will formed by joining DM and BN:

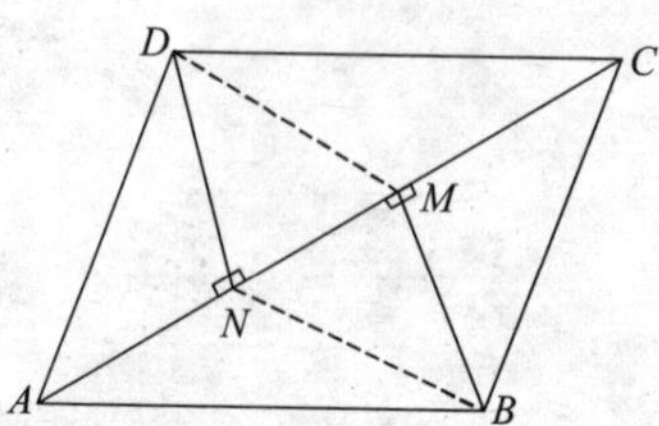

Figure 12.6

(A) rectangle (B) parallelogram
(C) Rhombus (D) None of these

12-10 In a triangle ABC, D and E are the mid points of AB and AC respectively. DP and EQ are perpendiculars from points D and E to BC respectively. If $DE = 4$ cm, then $1/2\ PQ = ?$

(A) 2 cm

(B) 1 cm

(C) 3 cm

(D) None of these

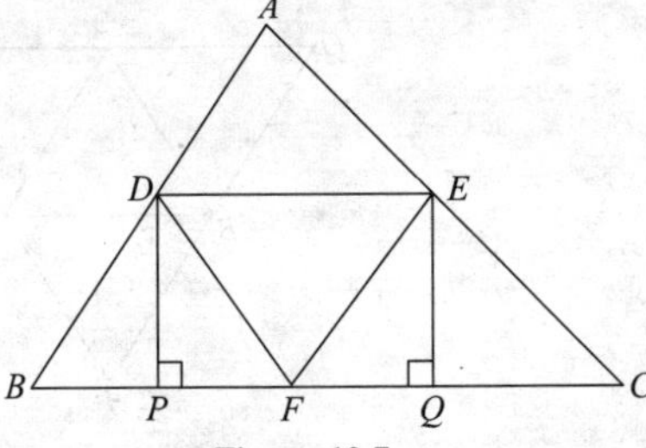

Figure 12.7

12-11 D, E and F are the midpoint of sides AB, AC and BC of ΔABC in which $AB = 7$ cm and $BC = 8$ cm. The perimeter of the quadrilateral formed by a vertex B of the triangle and the three points is :

(A) 15 cm

(B) 7.5 cm

(C) 56 cm

(D) None of these

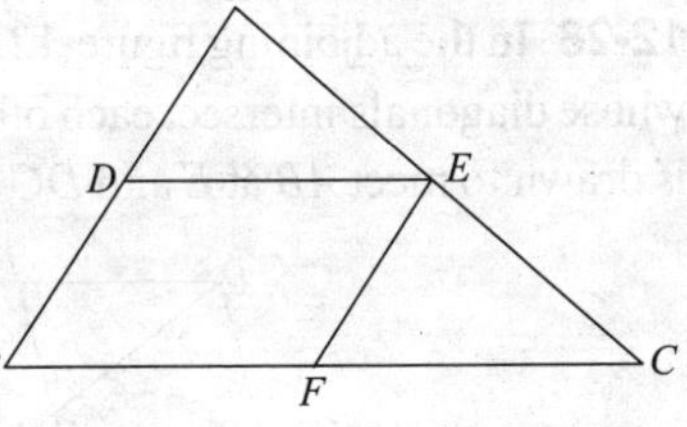

Figure 12.8

12-12 $ABCD$ is a parallelogram and AX, CY are bisectors of $\angle DAB$ and $\angle BCD$. If AX and CY are taken as mirrors and a ray emanating from gets reflected twice, then the incident ray and the reflected ray are :

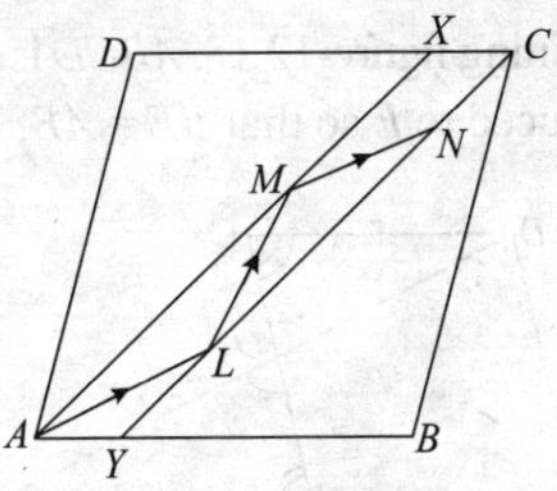

Figure 12.9

(A) Intersecting lines (B) Non parallel lines
(C) Parallel lines (D) None of these

12-13 In ΔABC if $PQ \parallel BC$ and P divides AB in the ratio 1 : 1 and $QR \parallel CD$. R divides AD in the ratio 1 : 2. Which one of the following statements is correct ?

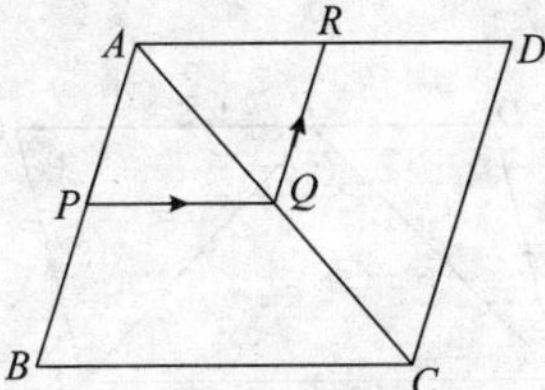

Figure 12.10

(A) It is always correct true (B) It is conditionally true
(C) It is not true (D) None of these

12-14 In the given figure-12.11 (not to scale), $\overline{AB} \parallel \overline{CD}$. If $\angle BAE = 25°$ and $\angle DCE = 30°$, then find $\angle AEC$:

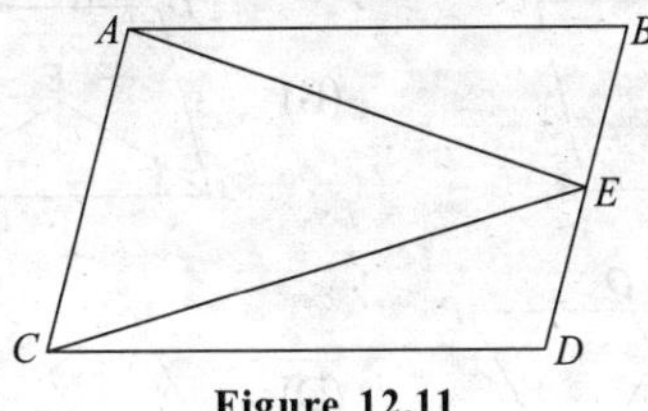

Figure 12.11

(A) 30° (B) 45°
(C) 50° (D) 55°

12-15 In a trapezium, E and F are respectively the midpoint of AD and BC, the non parallel sides. The longer side is 5 times the smaller side. The line segment EF is how many times the smaller side :

(A) 2 times (B) 3 times
(C) 4 times (D) none of these

12-16 A quadrilateral is formed by joining the mid points of the sides of a quadrilateral $PQRS$. If $AC = 12$ cm. What could be the length of SR or PQ :

(A) 7 cm to 9 cm (B) 5 cm to 6 cm
(C) 5 cm to 10 cm (D) None of these

12-17 In a parallelogram $ABCD$, $AD = BC = 4$ cm, P and Q are two points at distances 1 cm and 3 cm from D and C respectively on DA and CB. The perpendicular distance between AQ & CP is :

(A) Equal (B) Not equal
(C) 4 cm (D) none of these

12-18 In the given rectangle $ABCD$, the sum of the lengths of two diagonals is equal to 52 cm and E is a point in AB such that $\overline{OE}$ is perpendicular to $\overline{AB}$. Find the lengths of the sides of the rectangle, if $OE = 5$ cm :

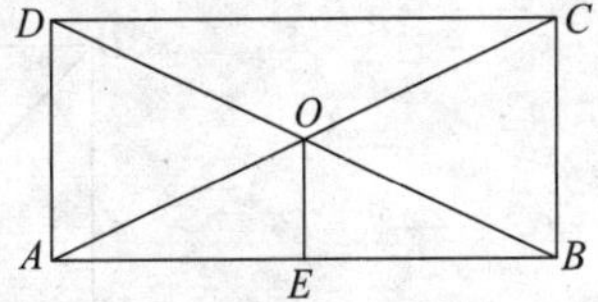

Figure 12.12

(A) 24 cm, 10 cm (B) 12 cm, 10 cm
(C) 24 cm, 5 cm (D) 12 cm, 15 cm

12-19 In the following figure-12.13, $ABCD$ is a square and AED is an equilateral triangle. Find the value of a :

(A) 30°

(B) 45°

(C) 60°

(D) 75°

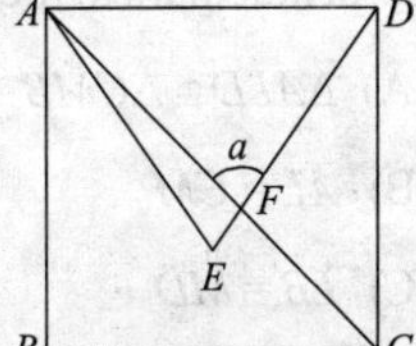

Figure 12.13

12-20 In which of the following figures, you find polygons on the same base and between the same parallels ?

(A) 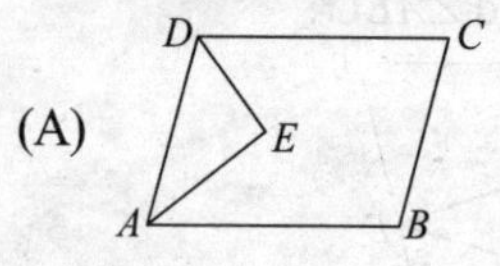

(B) 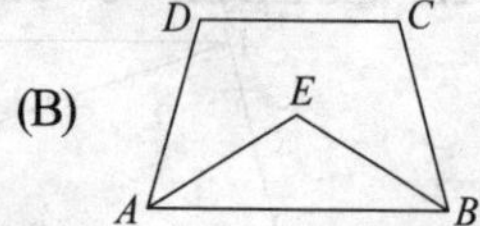

(C) 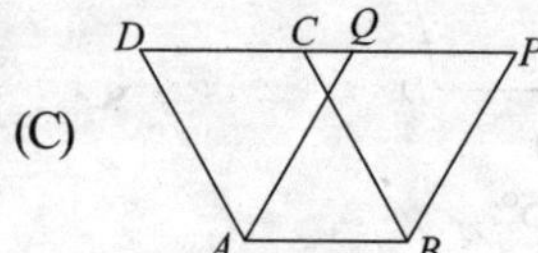

(D) 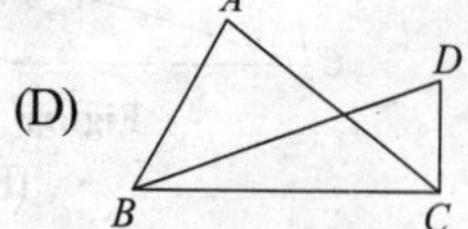

12-21 BD is a median of a ΔABC. F is a point on AB such that CF intersects BD at E and $BE = ED$. If $BF = 5$ cm then $BA =$

(A) 10 cm (B) 12 cm
(C) 15 cm (D) 17 cm

12-22 The figure formed by joining the consecutive mid points of the sides of a quadrilateral $ABCD$ is a rhombus if and only if $ABCD$ is *a* :

(A) Rectangle (B) Rhombus
(C) Trapezium (D) Can't say

12-23 In a parallelogram $ABCD$, $AE \perp DC$ and $CF \perp AD$. If $AD = 6$ cm, $CF = 10$ cm and $AE = 8$ cm, then CD is :

(A) 7.5 cm (B) 12.5 cm
(C) 16 cm (D) 2.5 cm

12-24 Each side of a rhombus is 10 cm long and one of its diagonals measures 16 cm. Then the length of the other diagonal and the area of the rhombus is:

(A) 12 cm, 96 cm^2 (B) 13 cm, 100 cm^2
(C) 14 cm, 80 cm^2 (D) 11 cm, 70 cm^2

12-25 In the adjoining figure-12.14, $ABCD$ is a square. A line segment CX cuts AB at X and the diagonal BD at O such that $\angle COD = 80°$ and $\angle OXA = x°$, then the value of x is :

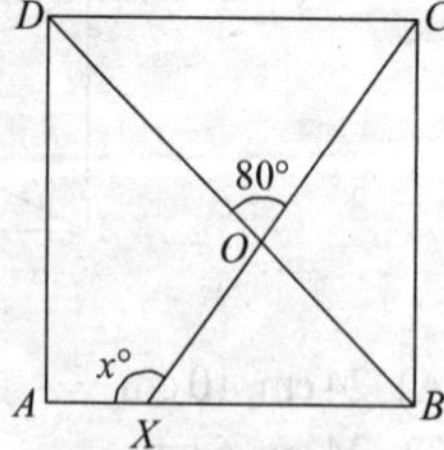

Figure 12.14

(A) 125°
(B) 120°
(C) 130°
(D) 140°

12-26 In the adjoining figure-12.15, AL and CM are perpendiculars to the diagonal BD of a || gm $ABCD$. Then :

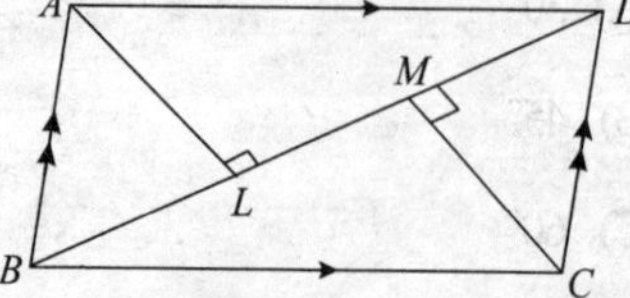

Figure 12.15

(A) $\Delta ALD \cong \Delta CMB$
(B) $AL = CM$
(C) $LB = MD$
(D) All of these

12-27 A ΔABC is given. If lines are drawn through A, B, C, parallel to the sides BC, CA and AB respectively, forming ΔPQR, as shown in the adjoining figure-12.16, Then :

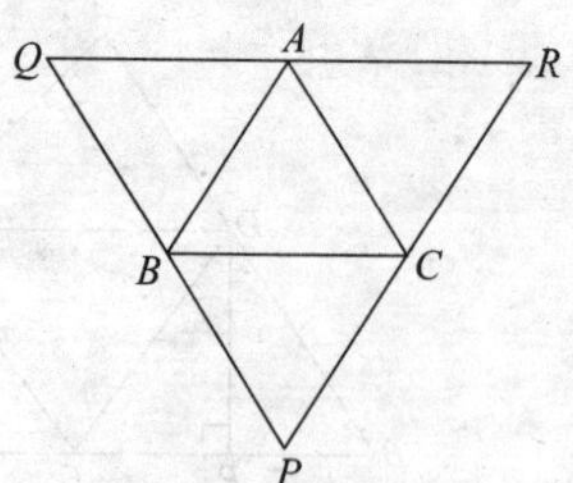

Figure 12.16

(A) $AB = PR$ (B) $AR = PQ$
(C) $AB = QR$ (D) $BC = \frac{1}{2} QR$

12-28 In the adjoining figure-12.17, $ABCD$ is a parallelogram whose diagonals intersect each other at O. A line segment EOF is drawn to meet AB at E and DC at F. Then :

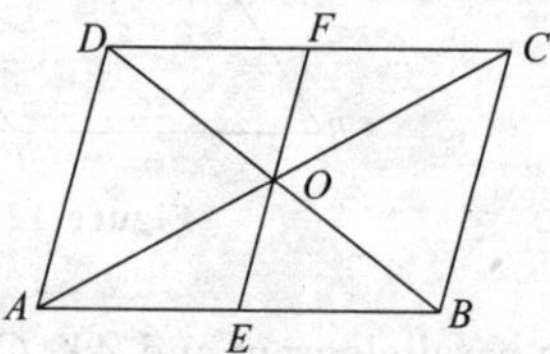

Figure 12.17

(A) $OE = OC$ (B) $OE = OF$
(C) $AB = FC$ (D) $CD = AE$

12-29 In the adjoining figure-12.18, $ABCD$ is a parallelogram in which AB is produced to E so that $BE = AB$. Then :

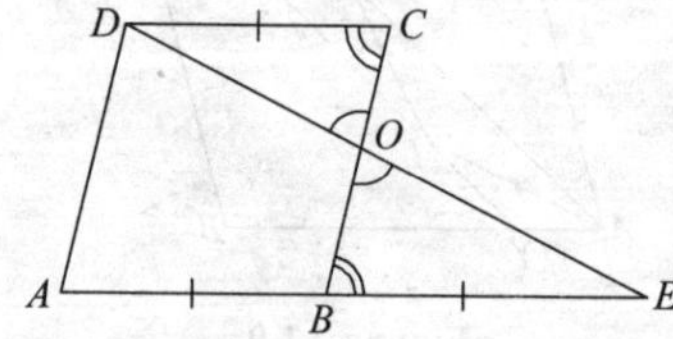

Figure 12.18

(A) $OB = OC$ (B) $AB = OD$
(C) $AE = OB$ (D) Can't say

12-30 In the adjoining figure-12.19, $ABCD$ is a parallelogram in which $\angle A = 60°$. If the bisectors of $\angle A$ and $\angle B$ meet DC at P, Then :

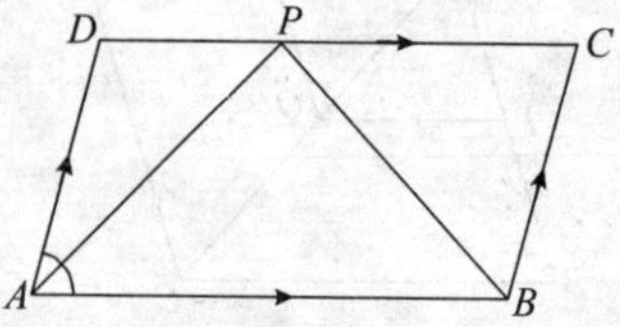

Figure 12.19

(A) $\angle APB = 90°$ (B) $AD = DP$
(C) $DC = 2AD$ (D) All of these

12-31 Which of the following properties are not true for a parallelogram:
(A) Its diagonals are equal
(B) Its diagonals are perpendicular to each other
(C) The diagonals divide the figure into four congruent triangles
(D) All the above

12-32 A quadrilateral is a rhombus but not a square if:
(A) Its diagonals do not bisect each other
(B) Its diagonals are not perpendicular
(C) Opposite angles are not equal
(D) The length of diagonals are not equal

12-33 If the diagonals of a quadrilateral intersect each other proportionally, the quadrilateral is a :
(A) Parallelogram (B) Rhombus
(C) Trapezium (D) Rectangle

12-34 The figure formed by joining the consecutive mid-points of any rhombus is always :
(A) A square (B) A rectangle
(C) A parallelogram (D) None of the above

12-35 If each interior angle of a regular polygon is 178°, then the number of sides of that polygon is :
(A) 180 sides
(B) 360 sides
(C) 10 sides
(D) 178 sides

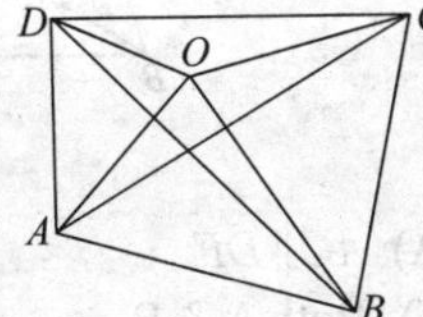

Figure 12.20

12-36 In a || gm $ABCD$, $\angle A=60°$. If the bisectors of $\angle A$ and $\angle B$ meet DC at P then ΔBCP is :
(A) An isosceles triangle
(B) A right triangle
(C) An isosceles right triangle
(D) An equilateral triangle

12-37 The sides of a parallelogram are 12 cm and 8 cm long and one of the diagonals is 10 cm long. If d is the length of other diagonal, then which one of the following is correct?
(A) $d<8$ cm (B) 8 cm $<d<$ 10 cm
(C) 10 cm $<d<$ 12 cm (D) $d>$ 12 cm

12-38 A parallelogram and a rectangle are on the same base and between the same parallel lines. Then the perimeter of the rectangle is :
(A) Equal to the perimeter of the parallelogram
(B) Greater than the perimeter of the parallelogram
(C) Less than the perimeter of the parallelogram
(D) None of these

12-39 $ABCD$ is a trapezium in which $AB \parallel DC$ and $DC=40$ cm and $AB=60$ cm. If X and Y are respectively, the mid points of AD and BC then area of trapezium $DCYX$:
(A) $\frac{6}{11} ar(\text{trap. } XYBA)$ (B) $\frac{7}{11} ar(\text{trap. } XYBA)$
(C) $\frac{8}{11} ar(\text{trap. } XYBA)$ (D) $\frac{9}{11} ar(\text{trap. } XYBA)$

12-40 Which of the following statements is true ?
(A) All the angles of a parallelogram can be acute
(B) If the diagonals of a quadrilateral are at right angles, it is a rhombus
(C) If the diagonals of a quadrilateral are at right angles, the figure formed by joining the mid-points of adjacent sides is a rectangle
(D) If one pair of opposite sides is parallel and the other pair of opposite sides is equal in a quadrilateral, then the quadrilateral is a parallelogram

12-41 $ABCD$ is a parallelogram. G is a point on AB such that $AG=2\,GB$, E is a point on DC such that $CE=2DE$ and F is a point on BC such that $BF=2FC$ then ar (quadrilateral $ADEG$) =
(A) $\frac{1}{2}$ ar(□$GBCE$) (B) ar(□$GBCE$)
(C) $\frac{1}{3}$ ar(□$GBCE$) (D) None of these

12-42 $ABCD$ is a parallelogram. G is a point on AB such that $AG=2GB$, E is a point on DC such that $CE=2DE$ and F is a point on BC such that $BF=2FC$ then ar (ΔEFG) : ar (||gm $ABCD$) =
(A) 5 : 13 (B) 5 : 18
(C) 7 : 13 (D) 7 : 18

12-43 In the figure-12.21, the area of square $ABCD$ is 4 cm^2 and E any point on AB. F, G, H and K are the mid-point of DE, CF, DG and CH respectively. The area of ΔKDC is :

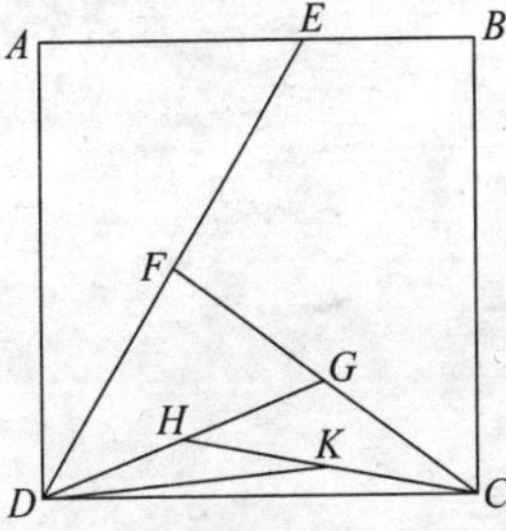

Figure 12.21

(A) $\frac{1}{4}$ cm^2 (B) $\frac{1}{8}$ cm^2
(C) $\frac{1}{16}$ cm^2 (D) $\frac{1}{32}$ cm^2

12-44 In the adjoining figure-12.22, $ABCD$ is a parallelogram. E is the midpoint of DC and through D, a line segment is drawn parallel to EB to meet CB produced at G and it cuts AB at F. Then :

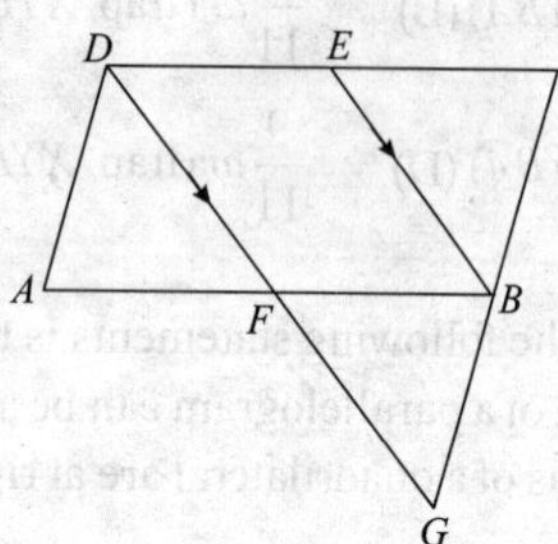

Figure 12.22

(A) AD$=\frac{1}{2}GC$ (B) $DG=2.EB$
(C) Both (A) & (B) (D) None of these

8-45 D is the mid point of side AB of the ΔABC, E is mid point of CD and F is mid point of AE. Area of $\Delta AFD=$
(A) $2\times$ area (ΔABC) (B) $1/8\times$ area (ΔABC)
(C) $1/2\times$ area (ΔABC) (D) $1/4\times$ area (ΔABC)

8-46 In the parallelogram $ABCD$, the side AB is produced to the point X, so that $BX=AB$. The line DX cuts BC at E. Area of $\Delta AED=$
(A) $2\times$ area (ΔCEX) (B) $1/2\times$ area (ΔCEX)
(C) area (ΔCEX) (D) $1/3\times$ area (ΔCEX)

7-47 $ABCD$ is a parallelogram, X and Y are the mid points of BC and CD respectively. Then ar (ΔAXY) :

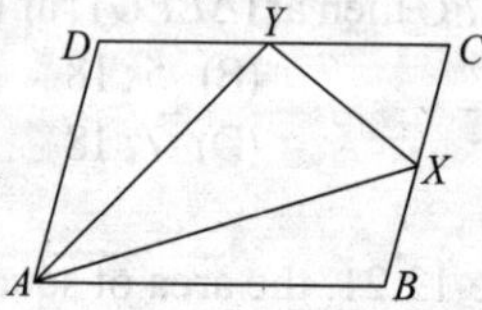

Figure 12.23

(A) $\frac{2}{8}$ ar ($\|^{gm}$ $ABCD$) (B) $\frac{1}{8}$ ar ($\|^{gm}$ $ABCD$)
(C) $\frac{3}{8}$ ar ($\|^{gm}$ $ABCD$) (D) None

7-48 $ABCD$ is a square with diagonals AC and BD intersecting at O. Y is any point on DO, BZ is drawn perpendicular to AY to cut AO in X, then $AX=$
(A) AY (B) DY
(C) AZ (D) Can't be determined

12-49 One side of a parallelogram has length 3, and another side has length 4. Let a and b denote the lengths of the diagonals of the parallelogram. Which of the following quantities can be determined from the given information ?
I $a+b$ II a^2+b^2 III a^3+b^3
(A) Only I (B) Only II
(C) Only III (D) Only I and II

12-50 Let ΔABC and ΔDEF be two triangles given in such a way that $AB \parallel DE$, $AB=DE$; $BC \parallel EF$ and $BC=EF$. Then :

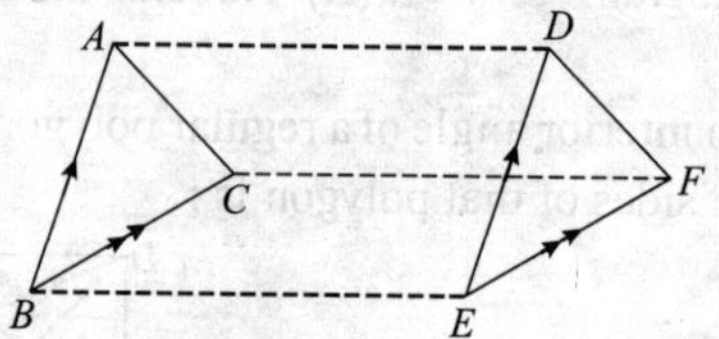

Figure 12.24

(A) $AC \parallel DF$ (B) $AC=DF$
(C) Both A & B (D) None of these

* * * * *

PRACTICE EXERCISE - 12.2

12-1 $ABCD$ is a parallelogram in which AO and BO are the bisectors of $\angle A$ and $\angle B$ and RO is the bisector of $\angle POQ$. The complement of $\angle POR$ is :

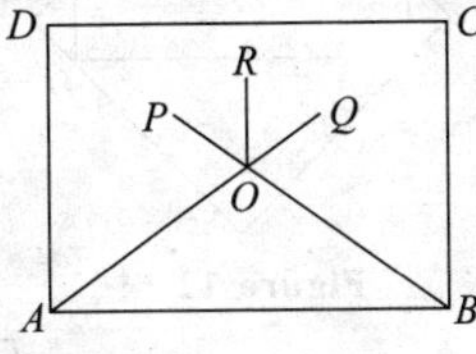

Figure 12.25

(A) 45°
(B) 90°
(C) 30°
(D) None of these

12-2 $ABCD$ is a parallelogram in which PA and PB are angle bisectors of $\angle DAB$ and $\angle CBA$ and $PL \| BC$. The measure of $\angle LPA + \angle LPB$:

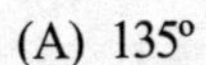

(A) 135°

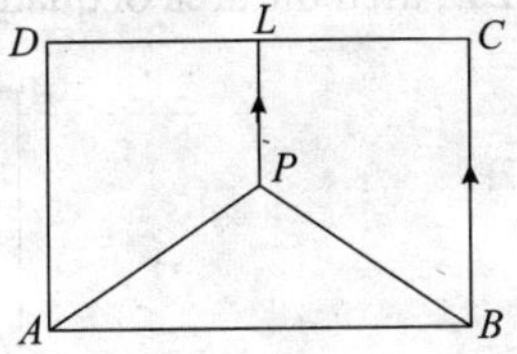

Figure 12.26

(B) 210°

(C) 270°

(D) None of these

12-3 AC bisects $\angle DAB$ of parallelogram $ABCD$. Taking B as centre a circle is drawn. The measure of $\angle AEB = ?$

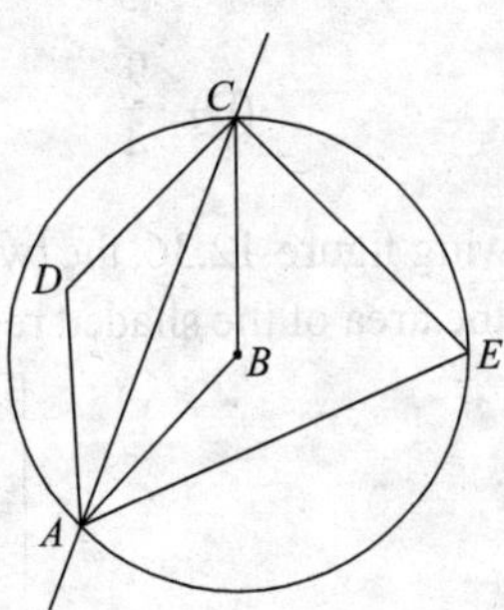

Figure 12.27

(A) $90° + x$
(B) $90° - x$
(C) $180° - x$
(D) None of these

12-4 In the given figure-12.28, $ABCD$ is a rhombus in which diagonals AC and BD intersect each other at point O such that $\angle OAD = 30°$. The sum of the lengths of any pair of adjacent sides is :

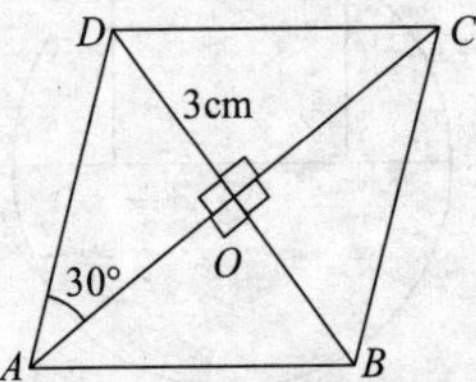

Figure 12.28

(A) 10 cm
(B) 12 cm
(C) 6 cm
(D) None of these

12-5 In a parallelogram, a pair of lines divides a pair of adjacent angles in the ratio 1 : 3. Again another pair of lines divides the same pair of angles in the ratio 1 : 1. Find the difference between the angles formed by the first pair of lines and the second pair of lines :

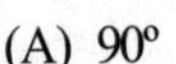

(A) 90°

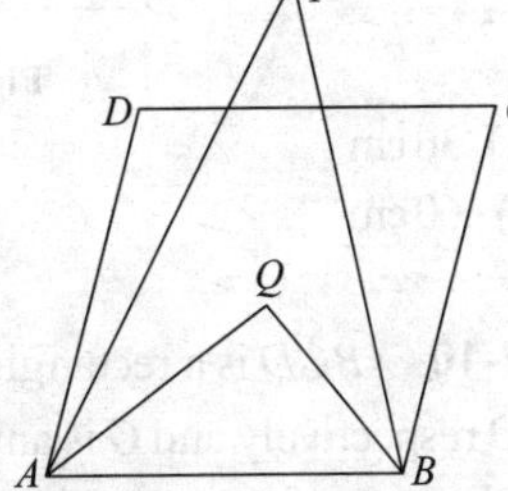

Figure 12.29

(B) 120°

(C) 30°

(D) None of these

12-6 In a cyclic parallelogram, perpendiculars are drawn from centre to the sides. What is the length of the side of the new quadrilateral formed if the length of the diagonal of the cyclic parallelogram is 8 cm :

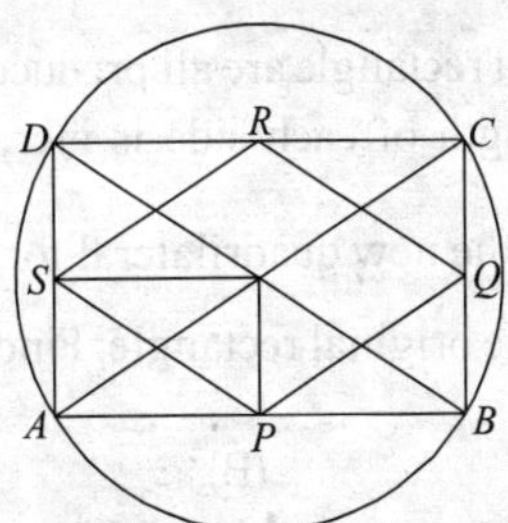

Figure 12.30

(A) 4 cm
(B) 2 cm
(C) 6 cm
(D) None of these

12-7 In ΔABC, AD is median and P is a point in AD such that $AP : PD = 1 : 2$ then area of $\Delta ABP =$

(A) $\frac{1}{2} ar(\Delta ABC)$
(B) $\frac{2}{3} ar(\Delta ABC)$
(C) $\frac{1}{3} ar(\Delta ABC)$
(D) $\frac{1}{6} ar(\Delta ABC)$

12-8 In the adjoining figure-12.31, AD and BE are the medians of ΔABC and $DF \| BE$. Then :

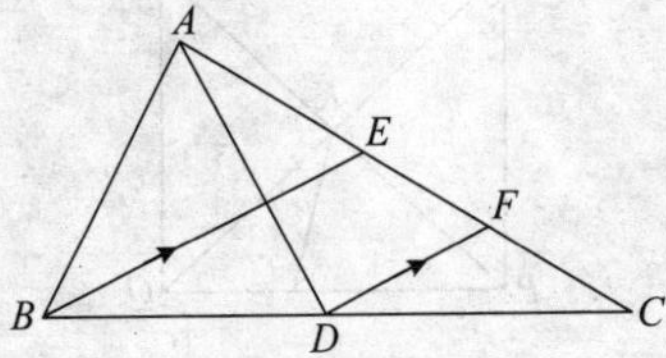

Figure 12.31

(A) $AB = DF$
(B) $CF = 2.BC$
(C) $CF = BC$
(D) $CF = \frac{1}{4} AC$

12-9 In figure-12.32, $AB \parallel CD \parallel EF \parallel GH$ and $AP = PQ = QH$. If $BD = 24$ cm then $BH =$

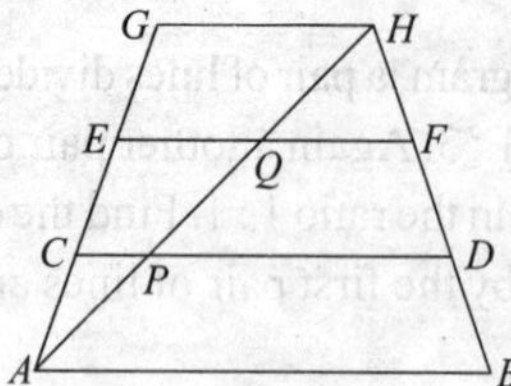

Figure 12.32

(A) 36 cm (B) 48 cm
(C) 60 cm (D) 72 cm

12-10 $ABCD$ is a rectangle. E, F are the mid points of BC and AD respectively and G is any point on EF, then ar ΔGAB equals to the area of :

(A) $\frac{1}{2}(\|^{r}_{gm} ABCD)$ (B) $\frac{1}{3}(\|^{r}_{gm} ABCD)$
(C) $\frac{1}{4}(\|^{r}_{gm} ABCD)$ (D) $\frac{1}{6}(\|^{r}_{gm} ABCD)$

12-11 The sides of rectangle are all produced in order, in such a way that the length of each side is increased by 'k' times itself. The area of the new quadrilateral formed becomes $2\frac{1}{2}$ times the area of the original rectangle. Find the value of 'k' :

(A) $\frac{1}{2}$ (B) $\frac{5}{2}$
(C) $\frac{3}{2}$ (D) None of these

12-12 If O is a point within a quadrilateral then,
(A) $OA < OB$
(B) $2.OB = AO.OD$
(C) $OA^2 = OB^2 + OC^2$
(D) $OA + OB + OC + OD > AC + BD$

12-13 In figure-12.33, $PQRS$ is a square. The diagonals RP and SQ intersect each other at K. T is a point on PQ such that $PK = PT$, then $\angle TKQ =$

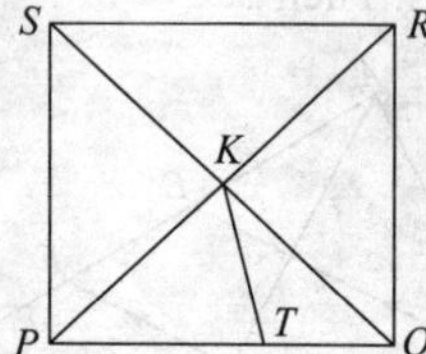

Figure 12.33

(A) $67\frac{1}{2}°$ (B) $22\frac{1}{2}°$
(C) 30° (D) 60°

12-14 Equilateral triangles are formed on the sides of a rectangle $ABCD$ with $AB = 5$ cm and $BC = 6$ cm. The total area of the figure-12.34 (in cm²) is :

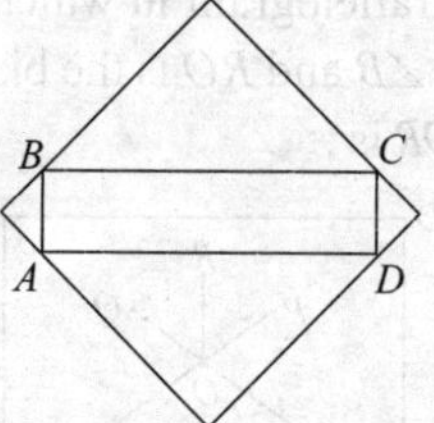

Figure 12.34

(A) $30 + \frac{\sqrt{3}}{2} \times 57$ (B) $30 + \frac{\sqrt{3}}{2} \times 61$
(C) $30 + \sqrt{3} \times 18$ (D) $30 + \sqrt{3} \times 27$

12-15 In the figure-12.35 $ABCD$ is a 2×2 square. E is the midpoint of AD, and F is on BE. If CF is the perpendicular to BE, then the area of quadrilateral $CDEF$ is :

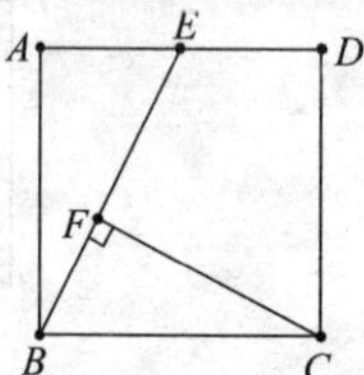

Figure 12.35

(A) $3 - \frac{\sqrt{3}}{2}$ (B) $\frac{11}{5}$
(C) $\sqrt{5}$ (D) $\frac{9}{4}$

12-16 In the following figure-12.36, the two square have same centre point. Find the area of the shaded region :

(A) 300
(B) 450
(C) 600
(D) 225

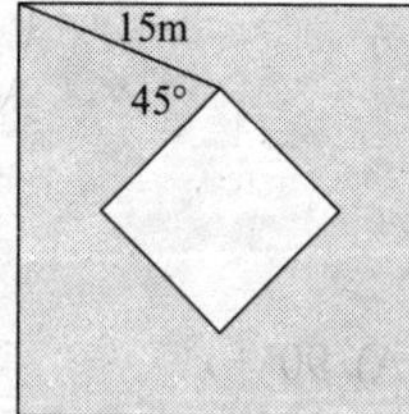

Figure 12.36

12-17 A square of area 20 cm² fits inside a semicircle as shown. Find the area of the largest square that will fit inside the full circle :

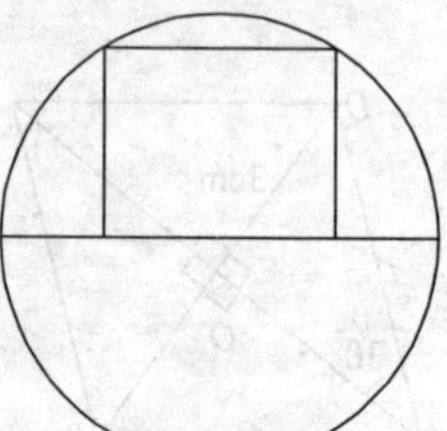
Figure 12.37

(A) 40 (B) 100
(C) 50 (D) 25

12-18 A square of side 13 is inscribed in a square of side 17 as shown in the figure-12.38. The greatest distance between a vertex of inner square and a vertex of outer square :

(A) 17

(B) $\sqrt{314}$

(C) $\sqrt{433}$

(D) 22

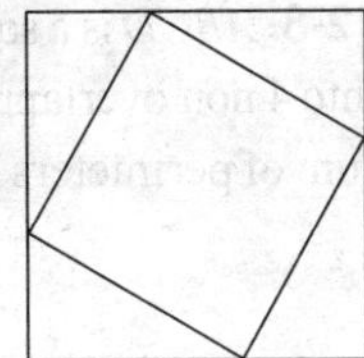

Figure 12.38

12-19 In the adjoining figure-12.39, ABC and DBC are two triangles on the same base BC, $AL \perp BC$ and $DM \perp BC$. Then, $\frac{\text{area}(\Delta ABC)}{\text{area}(\Delta DBC)}$ is equal to :

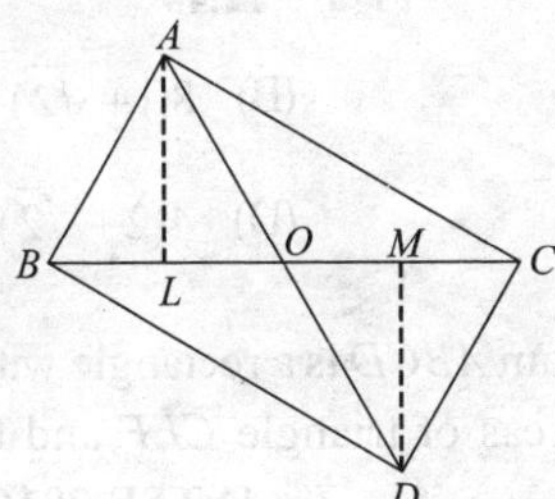

Figure 12.39

(A) $\frac{AO}{OD}$ (B) $\frac{AO^2}{OD^2}$

(C) $\frac{AO}{AD}$ (D) $\frac{OD^2}{AO^2}$

12-20 In the adjoining figure-12.40, $\frac{AO}{OC} = \frac{BO}{OD} = \frac{1}{3}$ and $AB = 5$ cm, then DC equals :

(A) 15cm

(B) 10cm

(C) 2.5cm

(D) 20cm

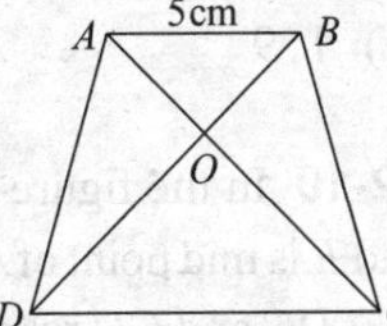

Figure 12.40

12-21 A square board side 10 centimeters, standing vertically, is tilted to the left so that the bottom-right corner is raised 6 centimeters from the ground.

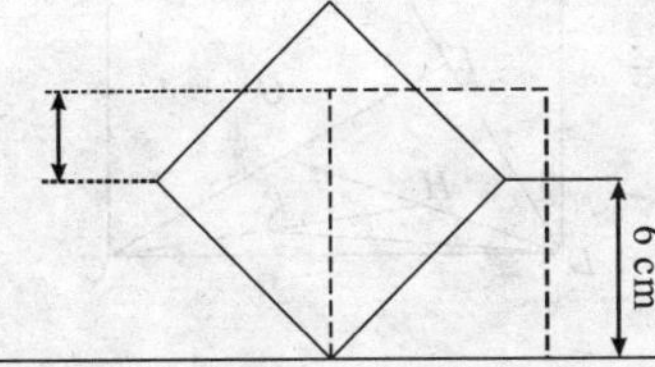

Figure 12.41

By what distance is the top-left corner lowered from its original position ?

(A) 1 cm (B) 2 cm

(C) 3 cm (D) 0.5 cm

12-22 ABC is an equilateral triangle of side 3cm. Three squares $ASTB$, $AMNC$ and $BCED$ are drawn on the sides, outside the triangle as shown in the figure-12.42, Then the area of triangle PQR is :

(A) $\frac{\sqrt{3}}{4}(96+36\sqrt{3})\ \text{cm}^2$

(B) $\frac{\sqrt{3}}{4}(108+18\sqrt{3})\ \text{cm}^2$

(C) $\left(\frac{117\sqrt{3}}{4}+27\right)\ \text{cm}^2$

(D) None of these

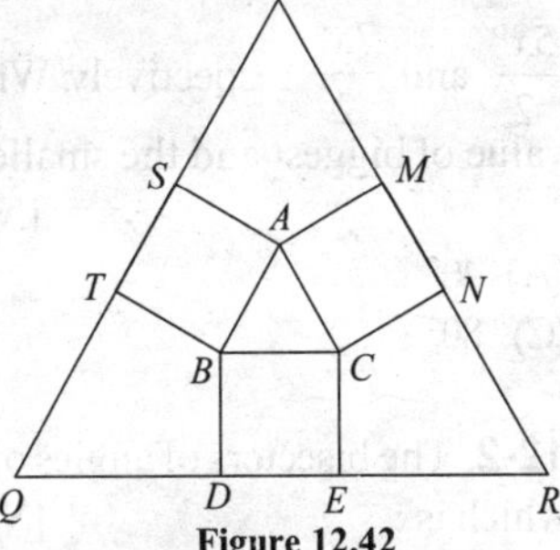

Figure 12.42

12-23 $FBED$ is a parallelogram. $EC = \frac{1}{3}BC$. area of ΔAEC = area (parallelogram $FBED$). Find the ratio of the height of the parallelogram to the triangle :

(A) 3 : 2

(B) 1 : 4

(C) 2 : 5

(D) 1 : 3

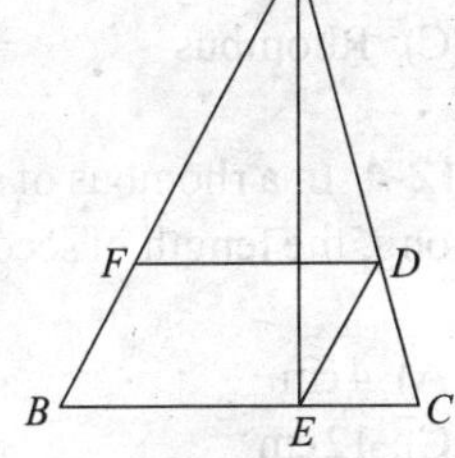

Figure 12.43

12-24 In the adjoining figure-12.44, $ABCD$ is a trapezium in which $AB \parallel DC$ and P, Q are the midpoints of AD and BC respectively. DQ and AB when produced meet at E. Also, AC and PQ intersect at R, then :

(A) $DQ = QE$

(B) $PR \parallel AB$

(C) $AR = RC$

(D) All of these

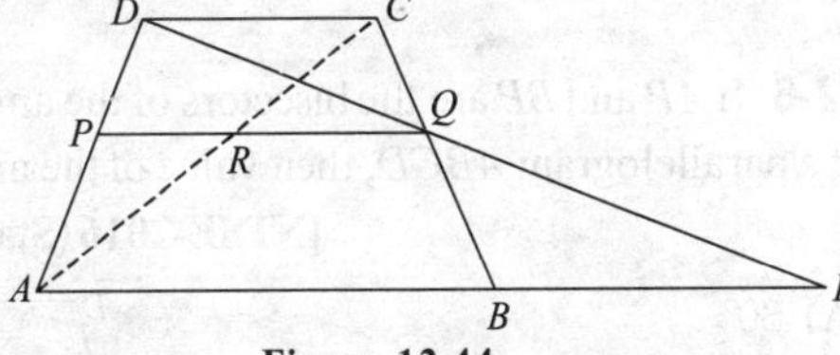

Figure 12.44

12-25 D, E, F are mid points of BC, AC and AB respectively. G, H, I, are again mid points of sides FD, DE, EF respectively, then ar (quad $GHIF$) : ar (quad $AEDB$) =

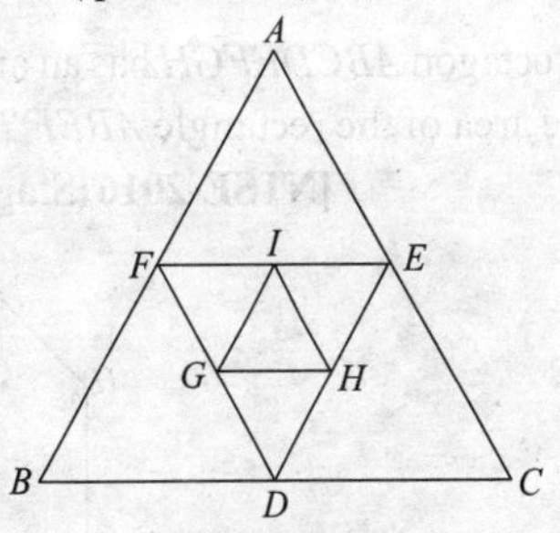

Figure 12.45

(A) 1 : 3 (B) 1 : 6

(C) 1 : 4 (D) 1 : 16

* * * * *

PRACTICE EXERCISE - 12.3

12-1 A quadrilateral *ABCD* has four angles $x°$, $2x°$, $\frac{5x°}{2}$ and $\frac{7x°}{2}$ respectively. What is the difference between the value of biggest and the smallest angles :

[NTSE-2012 (Stage-I) Rajasthan]

(A) 40° (B) 100°
(C) 80° (D) 20°

12-2 The bisectors of angles of a parallelogram makes a figure which is : **[NTSE-2013 (Stage-I) Rajasthan]**

(A) Rectangle (B) Circle
(C) Pentagon (D) Octagon

12-3 The line segment joining the mid-points of the adjacent sides of a quadrilateral : **[NTSE-2015 (Stage-I) MP]**

(A) Parallelogram (B) Square
(C) Rhombus (D) Rectangle

12-4 In a rhombus of side 10 cm, one of the diagonal is 12 cm long, the length of second diagonal will be :

[NTSE-2015 (Stage-I) MP]

(A) 4 cm (B) 8 cm
(C) 12 cm (D) 16 cm

12-5 If the diagonals of a rhombus are 30 cm and 40 cm, then the length of side of rhombus is :

[NTSE-2015 (Stage-I) Chennai]

(A) 20 cm (B) 22 cm
(C) 25 cm (D) 45 cm

12-6 If *AP* and *BP* are the bisectors of the angle *A* and angle *B* of a parallelogram *ABCD*, then value of the angle *APB* is :

[NTSE-2016 (Stage-I) Rajasthan]

(A) 30°

(B) 45°

(C) 60°

(D) 90°

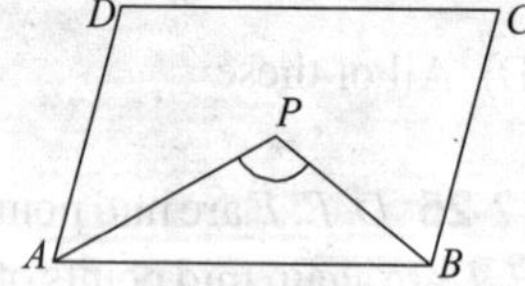

Figure 12.46

12-7 A regular octagon *ABCDEFGH* has an area of one square unit. What is the area of the rectangle *ABEF* ?

[NTSE-2016 (Stage-I) Telangana]

(A) $1-\frac{\sqrt{2}}{2}$

(B) $\frac{\sqrt{2}}{4}$

(C) $\sqrt{2}-1$

(D) $\frac{1}{2}$

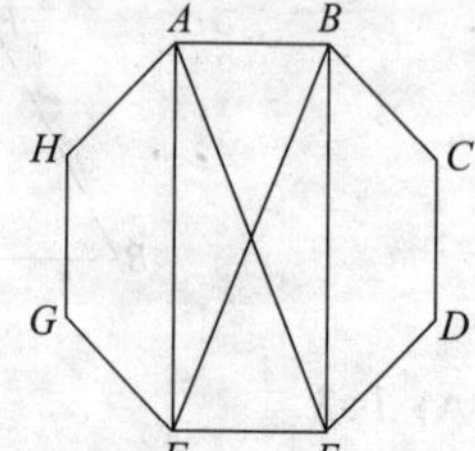

Figure 12.47

12-8 *ABCD* is a square of area of 4 square units which is divided into 4 non overlapping triangles as shown in figure-12.48, then sum of perimeters of the triangles so formed is :

[NTSE-2016 (Stage-I) Delhi]

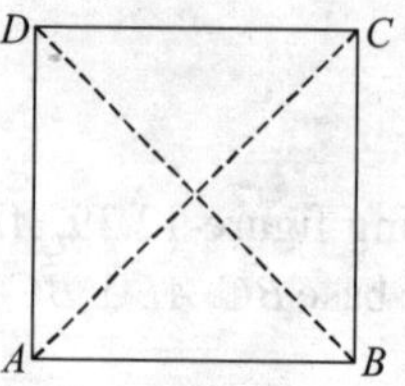

Figure 12.48

(A) $8(2+\sqrt{2})$ (B) $8(1+\sqrt{2})$
(C) $4(1+\sqrt{2})$ (D) $4(2+\sqrt{2})$

12-9 In the diagram *ABCD* is a rectangle with $AE = EF = FB$, the ratio of the areas of triangle *CEF* and that of rectangle *ABCD* is : **[NTSE-2016 (Stage-I) Delhi]**

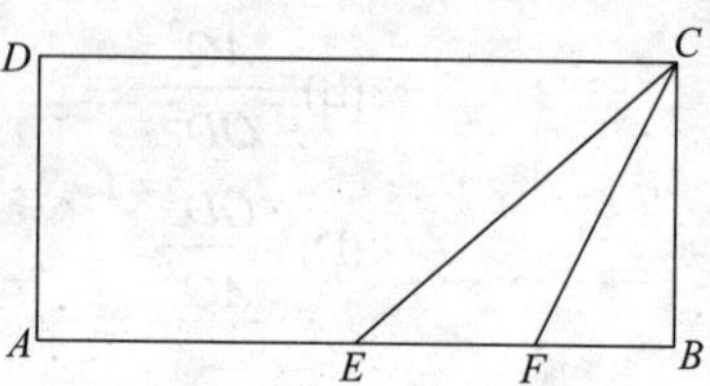

Figure 12.49

(A) 1 : 6 (B) 1 : 8
(C) 1 : 9 (D) 1 : 10

12-10 In the figure-12.50, the area of square *ABCD* is 4 cm² and *E* is mid point of *AB*; *F*, *G*, *H* and *K* are the mid points of *DE*, *CF*, *DG* and *CH* respectively. The area of ΔKDC is :

[NTSE-2016 (Stage-I) Delhi]

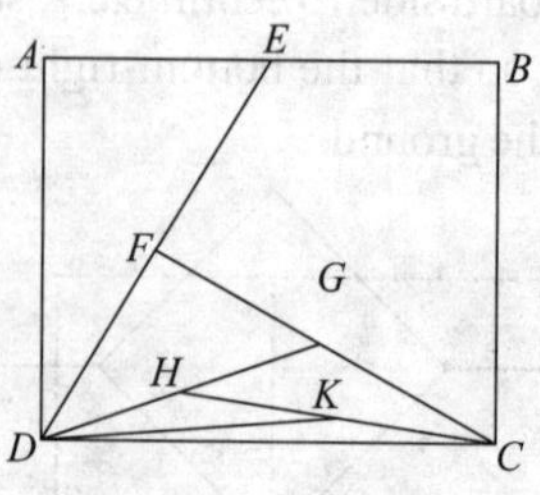

Figure 12.50

(A) $\frac{1}{4}$ cm² (B) $\frac{1}{8}$ cm²
(C) $\frac{1}{16}$ cm² (D) $\frac{1}{32}$ cm²

12-11 In the given figure-12.51, $ABCD$ is trapezium in which $AB \parallel CD$ and its diagonals intersect at O. If $AO = (3x - 1)$ cm, $OC = (5x - 3)$ cm, $BO = (2x + 1)$ cm and $OD = (6x - 5)$ cm, find the value of x : **[NTSE-2016 (Stage-I) Jharkhand]**

(A) 1/2

(B) 3

(C) 4

(D) 2

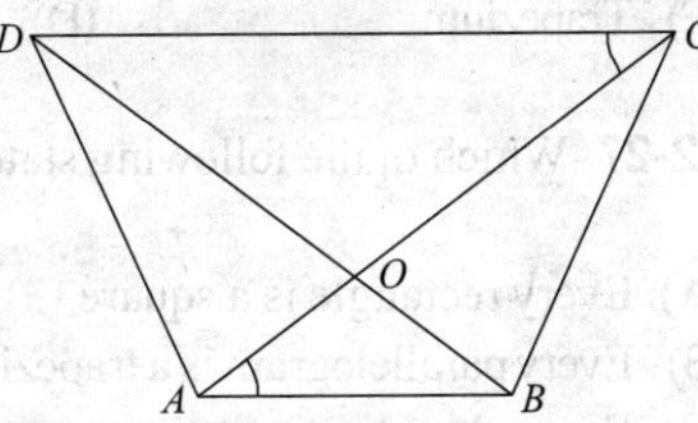

Figure 12.51

12-12 If diagonals of a quadrilateral are not congruent and bisect at right angle, then such quadrilateral is known as —: **[NTSE-2017 (Stage-I) Gujarat]**

(A) Square (B) Rectangle
(C) Trapezium (D) Rhombus

12-13 □$ABCD$ is a rhombus. If are $ABCD = 160$ and $AC = 16$ then BD = —: **[NTSE-2017 (Stage-I) Gujarat]**

(A) 10 (B) 20
(C) 15 (D) 25

12-14 In the adjoining figure-12.52 □$ABCD$ and □$PBCQ$ are parallelogram $BC = 12$ cm $PR = 8$ cm. Find $A(\Delta PSB)$: **[NTSE-2017 (Stage-I) Maharashtra]**

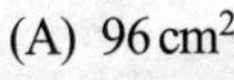
(A) 96 cm^2

(B) 72 cm^2

(C) 48 cm^2

(D) 36 cm^2

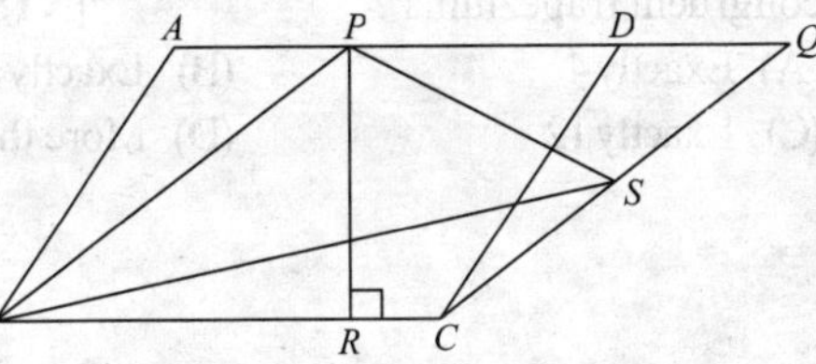

Figure 12.52

12-15 The figure obtained by joining the mid-points of the adjacent sides of a rectangle of 10 cm, 6 cm, is : **[NTSE-2017 (Stage-I) Tamilnadu]**

(A) A rectangle of area 30 cm^2
(B) A square of area 25 cm^2
(C) A trapezium of area 30 cm^2
(D) A rhombus of area 30 cm^2

12-16 In figure-12.53 $PQ \perp PS$, $PQ \parallel SR$, $\angle SQR = 28°$ and $\angle QRT = 65°$ then $x°$ and $y°$ will be : **[NTSE-2017 (Stage-I) Uttrakhand]**

(A) $x° = 37°, y° = 53°$

(B) $x° = 53°, y° = 37°$

(C) $x° = 57°, y° = 53°$

(D) $x° = 33°, y° = 57°$

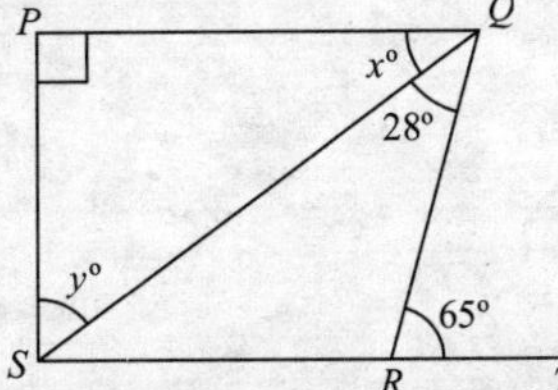

Figure 12.53

12-17 The diagonals of rectangle $ABCD$ intersect each other at O. If $\angle BOC = 44°$ the value of $\angle OAD$ will be : **[NTSE-2017 (Stage-I) Uttrakhand]**

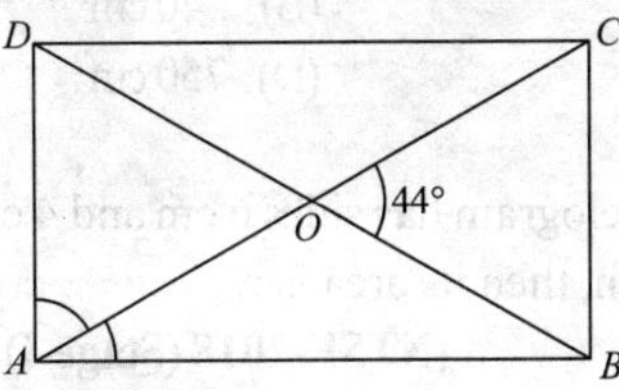

Figure 12.54

(A) 120° (B) 68°
(C) 90° (D) 44°

12-18 The length of the side of a rhombus is 4 cm. If one of the diagonals is equal to the side of rhombus, then the length of other diagonal in cm will be : **[NTSE-2018 (Stage-I) Rajasthan]**

(A) $\frac{\sqrt{3}}{2}$ (B) $\sqrt{3}$

(C) $2\sqrt{3}$ (D) $4\sqrt{3}$

12-19 Which of the following statements is false for the quadrilateral $ABCD$: **[NTSE-2018 (Stage-I) Rajasthan]**

(A) $AB + BC + CD + DA > AC$
(B) $AB + BC + CD + DA > AC + AC$
(C) $AB + BC + CD + DA > AC + BD$
(D) $AB + BC + CD + DA < 2AC$

12-20 The diagonals of a quadrilateral $ABCD$ are perpendicular to each other. Then the quadrilateral formed by joining the mid-points of its sides (in order) is a : **[NTSE-2018 (Stage-I) Haryana]**

(A) kite (B) rectangle
(C) rhombus (D) square

12-21 If $PQRS$ is a square whose vertices P, Q, R and S are on the mid point of side AB, BC, CD and DA of a square $ABCD$ respectively. Then the ratio of the areas of square $PQRS$ to square $ABCD$ is : **[NTSE-2018 (Stage-I) Karnataka]**

(A) $1:2$ (B) $1:\sqrt{2}$

(C) $2:1$ (D) $\sqrt{2}:1$

12-22 Choose the correct figure that has all the following properties :

(a) Both the diagonals are congrent
(b) It is called a rectangle
(c) The perimeter of the figure is four times its length or breadth
(d) It is a rhombus **[NTSE-2018 (Stage-I) Maharashtra]**

(A) Rhombus (B) Rectangle
(C) Trapezium (D) Square

12-23 There is a rhombus of one side 17 cm and one diagonal 30 cm. The area of the rhombus will be : **[NTSE-2018 (Stage-I) Telangana]**

(A) $60\ cm^2$ (B) $240\ cm^2$

(C) $305\ cm^2$ (D) $750\ cm^2$

12-24 A parallelogram has sides 6 cm and 4 cm and one of its diagonals is 8 cm, then its area is : **[NTSE-2018 (Stage-I) Uttar Pradesh]**

(A) $36\ cm^2$ (B) $3\sqrt{15}\ cm^2$

(C) $6\sqrt{15}\ cm^2$ (D) $12\sqrt{210}\ cm^2$

12-25 In the given figure-12.55 *ABCD* is a rhombus in which $\angle C = 60°$ then $AC : BD$ will be : **[NTSE-2018 (Stage-I) Uttarakhandh]**

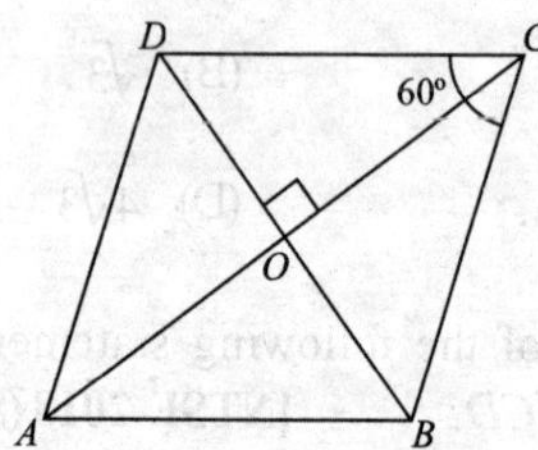

Figure 12.55

(A) $\sqrt{3}:1$ (B) $\sqrt{3}:\sqrt{2}$

(C) 3 : 1 (D) 3 : 2

12-26 If the angles *A*, *B*, *C* and *D* of a quadrilateral *ABCD* in the same order are in the ratio 3 : 7 : 6 : 4, then *ABCD* is a : **[NTSE-2012 (Stage-II)]**

(A) Parallelogram (B) Rhombus

(C) Trapezium (D) Kite

12-27 Which of the following statements holds always true ? **[NTSE-2013 (Stage-II)]**

(A) Every rectangle is a square

(B) Every parallelogram is a trapezium

(C) Every rhombus is a square

(D) Every parallelogram is a rectangle

12-28 Which of the following polygons are uniquely determined when all the sides are given ? **[NTSE-2013 (Stage-II)]**

(A) Quadrilateral (B) Triangle

(C) Pentagon (D) Haxagon

12-29 If the line segments joining the midpoints of the consecutive side of a quadrilateral *ABCD* form a rectangle then □*ABCD* must be a : **[NTSE-2014 (Stage-II)]**

(A) Rhombus (B) Square

(C) Kite (D) All of the above

12-30 In how many ways can a given square by cut into two congruent trapeziums ? **[NTSE-2014 (Stage-II)]**

(A) Exactly 4 (B) Exactly 8

(C) Exactly 12 (D) More than 12

* * * * *

ANSWERS

PRACTICE EXERCISE-12.1

1	(A)	2	(A)	3	(A)
4	(C)	5	(A)	6	(B)
7	(D)	8	(B)	9	(B)
10	(A)	11	(A)	12	(C)
13	(C)	14	(D)	15	(B)
16	(C)	17	(A)	18	(A)
19	(D)	20	(C)	21	(C)
22	(A)	23	(A)	24	(A)
25	(A)	26	(D)	27	(D)
28	(B)	29	(A)	30	(D)
31	(D)	32	(D)	33	(C)
34	(B)	35	(A)	36	(D)
37	(D)	38	(C)	39	(D)
40	(C)	41	(B)	42	(B)
43	(B)	44	(C)	45	(B)
46	(A)	47	(C)	48	(B)
49	(B)	50	(C)		

PRACTICE EXERCISE-12.2

1	(A)	2	(C)	3	(B)
4	(B)	5	(C)	6	(A)
7	(D)	8	(D)	9	(D)
10	(C)	11	(B)	12	(D)
13	(B)	14	(B)	15	(B)
16	(B)	17	(C)	18	(C)
19	(A)	20	(A)	21	(B)
22	(C)	23	(B)	24	(D)
25	(B)				

PRACTICE EXERCISE-12.3

1	(B)	2	(A)	3	(A)
4	(D)	5	(C)	6	(D)
7	(D)	8	(B)	9	(A)
10	(B)	11	(D)	12	(D)
13	(B)	14	(C)	15	(D)
16	(A)	17	(A)	18	(D)
19	(D)	20	(B)	21	(A)
22	(D)	23	(B)	24	(C)
25	(A)	26	(C)	27	(B)
28	(B)	29	(D)	30	(D)

Solutions of PRACTICE EXERCISE-12.1

Sol. 1 (A) Given *ABCD* is a parallelogram, their diagonals bisect each other.

$\Rightarrow \quad AC = 2 \times OA = 2 \times 4 = 8$ cm

$BD = 2OD = 2 \times 3 = 6$ cm

$\Rightarrow \quad AC^2 - 2AC.\,BD + BD^2$

$(AC - BD)^2 = (8 - 6)^2$

$= 2^2 = 4$ cm

Hence Ans is (A)

Sol. 2 (A) From the figure it is clear that

$\angle A + \angle 5 + \angle 6 = 180^\circ$ ...(1)

$\angle B + \angle 4 + \angle 3 = 180^\circ$ ...(2)

$\angle C + \angle 1 + \angle 2 = 180^\circ$ ...(3)

$\angle D + \angle 7 + \angle 8 = 180^\circ$ ...(4)

On adding (1), (2), (3) and (4)

$\angle A + \angle B + \angle C + \angle D + \angle 1 + \angle 2 + \angle 3 + \angle 4 + \angle 5 + \angle 6 + \angle 7 + \angle 8 = 720^\circ$

$\Rightarrow \quad 360^\circ + (\angle 1 + \angle 2 + \angle 3 + \angle 4 + \angle 5 + \angle 6 + \angle 7 + \angle 8) = 720^\circ$

$[\because \angle A + \angle B + \angle C + \angle D = 360]$

$\Rightarrow \quad \angle 1 + \angle 2 + \angle 3 + \angle 4 + \angle 5 + \angle 6 + \angle 7 + \angle 8 = 360^\circ$

Hence Ans is (A)

Sol. 3 (A)

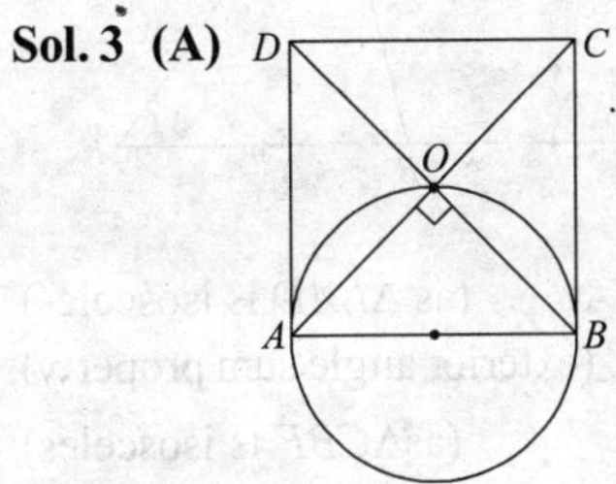

Since $\angle AOB = 90^\circ$

(diagonals of a quadrilateral rhombus bisect each other at right angle)

Taking *AB* as diameter the circle will definitely pass through the point '*O*'

Hence Ans is (A)

Sol. 4 (C)

D C

A B

The pairs of adjacent sides are *AD*, *AB*; *AB*, *BC*; *BC*, *CD* and *CD*, *DA*

Hence Ans is (C)

Sol. 5 (A)

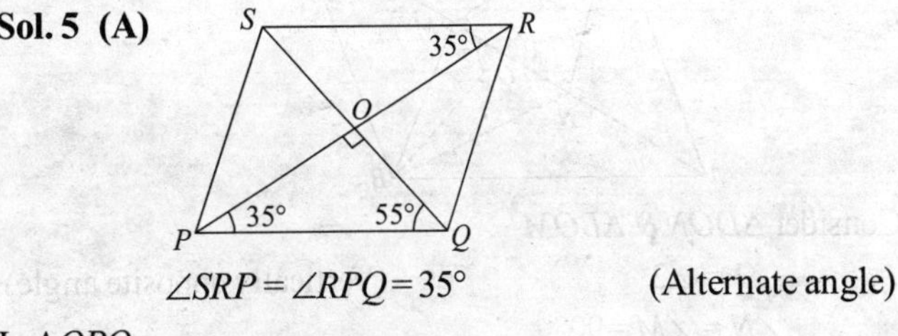

$\angle SRP = \angle RPQ = 35^\circ$ (Alternate angle)

In ΔOPQ,

$\angle POQ = 90^\circ$ (diagonal of a rhombus bisect at 90°)

$\angle OQP = 55^\circ$ (Angle sum property of triangle)

Hence $\angle OQP + \angle ORS = 55^\circ + 35^\circ = 90^\circ$

Hence Ans is (A)

Sol. 6 (B) From the figure

$\alpha = \angle 1$ ...vertically opposite angle

$\beta = \angle 2$ (vertically opposite angle)

$\alpha + \beta = \angle 1 + \angle 2$

$\Rightarrow \alpha + \beta = 180^\circ$

(Sum of the interior angles on the same side of the transversal)

Hence Ans is (B)

Sol. 7 (D) A quadrilateral in which all its vertices are concyclic must be either a rectangle or a square because sum of each pair of opposite angles is 180°

Hence Ans is (D)

Sol. 8 (B)

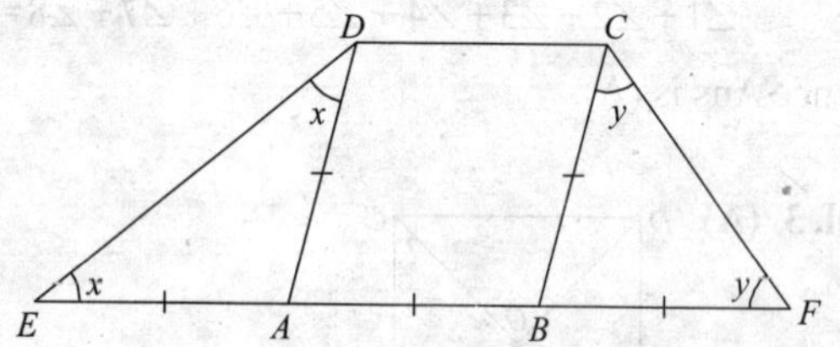

In the figure

$\angle E = \angle D = x$ (as ΔEAD is isosceles)

$\angle DAB = x + x = 2x$ (exterior angle sum property)

$\angle F = \angle C = y$ (as ΔCBF is isosceles)

and $\angle CBA = y + y = 2y$ (exterior angle sum property)

$\Rightarrow 2x + 2y = 180^\circ$

(adjacent angle of a rhombus are supplementary)

$\Rightarrow 2|x + y| = 180^\circ$

$\Rightarrow x + y = 90^\circ$ ...(1)

Now $(y - x)^2 = (x + y)^2 - 4xy$

$= (90^\circ)^2 - 4.1800$

$= 8100 - 7200$

$= 900$

$\Rightarrow y - x = \sqrt{900} = 30^\circ$

Hence Ans is (B)

Sol. 9 (B)

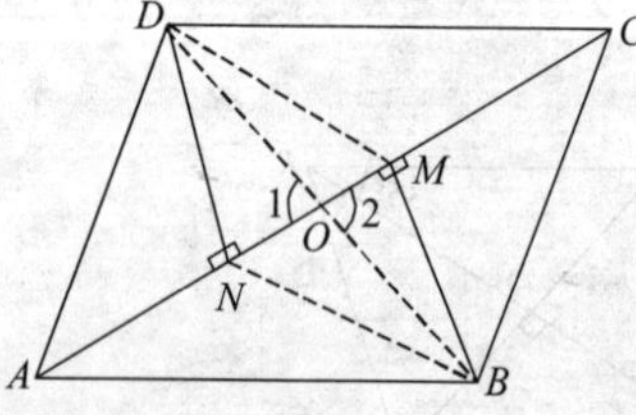

Consider ΔDON & ΔBOM

$\angle 1 = \angle 2$ (Vertically opposite angle)

$\angle N = \angle M = 90^\circ$

$DO = OB$(Diagonal of a parallelogram bisect each other)

$\Rightarrow \Delta DON \cong \Delta BOM$ (By AAS)

Hence $BO = OM$

So $DNBM$ is a parallelogram as its diagonal bisect each other

Hence Ans is (B)

Sol. 10 (A) Given D and E are midpoints of AB and AC.

$\Rightarrow DE \parallel BC$ (By mid-point theorem)

and $DP \parallel EQ$

$\Rightarrow DEQP$ is a parallelogram.

$\Rightarrow DE = PQ$

$\Rightarrow PQ = 4$

$\Rightarrow \frac{1}{2} PQ = 2$ cm

Hence Ans is (A)

Sol. 11 (A)

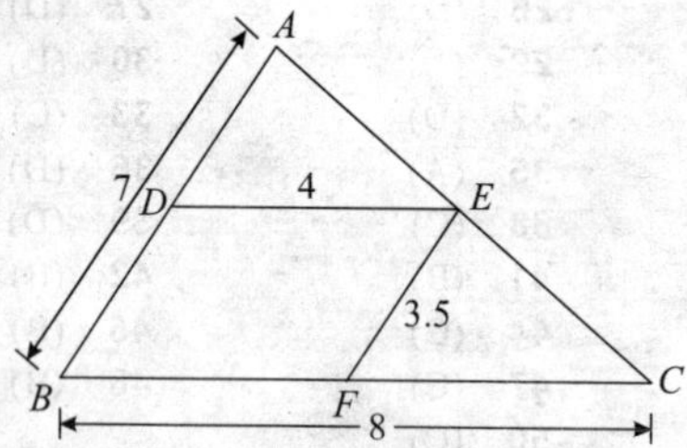

D and E are the midpoint of sides AB, AC hence by mid-point theorem DE is parallel to BC and half of BC

$\Rightarrow DE = BF$ (as F is the mid-point of BC)

and $DE \parallel BF$

$\Rightarrow BFED$ is a parallelogram.

$DE = \frac{1}{2} BC$

$= \frac{1}{2} \times 8 = 4$ cm

Similarly $EF = \frac{1}{2} AB = \frac{1}{2} \times 7$ cm

$= 3.5$ cm

$\Rightarrow$ Perimeter of $BFED = 2 \times (EF + DE)$

$= 2 \times (4 + 3.5)$

$= 2 \times 7.5$

$= 15$ cm

Hence Ans is (A)

Sol. 12 (C)

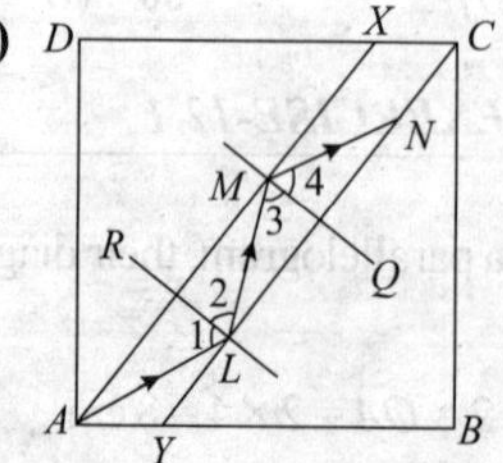

$\angle 1 = \angle 2$ (Angle of incidence = angle of reflection)

$\angle 2 = \angle 3$ (Alternate angle $LR \parallel MQ$)

$\angle 3 = \angle 4$ (Angle of incidence = angle of reflection)

$\Rightarrow \angle 1 = \angle 4$

Hence Ans is (C)

Sol. 13 (C) As per converse of midpoint theorem Q has to be the midpoint of AC

And similarly R has to be the midpoint of AD.

$\Rightarrow$ R divides AD in the ratio 1 : 1.

Hence Ans is (C)

Sol. 14 (D)

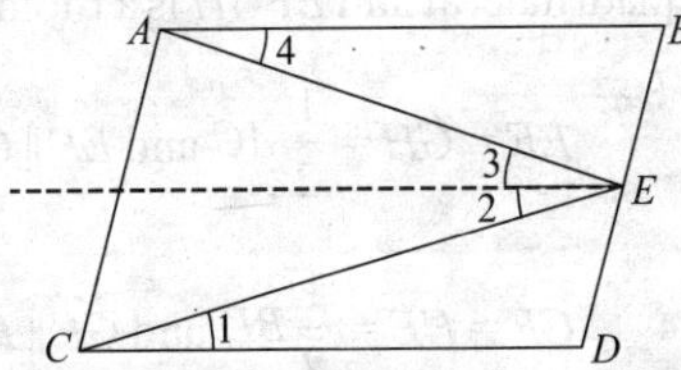

From the figure

$$\angle 1 = \angle 2 = 30° \quad \text{(Alternate angle)}$$

$$\angle 3 = \angle 4 = 25° \quad \text{(Alternate angle)}$$

$$\angle AEC = \angle 2 + \angle 3 = 30° + 25° = 55°.$$

Hence Ans is (D)

Sol. 15 (B)

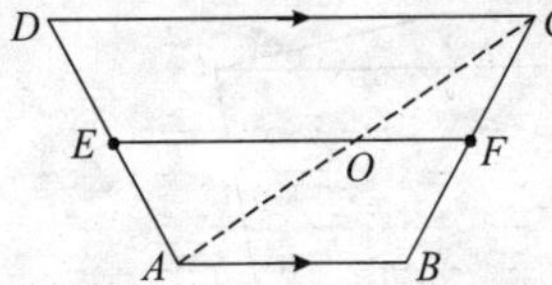

Given $DC \parallel AB$

Now it is given that AD and BC are the non parallel side.

E and F are the a midpoints of them.

$\Rightarrow$ $EF \parallel DC \parallel AB$(By intercept theorem)

Let AB be the smaller side $= x$

$\Rightarrow$ The longer side $DC = 5x$

In ΔADC, E is a mid-point of AD and $EO \parallel DC$

So by mid-point theorem

$$EO = \frac{1}{2}DC \quad \ldots(1)$$

Similarly $$OF = \frac{1}{2}AB \quad \ldots(2)$$

Adding equation-(1) & equation-(2)

$$EF = \frac{1}{2}DC + \frac{1}{2}AB$$

$$\Rightarrow \quad EF = \frac{1}{2} \times (5x + x)$$

$$\Rightarrow \quad EF = \frac{1}{2} \times 6x = 3x$$

$$\Rightarrow \quad \frac{EF}{AB} = \frac{3x}{x}$$

$$\Rightarrow \quad EF = 3AB$$

Hence Ans is (B)

Sol. 16 (C)

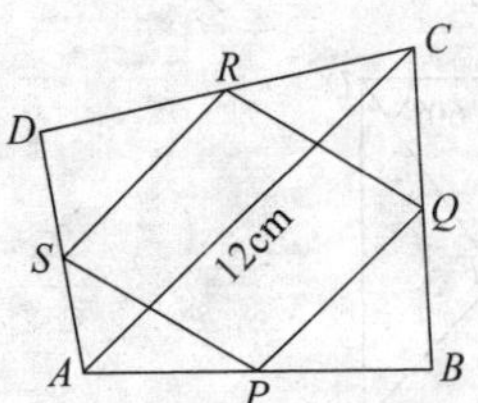

Since $SPQR$ is a parallelogram because it is a quadrilateral formed by joining the mid points of the sides of a quadrilateral $ABCD$. Now in ΔDAC. S and R are the mid points of sides DA and DC of the triangle.

$$\Rightarrow \quad SR = \frac{1}{2}AC \quad \text{(by mid point theorem)}$$

$$\Rightarrow \quad SR \text{ or } PQ = \frac{1}{2} \times 12$$

$\Rightarrow$ The length will be between 5cm to 10 cm

Hence Ans is (C)

Sol. 17 (A)

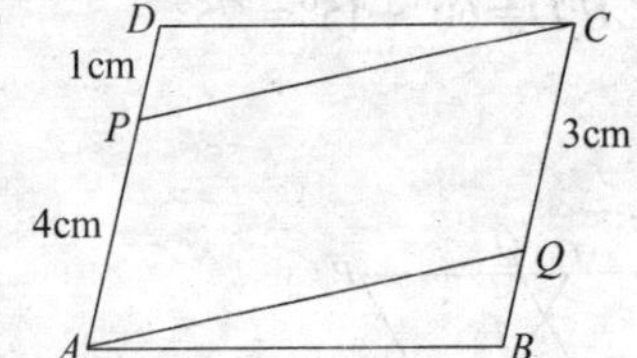

ΔDPC and ΔBQA are congruent (by SAS)

$$\Rightarrow \quad PC = AQ$$

and $$AP = CQ \;\&\; AP \parallel CQ$$

$\Rightarrow$ $APCQ$ is a parallelogram

$\Rightarrow$ The perpendicular distance between AQ and CP is always equal

Hence Ans is (A)

Sol. 18 (A) Length of diagonal AC & BD are equal in rectangle

$$\Rightarrow \quad AC = BD = 26$$

Diagonal bisect at O

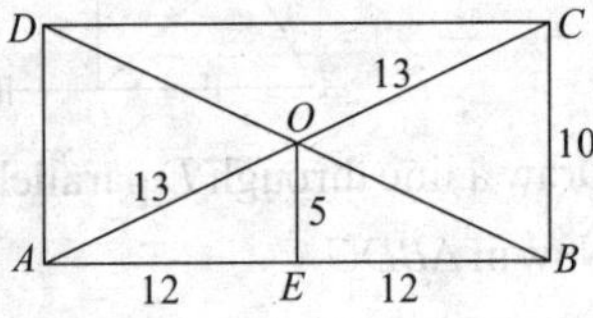

$$\Rightarrow \quad BO = 13$$

Given $OE \perp AB$

So by pythgoras theorem

$$AE^2 = AO^2 - OE^2$$

$$\Rightarrow \quad AE^2 = 13^2 - 5^2 = 169 - 25$$

$$= 144$$

$$\Rightarrow \quad AE = 12$$

Hence $$AB = 24$$

Now in ΔABC

$$BC^2 = AC^2 - AB^2$$

$$= 26^2 - 24^2$$

$$BC^2 = 100$$

$$\Rightarrow \quad BC = 10 \text{ cm}$$

Hence Ans is (A)

Sol. 19 (D)

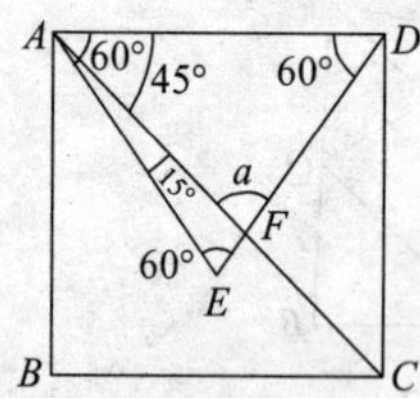

In ΔADE $\quad \angle DAE = 60° = \angle AED = \angle ADE$

[Equal angles of a equilateral angle]

$\angle CAD = 45°$

(Diagonal of a square bisect vertex angle)

$\angle EAF = \angle DAE - \angle CAD$

$= 60° - 45° = 15°$

$\angle AFD = \angle EAF + \angle AED$

(Exterior angle property of a triangle)

$\angle AFD = 60° + 15° = 75°$

Hence Ans is (D)

Sol. 20 (C)

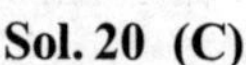

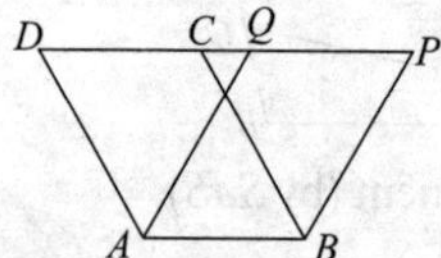

Here 'AB' is the common base and polygons are between the same parallels AB & PD

Hence Ans is (C)

Sol. 21 (C)

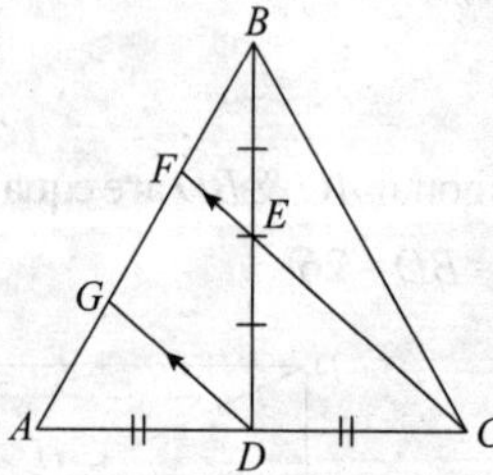

Draw a line through D parallel to CF. Intersects BA at G

Now in ΔBDG

$FE \parallel GD$ & E is the mid-point of BD

$\Rightarrow$ F will be mid point of BG

(by converse of mid-point theorem)

so that $\quad BF = GF = 5$

Now again in ΔACF

$GD \parallel FC$ & D is a mid-point of AC

$\Rightarrow$ G will be mid-point of AF

$GA = GF = 5$

Now $\quad BA = GA + FG + BF$

$= 5 + 5 + 5$

$= 15$ cm

Hence Ans is (C)

Sol. 22 (A)

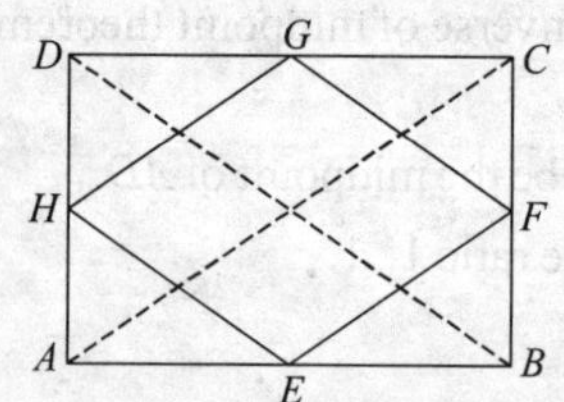

If $ABCD$ is any quadrilateral and $EFGH$ is a rhombus.

then $\quad EF = GH = \frac{1}{2}AC$ and $EF \parallel GH \parallel AC$

$GF = HE = \frac{1}{2}BD$ and $GF \parallel HE \parallel BD$

$EF = GH = GF = HE$ (sides of rhombus)

i.e. $\quad AC = BD$

$\Rightarrow$ $ABCD$ is a rectangle

Hence Ans is (A)

Sol. 23 (A)

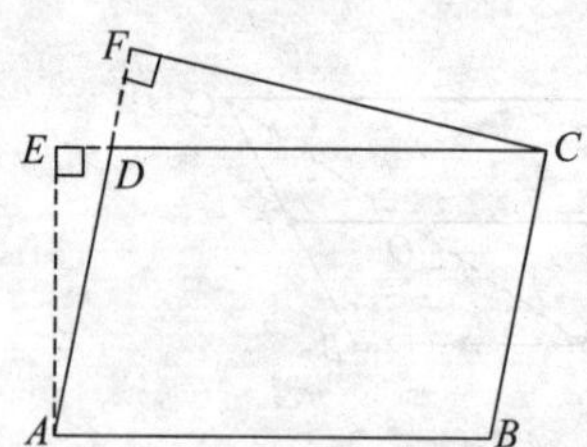

We know

Area of parallelogram = base × height

$\Rightarrow \quad AE \times CD = CF \times AD$

$\Rightarrow \quad 8 \times CD = 10 \times 6$

$\Rightarrow \quad CD = \frac{60}{8} = \frac{30}{4} = 7.5$ cm

Hence Ans is (A)

Sol. 24 (A)

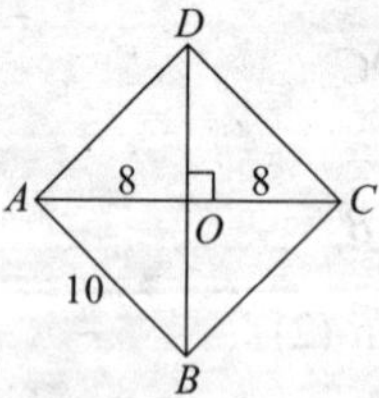

Given $ABCD$ is a Rhombus

In ΔAOB

$BO^2 = AB^2 - AO^2$

$= 100 - 64 = 36$

$\Rightarrow \quad BO = 6$ cm

i.e. other diagonal

$= 12$ cm

Area of rhombus $\quad = \frac{1}{2}d_1 \times d_2 = \frac{1}{2} \times 16 \times 12$

$= 96$ cm^2

Hence Ans is (A)

Sol. 25 (A)

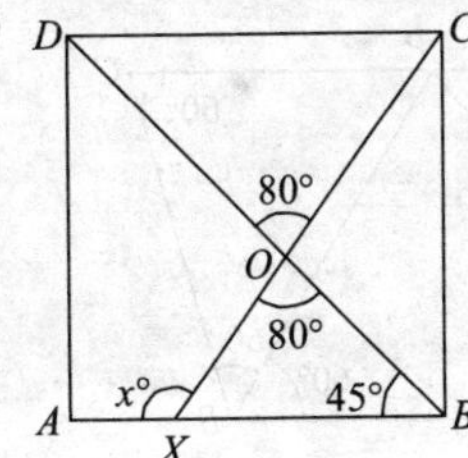

From the figure

$\angle XOB = 80°$ (Vertically opposite angle)

and $\angle ABD = 45°$

i.e. $x = 80° + 45° = 125°$

(Exterior angle is equal to sum of interior opposite angle)

Hence Ans is (A)

Sol. 26 (D)

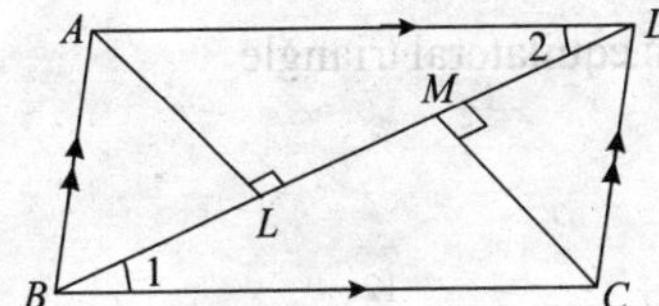

In right angle ΔALD & ΔCMB

$\angle 2 = \angle 1$

and $\angle ALD = \angle CMB = 90°$

$AD = BC$ (opposite side of a $||^r$ gm)

$\Rightarrow$ $\Delta ALD \cong \Delta CMB$

Hence $AL = CM$

Similarly $\Delta ALB \cong \Delta CMD$ (by RHS)

Hence $LB = MD$

Hence Ans is (D)

Sol. 27 (D) According to mid-point theorem

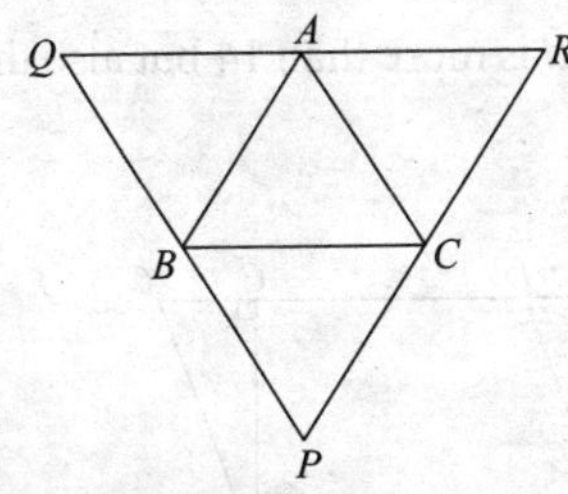

Here $PQ \parallel AC$, $QR \parallel BC$, $RP \parallel AB$

$\Rightarrow$ $AQ \parallel BC$ & $QB \parallel AC$

$\Rightarrow$ $AQBC$ is a parallelogram

similarly $ARCB$ is also a parallelogram

$\Rightarrow$ $BC = QA = AR$

$BC = \frac{1}{2} QR$

i.e. all four triangle are congruent to each other.

Hence Ans is (D)

Sol. 28 (B)

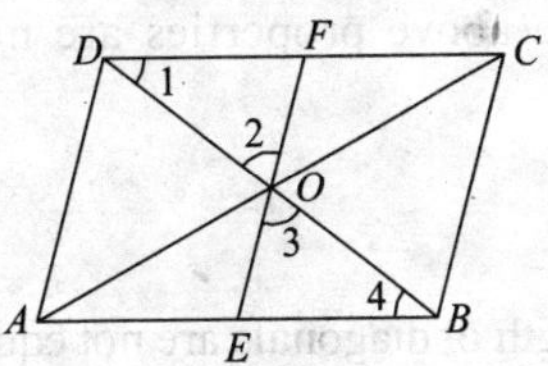

In ΔDOF and ΔBOE

$\angle 1 = \angle 4$ (Alternet angle)

$\angle 2 = \angle 3$ (Vertically opposite angle)

$OD = BO$ (Diagonal bisect at O)

$\Rightarrow$ $\Delta DOF \cong \Delta BOE$

then $OE = OF$ (By c.p.c.t.)

Hence Ans is (B)

Sol. 29 (A)

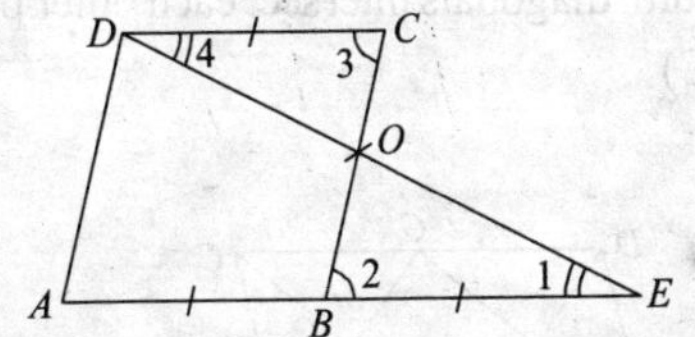

In ΔBOE & COD

$\angle 1 = \angle 4$ (Alternate angle)

$\angle 2 = \angle 3$ (Alternate angle)

$BE = CD$ (Given $BE = AB$)

Hence, $\Delta BOE \cong \Delta COD$ (ASA)

$BO = CO$ (c.p.c.t.)

Hence Ans is (A)

Sol. 30 (D)

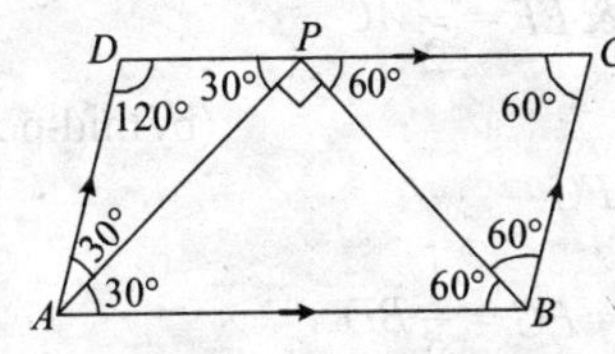

$\angle A = 60°$ (Given)

i.e. $\angle B = 120°$

(Adjacent angle of a $||^r$ gm are supplementary)

$\angle APB = 180° - 30° - 60° = 90°$

(Angle sum property of a triangle)

$\angle DPA = \angle PAB$ (Alternet angle)

i.e. $AD = DP$

(Being side of isocesles triangle)

similarly $BC = CP$ (Side of equilateral triangle)

i.e. $CD = DP + PC$

$= AD + BC (AD = BC)$

$CD = 2AD = 2BC$

Hence Ans is (D)

Sol. 31 (D) All the above properties are not true for a parallelogram

Hence Ans is (D)

Sol. 32 (D) The length of diagonals are not equal

Hence Ans is (D)

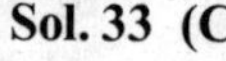

Sol. 33 (C)

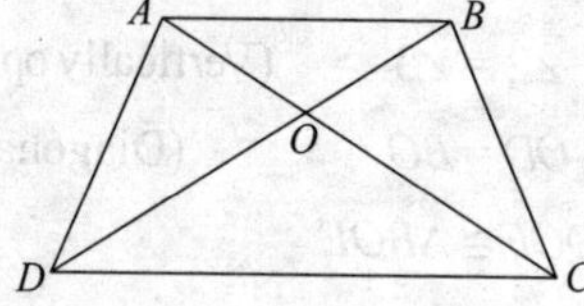

Given $\frac{OA}{OC} = \frac{OB}{OD}$

So, in a trapezium, diagonals intersect each other proportionally

Hence Ans is (C)

Sol. 34 (B)

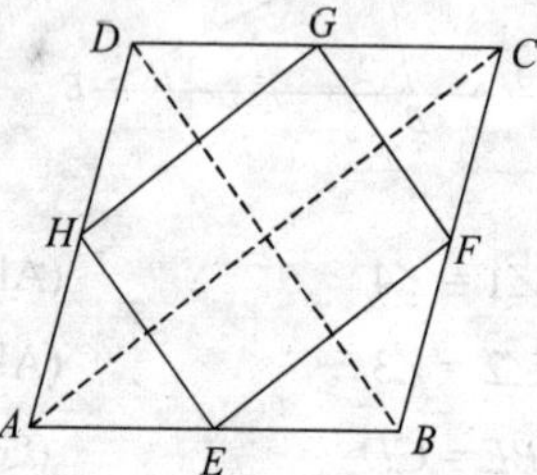

$$HG \parallel AC \;\&\; HG = \frac{1}{2}AC$$

(by mid-point theorem)

Similarly $EF \parallel AC \;\&\; EF = \frac{1}{2}AC$

(by mid-point theorem)

Similarly $EH \parallel BD \parallel FG$

& $\quad EH = FG = \frac{1}{2}BD$

Since in rhombus $AC \neq BD$

Hence the figure formed by joining the consecutive mid points of any rhombus is always a rectangle

Hence Ans is (B)

Sol. 35 (A) Each exterior angle of a polygon

$= 180° -$ each interior angle

$= (180° - 178°)$

$= 2°$

number of sides $= \frac{360°}{\text{each exterior angle}}$

$\frac{360°}{2°} = 180$

Hence Ans is (A)

Sol. 36 (D)

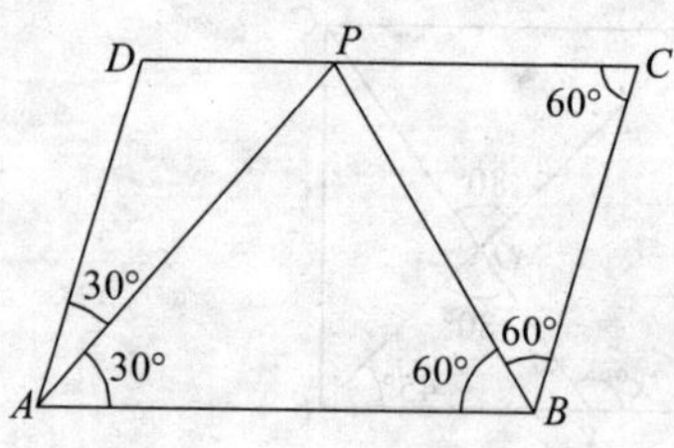

Given $\qquad \angle A = \angle C = 60°$

(opposite angle of a parallelogram are equal)

$\angle B + \angle C = 180°$

$\angle B + 60° = 180°$

$\angle B = 120°$

$\angle CBP = \angle ABP = 60°$

$(\angle BPC = 180° - 120° = 60°)$

Hence ΔBCP is an equilateral triangle

Hence Ans is (D)

Sol. 37 (D)

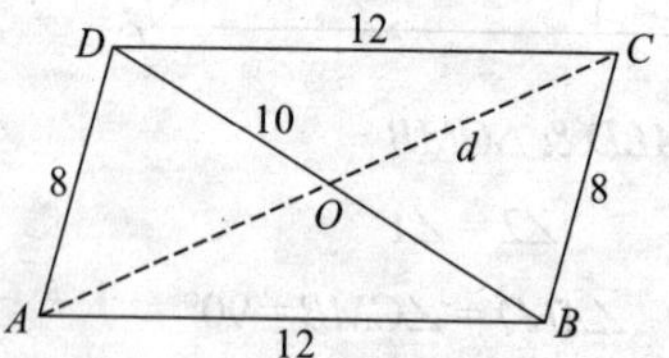

In triangle ABC

$$AC < AB + BC$$

$\Rightarrow \quad d < 12 + 8$

$\Rightarrow \quad d < 20$

In ΔOAB

$$OA + OB > AB$$

$$\frac{d}{2} + 5 > 12$$

$\Rightarrow \quad d > 14$

$\Rightarrow$ The value of d is more than 14 but also than 20.

Hence Ans is (D).

Sol. 38 (C)

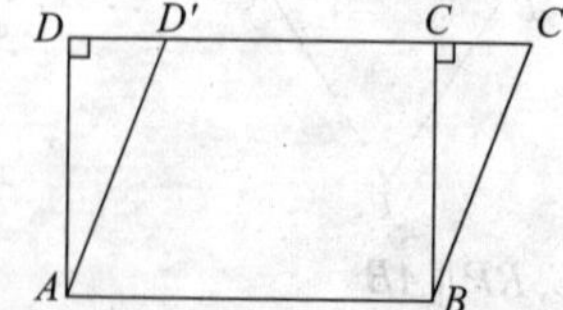

In right angle $\Delta ADD'$

$$AD' > AD$$

(hypotenuse is the greatest sides in a right angle triangle)

$$2AD' > 2AD$$

$$2AD' + 2AB > 2AD + 2AB$$

$$AD' + BC' + AB + C'D' > AB + BC + CD + AD$$

Perimeter of parallelogram $ABC'D'$ > Perimeter rectangle $ABCD$

Hence Ans is (C)

Sol. 39 (D)

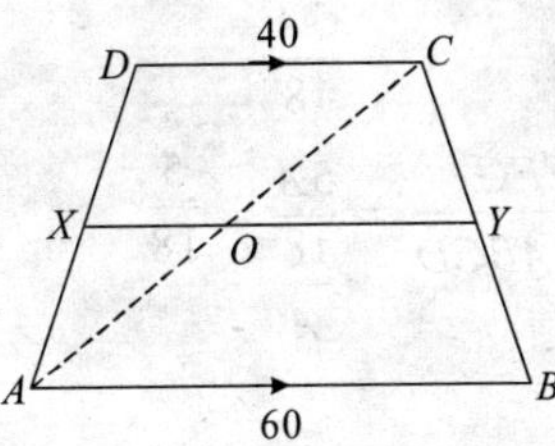

In ΔADC X is the mid-point of AD & $XO \parallel^r DC$

so, by converse of basic propotionality theorem

$$XO \parallel DC \;\&\; XO = \frac{1}{2}DC = \frac{1}{2} \times 40 = 20$$

Similarly in ΔBCA

$$YO = \frac{1}{2}AB = \frac{1}{2} \times 60 = 30$$

So $\qquad XY = XO + OY = 20 + 30 = 50$

ar trapezium $\qquad YXCD = \frac{1}{2}(DC + XY) \times h$

$$= \frac{1}{2}(40 + 50) \times h$$

$$= \frac{1}{2} \times 90 \times h$$

area of trapezium $XYBA = \frac{1}{2}(AB + XY) \times h$

$$= \frac{1}{2}(50 + 60) \times h$$

$$= \frac{1}{2} \times 110 \times h$$

$$\frac{\text{area of trapezium } DCYX}{\text{area of trapezium } XYBA} = \frac{\frac{1}{2}90 \times h}{\frac{1}{2} \times 110 \times h} = \frac{9}{11}$$

ar trapezium $DCYX = \frac{9}{11}$ ar trapezium $(XYBA)$

Hence Ans is (D)

Sol. 40 (C) In the ΔABD

S & R are mid-points of AB & AD respectively

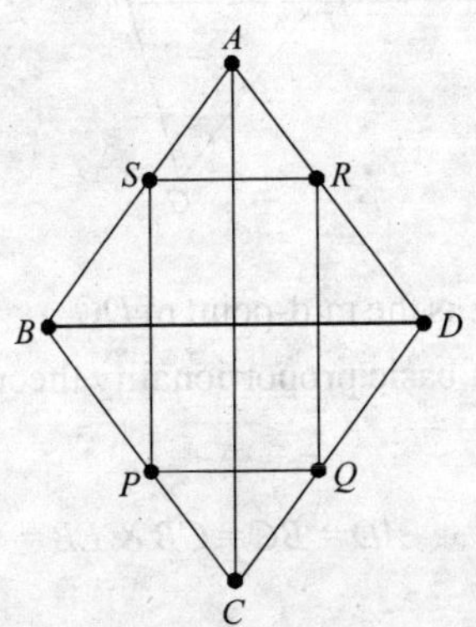

$$\Rightarrow \qquad SR = \frac{1}{2}BD \;\&\; SR \parallel BD \qquad \ldots(1)$$

Again in the ΔCBD

point P & Q are mid-points of BC & CD respectively

$$\Rightarrow \qquad PQ = \frac{1}{2}BD \;\&\; PQ \parallel BD \qquad \ldots(2)$$

by (1) & (2)

$$PQ = SR \text{ and } PQ \parallel SR$$

Similarly for ΔADC & ΔABC

$$SP = QR \;\&\; SP \parallel QR \qquad \ldots(3)$$

Now $AC \perp BD \;\Rightarrow\; SP \perp PQ$

Hence, $\qquad \angle SPQ = 90°$

$\Rightarrow$ $PQRS$ is rectangle

Hence Ans is (C)

Sol. 41 (B)

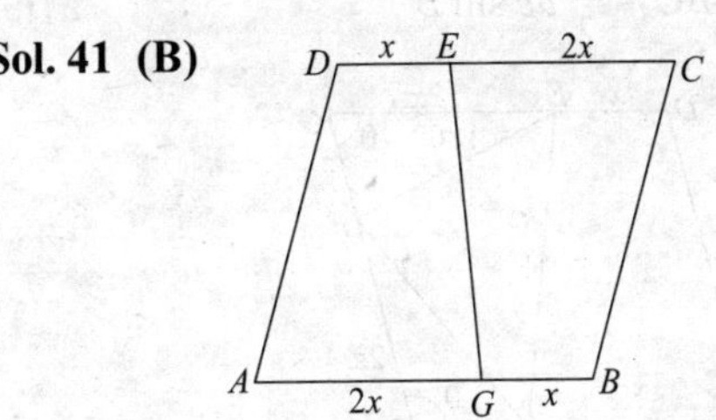

Let the distance between parallel AB & DC be h then area of parallelogram

$$ABCD = 3x \times h = A \qquad \ldots(1)$$

area of trapezium $ADEG = \frac{1}{2}(AG + DE) \times h$

$$= \frac{1}{2} \times (2x + x) \times h = \frac{1}{2} \times 3x \times h = \frac{A}{2}$$

(Using (1))

Similarly area of trapezium

$$GBCE = \frac{A}{2}$$

Hence Ans is (B)

Sol. 42 (B)

Let the distance between parallel AB & DC be h

then area of parallelogram

$$ABCD = 3x \times h = A \qquad \ldots(1)$$

area of trapezium

$$ADEG = \frac{1}{2}(AG + DE) \times h$$

$$= \frac{1}{2} \times (2x + x) \times h$$

$$= \frac{1}{2} \times 3x \times h = \frac{A}{2} \quad \ldots(2)$$

(Using (1))

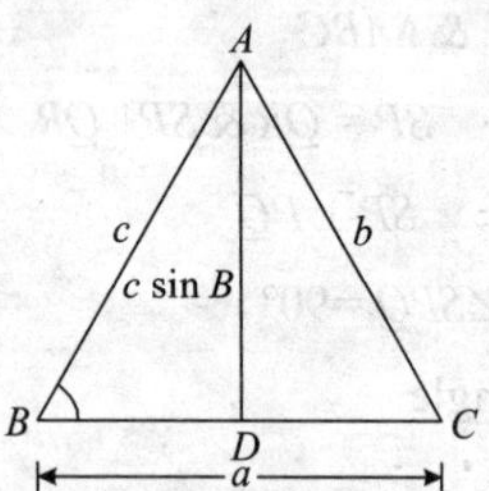

Area of $\Delta ABC = \frac{1}{2} ac \sin B \quad \ldots(3)$

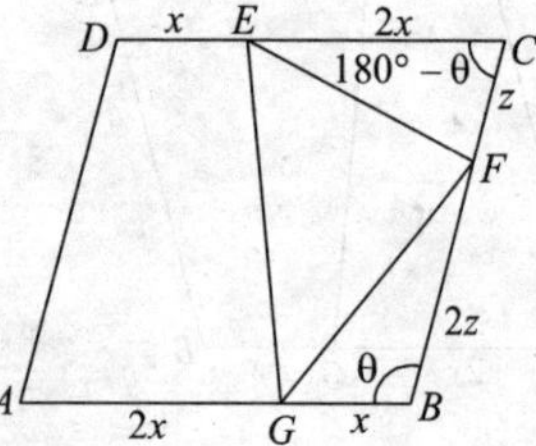

Area of parallelogram

$$ABCD = 3x \times 3z \sin\theta = A \quad \ldots(4)$$

Area of $\Delta ECF = \frac{1}{2} 2x \times z \times \sin(180 - \theta)$

(Using equation-(3))

$$= xz \sin\theta = \frac{A}{9}$$

(Using equation-(4)) ...(5)

Similarly area of triangle

$$BFC = \frac{1}{2} 2xz \sin\theta \quad \text{(Using equation-(3))}$$

$$= xz \sin\theta = \frac{A}{9} \quad \text{(Using equation-(4))} \quad \ldots(6)$$

Area of ΔEFG

= Area of trapezium $EGBC$ – Area of ΔECF – Area of ΔBGF

$$= \frac{A}{2} - \frac{A}{9} - \frac{A}{9} \quad \text{(Using eq. (2), eq. (5), eq. (6))}$$

$$= \frac{9A - 2A - 2A}{18}$$

$$= \frac{9A - 4A}{18}$$

$$= \frac{5A}{18} \quad \ldots(7)$$

$$\frac{\text{Area of } \Delta EFG}{\text{Area of } \|^{r}\text{gm } ABCD} = \frac{\frac{5A}{18}}{A} = \frac{5}{18}$$

Hence Ans is (B)

Sol. 43 (B)

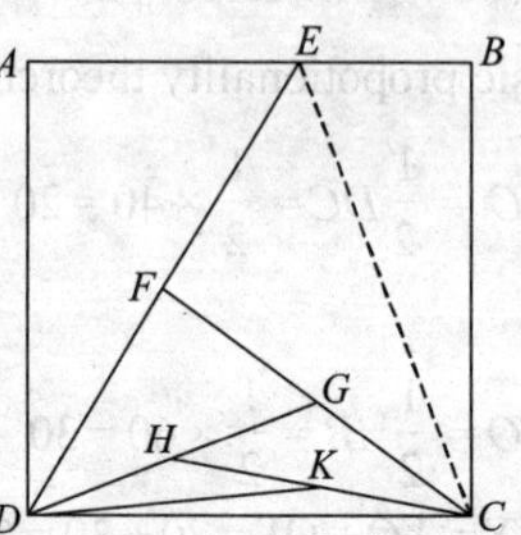

As we know that median divides the Δ in to two part having same area

So let *ar* of $\Delta KDC = A$

As DK is median to ΔHDC

$\Rightarrow \quad ar\,\Delta HDK = A$

$\Rightarrow \quad ar\,\Delta HDC = 2A = ar\,\Delta HGC$

$\Rightarrow \quad ar\,\Delta DGC = 4A = ar\,\Delta FGD$

$\Rightarrow \quad ar\,\Delta FDC = 8 = \text{ar}\,\Delta AFC$

Join EC

$\Rightarrow \quad ar\,\Delta EDC = 16A$

Which is $\frac{1}{2}$ *ar* of square $ABCD$

$\Rightarrow \quad ar\,\Delta EDC = \frac{1}{2} \times 4$

$\Rightarrow \quad 16A = 2$

$\Rightarrow \quad A = \frac{2}{16} = \frac{1}{8}$

Hence Ans is (B)

Sol. 44 (C)

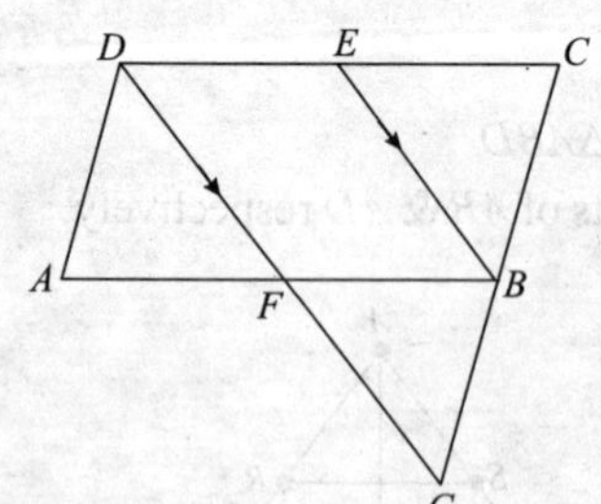

In ΔCDG

$EB \parallel DG$ & E is the mid-point of DC

so by converse of basic proportionality theorem B will be the mid-point of CG

Hence $\quad AD = BC = GB$ & $EB = \frac{1}{2} DG$

Hence Ans is (C)

Sol. 45 (B)

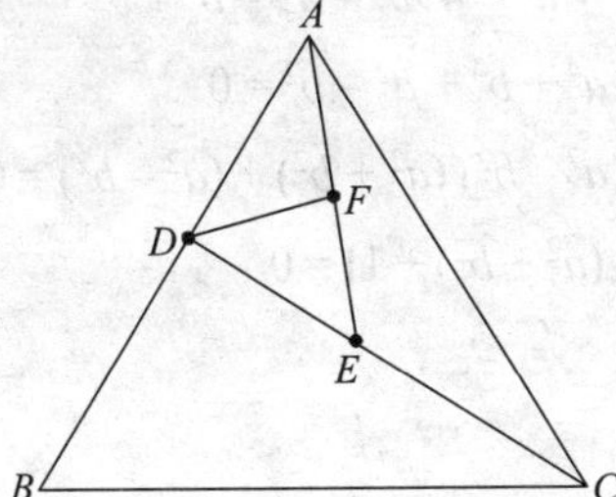

Medians divides the triangle in two parts having same area

Let $ar\Delta AFD = ar\Delta FDE = A$

$\Rightarrow \quad ar\Delta AED = 2A = ar\Delta AEC$

$\Rightarrow \quad ar\Delta ACD = 4A = ar\Delta BDC$

$\Rightarrow \quad ar\Delta ABC = 8A$

$$\Rightarrow \quad \frac{ar\Delta AFD}{ar\Delta ABC} = \frac{A}{8A}$$

$$\Rightarrow \quad ar\Delta AFD = \frac{1}{8}\ ar\Delta ABC$$

Hence Ans is (B)

Sol. 46 (A)

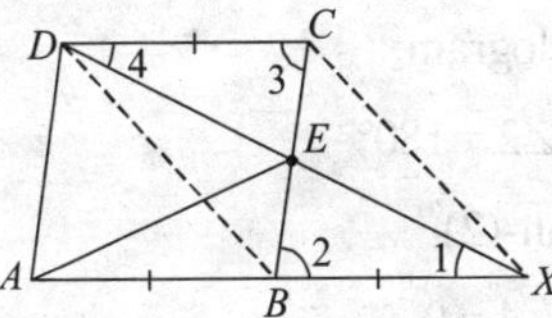

In ΔBEX & ΔCED

$\angle 1 = \angle 4$ (alternate angle)

$\angle 2 = \angle 3$ (alternate angle)

$BX = DC$

(as $AB = BC$ and given $AB = BX$)

$\Rightarrow \quad \Delta BEX \cong \Delta CED$

$\Rightarrow \quad EC = EB$ & $ED = EX$

$\Rightarrow$ $BXCD$ is a parallelogram

area of parallelogram

$ABCD$ = area of parallelogram $BXCD$ ... (A)

As they are on same base & between same parallel lines

Now

$$ar\ \Delta AED = \frac{1}{2} \text{ are of parallelogram } ABCD \ldots (1)$$

$$ar\ \Delta CEX = \frac{1}{2}\ ar\ \Delta CDX$$

$$= \frac{1}{4} \text{ area parallelogram } CXBD \quad \ldots (2)$$

$\Rightarrow \quad ar\Delta AED = 2\ ar\ \Delta CEX$

Using (A) (1) & (2)

Hence Ans is (A)

Sol. 47 (C)

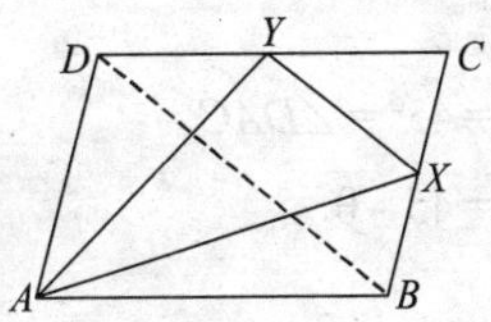

Let area of parallelogram $ABCD = 8$

then $ar\ \Delta BCD = 4$

(As diagonal of parallelogram divides it into two triangle having same area)

$\Delta CYX \sim \Delta CDB$ (as $XY \parallel BD$)

So ratio of area of two similar triangle is equal to ratio of square of there corresponding sides

$$\frac{\text{area of } \Delta CYX}{\text{area of } \Delta CDB} = \left(\frac{CX}{CB}\right)^2 = \left(\frac{CX}{2 \times CX}\right)^2$$

$$\frac{\text{area of } \Delta CYX}{4} = \frac{1}{4}$$

$$\Rightarrow \quad ar\ \Delta CYX = \frac{1}{4} \times 4$$

$$= 1$$

In ΔDAC DY is median then as median divides the triangle in to two parts having same area

So, $\text{area of } \Delta AYC = \frac{1}{2} \text{ area of } \Delta DAC$

$$= \frac{1}{2} \times 4 = 2$$

Similarly area of

$\Delta AXC = 2$

So $ar\Delta AYX = ar\ \Delta AYC + ar\ \Delta AXC - ar\ \Delta CYX$

$= 2 + 2 - 1$

$= 3$

$$\text{Hence } \frac{ar\Delta AYX}{ar \text{ parallelogram } ABCD} = \frac{3}{8}$$

$$ar\ \Delta AYX = \frac{3}{8}\ ar \text{ parallelogram } ABCD$$

Hence Ans is (C)

Sol. 48 (B)

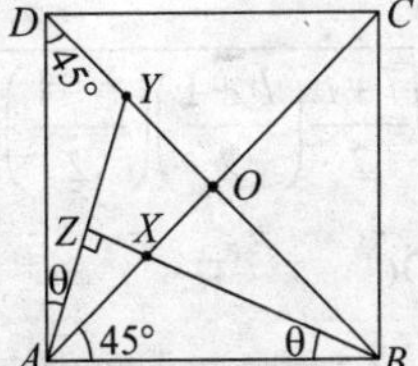

Let $\angle DAY = \theta$

& We know that

$$\angle ADY = 45° = \angle DAC$$

Now $\angle YAO = 45 - \theta$

So in ΔAZB

$$\angle ZBA = \theta$$

Now consider ΔAXB & ΔDYA

$\angle ADY = \angle BAX = 45°$

$AD = AB$ (being side of square)

$\angle ABX = \angle DAY = \theta$ (we assume)

So $\Delta AXB \cong \Delta DYA$

Hence by c.p.c.t. $AX = DY$

Hence Ans is (B)

Sol. 49 (B)

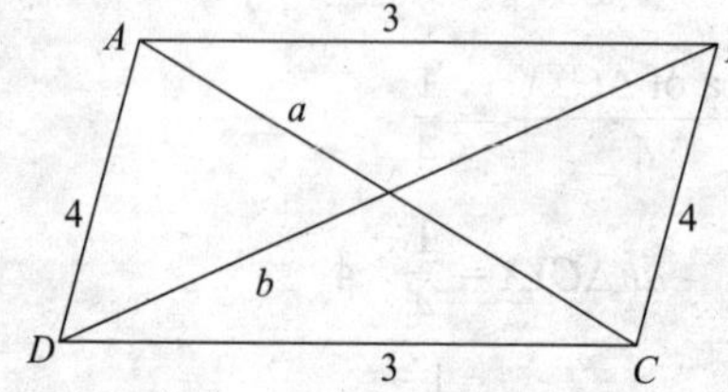

Area of $\Delta ABC = \sqrt{s(s-a)(s-b)(s-c)}$

when

$$s = \frac{3+4+a}{2}$$

$$s = \frac{7+a}{2}$$

Area of

$$\Delta ABC = \sqrt{\frac{7+a}{2}\left(\frac{a+1}{2}\right)\left(\frac{a-1}{2}\right)\left(\frac{7-a}{2}\right)}$$

$$= \frac{1}{4}\sqrt{(49-a^2)(a^2-1)}$$

Similarly area of

$$\Delta ABC = \sqrt{s'(s'-a)(s'-b)(s'-c)}$$

$$s' = \frac{3+4+b}{2}$$

$$s' = \frac{7+b}{2}$$

$$D = \sqrt{\frac{7+b}{2}\left(\frac{b+1}{2}\right)\left(\frac{b-1}{2}\right)\left(\frac{7-b}{2}\right)}$$

Area of ΔABC = Area of ΔADC

$$= \frac{1}{4}\sqrt{(49-b^2)(b^2-1)}$$

$\Rightarrow 49a^2 - 49 - a^4 + a^2 = 49b^2 - 49 - b^4 + b^2$

$\Rightarrow 49a^2 - 49b^2 - a^4 + b^4 + a^2 - b^2 = 0$

$\Rightarrow 49(a^2 - b^2) - (a^2 - b^2)(a^2 + b^2) + (a^2 - b^2) = 0$

$\Rightarrow (a^2 - b^2)[49 - (a^2 + b^2) + 1] = 0$

$\Rightarrow a^2 - b^2 = 0$

or $a^2 + b^2 = 48$

Hence Ans is (B)

Sol. 50 (C)

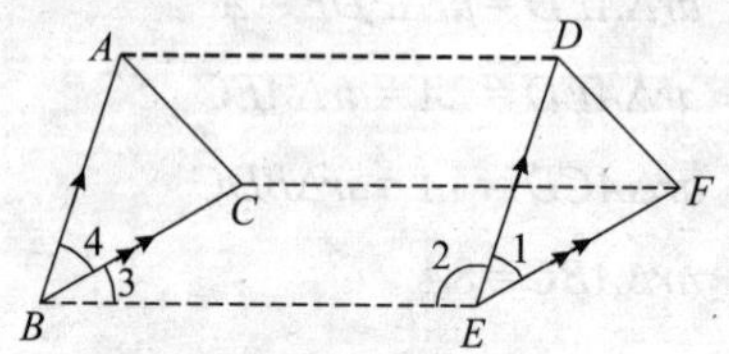

Given $BC \parallel EF$ & $BC = EF$

$\Rightarrow$ $BCFE$ is a parallelogram

Hence $\angle 3 + \angle 2 + \angle 1 = 180°$ ...(1)

(Adjacent angle of a parallelogram are supplementary)

Similarly $AB \parallel DE$ & $AB = DE$

$\Rightarrow$ $ABED$ is a parallelogram

Hence $\angle 4 + \angle 3 + \angle 2 = 180°$ ...(2)

equation-(1) – equation-(2)

$$\angle 1 - \angle 4 = 0$$

$$\angle 1 = \angle 4$$

$\Delta ABC \cong \Delta DEF$ (*SAS* congreuncy)

i.e. $AC = DF$ and $AC \parallel DF$

Hence Ans is (C)

Solutions of PRACTICE EXERCISE-12.2

Sol. 1 (A) $ABCD$ is a parallelogram

$\Rightarrow$ $\angle A + \angle B = 180°$

$\Rightarrow$ $\frac{\angle A + \angle B}{2} = \frac{180°}{2}$

$\Rightarrow$ $\frac{1}{2}\angle A + \frac{1}{2}\angle B = 90°$ ...(1)

Now in ΔAOB

$\frac{1}{2}\angle A + \angle AOB + \frac{1}{2}\angle B = 180°$

$\Rightarrow$ $\frac{1}{2}\angle A + \frac{1}{2}\angle B + \angle AOB = 180°$

$\Rightarrow$ $90° + \angle AOB = 180°$

$\Rightarrow$ $\angle AOB = 180° - 90° = 90°$

$\Rightarrow$ $\angle POQ = \angle AOB = 90°$

(Vertically opposite angles)

$\Rightarrow \quad \angle POR = \frac{1}{2}\angle POQ = 45^\circ$

$\Rightarrow$ Complement of

$\angle POR = 90^\circ - 45^\circ$

$= 45^\circ$

Hence Ans is (A)

Sol. 2 (C) Since $ABCD$ is a ||^r gm

$\Rightarrow \quad 2\angle PAB + 2\angle PBA = 180^\circ$

$\Rightarrow \quad \angle PAB + \angle PBA = 90^\circ \quad \ldots(1)$

In ΔPAB

$\angle PAB + \angle PBA + \angle APB = 180^\circ$

$90 + \angle APB = 180^\circ$ (Using equation-(1))

$\Rightarrow \quad \angle APB = 90^\circ \quad \ldots(2)$

Now $\quad \angle LPA + \angle LPB + \angle APB = 360^\circ$

$\Rightarrow \quad \angle LPA + \angle LPB + 90^\circ = 360^\circ$ (Using equation-(2))

$\Rightarrow \quad \angle LPA + \angle LPB = 360^\circ - 90^\circ = 270^\circ$

Hence Ans is (C)

Sol. 3 (B)

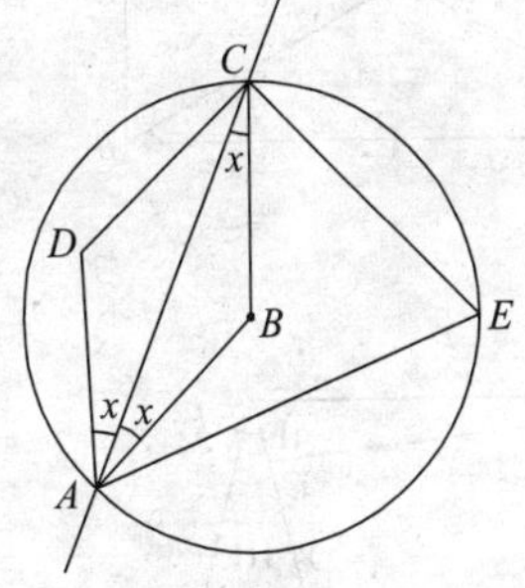

$ABCD$ is parallelogram

$\Rightarrow AD \parallel BC$ and AC is a transversal

$\Rightarrow \angle DAC = \angle ACB = x$

Now in ΔABC,

$x + \angle ABC + x = 180^\circ$

$\Rightarrow \quad \angle ABC = 180^\circ - 2x$

Now $\quad \angle ABC = 2\angle AEB$

$\Rightarrow \quad 180^\circ - 2x = 2\angle AEB$

$\Rightarrow \quad \angle AEB = 1/2\,(180^\circ - 2x)$

$= 1/2 \times 2\,(90^\circ - x)$

$= (90^\circ - x)$

Hence Ans is (B)

Sol. 4 (B) Given $ABCD$ is a rhombus.

$\Rightarrow$ its diagonals are perpendicular to each other.

$\Rightarrow \quad \angle AOD = 90^\circ$

Now, In rt. ΔAOD

$$\sin 30^\circ = \frac{OD}{AD}$$

$\Rightarrow \quad \frac{1}{2} = \frac{3}{AD}$

$\Rightarrow \quad AD = 6\text{ cm}$

So $\quad AD + DC = 6\text{ cm} + 6\text{ cm}$

$= 12\text{ cm}$

Hence Ans is (B)

Sol. 5 (C) AP and BP divide $\angle A$ and $\angle B$ in the ratio 1 : 3.

$\Rightarrow \quad \angle PAB = 2/3\ \angle DAB$

$\angle PBA = 2/3\ \angle CBA$

Now in ΔPAB,

$\angle PAB + \angle APB + \angle PBA = 180^\circ$

$\Rightarrow \quad \frac{2}{3}\angle DAB + \frac{2}{3}\angle CBA + \angle APB = 180^\circ$

$\Rightarrow \quad \frac{2}{3} \times (\angle DAB + \angle CBA) + \angle APB = 180^\circ$

$\Rightarrow \quad \frac{2}{3} \times 180 + \angle APB = 180^\circ$

$\Rightarrow \quad \angle APB = 180^\circ - 120^\circ = 60^\circ$

Now $\quad \angle AQB = 180^\circ - \frac{1}{2}$

$(\angle DAB + \angle CBA)$

$= 180^\circ - \frac{1}{2} \times 180^\circ = 90^\circ$

$\Rightarrow \quad \angle AQB - \angle APB = 90^\circ - 60^\circ = 30^\circ$

Hence Ans is (C)

Sol. 6 (A) Cyclic parallelogram will either a square or a rectangle so quadrilateral formed by joining the mid-point of such cyclic parallelogram will be a square.

$\Rightarrow \quad SP \parallel BD$

and $\quad SP = \frac{1}{2} BD \quad$ (by mid point theorem)

$= \frac{1}{2} \times 8 = 4\text{ cm}$

Hence Ans is (A)

Sol. 7 (D) Let $AP = x$, then $PD = 2x$

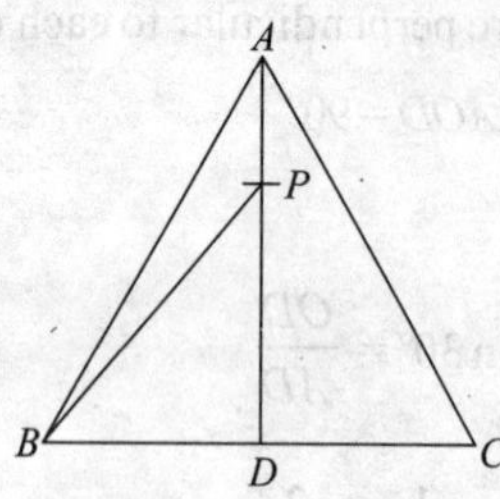

Now $\quad ar(ABD) = \frac{1}{2} ar(ABC)$

(as median divides the triangle in to two parts having same area)

$$ar(ABP) = \frac{1}{2} \times x \times h$$

and $\quad ar(ABD) = \frac{1}{2} \times 3x \times h = 3\left(\frac{1}{2} \times x \times h\right)$

$\Rightarrow \quad ar(ABP) = \frac{1}{3} ar(ABD)$

Also $\quad ar(ABP) = \frac{1}{3} \times \frac{1}{2} ar(ABC)$

$$= \frac{1}{6} ar(ABC)$$

Hence Ans is (D)

Sol. 8 (D) $DF \parallel BE$ and D is mid-point of BC so by converse of mid-point theorem F will be mid-point of CE.

$$CF = EF$$

and $\quad CE = AE$

(Given BE is a median of a ΔABC)

$$CE = AE = \frac{1}{2} AC$$

$$CE = \frac{1}{2} AC$$

$$2CF = \frac{1}{2} AC$$

$$CF = \frac{1}{4} AC$$

Hence Ans is (D)

Sol. 9 (D) In ΔHAB,

PD is $\parallel^r$ to AB and $HA : AP = 3 : 1$

so apply basic proportionality theorem in ΔHAB

$\Rightarrow \quad \frac{HA}{PA} = \frac{HB}{BD}$

$\Rightarrow \quad \frac{3}{1} = \frac{HB}{24}$

$\Rightarrow \quad BH = 24 \times 3$

$$= 72 \text{ cm}$$

Hence Ans is (D)

Sol. 10 (C) $ar \parallel^r_{gm} AFEB = \frac{1}{2} ar.(\parallel^r_{gm} ABCD)$ $\quad \ldots(1)$

(EF divides $\parallel^r_{gm}$ in to two parts having same area)

$ar\Delta GAB = \frac{1}{2} ar.(\parallel^r_{gm} AFEB)$ $\quad \ldots(2)$

(If a triangle and $\parallel^r_{gm}$ are on the same base and between same $\parallel^r$ then area of triangle is half the area of $\parallel^r_{gm}$)

$\Rightarrow \quad ar\Delta GAB = \frac{1}{4} ar(\parallel^r_{gm} ABCD)$

[From (1) and (2)]

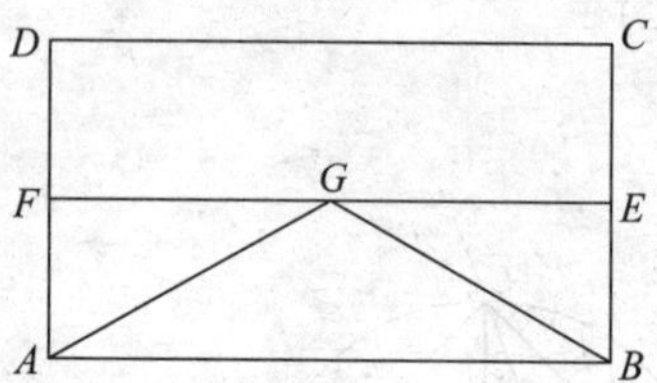

Hence Ans is (C)

Sol. 11 (B)

The new figure obtained is made up of the original rectangle and four additional triangles, I, II, III, IV, as marked in the figure in which, I = II and III = IV. If x and y are the sides of the original rectangle, the sides of triangle I or II are $x(1 + k)$, ky and of Areas of I + II + III + IV are $y(1 + k)$, kx.
Areas of I + II + III + IV

$$= 2[\frac{1}{2}x(1+k)ky + \frac{1}{2}y(1+k)kx]$$

$$= k(1+k)ky + k(1+k)xy = 2k(1+k)xy$$

The area of the new quadrilateral

$$= 2k(1+k)xy + xy = \frac{5}{2}xy \text{ (given)}$$

So, $\quad 2k(1+k) + 1 = \frac{5}{2}$ given $k(k+1) = \frac{3}{4}$, i.e. $k = \frac{1}{2}$ or $-\frac{3}{2}$

Which is impossible. Hence the required

$$k = \frac{1}{2}$$

Hence Ans is (A)

Sol. 12 (D)

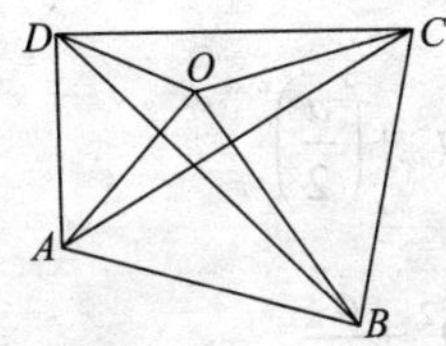

In ΔAOC and ΔBOD,

$$OA + OC > AC \quad \ldots(1)$$

(by triangle inequality)

and in ΔBOD,

$$OB + OD > BD \quad \ldots(2)$$

(by triangle inequality)

equation-(1) + equation-(2)

Hence,

$$OA + OB + OC + OD > AC + BD$$

Hence Ans is (D)

Sol. 13 (B)

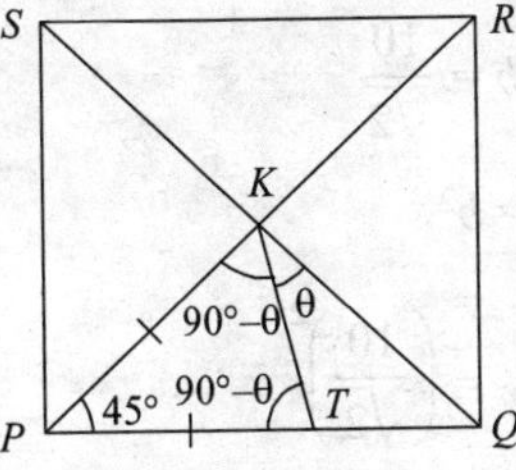

Let $\angle TKQ = \theta°$

Diagonal of a square bisect at 90°

So $\angle PKT = 90° - \theta$

Given $PK = PT$

$\Rightarrow \angle PTK = 90° - \theta$

So now in ΔPKT we have

$$\angle TPK + \angle PKT + \angle PTK = 180°$$

$$45 + 90 - \theta + 90 - \theta = 180°$$

$$45 - 2\theta = 0$$

$$\theta = 22.5$$

Hence Ans is (B)

Sol. 14 (B) Area of equilateral triangle $= \frac{\sqrt{3}}{4}(\text{side})^2$

Area of rectangle = length × breadth

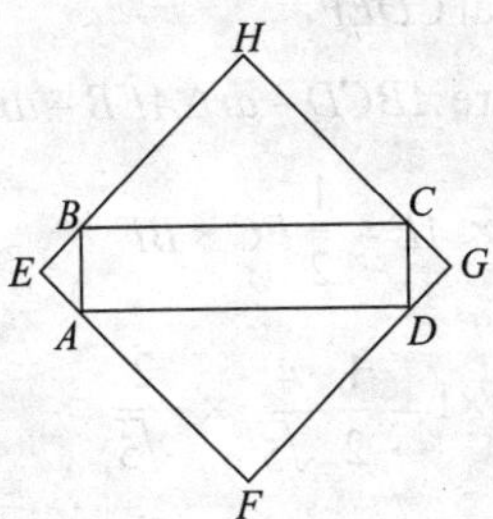

Area of the figure

$$= ar\Delta BEA + ar\Delta CGD + ar\Delta ADF + ar\Delta BCH + ar\square ABCD$$

$$= \frac{\sqrt{3}}{4}(5)^2 + \frac{\sqrt{3}}{4}(5)^2 + \frac{\sqrt{3}}{4}(6)^2 + \frac{\sqrt{3}}{4}(6)^2 + 6 \times 5$$

$$= 2\left(\frac{\sqrt{3}}{4} \times 5^2 + \frac{\sqrt{3}}{4} \times 6^2\right) + 5 \times 6$$

$$= 30 + \frac{\sqrt{3}}{2}[25 + 36]$$

$$= 30 + \frac{\sqrt{3}}{2} \times 61$$

Hence Ans is (B)

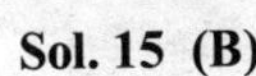

Sol. 15 (B)

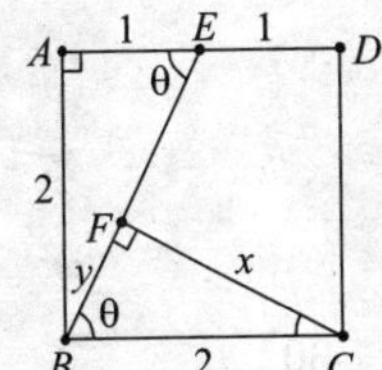

Let $\angle AEB = \angle EBC = \theta$

$$BF = y \ \& \ FC = x$$

$$BE^2 = AE^2 + AB^2 = 1^2 + 2^2 = 1 + 4 = 5$$

$$BE^2 = 5$$

$$BE = \sqrt{5}$$

Since $\Delta BFC \sim \Delta EAB$ (*AA* similarity)

So ratio of the corresponding sides of a similar triangle are equal

$$\frac{AB}{FC} = \frac{AE}{FB} = \frac{BE}{BC}$$

$$\frac{2}{x} = \frac{1}{y} = \frac{\sqrt{5}}{2}$$

$$x = \frac{4}{\sqrt{5}}, y = \frac{2}{\sqrt{5}}$$

Area of quadrilateral $CDEF$

$= \text{Area of square } ABCD - ar\Delta AEB - ar\Delta BFC$

$= AB^2 - \frac{1}{2}AB \times AE - \frac{1}{2}FC \times BF$

$= 2 \times 2 - \frac{1}{2} \times 2 \times 1 - \frac{1}{2}\frac{4}{\sqrt{5}} \times \frac{2}{\sqrt{5}}$

$= 4 - 1 - \frac{4}{5} = \frac{11}{5}$

Hence Ans is (B)

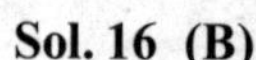

Sol. 16 (B)

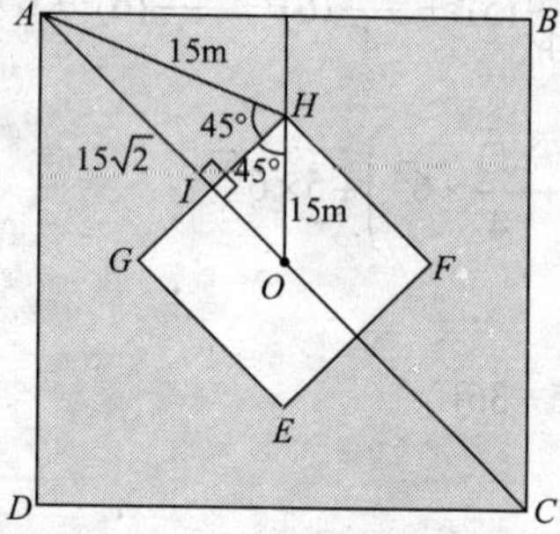

In ΔAIH

$$\frac{IH}{AH} = \cos 45°$$

$$\frac{IH}{15} = \frac{1}{\sqrt{2}}$$

$$IH = \frac{15}{\sqrt{2}}$$

$$\Rightarrow \quad GH = 2IH = \frac{30}{\sqrt{2}}$$

In ΔAHO

$$AH^2 + HO^2 = AO^2$$

$$\Rightarrow \quad 15^2 + 15^2 = AO^2$$

$$\Rightarrow \quad AO = 15\sqrt{2}$$

$$\Rightarrow \quad AC = 30\sqrt{2} = AB\sqrt{2}$$

$$\Rightarrow \quad AB = 30$$

Now area of shaded region

$= \text{area of square } ABCD - \text{area of square } EFGH$

$= AB^2 - GH^2$

$= 30^2 - \left(\frac{30}{\sqrt{2}}\right)^2 = 900 - \frac{900}{2} = 900 - 450 = 450$

Hence Ans is (B)

Sol. 17 (C)

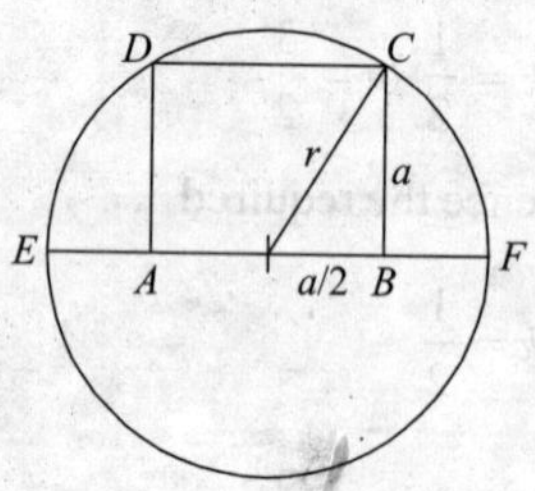

Let the side of square be a & radius of circle be 'r'

From figure it is clear that

$$r^2 = a^2 + \left(\frac{a}{2}\right)^2$$

$$r^2 = a^2 + \frac{a^2}{4}$$

$$r^2 = \frac{5a^2}{4}$$

$$r^2 = \frac{5}{4} \times 20 \quad (\text{as } a^2 = 20) \text{ (given)}$$

$$r^2 = 25$$

$$r = 5$$

Diagonal of largest square of side b will be the diameter of circle.

$$\Rightarrow \quad b\sqrt{2} = 2 \times r$$

$$\Rightarrow \quad b\sqrt{2} = 5 \times 2 = 10$$

$$\Rightarrow \quad b = \frac{10}{\sqrt{2}}$$

Area of largest square $= b^2$

$$= \left(\frac{10}{\sqrt{2}}\right)^2$$

$$= \frac{100}{2} = 50 \text{ sq.}$$

Hence Ans is (C)

Sol. 18 (C)

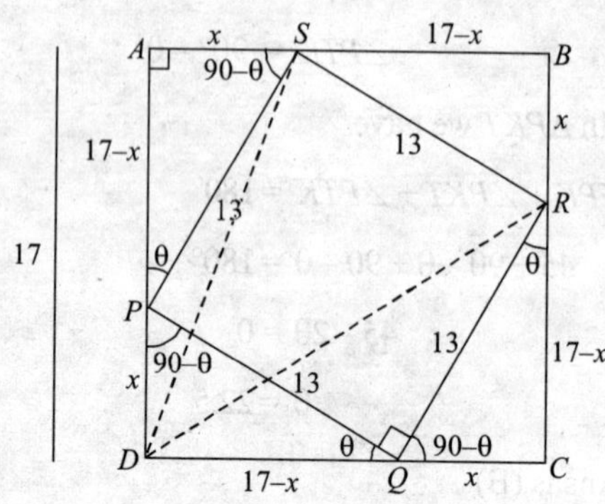

$$\Delta PSA \cong \Delta RQC \quad \text{(by } ASA)$$

$\Rightarrow \quad AS = QC = x$

Now in ΔPDQ

$$PD^2 + DQ^2 = PQ^2$$

$$x^2 + (17-x)^2 = 13^2$$

$$x^2 + 289 - 34x + x^2 = 169$$

$$2x^2 - 34x + 120 = 0$$

$$x^2 - 17x + 60 = 0$$

$$(x-5)(x-12) = 0$$

$$x = 5$$

or $\quad x = 12$

Greatest distance between a vertex of inner square & outer square will be either.

DS or DR

$\Rightarrow \quad DS^2 = DA^2 + AS^2 \quad$ or $\quad DR^2 = DC^2 + RC^2$

$\Rightarrow \quad DS^2 = 17^2 + 5^2 \quad$ or $\quad DR^2 = 17^2 + 12^2$

$\Rightarrow \quad DS^2 = 289 + 25 \quad$ or $\quad DR^2 = 289 + 144$

$\Rightarrow \quad DS = \sqrt{314} \quad$ or $\quad DR^2 = 433$

$$DR = \sqrt{433}$$

Hence Ans is (C)

Sol. 19 (A)

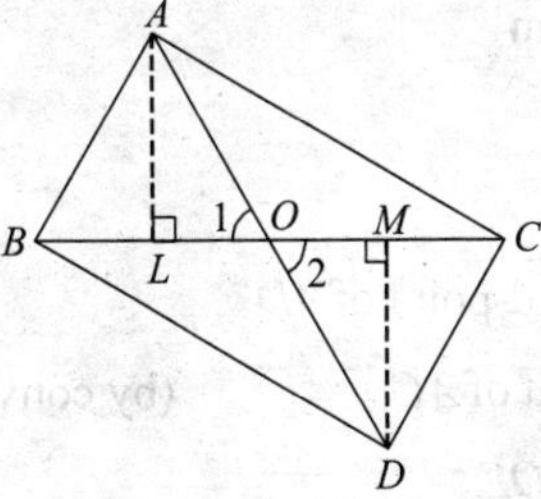

In ΔALO & ΔDMO

$\angle M = \angle L = 90°$ (each)

$\angle 1 = \angle 2$ (vertically opposit angle)

$\Rightarrow \quad \Delta ALO \sim \Delta DMO$

$$\Rightarrow \quad \frac{AL}{DM} = \frac{AO}{OD} \quad \ldots(1)$$

$$\Rightarrow \quad \frac{ar \text{ of } \Delta ABC}{ar \text{ of } \Delta BDC} = \frac{\frac{1}{2} \times BC \times AL}{\frac{1}{2} BC \times DM}$$

$$\Rightarrow \quad \frac{ar \text{ of } \Delta ABC}{ar \text{ of } \Delta BDC} = \frac{AL}{DM} = \frac{AO}{OD} \quad \text{(Using (1))}$$

Hence Ans is (A)

Sol. 20 (A)

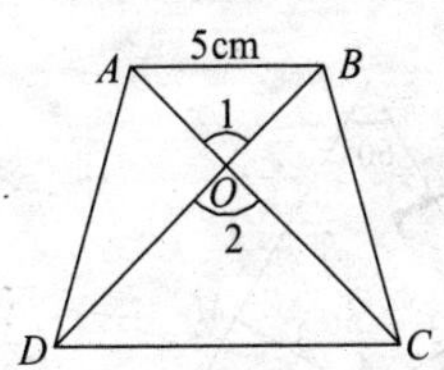

Consider ΔAOB & ΔCOD

We have $\quad \dfrac{AO}{OC} = \dfrac{BO}{OD} = \dfrac{1}{3}$

& $\quad \angle 1 = \angle 2 \quad$ (vertically opposite angle)

$\Rightarrow \quad \Delta AOB \sim \Delta COD$

$$\Rightarrow \quad \frac{AB}{DC} = \frac{1}{3}$$

$$\Rightarrow \quad \frac{5}{DC} = \frac{1}{3}$$

$\Rightarrow \quad DC = 15$

Hence Ans is (A)

Sol. 21 (B)

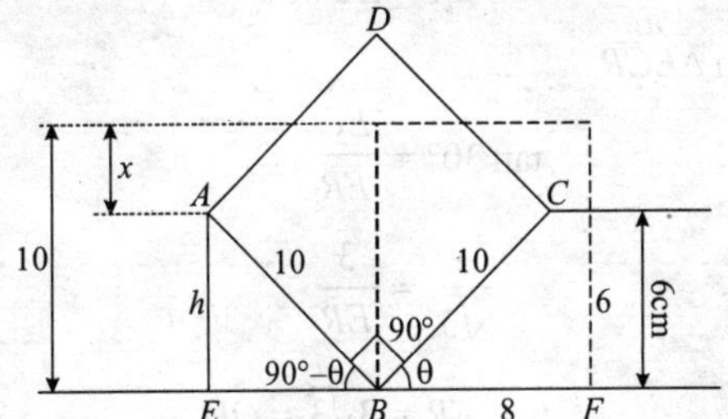

We have

$\angle ABC = 90°$

Let $\quad \angle CBF = \theta \quad \ldots(1)$

In ΔCBF, $\quad \angle BCF = 90 - \theta \; \{\angle F = 90°\} \quad \ldots(2)$

Now $\angle ABE + \angle ABC + \angle CBF = 180°$

$\angle ABE + 90° + \theta = 180°$

$\Rightarrow \quad \angle ABE = 90° - \theta \quad \ldots(3)$

so in ΔABE, $\quad \angle EAB = \theta \quad \ldots(4)$

Now in ΔABE and ΔBCF

$\angle ABE = \angle BCF = 90 - \theta$

{From (1) and (3)}

$\angle BAE = \angle CBF = \theta \quad$ {From (2) and (4)}

$AB = BC = 10$

$\Rightarrow \quad DABE \cong DCBF \quad$ [By ASA]

So $\quad BE = CF = 6$ cm $\quad$ (c.p.c.t)

In triangle $ABE \quad AB^2 = AE^2 + BE^2$

$10^2 = AE^2 + 6^2$

$\Rightarrow \quad AE = 8$ cm

So $\quad x = 10 - AE = 10 - 8 = 2$ cm

Hence Ans is (B)

Sol. 22 (C)

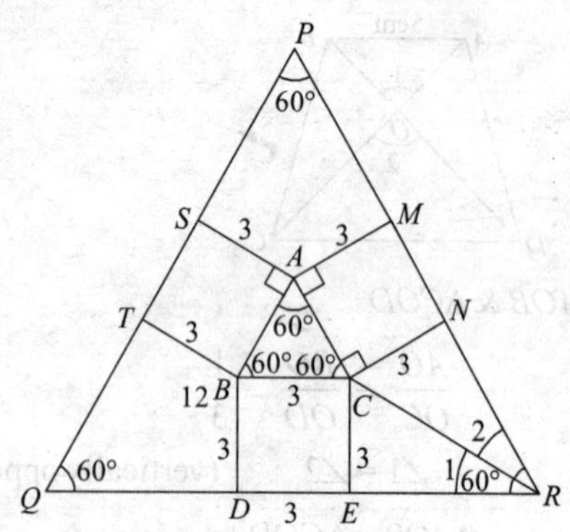

Consider ΔECR & NCR

We have

$\angle E = \angle N = 90$ (each)

$EC = NC = 3\text{cm}$ (each)

$RC = RC$ (common)

$\Rightarrow \quad \Delta ECR \cong \Delta NCR$ (by RHS)

$\Rightarrow \quad \angle 1 = \angle 2 = 30°$

Now in ΔECR

$$\tan 30° = \frac{EC}{ER}$$

$$\frac{1}{\sqrt{3}} = \frac{3}{ER}$$

$$\Rightarrow \quad ER = 3\sqrt{3} = QD$$

$$\Rightarrow \quad QR = QD + DE + ER = 3 + 6\sqrt{3}$$

$$ar \text{ of } \Delta PQR = \frac{\sqrt{3}}{4}(QR)^2$$

$$= \frac{\sqrt{3}}{4}(3+6\sqrt{3})^2$$

$$= \frac{\sqrt{3}}{4}(9+108+36\sqrt{3})$$

$$= \frac{117\sqrt{3}}{4} + 27$$

Hence Ans is (C)

Sol. 23 (B)

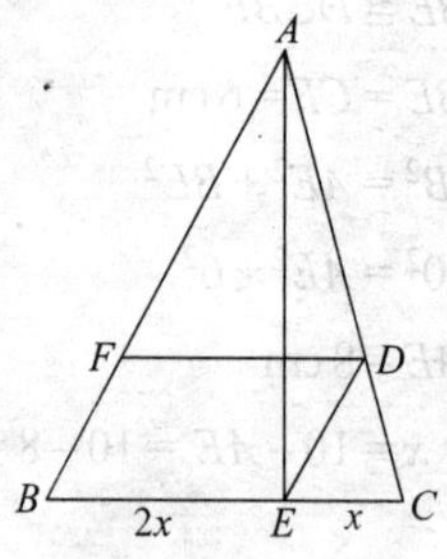

Let $\quad BC = 3x$

$$\Rightarrow \quad EC = \frac{1}{3}3x = x \;\&\; BE = 2x$$

Let the length of altitude between $\|^r$ lines FD & BE be h_1, & from vertex A to EC be h_2

So as per question

$$ar\, \Delta AEC = \text{area of parallelogram } FBED$$

$$\Rightarrow \quad \frac{1}{2} \times \text{base} \times \text{height} = \text{Base} \times \text{height}$$

$$\Rightarrow \quad \frac{1}{2} \times x \times h_2 = 2x \times h_1$$

$$\Rightarrow \quad \frac{h_1}{h_2} = \frac{1}{4}$$

Hence Ans is (B)

Sol. 24 (D)

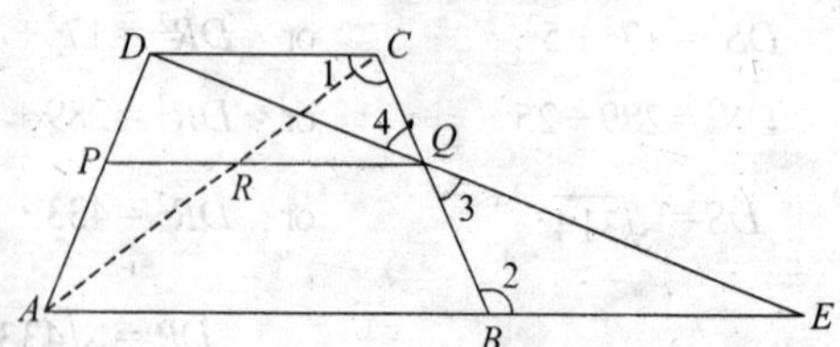

Since $ABCD$ is a trapezium & P & Q are mid-point of AD & BC respectively.

So by intercept theorem

$PQ \| DC \| AB$

Now In ΔADC

$PR \| DC$ & P is mid-point of AD

$\Rightarrow$ R is also mid-point of AC (by converse of BPT)

Consider ΔDQC & ΔBQE

$\angle 1 = \angle 2$ (Alternate angle)

$\angle 3 = \angle 4$ (Vertically opposite angle)

& $\quad BQ = QC$ (Given)

$\Rightarrow \quad \Delta DQC \cong \Delta EQB$

Hence by c.p.c.t

$DQ = QE$

Hence Ans is (D)

Sol. 25 (B) Since G, H, I are mid-point of DF, DE, EF respectively.

So be using mid-point theorem

We have that

$$GH \| EF \;\&\; GH = \frac{1}{2}EF$$

$$\Rightarrow \quad GH \| FI \;\&\; GH = FI$$

So $GHIF$ is a $||^r$gm

GI is diagonal of $GHIF$

So it divides the parallelogram in to two triangle having same area.

$$ar \text{ of } \Delta GIF = \text{ar } \Delta GHI = A$$

Similarly $\quad ar \text{ of } \Delta IHE = A = ar \text{ of } \Delta GHD$

Similarly. $EF \parallel BD$ & $EF = BD$

So we have

$$ar \text{ of } \Delta BDF = ar\, \Delta \text{ of } FED = 4A$$

$$= ar \text{ of } \Delta AFE = ar \text{ of } \Delta DEC$$

$$\frac{ar(\text{quad } GHIF)}{ar(\text{quad } AEDB)} = \frac{2A}{12A} = \frac{1}{6}$$

Hence Ans is (B)

Solutions of PRACTICE EXERCISE-12.3

Sol. 1 (B) By angle sum property of quadrilateral, we have

$$x + 2x + \frac{5x}{2} + \frac{7x}{2} = 360°$$

$$\Rightarrow \quad 3x + 6x = 360°$$

$$\Rightarrow \quad 9x = 360°$$

$$\Rightarrow \quad x = 40°,$$

$$\Rightarrow \quad 2x = 80°,$$

and $\quad \frac{5x°}{2} = 100°$

and $\quad \frac{7x°}{2} = 140°$

So the required difference between the biggest & the smallest angle is $140 - 40 = 100°$.

Hence Ans is (D)

Sol. 2 (A)

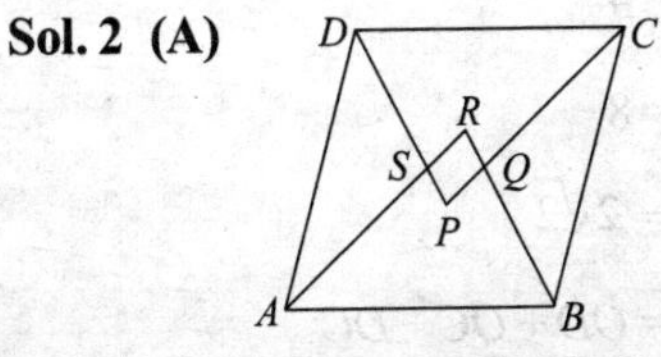

$$\angle A + \angle B = 180°$$

As A & B are adjacent angle of parallelogram.

$$\frac{1}{2}\angle A + \frac{1}{2}\angle B = 90°$$

So $\quad \angle SPQ = 90°$

So $\quad \angle PSR = 90°$

So $\quad \angle PQR = 90°$

Hence Ans is (A)

Sol. 3 (A)

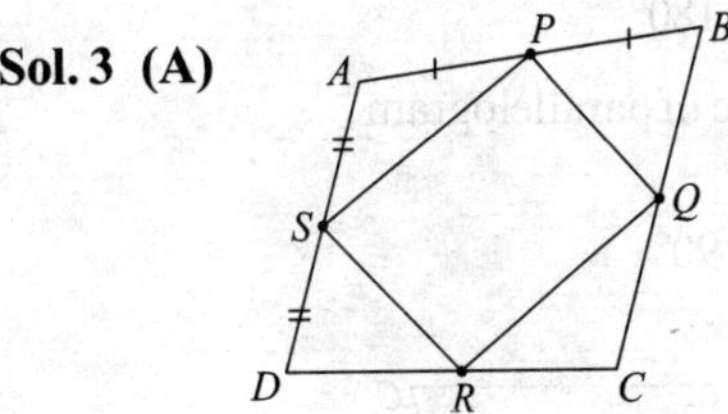

It will be a parallelogram by mid point theorm.

Hence Ans is (A)

Sol. 4 (D)

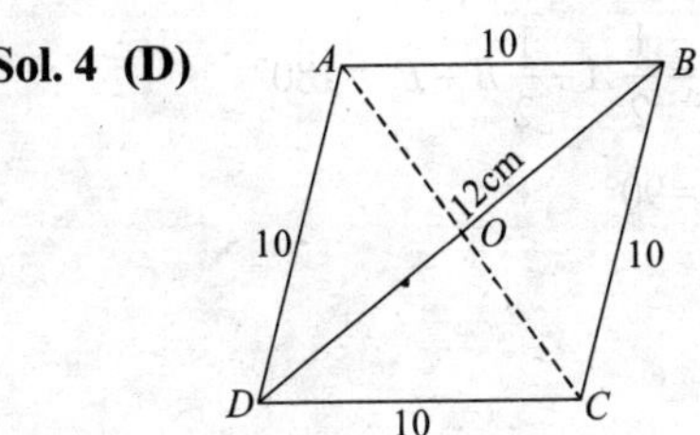

In Rhombus, diagonals bisect each other at 90°

In ΔAOB

$$AB^2 = AO^2 + OB^2$$

$$(10)^2 = AO^2 + 6^2$$

$$AO^2 = 64$$

$$AO = 8$$

$\Rightarrow$ Diagonal

$$AC = 2(AO)$$

$$= 16 \text{ cm}$$

Hence Ans is (D)

Sol. 5 (C)

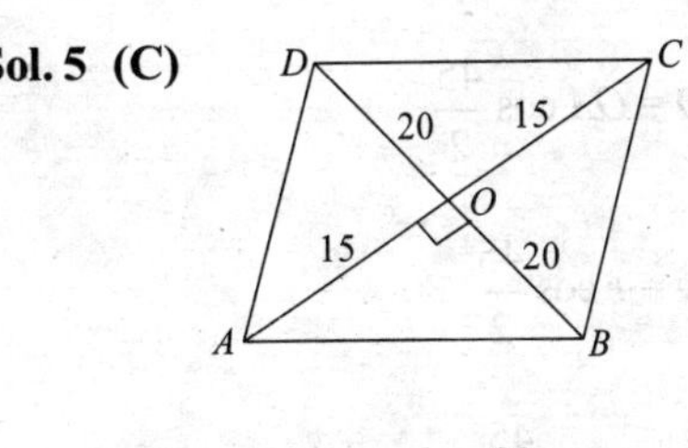

$$d_1 = 30 \text{ cm}$$

$$d_2 = 40 \text{ cm}$$

Diagonal of rhombus bisect each other at 90°

$$\Rightarrow \quad OA^2 + OB^2 = AB^2$$

$$\Rightarrow \quad 15^2 + 20^2 = AB^2$$

$$\Rightarrow \quad 225 + 400 = AB^2$$

$$\Rightarrow \quad AB^2 = 625$$

$$\Rightarrow \quad AB = 25 \text{ cm}$$

Hence Ans is (C)

Sol. 6 (D) $\angle A + \angle B = 180°$

as A & B are adjacent angle of parallelogram

$$\frac{1}{2}\angle A + \frac{1}{2}\angle B = 90°$$

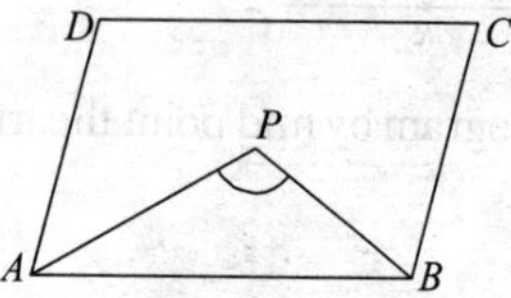

Now in $\Delta APB = \frac{1}{2}A + \frac{1}{2}B + P = 180°$

$$P = 90°$$

Hence Ans is (D)

Sol. 7 (D)

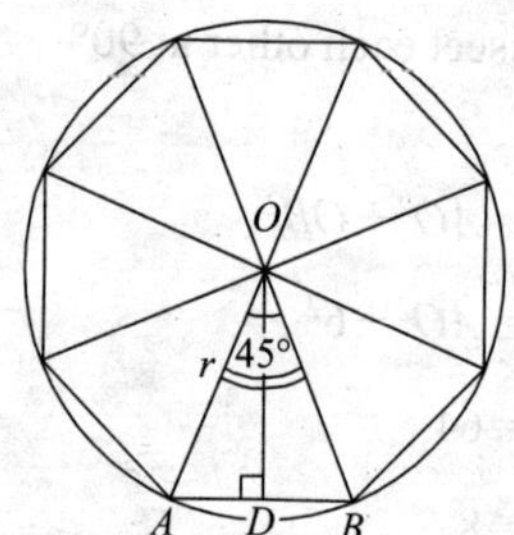

Angle subtended by each chord at the centre = 45.

Let each side be of $2x$ unit

then $AD = x$

Let $OD = y$

& $OA = r$

$\Rightarrow$ $OD = OA\cos\frac{45}{2}$

$\Rightarrow$ $y = r\cos\frac{45}{2}$

$\Rightarrow$ $x = r\sin\frac{45}{2}$

Given

Area of octagon $= 8\left(\frac{1}{2}r^2 \cdot \sin 45\right) = 1$

$\Rightarrow$ $r^2 \sin 45 = \frac{1}{4}$ ...(1)

Now area of rectangle $ABEF$

$\Rightarrow$ $\therefore AB \times BE = 2x \times 2y$

$= 4xy$

$$= 4 \times r.\sin\frac{45}{2} \cdot r\cos\frac{45}{2}$$

$$= \frac{1}{2} 4 \cdot r^2\, 2\sin\frac{45}{2} \cdot \cos\frac{45}{2}$$

$$= \frac{1}{2} \cdot 4 \cdot r^2 \sin 45$$

$$= \frac{1}{2} \cdot 4 \cdot \frac{1}{4} \text{ Using (1)}$$

$$= \frac{1}{2}$$

Hence Ans is (D)

Sol. 8 (B)

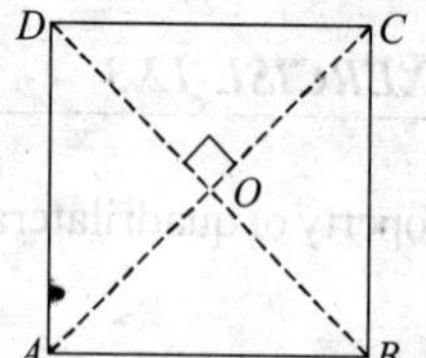

Let the side of square $ABCD$ be 'a'

then $a^2 = 4$

$\Rightarrow$ $a = 2$

Given $AC = BD = d$

$\Rightarrow$ $OC = OD = \frac{d}{2}$

In right angle triangle

ΔODC & $OC^2 + OD^2 = DC^2$

$$\frac{d^2}{4} + \frac{d^2}{4} = (2)^2$$

$\Rightarrow$ $2\frac{d^2}{4} = 4$

$\Rightarrow$ $d^2 = 8$

$\Rightarrow$ $d = 2\sqrt{2}$

Perimeter of $\Delta ODC = OD + OC + DC$

$$= (4\sqrt{2} + 2)$$

Sum of perimeter of all

$$\Delta = 4\sqrt{2} + 2 + 4\sqrt{2} + 6$$

$$= 8\sqrt{2} + 8$$

$$= 8(\sqrt{2} + 1)$$

Hence Ans is (B)

Sol. 9 (A)

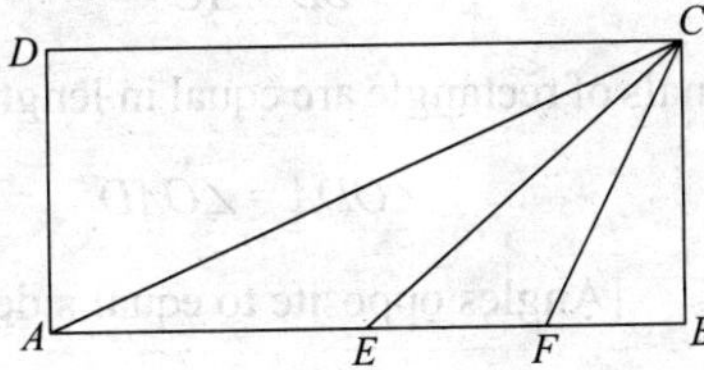

Given $AE = EF = FB$

So ratio of area of ΔAEC

$\Delta ECF : ar\,\Delta FCB = AE : EF : FB$

Let ar of $\Delta AEC = X$

$\Rightarrow$ ar of $\Delta EFC = X$

$\Rightarrow$ $ar\,\Delta ABC = 3X$

So ar of rectangle

$ABCD = 6X$

So ratio of ar of ΔECF to ar of $ABCD = \dfrac{X}{6X} = \dfrac{1}{6}$

Hence Ans is (A)

Sol. 10 (B) Median divide the triangle in two equal half having same area join EC.

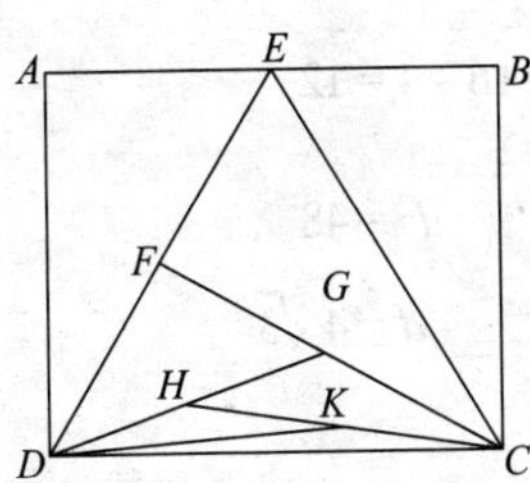

Let area of

$\Delta KDC = A$

$\Rightarrow$ ar of $\Delta HDC = 2A$

$\Rightarrow$ ar of $\Delta DGC = 4A$

$\Rightarrow$ ar of $\Delta DFC = 8A$

$\Rightarrow$ ar of $\Delta EDC = 16A$

$= \dfrac{1}{2}$ ar of $ABCD$

$\Rightarrow$ $16A = \dfrac{1}{2} \times 4$

$\Rightarrow$ $A = \dfrac{2}{16} = \dfrac{1}{8}$

Hence Ans is (B)

Sol. 11 (D)

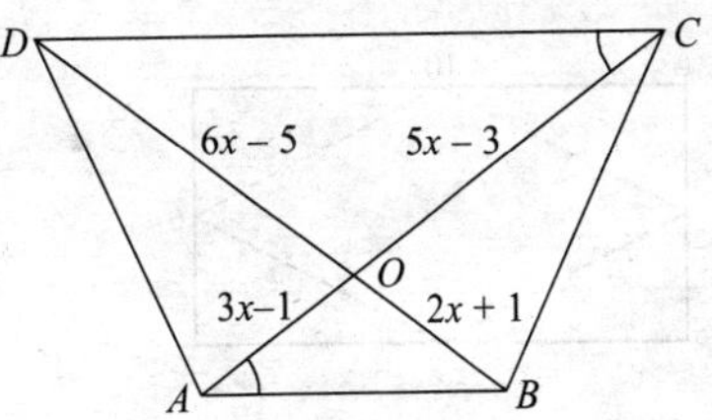

Given

$\Delta AOB \sim \Delta COD$

by AA similarity

$\dfrac{AO}{OC} = \dfrac{OB}{OD}$

$\dfrac{3x-1}{5x-3} = \dfrac{2x+1}{6x-5}$

$(3x-1)(6x-5) = (5x-3)(2x+1)$

$18x^2 - 15x - 6x + 5 = 10x^2 + 5x - 6x - 3$

$8x^2 - 20x + 8 = 0$

$4x^2 - 10x + 4 = 0$

$4x^2 - 8x - 2x + 4 = 0$

$4x(x-2) - 2(x-2) = 0$

$(x-2)(2x-1) = 0$

$x = 2, \dfrac{1}{2}$

$x \neq \dfrac{1}{2}$

$\Rightarrow$ $x = 2$

Hence Ans is (D)

Sol. 12 (D) Trapezium

Hence Ans is (D)

Sol. 13 (B) $\dfrac{1}{2} d_1\, d_2 = 160$

$\dfrac{1}{2}\, X\, 16\, X\, BD = 160$

Hence Ans is (B)

Sol. 14 (C) $ar\,(ABCD) = ar\,(PQCB)$

$ar\,(\Delta PSB) = \dfrac{1}{2}\, ar\,(PQCB)$

and, $ar\,(PQCB) = 12 \times 8 = 96\text{ cm}^2$

$\Rightarrow$ $ar\,(\Delta PSB) = \dfrac{1}{2}$ are $(PQCB)$ $\dfrac{1}{2} \times 96 = 48\text{ cm}^2$

Hence Ans is (C)

Sol. 15 (D)

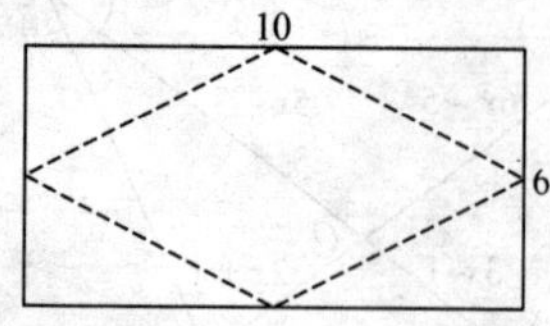

$$ar\text{ (Rhombus)} = \frac{1}{2} \times d_1 \times d_2$$

$$= \frac{1}{2} \times 10 \times 6$$

$$= 30$$

Hence Ans is (D)

Sol. 16 (A)

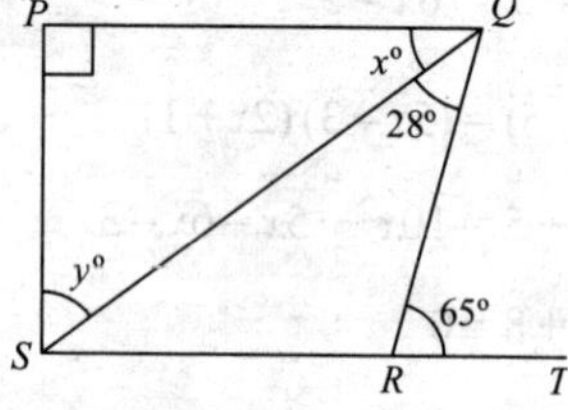

Given : $PQ \| SR$ and $PS \perp PQ$

$\angle PQR = \angle QRT$ [Alternate angles]

$65° = x° + 28°$

$x° = 65 - 28 = 37°$

and $\angle PQS = 37°$

$\angle QPS = 90°$ (given)

In ΔPQS

$90° + x° + y° = 180°$

$90° + 37° + y° = 180°$

$\Rightarrow$ $y° = 53°$

So $x° = 37°$

and $y° = 53°$

Hence Ans is (A)

Sol. 17 (A)

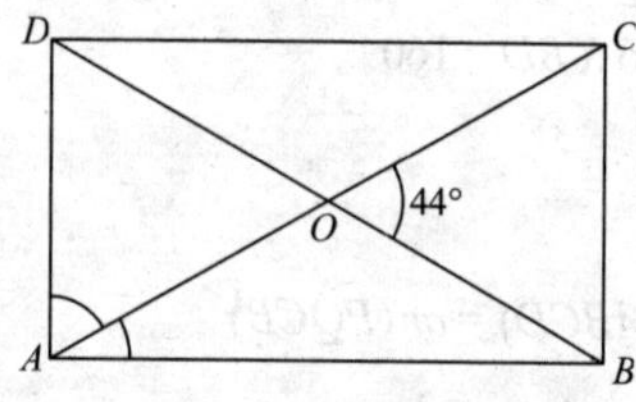

$ABCD$ is a rectangle

$\angle DOA = 44° = \angle COB$

[Vertically opposite angle]

$$OD = OA,\ OD = \frac{1}{2}BD,\ OA = \frac{1}{2}AC$$

and $BD = AC$

[Because diagonals of rectangle are equal in length]

$\Rightarrow$ $\angle ODA = \angle OAD$

[Angles opposite to equal sides are equal]

In ΔOAD

$\angle ODA + \angle OAD + \angle DOA = 180°$

$2\angle OAD = 180° - 44°$

$\angle AOD = 68°$

Hence Ans is (A)

Sol. 18 (D)

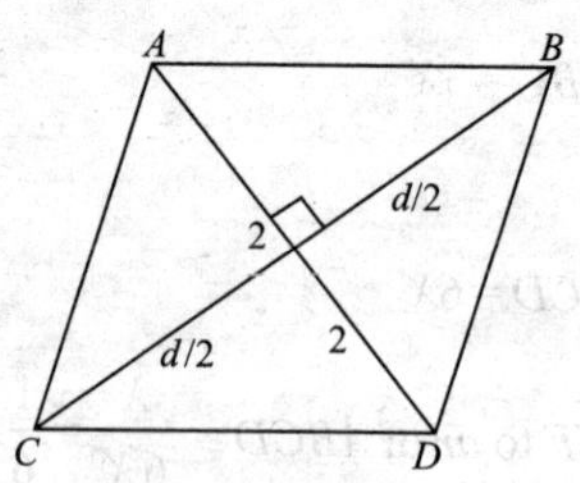

Let other diagonal be d

So, $(2)^2 + \left(\frac{d}{2}\right)^2 = (4)^2$

$$\frac{d^2}{4} = 16 - 4 = 12$$

$$d^2 = 48$$

$$d = 4\sqrt{3}$$

Hence Ans is (D)

Sol. 19 (D) In ΔABC,

$$AB + BC > AC \quad \ldots(1)$$

& In ΔADC

$$AD + CD > AC \quad \ldots(2)$$

Add (1) & (2), we get

$\Rightarrow$ $AB + BC + CD + DA < 2AC$

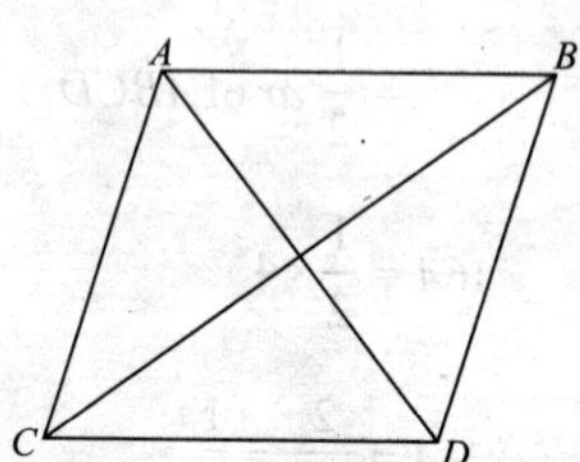

Hence Ans is (D)

Sol. 20 (B)

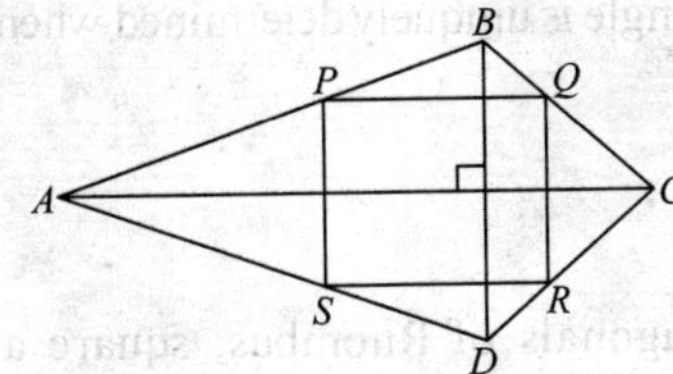

By Mid-point Theorem :

$PQ \parallel AC$ and $SR \parallel AC$

Also $PS \parallel BD$ and $QR \parallel BD$

Also angle between PQ and PS = angle between AC and BD

(since angle between lines = angle between their parallels)

$\Rightarrow \quad \angle P = 90^\circ$

Similarily

$$\angle Q = \angle R = \angle S = 90^\circ$$

$\Rightarrow$ $PQRS$ is a rectangle

Hence Ans is (B)

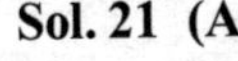

Sol. 21 (A)

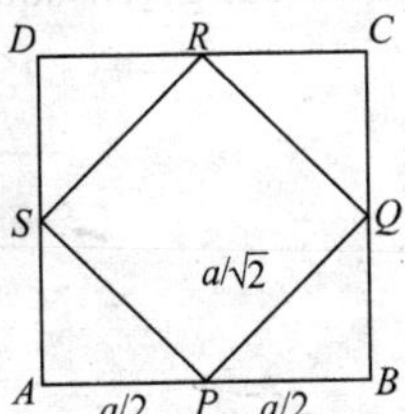

$$\frac{ArPQRS}{ArABCD} = \frac{\frac{a^2}{2}}{a^2} = \frac{1}{2}$$

Hence Ans is (A)

Sol. 22 (D) Theoretical questions.

Sol. 23 (B)

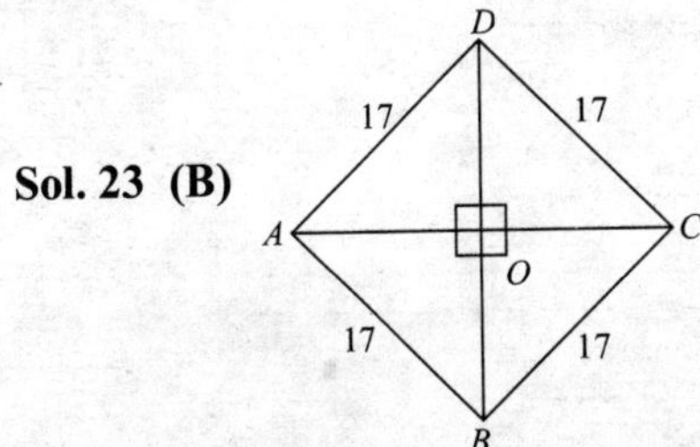

By pythagoras theorem ΔAOD

$$OA^2 = 17^2 - 15^2$$

$$= (17-15)(17+15)$$

$$OA^2 = 64$$

$$\Rightarrow \quad OA = 8$$

Area (rhombus) $= \frac{1}{2} \times 16 \times 30 \text{ cm}^2$

$= 240 \text{ cm}^2$

Hence Ans is (B)

Sol. 24 (C)

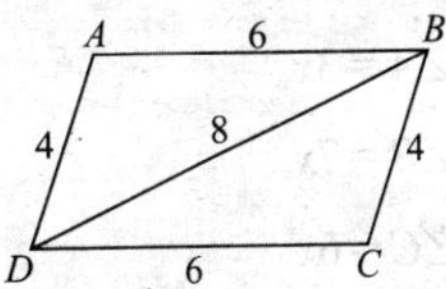

If sides 6 cm, 4 cm and diagonal is 8 cm then

Area of triangle

$$= \sqrt{s(s-a)(s-b)(s-c)}$$

where $s = \frac{a+b+c}{2}$

then $s = \frac{4+6+8}{2} = 9$

area of $\Delta ADB = \sqrt{9(9-4)(9-6)(9-8)}$

$$= \sqrt{9 \times 5 \times 3 \times 1}$$

$$= 3\sqrt{15} \text{ cm}^2$$

Then Area of Parallelogram

$$= 2 \times 3\sqrt{15} = 6\sqrt{15} \text{ cm}^2$$

Hence Ans is (C)

Sol. 25 (A) As we know, diagonals, bisect each other at right angle.

Also diagonals bisect the interior angles of rhombus.

$\Rightarrow \quad \angle DOC = \frac{1}{2}$ of $60^\circ = 30^\circ$

In ΔDOC

$$\tan 30^\circ = \frac{OD}{OC}$$

$$\frac{1}{\sqrt{3}} = \frac{OD}{OC}$$

$$\Rightarrow \quad \frac{\sqrt{3}}{1} = \frac{OC}{OD}$$

$$\Rightarrow \quad \frac{\sqrt{3}}{1} = \frac{2 \times OC}{2 \times OD}$$

$$\frac{\sqrt{3}}{1} = \frac{AC}{BD}$$

$$\Rightarrow \quad \sqrt{3} : 1 = AC : BD$$

Hence Ans is (A)

Sol. 26 (C)

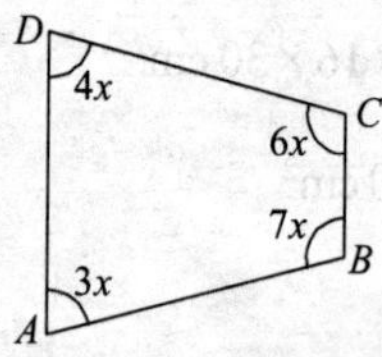

Let $\angle A = 3x,$

$\angle B = 7x,$

$\angle C = 6x$

& $\angle D = 4x$

Sum of all angle of quadrilateral = 360°

$$\angle A + \angle B + \angle C + \angle D = 360°$$

$$3x + 7x + 6x + 4x = 360°$$

$$20x = 360°$$

$$x = 18°$$

Now since $\angle A + \angle B = 10x = 180°$

& also $\angle C + \angle D = 10x = 180°$

Hence quadrilateral $ABCD$ is a trapezium.

Hence Ans is (C)

Sol. 27 (B) Every parallelogram is a trapezium

Hence Ans is (B)

Sol. 28 (B) Triangle is uniquely determined when all sides are given

Hence Ans is (B)

Sol. 29 (D) Diagonals of Rhombus, square and kite are intersecting at right angle, so quadrilateral formed by joining the mid-points is always rectangle

Hence Ans is (D)

Sol. 30 (D)

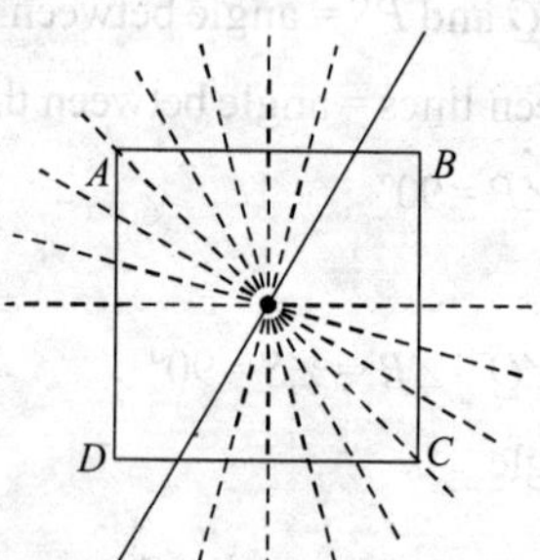

i.e. There are so many ways to cut given square into two congruent trapeziums.

Hence Ans is (D)

* * * * *

Statistics 13

Introduction :

It is the science which deals with the collection, presentation, analysis and interpretation of numerical data.

In singular form, statistics is taken as a subject. And, in plural form, statistics means data.

Collection of data :

The word data means a set of given facts in numerical figures.

Fundamental characteristics of data :

(i) Numerical facts alone form data. Qualitative characteristics, like honesty, poverty, etc., which cannot be measured numerically do not form data.

(ii) Data are aggregate of facts. A single observation does not form data.

(iii) Data collected for a definite purpose may not be suitable for another purpose.

Types of data :

(i) Primary Data :

The data collected by the investigator himself with a definite plan in mind are known as primary data.

(ii) Secondary Data :

The data collected by someone, other than the investigator, are known as secondary data.

Presentation of data :

Raw or ungrouped data

The data obtained in original form are called raw data or ungrouped data.

Ex. The marks obtained by 25 students in a class in a certain examination are given below : 25, 8, 37, 16, 45, 40, 29, 12, 42, 40, 25, 14, 16, 16, 20, 10, 36, 33, 24, 25, 35, 11, 30, 45, 48.

This is the raw data.

Array :

An arrangement of raw data in ascending or descending order of magnitude is called an array. Arranging the marks of 25 students in ascending order, we get the following array.

8, 10, 11, 12, 14, 16, 16, 16, 20, 24, 25, 25, 25, 29, 30, 33, 35, 36, 37, 40, 40, 42, 45, 45, 48.

To prepare a frequency distribution table for raw data using tally marks :

We take each observation from the data, one at a time, and indicate the frequency (the number of times the observation has occurred in the data) by small lines, called tally marks. For convenience, we write tally marks in bunches of five, the fifth one crossing the fourth diagonally. In the table so formed, the sum of all the frequencies is equal to the total number of observations in the given data.

Grouped data :

To put the data in a more condensed form, we make groups of suitable size, and mention the frequency of each group. Such a table is called a grouped frequency distribution table.

Class interval :

Each group into which the raw data is condensed, is called a class-interval.

Each class is bounded by two figures, which are called **class limits**. The figure on the left side of a class is called its **lower limit** and that on its right is called its **upper limit**.

Types of grouped frequency distribution :

1. Exclusive form (or continuous interval form) :

A frequency distribution in which the upper limit of each class is excluded and lower limit is included, is called an exclusive form.

Ex. Suppose the marks obtained by some students in an examination are given.

We may consider the classes 0 – 10, 10 – 20 etc. In class 0 – 10, we include 0 and exclude 10. In class 10 – 20, we include 10 and exclude 20.

Inclusive form (or discontinuous interval form) :

A frequency distribution in which each upper limit as well as lower limit is included, is called an inclusive form. Thus, we have classes of the form 0 – 10, 11 – 20, 21 – 30 etc. In 0 – 10, both 0 and 10 are included.

Important terms related to grouped data :

Class boundaries or true upper and true lower limits:

(i) In the exclusive form, the upper and lower limits of a class are respectively known as the true upper limit and true lower limit.

(ii) In the inclusive form, the number midway between the upper limit of a class and lower limit of the subsequent class gives the true upper limit of the class and the true lower limit of the subsequent class.

Thus, in the above table of inclusive form, we have:

true upper limit of class 1 – 10 is $\left(\frac{10+11}{2}\right) = 10.5$, and, true lower limit of class 11 – 20 is 10.5.

Similarly, true upper limit of class 11 – 20 is $\left(\frac{20+21}{2}\right) = 20.5$, and true lower limit of class 21 – 30 is 20.5.

Class size :

The difference between the true upper limit and the true lower limit of a class is called its class size.

Class mark of a class :

$$\text{Class mark} = \left(\frac{\text{True upper limit} + \text{True lower limit}}{2}\right)$$

The difference between any two successive class marks gives the class size.

Method of forming classes of a data :

1. Determine the maximum and minimum values of the variate occurring in the data.
2. Decide upon the number of classes to be formed.
3. Find the range, i.e., the difference between the maximum value and the minimum value. Divide the range by the number of classes to be formed to get the class-size.
4. Be sure that there must be classes having minimum and maximum values occurring in the data.
5. By counting, we obtain the frequency of each class.

Graphical representation of statistical data :

The tabular representation of data is an ideal way of presenting them in a systematic manner. When these numerical figures are represented pictorially or graphically, they become more noticeable and easily intelligible, leaving a more lasting effect on the mind of the observer. With the help of these pictures or graphs, data can be compared easily.

There are various types of graphs. In this chapter, we shall be dealing with the following graphs:

1. Bar graphs
2. Histogram
3. Frequency polygon

Bar graph (or column graph or bar chart) : A bar graph is a pictorial representation of numerical data in the form of rectangles (or bars) of equal width and varying heights. These rectangles are drawn either vertically or horizontally. The height of a bar represents the frequency of the corresponding observation. The gap between two bars is kept the same.

Histogram :

A histogram is a graphical representation of a frequency distribution in an exclusive form in the form of rectangles with class intervals as bases and the corresponding frequencies as heights, there being no gap between any two successive rectangles.

Method of drawing a histogram of uniform class width :

Step-1 : If the given frequency distribution is in inclusive form, convert it into an exclusive form.

Step-2 : Taking suitable scales, mark the class-intervals along x-axis and frequencies along y-axis. Note that the scales chosen for both the axes need not be the same.

Step-3 : Construct rectangles with class-intervals as bases and the corresponding frequencies as heights.

Method of drawing a histogram of non-uniform class width. In this case we adjust the frequencies as given in the following steps :

Step-1 : Take a graph paper and draw two perpendicular lines, one horizontal and one vertical, intersecting at O (say). Mark them as OX and OY.

Step-2 : Take horizontal line OX as X-axis and vertical line OY as Y-axis.

Step-3 : Choose a suitable scale along X-axis and represent class-limits on it.

Step-4 : Determine a class-interval which has the minimum class size. Let the minimum class size be h.

Step-5 : Compute the adjusted frequencies of each class by using the following formula :

$$\text{Adjusted frequency of a class} = \frac{h}{\text{Class size}} \times \text{Frequency of the class.}$$

These adjusted frequencies are the heights of each rectangle of histogram but width will be according to class limits.

Step-6 : Choose a suitable scale for Y-axis and mark adjusted frequencies along Y-axis.

Step-7 : Construct rectangles with class intervals as bases and respective adjusted frequencies as heights.

The histogram so obtained is the desired histogram of the given frequency distribution.

Frequency Polygon :

Let $x_1, x_2, \ldots, x_n$ be the class marks (i.e., mid points) of the given frequency distribution and let $f_1, f_2, \ldots f_n$ be the corresponding frequencies. We plot the points (x_1, f_1), (x_2, f_2),..., (x_n, f_n) on a graph paper and join these points by line segments. We complete the diagram in the form of a polygon by taking two more classes (called imagined classes), one at the beginning and the other at the end, each with frequency zero. This polygon is known as the frequency polygon of the given frequency distribution.

Measures of central tendency :

Arithmetic mean :

The average of numbers in arithmetic is known as the Arithmetic Mean or simply the mean of these numbers in statistics.

$$\text{Mean} = \frac{\text{Sum of observations}}{\text{Number of observations}}$$

Mean of ungrouped Data :

The mean of n observations $x_1, x_2, \ldots, x_n$ is given by

$$\text{Mean, } \bar{x} = \frac{(x_1 + x_2 + x_3 + \ldots\ldots + x_n)}{n} = \frac{\Sigma x_i}{n}$$

where the symbol Σ, called sigma stands for the summation of the terms.

Mean for an ungrouped frequency distribution :

Direct method :

Let n observations consist of values $x_1, x_2, \ldots, x_n$ of a variable x, occurring with frequencies $f_1, f_2, \ldots, f_n$ respectively.

Then, the mean of these observations is given by:

$$\text{Mean, } \bar{x} = \frac{(f_1x_1 + f_2x_2 + \ldots + f_nx_n)}{(f_1 + f_2 + \ldots\ldots + f_n)} = \frac{\Sigma f_i x_i}{\Sigma f_i}$$

Properties of Arithmetic Mean :

1. If $\overline{X}$ is the mean of n observation $x_1, x_2, \ldots x_n$, then $\sum_{i=1}^{n}(x_i - \overline{X}) = 0$ i.e. the algebraic sum of deviations from mean is zero.

2. If $\overline{X}$ is the mean of n observations $x_1, x_2, \ldots x_n$, then the mean of the observations $x_1 + a, x_2 + a, \ldots x_n + a$. i.e. if each observation is increased by a, then the mean is also increased by a.

3. If $\overline{X}$ is the mean of $x_1, x_2, \ldots x_n$, then the mean of $ax_1, ax_2, \ldots ax_n$ is a $(\overline{X})$, where a is any number different from zero i.e. if each observation is multiplied by a non-zero number a, then the mean is also multiplied by a.

4. If $\overline{X}$ is the mean of n observation $x_1, x_2, x_3, \ldots x_n$, then the mean of $\frac{x_1}{a}, \frac{x_2}{a}, \frac{x_3}{a} \ldots \frac{x_n}{a}$ is $\frac{\overline{X}}{a}$, where a is any non-zero number.

5. If $\overline{X}$ is the mean of n observations $x_1, x_2, \ldots x_n$, then the mean of $x_1 - a, x_2 - a, \ldots, x_n - a$ is $\overline{X} - a$, where a is any real number.

Median of ungrouped data :

After arranging the given data in an ascending or a descending order of magnitude, the value of the middle-most observation is called the median of the data.

Method for finding the median of an ungrouped data:

Arrange the given data in an increasing or decreasing order of magnitude. Let the total number of observations be n.

(i) If n is odd, then median = value of $\left(\frac{n+1}{2}\right)^{th}$ observation.

(ii) If n is even, then median

$$= \frac{1}{2}\left\{\left(\frac{n}{2}\right)^{th} \text{observation} + \left(\frac{n}{2}+1\right)^{th} \text{observation}\right\}$$

Mode of ungrouped data :

The mode is that value of the observation which occurs most frequently, i.e., an observation with the maximum frequency is called the mode. The ready made garment and shoe industries make great use of this measure of central tendency. Using the knowledge of mode, these industries decide which size of the product should be produced in large numbers.

* * * * *

PRACTICE EXERCISE - 13.1

13-1 The weight (in kg) of 5 men are 62, 65, 69, 66 and 61. The median is :

(A) 45 kg (B) 66 kg
(C) 65 kg (D) 55 kg

13-2 The mean of $x, x+3, x+6, x+9$ and $x+12$ is :

(A) $x+6$ (B) $x+3$
(C) $x+9$ (D) $x+12$

13-3 The mean of a data is 'p'. If each observation is multiplied by 3 and then 1 is added to each result, then the mean of the new observations so obtained is :

(A) p (B) $3p$
(C) $p+1$ (D) $3p+1$

13-4 The mean of 20 observations is 12.5. By error, one observation was noted as – 15 instead of 15. Then the correct mean is :

(A) 11.75 (B) 11
(C) 14 (D) None of these

13-5 The average age of 5 teachers is 28 years. If one teacher is excluded the mean gets reduced by 2 years. The age of the excluded teacher is :

(A) 26 years (B) 33 years
(C) 36 years (D) None of these

13-6 Which of the following is not a measure of central tendency ?

(A) Mean (B) Median
(C) Mode (D) Standard deviation

13-7 The true statement for the data : 1, –1, 0, 2, 3, 5, 5, 6, 8, 10 and 11 is :

(A) Mean = Mode = Median (B) Mode = Median = 5
(C) Mean = Median = 5 (D) Mean = Mode = 5

13-8 The mean weight of a class of 34 students is 46.5 kg. If the weight of the teacher is included, the mean rises by 500 g. Then the weight of the teacher is :

(A) 175 kg (B) 62 kg
(C) 64 kg (D) 72 kg

13-9 If in a data, 10 numbers arranged in increasing order. If the 7th entry is increased by 4, then the median increases by :

(A) Zero (B) 4
(C) 6 (D) 5

13-10 20 years ago, when my parents got married, their average age was 23 years, now the average age of my family, consisting of myself and my parents only is 35 years. My present age is :

(A) 34 years (B) 42 years
(C) 24 years (D) 19 years

13-11 The median of the series –5, 11, 10, –3, 5, 5, 8, –8, 3, –10 is :

(A) 2 (B) 3
(C) 4 (D) 5

13-12 Histogram is useful to determine graphically the value of :

(A) Arithmetic Mean (B) Median
(C) Mode (D) None of these

13-13 A histogram is a n-dimensional diagram where n is equal to :

(A) 0 (B) 1
(C) 2 (D) 3

13-14 A student got marks in 5 subjects in a monthly test is given as 2, 3, 4, 5, 6. In these obtained marks, 4 is the :

(A) Mean and median (B) Mean but no median
(C) Median but no mean (D) Mode

13-15 In an examination, 10 students scored the following marks in Mathematics 35, 19, 28, 32, 63, 02, 47, 31, 13, 98 Its range is :

(A) 2 (B) 96
(C) 98 (D) 50

13-16 In a frequency distribution, the mid value of a class is 15 and the class interval is 4. The lower limit of the class is :

(A) 10 (B) 12
(C) 13 (D) 14

13-17 The mid value of a class interval is 42. If the class size is 10, then the upper and lower limits of the class are :

(A) 47 & 37 (B) 37 & 47
(C) 37.5 & 47.5 (D) 47.5 & 37.5

13-18 The following marks were obtained by the students in a test :

81, 72, 90, 90, 86, 85, 92, 70, 71, 83, 89, 95, 85, 79, 62,

The range of the marks is :

(A) 9 (B) 17
(C) 27 (D) 33

13-19 Find the mode of the following data :
8, 12, 9, 18, 11, 15, 12, 10, 16, 12, 15
(A) 12 (B) 15
(C) 10 (D) 8

13-20 The median of a given frequency distribution is found graphically with the help of :
(A) Histogram (B) Frequency curve
(C) Frequency polygon (D) Ogive

13-21 The mode of a frequency distribution can be determined graphically from :
(A) Histogram (B) Frequency polygon
(C) Ogive (D) Frequency curve

13-22. The mean of a data is 'p'. If each observation is multiplied by 4 and then 3 is added to each result, then the mean of the new observations so obtained is :
(A) $4p$ (B) $4p+1$
(C) $4p+3$ (D) $3p+1$

13-23 Which of the following is true :
(A) Mode = 2 Median – 3 Mean
(B) Mean = Mode + $\frac{2}{3}$(Median – Mode)
(C) Median = 2 Mode – 3 Mean
(D) Median = Mode + $\frac{2}{3}$(Mean – Mode)

13-24 A set of numbers consists of three 4*s*, five 5*s*, six 6*s*, eight 8*s* nine 9*s* and seven 10*s*. The mode of this set of numbers is :
(A) 6 (B) 9
(C) 8 (D) 10

13-25 The mean of $x_1, x_2, \ldots, x_{50}$ is M if each x_i where $i = 1, 2, \ldots, 50$ is replaced by $x_i/50$ then new mean is :
(A) M (B) $M + \frac{1}{50}$
(C) $50M$ (D) $\frac{M}{50}$

13-26 The average income of Sambhu and Ganesh is Rs. 3000 and that of Arun and Vinay is Rs. 500. What is the average income of Sambhu, Ganesh, Arun and Vinay ?
(A) Rs. 1750 (B) Rs. 1850
(C) Rs. 1000 (D) Rs. 2500

13-27 If the arithmetic mean of n numbers of a series is $\bar{x}$ and the sum of first $(n-1)$ numbers is K, then the nth number is :
(A) $n+k$ (B) $n\bar{x}+k$
(C) $n\bar{x}-k$ (D) $n-k$

13-28 The numbers 3, 5, 6, and 4 have frequencies of $x, x+2, x-8$ and $x+6$ respectively. If their mean is 4 then find x :
(A) 5 (B) 6
(C) 7 (D) 8

13-29 The mean of weight of 100 persons is 46 kg. The mean of weight of males being 50 kg and of females being 40 kg then the number of males is :
(A) 50 (B) 60
(C) 55 (D) 65

13-30 The mean weight of a class of 34 students is 47 kg. If the weight of the teacher is included, the mean rises by 1 kg. Then the weight of the teacher is:
(A) 82 kg (B) 62 kg
(C) 64 kg (D) 72 kg

13-31 The average age of 5 teachers is 30 years. If one teacher is excluded the mean gets reduced by 4 years. The age of the excluded teacher is :
(A) 26 years (B) 33 years
(C) 36 years (D) 46 years

13-32 If the mean and median of a set of numbers are 8.7 and 8.8 respectively, then the mode will be :
(A) 8.2 (B) 9
(C) 9.2 (D) Can't be determined

13-33 The median of a set of 11 distinct observations is 21.5. If each of the largest 5 observations of the set is increased by 2, then the median of the new set :
(A) Is increased by 2
(B) Is decreased by 2
(C) Is two times the original median
(D) Remains the same as that of the original set.

13-34 The median of the following incomplete frequency distribution is 4.

x	1	2	3	4	5	6	7	8
Frequncy (f)	2	3	4	1	2	4	2	–

The frequency of 8 is :
(A) 1 (B) 2
(C) 3 (D) 4

13-35 The average value of the median of 2, 8, 3, 7, 4, 6, 7 and the mode of 2, 9, 3, 4, 9, 6, 9 is :
(A) 9 (B) 8
(C) 7.5 (D) 6

13-36 A, B, C are three sets of value of x :

$A: 2, 3, 7, 1, 3, 2, 3$

$B: 7, 5, 9, 12, 5, 3, 8$

$C: 4, 4, 11, 7, 2, 3, 4$

Select the correct statement from among the following :

(A) Mean of A is equal to mode of C

(B) Mean of C is equal to median of B

(C) Median of B is equal to mode of A

(D) Mean, median and mode of A are same

13-37 The mean of 20 observations is 15. By error, one observation was noted as – 15 instead of 15. Then the correct mean is :

(A) 11.75 (B) 16.5

(C) 14 (D) 13.5

13-38 Find the range of the following frequency distribution :

Class Interval	Frequency
0 – 5	6
5 – 10	8
10 – 15	12
15 – 20	5
20 – 25	4

(A) 20 (B) 21

(C) 22.5 (D) 19.5

13-39 If the mean of 6, 4, 7, P and 10 is 8 find P:

(A) 12 (B) 13

(C) 10 (D) 9

13-40 Find the median of the following values :

37, 31, 42, 43, 46, 25, 39, 45, 32.

(A) 32 (B) 46

(C) 39 (D) 43

13-41 The weight of 6 mens are 30, 75, 28, 85, 23, 21. The median is :

(A) 56.5 (B) 30

(C) 29 (D) 75

13-42 The mean of $x + 2, x, x + 3, x + 4, x + 1$ is 20 then Find x :

(A) 3 (B) 12

(C) 18 (D) 1

13-43 The average of 5 men is 25 if a new men of age 19 join then find new average :

(A) 25 (B) 24

(C) 19 (D) 20

13-44 Find the mode of the distribution 4, –1, 1, 1, 2, 3, 1, –1, 4, 5, 4, 5, 1 :

(A) 1 (B) –1

(C) 4 (D) 5

13-45 The mean of 10 observation is 50, By error the observation was noted as –30 instead of 50, Then correct mean is :

(A) 48 (B) 58

(C) 54 (D) 52

13-46 The true statement for observation is 1, 5, 4, 3, 2, 7, 10, 9, 5 :

(A) Mean = 5 (B) Median = 5.5

(C) Mode = Median = 5 (D) Mode = 1

13-47 The mean weight of class of 20 student is 50 kg if the weight of teacher is included the mean rised by 2 kg. The weight of teacher is :

(A) 82 kg (B) 72 kg

(C) 92 kg (D) 91 kg

13-48 If 12 data arranged in increasing order. If the 8th entry is increased by 4, then median increased by :

(A) 4 (B) 1

(C) 0 (D) 2

13-49 The average income of Ajay & Vijay is Rs. 500 and average of Ajay & Manish is Rs. 800 and their total income is Rs. 2200 then find Ajay income :

(A) Rs. 300 (B) Rs. 400

(C) Rs. 500 (D) Rs. 600

13-50 The average age of 6 teacher is 30 years. If one teacher is excluded the mean gets reduced by 4 years. The age of excluded teacher is :

(A) 40 yrs. (B) 45 yrs.

(C) 50 yrs. (D) 52 yrs.

* * * * *

PRACTICE EXERCISE - 13.2

13-1 If the arithmetic mean of the observations $x_1, x_2, x_3 \ldots x_n$ is 1, then the arithmetic mean of $\frac{x_1}{k}, \frac{x_2}{k}, \frac{x_3}{k}, \ldots \frac{x_n}{k} (k > 0)$ is :

(A) Greater than 1 (B) Less than 1
(C) Equal to 1 (D) None of these

13-2 If the arithmetic mean of 7, 5, 13, x and 9 be 10, then the value of x is :

(A) 10 (B) 12
(C) 14 (D) 16

13-3 In a monthly test, the marks obtained in mathematics by 16 students of a class are as follows :

0, 0, 2, 2, 3, 3, 3, 4, 5, 5, 5, 5, 6, 6, 7, 8

The arithmetic mean of the marks obtained is :

(A) 3 (B) 4
(C) 5 (D) 6

13-4 The mean of first n natural numbers is $\frac{5n}{9}$. Find n.

(A) 5 (B) 4
(C) 9 (D) None of these

13-5 Mean of a certain number of observation is m. If each observation is divided by $x (x \neq 0)$ and increased by y, then the mean of new observation is :

(A) $mx + y$ (B) $\frac{mx + y}{x}$
(C) $\frac{m + xy}{x}$ (D) $m + xy$

13-6 If the difference of mode and median of a data is 24, then the difference of median and mean is :

(A) 12 (B) 24
(C) 8 (D) 36

13-7 The mode of the observation $2x + 3, 3x - 2, 4x + 3, x - 1, 3x - 1, 5x + 2$ (x is a positive integer) can be :

(A) 3 (B) 5
(C) 7 (D) 9

13-8 The median of 21 observations is 18. If two observations 15 and 24 are included to the observation, then the median of new series is :

(A) 15 (B) 18
(C) 24 (D) 16

13-9 Range of 14, 12, 17, 18, 16 and x is 20. Find $x (x > 0)$:

(A) 2 (B) 28
(C) 32 (D) Cannot be determined

13-10 The mean of a set of observation is a. If each observation is multiplied by b and each product is decreased by c, then the mean of new set of observation is :

(A) $\frac{a}{b} + c$ (B) $ab - c$
(C) $\frac{a}{b} - c$ (D) $ab + c$

13-11 The mean of data is x. If each observation is multiplied by 5 and 2 is subtracted from each observation then new mean is :

(A) x (B) $5x + 2$
(C) $5x - 2$ (D) $5x + 1$

11-12 Find the mean of $x, x + 8, x + 11, x + 1$:

(A) $x + 4$ (B) $x + 5$
(C) $2x + 9$ (D) $x + 6$

11-13 The arithmetic mean of distribution is 25 then find P :

Class	Frequency
0 – 10	5
10 – 20	18
20 – 30	15
30 – 40	P
40 – 50	6

(A) 10 (B) 12
(C) 16 (D) 18

11-14 Find the average of first 40 natural no :

(A) 21 (B) 20.5
(C) 21.5 (D) 19.5

11-15 The average of 11 result is 60. If average of first six result is 58 and that of last six is 63. Find sixth result :

(A) 56 (B) 62
(C) 66 (D) 68

11-16 The average weight of A, B, C is 45 kg. If average of A & B is 40 kg a that of B & C is 43 kg. Find weight of B :

(A) 32 kg (B) 31 kg
(C) 30 kg (D) 29 kg

11-17 A batsman makes a score of 87 runs in 17th inning & thus increases his average by 3. Find his average after 17th inning :

(A) 39 (B) 40
(C) 35 (D) 29

11-18 The mean of 2, 7, 6, x is 5 & the average of 18, 1, 6, x, y is 10. Find x & y :

(A) 20, 5 (B) 5, 20
(C) 15, 10 (D) 10, 15

11-19 Three year ago average age of A & B was 18 yrs. and now C joins then average age become 22 years. How old is C?

(A) 24 yrs (B) 27 yrs
(C) 28 yrs (D) 30 yrs

11-20 If the mean & median of set of number is 8 & 9 respectively then there mode is :

(A) 12 (B) 10
(C) 11 (D) 13

11-21 The mean of $x+3, x+6, x+9$ and $x+12$ is :

(A) $x+7.5$ (B) $x+3.5$
(C) $x+9.5$ (D) $x+12.5$

11-22 For an arranged series of n observations. If n is odd, the median is given by the value of :

(A) $\frac{n}{2}$ th term

(B) $\left(\frac{n+1}{2}\right)^{\text{th}}$ term

(C) $\left(\frac{n+2}{2}\right)^{\text{th}}$ term

(D) $\frac{1}{2}\left[\left(\frac{1}{2}\right)^{\text{th}} \text{term} + \left(\frac{n+2}{2}\right)^{\text{th}} \text{term}\right]$

11-23 The mode of a continous series is computed by the formula :

(A) Mode $= l + \frac{f-f_1}{2f-f_1-f_2} \times h$

(B) Mode $= l - \frac{f+f_1}{2f-f_1-f_2} \times h$

(C) Mode $= l - \frac{f+f_1}{2f-f_1-f_2} \times h$

(D) Mode $= l + \frac{f+f_1}{2f-f_1-f_2} \times h$

11-24 For a continuous series in ascending order of magnitude the median is given by :

(A) Median $= 1 - \frac{\frac{N}{2}+C}{f} \times h$ (B) Median $= 1 + \frac{\frac{N}{2}+C}{f} \times h$

(C) Median $= 1 - \frac{\frac{N}{2}-C}{f} \times h$ (D) Median $= 1 + \frac{\frac{N}{2}-C}{f} \times h$

11-25 In a class test in English 10 students scored 75 marks, 12 students scored 60 marks, 8 scored 40 marks and 3 scored 30 marks, the mode for their score is :

(A) 75 (B) 30
(C) 60 (D) 25

* * * * *

PRACTICE EXERCISE - 13.3

13-1 The adjoining Pie Chart shows the marks scored in an examination by a student in Hindi, English, Mathematics, Social Science and Science. If the total marks obtained by the Student were 540. How many more marks were obtained by the student in mathematics than in Hindi?

[NTSE-2012 (Stage-I) Rajasthan]

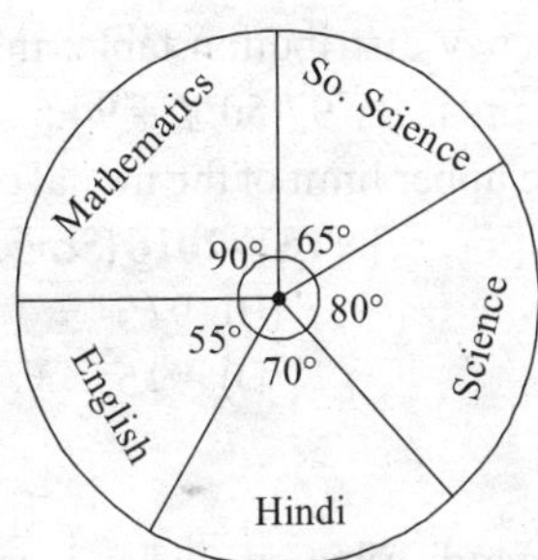

Figure 13.1

(A) 30 Marks (B) 10 Marks
(C) 20 Marks (D) 50 Marks

13-2 The median and mode of a frequency distribution are 525 and 500 then mean of same frequency distribution is :

[NTSE-2013 (Stage-I) Rajasthan]

(A) 75 (B) 107.5
(C) 527.5 (D) 537.5

13-3 The median of first 12 prime numbers is :

[NTSE-2014 (Stage-I) Rajasthan]

(A) 13 (B) 14
(C) 15 (D) 17

13-4 The mean of the first ten even natural numbers is :

[NTSE-2015 (Stage-I) Rajasthan]

(A) 10 (B) 11
(C) 12 (D) 13

13-5 The median of 29, 32, 48, 50, x, $x+2$, 72, 78, 84, 95 is 63 the value of x is : **[NTSE-2015 (Stage-I) Tamilnadu]**

(A) 124 (B) 29.5
(C) 62 (D) 64

13-6 The sum of seven consecutive natural numbers is 1617. How may of these are prime? **[NTSE-2015 (Stage-I) Delhi]**

(A) 4 (B) 5
(C) 2 (D) 4

13-7 The mean of 100 observations is 24. If 4 is added to each of the observation and then each of them is multiplied by 2.5 then new mean is : **[NTSE-2015 (Stage-I) Delhi]**

(A) 70 (B) 80
(C) 65 (D) 75

13-8 Given that $a^2+b^2=1$, $c^2+d^2=1$, $p^2+q^2=1$, where a, b, c, d, p, q are all real numbers, then :

[NTSE-2015 (Stage-I) Delhi]

(A) $ab+cd+pq \geq 1$ (B) $ab+cd+pq \geq 3$
(C) $ab+cd+pq < 3$ (D) $ab+cd+pq \leq \frac{3}{2}$

13-9 If mean of 5, 10, 15, P, 20, 35, 40 is 21. Then the value of P will be : **[NTSE-2015 (Stage-I) UP]**

(A) 18 (B) 22
(C) 25 (D) 30

13-10 The median of first 10 prime numbers will be.

[NTSE-2015 (Stage-I) UP]

(A) 5 (B) 11
(C) 12 (D) 13

13-11 If mode of any series is 9 and median is 7 then mean of that series will be : **[NTSE-2015 (Stage-I) UP]**

(A) -6 (B) 6
(C) $-5/3$ (D) 5/3

13-12 The mean of eight number is 6. If each number is multiplied by 2, the new mean will be :

[NTSE-2015 (Stage-I) Chhatisgarh]

(A) 3 (B) 6
(C) 12 (D) 96

13-13 Marks secured by a student in various subjects are 25, 26, 27, 28 and 29. What does the mark '27' denotes ?

[NTSE-2015 (Stage-I) Chhatisgarh]

(A) Mode (B) Mode and median
(C) Mean and median (D) Mean, median and Mode

13-14 The sum of 'n' terms of series

$$\left(1-\frac{1}{n}\right)+\left(1-\frac{2}{n}\right)+\left(1-\frac{3}{n}\right)+\ldots \text{ will be.}$$

[NTSE-2015 (Stage-I) Chhatisgarh]

(A) $\frac{1}{n}(n+1)$ (B) $\frac{1}{n}(n-1)$
(C) $\frac{1}{2}(n+1)$ (D) $\frac{1}{2}(n-1)$

13-15 If mode of any series is 5 and median is 3 then mean of that series is : **[NTSE-2016 (Stage-I) Rajasthan]**

(A) 1 (B) 2
(C) 3 (D) 4

13-16 The sum of 49 consecutive integers is 7^5, what their median ? **[NTSE-2016 (Stage-I) Telangana]**

(A) 7 (B) 7^3
(C) 7^2 (D) 7^4

13-17 If the mean of x and $1/x$ is M, then mean of x^3 and $1/x^3$ is : **[NTSE-2016 (Stage-I) Chandigarh]**

(A) $\frac{M^2-3}{2}$ (B) $M(4M^2-3)$
(C) M^3 (D) M^3+3

13-18 The average weight (in kg) of all the students in a class equals the number of students in the class. The increase in the average weight when a teacher to 21 kg is included equals the decrease in average weight when a student of 19 kg is included. The strength of the class is : **[NTSE-2016 (Stage-I) Delhi]**

(A) 15 (B) 10
(C) 20 (D) 17

13-19 The total number of squares on a chessboard is : **[NTSE-2016 (Stage-I) Delhi]**

(A) 206 (B) 205
(C) 204 (D) 202

13-20 The mean and mode of a frequency distribution are 28 and 16 respectively, then the median is : **[NTSE-2016 (Stage-I) Jharkhand]**

(A) 23.5 (B) 22
(C) 24 (D) 24.5

13-21 If A and G are AM and GM of two given positive numbers 'a' and 'b', then $\left(\frac{\sqrt{a}-\sqrt{b}}{\sqrt{2}}\right)^2=$ **[NTSE-2016 (Stage-I) Karnatka]**

(A) $A+G$ (B) $A-G$
(C) $A\times G$ (D) $A\div G$

13-22 The mean and mode of a set of data are respectively $2n$ and $5n$. The median of same data is : **[NTSE-2016 (Stage-I) Karnatka]**

(A) $9n$ (B) $7n$
(C) $5n$ (D) $3n$

13-23 What is the correct relation in the given data?
2, 3, 0, – 1, 1, 5, 6, 4, 5, 8, 11 **[NTSE-2016 (Stage-I) Chhatisgarh]**

(A) Mean = Median (B) Mean = 5
(C) Median = Mode (D) Median = Mean + Mode

13-24 There are 20 students in a class. The mean value of their scores is 135. On rechecking, two mistakes were found. After correction, the marks of one student was increased by 35 and the marks of the other was decreased by 15. What is the mean value of the marks after correction? **[NTSE-2016 (Stage-I) Chhatisgarh]**

(A) 135.5 (B) 136
(C) 155 (D) 134.5

13-25 In a frequency distribution table, modal value of the wages of 130 workers is Rs. 97.50. $L=94.5, f_m=x+15; f_1=x; f_2=x+5$. Find the upper limit of the modal class : **[NTSE-2016 (Stage-I) Chhatisgarh]**

(A) 96.5 (B) 97.5
(C) 98.5 (D) 99.5

13-26 In a frequency distribution median is $\frac{11}{10}$ times the mean, and mode is 5.2. Find the median : **[NTSE-2016 (Stage-I) Chhatisgarh]**

(A) 4.4 (B) 4.3
(C) 4.1 (D) 4.0

13-27 The average of 9 numbers is 18. If the average of first five numbers is 19 and the average of last 5 numbers is 17, find the 5th number : **[NTSE-2017 (Stage-I) Chandigarh]**

(A) 16 (B) 20
(C) 18 (D) 22

13-28 If × means –, + means ÷, – means × and ÷ means + then $15-2\div900+90\times100=?$ **[NTSE-2017 (Stage-I) Delhi]**

(A) 190 (B) 180
(C) 90 (D) –60

13-29 Upper limit of class '41 – 50' is — : **[NTSE-2017 (Stage-I) Gujarat]**

(A) 41 (B) 50
(C) 45 (D) 91

13-30 The mean of certain number of observations is 46. If four observation whose mean is 52 are removed, the mean becomes 44.5. The original number of observation is : **[NTSE-2017 (Stage-I) Haryana]**

(A) 35 (B) 20
(C) 15 (D) 12

13-31 The median of certain observations 17, 18, 23, 27, $x-3$, $x+5$, 45, 49, 74 and 85, arranged in an ascending order is 35. Later on, it was found that one observation 72 was misread as 27 by mistake. The correct median of the data is : **[NTSE-2017 (Stage-I) Haryana]**

(A) 36 (B) 38
(C) 42 (D) 47

13-32 The mean, mode and the median of the observation 7, 7, 5, 7 and x are the same. Then the observation x is : **[NTSE-2017 (Stage-I) Haryana]**

(A) 10 (B) 9
(C) 8 (D) 7

13-33 Following table gives the number of trees planted by the students in a school on 'Environment Day'. Observe the table and find mode of the trees planted by the students :

Number of plants	0 – 10	10 – 20	20 – 30	30 – 40	40 – 50	50 – 60
Number of students	30	42	50	80	50	40

[NTSE-2017 (Stage-I) Maharashtra]

(A) 80 (B) 50
(C) 45 (D) 35

13-34 The mean temperature of Monday to Wednesday was 37°C and of Tuesday to Thursday was 34°C. If the temperature on Thursday was 4/5th the of Monday. Then the temperature of Thursday was : **[NTSE-2017 (Stage-I) Punjab]**

(A) 35.5° C (B) 34° C
(C) 36.5° (D) 36° C

13-35 If mean of ten consecutive odd numbers is 120, then the mean of first five odd numbers among them is : **[NTSE-2017 (Stage-I) Rajasthan]**

(A) 113 (B) 115
(C) 114 (D) 116

13-36 If the mode is of the data 23, 15, 24, 40, 27, 26, 22, 25, 20, x is 25 then the value of x is : **[NTSE-2017 (Stage-I) Tamilnadu]**

(A) 26 (B) 24
(C) 20 (D) 25

13-37 The mean height of group of 8 students is 152 cm. Two more students of heights 143 cm and 156 cm join the group. The new mean height of the group is : **[NTSE-2017 (Stage-I) Uttar Pradesh]**

(A) 151.5 cm (B) 115 cm
(C) 152 cm (D) 200 cm

13-38 Observations 11, 12, 14, 18, $x+2$, $x+4$, 30, 32, 35, 41 have been arranged in ascending order. If median is 24 then the value of x will be : **[NTSE-2017 (Stage-I) Uttrakhand]**

(A) 22 (B) 21
(C) 24 (D) None of these

13-39 $(x+2)$, x and $(x-1)$ are the frequencies of the numbers 12, 15 and 20 respectively. If the mean of the distribution is 14.5, the value of x is : **[NTSE-2017 (Stage-I) West Bengal]**

(A) 2 (B) 3
(C) 4 (D) 5

13-40 The mean of first seventeen whole numbers is : **[NTSE-2018 (Stage-I) Rajasthan]**

(A) 8 (B) 7.5
(C) 8.5 (D) 18

13-41 If the number of observation n is even, than median is : **[NTSE-2018 (Stage-I) Andhra Pradesh]**

(A) average of nth and $(n+1)^{th}$ observation

(B) average of $\left(\frac{n}{2}\right)^{th}$ and $\left(\frac{n-1}{2}\right)^{th}$ Observation

(C) average of $\left(\frac{n}{2}\right)^{th}$ and $\left(\frac{n+1}{2}\right)^{th}$ Observation

(D) average of $\left(\frac{n}{2}\right)^{th}$ and $\left(\frac{n}{2}+1\right)^{th}$ Observation

13-42 The mean of 25 observation is 36. If the mean of the first 13 observation is 32 and that of the last 13 observations is 39 then the 13th observation is : **[NTSE-2018 (Stage-I) Bihar]**

(A) 32 (B) 30
(C) 28 (D) 23

13-43 The average weight of pupils of a class is 46 Kg. The average weights of boys and girls are respectively 50 Kg and 40 Kg. The ratio of the number of boys to the number of girls is .... **[NTSE-2018 (Stage-I) Bihar]**

(A) 2 : 3 (B) 3 : 2
(C) 2 : 5 (D) 5 : 2

13-44 The mode of the given series is 36. Find the value of K : **[NTSE-2018 (Stage-I) Chandigarh]**

Class interval	0-10	10-20	20-30	30-40	40-50	50-60	60-70
Frequency	7	6	K	16	12	8	10

(A) 10 (B) 15
(C) 20 (D) 30

13-45 If mode of the 64, 60, 48, x, 43, 48, 43, 34 is 43. Then the value of x is : **[NTSE-2018 (Stage-I) Chhattisgarh]**

(A) 60 (B) 40
(C) 43 (D) 48

13-46 The width of the class 55.5 – 60.5 is ______. **[NTSE-2018 (Stage-I) Gujarat]**

(A) 10 (B) 5
(C) 2.5 (D) 7

13-47 The average monthly income of four earning members of a family Rs. 7350. One member passes away and the average monthly income becomes Rs. 6500. What was the monthly income of the person, who is no more :

[NTSE-2018 (Stage-I) Jharkhand]

(A) Rs. 6928 (B) Rs. 8200
(C) Rs. 9900 (D) Rs. 13850

13-48 A class is divided into two sections A and B. Passing average of 20 of students of section A is 80% and passing average of 30 students of section B is 70%. What is the passing average of both of the sections :

[NTSE-2018 (Stage-I) Jharkhand]

(A) 72% (B) 74%
(C) 75% (D) 77%

13-49 The mean age of a combined group of men and women is 25 years. If mean age of men is 26 and that of women is 21, then the percentage of men and women in the group is :

[NTSE-2018 (Stage-I) Jharkhand]

(A) 60, 40 (B) 80, 20
(C) 20, 80 (D) 30, 70

13-50 If the number of observations n is even, then median is :

[NTSE-2018 (Stage-I) Madhya Prasesh]

(A) $\left(\frac{n+1}{2}\right)^{th}$ term

(B) $\left(\frac{n}{2}\right)^{th}$ term

(C) Mean of $\left(\frac{n}{2}\right)^{th}$ and $\left(\frac{n+1}{2}\right)^{th}$ term

(D) None of these

13-51 Mean of first n natural numbers is :

[NTSE-2018 (Stage-I) Madhya Prasesh]

(A) $\frac{n(n+1)}{2}$ (B) $\frac{n+1}{2}$

(C) $\frac{n}{2}$ (D) $\frac{n(n-1)}{2}$

13-52 If $N = 70$, $h = 10$, $c.f = 22$, $f = 10$, $L = 30$ then using this information find median :

[NTSE-2018 (Stage-I) Madhya Prasesh]

(A) 42 (B) 45
(C) 43 (D) 34

13-53 Numbers 50, 42, 35, $2x+10$, $2x-8$, 12, 11, 8 are written in descending order and their median is 25 find x :

[NTSE-2018 (Stage-I) Telangana]

(A) 20 (B) 25
(C) 12 (D) 11

13-54 Mean of 35 observation is 75. The mean of first 18 observation is 70 and the mean of last 18 observation is 80 find the 18th observation : **[NTSE-2018 (Stage-I) Uttar Pradesh]**

(A) 80 (B) 70
(C) 68 (D) 75

13-55 Find mean of $x+1, x+3, x+4, x+8$ is :

[NTSE-2018 (Stage-I) Uttar Pradesh]

(A) $(x+1)$ (B) $(x+3)$
(C) $(x+4)$ (D) $(x+8)$

13-56 In a frequency distribution, the mid value of a class is 10 and its width is 6 then the lower limit of the class will be :

[NTSE-2018 (Stage-I) Uttarakhandh]

(A) 6 (B) 7
(C) 8 (D) 12

13-57 Which of the following statement is true for the value of central tendency : **[NTSE-2018 (Stage-I) Uttarakhandh]**

(A) 2 median = mode + 2 mean
(B) mode = mean − median
(C) 3 median = mode + 2 mean
(D) None of the above

13-58 The mean of the median, the mode and the range of the following data :
84, 56, 39, 45, 54, 39, 56, 54, 84, 21, 77, 56 is :

[NTSE-2012 (Stage-II)]

(A) 55 (B) 56
(C) 58 (D) 63

13-59 If tax on a commodity is decreased by 15% and its consumption increases by 10% then the percentage decrease in the revenue is : **[NTSE-2012 (Stage-II)]**

(A) 15 (B) $8\frac{1}{2}$

(C) $6\frac{1}{2}$ (D) 5

13-60 The mean of three positive numbers is 10 more than the smallest of the numbers and 15 less than the largest of the three. If the median of the three numbers is 5, then the mean of squares of the numbers is : **[NTSE-2015 (Stage-II)]**

(A) $108\frac{2}{3}$ (B) $116\frac{2}{3}$

(C) $208\frac{1}{3}$ (D) $216\frac{2}{3}$

13-61 Positive integers from 1 to 21 are arranged in 3 groups of 7 integers each, in some particular order. Then the highest possible mean of the medians of these 3 groups is :

[NTSE-2016 (Stage-II)]

(A) 16 (B) 12.5

(C) 11 (D) 14

13-62 The mean of a group of eleven consecutive natural numbers is m. What will be the percentage change in the mean when next six consecutive natural numbers are included in the group ?

[NTSE-2017 (Stage-II)]

(A) $m\%$ (B) $\frac{m}{3}\%$

(C) $\frac{m}{300}\%$ (D) $\frac{300}{m}\%$

* * * * *

ANSWERS

PRACTICE EXERCISE-13.1

1	(C)	2	(A)	3	(D)
4	(C)	5	(C)	6	(D)
7	(B)	8	(C)	9	(A)
10	(D)	11	(C)	12	(C)
13	(C)	14	(A)	15	(B)
16	(C)	17	(A)	18	(D)
19	(A)	20	(D)	21	(A)
22	(C)	23	(D)	24	(B)
25	(D)	26	(A)	27	(C)
28	(C)	29	(B)	30	(A)
31	(D)	32	(B)	33	(D)
34	(A)	35	(C)	36	(D)
37	(B)	38	(A)	39	(B)
40	(C)	41	(C)	42	(C)
43	(B)	44	(A)	45	(B)
46	(C)	47	(C)	48	(C)
49	(B)	50	(C)		

PRACTICE EXERCISE-13.2

1	(B)	2	(D)	3	(B)
4	(C)	5	(C)	6	(A)
7	(C)	8	(B)	9	(C)
10	(B)	11	(C)	12	(B)
13	(C)	14	(B)	15	(C)
16	(B)	17	(A)	18	(B)
19	(A)	20	(C)	21	(A)
22	(B)	23	(A)	24	(D)
25	(C)				

PRACTICE EXERCISE-13.3

1	(A)	2	(D)	3	(C)
4	(B)	5	(C)	6	(C)
7	(A)	8	(D)	9	(B)
10	(C)	11	(B)	12	(C)
13	(C)	14	(D)	15	(B)
16	(B)	17	(B)	18	(C)
19	(C)	20	(C)	21	(B)
22	(D)	23	(A)	24	(B)
25	(D)	26	(D)	27	(C)
28	(D)	29	(B)	30	(B)
31	(C)	32	(B)	33	(D)
34	(D)	35	(B)	36	(D)
37	(A)	38	(B)	39	(B)
40	(A)	41	(D)	42	(D)
43	(B)	44	(A)	45	(C)
46	(B)	47	(C)	48	(B)
49	(B)	50	(C)	51	(B)
52	(C)	53	(C)	54	(D)
55	(C)	56	(B)	57	(C)
58	(C)	59	(C)	60	(D)
61	(D)	62	(D)		

Solutions of PRACTICE EXERCISE-13.1

Sol. 1 (C) Arrange in ascending order 61, 62, $\boxed{65}$, 66, 69

Hence no. of item = 5

Hence median is $\left(\frac{5+1}{2}\right)^{th}$ term = 3rd term

$\Rightarrow$ 65 is the median

Hence Ans is (C)

Sol. 2 (A) Mean

$$= \frac{x+(x+3)+(x+6)+(x+9)+(x+12)}{5}$$

$$= \frac{5x+30}{5} = \frac{5(x+6)}{5} = x+6$$

Hence Ans is (A)

Sol. 3 (D) If all the observation are multiplied by same number and added with same number. Mean gets changed by same.
i.e. new mean is $3p+1$

Hence Ans is (D)

Sol. 4 (C) New mean

$$= \frac{20\times 12.5-(-15)+15}{20} = \frac{280}{20} = 14$$

Hence Ans is (C)

Sol. 5 (C) $26 = \frac{140-x}{4}$

$\Rightarrow$ $x = 36$ year

Hence Ans is (C)

Sol. 6 (D) Standard deviation

Hence Ans is (D)

Sol. 7 (B) −1, 0, 1, 2, 3, 5, 5, 6, 8, 10, 11

Mode is 5

Median = 5

$$\text{Mean} = \frac{\text{Sum}}{11} = \frac{50}{11} < 5$$

Hence Ans is (B)

Sol. 8 (C) Here weight of teacher

$$= 46.5 + 500\text{ g} \times 35$$
$$= 46.5 + 17.5 = 64.0\text{ kg}$$

i.e. 500 g is distributed over 35 people now (including teacher).

Hence Ans is (C)

Sol. 9 (A) Since median is here 5th & 6th data/observation.
Hence it is not affected by 7th entry
Hence Ans is (A)

Sol. 10 (D) Now total age of parents

$$= 23 \times 2 + 20 \times 2$$
$$= 46 + 40 = 86 \text{ years}$$

$$\Rightarrow \quad 35 = \frac{86 + x}{3}$$

$$\Rightarrow \quad x = 19$$

Hence Ans is (D)

Sol. 11 (C) Median of $-10, -8, -5, -3, 3, 5, 5, 8, 10, 11$

$$\text{Median} = \left(\frac{5^{th} + 6^{th}}{2}\right)$$

$$= \frac{3+5}{2} = 4$$

Hence Ans is (C)

Sol. 12 (C) Histrogram is used to find mode
Hence Ans is (C)

Sol. 13 (C) A histogram is a 2-dimensional diagram
Hence Ans is (C)

Sol. 14 (A) 2, 3, 4, 5, 6

$$\text{Mean} = \frac{20}{5} = 4$$

$$\text{Median} = 4$$

$$\text{Mean} = \text{Median} = 4$$

Hence Ans is (A)

Sol. 15 (B) 02, 13, 19, 28, 31, 32, 35, 47, 63, 98

$$\text{Range} = \text{Upper limit} - \text{lower limit}$$

$$= 98 - 2 = 96$$

Hence Ans is (B)

Sol. 16 (C) Mid value of a class is 15 and class interval is 4

So Range is 13 – 17

So, 13 will be lower limit and 17 is upper limit

Hence Ans is (C)

Sol. 17 (A) Mid value is 42 and class size is 10.

So, class range should be 37 – 47

So lower and upper limit is 37 and 47

Hence Ans is (A)

Sol. 18 (D) Range = upper limit – lower limit

$$= 95 - 62 = 33$$

Hence Ans is (D)

Sol. 19 (A) Mode of the 8, 12, 9, 18, 11, 15, 12, 10, 16, 15, 12

Mode = 12 which occur 3 times

Hence Ans is (A)

Sol. 20 (D) Median can be find by ogive

Hence Ans is (D)

Sol. 21 (A) Histogram is used to find mode

Hence Ans is (A)

Sol. 22 (C) Mean is P

It each observation is multiplied by 4 & then 3 is added to each result then the new mean is $(4p + 3)$

Hence Ans is (C)

Sol. 23 (D) Mode = 3 median – 2 mean (it is an empirical relation)

Hence Ans is (D)

Sol. 24 (B) Mode = 9 as 9 occurs 9 times which is maximum

Hence Ans is (B)

Sol. 25 (D) Mean of $x_1, x_2 \ldots x_{50}$ is M.

If each no. is divided by 50 then the new mean will be $\frac{M}{50}$

Hence Ans is (D)

Sol. 26 (A) Sum of Income of Sambhu & Ganesh

$$= 2 \times 300 = \text{Rs. } 6000$$

Sum of Income of Arun & Vinay

$$= 2 \times 500 = \text{Rs. } 1000$$

Average Income of all

$$= \frac{7000}{4} = \text{Rs. } 1750$$

Hence Ans is (A)

Sol. 27 (C) Sum of the n number $= n\bar{x}$

Sum of the first $(n - 1)$ number $= k$ then the nth number is

$$= (n\bar{x} - k)$$

Hence Ans is (C)

Sol. 28 (C) The numbers are 3, 5, 6 & of frequencies $x, x+2$, $x-8$ & $x+6$

$$\text{Mean} = \frac{3x+5(x+2)+6(x-8)+4(x+6)}{x+x+2+x-8+x+6}$$

$$= \frac{3x+5x+10+6x-48+4x+24}{4x}$$

$$\text{Mean} = 4 = \frac{18x-14}{4x}$$

$\Rightarrow$ $2x = 14$

$x = 7$

Hence Ans is (C)

Sol. 29 (B) Let number of Boys

$= x$ and girls $= (100-x)$

Total sum of weight

$= 100 \times 46 = 4600$ kg

Sum of weight of Boys

$= 50x$

Sum of weight of girls

$= 40(100-x)$

$4600 = 50x + (4000 - 40x)$

$\Rightarrow$ $600 = 10x$

$\Rightarrow$ $x = 60$

Number of Males $= 60$

Hence Ans is (B)

Sol. 30 (A) Total weight of a class

$= 34 \times 47 = 1598$ kg

Total weight of a class including teacher

$= 35 \times 48 = 1680$ kg

Weight of teacher

$= (1680 - 1598) = 82$ kg

Hence Ans is (A)

Sol. 31 (D) $5 \times 30 = 150 =$ sum of ages of five teachers

$4 \times 26 = 104$

$=$ sum of ages of four teachers

Age of the excluded teacher

$= (150 - 104) = 46$ years

Hence Ans is (D)

Sol. 32 (B) Mode $= 3$ median $- 2$ mean

$= 3 \times 8.8 - 2 \times 8.7$

$= 26.4 - 17.4$

Mode $= 9$

Hence Ans is (B)

Sol. 33 (D) In odd number like 11 number median is $\left(\frac{11+1}{2}\right) = 6^{\text{th}}$ term so median will not get change in changing the largest observation

Hence Ans is (D)

Sol. 34 (A)

X	F	CF
1	2	2
2	3	5
3	4	9
4	1	10
5	2	12
6	4	16
7	2	18
8	F	$18+F$

As median is 4 so its $CF = 10$

As so $\frac{18+F+1}{2} = 10$

$19 + F = 20$

$F = 20 - 19$

Value of $F = 1$

Hence Ans is (A)

Sol. 35 (C) Median of 2, 3, 4, 6, 7, 7, 8 is 6 and mode of 2, 9, 3, 4, 9, 6, 9 is 9

So $\frac{9+6}{2} = \frac{15}{2} = 7.5$

Hence Ans is (C)

Sol. 36 (D) Arrange the data in ascending order

$A: \rightarrow 1, 2, 2, 3, 3, 3, 7$

$B: \rightarrow 3, 5, 5, 7, 8, 9, 12$

$C: \rightarrow 2, 3, 4, 4, 4, 7, 11$

Mean of A is 3, Mode is 3 and Median is 3

So, mean $=$ mode $=$ median $= 3$

Hence Ans is (D)

Sol. 37 (B) Number of observations $= 20$

Mean $= 15$

Sum $= 15 \times 20$

$$\text{New mean} = \frac{15 \times 20 + 15 + 15}{20}$$

$$= \frac{300+30}{20} = \frac{330}{20}$$

$= 16.5$

Hence Ans is (B)

Sol. 38 (A) The range is the difference between the mid value of the least class-interval and the greatest class interval.
Mid value of least class interval

$$= \frac{0+5}{2} = 2.5$$

Mid value of greatest class interval

$$= \frac{20+25}{2} = 22.5$$

$\Rightarrow$ Range $= 22.5 - 2.5 = 20$

Hence Ans is (A)

Sol. 39 (B) $\frac{6+4+7+P+10}{5} = 8$

$\Rightarrow$ $P = 13$

Hence Ans is (B)

Sol. 40 (C) Arranging the data in ascending order, we have
25, 31, 32, 37, 39, 42, 43, 45, 46
Here the number of observation $n = 9$ (odd)

$$\Rightarrow \quad \text{Median} = \text{Value of } \left(\frac{9+1}{2}\right)^{th} \text{ observation}$$

$= \text{Value of } 5^{th}$ observation
$= 39$

Hence Ans is (C)

Sol. 41 (C) Arrange in ascending order 21, 23, 28, 30, 75, 85

$$\text{Median} = \frac{28+30}{2} = \frac{58}{2} = 29$$

Hence Ans is (C)

Sol. 42 (C) $\text{Mean} = \frac{5x+10}{5}$

$$20 = \frac{5x+10}{5}$$

$$90 = 5x$$

$$18 = x$$

Hence Ans is (C)

Sol. 43 (B) $\text{New average} = \frac{25\times5+19}{6}$

$$= \frac{144}{6} = 24$$

Hence Ans is (B)

Sol. 44 (A) Mode = Highest number of frequency = 1

Hence Ans is (A)

Sol. 45 (B) $\text{New mean} = \frac{50\times10-(-30)+50}{10}$

$$= \frac{500+80}{10} = 58$$

Hence Ans is (B)

Sol. 46 (C) 1, 2, 3, 4, 5, 5, 7, 9, 10

i.e. Mode = 5,

Median = 5,

and $\text{Mean} = \frac{46}{9} > 5$

Hence Ans is (C)

Sol. 47 (C) Given mean weight of 20 students = 50
Let 'x' be the weight of the teacher.

$$\frac{20\times50+x}{21} = 52$$

$$x = 52\times21-1000$$

$$= 1092-1000 = 92 \text{ kg}$$

Hence Ans is (C)

Sol. 48 (C) Since median is 6th & 7th observation. Hence no change
Hence then Ans is (C)

Sol. 49 (B) Given

Ajay's income + Vijay's income = 1000

Ajay's income + Manish's income = 1600

Their Total income = 2200

Ajay's income = 2600 – 2200 = Rs.400

Hence Ans is (B)

Sol. 50 (C) Given

$$\frac{6\times30-x}{5} = 26$$

$$180-x = 130$$

$$x = 50 \text{ yrs}$$

Hence Ans is (C)

Solutions of PRACTICE EXERCISE-13.2

Sol. 1 (B) Given : $\frac{x_1+x_2+x_3+\ldots x_n}{n} = 1$

Then the mean of $\frac{x_1}{k}, \frac{x_2}{k}, \frac{x_3}{k}, \ldots \frac{x_n}{k} = \frac{1}{k}$

Since $k > 0$, so mean will be less than 1

Hence Ans is (B)

Sol. 2 (D) Given $\frac{7+5+13+x+9}{5} = 10 \Leftrightarrow x = 16$

Hence Ans is (D)

Sol. 3 (B)

Marks x	Frequency f	$f \times x$
0	2	0
2	2	4
3	3	9
4	1	4
5	4	20
6	2	12
7	1	7
8	1	8
	$\Sigma f = 16$	$\Sigma(f \times x) = 64$

$$\text{A.M.} = \frac{\sum(f+x)}{\sum f} = \frac{64}{16} = 4$$

Hence Ans is (B)

Sol. 4 (C) Sum of first n natural numbers $= \frac{n(n+1)}{2}$

Given : Mean of first n natural numbers $= \frac{5n}{9}$

So, $\frac{n(n+1)}{2n} = \frac{5n}{9}$

$\Rightarrow \quad 9n + 9 = 10n$

$\Rightarrow \quad n = 9$

Hence Ans is (C)

Sol. 5 (C) Given mean $= m$

If each observation is divided by x and increased by y, then

new mean $= \frac{m}{x} + y = \frac{m+xy}{x}$

Hence Ans is (C)

Sol. 6 (A) Mode – Median = 24

$\Rightarrow$ Mode = Median + 24

Now, Mode = 3 median – 2 Mean

$\Rightarrow$ Median + 24 = 3 Median – 2 Mean

$\Rightarrow$ 2 Median – 2 Mean = 24

$\Rightarrow$ Median – Mean = 12

Hence Ans is (A)

Sol. 7 (C) When $x = 1$

Observations will be :

$2(1)+3, 3(1)-2, 4(1)+3, 1-1, 3(1)-1, 5(1)+2, 5, 1, 7, 0, 2, 7$

So, Mode = 7

Hence Ans is (C)

Sol. 8 (B) Median will remains same i.e. 18

Hence Ans is (B)

Sol. 9 (C) Given range = 20

So, $x - 12 = 20$

$x = 32$

Hence Ans is (C)

Sol. 10 (B) New mean $= ab - c$

Hence Ans is (B)

Sol. 11 (C) Let $x_1, x_2, x_3 \ldots x_n$ are n observation

$$x_1 + x_2 + x_3 + \ldots + x_n = nx$$

$$\text{New mean} = \frac{(5x_1-2)+(5x_2-2)+\ldots+(5x_n-2)}{n}$$

$$= \frac{5(x_1+x_2+x_3+\ldots+x_n)-2(n)}{n}$$

$$= \frac{5nx-2n}{n} = 5x-2$$

Hence Ans is (C)

Sol. 12 (B) Mean $= \frac{x+x+8+x+11+x+1}{4}$

$$= \frac{4x+20}{4}$$

$$= x+5$$

Hence Ans is (B)

Sol. 13 (C)

x_i	F_i	X_iF_i
5	5	25
15	18	270
25	15	375
35	P	$35P$
45	6	270

$\Sigma F_i = 44 + P$

and $\Sigma F_i x_i = 940 + 35P$

$$\text{Mean} = \frac{940+35P}{44+P} = 25$$

$$1100 + 25P = 940 + 35P$$

$$160 = 10P$$

$$16 = P$$

Hence Ans is (C)

Sol. 14 (B) $\text{Sum} = \dfrac{n(n+1)}{2}$

$= \dfrac{40 \times 41}{2} = 820$

$\text{Average} = \dfrac{820}{40} = 20.5$

Hence Ans is (B)

Sol. 15 (C) Let $x_1, x_2, x_3 \ldots x_{11}$ are 11 results

$x_1 + x_2 + x_3 + x_4 + x_5 + x_6 = 58 \times 6$ ...(1)

$x_6 + x_7 + x_8 + x_9 + x_{10} + x_{11} = 63 \times 6$ ...(2)

$x_1 + x_2 + \ldots + x_{11} = 60 \times 11$ ...(3)

$x_6 = 58 \times 6 + 63 \times 6 - 60 \times 11$

$x_6 = 348 + 378 - 660 = 66$

Hence Ans is (C)

Sol. 16 (B) Given

$A + B + C = 135$

$A + B = 80$

$B + C = 86$

$\Rightarrow \quad B = 166 - 135 = 31$ kg

Hence Ans is (B)

Sol. 17 (A) Let the average of 16 innings is x then sum of 16 innings is $16x$

$\Rightarrow \quad \dfrac{16x + 87}{17} = (x + 3)$

$16x + 87 = 17x + 51$

$36 = x$

So average of 17 innings is $36 + 3 = 39$

Hence Ans is (A)

Sol. 18 (B) Given

$\dfrac{2 + 7 + 6 + x}{4} = 5 \times 4$

$\Rightarrow \quad x = 20 - 15 = 5$ ...(1)

and $\dfrac{18 + 1 + 6 + x + y}{5} = 10$

$\Rightarrow \quad x + y = 50 - 25 = 25$ [using (1)]

$\Rightarrow \quad y = 25 - x = 25 - 5 = 20$

Hence Ans is (B)

Sol. 19 (A) Present age of $(A + B) = 18 \times 2 + 2 \times 3 = 42$ yrs.

Present age of $(A + B + C) = 66$ yrs.

C's age $= 66 - 42 = 24$ yrs

Hence Ans is (A)

Sol. 20 (C) Mode = 3 median – 2 mean

$= 3 \times 9 - 2 \times 8$

$= 27 - 16 = 11$

Hence Ans is (C)

Sol. 21 (A) Mean $\bar{X}$

$= \dfrac{\text{Sum of observations}}{\text{No of observations}} = \dfrac{4x + 30}{4}$

$\Rightarrow \quad \dfrac{4x + 30}{4} = x + 7.5$

Hence Ans is (A)

Sol. 22 (B) Median $= \left(\dfrac{n+1}{2}\right)^{th}$ term (if n is odd)

Hence Ans is (B)

Sol. 23 (A) $\text{Mode} = 1 + \dfrac{f - f_1}{2f - f_1 - f_2} \times h$

where l is lower limit of median class and f is frequency of median class

Hence Ans is (A)

Sol. 24 (D) $\text{Median} = l + \dfrac{\frac{N}{2} - C}{f} \times h$

$\dfrac{N}{2}$ = Cumulative frequency/2 l is lower limit of median class and h is class interval.

$f \rightarrow$ is frequency of median class

$c \rightarrow$ C.F. of upper median class

Hence Ans is (D)

Sol. 25 (C) Mode of the class is 60 which occurs maximum time i.e. 12

Hence Ans is (C)

Solutions of PRACTICE EXERCISE-13.3

Sol. 1 (A) $\dfrac{20°}{360°} \times 540 = 30$ marks

Hence Ans is (A)

Sol. 2 (D) Mode = 3 Median – 2 Mean

$500 = 3 \times 525 - 2$ Mean

Mean $= 537.5$

Hence Ans is (D)

Sol. 3 (C) First 12 prime numbers are

2, 3, 5, 7, 11, 13, 17, 19, 23, 29, 31, 37

$$\text{Median} = \frac{1}{2}\left[\left(\frac{n}{2}\right)^{th}\text{term} + \left(\frac{n}{2}+1\right)^{th}\text{term}\right]$$

$$\text{Median} = \frac{1}{2}\left[\left(\frac{12}{2}\right)^{th}\text{term} + \left(\frac{12}{2}+1\right)^{th}\text{term}\right]$$

$$\text{Median} = \frac{1}{2}[(6)^{\text{th}}\text{term} + (7)^{\text{th}}\text{term}]$$

$$\text{Median} = \frac{13+17}{2} = 15$$

Hence Ans is (C)

Sol. 4 (B) First ten even natural number are :

2, 4, 6, 8, 10, 12, 14, 16, 18, 20

$$\Rightarrow \quad \text{Mean} = \frac{2+4+6+\ldots+20}{10}$$

$$= \frac{10\times 11}{10}$$

[As sum of first n even natural number is $n \times (n+1)$]

$$\Rightarrow \quad \text{Mean} = 11$$

Hence Ans is (B)

Sol. 5 (C) Here total number of term (n) are 10.
So median

$$= \frac{1}{2}\left[\left(\frac{n}{2}\right)^{\text{th}}\text{term} + \left(\frac{n}{2}+1\right)^{\text{th}}\text{term}\right]$$

$$63 = \frac{1}{2}\left[\left(\frac{10}{2}\right)^{\text{th}}\text{term} + \left(\frac{10}{2}+1\right)^{\text{th}}\text{term}\right]$$

$$63 = \frac{1}{2}[5^{\text{th}}\text{term} + 6^{\text{th}}\text{term}]$$

$$126 = x + x + 2$$

$$2x + 2 = 126$$

$$x = 62$$

Hence Ans is (C)

Sol. 6 (C) Let the first number be 'n'

then $\quad n + n+1 + n+2 \ldots + n+6 = 1617$

$$7n = 1617 - 21$$

$$7n = 1596$$

$$n = \frac{1596}{7}$$

$$n = 228$$

So number are

228, 229, 230, 231, 232, 233, 234

So there are 2 prime

Hence Ans is (C)

Sol. 7 (A) Given

$$\frac{x_1 + x_2 + \ldots x_{100}}{100} = 24$$

$$\sum_{i=1}^{100} x_i = 2400$$

$$\sum_{i=1}^{100} x_i + 4\times 100 = 2800$$

$$\sum_{i=1}^{100} (x_i + 400)\times 2.5 = 2800\times 25$$

Now mean

$$\sum_{i=1}^{100} \frac{(x_i+400)\times 2.5}{100} = \frac{2800\times 25}{100}$$

$$= 70$$

Hence Ans is (A)

Sol. 8 (D) Given

$$a^2 + b^2 = 1$$

$\Rightarrow$ By A.M.G.M property

$$\frac{a^2+b^2}{2} \geq \sqrt{a^2b^2}$$

$$\Rightarrow \quad ab \leq \frac{1}{2}$$

Similarly $\quad cd \leq \frac{1}{2}$ & $pq \leq \frac{1}{2}$

$$\Rightarrow \quad ab + cd + pq \leq \frac{3}{2}$$

Hence Ans is (D)

Sol. 9 (B) $\quad \text{Mean} = \dfrac{5+10+15+P+20+35+40}{7}$

$$\Rightarrow \quad 21\times 7 = 125 + P$$

$$\Rightarrow \quad 147 - 125 = P$$

$$\Rightarrow \quad P = 22$$

Hence Ans is (B)

Sol. 10 (C) First 10 prime numbers are

2, 3, 5, 7, 11, 13, 17, 19, 23, 29

$$\text{Median} = \frac{\left(\frac{10}{2}\right)^{\text{th}} + \left(\frac{10}{2}+1\right)^{\text{th}}}{2}$$

$$= \frac{5^{\text{th}} + 6^{\text{th}}}{2} = \frac{11+13}{2} = 12$$

Hence Ans is (C)

Sol. 11 (B) Using empirical formula

$$\text{mode} = 3\text{ median} - 2\text{ mean}$$

$$\Rightarrow \quad 2\text{ mean} = 3\text{ median} - \text{mode}$$

$$\Rightarrow \quad \text{mean} = \frac{3\times 7 - 9}{2}$$

$$\Rightarrow \quad \text{mean} = 6$$

Hence Ans is (B)

Sol. 12 (C) If each number is multiplied by 2 then the new mean will also get multiplied by same real number.

Hence new mean = 2 × 6 = 12

Hence Ans is (C)

Sol. 13 (C) Given 25, 26, 27, 28, 29, clearly median = 27 & also mean

Hence Ans is (C)

Sol. 14 (D) $\left(1-\frac{1}{n}\right)+\left(1-\frac{2}{n}\right)+\left(1-\frac{3}{n}\right)+\ldots$

$$\frac{(n-1)}{n}+\frac{n-2}{n}+\frac{n-3}{n}\ldots$$

$$= \frac{(n-1)+(n-2)+(n-3)+\ldots}{n}$$

$$= \frac{(n-1)(n-1+1)/2}{n} \quad \text{as } \Sigma n = \frac{n(n+1)}{2}$$

$$= \frac{(n-1)(n)}{2\cdot n}$$

$$= \frac{1}{2}(n-1)$$

Hence Ans is (D)

Sol. 15 (B) We know

$$\text{Mode} = 3\text{ median} - 2\text{ mean}$$

$$5 = 3\times 3 - 2\text{ mean}$$

$$2\times\text{mean} = 9 - 5 = 4$$

$$\Rightarrow \quad \text{mean} = 2$$

Hence Ans is (B)

Sol. 16 (B) Given sum of 49 consecutive integers = 7^5 median & mean for first consecutive 49 integer will be same. And we know also that consecutive integer from an A.P. in which first term & last term sum is constant and also the second & second last term & so on & it is equal to 2 times mean/median (in case of odd number of term)

So $\quad T_1 + T_2 + \ldots T_{25} + \ldots T_{49} = 7^5$

Let $\quad T_{25} = x$

$$(T_1 + T_{49}) + (T_2 + T_{48}) + \ldots + T_{25} = 7^5$$

$$2x + 2x + \ldots + x = 7^5$$

$$\Rightarrow \quad 49x = 7^5 \Rightarrow x = 7^3$$

Hence Ans is (B)

Sol. 17 (B) Given

$$\frac{x+\frac{1}{x}}{2} = M$$

$$\Rightarrow \quad x + \frac{1}{x} = 2M \qquad \ldots(1)$$

Cube on both side

$$\Rightarrow \quad x^3 + \frac{1}{x^3} + 3.x\times\frac{1}{x}\left(x+\frac{1}{x}\right) = 8M^3$$

$$\Rightarrow \quad x^3 + \frac{1}{x^3} = 8M^3 - 3.2M$$

$$\Rightarrow \quad \frac{x^3 + \frac{1}{x^3}}{2} = \frac{8M^3 - 6M}{2}$$

$$= 4M^3 - 3M$$

$$= M(4M^2 - 3)$$

Hence Ans is (B)

Sol. 18 (C) Let the number of student in class be n then

$$\text{Av. weight} = \frac{\text{sum of weight of all student}}{\text{number of students}}$$

$$n = \frac{\text{sum of weight}}{n}$$

$\Rightarrow$ Sum of weight = n^2

Now let k be increase/decrease as per question.

$$Av. + k = \frac{n^2 + 21}{n+1} \qquad \ldots(1)$$

$$Av. - k = \frac{n^2 + 19}{n+1} \qquad \ldots(2)$$

Adding (1) & (2)

$$2Av. = \frac{2n^2 + 40}{n+1}$$

$$\Rightarrow \quad 2n(n+1) = 2n^2 + 40$$

$$\Rightarrow \quad n = 20$$

Hence Ans is (C)

Sol. 19 **(C)** Total number of square in a chessboard

$1^2+2^2+3^2+4^2+5^2+6^2+7^2+8^2$

$$\Rightarrow \frac{8(8+1)(2\times 8+1)}{6}=\frac{8\times 9\times 17}{6}=204$$

Using formula $\Sigma n^2=\frac{n(n+1)(2n+1)}{6}$

Hence Ans is (C)

Sol. 20 **(C)** We have

$$\text{Mode} = 3\text{ median} - 2\text{ mean}$$

$$16 = 3\text{ median} - 2\times 28$$

$$16+56 = 3\text{ median}$$

$$3\text{ median} = 72$$

$$\text{median} = \frac{72}{3} = 24$$

Hence ans is (C)

Sol. 21 **(B)** Given

$$A=\frac{a+b}{2},\ G=\sqrt{ab}$$

$$\left(\frac{\sqrt{a}-\sqrt{b}}{\sqrt{2}}\right)^2$$

$$\frac{a+b-2\sqrt{ab}}{2}$$

$$\frac{a+b}{2}-\sqrt{ab}$$

$$A-G$$

Hence Ans is (B)

Sol. 22 **(D)** Mode = 3 median − 2mean

$$5n = 3\text{median} - 2\times 2n$$

$$5n+4n = 3\text{ median}$$

$$\text{median} = 3n$$

Hence Ans is (D)

Sol. 23 **(A)** −1, 0, 1, 2, 3, 4, 5, 6, 8, 11

$$\text{Mean} = \frac{-1+0+1+2+3+4+5+5+6+8+11}{11}$$

$$=\frac{44}{11}=4$$

$$\text{Median} = \left(\frac{n+1}{2}\right)^{th}\text{ term} = \left(\frac{12}{2}\right)=6^{th}$$

$$=6^{th}$$

$$=4$$

Hence Ans is (A)

Sol. 24 **(B)** Sum of marks before correction

$$= \text{mean} \times \text{number of students}$$

$$=135\times 20 = 2700$$

Sum of marks after correction

$$=2700+35-15$$

$$=2720$$

$$\text{New mean} = \frac{2720}{20}=136$$

Hence Ans is (B)

Sol. 25 **(D)** From formulae,

$$97.5 = 94.5 + h\left(\frac{x+15-x}{2(x+15)-x-(x+5)}\right)$$

$$\Rightarrow 3 = h\left(\frac{15}{25}\right)=\frac{3h}{5}$$

$$\Rightarrow h=5$$

$\Rightarrow$ upper limit $94.5+5=99.5$

Hence Ans is (D)

Sol. 26 **(D)** Mode = 3 Median − 2 Mean

$$\Rightarrow 5.2 = 3\times\left(\frac{11}{10}\times\text{Mean}\right)-2\text{ Mean}$$

$$=\left(\frac{33}{10}-2\right)\times\text{Mean}$$

$$=\frac{13}{10}\times\text{Mean}$$

$$\Rightarrow \text{Mean}=4$$

Hence Ans is (D)

Sol. 27 **(C)** Let $x_1, x_2, x_3, \ldots, x_8, x_9$ be the numbers

$$\frac{x_1+x_2+x_3+x_4+x_5}{5}=19$$

$$\Rightarrow x_1+x_2+x_3+x_4+x_5=95 \quad \ldots(1)$$

$$\frac{x_5+x_6+x_7+x_8+x_9}{5}=17$$

$$\Rightarrow x_5+x_6+x_7+x_8+x_9=85 \quad \ldots(2)$$

$$\frac{x_1+x_2+x_3+x_4+x_5+x_6+x_7+x_8+x_9}{9}=18$$

$$\Rightarrow x_1+x_2+x_3+x_4+x_5+x_6+x_7+x_8+x_9=162 \quad \ldots(3)$$

Adding equations-(1) and (2) and then subtracting equation-(3) from it, we get

$$x_5=18$$

Hence Ans is (C)

Sol. 28 (D) $15\times 2+900\div 90-100$

$\Rightarrow\quad 30+10-100$

$\Rightarrow\quad 40-100=-60$

Hence Ans is (D)

Sol. 29 (B) From the question upper limit = 50.

Hence Ans is (B)

Sol. 30 (B) $\dfrac{x_1+x_2+---x_n}{n}=46$

$\Rightarrow\quad x_1+x_2+---x_n=46n \quad \ldots(1)$

$\dfrac{x_1+x_2+x_3+x_4}{4}=52$

$\Rightarrow\quad x_1+x_2+x_3+x_4=208 \quad \ldots(2)$

$\dfrac{x_5+x_6+---x_n}{n-4}=44.5$

$\Rightarrow\quad x_5+x_6+---x_n=44.5\,(n-4) \quad \ldots(3)$

from (1), (2) and (3)

$208+44.5\,(n-4)=46n$

$\Rightarrow\quad n=20$

Hence Ans is (B)

Sol. 31 (C) Data in ascending order

17, 18, 23, 27, $x-3$, $x+5$, 45, 49, 74, 85

median = 35

$\dfrac{x-3+x+5}{2}=35$

$\dfrac{2x+2}{2}=35$

$x+1=35$

$x=34$

17, 18, 23, 31, 39, 45, 49, 74, 85

Corrected data

17, 18, 23, 31, 39, 45, 49, 72, 74, 85

$\Rightarrow\quad \text{Median}=\dfrac{39+45}{2}=\dfrac{84}{2}=42$

Hence Ans is (C)

Sol. 32 (B) mean, mode, median of the observation is

7, 7, 5, 7 & x are same

$\Rightarrow\quad \text{mode}=7$

$\text{median}=7$

for mean

$\dfrac{7+7+5+7+x}{5}=7$

$26+x=35$

$x=35-26$

$x=9$

Hence Ans is (B)

Sol. 33 (D) $\text{Mode}=l+\dfrac{f_m-f_1}{2f_m-f_1-f_2}\times h$

given $f_m=80, f_1=50, f_2=50, l=30$

and $h=10$

$=30+\dfrac{80-50}{2\times 80-50-50}\times 10$

$=30+\dfrac{30}{60}\times 10$

$=30+5$

$=35$

Hence Ans is (D)

Sol. 34 (D) Let temperatures be

Monday $\rightarrow a°$

Tuesday $\rightarrow b°$

Wednesday $\rightarrow c°$

Thursday $\rightarrow \dfrac{4}{5}a°$

$\dfrac{a+b+c}{3}=37$

$\Rightarrow\quad a+b+c=111 \quad \ldots(1)$

$\dfrac{4}{5}a+b+c=102 \quad \ldots(2)$

from (1) and (2) $\dfrac{a}{5}=9 \Rightarrow a=45$

Hence on Thursday

$\Rightarrow\quad \dfrac{4}{5}\times 45=36°$

Hence Ans is (D)

Sol. 35 (B) $n+1, n+3, n+5, \ldots \rightarrow$ 10 consecutive odd number

$120=\dfrac{10n+100}{10} \Rightarrow 120\,n+10$

$n=110$

$=\dfrac{(n+1)+(n+3)+(n+5)+(n+7)+(n+9)}{5}$

$=\dfrac{5n+25}{5}=n+5=115$

Hence Ans is (B)

Sol. 36 (D) By definition

Hence Ans is (D)

Sol. 37 (A) Mean of 8 student

$$= 152 \text{ cm}$$

Sum of height of 8 student

$$= 152 \times 8 = 1216$$

Sum of height of 10 students

$$= 1216 + 143 + 156 = 1515$$

Mean height of 10 student

$$= \frac{1515}{10} = 151.5 \text{ cm}$$

Hence Ans is (A)

Sol. 38 (B) Observations 11, 12, 14, 18, $x+2$, $x+4$, 30, 32, 35, 41 are in ascending order

Total Number of observation = 10

$$\text{Median} = \frac{(5^{th})\text{observation} + (6^{th})\text{observation}}{2}$$

$$24 = \frac{x+2+x+4}{2}$$

$$48 = 2x+6$$

$$42 = 2x$$

$$x = 21$$

Hence Ans is (B)

Sol. 39 (B) $\dfrac{12(x+2)+15x+20(x-1)}{3x+1} = \dfrac{29}{2}$

$\Rightarrow$ $x = 3$

Hence Ans is (B)

Sol. 40 (A) Mean of 1st seventeen whole number

$$\overline{x} = \frac{0+1+2.......16}{17}$$

$$= \frac{\frac{16\times17}{2}}{17} = 8$$

Hence Ans is (A)

Sol. 41 (D)

$$\text{Median} = \frac{\left(\frac{n}{2}\right)^{th} \text{observation} + \left(\frac{n}{2}+1\right)^{th} \text{observation}}{2}$$

Hence Ans is (D)

Sol. 42 (D) The mean of 25 observation is 36

$$x = \frac{\text{sum}}{\text{n}}$$

$$\text{sum} = 36 \times 25 = 900 \qquad \ldots(1)$$

If the mean of the first 13 observations is 32

$$\text{sum} = 13 \times 32 = 416 \qquad \ldots(2)$$

and that of last 13 observation is 39

again, $$\text{sum} = 13 \times 39 = 507 \qquad \ldots(3)$$

equation (2) + (3)

$$13\times32 + 13\times39 = 13\,(32+39) = 13\times71 = 923 \qquad \ldots(4)$$

13th observation = equation-(4) – (1)

$$923 - 900 = 23$$

then the 13th observation is 23.

Hence Ans is (D)

Sol. 43 (B) Let the number of boys x and number of girls y

$$\Rightarrow \quad \frac{50x+40y}{x+y} = 46$$

$$50x + 40y = 46x + 46y$$

$$4x = 6y$$

$$\frac{x}{y} = \frac{6}{4}$$

$$x : y = 3 : 2$$

Hence, the number of boys to the number of girls is 3 : 2.

Hence Ans is (B)

Sol. 44 (A) $\text{Mode} = l + h\left\{\dfrac{fm - f_1}{2\,fm - f_1 - f_2}\right\}$

Modal class = 30 – 40

$$36 = 30 + 10\left\{\frac{16-k}{32-k-12}\right\}$$

$$\frac{6}{10} = \frac{16-k}{20-k} \Rightarrow \frac{3}{5} = \frac{16-k}{20-k}$$

$$\Rightarrow \quad 60 - 3k = 80 - 5k$$

$$2k = 20 \Rightarrow k = 10$$

Hence Ans is (A)

Sol. 45 (C)

Observation	Frequency
64	1
60	1
48	2
43	2
34	1

Now, mode to be 43, highest frequency must be of observation 43.

So, $x = 43$

Hence Ans is (C)

Sol. 46 (B) Class width $= 60.5 - 55.5 = 5$

Hence Ans is (B)

Sol. 47 (C) Total monthly income of four earning number will be $4 \times 7350 = 29400$, when one member passes away, then total monthly income of 3 earning member will be $3 \times 6500 = 19500$.

$\Rightarrow$ Monthly income of person who is no more is

$29400 - 19500 = 9900$

Hence Ans is (C)

Sol. 48 (B) Required % $= \frac{20 \times 80 + 30 \times 70}{50}$

$= \frac{1600 + 2100}{50}$

$= \frac{3700}{50}$

$= 74\%$

Hence Ans is (B)

Sol. 49 (B) Let the number of men be x and the number of women be y then as per question

$$26x + 21y = 25(x + y)$$

$$26x + 21y = 25x + 25y$$

$$x = 4y$$

$$\% \text{ man} = \frac{x}{x+y} \times 100 = 80\%$$

$$\% \text{ women} = \frac{y}{x+y} \times 100 = 20\%$$

Hence Ans is (B)

Sol. 50 (C) Number of observations is even

$\Rightarrow$ median will be $\dfrac{\left(\frac{n}{2}\right)^{th} \text{term} + \left(\frac{n}{2}+1\right)^{th} \text{term}}{2}$

$\Rightarrow$ mean of $\left[\left(\frac{n}{2}\right)^{th} \text{term} + \left(\frac{n}{2}+1\right)^{th} \text{term}\right]$

Hence Ans is (C)

Sol. 51 (B) Mean of first n natural numbers is $= \frac{n+1}{2}$

because sum of n natural number $= \frac{n(n+1)}{2}$

Total number of terms $= n$

$$\text{mean} = \frac{\text{sum of all observation}}{\text{Total number of observation}} = \frac{n+1}{2}$$

Hence Ans is (B)

Sol. 52 (C) $N = 70, h = 10, c.f = 22, f = 10, L = 30$

$$\text{Median} = L + \frac{\left(\frac{N}{2} - cf\right)h}{f}$$

$$= 30 + \frac{(35-22)}{10} \times 10$$

$$\text{Median} = 43$$

Hence Ans is (C)

Sol. 53 (C) $50, 42, 35, 2x + 10, 2x - 8, 12, 11, 8$

$$\text{Median} = \frac{2x + 10 + 2x - 8}{2} = 25$$

$\Rightarrow$ $4x + 2 = 50$

$$4x = 50$$

$$x = 12$$

Hence Ans is (C)

Sol. 54 (D) Sum of first 18 observations

$= 70 \times 18 = 1260$

Sum of last 18 observations

$= 80 \times 18 = 1440$

Sum of all 35 observations

$= 75 \times 35 = 2625$

18th observation

$= 1260 + 1440 - 2625 = 75$

Hence Ans is (D)

Sol. 55 (C) $\text{Mean} = \frac{(x+1)+(x+3)+(x+4)+(x+8)}{4}$

$= \frac{4x+16}{4}$

$= x + 4$

Hence Ans is (C)

Sol. 56 (B) Lower limit $= 10 - 3 = 7$

Hence Ans is (B)

Sol. 57 (C) Theoretical question.

Sol. 58 (C) Arrange the array in an ascending order

21, 39, 39, 45, 54, 54, 56, 56, 56, 77, 84, 84

$$\text{Median} = \frac{1}{2}\left[\left(\frac{n}{2}\right)^{th} \text{term} + \left(\frac{n}{2}+1\right)^{th} \text{term}\right]$$

$$\text{Median} = \frac{1}{2}\left[\left(\frac{12}{2}\right)^{th} \text{term} + \left(\frac{12}{2}+1\right)^{th} \text{term}\right]$$

$$\text{Median} = \frac{1}{2}[(6)^{\text{th}}\text{ term} + (7)^{\text{th}}\text{term}]$$

$$\text{Median} = \frac{1}{2}(54+56) = \frac{1}{2}(110) = 55$$

$$\text{Mode} = \text{highest frequency element} = 56$$

$$\text{Range} = 84 - 21 = 63$$

Mean of median mode and range is equal to

$$\frac{55+56+63}{3} = 174 \div 3 = 58$$

Hence Ans is (C)

Sol. 59 (C) Let the tax on commodity be x and consumption be y

Then revenue $= xy$

$$\%\text{decrease in revenue will be } \frac{xy - .85x \times 1.1y}{xy} \times 100$$

$$(1 - .935) \times 100 = 6.5.$$

Hence Ans is (C)

Sol. 60 (D) Let three numbers are x, 5, y

As per the first condition of the question

$$\frac{x+5+y}{3} = x+10$$

$$x+5+y = 3x+30$$

$$y = 2x+25 \qquad \ldots(1)$$

As per the second condition of the question

$$\frac{x+5+y}{3} = y-15$$

$$x+5+y = 3y-45$$

$$x+5 = 2y-45$$

$$x+5 = 2(2x+25)-45 \qquad \text{(using equation-(1))}$$

$$x+5 = 4x+50-45$$

$$x = 0$$

$$\Rightarrow \qquad y = 25$$

$$\text{Required Mean} = \frac{0^2+5^2+25^2}{3} = \frac{650}{3}$$

$$= 216\frac{2}{3}$$

Hence Ans is (D)

Sol. 61 (D) Possible group

1st group =	1	2	3	18	19	20	21
2nd group=	4	3	6	14	15	16	17
3rd group =	7	8	9	10	11	12	13

$$\text{Mean} = \frac{18+14+10}{3} = \frac{42}{3} \Rightarrow 14$$

Hence Ans is (D)

Sol. 62 (D) Let the 11 consecutive natural numbers be $n, n+1, n+2, \ldots, n+10$

$$\Rightarrow \qquad \text{Mean} = \frac{n+n+1+n+2+\ldots+n+10}{11}$$

$$= \frac{11n + \frac{10\times 11}{2}}{11} = n+5 = m \qquad \text{(Given)}$$

Further, mean of 17 consecutive natural

$$\text{numbers} = \frac{n+n+1+\ldots+n+16}{17}$$

$$= \frac{17n + \frac{16(17)}{2}}{17}$$

$$= n+8$$

$$\%\text{ difference} = \frac{n+8-n-5}{m} \times 100\%$$

$$= \frac{3}{m} \times 100$$

$$= \frac{300}{m}\%$$

Hence Ans is (D)

* * * * *

14 Miscellaneous

Logarithm-Theory

1. Definition : If $a^x = N$

then $\log_a N = x$, provided $N > 0$, $a > 0$ and $a \neq 1$.

2. Common results :

(a) $\log_a(mn) = \log_a m + \log_a n$

(b) $\log_a(m/n) = \log_a m - \log_a n$

(c) $\log_a m^n = n \log_a m$

(d) $\log_{a^k} m = \frac{1}{k}\log_a m$

(e) $\log_b a = \frac{1}{\log_a b}$ (Interchange formula)

(f) $\log_b a = \frac{\log_c a}{\log_c b} = \log_b e.\log_e a$

(Base change formula)

(g) $a^x = e^{x\log_e a}$

(h) $a^{\log_a x} = x$

(i) $\log_a a = 1$

(j) $\log_a 1 = 0$

Fundamental Principle of Counting :

If an operation can be performed in '*m*' different ways and another operation in '*n*' different ways then these two operations can be performed one after the other in '*mn*' ways.

If an operation can be performed in '*m*' different ways and another operation in '*n*' different ways then either of these two operations can be performed in '*m* + *n*' ways. (provided only one has to be done)

This principle can be extended to any number of operations

FACTORIAL '*n*'

The continuous product of the first '*n*' natural numbers is called factorial *n* and is denoted by $n!$ i.e. $n! = 1 \times 2 \times 3 \times \ldots \times (n-1) \times n$.

Permutation :

An arrangement that can be formed by taking some or all of a finite set of things (or objects) is called a **Permutation.**

Order of the things is very important in case of permutation. A permutation is said to be a **Linear Permutation** if the objects are arranged in a line. A linear permutation is simply called as a permutation. A permutation is said to be a **Circular Permutation** if the object are arranged in the form of a circle. The number of (linear) permutations that can be formed by taking *r* things at a time from a set of *n* distinct things ($r \leq n$) is denoted by ^nP_r or $P(n, r)$. $^nP_r = n(n-1)(n-2)(n-3)\ldots(n-r+1) = \frac{n!}{(n-r)!}$.

Number of Permutations Under Certain Conditions :

1. Number of permutations of *n* different things, taken *r* at a time, when a particular thing is to be always included in each arrangement, is $r(^{n-1}P_{r-1})$.

2. Number of permutations of *n* different things, taken *r* at a time, when a particular thing is never taken in each arrangement is $^{n-1}P_r$.

3. Number of permutations of *n* different things, taken all at a time, when *m* specified things always come together is $m!\,(n-m+1)!$.

4. Number of permutations of *n* different things, taken all at a time, when *m* specified never come together is $n! - [m!\,(n-m+1)!]$.

5. The number of permutations of *n* dissimilar things taken *r* at a time when *k* (< *r*) particular things always occur is $[^{n-k}P_{r-k}]\cdot[^rP_k]$.

6. The number of permutations of *n* dissimilar things taken *r* at a time when *k* particular things never occur is $^{n-k}P_r$.

7. The number of permutations of *n* dissimilar things taken *r* at a time when repetition of things is allowed any number of times is n^r.

8. The number of permutations of *n* different things, taken not more than *r* at a time, when each thing may occur any number of times is

$$n + n^2 + n^3 + \ldots + n^r = \frac{n(n^r - 1)}{n-1}.$$

9. The number of permutations of *n* different things taken not more than *r* at a time

$$^nP_1 + {}^nP_2 + {}^nP_3 + \ldots {}^nP_r.$$

Permutations of Similar Things :

The number of permutations of *n* things taken all at a time when *p* of them are all alike and the rest are all different is $\frac{n!}{p!}$.

If p things are alike of one type, q things are alike of other type, r things are alike of another type, then the number of permutations with $p+q+r$ things is $\frac{(p+q+r)!}{p!q!r!}$.

Circular Permutations :

1. The number of circular permutations of n dissimilar things taken r at a time is $\frac{{}^nP_r}{r}$.

2. The number of circular permutations of n dissimilar things taken all at a time is $(n-1)!$.

4. The number of circular permutations of n dissimilar things in clock-wise direction = Number of permutations in anticlock-wise direction = $\frac{(n-1)!}{2}$.

Combination :

A selection that can be formed by taking some or all of a finite set of things (or objects) is called a **Combination.**

The number of combinations of n dissimilar things taken r at a time is denoted by ${}^nC_r$ or $C(n, r)$ or $\binom{n}{r}$.

1. ${}^nC_r = \frac{n!}{r!(n-r)!}$

2. ${}^nC_r = {}^nC_{r-1}$

3. ${}^nC_r + {}^nC_{r-1} = {}^{n+1}C_r$

4. If ${}^nC_r = {}^nC_s \Rightarrow r = s$ or $n = r+s$

5. The number of combinations of n things taken r at a time in which

(a) s particular things will always occur is ${}^{n-s}C_{r-s}$.

(b) s particular things will never occur is ${}^{n-s}C_r$.

(c) s particular things always occurs and p particular things never occur is ${}^{n-p-s}C_{r-s}$.

Total Number of Combinations :

1. The total number of combinations of $(p_1 + p_2 + \ldots + p_k)$ things taken any number at a time when p_1 things are alike of one kind, p_2 things are alike of second kind ... p_k things are alike of kth kind, is $(p_1 + 1)(p_2 + 1) \ldots (p_k + 1)$.

2. The total number of combinations of $(p_1 + p_2 + \ldots + p_k)$ things taken one or more at a time when p_1 things are alike of one kind, p_2 things are alike of second kind ... p_k things are alike of kth kind, is $(p_1 + 1)(p_2 + 1) \ldots (p_k + 1) - 1$.

* * * * *

PRACTICE EXERCISE - 14.1

14-1 In a flight of 600 km an aeroplane was slowed down due to a bad weather. If the average speed for the trip was reduced by 200 Km/h and the time of flight increased by 30 minutes, then the duration of flight is : **[NTSE-2015 (Stage-I) Chandigarh]**

(A) 1 hr (B) 2 hrs
(C) 3 hrs (D) 4 hrs

14-2 If U is any universal set and A is the subset of U, then $AUA'=$ **[NTSE-2015 (Stage-I) MP]**

(A) U (B) ϕ
(C) A (D) A'

14-3 The cost price of a horse is Rs. 27,000 = 00 and transportation charges are Rs. 2,400 = 00. If horse is sold in Rs. 33,810 = 00. The percentage of profit will be : **[NTSE-2015 (Stage-I) MP]**

(A) 5% (B) 10%
(C) 15% (D) 20%

14-4 The length of line segment is 3 which is perpendicular on line $4x+3y+C=0$ from the origin. Then value of c will be : **[NTSE-2015 (Stage-I) UP]**

(A) 0 (B) 7
(C) 10 (D) 15

14-5 If $\frac{a}{x+y}=\frac{b}{y+z}=\frac{c}{z-x}$, then which of the following equation is true ? **[NTSE-2015 (Stage-I) Maharashtra]**

(A) $a=b+c$ (B) $c=a+b$
(C) $b=a\times c$ (D) $b=a+c$

14-6 The marks scored by a student in an examination of 600 marks is shown in the following pie diagram. If he scored 60 marks in Mathematics, then find the percentage of marks that he secured in the examination : **[NTSE-2015 (Stage-I) Maharashtra]**

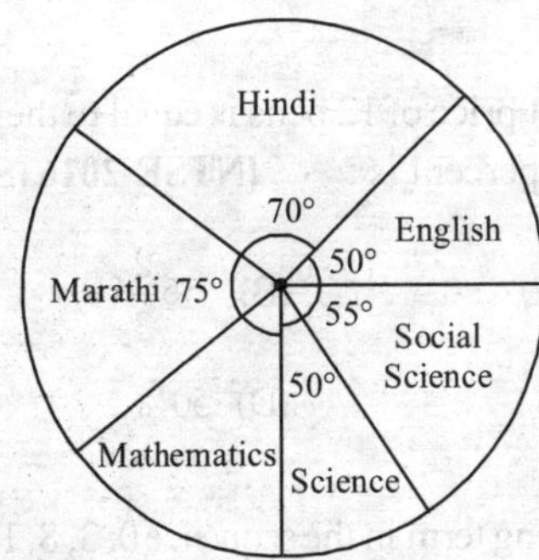

Figure 14.1

(A) 60% (B) 50%
(C) 75% (D) 5%

14-7 Side of a cube is increased by 50%, then what percent increases will be in the area of the vertical faces of the cube? **[NTSE-2015 (Stage-I) Maharashtra]**

(A) 125% (B) 150%
(C) 100% (D) 50%

14-8 $P\equiv(1,-9), Q\equiv(2,5)$ and $R\equiv(6,7)$ are the co-ordinates of the vertices of ΔPQR, then find the co-ordinates of the centroid from the following alternative given? **[NTSE-2015 (Stage-I) Maharashtra]**

(A) $\left(\frac{10}{3} m \frac{-17}{3}\right)$ (B) $(1,3)$
(C) $(3,1)$ (D) $(-3,1)$

14-9 If A and B are two non empty sets, then $A\cup B=$ **[NTSE-2015 (Stage-I) MP]**

(A) $\{x \mid x\in A \text{ and } x\in B\}$ (B) $\{x \mid x\in A \text{ or } x\in B\}$
(C) $\{x \mid x\in A \text{ and } x\notin B\}$ (D) $\{x \mid x\notin A \text{ and } x\in B|\}$

14-10 Selling price of one things is $\frac{3}{2}$ times of its cost price. What will be the percentage of profit? **[NTSE-2015 (Stage-I) MP]**

(A) $20\frac{1}{2}$ (B) $25\frac{1}{4}$
(C) $33\frac{1}{3}$ (D) 50

14-11 A sold a bicycle to B on 20% profit. B sold it to C on 25% profit. If C paid Rs. 225 for it, then what was the cost price of bicycle to A? **[NTSE-2015 (Stage-I) MP]**

(A) 110 (B) 125
(C) 120 (D) 150

14-12 $A:B=2:3, B:C=4:5$ and $C:D=6:7$ then the value of $A:D$ will be : **[NTSE-2015 (Stage-I) Chhatisgarh]**

(A) $\frac{2}{7}$ (B) $\frac{9}{7}$
(C) $\frac{7}{9}$ (D) $\frac{16}{35}$

14-13 Number of axis of symmetry in the following figure-14.2 is : **[NTSE-2015 (Stage-I) Chhatisgarh]**

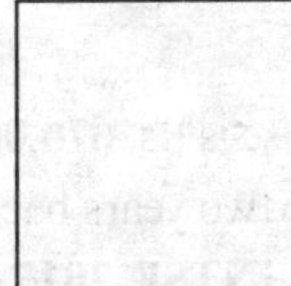

Figure 14.2

(A) 2 (B) 4
(C) 1 (D) 0

14-14 If $3y - 2x = 4$ and $4y - px = 2$ are perpendicular to each other the value of p will be :

[NTSE-2015 (Stage-I) Chhatisgarh]

(A) $\frac{3}{2}$ (B) $\frac{8}{3}$

(C) 6 (D) -6

14-15 The length of minute needle of a watch is 7 cm. The area swept by it during 9 : 10 to 9 : 25 will be :

[NTSE-2015 (Stage-I) Chhatisgarh]

(A) 154 cm^2 (B) 77 cm^2

(C) $\frac{77}{2}$ cm^2 (D) $\frac{77}{4}$ cm^2

14-16 If $f\left(2x+\frac{1}{x}\right) = x^2 + \frac{1}{4x^2} + 1, (x \neq 0)$, the value of $f(x)$ is :

[NTSE-2015 (Stage-I) West Bengal]

(A) $4x^2$ (B) $\frac{1}{4}\left(2x+\frac{1}{x}\right)^2$

(C) $\frac{1}{4}x^2$ (D) $4\left(2x+\frac{1}{x}\right)^2$

14-17 If $x(x^3 - 1) < 0$, then :

[NTSE-2015 (Stage-I) West Bengal]

(A) $x < 0$ (B) $0 < x < 1$

(C) $x > 1$ (D) None of the above

14-18 When the rate of interest being increased from 10% to $12\frac{1}{2}\%$, the yearly income of a person increases by Rs. 1,250. The principal amount was :

[NTSE-2015 (Stage-I) West Bengal]

(A) Rs. 50,000 (B) Rs. 5,000

(C) Rs. 15,000 (D) 37,500

14-19 A man sells two articles each at Rs. 198. He makes a profit of 10% on one article and a loss of 10% on the other. Net profit or loss of the person :

[NTSE-2015 (Stage-I) West Bengal]

(A) 2% profit (B) 2% loss

(C) 1% profit (D) 1% loss

14-20 The price of a house is Rs. 676,000. If the price increases every year by 4%, before two years back the price of the house was :

[NTSE-2015 (Stage-I) West Bengal]

(A) Rs. 6,00,000 (B) Rs. 6,25,000

(C) Rs. 6,50,000 (D) Rs. 5,75,000

14-21 If the edge of a regular tetrahedron is 1 cm, then its volume is :

[NTSE-2015 (Stage-I) West Bengal]

(A) $\frac{1}{12}$ cm^3 (B) $\frac{\sqrt{2}}{6}$ cm^3

(C) $\frac{\sqrt{2}}{12}$ cm^3 (D) $\frac{\sqrt{2}}{4}$ cm^3

14-22 The least value of $2^{\sin^2 x} + 2^{\cos^2 x}$ is :

[NTSE-2015 (Stage-I) West Bengal]

(A) 4 (B) $2\sqrt{2}$

(C) 2 (D) $\sqrt{2}$

14-23 If $\log(xy^3) = 1$ and $\log(x^2y) = 1$, then $\log(xy) = ?$

[NTSE-2016 (Stage-I) Telangana]

(A) $\frac{3}{5}$ (B) 0

(C) $\frac{1}{2}$ (D) $-\frac{1}{2}$

14-24 The area enclosed by the curve $|x| + |y| = 1$ is...

$$\left\{\begin{matrix} |x| = x & \text{for} & x > 0 \\ -x & \text{for} & x < 0 \\ 0 & \text{for} & x = 0 \end{matrix}\right\}$$

[NTSE-2016 (Stage-I) Andhara Pradesh]

(A) 1 square unit (B) 2 square units

(C) 3 square units (D) 4 square units

14-25 How many seconds will a 500 m long train to cross a man, walking with a speed of 3 km/h, in the direction of the moving train if the speed of the train is 63 km/h?

[NTSE-2016 (Stage-I) Bihar]

(A) 25 sec (B) 30 sec

(C) 40 sec (D) 45 sec

14-26 If the cost price of 12 pens is equal to the selling price of 8 pens, the gain percent is : **[NTSE-2016 (Stage-I) Bihar]**

(A) $33\frac{1}{3}\%$ (B) $66\frac{2}{3}\%$

(C) 25% (D) 50%

14-27 The missing term in the sequence 0, 3, 8, 15, 24,… ,48 is :

[NTSE-2016 (Stage-I) Bihar]

(A) 35 (B) 30

(C) 36 (D) 39

14-28 If 70% of the students in a school are boys and the number of girls be 504, the number of boys is : **[NTSE-2016 (Stage-I) Bihar]**

(A) 1176 (B) 1008
(C) 1208 (D) 3024

14-29 The mess charges for 35 students for 24 days is Rs. 6300. In how many days will the mess charge be Rs 3375 for 25 students : **[NTSE-2016 (Stage-I) Bihar]**

(A) 12 (B) 15
(C) 18 (D) 21

14-30 7 Oranges are bought for Rs 3. At what rate per hundred must be sold to gain 33% : **[NTSE-2016 (Stage-I) Bihar]**

(A) Rs 56 (B) Rs 60
(C) Rs 58 (D) Rs 57

14-31 If the side of a square is increased by 25% then, how much percent does its area gets increased : **[NTSE-2016 (Stage-I) Bihar]**

(A) 56.25% (B) 50%
(C) 12.5% (D) 156.25%

14-32 If x% of y is equal to 1% of z, y% of z is equal to 1% of x and z% of x is equal to 1% of y, then the value of $xy + yz + zx$ is : **[NTSE-2016 (Stage-I) Delhi]**

(A) 1 (B) 2
(C) 3 (D) 4

14-33 The line containing the points $(c, 8)$ and $(a, 0)$ is perpendicular to the line containing the points $(-c, c)$ and $(3c, a)$. If $a = 10$, then what is the value of $a + c$? **[NTSE-2016 (Stage-I) Odisha]**

(A) 22 (B) 12
(C) 10 (D) 6

14-34 The roots of the quadratic equation $x^2 - 4x - \log_3 a = 0$ are real. Then what is the least value of a? **[NTSE-2016 (Stage-I) Odisha]**

(A) 64 (B) $\frac{1}{81}$
(C) $\frac{1}{64}$ (D) 81

14-35 The maximum number of non-empty subsets of set $\{0, 1, 2, 3\}$ is : **[NTSE-2016 (Stage-I) Karnatka]**

(A) 7 (B) 8
(C) 15 (D) 16

14-36 The number of arrangements of all the letters of the word "GOURI", so that all vowels do not occur together will be : **[NTSE-2016 (Stage-I) Karnatka]**

(A) 36 (B) 84
(C) 108 (D) 120

14-37 If ${}^{2n}C_3 : {}^{n}C_3 = 12 : 1$ then the value of 'n' is : **[NTSE-2016 (Stage-I) Karnatka]**

(A) 5 (B) 6
(C) 10 (D) 11

14-38 Out of 30 consecutive positive numbers 2 are choose at random. The probability that their sum is odd is : **[NTSE-2016 (Stage-I) Karnatka]**

(A) $\frac{10}{29}$ (B) $\frac{14}{29}$
(C) $\frac{15}{29}$ (D) $\frac{16}{29}$

14-39 $22\frac{1}{2}$ has how many $\frac{1}{4}$? **[NTSE-2016 (Stage-I) Chhatisgarh]**

(A) 22 (B) 44
(C) 45 (D) 90

14-40 Some people complete a work in 20 days. If the number of people is doubled and work in halved, in how many days will they complete it ? **[NTSE-2016 (Stage-I) Chhatisgarh]**

(A) 5 (B) 10
(C) 20 (D) 40

14-41 If $3\sqrt{3} \times 3^3 \div 3^{-3/2} = 3^{n+2}$, then $a = ?$ **[NTSE-2016 (Stage-I) Chhatisgarh]**

(A) 2 (B) 1/2
(C) 4 (D) 0

14-42 If $3A = 4B = 6C$ then $A : B : C$ will be : **[NTSE-2016 (Stage-I) Chhatisgarh]**

(A) $3:4:6$ (B) $\frac{1}{4}:\frac{1}{3}:\frac{1}{2}$
(C) $6:4:3$ (D) $4:3:2$

14-43 $\frac{8}{40}$ is equivalent to : **[NTSE-2016 (Stage-I) Chhatisgarh]**

(A) 20% (B) 40%
(C) 25% (D) 8%

14-44 Given the equality of the following determinants. Find the value of $(a + b)$

$$\begin{vmatrix} 4 & 3 \\ 6 & a \end{vmatrix} = \begin{vmatrix} 6 & b \\ 4 & 5 \end{vmatrix}$$

[NTSE-2016 (Stage-I) Chhatisgarh]

(A) 8 (B) 12
(C) 14 (D) 16

14-45 If in a business, Alok gains 75% more profit than Akash, then by what percentage profit of Akash is less than the profit of Alok ? **[NTSE-2017 (Stage-I) Delhi]**

(A) 25% (B) 12.63%
(C) 30.8% (D) 42.85%

14-46 If $\sin\alpha, \cos\alpha, \tan\alpha$ are in *GP*, *GP* means $\cos^2\alpha = \sin\alpha.\tan\alpha$ $\cot^6\alpha - \cot^2\alpha =$: **[NTSE-2017 (Stage-I) Delhi]**

(A) 1 (B) 0
(C) 4 (D) 2

14-47 Eight members of a group shake hand with one another once. How many hand shakes were done altogether ? **[NTSE-2017 (Stage-I) Delhi]**

(A) 64 (B) 16
(C) 28 (D) 18

14-48 Three of the six vertices of a regular hexagon are chosen at random. The probability that triangle formed by these vertices is equilateral is : **[NTSE-2017 (Stage-I) Delhi]**

(A) $\frac{1}{20}$ (B) $\frac{1}{10}$
(C) $\frac{1}{5}$ (D) $\frac{1}{2}$

14-49 Preeti, Isha and Shruti divided some number of chocolates among themselves in the ratio 14 : 40 : 27. Since Isha was not happy with the division, they revised the division to 19 : 55 : 37. How many chocolates did Shruti got more from the division ? **[NTSE-2017 (Stage-I) Goa]**

(A) 19 (B) 27
(C) 0 (D) 37

14-50 The total cost price of two items is Rs. 10200 and their selling prices are equal. If one of the item is sold at loss of 12% and another at a loss of 18%, then the cost price of an item which is sold at a loss of 18% is : **[NTSE-2017 (Stage-I) Goa]**

(A) Rs. 4920 (B) Rs. 5280
(C) Rs. 6400 (D) Rs. 300

14-51 The slope of a line $3x - 5y = 8$ is : **[NTSE-2017 (Stage-I) Goa]**

(A) 0.6 (B) $-1\frac{2}{3}$
(C) $2\frac{2}{3}$ (D) –1.6

14-52 If $U = \{x \mid x \in N, x < 5\}, A = \{x \mid x \in N, x \leq 2\}$ then $A' =$: **[NTSE-2017 (Stage-I) Gujarat]**

(A) $\{1, 2\}$ (B) $\{1, 2, 3, 4, 5\}$
(C) $\{3, 4\}$ (D) $\{3, 4, 5\}$

14-53 — was the most logical and abstract creator of Euclid's geometry approach : **[NTSE-2017 (Stage-I) Gujarat]**

(A) Hilbert (B) Bhaskaracharya
(C) Thelus (D) Pythagoras

14-54 If the letters of the word "*FATE*" are arranged as in a dictionary without repetition, then the rank of the arrangement of "*FAET*" is : **[NTSE-2017 (Stage-I) Karnataka]**

(A) 12 (B) 13
(C) 14 (D) 15

14-55 There are 12 points in a plane of which 4 are collinear. The number of straight lines and triangles can be formed from these points are respectively : **[NTSE-2017 (Stage-I) Karnataka]**

(A) 60 and 220 (B) 66 and 220
(C) 65 and 216 (D) 61 and 216

14-56 The correct relation is

	A		B
I.	*a*, *b*, *c* are in G.P.	a.	$2b = a + c$
II.	*a*, *b*, *c* are in A.P.	b.	$a + c = \frac{2ac}{b}$
III.	*a*, *b*, *c* are in H.P.	c.	$b^{1/2} = ca$
		d.	$b = (ac)^{1/2}$

[NTSE-2017 (Stage-I) Karnataka]

(A) I-c, II-b, III-a (B) I-c, II-a, III-d
(C) I-d, II-a, III-b (D) I-d, II-b, III-c

14-57 If $y = a + a^2 + a^3 + ... \infty$ where $|a| < 1$ then, the value of '*a*' is : **[NTSE-2017 (Stage-I) Karnataka]**

(A) $\frac{y}{1+y}$ (B) $\frac{y}{1-y}$
(C) $\frac{1+y}{y}$ (D) $\frac{1-y}{y}$

14-58 If *A* and *B* are two non empty sets then $(A \cup B)^C =$: **[NTSE-2017 (Stage-I) Madhya Pradesh]**

(A) $A^C \cup B^C$ (B) $A^C \cap B^C$
(C) $A \cup B^C$ (D)

14-59 The expenditure incurred on different items in a family is shown in the adjacent pie diagram. If the amount of house rent is 10,000 then find the amount incurred on education : **[NTSE-2017 (Stage-I) Maharashtra]**

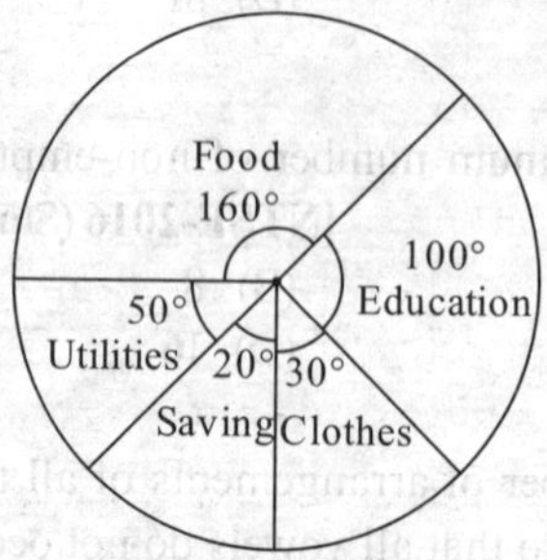

Figure 14.3

(A) Rs. 20, 000 (B) Rs. 32, 000
(C) Rs. 72, 000 (D) Rs. 30, 000

14-60 If $F_1 = F_2 = 1$ and $F_n = F_{n-1} + F_{n-2}$, then the value of F_3 : **[NTSE-2017 (Stage-I) Tamilnadu]**

(A) 1 (B) 2
(C) 3 (D) 4

14-61 If $\log_3[\log_4(\log_2 x)] = 0$ then the value of x is : **[NTSE-2017 (Stage-I) Uttar Pradesh]**

(A) 16 (B) 8
(C) 64 (D) 32

14-62 The present population of a city is 8000 if it increases by 10% during the first year and by 20% during the second year. Then population after two years will be : **[NTSE-2017 (Stage-I) Uttar Pradesh]**

(A) 12400 (B) 14400
(C) 10560 (D) None of these

14-63 If $\log_4[\log_4\{\log_4 \cdot (\log_4 . x)\}] = 0$, '$x$' is equal to : **[NTSE-2017 (Stage-I) West Bengal]**

(A) 256 (B) 4^{16}
(C) 2^{512} (D) 256^4

14-64 If $x^2 + y^2 = z^2$, the value of $\dfrac{1}{\log_{z-y} x} + \dfrac{1}{\log_{z+y} x}$ is : **[NTSE-2017 (Stage-I) West Bengal]**

(A) x (B) y
(C) $x+y$ (D) 2

14-65 The compound interest for two years of the amount Rs. 75000 at the rate of 8% per annum would be : **[NTSE-2017 (Stage-I) West Bengal]**

(A) Rs. 1,248 (B) Rs. 1,260
(C) Rs. 1,300 (D) Rs. 1, 352

14-66 A businessman fixed the selling price of an article after increasing the cost price by 40%. Then he allowed his customer a discount of 20% and gained Rs. 48. The cost price of the article is : **[NTSE-2017 (Stage-I) West Bengal]**

(A) Rs. 200 (B) Rs. 248
(C) Rs. 400 (D) Rs. 448

14-67 What is the number you get on simplifying the sum

$$\frac{1}{3} + \frac{1}{3^2} + \frac{1}{3^3} + \ldots + \frac{1}{3^{10}} + \frac{1}{2 \times 3^{10}} ?$$

[NTSE-2017 (Stage-I) Kerala]

(A) 1 (B) $\frac{2}{3}$
(C) $\frac{1}{2}$ (D) $\frac{1}{3}$

14-68 If $a^x = b^{y+z}$ then : **[NTSE-2018 (Stage-I) Andhra Pradesh]**

(A) $\dfrac{\log a}{\log b} = \dfrac{x}{y+z}$ (B) $\dfrac{\log b}{\log a} = \dfrac{y+z}{x}$

(C) $\dfrac{\log a}{\log b} = \dfrac{y+z}{x}$ (D) $x \log a = yz \log b$

14-69 The solution of

$$\log\frac{x}{\sqrt{3}} + \log\frac{x}{\sqrt[4]{3}} + \log\frac{x}{\sqrt[8]{3}} + \ldots.. + \log\frac{x}{\sqrt[16]{3}}. \text{ Find } x:$$

[NTSE-2018 (Stage-I) Bihar]

(A) $x = 3$ (B) $x = \sqrt{3}$
(C) $x = \sqrt[4]{3}$ (D) $x = 9$

14-70 Rahim sells apples to his customers at the cost price itself but uses a weight of 800g instead of 1 kg weight. Find his profit % : **[NTSE-2018 (Stage-I) Chandigarh]**

(A) 25% (B) 20%
(C) 15% (D) 30%

14-71 Rajat's salary in 2017 is Rs.1,77, 100. His salary from 2014 has risen by 10, 15 and 40 percent respectively to reach 2017 salary figures. What was his salary in 2014 : **[NTSE-2018 (Stage-I) Chandigarh]**

(A) 95,000 (B) 1, 15, 000
(C) 1, 20, 000 (D) 1, 00, 000

14-72 A work is completed in 9 days by 25 persons for 6 hrs daily. Then the same work will be completed by 15 persons for 9 hrs daily in how many days : **[NTSE-2018 (Stage-I) Chhattisgarh]**

(A) 25 (B) 9
(C) 10 (D) 6

14-73 If $f(x) = 2x + 1$ then number of real values of x for which three unequal functions $f(x), f(2x), f(4x)$ are in G.P. : **[NTSE-2018 (Stage-I) Himachal Pradesh]**

(A) 0 (B) 1
(C) 2 (D) 3

14-74 In a hostel 60% of students read Hindi newspapers, 40% read English and 20% read both. A student is selected at random. Find the probalility that she reads neither Hindi nor English newspaper : **[NTSE-2018 (Stage-I) Himachal Pradesh]**

(A) 0

(B) $\frac{1}{5}$

(C) $\frac{1}{3}$

(D) $\frac{1}{2}$

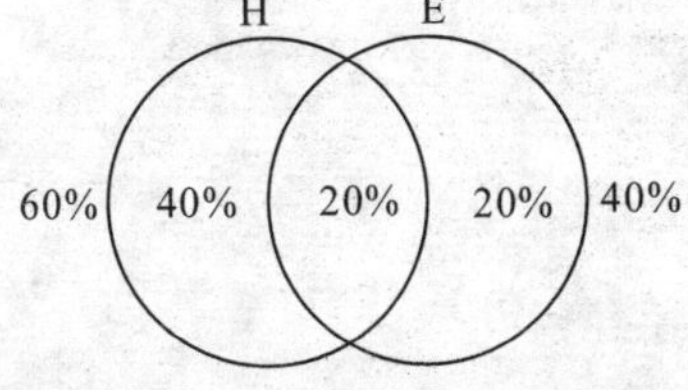

Figure 14.4

14-75 Five ninth of 60% of a number is equal to 2790. What is the number : **[NTSE-2018 (Stage-I) Jharkhand]**

(A) 8100 (B) 7200
(C) 6300 (D) None of these

14-76 Indian Mathematician Varahmihir wrote the : **[NTSE-2018 (Stage-I) Madhya Prasesh]**

(A) Arya Bhattiyam (B) Panch Siddhantika
(C) Ganitsaar Sangrah (D) Leelawati

14-77 Read the following statement carefully and choose the correct alternative :

(a) The slope of the line parallel to X-axis can be derived by the formula $\frac{x_2 - x_1}{y_2 - y_1}$

(b) The slope of the line parallel to Y-axis is 1

(c) The cotangent ratio of an angle made by the line with the positive direction of X- axis is called the slope of that line

(d) The slope of the line which makes acute angle with X-axis is less than zero and the slope of the line making obtuse angle with X-axis is greater than zero

[NTSE-2018 (Stage-I) Maharashtra]

(A) Statements a and b correct
(B) Statements c and d correct
(C) Only statement c is wrong
(D) All statements are worng

14-78 If $\log_4 7 = x$, then the value of $\log_7 16$ will be : **[NTSE-2018 (Stage-I) Telangana]**

(A) x^2 (B) $2x$
(C) x (D) $\frac{2}{x}$

* * * * *

ANSWERS

PRACTICE EXERCISE-14.1

1	(A)	2	(A)	3	(C)
4	(D)	5	(D)	6	(A)
7	(A)	8	(C)	9	(B)
10	(D)	11	(D)	12	(D)
13	(B)	14	(D)	15	(C)
16	(C)	17	(B)	18	(A)
19	(D)	20	(B)	21	(C)
22	(B)	23	(A)	24	(B)
25	(B)	26	(D)	27	(A)
28	(A)	29	(C)	30	(D)
31	(A)	32	(C)	33	(B)
34	(B)	35	(C)	36	(B)
37	(A)	38	(C)	39	(D)
40	(A)	41	(C)	42	(D)
43	(A)	44	(B)	45	(D)
46	(A)	47	(C)	48	(B)
49	(C)	50	(B)	51	(A)
52	(C)	53	(A)	54	(B)
55	(D)	56	(C)	57	(A)
58	(B)	59	(A)	60	(B)
61	(A)	62	(C)	63	(C)
64	(D)	65	(A)	66	(C)
67	(C)	68	(C)	69	(B)
70	(A)	71	(D)	72	(C)
73	(B)	74	(B)	75	(D)
76	(B)	77	(D)	78	(D)

Solutions of PRACTICE EXERCISE-14.1

Sol. 1 (A) Let the initial speed of aeroplane be x km/H. then initial time

$$\text{time} = \frac{\text{Distance}}{\text{Speed}}$$

$$= \frac{600}{x}$$

But when speed is reduced by 200 km/H, then time taken by the aeroplane

$$t_1 = \frac{600}{x-200}$$

$$t_1 - t = 30 \text{ min}$$

$$\frac{600}{x-200} - \frac{600}{x} = \frac{1}{2}$$

$$\frac{x-x+200}{x(x-200)} = \frac{1}{1200}$$

$$x^2 - 200x = 240000$$

$$x^2 - 200x - 240000 = 0$$

$$(x+400)(x-600) = 0$$

$$\Rightarrow \quad x = 600$$

So initial time, taken by aeroplane will be

$$t = \frac{600}{600} = 1 \text{ hr}$$

Hence Ans is (A)

Sol. 2 (A) Given,

'U' is the universal set

'A' is the subset of 'U'

there AUA'

$$= AU(U-A)$$

$$= U$$

Hence Ans is (A)

Sol. 3 (C) Total cost price

$$= \text{Rs. } 27{,}000 + \text{Rs. } 2{,}400$$

$$= \text{Rs. } 29{,}400$$

$$\text{Selling price} = \text{Rs. } 33{,}810$$

$$\text{Proft} = \text{S.P.} - \text{C.P.}$$

$$= \text{Rs. } 33{,}810 - \text{Rs. } 29{,}400$$

$$= \text{Rs. } 4{,}410$$

$$\%\ \text{profit} = \frac{4{,}410}{29{,}400} \times 100$$

$$= 15$$

Hence Ans is (C)

Sol. 4 (D) Length of perpendicular from point $P(x_1, y_1)$ to line $ax + by + c$ is given by

$$d = \frac{ax_1 + by_1 + c}{\sqrt{a^2 + b^2}}$$

$$d = 3,$$

point (0, 0)

line $\quad 4x + 3y + c = 0$

$$\Rightarrow \quad 3 = \frac{4\times 0 + 3\times 0 + c}{\sqrt{3^2 + 4^2}}$$

$$\Rightarrow \quad 3 = \frac{c}{\sqrt{25}} = \boxed{c = 15}$$

Hence Ans is (D)

Sol. 5 (D) Let $\frac{a}{x+y} = \frac{b}{y+z} = \frac{c}{z-x} = k$

$\Rightarrow \quad a = kx + ky \quad \ldots(1)$

$b = ky + kz \quad \ldots(2)$

$c = kz - kx \quad \ldots(3)$

Adding-(1) & (2)
We get

$a + c = ky + kz$

$a + c = b \quad$ [from (2)]

Here Ans is (D)

Sol. 6 (A)

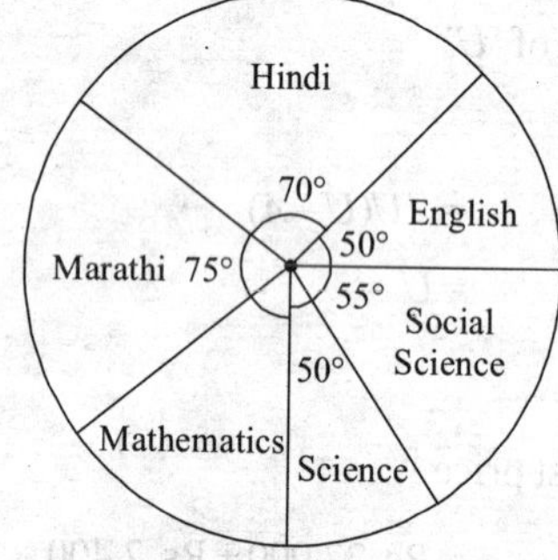

Let $x°$ represents maths in the given pi-diagram

$\Rightarrow \quad x + 75 + 70 + 55° + 50 + 50 = 360°$

$\Rightarrow \quad x = 360 - 300$

$\Rightarrow \quad x = 60°$

Also given Marks scored in Maths = 60

$\Rightarrow \quad 1° = 1$ mark

$\Rightarrow$ Total marks scored by the student

$= 60 + 75 + 70 + 55 + 50 + 50$

$= 360$ marks

$\Rightarrow \quad$ Percentage $= \frac{360}{600} \times 100$

$= 60\%$

Hence Ans is (A)

Sol. 7 (A)

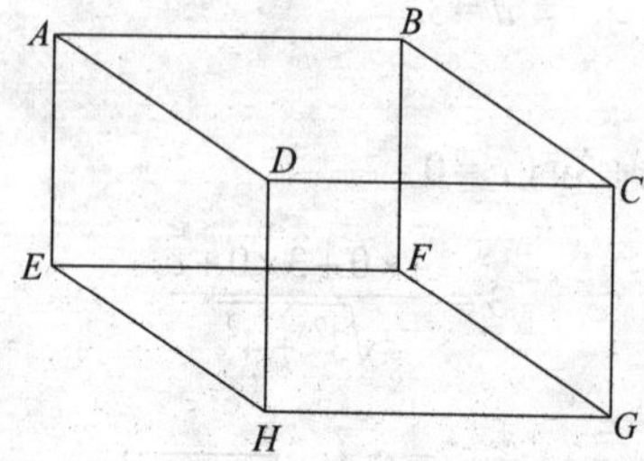

Let the side of the cube be '*a*' units

given it is increased by 50%

$\Rightarrow$ Now, new side $= \frac{3a}{2}$ units

Area of the vertical faces of cube of side

$d = 4 \times a^2$

$= 4a^2$

New area $\quad = 4 \times \left(\frac{3a}{2}\right)^2$

$= 9a^2$

% increase $= \left(\frac{9a^2 - 4a^2}{4a^2}\right) \times 100 = \frac{5a^2}{4a^2} \times 100$

$= 1.25$

$= 125\%$

Hence Ans is (A)

Sol. 8 (C)

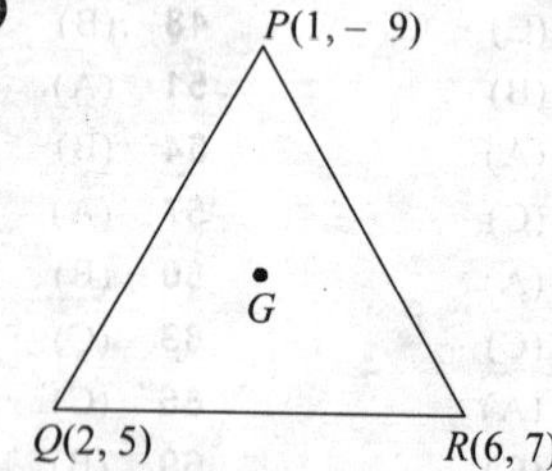

We know co-ordinates of centroid '*G*' are given as

$\left(\frac{x_1 + x_2 + x_3}{3}, \frac{y_1 + y_2 + y_3}{3}\right)$

$\Rightarrow \left(\frac{1+2+6}{3}, \frac{-9+5+7}{3}\right)$

$\Rightarrow$ (3, 1)

Hence Ans is (C)

Sol. 9 (B) By Definition

Hence Ans is (B)

Sol. 10 (D) Given,

S.P. $= \frac{3}{2}$ C.P.

%profit $= \frac{SP - CP}{CP} \times 100$

$= \frac{\frac{3}{2}CP - CP}{CP} \times 100$

$= \frac{1}{2} \times 100$

$= 50\%$

Hence Ans is (D)

Sol. 11 (D) Let the cost price of the bicycle = Rs. x

Given

A sold a bicycle to B on 20% profit

$\Rightarrow$ $\quad$ S.P. $= x + 0.2x$

$= 1.2x$

Now B sold it to C on 25% profit

$\Rightarrow$ $\quad SP = 1.25 \times 1.2x$

Given C paid Rs. 225

$\Rightarrow$ $\quad 1.25 \times 1.2x = 225$

$\Rightarrow$ $\quad x = \dfrac{225}{1.25 \times 1.2}$

$\Rightarrow$ $\quad x = 150$

Hence Ans is (D)

Sol. 12 (D) $\quad A : B = 2 : 3$

$B : C = 4 : 5$

& $\quad C : D = 6 : 7$

$$\frac{A}{B} \times \frac{B}{C} \times \frac{C}{D} = \frac{2}{3} \times \frac{4}{5} \times \frac{6}{7}$$

$$A : D = 16 : 35$$

Hence Ans is (D)

Sol. 13 (B)

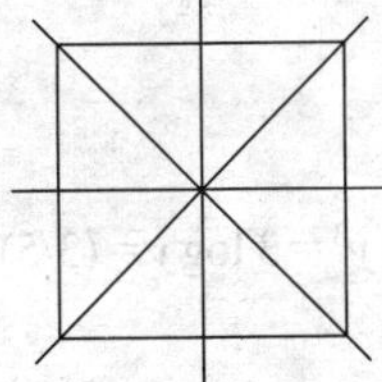

So four lines of symmetry are there

Hence Ans is (B)

Sol. 14 (D) $\quad 3y - 2x = 4 \quad \ldots(1)$

slope of the line-(1)

$$m_1 = -\frac{\text{coefficient of } x}{\text{coefficient of } y}$$

$$m_1 = \frac{-(-2)}{3} = \frac{2}{3}$$

Now slope of line

$$4y - px = 2$$

$$m_2 = -\frac{\text{coefficient of } x}{\text{coefficient of } y}$$

$$m_2 = \frac{-(-p)}{4} = \frac{p}{4}$$

Now since line (1) & line (2) are so perpendicular

$\Rightarrow$ $\quad m_1 m_2 = -1$

$\Rightarrow$ $\quad \dfrac{2p}{12} = -1$

$\Rightarrow$ $\quad p = -6$

Hence Ans is (D)

Sol. 15 (C)

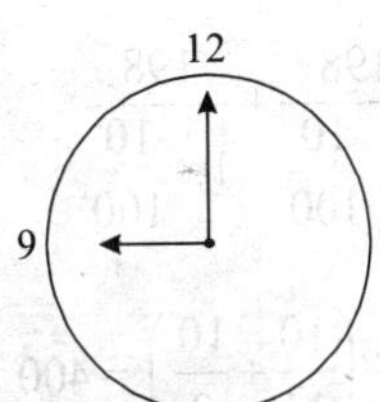

Minute hand cover 360° in 60 minute.

So in one minute it will cover 6°.

So from 9 : 10 to 9 : 25 means is 15 min. it will cover 90°.

So area covered by needle

$$= \pi r^2 . \frac{\theta}{360°}$$

$$= \frac{22}{7} \times 7 \times \frac{90}{360}$$

$$= \frac{77}{2} \text{ cm}^2$$

Hence Ans is (C)

Sol. 16 (C) $\quad f\left(2x + \dfrac{1}{x}\right) = x^2 + \dfrac{1}{4x^2} + 1$

$\Rightarrow$ $\quad f\left(2x + \dfrac{1}{x}\right) = \left(x + \dfrac{1}{2x}\right)^2$

$\Rightarrow$ $\quad f\left(2x + \dfrac{1}{x}\right) = \dfrac{1}{4}\left(2x + \dfrac{1}{x}\right)^2$

$\Rightarrow$ $\quad f(x) = \dfrac{1}{4}x^2$

Hence Ans is (C)

Sol. 17 (B) $\quad x(x^3 - 1) < 0$

$x(x - 1)(x^2 + x + 1) < 0$

$x^2 + x + 1 > 0$

because discriminant < 0

$x(x - 1) < 0$

$\Rightarrow$ $\quad 0 < x < 1$

Hence Ans is (B)

Sol. 18 (A) Let the principal amount be A

then $\frac{A\times 25/2\times 1}{100}-\frac{A\times 10\times 1}{100}=1250$

$\Rightarrow \quad A=50{,}000$

Hence Ans is (A)

Sol. 19 (D) Net cost price

$$=\frac{198}{1+\frac{10}{100}}+\frac{198}{1-\frac{10}{100}}$$

$$=198\left(\frac{10}{11}+\frac{10}{9}\right)=400$$

Selling price $=2\times 198=396$

loss $=400-396=4$

$$\%\text{loss}=\frac{4}{400}\times 100=1$$

Hence Ans is (D)

Sol. 20 (B) Let the price two year before be P

So current price will be $P\left(1+\frac{4}{100}\right)^2$

$$\Rightarrow \quad P\left(1+\frac{4}{100}\right)^2=676000$$

$$\Rightarrow \quad P\left(\frac{26}{25}\right)^2=676000$$

$$\Rightarrow \quad P\times\frac{676}{625}=676000$$

$$\Rightarrow \quad P=625000$$

Hence Ans is (B)

Sol. 21 (C) Volume of tetrahedron

$$=\frac{a^3}{6\sqrt{2}}$$

$$=\frac{1^3}{6\sqrt{2}}=\frac{\sqrt{2}}{12}$$

Hence Ans is (C)

Sol. 22 (B) $2^{\sin^2 x}+2^{\cos^2 x}$

$$2^{\sin^2 x}+\frac{2}{2^{\sin^2 x}}$$

Apply A.M. & G.M.

$$\frac{2^{\sin^2 x}+\frac{2}{2^{\sin^2 x}}}{2}\geq\sqrt{2^{\sin^2 x}\cdot\frac{2}{2^{\sin^2 x}}}$$

$$2^{\sin^2 x}+\frac{2}{2^{\sin^2 x}}\geq 2\sqrt{2}$$

Hence Ans is (B)

Sol. 23 (A) Given

$$\log xy^3=1$$

& $$\log x^2y=1$$

$$\log x+\log y^3=1$$

& $$\log x^2+\log y=1$$

$$\log x+3\log y=1 \quad \ldots(1)$$

& $$2\log x+\log y=1 \quad \ldots(2)$$

Equating equation-(1) & equation-(2)

$$\log x+3\log y=2\log x+\log y$$

$$\Rightarrow \quad \log x=2\log y$$

$$\Rightarrow \quad x=y^2 \quad \ldots(3)$$

Using (3) & (1)

We have

$$\Rightarrow \quad \log y^2+3\log y=1$$

$$\Rightarrow \quad 2\log y+3\log y=1$$

$$\Rightarrow \quad 5\log y=1$$

$$\Rightarrow \quad \log y=1/5 \quad \ldots(4)$$

Now $\log xy=\log y^3=3\log y=(3/5)$

Hence Ans is (A)

Sol. 24 (B) $|x|+|y|=1$

We get st. lines

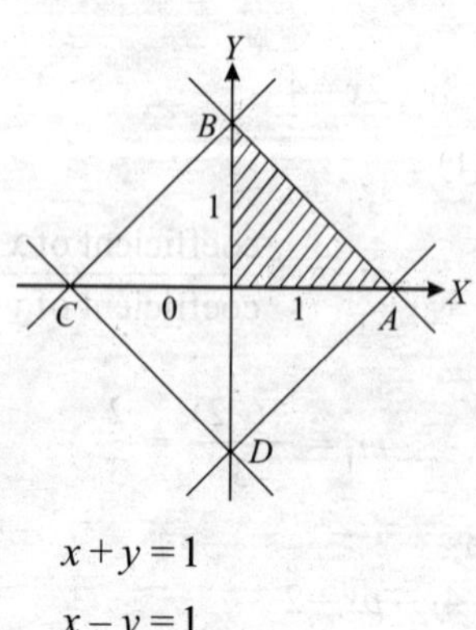

$$x+y=1$$

$$x-y=1$$

$$-x+y=1$$

$$-x-y=1$$

$$Ar(ABCD)=\tfrac{1}{2}+\tfrac{1}{2}+\tfrac{1}{2}+\tfrac{1}{2}=2$$

Hence Ans is (B)

Sol. 25 (B) Length of the train = 500 m
Speed of the man = 3 km/h

$$= 3\times\frac{5}{18}\text{ m/s}$$

$$= \frac{5}{6}\text{ m/s}$$

Speed of the train = 63 km/h

$$= 63\times\frac{5}{18} = \frac{35}{2}\text{ m/s}$$

Train $\xrightarrow[35/2\text{m/s}]{}$ $\xrightarrow{5/6\text{ m/s}}$ man

Distance travelled by train is equal to length of the train & relative speed of the train

$$= \frac{35}{2} - \frac{5}{6}$$

$$= \frac{105-5}{6} = \frac{100}{6} = \frac{50}{3}\text{ m/s}$$

Time taken to cover a distance of 500 m with a speed of $\frac{50}{3}$ m/s is equal to

$$t = \frac{500}{50/3} = 30\text{ sec}$$

Hence Ans is (B)

Sol. 26 (D) Given

C.P. of 12 pens = S.P. of 8 pens

$$\Rightarrow \quad 12\text{ C.P} = 8\text{ S.P.}$$

$$= \frac{CP}{SP} = \frac{8}{12} = \frac{2}{3}$$

$$\text{gain\%} = \frac{S.P.-C.P}{C.P} = \frac{3-2}{2}\times 100$$

$$\text{gain} = 50\%$$

Hence Ans is (D)

Sol. 27 (A) Given 0, 3, 8, 15, 24, – 48 is here by observation we can see that sequence is $n^2 - 1$

So ans is 35

Hence Ans is (A)

Sol. 28 (A) Given 70% of the students in a school are boys

⇒ 30% of student are girl

Let number of student be x

$$\Rightarrow \quad 30\% \text{ of } x = 504$$

$$\frac{30}{100}\times x = 504$$

$$x = 1680$$

Number of boys = 1680 – 504 = 1176

Hence Ans is (A)

Sol. 29 (C) Given

Mess charge per 35 student for 24 days = 6300

⇒ Mess charge for 25 students for 24 days

$$= \frac{6300}{35}\times 25$$

$$= 4500$$

Per day cost for 25 student

$$= \frac{4500}{24}$$

Given certain day (x) cost for 25 student = 3375

Per day cost for 25 student

$$= \frac{3375}{x}$$

So we have

$$\frac{4500}{24} = \frac{3375}{x}$$

$$x = \frac{3375\times 24}{4500}$$

$$x = 18$$

Hence Ans is (C)

Sol. 30 (D) Cost of 1 orange = $\frac{3}{7}$

$$\text{Cost of 100 orange} = \frac{3}{7}\times 100$$

$$\text{gain\%} = 33\%$$

$$\Rightarrow \quad \text{S.P.} = 1.33\times\text{C.P.}$$

$$= 1.33\times\frac{3}{7}\times 100$$

$$= 133\times\frac{3}{7}$$

$$= 57\text{ Rs.}$$

Hence Ans is (D)

Sol. 31 (A) Since change in area is a successive change. So use the formula

$$\left(a+b+\frac{ab}{100}\right)\%$$

$$\Rightarrow \quad 25+25+\frac{25\times 25}{100}$$

$$\Rightarrow \quad 50+\frac{625}{100}$$

$$= 56.25\%\text{ increase}$$

Hence Ans is (A)

Sol. 32 (C) Given

$$x\% \text{ of } y = 1\% \text{ of } z$$

$$\frac{xy}{100} = \frac{z}{100}$$

$\Rightarrow$ $xy = z$ ...(1)

$$y\% \text{ of } z = 1\% \text{ of } x$$

$\Rightarrow$ $yz = x$ ...(2)

$$z\% \text{ of } x = 1\% \text{ of } y$$

$\Rightarrow$ $xz = y$ ...(3)

$$xy + yz + zx = x + y + z$$

Multiply (2) & (3)

$$x^2 y^2 z^2 = xyz$$

$$xyz = 1$$

$$z^2 = 1 \Rightarrow z = 1$$

Similarly $x = 1 \;\&\; y = 1$

$\Rightarrow$ $xy + yz + zx = 3$

Hence Ans is (B)

Sol. 33 (B) $A(c, 8), B(a, 0), C(-c, c), D(3c, a)$

Slope of (AB) × slope of $CD = -1$

$$\frac{0-8}{a-c} \times \frac{a-c}{3c+c} = -1$$

$\Rightarrow$ $c = 2$

$\Rightarrow$ $a + c = 12$

Hence Ans is (B)

Sol. 34 (B) $D \geq 0$

$\Rightarrow$ $16 + 4\log_3 a \geq 0$

$\Rightarrow$ $\log_3 a \geq -4$

$\Rightarrow$ $a \geq 3^{-4}$

Hence Ans is (B)

Sol. 35 (C) Total number of subset of

$$A \equiv \{0, 1, 2, 3\}$$

$$2^4 - 1 = 15$$

Hence Ans is (C)

Sol. 36 (B) Total number of word using all the letter of the word GOURI = 5! = 120

Now when all three vowel together

$GR\boxed{IOU}$

$3! \times 3! = 36$

Total number of word in which all vowels do not occur together $= 120 - 36 = 84$

Hence Ans is (B)

Sol. 37 (A) ${}^{2n}C_3 : {}^{n}C_3 = 12 : 1$

$$\frac{2n!}{3! \times (2n-3)!} : \frac{n!}{3!(n-3)!} = \frac{12}{1}$$

$\Rightarrow$ $$\frac{2n!}{3! \times (2n-3)!} \times \frac{3!(n-3)!}{n!} = \frac{12}{1}$$

$\Rightarrow$ $$\frac{2n(2n-1)(2n-2)}{n(n-1)(n-2)} = \frac{12}{1}$$

$\Rightarrow$ $$\frac{4(2n-1)(n-1)}{(n-1)(n-2)} = \frac{12}{1}$$

$\Rightarrow$ $$\frac{(2n-1)}{(n-2)} = \frac{3}{1}$$

$\Rightarrow$ $2n - 1 = 3n - 6$

$\Rightarrow$ $\boxed{n = 5}$

Hence Ans is (A)

Sol. 38 (C) If 30 consecutive integers are there, then 15 are odd & 15 are even the sum of two integer is odd when one is even & one is odd.

$\Rightarrow$ Probability for sum being odd $= \dfrac{{}^{15}C_1 \cdot {}^{15}C_1}{{}^{30}C_2}$

$$= \frac{15 \times 15 \times 2}{30 \times 29} = \frac{15}{29}$$

Hence Ans is (C)

Sol. 39 (D) Let $n \frac{1}{4}$ are there

$\Rightarrow$ $$\frac{1}{4} \times n = 22\frac{1}{2}$$

$\Rightarrow$ $$n = \frac{45/2}{1/4} = 90$$

Hence Ans is (D)

Sol. 40 (A) $\dfrac{m_1 D_1}{w_1} = \dfrac{m_2 D_2}{w_2}$

Let m people complete w task in 20 days

then $$\frac{m \times 20}{w} = \frac{2m \times D}{w/2}$$

$\Rightarrow$ $4D = 20$

$\Rightarrow$ $D = 5$

Hence Ans is (A)

Sol. 41 (C) Given $3\sqrt{3}\times 3^3 \div 3^{-3/2} = 3^{n+2}$

$$3^{1+\frac{1}{2}+3+\frac{3}{2}} = 3^{n+2}$$

$$n+2=4+2$$

$$n=4$$

Hence Ans is (C)

Sol. 42 (D) $3A=4B=6C$

$$\frac{3A}{12}=\frac{4B}{12}=\frac{6C}{12}$$

$$\frac{A}{4}=\frac{B}{3}=\frac{C}{2}$$

$$A:B:C=4:3:2$$

Hence Ans is (D)

Sol. 43 (A) $\frac{8}{40}\times 100=20\%$

Hence Ans is (A)

Sol. 44 (B) By expanding the determinants, we get

$$4a-18=30-4b$$

$\Rightarrow$ $4(a+b)=48$

$\Rightarrow$ $a+b=12$

Hence Ans is (B)

Sol. 45 (D) Profit of Akash $=x$

Profit of Alok $=x+\frac{75}{100}x=\frac{7x}{4}$

$\Rightarrow$ $\dfrac{\frac{7x}{4}-x}{\frac{7x}{4}}\times 100$

$$\frac{3}{7}\times 100=42.85\%$$

Hence Ans is (D)

Sol. 46 (A) $\cos^2\alpha=\sin\alpha\tan\alpha$

$$\cos^3\alpha=\sin^2\alpha$$

$$\cos^6\alpha=\sin^4\alpha$$

$\Rightarrow$ $\cot^6\alpha-\cot^2\alpha$

$\Rightarrow$ $\dfrac{\cos^6\alpha}{\sin^6\alpha}-\cot^2\alpha$

$\Rightarrow$ $\dfrac{1}{\sin^2\alpha}-\dfrac{\cos^2\alpha}{\sin^2\alpha}=\dfrac{1-\cos^2\alpha}{\sin^2\alpha}=\dfrac{\sin^2\alpha}{\sin^2\alpha}=1$

Hence Ans is (A)

Sol. 47 (C) Number of hand shakes $={}^8C_2=\frac{8\times 7}{2}=28$

Hence Ans is (C)

Sol. 48 (B)

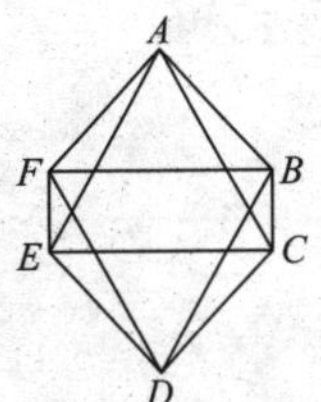

AEC and DBF are equilateral triangles

$$P(E)=\frac{2}{{}^6C_3}=\frac{2}{20}=\frac{1}{10}$$

Hence Ans is (B)

Sol. 49 (C) Case-I :

$14x+40x+27x=y$ (number of chocolates)

$$81x=y$$

$$x=\frac{y}{81}$$

Number of chocolates with Shruti

$$=27x=27\frac{y}{81}=\frac{y}{3}$$

Case-II : $19a+55a+37a=y$

(number of chocolates being same)

$$111a=y$$

$$a=\frac{y}{111}$$

Number of chocolates Shruti now has

$$37\times\frac{y}{111}=\frac{y}{3}$$

Hence no changes

Hence Ans is (C)

Sol. 50 (B) Let one be x other be $(10200-x)$

$$x-\frac{12}{100}x=(10200-x)-\frac{18}{100}(10200-x)$$

Solving $x=$ Rs. 4920

Hence required answer = Rs. 5280

Hence Ans is (B)

Sol. 51 (A) $Y = \frac{3}{5}x - \frac{8}{5}$

$$\text{Slope} = \frac{3}{5} = 0.6$$

Hence Ans is (A)

Sol. 52 (C) $U = \{1, 2, 3, 4\},$

$A = \{1, 2\}$

$A = \{3, 4\}$

Hence Ans is (C)

Sol. 53 (A) Hilbert

Hence Ans is (A)

Sol. 54 (B) FATE

A □□□ $\Rightarrow 3! = 6$

E □□□ $\Rightarrow 3! = 6$

F A E T $\Rightarrow = 1$

Rank $= 6 + 6 + 1 = 13$

Hence Ans is (B)

Sol. 55 (D) Total number of points '12' out of which 4 are collinear

No. of St. lines are $12C_2 - 4C_2 + 1$

$= 66 - 6 + 1 = 61$

No. of triangles are $= 12C_3 - 4C_3$

$= 216$

Hence Ans is (D)

Sol. 56 (C) a, b, c are in G.P. then $b^2 = ac$

$b = (ac)^{1/2}$

a, b, c are in H.P. then

$\Rightarrow \frac{1}{c} + \frac{1}{b} + \frac{2}{b}$

Hence Ans is (C)

Sol. 57 (A) $y = a + a^2 + a^3 \ldots, |a| < 1$

$\Rightarrow \quad y = \frac{a}{1-a}$

$\Rightarrow \quad y - ay = a$

$\Rightarrow \quad y = (y+1)a$

$a = \frac{y}{y+1}$

Hence Ans is (A)

Sol. 58 (B) $(A \cup B)^C = A^C \cap B^C$

Hence Ans is (B)

Sol. 59 (A) $50 = \frac{10000}{x} \times 360$

$\Rightarrow \quad x = \frac{10000}{50} \times 360 = 72000$

$\Rightarrow$ Amount incurred on education

$= \frac{100°}{360°} \times 72000$

$\Rightarrow \quad x = 20000$

Hence Ans is (A)

Sol. 60 (B) $F_3 = F_2 + F_1 = 2$

Hence Ans is (B)

Sol. 61 (A) $\log_3 \log_4 \log_2 x = 0$

$\Rightarrow \quad \log_4 \log_2 x = 1$

$\Rightarrow \quad \log_2 x = 4$

$\Rightarrow \quad x = 2^4$

$\Rightarrow \quad x = 16$

Hence Ans is (A)

Sol. 62 (C) Population after two year

$= 8000\left(1 + \frac{10}{100}\right)\left(1 + \frac{20}{100}\right)$

$= 10560$

Hence Ans is (C)

Sol. 63 (C) $\log_4 [\log_4\{\log_4 (\log_4 x)\}]$

$\Rightarrow \quad \log_4 \{\log_4 (\log_4 x)\} = 1$

$\Rightarrow \quad \log_4 (\log_4 x) = 4$

$\Rightarrow \quad \log_4 x = 4^4$

$\Rightarrow \quad \log_4 x = 256$

$x = 4^{256} = 2^{51}$

Hence Ans is (C)

Sol. 64 (D) $\frac{1}{\log_{z-y} x} + \frac{1}{\log_{z+y} x}$

$= \log_x (z-y) + \log_x (z+y)$

$= \log_x (z^2 - y^2) = \log_x x^2 = 2$

Hence Ans is (D)

Sol. 65 (A) $CI = 7500\left(1+\frac{8}{100}\right)^2 - 7500$

$= \text{Rs. } 1248$

Hence Ans is (A)

Sol. 66 (C) Let $CP = x$

$$SP = \frac{7x}{5}$$

Price after discount

$$= \frac{7x}{5} - 20\% \text{ of } \frac{7x}{5} = \frac{28x}{25}$$

Gain = 48

$$\Rightarrow \frac{28x}{25} - x = 48$$

$$\Rightarrow \frac{3x}{25} = 48$$

$$\Rightarrow x = \text{Rs. } 400$$

Hence Ans is (C)

Sol. 67 (C) $\frac{1}{3} + \frac{1}{3^2} + \frac{1}{3^3} + \ldots + \frac{1}{3^{10}} + \frac{1}{2\cdot 3^{10}}$

$$\frac{1}{3}\left(1+\frac{1}{3}+\frac{1}{3^2}+\ldots\frac{1}{39}\right) + \frac{1}{2\cdot 3^{10}} \quad \ldots(1)$$

Now we know the sum of n term of G.P. is given by

$$S_n = \frac{a(1-r^n)}{1-r}$$

Where r = common ratio

Here $r = \frac{1}{3}$

Now from (1)

$$\frac{1}{3}\left[\frac{1\cdot\left(1-\left(\frac{1}{3}\right)^{10}\right)}{1-\frac{1}{3}}\right] + \frac{1}{2\cdot 3^{10}}$$

$$\frac{1}{3}\left[\frac{3}{2}\left(1-\left(\frac{1}{3}\right)^{10}\right)\right] + \frac{1}{2\cdot 3^{10}}$$

$$\frac{1}{2} - \frac{1}{2\cdot 3^{10}} + \frac{1}{2\cdot 3^{10}} = \frac{1}{2}$$

Hence Ans is (C)

Sol. 68 (C) $a^x = b^{y+z}$

By taking log both side

$$x \log a = (y+z) \log b$$

$$\frac{\log a}{\log b} = \left(\frac{y+z}{x}\right)$$

Hence Ans is (C)

Sol. 69 (B) $\log\frac{x}{\sqrt{3}} + \log\frac{x}{\sqrt[4]{3}} + \log\frac{x}{\sqrt[6]{3}} + \ldots.. + \log\frac{x}{\sqrt[16]{3}} = 36$

$$\Rightarrow 2\log_3 x + 4\log x_3 + \ldots.. + 16\log_3 x = 36$$

$$(\log \sqrt[m]{a}\, x = m\log_a x)$$

$$\Rightarrow \log_3 x^{(2+4+\ldots+16)} = 36$$

$$\Rightarrow \log_3 x^{(72)} = 36$$

$$\Rightarrow \log_3 x = \frac{1}{2} \quad \text{[by defination]}$$

$$\Rightarrow x = 3^{\frac{1}{2}}$$

$$\Rightarrow x = \sqrt{3}$$

Hence Ans is (B)

Sol. 70 (A) Profit = Price

of 200gm = 200x

CP = 800x

$$\Rightarrow \text{Profit}(\%) = \frac{\text{Profit}}{\text{CP}} \times 100\%$$

$$= \frac{200x}{800x} \times 100\%$$

$$= 25\%$$

Hence Ans is (A)

Sol. 71 (D) Let his salary be Rs. x in 2014

Salary in $2015 = x \times \frac{110}{100}$

Salary in $2016 = x \times \frac{110}{100} \times \frac{115}{100}$

Salary in $2016 = x \times \frac{110}{100} \times \frac{115}{100} \times \frac{140}{100}$

$$x \times \frac{110}{100} \times \frac{115}{100} \times \frac{140}{100} = 1{,}77{,}100$$

$$\Rightarrow = \frac{1{,}77{,}100 \times 1000}{11 \times 23 \times 7} = 1{,}00{,}000$$

Hence Ans is (D)

Sol. 72 (C) $D_1 = 9$ days $D_2 = ?$

$M_1 = 25$ persons

$M_2 = 15$ persons

$T_1 = 6$ hrs

$T_2 = 9$ hrs

$M_1D_1T_1 = M_2D_2T_2$

$\Rightarrow \quad 25 \times 9 \times 6 = 15 \times D_2 \times 9$

$\Rightarrow \quad D_2 = 10$ days

Hence Ans is (C)

Sol. 73 (B) $f(x), f(4x) = [f(2x)]^2$

$\Rightarrow \quad (2x+(1))\,(8x+(1)) = (4x+(1))^2$

$\Rightarrow \quad 16x^2 + 10x + 1 = 16x^2 + 8x + 1$

$\Rightarrow \quad x = 0$

Only one value

Hence Ans is (B)

Sol. 74 (B) Student who read Hindi news paper $= \dfrac{60}{100}$

Student who read English news paper $= \dfrac{40}{100}$

Student who read both news paper $= \dfrac{20}{100}$

Student who read Hindi or English news paper

$= P(H) + P(E) - P(H \cap E) = \dfrac{80}{100}$

Students who read neither Hindi nor English news paper $= \dfrac{20}{100}$

Probability of students who read neither Hindi nor English $= \dfrac{1}{5}$

Hence Ans is (B)

Sol. 75 (D) Required no is

$$\frac{5}{9} \times \frac{60}{100} \times x = 2790$$

$\Rightarrow \quad x = 8370$

Hence Ans is (D)

Sol. 76 (B) Panch Siddhantika

Hence Ans is (B)

Sol. 77 (D) Verify all the options

$A \Rightarrow$ Slope of x-axis $\dfrac{x_2 - x_1}{y_2 - y_1}$ [False]

$B \Rightarrow$ Slope of y-axis $= 1$ [False]

$C \Rightarrow$ Slope $= \cot\theta$

$D \Rightarrow$ False

Hence Ans is (D)

Sol. 78 (D) Consider

$\log_4 7 = x$

$7 = 4^x$ ...(1)

$= \log_4 16$

$\Rightarrow \quad \log_{4^x} 4^2 = \dfrac{2}{x}$

Hence Ans is (D)

* * * * *